THE
TEXAS
GOLF
BIBLE

JASON STONE

fandango
PUBLISHING CO.
DALLAS, TEXAS

THE TEXAS GOLF BIBLE
Jason Stone

Published by:

Fandango Publishing Company
P.O. Box 7776
Dallas, Texas 75209
www.texasgolfbible.com
Please report errors and changes to: *feedback@texasgolfbible.com*

Printed by:
Sandford Press
Dallas, TX
Copyright © 2003 by Jason Stone
Editor: Regan Brown
Production Artist: Mary Catherine Kozusko
Cover design: Linda Griffith

ISBN: 0-9724707-0-0

Library of Congress Control Number: 2003104570

First edition
Printed and bound in the United States of America

To Mom, Dad, Robin, Sam, & Charlie

CONTENTS

TEXAS GOLF ESSAYS

*Handicapping • Scoring • Statistics • Rules • Etiquette • Statistics •
Gamesmanship • Wagering • Games • Style • Etc.*

APPENDICES

INDEX

PUBLISHER'S ACKNOWLEDGMENTS

The following people helped bring this book to market:

Senior Project Editor: Regan Brown

Copy Editor and Technical Reviewers: Robin Stone, Reid Slaughter, Regan Brown

General Reviewers and Proofreaders: Julie Jackson, Robin Stone, Chase Perry, Regan Brown, the Boyer family, and the Stone family

Indexer: Regan Brown

Design and Layout: Mary Catherine Kozusko

Cover design: Linda Griffith

Mileage Chart Data: Andy Neyhart

Photo credits: Dallas Public Library; Houston Public Library; Carlton Woods photos courtesy of the Woodlands Operating Company, L.P.; Ambush at Lajitas photo courtesy of Lajitas Resort.

AUTHOR'S ACKNOWLEDGMENTS

My soul mate, Robin, who patiently persevered and took care of our family while I journeyed through this process of discovery. Thank you for listening, talking, and helping me stay focused. I love you.

I had some valuable assistance throughout this marathon and I'm grateful to everyone who has helped see this through. The "venerable" Regan Brown, editor of the book, for learning the golf lingo and racking up the hours going through city after city, and course after course. To Shannon Lekas and Andy Neyhart: thank you for the support. Reid Slaughter, a talented writer who served as my teacher and inspiration for many different aspects of this project. And to Mary Catherine Kozusko for taking the time to help a friend in need! To Joyce Griffith, Carol Burrel, Rebecca Price, and Carol Grosvenor for teaching me some very expensive lessons about people, communication, and business.

Many thanks to the hundreds of friendly small-town Texans that I encountered who assisted in helping me bring out colorful information that is the backbone of this book. This includes the hundreds of chambers of commerce, as well as the folks who work in the golf shops across Texas.

Many more thanks to the Texas golf community for assisting with interviews and providing valuable information about their facilities.

Encouragement, suggestions, criticism and more: Shannon Lekas, Andy Neyhart, Eric O'Keefe, Herb Allen, Chase Perry, Ben Arnold, Randy Touchstone, Kimberly Pflaum.

One of the reasons why I, a medical man, decided to give up medicine and take to golf architecture was my firm conviction of the extraordinary influence on health of pleasurable excitement, especially when combined with fresh air and exercise.

Dr. Alister Mackenzie

I always try to think positive. I try not to take anything too serious— I try not to get too happy or too sad. A good attitude is to live in the present as much as I can—not worry about yesterday or tomorrow. I think that's healthy.

Willie Nelson

INTRODUCTION

A Different Kind of Golf Travel Guidebook

The Texas Golf Bible springs from the desire to play golf and travel the open roads of Texas. In the old days, people were content to limit their enjoyment of the game to their home course. No longer. Golf is exploding, and the dazzling new courses out there are just one reason to take off and explore new territory. Another reason is the one-of-a-kind travel opportunity that awaits you through a Texas golf road trip. Take one described in this book, and you'll discover a whole new aspect of the Lone Star State.

Just for a moment, forget Disneyland and the Hawaiian resort. Think about a trip much closer to home—far less expensive and much deeper in memorable experiences. Something you can do with a buddy or with the whole family. It all begins at the end of your driveway.

Until now, such a trip was a hit-or-miss venture since no one has compiled detailed information about playing golf in small Texas towns like Alpine, Marshall, and McAllen. *The Texas Golf Bible* fills that gap by providing accurate, colorful, and valuable information about all Texas courses, including the off-the-beaten-path tracks that are seldom mentioned.

Most golf guidebooks are more like directories than actual guides: boring compilations of addresses, holes, names, and phone numbers, along with a few tidbits about the layout of a course (if they even offer that). This book is different. It's about the entire experience.

This book covers every course in Texas—over 900 of them. We cover the best golf destinations and the not-so-best, as well as non-golf activities, dining and travel. With this book in your truck you can road-trip through Texas and find gorgeous scenery, fresh air, mental and physical rejuvenation, and the renewal of your love affair with the game itself.

In small towns across Texas, the game holds a special meaning. It's cow pasture pool on 9-hole courses and golf in its most basic form. When you're in the rough, you know it's rough. When the wind blows, it really blows.

We've included private courses because, well, at some point you'll find yourself on a private course. This is about every available experience, not just the public courses. And it's about the little details that can maximize your fun. It's helpful to know that the new course outside of Waco, Bear Ridge Golf Club, doesn't sell cold beer. We give you that warning and mention that the HEB down the highway can help you out if that's what you need for that particular round.

It wouldn't be any fun to write a book about Texas golf and not include other details about the intangibles of the game. To make the most of your reading experience, we've included bonus material here that you'll want to refer to regularly. We touch on subjects such as Hunting, Fishing, & Golf; Romance &

Golf; and Camping & Golf. We provide sample Texas golf road trips for you to dream about or duplicate.

This book is not written solely for the avid Texas golfer. Remember that one of the best things you can do to improve your game is playing a quick round of par 3 golf. This lets you hone in your short irons and work out the kinks in your game. Whenever I go toe-to-toe with the evil demons of the shanks, I always find that I can work through it by spending time at a par 3 course. There's just something about it, and Texas has a multitude of quality par 3 layouts. We cover these facilities, along with the driving ranges for each destination. So if you're in Wichita Falls visiting the Griswolds over Thanksgiving, you'll know where you can work on your game. Texas offers an endless variety of golf experiences. The Texas golf journey is wide open. There are no limits.

We're going to provide you with information and inspiration, but what you do with that is the key. Fill up the ice chest, spread out the maps, throw the clubs in the back of the truck, and head down the road for your own Texas golf adventure.

Jason Stone
Dallas, Texas
April 2003

BEFORE YOU TEE UP: A GUIDE TO THIS GUIDE

Some books, like the ones you were supposed to read in high school but bought the Cliff Notes for instead, look good on a shelf. This book, on the other hand, is meant to be used. Read it for fun or use it as a reference. Write in it. Waterproof it. Throw it in your truck. Spill beer on it. And yes, feel free to ignore a section if you like. You may not even play enough golf to have a handicap, but that may change, so keep *The Texas Golf Bible* handy.

Attempting to "rank" more than 900 courses is a fool's errand, and we don't attempt it. Instead, we toss all that subjectivity out the window and describe the courses in more detail than has ever been attempted before. Then you can decide what's right for you. After all, every course is different, and every experience is unique. Some of you may enjoy a heavily wooded setting, while others long for the treeless plains. We've done the research so you can call the shots—and create your own golf experience.

Having read a lot of other golf books, we were determined not to regurgitate volumes of generic "golfspeak" regarding hole after hole after hole. Our focus is giving you a feel for the course, and knowing that the signature hole is a "dogleg right with an uphill tee shot over water" doesn't always do the trick. Okay, occasionally we get into the detail of a hole, but only if it helps shape your overall perception of the potential golf experience.

What good is a fax number to the discriminating traveler? Why do you need to know the name of the pro? How does it help you when the so-called golf guidebooks give you a P.O. Box for an address to plug into your GPS or map software to determine directions? And if you need to know what the dress code is, you shouldn't be reading this book. Does it do you any good to know that you can't wear cut-off shorts and a tank top?

The Texas Golf Bible gives you information you can sink your teeth into—like where to eat in just about every town. Because you'll generally be passing through these spots, we decided against cramming in hotel information for every spot. If a place stands out and is worth consideration, we mention it. If the town is too small and you're better off moving on, we'll recommend another destination.

We do not list specific pricing for each course; instead, we give you a feel for the overall quality and point out any extremes as necessary. There are bottom-liners who are particular about green fees, but a true golf bum ignores the price and pursues the experience, regardless of cost. That said, if a high-end course charging $100 a round is clearly not worth it, we'll tell you. And by the way, just because a course is named "country club" doesn't mean that it's a ritzy private course.

If we had covered every course in multi-page detail, you wouldn't be able to lift this book. Still, The Texas Golf Bible aims to be the most comprehensive and interesting tour guide to Texas golf available. To do that, we could use your input since this is only the first of many editions: a living, breathing organism that will keep evolving just as the game and our enjoyment of it has evolved. So help us out. Jot down notes about places to eat and things to do on your golf travels, and drop us a line at authors@texasgolfbible.com. Now start planning your next round!

Course Price Legend – Due to the constant fluctuation in green fee pricing, as well as the various rates one might pay based on a particular day of the week or time of day, the following price legend depicts an approximate green fee with cart during peak times. Note that these figures do not depict any sort of course rating, and are not official price guides to each facility, but are presented to give the reader a feel for the approximate cost to play with a cart.

$	$0 - $24
$$	$25 - $49
$$$	$50 - $74
$$$$	$100 +

The fellas at Dallas Country Club circa 1925

TEXAS GOLF: A BRIEF HISTORY

In 1900, Sigmund Freud was developing psychoanalysis, the first Zeppelin took flight, and there were only five golf courses in Texas. Today, the zeppelin is now a Goodyear Blimp, there are more than 900 golf courses in Texas, and psychoanalysis is used to help nervous golfers conquer their fears of "yips," three-puts and other links-related maladies. Clearly golf has prospered. The state's vast, wide-open spaces and warm climate have enabled the sport to boom here over the past 100 years. It's been reported that up to six million people now regularly enjoy the game of golf in Texas.

1895   Englishmen H.L. Edwards and Richard Potter build a 6-hole course on a farm at the corner of Haskell and Cole streets in Dallas.

1896   Dallas Golf & Country Club, a 9-hole course with sand greens, opens along Oak Lawn Avenue.

1898   Galveston Country Club opens a 9-hole course with sand greens where the San Luis Hotel now stands.

1898   Austin Mayor Lewis Hancock leads a group that builds a 9-hole course on the banks of Waller Creek in Austin, the first of many locations for the Austin Country Club.

1903   Houston Country Club is founded.

1906   Men's amateur organizations and state championships are established. Beaumont Country Club opens.

★

From 1937–1957, five PGA champions were Texans.

1907   San Antonio Country Club founded.

1910   El Paso and Corpus Christi Country Clubs founded.

1911   Tom Bendelow builds Rivercrest Country Club in Fort Worth

1912   Tom Bendelow builds Lakewood Country Club in Dallas. Glen Garden in Fort Worth opens.

1914   Corsicana Country Club opens. Temple and Taylor Country Clubs are formed.

1916   Women's amateur organizations and state championships established. Texas' first public golf course opens in San Antonio with A.W. Tillinghast's Brackenridge Park.

1918   Paris Country Club opens (Paris, TX). San Antonio's Riverside Park course opens.

1919   A.W. Tillinghast designs Cedar Crest Country Club in Dallas.

1921   A.W. Tillinghast designs Brook Hollow Golf Club in Dallas.

1922   Texas PGA formed by John Bredemus and Willie Maguire. Inaugural Texas Open held in San Antonio at Breckenridge Park. First prize is $5,000.

1923   Houston opens the public 16-hole Hermann Park Golf Course.

1924   Tenison Park and Stevens Park public courses open in Dallas.

1927   PGA Championship held in Dallas at Cedar Crest Country Club.

1936   Fort Worth's Colonial Country opens after magnate Marvin Leonard hires John Bredemus.

1941   Colonial Country Club in Fort Worth becomes the first Texas venue to host the U.S. Open.

1944   Dallas' Lakewood CC hosts the first Dallas Open, won by Byron Nelson.

1945   Byron Nelson wins 11 consecutive tournaments and becomes the AP's Athlete of the Year for the second straight year. Houston Golf Association created.

1946   First Houston Open is held at River Oaks Country Club, won by Byron Nelson over Ben Hogan.

1948   The golf cart is invented at Houston Country Club.

1949   North Texas State University, led by coach Fred Cobb, wins the first of four NCAA championships.

1951   LPGA hosts Weathervane Women's Open tournament at Dallas' Lakewood CC. First prize is $750.

1952   Dallas' Northwood CC hosts U.S. Open, won by Julius Boros.

1954   Houston businessman Charles Washington takes first golf shot by a black man at Memorial Park, breaking the color barrier.

⭐

The lore of the game, the story of its development and the stirring deeds of the great players of the past must always command the respectful attention of all who play golf regularly. To be reasonably knowledgeable in such matters comes close to being an obligation to a true golfer. Bobby Jones

1955   Former Duke fullback Mike Souchak breaks PGA's 72-hole record with a 27-under-par 257 in the Texas Open at Brackenridge Park, San Antonio.

1959   Ben Hogan wins his final PGA Tour victory at Colonial.

1963   23-year-old Jack Nicklaus endures a heat wave to win the PGA Championship at Dallas Athletic Club.

1967   Ryder Cup matches held in Houston at Champions Golf Club.

1968   Lee Trevino wins the U.S. Open, the first of his five major championships. San Antonio's Pecan Valley hosts PGA Championship, won by Julius Boros. First prize is $25,000.

1969   U.S. Open is hosted at Houston's Champions Golf Club, won by Orville Moody.

1971   Ben Hogan plays his last round as a professional when he injures his knee at the Houston Champions International.

1975   Texas Lee Elder is the first black man to play in the Masters tournament in Augusta, GA. Texas Golf Hall of Fame established in Woodlands, TX.

1978   Seeds for Senior PGA Tour established via the Legends of Golf tournament organized by Jimmie Demaret and Fred Raphael.

1984   Ben Crenshaw wins the first of his two Masters titles.

1985   LPGA Hall of Fame opens in Sugarland, TX.

1987   University of Houston's legendary golf coach Dave Williams retires after producing more than 80 professional golfers.

1992   Tom Kite wins U.S. Open.

1995   Legendary Austin CC pro and golf's most famous teacher, Harvey Penick, passes on, spurring Ben Crenshaw to his miraculous second Masters title.

1997   Justin Leonard wins the British Open.

2002   Despite the economic downturn, Texas added 33 new golf courses to its resumé.

2003   The National Golf Foundation lists 83 golf course projects either in planning or under construction in Texas.

Some people don't realize this was the tournament (Texas Open) which helped launch the PGA Tour. The pros played in San Antonio and moved on to Los Angeles or over to Shreveport, New Orleans, and Florida. Harvey Penick

JOHN BREDEMUS' TEXAS COURSES

BraeBurn Country Club – Houston TX
Colonial Country Club – Fort Worth TX
Flying L. Guest Ranch – Bandera TX
Glen Garden Golf & Country Club – Fort Worth TX
Memorial Park Golf Course – Houston TX
Rockwood Municipal Golf Club – Fort Worth TX
San Angelo Country Club – San Angelo TX
San Felipe Country Club – Del Rio TX
Scott Schriener Municipal Golf Course – Kerrville TX
Starcke Park Golf Club – Seguin TX
Temple College Golf Course – Temple TX
Victoria Country Club – Victoria TX

A.W. TILLINGHAST'S TEXAS COURSES

Brackenridge Park Golf Course – San Antonio TX
Brook Hollow Golf Club – Dallas TX
Cedar Crest Golf Course – Dallas TX
Corsicana Country Club – Corsicana TX
Fort Sam Houston Golf Course – San Antonio TX
Oak Hills Country Club – San Antonio TX

TEXAS GOLF:
OVERVIEW & ARCHITECTURE

Before we get into the architecture of Texas courses, let's debunk a classic golf myth that goes something like this: "The 100 Greatest Golf Courses in America are chosen because they provide the avid golfer with the 100 greatest golf experiences." Bull's wool. Nothing could be farther from the truth. That list, named each year by Golf Digest magazine, reflects the average golfer's tastes as accurately as, say, the Academy Awards reflect the true feelings of the movie-going public.

They are all great courses, to be sure, but a better name for that list might be "The 100 Toughest Courses to Get a Tee Time On." For most of us, the odds of getting to play Augusta, Pine Valley, or Spyglass are roughly the same as making People Magazine's "50 Most Beautiful People" issue: very long indeed. Fortunately, the odds of playing almost any course in Texas are much better. What the state's courses don't offer in terms of history and major tournament lore, they make up for in accessibility.

It's interesting to note that only 25 of Golf Digest's 100 honorees were built in the last 30 years. In the old days, technology wasn't available to move massive pieces of earth and trees, putting a premium on natural, parkland-style settings, which were not common in Texas. For the most part, Texas is flat and doesn't offer the traditional terrain that has defined the classic courses. By the way, Colonial Country Club in Fort Worth is the only Texas course on Golf Digest's current top 100, coming in at No. 35. Other Texas courses to make past lists include: Barton Creek in Austin (Tom Fazio, designer), Preston Trail in Dallas (Ralph Plummer, Byron Nelson), and Champions Golf Course in Houston (George Fazio, Jimmy Demaret, and Jack Burke, Jr.).

When the famous boom of golf course architecture occurred, two of the game's most noted designers spent some time in Texas. Yet A.W. Tillinghast and Scotland's Donald Ross mostly made their reputations elsewhere. Pete Dye, Jack Nicklaus, Robert Trent Jones, Sr., and Ralph Plummer have created gems in Texas, yet still the state isn't considered among "the elite regions" in terms of world-class golf courses. So is Texas, known far and wide for producing great golfers, destined to lag behind in producing great golf courses?

Not at all. Texas has two enormous advantages on its side when it comes to golf course creation. First, it has space! As the price of prime real estate continues to soar all over the country, the Lone Star State has room to spare. Second, modern technology allows imaginative course architects to realize even their most far-fetched dreams. Hills can be built, groves of trees planted, streams re-routed, and waterfalls added. State-of-the-art irrigation systems keep fairways and greens lush, even under blistering Southwest sun.

The next chapter of truly inspired course design is being written right now. The Ambush Golf Course designed by Roy Bechtol and Randy Russell in

---

Lajitas is a marvel, and Tom Fazio's new Dallas National Golf Club, built at a cost of $30 million, will doubtless become one of the American golfing landmarks in short time. Designers like Jay Morrish, Bill Johnston, Robert Von Hagge, Bruce Devlin, Tom Weiskopf, and native son Ben Crenshaw are all bringing fresh new ideas to the state's golfing environment. Texas may be late to the party, but the next round is on us.

Gene Sarazen displays his fine form for spectators at Dallas Country Club.

TEXAS GOLF ROAD TRIPS

"Not a shred of evidence exists that wandering is irresponsible. One trip can change everything, and every trip should try."
Bruce Northam, Globetrotter Dogma

It's a clear spring morning. I am young, still on the optimistic side of 20. I wake up and find myself sprawled across the back seat of my Jeep, surrounded by golf clubs, guns, fishing gear, fast-food wrappers, empty beer bottles, and an old sleeping bag I evidently neglected to use. The jeep is moving—roaring, actually—down the highway at what feels like 80 miles an hour. Squinting painfully, I see the outline of my buddy's head against the yellow glow of sunrise, his hair whipping in the wind. One hand is on the wheel, the other tapping to the sound of Willie Nelson's "Red Headed Stranger" blaring out of the radio and infusing itself into the perfect blue Texas morning. I am not well. My head hurts, I have no idea where I am, I reek of strip joint perfume, and if I don't hit a restroom in the next 90 seconds, we're all doomed. Suddenly, it comes to me, a memory from the beer-soaked cellar of my brain, two words that answer all my unasked questions: road trip.

Five hours later, I felt lighter and livelier and we were another 300 miles down the road. At midday we pulled into a private Hill Country ranch with an impressive rock cabin and a 20-acre spring-fed bass lake. Over the next 14 hours we drank beer and caught lunkers under the warm spring sun, pausing only for quick hikes into the hills for glimpses of wild turkey or wandering Barbados sheep. We even worked in a quick 9-hole jaunt around the local goat track.

We had the place to ourselves until the arrival of the proprietors persuaded us to venture into the night. After glancing at a map we maneuvered our way through the clear cool night and rambling roads that weave through some of Texas' most beautiful terrain. Vanderpool, Leakey, Camp Wood, Barksdale, Rocksprings, Del Rio, Acuna. Yes, Acuna. As in Mexico. We were smart enough to pull over and ditch our gear behind a few big yuccas somewhere off an unmarked back dirt road. By then the binge was in its advanced stages. The neighboring country brought music, booze, dominoes, and even love into the equation, and we wrapped up our activities just in time to stumble upon a friendly local gang smashing out the Jeep's passenger-side window.

They ran and we got the hell out of Dodge. My partner passed out while I struggled to find our gear, so it figured it was my turn to drive. With the missing window the passing night was cold and loud, and the road back was dark and lonely except for all the deer. We lost the radiator to an attack deer, and luckily had enough juice to make it the last few miles to I-10. The wreck didn't even stir my buddy, and I couldn't wake him to let him know that I was hitch-

---

hiking into Kerrville for help. After a mile of jogging, a cross-country road-tripper in an old smoke-filled Trans Am took me that last few miles into Kerrville with James Brown blaring wildly as the sun climbed in the sky. Once we rounded up a tow service and made back to the Jeep, my traveling companion was nowhere to be found. We finally found him a hundred yards off the roadside curled up inside the sleeping bag in a ditch.

Golf and Travel in Texas

Everyone has their own idea of a good road trip, but the general idea is usually to get away completely and forget everything. The best trips have nothing to do with planning. It is in this spirit that we recommend a few golf excursions for you to consider.

Roads and Highways

Texas has America's largest highway system with more than 250,000 miles of roads and streets. Almost anywhere you go in Texas, the roads are well maintained. Even the farm and ranch roads are generally paved, well marked, and a great option if you're interested in getting off the beaten path.

Texas is as large as all of New England, New York, Pennsylvania, Ohio and North Carolina combined – the perfect place to explore. The state's area consists of 261,914 square miles of land and 5,363 square miles of water. Texas occupies about 7 percent of the total water and land area of the United States. Second in size among the states, Texas, according to the 1996 Statistical Abstract of the United States, has a land and water area of 267,277 square miles as compared with Alaska's 615,230 square miles. California, third largest state, has 158,869 square miles.

Length and Breadth of Texas

The longest straight-line distance in a general north-south direction is 801 miles from the northwest corner of the Panhandle to the extreme southern tip of Texas on the Rio Grande below Brownsville. The greatest east-west distance is 773 miles from the extreme eastward bend in the Sabine River in Newton County to the extreme western bulge of the Rio Grande just above El Paso

Both golf and traveling in Texas embrace the Zen-like notion that the journey itself, rather than the destination, is the thing. Texans have always been highly susceptible to the call of the open road. Texas is rich in diverse routes, unique cities, and outstanding golf courses. When you're in your car traveling down the open road, you have the independence to do whatever you want to do, see what you can see, and generally enjoy yourself.

★

I never rooted against an opponent, but I never rooted for him either. Arnold Palmer

The Rules

Some wise sage wrote that the best trips have nothing to do with planning, and it's absolutely true. Let your imagination run wild. Adventure is often synonymous with "expedition," and we sometimes mistakenly succumb to the idea that true adventures require preparation and planning.

There are few things in life more exhilarating than taking off on a road trip. Sometimes the solitude of the road is appropriate, while other times good company is preferred. The adventure begins when Plan A fails.

Money

In my own fantasy world, money is no object. I'd like to think that I can convince most of you to avoid financial issues altogether and focus on the task at hand: your golf adventure. You can' t always take this approach, but try it at least once. The game of golf transcends the concept of monetary value. Trust me, it all works out in the end. Some days you'll stumble across an unexpected jewel of a course, in perfect condition and surprisingly inexpensive. Other days you'll plan accordingly for your round at a top-flight course, only to discover that they've sanded the greens and their promotional message quotes a golf writer who was paid off three years ago: "Rated the best public daily fee course in Texas." It's all in the experience and you'll never enjoy it if you're worried about every dime you spend in your golf adventures. Go ahead, you have my permission to indulge yourself a little. Buy yourself a shirt in the pro shop. Spend a little extra on the premium imported beers. Get a little loose with your partners and challenge them to a substantial wager. Tip the cart girl too much and write it off to the pleasure of seeing such an attractive girl. Splurge a little and enjoy yourself. Life is too short to do otherwise.

POSSIBLE TEXAS GOLF ROAD TRIPS

To set the mood, here a just a few random ideas to get your brain-pan working on the possibilities of golf and travel in Texas. The hardcore details of these cities and courses can be found in one of the eight regional chapters that follow this page. You've got the entire state, an unbelievable highway system, generally outstanding weather, and the always handy Southwest Airlines to help you hop from one side of the state to the other when it's affordable and convenient.

The Big Country Loop

Seven 9-hole courses on a 160 miles round trip excursion. Haskell, Stamford, Anson, Hamlin, Rotan, Jayton, and Aspermont all await the restless golfer just north of Abilene. This one keys off of the small-town experience,

---

My worst day on the golf course still beats my best day in the office. John Hallsey

with the largest population totaling only 3,500 folks. Get ready for Dairy Queen, friendly people, and wide-open blue Texas skies.

Hill Country Triangle

Outline this route on your map and fantasize about the road trip possibilities. Austin, Kyle, San Marcos, New Braunfels, San Antonio, Comfort, Fredericksburg, back to Austin, and all points in between; a total of 230 miles if you push this one round trip. Take a look at what lies in the middle of the triangle: hard core hill country roads, historic, small-town cities, bed and breakfasts, and dance-hall beer joints galore. If your home base is Austin or San Antonio, you're always relatively close to home in case of a legitimate business responsibility that requires your presence.

Random High Plains Fandango

Get to Lubbock and use that as your home base (see Southwest Airlines), then make a point to play as many small town 9 hole tracks that you can work in during your stay. The Panhandle region serves up an impressive 38 nine holers and some of the most affordable golf in Texas.

High Plains Bermuda Triangle Golf Challenge

This one is for the remote-minded. Get away from it all and mosey up to the one of the most remote areas of Texas. The thriving metropolises of Muleshoe, Farwell, Friona form the equivalent of golf's Bermuda Triangle (73 miles round trip), where you can escape and have golf-fun without the crowds.

East Bound and Down Shreveport Golf Orgy

From Dallas, hit I-20 east towards Shreveport, LA, the Las Vegas of the south, and make it a point to hit the small-town courses within easy range of the interstate. Towns like Canton, Lindale, Mineola, Big Sandy, Gladewater, Kilgore, Marshall, Longview, etc. all offer Northeast Texas golf at its finest. Huge pine trees, the lush conditions of the Piney Woods, and terrain that will make you feel like you're next door to Augusta National.

The Gulf Coast Golf Trail

Take your state map along with this book and circle the golf towns of the Texas Riviera. All told there are 367 miles of Texas surf and plenty of golf along the way. Fly to the tip of Texas and start off on Texas' southernmost course, the outstanding South Padre Island Golf Club, then work your way up through Corpus Christi to Portland's unbelievable country club, then Rockport, Port Lavaca, Palacios, Freeport, Galveston, and eventually Orange.

★

Long ago I learned that no put is short enough to take for granted. Bobby Jones

Texas Regional Map

WEST TEXAS
REGIONAL WEATHER

	Average Precipitation	Average Temperature (F)
January	0.4	42.5
February	0.62	47.1
March	0.58	55.7
April	0.83	64.6
May	1.98	72.8
June	1.55	79.6
July	1.7	82
August	1.69	80.8
September	2.62	73.3
October	1.74	64
November	0.69	52.6
December	0.56	44.6

WEST TEXAS

Flat land, open skies, and empty spaces. The West Texas hori-zon dwarfs the low-slung mountain ranges that litter the landscape. Nowhere else does a cold front look as ominous as one that is bearing down on the West Texas plains. The air is dusty, sensual, sweltering, and refreshing in this phenomenal climate, where most cities boast over 300 days of sunshine per year. If you believe that the dry desert heat is more bearable than the humidity that dominates other regions of Texas, the 100-degree summer days here aren't so bad.

Out here you'll find some of the most remote golf courses in the world. West Texas is "off the beaten path" at its finest, and since no one has covered these courses, few people know about them.

The golf map in West Texas consists of 27 cities, 51 courses, and upwards of 740 golf holes. Of the region's 29 counties, six do not have golf courses. Of the 51 courses you could possibly play, a number of general statements apply to the game in West Texas.

For one, the winds change the game drastically. You could tee off after sun-rise on a March morning and experience only a slight breeze on the first few holes, only to be bombarded by 30-40 mph winds for the remainder of the round. The West Texas winds, much like in the Panhandle, dominate the game in this region.

For the smaller facilities, your green fee allows you to play all day. Because of the simple layouts and lack of championship courses that are so prevalent in the big cities, West Texas is where the average golfer has the opportunity for career-low rounds. When playing golf out here, expect to find firm, dry fair-ways that roll, short courses, sometimes higher elevations that add distance to your shots, a lack of bunkers and water hazards, and generally old-school, basic tracks.

Some courses are long (Midland Country Club), and there is the rare excep-tion of an extremely difficult course (Quicksand in San Angelo), but for the most part you'll play at least a few strokes higher than your handicap.

One of the true highlights of any West Texas golf tour should be the wild 9-hole courses scattered across the open plains. Towns like McCamey, Big Lake, Iraan, and Kermit generally have only a few thousand residents and mostly seem more like living ghost towns than active communities. Drive through Rankin at 4 p.m. on a sweltering August afternoon, or ramble through Crane in the dead of winter, and you'll be able to taste the loneliness.

We've provided information about non-golf activities for every golf destina-tion, but expect most of these towns to be short breaks in the midst of a big-ger golf adventure. Yes, it's possible to relax and enjoy your after-round

---

The cardinal principle of all golf shot-making is that if you move your head,
you ruin body action. Tommy Armour

festivities in Big Lake (pop. 2,752), but you're probably better off stopping at the Town & Country for burritos and beer to-go before heading on down the road to your next destination. The beauty of playing the game in West Texas is that you don't have to fight the crowds and time seems to move at a slower pace. You notice wildlife you wouldn't see on a high-dollar city course. The fees are unbelievably cheap. The highways are desolate and you can hop from town to town on a golf adventure like no other.

In certain respects, you can compare West Texas golf to the European links-style philosophies that date back 500 years–not necessarily in the traditional sense of seaside terrain with high grasses and rolling hills, but at least in the notion that golf requires a spirit of improvisation. In the small towns spread across the region, the courses are not perfectly manicured. You hit whatever shot is required, not the shot you want. The game is characterized by severe winds that require a different type of shot and small, elevated, fast greens. Much like the European golfer who accepts the winds as something that intensifies the flavor of the game, the West Texas golfer accepts and deals with his surroundings.

West Texas golf means crusty codgers who've been hardened by the dry heat and wind. Hustlers who wouldn't think of stepping onto a course without their bottle of Crown Royal, cooler of cold beer, and packs of Marlboro Reds. Wrangler jeans instead of golf slacks. Old velour 1950s golf bags. Ancient, no-name clubs with grips as thick as a baseball bat. Carrying a pistol to protect yourself while searching for errant golf balls in mesquite fields littered with rattlers. West Texas golf is coaching shorts instead of Bermudas. It's the untucked Western-style golf shirt. Ranchers who wear boots with spikes. Cussing, spitting, gambling, farting. Accents so unique that the vernacular could be considered its very own language. West Texas is a world of its own, and so is the golf.

The Ambush at Lajitas' No. 11, which plays across the Rio Grande into Mexico.

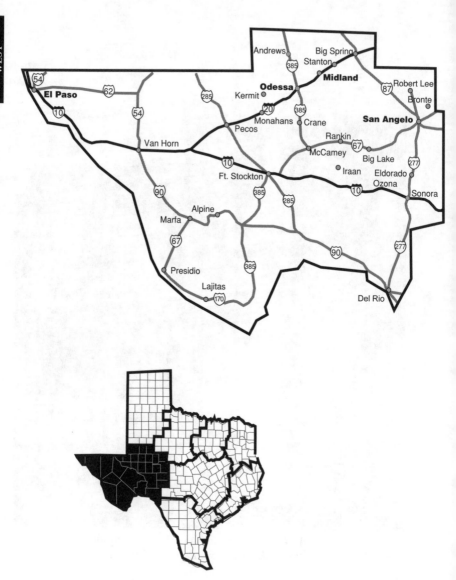

West Texas Mileage Chart

From \ To	Alpine	Andrews	Big Lake	Big Spring	Bronte	Crane	Del Rio	El Paso	Eldorado	Fort Stockton	Iraan	Kermit	Lajitas	Marfa	McCamey	Midland	Monahans	Odessa	Ozona	Pecos	Presidio	Rankin	Robert Lee	San Angelo	Sonora	Stanton
Andrews	173																									
Big Lake	155	120																								
Big Spring	202	63	76																							
Bronte	258	153	103	90																						
Crane	117	66	61	164	209																					
Del Rio	204	271	152	227	188	209																				
El Paso	216	264	327	327	404	279	419																			
Eldorado	203	187	61	131	77	128	111	375																		
Fort Stockton	62	117	93	143	196	55	185	234	141																	
Iraan	124	49	120	145	50	159	296	195	79	62																
Kermit	127	46	104	180	67	258	225	229	173	50	103															
Lajitas	95	117	284	283	242	288	144	108	88	81	229	133														
Marfa	26	190	364	303	269	280	108	229	46	29	213	144	72													
McCamey	107	181	233	143	303	195	88	65	23	284	189	110	55	133												
Midland	163	47	180	67	230	288	144	81	217	133	189	55	140	119	38											
Monahans	108	42	115	45	235	242	173	50	133	65	20	53	79	93	36	74										
Odessa	143	69	150	51	229	188	108	103	46	29	88	45	84	83	45	119	140	133								
Ozona	168	34	21	188	280	144	173	50	84	163	274	194	169	92	79	192	228	254	159							
Pecos	99	161	110	341	47	107	50	163	48	220	96	79	38	74	133	155										
Presidio	85	95	114	100	52	114	96	93	92	140	159	155	88													
Rankin	126	249	208	238	205	193	52	209	96	48	220	248	192	228	254	211	130	99	32	66						
Robert Lee	256	96	76	289	288	147	114	203	59	193	50	19	55	77	62	70	109	196	341	97	283	281				
San Angelo	225	141	343	202	249	193	209	50	220	19	59	152	19	158	123	112	204	289	106	73	97	105	260			
Sonora	203	149	287	343	205	288	52	114	203	274	194	229	75	168	34	194	267	182	150	200						
Stanton	182	197	240	133	76	238	193	52	96	48	79	53	75	40	114	112	105									
Van Horn	100	54	137	208	100	205	259	118	180	136	184	74	164	181	125	161	225	88	133	182	283	281	260	150	200	

ALPINE

Elev. 4,481   Pop. 5,488

Located in the foothills of the Davis Mountains in northwest Brewster County, this mountain town is sometimes referred to as the "Alps of Texas" and is unquestionably the region's cultural hot spot. Alpine is the seat of Brewster County, a vast mountainous area of 5,935 square miles that's the largest county in Texas and larger than the state of Connecticut.

Originally named Osborne, the town began in 1882 when railroad workers set up camp along a small spring-fed creek at the foot of what is known today as "A" Mountain. To gain control of the springs as a source of water for steam engines, the railroad negotiated a deal with the Murphy family and changed the name to Murphyville. By 1888 the town consisted of three saloons, a hotel and boarding house, livery stable, butcher shop, drug store, and post office. Thankfully the residents petitioned to change the name to Alpine.

Today's Alpine is the hub of a huge ranching area, home to Sul Ross State University, and a jumping-off point for excursions into Big Bend National Park. Recent growth has been fueled by an influx of affluent retired people who take advantage of Alpine's ranking as one of the 50 safest and most economical places for retirement in the United States. The climate and remote location make Alpine a popular vacation spot.

ALPINE COUNTRY CLUB

The golf   The Alpine CC is a charming 9-hole course that is routed around the pesky Kokernut Creek, which doesn't have much water in it. But the club is surrounded by a Grand Canyon-esque gorge that sucks in golf balls like a magnet.

This short course dates back to the 1940s and is highlighted by its greens, which are extremely small, dome-shaped, and in superb condition. Their unique shape means that no matter where they cut the hole, you'll never have a simple pin placement. The key is being aware that your bail-out area is always short of the green, enabling a chip from below the hole rather than from the side or behind the green. Chip shots that are close to being perfect, but not quite there, will skim by the hole and roll down off the green, often into a bunker, leaving a more pitiful predicament out of the sand.

No. 1 hits over the creek and plays straight away to the first mounded green. First-timers are more likely to struggle with the par 5 No. 3, since it's impossible to determine how to negotiate the creek and its surrounding gorge. Lay it up close and be ready to hit a solid second shot to carry it. Holes 7 and 8 offer back-to-back par 3s, with No. 8 being a tad bit better because it plays more downhill to a challenging target. No. 9 is the perfect finishing hole–a tight fairway lined by danger, playing into a larger green with tons of subtle undulations.

Much of the charm comes from the natural-rock clubhouse that sits below the hills and beside the wide Kokernut Creek bed. In those hills to the east lie a few interesting houses that overlook the course.

★

Continuing to trust your stroke as you practice is part
of the discipline you must learn. Dr. Bob Rotella

Alpine's pro shop is closet-sized but functional, offering only the basic amenities and cold beers for $1.50. The bar next door has a rowdy edge to it that must be experienced by any traveling golfer.

The details   915-837-2752. 1601 N. Loop Rd., Alpine, TX 79830.

- 1947. Par 35. Back – 2,788 (33.7/115). Forward – 2,135 (34.3/109). Price - $.

Getting there The clubhouse is located on Loop 223 (North Harrison St.), which intersects East Ave. E. (US 90) and Texas 118 (heading toward Fort Davis). The clubhouse and course are clearly visible from Loop 223 to the west.

ALPINE NOTES   If your timing is right, catch a baseball game at historic **Kokernut Field**, which sits on the banks of the creek of the same name and is adjacent to the golf course. Or explore the craggy West Texas mountains 26 miles south on TX 118, where the **Elephant Mountain Wildlife Management Area** offers six-mile drive-through tours that give you the chance to see the rare desert bighorn sheep. **The Reata** gets the headlines with its fancy Southwestern cuisine, but the savvy traveler joins the locals at **La Casita** for tasty Mexican food. If staying, go old-school funky at the 1912 **Holland Hotel**, where the fourth-floor penthouse sports a rooftop deck. Don't forget your earplugs: the train rolls by all night long.

ANDREWS
Elev. 3,190   Pop. 9,617

Andrews, the seat of Andrews County, was founded around 1908 and named after Richard Andrews, the first man to die in the war for Texas independence. The only town in Andrews County, this community of 10,000 sits on Hwy. 385 in the mesquite-dotted oil fields 34 miles north of Odessa. Andrews has survived the ups and downs of the oil industry, spurred originally by the Deep Rock Oil Company's first area strike in 1929. Luckily for locals and residents of nearby towns such as Midland and Odessa, Andrews is home to an excellent 18-hole West Texas layout.

ANDREWS COUNTY GOLF COURSE

The golf Don't be misled by the isolated rural location of this small-town municipal golf course. The par 70, 6,064-yard layout, designed by Warren Cantrell in 1955, is a hidden gem in the west Texas oilfields. With mature trees lining the somewhat narrow fairways, fast greens in superb condition (with the exception of problems in 2001 that have since been resolved), and water in play on over half of the holes, it's a challenging test of golf.

Let your attitude determine your golf game.
Don't let your golf game determine your attitude. Davis Love, Jr.

With only two par 5s, the course is enjoyable for the average hack because of its short length. Out-of-bounds comes into play on eight holes due to the boundaries of the course's driving range and the town's airport. The front nine is highlighted by a dicey par 3. Ladies play to par 72 and do not get much of an advantage on most holes due to the proximity of the differing tees.

Like other West Texas municipals, the fairways are susceptible to the lack of rain as well as the extensive use of carts; therefore, the fairways are sometimes a little beaten-down and dry. The advantage is that your ball will roll farther on what is already a short course.

Overall, a good value course. Locals praise the service of the club since Jerod Lee took over operations a few years back. The pro shop is small but has a decent selection of clubs and accessories.

The details 915-524-1462. 920 Golf Course Rd., Andrews, TX 79714.

- 1955. Warren Cantrell. 18 holes. Back – 6,300. Par 70 (68.9/116). Forward – 5,331. Par 72 (69.7/116). Price - $$.

Getting there Heading north on 385, turn left at Big Springs Hwy. Take the Broadway exit and turn right on Mustang Dr. The course is just down the road.

ANDREWS NOTES If you don't grab a bite at the course, your best options are **Grumpy's BBQ** (915-523-4125) for sliced beef, or **Buddy's Drive-In** (915-523-2840), where the steak fingers have become world famous. If you must stay, there are a few local motels, but you're better off heading back to Midland or Odessa. For kicks head 37 miles northwest to **Eunice, New Mexico** and play the desert-like 9-hole municipal course.

BIG LAKE
Elev. 2,678   Pop. 2,752

Named after what was once a water-filled depression that was the only fresh water between the Concho River and Comanche Springs in Fort Stockton, Big Lake is on Texas 137 and US 67 in south-central Reagan County. The town was originally established for the arrival of the railroad, but boomed in 1923 with the nearby discovery of oil on land owned by the University of Texas (whose subsequent revenues made it one of the richest universities in the country). Throughout the oil booms over the years, Big Lake has established itself as a supply town for the local oil industry.

★

In golf, as in other sports, youth is a great helper, but if you cannot start at three, or twelve, or even thirty-five, start at forty-five or fifty. Remember that it's better to have golfed and foozled than never golfed at all. Jerome Travers

BIG LAKE COUNTRY CLUB

The golf This semi-private 9-hole "country club" is a hacker's dream in terms of difficulty with flat, wide fairways, no water, no bunkers, and a short layout.

The wind and rugged conditions can get you, but the highlight of this facility is not the golf course–it's the other golfers you'll share the experience with. There's something special about playing the great game with an oilman who's sporting a six-beer buzz, spitting tobacco, sipping on whiskey, and teaching you the art of profanity and golf.

Pay once and play all day. There are two sets of tees for a different look the second time around. Refrain from outfitting yourself in the big-city garb of khakis and a polo, as the locals could be wearing Wrangler jeans, multi-colored Western shirts (if at all), and either cowboy boots or tennis shoes.

The details 915-884-2623. W. Hwy. 67, Big Lake, TX 76932

• Par 36. Back – 2,848 (32.8/95). Forward – 2,245 (33.8/99). Price - $.

Getting there Take Hwy. 67 west out of Big Lake.

BIG LAKE NOTES Before you load up at the local convenience store and take the scenic drive to the town of Ozona, TX take a look at the **1927 Reagan County Courthouse**, built of brick in the Texas Renaissance Style. The ghost town of **Stiles** still sports the remnants of the 1904 courthouse that was gutted by fire on Christmas Eve in 1999. Also find Santa Rita No. 1 13 miles west of town, just south of 67 on FM 1675–the most famous remnant of the oil boom.

BIG SPRING

Elev. 2,397 Pop. 25,477

On a warm west Texas night with the right music and perhaps a few beers to facilitate the appropriate mood, you might consider Big Spring a picturesque town. After all, it was founded in 1882 at the source of the historic springs that provided life-sustaining water for settlers and Indians traveling across the dry country. The 15-story Settles Hotel dominates the skyline, just as it did when Jon Voight was here for Midnight Cowboy. And the flat cotton fields that surround the town actually do have a few elevation changes, some of which impact the two 18-hole golf courses located south of town.

BIG SPRING COUNTRY CLUB

The golf Big Spring's country club is an 18-hole private course that dates back to the early 1960s. Its design features open fairways that are flat and easy

---

I have not the slightest hesitation in saying that beauty means a great deal on a golf course; even a man who emphatically states that he does not care a hang for beauty is subconsciously influenced by his surroundings. Dr. Alister Mackenzie

to walk, and offer the chance to shoot a career-low round. Water hazards are not predominant but do come into play on a few holes. The greens are considered fast, and as always out here, wind can be an issue when it's howling 20-30 mph.

The details   915-267-5354. East Driver Rd., Big Spring, TX 79721

* 1960. Back – 6,920 (71/117). Middle – 6,156 (69/113). Forward – 5,455 yards. Price - $$.

Getting there The course is located south of town on US 87. Turn left on Driver Rd.

COMANCHE TRAIL GOLF COURSE

The golf   Comanche Trail boasts that it's the only "rolling hills" course in West Texas. Nestled in the hills just south of town, this course has tight, hilly fairways and bent grass greens. Given the variations in elevation, it is actually quite scenic compared to other courses in this region. No. 7 is the signature hole, a 537-yard, par 5 that features a great view of the entire back nine.

Just a word of caution regarding the opinion of some golfers we talked to in Big Spring. While some were satisfied with the course, others complained of the value, stating that the green fee is overpriced considering the condition. One golfer complained of dry fairways, the poor shape of the greens, roots sprouting on greens, and rocks throughout the course.

The details   915-264-2366. 800 Comanche Park Rd., Big Spring, TX 79720

* 1934. 18 holes. Par 71. Back – 6,327 (69.8/112). Middle – 6,014 (68.4/109). Forward – 5,098 (66.1/101). Price - $$.

Getting there Located south of town on US 87. Take the Comanche Trail Park exit and follow the signs to the course.

BIG SPRING NOTES   Grab breakfast before your round at **Herman's Restaurant** (915-267-3281). **The Carlos Restaurant and Bar** (915-267-9141) is a West Texas tradition, offering excellent, basic Mexican food and cold beer. If it's too crowded find **Casa Blanca Restaurant** (915-263-1162). One of West Texas' best examples of Victorian architecture, the **Potton House** (1901) is on 2nd St. and Gregg. Your best bet for lodging is the **Best Western** (915-267-1601) on Hwy. 87.

BRONTE

Elev. 1,893   Pop. 1,057

Located just north of San Angelo on US 277 at its junction with Texas 158 in east central Coke County, Bronte was founded in the late 1880s and named for the English novelist Charlotte Brontë. Bronte is something of a retirement village, popular for its laid-back demeanor. Downtown houses the historic Texas Theatre and a few quaint shops.

SINGING WINDS GOLF COURSE

The golf   Singing Winds is a 9-hole public course set in the rolling terrain on the edge of West Texas. This is a short course with tree-lined fairways, no bunkers, and small greens. The signature hole is No. 6, a 185-yard par 3 over water.

If you catch this track during dry conditions, the fairways might be brown, but the grass is good enough to give you a good lie. Use your irons and keep it in the fairway, because the rough is hard-panned dirt and rocks.

The details   915-473-2156. E. Oliver, Bronte, TX 76933

- 1960. 9 holes. Par 36. Back – 2,896 (34.1/118). Forward – 2,330 (33.1/107). Price - $.

Getting there Located on Hwy. 277 halfway between Abilene and San Angelo. Look for the signs to the course.

BRONTE NOTES   Ten miles north of Bronte on US 277 lies the **Fort Chadbourne Cemetery**, established in 1852 but abandoned in 1867 when troops were transferred to nearby Fort Concho. **Lake Spence** is nearby, as is the ghost of the former Oak Creek Lake, which has, sadly, been sucked dry. Drive by it and envision the old lake filled with water and lunker fish. For eats look to **Hidalgo's** for Mexican Food, or the **Town & Country** for hamburgers. You might also check on the **BBQ Barn**, although it's not always open.

CRANE

Elev. 2,555   Pop. 2,961

The town of Crane (est. 1908) sits on US 385 and Texas 329 due south of Odessa. Named for former Baylor University president William C. Crane, it's the only town in the county. The discovery of oil in the 1920s spurred the development of the town, and Crane has served as a service center for the region's oil industry ever since. Crane is desolate, lonely, and just plain ugly. The wind blows hard and the outskirts of town are scattered with oilfield supplies.

Like other nearby oil boomtowns (Rankin, McCamey, Iraan, and Big Lake), Crane is home to a 9-hole golf course that serves the local community.

Golf is a game with the soul of a 1956 Rotarian. Bill Mandel

WEST

CRANE COUNTRY CLUB

The golf   "CCC" is another simple, semi-private, small-town golf course that features wide-open fairways, no water, and tiny "postage stamp" greens that are generally surrounded by bunkers. Unless your approach is perfect, your short game needs to be on in order to get up-and-down on these small, humpbacked greens. The most difficult hole is No. 5 (193 yards, par 3), where the wind can render it almost impossible to get the ball to land on the very small green.

The details   915-558-2651. 230 Golf Course Rd., Crane, TX 79731

• 1956. 9 holes. Par 36. Back – 3,092. Forward – 2,550. Price - $.

Getting there The course is 2.5 miles north of town on Hwy. 385.

CRANE NOTES   Check out **Horsehead Crossing** 7 miles south of town–it was once the only logical low-water crossing of the Pecos River for Indians and cattle herds. You'll get a feel for the desolate nature of the land thinking about hundreds of horse and mule skulls lying around as a result of animals drinking water too quickly. Before you leave town, try **Big Deal Burritos** (915-558-3445) for greasy, gas-inducing burritos to-go.

DEL RIO

Elev. 948   Pop. 34,631

Del Rio lies in the arid vastness of southwest Texas, and has a unique character based on its ranching and agricultural heritage, the nearby military base, and a reputation as a spunky border town. The seat of Val Verde County, the town sits on US 90 at the confluence of the Rio Grande River and San Felipe Creek.

As you might expect, Del Rio is not the golf hotbed of the state. We recommend that your golf experiences out here be approached as sideline activities to break up the other adventurous possibilities. Most come here for the water recreation and Ciudad Acuna. The western, desert-like beauty of Lake Amistad is the closest thing to Utah's Lake Powell that you'll find just about anywhere other than Nevada or Arizona. And the state's purest river, the Devil's River, offers wild river trips and outstanding fly fishing, particularly for small-mouth bass.

It can be hard to make time for golf in Del Rio when you're tempted by the lure of a day on the water followed up by lurid excursions across the border. However, the golf aficionado might be intrigued by the John Bredemus-designed 9-hole San Felipe Country Club or the 18-hole Leaning Pines Golf Course.

You can't take a car from a dead start and put it immediately up to 70 miles an hour. No matter how powerful your engine, you must have a gradual acceleration of speed. So it is in a golf swing. Mickey Wright

WEST TEXAS GHOST COURSE

Somewhere south of Sheffield, TX near the Pecos River lies the old Joe Chandler's Guest Ranch, which is now known as the Chandler Ranch and no longer is open to the public. The ranch primarily serves hunters now, but back in the day, possibly 20-30 years ago, a 9-hole golf course served as the centerpiece of this dude ranch/B&B getaway. Remnants of the course are barely visible now, but you can see where people once tried to farm the flat river bottoms of the Pecos. This dry, rugged country, not too far northwest of Del Rio, features spectacular terrain highlighted by the spring-fed Independence Creek that runs through the property. It must have been fun to hack away on what was surely a unique, entertaining desert-like course.

LEANING PINE GOLF COURSE

The golf   Laid out on the grounds of Laughlin Air Force Base, this is long compared to other 9-hole courses in the region, and is generally open for play only to the military. Despite the "private" classification, it's worth a shot to place a friendly call to the pro shop and enquire about working your way onto the course.

Leaning Pine has two sets of tees if you're interested in playing 18 holes. On this fairly wide-open course, there are a few trees that can affect play, and the course has four water holes, two of which require shots over the hazards. Grass and sand bunkers dot the course.

The details   830-298-5451, Bldg. 494, Laughlin AFB, Del Rio, TX 78840

• 1964. 9 holes. Back – 3,181 (35.6/115). Forward - 2,778 yards. Price - $.

Getting there Located on the grounds of Laughlin Air Force Base 7 miles east of Del Rio off of Hwy. 90.

SAN FELIPE COUNTRY CLUB

The golf   Designed by the legendary John Bredemus (Fort Worth's Colonial CC), San Felipe is a semi-private course despite its country club label. It's named after the San Felipe Springs, which give life to the San Felipe River that runs through most of this 9-hole track. This course has tight, narrow fairways lined with trees, and bunkers that test your shot-making ability. Your short game needs to be solid because most approaches will be into small

It is much too large a subject to go into the question of the placing of hazards,
but I would like to emphasize a fundamental principle. It is that no hazard
is unfair wherever it is placed. Alister Mackenzie

greens, and a slight miss will require an up-and-down for par.

The details   830-775-3953. Hwy. 90 East, Del Rio, TX 78841

- 1930. John Bredemus. Back – Par 36. 2,988 (34.5/116). Ladies – Par 35. 2,318 (34.6/119). Price - $.

Getting there Two miles east of town on Hwy. 90.

DEL RIO NOTES   Work your golf around time on beautiful **Lake Amistad.** Stay at the **La Quinta** (830-775-7591), **1890 House B&B** (830-775-8061), or the enchanting **Villa Del Rio B&B** (830-768-1100) Cross the border to **Ciudad Acuna** for shopping, nightlife, and cold beers along the main avenue. Find the **Corona Club** in the late afternoon for domino matches with the locals. For dinner roll into either **Crosby's,** where the character of this 1930s joint goes well with the outstanding food, or **Lando's Restaurant and Bar,** which is a little more upscale. Depending on your mood and spiritual convictions, "Boys Town," Acuna's red-light district, is always an option for late-night debauchery.

EL PASO   Elev. 3,762 Pop. 615,032

As Texas' fourth-largest and westernmost city, located halfway between Houston and Los Angeles, El Paso offers so much for the avid golfer that it should probably be marketed more as a premier golf destination with the likes of Phoenix or San Antonio. Out here the desert offers over 300 days of sunshine per year, outstanding shopping, authentic Mexican food, impressively old historic sites, and plenty of adventures across the border.

Five public facilities with a total of 117 golf holes are available in El Paso, highlighted by the spectacular **Painted Dunes** course that is consistently ranked as one of the top public facilities in the state. The more connected golfer has the option of playing three quality private courses, with the famed **El Paso Country Club** heading the top of the list. However, a golf excursion to El Paso isn't complete without side trips to Las Cruces, NM and Juarez, Mexico, both of which offer outstanding golf for unbelievable values.

ASCARATE MUNICIPAL GOLF COURSE

The golf   Ascarate opened in 1958 and was the first solo project of George Hoffman, who moved to West Texas from New Jersey when his family bought a ranch. It has long been considered one of the toughest courses in El Paso. The 18-hole course is accompanied by the much easier 9-hole **Delta Nine Course,** which caters to beginners and overflow traffic.

★

A "weak" or "strong" grip is not about how tight you hold the club, but about where you place your hands on the handle. Whichever grip you use, be sure it fits the rest of your swing. Butch Harmon

The **Ascarate Course** is mostly flat with only sporadic mounding. The design features undulating greens, plenty of trees to get in the way, and water on six of nine holes on the back.

Two holes stand out on the front nine: The 415-yard No. 4, which requires a bomb of a tee shot to set up a decent approach into a narrow green, and No. 5, a 217-yard par 3 that plays downhill from an elevated tee.

On the back, No. 11 is a butt-pucker hole playing 190 yards over a lake, and Ascarate's signature hole is the long par 4 18th.

If you need to build your confidence or the Ascarate course is too crowded, the **Delta Nine Course** is the place to spend some time working on your game. A short course that still requires some accuracy, it is easy to walk and never too crowded.

The details 915-772-7381. 6900 Delta Dr., El Paso, TX 79905

- Ascarate Course: George Hoffman. 1958. 18 holes. Par 71. Back – 6,565 (69.4/114). Middle – 6,185 (67.7/110). Forward – 5,650 (66.2/107). Price - $$.

- Delta Nine Course: 2,677 yards. Par 36. Price - $.

Getting there From I-10, get on Throwbridge and follow it to Delta Dr.

CIELO VISTA MUNICIPAL GOLF COURSE

The golf Formally known as Del Norde Country Club, this basic, flat course has long been known as the easiest course in El Paso. This short lay-out features wide-open fairways, large bent-grass greens, and minimal bunkering and water hazards. Yet there are a few spots where scores can add up, as many of the fairways dogleg, and more than a few approaches offer minimal views of the green because of the trees that have been added over the years.

In terms of notable holes, the signature is the 435-yard par 4 No. 2, tough because of its length and approach into a narrow, multi-level green. Be ready for No. 11, a 575-yard par 5 that features a long dogleg left with loads of trouble along that side. Big hitters might be able to cut the corner on this hole. No. 18 features a lake in the corner of the dogleg left that impacts both the tee shot and approach on this 380-yard hole.

The details 915-591-4927. 1510 Hawkins Blvd., El Paso, TX 79925

- 1977. Marvin Ferguson. 18 holes. Par 71. Back – 6,505 (69.4/122). Middle – 6,126 (68.4/120). Forward – 5,421 (69.4/113). Price - $$.

Getting there Adjacent to the El Paso Airport. From I-10 heading east, exit Hawkins and drive north. The course is on the right side of the street.

I felt a fly on my chin. When I went to brush it off there was no fly. It was drool.
You know you're close to retirement when you can't swallow
your own saliva. Lee Trevino

CORONADO COUNTRY CLUB

The golf Located on the west side of the Franklin Mountains at an elevation of almost 4,000 feet, Coronado Country Club is a scenic course that offers panoramic views of Mexico, New Mexico, and Texas to the southeast. This course resembles the desert tracks of Arizona and features plush fairways and greens that are considered some of the fastest in the nation. In fact, pros have prepared for the Masters here, and Nike Tour events have been hosted despite the rather short layout.

The par 70 route features only two par 5s, but challenges with four par 4s over 400 yards, and a 212-yard par 3. While there are no water hazards, at least 14 out-of-bounds areas await wayward shots.

The details 915-584-3841. 1044 Broadmoor Dr., El Paso, TX 79912

- 1956. Marvin Ferguson. 18 holes. Par 70. Back – 6,485 (70.9/129). Middle – 6,142 (69.5/125). Forward – 5,404 (70.3/125). Price - $$.

Getting there Take the Sunland Park exit off of I-10 to Thunderbird Rd. Turn left on Thunderbird and drive to Broadmoor. Turn left and after a short distance, the clubhouse is on the right side of the road.

EL PASO COUNTRY CLUB

The golf The crown jewel of golf out here is the El Paso Country Club, with its old-school charm and a burgeoning reputation as a proving ground for future PGA stars. Built along the Rio Grande River, this course is the oldest in West Texas, dating back to 1910. It has gained recent acclaim since former employee Rich Beem burst onto the scene with his victory at the 2002 PGA Championship. The colorful tales of the Friday game at EPCC paint a vivid picture of how the former cell phone salesman honed his gamesmanship and confidence to the level of a major champion.

Tom Bendelow's original design was modified in 1920 by Jack Harden, then again via a $1.5 million Ron Fream renovation. The traditional layout is not long (6,781 yards), but requires pro-like accuracy on approach shots, and the bentgrass greens feature the speed and quickness characteristic of any pro setup.

No. 15 is the feature hole. It's a short par 4 that requires accuracy to avoid the fairway bunkers and trees off the tee, then a little savvy to deal with the approach shot into a super-slick green covered by more bunkers.

The details 915-584-0511. 5000 Country Club Place, El Paso, TX 79922.

- www.elpasocountryclub.com

- 1910. Tom Bendelow. Modified in 1920 by Jack Harden. Redesigned in 1984 by Ron Fream. 18 holes. Par 71. Back – 6,781 (72.2/130). Middle – 6,362 (70.3/126). Forward – 5,363 (71.1/122). Price - $$$.

Getting there From I-10 west take Exit 11 and make a left turn onto Mesa.

If you are in the woods, don't act like a seamstress. Your job is not to thread needles but to get the ball back into the fairway. Arnold Palmer

Drive over the railroad tracks, then turn left onto Country Club, which will lead you directly to the course.

EMERALD SPRINGS
RESORT & CONFERENCE CENTER

The golf   Emerald Springs is the place where Lee Trevino honed his trade in the big-money El Paso games of the 1960s. The layout winds through a housing community and features wide fairways and large, well-maintained greens.

No. 2 is the most interesting hole on the front: 450 yards lined by out-of-bounds on the left and water fronting the green. On the back, hole 13 is 463 yards with water on the right side of a dogleg right, and a green that slopes towards the water.

The club is currently entertaining ideas of adding 18 holes.

The details   915-852-9110. 16000 Ashford St., El Paso, TX 79928

- 1962. 18 holes. Par 70. Back – 6,759 (71.5/122). Middle – 6,032 (67.8/119). Forward – 4,896 (64.3/108). Price - $$.

Getting there From I-10 east, exit Horizon, then drive north to Ashford St. Turn left and you'll see the course on the right.

PAINTED DUNES DESERT GOLF COURSE

The golf   One of the only true desert-style golf courses in the state, this city-owned municipal is one of the most unusual golf courses in Texas. Set in the foothills of the Franklin Mountains and surrounded by native cacti and creosote bushes, Painted Dunes has received much well-deserved acclaim since its opening in 1991.

Ken Dye, of New Mexico's Paa-Ko Ridge and Pinon Hills design fame, set the course up with open areas off the tee, but ample mounding and fairway bunkers present problems. The hourglass fairways weave their way to multi-level greens. The approach shots are difficult, as a wayward iron often finds deep, penalizing bunkers or bounces precariously away from the target after creating the illusion of a perfectly executed golf shot.

Two par 3s stand out at Painted Dunes. Hole 2 on the West plays 173 yards over a pond and is tricky because of the obscured view from the tee, making club selection critical. Also on the West, No. 8 plays 149 yards into a large green guarded by water on the left side. A tough bunker looms for those considering the bail-out area. All par 5s are well over 500 yards. The most difficult hole might be the long, 446-yard No. 5.

Last but not least, the inexpensive aspect of Painted Dunes is its greatest asset. For $35 visitors can walk the course on the weekends (residents pay less), and using a cart is only $10 more.

Other notes: Painted Dunes has been ranked as high as 14th in the state by *Golf Digest,* including private facilities. The PGA Tour hosted their Q-School

---

⭐

It is an invariable rule that if you start the arms first—either at the beginning or at the top of the swing—the result is bad. Harry Vardon

tournament here from 1994-1996. In 1998 Painted Dunes opened a third nine designed by Jeff Brauer, allowing the popular course the flexibility to serve more golfers.

The details   915-821-2122. 12000 McCombs St., El Paso, TX 79934

- www.painteddunes.com

- 1991. Ken Dye. 18 holes. Par 72. Back – 6,925 (74.0/137). Middle – 6,497 (71.2/133). Forward – 5,717 (74.5/123). Price - $$.

- New North Nine: 3,460 yards. Par 36.

Getting there Located east of El Paso on 54E, 10 miles from I-10. Turn left on McCombs; the course is 1 mile farther on the right.

UNDERWOOD GOLF COMPLEX

The golf   Set on the grounds of Fort Bliss, Underwood sells itself as an affordable alternative to the other El Paso courses, as well as a place for the high handicapper to learn the game. This facility has two regulation 18-hole courses: the Sunset, a parkland-style track, and the Sunrise, a newer, desert-style course.

Sunset, built in 1957, is an easier, flat course, void of water hazards. The front nine is loaded with three par 5s over 500 yards, including the monster 574-yard No. 9. The back nine plays shorter with three par 3s and two par 5s. Hole 11 is the toughest par 4, a 452-yard dogleg right, but the other 4-pars are all under 400 yards.

Sunrise opened in April of 1995, bringing a more modern layout to the Underwood facility. Ken Dye (Painted Dunes) built the course as sort of a Scottish links/desert-style track with undulating fairways and a multitude of water hazards. Quite a bit of dirt was moved to sculpt the flat terrain.

On the front No. 5 stands out because it plays as a 465-yard par 4, but No. 9 is the most difficult because of its even greater length–a 587-yard par 5. Holes of note on the back are the 302-yard No. 11, which offers a great chance for birdie; another long par 4 in No. 13 (452 yards); and the mean 18th, a 441-yard dogleg right.

The details   915-562-1273. 3200 Coe Ave., El Paso 79904

- Sunrise – 1995. Ken Dye. 18 holes. Par 72. 6,942 yards. Gold (73.1/126), Blue (70.4/117), White (68.1/113), Red (71.1/124). Price - $$.

- Sunset – 18 holes. Par 72. Back – 6,629 (70.4/120). Middle – 6,328 (68.9/117). Forward – 5,531 (70.4/109). Price - $$.

Getting there Located off I-10 and Gateway. From I-10 east, take US Hwy. 54 north and exit Ellerthorpe. Turn right and drive down the road into the housing development, where you will eventually see the clubhouse.

✩

Real men don't use old balls on water holes. West Texas rancher

VISTA HILLS COUNTRY CLUB

The golf   Vista Hills is a private track built by Bruce Devlin and Robert von Hagge in 1973. This is a fairly long, desert-style course that winds through a residential subdivision with out-of-bounds lining narrow fairways on many holes. Some holes have slight elevation changes and can leave you with uneven lies.

Hole 4 offers a nice touch: a 384-yard par 4 with an outstanding view of El Paso and Mexico. The long No. 17 has out-of-bounds on either side of the fairway, and a water hazard 100 yards out from the green. At 450 yards even a big drive leaves you with a long approach. The 13th hole is only 307 yards and doglegs right, which tempts you to cut the corner over the apartments.

The details   915-592-6565. 2210 Trawood Dr., El Paso, TX 79935.

- 1973. Robert Van Hagge-Bruce Devlin. Par 72. Back – 7,032 (72.7/129). Middle – 6,608 (70.6/128). Forward – 5,398 (69.9/118). Closed Mondays. Price - $$.

Getting there Take the Lee Trevino exit off of I-10. Turn left, and make another left when you come to Trawood St. The clubhouse is on the left side of the street.

EL PASO NOTES There's always adventure to be had across the line in Juarez, Mexico. Take the downtown trolley, then start off in the bustling central market place. You can even golf at the immaculate **Campestre Juarez Country Club** (see "Border Crossings" at the end of the region). In El Paso the best barbecue in town is at **The State Line Bar-B-Q** (915-581-3371), where you'll get an entire loaf of bread with your generous portions, and **Aceitunas** is a dive with mariachis on spring and summer evenings. Also, **Cafe Central** (915-545-2233) has a cozy bar and a solid menu, and **La Nortena** (915-533-0533) features a great bar and items such as grilled quail and green chicken tamales. **Leo's Mexican Food Restaurant** (915-544-1001), a downtown establishment since the 1940s, has a bustling scene for breakfast and lunch. If you're heading north towards New Mexico for golf, stop off in Canutillo, TX for flautas and gorditas at the **Little Diner** (915-877-2176). Finally for lodging: The **Camino Real** (915-534-3000) downtown is as good as it gets, and the **Marriott** (915-779-3300) and Hilton (915-778-4241) at the airport aren't far behind. For a B&B experience look to the **Sunset Heights B&B** (915-544-1743).

ELDORADO   Elev. 2,410   Pop. 1,977

The seat of Schleicher County and its only town, Eldorado was established in 1895. This scrubby little West Texas town is scenic and rugged, perched on the edge of the Texas hill country 45 miles south of San Angelo–it's a remote

---

place that you'll most likely experience passing through to your final destination. Eldorado is a center for oil field service and supply firms, headquarters for a large ranching area (sheep and goats), and a popular spot to hunt white-tailed deer.

ELDORADO GOLF CLUB

The golf   This unique course is highlighted by five par 3s and small greens, making this a great place to work on your short game. Known for its excellent condition, the fairways are plush and the greens and tees are always in great shape. You will only need your driver if you're planning on trying to drive the short par 4s; otherwise, play your irons off the tee. The only par 5 (hole 3) plays just 464 yards. There is no water on the course. The price is right, and you can pay once and play all day. Use the second set of tees for an 18-hole round.

The details   915-853-2036. Hwy. 109, Eldorado, TX 76936

- 1965. 9 holes. Par 32. Back – 2,104. Forward – 1,766. Price - $.

Getting there Head south through town on Hwy. 277 until you reach Hwy. 109. Turn right, proceed one block, then turn right and drive three blocks to the course. Look for signs.

ELDORADO NOTES If you're killing time, visit the **Schleicher County Museum** and check out the rustic paraphernalia from the early ranching communities. If lunch is a priority, **Granny Netts BBQ** (915-853-3830) will do you right. The **X Bar Ranch** (915-853-2688) offers accommodations, hiking, ranch tours, and stargazing.

FORT STOCKTON   Elev. 2,954   Pop. 7,693

Fort Stockton dates back to the 1850s, when the US Army established a fort on the banks of the Comanche Creek to protect settlers and travelers from Indians.

Unless you live in the general vicinity, you will most likely experience Fort Stockton driving through on your way to Big Bend National Park. You can sense the transition into the differing terrain to the southwest; the city sits at the northern edge of the Chihuahuan Desert at an elevation of almost 3,000 feet. This is a sunny climate, with temperatures above 90 degrees an average of 127 days per year, but the desert setting and elevation result in cool nights.

The economy of Fort Stockton is primarily based upon oil and gas production, ranching, and farming.

WEST

PECOS COUNTY MUNICIPAL GOLF COURSE

The golf   Although you wouldn't expect many PGA Tour professionals to come from this region, Blaine McCallister, whose course record 61 scorecard sits prominently displayed in the pro shop, honed his game here and has proved his mettle on tour.

This traditional West Texas course is well maintained. There are mature trees, but they're spread out enough to allow the wind to be a major factor. The 18-hole layout looked quite lush during our visit on a 95-degree September day at the end of a summer of drought conditions.

Although not too terribly long, the course has several water hazards that front greens, and the bent-grass greens are triple-tiered and easy to three-putt.

For its location, this course is well kept and if you stay in the fairways, grass isn't a problem. The layout requires decent length on your shots, but it is a good test overall.

The details   915-336-2050. N. Hwy. 285 Airport Rd., Fort Stockton, TX 79735.

- 18 holes. Par 72. Back - 6,186. Middle – 6,544 (70.8/114). Forward – 4,949 (68.5/98). Price - $$.

Getting there From I-10 west, exit N. Hwy. 285 and head straight to the course.

FORT STOCKTON NOTES It's easy to burn daylight in this historic town. Venture to old downtown and check out the old **Grey Mule Saloon** (just a building now), then mosey toward the myriad of historic buildings, including the **Annie Riggs Museum**. Work your schedule for a chips and salsa session at **Sarah's Cafe** (915-336-7700), where you'll get a feel for the cafe's long history by reading the framed articles that line the walls. Enjoy the sunset while driving south to **Marathon, TX** for a night at the **Gage Hotel**, the perfect jumping-off point for a road trip to Big Bend National Park.

IRAAN   Elev. 2,590   Pop. 1,350

Iraan is a remote, clean-looking little town at the intersection of US 190 and Texas 349, not far from the Pecos River in eastern Pecos County. The town was born when oil was discovered on the ranch of Ira Yates. A contest was held to name the town, and the genius who combined the name of Ira and his wife Ann won a town lot as a prize. Iraan is a close-knit community that takes pride in their youth and enjoys their "spectacular" 9-hole golf course.

⭐

It sometimes makes sense to play aggressively, but it always makes good sense to play smart. Jim Flick

WEST

IRAAN GOLF CLUB

The golf   Iraan is isolated, and you won't generally pass through here on the way to somewhere else. Even so, we recommend that you make a special trip here to play one of the gems of West Texas golf. An oasis in an otherwise desolate place, it's in outstanding condition for a small-town course. We heard of a group of about 15 San Antonio golfers who annually make the pilgrimage to Iraan for a one-week, nonstop golf orgy. The course must be good to warrant a week in a West Texas oil town of 1,300 where your amenities consist of the trailer park up the road! Another benefit was the surprisingly fast pace of play by the locals.

The very clean club house sells cold beers for $1.25. Call ahead to ensure course availability. They were having a cross-country meet on the course the Saturday we were there, and the course did not open until they were finished.

The details   915-639-8892. W. Hwy. 349, Iraan, TX 79744

• 1950. 9 holes. Back – 3,122 (33.8). Forward – 2,617 (33.6). Price - $.

Getting there Located off Hwy. 349 on the north side of the road.

IRAAN NOTES   You must eat at **Yulebebak's Bar B Q** at the main intersection in town. The sliced beef sandwich was truly the best we've ever had. The iced tea was cold, crisp, and very tasty. When we asked where everyone went for a cold beer, the answer was the golf course. And the drive to McCamey, TX is surprisingly scenic. Take US 190 for 10 miles, then turn right on RR 305.

KERMIT   Elev. 2,890   Pop. 5,586

Kermit, located in central Winkler County and only 10 miles from New Mexico, began as a supply post for the scattered ranches in the area. The town is named after the son of President Theodore Roosevelt, who visited the T Bar Ranch to hunt antelope. The oil boom hit Kermit in 1926 and the town has served the oil industry ever since.

WINKLER COUNTY GOLF COURSE

The golf   This is a 9-hole public course that serves the entire county. Tee it up and swing away into the wide-open, hard-panned fairways that are flat and let your ball roll for miles. The greens are elevated, fairly large, and undulating. Winkler County is a simple course with few trees and random bunkers scattered throughout the design.

If you can throw a wadded-up piece of paper into a garbage can, or toss a golf ball to a person 10 feet away, you've got touch. Don't sell yourself short. Phil Rodgers

The details   915-586-9243. 1010 E. Tascosa, Kermit, TX 79745.

- 1940. 9 holes. Par 36. Back – 3,128 (34.6/105). Forward – 2,584 (33.7/98). Price - $.

Getting there Located on Hwy. 302 seven miles west of town on the north side of the road.

KERMIT NOTES   This is a pass-through town so you shouldn't have any need for lodging. For food hit the **Dairy Queen** or **Town & Country** "to go" then get out of town and find your way to **Red Bluff Lake** on the New Mexico border where the Pecos River flows out of the bottom of the dam. The back roads will lead you to a bridge that crosses the river about a half mile below the dam, where you'll find hybrid white bass pounding the surface of the water. Light tackle or a fly rod will enhance the experience. Watch out for the authorities, who frown upon fishing from this spot. On the way, you might stop off in Mentone, TX at **The Boot Track Cafe**, order a beer, and discuss politics with the locals.

LAJITAS - TERLINGUA   Elev. 2,440   Pop. 100

Times have changed since the late 1800s, when macho Black Jack Pershing commanded his troops in pursuit of bandit Pancho Villa. Lajitas was a US Army Calvary post then, and remained one of the loneliest places on the planet. Along with the quicksilver town of Terlingua, the towns have served as an outpost for adventurers to Big Bend state and national parks.

Today, Lajitas is in the midst of a wild transformation that stems from a $100 million cash infusion from entrepreneur Steve Smith, whose vision to transform this portion of the Texas desert into the next Palm Springs has generated much publicity. Its neighbor, the ghost town of Terlingua, is booming around the ruins of the old mercury mine, offering quality restaurants, lively bars, shops, and adventure outfitters.

This means that the addicted golfer visiting this region no longer has to sweat it out playing round after round on the old 9-hole Lajitas course. Now Lajitas offers the golf vacation of a lifetime, with a 7,100-yard oasis course, a hunting club, equestrian center, world-class spa, and a spectacular restaurant.

THE AMBUSH

The golf   Located within 22,000 acres of Chihuahuan Desert at the foothills of the Chisos Mountains, The Ambush is a golf oasis in a barren land of nothingness. Designed by Austin-based architects Roy Bechtol and Randy Russell, this par 71 championship course is spectacular, to say the least.

Before you build a course with deep bunkers, railroad ties, forced carries and water everywhere, just remember that no Donald Ross course has ever gone Chapter 11. Lee Trevino

For starters, over 100 bunkers litter a layout that routes you through lakes, wetlands, waterfalls, and even the Rio Grande River. The course might be the world's first international golf course–the 19th hole (11-A) plays 110 yards over the river into Mexico with a green tilted toward the hole, creating a decent shot for a hole in one. The greens average 6,500 square feet in size.

The design theory involved laying out the course so that the holes slowly build in intensity, reaching a crescendo at the end. The course is heavily contoured to fit the area's mountainous ridges, with peaks climbing upwards of 8,000 feet.

The back nine is more scenic, with natural creeks cutting across several holes and the Chisos Mountains as the backdrop for most shots. Holes 11-13 make up a enjoyable stretch of golf. No. 11 is a long par 4 with the Rio Grande on the right. Hole 12 is a dogleg left towards the mountains, and No. 13 is a short par 3 backing up to the park.

Since hardly anyone plays the course, conditions are superb. Everything is first class, from Titleist Pro V1s on the driving range to the most upscale merchandise. Caddies are available if you're willing to put up with minor language barriers. Access to the course is limited to resort guests.

Other notes: A second course has been planned, The Outlaw, which will be routed more into the mountains and feature elevated tees with spectacular views.

The details   915-424-5080. 1 Main St., Lajitas, TX 79852.

• 18 holes. Par 72. El Jefe – 7,042 (72.9/129). Gambler – 6,619 (71.0/122). Caballero – 6,104 (68.7/115). Bandito – 5,663. Rustler – 5,082. Caddies available. Price - $$$$.

Getting there Lajitas is so small that you will not miss the course. There is one main turnoff into the town and you'll be able to see the golf course from the road. Turn on that road and weave your way to the pro shop.

LAJITAS NOTES   To play the course, you must stay at the resort. Don't worry, though, you'll be taken care of quite nicely. Before your round, find the latest generation of the beer-drinking, mayoral Henry family and buy him a beer for good luck (Clay Henry is a goat). November is a good time of year because of the **Terlingua Chili Cook-Off** (held since 1967). Away from the resort, Terlingua provides variety via the **Boathouse Bar and Grill** (915-371-2219), a funky hangout with good eats, an internet cafe, and eccentric locals who stack the bar, as well as the **Starlight Theatre** (915-371-2326), or the **Phoenix Cafe** (915-371-2251).

Big Bend National Park offers up any kind of adventure you can imagine. Raft, mountain bike, hike, camp and gaze at the stars, or cross the border for cold beers and tacos at **Boquillas**. For kicks strum up a game of **desert golf**. Take a few clubs and some scuffed-up balls, along with a sheet of fake grass, a portable radio, and a small cooler of cold beverages, then stroll along Texas 118 near **Study Butte**. You can make up your own variation of the rules. Just

---

drop the ball on the turf and give it a whack. Then track it down and do it again. One game involves picking mileage signs as your start and end points, then seeing who can get the ball to the finish in the least amount of strokes. Wear sunscreen and watch for cars.

MARFA   Elev. 4,688   Pop. 2,078

Scenic, healthy, and absolutely remote, Marfa sits on a high desert plateau at an elevation of 4,830 feet, with the scenic Davis Mountains looming to the north. The climate is superb, with summer highs rarely reaching 90 and evening temps in the 60s. Originally just a water stop on the railroad, Marfa experienced its pinnacle in the 1940s and 50s, when ranching empires sprang up and Hollywood brought Rock Hudson, Elizabeth Taylor, and James Dean to the El Paisano Hotel to film the movie *Giant*. Once labeled as on of the "10 Best Small Towns in America", Marfa has more to offer the wayward golfer than just the highest course in Texas.

MARFA MUNICIPAL GOLF COURSE

The golf   Playing the highest course in Texas is a special experience. Wide-open, firm fairways that enhance roll, shots that travel farther because of the altitude, and some of the best greens you'll ever play on . . . this course is a must-play if you're traveling in this remote region. While we didn't have time to walk the course, we teed off before 9 a.m. and finished our round in under an hour.

In terms of hazards, water comes into play on two of the nine holes, and the common Bermuda rough can be thick in the summer. There are not a ton of trees, but what's there is mature and there seem to be just enough to get in the way if you stray from the middle of the fairway.

One word of caution: Don't let the bitter attitude of the course manager negatively affect your experience or impressions of this golf course. Perhaps it was because we were not locals, or caught him too early on a bad day, but we were surprised by his lack of small-town hospitality–usually a given in this part of the world.

The details   915-729-4043. Golf Course Rd., Marfa, TX 79843.

• 1961. 9 holes. Par 36. Back – 3,265 (35.0/115). Forward – 2,893 (35.1/110). Price - $$.

Getting there Turn right (north) off of Hwy. 90 at the traffic light in Marfa. A few blocks down past the post office find FM 1112, then turn right. Drive 2 miles east and wind your way back to the course.

⭐

To find a man's true character, play golf with him. P. G. Wodehouse

WEST

MARFA NOTES Check into the newly restored 1930 **Hotel Paisano** (866-729-3669) and take a gander at the plush suites that hosted Hollywood during the filming of *Giant*. Grab a bite to eat on the patio downstairs, or mosey over to the lively **Borunda's Bar & Grill** (915-729-8163), just down the street from the original Borunda's where James Dean ate a few meals (now a gift shop). **Carmen's Café** is a tasty breakfast spot, **Mike's Place** is the place for burgers, and **Patsy's Thunderbird** can fill you up with home cookin'. After supper, cruise into the eclectic **Marfa Book Company** for some wine and intellectual stimulation, then take a late-night drive to find the mystical Marfa Lights, now viewable via a brand-new visitors center east of town. Other accommodations include the **Holiday Capri Inn** (915-729-4326) and the **Arcon Inn** (915-729-4826), a quaint B&B on N. Austin St.

McCAMEY   Elev. 2,441   Pop. 1,707

Unlike Alpine, just 112 miles to the southwest, McCamey is not in the running for one of the most beautiful towns in America. The country here is still barren, hard-core Permian Basin oil field. Southeast of town, perched atop King Mountain and the surrounding mesas, giant windmills harness the West Texas wind. With blades up to 90 feet long that slice above the countryside, they're an impressive sight.

McCamey is located on US 67 five miles east of the Pecos River on the windswept frontier of southwestern Upton County. When wildcatter George McCamey hit Baker No. 1 in 1925, the town boomed and became overloaded with 10,000 residents and a sea of tents. McCamey is home to tough, hardy people who make their living in the oil, farming, and ranching industries; the 9-hole McCamey Country Club exudes the rugged persona of those people.

McCAMEY COUNTRY CLUB

The golf   The course here is private but you should be able to talk your way on. You should: it's a good course with great bent-grass greens, though the conditions would be a lot better if they ever had any rain out here. Take your lip balm, because the wind will be blowing. You'll probably want to leave your camera behind because there's nothing really too picturesque about this golf course. The tees are slightly elevated and there is no water. The bent-grass greens are in unbelievable condition given the circumstances. There are two sets of tees for an 18-hole round.

The No. 1 tee box sits directly in front of the clubhouse and is shaded by a large tree and a pavilion. The opening shot is over the road that leads to the clubhouse.

The primary reason players often make spectacular trouble shots, causing the ball to go under, around, and over obstacles, is that they work harder on visualizing these shots that on those from less demanding positions. Gary Wiren

The scene here is surreal. Ancient golf carts from the 1960s are littered with Crown Royal bottles, empty beer cans, cigarettes, haggard, well-used clubs with worn grips, and other random paraphernalia. Inside the clubhouse, their owners sit partaking of cold beers, smokes, dice, and a football game on the television.

The details   915-652-8904. Bakersfield Hwy. McCamey, TX 79752

• 1928. 9 holes. Par 36. Back – 3,107. Forward – 2,263. Price - $.

Getting there Located south of town on FM 1901.

McCAMEY NOTES This "Wind Energy Capital of Texas" is a pass-through town...don't stay. Eat at the Dairy Queen and move on. Inquire locally about the scenic drive along back road routes across King Mountain and the surrounding mesas. Ten miles north of town, legend has it that a gap in the mountains was a popular crossing place for expeditions, and that the explorer Maximillian buried his treasure in a place called Castle Gap. On your way west down 67 you'll cross the Pecos River and run through the post-office-bar town of Girvin, TX where you can't miss the **Girvin Social Club** on the north side of the road. It might be shut down during the day, but this might be one of the most eclectic joints in Texas to have a beer in the evenings.

MIDLAND
Elev. 2,779   Pop. 99,621

Before the railroad came in 1881, Midland was the site of the last Comanche raid into Texas. Cattlemen came and the county held on until the 1920s, when oil was discovered in the Permian Basin and Midland became the headquarters for the region that produces 22% of the nation's oil reserves. In the 1980s the "Tall City," named for its imposing skyline over the barren, mesquite-laden land, was the fastest-growing city in the nation, increasing its population by 38% in only five years.

Positioned halfway between Fort Worth and El Paso on I-20, the flat, desolate terrain is balanced by 326 days of sunshine per year, horizons that have no end, and spectacular sunsets. The public golf has improved in recent years with the completion of an additional nine holes at the long-standing municipal, **Hogan Park Golf Course** (now 36 holes), as well as the newer upscale facility, **Nueva Vista**. Midland also boasts three outstanding private clubs: the old, traditional **Midland** and **Ranchland Hills Country Clubs**, and the newer, more modern **Green Tree Country Club**.

GREEN TREE COUNTRY CLUB

The golf   Laid out in a residential community northwest of town, Green

Some days you're on the range, and it hooks or slices, and you go out on the course, it hooks or slices. So let it hook or slice, don't try to fix it once you're in the game. Score with what you've got that day. Gloria Armstrong

Tree Country Club offers three separate 9-hole courses that are rotated to play as 18-hole combinations. The club was built back in the 1980s, and the 6,000 trees that were brought in to spice up the barren West Texas prairie have matured enough to give the course character. High winds, fast greens, a good amount of water, and out-of-bounds present on just about every hole because of the houses make Green Tree a very challenging test of golf.

The details   915-694-7726. 4900 Green Tree Blvd., Midland, TX 79707

- West-East: 1980. 18 holes. Par 71. Back – 6,524 (71.8/117). Middle – 6,006 (69.3/114). Forward – 5,245 (71.5/118). Price - $$$.
- North-West: 18 holes. Par 71. Back – 6,523 (71.8/117). Middle – 5,955 (69.2/115). Forward – 5,051 (69.5/114). Price - $$$.
- North-East: 18 holes. Par 72. Back – 6,811 (73.2/121). Middle – 6,312 (70.8/119). Forward – 5,358 (71.8/118). Price - $$$.

Getting there From I-20, exit Midland Dr. and turn north. When you come to Green Tree Blvd., turn left. The clubhouse is on the left side of the street.

HOGAN PARK GOLF COURSE

The golf   Hogan Park has been the long-time Midland institution for the Tall City layman, since it was the only public facility in town until Nueva Vista recently opened their daily-fee course on the west side. This facility originally opened in 1959, but upgraded with a 9-hole addition in 1983, and again in 1998, making 36 holes available to Midland's hacks.

The two courses are surprisingly different considering the terrain in this part of the world. The old course is more of a flat, traditional layout with narrow fairways and large, undulating greens. The trees that were planted back in the 1950s have grown up, providing some character to the otherwise flat, desert landscape. The toughest hole on this track is the 445-yard, par 4 No. 4, which plays uphill through a chute of trees, then doglegs right into a multi-tiered green protected by water. Multi-tiered is an understatement since there is a four-foot difference between the top and bottom levels.

The newer 18, built by Ron Kirby, is a links-style layout with minimal trees and more rolling terrain. You'll still need to keep it in the fairway because each hole is carved out of the nasty, mesquite-covered wastelands so typical of this area.

The details   915-685-7360. 3600 North Fairgrounds Rd., Midland, TX 79705

- Roadrunner: 1983. New 9: 1998. Ron Kirby. Blue - 6,925 (72/113). Red - 6,425 (71/110). White - 5,470 (71.3/112). Gold - 5,875. Price - $$.
- Quail (Old Course): 1950s. 18 holes. Blue – 6,595 (71/110). Red – 6,310 (69.3/108). White – 5,770 (72.3/111). Gold - 5,920. Price - $$.

Getting there On the east side of Midland, find Fairgrounds Rd. and look for the golf course sign about one mile south of the Loop.

Nobody ever swung a club too slowly. Bobby Jones

MIDLAND COUNTRY CLUB

The golf   MCC has served as the home of the elite in Midland since 1927. Since moving to its current location in 1954, it's maintained the reputation as one of the best and longest in the state. Designer Ralph Plummer must have been caught in some sort of a West Texas oil-patch pissing match in the midst of macho oil men when his ego prompted him to create a 7,354-yard monstrosity in an area that often is bombarded with 30-40 mph winds!

On hole after hole, golfers face long, narrow fairways lined with thick, mature trees, which themselves are lined with the famous rattlesnake-infested mesquite "jungles" that suck golf balls out of the West Texas wind. Crushed drives that find the fairway don't necessarily warrant pats on the back, as a long iron or even a 3-wood off the deck awaits the over-confident hack on his approach. Water comes into play in strategic places (7 holes), wreaking even more havoc on your round. The bent-grass greens are large and sometimes impossible to handle because of their speed.

Every hole is impressive, but the 601-yard 15th stands out, snaking its way right off the tee, then left for the second shot, and finally back to the right again into a massive, bowl-shaped, elevated green. Tiger Woods could not reach this hole in two.

Other notes: Ron Kirby redesigned the course in 1979, followed by Dick Nugent in 1985. This club hosted the 1997 Texas State Amateur. The club currently has plans for extensive renovation of the clubhouse.

The details   915-683-3621. 6101 N. Hwy. 349, Midland, TX 79705

- 1954. Ralph Plummer. Redesigned in 1979 by Ron Kirby, and again in 1985 by Dick Nugent. Par 72. Tournament – 7,354 (74.5/131). Blue – 6,936 (73.2/128). Gold – 6,577 (71.4/125). White – 5,430 (69.8/116). Yellow – 5,430 (69.8/116). Price - $$$.

Getting there Drive north out of Midland toward Lubbock on Hwy. 349. The entrance is 1.5 miles on the left side of the road.

RANCHLAND HILLS COUNTRY CLUB

The golf   Ranchland is the private version of Hogan Park, void of the mesquite-dotted scrub that lines each hole. Here you'll find narrow fairways bordered by the standard cut of rough and large, mature trees. Built circa 1950, the flat, traditional layout plays to a par 70 and has water on nine holes.

Notable holes on the front include the 604-yard opening hole, and No. 6, a 444-yard par 4. The back 9 features only one par 5, which plays only 487 yards, and several par 4s that play well under 400 yards. However, those are well-balanced with two mean par 3s that require long irons (or even a 3-wood) and the difficult finishing hole: a 400-yard-plus par 4.

⭐

Today, commit to loving your putter. Dr. Bob Rotella

The details 915-683-2041. 1600 E. Wadley Ave., Midland, TX 79705

- 1948. 18 holes. Men's – Par 70. Back – 6,560 (71.7/121). Middle – 6,030 (69.2/116). Forward – Par 71. 5,353 (71.5/124). Price - $$$.

Getting there Exit Business 80 off of I-20 and drive north on Fairgrounds Rd. Turn left on Wadley and drive a short distance to the course.

NUEVA VISTA GOLF CLUB

The golf Midland's newest course, the centerpiece of a residential community named Grassland Estates, opened for play in October 1999. The course is open, void of trees, and designed with the prevailing West Texas winds in mind, which give the layout a definite Scottish-links-style feel.

While the course is not overly difficult, playing just over 6,200 yards from the middle tees, low handicappers will be challenged from the tips, especially if they catch the course on a gusty day. There is nothing to protect the course from the wind, and the 6,900 back tees can play more like 7,500 in howling conditions.

The details 915-520-0500. 6101 Wadley Ave., Midland, TX 79707

- www.nuevavistagolf.com
- 1999. 18 holes. Par 72. Back – 6,900 (71.7/68.4). Middle – 6,215 (68.4/113). Forward – 5,270 (67.5/112). Price - $$.

Getting there Take Business Hwy. 20 East to Loop 250. Go north on Loop 250 to Wadley Ave. Take a left on Wadley and follow until it dead-ends into the golf course.

MIDLAND NOTES Lodging is everywhere, but the best choice downtown is the **Midland Hilton** (915-683-6131). For good eats, try lunch downtown at Midland tradition **Johnny's BBQ**, then later go for frosty-mugged beers, oysters on the half-shell, and steaks at **Wall Street**. Another option is to track down one of the many local Tex-Mex eateries, where Coronas and nachos always mix well (consider old-school **Tampico's**). Driving the farm roads west of town in search of sunsets and stars isn't a bad way to spend a summer night.

MONAHANS Elev. 2,613   Pop. 6,647

Spanish explorers crossed areas of present Ward County more than 400 years ago, but it remained the undisturbed habitat of Indians until the mid-1800s, when John Thomas Monahans found a plentiful supply of water. Today this Ward County seat is a trading center for more than 800 square miles of cattle and oil country. The importance of oil is evident today just outside of

---

⭐

They say golf is like life, but don't believe them. It's more complicated than that.
Gardner Dickinson

downtown off Texas 18, where several pumpjacks draw oil from slant wells beneath the city hall, courthouse, and banks of Monahans.

There are two attractions for those looking for fun in the outdoors: 4,000 acres of white, wind-sculpted sand dunes at the Monohans Sandhill State Park and the rugged-but-interesting Ward County Golf Course.

WARD COUNTY GOLF COURSE

The golf   This 18-hole public layout's claim to fame is that Kathy Whitworth, LPGA Hall of Famer, learned the game here. With more hills than you might expect for this desert region, this track has a nice variety of holes. Big, dangerous water hazards are sprinkled about the course. The par 3s are extremely tough, and the greens vary in size. Pay attention to your club selection when the wind is blowing.

Over the years this facility has gained a reputation of continuously being in poor condition; however, a new management team took over in the late 1990s, and they have made significant strides in improving the quality of the course.

The details   915-943-5044. N. Hwy. 18, Monahans, TX 79756

- Par 72. Back – 6,669 (69.6/115). Middle – 6,188 (67.8/110). Forward – 5,322 (108). Price - $$.

Getting there Located 2 miles north of town on Hwy. 18.

MONAHANS NOTES Fred's Bar B Q (915-943-2885) is the place for a sliced beef sandwich, and the **Jelisco Restaurant** (915-943-6636) has Tex-Mex. The **Monahans Sandhills State Park** is worth a look if you're not from the area: it's the West Texas version of the Sahara with 4,000 desolate acres of sand dunes. The **Best Western** on I-20 is a convenient place to crash.

ODESSA
Elev. 2,890   Pop. 91,572

Named by Russian rail workers for its resemblance to the barren wastelands in their Ukranian hometown, Odessa isn't the place to visit for the scenery or the culture. This ugly oil-hand city grew from the large Permian Basin oil and gas discoveries of the 1920s, and since I'm from Midland just 20 miles east, I can joke that Rand McNally once listed Odessa as one of the 10 worst places to live in the U.S., which perhaps explains why for decades the primary passion of its residents has been the local high school football team.

The city has pushed hard to make itself more attractive to visitors by establishing several cultural and performing arts centers, and golfers passing through will benefit from the variety of courses available in Odessa. **Ratliff Ranch Golf Links** is one of the top public courses in Texas, and the public

---

Think less about starting your putts on line and more about striking the ball solidly.
Johnny Miller

Sunset Country Club allows you to experience West Texas oil field golf at its finest. For those with enough pull to obtain access to the private clubs, **Odessa Country Club** and its recently acquired **Mission Dorado** course are first-class facilities that will round out your golf experience in Odessa.

COURSE RESEARCH

We received pretty interesting feedback when researching these courses, but this description of golf in Odessa is classic: "Suckset is a strange little course, very old. It has no sand traps because (you may want to validate this) I think it was the 1st course in Odessa and it had traps at first but the sand kept getting blown out of the bunkers and they became dirt traps (and you know how the dirt is out there, like a rock). Also, they have a 9-hole par 3 course that is very popular among the blue-jean, shirtless golfers. Ratliff, lighted driving range and hole 2, I have eagled twice, so you may be able to say that it is a fairly easy par 5. No.13 at Mission is a great par 3 for West Texas, about 150-160 yds and a pond covers most of the "fairway" jutting in from the left. The green has a big trap with those railroad ties creating a wall next to the green (looks nice and can screw you badly if you hit the trap). The green has raised wall-like banks of the rough around the back, so you feel like you can really fire at the pin. However the green has 2 or 3 levels and if the pin is on the higher, smaller level, it is a very hard hole. Fun as hell to play, especially in the West Texas wind. Don't know much about OCC as I have only played there twice in my life. Oh yea, Suckset has really good food. Like an old greasy diner. Cheeseburgers are great. Mission and OCC are under the same ownership now, I believe. Ratliff is fun to play. I don't think it has trees, only mesquite. It is like the Scottish links courses, which works out where it is and that wind."

THE CLUB AT MISSION DORADO

The golf Mission is a difficult, 18-hole championship layout that has recently been acquired by Odessa Country Club. This is a links-style course perfectly suited to the West Texas winds. The course features mounded fairways and the style of fast greens suited to the more advanced golfer. In fact, the Nike Tour hosted a tournament here throughout the 1990s.

This is a place where average golfers might enjoy themselves more by playing from the white tees. Even playing from the 6,660-yard blues, length is required off the tees, and combined with the wind, the course can beat even a

---

It's OK to have butterflies. Just get them flying in formation. Francisco Lopez

good golfer down. The par 5s are monstrous, and most of the par 4s will require long irons into the green.

The number one handicap is No. 3, which plays 585 yards from the tips and 560 yards from the blues. No. 17 is probably the best bet for a birdie, playing only 145 yards from the blues.

The details   915-563-0980. 1 Mission Blvd. Odessa, TX 79765

- 1984. 18 holes. Par 72. Back – 7,229 (73.7/130). Middle – 6,660 (71.4/125). Forward – 5,595 (72.3/127). Price - $$$.

Getting there Located on Mission Blvd. between Loop 588 and Hwy. 80. From 80 going west, turn right onto Faudree Rd., then drive 1 mile to the course. The entrance is on the right side of the street.

ODESSA COUNTRY CLUB

The golf   John Bredemus built this course in the late 1930s, and his design makes the most of the flat West Texas terrain. This is an old-school golf course with tree-lined fairways and undulating bent-grass greens. The fairways are wide and the course is a fair test of golf. When the wind blows the course can play difficult, but with only a smattering of water hazards, it's not too tough.

The signature hole is the 215-yard par 3 No. 9. The long shot into the shallow green is challenging, and the swale in the green makes it hard to hold. Other feature holes here are the 560-yard No. 7 that seems to always play into the wind. Off the tee you'll see water right and out-of-bounds left, with a narrow landing area. On the back 9, hole 14 is a 430-yard par 4 with another tee shot into a tight landing area, which generally leaves a long approach into an elevated green.

The details   915-366-4445. 7184 Club Dr., Odessa, TX 79760

- 1939. John Bredemus. 18 holes. Par 72. Back – 6,940 (71.8/118). Middle – 6,188 (68.3/114). Forward – 5,245 (69.7/110). Price - $$$.

Getting there Located east of town. Exit Business 80 off of I-20, then drive a few miles and look for the course.

RATLIFF RANCH GOLF LINKS

The golf   In 1988 Jeff Brauer, who has since become a nationally renowned architect, sculpted this West Texas wasteland into a links-style course reminiscent of the great courses overseas. The flat terrain has been modified with mounding and features plush fairways surrounded by large, immaculate bent-grass greens and extreme rough.

Brauer didn't incorporate many water hazards into the layout (only four holes) but, like the great links courses of Scotland, the difficulty of the course is often determined by the weather conditions–when the wind blows hard and

---

Swing like you were being paid by the hour, not the job. Davis Love, Jr.

WEST

blows your ball into the thick rough, scores add up quickly. Subtle mounding is evident throughout to add to the links-style feel. There are a few difficult par 4s on the course. No. 18 is the number one handicap at 412 yards, but holes 5 and 8 are around 450 yards. No. 14 is a drive-able par 4 at 285 yards.

The details   915-550-8181. 7500 N. Grandview Ave., Odessa, TX 79768

- 1988. Jeff Brauer. 18 holes. Par 72. 6,797 (73.0/122). Middle – 6,243 (70.5/117). Forward – 4,887 (68.9/110). Price - $$.

Getting there Take I-20 west to Loop 338 (exit 121). Go north on Loop 338 approximately 5 miles to Grandview. Turn left onto Grandview, and the clubhouse will be approximately .5 mile down on your left.

SUNSET COUNTRY CLUB

The golf   Not every facility is of championship caliber, but others still serve a purpose in fulfilling the needs of the golfing public. Sunset is a semi-private facility that features a regulation 18-hole course, as well as a 9-hole par 3 course with holes ranging from 50 to 165 yards. So while the conditions may not be the greatest, it's hard to complain about the availability of a quick practice round on the par 3 course prior to teeing off on the big course.

When you look at the score card for the regulation course, you'll quickly determine that the back nine is much easier than the front. The front features the five easiest holes, while the back nine challenges you with significant length and the three most difficult holes. The finisher isn't considered among those holes, but is still tough at 573 yards from the back tees.

The details   915-366-1061. 9301 Andrews Hwy., Odessa, TX 79760

- 18 holes. Par 72. Back – 6,665 yards. Middle – 6,230 (69.5/112). Forward – 5,083 (66.7/101). Price - $$.

Getting there Exit 385 off of I-20 and take Hwy. 385 north. Continue 12 miles and the course is on the left.

ODESSA NOTES Odessa is the "Jackrabbit-Roping Capital of Texas," so you might inquire as to how you might experience that sort of exciting outdoor activity. Breakfast enthusiasts should head to 40-year old **Pancake Alley # 10** (915-580-4015) on E. 2nd for an enjoyable first meal with the Odessa locals. Downtown, the **Barn Door** (915-337-4142) will cook your steak on the grill in the middle of the dining room. Over beers, talk high school football at **Marie's Lounge**. Or better yet, get creative and take a side trip to Goldsmith, TX (385 north, then west on SR-158), and see if anything is going on at the **Goldsmith Men's Club**. Whether you hunt or not, consider staying at the **K-Bar Ranch Hunting Lodge** (915-580-5880) south of town, where for $75

---

you'll get breakfast and an evening meal with your lodging. They offer a variety of hunting packages as well. There is also a nice **Radisson** on University Blvd.

OZONA Elev. 2,348   Pop. 3,444

Ozona is a tree-shaded little town with remarkable architecture quarried from local limestone. Texas' largest unincorporated town, it is the seat of and the only town in Crockett County, a vast ranching and oil area of over 3,000 square miles.

We realized why they named the town after the quantity of open air as we passed through on a surprisingly cool September day. The air was fresh, the city felt clean, and it felt good to be outside. Since the town is conveniently located on Interstate 10, it makes for a convenient stopping point, especially if you have the urge to tee it up.

OZONA COUNTRY CLUB

The golf   This "private" 9-hole course allows out-of-town visitors to play the course. Ozona Country Club is a typical small-town course that does not require length off the tee and has no water hazards or bunkers. However, you need to hit the ball straight because there are out-of-bounds stakes lining every fairway and large trees dotting the course throughout. The small bent-grass greens make for a tough target.

OCC plays around 3,000 yards, which is difficult for the ladies because there is only one set of tees. The layout consists of one par 5 (545 yards), two par 3s, and six par 4s that all play under 400 yards. Pay once and play all day.

The details   915-392-2520. Hwy. 163, Ozona, TX 76943

• 1954. 9 holes. Par 35. 3,001 yards. Price - $.

Getting there Located north of town on Hwy. 163.

OZONA NOTES   When pondering further adventures, sit down at Pepe's Cafe (915-392-2923) for sloppy, greasy, delicious enchiladas and a cold drink, then decide whether or not to head east to the Hill Country or south to the border. If you're on the way to Del Rio, take your time for a pit stop at the abandoned **Mayfield's General Store**, once one of the best cold-beer serving gas station convenience stores in Texas. There are three hotels in Ozona. But the **Best Western Ozona Inn** (915-392-5277) is your best option for lodging.

WEST

PECOS

Elev. 2,580   Pop. 9,157

Back in the 1880s, to "pecos" someone meant that you shot them and dumped them in the Pecos River. Once one of the roughest frontier towns in the Old West, Pecos started as a stop on the Texas and Pacific Railroad and soon became the hangout of rowdy cowboys of the day. If you come to town in July or August, vendors scatter along US 285 and other spots around town selling the sweetest cantaloupes known to man. The alluvial plains of the Pecos River are remarkably fertile, and the surrounding county also produces watermelons, cotton, onions, and bell peppers.

Ranching and oil are also important economically for this town that serves as a travel hub for east-west road trippers along I-20. For golfers driving through this area, the soon-to-be 18-hole golf course that sits just south of I-20 is a convenient place for a pit stop when traveling the long road to El Paso. The crowds are small, the price is right, and a dedicated hack could work in 9 holes in just over an hour, which is much better than killing time at the Dairy Queen after a stop for gas and supplies.

REEVES COUNTY GOLF COURSE

The golf   As you drive up to the course, Reeves County has a remarkable resemblance to the municipal in Fort Stockton. It's a typical West Texas layout that is built on flat terrain and over the years has gained character from the growth of trees planted along the fairway. The greens are small, with subtle undulations, and the course has no bunkers. Not a championship layout, but a basic course kept in reasonable condition that provides the locals the opportunity to enjoy the game.

For years this has been an 11-hole layout, with golfers working in 18 by playing the back holes of 1, 2, 12, 14, 4, skipping 5, then finishing with 6-9. However, the club is currently in the process of expanding the facility to a complete 18 holes. The plan involves adding two holes inside the existing course, and another five holes outside of the layout.

The details   915-447-2858. 88 Stanley Dr., Pecos, TX 79772

- 1942. 11 holes available. Par 35 for 9 holes. Back – 3,130 (34.4/104). Middle – 2,992 (33.7/100). Forward – 2,434 (34.3/93). Price - $.

Getting there Located just south of I-20 in Pecos. You can see the course from I-20.

MORE GOLF

A 9-hole executive course that has been temporarily shut down, the **Chaparral Village Golf Course** has suffered from the lack of water in this dry region. A phone call to the course in August 2002 was answered by an older gentleman who cussed the drought conditions and claimed that the course would re-open when the water issues were resolved.

⭐

The mind messes up more shots than the body. Tommy Bolt

PECOS NOTES   The lodging options are limited, but there are rooms at the **Best Western** on I-20. For a little Old West history visit **The West of the Pecos Museum** in the historic **Orient Hotel**. The saloon here was the scene of a murder, and bulletholes show the details of the event. When dining in Pecos, don't miss **La Norteña Tortilla and Tamale Factory** on 3rd St., and **Alfredo's** (915-445-7776) is the Gomez family's traditional Mexican eatery that serves authentic chicken chalupas and a wine margarita that hits the spot. For shopping, stop in the **Pecos Saddle Shop** (915-445-3125) for customized leather goods and cowboy gear.

PRESIDIO   Elev. 2,594   Pop. 4,334

This 300-year-old-plus town is wild and remote, and you will definitely not be bothered by crowds out here. Presidio sits across the border from Ojinaga, a rugged, historical city known for its outlaw image. Pancho Villa's band of rebels fought Mexican Federales here, and the town is notorious as an entry port for the Mexican drug cartels.

An important gateway to Big Bend state and national parks, Presidio is a popular starting point for tours into Mexico's Copper Canyon and the Camino del Rio, an unbelievable drive along the Rio Grande to Lajitas.

Be prepared for the heat when traveling here in the summer months. Presidio is often noted as one of the hottest spots in the country, with the average June high at 103 degrees F.

LOMA PALOMA GOLF CLUB

The golf   The LPGC is an 18-hole course that is as remote as it gets. Set in a valley with panoramic views of the mountains all around, this is a flat, desert course that is void of water hazards, and features bunkers only on the par 3 holes. The greens were renovated in November 2002.

The details   915-229-2992, Hwy. 170 E., Presidio, TX 79845

• 18 holes. Back – 5,998. Forward – 4,778. Price - $.

Getting there Take 170 east toward Big Bend about 5 miles outside of Presidio.

PRESIDIO NOTES   El Patio (915-229-4409) has good salsa and cold beer. The scenic drive down RR 170 is without a doubt the most spectacular in Texas. Stay at **Cibolo Creek Ranch** (915-229-3737, www.cibolocreekranch.com). If you're feeling adventurous, cross the border and look around Ojinaga. **El Bucanero** is a thatch-covered restaurant that specializes in seafood, and **Mariscos Lalo** is a popular gringo spot as well. Shop at **Fausto's Art Gallery** on Calle Juarez, take in a semi-pro baseball game, have a beer and a steak at **Los**

Ninety percent of putts that are short don't go in. Yogi Berra

Comales downtown, then venture into **La Zona Rosa**, OJ's red-light district, for a trip back to the wild West when liquor was plenty and women were wanton. For a Mexican view of Big Bend take the Chihuahua Hwy. 25 miles outside of Ojinaga ($40 roundtrip taxi ride) and gaze at the 2,000-foot-deep **Peguis Canyon**. Watch yourself, though…have some savvy as a gringo traveling across the border. For lodging in Presidio look to **La Siesta Motel** (915-229-3611) and **Three Palms Inn** (915-229-3211).

RANKIN   Elev. 2,595   Pop. 764

Out of the nothingness 55 miles south of Midland springs Rankin, the seat of Upton County. The heart of the Permian Basin at the junction of US 67 and Texas 349. Rankin was born sometime around 1910 and grew during the early oil boom days. Not much oil was originally discovered, and the Great Depression took its toll. But in the 1940s the Benedum field north of town came in and another boom period hit. This second boom gave life to Rankin Country Club, and the 9-hole course eventually produced some of the best high school golfers in the state. One would never imagine it from looking at the course today, but Rankin won five state golf championships in the 1970s.

UPTON COUNTY GOLF COURSE
The golf   The Rankin "Country Club" is not the stuff golf dreams are made of. If there is such a thing as a "ghost course" in the same sense as a "ghost town," Rankin Country Club fits the image perfectly. Set on the east side of town, there are no fairways and the clubhouse looks like it hasn't been used in a long, long, long time.

Pay your $5 green fee by inserting your cash into a customized RCC envelope and dropping it in the lock box by the first tee. If the sprinkler and hose are in your way on the first tee, pull it out of the way if you can't muster the nerve to ignore it.

The "fairways," which wasted away in the heat many moons ago, are hardpanned West Texas sand with a rare cactus or weed sprinkled about. The good news is that you do not need your driver, and every shot will roll significantly. The real challenge is to somehow get your approach on the green, or at the very least the "frog hair" that surrounds it, to leave you with a reasonable chip shot. Otherwise die-hard golfers that are "playing it down" will face a miserable sand save opportunity from the dusty surfaces where grass no longer grows.

The par 5 No. 8 hole is enjoyable because it plays with the prevailing south summer wind, and the roll of the fairway makes it possible to get there in two. The trick is the pin placement. The green is two-tiered with an extreme slope from back to front.

☆

There is no similarity between golf and putting; they are two different games—
one is played in the air, and the other on the ground. Ben Hogan

We were fortunate enough to meet the Head Pro, Director of Golf, Head Greenskeeper, Tournament Coordinator, and janitor, Gary Smith, who we found driving across the "fairways" in his old truck to take care of the greens (which by the way, are in great shape).

The details Country Club Rd., Rankin, TX 79778

• 1953. 9 holes. Par 36. 3,141 yards. Price - $.

Getting there Located off Hwy. 67 east of Rankin.

RANKIN NOTES The restored Yates Hotel (c. 1927) houses the **Rankin Museum**, and there is a nice little local cafe on the main drag in town, as well as a Mexican food joint on the road heading west out of town. We didn't, but you could, head up to Midkiff and find the remains of a 6-hole layout that apparently entertained the locals for years.

ROBERT LEE   Elev. 1,780   Pop. 1,134

Robert Lee, like nearby Bronte, is a tiny town with a 9-hole golf course north of San Angelo near the Colorado River. The county seat of Coke County, it lies at the junction of Texas 158 and 208. Robert Lee is the region's oil field supply center, as well as the commercial and legal center of the county. With the 9-hole course at Bronte nearby and proximity to Lake E.V. Spence, a unique desert-like lake that is the premier spot in West Texas for striped bass, this is an interesting place to combine fishing and golf on a weekend getaway.

MOUNTAIN CREEK GOLF CLUB

The golf This short, 9-hole, semi-private course is named after Mountain Creek, which runs through the layout and impacts three holes. Set in the scenic hills of central Coke County, there are a few hills on this track, and a total of five water hazards. The fairways are mostly flat and offer generous landing areas. A low score is a definite possibility. Start off with a birdie on No. 1, a 287-yard par 4, then use your confidence to go low because every par 4 is under 400 yards, and both par 5s are under 500 yards. The number 1 handicap is the par 5 No. 7, which plays 482 yards. Pay once and play all day. There are two sets of tees for a different look the second time around.

The details 915-453-2317. Park Rd., Robert Lee, TX 76945

• 9 holes. Par 36. Back – 2,859. Forward – 2,188. Price - $$.

Getting there Located in the county park, 1 mile west of Hwys. 208 and 158.

Golfers who carry ball retrievers are gatherers, not hunters. . . . Their dreams are no longer of conquest, but only of salvage. David Owen

WEST

ROBERT LEE NOTES The best part about a spot like this is that it's easy on the wallet. Book a room and striper guide service at the **Wildcat Marina** (915-453-2801), and work your rounds of golf at Robert Lee, Bronte, and even San Angelo around your time on the lake.

SAN ANGELO
Elev. 1,847   Pop. 88,608

Established in 1867 at the junction of the north and middle branches of the Concho River, this community grew as the rowdy frontier site of Fort Concho. When the original county seat and rival town, Ben Ficklin, washed away in a flood, San Angelo became the ranching center for cattle and sheep and the primary place for business in the region. Today it is the country's primary wool and mohair market and a major livestock auction center, as well as a regional hub for cotton, grain, and pecan production.

The city of San Angelo is located in an ideal spot in West Central Texas between the Hill Country to the southeast, the Chihuahan desert to the west, and the rolling plains to the northwest. US Highways 67, 87, and 277 merge here, and US Interstates 10 and 20 are within about an hour's drive. San Angelo is a great jumping-off point for excursions to the three area lakes, or into other parts of Texas (Hill Country, Del Rio, far west Texas) and an outstanding place to experience West Texas golf.

San Angelo is home to two private clubs, **San Angelo Country Club** and **Bentwood Country Club**, and offers 54 holes of public golf. One could make the case that **Quicksand Golf Course** is the toughest track in the west region, and one of the most punishing in the entire state. **Riverside** is fun and affordable, and **Santa Fe** is a charming 9-hole course set along the river in the middle of downtown.

BENTWOOD COUNTRY CLUB

The golf   Bentwood opened in 1979 and is an 18-hole private course laid out through a residential community. The course can be difficult when the wind is blowing, especially with its somewhat lengthy layout (almost 7,000 yards from the tips) and out-of-bounds on most holes. Four sets of tees provide options for every skill level. The fairways and roughs consist of the durable 419 Bermuda grass, and the large, undulating greens are Champion Dwarf Bermuda.

The front nine gives you the chance to start well with several par 4s under 400 yards, and a 523-yard par 5 that is a definite birdie opportunity when the wind is at your back.

The feature hole is No. 8, which has out-of-bounds on the right and usually plays into the prevailing south wind. At 464 yards it plays more like a par 5,

I can't tell you how much I hated practicing my putting. It bored me silly. I loved to hit balls, though. Golfers tend to practice the things they're already good at. Tom Weiskopf

and starts a difficult stretch of golf that extends through the 13th hole. Holes 9 and 10 play just over 400 yards, with the latter a dogleg left with water on the right and out-of-bounds on the left. The approach on No. 10 is into an elevated green surrounded by bunkers. Eleven is a 517-yard par 5, followed by a monster par 3 (224 yards), and another relatively long par 4 No. 13 (420 yards).

The details   915-944-8575. 2111 Club House Ln., San Angelo, TX 76904

- 1979. Billy Martindale. 18 holes. Par 72. Back – 6,932 (73.4/124). Middle – 6,590 (71.8/122). Forward – 5,269 (70.6/114). Price - $$$.

Getting there Located on the southwest side of town off Loop 306. From the Airport, take Knickerbocker Rd. going north for 5 miles to the course.

QUICKSAND GOLF COURSE

The golf   Overlooking the Concho River, Quicksand is named appropriately with its combination of desert and links-style architecture, and its prominent use of sand. Five tees, ranging from 5,023 yards to 7,171 yards, give the West Texas hacker lots of options on this unusually difficult course.

Nos. 5 and 7 are the holes of note on the front side–the 5th known for its elevated island green (surrounded by sand, not water), and the 7th famous as the toughest hole on the course. The signature No. 7 goes 621 yards and has the always-pleasing double dogleg feature, and is only lined by 22 bunkers. Yes . . . 22 bunkers!

The back features three difficult finishing holes. No. 16 features an approach over water to a tiny green, No. 17 requires a 200-yard carry over water. The ender is a long par 4 that features a tee shot into a fairway lined by water on the left, and a difficult approach into another island-like green, this time surrounded by water.

Other notes   Walking is not allowed on the weekends. The facility is considering adding another nine holes.

The details   915-482-8337. 2305 Pulliam St., San Angelo, TX 76905.

- www.quicksandgc.com

- 1995. Michael Hurdzen. 18 holes. Par 72. Black – 7,171 (75.0/140). Gold – 6,693 (72.3/131). Blue – 6,120 (70.1/124). White – 5,606 (67.7/117). Red – 5,023 (69.5/121). Price - $$$.

Getting there Heading east on Hwy. 67/277, take the 306 Loop Exit onto Smith Blvd. and the course is directly ahead.

Some golfers seem to have no genius for figures. They cannot count correctly and, unfortunately, their general tendency is to be one stroke shy rather than one too many. Jerome Travers

WEST

RIVERSIDE GOLF COURSE

The golf   Riverside Golf Course is an 18-hole public course along the Concho River. A short course at only 6,396 yards from the back tees, it is a great place to build your confidence before you try your game at San Angelo's impossible Quicksand Golf Course. The fairways here are flat and there are no bunkers. Despite the presence of the river, there is only water on six holes. Act like a pro and play from the tips, or work on your short iron approaches by teeing off one the two shorter sets of tees (5,922 and 5,297 yards).

The details   915-653-6130. 2600 MLK, San Angelo, TX 76902

- 1965. 18 holes. Par 72. Back – 6,396 (70.5/113). Middle – 5,922 (68.3/108). Forward – 5,297 (69.2/105). Price - $$.

Getting there Located of US 87 N. on W. 29th St.

SAN ANGELO COUNTRY CLUB

The golf   This historic course was built in 1920s by John Bredemus, and has the distinction of being the first course in Texas to have bent-grass greens. Bredemus' traditional layout is set along the Concho River with unusually hilly terrain for the region, with narrow fairways, mature trees, and a few lakes. Two creeks run through the course, which often require lay-up tee shots, but there is not much out-of-bounds.

The two notable holes at San Angelo Country Club are par 3s: The 173-yard No. 2, which requires a tee shot over water to a well-bunkered green, and No. 10, the signature hole that features an elevated tee box overlooking the Concho River, 169 yards over water down to the green.

The details   915-651-7395. 1609 Country Club Rd., San Angelo, TX 76904

- 1920s. John Bredemus. 18 holes. Par 71. Back - 6,658 (72.3/127). Forward - 6,154 (76.9/139). Price - $$$.

Getting there Located on US 87. From Hwy. 87 south, take Loop 306 and exit Ben Fickland. Turn right and drive a short distance to the clubhouse.

SANTA FE PARK GOLF COURSE

The golf   Santa Fe Park Golf Course is a city-owned track set along the Concho River in downtown San Angelo. It's the perfect place to work in a leisurely round in a short amount of time and practice your game. A short course at only 2,450 yards, its only hazards are the greenside grass bunkers.

The details   915-657-4485. 111 W. River Dr., San Angelo, TX 76902

- 1920. 9 holes. Par 34. 2,453 yards. Price - $.

Getting there Turn left on Beauregard, then left again on River Dr. to the course entrance.

Playing golf is just like going to a strip club. You're all revved up, ready to go. But three hours later, you're depressed, plastered, and most of your balls are missing. James Clark

MORE GOLF

Arden Road Driving Range – 4601 Arden Rd., 915-942-9599.
College Hills Driving Range – 2838 College Hills Blvd., 915-944-9683

SAN ANGELO NOTES Treasure hunt for the famous Concho River freshwater pearls and take them to the local jeweler to mount for your special gal. Five lakes are nearby with excellent fishing. The historic district downtown on Concho St. offers shopping and the landmark **Miss Hattie's Museum,** where ladies of ill repute once welcomed soldiers from Fort Concho. Three hometown barbecue spots rank with the best: **Old Time Pit Bar-B-Que** (915-655-2771), **Mule Creek Bar-B-Q** (915-658-2740), and **Packsaddle Bar-B-Que** (915-949-0616). An evening of romance can be had at **Damo's Café Italiano** (915-835-4103), where the food is superb and served generously. More high-toned grub can be had at a place called **Peasant Village** (915-655-4811), a quaint, upscale spot in a remodeled old home. Outside of town is the **Twin Mountain Steak House** (915-949-4239), where you should ask for the signature "Scraps" steak dish.

SONORA
Elev. 2,120   Pop. 2,977

Sonora has a unique feel to it. Located on the western edge of the Edwards Plateau and the eastern edge of the West Texas region, it's sort of West Texas, Hill Country, and South Texas merged into one. As seat of Sutton County, it is the leading wool and mohair center of the state, and has always maintained its western heritage. The town began as a trade post in 1890 on the Old San Antonio-El Paso road, and was connected by stage coach to San Angelo until the early 1900s. The longest fenced cattle trail in the world ended here: a 250-foot-wide path fenced for the entire 100 miles from Brady, TX. Hunting for deer and turkey is a passion for locals, and they take great pride in their unique little golf course that has been rated as one of the top 9-hole layouts in the state.

SONORA GOLF CLUB

The golf   Unlike other small town courses in this region, the Sonora Golf Club has extremely large greens (only one that is elevated) that make it much easier to rack up the Greens in Regulation (G.I.R.) stats. If you've been playing courses like Alpine and Marfa with tiny postage-stamp greens, you will gladly welcome these larger targets. The course is generally flat, but its location on the edge of the Hill Country provides some hilly terrain. Water comes

Think like the underdog. The underdog always has the advantage . . . The favorite, meanwhile, is prone to negativism, worrying about how embarrassing it would be to lose. Dr. Bob Rotella

into play on only three holes, and there are plenty of trees that can cause problems if your game is off.

The details   915-387-3680. 1612 Golf Course Rd., Sonora, TX 76950

- 1973. 9 holes. Par 36. Back – 3,225 (34.7/114). Forward – 2,786 (35.7/125). Price - $.

Getting there   From I-10, take the second Sonora exit. Make a left, go under the highway, then turn left again. Look for Golf Course Rd. and turn right, where you'll find the course at the end of the road.

SONORA NOTES   Sonora is a good jumping-off point to head south to Del Rio, Lake Amistad, and the Mexican border. But first take a look at the architecture on the 1891 courthouse, and it's worth a trip 15 miles outside of town to the **Caverns of Sonora**. For food, avoid the chains and try the local Mexican food options or the **Sutton County Steakhouse** (915-387-3833). Three lodging options: **The Best Western Sonora Inn** (915-387-9111) the **Devil's River Days Inn** (800-329-7666) or the **Twin Oaks Motel** (915-573-2551).

STANTON
Elev. 2,664   Pop. 2,552

The county seat of Martin County dates back to 1881, when the Texas and Pacific Railway built a two-story section house, a pump, and a water tank at a small settlement in Martin County then known as Grelton. The town was officially named Stanton after Abraham Lincoln's Secretary of War and Supreme Court Justice Edwin McMasters Stanton.

MARTIN COUNTY COUNTRY CLUB

The golf   This semi-private, small-town West Texas course is wide-open and difficult when the wind is beating you down. You can score well here because the flat terrain has no bunkers. The fairways are lined with mesquite, mulberry, and cypress trees that are relatively immature, leaving room to work even if you miss the generous landing areas. The bent-grass greens have a reputation for being difficult, as they are small and vary in undulation and speed. Water comes into play on only one hole.

The details   915-756-2556. 303 W. Bell St., Stanton, TX 79782

- 1969. 9 holes. Par 36. Back – 3,263 yards (36.1/122). Middle – 3,005 yards (34.9/113). Forward – 2,338 yards. Price - $.

Nothing cures a hangover like a milkshake followed by a cheeseburger, the greasier the better. First you drink the milkshake; it coats your stomach, and the sugar does you good. Then you eat the cheeseburger, slowly. The grease helps replace oxygen in your blood, the bread soaks up whatever's left of the alcohol, and the whole thing sits well in your stomach. Tom Weiskopf

Getting there Take the Stanton exit off of I-20 and turn south. When you come to Hwy. 80, go south and make a right on Bell Rd.

STANTON NOTES On the second weekends in April, June, and October, Stanton is host to **The Old Sorehead Trade Days**, a perfect opportunity for the ladies to shop for antiques, arts, and jewelry while the fellas experience the golf course. If you're a history buff, visit the restored **Old Jail** (1908) on the courthouse square, or take in the **Martin County Historical Museum**, which features the county's Indian, ranching, oil, and railroad history. On Convent St. you can find the old abandoned convent boarding school that was destroyed by a tornado in 1938. For digs and eats, your best bet is to hit the **Sonic** for two chili dogs and a malt, and move on down the road to Midland for some semblance of a night life.

VAN HORN   Elev. 4,010   Pop. 2,310

Van Horn sits at the junction of Interstate 10, US 90, and Texas 54 in the southwest portion of Culberson County, which is home to seven peaks with elevations over 8,000 feet. Once a junction on the Bankhead Hwy. and historic Old Spanish Trail from San Antonio to California in the mid-1800s, the town is still a hub for state and national parks, surrounded by the Van Horn, Sierra Diablo, and Apache Mountains.

Van Horn has a sunny climate that is ideal for outdoor recreation and golf. Outdoorsmen who come to town to hunt white-tailed deer, mule deer, pronghorn antelope, or upland game birds should definitely test their golf game at Van Horn's quality 9-hole layout surrounded by scenic West Texas mountains.

MOUNTAIN VIEW VALLEY GOLF COURSE

The golf Mountain View was built in 1976 as a cooperative effort between officials of both Reeves and Culberson counties. At over 4,000 feet, this is one of only a few true Texas mountain golf experiences.

Tee shots soar, and approaches to the green must be hit with one club less than routinely played from other Texas courses. Length off the tee is simply not required. The fairways are generous and are generally firm to provide more roll, and the two par 5s are well under 500 yards. The toughest test on this course is the par 3s (Nos. 3 and 8), which have been lengthened recently and now play at around 200 yards. The greens are bent-grass, and in great condition.

The pro shop offers drinks, snacks (no beer), and basic golf amenities.

The details 915-283-2628. Golf Course Rd., Van Horn, TX 79855

- 1970. 9 holes. Par 36. Back – 3,024 (68.2). Forward – 2,459 (66.8). Price - $.

I never exaggerate. I just remember big. Chi Chi Rodriguez

Getting there Exit Golf Course Rd. and drive 1 mile south of town on I-10.

VAN HORN NOTES Smack in the middle of the Guadalupe Mountains, Big Bend, and Davis Mountains, you have your choice of parks to visit and desert outdoor activities. Rock climb, hike, mountain bike, or hunt. Eat at **Chuy's**, one of NFL broadcaster John Madden's favorite restaurants. The **Best Western Inn of Van Horn** (800-367-7589) has the best accommodations, but you can also opt for the Days, Comfort, and Best Western American Inns. Ask them about golf packages—we've heard that some locations will offer free greens fees with your stay. The **Sierra Diablo Wildlife Refuge**, home to the resurgent Texas bighorn sheep, is north on Texas 54.

WEST TEXAS BORDER CROSSINGS

JUAREZ, MEXICO   Across the border from El Paso, TX

Our knowledge is curiously limited at this point, but we know that the **Campestre Country Club** is the preferred choice for golf, offering a par 72 6,846-yard track and the added option of a caddie. Some say there's a 9-hole **Juarez Racetrack Golf Course**, which sounds like an interesting proposition if it's coupled with nefarious Mexican horse racing, and we've heard there's another 18-holer called **Mision de los Lagos Country Club**. These two are unconfirmed, but it's always entertaining to wonder what lies beyond in the wilds of Mexico.

ANTHONY, NM   20 miles from El Paso, TX

Smack dab on the Texas-New Mexico border north of El Paso, Anthony is a town of about 7,600 souls and home to two golf courses.

The 1940s-era 9-hole **Anthony Country Club** (505-882-2723) is a private course that tips out at a par 35, 2,893 yards (33.6/114). However, the golf highlight of this town is the 18-hole **Dos Lagos Golf Course** (505-882-2830), which is popular with golfers from El Paso and often quite crowded. This par 71 tips out at 6,335 yards (69.9/119) and is known for its undulating greens.

LAS CRUCES, NM   45 miles from El Paso, TX

With four outstanding golf courses, ideal weather, and a nice-sized population of only about 170,000, Las Cruces might be one of the nation's most underrated golf destinations. Where else can you go to avoid big-city hassles and play your ass off for ridiculously low prices?

The 1929 **Las Cruces Country Club** (505-526-8731), a par 72 6,324-yard track (69.5/119), is famous for its tiny, unprotected greens and flat, generous fairways. The best hole is the opening 431-yard dogleg left that requires some testy shot-making because of the trees.

Highly touted **Picacho Hills Country Club** (505-523-2556) is always rated by the big boys as one of the best in New Mexico, and a top-rated course nationally as well. A late 1970s Joe Finger-designed valley track surrounded by mountains, the course is immaculate and challenging. The route goes 6,880 yards (72.9/126) and is a standard par 72. No. 3 is the signature, an almost 400-yarder that is dominated by two beautiful lakes.

The **Sonoma Ranch Golf Course** (505-521-1818) is a newish 7,001-yard par 97 track that weaves through a residential community. The signature here is the superb condition of the fairways.

Floyd Farley built the **New Mexico State University Golf Course** (505-646-3219) in 1961, and over the years this quality track has hosted a few NCAA championship tourneys. Highly regarded as one of America's most popular and affordable courses, its desert beauty gives it a unique character. Tipped out at just over 7,000 yards (74.1/133), the course plays to a par 72 and serves up one of its most difficult holes as the opener. No. 1 goes 500 yards, and is rated as the second most difficult hole on the course.

JAL, NM
20 miles from Kermit, TX

Friendly little **Jal Country Club** (505-395-2330) routes 3,164 yards and plays to a par 36. Water is in play on two holes, and the regulars brag about the great condition of the slick greens. On this one you can walk and play all day for $10 on the weekends.

EUNICE, NM
37 miles from Andrews, TX

The scenic 9-hole **Eunice Municipal Golf Course** (505-394-2881) sports the typical desert-like fauna over its 3,228-yard, par 36 route. It's flat and wide-open, just like you like it, and you can walk for around $10 on the weekends.

The greatest of champions have all been ex-chokers. Peter Dobereiner

TEXAS TORNADO FREQUENCY
(1959-2000)

PANHANDLE

	Jan.	Feb.	March	April	May	June	July	Aug.	Sept.	Oct.	Nov.	Dec.	Annual
1959	0	0	8	4	32	14	10	3	4	5	6	0	86
1960	4	1	0	8	29	14	3	4	2	11	1	0	77
1961	0	1	21	15	24	30	9	2	12	0	10	0	124
1962	0	4	12	9	25	56	12	15	7	2	0	1	143
1963	0	0	3	9	19	24	8	4	6	4	5	0	82
1964	0	1	6	22	15	11	9	7	3	1	3	0	78
1965	2	5	3	7	43	24	2	9	4	6	0	3	108
1966	0	4	1	21	22	15	3	8	3	0	0	0	77
1967	0	2	11	17	34	22	10	5	124	2	0	5	232
1968	2	1	3	13	47	21	4	8	5	8	11	16	139
1969	0	1	1	16	65	16	6	7	6	8	1	0	127
1970	1	3	5	23	23	9	5	20	9	20	0	3	121
1971	0	20	10	24	27	33	7	20	7	16	14	23	191
1972	1	0	19	13	43	12	19	13	8	9	7	0	144
1973	14	1	29	25	21	24	4	8	5	3	9	4	147
1974	2	1	8	19	18	26	3	9	6	22	2	0	116
1975	5	2	9	12	50	18	10	3	3	3	1	1	117
1976	1	1	8	53	63	11	16	6	13	4	0	0	176
1977	0	0	3	34	50	4	5	5	12	0	6	4	123
1978	0	0	0	34	65	10	13	6	6	1	2	0	137
1979	1	2	24	33	39	14	12	10	4	15	3	0	157
1980	0	2	7	26	44	21	2	34	10	5	0	2	153
1981	0	7	7	9	71	26	5	20	5	23	3	0	176
1982	0	0	6	27	123	36	4	0	3	0	3	1	203
1983	5	7	24	1	62	35	4	22	5	0	7	14	186
1984	0	13	9	18	19	19	0	4	1	5	2	5	95
1985	0	0	5	41	28	5	3	1	1	3	1	2	90
1986	0	12	4	21	50	24	3	5	4	7	1	0	131
1987	1	1	7	0	54	19	11	3	8	0	16	4	124
1988	0	0	0	11	7	7	6	2	42	4	10	0	89
1989	3	0	5	3	70	63	0	6	3	6	1	0	160
1990	3	3	4	56	62	20	5	2	3	0	0	0	158
1991	20	5	2	39	72	36	1	2	3	8	4	0	192
1992	0	5	13	22	43	66	4	4	4	7	21	0	189
1993	1	4	5	17	39	4	4	0	12	23	8	0	117
1994	0	1	1	48	88	2	1	4	3	9	8	0	165
1995	6	0	13	36	66	75	11	3	2	1	0	10	223
1996	7	1	2	21	33	9	3	8	33	8	4	1	130
1997	0	6	7	31	59	50	2	2	1	16	3	0	177
1998	24	15	4	9	11	6	3	5	3	28	1	0	109
1999	22	0	22	23	70	26	3	8	0	0	0	4	178
2000	0	7	49	33	23	8	3	0	0	10	20	1	154

Source: Office of State Climatologist

THE PANHANDLE

Several years ago I met a cotton farmer from the northern Panhandle who was vacationing in the Big Bend region with his wife. After a few post-round beers in the crusty bar of a tiny West Texas "country club," he began articulatin' about the attractions of life in the High Plains, describing a paradise like no other in the landscape of Texas.

"What makes it so much better?" I asked, feeling a bit patriotic towards my own native West Texas.

"Better?" he drawled, "Well, lemme tell ya." He swigged his cold beer and savored the flavor as if it were a fine wine, then slammed it back down on the counter. "Up in our neck of the woods cowboys wave to passers-by from mud-splattered pickups, windmills are an art form, the two-lane blacktop shimmers and stretches towards the horizon, everything is exposed, the wind blows for free, and the people are humble, honest, and forthright."

Since it sounded a lot like West Texas to me, I figured I'd avoid confrontation and shift the subject to golf. "What about your courses up there—how do they compare to what you've seen down here?"

He shifted in his seat and swug another. "There's Lubbock . . . and there's Amarillo, and that's really 'bout it in terms of big-time courses. But once you hit the road, man . . . there's courses out there like none other. It's like a whole 'nother country!"

Even though it still sounded a lot like West Texas, I understood what he was getting at. Panhandle golf is distinctly different. The Panhandle, like West Texas, is where you're most likely to encounter the quick one-finger wave shared by country travelers on desolate back roads. The Panhandle is not where you'll find big-city golf.

Up here in the Big Nothing, Lubbock and Amarillo are the only cities with a significant population. Second only to Southern Arizona for the number of days of sunshine annually, this most northwestern outpost of Texas is the quintessential plains region on earth. The terrain sprawls out from the Caprock, sliced by mesas, canyons, and dramatic geography found nowhere else in Texas.

There are 48 cities, 70 golf courses, and 900 golf holes. Over 90% of the facilities are open to the public. Of the 48 cities, few have populations of over several thousand or anything beyond a single 9-hole golf course. And you won't find many sand bunkers—the high winds would just blow the sand away.

There should be no excessive wrist action for this [chipping] stroke. The simplest, most straightforward way to play these shots is without spin. With shorter chip shots, you do this by taking your wrists out of the shot. Try not cocking your wrists. Ben Crenshaw

THE PANHANDLE
REGIONAL WEATHER

	Average Precipitation	Average Temperature (F)
January	0.39	38.8
February	0.68	43.1
March	0.89	51.2
April	0.97	61.1
May	2.35	69.4
June	2.75	77.2
July	2.37	80
August	2.51	77.9
September	2.6	71.1
October	1.86	61.4
November	0.75	49.8
December	0.53	40.6

PANHANDLE

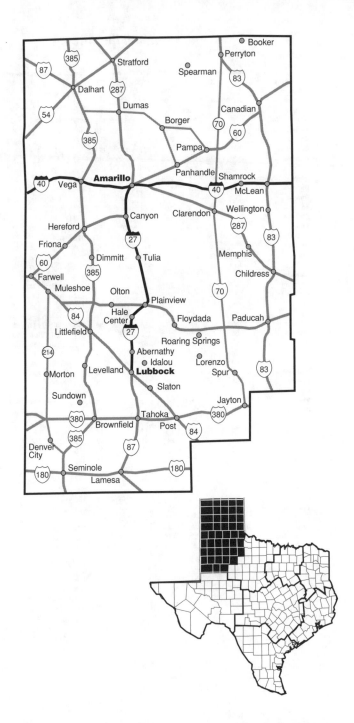

Panhandle Mileage

	Abernathy	Amarillo	Booker	Borger	Brownfield	Canadian	Canyon	Childress	Clarendon	Dalhart	Denver Ci.	Dimmitt	Dumas	Farwell	Floydada
Abernathy		103	232	149	57	198	86	127	122	179	97	64	149	84	40
Amarillo	103		130	49	159	99	19	115	59	81	189	66	47	95	101
Booker	232	130		84	288	44	149	151	125	125	320	196	100	225	209
Borger	149	49	84		206	74	67	127	70	80	238	114	41	144	127
Brownfield	57	159	288	206		255	141	177	176	214	40	98	206	107	90
Canadian	198	99	44	74	255		118	107	92	134	288	165	110	194	176
Canyon	86	19	149	67	141	118		127	70	93	172	48	66	77	84
Childress	127	115	151	127	177	107	127		57	196	217	131	162	174	88
Clarendon	122	59	125	70	176	92	70	57		139	216	110	106	147	86
Dalhart	179	81	125	80	214	134	93	196	139		236	116	39	142	178
Denver City	97	189	320	238	40	288	172	217	216	236		133	236	111	130
Dimmitt	64	66	196	114	98	165	48	131	110	116	133		113	45	71
Dumas	149	47	100	41	206	110	66	162	106	39	236	113		141	148
Farwell	84	95	225	144	107	194	77	174	147	142	111	45	141		108
Floydada	40	101	209	127	90	176	84	88	86	178	130	71	148	108	
Friona	92	71	202	120	115	170	54	163	123	118	119	31	118	24	102
Hale Center	17	86	215	133	73	182	69	120	105	163	113	48	133	82	34
Hereford	85	48	178	97	119	147	30	152	100	95	141	21	95	47	92
Idalou	22	112	240	158	51	207	95	126	125	188	91	82	159	98	39
Jayton	101	183	256	202	105	217	166	112	132	259	145	153	230	179	82
Lamesa	80	181	309	227	37	276	164	195	193	251	59	135	228	144	107
Levelland	45	134	265	183	30	233	117	169	166	184	69	68	181	77	81
Littlefield	31	110	241	159	54	209	93	152	143	160	92	44	157	53	65
Lorenzo	29	119	235	153	60	202	102	118	117	195	100	88	166	107	31
Lubbock	19	121	250	168	39	216	104	138	137	196	79	81	168	90	51
McLean	159	72	101	63	213	57	88	69	37	143	253	136	105	165	123
Memphis	124	85	139	97	175	95	97	31	26	165	215	113	132	157	85
Morton	59	134	265	183	57	233	117	185	180	181	55	78	181	56	98
Muleshoe	63	100	230	148	85	199	82	166	149	147	90	44	146	22	86
Olton	40	85	215	133	74	184	67	132	116	146	114	31	132	57	52
Paducah	101	143	181	155	151	137	142	32	85	224	191	133	190	170	62
Pampa	154	54	79	29	210	46	73	103	47	109	244	120	71	149	131
Panhandle	127	27	106	23	183	73	46	104	48	102	217	93	64	122	104
Perryton	216	115	16	68	272	47	133	154	109	109	304	181	85	210	193
Plainview	30	74	203	121	86	170	58	109	94	151	126	42	121	79	29
Post	58	151	265	183	52	232	134	138	143	228	92	121	198	130	57
Roaring Springs	72	134	203	148	114	167	117	66	78	211	154	104	181	141	33
Seminole	98	200	329	247	41	296	183	219	218	254	22	139	247	132	131
Shamrock	173	91	94	83	223	50	108	58	56	163	263	155	124	184	134
Slaton	34	127	255	173	49	222	111	141	140	204	89	97	174	106	53
Spearman	192	89	42	42	248	58	108	165	113	83	278	155	59	184	169
Spur	77	159	233	178	95	197	142	96	108	235	135	129	206	155	58
Stratford	183	80	94	75	239	110	99	195	139	31	265	145	33	171	181
Sundown	60	149	279	198	27	248	131	180	179	199	54	83	196	86	93
Tahoka	48	149	277	195	28	244	132	163	162	225	68	110	196	119	75
Tulia	55	50	180	99	111	149	33	99	78	127	151	32	97	76	53
Vega	114	35	165	84	148	134	43	148	92	65	171	50	65	77	121
Wellington	151	101	121	110	202	77	113	32	43	182	242	140	148	184	112

PANHANDLE

Panhandle Mileage

na	Hale Cntr.	Hereford	Idalou	Jayton	Lamesa	Levelland	Littlefield	Lorenzo	Lubbock	McLean	Memphis	Morton	Muleshoe	Olton	Paducah	Pampa
92	17	85	22	101	80	45	31	29	19	159	124	59	63	40	101	154
71	86	48	112	183	181	134	110	119	121	72	85	134	100	85	143	54
42	215	178	240	256	309	265	241	235	250	101	139	265	230	215	181	79
20	133	97	158	202	227	183	159	153	168	63	97	183	148	133	155	29
45	73	119	51	105	37	30	54	60	39	213	175	57	85	74	151	210
70	182	147	207	217	276	233	209	202	216	57	95	233	199	184	137	46
54	69	30	95	166	164	117	93	102	104	88	97	117	82	67	142	73
53	120	152	126	112	195	169	152	118	138	69	31	185	166	132	32	103
23	105	100	125	132	193	166	143	117	137	37	26	180	149	116	85	47
18	163	95	188	259	251	184	160	195	196	143	165	181	147	146	224	109
19	113	141	91	145	59	69	92	100	79	253	215	55	90	114	191	244
31	48	21	82	153	135	68	44	88	81	136	113	78	44	31	133	120
48	133	95	159	230	228	181	157	166	168	105	132	181	146	132	190	71
24	82	47	98	179	144	77	53	107	90	165	157	56	22	57	170	149
02	34	92	39	82	107	81	65	31	51	123	85	98	86	52	62	131
	79	23	105	184	152	85	61	114	97	141	144	64	29	61	164	126
79		69	37	116	96	61	37	44	35	142	109	74	60	25	96	137
23	69		102	173	156	89	65	109	101	118	126	86	52	51	154	102
05	37	102		81	71	42	45	9	12	162	124	68	76	59	100	162
84	116	173	81		109	122	126	73	92	165	126	148	157	134	80	178
52	96	156	71	109		67	91	77	61	230	192	94	123	110	168	231
85	61	89	42	122	67		24	51	30	203	166	27	56	52	142	189
61	37	65	45	126	91	24		54	37	179	146	37	32	28	126	165
14	44	109	9	73	77	51	54		21	154	116	77	85	68	92	157
97	35	101	12	92	61	30	37	21		174	136	56	68	51	112	172
41	142	118	162	165	230	203	179	154	174		39	204	169	153	97	36
44	109	126	124	126	192	166	146	116	136	39		183	152	120	59	73
64	74	86	68	148	94	27	37	77	56	204	183		35	65	159	189
29	60	52	76	157	123	56	32	85	68	169	152	35		35	148	154
61	25	51	59	134	110	52	28	68	51	153	120	65	35		114	139
64	96	154	100	80	168	142	126	92	112	97	59	159	148	114		131
26	137	102	162	178	231	189	165	157	172	36	73	189	154	139	131	
99	110	75	135	179	204	162	138	130	145	55	74	162	127	112	132	28
86	200	163	224	241	293	249	225	219	234	92	129	249	214	199	184	64
73	13	63	39	110	108	74	51	46	48	130	97	88	59	24	91	125
37	74	142	41	53	56	71	77	42	40	180	142	96	108	91	112	188
35	67	125	63	54	129	105	97	55	75	111	72	130	119	85	40	125
39	114	159	92	146	40	71	94	101	80	254	216	76	110	116	192	251
61	157	137	173	167	241	215	195	164	185	20	49	223	189	168	87	55
14	50	118	17	77	54	47	53	23	17	177	139	73	84	67	115	177
60	175	137	200	244	269	223	199	195	210	98	136	223	189	174	194	70
60	92	149	57	24	99	98	102	49	68	141	102	124	133	110	69	155
47	166	125	192	263	261	213	189	199	201	138	165	210	176	165	223	104
93	76	104	54	128	64	15	39	63	42	216	178	30	64	67	154	203
26	64	131	39	77	32	58	66	45	29	198	160	84	97	80	136	199
63	38	53	64	135	133	97	73	71	73	111	81	110	75	45	109	104
53	98	30	132	203	186	119	95	139	131	105	118	116	81	81	176	90
66	136	143	151	142	219	193	173	143	163	47	27	210	179	147	61	82

Panhandle Mileage

	Panhandle	Perryton	Plainview	Post	Roaring Sp.	Seminole	Shamrock	Slaton	Spearman	Spur	Stratford	Sundown	Tahoka	Tulia	Vega	Wellington
Abernathy	127	216	30	58	72	98	173	34	192	77	183	60	48	55	114	151
Amarillo	27	115	74	151	134	200	91	127	89	159	80	149	149	50	35	101
Booker	106	16	203	265	203	329	94	255	42	233	94	279	277	180	165	121
Borger	23	68	121	183	148	247	83	173	42	178	75	198	195	99	84	110
Brownfield	183	272	86	52	114	41	223	49	248	95	239	27	28	111	148	202
Canadian	73	47	170	232	167	296	50	222	58	197	110	248	244	149	134	77
Canyon	46	133	58	134	117	183	108	111	108	142	99	131	132	33	43	113
Childress	104	154	109	138	66	219	58	141	165	96	195	180	163	99	148	32
Clarendon	48	109	94	143	78	218	56	140	113	108	139	179	162	78	92	43
Dalhart	102	109	151	228	211	254	163	204	83	235	31	199	225	127	65	182
Denver City	217	304	126	92	154	22	263	89	278	135	265	54	68	151	171	242
Dimmitt	93	181	42	121	104	139	155	97	155	129	145	83	110	32	50	140
Dumas	64	85	121	198	181	247	124	174	59	206	33	196	196	97	65	148
Farwell	122	210	79	130	141	132	184	106	184	155	171	86	119	76	77	184
Floydada	104	193	29	57	33	131	134	53	169	58	181	93	75	53	121	112
Friona	99	186	73	137	135	139	161	114	160	160	147	93	126	63	53	166
Hale Center	110	200	13	74	67	114	157	50	175	92	166	76	64	38	98	136
Hereford	75	163	63	142	125	159	137	118	137	149	125	104	131	53	30	143
Idalou	135	224	39	41	63	92	173	17	200	57	192	54	39	64	132	151
Jayton	179	241	110	53	54	146	167	77	244	24	263	128	77	135	203	142
Lamesa	204	293	108	56	129	40	241	54	269	99	261	64	32	133	186	219
Levelland	162	249	74	71	105	71	215	47	223	98	213	15	58	97	119	193
Littlefield	138	225	51	77	97	94	195	53	199	102	189	39	66	73	95	173
Lorenzo	130	219	42	42	55	101	164	23	195	49	199	63	45	71	139	143
Lubbock	145	234	48	40	75	80	185	17	210	68	201	42	29	73	131	163
McLean	55	92	130	180	111	254	20	177	98	141	138	216	198	111	105	47
Memphis	74	129	97	142	72	216	49	139	136	102	165	178	160	81	118	27
Morton	162	249	88	96	130	76	223	73	223	124	210	30	84	110	116	210
Muleshoe	127	214	59	108	119	110	189	84	189	133	176	64	97	75	81	179
Olton	112	199	24	91	85	116	168	67	174	110	165	67	80	45	81	147
Paducah	132	184	91	112	40	192	87	115	194	69	223	154	136	109	176	61
Pampa	28	64	125	188	125	251	55	177	70	155	104	203	199	104	90	82
Panhandle		91	98	161	125	224	74	150	65	155	97	176	172	77	63	90
Perryton	91		188	250	187	314	96	240	26	217	78	264	261	165	150	123
Plainview	98	188		79	62	128	146	55	163	86	155	89	76	26	93	124
Post	161	250	79		73	94	190	24	226	43	231	75	24	103	171	167
Roaring Springs	125	187	62	73		155	121	78	191	30	214	117	97	86	154	95
Seminole	224	314	128	94	155		265	90	289	136	280	64	69	152	189	243
Shamrock	74	96	146	190	121	265		187	107	151	158	226	209	130	125	27
Slaton	150	240	55	24	78	90	187		216	66	207	52	22	79	148	166
Spearman	65	26	163	226	191	289	107	216		221	53	238	237	139	124	134
Spur	155	217	86	43	30	136	151	66	221		239	109	67	111	179	125
Stratford	97	78	155	231	214	280	158	207	53	239		228	229	130	94	181
Sundown	176	264	89	75	117	64	226	52	238	109	228		55	112	134	205
Tahoka	172	261	76	24	97	69	209	22	237	67	229	55		101	160	187
Tulia	77	165	26	103	86	152	130	79	139	111	130	112	101		77	108
Vega	63	150	93	171	154	189	125	148	124	179	94	134	160	77		134
Wellington	90	123	124	167	95	243	27	166	134	125	181	205	187	108	134	

PANHANDLE

ABERNATHY

Elev. 3,327   Pop. 2,850

Like Idalou and Slaton, Abernathy is a "suburb" of Lubbock. It's 18 miles from town on Interstate Highway 27 and US 87, barely across the border in Hale County. Named after M.G. Abernathy, the town was founded in 1909 by the South Plains Investment Company as the Santa Fe Railroad made its way from Plainview to Lubbock.

ABERNATHY COUNTRY CLUB

The golf   Like so many other small-town courses in the Panhandle, this "country club" is a 9-hole, semi-private course that allows anyone to play. With only one water hazard (hole 9), no bunkers, and flat terrain, this course is very fair, good for the ego, and fun for the high handicapper. This course is best experienced as a day trip from Lubbock.

The fairways are lined with trees and sport rare mounds that result in uneven lies. Both par 5s have dogleg fairways. The toughest hole is a 226-yard, par 3 into a green framed by mature trees; it's particularly difficult when the winds are howling. Pay once and play all day. For the second round use the additional set of tees for a different look.

The details   806-328-5261. FM 2060, Abernathy, TX 79311

- 1960. 9 holes. Back – 3,170 yards, par 36 (34.5 rating). Forward – 2,638 yards, par 36 (35.1). Price - $.

Getting there Exit FM 2060 off of I-27 and head east 4.5 miles to the course.

ABERNATHY NOTES There are no hotels, so head to Lubbock for the night. For eats, **Vecchio's** specializes in sloppy home-style burritos. The **Pizza Station** has outstanding pizza.

AMARILLO

Elev. 3,676 Pop. 176,066

The cowboy town of Amarillo dates back to 1887, when railroading and cattle dominated the economy. Once the fencing of ranges began, the town became the world's leading cattle shipping market, and wheat farmers turned Amarillo into a major wheat belt. Here in the northern reaches of the Texas Panhandle, the skies are bluer and the air is pristine–cleaner than any in the nation for a city of its size.

Amarillo has a unique Western heritage, excellent shopping, famous dining, and plenty of quality golf without the big-city crowds.

To hit the ball farther, think of creating your maximum clubhead speed past the ball—not at it, and certainly not before it. Randy Smith

AMARILLO COUNTRY CLUB

The golf   North of town lies the Amarillo Country Club, a private 18-hole layout that's considered one of the best courses in the Panhandle. William McConnell designed the course way back in 1919, and renovations occurred in 1960 (Warren Cantrell), and again in 1983 (Jay Morrish).

Tree-lined fairways, various hills, and several out-of-bounds make this a tough course, even though it's relatively short and there are minimal water hazards. The course has a good variety of holes, with several par 4s over 400 yards and only three par 5s. The feature hole is No. 6, a 349-yard par 4 that requires an approach shot over a lake into a green surrounded by bunkers.

The details   806-355-5021. 4800 Bushland Blvd., Amarillo, TX 79106

- 1919. William A. McConnell. 18 holes. Par 71. Back – 6,501 (71.1/127). Middle – 6,078 (69.2/123). Forward – 5,542 (72.1/123). Price - $$.

Getting there North of town on I-40 going west, take the Western Ave. exit and turn left. When you come to Bushland Rd., turn left; the entrance is on the right side of the road.

COMANCHE TRAIL GOLF COURSE

The golf   Owned by the city of Amarillo, Comanche Trail offers 36 holes of championship links-style golf at a very affordable price.

The original **Tomahawk** course, which opened in 1990, features a drainage ditch that runs through the layout and impacts holes 2-7. There are no trees and the wind can really affect your round, but the fairways are generous and the large greens are welcome targets when facing a stiff cross wind. Watch out for the water, which impacts 14 holes.

Tomahawk's signature hole is the dogleg-left No. 5. Playing it right to avoid the ditch spanning the entire left side of the fairway leaves a long iron approach. However, trying to carry the ditch leaves a short wedge into the green. Hole 9 is tough because of the narrow fairway and length (445 yards).

Robert Cupp designed the **Arrowhead** course, which features long rough and plenty of water and sand. No. 9 is a difficult par 5, only playing 484 yards from the blue tees, but water looms along the left of the fairway all the way around to the back of a well-bunkered green. Big hitters might want to go for the green in two following a solid tee shot. Hole 4, a 427-yard par 4, is rated the most difficult, featuring a tee shot over a small pond into a dogleg-left fairway.

The details   806-378-4281. 4200 S. Grand St., Amarillo, TX 79103

- www.comanchetrail.com

You ought to be able to kick the putter out of your hands at any time just by tapping it with the toe of your shoe. Bobby Jones

- Tomahawk: 1990. Charles Howard. 18 holes. Black – 7,180 (72.9/117). Blue – 6,748 (70.9/113). Red – 6,259 (68.7/108). White – 5,524 (70.0/108). Price - $$.
- Arrowhead: 1999. Bob Cupp. 18 holes. Par 72. Black – 6,940 (71.9/121). Blue (69.4/116). Red – 6,018 (67.4/112). White – 5,279 (70.2/118). Price - $$.

Getting there From Amarillo, take I-40 east and get off at the Grand exit. Then head south for about 3 miles to the course.

LA PALOMA GOLF CLUB

The golf Some maintain that the scenery around Amarillo is flat and mundane, yet set in the rolling plains around Amarillo Creek you'll find an impressive links-style course with dramatic elevation changes, three lakes, a creek, a natural waterfall, and a track that totally envelops its natural surroundings.

Many say La Paloma is the most difficult course in the area. The superbly conditioned bent-grass greens are lightning-fast. For a links course the fairways are surprisingly narrow, and loaded with fairway bunkers. Most greens are surrounded by water and/or bunkers.

The drab Panhandle scenery livens up on the back with a multitude of natural rock outcroppings. Hole 16 is the most spectacular: a 220-yard par 3 that requires a full carry over the water hazard to a big green fronted by a rock wall.

Play La Paloma while you can, as the facility has plans to go private. You won't be disappointed–this is one you'll want to play pretty much regardless of price.

The details 806-342-3051. 4302 Fairway Dr., Amarillo, TX 79124

- 1985. Robert Von Hagge. 18 holes. Par 71. Champs – 6,676 (72.4/131). Intermediate – 6,132 (70.2/124). Regular – 5,622 (68.4/117). Forward - 5,095 (70.5/116). Price - $$.

Getting there From I-40 west, exit Western St. and drive north 5 miles to Fairway Dr. Turn left and continue .75 mile to the course entrance on the right side of the street.

TASCOSA COUNTRY CLUB

The golf It's unfortunate that more clubs don't take the time to detail their history for the golfing public. Thanks to Morris Loewenstern, a member of the first foursome to tee off on the course, we know a little more about Tascosa Country Club.

─────────── ☆ ───────────

Let your love of winning drive your practice habits. Practice shouldn't be viewed as an exercise in self-denial or sacrifice. It should be viewed as an integral part of the process of improvement. Dr. Bob Rotella

Mr. Loewenstern was kind enough to leave behind a few notes detailing things like how his playing partner on the first hole, Stanley Blackburn, hit the opening shot into the swimming pool, and how the second ball "exploded." He also mentions that the club purchased the original 200 acres of land in 1954 at a price of $250 per acre, and that the original deed stated that the Humble Oil Co. had the right to drill for oil and gas.

Pampa-based Warren Cantrell designed the course, and volunteer groups manually cleared the land of rocks and debris. The original 10,000-square-foot clubhouse was built by member Dale Andrews, a local contractor, for a total cost of just over $200,000.

While not a long course, the fairways are lined with trees and the undulating bent-grass greens make three-putts a possibility. The course is loaded with bunkers, and high berms dot the fairways. The toughest stretch is holes 15 and 16–a long, testy par 3 followed by a long par 4.

The details   806-374-2351. 2300 Western St., Amarillo, TX 79116

- www.tascosacc.org

- 1955. Warren Cantrell. 18 holes. Par 72. Blue – 6,492 (71.6/121). Red – 6,104 (69.5/ 116). White – 5,401 (70./1/114). Gold – 5,200 (68.4/111). Price - $$.

Getting there From I-40 west, take the Western St. exit and go north. Drive 4 miles to the course and look for the entrance on the left side of the street.

ROSS ROGERS MUNICIPAL GOLF COURSE

The golf   Ross Rogers offers two basic, 18-hole courses of similar design, referred to as the East and West courses. For over 50 years the course has been the site of the annual Budweiser Partnership Tournament, a low ball/low total match play event that draws visitors from all over the area.

The **East Course**, originally a 9-hole track but expanded to 18 holes in 1981, features generous fairways, flat greens of average speed, and three small lakes. Holes of note are the par 3 No. 6, which forces a carry over water to an elevated green, and No. 12, which offers a lake cutting into the fairway that can only be carried with a drive over 200 yards.

Holes 15-17 provide a tough stretch of golf with two long par 4s and a difficult par 3. However, No. 18 offers a chance for birdie with a 483-yard par 5 with a dogleg right that can shorten the hole even more.

Built in 1977, The **West Course** is shorter than the East but very similar in design and layout. The design features little water, and the parallel fairways are characteristic of a course that was jammed into an area too small for 36 holes, but still needed to meet the demands of the golfing public. The back nine

The chief reaction among amateurs to poor putting, it seems to me, is exasperation, combined with a sort of vague hope that, by some kind of mini-miracle, it will all have gotten better by the next time they play. Jack Nicklaus

boasts two of the better holes: the 201-yard, par 3 No. 11 and the difficult, 425-yard No. 14.

The details   806-378-3086. 722 NW 24th Ave., Amarillo, TX 79107

- East Course: 1968. Leon Howard. 18 holes. Par 72. Back – 6,858 (70.8/112). Middle – 6,486 (69.2/109). Forward – 5,528 (69.5/111). Price - $$.
- West Course: 1977. 18 holes. Par 72. Back – 6,602 (69.2/110). Middle – 6,361 (68.1/107). Forward – 5,392 (68.2/108). Price - $$.

Getting there From I-40 east, take I-87 north to 24th St. Turn left and the course is 1 mile down on the right. Price - $$.

PRESTON WEST PAR 3 GOLF COURSE

The golf   Owned by one of the most famous professional poker players ever, Amarillo Slim, this is the place to work in a quick practice round when you're bordering on the shanks and need to get back to basics. The course is lighted after dark in the spring and summer, making it a nice place to have a few beers and work in a practice round. Unlike most par 3 courses, this one has enough water to make you think.

The details   806-353-7003. 9101 S. Coulter Rd., Amarillo, TX 79119

- 1993. T. A. Preston. 9 holes. Par 27. 972 yards. Price - $.

Getting there From Amarillo, head south on Hwy. 87, then take the Hollywood Rd. exit and turn right.

AMARILLO NOTES During the summer months High Plains evenings can be spent watching the great game of baseball, which is even better when it's the minors, by strolling into the **Amarillo Dillas'** ballpark (806-342-3455) for hot dogs and cold beers. Piddle around for macho-wear in **Amarillo's** boot and saddle shops. **Rancher Farmer Supply Company, Horse & Rider,** and **Oliver Brothers Saddle Shop** all offer tack, boots, and other odds and ends. For your meals, consider the Pig Hip Sandwich at **Cee's N Dee's Bar-B-Que** (806-342-4014), at the site of the old **Twing's Drive Inn. Ruby Tequila's Mexican Kitchen** (806-358-7829) serves Tex-Mex, and the **Stockyard Cafe** (806-342-9411) serves down-home meals. You decide which, but live music can be heard at **Brewster's Pub, The Caravan,** the **Golden Light Café,** or **Midnight Rodeo.** For lodging call the **Ambassador Hotel** (806-358-6161) for deluxe digs, or the colorful western-style **Big Texan Hotel** (806-372-5000) for more affordable rooms. There are also five B&Bs if that's your thing – try **La Casita del Sol** (806-342-3444) on S. Harrison.

⭐

I'm very tightly wound. All that jabbering is a
pressure valve. I couldn't do without it. Lee Trevino

BOOKER

Elev. 2,834   Pop. 1,279

Borders have never meant much to the town of Booker, which sits way the hell up there in the northeast corner of the Texas Panhandle. The town originated 7 miles to the northwest in 1909 as La Kemp, Oklahoma, and it now sits on the county lines of Lipscomb and Ochiltree, with residents living on either side of the county line. Booker's economy is based upon wheat, cattle, oil, and gas production, and their golf course is called Booker Country Club.

BOOKER COUNTRY CLUB

The golf   Unique in that it is the northernmost course in Texas, BCC is a nice little layout with a few trees lining wide fairways. The greens here are rarely guarded by anything other than the occasional bunker, so the design incorporates elevated greens with subtle sloping to cause problems. Hole 4 is the feature hole: a 382-yard par 4 with out-of-bounds staked by a barbed wire fence on the left and trees on the right.

The details   806-658-9663. W. Santa Fe, Booker, TX 79005

* 1960. 9 holes. Par 36. Back – 3,033 (33.2/90). Forward – 2,520 (32.5/90). No driving range. No alcohol served. Snack food only. Price - $.

Getting there From Booker, take Hwy. 15 to Main St. and drive north for 1 block. Turn left on West Santa Fe; the road dead-ends at the entrance to the course.

BOOKER NOTES   Go for the local feel at **Partner's Family Restaurant** (806-658-4859), where you can ponder the fact that Booker is farther north than Santa Fe, NM. If it's raining hard watch the playa lakes fill up with water; otherwise drive across the border and fart around in Oklahoma. If you need a room find the **Santa Fe Motel** on Industrial (806-658-9704).

BORGER

Elev. 3,116   Pop. 14,169

Borger boomed in the 1920s with the discovery of the Panhandle Oil Field, bringing some 40,000 residents who toughed it out in oil field shanties strung across the open land. After the degenerates were pushed out of the city, the community redesigned the town and established itself as an orderly center for oil, chemicals, and cattle. Surprisingly for a city of only 14,000, Borger is home to two quality 18-hole golf courses.

If you dub a shot, don't berate yourself unduly. Golf is supposed to cure ulcers, not create them. Arnold Palmer

BORGER COUNTRY CLUB

The golf   Borger Country Club is a semi-private facility that is priced well (under $50) for a full round of golf with cart. The layout is typical of the rolling terrain around Borger, and the greens are in good condition. The front nine is flatter than the back, which has slight undulations. Two lakes impact play on a few holes.

The details   806-273-2231. 599 Broadmoor St., Borger, TX 79007

- 1932. 18 holes. Par 72. Back – 6,199 (68.9/105). Forward – 4,835 (66.2/100). Price - $$.

Getting there From Hwy. 136 north, take the Borger exit (at Spur 1551) and turn right. When you come to Broadmoor, turn right and drive to the end of the street. The course is on the right.

PHILLIPS MUNICIPAL GOLF COURSE

The golf   Phillips Municipal offers wide-open fairways with generous landing areas, and greens that are in solid condition. This is an enjoyable course to play for the average golfer because of its reasonable length. Four par 4s are just over 300 yards. The signature hole is No. 8, a 373-yard par 4 that requires a blind tee shot over a hill. Nos. 7 and 13, both short par 3s, offer good birdie opportunities in addition to the par 4s.

The details   806-274-6812. 1609 N. Sterling, Borger, TX 79707.

- 1941. 18 holes. Par 72. Back – 6,071 (68.1/100). Forward – 5,212 (68.5/105). Price - $$.

Getting there From Hwy. 207 driving south, take Country Club Rd. west 3 blocks to the course.

BORGER NOTES   15 miles outside of town is the **Alibates Flint Quarries,** a National Historic Monument that pays tribute to 12,000 years of flint cliffs that were the Indians' source of hard stone to make their weapons. Take the 25-mile **scenic drive** west and north to Stinnett, which crosses rough, canyon-cut landscapes of the Canadian River brakes and leads across the dam impounding **Lake Meredith** (Texas 136 west, FM 1319, and FM 687 north). For eats in town, consider **Old Sutphen's BBQ** (806-273-6442) for lunch, and either **Lorene's Mexican Kitchen** (806-273-7106) or **The Nu-Way Cafe** (806-273-5321), both on Main St. For lodging there's the Royal and Budget Inns, but everyone will generally point you towards Borger's **Best Western Inn** (806-274-7050).

If you haven't had any instruction, it's almost certain that the first things you presently position are your feet, plonking them down in what you hope are the right locations, followed by the clubhead. Break that habit as fast as you can. Because you must align everything else relative to where it faces, always—repeat, always—aim the clubhead first. John Jacobs

PANHANDLE

BROWNFIELD

Elev. 3,312   Pop. 9,218

Brownfield is a neat, orderly little city that was established as the Terry County seat in 1904 and named for Col. Benjamin Franklin Terry, Confederate leader of Terry's Texas Rangers. Situated at the intersection of five highway routes, Brownfield is the hub for the area's farming, livestock, and oil production.

BROWNFIELD GOLF CLUB

The golf   Brownfield's course is a simple little layout featuring wide-open fairways and medium-sized greens. Wind can be a factor here, and there are a few drainage ditches that serve as water hazards.

Among the toughest holes are No. 3, a 195-yard par 3, and the 418-yard par 4 No. 5. Both par 5s are well under 500 yards, and holes 2 and 4 are short par 4s that are good birdie opportunities as well. Two sets of tees allow for an 18-hole round. Pay once and play all day.

The details   806-637-3656. Country Club Dr., Brownfield, TX 79316

- 1950. 9 holes. Par 36. Back – 3,170 (34.0). Forward – 2,656 (35.0). Price - $$.

Getting there From Hwy. 380 driving east, turn right on Country Club Rd. and drive about 2.5 miles. The entrance is on the left side of the road.

BROWNFIELD NOTES Brownfield has several great local eateries, including **The Cub Drive-In** (806-637-8297), where old-fashioned burgers are the specialty. **J.B. Steaks** (806-637-7471) is the place for sit-down sirloins, and two Tex-Mex joints stand out – **El Palacio** (806-637-0276). There are four motel/hotel options, highlighted by the **Best Western** (806-637-9471). Outside of town, ponder the death of the plains settlement of Gomez (6 miles west), which dwindled away in 1904 after Brownfield won the Terry County seat election from Gomez by 5 votes. The **Terry County Historical Museum** showcases the old pioneering times.

CANADIAN

Elev. 2,339   Pop. 2,173

The surreal beauty of the sand-sage prairie is hidden away in one of the outlying areas of Texas that most folks never get to experience. Up here at the far end of US 83, high in the northeast portion of the Panhandle, the weather in

The mere test of strength or of skill is one of the most subordinate of the elements of golf; much more important is the test of what goes by the name of "nerve," that quiet self confidence which no ghastly phantasms can shake ... So many golfers forget this. "If I had not done this, that, or the other stupid thing," they say, "my score would have been so-and-so." My dear sire, it is just those stupid things that make the game. Arnold Haultain

March might turn from 60 degrees and clear into a frozen winter wasteland in hours. In fact, the ecosystem here is so unique that Hemphill County is one of the last remaining strongholds of the Lesser Prairie Chicken, a bird now reduced from a population of millions to a few hundred specimens. Ranching and oil drive the economy, and Canadian serves as the hub of those operations.

CANADIAN GOLF CLUB

The golf   The Canadian Golf Club is a 9-hole, semi-private course that features tight, tree-lined fairways and small, fast greens. Not a difficult course–a few water hazards come into play, and the course is relatively short.

Get your pars in the early part of the round, as the finisher is a classic. This long par 4 features two blind tee shots onto a fairway with out-of-bounds on either side. Two sets of tees make for a full round, and you can pay once and play all day.

The details   806-323-5512. Hwy. 83 North, Canadian, TX 79014

- 1976. 9 holes. Par 36. Back – 2,942 (33.9/120). Forward – 2,497 (33.5/115). Price - $.

Getting there From Hwy. 60 going north, turn left on Hwy. 83 and the course is less than a mile away.

CANADIAN NOTES   Study the history of Canadian and Hemphill Counties at the quaint little **River Valley Pioneer Museum**. Northwest of Canadian is the **Black Kettle National Grasslands**, with nature trails, fishing at Lake Marvin, and places to picnic and camp. Don't miss the sandwiches at **Alexander's Grocery & Deli** (806-323-8853). For rooms call the **Emerald House** (806-323-5827) or the **Thicket B&B** (806-323-8118).

CANYON   Elev. 3,566   Pop. 13,245

The seat of Randall County and gateway to Palo Duro Canyon, this town originated in 1878 as headquarters for the huge T Anchor Ranch. Canyon sits just 18 miles south of Amarillo, and is home to an 18-hole public golf course and a 9-hole private country club.

CANYON COUNTRY CLUB

The golf   Canyon Country Club ranks at the top of the list in terms of small-town 9-hole courses the traveling golfer should experience. Set in the bottom of a canyon outside of town, this is an unassuming semi-private facil-

---

⭐

Fact: Walter P. Chrysler served as general foreman of the Childress railroad shops in 1905 and 1906 before working as a master mechanic in Iowa and eventually founding the Chrysler Motor Corporation.

ity with a gem of a golf course. Pristine fairways, bent-grass greens that are flawless, and creeks running throughout the course all add to the fun experience.

The design features short par 4s that dogleg, tempting the aggressive player to cut the corner and go for the green. A few of the greens are elevated, and the undulations make them tricky to get a good read.

The details   806-499-3397. Hereford Hwy. (Route 1), Canyon, TX 79015

- 9 holes. Par 35. Back – 2,808 (33.9/107). Forward – 2,340 (35.1/113). Price - $.

Getting there From I-27, get off at the Buffalo Stadium Rd. exit and go west to Route 1.

PALO DURO CREEK GOLF CLUB

The golf   Palo Duro Creek is a wonderful course that is sometimes maligned by the locals for being in less-than-perfect condition. Out-of-bounds squeezes the narrow fairways on most holes on the front nine as it winds through a residential community. Then water becomes the predominant hazard on the back, impacting almost every hole. Your approaches will find fast, undulating bent-grass greens.

The design features two challenging par 5s: The 549-yard No. 5 plays uphill into the prevailing wind, and No. 12 plays almost 600 yards with a tee shot through a chute of trees, and two more shots over water, including the approach into a green that is surrounded by the wet stuff. Another tough hole is No. 14, a 225-yard par 3 that requires a solid shot to carry the water.

The details   806-655-1106. 50 Country Club Dr., Canyon, TX 79015

- 18 holes. Par 72. Gold – 6,865 (72.1/117). Blue – 6,385 (69.8/112). White – 5,684 (67.6/108). Red – 4,981 (66.9/105). Price - $$.

Getting there From I-27 south, exit Hunsley and go west. When you get to Country Club Dr., turn south and the course is about a mile away.

CANYON NOTES   In town eat at the **Cowboy Cafe** (806-655-1124) or the **Texas Star Restaurant** (806-655-9379). Call to make sure it's open, but it's worth a trip to Umbarger for the specials at **Rafter G Bar-B-Que** (806-499-3347). Some of their specialties are Thursday steak, Friday catfish, and Saturday brisket and pork ribs. The **Hudspeth House** (806-655-9800) is one of the state's oldest bed and breakfasts. The **Panhandle-Plains Historical Museum** (806-651-2244) on the campus of West Texas A&M University is a fabulous 300,000-square-foot museum that covers Panhandle history all the way back to the Jurassic Period, 160 million years ago. For outdoor activities check out

---

The hands are the key to transmitting power from the body to the club. The club shaft is held more in the fingers than in the palms of your hands. In the palm, it is impossible to get any zip into the shot. Sam Snead

the 15,000-plus acres of scenic landscape at **Palo Duro Canyon State Park,** where the Red River has carved through the tabletop expanse of the High Plains and walls plunge a thousand feet to the canyon floor. Also find one of the major waterfowl refuges on the Central Flyway in **Buffalo Lake National Wildlife Refuge,** a winter haven for over a million ducks and around 80,000 geese.

CHILDRESS   Elev. 1,877   Pop. 6,861

Of the 7,700-some-odd folks who live in Childress County, almost 90 percent of them live in this town founded by attorney George C. Childress, author of the Texas Declaration of Independence.

Located on US 287 between Wichita Falls and Amarillo, Childress is referred to as the "Gateway to the Panhandle" and has long served as the agribusiness center for the surrounding area.

CHILDRESS COUNTRY CLUB

The golf   This is a private, 9-hole course with two sets of tees for a full round. The rolling terrain of the region offers many uneven lies, and the wind is always a factor here. The design features five par 4s, two par 3s, and one par 5. Both par 3s are short and offer good birdie opportunities.

The details   940-937-8552. Route 1, Childress, TX 79201

• 1930. 9 holes. Par 35. Back - 2,641. Forward – 2,307. Price - $.

Getting there From Hwy. 83 south, exit Country Club Dr. and proceed 5 blocks to the course.

MORE GOLF

With the assistance of a grant from the Texas Parks and Wildlife Department, the city of Childress is currently in the process of developing the 18-hole **Childress Municipal Golf Course.** Williams, Gill, & Associates out of Abilene, TX (Nueva Vista in Midland, Links at Lands End in Yantis, Coyote Ridge in Dallas) has been chosen to design the course, and the city is currently assessing the value of the proposed land. Locals state that the project is realistically 4-5 years away from completion, and they joke about the recent spike in property values once word of the project spread throughout the community.

CHILDRESS NOTES   Bass fishing is huge on **Lake Childress** and **Baylor Lake,** where it isn't crowded and you won't find many personal watercraft. Don't miss the opportunity to have a meal at the **Ranch Hand Cafe** (940-937-8309),

You've just got one problem. You stand too close to the ball after you've hit it. Sam Snead

where the excellent food is complemented by friendly service. Another good bet is **Fat Jack's Mesquite Grill & Mercantile** (940-937-3066). The **Childress County Heritage Museum** holds the keys to the city's history.

PANHANDLE

CLARENDON   Elev. 2,727   Pop. 1,878

Unlike typical boomtowns of the late 1800s, Clarendon was established by a Methodist minister as a "sobriety settlement" for local cowboys, who called the place "Saints Roost." Clarendon is the seat of Donley County and the oldest thriving town in the Panhandle. As you might expect, farming and ranching form the economy.

CLARENDON COUNTRY CLUB

The golf   A hidden treasure, Clarendon Country Club is an 18-hole, semi-private course that's set up as a fair test of golf for every skill level. A basic course that isn't tricked up with hidden hazards, it can be challenging from the back tees (6,745 yards), but very manageable for the average golfer from the middle tees (6,285 yards). Locals brag that the greens are some of the best around. The view over the lake here is quite scenic considering the remote, barren locale.

The signature hole is No. 9, a 448-yard par 4 requiring a straight, downhill tee shot directly into the wind, leaving the golfer with a long iron or possibly even a fairway wood to the green.

The details   806-874-2166. Country Club Dr., Clarendon, TX 79226

*   1968. 18 holes. Par 72. Back – 6,745 (69.8/111). Middle – 6,285 (68.1/108). Forward – 4,900 (66.2/103). Price - $$.

Getting there The golf course is visible from Hwy. 70. Look for the entrance off Star Route 2.

CLARENDON NOTES Cornelia Adair formed the Adair Hospital in 1910, which is now home to the **Saints Roost Museum** housing heirlooms from area ranches, farms, and businesses. The only place in town we found for Tex-Mex was the authentic **Amigo's Mexican Cafe**. The hub of Clarendon's social activity, **King's Kountry Kafe**, also serves outstanding home cooking, and is the place you're most likely to gather tips on how to play the golf course. For quick lunches to-go, grab a sandwich at the **Outpost Deli**. For weekenders Clarendon boasts some very unique, affordable lodging. One of the coziest cabins you'll ever find is at the **Coyote Ridge Ranch** (806-856-6200), and the **Finch Ranch Lodge** (906-856-5930) offers 10,000 acres of ranchland for roaming in addition to their comfortable rooms. And don't forget the **Ace #8 B&B** (806-874-

---

9787), with its hardwood floors and great location across from the **Taylor Lakes Wildlife Management Area.**

DALHART
Elev. 3,985   Pop. 7,210

Vast emptiness. The coldest place in the state. The mysticism of Midwesterners rebuilding the torched state capitol in exchange for three million acres of ranch land. Building 6,000 miles of fence and then going broke. Rolling plains stretching into the distance, every square foot covered with cows. Feedlots emanating the stench of bovine. Cropdusting planes and their acrobatics. A cowtown with king cab pickup trucks staining the streets with a red clay mud, then parking at the immaculate Dalhart Country Club to partake in the greatest game of all.

DALHART COUNTRY CLUB

The golf   This wide-open course features a scenic view of Rabbit Ears Mountain. This small-town private club only has 300 members. Since the elevation is almost 4,000 feet, you have the psychological advantage that your ball might carry just a bit longer than normal.

The details   806-244-5596. 3139 Hwy. 54 West, Dalhart, TX 79022

- 1960. 18 holes. Back – Par 72. 6,539 yards (69.5/112). Forward – Par 73. 5,556 yards (69.9/113). Practice putting green. Pro shop with grill. Beer available. Price - $.

Getting there From Hwy. 385 north, take Exit 54 and turn west. The course is 2 miles down the road, and the clubhouse is on the right side of the road.

DALHART NOTES   For lodging it's hard to beat the spotless **Days Inn** (806-244-5246), but another solid choice is **Carroll's Bed & Breakfast** (806-249-6407), built in a 12,000-square-foot former lumberyard, and the **XIT Ranch Motel** (806-244-3590) will help you soak in the mood of the town. It seems like every Panhandle town has at least one mucho authentic Tex-Mex joint, and the place in here is called **La Espanola II**. The only barbecue joint is **Hodies** and the best place to sit down after 36 holes at the DCC is the **Bar-H Steak House.**

★

Fact: Dalhart is 1,765 miles from New York City and 691 miles from Houston.

DENVER CITY

Elev. 3,550   Pop. 3,903

Located on Highway 83 about 70 miles southwest of Lubbock, Denver City is the largest town in Yoakum County and headquarters for most of the county's oil and ranch-related interests. When the Wasson oil pool was discovered in 1939, the town became the major oilfield supply point for the area.

YOAKUM COUNTY GOLF COURSE

The golf   Located between Denver City and Plains, Yoakum County is a wide-open course that was built on moderately rolling terrain. Water hazards (ponds, lakes, creeks, and streams) come into play on over half the holes, which is surprising for a course in this region. Avoid the driver if you can, as the course is short enough to score well without it. (You might need the driver, though, on the number-one handicap, a 440-yard, par 4 No. 14.)

Watch for storms blowing in quickly on hot, summer afternoons. The course gained a few moments of fame one recent June when newscasts captured winds upwards of 100 mph that took out whole trees and blew roofs off buildings.

The details   806-592-2947. Plains Hwy., Denver City, TX 79323

• 1964. 18 holes. Back – 6,232 yards. Par 70. Middle – 5,935. Forward – 5,146 yards. Price - $.

Getting there From Lubbock drive through Brownfield; 12 miles south is Wellman. Take a right on Hwy. 213. The course is 23 miles west of Wellman on the south side of the road. Turn left at the stop sign and button-hook back through the park.

DENVER CITY NOTES   Minimal lodging options can be found at the **Crown Inn** (806-592-8561) or the **Denver City Motel** (806-592-8541). You might disguise yourself as a local and visit the bowling alley for people-watching and cold beers. Otherwise, play the course and move to another town, perhaps across the border into New Mexico.

DIMMITT

Elev. 3,854   Pop. 4,213

Home to large farms and feedlots, as well as the golf mecca and seat of Castro County, Dimmitt is on US Highway 385 in the central part of the county, 31 miles southwest of Amarillo. In March 1890 the Bedford Town and Land Company, headquartered at Sherman in Grayson County, bought a section of land near the center of the county and laid out the town site.

When I was in high school, I used to walk down the hallways to
my locker with my clubs on my shoulder, wearing cords, and people used to
throw things at me. I was a LOSER! Now everyone plays golf. Peter Jacobsen

PANHANDLE

COUNTRY CLUB OF DIMMITT

The golf   Also referred to as Castro County Country Club, this is a fairly long links-style course with wide-open fairways and extremely large greens. Locals mentioned the added bonus of wildlife-watching, particularly for various species of fowl.

The course offers the chance to start your round well, with a 350-yard, par 4 opening hole, followed by a short par 3. Hole 4 is the most difficult: a 550-yard par 5 that can get really get to you when the wind is blowing.

The details   806-647-4502. West Halsell St., Dimmitt, TX 79027

- 1968. 9 holes. Par 36. Back – 3,340 yards (35/108). Forward – 2,705 yards (34.3/105). Price - $.

Getting there From Amarillo, take I-25 south and travel 35 miles to Hwy 60. Turn west and drive to Hwy 385. Turn south on 285 and travel 25 miles to West Hassel St. Turn west again and drive 1 mile to the course.

DIMMITT NOTES   Lodging is limited to a few local motels. **The Pancake House** (806-647-2065) is the place for breakfast, and **Ernie's Barbecue** (806-647-2231) is the best spot for lunch.

DUMAS   Elev. 3,668   Pop. 14,169

Set in the heart of the state's leading grain sorghum-producing region, Dumas is 50 miles north of Amarillo on US 287. This Moore County seat, founded in 1891, also produces large quantities of natural gas and two-thirds of the nation's helium. As you drive north into Dumas from Amarillo, the rugged country around the Canadian River flattens out into vast farmlands dotted by feedlots and grain elevators.

PHEASANT TRAILS GOLF COURSE

The golf   Set in the rugged canyon hills of the Canadian River area, Pheasant Trails was built around 1950 and is one of the better small-town courses in the region. This great-value course (*Golf Digest* has rated it one of the best values in Texas) features bent-grass greens, bunkers, water hazards, and mature, tree-lined fairways with narrow landing areas bordered by thick rough. Since it's one of the only courses in the area that waters its fairways, the condition of the course is excellent.

The front nine on this course features a Scottish-links design with newly

I love to play—I love fishing and hunting and trapshooting and Ping-Pong and chess and pool and billiards and driving a motor car, and at times I love golf, when I can get the shots going somewhere near right. It seems I love almost any pursuit except work. Bobby Jones

planted trees and a deep cut of rough bordering the flat fairways. The back nine is shorter and takes on more of a West Texas design with large, established trees lining the fairways.

The details   806-935-7375. 11352 Schuman Rd., Dumas, TX 79029

- 1950. 18 holes. Par 71. Back – 6,481 (69.5/111). Middle – 5,985 (67.2/106). Forward – 5,292 (70.5/117). Price - $$.

Getting there Driving north on I-87, head 4 miles past Dumas, then exit onto FM 119 and turn right. When you come to Country Club Terrace make a left and drive a short distance to the course. The clubhouse is on the right side of the street.

DUMAS NOTES   Close to the golf course is **The Branding Iron** (806-935-3424). For barbecue try **Paula's Bar B Q** (806-935-7425). If you need to sleep, there are a few chain hotels and local motels or the quaint little **Serendipity House B&B** (806-935-0339). **The Moore County Historical Museum,** housed in a former hotel, features memorabilia and displays of local history, area wildlife, Indian artifacts, and changing exhibits.

FARWELL   Elev. 4,375   Pop. 1,313

Perhaps one of the most remote outposts in Texas, Farwell is situated on the New Mexico border 90 miles from Lubbock and 10 miles from Clovis, NM. Agriculture is king here. Feedlots, a fertilizer plant, and grain elevators dot the landscape. The town sprang up from the lands once owned by the XIT Ranch as the railroad entered New Mexico, and today serves as the seat for Parmer County.

FARWELL COUNTRY CLUB

The golf   Farwell Country Club, an outstanding little course set in the middle of farm country, opened for play in the 1960s. The signature of this course is the large, undulating greens that are kept in perfect condition. The fairways are wide open and are lined by trees and a standard cut of rough. Although there are no sand bunkers, grass bunkers are scattered throughout and a lake comes into play on two holes. Two sets of tees make for an 18-hole round, and you'll be pleasantly surprised at how differently the course plays on that second nine.

The details   806-481-9210. RR 2, Farwell, TX 79325

- 1966. 9 holes. Back – Par 36. 3,165 yards (35/109). Forward – Par 37. 2,843 yards (35.8/105). Price - $.

Find out what he thinks he excels at and capitalize on it. Let a guy pick a game he can do— he has to feel some sense of superiority—and then find a way to beat it. Just 'cause he smells like ape shit don't mean he's Tarzan. Amarillo Slim

Getting there From Lubbock take Hwy. 84 west to Farwell. At the Dairy Queen turn right, then head over to Amarillo Hwy. and turn left. Drive .25 mile to the course and look for the entrance on the right side of the road.

FARWELL NOTES There isn't much in Farwell, so have lunch at **Barb's Cafe** (806-481-9690) after your round, then make it a golf pilgrimage by crossing the border into New Mexico for rounds in Clovis and Portales. The annual **Border Town Days** is held the last weekend in July.

FLOYDADA
Elev. 3,179   Pop. 3,617

Floydada, the seat of Floyd County and Pumpkin Capital of the US, lies 30 miles east of I-27 as you head between Plainview and Lubbock. A charming little town surrounded by farms, this is one place you don't want to miss if you're touring the High Plains for golf.

FLOYDADA COUNTRY CLUB

The golf A 9-hole, semi-private course located 8 miles south of town in Blanco Canyon, with elevation changes of as much as 150 feet, this is an outstanding little course with greens as good as any in Texas. The design features a dry creek that runs through the middle of the course that only comes into play after heavy rains. Two other ponds impact play on one hole.

Ladies and men tee off from the same set of tees. Pay once and play all day.

The details 806-983-2769. Hwy. 62, Floydada, TX 79235

- 9 holes. Par 36. 3,165 yards. Price - $.

Getting there Take Hwy. 62 south for 8 miles, then look for the course sign and turn right down a private road. Drive .5 mile to the course.

FLOYDADA NOTES Plan your trip for the early fall and set up a pheasant hunt on one of the nearby farms. Play the course and hunt as necessary. For entertainment cruise Main St. at night and watch the locals in action. The historic **Mott Creek Ranch** (806-787-0592), once owned by the famous Matador Land & Cattle Company, offers bed and breakfast accommodations, trail rides, and ranch tours.

Certainly the older golfer can't hit the ball as far as the young, flat-bellied player. But once you reach the fringe of the green, you and the younger player become no worse than equals. And you can even have the advantage if you are faithful in practicing your short game. Harvey Penick

FRIONA

Elev. 4,022   Pop. 3,812

Friona sits on a lonely stretch of US 60 just 26 miles from the New Mexico border. The town was established by the Capitol Freehold Land and Investment Co. in 1898 as a shipping station, and was originally named Frio after the Frio Draw that runs just south of town. Driving into town from the southwest, the green fairways and mature trees make Friona seem like an oasis in the middle of the barren High Plains Panhandle.

PANHANDLE

FRIONA COUNTRY CLUB

The golf   Friona's 9-hole semi-private track is the quintessential small-town golf experience.

Mature willow, oak, and elm trees choke the fairway and squeeze landing areas down to as little as 30 yards. And while this isn't a long course, those trees, combined with a draw that winds its way through the layout, provide many precarious shots. After rains the creek fills with water, making the course a bit more difficult.

The large, immaculate bent-grass greens generally slope back-to-front, so it's wise to keep the approach shots below the hole. The course is void of sand bunkers, but grass bunkers are sprinkled throughout.

The hardest rated hole is the long, narrow, 400-yard, par 4 No. 6; however, the locals will tell you that the par 5 No. 3 plays the toughest. While it's not long at only 468 yards from the tips, out-of-bounds borders either side of the fairway and the landing area is only about 40 yards wide. Suffice it to say that this is the hole that will destroy your round.

Karen Harrelson manages the course and will gladly give you the low-down on how to play each hole. Let her know if you're interested in setting up a match with any of the local hustlers–it might make the day more enjoyable.

Last but not least, the golf course is the only place in dry Parmer County to buy beer, so don't be alarmed if you see 18-wheelers in the parking lot and truckers hustling for a pass to buy a cold one.

The details   806-250-3125. 1505 West 5th St., Friona, TX 79035

- 1959. Jim Terry. 9 holes. Par 36. Back – 3,030. Middle – 2,911. Forward – 2,363. Course rating for 18 holes – 67.5. Price - $.

Getting there Located southwest of town on Hwy. 60.

FRIONA NOTES   Other than the **Sonic** and **Dairy Queen**, you might try **Holly's Cafe** (806-250-5800) or **The Chuckwagon** (806-247-2862) for a hot meal. If an early blizzard blows in and forces you to take cover, check into the **Friona Inn** (806-250-2784) for the night.

Prominent Houston businessman R.E. "Bob" Smith and his wife Vivian loved the game of golf enough to build a 5-hole course near their hunting lodge in Palacios, TX.

HALE CENTER

Elev. 3,423   Pop. 2,132

You'll bump into Hale Center driving due north out of Lubbock through some of the best agricultural lands in the world. Hale Center dates back to the late 1800s and sits just south of Plainview on US 87, surrounded by massive cotton, corn, and sunflower fields.

HILLSIDE ACRES COUNTRY CLUB

The golf   Hillside Acres is a 9-hole, semi-private course that features tight fairways, mature trees, and small greens. The course has recently undergone a transition to new management, who have high hopes of improving the facility. The greens are in great condition and make this course worth playing; however, the fairways need water and the track could generally use some tender loving care.

Hillside has replaced all of the old equipment with new state-of-the-art machinery. Potential improvements under consideration include re-opening the club's pool, renovating the clubhouse, making food and alcohol available, and improving a house on the premises to make it available for tournaments and family reunions.

The course does not serve alcohol but allows golfers to bring their own cold beverages. There is a slot to leave your funds if no one is around in the pro shop. Golfers can pay once and play all day, and carts are available. Thursday is discount day for seniors.

The details   806-839-2188. 1840 County Rd. M, Hale Center, TX 79041

• 9 holes. Par 36. Back – 3,019 yards. Forward – 2,700 yards. Price - $.

Getting there The course is 2.5 miles west of town. From I-27 north, take the Hale Center exit, and go to the main light. Turn west and drive to the course.

HALE CENTER NOTES   If it's late in the day, take in one of the spectacular sunsets, then head to Plainview or Lubbock for more metropolitan action. If you're forced to kill time in Hale Center, you can grab a bite and piddle around the stores downtown, or visit the **Hale County Farm and Ranch Museum**. The two local restaurants are **Alonzo's Cafe** and the **Owl's Cafe**.

✦

The devoted golfer is an anguished soul who has learned a lot about putting, just as an avalanche victim has learned a lot about snow. Dan Jenkins

HEREFORD

Elev. 3,806   Pop. 14,391

Hereford calls itself the Cattle Capital of the World: a fitting name for a place that moves over 3 million head of cattle through its feedlots every year. There are more feed yards per capita here than anywhere else in the US. Hereford takes its name from the white-faced cattle introduced by Charles Goodnight in the late 1800s. Just west of the city at Buffalo Lake, the massive XIT Ranch once took advantage of the area's rich agricultural lands, as well as the oil fields that eventually tapped its fertile soil.

PITTMAN MUNICIPAL GOLF COURSE

The golf   Hereford offers an 18-hole municipal course that is easy to play and is in good condition. The staff at Pittman has a reputation for continuously trying to improve the course, so the golf experience gets better and better. This beautiful little layout features wide-open fairways and small greens of medium speed. Water comes into play on only a few holes.

The details   806-363-7139. South Main St., Hereford, TX 79045

- 1939. 18 holes. Par 71. Back – 6,545 (69.6/113). Middle – 6,130 (67.5/113). Forward – 4,870 (66.2/113). Snack bar but no booze. Price - $$.

Getting there From I-27 south, take I-60 west and exit Main St. Look for the course on the right side of the street.

HEREFORD NOTES   After golf, dig into a real Texas barbecue dinner at the **Cattle Call Restaurant,** then ask around for the best cowboy honkytonk. The tamer approach is to tour the **Deaf Smith County Historical Museum** for miscellaneous pioneer recollections, or visit the **National Cowgirl Hall of Fame** and try to convince your wife that she would look good in Rocky Mountain jeans. **The Best Western Red Carpet Inn** (800-528-1234) is the place to stay.

IDALOU

Elev. 3,193   Pop. 2,166

What we know is that back in the day, a man named Ida and a woman named Lou decided they liked this little spot 12 miles northeast of Lubbock as much as they liked each other. They settled, they farmed, and eventually a community that relied on the small train depot and the farming grew up around them. What we don't know is whether it was Lou and Ida Bacon or Lou and Ida Bassett.

Either way, this tiny town is now home to one of the newest High Plains 9-hole courses, and it's a perfect day trip for rural golf when visiting Lubbock.

My wife and my children came first, then my legal profession. Finally, and
never in a life by itself, came golf. Bobby Jones

ISLAND OAKS GOLF CLUB

The golf   Island Oaks is one of the newest small-town Panhandle courses. Built in 1991 by Terry McNeil, this 9-hole public course features grass bunkers and ponds on many holes. The course is brutal from the back tees, playing over 3,600 yards–which can easily feel like 4,000 when the wind is howling.

The less macho golfer should play the more reasonable middle tees, where you'll still face a few long par 4s. Your best chances to score are on holes 6 and 9. No. 6 is a par 3 that requires only a wedge, and No. 9 is a 482-yard par 5.

The details   806-892-2839. County Rd. 33, Idalou, TX 79329

- 1991. Terry McNeill. 9 holes. Par 36. Back – 3,614 (36.7/114). Middle – 3,194 (34.7/104). Forward – 2,810 (32.9/98). Pro shop. Driving range. Putting and chipping green. Snack bar. No beer. Price - $$.

Getting there From Lubbock take Loop 289 east, then turn left on Hwy. 62. Drive to Walnut St. and turn right again, then continue on until the street dead-ends. Turn right on CR 33 and drive 1 mile to the course. The entrance is on the right side of the street.

IDALOU NOTES   Before you head back to the city, have lunch at rustic Muther's (806-744-8400), which offers peppery German garlic sausage and smoked brisket as well as other Texas favorites.

JAYTON   Elev. 2,005   Pop. 508

Jayton, the seat of Kent County, is sandwiched between the towns of Aspermont and Post just north of US 380. The town is named after the Jay family, early ranchers in the area. Zane Grey visited here in the early 1900s and used the setting for his novel *The Thundering Herd*. Grey, along with many other writers and artists, was attracted to Putoff Canyon 3 miles north of town.

Jayton is real small, with barely 500 residents, but golfers drive from miles around to play the immaculate little 9-hole track called the Kent County Golf Course.

KENT COUNTY GOLF COURSE

The golf   Owned by Kent County, this short, fun 9-hole course is better funded than other nearby city-owned facilities, which is most evident here in the quality, bent-grass greens. There are no bunkers or water hazards, but the design incorporates a scenic canyon as well as a few mature trees that can get

---

in the way of wayward shots. The best hole is No. 2, which requires a drive across the canyon. The par 5s are short so the longer knocker has the chance for easy birdies. Watch out for the par 3 on the west side of the course with deceptive undulations in the green.

For a mere $10, you can play sunup to sundown at Kent County. And since this course is in the middle of nowhere, you'll frequently find it void of golfers and staff. The clubhouse has envelopes for paying your fee when no one is around; definitely pay up because despite their friendly nature, the locals will ask you to leave if your green fee is missing.

Lastly, the course offers camping facilities. If you pay to play golf, the accommodations are free of charge, including the showers and bathrooms in the clubhouse–something the stinky, wayfaring golfer can always use after a long day on a wind-blown course.

The details   806-237-4970. Kenneth Curry runs the golf shop.

• 1959. 9 holes. Rental carts available. Price - $.

Getting there The course is 2 miles west of Jayton on FM 1083. In town, turn west at the courthouse.

JAYTON NOTES   There are three dining options as you pass through Jayton after your round of golf. The **Jay Birds Nest, Jayton Cafe**, and **Mitzie's Home Cooking** are all on Main St. The **Bunkhouse** (806-237-2700) is a hunting lodge on the Kyle Ranch worth investigating for outdoor excursions.

LAMESA Elev. 2,975   Pop. 9,822

Lamesa marks the edge of the High Plains and the start of West Texas. This town, named after "the table," is the halfway point between Midland and Lubbock. When the wind blows here in the flat cotton farmlands around town, the haze of dust that envelops the countryside is indescribable, potentially turning a pleasant round of golf into one of the most outrageous links experiences ever.

LAMESA COUNTRY CLUB

The golf   Lamesa's semi-private country club recently underwent a complete renovation that modernized the course and significantly improved the greens. Despite the ragged look of the clubhouse due to ongoing construction, this is a nice facility that offers 9 holes of pure wind-blown pleasure.

This flat course is loaded with trees, but for some reason that doesn't stop the wind from beating down even the most macho golfer. The new design features four water holes and almost 30 bunkers. The feature holes are No. 4, a 190-

---

Attitude is the one place an older golfer has an advantage. By age fifty, a golfer has perspective and wisdom that should give him a formidable mental game. Raymond Floyd

yard par 3 with water on the right (not the most ideal par 3 for tornado-like conditions), and the mammoth 435-yard No. 7, which plays into the prevailing southwest wind.

The details   806-872-3059. 2009 S. Hwy. 87, Lamesa, TX 79331

• 9 holes. Back – 3,160. Forward – 2,562. Price - $.

Getting there Driving north from Midland on Hwy. 349, take the Snyder-Lubbock Rd. to the right, then drive 2 miles to Radio Rd. Turn left on Radio and it will take you straight to the course.

PLAINS FAIRWAYS GOLF COURSE

The golf   Another simple, small-town course that is great for the average hack. There are no bunkers, but the course has two water holes, along with tight, tree-lined fairways that provide some challenges. As they told us in the pro shop, though, "You have to be real bad to hit the water hazards." The greens, and the course in general, have a reputation for being in good condition. This is also a great course to walk because it's flat.

The toughest hole is No. 3, a tree-lined par 4 that requires your approach thread the needle of a 15-yard opening between the mature, old trees that protect the green.

The details   806-872-8100. 201 South Ave. N., Lamesa, TX 79331

• 1950s. 9 holes. Par 35. Back – 3,150 yards. Forward – 2,375. Price - $.

Getting there Driving north from Midland on Hwy. 349, turn left at the first stop light (South 1st St.), and drive 10 blocks.

LAMESA NOTES   Cover yourself in grease while eating the famous Chihuahua Sandwich at the 1948 **Sky-Vue Drive-In**, a Truman-era drive-in movie theater. Tune the sound in via your FM dial and watch a movie in the small-town High Plains night. Lamesa has a few local motels, but **Waldrop's Well** (806-497-6421) is the best option: a country inn setting with meals as needed in a 9,000-square-foot home.

LEVELLAND   Elev. 3,523   Pop. 13,596

The land is indeed level up here just 30 miles west of Lubbock, where the water table is sucked dry by the rolling sprinklers that water the cotton and wheat. Cereal king C.W. Post laid the town out in the early 1900s, and eventually the ranch lands were sold off and converted into farms. Farmers came,

Golf is the hardest game in the world. There is no way you can ever get it. Just when you think you do, the game jumps up and puts you in your place. Ben Crenshaw

families grew, schools and roads popped up, and the townsmen built a traditional downtown square and a handsome courthouse. Cowboy culture is strong here, mosaics decorate the city buildings, and there's a college that specializes in music.

There's much to do, but technically the touring avid golfer can only play golf here during the week, as the **Levelland Country Club** only allows members access on weekends.

LEVELLAND COUNTRY CLUB

The golf   Tight fairways and subtle mounding define the layout at LCC. The signature hole is No. 8, which features a short dogleg-left fairway, an approach over water in front of the green, and out-of-bounds stakes behind the green.

The details   806-894-3288. 700 Country Club Ln., Levelland, TX 79336

- 1946. 9 holes. Par 36. Back – 3,240 (34.5/113). Forward – 2,730 (33.9/110). Pro shop and practice facilities. Restaurant and bar. Price - $.

Getting there From Lubbock take Hwy. 114 west for about 25 miles, then exit College Ave. and turn south. Drive 1.5 miles to the course, and look for the entrance on the right side of the road.

LEVELLAND NOTES   Warm up after a chilly fall round with a chile relleño at **Savannah's Mexican Food** (806-894-5699). Or for a little livelier action with an attitude, hit the **Mean Woman Grill** (806-897-0006), which has fast, friendly service, good food, and live music on the weekends. The **Levelland Motel** (806-894-7335) provides basic, clean rooms near the university.

LITTLEFIELD   Elev. 3,556   Pop. 6,567

Probably best known as the hometown of country music legend Waylon Jennings, Littlefield got its start in 1913 as a railroad station. Cattle baron George Washington Littlefield founded the town, which serves as the commercial and manufacturing center of Lamb County.

LITTLEFIELD COUNTRY CLUB

The golf   Built in the 1950s, semi-private Littlefield Country Club is a well-manicured course that features many mature trees. The fairways are open with generous landing areas, and the greens are small. The signature hole is the

---

par 3 No. 5, which requires a tee shot over water. This is one where you can pay once and play all day.

The details 806-385-3309. Route 385, Littlefield, TX 79339

- 1950s. 9 holes. Par 36. Back – 3,150 (34.5). Pros shop, driving range, and putting green. Snack bar with beer. Price - $.

Getting there From Lubbock take Hwy 84 west, and turn north when you come to Hwy 385. Drive 3 miles to the course.

LITTLEFIELD NOTES If you roll through town early, don't miss the hometown breakfast at **White Kitchen**, which is downtown and as authentic as it gets. Have lunch or dinner at the new **Jay's Steaks**, which replaces the old Wildcat Country Cafe and is the talk of the town., then hit the road and pop Waylon in the CD player while exploring the old Comanche Indian campgrounds at Bull and Illusion Lakes just west of town. For lodging you can go Mom and Pop style at the **Plains Motel** (806-385-5724), or hit the larger **Crescent Park** (806-385-4464).

LORENZO

Elev. 3,167   Pop. 1,388

Heading east out of Lubbock on US 82 toward the Caprock, you'll drive 12 miles to Idalou, then another 9 miles to the bustling High Plains nerve center of Lorenzo. This cotton-country town was founded by the C.B. Livestock Company in 1911 and named after an employee of the company, Mr. Lorenzo Dow. Like the nearby Lubbock fringes of Slaton and Idalou, Lorenzo is a daytrip event from Lubbock for those interested in the High Plains countryside.

LORENZO COUNTRY CLUB

The golf Lorenzo's semi-private course offers the chance to score well, with a layout featuring par 4s either right at or under 400 yards, and back-to-back par 5s that are both under 500 yards. The par 3s offer a bit of a challenge because both require mid to long irons. Elevated greens and tree-lined fairways await the High Plains hacker. The number one handicap is hole 2, a 380-yard par 4. As always, pay them once and play till golf until you can't play anymore.

The details 806-634-5787. RR 1, Lorenzo, TX 79343

- 1960. 9 holes. Par 36. Back – 3,285 (36.9/120). Forward – 2,425 (33.8/107). Pro shop, driving range, and putting green. Snack bar with beer. Price - $.

Never trust a politician or golfer who has never experienced a hangover. Anonymous

Getting there From Lubbock, take Hwy. 82 east to Lorenzo. In town turn right at the blinking light (Route 1), and drive 1 mile to the course. The entrance is on the left side of the road.

LORENZO NOTES   Another Lubbock suburb, so make it a day trip. Grab lunch at **Galvan's Mexican Restaurant** (806-634-0025) before you head back to the big city.

LUBBOCK
Elev. 3,241 Pop. 190,974

There is a certain beauty in the geography, the weather, the isolation, and the starkness of this largest and most prominent High Plains city. The flat horizon will make you want to take a deep breath and really feel the air. Every street goes east and west or north and south—a city of squares surrounded by a circle. There's what is now becoming a major university in the middle of this little slice of cotton patch. The people are conservative and tough, and their farming and ranching heritage is strong.

Lubbock was the music capital of Texas before Austin, and they're finally trying to capitalize on that fact with their own version of Austin's 6th St.: The Depot District. It's cheaper out here than in metropolitan cities, and the residents lack the *haute* persona of the big cities.

The golf is outstanding here, especially if you can get used to the wind. Affordable public courses without the crowds are everywhere. Lubbock Country Club rivals any track in the state, and Texas Tech alums have spent generously to bring in big-name architect Tom Doak for their new Red Raider Golf Course that should open sometime in 2003. There's even a lighted golf course with a sports bar and grill (Stonegate), allowing pleasure seekers to play late into the summer nights and then step next door for cold ones and sporting events.

ELM GROVE GOLF COURSE

The golf   This longtime Lubbock favorite is an impeccably groomed course accompanied by a full-service facility. Its popularity stems not only from its reputation as a well-conditioned course, but also because of its vulnerability, especially when the wind is not blowing.

Playing only 6,400 yards, the elm tree-lined fairways have generous landing areas and a limited amount of water hazards. After finding the wide fairways, you'll feel confident over your approach because the targets are large, bentgrass greens in outstanding condition. Golfers who find their groove will score well, just as Roland Adams did in 1969 when he shot the course record 59.

---

*A good round of golf is if you can hit about three shots that turn out
exactly as you planned them.* Ben Hogan

The 454-yard hole 12 is the most difficult: a par-4 dogleg left that features a difficult tee shot because of the trees looming on the right. The length of the hole inevitably leaves you with a monster approach, and, because of problems around the greens, ups-and-downs are difficult to come by.

The details   806-799-7801. 23202 Milwaukee Ave., Lubbock, TX 79407

- www.elmgrovegolfcourse.com
- 1940. Warren Cantrell. Par: 72. Back - 6,401 (69.8 / 110). Middle – 6,022. Forward – 5,480 (72.0/108). Price - $$.

Getting there Exit 34th off of Loop 289, then go a short distance to the course entrance.

HILLCREST COUNTRY CLUB

The golf   After delays due to the Korean War, Hillcrest finally opened in 1953 with a traditional layout designed by the popular Warren Cantrell, who also supervised the construction of the clubhouse and served as the first golf pro, club manager, and superintendent.

The course is set on the north side of Lubbock in a rocky, caliche-laced field loaded with deep gullies. The layout stretches 6,842 yards from the tips and plays to a par 72. One of Hillcrest's highlights is the difficult par 3s. No. 17 stands out as the best: a 174-yarder into a well-bunkered green.

Each nine offers difficult stretches of holes. In fact holes 6-8 on the front and 12-14 on the back make up the six most challenging holes on the course. Hole 6 is one of the longest in West Texas, playing 577 yards uphill–an insane figure given the winds that often blow out here.

Other notes: Hillcrest is private but will allow you to play if you are a member of the USGA. In 1994, all of the greens were rebuilt, marking the first green renovation since the club's opening. When the club opened in 1953, the membership fee was $240 and the monthly dues were $10.

The details   806-765-5208. 4011 N. Canton Ave., Lubbock 79415

- www.hillcrestcc.com
- 1950s. 18 holes. Par 72. Back – 6,862 (72.6/126). Middle – 6,495 (71.1/123). Forward – 5,843 (74.0/126). Price - $$.

Getting there From N. Loop 289, take the University Ave. exit and turn right. When you come to Newcomb, turn left and continue down this road until it dead-ends at the clubhouse.

LAKE RIDGE COUNTRY CLUB

The golf   Lakeridge opened in 1979 as the centerpiece of an exclusive neighborhood. The flat design is built around two lakes and features tight fair-

When you're playing for five bucks and you've got two bucks in your pocket—that's pressure. Lee Trevino

ways, heavily bunkered greens, and either water or out-of-bounds on every hole.

Two holes stand out on the front. The first is No. 4, a 178-yard par 4 that features water to the front and left of an extremely sloped green. The next tough one is the 520-yard 6th hole, which features a fairway framed by a road on the right, a lake on the left, and a creek that bisects the fairway at 250 yards from the tee.

On the back you'll notice the dogleg-left 17th, a 453-yard monster with an undulating, tree-lined fairway and a bunker protecting the front right of the green.

The details   806-794-4445. 8802 Vicksburg Ave., Lubbock, TX 79424

- 1979. 18 holes. Par 72. Back – 6,762 (72.4/124). Middle – 6,358 (70.3/119). Forward – 5,475 (71.6/119). Price - $$.

Getting there From I-27 south, take the 82nd St. exit and turn right. When you come to Vicksburg, turn left and the parking lot is at the end of the street.

LUBBOCK COUNTRY CLUB

The golf   Members will proudly argue that this is one of the best courses in the state. Originally built as a golf, hunting, and fishing club, the course is laid out in uniquely beautiful terrain for this part of Texas. This rolling course, primarily designed by Warren Cantrell, is loaded with mature trees and is difficult because of the wind and the multitude of long par 4s.

Nos. 1, 4, and 9 stand out on the front. The opener is a 534-yard par 5 with out-of-bounds on the right. No. 4 doglegs left and is tricky because of out-of-bounds on the right. Hole 9 is the layout's signature hole–playing along an old creek bed with a large cottonwood jutting into the fairway, this 430-yard hole requires accuracy of the tee and a long approach into a well-bunkered green.

On the back, No. 11 is tough because of its length (543 yards). This hole doglegs right and has out-of-bounds on the left. No. 15 can get you at 395 yards, doglegging left around the lake.

The details   806-763-1871. 3400 Mesa Rd., Lubbock, TX 79403

- www.lubbockcc.com
- 1950s. Warren Cantrell. 18 holes. Gold – 6,911 (72.9/127). Blue – 6,524 (71.2/124). White – 6,073 (68.7/119). Red – 5,293 (70.4/114). Price - $$$.

Getting there From I-27 north, take Exit 7 (Yucca), then drive to N. Mesa Rd.

The man who can go into a patch of rough alone, with the knowledge that only God is watching him, and play his ball where it lies is the man who will serve you faithfully and well. P. G. Wodehouse

MEADOWBROOK MUNICIPAL GOLF COURSE

The golf   Meadowbrook, whose original 18 holes dates back to circa 1930, offers 36 holes of golf with its Canyon and Creek Courses. Ralph Plummer laid these out back in the 1940s, Warren Cantrell put his signature here in 1955, then Bob Lohmann came along for another renovation in 1988.

The **Canyon Course** is the original layout, with wide-open fairways and hardly any hazards. Designed more for the average golfer, Canyon features less water than the Creek Course, but more bunkers. Warm up before you tee off on Canyon because you'll need to be loose to reach the 585-yard, number-one-rated opener in regulation.

The more challenging **Creek Course** has narrow fairways and requires more shot-making than the Canyon Course. Hole 6 is the toughest hole–a par 3 playing 230 yards from the tips.

Unlike most big city municipals, Meadowbrook allows you to play all day for the same fee.

The details   806-765-6679. 601 Municipal Dr., Lubbock, TX 79403

- www.golfmeadowbrook.com
- Canyon Course: 18 holes. Par 72. Back – 6,445 (70.7/120). Middle – 6,083 (69.0/117). Forward – 5,511 (74.3/117). Price - $$.
- Creek Course: 18 holes. Par 70. Back – 6,276 (69.3/117). Middle – 5,876 (68.0/113). Forward – 5,011 (70.4/113). Price - $$.

Getting there From I-27 north, take Exit 4 and turn right at the traffic signal. From there follow the signs to MacKenzie State Park and the course.

PINE VALLEY GOLF COURSE

The golf   Pine Valley offers a unique golf experience because the front nine consists of all par 3 holes. The back nine is more traditional, featuring generous, tree-lined fairways and elevated greens. The best part? The course is lit in the summer months, making it a great option to push the golf day late if you just can't pull yourself away from the course.

The course hosts 3-man scrambles every Monday at 6 p.m. Pine Valley was developed by Walt Denzer, who also established Lubbock's similar Stonegate golf facility.

The details   806-748-1448. 111th St. & Indiana Ave., Lubbock, Texas

- 1993. Walt Denzer. 18 holes. Par 63. Back – 4,487. Middle – 4,227. Forward – 3,461. Price - $$.

Getting there Take I-27 south to the "S" Loop and turn west. Drive to Indiana Ave. and turn south, then 2 miles to the course.

Never bet with anyone you meet on the first tee who has a deep suntan,
a one iron in his bag and squinty eyes. Dave Marr

JERRY S. RAWLS RED RAIDER GOLF COURSE

Opening 2003   Apparently Texas Tech wants to be known for more than its basketball and football programs–alumnus Jerry Rawls has donated upwards of $9 million toward an estimated $15 million project that hopes to create "the best collegiate golf course in the country." Construction began in fall 2001, with a slated opening date sometime in 2003.

Architect Tom Doak's plans involve moving over a million cubic yards of West Texas sand to create elevation changes, artificial canyons, plateaus, and berms to encircle the perimeter. Located next to the university campus, the facility will offer a first-class practice facility, clubhouse, pro shop, grill, locker rooms–the whole shebang.

The planners have high hopes, including one day hosting the NCAA Championships. Perhaps the design will be ingenious enough to beautify the surrounding terrain on a windy fall day, but it's difficult to imagine the nation's premier collegiate golf event being held here in the midst of 40 mph winds that turn the horizon into a sea of brown haze.

REESE GOLF CENTER

The golf   Reese Air Force Base has closed its doors, but it's been reinvented and remodeled as Reese Center. This facility west of Lubbock is a center for research, education, and aviation as well as home to an 18-hole, 6,633-yard golf course.

Be ready for the prevailing wind here at Reese–it will seem like you're hitting every shot into the wind. The most demanding hole is No. 4, a 406-yard par 4 that can play more like a par 5 when the wind is howling.

Other notes: The course is adding trees to improve the course, and a GPS system has been added to the cart fleet. One paid green fee allows you to play all day.

The details   806-885-1247. 1406 Quitsna Ave., Lubbock, TX 79416

• Williams & Gill. 18 holes. 6,633 yards. Price - $$.

Getting there From Hwy. 87 south, travel 20 miles then get off the 4th St. exit and proceed straight for 2 miles. This street dead-ends at Reese AFB.

SHADOW HILLS GOLF COURSE

The golf   Shadow Hills is a flat, fun course with the undulating and mounded fairways of a links-style layout. A few streams and ponds spice up the round, but its lack of trees makes it wide open and appealing to the high-handicap hack.

Originally opened in the early 1980s and designed by Ray Kilgore, Shadow Hills was renovated in 1995 and has recently opened a new 4,500-square-foot clubhouse with a fully stocked pro shop, full service grill, and tournament room.

Notable holes on the front include No. 4, with its elevated, sloping green; No. 6 at 123 yards over water that can get you because of the winds; and the long, par 4 No. 7 that plays uphill with water on the right.

On the back, No. 10 is fun because it plays downwind and has a wide-open fairway. Also No. 11 is a tough par 5 loaded with water.

The details   806-793-9700. 6002 3rd St., Lubbock, TX 79499

- www.shadowhillsgolf.com

- 1981. Ray Kilgore. 18 holes. Par 72. Back – 6,777 (71.2). Middle – 6,414 (69.8). Forward – 5,594 (71.2). Price - $.

Getting there The course is located at the intersection of Loop 289 and W. 4th St.

STONEGATE GOLF COURSE

The golf   Walt Denzer was on to something 15 years ago when he combined a bustling sports bar and grill with a lighted 9-hole par 3 and 9-hole regulation course. Stonegate, on the south edge of Lubbock, is an extremely popular place to enjoy the game, whether you're up for a five-hour afternoon or a quick evening practice round.

The course design features large, elevated bent-grass greens and some surprisingly challenging holes. The regulation course is straightforward and easy, so good shots are rewarded. The par 3 course is particularly tough, however, and will really test your short game.

Holes 15-17 present the toughest challenge. No. 15 plays 155 yards over the water, No. 16 requires an accurate approach because you need to get close (the long green is narrow and sloped, making it difficult to score). No. 17 might be the toughest par because it plays 228 yards.

The details   806-748-1448. 11010 Indiana Ave., Lubbock, TX 79423

- 9-hole regulation course: Back – 3,112. Middle – 2,992. Forward – 2,395. Price - $.

- 9-hole par 3 course: Back – 1,375. Middle – 1,235. Forward – 1,066. Price - $.

Getting there Take the 98th St. exit off of Hwy. 87 and drive west to Indiana Ave. Turn left and the course is just down the block.

Retief Goosen won $900,000 for winning the 2001 U.S. Open.

MORE GOLF

Bulls-eye Driving Range - 806-866-2194, 98th St. and Upland Ave.

Driving Range - 806-745-5252, 9200 Tahoka Hwy.

The Golf Station - 806-745-0336, 115th St. and Indiana Ave.

PANHANDLE

LUBBOCK NOTES   For the high-toned, reserve a room at the pricey-but-worth-it **Barcelona Court** (806-794-5353), then explore the heart of Texas wine country. The **Cap Rock** (806-796-0701; www.caprockwinery.com) is the newest, and the more established **Llano Estacado** (806-745-2258; www.llanowine.com) and **Pheasant Ridge** (806-746-6033; www.pheasantridgewinery.com) wineries all offer tastings.

For the more casual, take in the campus atmosphere over lunch at the cultured **Grapevine Cafe and Wine Bar** (806-744-8246), or coed-loaded **Mesquites** (806-763-1159). **The County Line** (806-763-6001) is a Lubbock tradition for dinner. Check the schedule for live music if that's your thing. Another option is to road-trip it to **TC's** (806-832-4478) northwest of town in Shallowater, TX, a historic building with an impressive menu that features Texas Toothpicks (hand-battered jalapeño and onion strips) and a massive chicken-fried steak.

McLEAN   Elev. 2,812   Pop. 811

Established 1901, "Muhclane" was once known as the "uplift city" because of a local ladies' undergarment factory, and was also the former site of a World War II German prisoner-of-war camp. Today McLean is a ranch town that exudes a bit of charm with its downtown restoration, murals along Main St. that depict the history of the city, and a restored 1930s Phillips 66 station that lies on old westbound Route 66.

McLEAN COUNTRY CLUB

The golf   McLean's course is pasture golf at its finest, and the last sand greens in Texas. No clubhouse. No green fees. Sloping farmland and fairways mowed 50 yards wide through a wheat field. The good Lord waters the fairways and the greens have to be rotor-tilled to keep the sand loose. Most days the wind blows 10-15 mph with gusts up to 25 mph; however, it's blown as much as 60 mph so it's nice that the holes are short.

The facility has experimented with a few innovations in recent years. For example, the greens have a strip of outdoor carpet to putt on. At the pin there's

The first competitive golf I played was at the age of 6 years, when I won my first cup . . . I've 120 cups and vases now, and 30 medals, but there's one little cup that never fails of being kept well polished. Bobby Jones

a string to measure the ball around to the carpet. Also on the 9th hole they've installed a grass green that's cut with a regular mower.

The locals use their own carts, but we highly recommend that you soak up the unique atmosphere by walking the course. On the 1st and 5th holes there are two co-ed outhouses, and one water faucet on the 1st hole.

The details   N/A. Hwy. 273, McLean, TX 79057

- Local Rancher. 2,802 yards. No pro shop. No green fees. BYOB. Price - $.

Getting there 80 miles east of Amarillo on the north edge of town. From I-40 take Hwy. 273 south and the course is less than a mile away.

McLEAN NOTES   Join the locals for the Sunday and Tuesday scrambles. Drive north 7 miles on TX 273 to the site of the **Battle of McClellan's Creek**, where in 1874 Frank D. Baldwin encountered some 300 Cheyenne warriors over a small rise and was able to hustle his way out of the skirmish (and recover two captured white women to boot). The **Devil's Rope Museum** features a large barbed wire collection. If you're heading east and itching for another side trip, stop in Groom, TX at the **Golden Spread Grill** and the old ghost truck stop, featuring the largest cross in the Western Hemisphere.

MEMPHIS   Elev. 2,067   Pop. 2,496

On the edge of the High Plains, home to peanut dryers and cotton ware-houses, Memphis is the base for a multi-faceted agricultural area. The old buildings and brick-paved downtown streets provide character, and the Memphis Country Club is the place to play golf.

MEMPHIS COUNTRY CLUB

The golf   Known for its solid care and good condition (the club frequently waters the course), this 9-hole semi-private course is a joy to play. While some of the terrain is flat, parts of the layout have elevation changes that add char-acter. The fairways are wide and large, and a creek flows throughout the course. The greens are large and fast.

The details   806-259-3237. 517 S. 10th St., Memphis, TX 79245

- 9 holes. Par 34. Back – 2,678 yards. Forward – 2,543 yards. Price - $.

Getting there On Hwy. 287 heading south, take the 10th St. exit and turn right. The is a short distance down on the right.

You'll want to play in what I call the trusting mode. That is, when you're out on the golf course, don't think about the mechanics you've been working on. Think about your target, or ball flight, or a line. Dr. Bob Rotella

MEMPHIS NOTES Drive scenic Texas 256 west over rolling country cut by the Prairie Dog Town Fork of the Red River. It rolls through the broken remnants of the High Plains, then climbs the Cap Rock with spectacular views of cliffs and canyons. Find Bob Wills' hometown of Turkey, TX and stay at the historic **Hotel Turkey** (806-423-1151), a country bed and breakfast set in an old brick and stucco building built in 1927. In town try **Gloria's** on the square of **The Ivy Cottage** (806-259-3520) for lunch.

MORTON   Elev. 3,758   Pop. 2,249

Morton, a lonesome Panhandle town only 20 miles from the New Mexico border, was established when prominent cattleman C.C. Slaughter died in 1919 and his huge Slaughter Ranch was broken up. Morton J. Smith, who founded and named the town, served as a broker for the heirs of the Slaughter family. Today Morton serves as a banking and supply center for the ranches and farms that surround it.

MORTON COUNTRY CLUB

The golf   Like most of the simple 9-hole courses of the High Plains, Morton Country Club, a semi-private course open to the public, is a great place for the mid to high handicapper. With wide fairways, generous landing areas, no bunkers, and water hazards on only two holes, there isn't much to intimidate a duffer. The small greens are well maintained and are excellent targets.

The details   806-266-5941. Route 2, Morton, TX 79346

• 1946. 9 holes. Par 35. Back – 2,869. Forward – 2,809. Price - $.

Getting there Out of Lubbock take Hwy. 114 west for 60 miles. Turn north on Hwy. 1780 and drive 6 miles to the course.

MORTON NOTES   Visit the headquarters of the **C.C. Slaughter Ranch**, which is not on most maps. It's 2 miles south on Texas 214 and 1 mile west on FM 1169. This is the type of town where the best meals are found at the convenience stores, so consider the **Circle S** (806-266-0279) for surprisingly good steak fingers. **Allsup's** and **Uncle's** also serve short order–hit em' all and enjoy!

To the beginner putting seems the least interesting part of the game. Like other things, essentially foolish in themselves, such as preaching, putting becomes attractive in proportion to the skill acquired in it. Sir Walter Simpson

MULESHOE

Elev. 3,889   Pop. 4,432

Home to the only golf course in Bailey County, Muleshoe was founded in 1913 and named after the muleshoe-shaped brand of the famous early ranch. They call this country the Blackwater Valley: a sparsely settled area of enormous cattle ranches that eventually began to break up in the early 1900s. Farming was introduced next, and today the town is a center for the marketing and shipping of agricultural interests.

MULESHOE COUNTRY CLUB

The golf   Muleshoe's semi-private 9-hole course is scenic, with mature elm trees lining the fairways. The greens are of medium size and fast. Two sets of tees allow an 18-hole round, and you'll be able to play all day for one green fee.

The details   806-272-4250. 900 Country Club Dr., Muleshoe, TX 79347

• 1953. 9 holes. Par 35. Back – 2,917 (34.0/117). Forward – 2,567 (33.5/114). Putting green and chipping area. Restaurant with beer available. Price - $.

Getting there Drive into Muleshoe from Lubbock on Hwy. 84, turn right at the crossroads, then go 4 blocks. Turn right again, then another 2 blocks, and follow the winding Country Club Rd. to the course.

MULESHOE NOTES   Tino's Mexican Restaurant (806-272-7528) is a good place to eat. If you find yourself near Muleshoe for the Fourth of July, attend the **World Championship Muleshoe Pitching Contest** and gamble heavily with the locals. The **Muleshoe National Wildlife Refuge** (1935) is the oldest national wildlife refuge in Texas. It was established principally for the migratory waterfowl that take advantage of the three small rainwater lakes (unusual features up here on the plains). There are a few local motels as well as the **Heritage House Inn** (806-272-7575).

OLTON

Elev. 3,580   Pop. 2,325

Around 1900, Harry Baughn, T.F. Brown, and Luther Williams settled what is now Olton on state land surrounded by the C. C. Slaughter ranch. Located on US 70 and FM 168, 20 miles east of Plainview in northeast Lamb County, Olton became the county seat when the county was organized in 1908.

⭐

I never go out looking for a sucker; I look for a champion and try to make a
sucker out of him. A champion's got something to spend, and a sucker's generally
out scratching his broke ass. Amarillo Slim

OLTON COUNTRY CLUB

The golf   Unlike most Panhandle courses, Olton Country Club is not as flat and is a bit more difficult. Nicknamed "The Hill" by locals because of its hilltop location, the course has fairways lined with Chinese elms. There are no bunkers; the greens are quick, small, and have subtle undulations. The course is kept in excellent condition, and you can pay once and play all day.

The details   806-285-2595. FM Rd. 168, Olton, TX 79064

• 1957. 9 holes. Par 36. Back – 3,288. Forward – 2,885. Price - $.

Getting there Take Hwy. 70 east 23 miles from Plainview and turn south on Hwy 168. The course is 2 miles outside the town and on the right side of the road.

OLTON NOTES   The best place to stay is the **Wild Plum B&B** (806-285-3014). It's a great place to relax, as there are no phones or televisions, and the accommodations are perfect. Breakfast is included and they will cook for you on request. Other dining options include burgers at **Dairy Queen** or the **J&H Restaurant**, but **Anna's** serves great Mexican food if you're in the mood.

PADUCAH   Elev. 1,886   Pop. 1,392

Established in 1892 as the seat of newly created Cottle County, and still the only town in the county, Paducah was named for the Kentucky home of the county attorney and surveyor who helped develop the town. Paducah is located on a branch of Salt Creek about 115 miles from both Wichita Falls and Lubbock. Today the town serves as supply and distribution point for the region's petroleum and agribusiness interests.

PADUCAH COUNTRY CLUB

The golf   This lonely course receives little play, and if you hit this town early on a weekend morning you'll most likely be the only person on the course. It can be especially interesting during dove season as nearby hunters blast away, creating a unique ambience that you can't find in a big-city course. The fairways are firm due to a lack of water, and wind always affects the round. The slow greens are in decent shape for a small-town course.

The details   806-492-2245. Paducah, TX 79248

• 9 holes. Par 36. Price - $.

Getting there The club is 2 miles south of town off FM 1038.

PADUCAH NOTES The **Heritage Museum**, housed in a restored railroad depot, features farming and ranching artifacts. Northwest of town is the **Matador Wildlife Management Area**, a 28,000-acre range on the Middle and South Pease rivers. The **Town House Motel** (806-492-3595) is a good overnight option, and for meals look to the popular **Cracker's Steakouse** (806-492-3171), named after the fela who owns the place. Try the **Cottle Kitchen Drive In and Grill** (806-492-2880) for short orders, or also the **Cross Roads** convenience store - all good ole High Plains American-style good eats facilities.

PAMPA

Elev. 3,234 Pop. 17,659

Downtown Pampa is notable for its extremely wide streets, and the city spreads outward into immaculate residential areas and clean parks. Named Glasgow, Sutton, and finally Pampa, the town boomed in the 1920s and balances agriculture (wheat and cattle) with the oil industry as its economic base. The good news for golfers traveling through Pampa is that this tidy little town of 17,000 boasts three golf courses and 45 holes of golf. They're not all public, but it's amazing how a few friendly conversations can open doors in a town like Pampa.

HIDDEN HILLS MUNICIPAL GOLF COURSE

The golf Hidden Hills, an 18-hole layout designed by Ray Hardy, was built in 1990 to serve Pampa's growing population. The layout sets in two deep valleys, so golfers are faced with very few level lies as they traverse their way up and down the many hills. Water comes into play on seven holes, and out-of-bounds impacts a few holes.

Even from the back tees, just about all of the par 4s are under 400 yards. Two of the three par 5s are under 500 yards and present good birdie opportunities. Boom a drive on the dogleg-left No. 7 hole and you have a good chance to birdie the 335-yard par 4. The most difficult hole is No. 9, a 420-yard, par 4 dogleg left. No. 12 is tricky as well, featuring 203 yards of carry over a creek.

The details 806-669-5866. North Hwy. 70, Pampa, TX 79065

- 1990. Ray Hardy. 18 holes. Back – 6,463 (69.4/122). Middle – 5,981 (67.2/117). Forward – 5,196 (68.0/116). Price - $$.

Getting there On Hwy. 60 driving east, take Hwy. 70 north and drive a short distance to the course. The course entrance is on the right.

There are really two ways of increasing your distance. You can learn to swing the clubhead faster. Or you can learn to deliver it to the ball more accurately. Jack Nicklaus

PANHANDLE

PAMCEL GOLF COURSE

The golf Located on the grounds of the Celanese Chemical plant, this is a private course open only to employees of the company and their guests. In the event that you work your way onto the course–and there is a slight chance–bring enough golf balls because water is everywhere.

Built around 1960 by Celanese employees for their enjoyment, the course also functions as a means to rid the plant of wastewater. As a result, huge lakes that hold 20 million gallons of water await errant shots on holes 2-6. This impressive amount of water allows for the adequate irrigation of cool-season grasses, which is definitely unique for Texas. Even in the summer, golfers will find bluegrass fairways, gnarly fescue rough, and immaculate bent-grass greens. The course has bunkers on six of the nine holes and the fairways are tree-lined.

Hole 6 is rated the toughest, playing 510 yards into the wind with water along the left side of the fairway. No. 2 is another difficult hole: a par 4 featuring a big dogleg-left fairway and water impacting both the tee and the approach shot.

You might also want to note that if you hear a loud horn blow on No. 5, it's not a weather alert–it's a warning that heat radiation is resulting from the plant's daily operations. So watch out for the "heat radiation zone" on No. 5.

The details 806-663-4342. Hwy. 60 West, Pampa, TX

• 1960. 9 holes. 3,060 yards. Price - $.

Getting there Located 5 miles southwest of Pampa on Hwy. 60.

PAMPA COUNTRY CLUB

The golf Home of the Top of Texas amateur tournament for over 50 years, many of Texas' great players have flailed away on this course. This is an 18-hole, traditional layout with tree-lined fairways and solid greens; it has a few hills but not much water. If you live more than 50 miles away from Pampa, you do not have to be accompanied by a member to play the course.

Make sure that you're warmed up for the opening hole, a monster 597-yard par 5. The 422-yard par 4 No. 4 is the feature hole. This long par 4 doglegs left and involves an approach into an elevated green. Hole 11 is another long par 4 featuring a tight fairway that drops into a valley. No. 18 is a challenging finishing hole–441 yards into a tight, dogleg-left fairway.

The details 806-665-8431, 1701 E. Harvester Ave., Pampa, TX 79066

• 1928. Ray Hardy. 18 holes. Back – 6,295 (69.1/115). Middle – 6,030 (68.2/112). Forward – 5,225 (68.7/109). Price - $$.

Getting there From Downtown Pampa, take Duncan St. to E. Harvester, then drive east to the course.

I never did see the sense in keeping my head down. The only reason I play golf is to see where the ball goes. Charles Price

PAMPA NOTES   The original **Dyer's Bar-B-Que** (806-665-4401) location serves Panhandle barbecue at its finest. Get a room at the **Davis Hotel** (806-669-9115), and for nightlife find the **Pickin' Shack** (live bluegrass and country music) 10 miles southeast of town on Hwy. 27.

PANHANDLE   Elev. 3,451   Pop. 2,594

The town of Panhandle grew from the Four Sixes Ranch. Named for its location in the Texas Panhandle, it became the county seat when Carson County was organized in 1888. Wheat, cattle, and petroleum products are the major commodities from this marketing and shipping center.

PANHANDLE COUNTRY CLUB

The golf   Panhandle Country Club is a 9-hole semi-private course that offers a nice variety of holes, considering its flat basic layout. The course features narrow fairways and small greens, with a few water hazards and bunkers sprinkled throughout the design.

The best birdie opportunity is No. 5, which plays to a par 4 at only 255 yards. Another confidence builder is No. 8, where you'll need nothing more than a 9 iron. However, the finishing hole is the toughest: a 543-yard par 5.

Pay once and play all day. The course has two sets of tees for an 18-hole round.

The details   806-537-3300. 100 Pecan St., Panhandle, TX 79068

- 1962. 9 holes. Par 36. Back – 2,979 (34.1). Forward – 2,519 (33.4). Putting green but no driving range. Snack bar with alcohol served. Price - $.

Getting there From Amarillo take Hwy. 60 east for 125 miles. In Panhandle turn north onto Boarder St., then travel 2 blocks and turn right on Pecan St. Next, drive 1 block to Maple and you should be able to see the course.

PANHANDLE NOTES   Enjoy the **scenic drive** along FM 293 west to Texas 136, with views of the modern High Plains agriculture contrasted with the rolling grasslands of the Canadian River valley ranch lands. Find the historical marker 10 miles north on 136; it marks the trail from Fort Smith, AR to Santa Fe, NM with wagon ruts that are still visible. **Lake Meredith** is just up the road. The **Texan Hotel** (806-537-3372) offers rooms, and you can eat your fill at **The Butter Churn Restaurant** (806-537-5274).

Golf teaches success and failure. Neither lasts long. Glenn Kummer

PERRYTON

Elev. 2,942   Pop. 7,922

Located a whopping 545 miles from the state capitol in Austin, the "Wheatheart of the Nation" is a clean little town with wide streets. The towering grain elevators attest to the town's reputation as one of the nation's top wheat producing areas. Perryton was founded in 1919 and is home to the 18-hole Perryton Municipal Golf Course.

PERRYTON MUNICIPAL GOLF COURSE

The golf   Built in 1976, this is a tough course with more water hazards than usual for courses up this way. While there are no bunkers on the well-maintained greens, they feature subtle breaks that make it challenging to read.

The details   806-435-5381. 402 SE 24th Ave, Perryton, TX 79070

* 1976. Par 72. Back – 6,431 yards (69.2/116). Middle – 6,172 (66.9/113). Forward – 5,257 (67.0/111). Price - $$.

Getting there Driving north into Perryton on Hwy. 83, look for the course on the right side of the road.

PERRYTON NOTES   Visit the buried Indian city 15 miles south at **Wolf Creek Park,** which also has a campground and lake. The **Museum of the Plains** offers general history exhibits of the Texas and Oklahoma Panhandlers. Perryton has a few basic hotels, but your best bet is the **Casa Manana Ranch Bed & Breakfast** (806-435-7690) or the **Ambassador Inn** (806-435-9611). Savor the barbecue of Texas' northernmost county at **Money's Bar-B-Que** (806-435-3945) or **JoAnn's Bar-B-Que** (806-435-9552).

PLAINVIEW

Elev. 3,366   Pop. 22,257

Plainview was founded in the late 1800s and was named for its wide-open and spectacular view of the plains. The town is known for its abundant underground water supply and its position as a leader in cotton and grain production. Oil has also played a major part of the economy.

PLAINVIEW COUNTRY CLUB

The golf   Plainview Country Club is a short 18-hole course featuring tree-lined fairways and small greens, which have been expanded recently. A few small streams and ponds come into play on this course, which is otherwise void of major difficulty. Locals rave about the staff's commitment to improve the course and generally enhance the overall golf experience with their friendly demeanor.

No one who ever had lessons would have a swing like mine. Lee Trevino

The front nine has only one par 5, the opening hole, so there is the legitimate opportunity to start out with a birdie on this short 460-yard hole. The signature hole is No. 12, a 396-yard par 4.

The details   806-293-2445. 2902 W 4th, Plainview, TX 79072

* 1939. Par 71. Back – 6,287 (69/113). Middle – 5,827 (68.9). Forward – 5,298 (68.4). Price - $.

Getting there From I-27 driving north, take Exit 49 and turn east onto Hwy/70. Turn south on Canyon St. and it will lead you directly to the course.

PLAINVIEW NOTES   If you don't eat at the golf course, try **Chuck Wagon Barbecue** (806-296-9907) or the **Rockin' R Steakhouse** (806-293-0087). The **Llano Estacado Museum** is home to the remains of a prehistoric elephant skull known as the "Easter Elephant," which was discovered in the nearby community of Easter. The historic downtown has several antique stores for restless significant others. For a room call the **Harman-Y House B&B** (806-296-2505).

POST   Elev. 2,590   Pop. 3,800

Referred to as the "Gateway to the Plains" because of its setting by the Cap Rock Cliffs, this cowboy country attracted cereal magnate Charles Williams Post in 1907 as he searched for his dream city. Mr. Post found that the scenic Caprock escarpment, combined with the headwaters of the Brazos River, were too much to keep him away. Post is an eclectic town for the High Panhandle Plains. Its beauty is accompanied by a rich cultural community, including an arts scene that has developed in the city's original buildings.

CAPROCK GOLF COURSE

The golf   At press time, Post's 9-hole course was temporarily closed apparently due to irrigation issues and a general lack of water. This typical of the terrain that separates the flat Llano Estacado from the rolling hills and canyons to the east. The course features wide, rolling fairways that, despite their generous landing areas, require uphill and downhill shot-making into small, bentgrass greens. Four of the holes have blind tee shots.

The details   806-495-3029. P.O. Box 220, Post, TX 79356

* 1954. D.H. Bartlett. 9 holes. Par 35. Back – 2,876. Forward – 2,444. Price - $.

Getting there From Lubbock head northeast on Hwy. 84, then turn left on Golf Course Rd. Drive 1 mile north and look for the course sign.

Post has about 50-75 operating oil wells in the residential areas of the city.

PANHANDLE

POST NOTES   Shop on Main St. and then go for chicken-fried steak at **Holly's Drive-In** (806-495-2704), where you can dine inside or wait in your car. Plan your trip around the **Old Mill Trade Days**, where up to 500 vendors dot the foot of the majestic Caprock. On Main St. you'll find the **Hotel Garza** Historic B&B (806-495-3962), which offers excellent accommodations.

ROARING SPRINGS   Elev. 3,105   Pop. 274

If solitude is the thing for you, this town of 274 residents is one place you can get away from it all. Set on the South Pease River on Texas 70 and FM 684, this former camp of the Matador Ranch is the hub for the area's ranching and agricultural needs, and not much else. If you're an adventurous golfer looking for an out-of-the-way place to work on your game, however, their 9-hole course off Texas 70 does the trick.

ROARING SPRINGS RANCH GOLF COURSE

The golf   Here you'll find basic, small-town golf on what is hilly terrain for the flat High Plains. Mesquite trees dot the layout but there's nothing much else to bother your game. The greens are average-sized and flat. Two sets of tees offer a different look the second time around, and you can pay once and play all day.

The details   806-348-7267. Hwy. 70, Roaring Springs, TX 79256

• 1980. 9 holes. Par 36. Back – 2,845. Forward – 2,404. Price - $.

Getting there From Lubbock, take Hwy. 70 north and drive about 30 miles to the course.

ROARING SPRING NOTES Check out the old 1913 depot that is now a museum. They'll feed you at the **Roaring Springs Cafe** (806-348-7205), then you can drive up to Matador to tour the 1891 **Motley County Jail** and hangman's gallows.

SEMINOLE   Elev. 3,312   Pop. 5,867

The city was established and named county seat shortly after Gaines County organized in 1905, and was named for nearby Indian watering places. The county is among the state's leaders in petroleum production, cotton, and peanuts. Although there's not much to do in Seminole, the fabulous Gaines County Golf Course is one of the best courses in the Panhandle, and is definitely worth the drive from Midland or Lubbock.

A hot streak is simply a glimpse of a golfer's true potential. Dr. Bob Rotella

GAINES COUNTY GOLF COURSE

The golf   After you drive through this flat, barren region of cotton and oil production, you'll be stunned when you stumble upon this hidden Panhandle gem that played host to Jack Nicklaus and Arnold Palmer in a 1963 exhibition. Originally built as a 9-hole course by Jim Terry in 1953, the facility was updated with another nine holes in 1991.

The layout features good elevation and plenty of trees, especially considering the terrain. The most outstanding amenity is the greens, which are large, fast, and in excellent condition. Sometimes the fairways dry out and the condition is average, but that helps the ball roll and is definitely beneficial when the wind is blowing.

Every par 3 requires a long iron, but the demanding par 4s are the attention-getters. Two par 4s stand out among many that are above average in difficulty for courses in this remote area. The signature hole is No. 8: it's only 340 yards but requires an approach shot over a pond to a well-bunkered green. Hole 5 also plays tough as a 435-yard dogleg right with an approach into an elevated green. This hole is particularly long into the wind.

The details   915-758-3808. Seagraves Hwy. 385, Seminole, TX 79360

• 1954 by Jim Terry. 18 holes. Par 72. Back – 6,685 (70.7/110). Middle – 6,290 (69.0/107). Forward – 5,087. Price - $$.

Getting there Drive through Seminole north on Hwy. 385 and look for the signs to the course. The course is set in a large grove of trees on the left side of the highway.

SEMINOLE NOTES   For steaks, find **The Sand Pit** on south Main St. or the **K & S Steak Place** on Hobbs Hwy. across from the school. The local Tex-Mex eateries are **Rosita's** and the **Little Gomez Mexican Restaurant**. Finally, locals swear by the **Old Town Bakery**. If you can't get enough golf, the truly addicted linksman can head 30 miles west to **Hobbs, NM** and play their two courses, which happens to be the closest place to buy cold beer, since this town of 29 churches still votes dry. Lodging in town can be found at the **Seminole Inn** (915-758-9881) or the **Raymond Motor Inn** (915-758-3653). If you're heading north, make a point to eat and stay at the Cherry Blossom Inn in Seagraves, which resides in the old 1917 Hotel Texan/Simpson (806-387-1407; www.cherryblossom-inn.com).

Golf is an awkward set of bodily contortions designed to produce
a graceful result. Thomas Armour

PANHANDLE

SHAMROCK

Elev. 2,498   Pop. 1,959

You'll find Shamrock at the "Crossroads of America," where I-40 intersects US 83, the highway that stretches from Mexico to Canada. Located only 15 miles from the Oklahoma border, Shamrock is one of the tidiest little towns in the Panhandle.

The town was named by Irish sheep rancher George Nickel, who selected the good-luck name of Shamrock when he established the original post office back in 1890. Oil was discovered in the 1920s, and old US 66 once ran through Main St. In recent years natural gas has fueled the economy, and cattle, agriculture, and tourism continue to help the town thrive.

Since rounds are free at the 9-hole Shamrock Country Club with paid lodging at any of the hotels, Shamrock is a particularly favorable place for avid golfers.

SHAMROCK COUNTRY CLUB

The golf   Shamrock Country Club is a semi-private course where your tee shots from elevated boxes will find severely undulating fairways and bent-grass greens. There are no sand or grass bunkers, but the track features three ponds that come into play throughout the round. The signature hole is No. 4, which requires a tee shot of around 200 yards, with water to the left and out-of-bounds on the right. For the approach you'll need a mid-iron over a small lake to a green surrounded by trees. Play all day for under $20.

The details   806-256-5151. 900 S Wall, Shamrock, TX 79079

- 1952. 9 holes. Par 36. Back – 3,238 (35.3). Forward – 2,426 (33.9/106). Price - $.

Getting there   From I-40, take Hwy. 83 south, then travel 4 miles to the Shamrock Community Center. Turn right and drive 1 block west to the course.

SHAMROCK NOTES   For attractions check out the **Blarney Stone**, a piece of the original from the ruins of Blarney Castle in Ireland. Or take in the regional history at the **Pioneer West Museum**, which is housed in the former Reynolds Hotel. For sit-down dining consider the **Mitchell Steak House, Mesquite Steak House,** or **Hasty's**, the local favorite. Your best motel/hotel options are the **Best Western** or the **Irish Inn,** each of which has a pool. However, golfers tend to lean towards the Irish Inn since it's one of the only bars in dry Wheeler County.

A good pro should want to find out everything he can about a pupil—especially the pupil's goals. Does he or she just want to be able to feel comfortable playing an occasional round of golf with a client or customer? Or to win the club championship? Be sure your teaching pro knows your goals. Dr. Bob Rotella

SLATON
Elev. 3,085   Pop. 5,593

Located 18 miles southeast of Lubbock on the edge of the Caprock, Slaton is the perfect place for a quick golf adventure when venturing out of the big city. The town dates back to 1910 when O.L. Slaton helped bring the Santa Fe Railroad through town.

SLATON MUNICIPAL GOLF COURSE

The golf   Slaton Municipal's layout consists of one par 5 (503-yard hole 6), two par 3s, and five par 4s, the longest of which is the 440-yard first hole. The signature hole is No. 8, a 156-yard par 3 that requires a tee shot over a large canyon filled with water. Two sets of tees offer an 18-hole round.

The details   806-828-3269. Route 2, Box 158B, Slaton, TX 79364

• 1962. 9 holes. Par 36. Back – 3,045. Forward – 2,688. Price - $.

Getting there Take Hwy 84 east, then turn left at Golf Course Rd. and drive 2 miles to the course. The course is about 3 miles north of town.

SLATON NOTES   The must-do here is a tour north to Ransom Canyon, TX and the **Krackaknut Grill** (806-741-0900), where you can take your own beer and wallow in the smoked ribs while listening to the live music that plays almost every night on the backyard stage. Grab breakfast at the historic, old-fashioned 1923 **Slaton Bakery** (806-828-3253) overlooking the quaint historic downtown square and train station. For lodgin try the **Slaton Inn** (806-828-5831), the only place in town.

SPEARMAN
Elev. 3,105   Pop. 2,937

Spearman, the seat of Hansford County, resonates with the lonely beauty of rolling wheat fields. Established in the 1920s when the railroad came through, the town was named after an executive of the company building the track. The standard High Plains industries of grain storage, farming, cattle, and a few oil and gas businesses define the economy.

HANSFORD GOLF CLUB

The golf   The only course in Hansford County, this small-town 9-hole course has rolling fairways and bent-grass greens that are quick, tiny, and flat.

For tournament golf, I have a good, big dinner in my room the night before, prefaced by two good, stiff highballs, the first taken in a tub of hot water; the finest relaxing combination I know; and then a few cigarettes and a bit of conversation, and bed at 9 o'clock. And usually I sleep well, despite the curious strain that is always present in championship competition. Bobby Jones

Although there are not many hazards, a pond on the 4th hole fills up when it rains. Two sets of tees offer sometimes-extreme variety between holes (No. 3 plays as a 250-yard par 4 on the front and a 161-yard par 3 on the back), and you can pay once and play all day.

The details   806-659-2233. FM 2387, Spearman, TX 79081

• 1957. 9 holes. Par 36. Back – 3,295 (31.3/90). Forward – 2,777 (32.8). Price - $.

Getting there From Hwy. 15 driving south, take Hwy. 207 west and make a right at Hardesty Hwy. (FM 2387) exit.

SPEARMAN NOTES   Eat with the cowboys and wheat farmers at the **Cactus Cafe** (806-878-3181) or **Ivey's Hungry Cowboy** (806-659-5151). For an uppity meal go to the **Paloduro Supper Club** (806-659-2232). Ask the locals for directions and head south on FM 760 and other local roads to find the Adobe Walls battleground. If you need to stay, the **Newcomb House B&B** (806-659-3287) is the place.

SPUR
Elev. 2,291   Pop. 1,076

   As with so many little towns in the Panhandle, phrases like "remote," "desolate," or "in the middle of nowhere" come to mind. Spur is 60 miles east of Lubbock on Highway 70. Named after the Spur Ranch, the town is the central shipping point in Dickens County for cotton, wheat, and cattle.

SPUR GOLF COURSE

The golf   Only the basics here at this 9-hole public course built in the rugged country of the Salt Fork of the Brazos. This is a natural course, with mounding that results from the contour of the land. While passing through town, we decided that this facility is perfect for the beginner. There are no water hazards or bunkers; furthermore, there is no pressure because there are no people. Teach your wife to play here–her shots will roll forever because the fairways are not watered.

The details   806-271-4355. Swenson Park, Spur, TX 79370

• 1930s 9 holes. Par 36. Back – 3,076. Forward – 2,651. Price $.

Getting there In town find the Allsup Convenience Store, turn left, and the course is over the hill.

No matter what happens—never give up on a hole . . . In tossing in your cards after a bad beginning you also undermine your whole game, because to quit between tee and green is more habitforming that drinking a highball before breakfast. Sam Snead

SPUR NOTES   The 1914 **Spur Inn Bed & Breakfast** (806-271-3940) is a nice option to find in such a small town, and your best bet (and about your only option) for a meal is the local **Dairy Queen**.

STRATFORD

Elev. 3,695   Pop. 2,033

PANHANDLE

Stratford sprang up in secrecy during the middle of the night in 1901, when Sherman County records were hustled from the former county seat at Coldwater to land owned by Walter Colton along the new Rock Island Railroad route. Texas Rangers had to settle the dispute over the location of the county seat, and Coldwater went the way of the ghost town. Today, the Stratford skyline is made up of wheat elevators.

One of the best examples of the outrageous Texas weather occurred here in May 1978, when a storm that dropped 12 inches of snow on the course was followed by a tornado that came through the next day with 3 inches of hail.

STRATFORD COUNTRY CLUB

The golf   Built in the late 1960s, this is a scenic 9-hole country golf course. The fairways are wide-open and generally flat; however, there are some subtle hills throughout the course.

The details   806-396-2259. Hwy. 54, Stratford, TX 79084

- 1968. 9 holes. Par 36. Back – 3,172 (32.8/112). Forward – 2,801 (35.1/128). Price – $.

Getting there On Hwy. 287 heading north, exit Hwy 54 (Dalhart Rd.) and drive 3 miles to the course.

STRATFORD NOTES There are a few local restaurants in Stratford but we recommend you head down US 54 to Conlen, TX, where **Jerry's Fine Food** (806-384-2124) really is fine. Chef and owner Jerry Robinson, who used to run the Dalhart Country Club, attended the Institute of Culinary Arts in New Haven, CT and serves up a mean lobster tail. Learn about the local history at the **Sherman County Depot Museum**. There are about three local hotels in town for lodging. Finally, road-trippers can drive 38 miles up US 287 for the 9-hole course in **Boyse City, OK**. The **Stratford Inn** (806-366-5574) is the only place in town but has just been redone and is in good shape.

The waggle gives the golfer a running start. It blends right into the swing.
For all general points and purposes, the backswing is simply an extension of the way
the golfer takes the club back on the waggle. Ben Hogan

PANHANDLE

SUNDOWN

Elev. 3,500   Pop. 1,505

Sundown is not on a major highway, but instead straggles at the junction of farm roads 301 and 303, 15 miles southwest of Levelland. Originally part of the C.C. Slaughter ranch, its name supposedly comes from a long discussion among settlers that ended at sundown. Sundown became known as "Boomtown USA" and was famous as the tiny town with the 2.5-mile-long main street.

SUNDOWN MUNICIPAL GOLF COURSE

The golf   This 9-hole High Plains course is a bit different from other small-town Panhandle courses. It is longer (over 3,100 yards) with two par 5s over 500 yards, and the greens are extremely large. So large that the club puts two flagsticks on every hole to make the hole different from the second set of tees the second time you play. The builders of most courses out here didn't bother with bunkers, but Sundown has about a half-dozen that are sprinkled about the course. The flat terrain was molded slightly to cause uneven lies. Water is in play on three holes and, as you might expect, the wind can be a major factor. There are even a few trees along the fairways that can cause problems. Hole 9 is the number one handicap and plays 450 yards on the back nine.

The details   806-229-6186. 600 W. Richardson, Sundown, TX 79372

- 1982. Warren Cantrell. 9 holes. Par 35. Back – 3,116 (34.5/109). Forward – 2,588 (33.9/106). Price - $.

Getting there From Lubbock, take FM 1585 west and turn left when you get to CR 301. Turn right on Richardson and drive 8 blocks to the course.

SUNDOWN NOTES   Sundown is best experienced as a day trip from Lubbock, or to work in a quick nine on your way to play in Levelland or Brownfield. Try **D & J's Cafe** (806-229-3337) for lunch after your round.

TAHOKA

Elev. 3,090   Pop. 2,848

The seat of Lynn County since 1903, this little stop-off on the way to Lubbock is a cotton marketing and shipping point complete with gins and compresses. The town name comes from nearby Tahoka Lake, a natural spring-fed lake whose Indian name meant "fresh, clear water."

The best advice I can offer for playing a ball out of water is—don't. Tony Lema

T-BAR COUNTRY CLUB

The golf   Built in the late 1950s, the semi-private T-Bar is a flat course with minimal trees, so the wind bears down hard. Hole 6 is the signature at 411 yards, featuring a tee shot is into a narrow landing area. No. 7 is also difficult and requires some nifty short game work. The bent-grass greens are in nice shape and hold shots well. As you might expect, the fairways are firm and the grass can get bare in some areas. Overall, a fun course to play because of its open layout.

The details   806-998-5305. Hwy. 380, Tahoka, TX 79373

• 1957. 9 holes. Par 36.   Back – 3,090 yards. Forward – 2,872 yards. Price - $.

Getting there Turn west off of Hwy. 87 and take Hwy. 380 until you come to T-Bar Lane. Drive north 2 miles to the course.

TAHOKA NOTES   The best way to play T-Bar is to start the weekend in Midland, then drive north to Lubbock on a calm fall Saturday for an evening football game in Lubbock. Play the Lamesa courses and T-Bar on the way. Around Tahoka, tour the land that was once heavily camped by Comanche Indians and buffalo hunters in the 1870s, and look for the Tahoka Daisy, a lavender wildflower that blankets the plains. The **Pioneer Museum** in town offers nostalgic images of the old days.

TULIA   Elev. 3,501   Pop. 5,148

Settled along Tule Creek, a misspelling changed the name to Tulia. Located halfway between Amarillo and Lubbock, Tulia is the seat of Swisher County and the commercial center for abundant agricultural production featuring milo, wheat, cotton, and several large livestock feedlot operations.

TULE LAKE GOLF CLUB

The golf   Tule Lake is another small-town High Plains course with wide-open fairways and only a few hazards that affect play. This basic layout has a good variety of holes, with the standard two par 3s, two par 5s, and five par 4s. The longest hole is the 524-yard par 5 2nd hole, and the number one handicap is the 412-yard hole 6.

Two sets of tees can be used when playing an 18-hole round. Pay once and play all day.

The details   806-995-3400. Golf Course Rd., Tulia, TX 79088

• 1954. 9 holes. Par 36. Back – 3,120 yards. Forward – 2,603 yards. Price - $.

A hit must be perfectly timed, but a swing will time itself. Grantland Rice

Getting there About 3 miles northeast of Downtown Tulia, take Love Rd. east for 1 mile, then turn north onto the County Rd. and drive a short distance to the course.

TULIA NOTES   Test the local Mexican food at **El Camino** (806-995-4083). For a room find the **Select Inn** (806-0995-3248). Historic Downtown Tulia is experiencing a renaissance with an eclectic mix of shops and galleries, and the **Swisher County Museum** offers an excellent collection of pioneer ranch and farm artifacts.

VEGA

Elev. 4,030   Pop. 907

Vega, a sprawling cowtown that marks the turnoff onto US 385, is about the only sight between Adrian and Amarillo. It rests on the level prairie land broken by the Canadian River and its tributaries. Once part of the 3-million-acre XIT Ranch, which was granted in 1879 by the state to the Capital Land Syndicate in exchange for building the present-day capitol in Austin, Vega is the ranching center and seat of Oldham county. With a population of just over 2,000 folks, the county has more cattle than people, and nearly one square mile for each person. Each year over 90,000 head of cattle are fed in Oldham County, and the folks that facilitate that process get their golf in at the Oldham County Country Club.

OLDHAM COUNTY COUNTRY CLUB

The golf   For the golfer with time to kill while in Amarillo, the semi-private Oldham County Country Club is an interesting side trip for golf on Route 66. This simple 9-hole course features strategically placed sand bunkers and a few water hazards to provide minor challenges. The casual atmosphere makes this course a fun place to play.

The details   806-267-2595. Hwy. 385 South, Vega, TX 79092

- 1973. 9 holes. Par 36. Back – 3,259 (34.4/113). Forward – 2,782 yards. Price - $.

Getting there Head south outside of Vega down Hwy. 385 for 5 miles, then look for the course on the right side of the road.

VEGA NOTES   In 1937 Route 66 was paved and re-routed through Vega, but the old route has a few interesting spots. For grub, dig in at **Anita's Longhorn Cafe** or hit Adrian, TX for world-class barbecue at the **Antique Ranch**. For nostalgia, stay at the **Vega Motel**, a restored Route 66 motor court. For comfort, stay at the **Best Western Country Inn**.

A fifth at night...a 68 in the morning. Walter Hagen

WELLINGTON

Elev. 2,078   Pop. 2,233

Wellington is a farming community that sits on US 83 halfway between Childress and Shamrock. An offspring of the old Rocking Chair Ranch, the land was originally owned by English nobility. Wellington is home to the only golf course in Collingsworth County, the Wellington Country Club.

WELLINGTON COUNTRY CLUB

The golf   This small-town 9-hole course is built on the rolling, broken terrain that drains into the Red River forks. The simple design fits the locale, as just over 3,200 people live in the entire county. One lake affects play on three holes, but there isn't much else to get in the way of a low score. Every par 4 is well under 400 yards. The longest hole is the 500-yard par 5 No. 8.

Two sets of tees allow for a full day of golf. Pay once and play all day. You will enjoy the hospitality of the staff and patrons.

The details   806-447-5050. Hwy. 203, Wellington, TX 79095

- 1978. 9 holes. Par 36. Back - 3,050 yards. Forward - 2,492 yards. Price - $.

Getting there From downtown turn right on Mangum Hwy. When you come to Hwy. 203, turn east and drive 3 miles to the course.

WELLINGTON NOTES   Satisfy your Tex-Mex cravings at **Mona's Cocina** (806-447-2941), and gear up for a tour through the **Collingsworth County Museum** (806-447-5327). In 1933, Bonnie Parker and Clyde Barrow flew off a half-completed bridge 7 miles north of town. A gunfight ensued and two police officers were taken hostage. Bonnie's gloves are on display at the museum. One place to stay here: **The Cherokee Inn Motel** (806-447-2508) on Houston St.

PANHANDLE BORDER CROSSINGS

With other state borders to the west, north, and east, many towns in the Panhandle are within a reasonable driving distance to courses in New Mexico, Oklahoma, and believe it or not, Kansas.

PORTALES, NM

28 miles from Farwell, TX

The flat, 9-hole **Portales Country Club** (505-356-8943) dates back to the 1940s, and although it is private, out-of-towners are officially allowed to play during the week and can sometimes wiggle their way on during the weekends. Best to hit 'em straight here, since the fairways are generally only about 30 yards wide and are lined with thick rough. The course tips out at 3,297 yards (34.7/105) and a par 36.

CLOVIS, NM
10 miles from Farwell, TX

The 1920s-era **Clovis Municipal Golf Course** (505-769-7871) serves up a beginner-friendly 9-holer (983 yards) in addition to its par 70 regulation 18-hole course (6,083/68.0/112). A few old elm trees get in the way, but you'll have to be real hungover to avoid shooting a career-low round. The best hole is the 475-yard No. 5, which tempts you to go for this par 5 in two with its short yardage but guards the green with a water hazard.

The more difficult **Colonial Park Country Club** (505-762-4775) offers a similar setup to the Clovis Muni, with both a hilly, 708-yard, 9-hole par 3 course that opened in the 1990s, and a 1960s Warren Cantrell/Ray Hardy par 72 18-holer (6,856/71.2/111), which can burn you with its length when the wind is blowing. Water hazards impact four holes, one of which is the signature 520-yard No. 18–a dogleg right that features a mean approach over water of at least 200 yards.

CLAYTON, NM
47 miles from Dalhart, TX

The **Clayton Golf Club** (505-374-9957) is owned by the community, and allows you to pay via an honor system since there is no pro shop. The course is loaded with bunkers and kept in good condition, and tips out at 3,174 yards (34.6). Unusual for a small-town 9-holer, both par 5s on this par 36 track are over 500 yards.

TUCUMCARI, NM
77 miles from Vega, TX

Little Feat didn't write about this track in their truck driving song "Willin," but they could have. A golfer named Dr. Hoover routed the **Tucumcari Municipal Golf Course** (505-461-1849) all the way back in the late 1940s. Lots of hills here, and the generous fairways are lined by trees. This 9-holer goes 3,314 yards (35.3/113) and plays to a very do-able par 36.

HOBBS, NM
30 miles from Seminole, TX

The scrubby town of Hobbs has its own little country club, the aptly named **Hobbs Country Club** (505-393-5212). Warren Cantrell came through in the 1950s to upgrade this deceptive course to a 6,627-yard (71.8/121) 18-holer. The wind can be a problem, and the barren landscape somehow makes it difficult to judge distances.

The **Ocotillo Park Golf Course** (505-397-9297) is flat and wide open, tipping out at 6,716 yards (70.7/122). The greens are nice and usually protected by bunkers, water is in play on three holes, and every now and then you have to watch out for random trees that get in the way.

─────────────────────── ★ ───────────────────────

Golf is a game of motion and rhythm, not of position and mechanics. Martin Hall

LOVINGTON, NM
32 miles from Denver City, TX

The small-town **Lovington Country Club** (505-396-6619) is friendly and fun. It's wide-open, tree-lined, and treasured by the locals who take great pride in this 9-hole 2,962-yarder (par 35/33.5/110). One small lake spots the course, but you'll score well here as there are not many hazards.

GUYMON, OK
42 miles from Stratford, TX

The **Sunset Hills Golf Course** (580-338-7404) is a great little 6,236-yard (70.3/120) par 71 track popular because of its solid condition. Some of the fairways are narrow, and water comes into play on a few holes.

BEAVER, OK
27.9 miles from Booker, TX

Beaver Pioneer Park Golf Course (580-625-363) is proud of its friendly employees and comfortable atmosphere. This short course was refurbished during 1996. The most difficult hole is No. 7, a par 4 requiring an approach shot that must clear both the creek and the trees in order to hit the elevated green. The green fees are good for all-day play.

BOISE CITY, OK
38 miles from Stratford, TX

Cimarron County Golf Course (580-544-2589) is a relatively short course built primarily on flat terrain, but occasional mounds can cause uneven lies. The greens are large-sized, have medium speed, and are quite undulating. The tree-lined fairways vary between narrow and wide, and are fairly flat. There are no sand bunkers on this course, but a pond does come into play on one hole. There is an additional set of men's tees that can be used when playing an 18-hole round.

Shattuck Golf & Country Club (580-938-2445) The fairways on this course are manicured, and there is one lake that comes into play on two holes. The signature hole is No. 4, a 516-yard, par 5 requiring an approach shot to an elevated green that is well protected by trees. There are additional tees that can be used when playing an 18-hole round.

ELK CITY, OK
56 miles from Shamrock, TX

The **Elk City Golf & Country Club** (580-225-3556) opened around 1980 with a nice Donald Sechrist design that plays to a par 71, 6,208 yards (68.9/106). Sechrist used elevated greens and tees to give the golfer great views of the wide-open fairways below. The signature at Elk City is the large, undulating greens–good targets but easy to three-jack.

You get rewarded at the bottom end of the club by what you do at the top end. Jerry Barber

PANHANDLE

HOBART, OK
78 miles from Shamrock, TX

Hilly with water in play on only two holes, the **Hobart Country Club** (580-726-3534) has four dogleg fairways and some scattered trees that can alter your shots. The greens are large and undulating. The course is open to out-of-towners; however, residents of Hobart are not allowed to play the course.

MANGUM, OK
43 miles from Wellington, TX

The **Mangum Golf Course** (580-782-3676) is a short 9-holer, routing only 2,857 yards (32.0/70) to a par 35. The best part about this track is its lush condition, brought about by frequent watering.

SAYRE, OK
38 miles from Shamrock, TX

The **Sayre Golf Course** (580-928-9046) goes 3,098 yards to a par 36, with water in play on 3 of 9 holes. No. 4 is the best hole, a long par 3 (200 yards) over a valley to an elevated green.

SHATTUCK, OK
44 miles from Canadian, TX

The 1950s **Shattuck Golf & Country Club** (580-938-2445) tips out at 3,150 yards (33.8/110) over its 9 holes, with one lake coming into play on two holes. No. 4 is the most difficult, a 500-yard plus par 5 that plays into an elevated green.

ELKHART, KS
60 miles from Stratford, TX

The former Elkhart GC was bought by Morton County in the late 1990s, renovated, and morphed into the **Point Rock Golf Club** (316-697-1201). Now this old, 3,199-yard, par 36 track has two water holes, one of which is the signature 181-yard No. 5 that plays over the drink. The first two holes are both par 5s, the first fairly long (533 yards), but the second only around 450 yards.

LIBERAL, KS
47.8 miles from Perryton, TX

The 1920s **Liberal Country Club** (316-624-3992) is a 9-hole track with two sets of tees for a full round. It tips out at 3,197 yards (35.9/128), with water in play on three holes and narrow fairways that wind to tiny greens.

The **Willow Tree Golf Course** (316-626-0175) plays 6,329 yards from the tips (par 72/70.1/121), and is known for a having a decent amount of water and small, quick greens. And as its name implies, willow trees line the fairways.

We all choke. You just try to choke last. Tom Watson

★ NORTHWEST TEXAS ★

NORTHWEST

When the Good Lord created Northwest Texas, He didn't spend a lot of time on outward appearances. There's no denying that this is, for the most part, a desolate, unforgiving place. As if to compensate for its homely appearance, the Almighty gave the region a gift: under its crusty exterior lies one of the largest oil reserves in the world.

One might think that this liquid gold would translate into fashionable neighborhoods and the other outward signs of wealth, but it hasn't. All you see is the pumpjacks nodding rhythmically across the prairie. The fruits of their metronome-like labor aren't visible until you reach neighborhoods like River Oaks in Houston, Alamo Heights in San Antonio, or Highland Park in Dallas. Northwest Texas (Archer City, to be precise) is where The Last Picture Show was filmed, and the tumbleweeds and dust storms still blow through, slamming screen doors and sending newspapers and hamburger wrappers skittering down the empty streets.

Wichita Falls—which had the dubious distinction of being named "Most Average City in America" by Advertising Age in 2000—and Abilene serve as hub cities, both with populations around 140,000. Not counting those two mighty metropolises, the average population of the 38 remaining cities is well under 10,000. Want to own a big ranch? You can get all the land you want for $50 an acre. As one military official noted at the opening of nearby Sheppard Air Force Base, "There is lots of open land to fly over."

So why bother with Northwest Texas? Why not leave it to the ranchers? Two reasons: people and price. If you've had your fill of overpriced country club settings and snooty golf pros, this region is as far from snobby as it gets. The people embody Texas friendliness, and they welcome you with genuine heart. As for cost, try this on for size: on Thursday nights at the main course in Wichita Falls, $17.50 gets you a cart, green fee, hamburger, chips, beverage, and entry into the nightly scramble. This is small-town golf in spades, and you can play all you want for very little money.

This area is so far off the map that only the intrepid souls from *The Texas Golf Bible* were willing to explore it. *Golf Magazine's* recent course directory listed only one of the dozens of courses in this region. If you search the Internet for information on these courses, you'll find nothing more than minimal directory information—not one review. Another fairly complete resource on Texas golf courses produced in 1998, *Texas Golf: The Best of the Lone Star State*, categorizes the courses with starred ratings. For this region, 47 out of the 52 courses were listed as one-star courses, and were subsequently listed with basic directory information, void of any sort of course review.

When you look down at your grip and see wrinkles in your wrists, chances are you are reaching for the ball and not using the club the way it was designed. Tommy Armour

When you come to Northwest Texas, lower your expectations and bring your shotgun. No palm trees or waterfalls out here, but there is excellent quail hunting and many big-city sportsmen keep hunting leases in the area. Mostly, come to work on your game and enjoy the absence of traffic, congestion, and all the other things we city folk complain about.

NORTHWEST

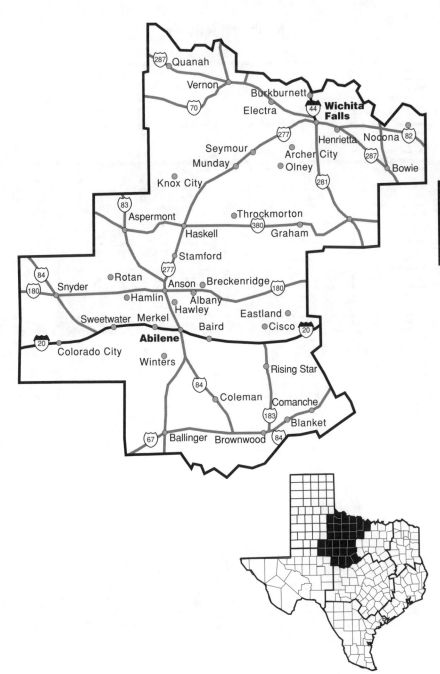

NORTHWEST

Northwest Mileage

	Abilene	Albany	Anson	Archer City	Aspermont	Baird	Ballinger	Blanket	Bowie	Brackenr.	Brownwood	Burkburnett	Cisco	Coleman	CO City	Comanche	Eastland	Electra	Graham
Abilene		38	24	120	60	24	57	87	156	61	81	158	48	54	64	86	58	149	94
Albany	38		37	82	67	26	90	82	118	24	83	121	35	66	101	81	43	113	57
Anson	24	37		111	36	42	79	106	155	61	101	138	67	76	73	106	77	125	94
Archer City	120	82	111		111	108	172	148	45	72	149	39	101	148	180	140	99	37	41
Aspermont	60	67	36	111		78	115	142	157	91	137	136	102	112	81	141	110	123	101
Baird	24	26	42	108	78		72	68	144	50	62	146	25	41	88	67	34	139	83
Ballinger	57	90	79	172	115	72		73	208	113	59	210	86	36	80	85	96	203	146
Blanket	87	82	106	148	142	68	73		154	76	15	183	47	43	151	13	55	185	109
Bowie	156	118	155	45	157	144	208	154		94	168	60	123	173	219	140	115	73	61
Breckenridge	61	24	61	72	91	50	113	76	94		77	107	29	79	125	72	27	109	33
Brownwood	81	83	101	149	137	62	59	15	168	77		184	48	30	139	27	56	186	110
Burkburnett	158	121	138	39	136	146	210	183	60	107	184		136	186	206	172	134	24	74
Cisco	48	35	67	101	102	25	86	47	123	29	48	136		51	113	46	10	138	62
Coleman	54	66	76	148	112	41	36	43	173	79	30	186	51		109	55	60	179	112
Colorado City	64	101	73	180	81	88	80	151	219	125	139	206	113	109		150	122	194	158
Comanche	86	81	106	140	141	67	85	13	140	72	27	172	46	55	150		45	177	98
Eastland	58	43	77	99	110	34	96	55	115	27	56	134	10	60	122	45		137	60
Electra	149	113	125	37	123	139	203	185	73	109	186	24	138	179	194	177	137		79
Graham	94	57	94	41	101	83	146	109	61	33	110	74	62	112	158	98	60	79	
Hamlin	42	54	17	116	18	60	97	124	161	78	119	142	84	94	64	123	94	130	106
Haskell	55	52	31	81	31	73	110	134	126	69	131	107	87	107	99	133	95	95	70
Hawley	13	43	11	122	47	31	68	95	161	67	90	149	56	65	71	94	65	136	100
Henrietta	160	122	145	40	143	148	212	162	28	101	176	33	130	179	214	148	123	46	68
Knox City	76	73	51	74	38	93	131	155	120	86	152	98	108	128	111	154	113	85	87
Merkel	13	50	26	132	51	37	67	100	168	74	94	163	61	67	51	99	71	151	107
Munday	76	71	52	62	50	94	131	150	107	74	151	86	103	128	121	146	101	73	75
Nocona	175	137	172	65	171	163	227	173	19	114	187	60	143	192	239	160	135	73	81
Olney	101	64	93	18	93	90	153	130	64	54	131	57	83	130	162	122	81	56	23
Quanah	138	130	114	89	101	156	193	209	125	133	210	72	162	190	174	205	160	52	124
Rising Star	59	54	79	120	115	40	75	27	143	49	29	156	20	40	124	27	28	158	82
Rotan	59	74	38	136	28	80	91	144	182	98	139	163	105	112	53	143	114	150	126
Seymour	100	65	76	38	74	90	154	143	83	68	145	61	97	131	145	139	95	49	58
Snyder	75	97	61	168	61	98	98	161	213	121	149	194	123	120	25	161	133	182	154
Stamford	39	37	15	96	30	57	94	118	141	60	116	123	71	91	84	118	80	110	86
Sweetwater	37	74	45	152	54	60	61	123	192	97	112	178	85	83	28	123	95	166	130
Throckmorton	71	34	63	48	63	60	123	113	94	37	114	87	66	100	132	109	64	80	38
Vernon	143	109	119	60	109	135	198	188	96	112	189	43	141	175	183	184	139	23	95
Wichita Falls	144	107	128	25	126	132	196	169	46	93	170	15	122	171	196	158	120	27	60
Winters	41	74	64	156	99	58	16	78	192	98	65	195	83	35	75	90	92	187	131

Northwest Mileage

Hamlin	Haskell	Hawley	Henrietta	Knox City	Merkel	Munday	Nocona	Olney	Quanah	Rising Star	Rotan	Seymour	Snyder	Stamford	Sweetwtr.	Throck.	Vernon	Wichita F.	Winter
42	55	13	160	76	13	76	175	101	138	59	59	100	75	39	37	71	143	144	41
54	52	43	122	73	50	71	137	64	130	54	74	65	97	37	74	34	109	107	74
17	31	11	145	51	26	52	172	93	114	79	38	76	61	15	45	63	119	128	64
116	81	122	40	74	132	62	65	18	89	120	136	38	168	96	152	48	60	25	156
18	31	47	143	38	51	50	171	93	101	115	28	74	61	30	54	63	109	126	99
60	73	31	148	93	37	94	163	90	156	40	80	90	98	57	60	60	135	132	58
97	110	68	212	131	67	131	227	153	193	75	91	154	98	94	61	123	198	196	16
124	134	95	162	155	100	150	173	130	209	27	144	143	161	118	123	113	188	169	78
161	126	161	28	120	168	107	19	64	125	143	182	83	213	141	192	94	96	46	192
78	69	67	101	86	74	74	114	54	133	49	98	68	121	60	97	37	112	93	98
119	131	90	176	152	94	151	187	131	210	29	139	145	149	116	112	114	189	170	65
142	107	149	33	98	163	86	60	57	72	156	163	61	194	123	178	87	43	15	195
84	87	56	130	108	61	103	143	83	162	20	105	97	123	71	85	66	141	122	83
94	107	65	179	128	67	128	192	130	190	40	112	131	120	91	83	100	175	171	35
64	99	71	214	111	51	121	239	162	174	124	53	145	25	84	28	132	183	196	75
123	133	94	148	154	99	146	160	122	205	27	143	139	161	118	123	109	184	158	90
94	95	65	123	113	71	101	135	81	160	28	114	95	133	80	95	64	139	120	92
130	95	136	46	85	151	73	73	56	52	158	150	49	182	110	166	80	23	27	187
106	70	100	68	87	107	75	81	23	124	82	126	58	154	86	130	38	95	60	131
35																			
29	42																		
150	115	156																	
48	23	63	105																
32	56	20	171	77															
57	21	63	93	12	78														
177	142	180	27	132	187	120													
98	62	104	59	70	114	58	83												
110	85	125	98	63	140	69	125	100											
96	106	68	149	127	72	122	162	102	182										
20	56	49	170	66	46	77	197	118	128	117									
81	46	87	69	36	102	24	96	35	66	116	101								
52	87	71	202	99	62	109	229	150	162	134	33	133							
20	16	26	130	36	41	37	157	78	99	91	40	61	72						
36	71	43	186	84	24	93	211	134	146	96	30	117	38	56					
68	32	74	89	49	84	37	113	30	96	85	88	31	120	48	104				
119	88	130	68	71	145	67	96	72	30	160	137	44	170	104	155	75			
132	97	139	19	88	153	76	46	43	79	141	153	51	184	112	168	73	50		
81	94	52	196	115	51	115	211	138	178	74	78	138	85	79	49	108	182	180	

ABILENE

Elev. 1,738 Pop. 108,257

Wide-open country. Farming and ranching. A few oil wells mixed in. Honest, genuine people who seal business deals with handshakes and laugh at the high-strung demeanor of city folks. Traveling west on I-20, Abilene marks the start of what some outsiders might consider the Old West.

Although Abilene began its existence as a rowdy frontier town and shipping point, it gained the reputation as a Bible Belt capital with three church-affiliated universities and a large number of churches. In addition to the solid, affordable accommodations and outstanding local food, Abilene offers 81 holes of golf and is the ideal jumping-off point for the "Big Country" courses located in small towns like Hawley, Anson, Albany, Baird, Merkel, Coleman, and Hamlin.

ABILENE COUNTRY CLUB

The golf   The par 71 Abilene Country Club dates back to 1920, but was redesigned in 1993 by George Williams and Garrett Gill, who reconstructed 10 holes. Pro golfers such as Tommy Bolt, Charles Coody, Don Cherry, Mike Standly, and Bob Estes have all spent time here.

The fairways are generous and the layout is loaded with bunkers. The track's first hole of note is the beautiful 360-yard par 4 No. 5, which doglegs left. Locals aim at the three oaks on the right side of the fairway and work their draw. The most difficult hole is the 390-yard par 4 ninth hole, which plays uphill into the wind with an approach that must carry water. Hole 14 (190 yards) is also tough, requiring a long iron with the wind–which makes it impossible at times to hold the green, and is especially treacherous with water front and left of the green.

The details   915-692-1855. 4039 S. Treadway Blvd., Abilene, TX 79602

- 1920s. 18 holes. Par 71. Back – 6,345 (70.1/125). Middle – 5,725 (67.0/116). Forward – 4,980 (68.8/117). Price - $$$.

Getting there From I-20 west, exit 83/84 and take the Buffalo Gap exit. Turn left onto Industrial, then turn right when you come to Treadway. The course is on the right side of the street.

FAIRWAY OAKS COUNTRY CLUB

The golf   Originally built in the 1970s by Ron Garl and Charles Coody, the club was purchased in the late 1990s and has been updated for the more modern game. Fairway Oaks is a long, challenging course that has hosted the Southwest Classic from 1981 to 1991. The layout incorporates many bunkers, and water dominates the back nine. In 1981 the LaJet Classic at Fairway Oaks

---

Golf and Racquet Club was added to the PGA tour.

The highlight of the course is the demanding nature of the finishing holes. Many a promising round has been tossed into the water that's present on each of the last five finishing holes. Survive the carries on 14 and 15, and deal with the par 3 hole 16 with water on the left, and your confidence will be strong enough to deal with the 448-yard par 4 17th, which requires a tee shot of at least 200 yards to reach the fairway. From the blue tees the par 5 18th is only 485 yards, but the lake runs the entire length of the fairway waiting to eat any fade or slice.

The details   915-695-1800. 34 Fairway Oaks Blvd., Abilene, TX 79606

- www.fairwayoaks.com
- 1970s. Ron Garl. 18 holes. Par 72. Blue – 7,020 (73.1/131). White – 6,424 (71.0/129). Gold – 5,756 (68.1/114). Red – 5,532 (72.3/121). Price - $$.

Getting there From Hwy. 83/84, exit Antilley Rd. and turn right. Turn right on Fairway Oaks Blvd. and the course is on the left.

MAXWELL GOLF COURSE

The golf   Maxwell is a great municipal course because it does not overwhelm the average duffer with difficulty. You can generally work your way onto the course at any time, and the greens have the reputation of being in outstanding condition. The design team of George Williams and Garrett Gill has worked on the course over the years.

The 526-yard par 5 2nd hole is the number one handicap, but No. 10 is another long par 5 that is tough. Hole 8 is tricky, featuring a severe dogleg left and trouble on the right. The back nine features short par 4s and two par 3s that require only an 8 or 9 iron at the most. Finish strong on 18, as it is only 326 yards from the middle tees.

The details   915-692-2737. 1002 S. 32nd St., Abilene, TX 79602

- 1940s. 18 holes. Par 71. Back – 6,129 yards (68.1/111). Middle – 5,877. Forward – 5,031. Price - $$.

Getting there Driving west on I-20, exit 83/84. Find the Buffalo Gap Rd. exit and head back under the freeway, turning right onto Industrial Blvd. Proceed to Treadway, then turn left. Stay to the right because the road veers onto South 32nd St.

DIAMONDBACK GOLF CLUB

The golf   This is an 18-hole daily fee championship golf course developed by Lytle Creek Golf Links, a company headed by Abilene resident and full-time Senior PGA player Charles Coody. Mr. Coody and Williams, Gill and

---

Every golfer has a little monster in him. It's just that type of sport. Fuzzy Zoeller

Associates designed the par 71, 6,975-yard course, which opened in November of 1999 and features bent-grass greens and Tifway (419) hybrid Bermuda grass fairways, roughs, and tees. Every June the course hosts the Diamondback SBC Charity Classic, a Senior PGA Tour pro-am.

Lytle Creek meanders throughout the site and comes into play on seven of the holes. Three additional lakes were also built on the site. Naturally occurring rock outcroppings on the site and native vegetation in the rough provide the course with unique character. Multiple tee locations on each hole allow golfers of all abilities to play a challenging and enjoyable round.

The details   915-690-9190. 1510 Industrial Blvd., Abilene, TX 79602

- 1999. 18 holes. Par 71. Champs – 6,977 yards (73.7/134). Regular – 6,516 yards (71.4/131). Legends – 6,009 (69.0/128). Forward – 5,006 (71.8/124). Price - $$$.

Getting there On Industrial Blvd., go 1 mile east of Loop 322.

MESQUITE GROVE GOLF COURSE

The golf   The course features elevated bent-grass greens and Bermuda fairways–it's a long course made longer by the wind. Although No. 6 is the signature hole (397 yards into a green fronted by water), the toughest test is No. 9 because it usually plays into the prevailing wind and is over 400 yards.

The details   915-696-5067. 766 Mesquite Trail, Dyess AFB, TX 79607

- 1960. 18 holes. Par 72. Back – 7,005 (71.1/116). Middle – 6,661 (69.9/114). Forward – 5,793 (71.2/114). Price - $$.

Getting there From I-20 east find the Winters Frwy. Take the South First St. exit and look for the signs to the course. Turn left on Arnold Blvd., which will lead you to the course.

WILLOW CREEK GOLF CENTER

The golf   This is the only par 3 course in the Big Country area, and the only one in West Texas for that matter. Lighted for practice and play at night, Willow Creek features bent-grass greens in excellent condition, as well as scramble every Monday night to help hone your competitive edge. The facility also has a practice putting green and driving range.

The details   915-691-0909. 1166 Ben Richey Dr., Abilene, TX

- 9 holes. Par 27. 1,163 yards. Price - $.

The property dictates what you put there, the topography, the drainage. A lot of designers get caught up in building for the pros, but the supporters of golf are the guys shooting in the 80s and 90s. You have to build so it's challenging for good players, but the average player isn't going back if he shoots too far over his handicap. Jay Riviere

Getting there In Abilene, take Treadway to the far south end of town. Go through the last light (Industrial Blvd.), and look for the Ben Richey Boys Ranch sign and Ben Richey Blvd.

ABILENE NOTES   Outstanding Texas food can be found at the **Royal Inn Smoke House** (915-692-3022), where you can dig into a rib-eye, home-style green beans, and a baked potato. Barbecue is available at Abilene mainstays **Joe Allen's Pit Bar B Que** (915-672-6082) or **Harold's Bar-B-Que** (915-672-4451). The most popular steakhouse is **Zentner's Daughter** (915-695-4290). For lodging there are a number of motels along I-20, or you can find the **Bolin Prairie Bed and Breakfast** (915-675-5855) and the restored **Mulberry House** (915-677-7890). Try to negotiate a better rate by mentioning golf packages when making reservations anywhere in town.

NORTHWEST

ALBANY

Elev. 1,429   Pop. 1,883

Albany, the county seat of Shackelford County, is 33 miles northeast of Abilene via Texas 351 and US 180. The town was an early supply point on the western trail to Dodge City, and is still an important ranching community. With the discovery of the Cook oil field in 1926, and later discoveries, Albany has grown into an oil drilling, production, and supply center. Despite the oil, the town slogan has been "Albany, the Home of the Hereford" since the cow was first introduced to the state here in the 1920s.

ALBANY GOLF COURSE

The golf   Along with panoramic views of the hills to the north and east of town, Albany's 9-hole track offers a great opportunity for simple, small-town golf. The course is wide open and has minimal hazards, but the best feature is the continued work of the staff to improve the condition of the course. The greens and tee boxes are in good condition. And while the fairways are by no means of championship quality, they get the job done and offer good lies to those who find the fairway.

This course is fun for the average hacker. The terrain is flat, and mature trees line the fairways. There are no bunkers and only four water hazards impact play. The feature hole is No. 5, a 437-yard par 5 that involves an uphill tee shot into a dogleg right fairway.

The details   915-762-2844. 1005 N. 3rd., Albany, TX 76430

- 1926. Ben Scott. 9 holes. Par 35. Back – 3,100. Forward – 2,720. Price - $.

The chief virtues of the links may briefly be summarized as being: first, that they should be difficult; secondly, that they should be pleasing to the eye; thirdly, that they should be strictly economical in design; and lastly, that to be truly admirable they will probably incur in the general opinion the accusation of being unfair. H. N. Wethered

Getting there From Abilene, take Hwy. 351 northwest to Albany. Turn north onto North Bird St., and the course is straight ahead.

ALBANY NOTES   Take a gander at one of the most spectacular court-houses in the state, the **Shackelford County Courthouse,** which is the focal point for the downtown district. Check the schedule for the **Fort Griffin Fandangle-Prairie Theatre** (915-762-3642), an outdoor cowboy show that's worth the time, or get into the local art scene at the **Old Jail Art Center** (915-762-2269). The **Fort Griffin General Merchandise Co.** (915-762-3034) has been lauded as the best small-town steakhouse in the state. In addition to steak, the menu includes oysters and mesquite-grilled red snapper.

OIL BELT SENIORS MEN'S GOLF ASSOCIATION
(The "Old Farts Tour")

Organized in the winter of 1991-92 by Bill "Ramrod" Gleason, the Oil Belt Seniors Men's Golf Association now consists of around 300 members who enjoy the game every two weeks at one of 13 small-town north Texas golf clubs, 9 of which are 9-hole courses. With no flatbellies in sight, the club offers active retired men the twin bene-fits of exercise and camaraderie. Oil Belt tournaments involve medal play with individual handicaps that give each golfer the chance to place in flights.

Participating courses span *The Texas Golf Bible's* Northwest and North Central regions, and include the following facilities: Archer City, Bowie CC, Bridgeport CC, Decatur, Graham, Henrietta, Horseshoe Bend (Weatherford), Jacksboro, Mineral Wells, Indian Oaks and Nocona Hills in Nocona, Olney, and Willow Springs (Haslet).

ANSON
Elev. 1,750   Pop. 2,426

Anson, the county seat of Jones County, is at the intersection of US 83/277 and 180 - some 20 miles north of Abilene. Named in honor of Anson Jones, the last president of the Republic of Texas, Anson is a typical Northwest Texas community with a wide main street and a beautiful courthouse that is the cen-terpiece of the downtown area.

You learn golf all the time, but you don't learn it all at once. Davis Love, Jr.

ANSON GOLF CLUB

The golf   Make the drive to Anson for a quality round of golf enhanced by the friendly locals, who are happy to coach you around the course and give you a feel for the area. The course is of average length, playing 3,049 yards from the back tees, but tends to play shorter than that because tee shots run forever on the hardpan fairways. Holes 5, 6, and 7 are the most challenging, and No. 9 is an interesting hole as well. The condition of the course is determined by the amount of recent rains in the area. Don't be surprised if the fairways are brown during drought conditions. However, the greens and tee boxes are generally in solid shape no matter how much rain has fallen. Two sets of tees make for an 18-hole round. For the price, it's worth the trip. Pay once and play all day.

The details   915-823-2822. 701 23rd St., Anson, TX 79501

• 1938. 9 holes. Par 36. Back – 3,049. Forward – 2,510. Price - $.

Getting there Four blocks east of Hwy. 277. Located in the city park near the middle of town.

ANSON NOTES   If you're in the area during October, play in the two-person scramble called the "Hoolie." It's named in memory of the late Hoolie White, who made a hole-in-one on the No. 6 hole in the 1940s and then again 50 years later at the age of 91. You'll find live music at the **Pioneer Hall**. Check out the **1907 Opera House**, once the largest and fanciest showplace between Fort Worth and Dallas. You might also plan your trip to Anson around the annual **Cowboy Christmas Ball**, which has been around since 1885.

ARCHER CITY   Elev. 1,041   Pop. 1,848

Archer City, the seat of Archer County, sits 25 miles southwest of Wichita Falls. Made famous by native son Larry McMurtry and his novel *The Last Picture Show*, this is an ultra-charming little town that is a must-stop for golfers in search of the ultimate small-town links experience. With the Archer City Country Club sitting at the edge of town, and cold beers that go for $1.25, it's hard to resist an afternoon on the links followed by an evening in town and a night at the Spur Hotel.

ARCHER CITY COUNTRY CLUB

The golf   Defining the outskirts of town, with ranchland beyond the mesquite-lined fairways, this 9-hole, semi-private course has unquestionable character. Rusted iron ladders have been placed on the barbed-wire fences surrounding the course, enabling one to track down shots that somehow don't find the fairway. The asphalt cart paths are cracked, the tee boxes are baked hard, and the bald Bermuda fairways shine like a bowling alley from the abuse of the sun and wind, enabling even the most incapable golfer to reach a par 5 in two.

The track features medium-length par 4s and a small lake that comes into play on a few holes. There are a few elevation changes, but the course is mostly flat. The greens are simple to read, a bit quick, and in good condition. Best of all, the price is right and the people are friendly.

The details   940-574-4322. 1007 S. Ash St., Archer City, TX 76351

• 9 holes. Par 35. Back – 2,855. Forward – 2,505. Price - $.

Getting there From Wichita Falls, take Texas 79 south to Archer City. Once in town, look for the signs leading to the course.

ARCHER CITY NOTES   After your round, enjoy cold beers with the locals in the relatively new clubhouse. Hit the **Dairy Queen** for burgers and then browse McMurtry's bookstores (**Booked Up** or **Three Dog Books**) before you hit the **Royal Theatre** (940-574-2489) for live music. Crash at the **The Spur Hotel** (940-574-2501), which typically houses hunters during season and sports a macho, cowboy ambience with squeaky-clean rooms.

ASPERMONT   Elev. 1,773   Pop. 1,092

Aspermont is at the junction of US 83 and 380 and FMs 610, 2211, and 1263; it's 59 miles north of Abilene in central Stonewall County. It was platted as a townsite in 1889 by A.L. Rhomberg, who provided the land and gave it the Latin name for "rough mountain." The annual rodeo is a feature event. Earlier area residents called the place Sunflower Flat.

ASPERMONT CITY GOLF COURSE

The golf   This 9-hole semi-private course opened for play in the early 1960s. The course is wide open, relatively easy, and perfect for the average player. The signature hole is No. 7, requiring a shot over water.

The details   940-989-3381. FM, Aspermont, TX 79502

• 1960. 9 holes. Par 36. Back – 2,766 (33.5). Forward – 2,124 (32.5). Price - $.

Getting there From Hwy. 83 south, take Hwy. 610 west. When you come to Golf Course Rd., turn left on the dirt road.

★

Any hole which must keep its green concealed from all parts of the fairway is open to severe criticism. A. W. Tillinghast

ASPERMONT NOTES   Dig in at the **Burger Barn** (940-989-2757). If you must, there are two local motels that are easy to find. At Double Mountain southwest of town, the ghost town of **Orient** shows the remnants of the 1900 boomtown based on silver mining. Just 35 miles north in near **Guthrie, TX** is the eclectic **6666 Supply House,** the only grocery and supply store within 30 miles and a must stop if you want to get into the character of this country.

BAIRD

Elev. 1,708   Pop. 1,610

NORTHWEST

The "Antique Capital of West Texas" lies at the junction of I-20 and US 283 just east of Abilene. Named for railroad surveyor and engineer Matthew Baird, the town is the center for local oil field supplies and ranching. In addition to the above-average 18-hole Shady Oaks Golf Course, Baird boasts more than 20 antique malls and shops representing more than 100 antique dealers.

SHADY OAKS GOLF COURSE

The golf   Shady Oaks is an outstanding facility for a town of 1,600 residents. In 1969 Leon Howard and Dave Bennett built this course, and a new nine was added in 1992. Over the years water hazards, trees, and subtle mounding have been incorporated into the layout to make it more difficult. This is a great-looking course that continues to improve, thanks to the constant work of the course staff.

No. 14 is the signature hole: a 430-yard par 4 that plays uphill into a tight fairway lined by oak trees. Your best chance for a hole-in-one is to knock your wedge into the short 13th hole that plays a little over 100 yards.

Be ready for the sometimes turtle-paced play of the locals. Then again, that's part of the character of the course–you shouldn't expect to experience a big-city round with low handicappers who are schooled in the proper etiquette of golf.

The details   915-854-1757. 3542 County Rd. 268, Baird, TX 79504

- 1969. Leon Howard and Dave Bennett. 18 holes. Par 70. Gold – 6,245 (67.2/112). Blue – 5,791. White – 5,337. Red – 4,587. Price - $$.

Getting there From I-20 east, exit 303 turn south (right) on Union Hill Rd. Take the first available left about a half-mile down the road.

BAIRD NOTES   You can eat at the clubhouse, or go for the **Caboose Bar BQ** (915-854-1309). Rough it at the **Baird Motor Inn** (915-854-2527), or splurge on **The Old Conner House B&B** (915-854-189).

I am a millionaire today and my wife deserves all of the credit. Before I met her I was a multi-millionaire. Chi Chi Rodriquez

BALLINGER

Elev. 1,637   Pop. 4,003

Ballinger began in 1886 where the Colorado River and Elm Creek converge, and surprisingly, became a hot spot that attracted crowds of drifters and gamblers who came to partake in the town's nine saloons and gambling halls. The nearby farms and ranches produce cotton, grain, sheep, cattle, and oil. Today Ballinger, the main shipping and distribution point for Runnels County, features restored historical homes and buildings, antique stores, a thriving downtown district, and the Ballinger Country Club for golfers traveling through the area.

BALLINGER COUNTRY CLUB

The golf   This 9-hole, semi-private course (open to out-of-towners) features a small creek and mildly undulating terrain. The creek impacts two holes, and there is only one hole with bunkers. No. 2 is the signature hole, a 379-yard par 4 with a tee shot over a canyon and out-of-bounds on either side of the fairway. Nothing too fancy here–both par 3s are well under 200 yards. The first hole is a 268-yard par 4, and No. 3 is listed as a par 5 at 426 yards.

The details   915-365-3214. Country Club Dr., Ballinger, TX 76821

• 1948. Par 36. Back – 2,876 (34.1). Forward – 2,172 (31.9). Price - $.

Getting there From the courthouse in town, turn left on Hwy. 158. Follow the road as it veers left over a hill. You'll see a nursing home hospital, and then eventually a green sign on the left for the city lake and country club. Take that road through one stop sign, then another four-way stop, then follow the main road 45 degrees due west to the course.

BALLINGER NOTES   Be here in August for the mid-month **Open Bass Tournament** at **Lake O.H. Ivie** 25 miles southwest of Ballinger. In the cotton fields between Ballinger and San Angelo you'll find the **Lowake Steak House** (915-442-3201), where famous folks and locals inhale T-bones. There are four local motels if you need to stay.

BLANKET

Elev. 1,619   Pop. 406

Blanket is a tiny town on US 67/377 ten miles northeast of Brownwood. Developed on the banks of Blanket Creek, the town takes its name from the early surveyors who spotted a group of Tonkawa Indians in a downpour spreading their blankets over sumac bushes for protection. Despite the small size of the town, Blanket offers an 18-hole golf course that can stand up to the tracks in the larger towns of this region.

Bad putting stems from thinking how instead of where. Jackie Burke, Jr.

SHADY CREEK GOLF COURSE

The golf Shady Creek is a tough, tree-lined course with its namesake creek running through the layout. In fact, water comes into play on six holes. The signature hole is the par 3 No. 7, which features an island green. Soon you'll be able to play a complete round, as a 9-hole addition is currently under construction.

The details 915-748-4404. 10955 Hwy. 377, Blanket, TX 76432

* 9 holes. Par 35. 2,923 yards. Price - $.

Getting there 10 miles east of Brownwood on Hwy. 67/377.

BLANKET NOTES After your round go for steaks at **Katy's** (915-748-3551) on Main St., which is only open Thursday-Saturday. The only other to-do in Blanket is to peruse the antique shops, but Brownwood is 8 miles away for more non-golf action.

BOWIE Elev. 1,145 Pop. 5,220

Bowie is on the way to Dallas in southwestern Montague County. After the railroad came through in 1882, the town became the financial center for farmers and ranchers between Fort Worth and Wichita Falls. Today the town is dotted with antique shops and art galleries, and offers a nice break from the road with its historic downtown area. Golfers get their kicks at the Top O' The Lake Country Club, which has recently drawn renewed interest with a new 9-hole addition.

TOP O' THE LAKE COUNTRY CLUB

The golf Originally built in the early 1960s by local volunteers, this private club recently upgraded by reworking its layout and adding an additional nine holes. The new 18 now plays to an extremely short 5,542 yards, but is lined with oak trees and has three water hazards on each nine.

The hole most complain about is No. 5, which requires a full carry over water to reach the green. Despite the complaints, this hole has seen three holes-in-one since the new course opened in 2002.

Located near Lake Amon Carter, this is a scenic, easy-to-medium course with narrow fairways and fast greens.

The details 940-872-5401. Rural Route 5, Bowie, TX 76230

* 1963. Frank Underwood. 18 holes. Par 70. Blue – 5,542. White – 5,097. Price - $$.

I don't know whether spikeless shoes help greens or not. I play in sneakers. Pete Dye

NORTHWEST

Getting there From Hwy. 287 north, take the FM 1125 exit and go left. Turn right at the Dean Stewart Cutting Horses sign and follow the road to the golf course gate.

BOWIE NOTES   Wise St. offers a variety of options if you're hungry. Try the **Kickapoo Catfish Hole** (940-872-5775), **Longhorn Cafe** (940-872-6466), or **Pepito's Mexican Food** (940-872-6666). For lodging in Bowie, try the **Day's Inn** (940-872-5426) or the **Gazebo B&B** (940-872-5775). For water sports, **Lake Amon Carter** is just southwest of town.

BRECKENRIDGE   Elev. 1,220   Pop. 5,974

The drive into Breckenridge is impressive. The town is surrounded by scrub oak and mesquite tree country, and from the south you'll see the town's skyscraper, the old Burch Hotel (now the First National Bank). In the late 1800s the population exploded from 1,600 to 20,000 in one year, when over 200 oil wells were put down inside the city limits. Gamblers, prostitutes, and booze provided the recreation then, but today residents enjoy the picturesque red-brick streets, great restaurants, and the charming little 9-hole Breckenridge Country Club.

BRECKENRIDGE COUNTRY CLUB

The golf   This semi-private club is known for being in great shape and offers a nice variety of holes, highlighted by a 625-yard par 6 hole (yes, a par 6), which is the only one of its kind in Texas. During the summer with a 20-30 mph south wind blowing in your face, you'll need everything you've got to reach the green in regulation.

This course sports small, dome-shaped greens that take some getting used to. Your short game needs to be on or you'll be sending chip shots rolling off the green. Water comes into play on seven holes. Two sets of tees offer a full day of golf. Pay once and play all day.

The details   254-559-3466. Rural Route 3, Box 53, Breckenridge, TX 76424

• 1935. 9 holes. Par 36. Back – 3,044 yards. Forward – 2,259. Price - $.

Getting there From I-20 east take Hwy. 180 east, and drive to Breckenridge - 58 miles away. The course entrance is on the right side of the highway.

BRECKENRIDGE NOTES   Drink beer and eat barbecue at the deer-camp-like **Double M Barbeque** (254-559-8016). **Pam's Cafe** has been around since the 1920s, and is the place to go for a pre-round breakfast. **Hubbard Creek**

I have the feeling when I'm taking my stance that someone has just pulled a chair from behind me and I'm waiting for him to put it back. Arnold Palmer

Lake is nearby. The **Blue Rose B&B** (254-559-2105) is quaint and has a great location on N. Rose St., and **The Keeping Room B&B** (254-559-8368) is becoming famous for their outstanding breakfast, served family-style around a huge table.

BROWNWOOD
Elev. 1,342   Pop. 19,400

Established in 1856 despite the fact that only two families lived here, Brownwood subsisted after the railroad came through and eventually boomed when oil became big in the 1920s. This Brown County seat was named after Captain Henry Brown, whose 1828 story of pursuing hostile Indians from his ranch in Gonzales to recover 500 stolen horses is the stuff of which legends are made.

While not a major destination for golf by any means, for years the Feather Bay resort has attempted to provide tourism potential for nearby Lake Brownwood. Things are bustling again on Feather Bay, with plans to open a hotel/marina and an additional nine holes. This gives area golfers an alternative to the 18-hole Brownwood Country Club.

BROWNWOOD COUNTRY CLUB

The golf   Best known for bent-grass greens in outstanding condition, Brownwood Country Club is a wide-open course with minimal trees. Only one water hazard comes into play (No. 12). The best hole is No. 4, a tricky 90-degree dogleg right that plays into a multi-level green that is surrounded by sand and grass bunkers.

The details   915-646-1086. 5825 County Rd. 225, Brownwood, TX 76804

- 1970. Leon Howard. 18 holes. Par 72. Blue – 6,288 yards (69.4/119). White – 5,972 (68.1/116). Red – 5,103 (69.9/110). Price - $$.

Getting there From Hwy. 36 south, take Hwy. 279 and exit Cross Plains. Turn onto Hwy. 377 and drive 4 miles to Hwy. 45. Turn left on 45 and the course is just down the road.

FEATHER BAY GOLF COURSE

The golf   Originally built in 1986, Feather Bay closed for more than 12 years due to financial problems. The course reopened in December 2001, and has undergone renovations to improve the layout. The facility has plans to open a hotel and marina as part of the resort as early as June 2003. In fact, construction of the new nine has been complete for some time, but only the original nine is open for play.

When a putter tries very hard not to three-putt, he generally winds up three-putting more often, and, at the very best, two-putting a lot. Dr. Bob Rotella

NORTHWEST

The details   915-784-4653. 6680 FM 2632, Feather Bay Blvd., Brownwood, TX 76801

- 18 holes built (9 holes currently open). Black – 3,570. Blue – 3,360. White – 3,235. Red – 2,635. Price - $$.

Getting there From Abilene take Hwy. 36 to Cross Plains. Take Hwy. 279 south to Lake Brownwood, cross the bridge, and turn left on FM 3021. It dead-ends into FM 2632. Turn right on FM 2632. The golf course is a quarter mile from that intersection on the left.

MORE GOLF

Golf Land – 915-643-5353. 2000 Hwy. 377 S., Brownwood, TX 76801

BROWNWOOD NOTES   The **Section Hand Steakhouse** (915-643-1581) and **Underwood's Cafeteria** (915-646-6110) are local mainstays that offer steaks and barbecue. Among the city's historic buildings, the **1902 Jail** is an interesting-looking structure, and the **1892 St. John's Episcopal Church** is worth a look. Twenty three miles out on TX 279 lies **Lake Brownwood State Park** for camping and fishing.

BURKBURNETT   Elev. 1,040   Pop. 10,963

Burkburnett is 10 miles north of Wichita Falls, just below the Red River and Oklahoma border. The first settlers established roots along Gilbert Creek in the 1860s, and in 1907 Joseph Kemp and Fran Kell bought a piece of the giant Samuel Burk Burnett 6666 Ranch to lay out the present townsite. Although the cowboys called it Nesterville, legend states that President Theodore personally requested that the town be named after Burnett, who hosted Roosevelt on a wolf hunt in the area.

RIVER CREEK PARK GOLF COURSE

The golf   With awesome views of the Red River and six greens actually on the north side of the border, not to mention the fact that the slope rating from the back tees is only 104, River Creek is worth playing. The course is scenic and has mature trees lining most of its wide-open fairways. The bent-grass greens are well manicured.

The signature hole could be No. 8 with its view of the river, or possibly No. 2: a 178-yard par 3 with water fronting the left side of the green. (Check out the sculpture carved from the large oak tree that died.) No. 12 is a 425-yard par 4 with a water hazard in front and on the right. No. 17 is a par 4 that heads south into the wind towards the pavilion.

Every golfer should establish his own par on a hole and play for that par. H. H. Ramsay

On Thursdays the club hosts its Hamburger Scramble at 6 pm, where your green fee includes a hamburger and drink.

The details   940-855-3361. 1177 S. FM 369, Burkburnett, TX 76354

- 1968. Richard Boyd and Buddy Pierson. 18 holes. Par 71. Back – 6,727 (69.9/104). Middle – 6,330 (67.8/100). Forward – 5,039. Price - $$.

Getting there From I-44, take Hwy. 240 east, then turn left on FM 1177. The course is 2.5 miles away on the left side.

BURKBURNETT NOTES   Circle H BBQ (940-569-8165) is the place for lunch. While there isn't a local hotel in Burkburnett, Wichita Falls is just south, and the little town of Randlett, OK is just across the river, offering the **Country Road B&B** (580-281-3626), as well as the brand new **Comanche Nations Casino**. The restless man might ask the locals where to find the **cock fights**. If you get into trouble, tell them you know Omar McClendon–the famous local Renaissance man who roamed these parts in the 1990s and is rumored to still have connections in the area.

CISCO   Elev. 1,608   Pop. 3,813

Cisco, at the intersection of US 183 and I-20, is another town that traces its roots to the railroad. Once called Red Gap, the town's name was changed to Cisco after John Cisco, the man who funded much of the Houston and Texas Central Railroad. We found Cisco a good place to take a break from a long road trip along I-20–we took advantage of its small size and proximity to I-20 by having lunch and taking in a quick nine holes to stretch our legs.

LAKE CISCO COUNTRY CLUB

The golf   Despite its label as a country club, this is a public course that's particularly fun for the average golfer. The short course has no bunkers and only one water hazard; the main challenge is negotiating the narrow, hilly fairways that are lined with mature oak trees. If you can hit your short irons well here, you can score. A solid, short game helps because the greens are small and you might often find yourself just off the green in regulation. Up-and-downs are easy to come by if you chip it close, because the greens have only average speed and are easy to read.

The details   254-442-2725. Rural Route 3, Box 44A, Cisco, TX 76437

- 1920. 9 holes. Par 34. Back – 2,609. Middle – 2,508. Forward – Par 36. 2,295. Price - $.

Getting there Heading east on I-20, take the second exit in Cisco and turn left on Ave. D (Conrad Hilton). Go under the highway and follow this road out of town, which turns into Route 6. Look for the course sign and follow the dirt road to the course.

CISCO NOTES   Tour the historic, preserved homes, or check out the place where hotel mogul Conrad Hilton began his career, the **Mobley Hotel**, which is now a museum and Chamber of Commerce office. The ghost town of **Red Gap** is north of town. You can stay at the **Best Western** (254-442-3735) or the **Oak Motel** (254-442-2100), and the places to eat are **Linda's Corner Cafe** (254-442-2666) and the famous **Spur & Sportsman Cafe** (254-442-4118). Note that the closest place to buy cold beer is the town of Putnam, TX.

COLEMAN   Elev. 1,710   Pop. 5,081

Located 54 miles southeast of Abilene, Coleman dates back to 1876 when it was founded along Hords Creek. The town boomed as a supply center for trail drivers road-tripping it to Dodge City, Kansas. Six lakes surround the community, and farming, ranching, oil and gas production drive the economy. Hunting and fishing are popular here, and the Coleman Country Club offers a great place to work in a round of rural golf in between trips afield.

COLEMAN COUNTRY CLUB

The golf   Coleman's semi-private, 9-hole course features a trio of par 3s, par 4s, and par 5s that add up to a 3,168-yard layout. Although it's a wide-open course, there are a few trees that can impact your shots. Two manmade lakes come into play on a few holes.

The signature is the 470-yard, par 5 No. 4, which requires a 200-yard tee shot over water. Your best birdie opportunity is the 158-yard No. 2.

The details   915-625-2922. San Angelo Hwy., Coleman, TX 76834

• 1927. 9 holes. Par 36. Back – 3,168. Middle – 3,076. Forward – 2,318. Price - $.

Getting there 5 miles south of Coleman on Hwy. 206. The course is on the right hand side of the road.

COLEMAN NOTES   The **Owl Pharmacy**, a clean, full-service soda fountain on the west side of Main, is an interesting stop. The night-time meal should be enjoyed at **Caroline's Coldwater Cattle Co. Steakhouse** (915-625-3664). **Camp Colorado** (10 miles north on TX 206) makes a good side trip; it was a cavalry outpost in the mid-1800s. And **Lake Coleman** and **Hords Creek** are available for fishing.

Putting greens are to golf courses what faces are to portraits. Charles Blair Macdonald

COLORADO CITY

Elev. 2,067   P op. 4,304

Colorado City, the first real boomtown of West Texas, once overflowed with 10,000 residents and boasted the finest hotel between El Paso and Fort Worth. The boom days are gone, but this little town on the Colorado River is still a handy road-trip destination for golfers pursuing off-the-beaten-path adventures. Located just north of I-20, Colorado City lets you cram 9 holes at Wolf Creek, followed by a quick lunch and boot shopping at the massive Woods Boots outlet, then be back on the road to your next destination in 2-3 hours.

WOLF CREEK GOLF LINKS

The golf   Named after Wolf Creek, which runs through the course and was once the site of an old Indian campground, this is a links-style course set in the rolling terrain north of town. Wide-open fairways lure you to use your driver off the tee, and drives that find the firm fairways will roll more than usual, setting up a short iron for the approach. Water hazards are on five of the nine holes. Pay once and play all day.

The details   915-728-5514. 1417 County Rd. 137, Colorado City, TX 79512

- 1927. 9 holes. Par 35. Back – 2,990 (67.8/109). Middle – 2,710. Forward – 2,365. Price - $.

Getting there From I-20, exit Country Club Rd. and drive north to the course.

COLORADO CITY NOTES   If you're committed to more than passing through, you owe it to yourself to rub elbows with the locals at **Al's Sportsman's Club Restaurant** (915-728-5324). Two lakes nearby: **Champion Creek Reservoir** to the south, and **Lake Colorado City State Park** to the southwest. The **Days Inn** (915-728-2638) offers acceptable lodging.

COMANCHE

Elev. 1,358   Pop. 4,480

Not too far from the geographic center of Texas, Comanche is located about 100 miles southwest of Fort Worth, and 90 miles southeast of Abilene. The town dates back to the mid-1800s and was named for the Comanche Indians who provided so many problems for the early settlers of the area.

With nearby Lake Proctor, which provides the setting for the outstanding local 18-hole golf course, Comanche is an excellent place to get into the heart of Texas for fishing, hunting, and golf.

My first rule is, "Distance without direction is worse than no distance at all." Nancy Lopez

P.A.R. COUNTRY CLUB

The golf   This course stands out among the small-town courses of this region for two reasons: it's very demanding, and it has one of the better layouts you'll find. The course rolls through the hills on the banks of Proctor Area Recreational Lake, and while the lake doesn't come into play on any holes, there are seven ponds scattered throughout the course, many strategically placed in front of greens. The medium-sized fairways are tree-lined and there are only a few dogleg fairways.

Your best scoring opportunities are on the much-more-forgiving front nine. The first two holes are among the easiest on the course. No. 1 is a 282-yard par 4 that offers the chance to drive the green, and No. 2 is a short par 3. Work your way through moderately difficult holes 3-7; the easier Nos. 8 and 9 will then give you the chance to wrap up the front in style.

The back nine can destroy your round, particularly holes 13 and 14. From the tips, No. 17 plays 583 yards and is listed as the number one handicap. By the time you reach 18, you'll be glad to see the short par 4 under 300 yards.

The only negative might be the average condition of the greens, but as a whole, this course is a must-play if you're in the area.

The details   254-879-2296. Route 1 PAR Box 1, Comanche, TX 76442

- 1963. 18 holes. Par 72. Back – 6,068 yards (67.9/108). Middle – 5,618 yards. Ladies – Par 70. 4,548 yards (67.4/110). Price - $.

Getting there From I-20 driving east, take Hwy. 36 east, then take Hwy. 377 (Hwy. 67) north. Turn left at the Proctor Dam and PAR sign and drive about 2 miles. Turn left on the paved road to the entrance gate.

COMANCHE NOTES   Do lunch at the historic **Grand Street Bakery and Tearoom** (915-356-1457) on the town square, then be sure and check out the oldest original courthouse still standing in Texas (**Old Cora**) and **The Fleming Oak**, an old oak tree that saved the life of Mart Fleming during the Indian raids. The **Comanche County Museum** can tell you more about those times.

EASTLAND   Elev. 1,421   Pop. 3,760

Traveling west on I-20 between Fort Worth and Abilene, the restless golfer will encounter an interesting temptation in this town, which is known for a horned toad that reportedly lived in the cornerstone of the 1897 courthouse for 31 years. Two quality lakeside golf courses run beside the lake and are void of the big-city crowds.

We all hit it into trouble at times. The key is to minimize the error and play smart.
As they say, a bogey is a lot better than a double bogey. David Leadbetter

LAKESIDE COUNTRY CLUB

The golf   Lakeside is a 9-hole, par 36 layout with seven par 4s, accompanied by a par 3 and par 5 hole. The course features tree-lined fairways, a creek that comes into play on four holes, and small greens.

Each of the par 4s is under 400 yards, with No. 7 being the shortest at 268 yards. The par 5 is long at 544 yards, but the only par 3 is only 155 yards.

A new irrigation system was installed in 1997 and a new nine is under construction, with a planned opening date sometime in summer 2003. For now, two sets of tees allow for an 18-hole round, and you can pay once and play all day.

The details   254-629-2892. 209 County Rd. 157, Eastland, TX 76448

• 9 holes. Par 36. White – 3,045. Blue – 3,156. Price - $.

Getting there The club is located 3 miles northwest of Eastland off FM 3101 on County Rd. 157.

LONE CEDAR COUNTRY CLUB

The golf   Lone Cedar is a flat, 9-hole course that's open to the public. Playing along Lake Leon, this wide-open course is scenic, and is highlighted by relatively new Champion Bermuda greens that putt true and allow you the chance to roll a few in.

The details   254-647-3613. County Rd. 570, Eastland, TX 76448

• 1950s. 9 holes. Back – 3,229. Forward – 2,507. Price - $.

Getting there From Abilene take I-20 east and exit at Lake Leon. Look for the signs to the lake and the course.

EASTLAND NOTES   Go for outstanding salsa and guacamole at **Cafe Rico** (254-631-0064), a quaint, family-owned joint. Or head to **Rip's Diner**, where menu items are named in honor of the horned toad, and the house special is known as a "Toadwich."

ELECTRA   Elev. 1,229   Pop. 3,152

Electra is on US 287 fifteen miles northwest of Wichita Falls. The railroad made its way through here in the 1880s, and the Waggoner family, of the famed Waggoner Ranch, persuaded officials to establish a switch along Beaver Creek. Residents chose to name the town Electra after the daughter of W.T. Waggoner. Golfers traveling from the DFW area to the Panhandle should take advantage of this little ranch town by stopping for lunch and stretching their legs on the 9-hole Crooked Creek course.

When Ben Hogan practiced, he didn't want to watch what anyone else was doing. He was working as hard as he could to monitor and refine what he was doing. Dr. Bob Rotella

CROOKED CREEK GOLF & COUNTRY CLUB

The golf   Crooked Creek is a flat, wide-open course that features a crooked creek winding its way throughout the layout. This is basic, small-town golf that lends itself to low scoring. But watch out for the tricky greens–they're loaded with subtle breaks and are difficult to read because of their average quality. No. 3 is the best hole, a challenging par 5 that involves crossing the creek three times. Pay once and play all day.

The details   940-495-3832. 13975 Hwy. 240 W., Electra, TX 76360

- 1950. 9 holes. Par 36. Back – 3,201. Forward – 2,487. Price - $.

Getting there From Hwy. 287 driving north, take Hwy. 25 north to Hwy. 240. Then turn right and the club is on the right less than a mile away.

ELECTRA NOTES   Time your trip around the annual **Goat Cook-Off,** which became famous when local oil company employees "bought some goats, got some beer, got drunk, got in a big fight, and everything got stuck." The main restaurant is the **Whistle Stop** on Hwy. 287, but there is a **Sonic** if you need it to-go.

GRAHAM   Elev. 1,045   Pop. 8,686

Graham is one of the prettiest towns in the state, located in an area of stunning beauty next to Possum Kingdom Lake, perhaps the most beautiful lake in Texas. The charm of this town is enhanced by the nation's largest downtown square, where shops, restaurants, and cultural activities lend a vibrant air to the community. Golfers with spouses lured by the bustling activity will be happy to know that the charming 9-hole Graham Country Club is just outside of town, providing the perfect alternative to incessant antique shopping.

GRAHAM COUNTRY CLUB

The golf   Fairways lined by large, ancient oak trees always provide character to a layout. That statement is definitely true for the scenic Graham Country Club, which features fast greens (replaced in 1997), narrow fairways, and water that comes into play on a few holes.

The design incorporates the traditional mixture of holes, with two par 3s, two par 5s, and five par 4s. The best birdie opportunity is the short, par 3, No. 5 (136 yards), but it's followed by the signature No. 6: a 435-yard par 4. You can play another round from a different set of tees, and they're nice enough not to charge you again.

The details   940-549-7721. Fort Belknap Rd., Graham, TX 76450

⭐

Why am I using a new putter? Because the last one didn't float too well. Craig Stadler

NORTHWEST

- 1962. 9 holes. Par 36. Back – 3,216 (35.3/116). Forward – 2,710 (35.6/113). Price - $.

Getting there From the Hwy. 380 Bypass driving west, take FM 61 (Fort Belknap Rd.) north, then turn left onto Country Club Dr. The entrance is on Country Club Dr. East.

GRAHAM NOTES   Take your time and tour the town square, where there is plenty of shopping and food available. Outside of town off FM 67 on Rosser Ranch Rd., try the **Backside Steakhouse** (940-549-9107). Take the scenic drives around Possum Kingdom Lake and you'll eventually run into **Lumpy's BBQ** (940-779-3535). Stay at **Cove Cabin Guest House** (940-549-6792) out on Lake Graham. On weekends the **Graham Drive-In Theatre** (940-549-8478) is a great way to spend a small-town Texas night. And book lovers can enjoy themselves in **Pratt's Books** (940-549-5341), one of the state's best used and rare book shops.

HAMLIN   Elev. 1,705   Pop. 2,196

Hamlin is on US 83 forty-three miles northwest of Abilene. The railroad gave life to the town back in the early 1900s, the oil boom kept it going in the 1920s, and the town has managed to hang on all these years as a center for manufacturing and farming. Like the surrounding towns of Aspermont, Stamford, Anson, and Rotan, Hamlin has its own little place in the golf world that provides locals and passersby with an adequate place to hack away.

HAMLIN GOLF COURSE

The golf   Hamlin's 9-hole course originally opened in 1938, but was shut down during World War II before reopening in the 1950s. Course conditions have improved recently with the installation of a new watering system. The size of the fairways varies, and most are lined with large, mature mesquite trees. Pay attention to your putting here. The greens have slight undulations and can be very tricky.

The details   915-576-3026. FM 2142, Hamlin, TX 79520

- 9 holes. Par 36. Back – 2,975 (70/117). Forward – 2,601. Price - $.

Getting there The course is 2.5 miles west of Hamlin on FM 2142. From Abilene, take Hwy. 83/277 north to Hwy. 83. Head northwest and follow the signs to the course.

Learning to wait patiently is important in playing golf successfully. Dr. Bob Rotella

NORTHWEST

HAMLIN NOTES　　Fill your belly at the **Country Corner Cafe,** then hit the back roads via TX 92 to the site of **Swedona,** a unique rural community farmed by Swedes well into the 1900s. **The Pied Piper Inn** (915-576-3627) offers lodging.

HASKELL　　　　　　　　　　　　　Elev. 1,553　　Pop. 3,084

　　Haskell, located at the junction of US 277 and 380, is the place to come and enjoy the ranch country and work in a little golf. Think of the explorers, Indians, and buffalo hunters who used to water here back when the place was called Willow Pond Springs, and a saloon called the Road to Ruin doubled as a church.

HASKELL COUNTY COUNTRY CLUB

The golf　　One of the area's oldest individual stroke play tournaments, the Bob Mobley Invitational, is played at this 9-hole, semi-private facility each year. This wide-open layout features no bunkers and minimal trees, which is made up for by a thick cut of rough bordering the fairways. Water hazards come into play on five holes.

　　Every fairway plays straightaway except for No. 5, a 400-yard par 4 that features a dogleg-left fairway surrounded by water and an approach into an elevated green.

The details　　940-864-3400. Rural Route 1 Box 190, Haskell, TX 79521

• 1962. 9 holes. Par 36. Back – 2,986 yards. Forward – 2,646. Price – $.

Getting there From Abilene, take Hwy. 277 north for 55 miles to Haskell. Turn east onto Country Club Rd. and drive 1 mile to the course. Turn right at the sign for the golf course and airport.

HASKELL NOTES　　Stay at the **Bevers House Bed & Breakfast** (940-864-3284) or the **Fieldan Inn** (940-864-2251). **Easterling's** serves barbecue and the **K&P Steakhouse** does steaks. Haskell is in excellent quail hunting country, so consider **Krooked River Ranch Outfitters** (915-773-2457) for guide service and lodging. Pricey ($450-$600 per person for a day's hunt and lodging with meals), and a decent trek from Haskell (22 miles), but the facility is first-class and the experience is worth it.

☆
The golfer who makes the best score has always done some very good putting. George Low

HAWLEY

Elev. 1,662   Pop. 591

Venturing north into the Big Country out of Abilene, US 287 first takes you to the tiny town of Hawley. In the past, there was never a reason for the avid golfer to stop off in this metropolis of almost 600. However, now that a first-class 18-hole golf course has been carved out of the mesquite and oak trees, hackers no longer pass through on their way to the secluded rural golf courses just up the road in Anson, Hamlin, and beyond.

TANGLE OAKS GOLF CLUB

The golf   Former Haskell Country Club superintendent Mark Bailey and his wife Gayle first broke ground for this course northeast of Hawley on New Year's Day, 1996. Two-and-a-half years later, the original nine holes opened. Construction on the next nine wrapped up in 2002, leaving 18 outstanding holes for the public.

Tangle Oaks is an appropriate name. The course is carved out of an extremely dense oak thicket, sometimes referred to as "the shinnery." In fact, the shinnery is so thick that it's played as a lateral hazard–players just drop from where the ball went into the briar-patch-like rough. Length is not imperative, but accuracy is key. The greens are elevated, tilt from back to front, and have a medium to high slope.

The fairways are quite tight, due to the oaks. The strategy is simple. Keep it straight or you'll get in trouble. Length is not important, but accuracy is a must.

The signature hole is No. 9, a 383-yard par 4 that plays into the teeth of the stiff West Texas wind. To further a golfer's sheer terror, the green is completely fronted by water and a formidable retaining wall. On the back the most notable hole is No. 13, which features an island green. Hole 18 is unique because of the split fairway.

Other notes: The county is dry, but Tangle Oaks allows you to bring your own beer. While most of the play comes from Abilene, many visiting hunters chase game afield early in the morning, then play golf in the afternoon.

The details   915-537-9023. 7932 Private Rd. 3521, Hawley, TX 79525

- 1998. 18 holes. Price - $$.

- Original nine: Gold – 3,032. Blue – 2,725. White – 2,473. New nine – N/A

Getting there Call the course for more detailed directions, as they may be able to give you a better feel for finding this out-of-the-way course. From Abilene, drive north on Hwy. 277 to Hawley. Go east at Exit 1226, and drive 6 miles to the course.

HAWLEY NOTES   There isn't much in Hawley, so you'll want to arrange lodging in Abilene. However, if you get the chance, order yourself a chicken-fried steak from **Debbie's Diner** downtown. Tour the countryside and take FM 1082 to 1851 **Fort Phantom Hill**, a desolate arrangement of chimneys that is home to many ghost legends.

HENRIETTA   Elev. 886   Pop. 3,267

Henrietta, the seat of Clay County, is on US 287 twenty miles southeast of Wichita Falls. The town dates back to pre-Civil-War days, but the frequent Indian hostilities often forced the settlers to hightail it to the safer confines of the military posts. In 1873 the residents reorganized the city and county; and for years it served as the only court of justice for a 300-mile area. Today, farming and agriculture fuel the economy and residents enjoy the great game of golf at the Clay County Country Club.

CLAY COUNTY COUNTRY CLUB

The golf   Clay County is a long, challenging course that breaks the mold of the simple, small-town architecture. Older than other courses in the area, this course was built in the 1970s and is more modern than most. Featuring long par 4s, many of which are over 400 yards, the track totals over 3,200 yards and has water on six of the nine holes. Trees line the fairways so you're not safe if you fail to hit it straight. Pay once and play all day.

The details   940-538-4339. Rural Route 1, Box 3A9, Henrietta, TX 76365

• 1971. 9 holes. Back – 3,245 (34.5). Forward – 2,835 (36.5). Price - $.

Getting there From Dallas, take Hwy. 287 west and exit Spur 510. Turn left and drive a quarter mile to the course. The entrance is on the right side of the road.

HENRIETTA NOTES   Of course there is a **Dairy Queen,** but for local flavor try **Original Joe's** (940-538-5888) or **Pepito's** (940-538-6644). The **Hillside Motel** (940-538-6551) has rooms. South on TX 148 and FM 2847 is **Lake Arrowhead State Park.**

KNOX CITY   Elev. 1,554   Pop. 1,161

Outside of Knox City, Highway 6 leaps the Brazos River and the landscape changes to the badlands of Red River country. Knox City is lonely and remote, out in the country 80 miles from Abilene, Lubbock, and Wichita Falls. Like so many of the towns in this area, Knox City was built for the coming of the railroad but now serves as a center for petroleum and agribusiness.

KNOX CITY COUNTRY CLUB

The golf   This nice 9-hole public course has open fairways, fairly new Princess Bermuda greens, and a par 4 (No. 4) that plays as a par 5 the second time around. In fact, No. 4 is the most difficult hole because it plays 450-yards into the wind. There are no bunkers or water hazards, and while the course is relatively simple, it plays to a long 3,360 yards, unusual for a small-town 9-hole track. Note the abundant mature mulberry trees that line the fairways.

The details   940-658-3911. 16035 S. Hwy. 6, Knox City, TX 79529

• 1962. 9 holes. Par 35. 3,360 yards. Price - $.

Getting there Located on Hwy. 6 south of town.

KNOX CITY NOTES   For a town of 1,200, there are more places to eat that you might think. **Bud's Cafe** (940-658-5100) is good for coffee and a meal, and **The Wild Flour Cafe** (940-658-3957) and **Brenda Jo's Cafe** (940-658-5100) are solid lunch options. The "Seedless Watermelon Capital of the World" holds an annual festival the last Saturday in July to celebrate that fact, complete with live music and good times. The **City Motel** (940-658-3541) can put you up if you don't want to road-trip it a few miles north to **Benjamin, TX** and stay at the old 1887 **Knox City Jail**. It's been restored by Texas artist Wyman Meinzer, who lives on the grounds with his family.

MERKEL   Elev. 1,872   Pop. 2,643

Merkel started as a shipping point in late 1881, when the railroad made it southwest through Abilene, and the community grew as a hub for farming and ranching activity. With an 18-hole golf course built into the scrubby West Texas mesquite 1 mile north of the interstate, Merkel makes for an interesting stop for the restless golfer traveling on I-20.

MERKEL GOLF CLUB

The golf   The Merkel Golf Club offers a short 18-hole, par 70 track that covers about 100 acres. Originally just a 9-hole course, the new nine opened in 1997. The course features bent-grass greens that are well maintained. The signature hole is No. 3, a 150-yard par 3 that requires a tee shot over water.

The details   915-928-3193. 200 Country Club Dr., Merkel, TX 79536

Learn to bear your ill fortune without appealing for sympathy. Harold H. Hilton

- 1958. 18 holes. Par 70. Back – 5,115. Forward – 4,156. Price - $

Getting there The course is 14 miles west of Abilene, 1 mile north of I-20 on FM 126. The entrance is on the left side of the road.

MERKEL NOTES   Grab a bite to eat at **Mesquite Bean BBQ** (915-928-5618). There are a few local motels in Merkel, but we recommend that you stay in Abilene or play this course as you're passing through to another destination.

MUNDAY
Elev. 1,460   Pop. 1,459

Originally called Maud for local resident, Maud Isbel, Munday is a quiet little city set along the edge of rugged Copper Breaks State Park. This agricultural community, located about 70 miles from Abilene and Wichita Falls, dates back to 1893 when a cotton gin and post office sprang up. Over the years the community has served as a hub for fertilizer and insecticide manufacturing, vegetable and cotton processing, as well as a petroleum center.

LAKE CREEK GOLF COURSE

The golf   A classic, rural Texas 9-hole, semi-private course. It's not very long but it has a few mesquite trees along the fairways, water hazards, and sometimes just a little bit of wind. The course has a reputation for being well-watered and in good condition, and it might get even better since they're working on a new irrigation system.

There is no pro shop but you can call City Hall (940-422-4331) to get pointed in the right direction. Pay the green fee by dropping your funds in the pay box.

The details   940-422-4331N/A. 121 East Main St., Munday, TX 76371

- 9 holes. Par 35. 3,300 yards. Price - $

Getting there Located 4 miles east of town on FM 222.

MUNDAY NOTES   Twelve miles southeast you'll find **Miller's Creek Reservoir,** which has a reputation for good fishing. During the winter, **goose hunting** is popular in the nearby peanut and wheat fields. Take the side trip 6 miles north to **Rhineland** (FM 267) and check out the tall, steepled church built by hand with 100,000 bricks from a local clay pit. Aside from the **Dairy Queen,** locally-owned **Mati's** has great home-cooking and Mexican food. The only place to stay is **Michael's Corner Inn.**

NORTHWEST

NOCONA

Elev. 988   Pop. 3,241

Nocona is an old cattle town founded in the 1870s by a local rancher who donated a section of his 22,000 acres to the city. It was named for Chief Peta Nocona, a Comanche chief and father of Quanah Parker, and served as a supply stop for cattle drives on their way to the Chisolm Trail at the Red River.

This is lonely country. Ranchland now covers the place where 30 businesses and residences once stood northwest in Belcherville. The terrain features more rolling hills and trees than you would think for an area that has the reputation of being flat and dry.

INDIAN OAKS GOLF CLUB

The golf   Indian Oaks is an old 18-hole course with wide fairways that flow along the hilly terrain of Nocona. The course is loaded with trees and bunkers, and water hazards are sprinkled throughout.

The architect provided a welcome opportunity to start off well by placing the easiest hole as the first (278-yard par 4). The signature hole is No. 15, a 346-yard par 4 with a severe dogleg fairway. The back nine plays a little more difficult, with particularly tough finishing holes. No. 17 is a 205-yard par 3, followed by a 500-yard-plus par 5 as the finisher.

The details   940-825-4213. 101 Cooke St., Nocona, TX 76255

- 1934. Earl Stone. 18 holes. Par 70. Back – 5,792. Forward – 4,232. Price – $.

Getting there From Wichita Falls, take Hwy. 82 east to Nocona. Once in town, look for the course entrance on the right side of the road.

NOCONA HILLS GOLF COURSE

The golf   Locals joke that Nocona Hills is the "premier course in Wichita Falls." This 18-hole layout is tight and challenging. Trees are everywhere, and out-of-bounds stakes loom on many holes. The condition of the course is excellent, and many claim that these are the best greens in North Texas.

Hole 3 is the most difficult: a 523-yard par 5 from the middle tees. However, the other par 5s are well under 500 yards. The par 4s are of average length, and the par 3s are reasonably short and offer excellent birdie opportunities.

The details   940-825-3444. 179 Country Club Dr., Nocona, TX 76255

- www.noconahills.com
- 1974. Leon and Charles Howard. 18 holes. Par 72. Back – 6,529. Middle – 6,155 (70.2/111). Forward – 4,971 (64.1/103). Price – $.

Getting there From I-82 east, exit Clay St. and turn left. When you come to

---

Golf is a game in which you yell "fore," shoot six and write down five. Paul Harvey

Hwy. 1956 turn right and proceed 7 miles. Next, turn left on Hwy. 3301, then drive 2 more miles to the course. Look for the gatehouse on the left side of the road.

NOCONA NOTES   Don't miss the opportunity to have a meal at the **Dairy Queen,** where you'll have the best chance to soak up the character of Nocona. After a meal and golf, head 17 miles north on FM 103 to **Spanish Fort** and tour the site of a Spanish-Indian battle that reversed the mission's colonization efforts in the late 1700s.

OLNEY
Elev. 1,184   Pop. 3,396

Olney is a small Northwest Texas town only 42 miles south of Wichita Falls and about 100 miles west of Fort Worth. The area around Olney was first discovered by cattlemen, who took advantage of the cool, clear lake and tall grasses to feed their stock. The Swastika Oil Field hit in the 1920s, kicking off a splurge of petroleum activity. Today the town still serves the oil industry, as well as agriculture, ranching, and hunting.

OLNEY COUNTRY CLUB

The golf   This is another small-town country club that's a joy for the average golfer because of the flat, open layout and lack of hazards. Only three holes have water and there are no bunkers. This basic course has the standard five par 4s, two par 3s, and two par 5s. Hole 9 is the longest par 4 at 399 yards. Pay once and play all day.

The details   940-564-2424. Bankhead Rd., Olney, TX 76374

• 1970 Leon Howard. 9 holes. Par 36. Back – 3,128. Forward – 2,525. Price - $$

Getting there From Wichita Falls, take Hwy. 79 south. When you come to Bankhead Rd., turn left and the course is just down the road.

OLNEY NOTES   Each year the Friday and Saturday after Labor Day offers a good chance to combine golf and hunting, when the annual **One-Armed Dove Hunt** takes place. The hunt started back in 1972 when Olney's one-armed citizens organized a hunt. For fine dining go for chicken-fried steak at **Gandy's Chicken & Bar-B-Q** (940-564-3539), a neat little diner with home-cooked food.

Every golfer is on his honor. Donald Ross

QUANAH

Elev. 1,568   Pop. 2,981

A charming town with tidy brick homes and shade-covered streets, Quanah lies on US 287 between the Red and Pease rivers. The town is named for Comanche chief Quanah Parker, whose white mother, Cynthia Ann Parker, was kidnapped and married into the Comanche Indians. Quanah's economic base of cattle, cotton, wheat, oats, and barley improved with the discovery of the Conley oilfield in 1959.

QUANAH COUNTRY CLUB

The golf   Quanah's 9-hole country club is another small-town course that's easy to play because of the flat terrain and lack of trees. Water impacts a few holes, with a creek, a pond, and another lake coming into play on three holes, but there are no bunkers. The course features basic greens that are small and generally flat.

The details   940-663-2069. Hwy. 287, Quanah, TX 79252

- 9 holes. Par 35. Back – 2,936. Middle – 2,888. Forward – 2,347. Private. Price - $.

Getting there From Hwy. 287 take FM 2568 north for 3.5 miles; the course is on the right.

QUANAH NOTES   Take Texas 6 south for 12 miles to **Copper Breaks State Park**. In addition to copper mining during the Civil War, the site is famous for the **Battle of the Pease River**, where in 1860 Cynthia Ann Parker was recaptured after living as an Indian. When you're hungry find **Ken's** for Mexican food and home cooking, or the **Medicine Man Depot** (940-663-5619) for red meat. About 8 miles west of town you can stay at the **Ole Towne Cotton Gin RV Park** (940-674-2477), featuring a hot tub, exercise room, pool, and breakfast.

RISING STAR

Elev. 1,625   Pop. 844

While there's not all that much to say about Rising Star, the one glaring positive is that this small agricultural community of under 1,000 residents offers 27 holes of public golf. Situated at the intersection of US Hwy. 183 and Texas 36, fifty-six miles southeast of Abilene in southwestern Eastland County, Rising Star began in 1876 when six families moved west from Gregg County to settle.

If you really want to get better at golf, go back and take it up at a much earlier age. Henry Beard

LAKEWOOD RECREATION CENTER

The golf   Built by Leon Howard around 1970, Lakewood is the hub of a retirement community. More of a traditional layout, the design incorporates a 30-acre lake that impacts play, and the large greens are tough because of the subtle undulations. Pay once and play all day.

The details   254-643-4602. Route 2, Rising Star, TX 76471

• 1970. Leon Howard. 9 holes. Par 36. Back – 2,874. Forward – 2,388. Price - $.

Getting there From I-20 west, take Hwy. 183 north. Travel 20 miles to Rising Star and head east 5 miles. Turn right at the course sign.

ROLLING OAKS GOLF CLUB

The golf   Rolling Oaks is an 18-hole, semi-private course that originally opened in 1992 with nine holes, followed by an additional nine in 1996. The layout features Tiff Bermuda greens and water hazards on two holes.

The feature hole is No. 7, a 506-yard par 5 with a large tree in the middle of the fairway. No. 18, a 484-yard par 5, offers the chance to finish strong.

The details   254-643-4563. County Rd. 266 S., Rising Star, TX 76471

• 1992/1996. 18 holes. Par 72. Gold – 6,487 (71.1/119). Blue – 6,095 (69.4/115). White – 5,609 (67.1/109). Red – 5,070 (69.5/114). Price - $$.

Getting there From Abilene, take Hwy. 36 south through the town of Cross Springs. When you come to CR 266, turn right. Follow the signs to the course.

RISING STAR NOTES   In town go for **Papa Smokey's Cafe** (254-643-1410), or head east to De Leon, TX and try the new **Blue Moon Cafe** (254-893-2455), which resides in the restored Higginbotham building. North Texas golfers traveling to the central part of the state should take this route down US 183 and plan a stop in Rising Star for a round of golf.

ROTAN   Elev. 1,952   Pop. 1,551

Rotan is noted as the home of Slingin' Sam Baugh, whom some consider to be the greatest quarterback ever to play the game. Baugh lives on a ranch outside of town and plays golf frequently at the local club and the surrounding area courses. The town is currently in the middle of a renovation project to revitalize the main street and some of the vacant buildings left empty in recent years.

Rhythm is best expressed in any swing directed at a cigar stump
or a dandelion head. Grantland Rice

ROTAN GOLF CLUB

The golf   Larry Hamlin, age 61, who caddied at the course as a youngster and is now one of the volunteers who helps keep the course in working condition, said it best: "My father is 87 years old, and there's another fella that's 92, and they both still play. These old-timers brought in a dump truck and filled up the water hazards. Then they had the city come out and cut down the trees that were in the way. We had one bunker but they filled that in, too."

Unlike other nearby courses that are owned by the county and have an easier time funding the maintenance of their golf course (like Kent County GC in Jayton), Rotan's course is owned by the city. The course is maintained by 12 volunteers who pay $100 per year to be members of the Rotan Golf Club. There is no pro shop and there are no carts. However, in the old days, locals used their cars in place of carts, and one member actually backed his "cart" into a tree. These days, members ride their carts from their homes to the course.

The green fee is $5, enforced by the Golf Gods. The small Bermuda greens are watered by hand, although the club is considering the installation of sprinkler heads around the greens. Hole 3 is the signature hole, a par 4 highlighted by an approach shot over a "ditch" to a small green.

The details   915-735-2210. 216 W. Sammy Baugh Ave., Rotan, TX 79546

- 1930s. 9 holes. Par 35. 2,453 yards. No carts. Price - $.

Getting there Located in the city park, with a Little League field and swimming pool nearby, the course is on the north side of Hwy. 92 east toward Hamlin (cross street is Lakeview).

ROTAN NOTES   When in need of a meal in Rotan, it's not hard to find **Casa Morales** (915-735-2658), which reeks of authentic Tex-Mex. For great burgers try **John's Place**, which has been open for over 75 years. Stay at **The Wind Word Inn** (915-735-3611), play a little golf, and let the **J&L Game Bird Farm** (915-776-2852) take you quail hunting.

SEYMOUR   Elev. 1,291   Pop. 2,904

Seymour is the only town and seat of Baylor County, about midway between Dallas-Fort Worth and the Lubbock and Amarillo areas. As you drive into town, the large farms and ranches are golden with wheat ready for harvest in spring, and loaded with grazing cattle in the fall and winter. Seymour serves as a base for farming, ranching, and oil businesses. Murals depicting the town's history take up most of a city block downtown, and the post office boasts a 1941 oil and canvas painting by Tom Lea, who was named an honorary citizen in 2000.

⭐

On August 12, 1936, Seymour recorded the hottest temperature in Texas—a whopping 120°.

Golfers traveling in this part of the state should definitely make it a point to stop off in this charming little town.

SALT FORK MUNICIPAL GOLF COMPLEX

The golf   Like so many other courses in this region, Salt Fork is a wide-open 9-hole course with minimal hazards (one pond impacts one hole). This somewhat hilly course features medium-sized, elevated greens that have severe undulations. While there is not a separate set of tees for ladies, there are two sets of tees to allow for an 18-hole round.

The details   940-889-2833. Throckmorton Hwy., Seymour, TX 76380

- 9 holes. Par 35. 2,820 yards. Price - $.

Getting there From the Adeline Hwy., take the Throckmorton exit and turn right. Look for and follow the signs to the course.

SEYMOUR NOTES   The **Old Chaps Supper Club** (940-889-2929) specializes in steaks, the **Rock Inn Cafe** (940-888-2322) serves up a mean meatloaf, and the locals swear by the club sandwich at **Maverick's Cafe** (940-889-3056). **Lake Kemp** is just north and hosts Fish Day every year on May 1, when the entire town shuts down to go fishing.

SNYDER   Elev. 2,316   Pop. 10,506

The county seat of Scurry County, Snyder is 87 miles southeast of Lubbock at the junction of US 84 and 180. It began in 1878, when a buffalo hunter and trader from Pennsylvania, William Henry "Pete" Snyder, built a trading post on the banks of Deep Creek. Other hunters came and their dubious character gave the town its first names: Hide Town and Robber's Roost.

SNYDER COUNTRY CLUB

The golf   This is a private, 9-hole track that features flat terrain, medium-sized fairways, and two sets of tees for an 18-hole round. The best part about playing here is the unique combination of holes: three par 3s, three par 4s, and three par 5s. If you have game, you'll score well here. The par 3s are short, and every par 5 is under 500 yards.

The details   915-573-0166. 557 N. US Hwy. 84, Snyder, TX 79550

- 1953. 9 holes. Par 36. Back – 3,043 (35.2/119). Forward – 2,548 (35.5/119). Price - $$.

The worst way to try to make a great stroke is by thinking about its mechanics when you putt the ball. It's something best left to your subconscious. Dr. Bob Rotella

Getting there From Lubbock, take Hwy. 84 south and take the first Snyder exit. Turn right and drive 2 miles to the course. The entrance is on the right side of the road.

WESTERN TEXAS COLLEGE GOLF COURSE

The golf Western Texas has been the municipal course of Snyder since the late 1970s. This 9-hole course, located on the grounds of Western Texas College, allows you to take full advantage of the West Texas winds, as most holes seem to play downwind. The layout sets nicely in the rolling terrain around Snyder, and the architect was able to incorporate several natural hazards as part of his design. When asked about the challenges of the course, locals most often referenced the tricky, undulating greens, which often cause the dreaded three-jack.

There is only one par 5, and all of the par 4s are under 400 yards, including the welcome 290-yard finishing hole (267 yards from the middle tees). The most difficult hole is No. 5, a 345-yard par 4. From the middle tees, go for birdies on the short par 3s, which shouldn't require anything more than an 8 iron.

The details 915-573-9291. 6200 College Ave., Snyder, TX 79549

- 1978. Jim Eagle. 9 holes. Par 35. Back – 3,016 (34.6/114). Middle – 2,754 (33.1/111). Forward – 2,250 (32.7). Price - $$.

Getting there From I-20 driving east, turn left on Hwy. 84 and drive about 23 miles to Snyder. In town make a left on Colorado City Hwy., travel to South College Ave., and make a right. The course is on the right side of the street.

SNYDER NOTES The best spot to add calories is **The Shack** (915-573-4921), the long-time Snyder tradition that serves up every kind of home-style cooking you can dream of. The **Scurry County Museum** offers Indian and local history artifacts, or find the 1908 **Mooar Mansion**, an impressive ranch house built by buffalo hunter J. Wright Mooar (who killed 20,000 buffalo in one decade). There are only small chain hotels for lodging; try the **Best Western** and **Days Inn**.

STAMFORD

Elev. 1,603   Pop. 3,530

Although not the "West Texas" that many claim, this country of brush, rolling ranchland, sweeping vistas, and random mesas has the unmistakable feel of the west. Lazy hills dot the horizon, the sky is wide, and there's a soothing feeling of emptiness.

Stamford is the home of the famous Texas Cowboy Reunion each July, and serves as the retail, banking and commercial center for a three-county area. The town's roots date back to 1899, when the railroad moved through the area. Today Stamford serves as the headquarters of the Swen R. Swenson Land and Cattle Company and is home to a nice little 9-hole country club.

STAMFORD GOLF & COUNTRY CLUB

The golf   Built in the 1930s, this course is known as the place where former Masters champion Charles Coody learned his game. The fairways are flat and lined with trees, and the landing areas are generous. A new irrigation system was installed in the 1990s, which makes the conditions more favorable. This scenic course is a pleasure to walk, fortunately–walking is mandatory because there are no carts. The only par 4 over 400 yards is No. 8, which is the number one handicap. The par 4 No. 4 hole is only 270 yards.

The details   915-773-5001. P.O. Box 289, Stamford, TX 79553

- 1930s. 9 holes. Back – Par 35, 2,914 yards (67.3/119). Forward – Par 36, 2,318 yards. Price - $.

Getting there From Fort Worth take Hwy. 6 down to Wells St. Turn left and drive straight to the course.

STAMFORD NOTES   Avoid the chains and try the **Cliff House Restaurant** (915-773-3431). Two lodging options are the **Deluxe Inn** (915-773-2751) and the **Great Western Inn** (915-773-2731). Located at the intersections of US 277 and Texas 6, the **Mackenzie Trail Monument** shows a large hand-carved marker erected by descendants of early rangers. The **Texas Cowboy Museum** (915-773-2411) displays paintings and prints from cowboy artists.

SWEETWATER   Elev. 2,164   Pop. 11,213

Before the ranchers arrived, the Kiowa Indians named this area Mobeetie, their word for "sweet water." Sweetwater lies just west of Abilene on land that rests on a divide between the Brazos and Colorado watersheds.

A store established in a dugout to accommodate buffalo hunters was the beginning of the city in 1877. Today it is the seat of Nolan County and is a banking and commercial center. Sweetwater offers two 18-hole golf courses. That's pretty impressive compared to another town of similar size in this region, Vernon, which musters up a measly 9 holes of private golf for residents and visitors who can work their way on.

However unlucky you may be, it really is not fair to expect your adversary's grief for your undeserved misfortunes to be as poignant as your own. Horace Hutchinson

SWEETWATER COUNTRY CLUB

The golf   Sweetwater's 18-hole semi-private country club course does not require length, as the middle tees play under 6,000 yards. Built on gently rolling terrain, the course features tree-lined fairways, water hazards that impact a few holes, and small Champion Bermuda greens that were installed in the mid-1990s.

The toughest hole is the par 4, 425-yard No. 8. However, many of the other par 4s are well under 400 yards. Not only are there birdie opportunities on the short par 4s, but all of the par 3s are under 200 yards, three of which should require no more than a medium-length iron. Hit the greens on the par 3s and you're assured of a respectable round.

The details   915-235-8093. 1900 Country Club Ln., Sweetwater, TX 79556

- 18 holes. Par 72. Back – 6,367 (68.6/115). Regular – 5,921. Forward – 5,038. Price - $$.

Getting there From I-20 west, exit Sweetwater Business and turn left on East Broadway. When you come to Hailey turn right, then proceed down to Woodruff. Turn left and this road leads directly to the course.

LAKE SWEETWATER MUNICIPAL GOLF COURSE

The golf   Originally built by the Civil Works Commission, Lake Sweetwater is a beautiful course that offers scenic views of the countryside. The track features wide-open fairways lined by a standard cut of rough. There are no bunkers, but water comes into play on almost half of the holes. The terrain is hilly, more so on the back nine than the front. Approach shots here find small, fast greens.

Some have complained about the conditions due to lack of water, but the course has recently installed a new irrigation system.

The details   915-235-8816. 2125 FM 1856, Sweetwater, TX 79556

- 18 holes. Par 71. Back – 6,185 (67.6/112). Forward – 5,194 (66.9/110). Price - $.

Getting there Lake Sweetwater is west of Abilene off of I-20. Exit FM 1856 and turn left. The course is 1 mile away on the left side of the road.

SWEETWATER NOTES   Sweetwater is known as the home of the largest rattlesnake convention in the world, held each March. The **Sweetwater Commercial Historic District**, listed on the National Register of Historic Places, includes more than 90 sites representing architectural styles from the 1900s and 1930s. Stare at the photograph files at the **Pioneer City County Museum**, which offers more than a dozen display rooms devoted to early pioneer life,

I learned how to put the money out of my mind and concentrate for 18 holes. I learned how to get the bet high enough so the guy I was playing would choke. Phil Rodgers

NORTHWEST

farm and ranch exhibits, and Indian artifacts. The B&Bs here are **Directly Under Heaven** or **The Guest House** (800-621-2932), and the **Comfort Inn** is the newest of the motel/hotel options. Lots of local restaurants here: Try **Casa Morales** for Tex-Mex, or **Buck's Steaks & BBQ** for American food.

THROCKMORTON
Elev. 1,441   Pop. 867

The county seat of Throckmorton County (population 1,850) is on US highways 380 and 183/283, 82 miles southwest of Wichita Falls. The valley Throckmorton sits in was once the site of a well-known campground on the old road west to California; it was notable for being the last stop on the way to New Mexico (300 miles away). Throckmorton started out as a Comanche Indian reservation (1854-1859), but eventually became a hub for the county's ranching and oil interests.

THROCKMORTON COUNTRY CLUB

The golf   Built around 1970, this 9-hole course is open to the public and is known for its extremely friendly employees. Set in the rolling plains between the Brazos River forks, the course features mesquite trees and a creek that runs throughout the layout. Four more ponds make water the predominant hazard, and a few of the greens are elevated. Pay once and play all day, as there are two sets of tees for an 18-hole round.

The details   940-849-5391. Lake Dr., Throckmorton, TX 76483

• 1970. Back – 2,806. Forward – 2,613. Price - $.

Getting there From Hwy. 380, turn south on Lake Dr. The course is on the left side of the street.

THROCKMORTON NOTES   What can you say about a town with 867 people? Eat at the **Ranchers Restaurant** (940-849-9761), stay at the **Cow Country Motel** (940-849-6131), play golf, and find out if there are fish in the nearby **Throckmorton Reservoir**.

As a young man, I couldn't accept the fact that golf is not a fair game. The game was my world, and if I didn't putt well, the injustice of it all would devour me. There were occasions during a round when I'd have to seek out one of those portable bathrooms and try to calm down. Tony Jacklin

VERNON

Elev. 1,205   Pop. 11,474

Vernon is the seat of Wilbarger County and the headquarters of the massive W.T. Waggoner Ranch. This town is the commercial center for a rich farming, ranching, and oil area, as well as the home of the only golf course in the county.

HILLCREST COUNTRY CLUB

The golf   Regarded as one of the nicer 9-hole courses in the state, Hillcrest is a straight course with only a few dogleg fairways. Visitors need to get their rounds in early or late, as members have full access between 11 a.m. and 4 p.m.

The details   940-552-5406. 4400 Country Club Rd., Vernon, TX 76384

• 9 holes. Par 35. Back – 3,024. Forward – 2,508. Price - $$.

Getting there Take the Crow Plains exit off US 287 and turn left. Go to the four-way stop and turn right, then proceed down to Country Club Rd. and turn left.

VERNON NOTES   About 15 miles north is Doan's Crossing, one of the most famous historic cattle crossings on the Red River. Shop for antiques or explore the 1881 **Doan's Adobe House**. Barbecue galore for a town of 11,000: try **Duncan's Smoke House** (940-552-2764). For lodging, the **Best Western Village Inn** (940-552-5417) is your best choice of eight hotels, and the **Victorian Rose** (940-552-5354) gives you a bed and breakfast alternative.

WICHITA FALLS

Elev. 946 Pop. 104,544

"Whiskeytaw Falls" began as a rail stop in the 1880s, and became a city of dancehalls and saloons that entertained the transient cowboys and cattle drovers of the day. The town was named for Wichita Indians, who lived near the waterfalls that were washed away in 1883 on what is now the Wichita River. Oil boomed the economy in the early 1900s, and still drives the economy today along with Sheppard Air Force Base and other manufacturing.

Although there is nothing overwhelming about the quality of golf in Wichita Falls, you can definitely play for a decent price and experience plenty of enjoyable golf holes.

If you start the downswing by first letting your weight shift onto your left foot and then unwinding your left hip ahead of your shoulders, your arms and hands will follow along naturally and the ball will simply get in the way of the clubface for longer, straighter shots. Butch Harmon

HAWK RIDGE GOLF CLUB

The golf   Formerly known as La Vista Golf Course, this is an 18-hole par 70 layout. Here you'll find several dogleg fairways that are protected by bunkers, and the course features a few water hazards that come into play, otherwise this is a basic municipal course that is somewhat outdated (1957) and in average condition. The course has a reputation for difficult pin placements, and locals complain about the constant problems with the greens.

The details   940-855-0771. 2000 N. Loop 11, Wichita Falls, TX 76306

- 1957. Wade Flat. 18 holes. Par 70. Back – 6,163 (68.8/112). Middle – 5,813 (69.5/114). Forward – 5,453 (67.0/105). Price - $$.

Getting there From Hwy. 287 north, exit Vernon/Amarillo and drive to the Beverly Drive/Loop 11 exit. Turn left and drive a short distance to the course. The entrance is on the right side of the street.

WEEKS PARK MUNICIPAL GOLF COURSE

The golf   Weeks Park is a quality municipal course that has received recognition in the past as one of the best public courses in the state (*Dallas Morning News* rated it as the 14th best in 1994). The course features greens that putt true, wide-open fairways, and creeks that come into play on 16 holes. Avoiding the water is key here for a good score.

No. 1 is a drivable, 279-yard par 4 with water along the left side of the fairway. The signature hole is the 212-yard No. 8, which features a winding creek that cuts into the fairway and around the green.

The back nine, renovated by Jeff Brauer, starts off with another tricky par 3, where you'll need to drive the tee shot over the water and into a green that slopes towards the drink. It is wise to keep the approach below the hole. The par 5 No. 15 also requires a tee shot over a creek, then into a dogleg-right fairway. The finishing hole is tricky (a 396-yard par 4) because it forces you to decide whether to lay up or go for it over the creek that crosses the fairway.

The details   940-767-6107. 4400 Lake Park Dr., Wichita Falls, TX 76302

- 1923. 18 holes. Back – Par 72. 6,470 (70.0/117). Forward – Par 73. 4,915 (67.8/109). Price - $$$.

Getting there From I-44, take Jacksboro Hwy. south. When you get to Western, drive 2 miles to Lake Park Dr.

WICHITA FALLS COUNTRY CLUB

The golf   Fred Cooper, a Scottish immigrant, failed to find a suitable place to pursue his passion for golf when he settled in Wichita Falls in the early 1900s. So in 1914, the Wichita Falls Golf Club was formed with a 9-hole course and clubhouse on Victory St.

The club prospered through the 1920s, then fell on hard times during the Depression and was eventually turned over to the mortgage company in 1935. After several attempts to reorganize the club, Solon Featherston bought the entire club, made many improvements (first bent-grass greens in North Texas), and brought the facility back to profitability–due in part to slot machines installed during his tenure.

The layout features a good mixture of holes, with a creek winding its way through the course and coming into play on more than half of the holes. A small lake also impacts a few holes. The fairways are tree-lined and there is a moderate amount of bunkering. While some tee shots require the precision for target golf, others are wide-open and offer generous landing areas.

In late 1994, holes 14 and 15 were renovated. Jeff Brauer and Ralph Plummer have done work here periodically over the years.

Make note of Ladies Day on Thursdays, as only ladies may tee off until 11:00 a.m.

The details   940-767-1486. 1701 Hamilton Blvd., Wichita Falls, TX 76308

- www.wichitafallscc.com
- 18 holes. Par 72. Back – 6,722 (72.5/132). Middle – 6,387 (71.0/126). Forward – 5,293 (71.1/128). Price - $$$.

Getting there From Hwy. 287 north, turn right at Midwestern, then drive 2 miles to the course. The entrance is on the right side of the street.

WIND CREEK GOLF COURSE

The golf   An outstanding course designed by Pete Dye in 1957, Wind Creek is located on the grounds of Sheppard Air Force Base outside of Wichita Falls. Although primarily open to military personnel, the pro shop welcomes civilian play, and will help golfers hook up with someone who can accompany them on the course as a guest.

Locals will tell you that it looks much easier that it actually plays. The course is characterized by wide landing areas off the tee, 40 bunkers, three ponds, and a creek that runs through the course and affects five holes on the back nine. The 434-yard par 4 No. 4 is listed as the number one handicap, but No. 17 is a 600-yard par 5 that is particularly testy in the wind. All par 5s are well over 500 yards. One great feature of the course is the 24-hour lighted driving range.

The details   940-676-6369. 900 First Ave., Bldg. 4490, Sheppard AFB, TX 76311

- 1957. Pete Dye. Back – 7,028 (72.6/123). Middle – 6,683 (71.3/120). Forward – 5,267 (69.4/116). Price - $$.

Getting there From Wichita Falls, take I-44 north to the exit for the Sheppard AFB. At the base entrance, ask the guard for directions to the course.

My favorite shots are the practice swing and the conceded putt.
The rest cannot be mastered. Lord Robertson

MORE GOLF

The **Loop 11 Driving Range** (940-855-9070) offers a place to hack away if you need to kill time on a hot summer night.

WICHITA FALLS NOTES   Eat at the popular **Fat McBride's Steakhouse** (940-696-0250), or the local favorite **Kemp Street BBQ** (940-723-7204). For lodging, try the **Harrison House B&B** (940-322-2299) on 11th St. Late-night enthusiasts can indulge themselves on the seedy side of Wichita Falls, the quality of which is rivaled perhaps only by the fine establishments of Odessa, TX. Local lore speaks of the famous Anita Samore (nice name), a 52 EEE dancer whose photos raise the always-important question of gender.

NORTHWEST

WINTERS   Elev. 1,860   Pop. 2,880

Winters is on US 83 in the rolling plains of northcentral Runnels County. It was first settled in 1880 in an area called Bluff Creek Valley and was named in honor of John Winters, a local rancher and land agent who donated land for the first school. Today the economy is based on agriculture and oil. Combined with the 9-hole course in Ballinger, Winters Country Club gives Runnels County 18 holes of golf.

WINTERS COUNTRY CLUB

The golf   This semi-private 9-hole course, which has been open for over 75 years, offers memberships to those who live 40 miles or farther from Winters ($128 per month; only $37.50 if you're a resident). A short course that measures under 2,700 yards, it has two sets of tees for 18 holes. Tuesday nights are reserved for the ladies starting at 5:30, and the club hosts a scramble every Wednesday.

The details   915-754-4679. Hwy. 83, Winters, TX 79567

• 9 holes. Par 34. Back – 2,698 (66.8/114). Forward – 2,242. Price - $.

Getting there Travel four miles south of Winters on Hwy. 83.

WINTERS NOTES   In town, find **Casa Cabana** (915-754-5796) for Tex-Mex. Make a weekend out of your trip to Winters by planning around the

---

A golf course is a field of maneuver and action, employing the military and engineering side of the game. It opens up a series of tactical and strategical opportunities, the implications of which it would be well for every golfer to grasp. It is important to emphasize the necessity for the golfer to use his head as much as his hands; or to make his mental agility match his physical ability. H. N. Wethered & Tom Simpson

Chili Superbowl held every Labor Day at the **Perini Ranch Steakhouse** (Buffalo Gap, 915-572-3339). **Motel Winters** has 14 rooms.

NORTHWEST TEXAS BORDER CROSSINGS

When traveling in this part of Texas, don't forget that there are eight courses in southwestern Oklahoma within an hour's drive of other Texas golf towns in our Northwest region.

WALTERS, OK   30 miles from Burkburnett, TX

Tree-lined and executive-like **Lakeside Park Golf Club** (580-875-3829) was upgraded with an additional nine in 1996, bringing the yardage all the way up to 5,146 (70.0/108). They give you 71 strokes to hit this in par, which seems easy because of the lack of bunkers, but it's difficult due to the numerous out-of-bounds areas. No. 7 is the best because it requires a testy tee shot over the drink into a narrow fairway.

FREDERICK, OK   30 miles from Vernon, TX

The **Frederick Golf & Country Club** (580-335-2911) is a rural 9-holer that tips out to a par 36, 3,120 yards and has water on only three holes. The best hole is No. 2, the longest par 4 at 395 yards.

LAWTON, OK   45 miles from Burkburnett, TX

Flat and tree-lined, the 18-hole **Lawton Country Club** (580-353-2073) tips out at a challenging 6,419 yards (70.7/123) and plays to a par 71. They saved the best for last, framing the 18th fairway with lakes.

The **Lawton Municipal Golf Course** (580-353-4493) is an 18-hole track that dates back to the 1950s, when Jack Greer laid out this flat, wide-open course. Greer used mounding to spice it up, but it's generally easy to score since there aren't that many trees. That generosity is compensated for by length—when the wind is blowing, this 7,142-yard (72.9/102), par 72 track can play extremely long. You'll feel that length the most on No. 14, a 600-yarder that plays into a narrowing, uphill fairway lined by out-of-bounds on the right.

Basically, all that matters is that, when you putt in competition, putt freely and with confidence, seeing your target and letting the stroke go. Remember to enjoy putting. Dr. Bob Rotella

ALTUS, OK
36 miles from Vernon, TX

The **Altus Air Force Base Golf Course** (580-481-7207), now an 18-hole, 6,963-yard, par 72 (72.8/120) track after an upgrade in 1997, features generous fairways that are open only to the military.

The **Elks Golf & Country Club** (580-477-0200) is pretty much out in the sticks, but a great spot to take it easy and play small-town 9-hole golf. This one is a par 36 and routes 3,238 yards (35.1/118), and the best hole is No. 6. Bring your fly rod, since there's lots of water and we've heard rumors of legendary bass lurking in the lakes and ponds that frame most holes.

DUNCAN, OK
65 miles from Nocona, TX

The **Duncan Golf & Country Club** (580-255-7706) is a classic—it's considered one of the better courses in Southern Oklahoma because of its great condition and outstanding layout. High dollar but worth it, this course plays 6,450 yards from the tips (par 71, 71.6/124) and you'll encounter plenty of water and bunkers. No. 15 is the butt-pucker hole, lined by water for its 447 yards. You have four shots to make par, and the approach must carry the drink that fronts the green.

Budget-minded hacks can look to the **Twin Oaks Golf Course** (580-252-4714) for a more laid-back, affordable round of golf. This 18-holer is a par 71 that tips out at 6,312 yards, and the best hole is the 200-yard No. 3 that plays uphill. Watch the pin placement, since the green is tough to see and is multilevel.

COMANCHE, OK
54 miles from Nocona, TX

At the **Comanche Golf Course** (580-439-8879) you'll find narrow, tree-lined fairways, zero bunkers, small greens, and water on three holes. The 9-hole route here traverses 3,072 yards, and they spot you 36 holes for par. The best feature of this course is the solid care provided by the owners, who generally keep the course in great condition.

NORTHWEST

CENTRAL TEXAS

> *"And lo, I command you, to getteth in thy car, and pack your clubs in the trunk, and drive to this land of milk and honey known as the Hill Country, for it is your Promised Land. And the golfing people did as they were told, and they saw the land, that it was good, and they rejoiced."*

—J. Stone 4:14

To fully appreciate why native Texans are so ga-ga over their own state, you have to come to Central Texas. With towering oaks, rolling fields, clear springs, limestone cliffs, gnarly ravines and the remainder of Texas squeezing against it, the Hill Country takes no prisoners when it comes to charm. In this land that's mostly free of cowboys, cattle, cotton, and oil, the air feels clean and healthy and the wildflowers seem to bloom more profusely than anywhere else. What's more, given the amount of courses situated near both Austin and San Antonio, this region is rapidly becoming the mecca of Texas golf.

The earliest to get caught up in the charms of the Edwards Plateau and the Balcones Fault were the German immigrants, and the settlements they made here—towns like Boerne, Comfort, Fredericksburg, and New Braunfels—still reflect an Old World Bavarian charm. Oktoberfest is the year's best party in these parts, and joining in are an eclectic array of urban escapees, hopeful artists, rambling college kids, high-tech wizards, and redneck-hippie free spirits. In these days of big cities, Central Texas and the Hill Country remain surprisingly small-town, with I-35 and I-10 the only major thoroughfares slicing through the countryside. Off-the-beaten-path fruit stands, barbecue shacks, dance halls, and wineries still thrive.

One good outcome of the area's recent population explosion is the investment in fabulous resorts and new golf courses. Some of the world's best architects have had a field day with this knobby terrain dominated by legendary oaks, meandering creeks, and unexpected waterfalls. The result is some of the most picturesque and challenging courses in the world.

People think about the yips in the context of putting, but that's nothing compared with chipping and pitching yips. I've seen professionals actually whiff chip shots by hitting the ground eight inches behind the ball. It's a scary thing to see. They're morbidly fascinated by their problem and want to show me again and again and again. Dr. Bob Rotella

CENTRAL

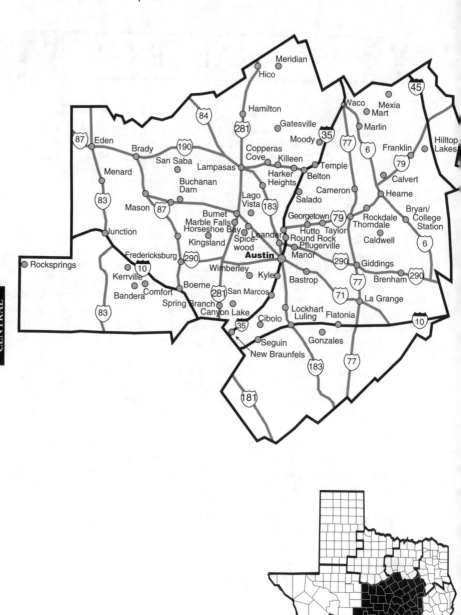

CENTRAL TEXAS
REGIONAL WEATHER

	Average Precipitation	Average Temperature (F)
January	1.71	48.8
February	2.17	52.8
March	1.87	61.5
April	2.56	69.6
May	4.78	75.6
June	3.72	81.3
July	2.05	84.5
August	2.04	84.8
September	3.3	80.2
October	3.43	71.1
November	2.37	60.9
December	1.88	51.6

CENTRAL

Central Texas Mileage

	Austin	Bandera	Bastrop	Belton	Boerne	Brady	Brenham	Bryan-C S	Buchanan	Burnet	Caldwell	Calvert	Cameron	Canyon Lk.	Cibolo	Comfort	Coppe
Austin		109	31	60	85	126	89	94	66	54	71	95	72	61	63	89	6
Bandera	109		128	167	25	116	187	200	104	111	177	204	181	58	61	29	15
Bastrop	31	128		72	104	155	59	73	95	82	50	89	69	78	76	115	9
Belton	60	167	72		143	123	97	80	73	59	64	57	35	120	122	147	28
Boerne	85	25	104	143		109	163	177	92	87	153	180	157	35	41	16	12
Brady	126	116	155	123	109		214	203	69	82	188	180	158	135	151	93	97
Brenham	89	187	59	97	163	214		42	146	133	33	67	62	137	129	174	12
Bryan-CS	94	200	73	80	177	203	42		142	128	23	28	47	151	149	183	10
Buchanan Dam	66	104	95	73	92	69	146	142		13	119	128	101	84	102	77	53
Burnet	54	111	82	59	87	82	133	128	13		106	115	88	80	97	88	40
Caldwell	71	177	50	64	153	188	33	23	119	106		40	30	128	126	160	92
Calvert	95	204	89	57	180	180	67	28	128	115	40		27	156	157	184	84
Cameron	72	181	69	35	157	158	62	47	101	88	30	27		133	134	161	62
Canyon Lake	61	58	78	120	35	135	137	151	84	80	128	156	133		31	51	11
Cibolo	63	61	76	122	41	151	129	149	102	97	126	157	134	31		57	12
Comfort	89	29	115	147	16	93	174	183	77	88	160	184	161	51	57		12
Copperas Cove	67	151	96	28	127	97	124	107	53	40	92	84	62	119	129	127	
Eden	158	129	187	155	135	32	246	235	101	114	220	212	190	165	176	119	12
Flatonia	68	130	38	110	108	193	60	95	133	120	74	113	93	85	69	124	13
Franklin	101	210	95	69	186	192	72	31	136	123	45	12	39	162	163	190	96
Fredericksburg	78	50	106	125	39	71	165	172	54	66	149	172	149	64	80	23	10
Gatesville	94	175	108	36	151	112	128	107	77	64	96	83	66	144	156	152	26
Georgetown	27	134	54	32	110	117	99	93	49	35	70	80	53	88	89	115	47
Giddings	55	153	25	83	129	180	34	54	112	99	31	71	51	103	102	140	11
Goldthwaite	104	142	133	83	131	63	178	156	70	59	145	132	116	138	156	115	56
Gonzales	61	112	50	118	90	182	88	120	123	113	97	137	116	66	51	106	12
Hamilton	113	177	139	68	155	97	159	138	81	68	127	114	98	147	165	149	57
Harker Heights	68	166	82	12	142	112	108	92	68	55	76	69	46	129	130	142	16
Hearne	87	196	81	60	172	183	58	20	123	110	32	9	28	148	149	177	87
Hico	134	198	153	81	176	115	151	102	88	141	123	111	168	185	170	72	
Hilltop Lakes	136	260	126	114	258	243	84	40	173	160	169	42	76	196	227	226	14
Horseshoe bay	51	102	81	77	80	89	140	142	25	18	119	129	102	72	89	80	58
Hutto	24	133	38	46	109	133	85	82	64	51	59	71	48	85	86	113	62
Junction	138	77	166	167	83	60	225	232	94	107	209	222	196	118	124	67	14
Kerrville	102	26	130	149	34	91	196		79	90	173	197	174	68	75	18	13
Killeen	69	162	86	15	138	108	112	95	64	51	80	72	50	130	131	139	12
Kingsland	59	104	89	78	85	71	148	147	7	19	125	134	107	77	95	77	58
Kyle	21	90	40	80	66	141	99	113	81	74	90	116	93	41	42	77	88
La Grange	62	152	32	103	130	186	38	73	126	113	52	91	71	106	90	143	12
Lago Vista	33	126	62	61	103	112	112	116	48	41	93	105	81	92	95	103	59
Lampasas	67	133	96	46	109	78	142	126	35	22	110	103	80	102	119	110	19
Leander	25	129	53	44	105	111	104	104	42	29	81	92	65	84	87	109	42
Llano	73	88	103	89	77	53	162	158	16	29	135	144	118	89	106	61	69
Lockhart	29	99	31	86	75	150	91	104	90	81	81	118	94	49	48	86	94
Luling	43	98	39	100	76	164	93	112	105	95	89	128	108	53	37	92	109
Manor	14	122	29	59	99	139	75	81	71	58	58	83	60	74	76	103	71
Marble Falls	46	98	76	72	75	84	135	137	20	13	114	124	97	67	84	75	53
Marlin	103	210	105	44	186	167	95	57	116	103	67	28	37	164	165	190	71
Mart	117	225	124	59	201	170	115	77	131	117	87	48	58	178	180	205	84
Mason	107	88	137	123	81	29	196	192	50	63	169	178	151	106	122	65	10
Menard	145	107	174	157	113	34	233	229	87	101	206	214	189	144	154	97	13
Meridian	127	211	139	68	189	131	156	130	115	101	124	101	94	181	189	183	71
Mexia	141	248	142	82	224	191	120	81	154	141	93	53	74	202	203	229	10
Moody	78	185	90	18	161	138	110	85	91	78	78	57	49	139	140	165	44
New Braunfels	48	65	64	107	41	142	123	137	92	87	114	142	119	18	16	57	11
Pflugerville	16	124	43	48	101	131	92	91	63	49	69	80	57	76	78	105	63
Rockdale	58	167	53	49	143	162	58	48	94	80	26	37	17	119	120	147	76
Rocksprings	174	100	202	213	107	106	261	268	141	154	245	269	242	142	149	91	19
Round Rock	18	125	46	41	102	125	94	91	56	43	68	80	57	79	80	106	56
Salado	51	158	66	9	134	129	104	88	64	50	72	65	43	112	113	138	34
San Marcos	30	81	47	89	57	140	106	120	89	83	96	125	102	31	33	68	97
San Saba	104	121	132	82	109	41	179	162	48	59	147	139	117	121	138	93	56
Seguin	53	78	61	112	56	157	114	134	106	101	111	147	124	33	17	72	119
Spicewood	36	105	63	98	83	128	127	149	35	28	127	138	117	64	92	80	68
Spring Branch	66	52	94	128	28	130	157	180	73	66	157	168	147	21	39	46	10
Taylor	33	141	34	38	118	138	79	74	69	56	51	62	39	93	95	122	64
Temple	66	173	74	7	150	130	94	73	79	66	62	50	32	127	128	154	35
Thorndale	45	154	46	46	130	150	71	61	82	68	38	50	27	106	107	134	73
Waco	100	207	106	41	183	150	111	84	113	99	79	56	50	161	162	187	65
Wimberley	37	79	59	95	55	128	118	131	78	72	108	132	109	27	41	62	100

Central Texas Mileage

Flatonia	Franklin	Frederick.	Gatesville	Georgetn	Giddings	Goldthwaite	Gonzales	Hamilton	Harker Hgts.	Hearne	Hico	Hilltop Lakes	Horseshoe Bay	Hutto	Junction	Kerrville
68	101	78	94	27	55	104	61	113	68	87	134	136	51	24	138	102
130	210	50	175	134	153	142	112	177	166	196	198	260	102	133	77	26
38	95	106	108	54	25	133	50	139	82	81	153	126	81	38	166	130
110	69	125	36	32	83	83	118	68	12	60	81	114	77	46	167	149
108	186	39	151	110	129	131	90	155	142	172	176	258	80	109	83	34
193	192	71	112	117	180	63	182	97	112	183	115	243	89	133	60	91
60	72	165	128	99	34	178	88	159	108	58	173	84	140	85	225	189
95	31	172	107	93	54	156	120	138	92	20	151	40	142	82	232	196
133	136	54	77	49	112	70	123	81	68	123	102	173	25	64	94	79
120	123	66	64	35	99	59	113	68	55	110	88	160	18	51	107	90
74	45	149	96	70	31	145	97	127	76	32	141	169	119	59	209	173
113	12	172	83	80	71	132	137	114	69	9	123	42	129	71	222	197
93	39	149	66	53	51	116	116	98	46	28	111	76	102	48	196	174
85	162	64	144	88	103	138	66	147	129	148	168	196	72	85	118	68
69	163	80	156	89	102	156	51	165	130	149	185	227	89	86	124	75
124	190	23	128	115	140	115	106	149	142	177	170	226	80	113	67	18
134	96	105	26	47	110	56	127	57	16	87	72	142	58	62	147	130
225	224	101	143	149	213	94	213	129	144	215	145	290	121	165	53	103
119	119	127	89	88	76	138	142	120	81	13	129	30	137	77	230	202
127	178	147	130	97	138	92	28	178	121	105	192	156	118	77	187	142
147	89	130	69	115	49	153	127	142	127	87	148	240	58	102	60	24
92	88	97	115	66	84	86	92	171	120	165	46	119	83	83	171	154
42	76	131	49	149	149	67	146	153	81	74	113	125	49	16	143	121
171	138	92	83	84	164	35	164	32	95	63	160	107	106	51	191	155
28	142	111	153	67	67	164	35	146	127	136	56	200	77	99	122	117
178	120	127	32	146	35	172	172	127	73	129	193	186	113	83	172	124
121	81	120	42	41	71	127	73	118	73	118	21	160	80	108	157	151
105	13	165	87	74	63	136	129	72	118	72	88	127	72	57	162	145
192	129	148	46	113	160	56	193	21	88	131	131	43	123	63	217	189
156	30	240	119	125	107	200	186	160	127	43	149	149	106	128	175	172
118	137	58	83	49	106	77	113	85	72	123	106	172	172	108	305	238
77	77	102	83	16	51	99	83	108	57	63	128	108	64	64	114	82
187	230	60	171	143	191	122	172	157	162	217	175	305	114	158	158	126
142	202	24	154	121	155	117	124	151	145	189	172	238	82	126	51	51
124	84	117	39	42	98	67	128	69	4	75	84	133	69	57	158	141
126	142	54	83	54	114	73	116	86	73	128	107	180	18	69	97	78
60	122	76	115	48	66	125	49	134	89	108	155	155	66	45	137	94
22	97	137	135	85	20	164	50	166	114	83	180	128	112	70	197	160
100	110	81	86	29	78	96	93	105	66	97	126	142	33	34	137	105
134	115	88	42	47	113	37	127	46	34	106	66	162	40	62	129	112
91	98	90	69	12	70	79	84	88	49	85	109	133	42	22	136	115
140	152	38	93	65	128	54	130	89	84	139	109	255	36	80	78	63
43	123	87	121	54	57	131	32	140	95	110	161	164	76	50	148	103
34	134	93	135	68	65	146	18	155	109	120	175	179	90	65	154	109
67	89	91	96	29	41	108	67	117	70	75	138	118	65	21	152	115
113	132	53	77	44	101	72	103	80	67	118	101	170	4	59	109	77
131	35	168	55	76	88	104	154	86	55	37	96	53	120	80	210	193
151	55	183	58	90	108	107	174	87	70	57	89	61	135	98	225	207
169	186	42	127	99	162	82	154	117	118	173	138	280	70	114	44	62
207	224	80	146	136	199	96	191	131	145	210	149	275	108	151	31	82
178	108	161	44	100	145	69	186	34	79	110	24	127	119	114	191	185
166	55	207	79	114	124	128	190	107	94	62	105	66	159	119	248	231
129	63	144	26	51	97	75	137	57	29	65	71	82	95	65	185	168
67	148	72	141	74	89	146	49	155	116	135	175	188	79	71	124	75
81	86	93	85	16	58	100	74	108	57	73	129	116	60	9	153	117
77	43	135	80	45	35	126	100	111	60	30	125	73	94	34	188	160
215	274	96	218	189	227	169	197	204	209	261	221	330	154	198	47	74
84	86	94	78	9	60	93	77	101	50	72	122	117	56	9	150	118
104	78	116	45	24	78	88	109	76	18	69	90	124	69	39	158	140
58	130	69	124	57	72	134	42	143	98	117	164	151	69	54	129	85
170	151	71	71	83	149	22	162	56	71	142	77	230	75	99	101	95
54	153	86	146	79	87	157	33	165	121	139	186	195	94	76	139	90
111	143	58	105	65	93	87	95	96	84	130	117	157	20	65	122	83
95	174	60	143	95	123	125	79	133	121	160	155	229	58	95	116	64
72	68	110	75	21	46	104	84	106	49	55	120	98	69	9	163	134
112	62	132	34	39	80	84	124	66	19	53	79	108	84	48	174	156
82	56	123	77	33	40	117	96	108	57	42	122	86	82	21	176	147
143	62	165	38	73	100	88	156	68	52	64	69	83	117	80	207	190
73	138	58	126	63	84	131	57	140	104	125	161	176	65	61	118	79

Central Texas Mileage

	Killeen	Kingsland	Kyle	La Grange	Lago Vista	Lampasas	Leander	Llano	Lockhart	Luling	Manor	Marble Falls	Marlin	Mart	Mason	Menard
Austin	69	59	21	62	33	67	25	73	29	43	14	46	103	117	107	145
Bandera	162	104	90	152	126	133	129	88	99	98	122	98	210	225	88	107
Bastrop	86	89	40	32	62	96	53	103	31	39	29	76	105	124	137	174
Belton	15	78	80	103	61	46	44	89	86	100	59	72	44	59	123	157
Boerne	138	85	66	130	103	109	105	77	75	76	99	75	186	201	81	113
Brady	108	71	141	186	112	78	111	53	150	164	139	84	167	170	29	34
Brenham	112	148	99	38	112	142	104	162	91	93	75	135	95	115	196	233
Bryan-CS	95	147	113	73	116	126	104	158	104	112	81	137	57	77	192	229
Buchanan Dam	64	7	81	126	48	35	42	16	90	105	71	20	116	131	50	87
Burnet	51	19	74	113	41	22	29	29	81	95	58	13	103	117	63	101
Caldwell	80	125	90	52	93	110	81	135	81	89	58	114	67	87	169	206
Calvert	72	134	116	91	105	103	92	144	118	128	83	124	28	48	178	214
Cameron	50	107	93	71	81	80	65	118	94	108	60	97	37	58	151	189
Canyon Lake	130	77	41	106	92	102	84	89	49	53	74	67	164	178	106	144
Cibolo	131	95	42	90	95	119	87	106	48	37	76	84	165	180	122	154
Comfort	139	77	77	143	103	110	109	61	86	92	103	75	190	205	65	97
Copperas Cove	12	58	88	127	59	19	42	69	94	109	71	53	71	84	103	130
Eden	140	103	173	218	144	110	143	85	182	195	171	116	198	201	59	22
Flatonia	124	126	60	22	100	134	91	140	43	34	67	113	131	151	169	207
Franklin	84	142	122	97	110	115	98	152	123	134	89	132	35	55	186	224
Fredericksburg	117	54	76	137	81	88	90	38	87	93	91	53	168	183	42	80
Gatesville	39	83	115	135	86	42	69	93	121	135	96	77	55	58	127	146
Georgetown	42	54	48	85	29	47	12	65	54	68	29	44	76	90	99	136
Giddings	98	114	66	20	78	113	70	128	57	65	41	101	88	108	162	199
Goldthwaite	67	73	125	164	96	37	79	54	131	146	108	72	104	107	82	96
Gonzales	128	116	49	50	93	127	84	130	32	18	67	103	154	174	154	191
Hamilton	69	86	134	166	105	46	88	89	140	155	117	80	86	87	117	131
Harker Heights	4	73	89	114	66	34	49	84	95	109	70	67	55	70	118	145
Hearne	75	128	108	83	97	106	85	139	110	120	75	118	37	57	173	210
Hico	84	107	155	180	126	66	109	109	161	175	138	101	96	89	138	149
Hilltop Lakes	133	180	155	128	142	162	133	255	164	179	118	170	53	61	280	275
Horseshoe bay	69	18	66	112	33	40	42	36	76	90	65	4	120	135	70	108
Hutto	57	69	45	70	34	62	22	80	50	65	21	59	80	98	114	151
Junction	158	97	137	197	137	129	136	78	148	154	152	109	210	225	44	31
Kerrville	141	78	94	160	105	112	115	63	103	109	115	77	193	207	62	82
Killeen		70	90	117	63	30	46	80	95	110	71	64	59	74	114	142
Kingsland	70		74	120	41	41	48	19	83	98	72	13	121	136	53	90
Kyle	90	74		71	54	88	46	88	17	31	34	61	124	138	119	156
La Grange	117	120	71		93	127	84	134	57	55	60	107	108	129	168	205
Lago Vista	63	41	54	93		59	17	59	60	75	37	28	104	119	93	131
Lampasas	30	41	88	127	59		43	51	95	109	71	35	89	99	85	111
Leander	46	48	46	84	17	43		58	52	66	29	37	88	102	92	130
Llano	80	19	88	134	59	51	58		97	112	87	31	132	147	34	71
Lockhart	95	83	17	57	60	95	52	97		15	35	71	128	144	129	167
Luling	110	98	31	55	75	109	66	112	15		49	85	142	158	136	173
Manor	71	72	34	60	37	71	29	87	35	49		60	93	111	121	158
Marble Falls	64	13	61	107	28	35	37	31	71	85	60		115	130	65	103
Marlin	59	121	124	108	104	89	88	132	128	142	93	115		21	166	201
Mart	74	136	138	129	119	99	102	147	144	158	111	130	21		181	203
Mason	114	53	119	168	93	85	92	34	129	136	121	65	166	181		38
Menard	142	90	156	205	131	111	130	71	167	173	158	103	201	203	38	
Meridian	97	160	162	144	143	121	126	170	167	181	132	154	39	29	204	225
Moody	33	97	99	117	79	63	63	107	104	119	78	91	29	41	141	172
New Braunfels	116	85	27	88	80	109	72	96	35	35	61	74	150	165	114	151
Pflugerville	58	68	36	74	30	63	21	79	42	56	17	55	89	106	113	150
Rockdale	64	99	79	55	68	90	56	110	81	92	46	89	54	74	143	181
Rocksprings	205	143	168	233	177	176	183	125	176	183	187	149	257	271	91	78
Round Rock	51	62	39	77	25	56	14	72	45	59	20	51	85	99	106	144
Salado	22	69	72	97	52	51	33	80	77	92	53	63	52	67	114	151
San Marcos	99	82	10	75	63	97	55	94	18	24	43	70	133	147	111	149
San Saba	67	51	120	163	92	37	79	32	130	144	108	64	126	128	61	75
Seguin	121	99	32	75	85	120	77	110	34	22	66	89	155	170	128	166
Spicewood	80	27	51	113	44	50	46	42	62	77	52	15	142	159	100	149
Spring Branch	118	65	54	123	81	88	87	75	63	62	82	53	173	251	103	143
Taylor	52	75	53	65	42	67	30	85	56	70	21	64	72	90	119	157
Temple	22	85	87	101	68	53	51	95	93	107	61	79	37	51	129	164
Thorndale	61	87	66	60	55	80	43	98	68	82	33	77	63	83	132	169
Waco	56	118	121	121	101	80	84	129	126	141	93	112	28	20	163	184
Wimberley	103	71	19	90	66	94	57	82	33	39	51	60	138	153	100	137

Central Texas Mileage

Moody	New Braun	Pflugervi	Rockdale	Rockspri	Round Rock	Salado	San Marcos	San Saba	Seguin	Spicewood	Spring Branch	Taylor	Temple	Thorndale	Waco	Wimberley
78	48	16	58	174	18	51	104	30	53	36	66	33	66	45	100	37
185	65	124	167	100	125	158	121	81	78	105	52	141	173	154	207	79
90	64	43	53	202	46	66	132	47	61	63	94	34	74	46	106	59
18	107	48	49	213	41	9	82	89	112	98	128	38	7	46	41	95
161	41	101	143	107	102	134	109	57	56	83	28	118	150	130	183	55
138	142	131	162	106	125	129	41	140	157	128	130	138	130	150	150	128
110	123	92	58	261	94	104	179	106	114	127	157	79	94	71	111	118
85	137	91	48	268	91	88	162	120	134	149	180	74	73	61	84	131
91	92	63	94	141	56	64	48	89	106	35	73	69	79	82	113	78
78	87	49	80	154	43	50	59	83	101	28	66	56	66	68	99	72
78	114	69	26	245	68	72	147	96	111	127	157	51	62	38	79	108
57	142	80	37	269	80	65	139	125	147	138	168	62	50	50	56	132
49	119	57	17	242	57	43	117	102	124	117	147	32	27	27	50	109
139	18	76	119	142	79	112	121	31	33	64	21	93	127	106	161	27
140	16	78	120	149	80	113	138	33	17	92	39	95	128	107	162	41
165	57	105	147	91	106	138	93	68	72	80	46	122	154	134	187	62
44	115	63	76	194	56	34	56	97	119	68	105	64	35	73	65	100
169	173	164	194	99	157	161	73	170	187	160	165	170	162	182	182	159
129	67	81	77	215	84	104	170	58	54	111	95	72	112	82	143	73
63	148	86	43	274	86	78	151	130	153	143	174	68	62	56	62	138
144	72	93	135	96	94	116	71	69	86	58	60	110	132	123	165	58
26	141	85	80	218	78	45	71	124	146	105	143	75	34	77	38	126
51	74	16	45	189	9	24	83	57	79	65	95	21	39	33	73	63
97	89	58	35	227	60	78	149	72	87	93	123	46	80	40	100	84
75	146	100	126	169	93	88	22	134	157	87	125	104	84	117	88	131
137	49	74	100	197	77	109	162	42	33	95	79	84	124	96	156	57
57	155	108	111	204	101	76	56	143	165	96	133	106	66	108	68	140
29	116	57	60	209	50	18	71	98	121	84	121	49	19	57	52	104
65	135	73	30	261	72	69	142	117	139	130	160	55	53	42	64	125
71	175	129	125	221	122	90	77	164	186	117	155	120	79	122	69	161
82	188	116	73	330	117	124	151	230	195	157	229	98	108	86	83	176
95	79	60	94	154	56	69	69	75	94	20	58	69	84	82	117	65
65	71	9	34	198	9	39	99	54	76	65	95	9	48	21	80	61
185	124	153	188	47	150	158	101	129	139	122	116	163	174	176	207	118
168	75	117	160	74	118	140	95	85	90	83	64	134	156	147	190	79
33	116	58	64	205	51	22	67	99	121	80	118	52	22	61	56	103
97	85	68	99	143	62	69	51	82	99	27	65	75	85	87	118	71
99	27	36	79	168	39	72	120	10	32	51	54	53	87	66	121	19
117	88	74	55	233	77	97	163	75	75	113	123	65	101	60	121	90
79	80	30	68	177	25	52	92	63	85	44	81	42	68	55	101	66
63	109	63	90	176	56	51	37	97	120	50	88	67	53	80	80	94
63	72	21	56	183	14	35	79	55	77	46	87	30	51	43	84	57
107	96	79	110	125	72	80	32	94	110	42	75	85	95	98	129	82
104	35	42	81	176	45	77	130	18	34	62	63	70	107	82	141	39
119	35	56	92	183	59	92	144	24	22	77	62	64	79	77	112	60
78	61	17	46	187	20	53	108	43	66	52	82	72	37	63	28	138
91	74	55	89	149	51	63	64	70	89	15	53	90	51	83	20	153
29	150	89	54	257	85	52	126	133	155	142	173	72	126	133	100	138
41	165	106	74	271	99	67	128	147	170	159	251	90	128	147	184	153
141	114	113	143	91	106	114	61	111	128	100	103	119	132	163	100	100
172	151	150	181	78	144	151	75	149	166	149	143	157	164	169	184	137
49	174	116	111	237	109	77	90	157	179	129	167	106	66	109	47	163
65	188	128	90	295	123	91	150	171	193	184	254	111	75	101	42	177
125		63	105	149	66	98	128	18	15	77	29	80	114	92	147	26
67	63		43	189	7	39	99	45	68	54	84	18	55	30	88	53
62	105	43		232	43	46	126	88	110	100	131	25	46	13	66	95
232	149	189	232		190	204	147	158	164	169	162	206	220	219	253	152
60	66	7	43	190		32	92	48	70	57	87	18	48	30	81	54
27	98	39	46	204	32		88	80	103	90	120	32	16	41	49	86
108	18	45	88	158	48	88		126	23	61	45	62	96	75	130	15
97	128	99	126	147	92	88	126		143	85	125	104	89	117	109	114
130	15	68	110	164	70	103	143	23		82	42	85	119	97	152	38
126	77	54	100	169	57	90	85	61	82		57	73	105	88	138	39
156	29	84	131	162	87	120	125	45	42	57		104	135	118	169	28
57	80	18	25	206	18	32	104	62	85	73	104		40	13	72	70
17	114	55	46	220	48	16	89	96	119	105	135	40		43	33	102
59	92	30	13	219	30	41	117	75	97	88	118	13	43		75	82
23	147	88	66	253	81	49	109	130	152	138	169	72	33	75		135
113	26	53	95	152	54	86	114	15	38	39	28	70	102	82	135	

AUSTIN
Elev. 550 Pop. 552,434

Though Spanish missionaries were a fleeting presence in the area around 1730, the town of Waterloo got its start in 1838 when a trader named Jake Harrell set up camp on the banks of the Colorado River. Other settlers joined him, a stockade was built, and Republic of Texas Vice President Mirabeau Bonaparte Lamar, a friend of Harrell's, came by for a buffalo shoot and liked the looks of the place. When Lamar became president, he decided to change the name of the town to Austin and make it the capital. The University of Texas started in 1883 and Austin remained a university and government town until the high-tech migration began in the mid-60s with Tracor and Texas Instruments, followed by hundreds of other tech firms over the years.

Say what you like about Austin—there's always something to do in this city where high-tech center, state capital, university town, and Live Music Capital of the World all come together. Even with the recent dot-com bust there's still plenty of techies to be found—in terms of per capita Internet connections, Austin is considered one of the most wired cities in the country. From the funkiness of South Austin to the midtown university scene to the high-tech corridors up north, this town is an amazing combination of historic and modern, laid-back and hustle-bustle, redneck and bohemian, all brought together in a beautiful setting of old oaks, clear lakes, rivers, rolling hills, and plenty of golf to go along with it.

CENTRAL

AUSTIN COUNTRY CLUB

The golf   Back around 1900, when the greater Austin area was only home to about 25,000 residents, Harvard Law School graduate and lifetime Austinite Lewis Hancock organized one of Texas' first formal country clubs, the venerable Austin Country Club.

The first 9-hole course, now known as Hancock Park, featured sand greens and a tiny two-room framed clubhouse. The club stayed put for half a century, noted for the presence of Harvey Penick. Then after a huge local debate, the facility was moved to Riverside Drive in East Austin. From there it made it another 35 years before moving to its current Davenport Ranch location.

The current ACC layout, designed by Pete Dye, rests on the shores of Lake Austin and the Colorado River. Dye didn't veer from his usual method of creating an impressively difficult track using his trademark railroad ties, deep pot bunkers, and huge undulations.

The opening holes play along Lake Austin, and are more of a links-style design. Afterwards the Hill Country takes effect, featuring canyons, ravines, creeks, and unbelievable views.

The back nine features many outstanding holes, including the 446-yard No. 11, which deceptively doglegs left along a canyon before requiring an approach over that same deep ravine. The par 3 No. 16 also stands out, featuring a long carry over another canyon.

You should want to hit the ball as far as you can; don't be ashamed of that. Davis Love, Jr.

The details   512-328-0030. 4408 Long Champ Dr., Austin, TX 78746

- www.austincountryclub.com
- 1899. 18 holes. Par 72. Back – 6,848 (73.5/135). Middle – 6,371 (71.1/126). Forward – 5,060 (69.1/120). Price - $$$.

Getting there The course is just east of Loop 360 and south of the lake. Take the Westlake Dr. exit and the entrance to the club is immediately on the left.

AVERY RANCH GOLF CLUB

The golf   Avery Ranch is one of Austin's newest courses–it's part of the Avery Ranch residential community, 20 minutes northwest of town, that was carved and blasted out of the rocky ranchlands along Brushy Creek. This historically significant area was once home to Indians and robbers, who were drawn to this beautiful setting thick with dense oaks, meandering creeks, and abundant wildlife.

The course was designed by former Jack Nicklaus designer Andy Raugust, who literally had to use dynamite to blast rock out of the landscape for five holes. His design features two potential signature holes on each nine.

No. 7 doglegs left, and features two scenic carries–one off the tee and another on the approach. The hole is rather short, providing the chance to be in good position for this most spectacular approach shot on the course. Staring at the multi-level green, you'll notice the huge rock wall fronting the green, the large bunker to the right, and the native cacti to the rear.

Hole 13 is sure to be considered one of the best par 3s in the area. The 161-yard par 3 features water on the right side, impressive, towering oaks in the back, and a unique ridge of rocks to the right of the green. The reasonable distance makes it a fun challenge, and the hole features a bail-out area in case of a miss.

The details   512-248-2442. 10500 Avery Club Dr., Austin, TX 78717

- www.averyranch.com
- Black (73.5/134). Gold (71.9/133). Blue (70.8/129). White (68.0/119). Green – N/A. Price - $$$.

Getting there From Austin, travel north on I-35 to Parmer Ln. Take Parmer Ln. west approximately 8 miles and the entrance to Avery Ranch is on your right. Follow the signs to the golf course.

BALCONES COUNTRY CLUB

The golf   Originally located in a remote part of the Hill Country that has now been absorbed by the Austin city limits, the BCC dates back to 1956 when it was only a 9-hole layout. Today the club boasts two totally distinct tracks, known as the Balcones Course and the Spicewood Course.

The original 9-holer transformed into the easier **Balcones Course**. With water on only two holes (15 and 16), it's just a friendlier layout that is enjoyable also because it plays fast. The signature hole is No. 6, a 456-yard par 4 highlighted by a magnificent old oak tree in the fairway.

In 1978 the club opened the more challenging **Spicewood Course**, featuring spectacular views amongst the more frequent elevation changes. On the front nine No. 3 is fun, featuring a tricky tee shot through a tunnel of oaks and a creek that cuts across the fairway. On the back, No. 11 is tough because of its 595 yards–virtually impossible to get there in two, and sometimes tough to get there in regulation.

The details   512-258-2775. 8600 Balcones Club Dr., Austin, TX 78750

- www.balconescountryclub.com

- Balcones Course (Old Course): 1961. Bill Cotton. 18 holes. Par 70. Back – 6,360 (69.9/114). Middle – 5,995 (67.9/111). Forward – Par 72. 5,128 (69.0/118). Price - $$$.

- Spicewood Course: 1970s. 18 holes. Par 72. Back – 6,769 (71.8/116). Middle – 6,331 (69.9/113). Forward – Par 73. 5,631 (71.5/121). Price - $$$.

Getting there From I-35 north, take Hwy. 183 north and take a right on Hunter's Chase Rd. Turn left, drive a little ways, and the course is on your left.

BARTON CREEK RESORT

The golf   The self-proclaimed "Golf Capital of Texas" is not only the premier golf destination in the state, but one of the most outstanding golf destinations in the world. Four championship golf courses grace the property of this four-star resort that is located just 20 minutes west of downtown Austin.

Palmer Lakeside Course   The former Hidden Hills Country Club opened in 1986, but was taken over by Barton Creek in 1989 and actually resides 25 miles west of the resort itself. The Arnold Palmer-designed course overlooks Lake Travis, with plenty of panoramic views of the lake and surrounding countryside.

While Palmer's design is surprisingly flat considering the terrain, No. 1 is an anomaly as it drops over 70 feet down to a tree-lined fairway. The remainder of the front is dominated by holes that require forced carries, including holes 2-4 that all force shots over water hazards. No. 3 plays 162 yards over water, and No. 4 doglegs downhill over water off the tee. Hole 6 is 565 yards, but No. 7 is the toughest hole, playing 403 yards, doglegging right into a canyon off the tee, and forcing a lay-up. The longish approach must carry the canyon to a green surrounded by trees.

The forced carries continue on the back, highlighted by the popular 201-yard No. 11, considered one of the most beautiful holes in Texas with its sce-

---

It often happens in match play when you least expect it. Don't get rattled when it does. Tom Watson

nic tee shot over a pond and creek-lined fairway. The view on No. 14 is nice as well, and you'll have the added bonus of being able to choose which green to hit into (the one on the right is shorter but the target is smaller).

The 17th is the last of Palmer's five par 3s, and carries 163 yards over water. The 18th is interesting because of the blind approach shot.

For excursions to Barton Creek, don't forget about Lakeside. If you've been tortured by being holed up at the resort for a few days, it's worthwhile to make the road trip into Spicewood for the day.

Crenshaw Cliffside Course Unlike the flashier Fazio Course, Crenshaw's work at Barton Creek typifies his traditionalist style, a tribute to his dedication as one of the game's great historians. There's more of a natural feel to playing on his courses, and more pure golf enjoyment for the layman because he actually has a chance to hit the wide fairways and monstrous greens.

In fact, the highlight of the Crenshaw course is the massive greens, which make it easier to reach in regulation, but often leave you with putts of 100 feet or more.

The Hill Country views, while not as dramatic as on the Fazio layout, are still prevalent on this track. The most scenic is the 125-yard No. 17, which plays over a huge valley into a green that slopes toward the drop-off.

Fazio Foothills Course This Fazio course features cliff-lined fairways, along with natural caves and waterfalls. Without delving into the monotonous details, suffice to say that Foothills is one of Texas' most highly acclaimed courses, receiving nationwide attention for its scenic layout that has often been called one of the top places to play in America.

Established in 1986, this course ranks at the top of all experts' lists. *Golfweek Magazine* rates the Foothills among America's 40 Best Resort Courses. The course is also named the Best Resort Course in Texas and has the distinction of consistently having several holes listed among the State's Best or Most Beautiful holes (holes 9, 10, 11, 16, and 18) recognized by The *Dallas Morning News.*

Fazio Canyons Course The newest addition to the Barton Creek golf mecca is known as The Canyons, a tipped-out 7,161-yard, par 72 Tom Fazio masterpiece that is actually 2 miles from the resort's clubhouse. Environmentally friendly like the other three tracks, this one was designated as a Certified Audubon Sanctuary System (one of the first in the country), which speaks to the level of care that went into preserving the natural environment.

At Fazio's disposal was the Short Springs Branch Creek, a scenic, limestone-bedded feature that rolls through the course and enhances the oak- and sycamore-laden fairways. The views on this one are just as tremendous as the others, and the golf community has already heaped heavy praise on the Canyons. *Golfweek Magazine* labeled it the No. 1 Course in Texas for 2002.

The ender is the signature—a 561-yarder that might be the best finishing

---

Even before you step up to the ball, have a full battle plan for the hole worked out. Arnold Palmer

hole at Barton Creek. The most difficult hole finishes off the front side, a 457-yard par 4.

The details   512-329-4000. 8212 Barton Club Dr., Austin, TX 78735

- www.bartoncreek.com
- Crenshaw Cliffside: Crenshaw-Coore. 18 holes. Par 71. Gold – 6,553 (71.0/124). Red – 4,850 (67.2/110). Price - $$$$.
- Palmer Lakeside: 1986. Arnold Palmer. 18 holes. Par 71. Gold – 6,668 (71.0/124). Red – 5,067. Price - $$$$.
- Fazio Foothills: 1986. Tom Fazio. 18 holes Par 72. Black – 6,956 (74.0/135). Red – 5,207 (70/124). Price - $$$$.
- Fazio Canyons: Tom Fazio. 18 holes. Par 72. Pro – 7,161. Black – 6,690. Gold – 6,370. Red – 5,078. Price - $$$$.

Getting there From I-35 south, take Hwy. 71 west (Ben White) and look for the entrance on the left side of the highway.

BLUEBONNET HILL GOLF COURSE

The golf   This course, designed by Jeff Brauer and opened in 1991, offers one of the more enjoyable experiences for the average golfer. The par 72 layout is only 6,500 yards and is void of trees, making it more of a links-style course. Mounding is prominent around the multi-tiered greens, making it difficult for ups and downs after approach miscues.

Two holes stand out, both on the back nine. The par 5 No. 12 is reachable in two at only 488 yards, but water guards the landing area off the tee and the green has three levels. No. 17 is a fun par 3, playing 195 yards over a lake.

Remember that the trick to Bluebonnet is the greens. Pay attention to the pin placements and try to find the right level of the green.

The details   512-272-4228. 9100 Decker Ln., Austin, TX 78724

- 1991. Jeff Brauer. 18 holes. Par 72. Back – 6,503 (70.0/113). Middle – 6,033 (67.7/105). Forward – 5,241 (69.4/115). Price - $$.

Getting there From 290 going west get off at the Decker Ln. exit, and drive about 1.5 miles to the course.

BUTLER PARK PITCH AND PUTT

The golf   Austinite Douglas Kinser approached the city in the late 1940s about improving the poor condition of the land occupied by the former Butler Brick Company. His wish was granted, and from the former clay mine he created a lush little 9-hole course that now graces a serene, landscaped setting just south of Town Lake. You can still see where the mine walls dropped down, as

Your arms should hang under your shoulders and feel relaxed. Your wrists will already be semi-cocked, so you can simply maintain that wrist cock as you swing back. Your hands are closer to your body for leverage. Tom Watson

holes 1 and 2 play down into the mine bottom. The design is simple and most of the holes require only a wedge. This includes the signature No. 7, which involves a pitch shot over a pond that fronts the green.

The central location of the course is ideal, making it the perfect place to kill some time on one of those outstanding spring days in Austin. Barton Springs, South Lamar, and downtown are all within a few minutes driving distance, so you definitely have plenty of post-round entertainment options. The green fee is $6, and the historic old clubhouse boasts a Hole-in-One Wall of Fame, old clubs in case you need to borrow a wedge and putter, and remnants of a shady murder that occurred in the shop in 1951.

The details   512-477-4430. 201 Lee Barton Dr., Austin, Texas 78704

• 1940s. Winston Kinzer. 9 holes. Par 27. 805 yards. Price - $.

Getting there From downtown Austin, take I-35 to Riverside Dr. and go right. Turn left on Lee Barton Dr. The course is 3 miles down on your left.

CEDARS OF BERGSTROM GOLF COURSE

The golf   When Bergstrom Air Force Base was shut down in 1993, the property was sold to the city of Austin, who subsequently went about renovating the 1960s Ralph Plummer design in conjunction with the new Austin airport.

The course isn't overly difficult, making it the perfect municipal track with its wide-open fairways and lack of hazards (only one water hazard). The new design plays 6,576 yards from the blue tees; it features long par 5s and five particularly difficult par 3s. The back nine is longer, and considered the more difficult of the two sides.

The feature hole is No. 12, a 560-yard behemoth that offers one of the better views on the course.

The details   512-530-4653. 10326 Golf Course Rd., Austin, TX 78719

• 1960s. Ralph Plummer. Par 71. 6,576 yards. Driving range, chipping green, and putting green. Back – 6,576 (69.5/115). Middle – 6,079 (67.6/109). Forward – 5,300 (70.5/116). Price - $$.

Getting there From I-35 south, take Hwy. 71 east to the Bergstrom Air Force Base exit. Turn right into the base and ask the guard for directions.

CIRCLE C COUNTRY CLUB

The golf   After years of construction delays and environmental hassles, Circle C's Jay Morrish design finally opened in 1993 just 20 minutes south of downtown Austin. Considered one of the best public courses in Austin, golfers are drawn to the Circle's proximity to the city, as well as the serene setting that

A good golf course is like good music or good anything else. It is not necessarily a course which appeals the first time one plays it, but one which grows on the player the more frequently they visit it. Dr. Alister Mackenzie

is void of houses.

Morrish's design is also popular because of its mostly flat, wide-open layout, which makes it fair for the laboring hack who struggles to keep it in the fairway. The generous fairways are lined with beautiful oaks, and the large, undulating greens provide welcome targets. Water isn't a big factor, coming into play on only 4 or 5 holes.

On the front, No. 3 is one of the only respites from the trees, but has a ravine lining the left side of the 193 yards of fairway and bunkers. Hole 4 is a tough par because it goes 446 yards, but No. 7 is rated the most difficult, playing 542 yards.

The back nine is known for its numerous doglegs. Every hole (even the par 3s) bends at least a little on the back, giving the advantage to shot-makers over long knockers. No. 11 stands out because of its 513-yard double dogleg that actually offers a decent birdie opportunity if you play it smart. Hole 13 is a nice hole, playing 168 yards over water, and it's followed by perhaps the most difficult hole on the course: the 591-yard No. 14. Your tee shot must be "pured" on 14 to put yourself in good position to attack the remainder of this long dogleg right.

Toward the very end of the round you'll finally have to face the water, with Nos. 16-18 all involving water hazards. Morrish didn't leave any room for error on the 200-yard-plus 16th hole, which requires a perfect tee shot to avoid a big number. The ender is the best hole, playing 386 yards with water on the right. It forces a painful risk-reward decision that will result in a long approach if you decide not to cut the corner.

Finally, note that only the die-hard walkers will want to face up to this one, as it is a particularly long, difficult 18-hole walk.

The details   512-288-4297. 7401 Hwy. 45, Austin, TX 78739

- Par 72. Gold – 6,859 (72.7/122). Blue – 6,333 (70.3/118). White – 5,702 (67.1/112). Red – 5,236 (69.9/120). Price - $$.

Getting there   From Mopac (Loop 1) south, turn left on Hwy. 45. When you come to Kendrick Blvd., turn left and head straight to the course.

THE CLUBS OF LAKEWAY

The golf   Lakeway opened in 1963 with two Leon Howard designs outside of Austin near Lake Travis.

The **Live Oak Course** is the closest to the lake, with holes 5 and 6 just off the marina. Howard stated that No. 3 was one of his all-time favorites. This beautiful hole plays over a canyon to a green that's real close to a huge cliff.

The **Yaupon Course** came along 12 years after Live Oak, and was particularly challenging for Howard's return to the area because of the rocky terrain. Due to the lack of soil, construction required 100,000 cubic yards of soil to be dredged from the lake bottom and spread over the entire course. Suffice it to say that those strings would never be pulled in today's environmentally conscious age.

Your weight should always be moving in the direction the clubhead is going. When you take the club back, your weight should move onto your back foot; as you swing forward, your weight should move onto your front foot. Butch Harmon

A few holes offer views of the lake, and the dramatic elevation changes make it difficult to judge distance. Enjoy the view from No. 18, where your tee shot will soar to the fairway that is more than 50 feet below. The second shot is a lay-up in front of the pond, and the approach must carry that pond to the elevated green.

The details 512-261-7173. 510 Lakeway Dr., Austin, TX 78734

- www.clubsoflakeway.com
- Live Oak Course: 1963. Leon Howard. Gold – 6,652 (71.6/121). Blue – 6,301 (70.1/119). White – 5,680 (66.9/110). Red 5,403 (71.8/122). Price - $$$.
- Yaupon Course: 1975. Leon Howard. Gold – 6,590 (71.5/123). Blue – 6,091 (69.8/119). White – 5,379 (66.0/110). Red – 5,032 (69.4/119). Price - $$$.

Getting there From Hwy. 620 west, drive about 6 miles past the dam and turn right on Lakeway Dr. Drive 2 miles and turn right at the second stop sign, then follow this road to the golf course.

EAST COMMUNITIES YMCA GOLF COURSE

Opening 2003 Austin's First Tee program, a World Golf foundation initiative dedicated to "providing affordable golf access for everyone, especially kids who might otherwise might not have an opportunity to play," was founded in 1999 and is currently in the process of building a new golf learning facility in East Austin.

The facility, which broke ground in summer 2002, will feature a 9-hole golf course, a 3-hole short course, a complete practice area with driving range, putting and chipping greens, all complemented by an interactive learning center. An ideal place for kids and beginners to learn the game, the course will have designated times just for families.

GREAT HILLS GOLF CLUB

The golf Great Hills rests atop one of the highest points in the Hill Country, featuring a Don January and Billy Martindale design that rolls through scenic hills and canyons.

Updates in 1990 lengthened the course, but it still plays a pedestrian 6,118 from the white tees. During the renovation, the last three holes of the more spectacular back nine were modified.

No. 16 is deceptively tough, playing only 378 yards but highlighted by huge oak trees and a hilly, rolling fairway before you get to the green. No. 17 is the most scenic par 3 on the course, a 183-yarder. And the par 5 No. 18 is one of the more welcome finishing holes that you'll come across, a definite birdie opportunity at only 477 yards.

The neatest thing about playing was my ability to surprise myself. Under pressure sometimes I'd face a real hard shot I'd never played before and pull it off just the way I envisioned it. Tom Weiskopf

The details   512-345-0505. 5914 Lost Horizon Dr., Austin, TX 78759

- www.greathillscc.org
- 1973. Billy Martindale-Don January. 6,637 (72.4/128). White – 6,118 (70.0/120). Gold – 5,346 (66.2/115). Red – 4,681 (68.4/117). Gold 2 – 5,346 (72.1/128). Price - $$.

Getting there   From Hwy. 183 north, take the Great Hills Trails exit and turn left. When you come to Rain Creek Pkwy., turn right, head over to Lost Horizon Dr., then turn left to the course.

HANCOCK GOLF COURSE

The golf   The original Austin Country Club, Hancock is named after famous Austinite Lewis Hancock, who organized the club in 1898 and brought the dream of one of Texas' first country clubs to fruition.

This course is steeped in history. Harvey Penick began caddying in 1913 on this 9-hole course that originally had sand greens. And since it's short, you'll want to walk, just as President Taft did when he played the course years ago.

The design features extremely small greens. Waller Creek comes into play on five holes, including the No. 1, which plays 152 yards over the hazard. Hole 9 is an interesting end to the round–a 264-yard par 4 with that isn't really driveable because of the creek fronting the green.

Other notes: Hancock is known as the oldest intact design in the state.

The details   512-453-0276. 811 E. 41st St., Austin, TX 78751

- 1899. Lewis Hancock. Par 35. Back - 2,633 (65.2/112). Forward – 2,427. Price - $.

Getting there   From I-35 take the Airport Rd. exit west and go south on the service road. When you get to 41st St., turn right (west), then turn left when you see the course entrance.

LAKEWAY COUNTRY CLUB – HILLS COURSE

The golf   The Hills opened in 1981 with a signature Jack Nicklaus design that is consistently ranked as one of the finest tracks in the state.

The Hills incorporates Hurst Creek, which is highlighted by waterfalls and comes into play on 13 holes. And while the tee shots are challenging, the course demands solid approaches, with narrow openings to the greens that require excellent short games. Along with stunning views of the area, this course is punctuated by the famous 7th hole. The hole plays as long as 165 yards from the tips, over water accented by a natural waterfall that fronts the green. On the back No. 18 stands out, offering 418 yards of water, out-of-bounds, sand, and trees.

The details   512-261-7272. 26 Club Estates Pkwy., Austin, TX 78738

- www.thehillscc.com

Forget about adding up your score, and live in the present moment. Dr. Bob Rotella

• 1981. Jack Nicklaus. Back – 6,954 (72.6/132). Middle – 6,306 (70.0/126). Forward – 5,123 (69.4/124). Price - $$$$.

Getting there   From I-35 going south, get off at the First St. exit and turn right. Head over to Mopac (Loop 1) and turn right onto Bee Caves Rd./2244. Continue on for approximately 15 miles until the road dead- ends at Hwy. 71. Turn right and head over to Hwy. 620. Once there, make another right and proceed up to Lakeway Blvd. Make a left and head over to Club Estates Pkwy. Make another left and drive a short distance to the course.

LAKEWAY C.C. – FLINTROCK FALLS COURSE

The golf   Recently opened in 2002, the Flintrock Falls course now enables Lakeway CC members the chance to play another fabulous Nicklaus design, this one co-designed by the elder Nicklaus and his son Jack II. Hurst Creek comes into play prominently again and, as with The Hills Course, Nicklaus had live oaks, cedars, and the natural Hill Country landscape at his disposal.

The signature hole is No. 11, highlighted by the creek and a natural waterfall.

The details   512-263-6090. 401 Jack Nicklaus Dr., Austin, TX 78738

• 2002. Jack Nicklaus. 7,051 yards (74.1/140). Price - $$$$.

Getting there   From I-35 going south, get off at the First St. exit and turn right. Head over to Mopac (Loop 1) and turn right onto Bee Caves Rd./2244. Continue on for approximately 15 miles until the road dead-ends at Hwy. 71. Turn right and head over to Hwy. 620. Once there, make another right and proceed up to Lakeway Blvd. Make a left and head over to Club Estates Pkwy. Make another left and drive a short distance to the course.

JIMMY CLAY–RAY KIZER MUNICIPAL GOLF COURSE

The golf   This is a 36-hole city-owned operation that features Austin's newest and best muni track, the Roy Kizer Course, which complements the 1970s Jimmy Clay layout. Austin's old water treatment facility was transformed by Randy Russell, who had over 80 acres of lakes and marshland at his disposal when he laid out the 200-acre site. Russell's links-style design is flat, burdened by the wind, and loaded with bunkers. The toughest par is No. 11, which rolls 468 yards into the wind and is shamefully listed as a par 4. Take your bogey on No. 11.

The **Jimmy Clay Course** opened in 1974 with a 6,857-yard Joe Finger design that incorporates Williamson Creek. This track is flat as well, and is noted for its generous fairways and large, elevated greens. The first and last holes are perhaps the most memorable. No. 1 serves up a blind approach shot over a hill into a skinny green, and the 400-yard doglegged 18th plays into the wind with water on the left side.

The details 512-444-0999. 5400 Jimmy Clay Dr., Austin, TX 78744

- Roy Kizer: 1994. Randolph Russell. 18 holes. Par 71. Back – 6,749 (71.6/125). Middle – 6,412 (69.9/120). Forward – 5,018 (67.4/109). Price - $$.

- Jimmy Clay: 1973. Joe Finger. 18 holes. Par 72. Back – 6,857 (72.4/124). Middle – 6,368 (70.5/119). Forward – 5,036 (69.3/114). Price - $$.

Getting there From I-35 south, take the Stassney exit and turn left. At about 2 miles you'll make a right on Jimmy Clay Dr., which will dead-end at the course.

LIONS MUNICIPAL GOLF COURSE

The golf   Lions upstaged the prestigious sand-greened Austin Country Club when it opened with Bermuda greens in 1923, and has been Austin's most beloved municipal ever since. Although no one knows for sure who officially designed this short, 6,000-yard classic, it appears that many members of Austin's golf scene were involved, including Harvey and Tom Penick, and perhaps even the legendary John Bredemus. Either way, the design is famously unique, jammed into an unusually small piece of oak and cedar-covered terrain north of Town Lake. The track features loads of trees, even more doglegs, and some subtleties that have stood the test of time.

Lions' colorful history is part of what attracts the 100,000-some-odd folks who cram the course every year. Ben Hogan teamed with Harvey Penick here in the 1950s for an exhibition match. He put on a show by stumbling around the first hole as if he'd spent the previous night partaking of drink, only to straighten it out and light up the course, much to the delight of the patrons. The story involves the No. 16 signature hole, which was No. 7 back then. Hogan was apparently a bit intimidated by the view from the tee. His question "Where's the fairway?" has been asked many times over the years as hacks prepare to negotiate the blind tee shot on this 381-yard par 4. And while the hole isn't as difficult today as it was back then, the approach is still testy over the water into a sloping, elevated green.

The details   512-477-6963. 2901 Enfield Rd., Austin, TX 78703

- www.ci.austin.tx.us/parks/lions.html
- 1934. 18 holes. Par 71. Back – 6,001 (68.9/118). Middle – 5,642 (67.2/115). Forward – 4,931 (67.6/109). Price - $$.

Getting there   From Mopac south, take the Enfield exit and turn right. Drive up the hill and make a left when you see the entrance to the course.

LOST CREEK COUNTRY CLUB

The golf   Lost Creek opened in 1971, featuring a 6,522-yard, par 72 layout that has hosted Sectional Playability Tests for aspiring PGA members over the years. The traditional design features narrow, tree-lined fairways, creeks that roll through the course and come into play on many holes, and well-conditioned greens.

The back nine is known for its two solid par 3s. No. 10 starts the side with a 147-yard carry over water, and the longer 18th finishes the round off with a 187-yard carry over water.

Other notes: Co-architect Terry Dill grew up in Fort Worth, graduated from UT Austin in 1962, then gave it a go as a pro golfer for over a decade. When that didn't work out, he went back to UT for his law degree and then became a professor at Texas A&M. In 1991, he got the urge for golf again and joined the Senior PGA Tour.

The details   512-892-2032. 2612 Lost Creek Blvd., Austin, TX 78746

- www.lostcreekclub.com
- 1971. 18 holes. Par 72. Back – 6,522 (71.4/127). Middle – 5,973 (68.6/119). Forward – 4,995 (68.2/118). Price - $$.

Getting there From I-35 north, take Ben White Blvd. exit and go west. This turns into Loop 360. Exit Lost Creek Blvd. and turn left. The course is 2.5 miles down the road, and the entrance is on the right.

FOR THE ROAD

For the slicing, dicing, and bumpy roads that connect the golf courses and parks and recreation sites of the state, order yourself one of Map Ventures' outstanding maps, which are clearly illustrated and done by the best in the business (www.gonetomorrow.com; 512-326-4141).

MORRIS WILLIAMS GOLF COURSE

The golf   The "Mo Willie," Austin's third municipal course, has some character: it served as the home of Harvey Penick's legendary golf teams, two of which won NCAA Championships back when Tom Kite and Ben Crenshaw graced the fairways. And it's named after Morris Williams, Jr. - one of the best golfers to ever come out of the city. Now Austin's airport has moved south, and this difficult Leon Howard design is a bit more peaceful.

Howard's layout requires all types of shots, and is known for its small, slightly elevated greens. The best hole on the front is the dogleg left, 540-yard No. 2, even though some would argue that the 187-yard No. 3 is one of Austin's all-time best. It drops 50 feet from tee to green over a pond. The back side is highlighted by water holes 11-14, with both 11 and 12 requiring approaches over the wet stuff.

The muttered hint, "Remember, you have a stroke here," freezes my joints like a blast from Siberia. John Updike

The details   512-926-1298. 4305 Manor Rd., Austin, TX 78723

- 1964. Leon Howard. 18 holes. Par 72. Back – 6,636 (71.0/121). Middle – 6,249 (69.6/119). Forward – 5,273 (69.0/117). Price - $$.

Getting there From the Austin Airport, turn left on Manor Rd. and the club-house is 100 yards down the street. The entrance is on the right.

ONION CREEK COUNTRY CLUB

The golf   Ravaged by floods, the sometimes 27-hole birthplace of the Senior PGA Tour is currently operating with 18 holes as the renovation of the other nine moves forward toward an opening date of August 2003. When the full 27 holes are available, the clubhouse determines which 18 is in play for the day, creating a confusing possibility of combinations that isn't worth detailing.

The bottom line is that Jimmy Demaret designed the original 18 holes which hosted the original Liberty Mutual Legends of Golf from 1979–1990. His route features the pesky Onion Creek, which unfortunately has a tendency to swell during intense rain, often wiping out certain portions of the course. The course isn't long, and is known as a shot-maker's course for its small greens and numerous bunkers, which spot the fairways and guard the greens. Ben Crenshaw and Bill Coore added the new nine in the mid-1990s, and it's designed similarly to Demaret's original track.

The details   512-282-2162. 2510 Onion Creek Pkwy., Austin, TX 78747

- www.onioncreekclub.com
- Demaret, Crenshaw, Coore: Back – 6,530 (70.3/124). Middle – 5,938 (67.9/122). Forward – 4,835 (67.6/114). Price - $$$.
- Original front nine under construction. Opening Spring 2003.

Getting there From I-35, take the Onion Creek Pkwy. exit (south of town), and look for the signs leading to the course.

RIVERSIDE GOLF COURSE

The golf   Riverside was the second home to the venerable Austin Country Club, designed by Press and Perry Maxwell and known primarily as Harvey Penick's domain; his home can still be seen from the 5th tee. Close to down-town, this beautiful layout is a local favorite that has been improved in recent years.

Giant oak trees are the primary hazard on this short track. Holes 1 and 14 are reachable par 4s at just over 300 yards. The signature is the 193-yard No. 5, which plays downhill and doesn't require as much club as you might origi-nally think when staring at the green.

The details   512-386-7077. 1020 Grove Blvd., Austin, TX 78741

The good player swings through the ball while the awkward player hits at it. Ken Venturi

The founder of Onion Creek, Jimmy Demaret, kicking back in some stylish sandals.

- www.americangolf.com
- 1950s. 18 holes. Par 71. 6,500 yards. Price - $$.

Getting there From I-35, get off at the Riverside exit. Go east for 2 miles, make a left on Grove Blvd., and look for the entrance on the left side of the road.

RIVER PLACE COUNTRY CLUB

The golf   River Place is finally established after years of financial problems that were resolved when Tom Kite and Roy Bechtol gave the facility new life with a redesign in the early 1990s. Located on the former Wilding Ranch between Lake Austin and RR 620, the Hill Country terrain is phenomenal, with a creek that dominates the front nine, and some dramatic slopes that never result in level lies.

The sloping is evident on No. 1, a 402-yard par 4 that requires a testy approach over a ravine from a downhill lie. No. 4 is tough because the creek rolls along the left side of the 561-yard hole before crossing in front of the green. And No. 7 is one of the toughest: a 430-yard doglegger that bends right around the creek.

The back side has a few ponds that come into play, but is void of the pesky creek. The one to watch for is No. 17, a 585-yard monster.

The details   512-346-1114. 4207 River Place Blvd., Austin, TX 78730

- 1991. Tom Kite and Roy Bechtol. Par 71. 6,611 (72/128). Price - $$$.

Getting there From Loop 360, take 2222 going west. In about 5 miles you'll come to River Place Blvd. Make a left and look for the entrance on the left side of the street.

SPANISH OAKS GOLF CLUB

The golf   Spanish Oaks is part of a huge master-planned community located in the scenic Hill Country along Texas 71 outside of Austin in Bee Caves. Membership in this private club will be limited to 350. Little Barton Creek rolls through the layout, which is cut by an impressive array of cliffs and rocky terrain. There is an unmistakable natural feel to the layout, and you'll definitely experience something special if you have the privilege of playing this course.

Since its opening in October 2001, accolades have come easy for this Bobby Weed-designed track. In fact, *Golf Digest* labeled the facility the "Best New Private Course in America" so it's not surprising that others now consider it one of the top ten in all of Texas.

Note that first-timers will greatly benefit from the club's outstanding caddie program, and the design is very walker-friendly, with short distances between each hole.

The details   512-421-8530. 13443 W. Hwy. 71, Austin, TX 78738

⭐

The biggest challenge you face on the tee—even before you decide what kind of shot you want to hit—is changing your mind-set from "driving range" to "on the course." Johnny Miller

- 2002. Bobby Weed. 18 holes. Par 72. 6,930 yards (73.3/136). Price - $$$$.

Getting there Located west of town on Texas 71 in the town of Bee Caves.

UNIVERSITY OF TEXAS GOLF CLUB AT STEINER RANCH

The golf   The UT Golf Club is under construction and slated for a November 2003 opening. Located at Steiner Ranch off of FM 620 in Northwest Austin, the project has been driven by prominent Dallas business executive and UT alum Mike Myers, who signed a 50-year licensing agreement with the university to use the school's name. The 7,008-yard, par 71 layout was designed by the Bechtol Russel Golf group, and will serve as the new home for UT's golf program. With the big names and money behind this project, this one should be spectacular. Three holes overlook Lake Austin, and former UT hacks have chipped in to collaborate on the design.

MORE AUSTIN GOLF

Ben White Golf Center: 512-462-2104. 714 Ben White Blvd., Austin, TX 78704

Golfsmith: 512-837-1810. 11000 N. I-35, Austin, TX 7875

Hank Haney Golf Ranch: 512-345-2013. 10515 N. Mopac Expy., Austin, TX 78759

Mr. Tee: 512-335-4444. 13910 RR 620 N., Austin, TX 78717

Mulligan's Golf: 512-282-1120. 11003 Manchaca Rd., Austin, TX 78748

Oak Hill Driving Range: 512-892-5634. 5243 W. Hwy. 290, Austin, TX 78735

Twin Creeks Range: 512-282-5725. 662 FM 1626, Austin, TX 78748

Woodland Greens: 512-250-5260. 11210 FM 620 N., Austin, TX 78726

CENTRAL

AUSTIN NOTES The heart of Austin, to many, is South Austin, and nowhere is the funky, eclectic spirit of the town more evident than the stretch of **South Congress** that runs south from Town Lake to Olthorf. **Guero's** (512-447-7688) is a classic Mexican joint with lots of character. The **Continental Club** (512-441-0202) serves up great Texas music every night—be sure to catch the legendary Toni Price on Tuesday evenings for Happy Hippie Hour, an Austin tradition. For South Austin lodging, the newly restored **San Jose Hotel** (512-693-9317) has beautiful, serene rooms in the heart of the South Congress scene of galleries, boutiques, and bistros. Another good place to stay is the downhome **Austin Motel** (512-441-1157) next door to the excellent Mexican cafe **El Soy y La Luna** (512-444-7770).

Many amateurs hit a putt too hard and turn away in disgust as the ball passes the hole. I watch closely as a putt goes by the hole to see how the comeback putt will break. Tom Watson

204 • *The Texas Golf Bible*

West a few blocks on South Lamar, a stop at the venerable **Broken Spoke** (512-442-6189) is close to obligatory. Even if you don't stick around to two-step to country music, have a chicken-fried steak and check out the musical memorabilia. Another nostalgic stop is **Threadgill's World Headquarters** on Riverside (512-472-9304) - there's also another Threadgill's on N. Lamar, (512-451-5440) - for world-class homestyle cooking and more trips down Memory Lane. Janis Joplin got her start at Threadgill's in the Austin jug band scene in the 60s. **Matt's El Rancho** on S. Lamar (512-462-8333) is another South Austin tradition for enchiladas and people-watching. **Curra's** on Olthorf is a great spot for Interior Mexico specialties. Also on Lamar, more towards campus, find the **Shoal Creek Saloon**, complete with shuffleboard, pool, and visits by the lively Earl Campbell family.

Between April and October, bat lovers gather at dusk at the Congress Avenue bridge on the Colorado River to watch one of the world's largest colonies of Mexican free-tail bats emerge. Take a stroll on the **Town Lake Hike and Bike Trail,** an 8-5-mile track that winds along the Colorado River past Zilker Park, the famous statue of late blues guitar legend Stevie Ray Vaughn, the year-round swimmers' mecca of **Barton Springs**, and the **Zilker Botanicial Garden**. Rent a canoe, kayak, or bicycles to get the full Town Lake experience.

No trip to Austin is complete without a nocturnal prowl on **Sixth Street**, the slightly surreal Texas version of Bourbon Street complete with tattoo parlors, panhandlers, shot bars, and live music blaring out of every door. The magnificent **Driskill Hotel** (512-474-5911) is a historic, upscale island of class amid the Sixth Street sleaze. **Las Manitas** (512-472-9357), on Congress is the place for morning-after migas, huevos rancheros, and breakfast tacos.

Far west on Sixth Street, on the other side of Mopac (Loop 1), you'll find the classic **Deep Eddy Cabaret** watering hole, one of Austin's traditions and the best place to hole up after rounds at Lions Municipal.

On the other side of Congress, the **Warehouse District** offers more genteel distractions and caters to an older crowd than Sixth Street. **Antone's, Home of the Blues** (512-320-8424) on 5th Street is the place to catch rising blues stars and established legends. **La Zona Rosa** (512-472-2293) books many national and local acts. **The Gingerman** on W. 4th (512-473-8801) and **Mother Egan's Irish Pub** (478-7747) offer serious international, cross-cultural beer appreciation in a pub atmosphere. Pick up an *Austin Chronicle* to find local music listings—if your taste runs to mellower sounds you'll enjoy the singer-songwriter scene at the **Cactus Cafe** on the UT campus. The late Texas troubador Townes Van Zandt considered this his home club, and many Texas legends have performed here over the years.

Historic sites of interest include the **Lyndon Baines Johnson Library and Museum** on the UT campus and the new **Bob Bullock Story of Texas Museum** between downtown and campus. The **Texas Capitol Building** is a must-see, and the Rotunda is open 24 hours a day.

70% of the population of Texas lives within 200 miles of Austin.

BASTROP
Elev. 374   Pop. 5,276

Located just east of Austin on Hwy. 71, Bastrop is part of an isolated, 70-square-mile forest of pine trees on the eastern edge of the Great Pine Belt. Driving from Austin toward Houston, the "Lost Pines of Texas" suddenly appear out of nowhere and, surprisingly, you find yourself out of the Hill Country and in the thick of the East Texas sticks. With the majestic pine trees and nearby Colorado River, the topography and terrain create the ideal setting for spectacular golf. Colo Vista and Pine Forest are absolutely breathtaking, and the Lost Pines course, located in Bastrop State Park, offers fabulous scenery and a much grander experience that one might expect from a state-run course. All told, if you're in the area, make it a point to play all three. You will not be disappointed.

COLOVISTA COUNTRY CLUB

The golf   Located in the Lost Pines area of Bastrop 30 minutes east of Austin, Colo Vista is a dramatic, immaculate course that's consistently rated one of the best in Texas. Some actually question whether it is in Texas, given the unusual terrain that the course flows through.

The highlight of the course is the now-famous 191-yard No. 15, which is perched on a bluff overlooking the Colorado River and has been called the prettiest par 3 in Texas. From a cliffside tee, the hole drops over 120 feet down to a green surrounded by bunkers and swales. Because of the wind, the best play is a hard punch shot that at least has the chance to lessen the impact of the breeze.

The front nine is more of a links-style track that definitely contrasts with what you'll see on the back. The opener is a tough, 468-yard par 4 that plays downhill.

The back nine, considered the better of the two, makes the most of the rugged terrain and extreme elevation changes. The view from the bluff is spectacular; giant pine trees line the fairways, and the 90-degree doglegs all add to the character of the nine.

Note that the club offers cottages that sleep two people for around $85 (866-366-6789 for reservations).

The details   512-303-4045. 1 Country Club Dr., Bastrop, TX 78602.

- www.colovista.com
- 1997. 18 holes. Par 72. Challenge – 6,966 (73.4/126). Tournament – 6,596 (71.4/122). Back – 6,112 (69.2/117). Forward – 5,452 (71.8/118). Speed – 4,803 (68.2/108). Price - $$$.

Getting there From Austin, take Hwy. 71 east to McAllister Rd. Turn right and follow the signs to the course, which is located 4 miles east of the river in Bastrop.

baffie: Old name for a 5-wood.

LOST PINES GOLF CLUB

The golf   Lost Pines, located in Bastrop State Park, was originally a 9-hole track designed by Leon Howard, but was upgraded to 18 holes in 1997 by Craig Metz. The course is scenic, and the main problem you'll have with stray golf shots is the abundant trees.

Cabins may be rented inside the park if you're interested in making a weekend of it.

The details   512-321-2327. Bastrop State Park, Bastrop, TX 78602

- Original 9 by Leon Howard (1973). New 9 by Craig Metz (1987). 18 holes. Par 71. Back – 6,199. Middle – 5,831. Forward – 5,426. Price - $$.

Getting there From Hwy. 71, turn right on Hwy. 95. The course is one mile up the hill.

PINE FOREST GOLF CLUB

The golf   While it hasn't received the same fanfare as Colo Vista, Pine Forest holds its own. The course provides a true golf adventure through sneaky elevation changes and red bluffs, with blind tee shots and holes along the Colorado River. Don January built it in 1979, and with a few improvements in conditioning his course could equal the more respected Colo Vista.

No. 3 is a picturesque par 3, playing 170 yards downhill, with a green framed by the red bluffs. On No. 6, keep the tee shot right to avoid a blind second shot, and watch out for the tough, two-tiered green. No. 7 plays along the Colorado, and is protected by a massive cottonwood tree on the left.

On the back, make note that the highest point on the course is the 11th green. For the home stretch, make the most of the two downhill par 3s. No. 12 plays 180 yards and you'll need to leave it below the hole. Hole 16 is longer at 225 yards and is protected by a beautiful oak tree on the left.

Don't forget to try this one when you're in Bastrop. During the week you can play for $25 with a cart, and the clubhouse has recently been renovated and expanded.

The details   512-321-1181. 636 Riverside Dr., Bastrop, TX 78602.

- www.pineforestgolfclub.com

- 18 holes. Par 72. Back – 6,569 (71.5/126). Middle – 6,048 (69.2/118). Forward – 4,946 (69.0/114). Price - $$.

Getting there From Hwy. 71 south, turn right on Tahitian. Approximately 3 miles later, turn right on Riverside and the course will be on your left.

BASTROP NOTES   For lodging, if you don't rough it at the state park, **Pine Forest** offers cottages that sleep two people for under $100, and the **Comfort Inn** is near the course. Be sure to have a meal at the **Bastrop BBQ and Meat Market**

I don't fear death . . . but I sure do hate those three footers for par. Chi Chi Rodriguez

(512-321-7719) on Main St., then go for dessert at **Lock's Drug**, one of Texas' oldest, before wandering around the downtown **Colorado Riverwalk**. If that isn't enough, venture to downtown **Smithville, TX** and take in the character of that neat, oak-shaded town.

BANDERA

Elev. 1,258   Pop. 1,311

The classic Hill Country town of Bandera, only 49 miles from San Antonio, is called the "Cowboy Capital of the World" and is one of the most intoxicating towns in the state because of its lazy, laidback feel. This cowboy-hip ranching community was originally a staging area for the cattle drives up Montana way, and today dude ranches dot the countryside. The Texas music scene has given the town even more character with the likes of natives Robert Keen, Kinky Friedman, Junior Brown, and the Robison brothers making their presence known. You can't plan it any better than spending the mornings at either the Flying L or Lost Valley courses, floating lazily in the afternoons in the streams and rivers that roll by, then hanging out in Bandera for cold beers, live music, and two-stepping at Arkie Blue's.

FLYING L GOLF COURSE

The golf   Set in the beautiful Medina Valley, The Flying L Golf Course serves as the centerpiece of a resort built by Colonel Jack Lapham, a San Antonian who was attracted to this remote, beautiful area back in the 1950s and 1960s. Nine holes were added to the existing layout in 1972, so the resort now offers 18 holes of quality golf that improves year after year as the facility continues to upgrade with more hazards and improved conditioning.

Water hazards impact play throughout the design, particularly on No. 4. Though it only plays around 300 yards, much of it is over water. No. 5 features water as well, a big dogleg left with out-of-bounds on the right and a lake protecting the left side of the green. Hole 9 is the signature hole, playing 435 yards uphill into an elevated green. The hole requires a tee shot into a narrow dogleg-left fairway that is protected on either side by trees.

If your golf game is suffering, you can still enjoy the views—especially the 13th hole, which overlooks the panoramic Medina Valley.

The details   830-796-8466. Hwy. 173 at Wharton Dock Rd., Bandera, TX 78003

- 1960s. 18 holes. Par 72. Back – 6,646 (71.0/123). Middle – 6,273 (69.3/119). Forward – 5,442 (69.9/109). Price - $$.

Getting there From Loop 1604, find Hwy. 16 (Bandera Rd.) and drive north. When 16 dead-ends, make a left on Hwy. 173. The course is 1 mile down on the left.

Remember to focus on target or ball flight on every shot that you hit. Dr. Bob Rotella

LOST VALLEY RESORT GOLF COURSE

The golf   Lost Valley was developed in the 1940s and originally opened as a 9-hole course, with an additional nine added in the 1970s. This is a fun, basic course with wide-open fairways, void of major difficulties. The front nine, more of a traditional layout, features old oak trees, flat, basic greens, and a classic Hill Country feel. Hole 3 is particularly tough on the front because of the lake around the green.

You can tell that the back nine is newer, as it's a bit more difficult with its undulating greens–it's more of a links-style layout. Water comes into play on the 200-yard, par 3 No. 14, and you'll also need to watch for the 615-yard 17th hole. Fortunately, the finisher provides the chance to score well, as it's only a 310-yard par 4.

The details   830-460-7958 Hwy. 16, Bandera, TX 78003

• 1962. 18 holes. Par 72. Back – 6,210. Forward – 5,905. Price - $$.

Getting there From San Antonio, take Hwy. 1604 south to Hwy. 16. Turn west and travel for 35 miles, where you'll see the course on your right.

BANDERA NOTES   Gear up for your round with breakfast at the **OST Restaurant,** an old joint with shrines to John Wayne, then consider **Busbee's Barbecue** (830-796-3153) for oak-smoked meats and corn on the cob for lunch. Afterwards, stroll the streets for live music and wander into legendary **Arkie Blue's Silver Dollar Saloon,** a basement honkytonk with sawdust floors made for dancing. George Jones once performed at the **Cabaret Cafe** and was booed off the stage in a drunken stupor. Dude ranches, fishing, and hunting are abundant in the area. Take the scenic drive (long way) to Kerrville through Medina and enjoy the unbelievable views along Hwy. 16, or drift in the gin-clear, lazy waters of the Medina River.

BELTON   Elev. 511   Pop. 15,639

You'll hardly notice Belton in the confusing mass of urbanity around I-35 between Killeen and Temple. Belton began as a small Texas Ranger fort in 1836, but its early growth was a result of its location on the Chisholm Trail cattle drives and the stagecoach route from Austin to Dallas. If you're adding courses to your golf resume, Leon Valley in Belton is one to consider when traveling between Dallas and Austin.

LEON VALLEY GOLF COURSE

The golf   Leon Valley has improved its facilities recently, with a new clubhouse, restaurant, and expanded pro shop. This 18-hole country course is out in the boonies, but worth the trip because of the interesting, and sometimes funky, layout. With water on only one hole, and only a few bunkers on the course, it plays easy. Holes 7 and 10 are par 4s that play under 300 yards, and the small greens make three-putts harder to come by.

Hole 16 stands out: a par 5 at almost 600 yards that generally plays into the prevailing wind. Some of the more difficult holes are 2, 9, and 11–all par 4s that play well over 400 yards.

The details   254-939-5271. 709 E. 24th Ave., Belton, TX 76513

- 18 holes. Par 72. Back – 6,552 (70.1/117). Middle – 5,691 (66.2/110). Forward – 5,370. Price - $.

Getting there Located 45 miles south of Waco. On I-35 south, take Exit 294 and drive north on Hwy. 317 (Main St). Turn east on 24th Ave. and continue to the golf course entrance.

BELTON NOTES   Before your round, consider **Kevin's** (512-780-1177) for breakfast tacos, or the **Hiedenheimer Coffee Co.** (254-933-2233) for a quick bite. The **Beef Barn** serves steaks and seafood. Go for sausage or slow-cooked brisket at **Schoepf's Bar-B-Que** (512-939-1151). Order a chicken-fried steak at the **Classic Cafe** (512-939-3995), housed in an old 1891 downtown building, then cruise by the Old Stone Jail on Pearl where nine horse thieves were shot by an angry mob in 1874. Also on the town square find **Gerd's Pfeffermuehle** (512-939-5239) for authentic German food. Out on Hwy. 36 there's Maggie's, which is perfect for Sunday brunch. For overnight accommodations, seek the **Best Western** (512-939-5711) on 6th or the **Glen Riddle Manor B&B** (800-899-4538) might work better than a motel.

BOERNE   Elev. 1,405   Pop. 6,170

Unlike Bandera, Boerne's location on I-10 has sucked it into the urban sprawl of San Antonio. Despite this, "Burn-ee" still remains a peaceful old town that offers a world-class golf course and quick access to the depths of the Hill Country on either side of the interstate. The historic town square is more than charming, highlighted by the 1859 Kendall Inn and the Kendall County Courthouse. The Guadalupe River State Park is nearby, as well as the famous caves of Cascade Caverns and other attractions. And–more important for the golf fans–some consider Tapatio Springs one of the most awesome golf experiences in the state.

FAIR OAKS RANCH GOLF & COUNTRY CLUB

The golf   Built in 1978 on Ralph Fair's ranch, the original Black Jack Course is the more difficult of the two Gary Player designs. Both are carved out of the Hill Country and feature narrow, tree-lined fairways and large greens. Ponds and creeks dot the landscape and impact play.

Everything with its head down gets eaten. Jackie Burke, Jr.

CENTRAL

CENTRAL

The **Blackjack Oak Course**, which opened in 1994, is more of a links-style layout that requires a bit more length from the tee. The opening hole is a long par 5 that rolls down into a Hill Country valley loaded with scenic holes and spotted by sand and water. The 18th is only 359 yards from the blue tees but runs straight uphill.

In 1993, Player collaborated with Ron Kirby on the **Live Oak Course**, which is considered the more scenic of the two tracks. The back nine offers one tough stretch of golf in holes 16 and 17. The par 3 No. 16 plays uphill to a difficult hill-topped green that is hard to hold. Less-than-perfect tee shots will find the bunker or ditch. No. 17 is just under 500 yards and requires a blind drive–and a layup iron to follow – before firing uphill on the final approach.

Fair Oaks has a nice practice area with three putting greens, a driving range, and a chipping green with practice bunkers.

The details   830-755-4216. 7900 Fair Oaks Pkwy. Fair Oaks, TX 78015

- Live Oak: 1993. Gary Player and Ron Kirby. Gold – 6,732 (73.1/131). Blue – 6,337 (70.9/124). White – 5,886 (68.4/119). Red – 5,197 (71.7/126). Price - $$$.

- Black Jack: 1978. Gary Player and Denis Griffith. Gold – 7,000 (73.5/131). Blue – 6,494 (70.5/121). White – 5,870 (67.7/115). Red – 5,236 (69.4/115). Price - $$$.

Getting there From I-10 east, take Exit 546 and turn right, then drive 2 miles to the course. The entrance is on the right.

TAPATIO SPRINGS

The golf   Consistently ranked as one of the top resort courses in the state, Tapatio Springs has three different combinations of outstanding Hill Country golf. The spectacular Ridge Course, added in 1999, now complements the Valley and Lakes courses.

The design of all three tracks ingeniously incorporates the rugged Hill Country terrain. Giant oaks line the fairways and the fabled Frederick Creek runs throughout the design. The most talked-about of the three nines is the newer, more difficult Ridge Course, which appears to be built into the cliffs of this rugged ranch country.

Many claim that the **Ridge** is the most unbelievable golf experience in the state, while others complain that it is a tricked-up, unfair test of golf for the average player. The tee boxes are elevated and the elevation changes are extreme. Thanks to problems caused by either water, trees, cliffs, or waste areas, you face the potential for lost balls on every hole. Fans of the blind golf shot will be pleased with this design, as there are numerous blind shots both off the tee and on the approaches. Use the tip sheet and follow their recommendations.

If you think you can hole a chip shot, take out the flagstick, because the flagstick never helped a perfect shot. Davis Love, Jr.

The elevated tee boxes provide awesome views, and it's not uncommon to be hitting your tee shot from high above down into a valley loaded with herds of axis or whitetail deer. There are three par 3s on the Ridge, all of them exciting holes because of the elevated tee boxes.

The **Valley** and **Lakes** courses have some similarities, but provide an interesting change of pace from the wild and wooly Ridge. The elevation changes aren't as severe, and you're more likely to find a flat lie when your drives find the fairway. The water hazards are the only major issues on the Valley. Both are tight and tough.

The Lakes features two memorable back-to-back par 4s. No. 5 plays 371 yards through a chute of trees off the tee down to a fairway at least 40 feet below, with Frederick Creek looming left. No. 6 is longer, almost 400 yards, featuring another downhill tee shot that must be long in order to give yourself a reasonable approach uphill over the trees and creek to the green.

The details   830-537-4611. 36 FM 473, Boerne, TX 78006

- www.tapatio.com
- 1981. Bill Johnston. 27 holes. Price - $$$.
- Lakes-Valley: 18 holes. Par 72. Gold – 6,504 (71.4/133). Blue – 6,114 (69.2/128). White – 5,702 (67.3/125). Red – 5,185 (70.4/127).
- Valley-Ridge: 18 holes. Par 72. Gold – 6,500 (71.7/133). Blue – 6,221 (70.2/131). White – 5,818 (68.5/127). Red – 5,122 (70.2/126).
- Ridge-Lakes: 18 holes. Par 70. Gold – 6,252 (70.5/130). Blue – 5,871 (68.4/125). White – 5,474 (66.6/122). Red – 4,757 (67.9/118).

Getting there From I-10 west, exit Johns Rd. and go left at the stop sign. The club is about 4 miles down the road.

BOERNE NOTES   Try the country-resort kitchen outside of town called the **Guadalupe River Ranch** (830-537-4837), and be sure to order yourself some s'mores by the outdoor fireplace for dessert. Another dining option is the **Limestone Grille** (830-249-9954) in the historic town square. You might not find a better meal in these parts, and their wine list is exhaustive. Seven miles north of town off of I-10 is the community of **Welfare, TX**, where locals jam into the **Welfare Cafe** (830-537-3700) for German meals and imported beers on a fantastic outdoor patio.

BRADY   Elev. 1,670   Pop. 5,879

Brady truly is the heart of Texas–it's 412 miles to the Panhandle border at Texline, 341 miles to the Louisiana border at Burkeville, 401 miles to Brownsville, and 437 miles to El Paso. Dating back to the 1850s, the longest fenced cattle trail in the world once extended from Brady to Sonora 105 miles away. You can't help but fall in love with Central Texas when you drive through Brady. The town serves as headquarters for hunters taking white-tailed deer and wild turkey from surrounding counties. It also offers beautiful parks and the city-owned lake and golf course.

BRADY MUNICIPAL GOLF COURSE

The golf   Located on the west side of town in a nice little Hill Country setting, the Brady Municipal Golf Course offers a 9-hole layout that features narrow fairways, mature trees, small greens, and water hazards on a few holes.

As you might expect, this small-town course offers a few great scoring opportunities. Holes 6 and 7 are par 4s that play 279 and 302 yards, respectively. No. 8 follows with a 138-yard par 3. If you can avoid blowing up on the opening holes (especially the 513-yard, par 5 No. 5), you can assure yourself of a nice round with this welcome stretch of holes.

Two sets of tees make for an 18-hole round on this 9-holer.

The details   915-597-6010. Hwy. 87 W., Brady, TX 76825

- www.bradytx.com/sites/golf.html
- 9 holes. Par 36. Back – 2,841 (33.9/117). Forward – 2,472 (34.6/110). Price - $.

Getting there From San Angelo, take Hwy. 87 south. Watch for the course when you are a few miles outside of Brady.

BRADY NOTES   A drive through Brady isn't complete without a stop for lunch at **The Club Cafe** (830-597-7522), a typical Texas cafe decorated with photos from the old days. Explore the back roads and find the community of **Calf Creek**, where James and Rezin Bowie were bombarded for eight days by Tawakoni Indians before they fought their way out. Finally, try to time your weekend with the **World Championship Barbecue Goat Cook-off** around Labor Day, where you can work on your goat dung tossing in the Goat Pill Flip-Off, an activity that is perfect for honing your short-game touch. For a place to stay, call the **Heart of Texas B&B** (915-597-0120), a historic home with a honeymoon cottage for romance, or there's the **Best Western Brady Inn** (915-597-3997) for more standard accommodations.

BRENHAM   Elev. 350   Pop. 13,661

Driving east on US 290 around Brenham, you'll sense the transition from central to southeast Texas. While Brenham isn't in the heart of the Big Thicket,

---

Whether you are playing a full driver or a five-iron or a wedge, you make no conscious variation in the way you perform your swing. Without your knowing it, your swing will change slightly as the length of the shaft of the club changes. Ben Hogan

you can feel that millions of acres of marshes, streams, and dense woodlands are just ahead. Farming is huge in the fertile lands around Brenham, but the town is best known as the home of Blue Bell ice cream. April is the best time to visit. With spring in the air and bluebonnets blanketing the landscape, you'll want to figure out how to work your way on for a round at Brenham CC before you head for the ice cream tour.

BRENHAM COUNTRY CLUB

The golf   Originally a 9-hole course, an additional nine holes were added in 1993, making this a very challenging 18-hole layout with a few monster holes from the back tees (6,721 yards). The course features wide, tree-lined fairways and small greens, as well as water that comes into play on almost half of the holes.

One local told us that short-iron play was important; however, that's hard to imagine considering the length of some of the holes. Three holes stand out from the tips: Two par 5s play 600 yards or better (No. 11 is 643 yards), and No. 3, a 247-yard par 3. The rest of the layout is of a more reasonable length, particularly from the middle tees, where there are a few short par 5s under 500 yards as well as par 4s around the 300-yard range.

Note: Since this is a private course, you must be accompanied by a member.

The details   979-836-1733. 4107 Hwy. 105, Brenham, TX 77833

- 18 holes. Par 72. Back – 6,721 (72.0/123). Middle – 6,135 (69.1/118). Forward – 4,930 (68.6/111). Price - $$.

Getting there From Houston, take Hwy. 290 west and turn right on FM 577. Turn right on Hwy. 105. The course is located 2.5 miles away on the left-hand side of the road.

MORE BRENHAM GOLF

Strike-Fore Driving Range – 979-830-8313

BRENHAM NOTES   Satisfy your barbecue cravings at **Tex's Barbecue** (979-836-5962), a screen-door joint that serves pork ribs, cole slaw, and green beans on picnic tables underneath tall pines. Then waddle to **Blue Bell,** which was founded back in 1907 and now makes the best ice cream in the world. For lodging, the **Comfort Suites** (979-421-8100) is solid, and the **Ant Street Inn** (800-481-1951) is cool because of its porch and rocking chairs that overlook the street.

You can tell a good bunker shot by the sound. From powdery sand, you want a "poof." From coarser sand, it should sound like you're tearing a linen sheet in half. Strive to make the right sound, and you'll be surprised at how fast you improve. Gary Player

BRYAN–COLLEGE STATION   Elev. 367 Pop. 118,505

Home of the Texas Agricultural and Mechanical College, now known as Texas A&M University, these twin cities have grown together. The surrounding Brazos River bottoms sustain the diversified agricultural industry, and every other business pretty much revolves around the university. The Aggies will tell you that there isn't much to do here, so they drive to Austin for a little culture. What they fail to mention is the impressive number of golf courses available for a piddly little college town. No less than six courses dot the landscape of Aggieland, with their pride and joy soon to open: the Traditions Golf Course and Country Club at University Ranch.

BRIARCREST COUNTRY CLUB

The golf   Scenic Briarcrest, designed by Marvin Ferguson, features tight fairways lined by old oak trees, at least six water hazards that come into play, and small greens. Ferguson's layout requires accuracy off the tee, especially for the long par 3s.

Watch out for the approach on No. 8, which is long and must carry a lake that looms left of the green and cuts into the fairway at the 150-yard marker.

The two holes that cause debate over which is most difficult are Nos. 11 and 15. The 11th has it all, playing 430 yards uphill into a dogleg right and elevated green, along with a creek on the right side of the fairway. The 15th is probably a little meaner, an almost 600-yard double dogleg protected by bunkers and lakes.

The details   979-776-1490. 1929 Country Club Dr., Bryan, TX 77802

- www.briarcrestcc.com
- Marvin Ferguson. 18 holes. Par 72. Back – 6,748 (72.3/125). Middle – 6,456 (70.6/120). Forward – 5,066 (69.8/124). Price – $$.

Getting there From Hwy. 6 out of Bryan, take the Briarcrest exit and look for the signs to the course.

BRYAN MUNICIPAL GOLF COURSE

The golf   Dating back to the 1920s, when it was known as the Bryan Country Club, this is an old, traditional course with narrow fairways, mature trees, and small greens that are known for being in solid condition. The course opened to the public in the 1940s when an additional nine was added. We know that Marvin Ferguson did some renovations in 1971, and a fellow named I.F. Mayberry also had a hand in molding the course.

The course plays only 6,243 from the tips; you'll want to keep the driver in the bag and ensure accuracy off the box, as hazards off the tee are the main reason for big numbers.

CENTRAL

You will hit the ball farther more frequently when you don't try to hit it far. Sam Snead

Two holes stand out–the par 3 No. 3 that plays 169 yards over water to a tiny green, and No. 17, tough because it goes 440 yards into the wind.

The details   979-823-0126. 206 W. Villa Maria Rd., Bryan, TX 77801

- www.americangolf.com
- 1920s. 18 holes. Par 70. Back – 6,243 (69.6/110). Middle – 5,857 (67.1/106). Forward – 4,589 (61.8/103). Price - $$.

Getting there From Hwy. 6 west, take the Briarcrest exit and turn left. This eventually turns into Villa Maria. The course is at the corner of College and Villa Maria.

MIRAMONT

The golf   Located on the east side of town near the center of Bryan's business district, Miramont is Bryan's first master-planned community. After official groundbreaking ceremonies in March 2001, the club announced plans to open its course in the summer of 2003. The facility will offer 22 holes of golf: 18 for the regulation course and another 4 practice holes.

The details   979-268-5520. FM 158 & 1179, Bryan, TX 77802

- Slated to open summer 2003.

Getting there Located on the east side of Bryan at FM 158 and FM 1179.

PEBBLE CREEK COUNTRY CLUB

The golf   Pebble Creek, named after the rocky stream of water that rolls through the layout, opened in 1992 after a slew of designers put their two cents in. Leon Howard kicked it off but left because of money issues. Next came Mike Sheridan, then Ken Dye, and eventually the facilities superintendent to finish it off. As a result, every hole has its own unique character.

The course is beautiful, though, with rolling fairways, lots of trees, and plenty of water. The greens are multi-tiered and challenging–good enough to host the Southwest Conference Championships back in the day.

The highlight of the layout is the excruciating final stretch of holes. No. 15, a long par 4, tempts you to cut the corner of the dogleg because of its length. If you miss it, out-of-bounds looms right. The 600-yard 16th plays downwind with a lake fronting the green. No. 17 plays 230 yards and features another lake. The 18th is the best, though–it plays into the wind at 450 yards and features a creek that cuts into the landing area off the tee.

The details   979-690-0996. 1302 Greens Prairie Rd., College Station, TX 77845

- 1992. B. Spann. 18 holes. Par 72. Maroon – 6,870 (72.4/125). Blue – 6,340 (70.1/122). White – 5,788 (67.1/112). Red – 4,954 (70.7/119). Price - $$.

Getting there From Hwy. 6 south, take the Green Prairie exit and turn left. Drive 1 mile to Pebble Creek Pkwy., turn right, and the entrance is on the left side of the road.

TEXAS A&M UNIVERSITY GOLF COURSE

The golf   This old Aggie course opened in 1950 and features a Ralph Plummer-designed track with wide fairways and large greens. Labeled as a course for the masses and not all that difficult, the course toughens itself up with prominent greenside bunkering and water on 15 of 18 holes. And if you haven't played the course, the greens can be especially deceptive.

Hole 9 is the best challenge, playing 212 yards into a long, skinny green that is surrounded by sand.

The details   979-845-1723. Bldg. 672 Bizzel St., College Station, TX 77843

- Ralph Plummer. 18 holes. Par 70. Back – 6,361 (70.2/122). Middle – 5,776 (68.8/118). Forward – 4,711 (71.4/111). Price - $$.

Getting there From Hwy. 6 north, exit University and turn left. When you come to Texas St., turn left; the first right is the entrance to Texas A & M. Turn left at the dead end and find Bizzel St. Turn left and the course is on the left.

TRADITIONS GOLF COURSE & COUNTRY CLUB AT UNIVERSITY RANCH

The golf   The new Aggie course is on schedule for a fall 2003 opening, and will be called The Traditions Golf and Country Club at University Ranch. Jack Nicklaus and his son are designing the course, and plans have been announced for a Traditions Hotel and Conference Center. For now, you can find membership information by calling 979-822-2582, or visiting www.universityranch.com.

AGGIE LAND NOTES If there's a game in town, you could stand in a crowd of 80,000-plus and chant and sway for four hours. Some Aggies say they head to Austin for the weekend, but there's a few joints worth investigation. One of them is **Los Nortenos Cafe** (979-779-7337) in Bryan, the mint-green cafe that serves great tacos and lets you bring your own ice-cold beer. Afterwards find the **Dixie Chicken** (979-846-2322) for pool, dominoes, beer drinking, and music. And next door is the laid-back **Cow Hop** for cheap burgers. In College Station you'll be drawn to the giant patio of **Garcia's Mexican Cafe** (979-696-5900), where the pinto beans are worth a second helping. Co-ed socializing can be had at **Carney's** (in Bryan) or **The Tap**, where there's always a good scene. Or find the **Messina Hof Wine Cellars**, where you can drink Texas wine, picnic, and

In my experience, no one is too old to learn. However, some older players tend to be less receptive to new ideas and new ways of doing things. Their minds become more inflexible than their bodies. But both mental and physical inflexibility can be changed. Dr. Bob Rotella

fish on their private lake. For lodging, try the affordable **Brazos Inn** (979-779-0020) or the more upscale **Courtyard Marriott** (979-695-8111).

BUCHANAN DAM   Elev. 1,025   Pop. 1,688

It's easy to get lost in the splendor of Central Texas around "Buck-anan" Dam. Here the Colorado River is plugged by the largest multi-arch dam in the country, forming the highest of the Highland Lakes and providing extensive recreational opportunities for retirees and Hill Country explorers alike. For weekend road warriors with the urge for affordable golf, the scenic little course along Inks Lake is a welcome treat.

HIGHLAND LAKES GOLF COURSE ON INKS LAKE

The golf   This scenic 9-hole course adjacent to Inks Lake was redesigned by Dave Bennett in 1990 and offers many breathtaking views, with five of the nine holes set along the lake. The course features mature oak and mesquite trees that impact play throughout the design. Water comes into play on seven holes. The medium-sized greens are basic and of average speed.

When rains are frequent, the fairways are plush and the greens are in good condition. However, if you catch this course during a summer road trip when temperatures consistently reach the high 90s, expect dry conditions and a more rugged feel to the course.

Given the scenery and the course, the price is right, and you can pay once and play all day.

The details   512-793-2859. Park Rd. 4, Buchanan Dam, TX 78609

- Dave Bennett. 1967. 9 holes. Back – 2,778. Middle – 2,701. Forward – 2,371. Price - $.

Getting there From Burnet, take Hwy. 29 west for 7 miles, then turn left on Park Rd. 4. Look for signs to the course.

BUCHANAN DAM NOTES   For beverages and meals sample the variety of lakeside roadhouses like the **Blue Bonnet Cafe and Tavern** (830-793-2906), where they specialize in freshwater catfish. Northwest of the lake is **Fall Creek Vineyards**, a 65-acre estate Texas winery. About 12 miles southeast is the former outlaw hideout now called the **Longhorn Cavern State Park**, with cave tours and nature trails.

In playing golf for more than 50 years, I don't believe there ever was a round in which I used more than six clubs . . . Today there's a stick in the sack for every shot . . . Golfers used to be made on the golf courses. Now they are made in the machine shops. Donald Ross

BURNET

Elev. 1,319   Pop. 4,563

The town of "Burn-it," due west of Lake Buchanan on US 281, grew up around the frontier Fort Croghan in the 1850s and is known for the famous bluebonnet fields and geological outcroppings that dot the countryside. The Bluebonnet Capital of Texas, as designated by the 67th Texas Legislature, also boasts an 18-hole championship layout that is one of the best bargains in Texas.

DELAWARE SPRINGS GOLF COURSE

The golf   Named after the springs that snake through the layout, Burnet's municipal course is a scenic links-style track that is one of the better values in Texas golf. The low prices and friendly service, combined with a picturesque and challenging golf course, make this a Hill Country favorite.

Architects Dave Axland and Dan Proctor built a natural-looking course that fits the terrain perfectly. The course is nestled into the rolling hills and oak trees along the Highland Lakes, playing 6,829 yards from the tips. During your round you'll encounter lush fairways frequently loaded with bunkers, large greens that slope severely, and numerous bump and run shots. The designers added a few original touches, such as the descriptive Scottish names for each hole (the 18th is called "Hame" for the home hole).

Another interesting design twist involved placing the signature hole as the opener. Playing 504 yards to a par 5, No. 1 is best attacked with an iron into the left side of a sloping, tree-lined fairway. The creek cuts into the landing area, making it a testy tee shot. The second shot must bend around the dogleg to the left and over the creek, and the approach is into the green shaded by large trees on the right.

Also note that the grill is famous for its hamburgers, and the course offers an annual dues option if you visit the area frequently.

The details   512-756-8471. Hwy. 281, Burnet, TX 78611

- www.delawaresprings.com
- 1999. Dave Axland and Dan Proctor. 18 holes. Par 72. Black – 6,819 (72.0/121). Blue – 6,239 (69.2/114). White – 5,770 (66.9/108). Red – 4,839 (66.5/107). Price - $$.

Getting there From Hwy. 29, take Hwy. 281 south for 12 miles. The course entrance is on the right-hand side of the highway.

BURNET NOTES   Non-golfers in the family might be interested in the antique shops on the historic town square. There's basic and affordable lodging in Burnet: **Howard Johnson** and **Airy Mount Bed & Breakfast** get the job done. Find tasty BBQ at **Burnet Country Bar-B-Que** on Hwy. 29 West, or dig

---

⭐

I tell players to push their right hand as far away from their head as possible at the top. From this position, all you have to do is let your arms and hands drop as you shift your weight toward the target to start the downswing. That's how to hit with power. Butch Harmon

in for chicken-fried steak at the **Riverwalk Cafe**. The restless can do some scenic driving and cruise Texas 29 west or RM 2341 northwest to see panoramic landscape views near the confluence of the Llano and Colorado Rivers. Or enjoy the drive to Spider Mountain which, according to legend, was an Indian burial ground.

CALDWELL
Elev. 406   Pop. 3,575

A Czech town formed in the rich Brazos River basin, Caldwell was named after macho Indian fighter Mathew "Old Paint" Caldwell, who was a signer of the Texas Declaration of Independence. Located just 26 miles west of College Station, today the "Kolache Capital of Texas" serves as the primary hub for surrounding farms and ranches. Golfers who find themselves on a road trip to Caldwell can partake of the great game at the Copperas Hollow Country Club.

COPPERAS HOLLOW COUNTRY CLUB

The golf   Copperas Hollow is a semi-private, 9-hole country club that is known for being in excellent condition. The track features rolling terrain with pine trees that can alter shots, generally wide-open fairways, and small, well-manicured greens.

Holes 5-7 are tough enough to test the most experienced golfers. The 560-yard, par 5 No. 6 is sandwiched between what are listed as the two toughest holes on the course (the two longest par 4s, which play almost 400 yards).

This is a great place to play, but beware of larger than normal groups, as a marshal is rarely on the course and it is not unusual to see groups with as many as five or six golfers. The price is right and you can pay once and play all day.

The details   979-567-4422. Country Club Dr., Caldwell, TX 77836

- 1964. 9 holes. Back – 3,190 (34.1/114). Middle – 3,135. Forward – 2,775 (35.1/115). Price – $$.

Getting there From Hwy. 36 west, turn right on County Rd. 316. Follow this road to the golf course, where you'll see the entrance off Route 5.

CALDWELL NOTES   Caldwell is home to an old oak tree, called the **Waugh Campground Oak**, which featured political debates back in the day. **Lake Somerville**, 18 miles away, is enjoyable because of the state park and lack of crowds. In town try the Victorian cottage-style 1891 **Kraitchar House** for lodging, and the **Lawyer's Landing** (979-567-3504) is "an uptown bed and breakfast" worthy of consideration.

Most amateurs don't take enough club. They presume they'll hit every shot perfectly and make their club selections based on the maximum distance, instead of the average distance, they hit each club. As a result, any shot that isn't flushed comes up short. Robert Baker

CALVERT

Elev. 335   Pop. 1,523

Calvert was once the fourth largest city in Texas, bustling with hotels, theaters, opera houses, expensive Victorian homes, and a population exceeding 10,000. Once the railroad came through, plantation owners made cotton king and displayed their wealth by building spectacular Victorian mansions in the Brazos River bottoms. Civil War heroes held reunions in Virginia Field Park, the largest cotton gin in the world was built, and times were good. Now you can come to Calvert to take your time, shop for antiques, absorb the history, and play golf at the 9-hole Calvert Country Club.

CALVERT COUNTRY CLUB

The golf   For golf addicts who find themselves in the thriving metropolis of Calvert, Calvert Country Club offers a short, 9-hole track that features medium-sized, elevated greens and five ponds that impact play on six holes. There is only one set of tees here, so this is one place where your scramble will not be ruined by the dreaded low-handicap female who can take advantage of playing forward tees, thus giving her team huge benefits off the tee. Then again, you probably won't be playing in a scramble in Calvert.

The details   979-364-8803. P.O. Box 244, Calvert, TX 77837

- 9 holes. Par 36. 2,741 yards. Price - $.

Getting there From Bryan going north, turn left on West Texas St., which turns into McCrary Rd. and curves to the right. Straight ahead you'll see a sign. The course is on the right.

CALVERT NOTES   Calvert has 37 blocks of homes listed on the National Historic Register. Get to know the town by touring the historic buildings, particularly the pre-1900 churches that dot the town. The 1872 **Calvert Hotel** (979-364-2430) has been restored: a plantation-style country inn that reeks of the Old South and features an outstanding chef for good eats. The best inn is the **Calvert Inn** (979-364-2868), where the honeymoon suite has clawfoot bathtubs in the bedroom for the true romantic. They say this is the Antique Capital of Texas, so rummage through **Cobb's Market** or **Rustique** on Main Street for eclectic trinkets. Out front you can grab a pre-round cup of joe at **Mojoe's Coffee Cart. Somewhere in Time** is open only on the weekends, but the rib-eyes are phenomenal. And every May, the **Maypole Festival** brings tourismos for art, bluegrass music, and fun.

Never practice your full swing when the wind is blowing at your back. If you're right-handed, this means the wind is left to right. The more you practice with the wind blowing left to right, the more you will be inclined to swing across the ball and hit from the top. Harvey Penick

CAMERON

Elev. 402   Pop. 5,951

Historic homes, wonderful restaurants, abundant rivers, lakes, trees, and wildlife–this tranquil town along the Little River 32 miles southeast of Temple has it all. It is known as the "Dewberry Capital of Texas." Imagine the romantic languages of Spanish, German, and Czech garbled with a Texas drawl, and you'll have a sense of the sounds in Cameron. The best place to hear that unique speak is at the Cameron Country Club, which is open to the public, easy to play, and friendly to out-of-towners.

CAMERON COUNTRY CLUB

The golf   Cameron Country Club is a private facility that offers 9 holes of wide fairways and small greens. No need to use your driver here because the course is short enough to use irons off the tee, and you'll want to avoid the dreaded slice due to the out-of-bounds right on every hole. No. 8 offers a nice hilltop view of the surrounding countryside.

The details   254-697-2371. Marlowe Rd., Cameron, TX 76520

* 1930s. 9 holes. Par 35. Back – 2,781 (34.1/103). Forward – 2,596. Price - $.

Getting there From I-35, take Hwy. 36 southeast. As you come into Cameron, turn left on Travis (Hwy. 77), then make a right on 22nd St. Stay on this street until you see the course. Look for E. Marlow Rd.

CAMERON NOTES   The 1895 **Magnolia House** is stunning, with every piece of lumber supposedly handpicked for authenticity and quality. And the **Milam County Museum** is the old three-story jailhouse that features a tower and hanging room. The last weekend in April is the **Dewberry Festival,** complete with a barbecue cook-off, spirits, and good times. In October there is a huge arts & crafts festival. The **Cameron Country Inn B&B (866-697-3160)** comes highly recommended. Eat at **The Texan** for steaks and burgers, but no beer. The **Rustic Corral** off Hwy. 77 serves beer, Tex-Mex and steaks, and **Guadalajara's** is the local authentic Mexican food joint.

CANYON LAKE

Elev. 720   Pop. 29,000

Long before it became a lake, the Guadalupe River ran through the land, giving life to the German farms and villages that dotted the countryside. Once the lake was built in the early 1960s, small communities named after those

Golf is a game to be played with two hands. Your left hand guides the club and keeps the face in the desired position for the hit, and power pours through the right hand and the club. Whack the hell out of the ball with the right hand. Tommy Armour

immigrants sprang up along the shores of the deep, clear waters. It's easy to make a day out of driving around the lake on the farm roads exploring small communities like Hancock, Startzville, and Sattler. Fly-fishing is excellent below the dam, and historic Gruene is just down the road with shopping, tubing, good eats, legendary live music, and cold beers. Before you go, though, play some golf at the scenic 18-hole course that overlooks Canyon Lake.

CANYON LAKE GOLF CLUB

The golf   With its lake views, rolling hills, elevation changes, huge oak trees, and tons of water, Canyon Lake is well worth the day trip despite its remote location.

The key to playing this course well is to be aware of the adjustments that need to be made to deal with the elevation changes. While some of the fairways are tight, there are a surprising number of holes with generous landing areas. The greens are not overly difficult but they do have some undulations.

No. 1 will get your attention: a 450-yard par 4 with a bending fairway. You'll be happy to open with a bogey.

On the back, two notable holes are Nos. 12 and 18. The par 5 No. 12 is just under 500 yards, but forces an approach over water to a green surrounded by bunkers. The ender is a longer par 5, playing 538 yards–you'll need a solid tee shot to reach the corner, which will set up a difficult second shot over a creek to a small landing area. Fortunately, the final approach is less risky: only a short wedge to the green.

The club has a quaint little lounge for post-round refreshments. And it's probably not a bad idea to ask about the use of their pool and condos if the family is with you.

The details   830-899-3301. 405 Watts Ln., Canyon Lake, TX 78133

- www.cedarpost.com/golf
- 18 holes. Par 72. Back – 6,528 (71.0/126). Middle – 6,037 (68.8/122). Forward – 4,726 (67.9/114). Price - $$.

Getting there From I-35 south, turn right at FM 306. After about 13 miles, turn left on FM 2673 then travel another 13 miles and turn right on Campbell Rd. The course is where Campbell Rd. dead-ends. Turn right on Watts Ln.

CANYON LAKE NOTES   This part of Texas is perfect for scenic back-road touring, especially if your destination is a crusty old dance hall like the 1870 **Twin Sisters Hall** (830-833-4808) or the beautiful **Kendalia Halle** (830-833-4902) in the town of the same name just south of Blanco. This 94-year-old hall features a 2,000-square-foot hardwood boot-scootin' floor, an old oak tree out front where borachos were chained until sobriety returned, and another big tree out back bent by Indians to mark their routes. Enjoy the views but watch out for DPS troopers, particularly on 46. Overnighters can call **Mary Ann's B&B** (830-

---

The most important shot in golf is the next one. Ben Hogan

964-2266) on the Guadalupe River, 4 miles from the lake, or the **Maricopa Ranch Resort** (830-964-3731), which has all sorts of things to do in addition to the lodging. Down by Gruene, TX find the **Gristmill** (830-629-5077), a great place to dine on a deck overlooking the Guadalupe River. Next door is the legendary Texas music emporium **Gruene Hall**, where every great name in Texas music turns up sooner or later. **Papa Dock's Cafe** (830-935-4335) and the **Old Sattler Baking Co.** (830-964-3033) are great local options for dining and hanging out around the lake.

CIBOLO   Elev. 706   Pop. 3,035

The town of Cibolo sits on FM 78 just northeast of San Antonio on the back road to Seguin, which is 16 miles east. Cibolo is Spanish for "buffalo" and the town's namesake, Cibolo Creek, features very steep banks that reportedly served as the means for Indians to stampede buffalo over the side, disabling them for slaughter.

Cibolo has been sucked in by the growth of San Antonio and the developments along I-35. The area has grown dramatically since the 1980s and the ensuing housing developments have brought golf course construction along in the area. Two of these communities, the older Northcliff and brand-new Century Oaks, both help fulfill the demand for golf in this outlying area of the Alamo City.

NORTHCLIFFE GOLF & COUNTRY CLUB

The golf   Northcliffe's beleaguered existence has set the stage for one of the best golf values in the San Antonio area. Originally designed in 1979 by Joe Finger to be the centerpiece of a housing community, the houses didn't sell and the course fell on hard financial times. In 1992 a group led by pro John Clay bought the facility and began the long process of improvement.

Those improvements have continued in recent years and the course now has an improved reputation among the golfing public. The new irrigation system, in particular, keeps the course in excellent condition. Now the fairways are plush and putts roll true.

Finger's links-style design features generous fairways and the prominent use of water, along with dry creek beds that snake through the course. The front nine is basically wide open and straight, with the exception of the bending par 5s. The back is more enjoyable with long par 3s, one of which requires a carry over water, and short par 5s that make for solid birdie opportunities. If you're spraying it, the dry creek beds will cause problems. Another notable hole on the back is No. 14, which rides downhill along I-35.

Other notes: Finger built an extra hole as a good-faith effort to build an additional nine holes once home sales improved. The homes never sold, how-

---

If football is a game of inches, how do you describe golf? Bob Rosburg

ever, and this 19th hole remains today. For food and drink, only the basics are offered.

The details   830-606-7351. 5301 Country Club Blvd., Cibolo, TX 78108

• 1978. Joe Finger Par 72. Back – 6,532 (71.0/119). Middle – 6,080 (68.9/115). Forward – 5,285 (70.4/115). Price - $$$.

Getting there From I-35 north, take Exit 178 and turn right onto Country Club Dr. The entrance to the course is on the right side of the street.

CIBOLO NOTES In nearby Selma you'll find **Retama Park** for nefarious speculations on the ponies and excellent machine-made frozen margaritas *con sal* to get you in the mood. Another option is to find the **Hangin' Tree Saloon** (210-651-5812) for cold beer and great live Texas music.

COMFORT
Elev. 1,437   Pop. 1,593

CENTRAL

Comfort's early founders fled the religious and political persecution of their German homelands, and brought their own sense of intellectual independence to this pastoral valley in the hills northwest of San Antonio. Organized religion wasn't necessarily a priority, and the town's founders preferred less government intervention–so much so that the town is still unincorporated today.

In Comfort you'll notice the preservation of the old town in the Comfort Historic District. Craftsmen and artisans make their home here. The Guadalupe River flows lazily south of town, and the Buckhorn Golf Course is the place to play golf.

BUCKHORN GOLF COURSE

The golf   The Buckhorn offers a basic, no-frills golf experience away from the urban hysteria in San Antonio. The course is wide-open and not overly difficult, but generally in excellent condition, highlighted by its challenging greens. Since it's a good drive from San Antonio, the crowds don't make it out this way and you'll never be rushed or have to wait for the group in front of you.

Since the basic layout provides minimal hazards, the real challenge at Buckhorn is in dealing with the greens. The greens are large and slick; many have three to four elevation changes. When analyzing your putt be sure to take a look from all angles, as there are subtle breaks that you'll fail to notice with just a passing glance.

The details   830-995-5351. 36 FM 473, Comfort, TX 78013

• 18 holes. Par 71. Forest – 6,648 (71.4/117). Blue – 6,155 (68.8/113). Stone

You can't go into a shop and buy a good game of golf. Sam Snead

– 5,561 (66.2/106). Red – 4,616 (66.0/109). Price - $$.

Getting there Take Exit 523 off of I-10 North, then turn left on FM 87 south. Go under I-10, turn left on FM 473, and the course is the next left.

COMFORT NOTES   For real adventure see if you can get into the private **Comfort Turn Verein** on Water St., the town's first social club, complete with a 1901 bowling alley that still uses pin boys to replace the pins. Past the river bridge is the home of the best burger around. **Bruno's Curve** (830-995-3547) is a colorful old joint with an outside beer garden (BYOB). In the evening, **Mimi's Cafe** (830-995-3470) is a good choice for bacon-wrapped filet mignon and a baked potato.

COPPERAS COVE   Elev. 1,086   Pop. 30,946

Copperas Cove is on US 190 between Killeen and Lampasas. In the 1950s, less than 5,000 residents lived here, but the coming of Fort Hood brought growth to the area and the city is now home to more than 30,000 people. Driving west from I-35, the highway is so developed it's hard to tell the difference among Belton, Killeen, or Copperas Cove. Rural Central Texas looms ahead, but you won't sense the Hill Country until you're on the western outskirts of Lampasas.

HILLS OF COVE MUNICIPAL GOLF COURSE

The golf   Operated by the city of Copperas Cove, Hills of Cove is a recently expanded 18-hole track that winds through the rolling hills northeast of town. Playing almost 6,300 yards from the tips to a par 71, the design features five challenging par 3s that range from 130 to 230 yards.

The original nine opened in 1972 and its flat, basic layout is a bit outdated but easy for the average golfer and a great way to start a full round. The newer back is more modern, featuring more hills, numerous blind shots, and multi-level greens.

Hole 18 is the feature hole, playing 420 yards and loaded with trees–it's particularly challenging without a solid drive. Long approaches are difficult because the green is protected on the left by a bunker.

Also note that the course has a full-service pro shop and lighted driving range.

The details   254-547-2606. 1405 Golf Course Rd., Copperas Cove, TX 76522

- 1972. 18 holes. Par 72. Back – 6,295. Middle – 5,745. Forward – 5,055. Price - $.

Properly fitted clubs are the only part of improved golf that anyone can buy. Tommy Armour

Getting there From Hwy. 190 west, drive into Copperas Cove and stay in the far right lane. Turn right at the Wal-Mart and McDonalds and follow this road to the first stoplight. Turn right, then make a right again on Golf Course Rd. When you come to the first street on the left, turn into the parking lot.

COPPERAS COVE NOTES   Try **Penni's BBQ** (254-547-6555) or **Aaron's Chopped Beef** (254-542-4670) for lunch. If you're forced to stay, the **Howard Johnson** and **Best Western** are nearby. It's hard to justify more goings-on in the Cove since random Hill Country adventures are so close by. Consider the side trip northwest of town on FM 1113 to see the countryside, and if the kids are with you be sure to check out the drive-through animal park.

EDEN Elev. 2,048   Pop. 1,607

Eden is on the edge of the Hill Country, 40 miles east of San Angelo, in the middle of some of Texas' best ranchland. The surrounding countryside is loaded with live oak, mesquite, pecan, and prickly pear, as well as cattle, sheep, mohair, antelope, and white-tail deer. Concho County has the greatest sheep density of any Texas county, and exotic Axis deer have proliferated on area ranches in recent years. Eden is often ignored by passers-by because of its small size, but with nearby Lake O.H. Ivie producing huge bass and the opening of a brand new 9-hole golf course, Texas travelers have started to pay a little more attention to this friendly little town.

CONCHO SPRINGS GOLF COURSE

The golf   After opening in November of 1998, Concho Springs has received rave reviews, particularly for its lush, green condition–a rarity for small town courses that border drought-prone West Texas. This is a 9-hole country track with wide-open fairways and large, quick greens. Brady Creek winds its way through the course, coming into play on a few holes. In fact, since the hazards are minimal on this basic little course, one of the biggest challenges is dealing with the surprisingly deceptive greens.

One of the best holes at Concho Springs is No. 3, a long par 5 with a tough dogleg fairway.

The details   915-869-8180. South Hwy. 83, Eden, TX 76837

- 1998. 9 holes. Par 36. Back – 3,358. Middle – 2,955. Forward – 2,542. Price - $.

I believe the natural, logical, and easiest way to teach golf is to start with the shortest swing and then increase it to a full swing. I strongly believe it's much easier to learn golf's basic elements—aiming the clubface and hitting the ball consistently in the middle of the clubface—by using a short rather than a long swing. Tom Watson

Getting there From San Angelo, drive east on US 87 into Eden. At the intersection of US 87 and 83, turn right onto US 83 and the course is ahead half a mile.

EDEN NOTES   After golf grab a quick lunch to-go (try **Dairy Queen**), then head north 22 miles to **Paint Rock**, described as the largest single collection of pictographs in the US. Take the tour boat up the Concho River and follow the foot trails to the bluffs that feature the paintings.

FLATONIA Elev. 1,377   Pop. 458

Flatonia, a tiny railroad town on I-10 halfway between Houston and San Antonio, is a quiet Czech community known for its blowout Czhilispeil celebration, antique shopping, and quaint bed and breakfasts. While this spot on I-10 is good for a weekend getaway anytime, late October is the best time to visit because of Czhilispeil–the second-largest chili cook-off in Texas. Highlights include the "World's Largest Tented Biergarten" and live Texas music.

FLATONIA GOLF COURSE

The golf   Built in the first half of the 1990s, this newer 9-hole track is a great place to work in a quick round if you're in the area. The fairways are narrow and the greens are elevated. Unlike many of the older rural, 9-hole courses in the state, Flatonia's course is a little longer (over 3,000 yards) and the holes tend to play more like the big-city courses.

No. 5 is the longest par 4 at 413 yards, and is listed as the number one handicap. Hole 7 is fun to play, a 114-yard par 3 that requires a carry over water to reach the green.

The details   361-865-2922. Hwy. 90E, Flatonia, TX 78941

- 1993. Bill Hassell and Lonnie Garbade. 9 holes. Par 36. Back – 3,056 (34.3/114). Forward – 2,638 (34.9/115). Price - $.

Getting there From Hwy. 609 driving south, take Hwy. 90 east and the course is about a mile away.

FLATONIA NOTES   Piddle around the 1878 **Arnim and Lane Mercantile**, a classic, enduring commercial building where you can buy just about any-

Many great players learned the short game first, then polished the long game. In an earlier era, they were caddies who spent their spare time playing chipping and putting games for pocket change. Develop your short game first so you will know you can score even when your long game is not in good shape. Dr. Bob Rotella

thing. One of the only sit-down places is **Grumpy's Restaurant** on I-10, a truck-stop cafe with good meals. For cheap cold beer and dominoes find the **Friendly Tavern** on Penn St.

FRANKLIN

Elev. 450   Pop. 1,337

Franklin is the seat of Robertson County, located north of College Station in the rolling hills that drain to the bottoms of the Brazos and Navasota Rivers. Robertson County has four towns and a population of only 16,000, but three of those towns have golf courses. Franklin is one of those towns where the business district didn't boom around the town square; residences still flank one side. The golf course here is called the Oak Grove Country Club.

OAK GROVE COUNTRY CLUB

CENTRAL

The golf   Private for the locals but open for the traveling hacker, the Oak Grove CC, famous for its two-day Blind Bogey Tournament held every April, is an improving little redneck course that can entertain you all day long for the low, low price of $22. That investment includes one of the three old-ass three-wheel golf carts, so it's even less expensive to attack on foot.

What you'll experience is a gem of a course, highlighted by a relatively new sprinkler system and some challenging, but extremely fair holes. Two of the nine holes are short par 3s, routing 460 and 495 yards respectively. The shorter one is the best: extremely tight, densely wooded, and spotted by a strategic pond that can be reached off the tee. The 495-yarder involves hitting over a pond on the second shot as well. The best hole is No. 2, a straight 350-yard par 4 that is tough because of its angled green.

Post-round in the 19th Hole, make a donation to the club and receive a cold beer for the effort. Note that the area is dry, but they don't mind if you bring your own cold beverages.

The details   979-828-2301. Hwy. 56, Franklin, TX 77856

• 1968. 9 holes. Par 36. 2,747 yards. Price - $.

Getting there From downtown Franklin drive north on Hwy. 56. Pass the Oak Grove Store 4 miles north of town and look for the course on the right hand side.

FRANKLIN NOTES   Stay in Hearne at the **Oak Tree Inn** (979-279-5599), but before you go don't miss **The Lone Star Burger Bar** (979-828-5000) in the courthouse section, which is open Friday through Sunday. For exploring, drive

When I hit a shot into trouble, I expect the worst . . . When I get there and find that I can actually hit the ball—which you usually can—it changes my mood for the better right away. Corey Pavin

four miles southeast of town on FM 2446 to the **Mt. Pleasant Church cemetery**. It's significant for housing the grave of Confederate soldier Walter Williams, who outlived all other veterans, both North and South, of the Civil War.

FREDERICKSBURG   Elev. 1,742   Pop. 8,847

The fascinating German town of Fredericksburg is one of Texas' most celebrated destinations. It's historic, clean, and quaint, with wide streets lined by hundreds of shops. The community is surrounded by charming country bed and breakfasts, wildflowers, orchards, vineyards, beer joints, oak trees, clear streams, and hills. John Meusebach led the town folk against the Comanches in 1846 and successfully established a lasting peace, and ever since there always seems to be something going on in and around Fredericksburg. Rustic Luckenbach looms nearby in the woods, old German customs such as Oktoberfest, Schuetzenfests, and Kinderfest are regularly celebrated, and quarter horse racing often takes place at the fairgrounds, which happens to be next door to the Lady Bird Johnson Park and the city's 18-hole municipal golf course.

LADY BIRD JOHNSON MUNICIPAL GOLF COURSE

The golf   Thankfully, Fredericksburg offers this facility as a respite from incessant *turista* shopping along the main drag. While not overly fancy, this little Hill Country course gets the job done while the shoppers in the family spend their days in town.

The Jeff Brauer-designed track plays around 6,400 yards from the tips and includes plenty of trees and water hazards that get in the way.

You'll notice the two par 5s on the front. No. 3 is the signature, playing 523 yards and forcing a shot over a creek, and another over a bluff. No. 5 is longer, a testy 578 yards from the back.

The most difficult rated hole is No. 9, a 425-yard par 4, but the regulars complain more about the challenging 18th, an even longer par 4 that plays 450 yards from the tips.

The details   830-997-4010. 341 Golfers Loop, Fredericksburg, TX 78624

- www.fbgtx.org/departments/ladybirdpark
- 1969. Jeff Brauer. 18 holes. Par 72. Gold – 6,432 (70.3/125). Blue – 6,054 (68.6/119). White – 5,672 (66.8/118). Red – 5,092 (68.0/112). Price - $$.

Getting there The course is just south of town on the west side of the road.

If rough is growing in the direction of the shot, the ball will come out easier and faster; if it is against that direction, the grass will resist the club, so you must swing harder. Raymond Floyd

FREDERICKSBURG NOTES Before you go, make your bed and breakfast reservations at **Gastehaus Schmidt** (830-997-5612). For lunch consider **Ken Hall's Barbecue Place** (830-997-2353) 3 miles south of town on US 87. It's worth stumbling through **Luckenbach** (888-311-8990) for cold beer, people watching, and the chance to hear live music under the huge oak trees. Just 10 miles northwest of town is the **Hill Top Cafe** (830-997-8922) where home cooking is taken to a gourmet level, accentuated by the atmosphere and live music. Further down the road, the 1889 **Cherry Springs Dance Hall** (830-833-4902) has seen them all (even Elvis) since it originally opened as a stop for cattle drives with a bunkhouse in the back. Finally, another fun outdoor activity is to find the 500-foot-high dome called **Enchanted Rock,** said to be the site of human sacrifices in Indian legends. Finally, if you're heading to Austin, don't forget the **Friendly Bar** (830-868-2347) in Johnson City, TX, a watering hole worthy of a visit. Pool, live music, domino tournaments, and general socializing are the activities of choice, and have been since this place opened as Kin Casparis Palace Saloon in 1916. If the timing is right and you need an upscale meal, go for poached salmon at the new **Silver K Cafe** (830-868-2911), which also prides itself on its weekend Texas music program.

SUPPORTING TEXAS

While you're traveling in Texas, you will inevitably stumble across a state park that you may want to investigate. Thanks to Texas Parks & Wildlife, you can obtain free entry to more than 120 state parks by paying $50 for a Texas Conservation Passport. The membership supports Texas State Parks, and you receive quarterly listings of special events. Available at any state park, or contact the TPWD at 800-792-1112 (www.tpwd.state.tx.us).

GATESVILLE

Elev. 795   Pop. 12,003

Driving west from Waco on US 84, the central prairies break off into the rougher landscapes of the Hill Country. The highway runs through the low hills into the Leon River Valley, straight through Gatesville and its weathered

It would be an insult to your good taste and intelligence to tell you how to behave on the links,
because it is only necessary to remember that for the time being the golf course is your garden and
the clubhouse is your temporary home. Henry Cotton

town square. Fort Gates was big in 1848, but is no longer. In the hills north of town the search still continues for the Lost Jim Bowie Mine. South of town is the main reason golfers should drive through Gatesville–the 18-hole Gatesville Country Club.

GATESVILLE COUNTRY CLUB

The golf   The GCC is an 18-hole Texas gem. The front nine features tree-lined fairways and two par 5s under 500 yards. This is a scenic little course with elevated tees and greens, a back nine design that incorporates a canyon, and water than comes into play on seven holes.

The details   254-865-6917. Straws Mill Rd., Gatesville, TX 76528

• 1947. 18 holes. Par 72. Back – 6,448. Forward – 5,029. Price - $.

Getting there From Hwy. 36 south, turn west on Golf Course Rd. The entrance is on the left.

GATESVILLE NOTES Some say the **1897 courthouse**, with its hand-cut limestone and copper-domed clock tower, is the best in Texas. Call the **Chateau-Ville** (254-865-2281) for lodging, and have your meals at local sit-down favorites **Andy's Restaurant** or **Rancher's Restaurant**. Out on Hwy. 36, there's a vintage drive-in picture show theatre for evening fun, or you can mosey into **The Horseshoe** for live music and spirits. On 36 to Temple, turn south on FM 1114 and find the village called **The Grove** (pp. 40), where the **Cocklebur Saloon** features live music on most weekend nights. Here more than 800 sets of antlers hang from the ceiling, and the old bar gives that true saloon-type feel.

CENTRAL

GEORGETOWN   Elev. 750   Pop. 28,790

Georgetown feels old and traditional, with its Victorian square, almost 200 old homes and buildings, and the quiet campus of 1840s Southwestern University, the oldest chartered university in Texas. The muddy farmlands and the Hill Country ranch lands merge here, proving its former worth as an agricultural trade center. Lately the city has transformed due to the growth of Austin and the influx of retired couples who crave the scenic locale and convenience of the nearby capital city.

For golfers interested in Georgetown, there is plenty to go around. A few old facilities show the character of Georgetown, but the news is being made by the

If you attend professional golf tournaments, it might help you to follow a good putter for a couple of rounds and notice how often he misses very remarkable putts. Then, watch his response and how, on his next putt, his routine stays the same. Dr. Bob Rotella

rapid pace of new golf course construction, with three high-end courses opening since 1996.

BERRY CREEK COUNTRY CLUB

The golf   Named after the creek that runs through the layout, this is an outstanding course with some of the state's premier holes.

A limestone quarry is incorporated into the design, which provides a spectacular backdrop to the tee shot over water on the 175-yard No. 8.

The front nine is more open than the tree-lined back, but both sides feature tight fairways. Water is in play on 10 holes, including the tricky 326-yard 9th, where the tee shot needs to clear the first lake and the approach must carry another.

The par 3 No. 12 is another beautiful hole. Your tee shot must slide through a narrow chute of trees and avoid the lake to the left of the skinny green.

The details   512-930-4615. 30500 Berry Creek Dr., Georgetown, TX 78628

- www.americangolf.com
- 18 holes. Par 72. Gold – 6,648 (71.6/126). Blue – 6,104 (69.1/119). White – 5,412 (65.9/108). Red – 5,110 (69.8/118). Price - $$.

Getting there From I-35 north, take Exit 266 and turn left. When you come to Berry Creek Dr., turn left again and drive 1.5 miles to the course.

CIMARRON HILLS GOLF CLUB

The golf   Cimarron Hills features an impressive Jack Nicklaus-designed course in a first-class country club setting, which is fortunately open for public play while the residential community builds itself out. Featuring bent-grass greens that are rare these days in Texas, Cimarron goes a mean 7,302 yards from the tips, but offers three other sets of tees that range from 6,800 to 6,276 yards.

The number one handicap hole resides on the front, the 474-yard, par 4 No. 4, which allows you to let it loose off the tee of this dogleg-left hole. Leave the tee shot on the right so you have a clear shot into the green. You'll need that view because it's probably going to be a 3-wood on the monster approach into an angled green guarded by bunkers.

No. 9 is one of the better par 3s, the second longest par 3 on the course. Watch the wind because you'll need to carry the 215 yards of native grasses and shrubs between the tee and green.

Cimarron has packaged their "Club Club Cottage Vacation Getaway," so don't forget to inquire about the details when you plan your trip to Georgetown.

The details   512-736-1800. 5850 Hwy. 29 W., Georgetown, TX 78628

- www.cimarronhills.com

Do not use your body to move the club. Let your body respond
to the moving of the club. Jim Flick

- 18 holes. Par 72. Bear – 7,302 (74.9/135). Outlaw – 6,803 (72.8/131). Cimarron – 6,429 (71.0/125). Legend – 6,276 (69.8/123). Rose – 5,059. Price - $$$.

Getting there From Austin, take I- 35 north to exit 261 in Georgetown. At the first stop light, turn left onto W. Hwy. 29. The club is located 5.8 miles on the right.

GEORGETOWN COUNTRY CLUB

The golf GCC is an old, private course, dating back to 1924 when it was a 9-hole layout. The second nine was added in the 1970s, and today the par 70 layout rolls through the San Gabriel River valley, with water coming into play on 11 holes.

The old nine is more basic, taking advantage of the natural terrain without as many modern, manmade hazards. The newer back is a bit more difficult, highlighted by the signature 13th, which plays 538 yards and crosses the San Gabriel twice.

The details 512-930-4577. 1500 Country Club Rd., Georgetown, TX 78627

- 1920s. 18 holes. Par 70. Back – 5,471 (66.2/111). Middle – 5,089 (64.5/107). Forward – 4,256 (65.2/106). Price - $$.

Getting there From I-35 north, take the Lake Georgetown/Andice exit and turn left. Drive over the overpass and turn left onto Country Club Rd. Look for the clubhouse on the left side of the road.

KURTH-LANDRUM GOLF COURSE

The golf Southwestern University is Georgetown's most recognized historic landmark. Chartered as Texas University by the Republic of Texas way back in 1840, it is the state's oldest college institution. The small campus has dignified charm, with white-stone buildings dotting the campus along with impressive new athletic facilities that have been added in recent years.

Part of the athletic expansion has unfortunately impacted the school's old golf course, as the new soccer field wiped out three of the original nine holes. And if the university's track record for expansion holds true, the remaining six will eventually be eliminated, despite reported plans to restore the 9-hole configuration.

Before World War II the course was apparently an 18-hole track, but was reduced to nine holes after the war. The school opened it to public play in the 1980s, and since then it has averaged around 10,000 rounds per year.

The six holes that remain are short and offer minimal challenges. The greens are some of the smallest you'll find, especially on the uphill, 326-yard No. 2. In fact, these greens reminded us of the burial-mound-like round tops in Alpine and Marfa, hazards in themselves because they're impossible to hit and leave

Golf is the worst drug in the world. You just keep coming back for more embarrassment. Deacon Jones

excruciatingly difficult ups and downs.

Another part of the character at Kurth-Landrum is the maze of campus that leads you to the final two holes. Dirt cart paths weave in many directions, so follow the scorecard and enjoy any potential detours.

These last two holes are both par 3s, the final one considered the best looking hole on the course. A creek fronts the green, and your 150-yard shot must thread the needle between trees that line the hole. And while this green also slopes back-to-front, it's larger than the others.

The details   512-863-1333. Hwy. 29 East, Georgetown, TX 78626

• 6 holes. Back – 2,710 (31.2/97). Price - $.

Getting there In Georgetown off of I-35, take Hwy. 29 east 4 miles to the Southwestern University campus. The course is on the left side.

LEGACY HILLS GOLF CLUB

The golf   Legacy Hills opened in fall 1996 and immediately gained the respect of the Central Texas golf community. Designed by Greg Cash and Billy Casper, the course blends in beautifully with the natural terrain, featuring rolling hills, old oak trees, ravines, and numerous elevation changes, both in the fairway and on the greens.

Berry Creek runs through the layout, and is integral to the signature par 5 18th hole, where you'll have two options off the tee. One side offers the more conservative lay-up, while the other option involves clearing the creek but gives you the chance to get home in two on this 520-yard hole. Fairway bunkers loom ominously, and the long green is extremely prone to a three-jack.

Before you get to that one, though, two par 3s stand out on each side. No. 4 plays 171 yards into a pond and a rock-guarded three-tiered green. No. 16 goes 216 yards into another multi-level green guarded by water and sand on the right.

No. 9 rivals the 18th as the signature—it plays 357 yards uphill, with a creek along the left and fairway bunkers waiting for your tee shot. The approach involves Legacy Hill's waterfall, but it's actually more scenic that it is difficult since a good drive leaves you with a short iron in.

The details   512-864-1222. 301 Del Webb Blvd., Georgetown, TX 78628

• www.legacyhillsgolfclub.com

• 1996. Greg Cash and Billy Casper. 18 holes. Par 72. Black – 7,088 (73.4/127). Gold – 6,693 (71.5/122). Blue – 6,179 (67.8/113). Red – 5,436 (70.5/118). Price - $$.

Getting there Off of I-35 north, take the 261A Exit (County Rd. 2338) and drive west for 5 miles. Turn right at the Del Webb Sun City Georgetown entrance. The course is 2 miles down on the right.

The stories you may have heard or read about "the perfect stroke"
are golf's equivalent of urban legends. Dr. Bob Rotella

WHITE WING GOLF CLUB

The golf   The second of Sun City's Billy Casper signature designs, White Wing first opened with 9 holes in June of 2000, and followed shortly thereafter with the complete package. Often compared to the nearby 1996 Legacy Hills, White Wing isn't quite as long, but is definitely more narrow, lined with massive old oak trees, some of which are located right in the middle of the fairway. Many times even if you "pure" the tee shot down the middle, you'll be forced to hustle a punch shot under one of these majestic trees.

Casper's design is known for its challenging par 5s, one of which is the signature finishing hole. No. 18 plays downhill into a split fairway, offering a more aggressive shot to the right that must clear Berry Creek at 210-yards out, which gives you the chance to get home in two. If you play it sissy-left, you'll need three good shots to get to the green, one of which will involve dealing with one of the huge oaks that looms in the fairway.

The most difficult hole is the par 4 No. 4, which requires an accurate tee shot between fairway bunkers, followed by an approach over a bunker into a multi-level green.

Interestingly, they used TifEagle greens at White Wing, which are quicker than the 328 Bermuda used next door at Legacy Hills. Be ready for the slickness, as they average about 10 on the stimpmeter.

The details   512-864-1244. 151 Dove Hollow Trail, Georgetown, TX 78628

- www.whitewinggolfclub.com
- 2000. Billy Casper. Back – 6,700 (71.6/126). Middle – 6,288 (69.8/122). Forward – 5,159 (70.1/118). Price - $$$.

Getting there Take exit 261-A if driving from Austin or exit 262 if driving in from the north. Driving 5 miles west on Williams Dr., and turn right on Del Webb Blvd. At the stop sign, turn left on Sun City Blvd., then right on Dove Hollow Trail.

GEORGETOWN NOTES   It's worth a call to investigate the Sun City vacation packages for prospective residents that include deals on green fees and good pricing on fully furnished model houses for lodging. Along the San Gabriel River is the **San Gabriel Motel**, with 19 rooms built in the 1930s. Also on the river is **San Gabriel Park**, former Tonkawa Indian village and site of political debate as well as the occasional hanging. For eats go off the beaten path to the farming town of **Walburg, TX** (exit 268 of I-35 and drive 4 miles down CR 972), where the **Walburg Restaurant** (512-863-8440) serves up Bavarian specialties like bratwurst and roasted pork loin.

It is not necessary to go back and through the same length. That's hogwash,
unless it happens to work for you. Jim McLean

CENTRAL

GIDDINGS
Elev. 520   Pop. 4,633

Giddings lies on the crest of a divide separating the Colorado and Brazos river basins, the ideal spot for the railroad which founded the town in 1872. Located on US 290 55 miles east of Austin and 100 miles west of Houston, Giddings offers plenty to do for the curious post-golf adventurer. Playing the 9-hole Giddings Country Club once before lunch, then once more after lunch, sets the stage for piddling around town and lazy backroads adventures into the surrounding countryside.

GIDDINGS COUNTRY CLUB

The golf   A typical small-town course with wide fairways, mature trees, minimal bunkers, and enough water to cause problems, Giddings Country Club offers an enjoyable round of golf. You can pay once and play all day, and you'll be able to score better once you get used to the small, mound-shaped greens that are hard to hit in regulation, and even harder to chip to and avoid having your ball roll down the other side. In the summer the rough can be thick, so keep it in the fairway if you can.

The details   979-542-3777. RR 2, Giddings, TX 78942

• 1974. 9 holes. Par 36. Back – 3,101. Middle – 2,855. Forward – 2,550. Price - $.

Getting there From Austin, take Hwy. 290 west for 48 miles to Giddings. Turn right at the Wal-Mart and drive 1.5 miles to the course. The entrance is on the left-hand side of the road.

GIDDINGS NOTES   In Giddings, the locals go to **Ernie's Cafe** for morning coffee-drinking philosophizing and the **City Meat Market** (979-968-3259) for barbecue at lunch. However, since golf in Giddings can be quick, you may be heading to another destination, and the place we recommend is south of US 290 at **Round Top, TX**, where you can lounge in the quaint biergarten of the **Landaus Ramsey German-American Kitchen** (979-249-2080) and sample the bratwurst. Another option here is the **Royers Round Top Cafe** (877-866-7437), with its fried jalapeños, pork tenderloin, and unique atmosphere.

GOLDTHWAITE
Elev. 1,580   Pop. 1,696

Located 90 miles west of Waco on US 84, Goldthwaite is the ranching and agricultural hub for Mills County. Like San Saba to the south, the production of wool, mohair, cattle, sheep, and pecans drives the economy of this quiet town of weathered rock. Indian fighting used to be prominent here in

This is really the whole secret of good match play—simply to play your best and steadiest, and not to care about the opponent's game until it is absolutely necessary to do so. James Braid

Comanche country, but those days faded with the coming of the railroad in 1885. To the south, the Colorado River offers good river fishing and the municipal golf course awaits the traveling hacker.

GOLDTHWAITE MUNICIPAL GOLF COURSE

The golf   With fairways lined with oak and pine trees, and enough water and sand hazards to make the day interesting, Goldthwaite's muni track is a nice place to work in a quick round. The course features small greens with tricky undulations.

The 333-yard 5th hole is a good birdie opportunity, as is the short, par 3, 128-yard No. 8. The par 4s are of standard length, ranging from 333 to 382 yards. Good drivers will spend their day hitting short irons into the tiny greens.

The details   915-938-5652. Hwy. 16, Goldthwaite, TX 76844

- 1988. 9 holes. Par 36. Back – 3,086 (33.2/112). Forward – 2,633 (32.8/111). Price - $.

Getting there From Austin, take Hwy. 183 north for 100 miles to Goldthwaite. On Hwy. 16 turn south and drive 3 miles south to the course.

GOLDTHWAITE NOTES   The famous **Regency Bridge** was featured on the 2000 Texas Highways map. The **Goldthwaite B & B** can put you up for the night, and there's an RV park for those who travel that way. Do **Texas Pride BBQ** for lunch and hit **Trevino's Fajita Junction** for mouth-watering fajitas at dinner time.

GONZALES   Elev. 292   Pop. 6,618

Gonzales holds a special place in Texas history as the site where, in 1835, Texans fired the first shot in the war against Mexico. Before that the settlers struggled constantly with the Comanche and Tonkawa Indians, and the town housed Fort Waul for the Confederacy during the Civil War. Normalcy eventually prevailed; cotton farming became the main force in the economy before cattle drives and railroads made their way through town.

Gonzales has streets that were planned by the Mexican government and named for saints. Magnificent oak and magnolia trees line these thoroughfares today, along with over 80 historical markers telling the tales of the revolution.

INDEPENDENCE GOLF COURSE

The golf   Set along the Guadalupe River and located in the city park, this is a beautiful, clean facility with wide-open fairways and immaculate, undulating greens.

For the long bunker shot, set up with the ball forward in your stance and plan for your club to enter the sand two or three inches behind the ball, as with any other bunker shot. Butch Harmon

The design features a few holes that offer very solid birdie opportunities for even the average golfer. Both par 5s are under 500 yards, the longest of the three par 3s plays only 150 yards, and the par 4s range from 285 to 360 yards.

Pay once and play all day here, and there are two sets of tees that make for an 18-hole round. Carts are available but you should walk this one and take in the scenery.

Note that frequent visitors to the area can buy an annual membership to the course for $185 for individuals and $240 for families.

The details   830-672-1324. Hwy. 183, Gonzales, TX 78629

- 1950. 9 holes. Par 35. Back – 2,690 (33.1/113). Forward – 2,330 (34.6/110). Price - $.

Getting there From I-10 east, turn left on Hwy. 304 to Gonzales. When you reach Hwy. 183, turn left (south) and the clubhouse is on the right side of the street.

GONZALES NOTES   Soak up the history of the revolutionary war against Mexico by visiting the downtown plazas named **Confederate Square** and **Texas Heroes Square.** You'll also find the **Old Jail Museum,** which houses cells, a dungeon, gallows, and jailer's quarters. **Independence Park** (home of the golf course) offers campsites and recreational facilities south of town on the banks of the Guadalupe. Have a family-style meal at the **Hernandez Cow Palace Restaurant** (830-672-4777). The **St. James Inn** (830-672-7066) is the place to stay–a quaint old home that's fitting for any trip to Gonzales.

HAMILTON
Elev. 1,154   Pop. 2,867

Hamilton is set in the middle of a rich farming area full of windmills, hay bales, and woods; hunters are a mainstay of the economy. About 70 miles west of Waco on north-south US 281, this prosperous-looking town of 2,800 exudes the feel of a place that hasn't changed since the 1950s.

PERRY COUNTRY CLUB

The golf   Perry Country Club is a private facility that allows non-resident golfers to play for a fee. Built in the 1930s, this old course features a traditional layout with hilly terrain and mature trees. The greens are small and sloped, but in excellent condition.

Warm up before you tee off because the first hole plays 588 yards. On a cool, windy, spring day, it feels like 688 yards. The two par 3s (2 and 5) offer good birdie opportunities, as does the 269-yard par 4 8th hole.

Everyone raves about the golf experience in the small town of Hamilton.

I'm not saying my golf game went bad, but if I grew tomatoes they
would have come up sliced. Lee Trevino

This place is a bargain that is made more enjoyable by the friendly nature of the staff and golfers.

The details 254-386-3383. Hwy. 36, Hamilton, TX 76531

- 1934. 9 holes. Par 36. Back – 3,110. Forward – 2,622. Price - $.

Getting there From Fort Worth, take I-35 south to Hwy. 67. Turn south again and proceed to Hwy. 281. Turn south again and find FM 218, where you'll turn west and drive 2 miles to the course. The entrance is on the right-hand side.

HAMILTON NOTES On the highway into town look for **Lazy T's BBQ** trailer and order a sliced-brisket sandwich. **Storm's Hamburgers** (254-386-3143) is the best place for juicy home-style burgs. **Pecan Creek Park** meanders over 10 blocks downtown and is the best way to soak in the feel of this quaint town. For lodging there are several nice bed and breakfasts. Try the **Pecan Creek Ranch B&B** (254-386-4419) or **The Hamiltonian** (254-386-8868).

HARKER HEIGHTS
Elev. 767   Pop. 17,872

Despite its size and rapid rate of growth, Harker Heights is a relatively unknown Texas city, hidden in the shadows of other Fort Hood area cities such as Copperas Cove, Temple, Belton, and Killeen. While the town has no major industry, it is closely integrated with Killeen and houses approximately 10% of the Fort Hood personnel living off base. Set in the rolling hills near Still House Hollow Lake and Lake Belton, Harker Heights offers scenic Central Texas views and ample recreation opportunities.

LAKEVIEW GOLF & COUNTRY CLUB

The golf Lakeview rests along Still House Hollow Lake and features spectacular views, plush fairways, and greens known for their outstanding condition. Unusual for a 9-hole facility, the course offers five sets of tees, ranging in yardage from 2,455 to 3,318 yards.

The finishing hole is listed as the number one handicap, even though it plays as a par 4 just over 300 yards. However, both par 5s play over 500 yards from the tips. The toughest hole might be No. 8, a challenging 205-yard par 3.

The details 254-698-4554. 1901 Valley Oaks Dr., Harker Heights, TX 76548

- 1971. 9 holes. Par 36. Black – 3,318 (71.0/120). Blue – 2,999. White – 2,855 (68.0/113). Yellow – 2,509. Red – 2,455. Ratings listed for 18-hole round. Price - $.

The shorter the shot, the more deliberate and carefully thought out your efforts must be. Henry Longhurst

Getting there From Killeen, take Hwy. 190 east, then exit FM 2410 and drive south. Go to the second flashing yellow light (Cedar Knob) and turn right. Drive 2.5 miles to Fuller Ln., turn left, and travel a short distance to Oakridge. Turn left on Oakridge and continue to Valley Oaks Dr. Turn right and the course is down the road on the right-hand side.

HARKER HEIGHTS NOTES   Harker Heights is Killeen. See Killeen. Don't stay. Just play golf, eat, and move on.

HEARNE
Elev. 305   Pop. 4,852

The agricultural town of Hearne spreads out over railroad crossings and highway junctions among the fertile farmlands just east of the Brazos River. Centrally located for weekend explorers from Austin, Houston, and Dallas, Hearne attracts the increasing number of folks who are traveling through on Hwy. 79 looking for out-of-the-way adventures. The old depot is restored, and there are a few old homes worth looking at, but if you find yourself with a little more time, work in a round at Hearne's municipal golf course.

HEARNE MUNICIPAL GOLF COURSE

The golf   Hit 'em straight, bring your short game, and get ready for some testy up-and-downs. This 9-hole track is lined with pine trees and is in excellent condition, but the dominating feature is the miniscule, elevated, mound-shaped greens. The design offers simplicity, with straight holes that can make it seem like you're playing the same hole over and over again. The pessimist will say it's a boring course, while the optimist will rave about the opportunity to work on your game on this simple course with tricky greens.

The details   979-279-3112. 405 Norwood Ln., Hearne, TX 77859

• 1935. 9 holes. Par 36. Back – 3,149 (34.9/118). Forward – 2,354 (31.4/99). Price - $.

Getting there From Bryan-College Station, take Hwy. 6 north to Wheelock Rd. Turn east and continue to Norwood Ln. Turn north and the course is straight ahead.

HEARNE NOTES   Get to know the locals and invite yourself on a **late-night coon hunt**, something that every discerning golfer should experience. If they don't ask you to stay over, call the **Oak Tree Inn** (888-897-9647), which is clean and new. Two recommended restaurants here: **The Dixie Cafe** on the

---

☆

Casual water: Water other than a water hazard on the course from which you can lift your ball without penalty.

corner of Hwy. 6 and 79, where pork chops are popular, and the super-authentic Mexican food joint known as **Ama's**.

HICO
Elev. 1,006   Pop. 1,289

Traffic is light around Hico (with a long 'i') as you roll through dairy, pecan, and peanut farms. Nothing much here, just famous pies at the local cafe and a museum with documentation stating that the late, local resident Brushy Bill was actually famous outlaw Billy the Kid. The country club is semi-private, though, so make it a point to get out and experience the course if you're driving through.

BLUEBONNET COUNTRY CLUB

The golf   Bluebonnet CC is a 9-hole, semi-private facility that features wide-open fairways, minimal trees, small greens, and a creek that is incorporated into the design. In fact, water impacts play on five of the nine holes. The layout also incorporates a few dogleg fairways that make strategy a little more important here than on other small-town courses. One of the best features, though, is the fact that for under $30 you can play and ride all day long.

The details   254-796-4122. 1581 Farm Rd. 1602, Hico, TX 76457

• 1925. 9 holes. Par 36. Men's – 3,090. Ladies – 2,176. Price - $.

Getting there From Stephenville, take Hwy. 281 east into Hico. Turn right at the blinking light. Once you reach the Ferry sign, turn left and drive 2 miles to the course. Look for the entrance on the right side of the road.

HICO NOTES   Try the rustic **Bout' Time' BBQ** (254-796-4300) for hot links and trimmings at lunch time. In the evenings roll into **Jersey Lilly's** (254-796-0999) for everything under the sun, including patio dining and entertainment. Weekenders should make reservations at the **Flying "P" Lodge** (254-796-4427) for game-bird hunting and sporting clays, which always go well with planned golf outings at the Bluebonnet Country Club.

HILLTOP LAKES
Elev. 465   Pop. 311

Centrally located about 130 miles from Houston, Austin, and Dallas, Hilltop Lakes is a retirement and resort community built around five lakes, with a variety of outdoor recreation available in addition to the golf course. The community started out as a ranch back in 1961, but was sold in the late 1990s to property owners.

Aggressive golf begins with an honest appraisal of your current ability with every club in the bag. Greg Norman

HILLTOP LAKES GOLF COURSE

The golf   With so many high-dollar resort courses available all over the state, the lack of affordable "stay and play" options can sometimes be frustrating. Hilltop Lakes solves that problem by offering a remote little hideaway with an extremely scenic 18-hole course.

The resort originally opened with 9 holes back in the early 1960s (Ralph Plummer design), but Leon Howard came along and added another 9 around 1970. The design incorporates a few water hazards, as well as some strategically placed bunkers as the course rolls through the residential community.

Most would classify this as an easy course, and if you can hit the ball a long ways you'll be in good position to score well with your short irons. The par 5s are all 500 yards or shorter, and with the exception of No. 9 (412 yards), all of the par 4s are under 400 yards. The course is also void of long par 3s. No. 14 plays tough: it's a 361-yard par 4 that requires a tee shot over a creek, followed by an approach shot over a small pond to the green.

The details   936-855-2100. 100 Golf Club Dr., Hilltop Lakes, TX 77871.

- www.hilltoplakes.com
- 1963. Ralph Plummer-Leon Howard. 18 holes. Par 72. Blue – 6,330 (69.1/114). White – 6,065 (70.1/115). Red – 5,635 (70.85/120). Price - $$.

Getting there From Austin take I-35 north to Round Rock. Turn right on W. Palm Valley Blvd. and drive 15 miles. Merge on to Hwy. 79 toward Rockdale. 5 miles outside of Ridge, turn right on Hwy. 3. Go 9 miles and the resort will be on the right.

HILLTOP LAKES NOTES   Because of its out-of-the-way location, Hilltop Lakes is one of those places that you'll visit for the full weekend, rather than a quick pass-through. The resort offers three lodging options with the **Mirror Lake Inn**, the **Hillside Villas**, and a campground. Hilltop's **Overlook Dining Room** has been recently renovated.

HORSESHOE BAY   Elev. 825   Pop. 3,337

Robert Trent Jones, Sr., said it best when he so eloquently described this impressive Hill Country resort: "I know of no area, including those known for several courses, that has a more interesting variety of golf than Horseshoe Bay. I rank this among the best in the world."

Everything is meant to be for the Texas golfer at Horseshoe Bay. Surrounded by the Hill Country within Texas' most ideal climactic region, the area will soon offer four spectacular courses along 150 miles of Lake LBJ shoreline, free of annoying housing developments. Combined with the world-class Horseshoe

Golf is based on honesty, where else would you admit to a seven on a par three? Jimmy Demaret

Bay Resort this adds up to one of Texas' premier golf destinations.

In the midst of the current golf boom, this spectacular resort has tended to get lost in the shuffle since it opened in the 1970s. That's unfortunate, and unwarranted. With the opening of the fourth course, Flintrock, Horseshoe Bay will become known again as one of the true treasures of Texas golf.

HORSESHOE BAY RESORT COURSES

The golf   The **Slick Rock Course** started it all in 1972 and is the oldest and most hacker-friendly. Giant oaks guard the somewhat generous fairways of this 6,839-yard layout. Water comes into play on 12 holes, but Mr. Jones lessened the impact of bunkering and created inviting targets with the large, rolling greens, which were completely rebuilt in 1997.

The longest par 4 is on the front, playing 421 yards as the 7th hole. This one is tricky because of the fairway bunker in the landing area off the tee.

Everyone talks about the 361-yard 14th hole, which requires a lovely little tee shot over a wide river valley that features waterfalls, lily pads, and the rare Guadalupe river bass. After the tee shot, the drive to the green makes the day, crossing the water near the waterfall and providing some relief to the summer heat.

The most difficult of the four, the **Ram Rock Course**, came along when the Slick Rock course couldn't stand up to the pros in one of the Texas State Opens. After complaints about Slick Rock's ease, Jones came in and built what is respected throughout Texas as one of the state's most difficult courses.

Rock outcroppings pingpong wayward shots, natural streams and waterfalls suck in golf balls, and the narrow fairways are enough to make the most virile of men crumble under pressure. Water is present on 10 holes and 60 bunkers dot the landscape.

Every hole stands out, but we'll mention the 488-yard par 4 No. 2, a ridiculous hole for a hack, and the island-greened, 191-yard No. 4.

There's an island green at No. 4, 191 yards from the rear, and the greens are slick-bent, the only Horseshoe Bay course that has retained this quick putting surface.

Note that former Texas Tech head football coach and all-around good-ole-boy Spike Dykes lives off hole 11.

After the **Applerock Course** opened in 1985, Golf Digest bestowed its "Best New Resort Course in America" ranking on the Robert Trent Jones track. This one is considered the most spectacular of the three existing courses at Horseshoe Bay. Nestled along the shores of Lake LBJ, it takes advantage of the highest elevations on the entire property to offer outstanding views of the countryside. Hole after hole is dramatic, with exciting elevation changes, magnificent oak and elm trees, and native granite-lined stream beds that cut through the course.

Holes 10-12 offer the best stretch of golf at Applerock. Starting with the

No matter how short the par 3, the drive is never a gimme. Henry Beard

back-to-back par 5s that roll downhill to the lake, and ending with the signature 179-yard No. 12 that rests along the lake, these holes take you from the highest point on the course down to the banks of the lake that surround the 12th green.

Jack Nicklaus has been commissioned to design Horseshoe Bay's fourth resort course, the **Saddle Rock Course,** which is currently under construction with a slated opening date sometime in summer 2003.

Also note that the resort's **Whitewater Putting Course** features 18 holes of bent-grass greens, complete with sand traps, water hazards, and lights for night-time putting with the dean's daughter (see *Caddyshack*). As you might expect, this added feature holds up well to the standard set by the regulation courses.

The details   830-598-2561. 1 Horseshoe Bay, Horseshoe Bay, TX 78657

- www.horseshoebaytexas.com
- Slick Rock Course: 18 holes. Par 72. Back – 6,834 (72.6/125). Middle – 6,354 (70.2/117). Forward – 5,438 (72.1/127). Price - $$$$.
- Ram Rock Course: 18 holes. Par 71. Back – 6,926 (74.5/140). Middle – 6,378 (71.8/130). Forward – 5,306 (72.5/129). Price - $$$$.
- Apple Rock Course: 18 holes. Par 72. Back – 6,999 (74.0/139). Middle – 6,536 (72.1/128). Forward – 5,509 (73.0/128). Price - $$$$.
- Saddle Rock Course: Jack Nicklaus. 18 holes. Under construction.

Getting there From Hwy. 71 west, take the Horseshoe Bay exit and follow the signs to the club.

HORSESHOE BAY NOTES   You definitely have options here along Lake LBJ, with hotel accommodations to luxury suites, most of which offer outstanding views of Lake LBJ. In addition to the golf, tennis, swimming, and volleyball, boating and fishing on the lake are the things to do here. You can get your workouts in at the **Bayside Club & Spa,** which gives you the option to truly indulge at one of the five restaurants and six lounges the resort has to offer. The nationally acclaimed **Members Club** allows you to go upscale, or you can take it easy at the **Waterfront Pub & Eatery** that overlooks the lake. Call 800-252-9363 for reservations, or visit www.horseshoebaytexas.com for more notes on what they have to offer.

HUTTO   Elev. 661   Pop. 1,250

As Austin's growth creeps up I-35 and sucks in Pflugerville, Round Rock, and Georgetown, small communities like Hutto, just 7 miles east of Round Rock, are inevitably drawn into the urbanization. That means big dollars, traf-

---

fic, sophisticated housing communities, and superb golf courses. Now the former railroad and cotton town, originally settled by German, Swedish, and Danish immigrants, is the site of the Timmerman Ranch development and The Golf Club at Star Ranch.

THE GOLF CLUB AT STAR RANCH

The golf   Hutto's been put on the golf map now that the first-class Star Ranch has opened up on what was once a cattle ranch, boasting a unique collaborative effort from the Morrish brothers (Jay and Carter) and the Bechtol-Russell design firm.

The course sits on a hill and is built around a centralized lake, featuring the typical spectacular Hill Country topography highlighted by plush, undulating fairways and bleached white sand bunkers.

No. 2 is one of the most difficult holes and the first real challenge of your golf day. The 417-yard par 4 has more of an open feel than some of the other holes, but its length generally means a rather long approach, and the green is surrounded by several massive bunkers.

The details   512-252-4653, 2500 FM 685, Hutto, TX 78634

- www.starranchgolf.com
- 18 holes. Par 71. Tour – 7,017. Champ – 6,341. Preferred – 5,678. Forward – 4,960. Price - $$$.

Getting there From Austin, take I-35 north and exit Parmer Ln. Turn right and go east on Parmer to Dessau Rd. Turn left and go north on Dessau, which becomes FM 685. Go 5 miles past FM 1825 in Pflugerville and the club is on the left.

HUTTO NOTES   Try lunch at **Bibs BBQ** (512-759-2677) on East St., then head back to Austin or continue the adventure down the backroads to the **Coupland Dance Hall** (512-856-2226). It features a carved, bullet-riddled bar dating back to 1886, a family-style restaurant if you're still hungry, and real-live true Texas music.

JUNCTION   Elev. 1,742   Pop. 2,696

Surrounded by hundreds of natural springs, Kimble County has more flowing streams than any other Texas county, earning it the moniker "Land of the Living Waters." The pristine little town of Junction serves as the county seat of this sparsely populated area, and is nationally known for the production of wool and mohair. Junction also serves as a hub for regional hunting and fishing activities.

Chili was officially named the "State Dish of Texas" in 1977.

CENTRAL

JUNCTION GOLF CLUB

The golf   Dating all the way back to 1927, this 9-hole course is set in the rugged Hill Country alongside the South Llano River and features Cedar Creek, which runs throughout the layout and comes into play on three holes. Over its 76-year history, the facility has received two major improvements, one of which was a project to convert the greens from sand to grass back in the 1980s. The land is owned by the Hill Country Fair Association and is leased to the Junction Golf Association, which keeps the course in good condition.

You might drive the green on No. 2, a 257-yard par 4, but you'll be faced with many challenging shots here. One of them is the tee shot over water on the 223-yard, par 3 hole 9.

We recommend that you plan your trip to Junction to coincide with one of the 8-10 two-day tournaments that are held annually. Food is included with the entry fee, and the friendly locals can help you negotiate the unfamiliar course layout.

The details   915-446-2968. FM 2169 West, Junction, TX 76849

- 1930. 9 holes. Par 35. Back – 2,827 (34.3/120). Middle – 2,582 (34.1/116). Forward – 2,141. Price - $.

Getting there From I-10, take the Junction City exit and head up the road for 1 mile to the course.

JUNCTION NOTES   Take advantage of the beautiful Texas scenery along US 377 southwest along the South Llano River, particularly the rest area overlook 22 miles south. Heading north on US 377, you'll run into the venerable **London Hall** (915-475-2921), with its large stone fireplace, cozy bar, pool tables, and shuffleboard. Supposedly there's been a dance here every Saturday night for a hundred years or more. Junction offers a few great dining options. **Coopers Bar-B-Q & Grill** (915-446-8664) does it all and specializes in cabrito, and the **Gonzales Cafe** (915-446-4202) is the place for cold Carta Blancas and nachos after a day of hunting, fishing, and golf. Also don't miss a meal at **Lum's** (915-446-3541), the spot for barbecue-deli fare on the patio. Reserve your rooms at either the **Shady Rest B&B** (915-446-4067) on 11th St. or the **South Llano River B&B** (915-446-3609).

KERRVILLE   Elev. 1,645   Pop. 21,031

Surrounded by scenic green valleys, clear streams, and rugged live-oak-covered hills, combined with perhaps the most ideal climate in the nation,

---

We all have particular quirks and faults in our golf swing we wish were not there.
We anguish over how to make them go away. But they never do and they never will.
It's all part of our "thumb print." Don't forsake your thumb print. It is who you are.
Work with it, not against it. Roger Maltbie

Kerrville has consistently been one of Texas' most sought-after Hill Country destinations. The city's history dates back to 1869 when Captain Charles Schreiner established his merchandising business and ranching operations here, eventually purchasing more than 600,000 acres of land by 1900.

The pleasant setting attracts not only visitors, but an interesting mix of affluent and somewhat international residents who give the city a little more culture than you might expect out this way. In fact, in the mid-1990s the *Wall Street Journal* listed Kerrville as one of the wealthiest small towns in America. Fortunately for the traveling golfer, that wealth has helped bring three outstanding golf courses to this town of just 21,000 residents.

THE CLUB AT COMANCHE TRACE

The golf   Comanche Trace is Kerrville's newest golf course, designed by Tom Kite as the centerpiece of a master-planned residential community that is truly spectacular. Kite worked with the design team of Roy Bechtol and Randy Russell to sculpt this track out of the Guadalupe River Valley. The course opened in December 2000.

Comanche Trace's signature and most famous aspect is the outstanding bent-grass greens. When you see the course, you'll immediately become entranced by their healthy, lush looks. And you'll need to–if the average hack doesn't pay attention in keeping the approaches in the correct position in relation to the pin, these greens will beat you down hole after hole. But if you're in the right spot, they roll true and are extremely fair.

In addition to the greens, the course has subtle macho characteristics that distinguish it from other new housing community courses. Everything flows here, such as the discreet placement of the 150-yard markers, and the 100-year old rock bar that was incorporated into the design between holes 5 and 6. The cart path rolls right through the barn, with bathrooms on one side and horse stalls on the other. The clubhouse sits atop the area's highest elevation, a former Comanche lookout that sports stunning views of the Hill Country.

If you hit them straight here, you'll be okay. Otherwise some punishment is in order, with deep bunkers sucking in wayward hacks and dreadlock-like rough framing the fairways.

You'll notice that most of the outstanding holes play uphill, including the almost ridiculous 9th hole, which plays 448 yards into the wind and is loaded with up to 10 bunkers.

Hole 14 is neat because of the split fairway. The recommended strategy is to take the higher right side instead of the longer left, which requires a blind approach.

You can't beat No. 18 as a finisher. At 525 yards, bunkers protect the dog-

The great anxiety of the moderate player when making his stroke is to get the ball properly lofted, and in some obstinate cases it seems to take several seasons of experience to convince him completely that the club has been specially made for the purpose, and, if fairly used, is quite adequate. Harry Vardon

leg right as you continually work your way uphill. At 100 yards out, the hole doglegs back left to a multi-level green.

Other notes: The elevation here means cooler summer temps than nearby San Antonio, sometimes as much as a 6-7 degree difference. The club has plans to add 9 more holes. Ask about the stay-and-play packages the course offers in conjunction with several area hotels and bed and breakfasts.

The details   830-792-6282. 3074 Bandera Hwy., Kerrville, TX 78028

- www.comanchetrace.com
- 2000. Tom Kite and Roy Bechtol. 18 holes. Par 72. Back – 7,103. Forward – 5,103. Price - $$$.

Getting there From I-10 west, connect with Hwy. 16 south and turn left on Country Club Dr.

RIVERHILL COUNTRY CLUB

The golf   Riverhill's architect, Joe Finger, was a well-traveled Renaissance man who has dabbled in everything from corrugated plastics and dairy farming to college golf and course development. So it says something that he chose Riverhill Country Club as his home. Consistently rated as one of the top courses in all of Texas, Riverhill is a scenic layout with major elevation changes; undulating, elevated greens; lots of water and tough Hill Country brush that wreaks havoc on errant balls.

Leon Howard designed the course originally as a 9-hole layout back in 1952, but members eventually commissioned Byron Nelson and Ralph Plummer to improve the layout. Plummer became ill, opening the door for Finger's contributions. One of his most challenging holes is No. 11, a par 3 that sometimes plays around 200 yards from the tips. With the wind blowing and water all along the right side, it's an intimidating tee shot when you're aiming at the tiny green.

Hole 4 is the most difficult rated hole, a 458-yard par 4. Another tough challenge is the long par 5 14th, which happens to be proceeded by another long par 5, creating a tough stretch of golf on the back side.

The details   830-792-1143. 100 Riverhill Club Ln., Kerrville, TX 78028

- www.riverhillcc.com
- 1952 by Leon Howard. 1970 by Joe Finger and Byron Nelson. 18 holes. Blue – 6,855 (73.8/130). White – 6,454 (71.0/126). Gold – 6,051 (70.0/118). Red – 5,301 (71.5/121). Price - $$$.

Getting there From I-10 west, take Hwy. 16 south. When you come to Hwy. 173, turn toward Bandera and drive to Riverhill Club Ln. Turn right and the course is just down the road.

Poor chipping is the primary reason the handicap of the average golfer has remained frozen. Corey Pavin

SCOTT SCHREINER MUNICIPAL GOLF COURSE

The golf   John Bredemus stopped off here in the 1920s to open up Kerrville's first golf course. Originally private when it opened in 1923, the course was acquired by the city in the 1930s and the course has remained public ever since.

Situated on gently rolling terrain, the course offers scenic views of the surrounding Texas hill country. R.D. Kizer and Joe Finger have had their hands in molding the layout, which features somewhat generous fairways and an interesting combination of mounded greens.

Bredemus designed the front nine, which is highlighted by the classic 592-yard par 5. This is a mean hole, with water cutting into the fairway twice and an elevated green that requires a perfect approach. The hole has character, with water along the right and an ominous-looking cliff framing the view. Another notable hole on the front is the dogleg-left No. 7, with trees dominating the left side.

The signature hole is No. 17, a 535-yard par 5. Water comes into play on the second shot and then again on the approach to the green, which is surrounded by water on three sides. A waterfall to the left of the green adds a pleasing aesthetic.

The back nine, which opened in 1977, is more forgiving than the front. The best hole is the tough, par 5 No. 17. If you survive the tee shot, water comes into play on both the second and third shots. The last shot is particularly pleasing because of the waterfall on the left side of the green.

The details   830-257-4982. 1 Country Club Dr., Kerrville, TX 78028

- www.kerrville.org
- 1920s. John Bredemus, then R.D. Kizer. 18 holes. Par 70. Back – 6,453. Middle – 6,000. Forward – 5,100. Price - $$.

Getting there From I-10 west, take Hwy. 16 south and turn left on Country Club Dr.

MORE GOLF

The **Las Lomas Golf Resort** is currently in the planning stages. **Golfland** (830-257-5997) offers the area's only par 3 golf course, as well as an excellent practice facility. For golf gear there is **Golf USA** (830-896-3330). The project once known as Quinlan Creek Golf Resort has been reborn as Whiskey Springs Golf Resort. Located on 800-acres near Texas 16 and I-10, Robert Von Hagge has been hired to route the course, and a hotel, conference center, and houses are slated to open around 2005.

Being a Scotsman, I am naturally opposed to water in its undiluted state. Dr. Alister Mackenzie

KERRVILLE NOTES   On the way to Ingram, TX on Texas 27, look for **Bill's Barbeque** (830-895-5733) and try the cabrito, or go for Tex-Mex at **Acapulco Restaurant** (830-895-2232), where the tacos al carbon are the specialty. Continue on to **Old Ingram**, where the historic business buildings now house art studios, galleries, antique shops, and restaurants. Back in Kerrville try some two-stepping to live music at **The Ol' Watering Hole**. For lodging, there's too much to cover for this Hill Country paradise, so call the chamber (800-221-7958) for a complete listing of their numerous hotels, inns, and B&Bs. Consider staying outside of the city in one of the charming lodges of Kerr County. One of these is the **Lazy Hills Guest Ranch** (830-367-5600), which offers many other outdoor activities. In town, the **Y.O. Ranch Hilton** (830-257-4440) is a solid option.

KILLEEN

Elev. 833   Pop. 80,720

Killeen is the military town of Fort Hood, the world's largest armor center, located just west of I-35 near Temple and Belton. Frank Killeen and the Gulf, Colorado, and Santa Fe Railroad brought business and typical frontier lawlessness to the area, but the town never amounted to much until World War II when Camp Hood opened. The population has grown since the 1,200 souls it housed back then, and the area now sports three golf courses to entertain the masses: two courses within the 217,000-acre Fort Hood facility, and Jay Riviere's Killeen Municipal Golf Club.

ANDERSON GOLF COURSE

The golf   Anderson is the older of the two Fort Hood courses, dating back to the 1940s when the Maxwell brothers laid it out. This is a simple course with wide fairways lined by mature trees, elevated greens, and water on only four or five holes.

The front has only one par 3 and one par 5, and the toughest hole is the 412-yard No. 3. The back features the more traditional combination of holes, but starts off with a 220-yard par 4. Holes 14 and 15 offer up back-to-back par 5s that are welcome birdie opportunities if you're hitting it well.

The details   254-287-6921. Building 5794, Fort Hood, TX 76544

- 1948. Perry and Press Maxwell. 18 holes. Par 71. Back – 6,447 (71.4/121). Middle – 6,230 (70.4/113). Forward – Par 71. 5,603 (72.1/113). Price - $$.

Getting there From I-35 in Temple, take Hwy. 190 west. Next take Hwy. 195 north and go to the dead end. Turn into the east entrance gate to the course.

There are no points for style when it comes to putting. It's getting the ball in the cup that counts. Brian Swarbrick

CLEAR CREEK GOLF COURSE

The golf   Clear Creek opened in 1970 with a Leon Howard design featuring elevation changes and its namesake creek coming into play throughout the course.

On the front, Nos. 7 and 8 are a tough stretch. The first is not too long but requires an approach over water. The second plays 427 yards as the most difficult-rated hole on the course.

Both par 5s on the back are challenging and play well over 500 yards.

The details   254-287-4130. Building 52831. Fort Hood, TX 76544

- 1970. Leon Howard. 18 holes. Par 72. Back – 6,768 (71.8/124). Middle – 6,315 (69.7/121). Forward – 5,864 (70.3/121). Price - $$.

Getting there From I-35 north, take Hwy. 190 west to the Clear Creek exit. Turn right, continue for 15 miles, then turn right onto Battalion Rd. Stay on Battalion until you come to the clubhouse.

KILLEEN MUNICIPAL GOLF CLUB

The golf   Jay Riviere built this course in the 1960s to offer a non-military alternative for golf in Killeen. The conditions have improved since the updated irrigation system was installed in the 1990s, and the greens are known for consistently being in solid condition. You'll face a good combination of tee shots at this muni, with both narrow and wide fairways.

Start off with some patience, if you can survive the more difficult front nine, you'll be confident and in good position for a low round when you face the easier back nine.

The details   254-699-6034. 406 S. Roy Reynolds Dr., Killeen, TX 76543

- 1966. Jay Riviere. 18 holes. Par 72. Back – 6,693 (70.5/109). Middle – 6,164 (68.1/105). Forward – 4,997 (69.5/117). Price - $$.

Getting there From I-35 north, take Hwy. 190 west and exit FM 2410. Turn right and look for Roy Reynolds Dr. Turn right again and look for the course on the left side of the road.

KILLEEN NOTES   The locals will point you towards two restaurants: **Shananagan's Grill** (254-634-4422), which serves just about everything, and the eclectic **Muncher Kind'l German Restaurant and Club** (254-634-1818), one of the best German joints in the state. No B&Bs to recommend here, so go with the chains if you're forced to stay. The Sheraton, La Quinta, Holiday Inn, and Hilton all have accommodations in Killeen. Hint: play the courses, consider lunch, then move on. There's just not much to this military town.

Understand that golf is neither a right-handed nor a left-handed game, but a two-handed one. Ernest Jones

KINGSLAND

Elev. 856   Pop. 4,584

Originally named Kingsville, this small Hill Country town at the confluence of the Colorado and Llano Rivers was popular for fishing long before the Highland Lakes were built. Since South Texas already had a Kingsville, the name was changed to Kingsland and the town became a shipping center with the arrival of the railroad around 1900. The Antlers Hotel–the first to bring tourists to the area–sprang up about the same time, While the old hotel has changed hands many times, it's now back on the list as an option for lodging when visiting this scenic area for fishing, water sports, and golf.

LEGENDS ON LAKE LBJ

The golf   This course, designed by Tom Kite and Bechtol-Russell, is slated to open for limited play in April 2003. Nine holes are complete and the grass has grown in. The clubhouse construction began in January 2003, and the additional nine could open as early as the summer.

The course is a semi-private facility on Lake LBJ that is the centerpiece of a residential community. Play will be open to the public on weekends only. The April opening is slated for Thursday-Sunday, with "property owners, members, and guests" having access to the course.

The temporary accommodations include a makeshift starters facility located at the Legends Park Area, with play beginning on hole 2 and finishing up on No. 9. In addition to the putting and chipping area, there is a temporary irons-only driving range in place.

The details   512-756-7444. 105 Rangeway Circle, Kingsland, TX 78639.

- 2002. Tom Kite and Bechtol-Russell. 18 holes. Par 72. 7,186 yards. Price - $$$.

Getting there Located minutes from Kingsland at the intersection of Hwy. 1431 and Hwy. 2342.

PACKSADDLE COUNTRY CLUB

The golf   Packsaddle came along before the prestigious Horseshoe Bay resort, with Leon Howard architecting the design back in 1968. As is typical of his philosophy, the course is fairly basic and surprisingly flat for this Hill Country setting.

While many complain about the lack of championship-style amenities ("the worst clubhouse in America") and average condition of the course ("the cart paths are dirt"), Pack Saddle has its advantages: it's less expensive and is always good for a quick 18 holes.

Rule number one of your short game goes something like this: minimum air time, maximum ground time. Rule number two: putt whenever you can, even if you're not on the green. When you can't putt, chip. When you can't chip, pitch. Mike Adams and T. J. Tomasi

Howard's layout is spiced up somewhat by water hazards that impact play on about half of the holes. Holes of note include the scenic No. 7, which plays uphill to an interesting-looking green surrounded by slabs of granite and thick trees. Holes 9 and 11 are tough par 5s because of their length and the creek that cuts into the fairway on both holes.

The details   512-388-3863. River Oaks Dr., Kingsland, TX 78639

- 1968. Leon Howard. Back – 7,133 (73.3/117). Middle – 6,636 (71.0/113). Forward – 5,286 (69.3/113). Price - $.

Getting there From Austin, take Hwy. 71 north to Route 2233, then turn right and find Route 2900. Turn left on 2900 and follow the signs to the course.

KINGSLAND NOTES   Hotel suites and cabins are available at **The Antlers Hotel** (800-383-0007), a turn-of-the-century railroad resort on Lake LBJ. Don't forget: Llano, Marble Falls, and Buchanan Dam are all just a short drive away for any dining option you might be craving. Take the back roads north of Lake Buchanan to **Tow, TX** and find the **Hi-Line Resort Rod & Reel Grille** (915-379-1065). Another worthwhile side trip is to the **Packsaddle Mountain** landmark just off Texas 71. Traces of gold and silver have been reported in the sands of Honey Creek, which rests at the foot of the mountain, and this spot was also the site of an Apache Indian battle in August 1873.

CENTRAL

KYLE

Elev. 714   Pop. 3,645

The small community of Kyle, just south of Austin barely off of I-35, exists because a 19th-century railroad magnate decided there should be a station between Austin and San Marcos. And up until recently, this quaint little town has been able to avoid the growth of Austin and maintain its position as a nice little day-trip destination. Now the ranchlands covered in bluebonnets are undergoing transformation, and more people are coming to this part of the world. One of the reasons is Plum Creek Golf Course.

PLUM CREEK GOLF COURSE

The golf   Even though it's just two miles west of I-35, Plum Creek is sort of an off-the-beaten-path place to play. Located in the wildflower pastures just south of Austin, Roy Bechtol designed this links-style track for Glenn and Mary Evans, who were developing their vision of the Plum Creek residential community.

Bechtol's layout is especially pleasing because of its natural appearance– the track rolls through the flowers that blanket the ranchland, with aesthetic water

I believe the lay-up second shot is one of the most overlooked in golf. When I think of good lay-up players, I think of Tom Kite. He pays close attention to his second shot on a par 5 so he leaves himself perfect sandwedge distance from which he is deadly accurate. Corey Pavin

features and grass mounds. The course has an open feel to it, and you'll never see an adjoining fairway. And while sand isn't a concern, the lack of trees and the course's hilltop location make it susceptible to the winds.

The most difficult hole at Plum Creek is the 659-yard No. 2, which should probably play like a par 7 when the wind is blowing. Natural brush lines this somewhat narrow fairway, and a creek cuts across the lane on your second shot. Later on the front comes the uphill 605-yard No. 9, where you won't be able to afford any duffs to make par.

Water comes into play more on the back side, including the pesky 382-yard No. 14. The hole doglegs right around a small lake and requires a solid drive to turn that corner. If it's too long, you're through the bend and will be forced to chip out before the approach over the creek fronting the green.

All told, there's a good mixture of holes at Plum Creek, and the outstanding service provided by the staff makes for a great day of golfin' Kyle.

The details   512-262-5555. 750 Kohler's Crossing Rd., Kyle, TX

- www.plumcreekgolf.com
- 1999. 18 holes. Black – 7,132 (74.0/125). Blue – 6,443 (71.3/120). White – 5,754 (67.5/113). Red – 4,876 (69.8/118). Price - $$$.

Getting there Head south from Austin on I-35 and take Exit 217. Turn right at the stop sign onto County Rd. 210. Follow the Plum Creek signs, turning right onto Kohler's Crossing.

KYLE NOTES   **The Auction Oak**, a unique place of historic business deals, is located inside Kyle on Sledge St. about two blocks south of Center St. **The Kyle Hanging Tree**, the spot where many have met their match, is a few miles down Old Post Rd. on your left. Take your own cervezas and roll into nearby **Buda, TX** for chips and salsa at **La Casa del Taco** (512-295-6327).

LA GRANGE

Elev. 272   Pop. 4,215

La Grange is a beautiful old historic town that dates back to 1819, when the legendary "Strap" Buckner set the example for frontier machismo and led the way for further settlement of this oak-infested area. The town is located just north of I-10 between San Antonio and Houston at the site where an old buffalo trail crossed the Colorado River. Giant oaks, one of which has served as the fatal defining moment for men in six different conflicts, line the town's square and streets. Historic structures, excellent restaurants and bakeries, and cozy places to drink beer lure travelers. The famous little whorehouse has been

Golf is twenty percent mechanics and technique. The other eighty percent is philosophy, humor, tragedy, romance, melodrama, companionship, camaraderie, cussedness, and conversation. Grantland Rice

shut down, but golfers can still indulge themselves, albeit while pursing a more accepted passion, at the Frisch Auf Valley Country Club.

FRISCH AUF VALLEY COUNTRY CLUB

The golf   Frisch Auf is a 9-hole, semi-private facility that features elevated tee boxes, a few hills sprinkled over the mostly flat layout, and large, raised greens that are protected by bunkers. Water comes into play on four holes. Also note that you can pay once and play all day.

The details   979-968-6113. 575 Country Club Dr., La Grange, TX 78945

- 1966. 9 holes. Par 36. Back – 3,089. Middle – 2,985 (34.0/114). Forward – 2,349 (32.6/111). Price - $.

Getting there Take Hwy. 71 west out of Austin toward Houston. Exit Country Club Dr. in La Grange and turn right. The course is 1.5 miles down the road.

LA GRANGE NOTES   For good eats you can try **Prause Meat Market** (979-968-3259) or **Tim's Cafe on the Square** (979-968-9665), a good place to relax and ponder your round. The side trip to the **Kreische Brewery** ruins might be worthwhile–it's the home of stonemason and brewer Heinreich L. Kreische and Texas' first commercial brewery. Also consider a scenic drive southwest to FM 2436 and Hostyn, TX, or the first roadside park on Texas 71 with its scenic overlook of the Colorado River Valley.

LAGO VISTA   Elev. 1,230   Pop. 4,507

Lago Vista sits on a bend in the Colorado River just north of Lake Travis, about a 30-minute drive from Austin. Developed in the 1960s as a lake resort area, the area has grown into a popular golf destination, especially since the beautiful hills around Lake Travis create the perfect setting for spectacular golf.

LAGO VISTA RESORT – HIGHLAND LAKES COURSE

The golf   Of the two courses at the Lago Vista, the Highland Lakes course is considered the more difficult. An unforgiving course that allows no room for error, it features dramatic elevation changes and the stunning topography so typical of courses in this area.

You'll feel squeezed from the first tee of this newer of the two Lago Vista courses that opened in 1980. No. 1 requires an almost perfect blind tee shot to reach the ridge that drops the ball to the green some 35 feet below. And No. 2 is just as tough with another blind shot.

Later on the front nine, No. 8 is a long, doglegging par 5 that can grab you.

If the average American player would only realize how much easier it is to play well when he is swinging along at a good rate, he would surely gird up his loins and walk a little faster. H. J. Whigham

Driver works well off the tee down into the valley, then the second shot works back up to a plateau before dropping back down again. The approach is nice, carrying the final valley into a green protected by bunkers and lined by a striking rock wall in the back.

The last hole on the front, which offers a panoramic view of Lake Travis, is the perfect warmup for one of the most spectacular holes in the state. No. 10 is the signature, and it's well deserved because of the 100-foot drop in elevation. The fairway stair steps down, then plays into a severely back-to-front sloping green.

All of the holes are awesome, but the double-dogleg No. 16 stands out a bit more. Lined by trees, it winds down to a green that rests a good 20-30 feet from where you'll be hitting the approach. Big hitters can reach it in two, but the twists and turns make for a very delightful golf hole.

The details   512-267-1685. 20552 Highland Lake, Lago Vista, TX 78645

- www.lagovistaclubs.com

- 1980. Dave Bennett. 18 holes. Par 72. Gold – 6,529 (71.0/129). Blue – 6,267 (69.8/127). White – 5,921 (68.2/123). Red – 5,146 (69.3/118). Price - $$$.

Getting there From Austin, take Hwy. 183 north to FM 1431, then turn west 11 miles. When you come to Lohmas Ford Rd., turn left and drive 3 miles, then turn right on Boggy Ford Rd. Veer to the right and follow the signs to the course.

LAGO VISTA RESORT – LAGO VISTA COURSE

The golf   The Lago Vista Course is the resort's original track, designed by Leon Howard in the late 1960s and renovated by Dave Bennett in 1992. The course has four water holes, over 40 bunkers, and dramatic elevation changes of up to 100 feet.

The course is known for its demanding par 3s, which all go right at 200 yards. No. 10 is fun because it can be reached in two: a 495-yard par 5 with a creek that looms right.

The details   512-267-1170. 4616 Rimrock Dr., Lago Vista, TX 78645

- www.lagovistaclubs.com

- 1967. Leon Howard and Dave Bennett. 18 holes. Par 72. Gold – 6,579 (70.0/118). Blue – 6,198 (68.2/115). White – 5,851 (66.6/112). Red – 5,212 (69.1/114). Price - $$$.

Getting there From Austin, take Hwy. 183 north to FM 1431, then turn west 11 miles. When you come to Lohmas Ford Rd., turn left and drive 3 miles, then turn right on Boggy Ford Rd. Veer to the right and follow the signs to the course.

If you accelerate the putter, your contact will be more consistent, even on mis-hits. Tom Watson

MORE GOLF

The **Marshall Ranch Golf Club**, a private club scheduled for a membership of just under 400, is scheduled to open sometime in the summer of 2003. The club will feature a Gary Player-designed, 7,252-yard par 72 layout on the north shore of Lake Travis, complete with 200-foot elevation changes and 600-yard holes. Should be a stunner, as Gary Player apparently has plans to build a home on the 8th green.

LAGO VISTA NOTES Make it a weekend on the lake by reserving rooms with the golf packages offered at either the **Shores at Lake Travis** (800-438-6493) or the **Travis Lake Resort** (866-525-3386). Both offer full-service dining and numerous non-golf activities, including guided fishing trips.

LAMPASAS   Elev. 1,025   Pop. 8,077

Taking US 183 out of Austin to the north leads you to the former cattle trail and current ranch town of Lampasas, with its broad streets, historic square, rock homes, and abundant water. The nearby Colorado and Lampasas Rivers offer ample outdoor recreation. Where the mineral springs still flow a half mile from the stone courthouse in Hancock Park, you'll find the city's only golf option.

HANCOCK PARK GOLF COURSE

The golf Hancock Park renovated and upgraded with an additional nine holes in 1996, providing locals and visitors with a full round of down-home golf. This country course features average-size fairways, numerous bunkering, and water hazards that impact play on seven holes. The greens are of average size and medium speed, with minimal undulations. A short course that plays just over 6,000 yards; it is generally susceptible to low scores unless the wind is blowing, which is often the case later in the day.

Most talk about No. 2, the 355-yard par 4 that features an island green. The tee shot must be accurate here as the fairway is lined by out-of-bounds on the left and thick trees on the right.

While No. 2 is rated as the most difficult, some argue that the more challenging hole is No. 17, a 221-yard, par 3 from the back tees, which are played most often since the middle tees are a very pedestrian 5,300 yards.

Unusual for an 18-hole course, Hancock allows you to pay one green fee and play all day long.

The details 512-556-3202. 700 Noruna Rd., Lampasas, TX 76550

• www.ci.lampasas.tx.us/golf

Show me a golfer who doesn't have a mean streak, and
I'll show you a weak competitor. Lee Trevino

- 18 holes. Par 72. Back – 6,029 (68.2/118). Middle – 5,288 (65.3/109). Forward – 4,782 (68.1/121). Price - $.

Getting there From Austin, take Hwy. 183 north, then continue to Lampasas for about an hour and you'll see the course near town.

LAMPASAS NOTES Make your reservations at the historic **Moses Hughes Ranch Bed and Breakfast** (512-556-5923), set in the stone house built by the founder of Lampasas. **Perk's Coffee Bar** (512-556-5704) has a little character worth investigating. On 3rd St. track down **Medina's Mexican Restaurant** (512-556-8412) for mouth-watering enchiladas, or head down Hwy. 281 and find the **Limestone Grill** (512-556-5399). They prepare burgers just right at **Martin's Restaurant** (512-556-3362), a place that takes you back to the 1950s.

LEANDER
Elev. 983   Pop. 15,000

Like Round Rock and Georgetown, this town just north of Austin on US 183 has grown at an amazing pace, booming from a population of 3,400 residents in 1990 to a whopping 15,000 folks today. Formerly known as Bagdad, this railroad town has been sucked into Austin's sprawl, becoming a commuter community for those who travel down 183 to earn their living in Austin.

THE GOLF CLUB AT CRYSTAL FALLS

The golf While it hasn't received as much publicity as the other Hill Country tracks since it opened around 1990, Crystal Falls is definitely worthy of praise. Highlighted by one of the greatest par 3s in Texas and some outstanding topography, this is one of those courses you'll want to play at least once, if only for the views.

In addition to the scenery, the main thing everyone talks about here is the severely sloping fairways that provide problems for those who hit the ball left-to-right.

The famous par 3 in question is the 192-yard No. 11, featuring a phenomenal view and a 200-yard drop to the green. Club selection is a crap-shoot at best, and the green is surrounded by mounds.

The next hole is probably the most difficult fairway on the entire course, and demonstrates Crystal Falls' most frequently criticized feature–the unfair slope to the fairways. A good drive can still roll off the side into the oblivion of cliffs or tall grass.

No. 18 plays 549 yards into another severely sloping fairway, yet berms have been put in place to prevent decent shots from rolling into the canyon. You'll need to lay up with a mid iron in front of the creek, then carry that hazard to the green.

As you walk down the fairway of life you must smell the roses, for you only get to play one round. Ben Hogan

The details   512-259-5855. 3400 Crystal Falls Park, Leander, TX 78646

- www.golfclubatcrystalfalls.com
- 1990. Jack Miller. 18 holes. Par 72. Back – 6,654 (72.3/126). Middle – 6,164 (70.1/122). Forward – 5,194 (70.0/123). Price - $$$.

Getting there From Loop 1, take Hwy. 183 north for 14 miles to the course. The entrance is off Crystal Falls Pkwy.

POINT VENTURE GOLF CLUB

The golf   Built along Lake Travis in 1971, Point Venture was the first course in Leander, but has been overshadowed since the opening of Crystal Falls. The course has 9 holes that meander through a residential development and is loaded with dogleg holes and mature trees.

Jimmy Demaret designed the course, and his layout features two nasty par 5s. The best hole on the course is No. 7–a scenic hole that starts from an elevated tee box and plays downhill to a green surrounded by a lake.

The details   512-267-2768. 422 Venture Blvd. S., Leander, TX 78645

- 1971. Jimmy Demaret. 9 holes. Par 36. Back – 3,038 (34.2/112). Middle – 2,815 (33.0/108). Forward – 2,455 (33.9/109). Price - $$.

Getting there From I-35, exit FM 1431 and drive west approximately 25 miles to Lago Vista. Turn left on Lohman Ford Rd. and drive 8 miles to the Point Venture guard gate.

LEANDER NOTES   If there's a sporting event involving a wagering interest and you can't wait to get back to Austin, step into **Elmo's Sports Bar** for adult beverages and sports-guy cravings. Otherwise get out of town and take advantage of being near the capital city. In other words, make this a day trip from Austin.

LLANO   Elev. 1,029   Pop. 3,357

Located 70 miles northwest of Austin on scenic Hwy. 71, Llano is a beautiful Hill Country town in the heart of farm and ranch country. The town was founded in 1855 along the spring-fed waters of the Llano River, and became the county seat in 1856.

Llano means "plain" in Spanish, but there is nothing ordinary about this picturesque town that calls itself the "Deer Capital of Texas" and is surrounded by the Highland Lakes. The entire downtown square is designated a National Historic District. The clear, spring-fed river and the rare pink granite called Llanite that is found here in the "Llano Uplift" all make Llano worth adding to your list of weekend road-trip explorations.

The ardent golfer would play Mount Everest if somebody would put a flagstick on top. Pete Dye

LLANO MUNICIPAL GOLF COURSE

The golf   Llano's municipal course has the wonderful distinction of being laid out along the scenic Llano River, with beautiful views and great golf. This course should be a must-play anytime you're touring through the immediate area.

In addition to the scenery, the most memorable feature of this course is the tiny, postage-stamp-sized greens that require pinpoint accuracy and a solid short game for pars. In fact, these well-manicured greens compare favorably to the tricky burial-mound greens of Alpine and Marfa, and are surely some of the smallest targets in the state.

Mature trees line the fairways, and water hazards come into play on only three holes.

The best birdie opportunity is the short, par 5 13th hole, playing only 437 yards. Good golfers can get there in two and give it a roll at an eagle putt. The ender is talked about as the signature, a difficult 502-yard par 5 with out-of-bounds along the left as well as behind the green.

The details   915-247-5100. 301 Main St., Llano, TX 78643

- www.llanotx.com/LlanoMunicipalGolfCourse.html
- 18 holes. Par 71. Back – 6,094 (69.1/123). Middle – 5,684 (67.4/118). Forward – 4,848 (70.0/113). Price - $$.

Getting there In Llano turn left on the north side of the courthouse and head out to the course.

LLANO NOTES   Stay at the **Badu House** (915-247-4304), built in 1891 and originally a bank, but now restored as an inn and restaurant. The place for lunch is the famous **Cooper's Barbecue** (915-247-5713), where you can select your meat from a fire pit before taking it inside to fix up for your liking. For morning eats there is a great little breakfast taco shack across from the convenience store at the intersection of Hwy. 29 & 16, and the **Hungry Hunter** serves sit-down home-style breakfast like no other.

LOCKHART   Elev. 518   Pop. 11,602

Lockhart is south of Austin on US 183 toward Luling and east-west US 90. The town is famous for the 1840 Battle of Plum Creek, where a volunteer force of settlers and Texas Rangers defeated a plundering Comanche war party. This marked the last time the Comanches attacked a coastal town or ranch.

The Chisolm Trail routed through Lockhart in the 1870s, and today the town is the hub for the area's farming and agricultural needs. Since US 183 is

Usually, the best way to learn a new swing movement does not require that you actually hit the ball. Dr. Bob Rotella

the less-traveled route south of Austin, we highly recommend a trip through the "BBQ Capital of Texas" for golf and good eats.

LOCKHART STATE PARK GOLF COURSE

The golf   As the name implies, this is a state-maintained and operated 9-hole golf course that dates back to 1938, when it was carved out of a 263-acre park. While definitely not a championship resort-style course, this might be one of the best values for golf anywhere in the state, offering all-day access for under $10.

The course is very well maintained, with a design that features wide-open fairways, no bunkers, and water hazards on a few holes. Even though the fairways offer generous landing areas, there are a few strategically placed trees that get in the way.

Clear Fork Creek comes into play on the first and last holes. And No. 3 is the most challenging–a long par 4 that plays downhill off the tee, then back uphill into a green surrounded by trees. Most of the par 4s are short, playing under 350 yards, including the 295-yard No. 5.

Other notes: While there is not a formal driving range, there is an area where you can hit a few balls to warm up (provided that you retrieve them when you're done).

The details   512-398-3479. 4179 State Park Rd., Lockhart, TX 78644

- www.tpwd.state.tx.us/park/lockhart/lockhart.htm
- 1939. 9 holes. Par 35. 2,989 yards (34.1/110). Price - $.

Getting there Off of Hwy. 183 S., turn right on FM 20, then drive 1.5 miles to the course. The entrance is on the left-hand side of the road.

LOCKHART NOTES   When you're in the BBQ Capital of Texas, don't even consider eating anything other than the messy stuff. Test your BBQ intake tolerance against elderly East Texas lovelies at **Smitty's Market** (512-398-9344), where you can stack your plate and share a long wooden table to stuff your face with the locals. Other options are **Black's Barbecue**, the oldest in Texas, **Kreuz Market**, where they don't offer sauce because "good barbecue doesn't need sauce," or the cafeteria-style **Chisolm Trail Bar-B.Q.**

LULING   Elev. 419   Pop. 5,279

Luling is more toned down today than it was in the old days when it was called "the toughest town in Texas." Rowdy cowhands once pushed cattle from Chihuahua, Mexico to this branch of the Southern Pacific Railroad. When oil was struck in 1922, thousands of oilfield hands bombarded what

---

I think of driving the ball through an imaginary goal post, especially when the landing area is tight. Tom Watson

was then a small agricultural community of 500, booming the town to over 5,000 roughnecks. Imagine makeshift saloons, a shooting gallery for entertainment, and temporary tent houses filling every vacant area.

Today the signs of the hard life are gone, but almost 200 pump jacks still remain within the city limits. Antique shopping is popular, the town boasts barbecue to rival Lockhart, and the famous Watermelon Thump is held annually. For golfers, the San Marcos River runs through town, providing a scenic locale for the 9-hole Luling Golf Club.

LULING GOLF CLUB

The golf Practice your fade, or even a slice, before your big round at the 9-hole Luling Golf Club, since the first five holes have out-of-bounds to the left and plenty of open spaces to the right. "Setting up well for a fade" is an understatement to say the least. This flat course has a few water hazards and bunkers on seven of nine holes. Despite its short length, it is a surprisingly tough challenge.

The most notable hole is No. 7. It plays around 340 yards from either set of tees, the river on the left cuts into the fairway, and you'll need a solid drive of around 200 yards to carry it.

Two sets of tees allow for an 18-hole round, and they're nice enough to allow you to pay once and play all day.

The details 830-875-5114. 1005 S. Magnolia, Luling, TX 78648

• 9 holes. Par 35. Back – 2,831. Forward – 2,343. Price - $.

Getting there Take the Luling exit to the north from I-10, cross the San Marcos River, and the course is on the right.

LULING NOTES Go for pork ribs at the **City Market** (512-875-9019), Luling's best spot for lunch, then take the scenic drive to Palmetto State Park 7 miles south of town on US 183. Here on the San Marcos River, the jungle-like terrain will startle the Hill Country traveler with an unbelievable tropical abundance of plants like no other. Camping, fishing, hiking, and swimming are all options.

MANOR
Elev. 538   Pop. 1,248

Manor, which has become a suburb of Austin just 12 miles away on US 290, is the gateway to the fertile, rolling pastures northeast of Austin. The railroad made it through in 1871, and the town has served as the commercial center for farmers using the railroad to ship livestock and dairy products. For years

CENTRAL

Manor's only true attraction was the rustic-but-entertaining quarter horse track known as Manor Downs. The community is growing, however, much to the delight of golfers who can now get an afternoon round in at the new Shadow Glen Golf Course before hitting the track for spirits and wagering.

SHADOW GLEN GOLF COURSE

The golf   If you've ever driven through Manor, you know that the terrain is predominantly flat, with the occasional rolling hill. You'll be surprised by the new 18-hole Shadow Glen Golf Course, which plays through several small ravines. The course, designed by the Bechtol-Russell firm, is slated for a spring 2003 opening with a very wallet-friendly green fee, which will include range balls and ProLink GPS with the cart rental.

The mostly traditional layout will feature two differing nines–one with more elevation changes and trees, and the other with lakes, creeks, and bunkers.

The details   512-278-1304. 12801 Lexington, Manor, TX 78653

- 2003. Bechtol-Russell. 18 holes. Par 72. 7,174 yards. 5 sets of tees. Price - $$$.

Getting there 9 miles east of I-35 on Hwy. 290. The course fronts Hwy. 290 on the north side of the road.

CENTRAL

MANOR NOTES   Well-rounded individuals must experience the thrill of betting on the ponies at **Manor Downs** (512-272-5581), despite the possible results. Even if live racing is not in season, the eclectic "jockey club" bar that adjoins the track is the perfect place to settle up on golf bets, grab a simple meal, drink beer, bond with wayward degenerates, and bet on simulcast racing. For lodging your money is more wisely spent in Austin, just a short drive away.

MARBLE FALLS   Elev. 764   Pop. 5,656

Marble Falls is 47 miles northwest of Austin in the middle of the Highland Lakes. Named for a spot on the Colorado River where waterfalls poured over marble outcroppings, the picturesque community has always been one of Texas' most popular Hill Country destinations. Horseshoe Bay is only minutes away with what will soon be four world-class golf courses. That, combined with the fact that Blue Lake might be the most beautiful 9-hole course in Texas, makes this area pure golf paradise.

★

A lesson is of very short duration, but will, if properly understood,
provide you with tasks for a week or more. Henry Cotton

BLUE LAKE GOLF CLUB

The golf   Often overshadowed by the high-dollar resorts and new championship layouts, Blue Lake is one of the lesser-known gems of the Highland Lake area. Exuding the old-school charm of its course designer, the crusty Jimmy Burke, this scenic track is loaded with wildlife and is generally a joy to play because of its simplicity.

Burke's par 32 layout consists of five par 3s, three par 4s, and only one par 5. There are no bunkers or water hazards. The course weaves in and out of a quaint housing community, and a few elevated tees offer views of Lake LBJ.

Notable holes include the 365-yard par 4 with out-of-bounds looming left and trees on the right, and the par 3 16th, which plays almost 200 yards.

Two sets of tees make for an 18-hole round, and you can pay once and play all day.

The details   830-598-5524. 214 W. Bluebonnet Dr., Marble Falls, TX

- 1963. Jimmy Burke. Back – Par 32. 2,336 yards (30.7 / 96). Forward – Par 33. 2,126 yards (31.7 / 104). Price - $.

Getting there From Hwy. 71 west, turn right on Blue Lake Deer Haven Dr., then drive 2 miles north to the course.

THE COUNTRY CLUB OF MEADOWLAKES

The golf   Meadowlakes opened in 1974: a Leon Howard design that cuts through a pecan grove on the front and what seems like an ocean of water on the back, creating two totally different golf experiences.

Howard uncharacteristically left out water on the tight, pecan-lined front, with the wet stuff in play on only one hole. However, this one pond plays a role in the best hole on the course, No. 4, which features a pond and waterfall in the landing area off the tee. No. 4 is rated as the most difficult.

The more open back nine is dominated by water. No. 10 starts off with a drive of 200-yards-plus over the pond fronting the tee. A small creek comes into play on the next three holes, which lead you to the other signature hole, No. 14. Water lines the left side of the 14th, and the approach is over a small pond.

If that's not enough, the final three holes all feature water in play off the tee. No. 16 is a par 4, and No. 17 a longish par 3. Then the 18th, which plays about 540 yards, requires a solid tee shot to carry the pond, but can't be too far because there are two more ponds that sit on each side of the dogleg. The approach is into an elevated green protected by mounding.

The details   830-693-3300. 220 Meadowlakes Dr., Marble Falls, TX 78654

- 1976. 18 holes. Par 72. Back – 6,582 (71.2/118). Middle – 6,254 (69.6/114). Forward – 5,378 (71.4/117). Price - $$.

The most valuable time to practice is right after your round, when your mistakes are fresh in your mind. Tom Watson

Getting there From Hwy. 71 north find US 281. Turn north again and drive 5 miles until you reach Marble Falls. After crossing the bridge, turn left and follow the signs to the course.

MARBLE FALLS NOTES The traditional eating establishment here is the **Bluebonnet Cafe** (830-693-2344), just north of the bridge on US 281. The recommended side trip is the scenic route down 1431, where you can take your lunch to the picnic area just north of town and stare at **Granite Mountain,** a massive dome of pink and red granite where the stone for the Texas Capitol was quarried. This road offers spectacular scenery in every direction as it winds and curves through the hills. Another scenic drive is down 2147 along the western shore of Lake Marble Falls.

MARLIN

Elev. 383   Pop. 6,344

A weekend here is easier on the wallet than Barton Springs, the hot springs are still around, and the golf course isn't crowded. Yet Marlin doesn't necessarily come to mind when you think of Central Texas golf destinations. However, this small town just southeast of Waco is worth consideration if you have some time to venture off of I-35 looking for golf. While not the classic resort and spa experience, the town was once famous for the curative hot artesian springs that made the town one of the early resort spas of Texas.

MARLIN COUNTRY CLUB

The golf Marlin offers nothing but 9 holes of basic, small-town golf. The layout features narrow fairways, a lake that comes into play on a few holes, and medium-sized greens with minor undulations. This is an easy course. Take your time and enjoy the laid-back atmosphere.

The details 254-803-6101. RR 1, Marlin, TX 76661

- 9 holes. Par 36. Back – 3,050 (34.9/109). Forward – 2,487 (34.0/104). Price - $.

Getting there Take Hwy. 6 south out of Waco and take the first Marlin exit. Find Drew Lumber and turn right. Drive to Rockdam Rd. and turn right, then drive until you see Country Club Dr. Take one more right and the course is just down the road.

MARLIN NOTES The beer is cold at the **Tap Room** and there's solid Tex-Mex at the **Cactus Mexican Restaurant** in the Falls Hotel. Also don't forget to try the **B&B Market** (254-803-3402), a longtime Marlin tradition. For a side trip, head 2 miles west of city, where **Falls on the Brazos Park** offers fishing, canoeing, swimming, and camping. One of the buildings to see in Marlin

---

With either a downhill lie or an uphill lie, always play the ball nearer the higher foot. Jackie Burke, Jr.

is the **Highlands Mansion,** located 1 mile northeast of town on FM 147.

MART
Elev. 523   Pop. 2,273

The old-timers who chose the name of Mart imagined the town becoming an important hub for commerce. They missed that prediction, though, and not many folks outside of Waco know much about this rural community.

Golfers will be glad to find the tiny town of Mart while exploring the back roads east of Waco. In the midst of cattle, farms, and ranchlands lies the unique Battle Lake Golf Course, an outstanding facility and definitely the primary reason to put Mart on your list of Texas golf excursions.

BATTLE LAKE GOLF COURSE

The golf   The venerable Battle Lake Golf Course puts the small town of Mart on the Texas golf map as a mandatory destination. Because it's out in the country, surrounded by cattle farms and ranchland, it's a totally different experience. The course was originally a 9-hole sand-green track, but expanded to 18 holes in the 1970s. The layout is not overly difficult, featuring generous fairways and a few ponds that come into play.

Notable holes include the difficult par 3 No. 3, which requires a 190-yard carry into the prevailing wind off the tee. A large oak covers the left side of the green on this 215-yard hole.

No. 16 is a fun one: a 415-yard par 4 with a blind tee shot and a downhill approach into a small green, with water looming behind it.

The feature hole is No. 17, a 370-yard par 4 that doglegs right around the lake.

Other notes: Springtime is the best time to play Battle Lake, since the bluebonnets are in full bloom. The golf shop earned praise as one of "America's 100 Best Golf Shops" in 1996, and the practice facility stands up to any of the big-time courses in Texas.

The details   254-876-2837. 4443 Battle Lake Rd., Mart, TX 76664

• www.battlelakegolf.com

• 18 holes. Par 72. Back – 6,601 (70.7/116). Middle – 6,113 (68.9/112). Front – Par 74 5,173 (69.3) Price - $$.

Getting there From I-35 south, take Hwy. 6 south and exit Battle Lake Rd. Turn left and drive 4.5 miles to the course.

MART NOTES   There's one motel in town, the **Western Motel** (254-876-

2412), but most stay in Waco. You can count on a solid meal at the **Lighthouse Cafe** (254-876-2606), the best place for lunch before you head back to town.

MASON
Elev. 1,550   Pop. 2,134

Driving into to Mason on a clear, warm summer morning for golf is something that every Texas golfer will remember. On the way in, the surrounding hillsides are blanketed with wildflowers and the ranchland is lined with picturesque rock fences. In town, the homes and businesses are made out of sandstone blocks from old Fort Mason, and the historic town square is surrounded by majestic pecan trees. The square is the perfect spot for morning coffee and breakfast before heading to the town's charming city park, where you'll find the 9-hole Comanche Creek Golf Course.

COMANCHE CREEK GOLF CLUB

The golf   Comanche Creek is a tidy 9-hole layout that rolls through Fort Mason Park, the same pleasant setting that is home to Mason's football stadium, community center, and rodeo arena. This is a simple track with minimal hazards that will build the confidence of the average golfer, and is a great place for those just learning the game. The course is well maintained and the fairways and greens are in excellent condition.

The terrain is mostly flat, but does feature some mounding. The greens are small and elevated. It's a great course to walk.

Hole 9 has the only water hazard, a 563-yard par 5 that features a pond fronting the green. Average golfers have good chances for birdie on holes 5-7. The stretch starts with a 454-yard par 5, and is followed by a 300-yard par 4 and a short par 3. You'll need to score well to give yourself some room for slip-ups on the difficult finisher.

The details   915-347-5798, Comanche Creek Rd., Mason, TX 76856

• 1986. 9 holes. Par 36. Back – 3,101 (34.7). Forward – 2,416. Price - $.

Getting there Located just off Hwy. 87 in the city park.

MASON NOTES Check out the crumbling remnants of **Fort Mason** and the restored main building five blocks south of the courthouse. The 1880s **Seaquist Home** is usually open for tours that show off the 17 rooms and 14 fireplaces. The **Willow Creek Cafe** (915-347-6124) on the town square or **Cooper's Pit Barbecue** (915-347-6897) are great lunch options. For post-round exploring, head 11 miles south on Hwy. 87 to the **Llano River** and **Keller's Riverside Store** (915-347-0055).

I am forced to conclude that God made Texas on his day off, for pure entertainment, just to prove that all that diversity could be crammed into one section of earth by a really top hand Mary Lasswell

CENTRAL

MENARD
Elev. 1,960   Pop. 1,676

First established in the mid-1700s as the Spanish mission of Santa Cruz de San Saba, Menard became an early trading post on the northwest cattle trails. Cowhands once held their cattle in the ruins of the old Spanish compound. Menard is a small, undiscovered town on the western edge of the Hill Country. Primarily a ranch town that serves the area's sheep and wool production, the town also boasts an attractive city park on the San Saba River and a quaint 9-hole golf course west of town.

PRESIDIO GOLF CLUB

The golf   Presidio rolls along the San Saba River and is named after the old Spanish mission on the back side of the course.

No. 5 is one of the better holes, a par 4 that is sort of a blind dogleg out of a chute of trees. The approach can get away from you with the river looming right.

Compared to other small-town 9-holers, this one is worth it but pricey, totaling $25 for the fee and cart.

The details   915-396-3319. Hwy. 190 W, Menard, TX 76859
• 9 holes. Price - $$.

Getting there From the middle of town, drive north over the river until you reach Hwy. 190. Turn left and drive a short distance until you see the course on your left.

MENARD NOTES   Ask the locals about the legend of the lost silver mine. Stuff your face at the **Branding Iron BBQ** or go for Tex-Mex at **Ojeda's. Hat Creek Cabins** (866-396-3399) can put you up and provide just about any kind of outdoor activity you could want. Also at nearby **Ft. McKavett,** the **Copperas Creek B&B** (915-446-3289) has rooms and proximity to that unique state park. Don't mill shuffleboard and beers at **The Fort Trading Post,** a crusty old watering hole next door to the state park. West of town on Texas 29, find the ruins of **Real Presidio de San Saba,** the Spanish fort dating back to 1751 that was the site of fierce Comanche Indian attacks.

MERIDIAN
Elev. 791   Pop. 1,415

Bosque County, just 70 miles southwest of Dallas and due west of Lake Whitney, marks the edge of the Hill Country with its scenic valley walls that

You will not improve very much, or very rapidly, if you confine your lessons to the practice tee and the full swing. To play the golf of your dreams, you'll need to take short-game lessons and playing lessons. Dr. Bob Rotella

surround the community. The town was established on July 4, 1854 in a log cabin, and today serves as the retail center for the surrounding agricultural activities. With the popular Meridian State Park, Lake Whitney, and pleasant Bosque Valley Golf Club nearby, Meridian is a great place to get away for the weekend.

BOSQUE VALLEY GOLF CLUB

The golf   Bosque Valley is a well-maintained 9-hole course that is mentioned at the top of the list for its kind in Texas. Situated 50 miles west of Waco, this quaint, casual course rests along the Bosque River and features mature oak trees lining its narrow fairways. The greens are small, of average speed, and putt true.

This 3,054-yard par 35 does not require length, but accuracy is important because of the overhanging trees. Water impacts play on two of the final three holes, and while the course starts out fairly open, you'll soon learn to be aware of the impact of the trees.

The details   254-435-2692. State Rd. 1991, Meridian, TX 76665

- 1971. 9 holes. Par 36. Back – 3,054 (34.0/114). Forward – 2,595 (33.6/109). Price - $.

Getting there From I-35, take Hwy. 22 west to Meridian. Look for signs to the course in town. Turn left on Hwy. 1991 and drive 2.5 miles to the course.

MERIDIAN NOTES   Two viable dining options in Meridian–just off the square is **Mary's**, where you can get a mean burger, and the Tex-Mex **El Jardin** is always delicious. Tour the countryside and view the limestone bluffs on the way to lunch in Clifton, TX, where a sausage sandwich from the **Bunkhouse Bar-Barbeque Restaurant** (254-675-8409) will tide you over while you take in the famous Western art at the Bosque Conservatory. Back in Meridian, check out the limestone courthouse that houses the Word family, one of the oldest small-town political dynasties in Texas. Up northwest near Lake Whitney is the town of Lakeside Village, TX, which sports the roadhouse-cafe called **Holly's**, known for chicken-fried steak, cheap cold beers, and jukebox pool hall fun. Also consider the **Lampman's Texaco** for provisions and supplies, because while you're there you can pick up a juicy home-style burger with fries to-go.

MEXIA   Elev. 534   Pop. 6,572

Pronounced *Muh-HEY-uh*, this former 1920s oil boom town is about 90 miles south of Dallas between I-35 and I-45, just east of Waco. This quiet city

Watch your opponent's (or partner's) ball and mark the spot carefully
if it should land in trouble . . . It is a great comfort to know that those
withyou will extend the same courtesy to you. Peter Dobereiner.

was established in 1871 and named for the family of Mexican General Jose Antonio Mexia, who donated the townsite. While it might be nice to dig into the community and investigate the absorbing intellectual roots of Mexia's most famous resident, Anna Nicole Smith, grizzled travelers should have their priorities straight and find fun at Mexia's 9-hole golf course instead.

OLDE OAKS GOLF CLUB

The golf   Mexia's 9-hole course lies over some fairly rugged, hilly terrain with mature oak trees that line the fairways. This is another of the many small-town Texas courses that offers basic golf, small greens, and a green fee that allows you to play all day. Olde Oaks' main feature is the water hazards that come into play on six holes.

The details   254-562-2391. Hwy. 39 South, Mexia, TX 76667

• 1929. 9 holes. Par 36. Back – 3,032. Forward – 2,639. Price - $.

Getting there From Waco, take Hwy. 84 east, then travel 40 miles to Hwy. 39. Turn south and drive 1 mile to the course.

MEXIA NOTES When it's time to eat and drink, head to the **Rockin' L Steakhouse** (254-562-9404) out by **Lake Mexia**. For lodging call the **Hamilton House B&B** (254-562-2005). At the **Old Fort Parker State Historic Site**, you can see where Cynthia Ann Parker, the mother of the last great Comanche chief, Quanah Parker, was taken captive in 1836 in a massive Indian attack. Also, the highest point between Houston and Dallas is at nearby **Tehuacana Hills**.

MOODY   Elev. 783   Pop. 1,400

Just 26 miles south of Waco and about 5 miles west of I-35, Moody was originally established in 1852 as Perry, TX, then renamed in honor of W.L. Moody, the director of the railroad that built through the town. For those interested enough to wander a little further than the normal gas stops along I-35, Moody offers a few buildings with interesting architecture, one of the oldest drug stores in Texas (1881 Moody Drug), and the 18-hole Greenbrier Golf Club.

GREENBRIER GOLF CLUB

The golf   Greenbrier dates back to the 1960s, when the Farm and Home Administration implemented a program to help rural communities create places for locals to play golf. The course survived for a while, but was shut down in the 1980s due to financial problems. After being bought at auction, the course has been gradually improved and sold again over the years.

Known for its well-conditioned greens, the 18-hole design features pretty Central Texas scenery, wide fairways, and lakes, ponds, and creeks that impact play on 14 holes.

While the front nine is more of an open links-style track, the back nine has more doglegs, hills, water, and a real estate development that has made the course much tighter.

The back nine boasts two of the more challenging holes. No. 12 is a 529-yard par 5 that requires accuracy due to the creek crossing the fairway and another pond. Hole 14 is the feature hole with a creek in the fairway and a ditch toward the right. Your approach must clear trees in the middle of the fairway from around 160 yards out.

The details   254-853-2927. 7810 S. Lone Star Pkwy., Moody, TX 76557

- 1968. 18 holes. Par 70. Back – 6,457 (70.3/113). Middle – 6,159 (68.9/110). Forward – 5,406 (70.1/111). Price - $$.

Getting there From I-35, take Hwy. 317 west for 7 miles. Look for the signs to the course.

MOODY NOTES   You can grab a bite at **Lucy's Cafe** (254-853-9302) before you head to Texas' first state park, known as **Mother Neff State Park,** located on a shady 260-acre site on the Leon River. Unless you're camping don't worry about lodging, as the wise plan involves heading back to Waco or another small town with more appealing B&B accomodations.

NEW BRAUNFELS   Elev. 620   Pop. 36,526

Established in 1845 when Prince Carl of Salms-Braunfels led a group of German settlers fleeing the troubles of their homeland, New Braunfels is a beautiful old town that has become the home base of frustrated urban escapees and restless, barbecue-loving river rats. There's something about the abundant waters of the Comal River, the good German food, the venerable dance halls that serve cold beer, and the laid-back lifestyle that draws you to this little piece of Texas paradise.

THE BANDIT GOLF CLUB

The golf   The Bandit is owned by Foresight Golf, the same group that owns The Buckhorn in Comfort, TX, as well as the Republic in San Antonio. Like The Buckhorn, this is an affordable, no-frills course that offers friendly

The principles of good putting will work for as long as your commitment to them stands. Dr. Bob Rotella

service and good golf.

Designed by Keith Foster, who has put his stamp on such notable Texas lay-outs as Texas Star in Euless, TX, and San Antonio's The Quarry, the layout rolls through spectacular Hill Country terrain that features drastic elevation changes, elevated greens, miles of creeks meandering through the course, and some very memorable holes. The greens are known for their great condition as well as their tricky angles.

No. 2 is named "Two Much Too Soon" because it plays 241 yards from the tips, definitely not the par 3 a hacker needs to start the day off right. A few holes later comes the 403-yard No. 5, a slight dogleg lined by a creek on the left, with the right side protected by a hill that can leave you with a precarious lie. And No. 9 is a mean par 4, going 459 yards uphill into an elevated green with a tee shot over a creek.

On the back you'll be ready to laugh after negotiating the 12th hole, a 468-yard par 4 soon to be followed by the 624-yard No. 15, which features out-of-bounds and a creek that crosses the fairway twice. But the highlight of the round is the signature No. 18, only 522 yards but loaded with danger. The hole plays from an elevated tee and rolls along the Guadalupe River on the right. Out-of-bounds is left, so there's no margin for error off the tee. The green is cut into the hill that houses the clubhouse, and a miss here means that your ball will roll into the water. Give yourself an extra stroke on 18 and play for bogey.

The details   830-609-4665. 6019 FM 725, New Braunfels, TX 78130

- 1997. Keith Foster. 18 holes. Par 72. Black – 6,928 (73.6/133). Blue – 6,405 (71.2/124). White – 5,991 (69.2/122). Red – 5,253 (70.3/126). Price - $$.

Getting there The Bandit is only 35 minutes from San Antonio's airport, less than an hour from Austin, and an easy 2.5 hour drive from Houston. Take the Lake McQueeney exit 187 off of I-35.

LANDA PARK MUNICIPAL GOLF COURSE

The golf   Landa Park is New Braunfel's most popular course. It's consis-tently in good condition, a great value with weekend fees under $30 with cart, and a relatively quick round considering the traffic. The other nice feature is that it's easy to score if you're striking it well.

The course opened in 1939 as a 9-holer, and was expanded in 1969 when Leon Howard and Dave Bennett came through. The course is nestled along the Comal River and is watered well. That fact, combined with the course's strict cart-path-only policy, keeps the fairways in lush condition. This is also one you won't mind walking because it's a flat track.

Water hazards come into play on several holes, and the Comal is involved in the layout. The fairways are wide, but lined with trees. The greens are small and undulating. The most difficult hole is No. 4, a long par 5 that goes 553 yards.

☆

Take responsibility for your own ball and your own score: the only things you have control over. Sam Snead

Note that there is no driving range, so some folks head to Sundance near Gruene for their warm-up.

The details   830-608-2174. 800 Landa Park Dr., New Braunfels, TX 78130

- 1939. 18 holes. Back – 6,103 (68.9/112). Middle – 5,585 (66.5/105). Forward – 4,919 (67.4/106). Price - $$.

Getting there From I-35 north, exit San Antonio St. and turn right. When you come to Seguin St., turn right and find Landa Park. Turn right again and you'll see the course just down the road.

LEE'S PAR 3 GOLF COURSE & DRIVING RANGE

The golf   Lee Maddox built this course on top of a hill in 1986, so you'll have more alluring views at this facility than at most par 3 driving range joints. Among the challenges are waste bunkers that impact play and sporadic water hazards. No. 5 is the most dangerous–you'll need a 7-iron to carry the water hazard to reach the tiny green.

The details   830-620-4653. 1450 Klein Rd., New Braunfels, TX 78130

- 1986. Lee Maddox. 9 holes. Par 27. Back – 1,095. Forward – 1,055. Price - $.

Getting there From I-35, get off at the McQueeny exit and head toward McQueeny. Drive 2 miles to the top of the hill, then turn on Klein Rd. and drive a short distance to the course.

SUNDANCE GOLF COURSE

The golf   Next door to Gruene, TX, making it the ideal place to combine golf and late-afternoon or evening roadhouse activities at Gruene Hall, Sundance is a par 58 executive course that has also been noted as being one of *Golf Magazine's* "Top Fifty Practice Facilities in the Nation."

The links-style design features water in play on seven holes, but has virtually no trees or sand. The best hole is No. 3, only a 337-yard par 4, but it bends around a large lake that comes into play on the next three holes as well.

The details   830-629-3817. 2294 Common St., New Braunfels, TX 78130

- www.sundancegolf.com
- 1995. 18 holes. Back – 3,600. Middle – 3,088. Forward – 2,519. Price - $$.

Getting there On I-35 north take Exit 191 and turn left onto Hwy. 306. Drive to the first stop sign and turn left on Common St. The course is on the left a short distance down the road.

NEW BRAUNFELS NOTES Most associate New Braunfels, a veritable beer-joint dancehall heaven on earth, with nearby **Gruene Hall** (www.gruene-hall.com). However, there is more to be experienced. The recently remodeled

A lot of guys who have have never choked, have never been in the position to do so. Tom Watson

River Road Icehouse (830-626-1335), complete with cabins for rent, tubing on the Comal River, good food, and great music, has been hosting some pretty big Texas music names of late. The 1870 **Clear Springs Cafe** (830-629-3777), "The Hill Country's Oldest Dance Hall," has also been restored and hosts the occasional live concert. Another spot is the **Freiheit Country Store** (830-625-9400), established in 1889 and home to cold, cold, cold beer and great food as well as frequent live music and a live radio broadcast that lets you be part of the audience (www.humbletime.com). And last but not least, **Saengerhalle** (830-625-4255) is just off I-35 with its expanded 10,000-square-foot dance floor and rustic, old-school aura.

PFLUGERVILLE   Elev. 713   Pop. 18,000

Pflugerville is 15 miles north of Austin on FM 1825, barely east of I-35. The town sprang up with the coming of the railroad around 1900 and maintained a population of under 1,000 residents until the community became absorbed by the expansion of Round Rock and Austin. Today this rural commuter community is the second-fastest-growing city in Texas with almost 18,000 residents.

BLACKHAWK GOLF CLUB

The golf   Blackhawk rests on the site of an old dairy farm, where the rolling terrain is suited for this links-style layout. This wide-open course features lots of water, loads of bunkers, and huge greens that are easy to three-putt if your approaches are off and you don't have that feel for lag putting.

Each side has a punishing finishing hole. No. 9 is a monstrous par 4 that plays 464 yards. Off the tee, the narrow landing area is not conducive for the necessary booming drive, and the water causes problems in the fairway and around the green.

Hole 18 plays 430 yards, requiring a tee shot into the dogleg-right fairway that must thread two bodies of water.

The club prefers that you walk only on weekdays.

The details   512-251-9000. 2714 Kelly Ln., Pflugerville, TX 78660

• www.blackhawkgolf.com

• 18 holes. Par 72. Black – 7,103 (73.3/123). Blue – 6,639 (71.2/121). White – 6,220 (69.6/119). Red – 5,538 (71.1/121). Price - $$$.

Getting there Take I-35 north out of Austin, then exit FM 1825 east. Drive 5 miles to Hwy. 685 and turn left. Drive another 2.5 miles to Kelly Ln. and turn right.

The first thing you should do when you see that your ball has settled in a divot is to tell yourself that it's a bad break, that it happens to everyone, and that you really have to concentrate on this shot . . . Oh, and you might also resolve never to leave a divot unrepaired yourself. Ken Venturi

PFLUGERVILLE NOTES   There are no B&Bs or motel/hotels in Pflugerville proper, so if you must stay close, check the chains along I-35 around the FM 1825 exit. **Charlie's Steakhouse** (512-251-5398) is a popular spot for lunch, as is **Smokey Mo's Bar-B-Q** (512-828-4050). For nighttime meals, queso lovers will be overjoyed to find the wonderful **El Rincon Mexican Restaurant** (512-990-0250). **Hanover Draught Haus** (512-670-9617) is the place for live Texana music if you're hanging around late. Remember, though, the capital city is just down the road so high-tail it back to Austin for the nightlife.

ROCKDALE

Elev. 467   Pop. 5,615

Rockdale, a clean, prosperous-looking town with wide, tree-lined streets and a tidy little business area, is on US 79 about 45 miles east of Round Rock. Texas' largest lignite coal reserves border the community, and many of the residents earn their living from the Alcoa aluminum plant. Near the plant lies Rockdale's no-hassle country club, which offers the typical mixture of Hill Country oaks and East Texas pines that you'd expect to find here on the eastern edge of Central Texas.

ROCKDALE COUNTRY CLUB

The golf   Located near Rockdale's Alcoa plant, the RCC is a semi-private track that offers no-hassle golf for the right price. The well-maintained design features wide fairways lined with both pine and oak trees, several lakes, and easy par 4s that play under 400 yards. You'll have the chance to start out well since the course opens up with a par 3 followed by a short par 5. The par 3s are good birdie chances since the longest one is only 162 yards.

Two sets of tees make for an 18-hole round, and they don't mind letting you play all day with your paid green fee.

The details   512-446-4013. Alcoa Lake Rd., Rockdale, TX 76567

- 1965. Leon Howard. 9 holes. Par 36. Back – 3,318. Forward – 2,635. Price - $.

Getting there From Hwy. 79, exit FM 487, then go 3 miles. Turn right on FM 16 and drive 2 miles to the club.

ROCKDALE NOTES   If you're in the area frequently, ask about the inexpensive monthly membership options. The clubhouse grill is a great place for food and drink if you're not in the mood to tour Rockdale. The club also offers

---

Taking the high road—playing more break rather than less—makes sense for many reasons:
A ball is more likely to fall down into the hole from the high side that fall
up from the low side; it also encourages rolling the ball at a slower speed,
meaning it is less likely to run too far past the hole should it miss. Dave Pelz

tennis, swimming, and a jogging/walking track that wraps around the course. For lodging in Rockdale try one of the oldest hotels in Texas–the newly renovated **Rainbow Courts Motel** (512-446-2361). For grub nearby call on **Po Boy BBQ** (512-446-2237), or across down by the Wal-Mart is local Tex-Mex heaven at **Mariachi's** (512-446-0276). If you really need some action, ask around and find out if there's a Saturday night dance at the **KC Hall** (Knights of Columbus).

ROCKSPRINGS

Elev. 2,450   Pop. 2,253

Rocksprings, a rugged little sheep-and-goat town on US 377 approximately 100 miles west of San Antonio, is the seat of Edwards County, one of the top producers of wool and mohair in the world. This is a pass-through town, with quick amenities for gassing up and moving on. Hunting and fishing generates 20% of the county's income, Del Rio and Ciudad Acuna are down the road, and the spectacular 400-foot-deep Devil's Sinkhole is to the east.

ROCKSPRINGS COUNTRY CLUB

The golf   As you drive through the rugged terrain around Rocksprings, you'll understand why an open mind is required to experience the golf at Rocksprings Country Club. This borderline pasture golf course was opened in 1976 by local rancher Joe Ball. Ball started with a driving range, then eventually built this 9-hole layout with sand greens. While there is no official water on the course, Ball ingeniously staked out an area and put up a "no fishing" sign with ceramic ducks, which serves as the only hazard.

Drive it straight because "cart paths" frame the fairways, and if your ball is outside of them, the ranchland rough is tough on your clubs. Bring an old iron to punch out of it. However, if you are in the fairway, the "natural prairie grasses" generally offer good lies.

The details   830-683-4224. Hwy. 55, Rocksprings, TX 78880

• 9 holes. Par 36. 2,900 yards. Price - $.

Getting there Located 6 miles south of Rocksprings on Hwy. 55. Turn right past the airport.

ROCKSPRINGS NOTES   You'll see your limitations for adventure in town, so head 25 miles south via Texas 55 to **Barksdale, TX**. Set in the Nueces Canyon, Indian caves dot the canyon walls, and fly-fishers can go crazy in the numerous clear streams. Take precautions and avoid the police, as we've burdened them before, being pulled over for speeding outside of town in the early stages of a binge. It was a close one that involved the officers driving our truck back into town for a blow on the wonder machine. The

Thinking must be the hardest thing to do in golf because we do so little of it. Harvey Penick

negative test and our subsequent freedom surely says something about their eager intentions.

ROUND ROCK

Elev. 720   Pop. 60,686

Round Rock is another old town that has been given new life by the expansion of Austin. It's popular both with commuters and retirees, who are attracted by the slightly lower cost of living. Located 20 miles north of the state capital, the city was established in 1850 and named for a large round rock in the bed of Brush Creek. Famous frontier outlaw Sam Bass and his gang wreaked havoc on stagecoaches and banks here in the 1870s, and his life ended in a bloody gun battle in Round Rock.

With the outstanding new Forest Creek and Teravista Golf Clubs, as well as two more new courses currently under construction, Round Rock's golf scene has kept up with the growing population.

FOREST CREEK GOLF CLUB

The golf   Designed by Dick Phelps, this highly touted track was named "Best Public Golf Course in Central Texas" by *Golf Digest* as well as "Golf Club of the Year" by Club Corporation of America. Phelps' design features plush, narrow fairways, and its namesake Forest Creek that comes into play on 11 holes. Many of the holes dogleg, and its most difficult holes are the long par 4s.

These holes are especially evident on the back nine, with holes 10, 15, and 18 all playing well over 400 yards. The 15th is the most difficult, playing a bogey-welcoming, par 5-like 472 yards.

Other notes: Former Head Pro J.L. Lewis honed his game here before finding success on the PGA Tour. His course record of 65 was set when the course first opened in 1991. Several small pro events have been held at Forest Creek. ParView GPS is utilized on all carts.

The details   512-388-2874. 99 Twin Ridge Pkwy., Round Rock, TX 78664

- Dick Phelps. 18 holes. Par 72. Gold – 7,147 (72.8/130). Blue – 6,405 (70.3/123). White - 6,059 (69.9/118). Red – 5,601 (71.9/124). Price - $$$.

Getting there From I-35 north in Round Rock, turn east on Hwy. 79, then drive 4.5 miles and turn right on County Rd. 122. When you reach Forest Creek Dr., turn left and the course is just down the road.

TERAVISTA GOLF CLUB

The golf   If you have the chance to play one of Troon Golf's facilities, you'll understand that there's just something special about the golf experiences they offer. Their courses are beautiful and in excellent condition. They've laid

---

The secret in the rough is to take a few dozen practice swings
with a 2-iron (a scythe is good, too). Tom Callahan

them out to be challenging from the tips, but also very playable for average hacks from the forward tees. The service is unparalleled, making it seem as if you're at a private club, with staff members greeting you to take your clubs and pampering you throughout the day.

Despite its Hill Country setting, this course has more of a links feel, with wide-open fairways and casually rolling mounds. About 60-70 white bunkers spot the layout, and water comes into play on 14 holes. The course is well marked and features the old-school barberpoles at every 150-yard marker. The Tiff Eagle greens are immaculate and amazing.

No. 17 is the number one handicap, playing a long 443 yards from the tips. The hole bends left toward a kidney-shaped green that is surrounded by three bunkers.

Other notes: Instead of GPS systems on the carts, you're given goodie bags with the more functional yardage charts. The course offers a beginner-friendly tee box that plays only 3,744 yards, making it enjoyable for any skill level.

The details 512-651-9850. 4333 Teravista Club Dr., Round Rock, TX 78664

- www.teravistagolf.com
- 18 holes. Par 72. Black – 7,039. Gold – 6,637. Silver – 6,250. Tan – 5,099. Jade – 3,744. Price - $$$.

Getting there From Austin, travel north on I-35 to Exit 256 and Chandler Rd. Turn right on Chandler and go approximately 1 mile to the main entrance on your left.

MORE GOLF

A new municipal that is in the planning stages is **Southwest Williamson County Golf Course** (512-248-3238), slated to be located at FM 1431 and CR 175. Another new construction project, the **Behrens Ranch Country Club** course, is located in the Behrens Ranch (pronounced 'burns') master-planned community, a former cattle ranch that is being transformed by Masonwood Development.

ROUND ROCK NOTES October is a good time to visit, since the weather is a bit more reasonable and the **Bluegrass & Acoustic Music Festival** is going on. Check out outlaw Sam Bass' grave at the **Round Rock Cemetery** 1 mile west of town on US 79. For meals hit the **Inn at Brushy Creek** (512-255-2555), featuring unique meals in an 1850 house. In the summer don't forget to take in a minor league baseball game in their new first-class stadium.

⭐

I learned the value of making a guy mad—push the right buttons and a guy can't play at all. Phil Rodgers

CENTRAL

SALADO

Elev. 695   Pop. 3,475

The charming town of Salado is the ideal couples get-away–a historic city loaded with antiques, art galleries, and clothing shops to keep the shopping aficionados at bay while the golfers play 27 holes at the Mill Creek golf resort. Located on I-35 halfway between Austin and Waco, Salado is within a few hours' driving distance of many areas of the state, making it easy to drive down on a Friday afternoon or evening, in time for dinner at some of the excellent restaurants, followed by a relaxing night preparing for the weekend activities.

MILL CREEK INN & COUNTRY CLUB

The golf   Golf came to Salado and Mill Creek in 1968, when an informal 9-hole course was opened as sort of an afterthought for the inn's guests. But golf didn't really become a prominent fixture until Robert Trent Jones, Jr. installed a 6,486-yard championship layout in 1979. Jones came back in 2000 to add the third nine, and now the resort has 27 holes carved out of this beautiful Hill Country setting.

Named Creek 1, Creek 2, and Creek 3, they all feature abundant water hazards, fabulous Bermuda greens, and tremendous oak and elm trees.

The details   254-947-5698. 1610 Club Circle, Salado, TX 76571

- www.millcreekgolfresort.com
- Creek 1: 9 holes. Par 36. Blue – 3,324. White – 3,122. Red – 2,836. Price - $$$.
- Creek 2: 9 holes. Par 35. Blue – 3,162. White – 2,930. Red – 2,514. Price - $$$.
- Creek 3: 9 holes. Par 34. Blue – 3,258. White – 2,992. Red – 2,503. Price - $$$.
- 18 hole ratings – Blue (72.1/128). White (70.0/124). Red (69.6/114).

Getting there From I-35 north take the Salado exit and look for signs in town to the course.

SALADO NOTES   You'll probably plan your trip around the resort's offerings, which include remodeled suites and townhomes as well as dining. Tour the quaint shops of Main Street or check out the remains of the 1860 **Salado College**. Salado Creek was Texas' first designated natural landmark. For other digs try the **Ho-Jo Motel** (817-947-5000) or the famous **Stagecoach Inn** (817-947-5111), which serves great steaks and has hosted the likes of George Custer, Robert E. Lee, Sam Houston, and Jesse James.

You know those two-foot downhill putts with a break? I'd rather see a rattlesnake. Sam Snead

SAN SABA
Elev. 1,210   Pop. 2,827

The "Pecan Capital of the World" was settled in the 1850s along the scenic San Saba River. Most know this spot 87 miles northwest of Austin as a great place to fish and hunt. The well-traveled golfer knows San Saba as one of the best-kept secrets of Texas golf.

SAN SABA MUNICIPAL GOLF COURSE

The golf   Carved out of pecan orchard along the San Saba River, this 18-hole gem is one you don't want to miss when you're within reasonable distance of this quaint little town. Over 600 pecan trees dominate the landscape, helping the course produce over 30,000 pounds of pecans each year.

Unlike other small-town courses, there is nothing easy about a golf round at San Saba. The front nine, built in 1972, is really tight, and anything that strays from the fairway will require imaginative recovery shots from the pecan trees. Most of the par 4s are close to 400 yards, the par 3s play over 170, and the two par 5s are extremely long, including No. 9 that goes 625 yards from the back.

The back nine, added in 1987, isn't as squeezed by the pecans, but has more water hazards that impact play. This side also has two long par 5s, but there are a few solid birdie chances, especially the 152-yard par 3 No. 13.

San Saba's muni is beautiful and challenging. You won't want to pass up an opportunity to grace the fairways of this fun course.

Other notes: Actor Tommy Lee Jones reportedly stops in the golf shop to buy gloves for his polo habit. The facility has a few trailer spots if you have the means, making this place the ideal working man's golf vacation destination. Fifty-four holes per day are possible for diehards.

The details   915-372-3212. Hwy. 190E, San Saba, TX 76877

• 1972. Sorrell Smith. 18 holes. Par 72. Back – 6,904 (72.5/119). Middle – 6,379 (70.5/113). Forward – 5,246 (69.5/110). Price - $.

Getting there From San Saba, take Hwy. 190 east, travel 3 miles and look for the signs leading to the clubhouse. The course is adjacent to Risien Park.

SAN SABA NOTES   Investigate the **Oliver Pecan Company** (915-372-5771) before hitting **Ma and Pa's Diner** (915-372-4035) for lunch. The highlight of the area is **Colorado Bend State Park**, where you can set up camp, hike along the scenic banks of the river, catch fish, and track down the spectacular **Gorman Falls**.

You have to play to your personality. If you're high strung, you want to play quickly, even though the whole world will tell you to slow down. If you play at a pace that doesn't fit you, or gamble when you're a conservative person by nature, or try not to talk when you're naturally extroverted, golf is going to be a battle. Phil Rodgers

SAN MARCOS

Elev. 581   Pop. 39,491

Folks have been enjoying the abundant natural springs of San Marcos for quite a while. An underwater archaeological dig has uncovered Indian artifacts dating back over 12,000 years. Spanish explorers stumbled across the springs on St. Mark's Day over three centuries ago and gave the name San Marcos to the springs and the river that flows up from them. After World War II, the tourist attraction of Aquarena Springs featured glass-bottomed boats, the Submarine Underwater Theater, live underwater "mermaids," and Ralph the Swimming Pig. Ralph and the mermaids are long gone, but you can still ride the boats. Southwest Texas University has taken over Aquarena Springs and runs it as an eco-attraction that highlights the area's many rare and endangered plants and fish.

Though growing by leaps and bounds, San Marcos is known primarily as a college town and home to a huge complex of outlet stores on I-35. As much as there is to do in and around San Marcos, the golf in the immediate vicinity is surprisingly lacking for a town of 40,000 that's known for its recreational opportunities.

QUAIL CREEK COUNTRY CLUB

The golf   Quail Creek opened around 1970 as a 9-hole course carved out of an old dairy farm, but was quickly enhanced with the addition of a second nine. Surprisingly, the course remains this college town's only regulation facility.

This semi-private track is known for its difficult greens that are sure three-putts if your game is not on. The fairways are not generous–they're lined with trees and are quite narrow. The back nine is a bit more forgiving than the front. Water hazards come into play on seven holes.

Holes of note include the three par 3s that play around 190 yards and carry water. The other par 3 in only 167 yards, but has character because of the giant pecan tree that dominates the left side.

The hole everyone talks about is No. 7, a scenic 312-yard par 4 that plays over a canyon. The most difficult hole (primarily because of its length) is hole 13, which goes 435 yards and forces fairway wood approaches into the smallest green on the course.

The details   512-353-1665. 2701 Airport Hwy. 21, San Marcos, TX 78667

- 1969-1970. 18 holes. Par 72. Back – 6,449 (70.3/116). Middle – 6,003 (68.5/111). Forward – 4,993 (68.4/107). Price - $$.

Getting there From I-35 south, take Exit 205/Hwy. 80 and turn left. When you come to Hwy. 21, turn left and drive 1.5 miles to the course. The entrance is

I have never seen a pocket billiards player lose his stroke. He's not thinking about his stroke. He's thinking about what's in front of him, as athletes in other sports do. His concern is moving the cue ball to a certain point with a certain amount of speed, not how he's holding the darn cue stick. Roger Maltbie

on the left side of the street.

SOUTHWEST TEXAS STATE GOLF COURSE

The golf   SWT's course is a 9-hole executive track that dates back to the 1920s, when it was originally envisioned as a big-time resort. The San Marcos River is nearby, and many spring-fed streams impact the layout. Pecans and oaks line the fairways, so you'll need to keep it straight

The course opens with a basic par 4 at about 380 yards that is loaded with trees and bunkers. The creek comes into play on holes 2-4. Of the remaining holes, the long par 3 6th is probably the most challenging because of its 194-yard length.

Note No. 9, originally a 660-yard par 5 that has thankfully been cut in half due to safety concerns. The tee box used to be behind the road, creating havoc for passersby, but has now been moved in front of the road.

Other notes: Ask about the Trifecta tournament, held every Thursday at 5:30 pm.

The details   512-245-7593. 601 University Dr., San Marcos, TX 7866

* www.campusrecreation.swt.edu/Golf/
* 1929. Arthur Rogers. 9 holes. Par 34. Back – 2,602 (32.6/103). Forward – 2,083. Price - $.

Getting there On Hwy. 21 in San Marcos.

SAN MARCOS NOTES   Drive through the historic oak-lined streets, particularly Belvin St., to see the magnificent old 19th-century homes. Around the town square you'll find new bars and restaurants for the college scene, but the most unique side trip options are outside of town, especially the scenic drive down the **Devil's Backbone** – take RM 12 northwest to RM 32 along the winding roads and ridges. Consider the side trip to **Uhland, TX** and the 1893 **Club 21 Dance Hall** for festivities, or to **Hunter, TX** and **Riley's Tavern** (512-392-3132) "Texas' First Tavern After Prohibition." For lodging in town there's plenty of options to fit your budget, but the **Crystal River Inn B&B** (512-396-3739) has more character than most.

SEGUIN

Elev. 520   Pop. 21,719

Tidy and tree-shaded, Seguin is 30 minutes west of San Antonio and equidistant from the coastal ports of Houston and Corpus Christi. Ancient oaks, some of which are have historical names and are estimated to be 1,000 years old, line the streets, and pecans are a major cash crop for the community. South of town the beauty of the community is enhanced by the green waters of the

---

For acceleration, swing the putter forward through the ball farther than you take it back. Tom Watson

Guadalupe River. Max Starcke Park is one of the finest in the state for its size and home to the only public golf course in Seguin.

CHAPARRAL COUNTRY CLUB

The golf   Seguin's country club dates back to the 1960s and features wide fairways lined with ash, oak, pecan, cottonwood, and mesquite trees, as well as large greens. Four lakes and a creek spot the rolling terrain, which is primarily noted for its long par 3s. The toughest par 3, No. 11, goes 250 yards with water guarding the left side of the green. And while No. 15 is fairly long at 178 yards, it has been taken for numerous holes-in-one over the years.

On the front, holes 5 and 6 require attention. The first is highlighted by a large lake, and No. 6 bends 450 yards uphill. On the back, the most difficult is No. 18, which plays almost 600 yards and features water on two occasions.

The details   830-379-6313. 300 Chapparral Dr., Seguin, TX 78155

- 1964. 18 holes. Par 72. Back – 7,008 (72.6/119). Middle – 6,570 (70.5/115). Forward – 5,560 (70.7/111). Price - $$.

Getting there In town turn right onto Hwy. 725, then continue on for another 4 miles and look for signs leading to the clubhouse.

STARCKE PARK GOLF CLUB

The golf   Max Starcke, former mayor of Seguin, has this great little municipal named after him. The course rolls along the Guadalupe River and is lined by giant pecans. John Bredemus designed the front nine in 1936 and Ralph Plummer added the second nine in 1979.

While the front is the easier of the two nines, it features one extremely difficult hole in the 457-yard No. 3: it plays uphill into a gentle dogleg left, with the left side also protected by a lake.

No. 18 is the signature on the back, but holes 11-13 offer a difficult stretch of golf. The par 5 No. 11 plays uphill, and is longer when facing the wind. Holes 12 and 13 both have elevated greens fronted by water. The 16th is known for its Texas-shaped (but not Texas-sized) green. The final hole plays 434 yards and demands an accurate tee shot down a skinny fairway that has a pond on the right side.

After post-round beers with the friendly locals, partake in the Starcke tradition of hitting wild drivers from the practice range in a desperate effort to reach the galvanized metal-sided cart barn some 300 yards away.

The details   830-401-2490. 1400 S. Guadalupe St., Seguin, TX 78156

- 1936. John Bredemus (9), 1979. Ralph Plummer (9). 18 holes. Par 71. Back – 6,725 (70.8/115). Middle – 6,424 (69.2/112). Forward – Par 72. 5,733 yards. Price - $$.

Get set up, take a last look at the target, and let the shot go without delay. Dr. Bob Rotella

Getting there From I-10, take the Austin St. exit, then head south for 5 miles to the course. Look for S. Guadalupe St.

SEGUIN NOTES Look for the old bar downtown called **The Oak** to take in the local flavor of Seguin, as well as a few games of pool. The place to eat is **El Ranchito**, where sloppy enchiladas go well with Mexican cervezas. Shop for macho cowboy garb at the huge **D&D Farm & Ranch**. Note the numerous concrete buildings, dating to the 1880s, that once gave Seguin the name "Cement City."

SPICEWOOD Elev. 764   Pop. 100

Located 9 miles southeast of Marble Falls, due west of Austin on winding Hwy. 71, Spicewood is a famous little lakeside conglomeration of food joints and weekend getaways, and really not much more than a post office. The area is home to three exclusive golf courses and spectacular golf, but the average golf explorer will be more interested in the toned-down Pedernales Country Club, which is owned by none other than Texas hero Willie Nelson.

AUSTIN GOLF CLUB

The golf Ultra old-school, the Austin Golf Club is just that: a golf club. No real estate, no country club amenities, just a spectacular course designed by Ben Crenshaw and Bill Coore. The course, which opened in 2000, has slipped under the publicity radar and is an exclusive, quiet club that simply serves as a place to play for its members.

While not much information is available about the course, AGC is unique because of its outstanding caddie program, and because it's one of the only courses in the area with Zoysia tees, fairways, and first cut of rough. Perhaps we'll be able work our way on in the future, but for now we can only drool over the lush bent-greens that Master Crenshaw created.

The details 512-264-9787. 25400 Hwy. 71, Spicewood, TX 78669

• 2000. Crenshaw-Coore. 7,000 yards. Par 70. Price - $$$$.

Getting there We're not exactly sure because the location is somewhat secret, but you could take Texas 71 west out of Austin for about 20 miles, then tour the back roads around Spicewood toward the lake looking for an ocean of green, lush Zoysia grass.

LAKECLIFF COUNTRY CLUB

The golf Arnold Palmer designed this new course, sometimes referred to as Lakecliff on Lake Travis, which features 12 man-made lakes, waterfalls, and spectacular Hill Country views. Laid out near the 165-mile chain of Hill Country lakes called the Highland Lakes, the course plays 6,754 yards to a par 71 and offers breathtaking, rolling terrain through the cliffs and ravines that plunge towards Lake Travis. The route has five par 3s and from all indications will be fairly user-friendly for the expected 475 members. The official opening date is scheduled for April of 2003.

The details No number yet. 25818 Haynie Flat Rd., Spicewood, TX 78669

- www.lakecliff.net
- Arnold Palmer. 18 holes. Par 71. 6,754 yards. Price - $$$$.

Getting there From Austin take Hwy. 71 west to the Hwy. 620 intersection. Turn right and drive 12 miles. You'll cross the Pedernales River and after a few miles, you will come upon Pale Face Ranch Rd. Turn right and drive 1 mile past the Barton Creek Lakeside entrance. Lakecliff's entrance is on the left.

PEDERNALES COUNTRY CLUB

The golf "Willie's Course" is officially called the Pedernales Country Club, but "Cut 'N Putt" is also printed on the scorecard. This rugged, almost pasture-golf-like course is known for its superb greens. It goes 3,330 yards and, despite its lack of formal hazards, is extremely challenging unless you've played it a few times.

The old sand bunkers have been covered by sprawling Bermuda. The fairways are hard–sometimes solid tee shots will roll and roll until they find the Hill Country scrub that lines the fairways.

Holes 4 and 7 have water. The fourth is notable because it requires a perfectly placed mid-iron into the dogleg-left fairway with water on the left, followed by an uphill approach over the drink to the green. They call the 7th hole the signature: the elevated tee offers one of the course's best views, and you'll have to deal with a severely sloping fairway that cuts right and requires another perfect tee shot to avoid having your ball slip off into oblivion.

Suffice it to say, this is required golf for any true Texan who dabbles in the great game. It's Willie's course and it's public. You can choose to play by his "cowboy-Zen" rules and save yourself a few strokes. Heck, he might even join you if he's on the premises.

Other notes: Charles Howard built the course and Willie took it over in 1979. Don't miss the clubhouse, which is just a small building with Willie paraphernalia littering the walls.

The details 512-264-1489. 807 Paisley Dr., Spicewood, TX 78669

- 1968. Frank Howard. 9 holes. Par 36. Back – 3,330 (36.0). Middle – 3,205 (35.0). Forward – 3,030 (36.0). Price - $.

Getting there From Austin, take Hwy. 71 west and turn right on County Rd.

2322. Drive 2 miles and turn right again at the Briarcliff St. sign. Drive up the hill past a security building and take the second right onto Paisley. The course is just up the hill.

SPICEWOOD NOTES You'll want to schedule some time at **Poodie's Hilltop Bar & Grill** (512-264-0318) for beer, food, and live music. Big names drop in to play at this famous joint on Hwy. 71.

WILLIE ON GOLF

In a recent national magazine interview, the Zen master of Texas mentioned his usual downtime activities after being on tour: chess, horseback riding, and poker. However, he elaborated a little more when the talk turned to golf:

"Mostly, though, I play golf. I've been playing for 25 years now. I didn't start until I was about 40, because I didn't think I'd like it. Back in those days, I was drinking all night and sleeping all day, so I didn't have time for swinging golf clubs. It's something you've really got to work at. The golf's extraordinary on Maui. Yesterday was a good golf day: In the morning I played nine holes with Kris Kristofferson, and in the afternoon I played nine with Clint Eastwood. I can beat Kris, but not Clint–he's pretty good."

SPRING BRANCH   Elev. 1,115   Pop. 200

The small community of Spring Branch, named for the spring that flows into the nearby Guadalupe River, is located just west of US 281 due north of San Antonio. Only 25 folks made Spring Branch home until Canyon Dam gave life to the lake just east of town, booming this town in the hills of Comal County to several hundred residents. Since this is less than 30 minutes from downtown San Antonio, the golf facilities here are often associated with the Alamo City. Make no mistake about it, though–this scenic region of the Hill Country, while offering the quality of big-city golf, is much more serene, peaceful, and remote than anything in town.

RAYNER RANCH GOLF CLUB

The golf   Formerly known as Rebecca Creek Golf Club, Rayner Ranch is a back-to-basics country course that has improved dramatically since the new

---

There is no shape nor size of body, no awkwardness nor ungainliness, which puts good golf beyond reach. There are good golfers with spectacles, with one eye, with one leg, even with one arm. In golf, while there is life there is hope. Sir Walter Simpson

ownership took over. The tee boxes have been redesigned and resodded, and several greens have been improved. New cart paths have been installed and the clubhouse and pro shop have been totally renovated.

Located near Rebecca Creek and Canyon Lake, the course is surprisingly void of water and bunkers, but is tight enough to cause problems if you're spraying the ball. The layout is carved out of the Hill Country, and the rolling fairways are lined by oak trees. Slicers will fare well here, since there always seems to be room for error to the right.

No. 3 is the rated the most difficult, a 552-yard dogleg left par 5, but the 18th is probably more challenging: a long par 4 with a long iron or fairway wood approach to a green fronted by a large body of water.

The staff's attitude reflects the club's bright future. Everyone is friendly, and you'll always see the beverage cart rolling around the course. For the price, this out-of-the way course is definitely worth a golf road trip.

The details   830-885-7495. 10101 Rebecca Creek, Spring Branch, TX 78070

- www.raynerranchgolf.com
- 18 holes. Black – 6,883 (73.5/129). Blue – 6,486 (72.0/122). White – 6,064 (69.0/119). Red – 5,325 (67.5/113). Price - $$.

Getting there From Hwy. 281 north, look for the large golf ball on the side of the Hwy. Turn right on Rebecca Creek Rd. and the course is 3 miles away.

RIVER CROSSING GOLF CLUB

The golf   River Crossing is an 18-hole public known for its serene setting, panoramic views, and outstanding, lightning fast tiff-eagle greens. The layout is fun because of the varied combination of holes. With a good mixture of short and long holes, as well as some blind tee shots, this track offers a complete golf experience and the opportunity to go low because of the wide fairways and large greens.

You'll have the chance to start strong in the early part of your round thanks to the more generous fairways, but the course eventually leads to some narrow, tree-lined holes that feature significant elevation changes. Errant tee shots will find the trees and creek beds that run parallel to the fairways. The back nine is considered more difficult because of the long par 4s.

Water is in play on four holes, with the par 3 No. 2 standing out because of the island green.

Other notes: The clubhouse is outstanding, and it's difficult to find anyone complaining about the food or service. If your round is on Sunday, plan on having the brunch.

The details   830-904-4653. 500 River Way, Spring Branch, TX 78070

Golf should be learned starting at the cup and progressing back toward the tee. . . . If a beginner tries to learn the game at the tee and move on toward the green, postponing the short game until last, this is one beginner who will be lucky to ever beat anybody. Harvey Penick

- www.rivercrossinggolfclub.com
- 18 holes. Black – 6,821 (72.5/132). Gold – 6,476 (70.9/126). Blue – 6,096 (68.7/124). Red – 5,588. Price - $$$.

Getting there River Crossing is about 15 miles north of 1604 on 281. The course is on the right.

SPRING BRANCH NOTES   If you can't strum up action in the bars, restaurants, and marinas around Canyon Lake, head to Bulverde, TX and find **Specht's Store Restaurant and Saloon** (830-980-7121) to enjoy onion rings, catfish filets, and live music. Other options are to head north on US 281 to **Blanco, TX** and the **Blanco Bowling Club Cafe** (830-833-4416), where you can chain smoke, drink beer, bowl, and eat chicken-fried steak with the area farmers and ranchers. Or hit **Oso's Mexican Grill & Cantina** (830-833-1304) in Blanco's historic Square. Tex-Mex is their specialty, and you'll want the Huevos de Oso (bear balls), which is a concoction of sopapillas, honey, ice cream, and pecans.

TAYLOR   Elev. 583   Pop. 14,690

Leaving Round Rock to the north on US 79, first there is Hutto, then Taylor–rival to Lockhart as the "BBQ Capital of Texas" and self-proclaimed "Barbecue Capital of the World." Settled by Germans and Czechs in 1876, this spick-and-span town serves the bustling agricultural and manufacturing community. Historic homes line the wide streets and the city hosts its International Barbecue Cookoff each August at shaded Murphy Park.

MUSTANG CREEK GOLF COURSE

The golf   Mustang Creek reportedly opened in 1915 as Taylor Country Club and remained private until 1989, when the course was brought public due to a lack of members. This course is easy to play, very affordable, and offers the chance for a quick 9-hole round of golf.

The layout sits in open, rolling terrain, so wind can be a factor when it's blowing hard. Uneven lies are common here, and you'll find yourself hitting many uphill and downhill shots. Water comes into play on two holes, particularly the opening hole, where water is everywhere.

The course isn't long, but the trick is to get used to the extremely small greens. To score well you'll need a few up and downs.

There is an extra hole that serves as the 18th hole when playing the second time around.

The details   512-365-1332. US 79, Taylor, TX 76574

- 1928. Dale Cummings. 9 holes. Par 34. Back – 2,523. Middle – 2,431

Let your left heel come off the ground if that helps you make a full backswing. Butch Harmon

(31.5/90). Forward – 2,120. Price - $$.

Getting there From Austin, take I-35 north, then turn north on Hwy. 79. Take the Loop Route (which is still Hwy. 79) and follow the signs to the course.

TAYLOR NOTES   Mix peppery potato salad, cold bottles of beer, and juicy pork ribs at **Louie Meuller Barbecue** (512-352-6206). Options that are often overlooked are the ribs at the **Taylor Cafe** (512-352-8475) or the burgers at the **Diamond Inn** (512-352-9043). For lodging there is a Regency Inn (512-352-2666), but we recommend that you call the **Minzenmayer Granger Lake Cabin** (512-365-5190) for a more well-rounded experience.

TEMPLE
Elev. 736   Pop. 49,427

This designated "Wildflower Capital of Texas" is a busy, rapidly growing city that has spread out around a compact business district. In the early years after the railroad came through town, Temple was a rough town dotted with saloons and brothels. Respectability eventually arrived with the help of citizens such as Dr. A.C. Scott, who was chief surgeon of the hospital from 1892 to 1940. With the help of his partner, Dr. R.R. White, the two helped Temple on its way to becoming what is now one of the leading medical centers in the nation.

The metro area that includes Temple, Belton, and Killeen is one of the fastest-growing in America. Temple itself offers two public golf courses, highlighted by the outstanding Sammons Park Golf Course, and one private facility, the scenic Wildflower Country Club.

SAMMONS PARK GOLF COURSE

The golf   Sammons Park is built around historic Lake Polk, which was originally formed way back in 1892 when the Santa Fe Railroad Co. dammed Bird's Creek to create a water supply for the area. The Lake Polk Association emerged, offering a private facility for boating, hunting, and fishing, and eventually morphed into the Lake Polk Golf and Country Club, with a 9-hole course that opened for play in 1922.

Those holes survived and were added to in the 1950s, when the facility was renamed the Temple Country Club. Another 30 years or so went by before the city took over and ran the course for a few years before selling out to golf course management company Evergreen Alliance Golf Limited. Evergreen brought in John Sammons to redesign the layout, and his course is still in place today, with the exception of some minor changes and a new location across the lake for the clubhouse.

Now it's a pesky 6,000-yard course with water on 15 of 18 holes, which is fairly prominent on the front, but especially dominating on the back side.

To fix a slice, grip the club much softer than you would shake someone's hand. Hank Haney

Holes 10 and 11 are back-to-back par 3s that play entirely over water, and rival each other as the signature holes on the course. No. 12 has water, and No. 13 offers a brief respite before the lake comes into play on holes 14 and 15. And it doesn't let up from there, as ponds dot the landscape on the final three holes. So do tributaries of the main lake, finishing off what must be one of the wettest 9 holes in the state.

The details   254-771-2030. 2727 W. Adams Ave., Temple, TX 76504

- 1986. John Sammons. Par 70. Back – 6,016 (69.6/129). Middle – 5,564 (67.2/120). Forward – 4,479 (65.8/110). Price - $.

Getting there From I-35 south take Exit 300 and turn right on 49th Street. 49th turns into W. Ave. D, and you'll see the course on the left side of the road.

TEMPLE JUNIOR COLLEGE GOLF COURSE

The golf   A college course that dates back to the 1940s, the design features tight fairways and small, undulating greens. This 9-hole public course has two sets of tees and plays to a par 34.

The details   254-773-0888. 2501 South 1st. St., Temple, TX 76505

- 1945. 9 holes. Par 34. Back – 2,763. Forward – 2,548. Price - $.

Getting there From I-35 north, turn on Loop 363 east, then exit 5th Street. Find Temple Junior College and look for South 1st Street.

WILDFLOWER COUNTRY CLUB

The golf   Wildflower opened in 1987, and is one of Leon Howard's better designs, featuring outstanding views of the central Texas landscapes, loads of water, and some of the best holes in this part of the state. While Howard established a reputation for basic, down-and-dirty courses in the 60s and 70s, this modern, challenging track is more of a complete golf experience.

The design incorporates numerous water hazards, including many natural ponds that grace the rolling terrain. The fairways are fairly generous, and most of the greens have deceptive undulations.

During the round you'll notice the long, challenging par 4s. Particularly the 405-yard No. 11, where a creek cuts into the fairway twice, framing the landing area off the tee. No. 3 is also tough, playing 446 yards and forcing another carry of a creek that cuts into the fairway. The 17th is another solid par 4–not as long, but picturesque because the green is completely surrounded by water.

Finally, the feature that rounds out the experience at Wildflower is the great condition of the course, enhanced by the new irrigation system that keeps the fairways lush and the greens healthy and rolling true.

The details   254-771-1177. 4902 Wildflower Ln., Temple, TX 76502

* www.wildflowerclub.com

* 18 holes. Par 72. Gold – 7,010 (74.3/127). Blue – 6,673 (72.5/122). White – 6,268 (69.5/115). Green – 5,921 (68.0/112). Red – 5,395 (71.0/124). Price - $$.

Getting there From I-35 north, exit Midway Dr. and turn left. Drive approximately 2 miles and turn right on Wildflower Ln.

TEMPLE NOTES   After golf, go for chicken-fried steak at the **Bluebonnet Cafe** (254-773-6644), a Temple institution that's famous for its good eats. Also consider the **Classic Cafe** (254-774-8701), set in a historic office building. There's lodging to be had at the **Holiday Inn** and tons of the standard traditional guidebook recommendations like city parks, museums, etc., to tour if you're dying to roam around Temple.

THORNDALE   Elev. 459   Pop. 1,134

About 30 miles west of Round Rock lies Thorndale, named after the region's mesquite thorn, sagebrush, and prickly pear. A vintage agricultural community, the town serves as the business hub for area farmers like Don and Beth Lackey, who've been kind enough to bring the glorious game of golf to the pastures of Milam County.

LACKEY FARMS PASTURE GOLF COURSE

The golf   Every now and then the discerning golfer needs to break out of the mold and do something different. Now, thanks to the Lackeys, the pastures of Thorndale provide the opportunity to play the game as it was in its beginnings 500 years ago.

At Lackey Farms they've created a course near their vineyard area, with fairways mowed out of the pastures and unimproved greens that feature two-foot-square sand holes to chip into. Leave your putter in the truck, but bring some apples for the horses that roam the fields.

The Lackeys have established their own unique set of rules that include provisions for dogs taking your balls, balls that roll down varmint holes, and the ingenious rule of allowing improved lies at any time. Grass fires are a hazard during drought conditions, so throw a fire extinguisher in your bag and pack out your smokes. There are no carts, but you can bring your 4-wheel-drive Mule if you have one. And bring your own beer while you're at it.

⭐

No matter how skillfully one may lay out the holes and diversify them, nevertheless one must get the thrill of nature. . . . The puny strivings of the architect do not quench our thirst for the ultimate. George Thomas, 1927

The design incorporates six par 4s, two par 3s, and one par 5. The par 35 layout plays just over 2,000 yards. The most notable hole is No. 8, a 180-yard (yes...180) par 4 that bends around a pond and offers the chance to reach the green in one if you can pull off the blind pitch over the dam and trees.

Don't miss this one–it's a hoot and only $7 to play.

The details   512-898-0600. 801 County Rd. 439, Thorndale, TX 76577

• Don Lackey. 9 holes. Par 35. 2,350 yards. No carts. Price - $.

Getting there From 79 east, take the loop around the south side of Taylor. Find FM 112, which veers to the right. Follow 112 about 8 miles. Turn right on FM 486 at Thorndale. Go approx 5 miles south on Hwy. 486. Turn right (west) at CR 451–an unpaved road for first .5 mile or so. It turns into CR 439 and becomes paved. Continue for 1.5 miles and Lackey Farms is on the right, atop the last hill on the road with a sign on the mailbox.

THORNDALE NOTES   **T-Bones** downtown comes highly recommended, or you can drive over to Granger Lake and find **The Cotton Club** for live music and adult beverages. Or track down the bump in the road called **San Gabriel** (FM 486 six miles north), where along the river lie the remnants of three **San Xavier missions** that date back to the 1750s, site of ill-fated Spanish religious efforts.

WACO
Elev. 427 Pop. 108,272

While it isn't the most popular vacation destination in Texas, Waco offers more than you might know from just speeding through on your way to Austin or Dallas. The town known for its five "Cs"–cattle, cotton, corn, collegians, and culture–is in the middle of a rich agricultural region of the Brazos River Valley that is loaded with outstanding golf courses.

President George W. Bush would know–he parks his plane at the former Connally Air Force Base for excursions to his ranch in Crawford, and he's been lured to the links of Waco more than once. His course of choice recently has been the Ridgewood Country Club. If he wanted to play with the common man, the newly opened Bear Ridge or the Cottonwood Creek municipal would stand out among Waco's six regulation public courses.

BEAR RIDGE GOLF COURSE

The golf   Part of the new generation of marathon-long championship layouts, Bear Ridge opened in November 2001. At the time it was the longest course in the state at 7,478 yards from the "Big Jake" tees. The moniker comes from one of the architects, PGA Tour funny-guy Peter Jacobsen, who partnered

The proper putting stroke cannot be contrived or manipulated
with the hands—it must be natural. Ben Crenshaw

with Jim Hardy to build this track southwest of Waco. The course is now the new home of Baylor University's men's and women's golf teams.

The duo's design weaves in and out of both forested Hill Country terrain and meadow-like open fields, offering a great variety of holes. Part of the variety lies in the potentially lengthy north-south holes that have the added flexibility of moving the tees based on the magnitude of the winds.

Much of the length lies in the par 5s. In fact Nos. 4, 8, 10, and 16 make up about 30% of the course's overall length. Both 4 and 10 play around the 600-yard range.

The signature hole is the par 3 No. 14, a spectacular 216-yard hole that drops almost 100 feet in elevation and involves a huge oak tree that can easily knock down less-than-perfect tee shots. No. 14 starts an impressive stretch of holes that takes you through the finish.

No. 15 is scary off the tee, lined by trees and the Bosque River on the left, and featuring a creek that crosses the fairway in front of the green. Next comes the shortest par 5, but is ironically the most difficult rated hole. This 16th plays from an elevated tee and features a creek that crosses the fairway at 100 yards out. The 17th is a manageable par 3 and the easiest of the final stretch, but the 18th is a man's hole, playing uphill with massive fairway bunkers and the creek again impacting the approach. If you're not on your game, these final holes will destroy your round.

The best part about this course, in addition to the affordability, is that it's relatively unknown and doesn't receive much traffic. We played on a warm spring day and had the entire course to ourselves, easily working in 36 holes and generally having a ball.

The details   254-848-7800. 1000 Bear Ridge Dr., Woodway, TX 76712

• 2001. Jacobsen and Hardy. 18 holes. Par 72. 7,478 yards. Price - $$.

Getting there Near the intersection of Hwy. 84 and Speegleville Rd. in southwest Waco.

BOGEY'S PAR 3 GOLF COURSE

The golf   Bogey's offers 18 holes of par 3 golf, with carts included if you like. The longest hole is 178 yards, and the design features two ponds, as well as several low areas that collect water during periods of frequent rain.

The details   254-754-4401. 5500 W. Old Steinbeck Bend, Waco, TX 76708

• 1992. Jesse Hancock. 18 holes. Par 54. Price - $.

Getting there Driving south from Dallas on I-35, exit Lake Shore and drive west until you pass Cargill Foods. Turn right at the next light and the course is on the second road on the left.

The flight of the ball ALWAYS tells you EVERYTHING you need to know to become a better player. John Jacobs

COTTONWOOD CREEK GOLF COURSE

The golf   Joe Finger teamed with Ken Dye to create Cottonwood Creek, which turned out to be one of Finger's last design projects. This links-style course features a good amount of cottonwood trees lining the fairways, and the appropriately named Cottonwood Creek meanders through the layout. Water is in play on over half the holes, and the Bermuda greens are generally elevated.

Two holes stand out on the front nine. The first is No. 5, a 435-yard par 4 that doglegs left between two creeks. The second is the 554-yard No. 7, which has the tightest fairway on the course.

The back nine starts out tough with another long doglegging par 4 with water backing the green. The next one to watch for is the double dogleg No. 15, which snakes 541 yards and has a green protected by water. Big, perfect drives force the consideration of cutting over the lake to reach the green in two.

And you'll need a solid drive on No. 16, a 453-yard par 4. Water is in play on the approach and off the tee.

Other notes: Cottonwood also has a 9-hole facility that serves as a nice little short-game practice area. The holes range from 37 to 90 yards, and the green fee is $5 for adults.

The details   254-745-6009. 5200 Bagby Ave., Waco, TX 76711

- 1985. Pete Dye and Joe Finger. 18 holes. Par 72. Champ – 7,140 (73.5/129). Blue – 6,606 (71.3/124). White – 6,304 (68.7/120). Red – 5,716. Price - $$$.

- Par 3 Course: 9 holes. Par 27. 1,070 yards. Price - $.

Getting there From I-35 south, exit New Rd. and turn right. When you get to Bagby Ave., turn left and the entrance is down on the right.

CREEKSIDE GOLF

The golf   Creekside is a 9-holer with holes ranging from 80-170 yards, with most playing somewhere between 100-120 yards. Water comes into play on only one hole, No. 4, which features the wet stuff behind the green. Beware of the winter hours, as they are only open on the weekends.

The details   254-848-9310. 6234 N. Hwy. 6, Waco, TX 76712

- 1970. 9 holes. Par 27. Approx 1,000 yards. Price - $.

Getting there From I-35 south, take Exit 330 (Hwy. 6 to Meridian), and drive 7 miles across the twin bridges of Lake Waco. Take the Speegleville exit, stay on the frontage, and the course is 1 mile down on the right.

My favorite key for slowing down the swing is to think of Sam Snead swinging a club.
All I have to do is picture his nice, flowing action, and my swing gets smoother.
He still has the best rhythm of anybody who has ever played the game. Sam's thought
for slowing down is to feel "oily" when he swings. I love that one. Tom Watson

JAMES CONNALLY MUNICIPAL GOLF COURSE

The golf   Waco's long-time favorite was designed by Ralph Plummer in the 1950s after Connally Air Force Base closed. Plummer's design is fairly long and features many long par 4s, plus water on 11 holes, but has the added benefit of generous fairways.

Holes 2, 4, 11, and 12 are all par 4s over 400 yards. The featured par 3 is No. 8, which plays 213 yards into an elevated green. The best par 5 is the 575-yard monster 16th, which plays uphill all the way.

The details   254-799-6561. 7900 Concord Rd., Waco, TX 76715

- 1955. Ralph Plummer. 18 holes. Par 72. Back – 6,966. Middle – 6,456. Forward – 5,763. Price - $$.

Getting there From Hwy. 35 south, turn left on Hwy. 84, then drive about 4 miles and make a right on Aviation Pkwy. The course is at the end of this road.

LAKE WACO GOLF & COUNTRY CLUB

The golf   Lake Waco opened to the public in 1964, but eventually became private in 1969 after several ownership changes. The club features a quality 18-hole track that annually hosts a qualifying tournament for the Texas State Open, as well as a nice little confidence-building executive course.

The designs offer the basics, with standard-width fairways that roll to medium size greens of average speed. A few lakes come into play on both courses.

On the **Main Course**, the most difficult holes are Nos. 7 and 8. The first goes 603 yards and plays like 800 into the wind. No. 8 is a scenic par 3, featuring a sloped green surrounded by water and majestic trees.

The **Executive Course** plays only 2,705 yards and features many short holes just over 200 yards. The greens are small, making this the place for members to work on their short game.

The details   254-772-2050. 5608 Flat Rock Rd., Waco, TX 76708

- Main Course: 1964. 18 holes. Par 72. Back – 6,640 (71.4/122). Middle – 6,125 (68.7/116). Forward – 5,581 (70.2/114). Price - $$.
- Executive Course: 18 holes. Par 54. Back – 2,705 (55.8). Forward – 2,378 (58.2). Price - $.

Getting there From I-35 south find Lake Shore exit, and turn west. Drive to Steinbeck Bend Rd. and turn right. When you reach Hwy. 1637, turn right and drive to Flat Rock Rd., where you'll turn left and see the course.

RIDGEWOOD COUNTRY CLUB

The golf   Ridgewood CC, which opened in 1947 and was redesigned by Ralph Plummer in 1962, once hosted the Southwest Conference tournament.

Golf enables me to dress like an idiot. Huey Lewis

A scenic course that overlooks Lake Waco, it opens with a difficult par 4 that plays off of the side of a large hill offering a panoramic view of the water.

Two holes stand out on the front: the 406-yard No. 6, which rolls to the lake and features an approach into a deep, massive green; and the 416-yard dogleg-right No. 8 with its sloping fairway.

No. 18 is a solid finisher at 558 yards, playing downhill to a tiny green.

The details   254-772-2050. 7301 Fish Pond Rd., Waco, TX 76714

• www.ridgewoodwaco.com

• Men's Champ – 6,469 (71.3/123). Men's White – 6,116 (69.7k/120). Ladies Gold – 5,705 (72.7/129). Ladies Red – 5,103 (69.4/121). Price - $$.

Getting there From Lakeshore Dr., take Valley Mills south. When you come to Cobbs St., turn right. Once you reach Fish Pond Rd., turn right again and drive approximately 4 miles to the course.

ROLLING OAKS GOLF CLUB

The golf   Rolling Oaks opened as the Western Oaks Country Club in 1978, became known as Heather Run in the 1990s, and is now known as the more descriptive Rolling Oaks. The course is built around many lakes that are known for holding outstanding lunker bass.

The front nine is more open and a bit less lengthy, while the back has more elevation changes and trees. The first notable hole is No. 6, which plays almost 200 yards into a severely sloping green.

Holes 12-15 make up the toughest stretch on the course. It starts with No. 12, a long par 5 with a tough green, followed by the signature No. 13, which plays 402 yards into a sloping, tree-lined fairway. This hole is known for the huge cliff on the right-hand side. No. 14 is tough because of the lake fronting the green, and No. 15 requires a tee shot over another lake.

The details   254-772-8100. 1600 Western Oaks Dr., Waco, TX 76712

• 1978. 18 holes. Par 70. Gold – 6,182 (70.7/122). Blue – 5,814 (68.7/117). White – 5,178 (69.6/124). Red – 4,840 (68.7/120). Price - $$$.

Getting there From I-35 south through Waco, turn north on Hwy. 6, then take the Bosque exit. Turn left and after 1 mile, turn right on Western Oaks Dr.. Turn right again and the course is at the end of the road.

WACO NOTES   Compare how you measure up to the machismos of Texas at the **Texas Ranger Museum**. For eats, **George's** (254-753-1421) is the place for fathers and sons to experience male bonding by partaking in giant-sized globes of beer and gazing at Baylor's beautiful co-eds. The **Lone Star Tavern** (254-799-0918) is one of the best steakhouses in Texas, and the **Elite Cafe** (254-754-4941) specializes in chicken-fried steak. Weekend golf orgy-goers

---

Golf is a game where white men can dress up as pimps and get away with it. Robin Williams

can go upscale at the **Waco Hilton** (254-754-8484), or more toned down at the **Old Main Lodge** (254-753-0316) near campus.

WIMBERLEY
Elev. 967   Pop. 3,797

The scenic Hill Country village of Wimberley, located in a remote spot just north of San Marcos, has grown as a resort destination, artists' haven, and retirement community over the years. There's something about this area that entrances everyone who finds their way here. Whether it's the crisp, clean air, the clear pools beneath the huge cypress trees, the cool waters of Cypress Creek and the Blanco River, or the stunning Hill Country views, everyone enjoys their stay in Wimberley.

QUICKSAND AT WOODCREEK COUNTRY CLUB

The golf   The game of golf came to Wimberley in the 1970s but never really achieved a true identity, due to shuffling ownership and poor maintenance. However, in May 2001 the Quicksand Golf Corporation, fresh from their successful Quicksand Golf Course in San Angelo, bought the existing property and began to make changes. The old Cypress Creek course was completely shut down, and the former Brookhollow and Eagle Rock 18 have been transformed into what is now referred to as Woodcreek.

The name of the game at Woodcreek is dogleg. On the front nine, every hole doglegs except the two par 3s, including the signature No. 8, a picturesque, 408-yard, par 4. This hole drops significantly off the tee, rounding the corner and funneling down to a small pond that fronts the green.

The back nine isn't as flat as the front side, with several holes featuring elevation changes similar to the signature 8th. Nos. 12, 13, and 17 all feature impressive views of the countryside as the hole drops down below.

The best hole on the back is No. 17, a 358-yarder that allows you to swing big off the tee. The tee shot must clear the ravine to set up the approach shot into the elevated green.

The details   512-847-9700. 1 Pro Ln., Wimberley, TX 78676

- 1971. Bruce Little. 18 Holes. Par 72. Back – 6,750 (71.8/121). Middle – 5,830 (68.1/111). Forward – 5,092 (69.7/114). Price - $$.

Getting there From I-35 south, take Hwy. 290 west and turn left on RR 12 in Dripping Springs. Drive 15 miles and the entrance is on the right side of the road.

Extremely large greens breed slovenly play. A.W. Tillinghast

MORE GOLF

On FM 12 towards Dripping Springs, TX, you'll find the rustic **Dripping Springs Instruction Center**, a little par-3 course/driving range on the east side of the road. The quaint golf shop is often left open, relying on golfers to slip their funds in a pay slot to cover the green fee or a bucket of balls ($3 large bucket). Basil Curry gives lessons out of this shop, and once you're done the chip-and-putt course is yours for no charge. Most of the holes are 40-60 yards, and they route through a grove of old oak trees whose branches overhang and cause problems for errant shots.

WIMBERLEY NOTES Shop away in this charming town–the misss will surely be proud to find herself here. Let her indulge herself and then take her to the famous **Cypress Creek Cafe** for a meal and possibly a show. Do your homework for the appropriate B&B accommodations, as there are many. One option is the **7A Ranch Resort** (512-847-2517) with its rustic cabins and river frontage with fishing and swimming. The back roads are stunning, and drives in any direction will reward the traveler with impressive views of the Hill Country. Make the drive to **Fischer, TX** and find the 1875 **Fischer Hall** (210-935-4800), with its hand-hewn beams and rafters, handset 9-pin bowling alley, cold beer, and live music.

CENTRAL

Those fairways are so narrow, you have to walk down them single file. Jimmy Demaret

NORTH CENTRAL TEXAS

For the married man with children, or even the unmarried man with a high-maintenance girlfriend, North Central Texas is a golfer's nirvana. For you, the region offers more than 3,500 golf holes that run the gamut from the greatness of Fort Worth's Colonial down to the niftiest little munis you've ever seen. For her, the Dallas/Fort Worth Metroplex is a bacchanalian feast of shopping on which to gorge. For the kids, there are theme parks and arcades of every size and type. So while you go out and take on TPC-Cottonwood Valley or Hyatt Bear Creek, she can explore the boutiques of Neiman-Marcus' flagship store while the kids run wild at Six Flags Over Texas. That night, everyone meets up at The Ballpark in Arlington for a Rangers game. With so much to do, everybody wins.

The multitude of activities reflects North Central Texas' multiple personalities. From Fort Worth's redneck cool to urban-uppity Dallas, you'll find Cadillac cowboys and busty big-haired blondes right out of a TV miniseries alongside sophisticated bankers and chic fashionistas. In Dallas' Soho-like Deep Ellum, you can slam dance with tattooed punkers or sip exquisite martinis with ultra-hip advertising execs. Forty miles west in the Stockyards of Cowtown, you can whoop 'n' holler to the strains of Charlie Daniels, Charlie Robison, and Junior Brown at Billy Bob's Texas, the World's Largest Honky Tonk. Hungry? Keep the jeans on and go for ribs at Sonny Bryan's Barbecue, or take a shower, put on your (looser-fitting) slacks, and take the family out to one of the area's renowned steakhouses for a "beef fest" you'll never forget.

Originally populated by outlaws and renegades, North Central Texas is a place where people know how to have fun.

Not surprisingly, you'll find lots of rabid sports fans in the Metroplex, as this area supports more major sports for its size than any city in the USA and has a winner's swagger to prove it. Vatican City may have the Pope on its roster, but has it ever won five Super Bowls? The North Central region also has more golf than any other in the state: a clear indication of how much this land-locked prairie population loves its links. In fact, no real estate developer worth his fat commission would even consider building a new development in North Texas without springing $2-$10 million for a nice golf course as part of the deal. It's almost expected.

If the big-city scene isn't what you're looking for, North Central Texas offers a wonderful array of diversions in quaint little towns scattered in a 60-mile radius of Dallas/Fort Worth. Towns like Denton, Waxahachie, Gainesville, and Granbury with their restored courthouse squares, antique shops, Victorian-era Main Streets and mom 'n' pop storefronts. Towns sprinkled around the mammoth lakes such as Lake Texoma, Lake Whitney, and Lake Grapevine.

ALWAYS – and I mean ALWAYS – tee the ball on par-3 holes, or any other time you play your opening shot with an iron. Jack Nicklaus

The highways and farm roads that lead to these little treasures are covered in bluebonnets and Indian paintbrushes most of the golfing season, adding color to the rural landscape.

You may be moving from a downtown hotel room to a bed & breakfast, but the quality of golf is still high. Just as New Yorkers flee Manhattan for Long Island each weekend and Bostonians head for Cape Cod, so Dallasites like to get away to any number of new developments springing up in the countryside. Here things move at a slower pace, cows outnumber people, and the guys in the pro shop are truly happy to see you.

I believe the real reason St. Andrews Old Course is infinitely superior to anything else is owing to the fact that it was constructed when non-one knew anything about the subject at all, and since then it has been considered too sacred to be touched. Dr. Alister Mackenzie

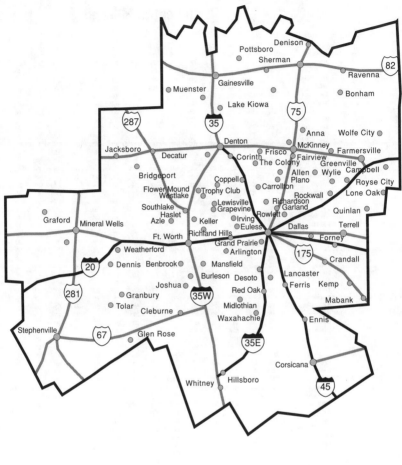

Denison
Pottsboro
Sherman
Ravenna
82
Gainesville
Muenster
Bonham
Lake Kiowa
287
75
35
Anna   Wolfe City
Denton
Jacksboro   Decatur   McKinney   Farmersville
Corinth   Frisco   Fairview
The Colony   Greenville   Campbell
Bridgeport   Allen   Wylie
Coppell   Plano   Royse City
Flower Mound   Trophy Club   Carrollton
Westlake   Rockwall   Lone Oak
Southlake   Lewisville   Richardson   Quinlan
Haslet   Grapevine   Garland
Graford   Azle   Keller   Irving   Rowlett   Terrell
Mineral Wells   Richland Hills   Euless   Dallas
Ft. Worth   Forney
Grand Prairie
Weatherford   Arlington   175   Crandall
20   Dennis   Benbrook   Mansfield
281   Burleson   Lancaster
Joshua   Desoto   Ferris   Kemp
Granbury   Red Oak   Mabank
Tolar   35W   Midlothian
Cleburne   Waxahachie   Ennis
Stephenville   67   Glen Rose   35E
Corsicana
Whitney   Hillsboro   45

North Central Mileage

	Aledo	Allen	Anna	Arlington	Azle	Benbrook	Bonham	Bridgeport	Burleson	Carrollton	Cleburne	The Colony	Coppell	Corinth	Corsicana	Crandal
Aledo		69	84	32	17	13	111	45	28	51	33	56	43	57	91	72
Allen	69		20	43	64	61	46	73	65	21	74	14	28	31	78	43
Anna	84	20		61	80	76	31	77	81	39	93	29	44	46	97	62
Arlington	32	43	61		30	23	88	57	24	24	38	33	19	34	69	42
Azle	17	64	80	30		22	106	29	32	46	46	51	38	50	92	71
Benbrook	13	61	76	23	22		103	51	18	42	31	48	35	49	80	62
Bonham	111	46	31	88	106	103		104	108	66	120	56	71	73	120	80
Bridgeport	45	73	77	57	29	51	104		60	59	75	61	51	46	120	92
Burleson	28	65	81	24	32	18	108	60		47	15	52	39	53	72	61
Carrollton	51	21	39	24	46	42	66	59	47		61	12	8	18	69	37
Cleburne	33	74	93	38	46	31	120	75	15	61		66	53	68	70	66
The Colony	56	14	29	33	51	48	56	61	52	12	66		15	17	78	47
Coppell	43	28	44	19	38	35	71	51	39	8	53	15		16	74	43
Corinth	57	31	46	34	50	49	73	46	53	18	68	17	16		86	55
Corsicana	91	78	97	69	92	80	120	120	72	69	70	78	74	86		48
Crandal	72	43	62	42	71	62	80	92	61	37	66	47	43	55	48	
Dallas	50	24	43	19	48	41	70	68	42	14	50	24	19	31	55	24
Decatur	42	62	66	50	26	46	93	11	54	51	68	50	45	35	114	85
Denison	112	49	31	89	104	104	27	90	108	66	122	57	71	70	127	91
Dennis	26	94	118	59	39	34	145	51	50	79	40	82	71	79	122	95
Denton	53	36	41	40	46	46	68	39	50	24	65	23	22	8	92	60
Desoto	52	39	58	23	51	41	84	79	37	27	39	37	31	43	50	28
Ennis	71	58	77	49	71	60	104	100	51	49	51	58	54	66	21	30
Euless	35	36	54	8	30	26	81	54	31	17	45	25	12	26	72	41
Fairview	71	5	15	47	66	63	42	72	67	25	78	16	30	33	83	47
Farmersville	89	24	22	61	84	81	36	84	84	42	91	34	48	50	91	48
Ferris	65	43	62	36	65	54	89	88	51	34	52	43	39	51	35	22
Flower Mound	51	30	45	29	44	43	72	50	47	14	62	16	11	16	82	51
Forney	70	34	52	39	68	61	69	88	62	32	67	40	39	50	58	14
Fort Worth	19	51	66	13	17	11	93	46	15	32	29	37	24	39	75	54
Frisco	64	13	26	41	59	56	53	61	60	19	75	9	23	25	81	49
Gainesville	80	62	48	71	65	75	58	50	79	56	94	53	54	40	123	92
Garland	66	14	32	36	61	58	59	77	60	18	67	22	26	35	68	29
Glen Rose	42	98	117	62	59	43	144	78	39	85	24	90	77	91	93	90
Graford	46	111	124	73	53	55	151	47	71	92	72	97	84	92	133	114
Granbury	26	87	102	49	43	27	129	61	37	69	29	74	61	75	98	88
Grand Prairie	37	37	56	6	36	29	83	62	29	20	43	29	17	30	65	36
Grapevine	36	35	50	11	31	28	77	50	32	16	46	21	8	23	77	46
Greenville	99	38	37	68	97	91	34	98	92	53	99	48	61	64	86	47
Haslet	31	46	61	27	24	25	88	33	31	31	46	33	23	27	91	63
Hillsboro	62	86	104	60	71	57	131	100	40	75	29	85	78	92	40	69
Irving	43	31	50	14	39	35	77	61	38	13	51	23	13	26	64	33
Jacksboro	57	98	103	74	44	65	130	28	76	87	82	87	79	72	136	115
Joshua	28	72	87	31	39	23	114	67	8	54	8	59	46	60	73	67
Keller	32	41	56	21	26	25	83	41	29	22	44	28	14	25	86	55
Kemp	92	61	79	62	91	82	89	112	81	57	84	67	63	75	35	21
Lake Kiowa	92	60	45	85	87	88	63	61	90	68	112	45	66	48	137	106
Lancaster	56	38	57	27	56	45	84	82	43	28	45	38	33	45	44	23
Lewisville	49	22	37	25	44	40	64	53	45	10	59	8	8	9	77	46
Lone Oak	108	53	53	77	106	100	49	113	101	64	108	63	72	77	86	47
Mabank	102	70	89	71	100	91	95	121	86	67	86	76	72	84	37	30
Mansfield	34	56	75	14	35	23	102	63	15	38	24	46	32	47	57	50
McKinney	73	8	12	50	68	65	38	69	69	27	81	18	32	34	86	50
Mesquite	63	29	47	32	61	54	70	81	55	26	61	34	32	44	56	16
Midlothian	45	49	68	23	45	34	95	74	25	36	26	46	37	50	47	40
Mineral Wells	33	98	113	60	39	41	140	45	57	79	58	84	71	85	120	101
Muenster	84	77	64	84	68	88	71	49	92	69	107	68	67	53	136	105
N. Richland Hills	29	43	58	14	24	21	85	45	26	24	40	29	16	30	81	51
Plano	64	6	25	37	60	56	52	71	60	15	68	15	23	27	72	37
Pottsboro	111	51	32	88	102	103	35	88	107	65	121	56	70	69	128	93
Prosper	69	17	22	46	64	61	49	58	65	24	80	14	28	28	86	54
Quinlan	92	44	51	60	90	83	50	105	84	48	91	54	56	66	70	31
Ravenna	141	53	38	98	136	137	10	110	139	75	130	67	76	79	133	105
Red Oak	59	44	62	30	59	48	89	87	43	33	43	43	38	50	44	28
Richardson	59	12	31	31	54	51	58	69	55	11	62	17	19	24	67	32
Rockwall	74	25	40	42	69	65	54	84	66	27	73	33	35	45	71	28
Rowlett	67	19	37	36	63	59	61	78	60	21	67	27	29	39	66	26
Royse City	81	29	40	50	78	73	49	94	74	37	81	40	44	53	75	34
Sherman	104	41	22	80	98	95	23	83	100	58	114	48	63	62	118	83
Southlake	39	35	50	19	33	30	77	43	35	17	49	22	9	23	80	49
Stephenville	56	117	132	79	70	57	159	86	67	98	53	103	90	105	120	118
Terrell	81	42	58	50	80	73	65	99	72	43	77	51	50	61	54	15
Tolar	35	95	111	58	52	35	138	69	45	77	37	82	69	83	107	97
Trophy Club	39	39	54	22	32	31	81	38	35	23	50	25	15	21	87	56
Waxahachie	57	52	71	35	57	46	98	86	37	42	37	51	46	58	36	37
Weatherford	14	79	94	41	20	22	121	36	38	60	39	65	52	66	101	82
Westlake	40	39	54	22	33	32	81	39	36	20	51	25	12	22	84	52
Whitney	63	99	118	68	76	61	145	105	45	89	30	96	83	98	54	83
Wolfe City	114	49	33	85	109	106	17	107	109	68	116	59	73	75	103	65
Wylie	73	14	29	42	68	65	53	81	66	24	73	24	32	37	74	36

North Central Mileage

	Decatur	Denison	Dennis	Denton	Desoto	Ennis	Euless	Fairview	Farmersville	Ferris	Flower Mound	Forney	Fort Worth	Frisco	Gainesville	Garland	Glen Rose
	42	112	26	53	52	71	35	71	89	65	51	70	19	64	80	66	42
	62	49	94	36	39	58	36	5	24	43	30	34	51	13	62	14	98
	66	31	118	41	58	77	54	15	22	62	45	52	66	26	48	32	117
	50	89	59	40	23	49	8	47	61	36	29	39	13	41	71	36	62
	26	104	39	46	51	71	30	66	84	65	44	68	17	59	65	61	59
	46	104	34	46	41	60	26	63	81	54	43	61	11	56	75	58	43
	93	27	145	68	84	104	81	42	36	89	72	69	93	53	58	59	144
	11	90	51	39	79	100	54	72	84	88	50	88	46	61	50	77	78
	54	108	50	50	37	51	31	67	84	51	47	62	15	60	79	60	39
	51	66	79	24	27	49	17	25	42	34	14	32	32	19	56	18	85
	68	122	40	65	39	51	45	78	91	52	62	67	29	75	94	67	24
	50	57	82	23	37	58	25	16	34	43	16	40	37	9	53	22	90
	45	71	71	22	31	54	12	30	48	39	11	39	24	23	54	26	77
	35	70	79	8	43	66	26	33	50	51	16	50	39	25	40	35	91
	114	127	122	92	50	21	72	83	91	35	82	58	75	81	123	68	93
	85	91	95	60	28	30	41	47	48	22	51	14	54	49	92	29	90
	61	73	79	37	15	35	18	28	42	20	27	20	31	27	68	18	74
	79		144	63	87	107	81	45	97	116	92	72	78	100	41	89	146
	51	144		76	73	101	58	97	116	87	72	56	35	24	31	41	88
	28	63	76		49	71	32	35	47	57	18	29	34	42	81	31	63
	73	87	73	49		30	27	43	56	15	39	41	54	61	103	48	75
	93	107	101	71	30		52	62	71	15	62	38	16	34	64	32	69
	47	81	58	32	27	52		40	56	37	21	38	53	13	61	18	102
	61	45	97	35	43	62	40		19	48	32	38	70	30	71	25	115
	72	45	116	47	56	71	56	19		56	49	34	47	46	88	33	76
	43	77	65	29	31	56	5	37	54		42	18	42	17	30	60	70
	87	53	132	61	63	70	67	33	16	62		64	40	80	44	81	123
	27	85	56	23	49	70	24	48	66	59	22		59	17	41	49	67
	93	134	91	89	49	39	67	90	102	51	87	73		54	88	119	53
	55	78	67	32	19	44	8	35	50	29	21	30	24		30	64	75
	37	116	56	65	95	115	74	98	109	109	78	112	61	86		76	84
	61	115	57	57	40	53	37	74	91	53	54	68	21	67	86		32
	35	83	56	21	43	66	17	43	60	51	18	51	15	36	52	40	
	105	104	114	81	48	33	62	65	61	42	71	27	74	68	112	47	108
	50	42	114	43	96	116	78	58	70	101	62	100	76	44	13	88	136
	75	87	77	51	6	24	31	43	54	9	41	24	38	16	46	26	82
	42	64	76	15	35	57	18	24	41	42	8	41	30	16	46	26	132
	102	68	144	76	71	70	76	48	30	68	76	43	89	59	96	47	110
	114	114	124	90	58	35	71	74	70	49	80	36	83	78	121	56	48
	57	102	57	51	23	36	21	60	74	36	42	51	18	54	82	49	84
	58	41	100	32	46	65	42	3	16	51	33	41	7	44	35	81	50
	74	77	91	50	23	36	31	33	36	21	40	7	44	28	88	42	57
	67	97	67	56	13	26	28	53	66	26	45	41	28	52	88	95	120
	55	134	24	81	80	99	63	100	117	94	79	98	48	92	95	95	63
	42	53	116	45	94	116	77	76	86	101	62	100	78	66	15	85	92
	39	85	51	29	36	60	10	45	62	47	25	48	11	37	60	40	145
	60	55	93	33	33	52	30	11	28	37	26	28	46	16	65	8	103
	77	8	138	62	88	108	80	46	53	93	71	84	92	49	38	64	115
	47	43	97	21	46	66	39	16	28	51	30	46	51	7	46	28	123
	98	70	127	72	55	54	60	45	29	52	62	27	72	55	98	32	67
	100	21	164	75	95	111	91	49	43	58	48	34	75	33	79	29	86
	80	92	81	56	8	24	35	48	60	9	46	31	41	46	87	36	97
	12	61	60	87	34	27	46	25	16	32	32	24	41	19	65	7	91
	61	60	87	34	27	46	25	16	32	32	36	14	54	34	83	11	105
	78	63	107	51	38	51	39	26	20	36	41	15	48	28	76	5	137
	72	67	100	45	31	45	33	23	27	31	35	22	62	41	88	20	73
	86	62	114	59	45	59	49	30	17	44	51	73	85	42	33	54	73
	72	11	137	54	79	73	36	41	83	45	64	18	45	20	30	52	30
	36	78	61	21	37	60	11	37	55	45	18	45	20	30	52	34	100
	97	159	47	102	91	104	82	119	136	104	99	117	67	112	126	114	17
	32	81	106	67	39	38	49	43	37	36	57	12	62	52	98	29	73
	70	138	33	80	75	88	61	97	115	89	77	96	45	90	109	93	61
	32	80	61	17	44	67	18	41	58	52	14	52	21	34	48	41	41
	28	79	101	79	64	16	40	57	69	18	54	40	40	55	96	45	74
	79	37	116	14	62	61	80	44	81	98	75	60	79	29	73	76	45
	37	29	33	81	61	18	40	63	15	41	58	49	15	49	22	33	140
	75	98	148	103	95	63	53	75	103	116	65	92	87	59	102	124	97
	67	96	43	150	70	81	88	83	44	30	79	74	57	95	55	71	
	24	70	59	110	43	38	54	38	15	18	39	36	26	54	25	74	6

North Central Mileage

	Graford	Granbury	Grand Prairie	Grapevine	Greenville	Haslet	Hillsboro	Irving	Jacksboro	Joshua	Keller	Kemp	Lake Kiowa	Lancaster	Lewisville
Aledo	46	26	37	36	99	31	62	43	57	28	32	92	92	56	49
Allen	111	87	37	35	38	46	86	31	98	72	41	61	60	38	22
Anna	124	102	56	50	37	61	104	50	103	87	56	79	45	57	37
Arlington	73	49	6	11	68	27	60	14	74	31	21	62	85	27	25
Azle	53	43	36	31	97	24	71	39	44	39	26	91	87	56	44
Benbrook	55	27	29	28	91	25	57	35	65	23	25	82	88	45	40
Bonham	151	129	83	77	34	88	131	77	130	114	83	89	63	84	64
Bridgeport	47	61	62	50	98	33	100	61	28	67	41	112	61	82	53
Burleson	71	37	29	32	92	31	40	38	76	8	29	81	90	43	45
Carrollton	92	69	20	16	53	31	75	13	87	54	22	57	68	28	10
Cleburne	72	29	43	46	99	46	29	51	82	8	44	84	112	45	59
The Colony	97	74	29	21	48	33	85	23	87	59	28	67	45	38	8
Coppell	84	61	17	8	61	23	78	13	79	46	14	63	66	33	8
Corinth	92	75	30	23	64	27	92	26	72	60	25	75	48	45	9
Corsicana	133	98	65	77	86	91	40	64	136	73	86	35	137	44	77
Crandal	114	88	36	46	47	63	69	33	115	67	55	21	106	23	46
Dallas	92	68	13	22	50	39	61	10	92	49	31	44	83	15	23
Decatur	58	61	56	43	87	27	93	55	37	61	35	105	50	75	42
Denison	136	130	85	77	53	85	134	78	116	115	83	104	42	87	64
Dennis	40	24	67	65	132	56	91	67	56	57	56	114	108	77	76
Denton	85	72	36	29	61	23	89	32	65	57	21	81	43	51	15
Desoto	93	67	18	31	63	49	49	19	95	40	43	48	96	6	35
Ennis	112	80	45	56	70	70	39	44	115	53	66	33	116	24	57
Euless	76	53	10	5	67	24	67	8	74	37	17	62	78	31	18
Fairview	113	89	41	37	33	48	90	35	98	74	43	65	58	43	24
Farmersville	130	107	55	54	16	66	102	50	109	91	60	61	70	54	41
Ferris	107	81	30	42	62	59	51	29	109	53	51	42	101	9	42
Flower Mound	92	69	25	18	64	22	87	21	78	54	18	71	62	41	8
Forney	112	88	33	42	40	59	73	30	112	68	51	27	100	24	41
Fort Worth	61	37	18	17	80	17	54	24	61	21	15	74	76	38	30
Frisco	106	82	37	30	44	41	88	30	86	67	36	68	44	41	16
Gainesville	97	100	68	60	81	49	119	64	76	86	52	112	13	82	46
Garland	108	84	30	33	35	48	78	25	104	66	40	47	88	30	26
Glen Rose	72	17	67	70	123	67	53	75	84	32	67	108	136	69	82
Graford		57	79	77	141	72	101	85	23	69	74	134	135	98	90
Granbury	57		55	54	117	51	58	61	68	30	51	109	114	72	66
Grand Prairie	79	55		15	62	32	64	8	80	36	26	56	87	23	22
Grapevine	77	54	15		68	21	71	13	75	39	13	66	70	36	14
Greenville	141	117	62	68		80	108	59	124	98	75	55	88	60	55
Haslet	72	51	32	21	80		71	32	60	38	8	83	62	53	25
Hillsboro	101	58	64	71	108	71		67	112	38	69	71	131	49	83
Irving	85	61	8	13	59	32	67		82	44	24	53	77	23	18
Jacksboro	23	68	80	75	124	60	112	82		80	69	135	88	100	79
Joshua	69	30	36	39	98	38	38	44	80		36	85	97	46	51
Keller	74	51	26	13	75	8	69	24	69	36		75	65	45	20
Kemp	134	109	56	66	55	83	71	53	135	85	75		126	43	66
Lake Kiowa	135	114	87	70	88	62	131	77	88	97	65	126		98	58
Lancaster	98	72	23	36	60	53	49	23	100	46	45	43	98		36
Lewisville	90	66	22	14	55	25	83	18	79	51	20	66	58	36	
Lone Oak	150	126	72	77	15	93	109	68	138	108	85	55	104	66	68
Mabank	143	115	65	75	61	92	73	63	144	88	84	9	135	52	75
Mansfield	76	48	19	25	81	34	46	27	79	21	31	69	97	29	39
McKinney	115	91	44	39	30	50	93	38	94	76	45	68	54	46	25
Mesquite	104	80	26	35	42	52	67	23	105	62	44	34	93	18	35
Midlothian	86	55	22	33	74	44	42	26	89	27	41	59	107	19	42
Mineral Wells	15	44	66	64	128	59	88	71	31	56	61	121	121	85	77
Muenster	88	104	81	73	94	63	132	77	66	99	65	125	27	95	59
N. Richland Hills	71	47	19	10	75	15	65	18	68	32	8	71	76	41	22
Plano	106	82	31	31	39	43	79	25	97	67	37	55	67	32	18
Pottsboro	134	129	84	77	61	84	135	77	113	114	83	111	37	88	63
Prosper	104	87	43	35	42	44	93	35	84	72	41	73	42	46	22
Quinlan	133	109	55	61	17	76	93	51	132	91	68	39	122	50	57
Ravenna	139	121	65	52	17	72	106	84	137	146	114	125	62	94	73
Red Oak	101	72	26	39	66	57	43	26	103	44	50	48	101	6	41
Richardson	101	77	25	25	43	41	74	19	97	61	33	51	80	27	20
Rockwall	115	91	37	40	27	56	82	33	112	73	47	41	102	34	37
Rowlett	109	85	30	34	34	50	77	26	105	66	41	42	95	28	30
Royse City	123	99	44	50	18	65	90	41	121	80	57	44	109	41	44
Sherman	130	121	77	69	49	77	125	70	109	106	75	100	35	78	56
Southlake	80	57	21	7	69	14	74	19	70	41	8	69	67	39	14
Stephenville	58	30	85	83	146	81	80	91	74	59	81	137	151	97	96
Terrell	123	99	45	54	32	71	78	41	123	78	62	23	112	34	52
Tolar	55	8	63	62	125	59	66	69	71	38	59	117	122	80	75
Trophy Club	80	57	28	14	73	10	75	25	66	42	6	76	62	46	17
Waxahachie	98	66	33	45	75	56	34	34	101	38	53	48	108	15	50
Weatherford	32	25	47	45	109	40	69	52	43	37	42	102	102	66	58
Westlake	81	58	25	11	72	11	76	22	67	43	7	73	62	42	18
Whitney	102	59	73	76	122	76	14	81	112	38	74	84	143	62	89
Wolfe City	153	132	80	79	17	91	125	76	132	116	85	73	80	77	66
Wylie	114	91	37	39	29	52	85	32	106	73	46	53	72	36	28

North Central Mileage

	Mabank	Mansfield	McKinney	Mesquite	Midlothian	Mineral Wells	Muenster	N. Richland Hills	Plano	Pottsboro	Prosper	Quinlan	Ravenna	Red Oak	Richardson	Rockwall	Rowlett
8	102	34	73	63	45	33	84	29	64	111	69	92	141	59	59	74	67
3	70	56	8	29	49	98	77	43	6	51	17	44	53	44	12	25	19
3	89	75	12	47	68	113	64	58	25	32	22	51	38	62	31	40	37
7	71	14	50	32	23	60	84	14	37	88	46	60	98	30	31	42	36
6	100	35	68	61	45	39	68	24	60	102	64	90	136	59	54	69	63
0	91	23	65	54	34	41	88	21	56	103	61	83	137	48	51	65	59
9	95	102	38	70	95	140	71	85	52	35	49	50	10	89	58	54	61
3	121	63	69	81	74	45	49	45	71	88	58	105	110	87	69	84	78
1	86	15	69	55	25	57	92	26	60	107	65	84	139	43	55	66	60
4	67	38	27	26	36	79	69	24	15	65	24	48	75	33	11	27	21
8	86	24	81	61	26	58	107	40	68	121	80	91	130	43	62	73	67
3	76	46	18	34	46	84	68	29	15	56	14	54	67	43	17	33	27
2	72	32	32	37		71	67	16	23	70	28	56	76	38	19	35	29
7	84	47	34	44	50	85	53	30	27	69	28	66	79	50	28	45	39
7	37	57	86	56	47	120	136	81	72	128	86	70	133	44	67	71	66
7	30	50	50	16	40	101	105	51	37	93	54	31	105	28	32	28	26
9	53	32	32	13	25	78	82	27	18	74	32	42	79	20	12	24	17
2	114	57	58	74	67	55	42	39	60	77	47	98	100	80	61	78	72
8	114	102	41	77	97	134	53	85	55	8	43	70	21	92	60	63	67
4	124	57	100	91	67	24	116	51	93	138	97	127	164	81	87	107	100
6	90	51	32	50	56	81	45	29	33	62	21	72	75	56	34	51	45
1	58	23	46	23	13	80	94	36	33	88	46	55	95	8	27	38	31
0	35	36	65	36	26	99	116	60	52	108	66	54	111	24	46	51	45
6	71	21	42	31	28	63	77	10	30	80	39	60	91	35	25	39	33
8	74	60	3	33	53	100	76	45	11	46	16	45	49	48	16	26	23
0	70	74	16	36	66	117	86	62	28	53	28	29	43	60	32	20	27
8	49	36	51	21	26	94	101	47	37	93	51	52	58	9	32	36	31
6	80	42	33	40	45	79	62	25	26	71	30	62	48	46	24	41	35
3	36	51	41	7	41	98	100	48	28	84	46	27	34	31	24	14	15
9	83	18	55	44	28	48	78	11	46	92	51	72	75	41	41	54	48
6	78	54	14	35	52	92	66	37	16	49	7	55	33	46	19	34	28
6	121	82	58	81	88	95	15	60	65	38	46	98	79	87	65	83	76
7	56	49	21	15	42	95	85	40	8	64	28	32	29	36	7	11	5
32	110	48	105	84	50	57	120	63	92	145	103	115	123	67	86	97	91
50	143	76	115	104	86	15	88	71	106	134	104	133	139	101	101	115	109
26	115	48	91	80	55	44	104	47	82	129	87	109	121	72	77	91	85
2	65	19	44	26	22	66	81	19	31	84	43	55	65	26	25	37	30
7	75	25	39	35	33	64	73	10	31	77	35	61	52	39	25	40	34
5	61	81	30	42	74	128	94	75	39	61	42	17	17	66	43	27	34
3	92	34	50	52	44	59	63	15	43	84	44	76	72	57	41	56	50
09	73	46	93	67	42	88	132	65	79	135	93	93	106	43	74	82	77
8	63	27	38	23	26	71	77	18	25	77	35	51	84	26	19	33	26
38	144	79	94	105	89	31	66	68	97	113	84	132	137	103	97	112	105
08	88	21	76	62	27	56	99	32	67	114	72	91	146	44	61	73	66
5	84	31	45	44	41	61	65	8	37	83	41	68	114	50	33	47	41
5	9	69	68	34	59	121	125	71	55	111	73	39	125	48	51	41	42
04	135	97	54	93	107	121	27	76	67	37	42	122	62	101	80	102	95
6	52	29	46	18	19	85	95	41	32	88	46	50	94	6	27	34	28
8	75	39	25	35	42	77	59	22	18	63	22	57	73	41	20	37	30
	53	90	45	50	83	137	109	85	50	76	57	18	59	72	54	37	44
3		71	77	43	61	130	134	80	64	120	83	45	135	57	60	50	51
0	71		63	44	10	63	95	24	50	101	59	73	112	28	44	55	49
5	77	63		36	56	101	73	46	14	43	13	43	45	51	19	29	26
0	43	44	36		35	91	94	40	23	78	40	34	89	25	18	16	11
3	61	10	56	35		73	101	34	43	98	57	66	103	18	37	48	41
7	130	63	101	91	73		93	58	93	132	98	120	74	88	88	102	96
09	134	95	73	94	101	93		73	78	50	61	111	109	100	79	96	90
5	80	24	46	40	34	58	73		38	84	43	69	34	44	33	48	42
0	64	50	14	23	43	93	78	38		56	21	39	45	37	6	19	13
6	120	101	43	78	98	132	50	84	56		42	77	100	93	62	71	69
7	83	59	13	40	57	98	61	43	21	42		56	58	51	24	39	33
8	45	73	43	34	66	120	111	69	39	77	56		61	56	38	21	28
9	135	112	45	89	103	74	109	34	45	100	58	60		99	66	74	73
2	57	28	51	25	18	88	100	44	37	93	51	56	99		32	40	34
0	60	44	19	18	37	88	79	33	6	62	24	38	66	32		18	12
7	50	55	29	16	48	102	96	48	19	71	39	21	74	40	18		7
4	51	49	26	11	41	96	90	42	13	69	33	28	73	34	12	7	
8	28	64	32	24	55	110	103	57	26	70	44	14	64	48	27	9	16
4	109	94	33	68	89	128	46	77	46	13	35	66	29	83	52	59	58
9	78	32	39	38	40	67	65	9	31	77	35	62	86	44	27	42	36
6	139	77	121	110	78	43	129	77	112	159	117	139	200	96	107	121	114
2	33	61	47	19	51	110	112	59	37	89	57	16	77	41	35	18	25
4	123	56	99	89	63	40	112	56	91	137	95	117	190	80	85	99	93
6	85	37	43	45	46	67	61	15	35	79	38	69	89	51	34	48	42
2	51	22	60	34	12	85	109	46	46	102	60	65	107	10	41	49	43
18	111	44	82	72	54	19	79	39	74	113	79	101	151	69	69	83	77
2	82	35	42	42	43	68	62	13	34	80	38	66	89	47	30	45	39
3	86	54	106	81	55	88	137	70	93	148	107	107	153	56	87	96	90
2	79	98	41	59	91	142	84	87	54	51	51	34	28	83	60	45	52
1	62	56	18	21	48	101	87	47	10	61	30	31	63	42	14	12	11

North Central Mileage

	Royse City	Sherman	Southlake	Stephenville	Terrell	Tolar	Trophy Club	Waxahac.	Weatherfd	Westlake	Whitney	Wolfe City	Wylie
Aledo	81	104	39	56	81	35	39	57	14	40	63	114	73
Allen	29	41	35	117	42	95	39	52	79	39	99	49	14
Anna	40	22	50	132	58	111	54	71	94	54	118	33	29
Arlington	50	80	19	79	50	58	25	35	41	22	68	85	42
Azle	78	98	33	70	80	52	32	57	20	33	76	109	68
Benbrook	73	95	30	57	73	35	31	46	22	32	61	106	65
Bonham	49	25	77	159	65	138	81	98	121	81	145	17	53
Bridgeport	94	83	43	86	99	69	38	86	36	39	105	107	81
Burleson	74	100	35	67	72	45	35	37	38	36	45	109	66
Carrollton	37	58	17	98	43	77	23	42	60	20	89	68	24
Cleburne	81	114	49	53	77	37	50	37	39	51	30	116	73
The Colony	40	48	22	103	51	82	25	51	65	25	96	59	24
Coppell	44	63	9	90	50	69	15	46	52	12	83	73	32
Corinth	53	62	23	105	61	83	21	58	66	22	98	75	37
Corsicana	75	118	80	120	54	107	87	36	101	84	54	103	74
Crandal	34	83	49	118	15	97	56	37	82	52	83	65	36
Dallas	32	64	25	97	32	76	32	28	59	29	75	67	24
Decatur	86	72	36	87	93	70	32	79	37	33	98	96	70
Denison	62	11	78	159	81	138	80	101	116	81	148	43	59
Dennis	114	137	61	47	106	33	61	79	14	61	103	150	110
Denton	59	54	21	102	67	80	17	64	62	18	95	70	43
Desoto	45	79	37	91	39	75	44	16	61	40	63	81	38
Ennis	59	98	60	104	38	88	67	16	80	63	53	88	54
Euless	49	73	11	82	49	61	18	40	44	15	75	83	38
Fairview	30	36	37	119	43	97	41	57	81	41	103	44	15
Farmersville	17	41	55	136	37	115	58	69	98	58	116	30	18
Ferris	44	83	45	104	36	89	52	18	75	49	65	79	39
Flower Mound	51	64	18	99	57	77	14	54	60	15	92	74	36
Forney	22	73	45	117	12	96	52	40	79	49	87	57	26
Fort Worth	62	85	20	67	62	45	21	40	29	22	59	95	54
Frisco	41	42	30	112	52	90	34	55	73	33	102	55	25
Gainesville	88	33	52	126	98	109	48	96	76	49	124	71	74
Garland	20	54	34	114	29	93	41	45	76	38	92	53	6
Glen Rose	105	137	73	30	100	17	73	61	41	74	45	140	97
Graford	123	130	80	58	123	55	80	98	32	81	102	153	114
Granbury	99	121	57	30	99	8	57	66	25	58	59	132	91
Grand Prairie	44	77	21	85	45	63	28	33	47	25	73	80	37
Grapevine	50	69	7	83	54	62	14	45	45	11	76	79	39
Greenville	18	49	69	146	32	125	73	75	109	72	122	17	29
Haslet	65	77	14	81	71	59	10	56	40	11	76	91	52
Hillsboro	90	125	74	80	78	66	75	34	69	76	14	125	85
Irving	41	70	19	91	41	69	25	34	52	22	81	76	32
Jacksboro	121	109	70	74	123	71	66	101	43	67	112	132	106
Joshua	80	106	41	59	78	38	42	38	37	43	38	116	73
Keller	57	75	8	81	62	59	6	53	42	7	74	85	46
Kemp	44	100	69	137	23	117	76	48	102	73	84	73	53
Lake Kiowa	109	35	67	151	112	12	62	108	102	62	143	80	72
Lancaster	41	78	39	97	34	80	46	15	66	42	62	77	36
Lewisville	44	56	14	96	52	75	17	50	58	18	89	66	28
Lone Oak	28	64	79	156	32	134	86	82	118	82	123	32	41
Mabank	54	109	78	139	33	123	85	51	111	82	86	79	62
Mansfield	63	94	32	77	61	56	37	22	44	35	54	98	56
McKinney	32	33	39	121	47	99	43	60	82	42	106	41	18
Mesquite	24	68	38	110	19	89	45	34	72	42	81	59	21
Midlothian	55	89	40	78	51	63	46	12	54	43	55	91	48
Mineral Wells	110	128	67	43	110	40	67	85	19	68	88	142	101
Muenster	103	46	65	129	112	112	61	109	79	62	137	84	87
N. Richland Hills	57	77	9	77	59	56	15	46	39	13	70	87	47
Plano	26	46	31	112	37	91	35	46	74	34	93	54	10
Pottsboro	70	13	77	159	89	137	79	102	113	80	148	51	61
Prosper	44	35	35	117	57	95	38	60	79	38	107	51	30
Quinlan	14	66	62	139	16	117	69	65	101	66	107	34	31
Ravenna	64	29	86	200	77	190	89	107	151	89	153	28	63
Red Oak	48	83	44	96	41	80	51	10	69	47	56	83	42
Richardson	27	52	27	107	35	85	34	41	69	30	87	60	14
Rockwall	9	59	42	121	18	99	48	49	83	45	96	45	12
Rowlett	16	58	36	114	25	93	42	43	77	39	90	52	11
Royse City		58	51	128	21	107	58	57	91	55	104	35	16
Sherman	58		69	151	77	130	71	92	109	72	139	39	51
Southlake	51	69		86	57	65	7	51	48	3	79	80	40
Stephenville	128	151	86		129	21	87	90	50	88	68	161	120
Terrell	21	77	57	129		107	63	50	91	60	91	49	29
Tolar	107	130	65	21	107		66	74	33	66	61	140	99
Trophy Club	58	71	7	87	63	66		58	48	3	80	83	45
Waxahachie	57	92	51	90	50	74	58		66	55	47	92	51
Weatherford	91	109	48	50	91	33	48	66		49	69	123	82
Westlake	55	72	3	88	60	66	3	55	49		81	83	44
Whitney	104	139	79	68	91	61	80	47	69	81		139	98
Wolfe City	35	39	80	161	49	140	83	92	123	83	139		46
Wylie	16	51	40	120	29	99	45	51	82	44	98	46	

NORTH CENTRAL TEXAS
REGIONAL WEATHER

	Average Precipitation	Average Temperature (F)
January	1.83	43.4
February	2.18	47.9
March	2.77	56.7
April	3.5	65.5
May	4.88	72.8
June	2.98	81
July	2.31	85.3
August	2.21	84.9
September	3.39	77.4
October	3.52	67.2
November	2.29	56.2
December	1.84	46.9

NORTH
CENTRAL

ALLEN

Elev. 637   Pop. 43,554

The railroad came through Allen in the 1880s, and the town was named after former Texas attorney general Ebenezer Allen. The town gained notoriety back when Denton badman Sam Bass committed the state's first train robbery in 1878.

Now Plano, Allen, and McKinney all seem to blur together, and from a 1990 population of under 20,000 Allen is well on its way to 50,000 residents as Collin County continues to bear the burden of Dallas' northward migration. Golf courses have popped up everywhere on this stretch of I-75, and Allen has been part of that golf boom with the Twin Creeks master-planned community and golf course.

TWIN CREEKS GOLF CLUB

The golf   Arnold Palmer and Ed Seay designed Twin Creeks (named after the two creeks that run through the layout) to integrate with five strategically placed lakes that come into play. For the most part, the fairways here are generous, rolling peacefully toward large, undulating greens seeded with Crenshaw Creeping Bentgrass.

Hole 11 is one of the best, a long, 383-yard par 4 with trees lining the fairway and a difficult green guarded by several giant pecan trees. No. 17, a 409-yarder with water on the right, requires a monster drive to carry the full body of water. The best play is to aim left even though the approach will be a bit longer.

Other notes: *Golf Digest* has rated Twin Creeks as high as 10th for the "Best Public Course" in the state. For now Twin Creeks is public, but the long-term plan is for the facility to become private after it's purchased by the homeowner's association.

The details   972-390-8888. 501 Twin Creeks Dr., Allen, TX 75013

- www.twincreeks.com
- 1995. Arnold Palmer and Ed Seay. 18 holes. Par 72. Gold – 6,840 (73.2/131). Blue – 6,288 (70.5/117). White – 5,651 (69.4/114). Red – 4,529 (66.5/107). Price - $$$.

Getting there Take I-75 north from Dallas, then exit McDermott (Exit 34). Turn left, drive 1.5 miles, and you should be able to see the signs leading to the course.

ALLEN NOTES   For Tex-Mex, **La Finca** (972-747-5060) is family-owned and authentic. And if your winnings from the round at Twin Creeks are burning a hole in your pocket, the **Allen Outlet Mall**, just north of Stacy Rd.

The score is important, of course. And the discovery that you are superior to another golfer is satisfying. But when your score is bad and the other fellow beats you, golf still has been a blessing to you. The score isn't the "be all and end all." Tommy Armour

on I-75, offers a better selection of quality shops than most. Pick up some golf slacks or business wear at the Polo outlet.

ANNA
Elev. 712   Pop. 1,225

Located 11 miles north of McKinney in the sticks just east of I-75, Anna is a former railroad town that has subsisted since 1873, when it had a population of 20. Sometimes lost in the shuffle of the numerous courses around booming McKinney is the 18-hole Hurricane Creek CC.

HURRICANE CREEK COUNTRY CLUB

The golf   Leon Howard built this course in 1968, which is named for the creek that traverses the terrain. Howard's design features wind and water and is known for three difficult holes.

The first mean hole is the 209-yard No. 5, which plays uphill to a green protected by a bunker on the right. Hopefully you'll have the wind at your back; otherwise a 3-wood is in order. On the back, another long par 3 is No. 15, which requires the carry of a pond and an accurate shot to avoid the bunkers. The last hole is one of the toughest par 4s on the course and considered the signature hole. No. 18 doglegs 430 yards to the right, with an uphill approach that always seems to play into the wind.

The details   972-924-3247. 1800 Fairway Ln., Anna, TX 75409

- 1968. Leon Howard. 18 holes. Par 72. Blue – 7,052 (73.7/123). White – 6,559 (71.1/117). Gold – 6,320 (69.1/113). Red – 5,248 (70.0/114). Price - $.

Getting there From I-75 north, take Exit 48 and turn left. Stay on the Northbound Service Road for 2 miles, and the entrance is on the left side of the road.

ANNA NOTES   Don't miss the club's outstanding bar and grill, which serves delicious burgers. Up the road in Van Alstyne, TX **La Colina** draws a big crowd for its fajitas and is the best place for Tex-Mex. Otherwise, make the drive back into McKinney for more robust entertainment options.

ARLINGTON
Elev. 616 Pop. 306,497

In the 1840s Arlington attracted farmers, who were drawn to the area's fertile blacklands and sandy loam watered by the Trinity River and its tributar-

The perfect shot is invariable rewarded; it is only right that the shot which is slightly imperfect should be weighed in the scales of providence. H.N. Wethered

ies. However, the area didn't truly open for white settlers until the Indians were defeated at Village Creek, near the site of Lake Arlington. The train came through, Dallas and Fort Worth grew exponentially, and the rest is history. Today the city is home to over 300,000 residents as well as six regulation golf courses.

CHESTER W. DITTO GOLF COURSE

The golf   The Ditto was Dick Nugent's first course in Texas, when he teamed with Ken Killian in 1982 to build this very functional 6,727-yard municipal layout. Both challenging and fun, the course plays to a very hacker-friendly 6,106 from the middle tees, and allows the erratic high handicapper to build momentum with a front side that's more wide open than the back. Nugent's design is dominated by wet stuff, with only six ponds coming into play on just a few holes.

No. 3 is the first difficult hole because of the swirling winds, which make club selection difficult on this 185-yard par 3. The front side also boasts the signature hole (No. 8), a mean 567-yard par 5 that plays into the wind.

On the back side No. 13 is noticeable–a rare par 4 double dogleg that goes 427 yards and requires a long approach into a green surrounded by trees.

The details   817-275-5941. 801 Brown Blvd., Arlington, TX 76011

- 1982. Ken Killian and Dick Nugent. 18 holes. Par 72. Back – 6,727 (70.8/117). Middle – 6,106 (68.5/112). Forward – 5,555 (71.3/118). Price - $$.

Getting there From Hwy. 360, take the Brown Blvd. exit and go west. The entrance is on the right.

LAKE ARLINGTON GOLF COURSE

The golf   Owned by the city of Arlington, this course has been around since 1963–it's located on the north edge of Lake Arlington and surrounded by native trees and wildflowers. Ralph Plummer designed this easy course, incorporating little water and no bunkers.

The first hole is one of the most difficult, playing over 400 yards into a dog-leg-left fairway dominated by a huge pecan tree. Holes 13 and 14 play near the lake–the 13th goes 389 yards uphill and doglegs right, and the 14th measures 240 yards downhill to a green protected by water on the left side. Even though it's a long par 3, there is a dramatic drop from tee to green.

The details   817-451-6101. 1516 W. Green Oaks Blvd., Arlington, TX 76013

- 18 holes. Back – 6,637 (70.7/117). Middle – 6,204 (68.5/111). Forward – 5,485 (71.0/114). Price - $$.

The player who expects a lesson to "take" without subsequent practice just isn't being honest with himself or fair to his professional. Gary Player

Getting there From Dallas, take I-30 west and exit East Chase Pkwy. Turn left, travel about 4 miles, and you'll come to the intersection of Spur 303 and Green Oaks Blvd.

MEADOWBROOK PARK GOLF COURSE

The golf   Meadowbrook is an old 9-hole executive track that some claim dates back to the 1920s. The par 33 layout plays to 2,062 yards from only one set of tees. The best hole is No. 3, which plays 151 yards into a scenic green surrounded by giant pecan trees.

The details   817-275-0221. 1300 E. Dugan St., Arlington, TX 76010

- 1920s. 9 holes. Par 33. 2,062 yards. Price - $.

Getting there From Hwy. 360 south find Abram and turn right (west). When you come to Willis, turn left, then look for the course on the left side of the road.

ROLLING HILLS COUNTRY CLUB

The golf   Rolling Hills is a traditional 1950s-style course that is known for its extremely short length. From the tips the course measures 6,117 yards, and it features par 5s that are all under 500 yards. Water in play on just seven holes.

Despite its relative ease, a few holes stand out because of their length. For example, the 2nd hole is a par 4 453-yarder that isn't too much shorter than the par 5s, and one of the toughest holes is No. 16, a 428-yard par 4 that doglegs left around a lake.

No. 6 is the signature even though it's only 355 yards. This hole requires a tee shot into a dogleg fairway lined by trees left and out-of-bounds to the right, followed by an approach over water to a well-bunkered green.

The details   817-261-6221. 401 E. Lamar Blvd., Arlington, TX 76011

- 1950s. C.M. Mimms. 18 holes. Par 71. Back – 6,117 (69.1/121). Forward – Par 72. 4,989 (68.3/116). Price - $$.

Getting there From Hwy. 360 west, take the Lamar exit and drive 4 miles to the clubhouse.

SHADY VALLEY GOLF CLUB

The golf   Shady Valley opened on Labor Day in 1960, and has matured into one of the best-kept secrets in DFW golf. Loaded with every kind of tree native to this terrain, and highlighted by pesky Rush Creek and other water hazards that come into play on 14 holes, this is a par 70 track that requires you to hit it straight.

Confidence, of couse, is an admirable asset to a golfer, but it should
be an unspoken confidence. It is perilous to put it into speech. The gods of golf lie in wait to
chasten the presumptuous. P.G. Wodehouse

Early in the round, the 526-yard No. 2 jumps out with a tee shot over water and out-of-bounds lining the fairway. Also on the front, Nos. 4 and 8 involve Rush Creek and are considered among the most difficult on the course.

Rest up at the turn and get ready for the challenging opening holes on the back nine. No. 10 goes 437 yards and doglegs to the right with water on each side. No. 11 plays the same distance and is squeezed by a narrow chute of trees. And there's no forgiveness on No. 12, which requires the navigation of another dogleg right around water.

The details   817-275-3092. 4001 W. Park Row Dr., Arlington, TX 76013

- www.shadyvalley.com
- 1960. 18 holes. Par 70. Back – 6,536 (71.3/128). Middle – 6,104 (69.3/117). Forward – 5,118 (69.9/118). Price - $$.

Getting there From I-30 west, turn onto the East Chase Pkwy., turn left, and when you come to Pioneer Pkwy., make another left. Drive over to Park Springs Rd. and turn left again. The clubhouse is 3 blocks down the street on the left side of the road.

TIERRA VERDE GOLF COURSE

The golf   Located in a remote southwest part of the city, Tierra Verde is the successful result of Arlington's Parks and Recreation Department's effort to provide an upscale, daily fee municipal to complement the other public golf options in town.

Labeled with the new and prestigious Audubon International Signature Certification, this course was the first in Texas and the first municipal course in the world to achieve that honor. The certification signifies that the course was "designed, constructed, and maintained using wildlife conservation and habitat enhancement, water quality management, and water conservation." What this means for the inconsistent hack is that sprayed shots are not out-of-bounds, but instead buried in a "protected environment." Unfortunately, the penalty still applies and you'll need to take your drop. The opening hole is a good example–it's a basic 355-yard hole, but anything sliced right will find a plum tree thicket, which is the same as hitting it into a lake.

In terms of strategy, you'll be able to enjoy the generous fairways, but the approaches will require much more precision. Look at the scorecard and get your pars in on the shorter holes, then manage your game to avoid huge numbers on the more difficult holes.

One of the better holes on the front is No. 8, a 518-yard doglegger left that bends hard enough to favor a severe hook. Watch out for the multi-level green and its deceptive turns.

Water is more prominent on the back, as you'll see on No. 9, a short par 4 that requires a tee shot over water. The narrow fairway squeezes toward the

Take a club that you can swing at 80 percent and still get to the hole. Conserve your energy; you have a long life ahead of you! Gary McCord

green, and it's nice to know that the green widens on the back side. The par 5 No. 13 is a birdie hole if you pay attention to the flag position on the huge figure 8 shaped green. This one has water off the tee, as does No. 12. In fact, if you're short on balls at the turn, you should stock up. Water impacts play time and time again. No. 18, a long par 4 at 437 yards, involves a creek in the fairway that must be carried on the approach.

Other notes: Another bonus at Tierra Verde is the club's three-hole practice course and lighted driving range.

The details 817-478-8500. 7005 Golf Club Dr., Arlington, TX 76001

- 1998. David Graham. 18 holes. Par 72. 6,975 yards. Five sets of tees. Price - $$.

Getting there Take US 287 south off of I-20. Find Eden Rd. and turn right. The entrance is on the left.

MORE ARLINGTON GOLF

The **Golf Center of Arlington** (817-261-6312) is a great place to introduce the family to the game. Featuring two 18-hole miniature golf courses, driving range, and short game practice area, there's plenty of golf here for everyone. PGA/LPGA lessons are available, and the facility includes a snack bar with beverages, a big-screen TV, and video games.

ARLINGTON NOTES Time your golf around games at the **Ballpark at Arlington,** home of the Texas Rangers, and afternoons at **Six Flags Over Texas.** Stay at the **Wyndham Arlington Hotel** (817-261-8200), where the **Xtra Innings Sports Bar** offers a place to lounge into the evening with food, beer, and sports-watching. The **Hilton Arlington** (817-640-3322) is another lodging option. Arlington has a **Trail Dust Steak House** (817-640-6411) with great steaks and live music, and **J. Gilligan's Bar & Grill** (817-274-8561) has been around since the 1970s, serving cold beers with live entertainment on the weekends. Another hot spot is **Stumpy's Blues Bar** (817-274-0406), especially for jam nights on Sundays, Wednesdays, and Thursdays.

AZLE

Elev. 709   Pop. 9,600

Azle is located on Texas 199 just east of Eagle Mountain Lake, and only 16 miles northwest of Fort Worth. The town grew in the early years as dairy farming became an important industry that supplied the creameries in Fort Worth. Azle's proximity to Fort Worth, as well as its position as "Gateway to Eagle Mountain Lake," have made it a popular commuter community for those who work in the town of the cow.

Every fresh hole we play should teach us some new possibility of using our strokes and suggest to us a further step in the progress of our golfing knowledge. John Low, 1903

CROSS TIMBERS GOLF COURSE

The golf   Cross Timbers rolls over rocky and rugged terrain, offering spectacular views that resemble the Hill Country. Jeff Brauer's design is loaded with trees and features numerous pot bunkers, as well as a significant amount of water.

The elevated tee helps make the 165-yard No. 7 one of the best–it plays to a green fronted by bunkers and lined with rocks in the back.

Other notes: Remember the Texas farmer who graced the fairways of the Senior Tour in the mid-1990s? His name was Robert Landers, and Cross Timbers was his home course.

The details   817-444-4940. 1181 S. Stewart St., Azle, TX 76020

- 1995. Jeff Brauer. 18 holes. Par 72. Gold – 6,734 (71.7 / 128). Blue – 6,417 (70.0 / 121). White – 6,015 (68.1 / 116). Red – 5,051 (68.2 / 113). Price - $$.

Getting there Take Hwy. 820 north from Fort Worth. When you come to Hwy. 199 (Jacksboro Hwy.), turn west. Travel 10 miles to Stewart St. and turn left. The course is 1.5 miles and the entrance is on the left.

AZLE NOTES   **El Paseo** comes highly recommended as the place for Tex-Mex. The **Best Western** in Lake Worth offers the town's only chain option, but The **Hilltop B&B** (817-238-7503) is a little more upscale with a pool, cabana, and grill.

NORTH CENTRAL

BENBROOK   Elev. 688   Pop. 20,208

One of the oldest communities in Tarrant County, Benbrook sits on I-20 just south of Fort Worth, where the confluence of the Clear Fork of the Trinity and Mary's Creek used to provide mighty fine amenities for Indians passing through on expeditions. Today the community has grown as a satellite city to Fort Worth, with most of its residents earning their wages up the road. Golf in Benbrook is relatively new, with a par 3 facility opening in 1993 and the newer Whitestone facility finally bringing an 18-hole championship layout to the town.

BENBROOK PAR 3

The golf   Benbrook Lake provides the perfect setting for this unique little 9-hole par 3. Excellent views and short holes with elevated greens draw the folks to Frank and Debbie Reynolds' place. Water comes into play on a few holes, and they've even gone to the trouble of spotting the course with several bunkers. No. 2 is the best: a full 8 iron with water looming left. You'll feel the

---

Few things draw two men together more surely than a mutual inability to master golf, coupled with an intense and ever-increasing love for the game. P.G. Wodehouse

*machismo*ness when you nail this green.

You can pay once and play all day, and even extend the golf orgy into the darkness of night, since they've lighted the course.

The details   817-249-3727. 1590 Beach Rd., Benbrook, TX 76126

• 1993. Frank and Debbie Reynolds. 9 holes. Par 27. 929 yards. Price - $.

Getting there Take I-30 west to Hwy. 820 and turn south. Drive 1 mile to Winscott Rd. and turn left. Beach Rd. is a half mile down. Turn right and you'll see the course.

WHITESTONE GOLF CLUB

The golf   The city of Benbrook and ClubCorp teamed to create this public-private venture that has resulted in a unique 7,100-yard Jeff Brauer design. Long and susceptible to the wind, WhiteStone rolls through an impressive Hill Country-like setting with huge oak trees, lots of rocks, and loads of native oaks, cacti, yucca, and wildflowers.

Bunkers are everywhere, and water comes into play on about seven holes. The key to scoring well is keeping the ball below the hole, avoiding nasty downhill putts on the extremely fast greens. The par 5s are tough, and average golfers should probably play them conservatively and be happy just getting there in three, since three out of four are fronted by hazards and require carries.

On the front No. 1 tests you early—it's a 555-yarder with a creek that crosses the fairway and forces a layup on the second shot. No. 9 is nice as well, a 360-yarder that should be played with a short iron to lay up in front of the creek. This hole features a nice dip in the center of the green that requires knowing the correct pin placement.

The back starts strong like the front, opening with a 580-yard par 5 with a sloping fairway that is cut by the creek on two occasions. No. 11 is the best par 3 on the course—a 200-yarder that plays downhill over a creek and into a creek surrounded by bunkers.

The details   817-249-9996. 10650 Hwy. 377 S., Benbrook TX 76126

• www.whitestonegolf.com

• Jeff Brauer. 18 holes. 7,100 yards. Price - $$$.

Getting there The course is 2.5 miles south of I-20 on Hwy. 377 S., on the right-hand side of the road.

BENBROOK NOTES Whitestone's grill, known as **McGregors Market Grille**, serves all sorts of awesome grub. Just down the road from Whitestone

It's Old Man Par and you, match or medal. And Old Man Par is a patient soul, who never shoots a birdie and never incurs a buzzard. He's a patient soul, Old Man Par. And if you would travel the long route with him, you must be patient, too. Bobby Jones

is **Riscky's Bar-B-Q**, a Fort Worth area tradition now for over 75 years. For greasy Mexican fare go to **Pulido's** or **Rio Mambo** , and the **Texas Grill** is the local favorite for delicious burgers. If lustful leanings dictate the immediate need for motel-style accommodations, the **Motel 6** or **Benbrook Inn & Suites** get the job done. Otherwise spend some money and head to Fort Worth.

BONHAM
Elev. 568   Pop. 7,306

Turn right on US 82 just before you get to Oklahoma and you'll run into Bonham, tree-shaded and old, known for its courthouse square statue of Alamo hero James Bonham and as the home of "Mr. Sam" Rayburn, the long-time dean of the US Congress. This area of Blackland Prairie south of the Red River has been home to one of Texas' oldest courses, the Bonham Country Club, but has recently added a spectacular new track called Legacy Ridge.

BONHAM GOLF & COUNTRY CLUB

The golf   Bonham's country club lays out around a creek that meanders through the course and comes into play as the primary obstacle on 8 out of 9 holes. The short course, void of bunkers, opens up with a nice, short par 3 that only requires a 9 iron at most. The remainder of the layout features short par 4s, and a series of back-to-back par 5s and par 3s on holes 4-8.

The toughest hole, which is the longest par 4, is the 395-yard No. 3, but it's followed by a 278-yard par 4.

Two sets of tees allow for an 18-hole round.

The details   903-583-8815. 501 W. Russell Ave., Bonham, TX 75418

• 1914. 9 holes. Par 35. Back – 2,831. Forward – 2,148. Price - $.

Getting there From Loop 121 north, turn right on Russell Ave. From Hwy.78, turn left on Russell Ave.

LEGACY RIDGE COUNTRY CLUB

The golf   Bonham's newest golf course has the natives all excited about their new Bill Johnston design, created to serve as the centerpiece of a unique residential community. With the benefit of several unique landscapes at his disposal, Johnston built a front nine that starts high and weaves through lakes and waterfalls, smoothly transitioning into a parkland-style route highlighted by pecans and oaks.

The par 5 No. 9 stands out on the front, taking you back up the ridge with an approach shot into an almost cliffside green nestled against the lake.

The wetlands of Bois d' Arc Creek line the back nine fairways, keeping water in play most of the nine. Johnston made this one fun with multiple approach

The smaller the target you have, the better the brain and body can function in getting the ball there. Dr. Bob Rotella

NORTH CENTRAL

shots over water, including one par 3 that plays into an island green.

Do what you can to work your way onto this course, because it's rare to experience a course of this quality course in such an enjoyable, rural setting.

The details   903-640-4500. 1200 Ranch Dr. Bonham, TX 75418

- www.legacyridge.com
- 18 holes. Par 72. 6,800 yards. Price - $$.

Getting there From McKinney, take US 75 north to the Bonham 121 exit. Hwy. 121 merges into Hwy. 56 south of Bonham. Turn right on Hwy. 82 E.

BONHAM NOTES   The **Carlton House B&B** (903-583-2779) is here, but Bonham wouldn't be Bonham unless you could crash at a place called **Granny Lou's** (800-997-7912). This area is unfortunately overlooked by DFW-ites seeking outdoor backroad adventures. Northeast are the **Caddo National Grasslands** and just south there's **Bonham State Park**, both great places to fish, camp, and enjoy the outdoors. Also 13 miles northwest find the ghost town of **Old Warren**, the first Fannin County seat. We'll elaborate here for those who like to eat–try the popular **Feed Mill Restaurant** (903-961-2711), west on US 82, where the chicken-fried steak is the specialty. For lunch on the square hit **The Green Onion** or **Hickory BBQ** . **JJC's** is across from Granny Lou's and serves pasta specialties. And if you have margarita cravings, find **Rolando's** by the **Days Inn**.

BRIDGEPORT

Elev. 754   Pop. 4,362

The old town of Bridgeport is near Decatur, northwest of Fort Worth, and the gateway to Lake Bridgeport. Once a coal miner's town after the railroad came through, tourism is popular because of the beautiful Runaway Bay resort, which also boasts an 18-hole Leon Howard design that complements Bridgeport's 9-hole country club.

BRIDGEPORT COUNTRY CLUB

The golf   Jack Johnson laid out Bridgeport's 9-holer back in the 1960s, taking advantage of the Trinity River to lay out his par 35, 3,058-yard track. This scenic, well-watered course features plush fairways and immaculate, undulating greens.

The best hole is No. 3, the signature 558-yard par 5 that weaves through trees and around the river. Thankfully, this course is one where you can pay once and play all day.

The details   940-683-9438. 2123 FM, Bridgeport, TX 76426

The important question is not how good your good shots are – it's how bad are your bad ones. Harvey Penick

- 1964. Jack Johnson. 9 holes. Par 35. Back – 3,058 (34.0/110). Middle – 2,925 (33.7/108). Forward – 2,221 (33.3/106). Price - $$.

Getting there From Hwy. 114 west, turn left on FM 2123. The clubhouse is on the right.

RUNAWAY BAY GOLF CLUB

The golf   Runaway Bay, located on Lake Bridgeport, opened in 1963 as a 9-hole course, and was upgraded with the additional nine in 1972. And although its reputation suffered, particularly in the early 1990s, course conditions have improved dramatically since the Wood family took over in 1995 (the greens were renovated in 1996-97).

Water is barely an issue, since it only comes into play on three holes. Each side has a standout hole. On the front, the par 5 No. 8 involves carrying the lake on the approach, and is particularly tough because of the sloped green. On the back nine, No. 10 is a stickler because they only give you four shots on this 465-yard monster, and the fairway isn't as generous as you'd like. No. 18 is nice because it involves the lake from tee to green.

The details   940-575-2225. 400 Half Moon Way, Bridgeport, TX 76426

- www.runawaybay.com

- Leon Howard. 18 holes. Par 72. Blue – 7,032 (73.1/124). White – 6,657 (71.3/120). Gold – 5,600 (66.1/108). Red – 5,446 (68.2/106). Price - $$$.

Getting there From Hwy. 380 west to Bridgeport, take Exit 5 and turn right. Drive to Half Moon Way and turn left.

BRIDGEPORT NOTES   For restless-man's side trips, take FM 1156 as it turns toward **Wizard Wells,** an old health spa built around mineral wells once popular with the Kiowa Indians. In town, make your reservations at the **Greystone Inn** , and enjoy every moment at the **Stevens Street Grill** by the First National Bank. **Dos Chiles** has been known to serve outstanding Mexican grub. Travelers tip: bring your own booze, because Bridgeport doesn't have any (at least none that we've found yet).

BURLESON   Elev. 710   Pop. 20,976

In 1882, when Burleson got its start, the local saloon also housed the first post office. The town's location on the railroad helped Burleson prosper as an agricultural community. Then in the 1920s, Texas 21 was built from Fort Worth to Alvarado, creating more opportunities for growth. A commuter community for Fort Worth today, Burleson is home to over 20,000 residents and two fabulous golf courses.

HIDDEN CREEK GOLF COURSE

The golf   Nestled along the banks of its namesake Hidden Creek, this is a links-style/traditional combination that rolls through oak and mesquite groves. The fairways are narrow and trees line every hole. The greens are fast and huge, and lakes come into play frequently along with numerous dogleg fairways. The course was designed by Stephen D. Plumer, who incorporated a few split fairways to spice up the layout.

The best hole is the 448-yard No. 8, which forces at least a 230-yard tee shot over water to a tight landing area and an approach down the dogleg-left fairway to a multi-tiered green.

The details   817-447-4444. 700 S. Burleson Blvd., Burleson, TX 76028

- www.hiddencreekgolfcourse.com
- Stephen Plumer. 18 holes. Par 72. Black – 6,753 (73.8/139). Blue – 6,307 (70.9/133). White – 5,698 (67.8/120). Gold – 4,968. Price - $$$.

Getting there From I-20, take I-35 south, and drive 10 miles to Renfro Rd. Stay on the access road and the course is on the right side.

SOUTHERN OAKS GOLF CLUB

The golf   Designed by PGA Pro and fomer Texas Longhorn Mark Brooks, Southern Oaks is a very tough test of golf. Tipping out at over 7,300 yards to a par 71, it has lightning-fast greens highlighted by very extreme undulations. And while multiple tees offer shorter distances, average golfers will still struggle to have decent rounds on Brooks' first design.

The greens are moderately undulating and fast. Although well-bunkered, the greens accommodate roll-up shots. Most of the fairways are open, with some holes lined by mature oaks.

The signature hole is No. 16, a 441-yard, par 4 that requires a demanding tee shot. A creek runs across the fairway approximately 60 yards short of the well-bunkered green.

Live oaks dot the landscape, and the course lays out over some impressively natural-looking terrain. Off the tee there aren't too many problems, and driver is probably the way to go given the length and lack of out-of-bounds.

The real challenge is dealing with the elevated greens, the sucker pin placements, and the deep-faced bunkers that guard them. One of the best-looking holes is the scenic 181-yard No. 3, which plays uphill and is guarded by four black-hole-like bunkers. The best hole on the front is the 49-yard No. 9, which is unfortunately a par 4 that usually plays into the wind.

I think we must agree that all a man can do is beat the people who are around at the same time he is. He cannot win from those who came before any more than he can from those who may come afterward. It is human, I suppose, for every man to think that his days were the best. Bobby Jones

On the back, No. 16 is rated the most difficult—a 440-yarder with a creek crossing the fairway and in front of the elevated green.

The details   817-426-2400. 13765 Southern Oaks Dr., Burleson, TX 76028

- www.southernoaksgolf.com
- Mark Brooks. 18 holes. Par 71. Back – 7,302. Middle – 6,551. Forward – 5,369. Price - $$$$.

Getting there Located 12 miles south of Fort Worth. Take I-35 south to the Alsbury Exit, then drive 1.5 miles. The course is across from Spinks Airport.

BURLESON NOTES   Besides the chains, there's **Lafayette**, which specializes in seafood in the home of the town's old steakhouse. **Antonio's** on Main is popular as well. The nicest hotel is the **Comfort Suites** (817-426-6666), where you can cozy up in the indoor hot tub with your evening companion. On the way back to Fort Worth, stop in Everman, TX at **Longoria's BBQ** (817-568-9494).

CARROLLTON
Elev. 470 Pop. 100,463

Carrollton was no-man's land back in 1950, when it was home to only 1,600 folks–a far cry from the 100,000-plus residents today. Settlers from Carrollton, Illinois came to the area in the mid-1800s, and eventually selected the present-day site after fleeing from an Indian raid. The railroad came through in 1872 and the city's been able to hang on since then, primarily serving baby boomers moving north from Dallas with their families.

COLUMBIAN COUNTRY CLUB OF DALLAS

The golf   Although not that well known, Columbian Country Club has been an exclusive all-Jewish Dallas-area club since the 1950s when Ralph Plummer was hired to build 9 holes as one of his first solo projects. Five years later Leon Howard rolled through to add the second nine, and sporadic renovations have been completed since then: one by Joe Finger in 1971, and another that was recently completed around 2000.

The collaborative efforts of all these well-known architects have produced a course that's known for its small, fast greens, and numerous water hazards. In all, water is in play on 15 holes, and that–combined with the mature, tree-lined fairways–makes the 6,760-yard layout plenty challenging. The most difficult hole is No. 11, a 437-yard par 4 that plays uphill against the wind.

NORTH CENTRAL

I always tell my students that if there is a road to good golf, nowhere on that road is there a slice. You can go from hooking to good golf. You can go from slicing to hooking to good golf. But you can't go from slicing to good golf. Hank Haney

The details   972-416-2131. 2525 Country Club Dr., Carrollton, TX 75006

- 1950s. Ralph Plummer and Leon Howard. 18 holes. Par 71. Back – 6,760 (73.1/129). White – 6,314 (70.9/122). Gold – 5,609 (67.7/110). Red – 4,984 (69.1/116). Price - $$$.

Getting there From I-35 north, exit Belt Line and drive east past Josey to Country Club Dr. The club is north of Belt Line.

COYOTE RIDGE GOLF CLUB

The golf   Carrollton's newest championship layout, opened in 1999, features some unusual holes that traverse a variety of unique terrain. Each nine is strikingly different–the front plays through a burgeoning residential community, is generally wide open and void of trees, and takes on the characteristics of a links-style course.

Water comes into play six times on the front, including the extremely difficult hole 9, which doglegs left around a lake that stretches all the way around the green. Survive the tee shot by bailing right if you have to, but consider laying up on the approach since the water bends all the way around and surrounds the green on three sides. You'll still have the chance for an up-and-down par, and playing for bogey is much better that rolling into the turn after a double-digit disaster.

Also on the front, No. 7 is a fun par 3 because of the 70-foot drop in elevation. The tee shot goes 165 yards over water into a very wide, challenging green.

The back nine rolls through an abandoned rock quarry along the Trinity River, featuring more trees and elevation changes.

Other notes: Walking is not allowed on weekends.

The details   972-939-0666. 1680 Bandera Dr., Carrollton, TX 75010

- www.coyoteridgegolf.com
- 1999. 18 holes. Par 71. Back – 6,795. Middle – 6,155. Forward – 4,995. Price - $$$.

Getting there From Dallas, take I-35 north and exit Hebron Pkwy. Drive east 3 miles, turn left on Hunt Dr., then turn right on Bandera Dr.

INDIAN CREEK GOLF COURSE

The golf   The city of Carrollton hired Dick Phelps to create 36 holes in the flood plain of Indian Creek and the Elm Fork of the Trinity River. His design features narrow fairways lined with cedar, oak, mesquite, and elm trees, as well as average-size greens of medium speed. The predominant hazard is water, which comes into play on and astounding 34 of 36 holes.

The first course at Indian Creek, the **Creeks Course**, is considered more difficult, and features water on all 18 holes. The 466-yard No. 6 is the feature

People often ask me, "Why can't I play golf the same every day?" Well, what can you do the same every day? I don't even get out of bed the same way. Jackie Burke, Jr.

hole–Indian Creek runs in front of the tee and down the right side, and the fairway has a grove of trees in the middle.

Only two holes lack water on the **Lakes Course**, designed by Phelps three years after the Creeks opened. No. 9 is the best hole, playing 453 yards with water coming into play off the tee and the approach. A pond protects the left bend of the dogleg and extends to the green. Bogey isn't bad on this difficult par 4.

The details   972-466-9850. 1650 W. Frankford Rd., Carrollton, TX 75007

- www.cityofcarrollton.com

- Creek Course: 1983. Dick Phelps and Brad Benz. 18 holes. Par 72. Gold – 7,218 (74.7/122). Blue – 6,620 (71.3/116). White – 6,094 (70.9/115). Red – 4,967 (68.2/114). Price - $$.

- Lake Course: 1987. Dick Phelps. 18 holes. Par 72. Gold – 7,060 (72.9/122). Blue – 6,635 (71.9/120). White – 6,102 (70.3/118). Red – 5,267 (69.9/114). Price - $$.

Getting there From I-35 south, take the Trinity Mills exit and turn left. When you come to Dixon, turn left, then look for Frankford. Turn left on Frankford and the course is 1 mile away.

MORE GOLF

Carrollton Golf Center: FM 544, Carrollton. 972-492-7677

Golden Bear Golf Center: 2538 Golden Bear Dr., Carrollton. 972-733-4111.

Marsh Lane Golf Center: 2308 Marsh, Carrollton. 972-418-7545.

CARROLLTON NOTES   When you're in Carrollton you're in the heart of DFW, so you have every option under the sun for food, drink, and entertainment. However, old downtown Carrollton is worth a stroll, with nice retail stores and a restaurant worth trying, the **Cafe on the Square** (972-446-7936). You might also pray to the golf gods at the 1846 **Union Baptist Church**, the first in Dallas County.

CLEBURNE
Elev. 764   Pop. 25,033

From the DFW area, you'll pass through Cleburne on your way to the heart of Texas. The seat of Johnson County, the city is named after Confederate General Pat Cleburne and is home to two adequate small-town courses. On the outskirts, the town shows its dirty, rural roots, with random businesses scattered along the highway. Downtown has some character, with its historic, pris-

There are really two ways of increasing your distance. You can learn to swing the clubhead faster. Or you can learn to deliver it to the ball more accurately. Jack Nicklaus

tine homes on Prairie and North Anglin streets. In addition to the agriculture, the city is home to the state's largest railroad construction and repair industry.

CLEBURNE MUNICIPAL GOLF COURSE

The golf   Cleburne's municipal track was built by Leon Howard, who designed the course in and around the hilly terrain of Lake Cleburne. The flat front nine plays to a par 34 and has some interesting holes, particularly the number one handicap No. 7, which plays to a mean par 4 at 460 yards. This nine has only one par 5 but three par 3s, including two that play over 200 yards from the tips.

The unusual back has more elevation changes and is dominated by eight par 4s that are each under 400 yards, including the opening two drive-able holes. The most difficult hole on the back is the 395-yard 18th.

The details   817-641-4501. 2500 Country Club Rd., Cleburne, TX 76033

- 18 holes. Par 71. Back – 6,326 (69.0). Middle – 5,968. Forward – 5,084. Price - $.

Getting there From Hwy. 67, exit Knoland River Rd. and turn left. Travel 1 mile to Country Club Rd., turn right, and the course is a mile away.

RIVERVIEW GOLF CLUB

The golf   The former Nolan River Country Club, once run by legendary pro Ben Hogan, is now open to the public, boasting pesky Buffalo Creek that winds through the layout on this beautiful, quiet, country course. Leon Howard built this track in the 1960s when Nolan River moved from its old location. His design features no bunkers, elevated greens, and water in play on 10 holes.

The 4th hole is famous on the front. Sneaky because of the small pond looming right of the fairway and hidden off the tee, this one goes 513 yards with a difficult approach that must thread two huge trees and carry the creek.

Two par 3s stand out: No. 8, which carries the creek, and the signature 13th, which plays 146 yards over water, with trouble behind the green.

The most difficult par 4 is No. 14, playing 418 yards and usually requiring a lay-up behind the creek–the approach over water is longer than you'd like.

The details   817-641-7818. 2501 S. Nolan River Rd., Cleburne, TX 76033

- 1964. Leon Howard. 18 holes. Par 72. Back – 6,605 (70.7/111). Middle – 6,207 (68.9/107). Forward – 5,069 (67.4/105). Price - $$.

Getting there From Hwy. 67 west, travel to Nolan River Rd. Turn left and the course is 3 miles away.

CLEBURNE NOTES   The **Anglin Rose B&B** (817-641-7433) is one of a few

---

The difference between winning and losing sometimes is what you think of yourself. I like to be the aggressor. In my youth, if I didn't have but $40, I put the whole $40 in front of me. I don't want a piece of pork – I want the whole hog. Amarillo Slim

choices for a night's stay, and the locals will point you toward the **Lone Star Cafe** (817-556-3098) for a place to eat. The chamber of commerce might point you to the **Layland Museum**, which is interesting because of its Indian artifacts and details on early Texana, as well as the **Johnson County Courthouse**, which sports an ornate, stained-glass dome. The road-trip types might be interested in the **ghost town** sites that dot the countryside around town, one of which is 5 miles northwest and was the original county seat.

THE COLONY
Elev. 593   Pop. 26,531

The Colony is next to Lake Lewisville 24 miles north of Dallas, and was established by real estate developers in the early 1970s. The actual location is noted as the site of the Hedgcoxe War in 1852, when armed settlers raided and burned the Texas Emigration and Land Company. It's more peaceful now, especially with the lake and the two nice golf courses that have been developed along the shores of the lake.

STEWART PENINSULA GOLF COURSE

The golf   Stewart Peninsula offers a 9-hole course along Lake Lewisville with dual greens on every hole. On the first round, you'll play from the red tees to the red flags, and on the back you'll go yellow to yellow.

After a straightforward opening hole where the only real problem is a pesky fairway bunker, Nos. 2 and 3 start a trend of interesting holes. No. 2 offers completely different looks from each set of tees. The right side pin placement presents problems because of the lake, and the left flag rests close to greenside mounding that will send balls bounding afar. Misses here should find the bunkers, as the recovery is not all that difficult from the sand. No. 3 is probably the signature, and a 250-yard drive will put you in prime position to go at the multi-tiered green. Avoid missing back right, as the up-and-down is especially difficult from that side.

The details   972-625-8700. 100 Cottonwood Springs Dr., The Colony, TX 75056

- www.stewartpeninsula.com

- 9 holes. Tripp Davis. Rating for 18 holes is 124.

Getting there From Hwy. 121 turn north on Main St. (Hwy. 423). Drive to North Colony and turn left, then turn right on Stewart Blvd., which jogs left quickly into Acacia Trail. From there turn right on Cottonwood Springs and look for the lighthouse.

Quiet hands respond on their own to the weight of the clubhead. Tight hands have to be told what to do. Jim Flick

THE TRIBUTE GOLF CLUB

The golf   A Scottish-themed, links-style track that plays along the shores of Lake Lewisville, The Tribute one-ups the Tour 18 approach of modeling the world's finest golf holes. Patterning his design after the revered holes of St. Andrews, Troon, Prestwick, etc., Tripp Davis created an immaculate track that rolls over terrain strikingly similar to the dunes and grasses over the Atlantic.

From the tips the course plays to a par 72 7,003 yards, but its most strikingly entertaining feature is its playability from the forward tees. In total, four sets of tees are available to even things out for the high handicappers.

St. Andrews is well represented on the first and last holes at The Tribute, where they offer the world's largest fairway as a great way to start and finish your round.

Other notes: Don't forget to inquire about the club's seven guest rooms and available stay-and-play packages. The facility has hopes of opening another 18 and an adjoining hotel sometime in the near future.

The details   972-370-5465. 1000 Boyd Rd., The Colony, TX 75056

- www.thetexasgolftrail.com
- 2000. Tripp Davis. 18 holes. Par 72. Back – 7,003 (73.2/128). Middle – 6,552 (71.0/122). Forward – 5,352 (65.6/111). Price - $$$$.

Getting there From 75, take Hwy. 121 west to 423 (main street of The Colony). Turn right (north) to Boyd Road. Turn left, then drive 2.5 miles to the clubhouse.

THE COLONY NOTES   The Tribute offers an upscale B&B experience, mainly used for post-wedding honeymooners but available to anyone. The **Comfort Suites** (972-668-5555) has free breakfast and is nicer than the **Budget Suites** (972-370-1111). Fast food is everywhere, but on the main road (423), family-owned **Angelina's** has great Tex-Mex and margaritas, and **Stan's Lakeview Tap House & Grill** offers more of a sports bar atmosphere. Both of these are fun, with indoor and outdoor dining.

COMMERCE   Elev. 551   Pop. 7,669

Traveling east on I-30, take a left after Greenville and you'll be heading up Texas 50 to the college town of Commerce. "Cow Hill" was established in the 1870s on the fertile prairies between the Middle and South Sulphur rivers, and was named the "Bois d'Arc Capital of Texas" because of its location in the middle of a thick grove of those trees. Here you can reserve B&B accommodations, mosey around the square for shops and antiques, and play some golf on their course that overlooks nearby Cooper Lake.

There is no type of miracle that can't happen at least once on a golf course. Grantland Rice

SAND HILLS GOLF & COUNTRY CLUB

The golf   Sand Hills overlooks Cooper Lake and is loaded with trees and water, but there are no bunkers on this course. Two holes stand out on the par 36 layout–the 270-yard, par 4 No. 6 and the most difficult hole, the 220-yard par 3 No. 8. Hole 4 is the best birdie opportunity, a 470-yard par 5 that should definitely be reached in two if you're hitting them well.

Two sets of tees allow for an 18-hole round. On the weekends, the course is open only to members between 11 a.m. and 3 p.m.

The details   903-886-4455. 5950 Sand Hills Dr., Commerce, TX 75429

• 1962. 9 holes. Par 36. Back – 3,000 (34.0). Forward – 2,459. Price - $.

Getting there From I-30, take Hwy. 50 north, then turn right on Maloy Rd.

COMMERCE NOTES   The town square, affectionately known as **The Square**, is the hub of activity, featuring a great little coffee shop for breakfast, antique shops for piddling around, and restaurants to keep you fed. Look for the **Cow Hill Express** and order yourself a slug of Cow Hill cappuccino. Commerce celebrates the **Bois d'Arc Bash** every September, which honors the second-largest bois d'arc tree in Texas. Ask for directions to the tree, known locally as "Max." There's a recently refurbished local motel for lodging.

COPPELL
Elev. 519   Pop. 35,958

Another of the DFW area's soccer mom havens, Coppell houses those who've proved their mettle on the way to middle management. Here in this extreme northwest corner of Dallas County, bordered by Irving, Grapevine, and Carrollton, the Elm Fork of the Trinity River sucks water in from Grapevine and Denton Creeks, creating some interesting terrain for golf. History-wise, manly Sam Houston and his Republic of Texas troops camped out on Grapevine Creek during important Indian negotiations that secured their aid to defend against attacks by Mexican troops.

RIVERCHASE GOLF COURSE

The golf   One of Jim Fazio's first solo projects, Riverchase is a surprisingly tough challenge given its lack of trees and relatively short length. The course runs through the bottomlands of the Elm Fork Trinity River and is loaded with water due to a chain of interconnecting lakes created to collect heavy rains and irrigate the course. While there are no forced carries, water comes into play on at least 12 holes, and out-of-bounds is a frequent concern because of the housing community that surrounds the course.

Golf, like the measles, should be caught young, for, if postponed to riper years, the results may be serious. P.G. Wodehouse

No. 5 is the most difficult rated hole–a long dogleg right par 4 that requires a solid tee shot to be in position to reach the green in two. The approach is long and uphill into a severely back-to-front sloping green with a lake on the right and out-of-bounds and bunkers on the left.

Two holes later, No. 7 is one of the toughest approaches in all of DFW. This par 4 hole plays due south into the prevailing wind, and the elevated green has a depth of only about 25 feet. Bunkers line the back, and the slope in front is significant. Ups and downs are difficult because of the slopes in the green. Take a look at the pin placement when you're teeing off on No. 4.

The good news is that other than out-of-bounds, the course is mostly wide open, so you'll generally have a shot if you just miss the fairway. The only thick spot for trees is along the creek on holes 14-16.

The details   972-462-8281. 700 Riverchase Dr., Coppell, TX 75019

- www.americagolf.com
- 1989. Jim Fazio. 18 holes. Par 71. Back – 6,593 (72.0/124). Middle – 6,041 (68.9/114). Forward – 5,125 (70.5/119). Price - $$$.

Getting there Take the Belt Line exit off of 635 and drive north to MacArthur. Turn right (east) and drive to Riverchase Dr., where you'll turn left. Look for the course on the right side of the road.

COPPELL NOTES   The **Coppell Deli** is a landmark old grocery-cafe type of place that's famous for hosting the Dallas Cowboys, whose workout facility at Valley Ranch is nearby. Some of the sandwiches are named after former players like Nate Newton, who used to eat several of the triple-decker breakfast sandwiches crammed with eggs, bacon, cheese, sausage, more eggs, and such. The place is covered with photos of Cowboys, and the burgers are some of the best around. The **Dairy Queen** here received national attention when the Dallas Mavericks' owner volunteered as a manager one day in 2002.

AMERICAN GOLF GIFT CERTIFICATES

Linksmen know that the gift of golf is the best thing going when it comes to birthdays, Father's Day, and Christmas, and American Golf (www.americangolf.com) offers the genius option of enabling gift buyers to purchase certificates in increments of $25 that work like cash for the avid Texas golfer. The certificates can be used to purchase green fees, cart fees, and even merchandise at any American Golf course. All you have to do is fill out their simple online form or call 877-GOLF-AGC to order and have them ship directly to the address of your choice.

There is no surer nor more painful way to learn a rule than to be penalized for breaking it. Tom Watson

CORINTH
Elev. 600   Pop. 11,325

Corinth is a commuter community on I-35 just southeast of Denton that celebrated its 100th anniversary in 1980. Formerly a railroad and farming town, it has grown over the years to accommodate the growing DFW population. Unless you're looking for it, you'll hardly notice Corinth as you drive up and down I-35.

OAKMONT COUNTRY CLUB

The golf   Don January came out of retirement in 1986 to build this nice little course in Corinth, which eventually fell on hard times and was absorbed by Club Corporation of America in 1992. His design requires the use of most clubs in your bag as it rolls through the mature oak trees and hilly terrain just west of I-35.

Water is in play on over half of the holes, and the course has a decent amount of bunkering. No. 14 is one of the easiest holes, reachable for the big hitters at 320 yards. However, three long par 4s are the holes to be aware of. Holes 9, 16, and 18 all play well over 400 yards, and are especially tough when the wind is blowing.

Other notes: The clubhouse was renovated recently and offers an outstanding view of the first and last holes.

The details   940-321-5599. 1200 Clubhouse Dr., Corinth, TX 76210

- www.oakmontclub.com
- Gold – 6,908. (72.7/123). Blue – 6,602 (71.1/120). White – 5,880 (66.0/107). Red – 5,097 (69.2/118). Price - $$.

Getting there From I-35 north take the Shady Shores exit (461) and turn left. Find Clubhouse Dr. and look for the entrance.

CORINTH NOTES   Take the Garden Ridge exit (454B) off of I-35 and head to Lake Lewisville and Eagle Point Marina. **Sneaky Pete's** (972-434-2500) is on the lake, with its large bar, great food, and lots of options for sun and fun. Down in Lake Dallas, also on the lake, the **Jolly Roger Boat Club** is the perfect shady lounge.

CORSICANA
Elev. 411   Pop. 23,184

Heading towards Houston from Dallas on I-45, you'll run into Corsicana about an hour down the road. The seat and largest town of Navarro County, the town dates back to 1848 when Texas Revolution hero Antonio Navarro suggested the name in honor of his parents' hometown on the island of Corsica.

Some players are never satisfied unless they are buying new clubs....This is not good for the player, but it is quite good for the clubmaker. James Braid

The traveling golfer has two options in this industrious town of the Northern blacklands–the 1914 country club, which has the proud distinction of being designed by the irreverent A.W. Tillinghast, and the more laid-back 9-hole Oak Trail Golf Club.

CORSICANA COUNTRY CLUB

The golf This links-style course features wide fairways. The golfer will rarely play from a flat lie due to the contour of the fairways. Water hazards (a pond and a lake) come into play on at least seven holes. The green on hole 18, a 403-yard par 4, is the only green not surrounded by sand bunkers. Designed by A.W. Tillinghast in 1914 during his Texas swing, this is a links-style course with tree-lined fairways built around a large lake. Amid the rolling hills and oak trees you'll find few level lies. No. 2 is a tough par 3 at 225 yards over water and a green surrounded by bunkers.

The details 903-874-2441. 500 Emhouse Rd., Corsicana, TX 75151

- 1914. 18 holes. Par 71. Back – 6,541 (70.2/116). Middle – 6,230 (69.1/114). Forward – 5,357 (76.9/136). Price - $$.

Getting there From I-45 south, take Exit 31 and turn right onto Beaton St. Look for the signs to the course.

OAK TRAIL GOLF CLUB

The golf Formerly known as New Oaks Golf Course, this is the more public, 9-hole alternative for golf in Corsicana. Short and well-maintained, it's the kind of course that makes for an enjoyable, affordable afternoon on the links. The design rolls through mature trees, creeks meander through the lay-out, and water comes into play on 7 of 9 holes. As you might expect on a simple muni like this, the greens are pretty basic–flat and of medium speed.

The details 903-872-1801. 2509 N. Business 45, Corsicana, TX 75110

- 9 holes. Par 36. Back – 3,120. Forward – 2,640. Price - $.

Getting there From I-45 south, take the first Corsicana Business 45 exit and drive north. The course is about 4 miles away off Hwy. 45.

CORSICANA NOTES The **Collin Street Bakery** (903-872-8111) has been around for over 100 years, and **Roy's Cafe** (903-874-6791) is the local favorite for lunch. **Dee's Place** (903-874-5891) has been around since 1905 and is supposedly the oldest continually operating soda fountain in Texas. It's worth a quick drive around town to see the old, historic homes. For lodging, The **Magnolia House** (903-872-2577) or **The Wicklow Inn** (903-872-7311) offer excellent B&B options.

Golf is a game that creates emotions that sometimes cannot be endured with the club still in your hands. Bobby Jones

CRANDALL

Elev. 424   Pop. 3,016

Crandall began with the railroad in 1880, and quickly became a shipping point for area farmers. Located a stone's throw southeast of Dallas on US 175, this little town is well on its way to becoming one of the many commuter communities of Big D. In fact, since it's only a 15-minute drive from downtown Dallas if you're moving well, 90% of the business at the Crandall's Creekview Golf Club comes from Dallasites who enjoy the small-town friendliness combined with good golf for the right price.

CREEKVIEW GOLF CLUB

The golf   The great game of golf was blessed upon Crandall in 1995 when Dick Phelps was hired to build the town's municipal track. With a population of barely 3,000 folks, Crandall is the smallest Texas town with its own municipally owned golf course.

Phelps did Crandall right with his 7,238-yard design. Far from the basic courses that typically dot Texas' small towns, this one has some bite, with plenty of trees, water, and sand, as well as first-class bent-grass greens. In fact, this course is legitimate enough to bring golfers in droves from the Dallas area, with over 80% of the course's revenue coming from visiting golfers. Crandall used to be known as a speed trap; now it's known for its golf.

Two holes stand out, one on each side. The signature is the 581-yard par 5, which doglegs left with a creek on the right. The fairway is spotted with bunkers, and the small green is a difficult target because it is surrounded by trees and water. On the back, No. 15 goes 210 yards over water—it can be difficult to hold a shot on the two-tiered green because it plays with the prevailing wind.

The details   972-427-3811. 1602 E. Hwy. 175, Crandall, TX 75114

- www.creekviewgolfclub.com

- 1995. Dick Phelps. 18 holes. Par 72. Gold – 7,238 (74.1/119). Blue – 6,770 (71.8/117). White – 6,161 (68.7/110). Red – 5,459 (71.2/115). Price - $$.

Getting there Take Hwy. 175 west towards Dallas for 9 miles. Exit FM 148 and turn left. Stay to the right and look for the driveway to the course.

CRANDALL NOTES   This one is a day trip from Dallas, or one you'll hit in the morning on your way out of town. Before you head down the road, grab a meal and an ice-cold bottle of beer at the authentic **Cotton Gin Restaurant and Club** (972-427-3883), where the famous hickory mushroom burger is a tough choice over the crispy chicken-fried steak.

In 1998, *The Sporting News* claimed the Dallas Metroplex may have "more sports bars than any metro area in the country."

DALLAS

Elev. 512   Pop. 1,750,894

The most expensive real estate in Dallas just happens to be a 10-foot-square log shack that is badly in need of updating. It is John Neely Bryan's cabin, and it sits on one square block of downtown. In 1840, Bryan came to the three forks area of the Trinity River from Arkansas to survey a spot for a possible trading post serving Indians and settlers, but liked the area enough to stay. From that humble beginning sprang the city of Dallas, most likely named for the U.S. vice president at the time, George Mifflin Dallas, although no one knows for sure.

Dallas didn't really expand until the coming of the railroads in the 1870s. With the arrival of the trains, the population increased from 3,000 in early 1872 to more than 7,000 in September of the same year. New businesses and buildings appeared daily and telegraph lines arrived, connecting Dallas with the outside world. Dallas was now a concentration point for raw materials, such as grain and cotton shipped to the South and East. Thanks to the railroads, Dallas became a major trading center for just about everything produced in Texas, and has stayed that way through the years. After World War II, Dallas mushroomed as a banking and insurance headquarters, with high tech, communications, medicine, aviation, and fashion all contributing to the economy.

As a frontier town, Dallas had a lively reputation among outlaws and other renegades. Belle Starr began her adventures in Dallas as a dance hall singer and dancer, and later sold stolen horses. Doc Holliday opened up a dentist's office in Dallas before returning to gambling. Sam Bass hid out here, and in the 1920s, the bank-robbing duo of Bonnie and Clyde began their legendary crime spree near Dallas.

For good and for bad, four major events shaped Dallas' image as a modern American city. The first was an epic tragedy: the assassination of President John F. Kennedy on November 22, 1963, just three blocks from John Neely Bryan's cabin. The Sixth Floor Museum, which evokes the feelings of that fateful day with haunting realism, remains a major tourist stop. The second event was the opening of Dallas/Fort Worth International Airport in 1974, the largest in the country at the time and still one of the busiest airports in the world. Also during the 1970s, professional sports fever took root with the amazing success of the Dallas Cowboys, dubbed "America's Team." Under the leadership of two legendary quarterbacks, Roger Staubach and Troy Aikman, the football dynasty won five Super Bowls. Dallas later added teams from the NBA (the Dallas Mavericks), the NHL (the 1999 Stanley Cup Champion Dallas Stars), Major League Baseball (the Texas Rangers) and Major League Soccer (the Dallas Sidekicks). Finally, and the city's residents turn their eyes up in disgust over this one, Dallas became a worldwide household name with the unprecedented success of the long-running hit TV show, *Dallas,* which still airs in syndication throughout Europe.

NORTH CENTRAL

★

Gambling is illegal at Bushwood, sir. And besides, I never slice!
Judge Smails (Ted Knight) in the film "Caddyshack"

Now the seventh largest city in America, Dallas is a sophisticated, dynamic metropolitan area with vast cultural resources and plenty of Western flavor. The money and the people mean golf, and there's lots to be found when you make Dallas the hub of your golf excursions in and around the DFW area.

BEAR CREEK GOLF CLUB

The golf   Conveniently located adjacent to the DFW Airport, Bear Creek serves up two Ted Robinson-designed 18-hole masterpieces that are known for their stunning topography and outstanding greens. And with both courses playing around 6,700 yards from the tips, golfers can hit long irons and fairway woods off the tee to keep it in the fairway, which is mandatory for a good round on these tight courses.

The **West Course** is demanding early, and is significantly more difficult on the front side. However, the back side opens up and allows some room for error, making this the track of choice for the high handicapper.

Nos. 6 and 7 stand out on the demanding front. No. 6 requires a blind tee shot and an approach over water, and No. 7 might be the most difficult on the course: a 380-yard par 4 that plays into the wind and also involves water. The back side has the signature hole, the scenic 180-yard No. 17 that plays along a lake.

The **East Course** is considered a tad more difficult, with tighter fairways and smaller greens. 14 of 18 holes dogleg, so its label as a target course is accurate. Elevation changes make club selection a challenge, and the par 5s are tough to reach in two.

No. 5 stands out on the front: a 385-yarder that doglegs left and involves an approach over water. No. 8 is longer (418 yards) and features water in the fairway landing area and along the right side.

On the back, No. 15 is the signature, playing 432 yards and tricky because of the blind approach shot.

The details   972-456-3200. 3500 Bear Creek Court, Dallas, TX 75261

- www.clubcorp.com

- West: 1981. Ted Robinson. 18 holes. Par 72. Back – 6,690 (72.7/130). Middle – 6,264 (71.8/125). Forward – 5,570 (72.5/122). Price - $$$.

- East: 1980. Ted Robinson. 18 holes. Par 72. Back – 6,670 (72.5/127). Middle – 6,282 (71.8/121). Forward – 5,620 (72.4/124). Price - $$$.

Getting there From I-35 west, take Hwy. 183 west and find Hwy. 36 north. Exit Mid-Cities Blvd. and turn right. At Airfield Dr., turn right and the course is on the right.

If there's one thing certain about putting, it is that it's an individual business. The great putters have used every conceivable type of grip, stance and stroke. Ben Crenshaw

BENT TREE GOLF CLUB

The golf   Located next to Dallas' exclusive Preston Trail Golf Club, Bent Tree opened in 1974 as the centerpiece for a 700-acre development headed by Dallas real estate investors Robert Folsom and John Murchison. The two hired the eclectic Scotsman Desmond Muirhead to design the course on 190 acres of former cotton fields.

In the 1980s, the LPGA and Senior PGA tours frequently hosted tournaments at Bent Tree, and the course was eventually renovated in 1990. The improvements focused on the front nine (which is still more open than the back), spicing up the layout with bunkering, tree additions, and adjustments to greens.

Water comes into play on 14 of 18 holes, and the course is quite long if you play from the tips. The best hole on the front is No. 3, a long par 5 that plays almost 600 yards. The narrow fairway chutes between water on the left and bunkers on the right, and the small green slopes severely to the water on the left side.

The more interesting back nine offers a nice stretch of golf on holes 13-15. No. 14 is the most scenic on the course because it plays downhill at least 75 feet to a green surrounded on three sides by water. The 387-yard 18th is the perfect finishing hole–not too long but plenty challenging.

The details   972-931-7326. 5201 Westgrove, Dallas, TX 75248

- 1972. 18 holes. Par 72. Champs – 7,113 (74.9/139). Price - $$$$.

BROOK HOLLOW GOLF CLUB

The golf   One of only a handful of A.W. Tillinghast-designed Texas courses, super-exclusive Brook Hollow Golf Club still has the charm of its original 1919 design, despite subtle revisions by Ben Crenshaw and Bill Coore in the early 1990s.

As you might expect, this traditional course, while not all that long, plays difficult because of the tight, tree-lined fairways and the small greens. No. 6 is the signature, a 400-yard-plus par 4 that is famous for its downhill approach shot.

If you can hustle your way onto the course, you deserve a post-round beverage and burger at **Club Schmitz** (214-350-3607), the long-time Dallas tradition just down the road on Harry Hines.

The details   214-637-1914. 8301 Harry Hines Blvd., Dallas, TX 75235

- 1919. A.W. Tillinghast. 18 holes. Par 71. Back – 6,703 (72.4/131). Middle – 6,250 (69.9/123). Forward – 5,232 (71.7/124). Price - $$$$.

Getting there From I-35 north, take the Regal Row exit and turn right. When you come to Harry Hines Blvd., turn right and the course is just down the road. The entrance is on the right side.

Would you like to know the fastest way to take several strokes off your game?
Spend two hours in a bunker. Greg Norman

Brook Hollow in 1940

BROOKHAVEN COUNTRY CLUB

The golf   One of the largest golf complexes in Texas when it was built in 1959, Brookhaven CC features three Press Maxwell-designed courses that offer a wonderful variety of golf.

The signature course of the facility is the **Master's Course**, which was renovated in the early 1990s by Jeff Brauer and now boasts a brand-new set of bent-grass greens from work done in 2002. The course is perfectly balanced—both challenging and fair—but is considered the most difficult of the three.

On the front the first real challenge is No. 4, a short par 5 that's tricky because it requires a perfect tee shot into the dogleg-left fairway. You'll need to lay up with a long iron or fairway wood, then hit a solid 3 wood over the creek for the second shot before firing into the huge, multi-level green. Two holes later, the long par 3 No. 6 can get you if you let the lake that fronts the green intimidate. Watch the pin placement on this huge green. Also on the front, the par 5 No. 8 is fun because of its unique dogleg right that enables you to cut the corner with a solid drive over the lake and trees. The green on No. 8 is difficult because it is elevated and fronted by bunkers.

On the back side, there's a 591-yard par 5 that is only tough because of its length, and a few straight-away par 4s that require accurate drives. All told, though, it's an easier stretch of golf than the front.

The **Championship Course** is not as difficult as the Master's, but offers plenty of challenging holes. No. 10 is the most difficult—a long par 4 that bends right, it requires a perfect drive to set up a reasonable approach over the lake to the green. Most of the par 3s are short and offer good scoring opportunities.

The **Presidents Course** was built to accommodate beginners, seniors, and

---

A rough should have high grass. When you go bowling they don't give you anything for landing in the gutter, do they? Lee Trevino

women, but is a great way for better golfers to work on their iron play. The par 4s are around 300 yards or less, and the par 5s are reachable in two. Use this one to build the confidence or break out of the shanks.

The details 972-241-2761. 3333 Golfing Green Dr., Dallas, TX 75234

- www.clubcorp.com
- Masters: 1959. Press Maxwell. 18 holes. Par 72. Back – 6,866 (72.2/131). Forward – 6,409 (77.0/126). Price - $$$.
- Champs: 1959. Press Maxwell. 18 holes. Par 72. Back – 6,535 (71.2/122). Middle – 6,223 (69.8/118). Forward – 5,839 (74.4/127). Price - $$$.
- Presidents: 1959. Press Maxwell. 18 holes. Par 72. Back – 5,527 (65.2/106). Forward – 4,811 (68.3/117). Price - $$$.

Getting there Turn north on Midway off of 635 and drive north a few miles to Country Club Dr. Turn left (west) and you'll eventually see the club entrance on the right.

CEDAR CREST GOLF CLUB

The golf The revered A.W. Tillinghast didn't do many Texas courses, but old 1919 Cedar Crest was one of them, a course that hosted the 1927 PGA Championship won by Walter Hagen. Tillie's design takes advantage of this unusually hilly area of Dallas, with generous tree-lined fairways that often leave you with uneven lies. The trick here is in dealing with the small, fast greens, which are hard to hold–especially on the long par 3s. Four of the five par 3s play over 200 yards from the tips.

The city of Dallas bought the course in 1947 for $130,000 and has owned it ever since. The clubhouse was renovated recently.

The details 214-670-7615. 1800 Southerland Ave., Dallas, TX 75203

- www.cedarcrestgolf.com
- 1913. A. W. Tillinghast. 18 holes. Par 71. Back – 6,550 (71.0/121). Middle – 6,140 (69.0/116). Forward – 5,594 (72.0/113). Price - $$.

Getting there From Hwy. 45 south, take the Martin Luther King Jr. exit and turn right. This road turns into Cedar Crest, which dead-ends at the course.

DALLAS ATHLETIC CLUB

The golf Jack Nicklaus and Arnold Palmer came here in 1963 to endure one of Texas' hottest weeks ever, with temperatures rising as high as 113 degrees during the PGA Championship tournament. Nicklaus prevailed that week, and eventually he returned to renovate Ralph Plummer's original layouts. Plummer's courses were mostly flat, with immature, basic greens. Nicklaus toughened them up with mounding, bent-grass greens, and other subtle features to make them more of a championship caliber.

The **Blue Course** was redesigned by Nicklaus in 1985, and was improved with more updated features such as mounding and grass bunkers. The greens were replaced with bent-grass, and waterfalls were added around holes 5 and 11.

Long considered the lesser of the two tracks, the **Gold Course** was redesigned by Nicklaus in 1989, bringing it up to the standards of the Blue. The design incorporates eight lakes and plays over 7,000 yards.

The details   972-279-6517. 4111 La Prada Dr., Dallas, TX 75228

- Blue Course: 1954. Gold – 6,766 (73.4/133). Blue – 6,293 (71.2/130). White – 6,007 (69.6/126). Red – 5,363 (71.8/119). Price - $$$$.
- Gold Course: 1962. Gold – 6,993 (73.5/136). Blue – 6,349 (70.4/126). White – 5,891 (67.8/118). Red – 5,197 (70.0/115). Price - $$$$.

Getting there From I-635, get off at the La Prada exit and turn right. The course is just down the road on the right side.

DALLAS COUNTRY CLUB

The golf   Located in the middle of Dallas' most prestigious area, the old DCC was formed in 1896, the oldest club in Texas and one of the oldest in the nation. It's hard to imagine the time when Highland Park was out in the country, way north of downtown, but this land along the banks of Turtle Creek was indeed out in the boonies, more a haven for cotton farming than a playground for Dallas businessmen.

Tom Bendelow (Medinah CC in Chicago), who made his living building courses for $25 per course, came through in 1908 to start what was his 500th some-odd project. A prairie-style clubhouse was built, and golf was on its way to becoming the game in Dallas.

In 2001, architect Jay Morrish totally redesigned the course, making "the easiest course in Dallas" much tougher for its blue blood membership. Tight in layout, DCC is a small gem that exhibits meticulous landscaping, making the most of Turtle Creek and an abundance of azaleas, tulips and dogwoods. Two beautiful par 3s back-to-back at 15 and 16. Thanks to its length, layout and setting, most visitors end their round saying, "That was a really fun course to play." Longtime pro Billy Harris knows everyone and runs one of the best pro shops in town.

The details   214-521-2151. 4100 Beverly Dr., Dallas, TX 75205

- 1912. Tom Bendelow. 18 holes. Par 70. Back – 6,266 (70.3/126). Middle – 5,868 (68.1/119). Forward – 5,411 (71.6/122). Price - $$$$.

Getting there From the North Dallas Tollway going south, take the Mockingbird exit and go east until you see the first driveway after Preston Rd. Note: Across the street is Highland Park Village, the city's most stylish shopping center with great restaurants—a dream for the "golf widow."

It's still good sportsmanship to not pick up lost balls while they are still rolling. Mark Twain

DALLAS NATIONAL GOLF CLUB

The golf   Referred to as "the best piece of land left in America close to a downtown" by architect Tom Fazio, ultra-exclusive Dallas National sets a new standard for golf in Dallas. Created with the aim of obtaining a major championship, the course opened in 2002 in an amazing spot just 6 miles southeast of downtown in old Oak Cliff.

The land itself was once owned by a cement company that was unable to effectively use the land, and the city of Dallas refused to zone the area because of an escarpment that slices the landscape. Result: the perfect opportunity to use the terrain for golf. But this isn't just your normal run-of-the-mill upscale daily-fee development. The big boys play here—guys like Tom Hicks and Roger Staubach—and there's a hefty price tag of $150,000 to become one of 350 members.

The $30 million cost to build, Fazio name, superb location, and stunning landscape combine to make one of the highest-profile facilities that has ever graced the great state of Texas. Dallasites would be shocked to learn of the spectacular elevation changes that reside so close to their flat city. Tipping out at over 7,300 yards, the par 72 track spreads out over almost 400 acres of limestone canyons, winding creek beds, and large plateaus, with up to 160 feet of elevation changes.

Every hole is a signature hole, with Fazio's signature bunkers defining the immaculate zoysia fairways. The natural appearance of the course is accentuated by the subtle reddish-tan cart paths, and artistic wooden bridges span the limestone ravines. Many holes offer elevated tees and impressive views of the city. On May 1, 2003, a massive fire burned the new clubhouse to the ground; however, owners said they would begin rebuilding immediately.

And while the USGA gave the course one of the highest slope ratings ever (155), which is sure to help the club attract a big-time tournament, wealthy hacks can enjoy themselves from one of the other six remaining sets of tees.

The details   214-331-6144. 1515 Knoxville Rd., Dallas, TX 75211

• 2002. Tom Fazio. 18 holes. Par 72. 7,326 yards (155). Price - $$$$.

Getting there Just east of Loop 12 between Keeneland Pkwy. and Jefferson Blvd. south of I-30.

HANK HANEY AT PARK LANE

The golf   Formerly known as the Dallas Family Golf Center, this was once primarily a miniature golf-batting cage facility with only a 4-hole short course. Hank Haney assumed ownership in recent years, expanding his umbrella of golf practice facilities.

This facility now features a grass driving range and a short game practice area and putting green, as well as a short par 3 pitch-and-putt course. The holes on the 9-hole course range from 48-78 yards, with water and sand spic-

---

Every rock'n'roll band I know, guys with long hair and tattoos, plays golf now. Alice Cooper, 47

ing up the layout. There are also three 18-hole miniature golf courses, a dozen batting cages, and a restaurant/meeting facility known as The Ranch on site.

The details 214-341-9600. 8787 Park Ln., Dallas, TX 75231

• 9 holes. Par 27. About 600 yards. Price - $.

Getting there Located 2 miles east of I-75 off of Park Ln.

KEETON PARK GOLF COURSE

The golf Built in 1979 in the floodplain of the Elm Fork Trinity River, this course was designed with the average golfer in mind. Numerous lakes and ponds require accurate shot-making. In fact, water is in play on all but 3 holes and often impacts both the tee and approach shots.

The tree-lined fairways are plush, and the greens are medium in size and speed. The signature hole is No. 3, a 538-yard par 5 that plays into the wind and features a double-dogleg fairway that is tree-lined on the left and offers a cluster of trees with a pond on the right. This hole veers left off the tee through a chute of trees and a pond on the right, then back to the left on the second shot as the fairway slides down to a green nestled in a thick grove of trees. Players need to hook the second shot in order to approach the small, elevated green.

No. 6 is tough as well: a sweeping dogleg with two ponds on the right side of the fairway. The approach is into an elevated green on a peninsula with water behind and on both sides.

The details 214-670-8784. 2323 N. Jim Miller Rd., Dallas, TX 75227

• www.keetonpark.com

• 1978. 18 holes. Par 72. Back – 6,511 (70.6/113). Middle – 6,062 (68.6/113). Forward – 5,504 (68.1/113). Price - $$.

Getting there From I-30 east, take the Jim Miller Rd. exit and go south for 2.5 miles. The course is on the right.

CHRISTMAS DAY GOLF

The city of Dallas opens their courses (free of charge) for play on Christmas Day. There are no tee times, the clubhouses are closed, so there is no food or drink. But on those fortunate Christmas days of 40-degree temps and clear skies, combined with a much-needed break from family holiday festivities, it's ideal to sneak out to walk nine holes and work on your game. Enjoy the minimal crowds, fresh air, and the chance to try out the new golf gear Santa brought you.

I'll always remember the day I broke ninety. I had a few beers in the clubhouse and was so excited I forgot to play the round. George Burns

L.B. HOUSTON PARK GOLF COURSE

The golf   L.B. Houston is a crusty old Dallas municipal that hosts upwards of 80,000 rounds per year. It's located in the floodplains of the Elm fork of the Trinity River just west of I-35 between Northwest Hwy. and Hwy. 635.

This municipal course has water hazards coming into play on the front nine, and many trees that can alter your shots on the back nine. In the process of building this course, Leon Howard had 300,000-plus yards of dirt moved, creating 11 lakes and ponds, and used the fill to elevate the greens and tees. Dave Bennett redesigned this course in 1982.

All four par 3s require a carry over water. The course plays to a strong finish with the 545-yard, par 5 17th hole and the 436-yard No. 18. No. 17 intimidates the average hacker when playing into the prevailing south wind. The hole narrows significantly to about 250 yards from the back tees, with the extremely small landing area framed by two huge trees and lies just in front of a creek that crosses the fairway. If the tee shot isn't perfect, you have no angle for a solid second shot.

The well-stocked pro shop and locker room facilities are nice amenities—ones you usually don't see at municipal courses. A nice-sized putting green helps pass the time while waiting to tee off. This is an easy walking course for those looking for some exercise—the wooded terrain makes you forget you're smack in the middle of Dallas.

The details   214-670-6322. 11223 Luna Rd., Dallas, TX 75229

- www.cedarcrestgolf.com

- 1969. Leon Howard and Dave Bennett. 18 holes. Par 72. Back – 6,705 (70.8/126). Middle – 6,290 (69.8/120). Forward – 5,596 (72.8/113). Price - $$.

Getting there From I-35 south, take Hwy. 635 west and exit Luna Rd. Drive south and the club is on the right.

LAKEWOOD COUNTRY CLUB

The golf   Dallas experienced the golf craze after Dallas Country Club opened around the turn of the century, enabling clubs like Lakewood, which was founded in 1912, to generate the necessary funds to become established and build golf courses. Located in one of Dallas' oldest and most beautiful areas, Lakewood was originally designed by Tom Bendelow. The course layout was later influenced by Ralph Plummer in the 1940s, then by Ben Crenshaw and Bill Coore in the mid-1990s. The Dallas Open, now known as the Byron Nelson Classic, began here, and this private course has always had the unique, old-school charm of the greats.

The course lulls you into a false sense of confidence with its average 330-yard downhill opener, which can be reachable by the big hitters and should

Golf tips are like aspirin. One may do you good, but if you swallow the whole bottle you will be
lucky to survive. Harvey Penick

definitely be attacked as a par hole. However, holes 2-4 are the toughest on the course and can destroy the round early if not handled appropriately. Hole 2 doglegs left for 432 yards along an out-of-bounds line into a green that is surrounded by bunkers. No. 3 is longer, again doglegging left, this time with bunkers and a creek on the lefty side. The 4th is a solid three shot par 5 for most golfers, playing 554 yards and not what you'll be looking for after Nos. 2 and 3.

Also on the front is No. 7, considered the signature by some: a long iron par 3 from an elevated tee over water to a scenic, well-bunkered green framed by old oak trees.

The shorter back side eases up some, with only one average length par 5 and a short par 3. This side features a few challenging holes however, particularly in the long 400-yard-plus par 4s.

The details   214-821-7690. 6430 Gaston Ave., Dallas, TX 75214

- 1912. 18 holes. Golf – 6,635 (72.1/127). Blue – 6,323 (70.5/122). White – 5,956 (68.7/117). Forward – 5,418 (71.2/119). Price - $$$.

Getting there From I-30 east, exit Munger St. exit and turn left. When you come to Columbia St., turn right and it will turn into Abrams St. The course is only a short distance away from the point where the street changes names, and is on the right-hand side.

NORTH TEXAS GOLF CENTER

The golf   Not many know it's there, but in the floodplains west of I-35 there is a little gem of a lighted 9-hole track, complete with $1 beer nights and a full practice facility that's the absolute best way to tune your game for weekend rounds. The course is kept in immaculate condition and presents just the right level of difficulty for short iron work. The holes range from around 65-135 yards, depending on where the tees are, and the winds can pick up to make things more difficult. Out-of-bounds comes into play on a few holes, but water isn't in play unless you crush irons way over the green on holes that back up to the small irrigation lake that borders the course.

The best hole is No. 9, a deceptive 130-yard hole that can play longer if they place the tees back on a peninsula-like the area near the lake. The green is somewhat elevated and bordered on the left by a huge bunker, creating an almost island-like look.

In addition to the course, the facility is the home of The Golf Institute golf school, which provides classes, clinics, and individual instruction.

The details   972-247-4653. 2101 Walnut Hill Ln. Dallas, TX 75229

- www.northtexasgolf.com
- 1992. 9 holes. Par 27. Back – 1,037. Forward – 812. Price - $.

A major swing change is a little like surgery. I don't know too many people who would elect to go under the knife before they tried the other, less drastic, alternatives for getting better. Dr. Bob Rotella

Getting there Take the Walnut Hill exit off of I-35 and drive west. This road will dead-end 1 mile down at the course, which is on the north side of the road.

NORTHWEST PAR 3 GOLF COURSE

The golf   Convenient if you're killing time around 635 and NW Hwy. in east Dallas and you need a place to work in a quick round, this 9-hole par 3 track has lights and a driving range to play into the night. The design offers a few holes that run alongside a creek, so hacks afflicted with the shanks could possibly get wet, but it's generally just straight-up pitch-and-putt, with the longest hole playing 84 yards. There are a few bunkers that dot this small track. While the course does not serve beer, they don't mind if you bring your own, provided you drink out of cold, cold, cans. Note that they prefer you use koozies because it's just a better way to drink beer and play golf.

The details   214-348-3693. 10726 E. NW Hwy., Dallas, TX 75238

- 1950. 9 holes. Par 27. 571 yards. Price - $.

Getting there From Hwy. 75, exit Northwest Hwy. and drive east past Plano Rd. The course is 300 yards past Plano Rd.

THE NORTHWOOD CLUB

The golf   Northwood is a private, traditional course that held the US Open won by Julius Boros in 1952. In 1947, a man named Bill Diddel came down from Indianapolis to design what ended up being his only Texas course. An amazing character, Diddel lettered in just about every sport except golf in college but went on to win the Indiana Amateur several times in the early 1900s. Incredibly, Diddel survived to the age of 101, bagging over 1,000 rounds of golf where he shot his age or better.

Diddel's track was updated in 1990 by Tom Weiskopf and Jay Morrish, and the new track consistently earns recognition for some of the toughest holes in the DFW area.

White Rock Creek winds through the course and comes into play on numerous holes, and loads of long par 4s beat down players who lack big-time length. The signature is perhaps the 213-yard No. 16, which tees through a chute of trees down a fairway lined by water on the left.

The details   972-934-0544. 6524 Alpha Rd., Dallas, TX 75240

- 1947. Bill Diddel. 18 holes. Par 71. Gold – 6,835 (72.9/131). Blue – 6,324 (70.4/127). White – 5,812 (67.7/123). Red – 5,314 (71.0/123). Price - $$$$.

Getting there From Hwy. 635 east, take the Preston Rd. exit and turn left. When you come to Alpha Rd., turn right and the course is just down the road on the right.

There are really two ways of increasing your distance. You can learn to swing the clubhead faster.
Or you can learn to deliver it to the ball more accurately. Jack Nicklaus

OAK CLIFF COUNTRY CLUB

The golf Press Maxwell came along in 1952 to mold this 171-acre tract highlighted by ancient oaks and Five Mile Creek into the course that eventually became home to the PGA Tour's Dallas Open. The tourney was held here from 1958-1962, then again from 1964-1967.

Maxwell's design features small greens and a few of the toughest holes in Dallas. Water hazards come into play on many holes, including the 176-yard No. 3. On the back, Nos. 10 and 13 stand out because of their challenges. No. 10 doglegs left and requires a perfect tee shot to set up the approach into the tiny green. This approach is intimidating because of the creek on the left side of the fairway. No. 13 requires a 3 wood from the tips, playing 226 yards into a sloping green that is covered by bunkers.

Other notes: The first club pro to win a PGA Tour event was Oak Cliff's Earl Stewart, who won the Dallas Open in 1961.

The details 214-333-3595. 2200 W. Red Bird Ln., Dallas, TX 75232

• www.oakcliffcc.com

• 1953. Press Maxwell. Blue – 6,630 (72.1/129). White – 6,167 (69.8/122). Gold – 5,763 (67.6/117). Red – 5,465 (72.0/123). Price - $$$.

Getting there From I-35 south take the Hwy. 67 split and head towards the Cleburne/Hampton Exit and turn left. Find Red Bird Ln. and turn left again. The course is on the right-hand side.

PRESTON TRAIL GOLF CLUB

The golf What makes this one of the best golf courses in the state? Let's list the reasons: Location: Far north Dallas, with White Rock Creek meandering through. Layout: Stunning and traditional, with tree-lined fairways, the right amount of water and bunkering, and huge, lightning-fast bent-grass greens. Feel: Cart paths run the way they should—from greens to tees, not the other way around. And caddies are always available to promote playing the game on foot. Mystique: Memorabilia of professional tour players who are also members is tastefully distributed throughout the clubhouse, and the shrine to Mickey Mantle (a longtime member) is awe-inspiring. You'll need serious connections to play this course, but here are some highlights.

The third hole is a 591-yard par 5 with a narrow tee shot that opens to a wide landing area. The homes lining the right side of the fairway no doubt shelter some of the most jealous people in the world. The second shot begins to run down the dramatic slope that ends in a huge green in front of the creek.

The next par 5, the 498-yard 6th, has a similar slope which begins in the landing area of your drive. If you really pop it and have the wind, you'll be at the base of the hill with about 175 yards left to the large, two-tiered green. Be careful, though–it's protected by dense woods on the left and back, and water

The devoted golfer is an anguished soul who has learned a lot about putting, just as an avalanche victim has learned a lot about snow. Dan Jenkins

on the front and right.

The 7th hole is the number one handicap. This 422-yard par 4 dogleg right requires a perfectly faded and long tee shot to get far enough into the throat to approach. You'll still be hitting a long iron or wood into the severely back-to-front sloped green, and good luck making the putt from above the hole.

The back nine is maybe the best anywhere, but two holes stand out above the rest. The 16th is a 428-yard par 4 with a slight dogleg left. The tee shot is elevated at least 100 yards above where the green sits. A big, high draw will put you about 150 yards away from the two-tiered green, which is protected by the creek in front. They really like to put the pin on the lower tier right in front of the creek, which gives you about 20 square yards to work with. It's a lay-up hole for all but the longest and bravest.

The 422-yard dogleg-right finishing hole is almost a mirror of the 16th–it's a long dogleg right, all uphill. The tee area is extremely narrow from the tips, and the fairway slopes to the left to make shaving the corner as hard as possible. This ends up being a 5 par for most, and the outcome of many Nassaus is changed on this hole.

It's hard to describe this course without gushing, not to mention that hearing about it just frustrates most people because they won't have a chance to see it for themselves. But keep your eyes and ears open for friends who may be members and schmooze them as much as possible–it will surely be worth the effort.

The details   972-380-0669. 17201 Preston Trail Dr., Dallas, TX 75248

- 1965. Ralph Plummer. 18 holes. Par 72. Back – 7,091 (73.8/133). Forward – 6,623 (72.1/129). Price - $$$$.

Getting there From downtown Dallas, take the Tollway north to Westgrove. Turn right and head down to Preston Trail Dr. Turn left and the course is straight ahead

PRESTONWOOD COUNTRY CLUB

The golf   When Dallas began to sprawl to the north in the 1960s, Prestonwood Country Club opened to serve the families that would inevitably follow the migration.

The **Creek Course** was the original track, carved out of the live oaks and pecans. Spotted with creeks and lakes, it is the tighter and more difficult of the two courses. Water comes into play on 16 of 18 holes, and many approaches require carries of the lakes and creeks. Four holes stand out on the Creeks, including the demanding 410-yard opener. Two long par 5s, Nos. 5 and 17, can eat you alive, and the 230-yard No. 17 has been the cause of many ruined rounds.

Everyone has had the experience and knows how annoying it is hearing the swish of a club behind him just as he is in the midst of his swing. He has to be very fond of the culprit to restrain a desire to bash him on the head with the club, even when he knows that the guilt is only of thoughtlessness. Bobby Jones

The **Hills Course,** built almost 20 years after the club opened, is a more forgiving links-style design with wide fairways and large greens. Dave Bennett designed the course, which features pot and grass bunkers, as well as tough, undulating greens. The feature hole on the Hills is the 217-yard No. 4.

The details   972-239-7111. 15909 Preston Rd., Dallas, TX 75248

- www.prestonwoodcc.org
- Creek Course: 1965. Ralph Plummer. 18 holes. Par 72. Back – 6,515 (72.9/128). Middle – 6,135 (71.8/122). Forward – 5,223 (70.5/126). Price - $$$$.
- Hills Course: 1986. Dave Bennett. 18 holes. Par 72. Back – 6,496 (71.5/126). Middle – 6,040 (70.5/120). Forward – 5,325 (70.7/128). Price - $$$$.

Getting there From I-635, exit Preston Rd. and turn left. The course is on the left side of the road.

ROYAL OAKS COUNTRY CLUB

The golf   Royal Oaks opened in 1969 with a difficult Don January and Billy Martindale design, which was made even more challenging with Jay Morrish's renovation in 1985. The course lays out in the floodplain of White Rock Creek just east of I-75 north of downtown Dallas, and was noted in the late 1990s as the home course for US Amateur and British Open Champion Justin Leonard.

Some of the most demanding holes in the DFW area reside here, including the signature 467-yard, par 4 13th–a truly a pro-only hole that features loads of trees and huge carries. No. 13 doglegs around White Rock Creek, and involves a tee shot over water, followed by a mammoth approach shot that must carry the creek again.

The details   214-691-0339. 7915 Greenville Ave., Dallas, TX 75231

- 1969. Martindale-January. 18 holes. Par 71. Back – 6,960 (74.2/141). Middle – 6,541 (72.3/133). Forward – 5,407 (72.7/128). Price - $$$$.

Getting there From I-635 east, take the Greenville Ave. exit and turn right. The course is 3 miles down the road on the right.

SLEEPY HOLLOW GOLF & COUNTRY CLUB

The golf   Once one of Dallas' hot spots for golf back in the 1950s and '60s, Sleepy Hollow has lost a little of its luster over the years, but still offers an interesting day of golf for those willing to slip south on I-45. The former private club is now a semi-private facility, with every amenity shut down except for the golf. It's like going back into the 1960s when you drive onto the

I like to see players turn putting practice into a game. Putting contests with a friend are far more beneficial than working on your stroke on the putting green. Dr. Bob Rotella

premises to search for the bare-bones pro shop.

While some consideration should be given to the fact that we played after a week of intense rain, creating wild, unkempt course conditions, there's no mistaking the ghost-town feel of what was once a bustling country club.

The **Lake Course** is the simpler layout of the two, playing only 6,052 yards from the tips with only one par 4 over 400 yards. Much of its length comes from the solid par 5s that average 550 yards. Two holes stand out on the front nine. No. 2 goes 529 yards into a sharp dogleg with a pond guarding the corner, and No. 7 is a long par 4, playing 425 yards with a lake along the entire left side.

The **River Course**, while unnoticed these days, is still one of the toughest golf courses in the DFW area. Extremely long with loads of trees, water, and bunkers, hole after hole is punishing and can beat down even the most accomplished golfer. Don't play this from the tips unless you have to. If you do, you'll be faced with a 634-yard par 5, followed by a 238-yard par 3 on the front.

The back nine is pure murder, featuring an island green and holes that get progressively more difficult as you plod your way through the round. The dogleg left, 435-yard No. 14 didn't yield a single birdie during one minor-league bush tournament, when 150 aspiring pros took their best shots. No. 16 is almost 600 yards, lined by the Trinity River and doglegging to the right. Hole 17 goes 205 yards through a tunnel of giant trees and is the last thing you'll be ready for when you're limping home.

Other notes: 1956 U.S. Open champion Cary Middlecoff was once the head pro at Sleepy Hollow, and SMU great Doak Walker was the club's first champion.

The details   214-371-3433. 4747 S. Loop 12, Dallas, TX 75216

- Lake: 1956. Press Maxwell. 18 holes. Par 70. Back – 6,052 (68.3/108). Middle – 5,650 (66.3/107). Forward – 5,210 (69.5/114). Price - $$.
- River: 1956. Press Maxwell. 18 holes. Par 71. Back – 7,031 (73.4/125). Middle – 6,450 (70.7/118). Forward – 5,878 (74.1/123). Price - $$.

Getting there From downtown Dallas, take I-45 south and find the South Loop 12 exit. Take Loop 12 east and the club is just down the road on the left.

STEVENS PARK GOLF COURSE

The golf   Stevens is another Dallas tradition that dates back to the 1920s–a tight course with unbelievably small greens and wild doglegged holes that laugh at drivers. Creeks and streams dot the landscape, and those tiny greens are fast.

No. 6 is listed as the most difficult hole, rolling 416 yards with out-of-bounds on the right. The approach must carry a swale and slide through a chute of trees to the table-top green. Hole 8 has some character at only 272

Walter Travis, probably the greatest putter the game has ever seen, always said that he visualized the putting stroke as an attempt to drive an imaginary tack into the back of the ball. Bobby Jones

yards, with the creek cutting across the fairway and the old-ass trees over-hanging and squeezing the fairway.

The ender is impossible to shorten because there's no way to carry the giant trees and cut the dogleg. That leaves you with a weak-minded long iron that must be played perfectly. Get the right club on your approach because the green has two levels.

Other notes: Arthur Davis redesigned this course in 1983.

The details   214-670-7506. 1005 N. Montclair Ave., Dallas, TX 75208

• 1922. 18 holes. Par 71. Back – 6,005 (69.2/120). Middle – 5,544 (68.5/114). Forward – 5,007 (68.0/118). Price - $$.

Getting there From I-30 east, take the Hampton exit and go south. Turn left on Colorado, then turn right on N. Montclair Ave.

TENISON PARK GOLF COURSE

The golf   Built by Dallas banker E.O. Tenison after World War I as a memorial to his son who died in the war, Tenison Park has a storied history as Texas' most infamous hustlers course—the place where guys like Titanic Thompson and Lee Trevino earned their livings and their reputations. The original West course was laid out by Jack Burke and Syd Cooper in 1925, and was followed by the Ralph Plummer-designed East course in the 1950s. Yet over the years, like the neighborhood around it, the course fell victim to neglect and its conditions deteriorated significantly.

However, in the 1990s the city renovated the musty old clubhouse with a fitting rock-walled design. The practice range across the road from the clubhouse was upgraded, and more signs of improvement were on the horizon. Then Dallas hired D.A. Weibring's design firm to replace the West course, which opened for play in 2000 with a completely different look and name.

Now known as the **Highlands Course**, this track is the upscale, modern alternative to the budget-minded Glens Course, which is the new name for the old East course that has not been updated. Though the course is still hilly like the old days, many of the old trees were knocked down, water was added, and the greens were replaced. Many of the new greens offer wicked multi-level three-jack opportunities (especially holes 9 and 14).

Bunkers were added to spice up the design as well—a much-needed update to the old, bunkerless track. One of those bunkers fronts the elevated par 3 No. 5 green, which usually plays as a long iron and is tricky because of the huge oak tree that looms left. Another good hole on the front side is the 332-yard No. 7, which is reachable for big hitters from the more forward tees but is lined by a lake on the left. The play on No. 7 is to hit a mid-iron past the 150-yard marker.

On the back, the best birdie opportunity is No. 13, a relatively short par 3

The best way to putt is the way you putt best. Old golf saying that plays over a pond. No. 14 plays straight up one of the steepest hills in Dallas—it's tough because of its three-level green and blind approach. No. 15 goes back down the hill, offering the chance to get a few strokes back with a long drive and short iron approach.

The ender is a great hole as well, doglegging right as a longish par 4. You'll need a good drive long and left to set up the approach over the massive swale to the green that is fronted by steep-sided bunkers.

White Rock Creek is the predominant feature of the **Glens Course**, snaking across the route and providing a haven for stragglers looking to cool off with a dip, bag a few spare balls to sell, or even catch a catfish or two for supper. It's hard to believe but we've seen them, swimming around like it was Caddy Day at Bushwood.

The creek comes into play on the par 5 No. 2, which offers a challenging test of target golf, and is a nice complement to the opening hole—also a par 5 but much easier because it plays straightaway downhill and is void of hazards. This track also finishes with a par 5, a long push up the hill back to the new clubhouse.

For now the Glens, despite its confusing new name, is your chance to relive the old days of Tenison. It still sports the look and feel of the old hustler days while providing a cheaper alternative to the Highlands.

The details   214-670-1402. 3501 Samuell Blvd., Dallas, TX 75223

- www.tenisonpark.com

- Glens: 1925. 18 holes. Par 72. Champ – 6,605 (71.2/122). Challenge – 6,287 (69.6/117). Standard – 5,877 (67.7/113). Forward – 5,107 (70.8/115). Price - $$.

- Highlands: 2000. D.A. Weibring. 18 holes. Par 72. Diamond – 7,078 (73.9/139). Gold – 6,610 (71.6/124). Silver – 5,905 (68.2/119). Pearl – 4,883. Price - $$$.

Getting there From I-30 east, take the Dolphin Rd. exit and turn left. Drive over the highway to Samuel Blvd. and turn right, then make a left into the park/course entrance.

DALLAS NOTES   Texas' most modern and metropolitan city offers anything and everything for the traveling golfer. When planning a trip to Big D, it's wise to pay attention to where you'll be playing, both in and around the city, and choose a lodging option with convenient access for hauling ass to any part of the metroplex. Downtown accommodations put you near the **Main Street District**, **Deep Ellum**, the **West End Historic District**, and **McKinney-Uptown-West Village** areas, each of which offers its own unique slice of Dallas, and make it relatively easy to hop on I-30, I-35, or the Dallas Tollway to head

Close in golf usually means one more putt. Bob Murphy

any direction quickly. Also nearby is **Lower Greenville**, with its 1920s atmosphere and funky establishments, and the **Knox-Henderson** area, a diverse 2-mile swath loaded with shopping and restaurants. High-toned Highland Park and its famous **Highland Park Village** are also just a short drive north of downtown.

Most don't know that Dallas boasts more restaurants per capita than New York City (over 7,000), but especially for the golfer we'll go against our non-chain tendency and recommend one of the city's three **Hooter's** establishments, always a welcome destination for the worn-down, sunburnt, beer-buzzed golfer. For the upscale, put the venerable **Bob's Steak & Chop House** (214-528-9446) on your list for high-dollar beef, wine, cigars, and socializing. On McKinney, the preferable seafood place is the **S&D Oyster Bar**, probably one of the best classy-casual establishments where they serve the coldest Heineken on tap in the world to go with their outstanding baked redfish. The best Italian food in town is **Café Italia** on Lovers Lane, and the scene is just right. Also on Lovers track down the Dallas institution of **Rafa's**, a quaint little Mexican cafe with a great bar for sports-watching. Other nearby watering holes are the **Inwood Tavern** and **Time Out Tavern**, which round out the eclectic Lovers-Inwood intersection nicely.

For live music consider the ultra cowboy-funky casual **Adair's** for late afternoons before you hit the bigger clubs around Deep Ellum. At the edge of Deep Ellum is the historic and well-worthwhile **Sons of Hermann Hall**, where you can partake of cheap cold beers and shuffleboard or pool downstairs before stumbling up to the dance floor above.

DECATUR

Elev. 1,097   Pop. 5,284

Pre-Civil War Decatur, the seat of Wise County, is on Hwy. 81 on the way to Wichita Falls from Fort Worth, on the edge of the Grand Prairies region that overlooks the Cross Timbers. Gamblers have no doubt heard the phrase "eighter from Decatur," supposedly coined here when the railroad made its way through town in the 1880s. The town prospered as a shipping point, and has hung on over the years and even managed a bit of growth since some of its residents commute into Fort Worth to earn their living. These folks get their golf in at the 9-hole Decatur Golf & Country Club, where you can work in a quick round if you're headed towards the Indian territory.

DECATUR GOLF & COUNTRY CLUB

The golf   Everyone in Decatur takes great pride in their beautiful little 9-hole golf course, and that positive attitude is definitely on display when you deal with the ultra-friendly folks at the golf course. Always helpful, with smiles on their faces, and particularly friendly to out-of-towners, it sure makes it a joy to play golf when you're treated with that sort of charming hospitality.

Golf is even better nowadays in Decatur because of the renovated greens,

I hate a hook. It nauseates me. I could vomit. It's like a rattlesnake in your pocket. Ben Hogan

which look pristine and roll true. This course is flat, with water in play on about 3 holes, and the par 36 design offers a good combination of holes. The opener is testy, and not an easy par–it plays 440 yards to a par 4. There are three par 3s, two of which require long irons, and three par 5s, one of which is listed as the number one handicap: the No. 6 hole at 542 yards.

The details   940-627-3789. 211 Country Club Rd., Decatur, TX 76234

- 1950. 9 holes. Par 36. Back – 3,233 (35.0/108). Middle – 3,122 (35.3/111). Forward – 2,597. Price - $.

Getting there From Hwy. 380 exit, take the Airport exit and cross over the highway. Veer right and turn left at the stop sign. Turn right on Country Club Dr.

DECATUR NOTES   Up the road on US 81 in Alvord, TX is **Brushy Creek Vineyards** (940-427-4747), where the tasting room offers samples of the local moonshine. B&B options are **The Heritage House** (940-627-3736), the **Grasslands Bed & Barn** (940-627-7176) out on the **LBJ National Grasslands**. By the railroad tracks there's the **Whistle Stop Cafe** or find **Yesterday's Texas** (940-627-5866) on 287, a nice 1950s-style joint. Beer drinkers need to eat at the **Cow Camp Steakhouse** (627-7741), where the food is outstanding, or the more lively **Frilly's** (940-626-1424), where the locals go to watch sporting events.

DENISON

Elev. 767   Pop. 22,170

Denison is a welcome spot to stop off and plan your adventures on Lake Texoma. Located on US 75 just south of the Oklahoma border, it has been called "The Gateway City" because of the amenities it provides for those traveling south into Texas. While Denison is a clean, vibrant town that has been designated a Texas Main Street City, it's titillating to imagine its rugged history as a railroad tent city inhabited by gamblers, whores, and places of ill-repute.

DENISON COUNTRY CLUB

The golf   DCC is a basic 18-hole track that features only one par 4 over 400 yards. The fairways are of standard width and are lined by mature trees, but what you'll remember after your round are the extremely small greens. If you can nail the approach shots, it's pretty much birdies galore here because the course is short and doesn't offer up too many hazards.

On the front, the most difficult hole is the long par 5 No. 9, which plays 572 yards from the back. The back nine, like the front, is loaded with short par 3s that play from 300 to 350 yards.

The common error is taking the club back too far and decelerating through impact, which is like a boxer pulling his punches. It causes all sorts of mishit and misdirected pitch shots. Tom Watson

The details   903-465-4488. Hwy. 84 N., Denison, TX 75020

- 18 holes. Par 71. Back – 6,149 (69.0/113). Middle – 5,991 (68.3/112). Forward – 4,958 (66.9/110). Price - $.

Getting there From Hwy. 75, take Hwy. 84 west to the course.

GRAYSON COLLEGE GOLF COURSE

The golf   Formerly an Air Force base, Grayson College serves up an 18-hole track known for its windy conditions. The front nine was designed by Joe Finger, which is evident because of the multitude of long par 4s that play right around 400 yards. The back nine isn't as lengthy, featuring a par 4 under 300 yards, and three par 5s that are solid birdie opportunities for good golfers.

The details   903-786-9719. 7109 Dinn St., Denison, TX 75020

- 18 holes. Par 72. Back – 6,633 (71.0/118). Middle – 6,220 (69.7/112). Forward – 4,818 (67.7/108). Price - $.

Getting there From Hwy. 75 north, take County Rd. 691 west (left). Before the water tower make the first two rights; the course is on the right.

DENISON NOTES   Main Street in historic downtown Denison has become a little artists' mecca, with galleries popping up in the quaint shops that line the neat-looking streets. Nearby the **Katy Depot**, the old railroad house that helped spur the town's growth, houses restaurants, shops, and local businesses. **Lake Texoma** is just up the road, one of the great lakes of Texas with all sorts of recreational opportunities. The best places to eat are the **Cotton Patch Cafe** (903-464-0067) on US 75, or the **Railhead Steak House & Club** (903-463-5289) on S. Austin.

DENNIS   Elev. 728   Pop. 201

There's just not much to Dennis, a town that rests on FM 1543 about 15 miles southwest of Weatherford and home to only a few hundred folks. The town's roots go back to an 1892 Brazos River bridge that gave rise to development, and the community grew to serve the area's farmers and ranchers. Restless golfers in the DFW area know about Dennis because of the outstanding little Sugar Tree golf course that rolls along the river. Rural and off-the-beaten-path, it's an affordable road trip destination that's worth the drive for any golfer.

SUGAR TREE GOLF & COUNTRY CLUB

The golf   Fort Worth area golfers know about Sugar Tree, but unfortunately the news hasn't spread much further about this must-play golfing gem laid out on the banks of the Brazos River. Built by Phil Lumsden on his ranch, this is a course easy to fall in love with because of its unique character and small-town charm. Every hole is memorable, with magnificent old oak trees, 55 bunkers in play, water in play on most of the holes, lots of interesting blind golf shots, and quality, average-size greens that putt true.

No. 1 is one of the better holes, a challenging, 402-yard par 4 with a creek along the left that cuts in front of the green. Hole 5 also stands out on the front, highlighted by the trees in the center of the fairway–you'll need to pay attention to your tee shot on this long par 5.

On the back the signature 210-yard No. 12 features a creek that runs from the left of the tee across the fairway, with a neat-looking water wheel by the green providing some country charm. On the 15th, Lumsden's old barn is next to the fairway, another example of Sugar Tree's rugged character.

The details   817-596-0020. Hwy. 1189, Dennis, TX 76439

- www.sugartreegolf.com
- 1987. Phil Lumsden. 18 holes. Par 71. Gold – 6,726 (72.8/138). Blue – 6,237 (69.8/126). White – 5,826 (67.8/124). Red – 5,254 (71.0/125). Price - $$.

Getting there From I-20 west, take Exit 403 and turn left. Drive 10 miles south until you cross the Brazos River. The course is only a short distance away after crossing the river, and the entrance is on the right side of the street.

DENNIS NOTES   The **La Quinta** in town is brand new, and a good place to grab a bite is **Baker's Ribs** . But the only way to do Sugar Tree right is renting one of their two houses on the river, called **The Retreat**, and bringing your own food to make a weekend of it. The best part is that those accommodations come with a **private 6-hole golf course** that allows for all sorts of creative golf games (try the blind shots over the houses), as well as river frontage for fishing and outdoor grill accommodations. In town, the old-school meat market **Hamilton's** can provide all of the meat you'll need. This is an option that truly makes Sugar Tree special. For reservations, call the club.

DENTON   Elev. 620   Pop. 76,933

Denton is starting to get sucked in by the sprawl of DFW. Once its own unique town, now it's hard to tell you've left Dallas when you head north on I-35. To see the city you have to venture off the highway into the streets of old Denton. Named after pioneer barrister and preacher John B. Denton, whose grave is on the stately Denton County Courthouse lawn, the town dates back to the 1850s when it became the seat of Denton County. Two universities call Denton home: the University of North Texas, home of the fighting mean green Eagles, and the largest college in the nation for women, Texas Woman's University.

DENTON COUNTRY CLUB

The golf   DCC opened in 1922, when members transformed their cow pasture into a 9-hole golf course with sand greens. The club closed during the Depression, then again during World War II, but eventually reopened and began a long process of improvements. Eventually the greens were replaced with grass and the club added an additional nine holes. In the 1980s, Dick Nugent came in to further modernize the old course.

Of the notable holes, No. 7 stands out as the most challenging–a slight dog-leg left with water all over the place. No. 13 has water as well, and players must carry the hazards twice on their way to the green. In addition to the creek that slices across the fairway, a bunker resides in the middle to create more havoc. Some say that No. 18 is the signature–it goes 300 yards from the tips, yet it's all uphill into an elevated green.

The details   940-387-2812. 1213 Country Club Rd., Denton, TX 76201

- Gold – 6,624 (71.4/128). Blue – 6,303 (70.0/125). White – 5,554 (66.4/114). Red – 5,054 (69.1/119). Price – $$$.

Getting there From I-35 north in Denton, turn left and drive 5 miles to Country Club Rd. The course entrance is on the left.

EAGLE POINT GOLF CLUB

The golf   Back when they called it North Texas State University, coach Fred Cobb assembled some of the greatest golf teams of all times, winning four consecutive NCAA titles from 1949 to 1952. Eagle Point, now associated with the Radisson Hotel, was the home course for those teams, but has since been improved with more water and bunker hazards, as well as enlarged Tifdwarf greens.

The fairways are firm and wide open here, and there are several short par 4s that can be reached with solid drives. One of the toughest holes is the 235-yard, par 3 No. 2, which is one difficult par when playing into the wind.

Note that since the golf course is generally run down, unprofitable, and the school needs room for expansion, the days of Eagle Point are numbered. Plans for the land include a 500-room dormitory, an athletic complex, and possibly even a new $30 million football stadium for a fighting Eagle program that somehow manages to get into bowl games despite losing records.

The details   940-565-8499. 2211 N. I-35, Denton, TX 76205

- 1940s. Par 72. Gold – 6,547 (71.2/119). Blue – 6,301 (70.1/118). White – 5,489 (66.5/107). Red – 5,056 (64.1/102). Price – $$.

Getting there From I-35 north, take the University of North Texas exit, and the course is next to the University.

NORTH
CENTRAL

Golf has probably kept more people sane than psychiatrists have. Harvey Penick

LANTANA GOLF CLUB

The golf   Lantana's golf course opened in June 2002 and has become known for its outstanding greens and black-hole-like bunkers. This Jay and Carter Morrish design combines both wide-open and tree-lined holes to present a 7,100-yard parkland-style layout in the rolling hills southwest of Denton.

The course is beautiful, highlighted by 87 hazardous bunkers and extremely thick rough. Unlike other tracks that are loaded with bunkers, these are true hazards–very deep with soft sand and high faces. Because of the varying terrain, you'll feel at times as though you're playing two different courses. Some holes route through the meadow-like rolling hills, while others are more densely wooded and feature elevation changes.

The signature hole is the downhill 165-yard No. 15, which plays into an island green.

The details   940-728-4653. 10185 Lantana Trail, Lantana, TX 76226

- www.lantanatexas.com
- 2002. Jay and Carter Morrish. 18 holes. Par 72. 7,147 yards. Price - $$$$.

Getting there From Dallas take I-35 north to FM 1171. Turn left (west) and drive 6 miles, then turn right on FM 2499. Finally, turn left on FM 407 and drive 1.5 miles.

TEXAS WOMEN'S UNIVERSITY GOLF COURSE

The golf   This old, executive-like course dates back to the 1920s and plays to a meager 5,676 yards. The design features tree-lined fairways, small, quick greens, and water in play on only a few holes.

The details   940-898-3163. Club House Dr., Denton, TX 76204

- www.twu.edu
- 1928. L. H. Moore. 18 holes. Par 69. Back – 5,676. Forward – 5,005. Price - $.

Getting there Driving west on Hwy. 380, take Ruddell to Mingo, then look for the entrance off Clubhouse Dr. The course is on the right side of the street.

WILDHORSE GOLF CLUB

The golf   The Wildhorse Golf Club is the first of three planned courses for the Robson Ranch Community outside of Denton. Designed by architect Gary Stephenson, the course opened the second nine in October 2002.

The signature hole is on the front, a 566-yard par 5 that requires a monster drive followed by two demanding approach shots.

The details   940-246-1001. 9450 Ed Robson Blvd., Denton, TX 76207

- Gary Stevenson. 18 holes. Par 72. Black – 6,892. Gold – 6,094. Burgundy – 5,612. Beige – 5,098. Price - $$$.

Nobody asked how you looked, just what you shot. Sam Snead

Getting there From Dallas take I-35 to Denton and look for the 35 W split. This takes you back toward the south to Fort Worth for 6 miles, where you'll take the Robson Ranch exit. Drive 1.5 miles west and look for the course.

DENTON NOTES   Around Denton's town square you'll find a few interesting lunch options–**Ruby's Diner** and **The Loophole** are where the locals eat. The **Oak-Hickory Historic District** displays some impressive Victorian homes and cottages, so take a look before heading out to the sticks and the town of Ponder, TX., where the **Ponder Boot Company** can help you with an investment in cowboy footwear. Then mosey to the **Ranchman's Cafe** (940-479-2221), also known as The Ponder Steakhouse, where high-toned maidens like Cindy Crawford have partaken in sirloin and live bluegrass music in this rustic setting. Don't forget to bring your own beer and call ahead to reserve a baked potato. Finally, only the most wayward golfer would make it through the town of Tioga, TX, but if you're roaming lost on the northeast side of lake Ray Roberts, **Clark's Outpost** is legendary for their country cooking.

DESOTO
Elev. 668   Pop. 37,646

Desoto, located 12 miles south of Dallas just off I-35, is a community of commuters with an estimated 90% of the population earning their living in Dallas and Grand Prairie. Ten Mile Creek runs through town, and the city limits are bordered by Cedar Hill to the west, Lancaster to the east, Duncanville and Dallas to the north, and the lesser-known Glenn Heights to the south. You'll be here for golf if you're invited to play at the mighty-fine Thorntree Country Club, which has hosted the first round of the PGA's Tour School as well as multiple Byron Nelson qualifiers over the years.

THORNTREE COUNTRY CLUB

The golf   Thorntree opened in 1984, and while it has changed ownership multiple times over the years, it remains one of the toughest courses in the DFW area. The course features six lakes and three spring-fed creeks that spice up the layout, as well as immaculate fairways and challenging bent-grass greens.

On the front, No. 5 stands out as one of the most difficult holes – a 400 yard-plus par 4 that runs through a chute of trees and doglegs right into a green sided by a pond.

The back is a bit more difficult, which you'll realize quickly due to the 666-yard double dogleg No. 10. The next hole is only a 382-yard par 4, but the approach is dicey into the shallow green. No. 13 is another nice hole–only 338 yards with another challenging approach into a green that's guarded by an old thorn tree.

Golf is a day spent in a round of strenuous idleness. William Wordsworth

The details 972-296-7317. 825 W. Wintergreen Rd., Desoto, TX 75115

- www.americangolf.com
- 1983. 18 holes. Par 72. Gold – 7,023 (74.2/140). Blue – 6,412 (71/130). White – 5,708 (67.8/121). Red – 5,170 (70/126). Green – 4,509 (66.3/111). Price - $$.

Getting there From I-35 south, take the Wintergreen Rd. exit and turn right. Drive 4 miles to the course, and the entrance is on the right side.

DESOTO NOTES Ojeda's serves great Mexican food, and Desoto could be considered chain restaurant heaven, with every possible type of food available. Take your pick, or do what we'd do and head back to Dallas or out in the sticks for true backwoods adventures.

ENNIS
Elev. 548   Pop. 15,902

Ennis, another former railroad community that dates back to the late 1800s, is located on I-45 about 20 minutes south of Dallas and is known as "The City of Bluebonnets." The town has an economy based on railroad and cotton, with over 150,000 bales ginned in 1920, eventually earning the moniker "Where Railroads and Cotton Fields Meet." Industry has worked its way into the economy, and the town is also somewhat of a bedroom community to Dallas and its southern suburbs.

ENNIS COUNTRY CLUB

The golf Formerly Lakeside Country Club, ECC is a "new" facility that continues to undergo changes as the new ownership rounds out their plans to make this the premier place for golf in Ennis.

In addition to the new nine, the original nine has been renovated. Trees have been brought in to line the fairways, so the rolling fairways are generally wide open. The highlight of the course is the large, challenging greens, many of which have severe breaks.

The details 972-875-3641. 2905 Country Club Rd., Ennis, TX 75119

- www.enniscc.com
- 1998. 18 holes. Par 71. Blue – 6,278. White – 5,866. Red – 4,890. Price - $$.

Getting there From Dallas drive south on I-45 to Hwy. 34. Turn right, drive to Jeter Rd., and turn right. The course is 2 miles down on the left.

THE SUMMIT GOLF CLUB

The golf   The Summit Golf Club is actually closer to the town of Palmer, but officially lists its address as Ennis. This blackland course is known for its lush fairways, lack of bunkers, and large, sloped greens. After construction in the late 1980s, financial problems forced delays and the club was eventually bought at auction in 1991.

The design offers a good combination of open and tree-lined holes, but is mostly a links-style course. Water is in play on 10 holes–it's the primary obstacle on this hillside track. The front nine features average-length par 4s but has two par 3s that play 220 yards, as well as the 602-yard No. 3. The back nine features the most difficult hole, the 540-yard No. 16.

The details   972-878-4653. 102 Crescent View Dr., Ennis, TX 75119

- 18 holes. Blue – 6,702 (72.1/118). White – 6,125 (69.2/113). Gold – 5,259. Red – 4,538 (65.6/97). Price - $$.

Getting there On I-45 south, take Exit 258 and turn left. Next, take the first right onto the service road and go 1 mile south. There are signs for the course.

ENNIS NOTES   Try the **Woodcreek Cafe** for margs and beers, or track down **Don Jose's**. **Marsala's** offers good Italian grub. If you've had too much to drink, buy yourself a night at the **Quality Inn** (972-875-9641) or **Best Western** (972-875-3390). Traveler's tip: Ennis is a bowling-alley kind of town, so make a night of it and splurge on some smooth lanes.

NORTH CENTRAL

EULESS
Elev. 603   Pop. 46,005

The bustling town of Euless is nestled between Fort Worth and Dallas on US 183. Originally a railroad and farming town that developed along the confluence of Big Bear and Little Bear Creeks, the community was popular during Prohibition as the spot to obtain illegal whiskey brewed by local entrepreneurs. Euless was put on the golf map by the spectacular Texas Star Golf Course, which opened in 1997 in the middle of Pipeline Road's industrial area.

TEXAS STAR GOLF COURSE

The golf   One of the best public facilities in Texas, Texas Star is ironically located in the middle of an industrial area, yet somehow sports the natural look and feel of the Hill Country. Designed by Keith Foster, this is a tough course with numerous hazards, immaculate conditions, and many unique holes.

Foster's design tips out at 6,936 yards and is a par 71. Hurricane Creek traverses the landscape, and the old oaks that line the course offer the perfect

---

Retire to what? I'm a golfer and a fisherman. I've got no place to retire to. Julius Boros

respite from the surrounding industrial community.

No. 15 is one of the better holes—a 37-yarder highlighted by a green-fronting pond and waterfall. The fairway is split due to the hazard, and a solid tee shot of at least 220 yards is required to carry the falls.

Another great hole is the scenic 179-yard No. 16, which plays downhill and is framed by a rock-lined creek on the right. No. 18 is a nice ender, going 535 yards with water everywhere. Leave yourself a short-iron approach, since the green is protected by a creek.

Note that the course is closed on Tuesdays, and in the summer the club is known to limit play to 100 golfers per day. And while some complain that it this is a cart-path-only course, the condition of the fairways more than makes up for the inconvenience.

The details   817-685-7888. 1400 Texas Star Pkwy., Euless, TX 76040

- www.texasstargolf.com
- 1997. Keith Foster. 18 holes. Par 71. Back – 6,936 (73.6/135). Middle – 6,529 (71.1/130). Forward – 4,962 (69.7/124). Price - $$$.

Getting there From the Dallas-Fort Worth Airport, take Hwy. 183 west to Hwy. 157. Drive south to Hwy. 10 and turn right. The entrance is 1 mile down and visible from the highway.

WESTDALE HILLS GOLF COURSE

The golf   Originally the "elite" Sotogrande Country Club, a fancy 1960s par 3 track that was the finest of its kind in Texas, Westdale Hills was given new life in the late 1990s after being run-down and abandoned. Part of the Westdale Hills apartment complex, the course plays around a lake, with water coming into play on most holes if you're really hacking it up. Only three holes force a carry of the water. no. 7 isn't one of those, but is considered the toughest because it plays the longest and features the complex' satellite dish in the middle of the fairway. A few bunkers allow you to work on your short game, and the well-kept Bermuda greens can get pretty quick depending on the time of year.

The details   817-267-3304. 1401 Sotogrande, Euless, TX 76040

- www.texasstargolf.com
- 1960s. 9 holes. Par 27. Blue – 2,678. White – 2,246. Price - $.

Getting there From Dallas-Fort Worth Airport, take Hwy. 183 to North Richland hills and exit Central. Dead-end at Pipeline and turn right. Drive about a half mile to El Camino Real, and turn left into the apartment complex.

EULESS NOTES   After the round, order a giant, sloppy, delicious chicken-fried steak to go with your pitcher of beer at the **Texas Star Raven's Grille**. Top off your weekend rounds in Euless at **North Main Barbecue** (817-

267-9101), where the specialty is their melt-in-your-mouth pulled pork. Open only on Fridays and Saturdays, this unique joint is located in a trucking company building on Main Street.

FAIRVIEW

Elev. 631   Pop. 2,644

Fairview, Dallas' newest bedroom community, is located on FM 1378 just 3 miles south of McKinney, and barely northeast of Plano. The growth of Plano has been the primary stimulant of Fairview's growth as a business community. Thirty-something Dallas-ites who are faced with the choice of high-dollar private schools or the gladiator academies of DISD are drawn to the rolling hills of Fairview and the appealing Heritage Ranch Golf & Country Club.

HERITAGE RANCH GOLF & COUNTRY CLUB

The golf   Heritage Ranch serves up an especially challenging par 72, 7,040-yard Arthur Hills design that rolls through the oaks and pecans just outside of Fairview. And while it's part of a gated, active-adult residential community, the course is open to the public and especially fun because it integrates well with the neighborhood. Houses line some fairways, but a fair number of holes provide that natural, rural feel that is always so welcome on a golf course.

While the course is not particularly demanding off the tees, the real challenge at Heritage Ranch comes from the mound-shaped greens. If your irons aren't dialed in, you'll be working hard for ups and downs.

No. 1 is a unique opener because it bends left down to a fairway and green that aren't visible from the tee. Big drives can get close, but the recommended play is to take a long iron and draw it over the hill.

The par 5s on the front are nice holes. No. 3 doglegs right and requires a good tee shot, followed by a relatively easy second shot into a widening fairway toward the hole. The trick is nailing the short iron (almost a blind shot) into the elevated green guarded by bunkers on the front. No. 7 is longer and offers a good chance for birdie, again because of its wide-open nature.

No. 16 is the signature hole: a par 3 masterpiece that plays along a natural spring waterfall. You'll need to nail a long iron over the valley and avoid the trees that overhang the fairway from the right.

No. 18 is a good finisher–it's a long par 4 that doglegs left around a few large fairway bunkers, then works its way uphill to an elevated, mound-shaped green surrounded by bunkers. Ups and downs are possible here if you miss the green back left, which is easy to do when you approach with a fairway wood.

The details   972-540-6633. 465 Scenic Ranch Circle, Fairview, TX 75069

The man who runs from his office to the golf club, gulps a sandwich, belches and races to the first tee has no business howling in anguish when he puts his first two shots in the woods, then tops a 3-iron into the pond. Tony Lema

- www.heritageranchgolf.com
- 2002. Arthur Hills. 18 holes. Par 72. Blue – 7,040. White – 6,472. Gold – 5,815. Red – 4,910. Price - $$$.

Getting there Only 20 miles northeast of Dallas, take I-75 north to the Stacy Rd. exit, then turn right and drive to the dead end. The road jogs to the left, then right, and continues as Stacy Rd. The entrance is 2 miles down on the left.

FAIRVIEW NOTES Lake Lavon isn't far away, so taking the back roads around the lake is a worthy side trip.The **Collin Park Marina** (972-442-3567) offers a restaurant and club, and can hook you up on any type of lake activity. Otherwise, that's pretty much it at this stage in the development of this new community. Allen, Plano, and McKinney are all nearby, with loads of options for having fun.

FARMERSVILLE   Elev. 651   Pop. 3,118

Not far from McKinney, but not totally established yet as a DFW commuter community, Farmersville is a quiet little town with quaint shops and historic buildings–it's just far enough away from the hustle and bustle of Dallas to go unnoticed. In its early days, Farmersville was a railroad shipping point for cattle and cotton. Dallas will grow here eventually, but for now it's just a great little spot for the always-needed golf day trip.

LEATHERWOOD RANCH

The golf Cal Merritt, a former real estate man, grabbed this 40-acre farm and rock quarry when times were good back before the real-estate crash in the late 1980s. The upkeep was a problem and he wasn't convinced that he was a cattle rancher, so following his passion for golf and building a golf course seemed like the perfect way to have some fun and make the place look pretty.

He's definitely succeeded with his new, self-architected Leatherwood Ranch golf course, which opened for play in 1999. Here you can escape the city, avoid the crowds, and play for a fraction of what the big city courses charge. The *Dallas Morning News* ranked Leatherwood as the 9th best 9-hole course in the state, and Leatherwood will surely grow in popularity over the years as the metroplex spreads and golfers find out about this little gem.

The design is impressively clever. It features 9 holes made up of seven par 4s and two par 3s, highlighted by small, dome-shaped greens that are extremely firm. A creek that comes into play several times, as well as a big rock quarry that adds character to the layout. The quarry comes into play on the signature hole, No. 7, which offers the risk-reward option of hitting over the quarry or laying up.

✦

Many men are more faithful to their golf partners than to their wives and have stuck with them longer. John Updike

There are no bunkers, but water comes into play quite a bit. The creek comes into play on holes 1-4. No. 6 has water on the left, and hole 8 sets up perfectly for a bad slice into the water. The hardest hole is the par 4 No. 9 because of its 334-yard length.

The best part about the day at Leatherwood is the casual, laid-back atmosphere. As Mr. Merritt states, "Blue jeans are expected." His theory that "denim is one of the most practical pairs of pants to play golf in" is something all the country club pretty boys might want to consider every now and then.

The details   972-784-7338. 607 E. Hwy. 380, Farmersville, TX 75442

• 1999. Cal Merritt. 9 holes. Par 34.Back –2,119. Forward –1,648. Price - $$.

Getting there Drive I-75 to 380 in McKinney and go east 18 miles. The course is just past the Dairy Queen on the north side.

FARMERSVILLE NOTES   Have a beer in Leatherwood's grill, which is cozy, overlooks the golf course, and is run by the attractive, vibrant daughter of the Merritts. You'll enjoy the regulars as they partake in post-round revelry that includes cold beers and karaoke. The grill offers hamburgers and hot dogs on the weekends, along with homemade desserts. For dinner, there is an all-you-can-eat catfish place on the way home in Princeton, or you can head to **Lake Lavon** and find **The Cove**. Loaded with fishing pics from the lake, it's a good spot for a deli sandwich and cold drink.

FERRIS
Elev. 468   Pop. 2,500

Ferris is south of Dallas on I-45, another former railroad town surrounded by rich mineral clays that are found in the soils. The clays of Ferris have made this a town of brick, earning the moniker "Brick Capital of the Nation" and enabling the creation of a unique golf course in the Old Brickyard.

OLD BRICKYARD GOLF COURSE

The golf   Some argue that the tricked-up golf course has no place in today's game, but they might change their mind after visiting the eclectic Old Brickyard. As the name implies, the course lays out in and around an old brickyard, featuring dramatic elevation changes, blind shots, and some unbelievable, almost impossible holes. This is one you'll want to play just to say you've seen it.

The opening holes are pretty basic as you traverse northward before turning into the meat of the course, where the dramatic elevation changes start wreaking havoc on your club selection. After about the third or fourth hole, every hole seems to have some unique feature.

The Old Brickyard Lake comes into play on holes 9-11, some of the most

---

Golf is good for the soul. You get so mad at yourself you forget to hate your enemies. Will Rogers

difficult holes you'll find anywhere. After you limp homeward suffering near-disasters on the tricky par 3 No. 8, which plays over water and seems to drop about 5 stories, and the demented 9th hole, which features a funky tee shot and challenging approach over water to a difficult green, No. 10 is not a welcome sight. Hole 10 plays from an elevated tee box, with water along the right. Water comes into play on the next two shots as well, since it cuts across the dogleg-right fairway. If you're struggling, this is a double-digit hole for sure.

There's no real break after No. 10, either. The 13th requires a precision short iron to a tiered green. More surprises await as you finish the round, so be prepared. The yard is a fun day of golf.

The details 972-842-8700. 605 N. I-45, Ferris, TX 75125

- www.oldbrickyardgolf.com
- 18 holes. Par 71. Gold – 6,486 (70.6/125). Blue – 6,056 (68.6/119). Price - $$.

Getting there Take I-45 south from Dallas to Ferris, then exit 267 and continue down the access road to the entrance on the right.

FERRIS NOTES Ferris has a **Dairy Queen** as well as a place called **Bea's Cafe** , which serves home cooking with a little more variety than DQ. The **Rocket Bar & Grill** in Rocket, TX is the perfect little backwoods bar if you're in the mood for exploration.

FLOWER MOUND Elev. 610 Pop. 50,702

Named after a 50-foot-high mound covered with Indian paintbrush, Flower Mound is the "burbs" northwest of Dallas along the shores of Lake Grapevine. After Sam Houston helped quell the Indian raids, permanent settlers moved in to take advantage of the quality soil. Unlike most Texas towns, Flower Mound was bypassed by the railroad, yet was still able to hang on as a farming and cattle-raising community. In terms of golf, this commuter town is blessed with two outstanding public courses–the famed Tour 18 and the fabulous Bridlewood Golf Course.

BRIDLEWOOD GOLF COURSE

The golf It takes a while to work your way through Lewisville's Main Street to eventually reach the back road route that rolls through the beautiful countryside west of I-35. But once you're finally able to see the lush fairways of Bridlewood just north of the road, you'll know it was worth the drive.

The course, designed by D.A. Weibring, features a spectacular combination of links-style and traditional features as it snakes its way through the flat farmlands and terrain that seems to have been specifically created for golf.

The uglier a man's legs are, the better he plays golf. It's almost a law. H. G. Wells

The front nine isn't as rugged as the back, and its first few holes feel more residential than the rest of the course. Two holes stand out. No. 8 is all carry over water at 195 yards, followed by the monster–a 463-yard par 4 that demands one helluva tee shot to avoid the water left and out-of-bounds right in finding the skinny fairway. Next comes a long, long approach that will have you begging for a bogey.

The details 972-355-4800. 4000 Windsor Dr., Flower Mound, TX 75028

• www.bridlewoodgolf.com

• D.A. Weibring. 18 holes. Par 72. Black – 7,036 (73.6/130). Blue – 6,557 (71.0/123). White – 6,061 (68.5/117). Red – 5,278 (70.7/120). Price - $$$$.

Getting there From Dallas take I-35 North to Lewisville and exit Main St. Drive west for about 7.5 miles and look for the course on the right side.

TOUR 18

The golf "America's Greatest Eighteen Holes" is an ingenious compilation of the greatest golf holes in the nation, giving golfers the chance to play replica holes from 16 top courses. This one is tough—not only because of the challenging and lengthy choice of holes that went into the design, but especially because of the lightning-fast greens and sometimes ridiculous pin placements. While the conditions are probably accurate in terms of what the pros face each week, it can be quite humbling to drop $100 on a green fee and shoot 15 strokes over your handicap because of 4- and 5-putts.

The most recognizable holes on this track are the Augusta National Amen Corner replicas, which make up the final stretch of holes 16-18. The 455-yard No. 16 starts it off, requiring a solid blind tee shot to set up the famous approach over the lake and to the green. No. 17 is the all-time classic, the famous par 3 where Tom Weiskopf once lost the tournament lead by blowing up with a 13. On the ender, a big drive can help you cut the corner of the 485-yard dogleg left, but the average golfer should lay up and prepare for a short iron into over the creek to the tough 18th green.

Other notes: Be aware that the club has a tendency to use shotgun starts in the summer months, which can load the course with hacks and slow play to 5- or 6-hour rounds—not a welcome occurrence when you're forking out such a high green fee.

The details 817-430-2000. 8718 Amen Corner, Flower Mound, TX 75022

• 18 holes. Par 72. Champs – 7,033 (74.3/138). Tournament – 6,611 (72.2/132). Men – 6,202 (69.9/127) Forward – 5,493 (66.3/119). Price - $$$$.

Getting there From Dallas take I-35 north to Lewisville and turn west on FM 1171. Drive 9.5 miles and look for the course on the right side of the road.

Love and putting are mysteries for the philosopher to solve.
Both subjects are beyond golfers. Tommy Armour

FLOWER MOUND NOTES Both golf shops here have more than adequate post-golf accommodations, so take advantage of these 19th holes before you head to your evening destination in Dallas or Fort Worth. In Flower Mound, **Cristina's Mexican Restaurant** is damn good and convenient if you need to eat before you get back on I-35.

FORNEY
Elev. 475   Pop. 6,271

Forney is new to the Texas golf map. Another old railroad and farming community located in the fertile blackland prairie east of Dallas, the town is on its way to becoming another bedroom community for Big D. The former Forney Reservoir, now known as Lake Ray Hubbard, is nearby, and the surrounding ranchlands produce cotton, corn, grain, and onions. There's never been golf in Forney, but that's changing with the Windmill Farms development centered around D.A. Weibring's 18-hole golf course.

WINDMILL FARMS

The golf D.A. Weibring's company, The Golf Resources Group, designer of Flower Mound's Bridlewood Golf Club and Prosper's Gentle Creek course, is overseeing the project in Forney, which is scheduled to open sometime in early 2004.

FORNEY NOTES Frustrated spouses can be appeased by promises of antique binges at places like **Philbeck's**. Forney is another of the many "Antique Capitals of Texas," and has several interesting stops just off the highway. For meals try the **Country Smokehouse** (972-564-1906) or **Madres' Cocina** (972-564-3287).

FORT WORTH
Elev. 670 Pop. 491,801

Fort Worth may be the perfect Texas city; it has all the elements you want, with not too much of anything. The city's appeal begins with a colorful history. A central point on the Chisholm Trail, Fort Worth in the late 1800s was home to legendary cowboys and outlaws alike, who ambled in and out of the town's famous saloons and brothels in a section appropriately named "Hell's Half Acre." Butch Cassidy, the Sundance Kid and Etta Place all called Fort Worth home, and with the coming of the railroad in 1876, the city was literally "on the map" to stay.

The oil boom brought millions to the city via generous city fathers, and the multi-billionaire Bass family has almost adopted the city like a needy child.

Go play golf. Go to the golf course. Hit the ball. Find the ball.
Repeat until the ball is in the hole. Have fun. The end. Chuck Hogan

Thanks to their leadership, the city has excellent planning, great architecture and an Arts District that is positively world class. With just 500,000 residents, Fort Worth is easy to navigate. The downtown area is friendly and has great nightlife circulating out from an area known as Sundance Square. In short, for a place nicknamed "Cowtown," Fort Worth possesses unexpected reserves of sophistication and culture.

Sam Houston gets credit for saying that "Fort Worth is where the West begins," and you can sense that when you drive through the huge ranch spreads west of town and end up in the Stockyards area, where the last real gunfight took place on Exchange Avenue. Here the local bar has saddles for stools, handmade boots are still an art form (check out **Leddy's** for the best selection) and the World's Largest Honky Tonk, **Billy Bob's Texas**, has top-drawer country music acts almost every weekend.

As the West was tamed, a generation of Fort Worth-based mavericks traded "six guns" for five irons, creating some of golf's history-making courses and characters. A couple of teenage caddies named Byron Nelson and Ben Hogan pulled bags around Glen Garden Country Club, competed against each other in caddie tournaments, and went on to rewrite the sport's record books. Marvin Leonard and John Bredemus built Colonial Country Club's National Invitational Tournament into one of the tour's most important events. And one old fart who couldn't hit straight but loved sports, golf, and Fort Worth more than life its ownself, Dan Jenkins, captured the essence of professional golf's quirky appeal in the book *Dead Solid Perfect*, a title that also fits the recreational atmosphere of his hometown.

CASINO BEACH GOLF ACADEMY

The golf   Located on Lake Worth, Casino Beach opened in 1986 and was renovated in the late 1990s. The course is known for its outstanding condition, which is always a nice feature when you pull into a par 3 course for a quick practice round. The key to scoring if your irons aren't on is to focus on accurate lag putts to avoid the dreaded three-jack. The greens are undulating and tricky if you've left the approach a ways away.

On this one you can pay once and play all day.

The details   817-237-3695. 7464 Jacksboro Hwy., Fort Worth, TX 76135

- 1986. Steve Champion. 9 holes. Par 27. Back – 1,244. Forward – 1,032. Price - $.

Getting there Take I-35 north, then take Loop 820 west and turn onto Hwy. 199. Drive over the Lake Worth Bridge and take the first exit after crossing the bridge, which will lead you directly to the course.

The EDS Byron Nelson Classic golf tournament, held at the Four Seasons Hotel and Resort, raises more money for charity (more than $5 million annually) than any other event on the PGA tour.

THE CREEKS AT BEECHWOOD

The golf   The Creeks has earned a reputation for its extreme difficulty, with one story stating that the designer himself, Greg Norman, rolled into town one day for a round and had trouble breaking par, even running out of balls in the process. And you'll do the same unless you make the less manly choice of playing from the more forward tees (copper is 5,532 yards).

Creeks literally dominate the layout, which roll through the hills on the north side of Fort Worth near Texas Motor Speedway. Elevation changes are subtle but effective, and the fairways are lined by 4-inch-thick rough and loads of oak trees, as well as the occasional outcropping.

The par 4 No. 17 is one of the most interesting holes. With creeks lining both sides and crossing the fairway twice on this 317-yard hole, you'll need to place the tee shot perfectly. The hole bends left and tempts the big hitter, especially from the forward tees.

The details   817-497-2582. 15801 Championship Pkwy., Fort Worth, TX 76177

- www.thecreeksatbeechwood.com
- Greg Norman. 18 holes. Par 72. Black – 7,133. Gold – 6,510. Copper – 5,532. Silver – 5,494. Jade – 4,949. Price - $$$$.

Getting there Located in Northeast Fort Worth, just across Hwy. 114 (across from the Texas Motor Speedway.)

COLONIAL COUNTRY CLUB

The golf   Known as one of the all-time Texas classics, Colonial Country Club opened in 1935 after Marvin Leonard hired John Bredemus to route 18 holes through the lush Trinity River bottoms and implement his newfound breed of bent-grass greens. Every honor that could be bestowed up a course has been lavished on Colonial, and the golf community has raved for over 60 years now. One of the PGA Tour's longest running tournaments, The Colonial, has been held here since 1938, and this revered monument was the first Southern club to host a US Open (1941).

The details   817-927-4221. 3735 Country Club Circle, Fort Worth, TX 76109

- Champs – 7,010 (73.7/132). Men's – 6,486 (70.9/126). Executive – 6,072 (68.8/122). Ladies – 5,745 (74.0/123). Price - $$$$.

Getting there From I-30 west, exit University and drive south. Turn right on Colonial Pkwy. and look for Country Club Circle. The course is on the right.

☆

Whitey Shafer, co-writer (with his wife, Lyndia) of George Strait's #1 hit country single, "All My Ex's Live in Texas," composed most of the song while playing golf in a local tournament.

DIAMOND OAKS GOLF & COUNTRY CLUB

The golf   Diamond Oaks dates back to 1960 when Charles Akey, who worked as the field engineer for Robert Trent Jones and Ralph Plummer, was hired to mold the densely wooded terrain around Fossil Creek. This long course is lined by oaks from tee to green, featuring water on seven holes and small greens.

Akey's design, which has been improved in recent years under the guidance of PGA Tour veteran and Fort Worth native Mark Brooks, features several menacing par 4s that are tough for any golfer. Nos. 9, 10, and 11 each play right at 450 yards. Hole 10 doglegs right over water, while No. 11 bends left with water on the right. The back nine is longer and more difficult. Following the opening two holes on the back are a 200-yard-plus par 3 and a 609-yard par 5 sandwiched between two more monstrous par 4s.

The details   817-834-6261. 5821 Diamond Oaks Dr., Fort Worth, TX 76117

• www.americangolf.com

• 1960. 18 holes. Par 70. Champs – 6,941 (72.5/120). Back – 6,719 (71.4/118). Middle – 6,467 (70.3/112). Forward – Par 72. 5,760 (73.8/126). Price - $$$.

Getting there From Loop 820 west, take Hwy. 377 south and exit at Diamond Oaks Dr., which will lead you to the course.

EAGLE MOUNTAIN COUNTRY CLUB

The golf   Don January was hired to mold this terrain along Eagle Mountain Lake, building a course once known by the wildly confusing name of Lake Country Country Club. Nine holes opened in the 1970s, and the layout was eventually expanded to 18. The course features elevation changes, tight fairways, and water hazards on 8 holes, as well as an abundance of out-of-bounds markers.

The most difficult hole is the long par 4 No. 3, which plays 428 yards. The back nine features only one par 3 and one par 5, but every par 4 plays under 400 yards.

The details   817-236-3400. 7200 Golf Club Dr., Fort Worth, TX 76179

• 1968. Don January. 18 holes. Par 72. Back – 6,550 (73.4/129). Middle – 6,279 (72.2/126). Forward – Par 74. 5,614 (74.5/127). Price - $$$.

Getting there Take Loop 820 west to the Azle Ave. exit and turn right. Travel to Boat Club Rd. and turn right, then proceed 4 miles until you see a sign.

FOSSIL CREEK GOLF COURSE

The golf   The links-style Fossil Creek was nominated by *Golf Digest* as one of the "Best New Public Courses" in the state when it opened in 1988, and

After every round, ask yourself if you feel as though you just played a game that you love. Dr. Bob Rotella

has lived up to that advance billing since then. The course is scenic, with massive trees, limestone bluffs, bubbling creeks, and numerous lakes that bring water into play on 15 of 18 holes.

The details 817-847-1900. 3401 Club Gate Dr., Fort Worth, TX 76137

- www.fossil-creek.com
- 1987. Arnold Palmer. 18 holes. Par 72. Price - $$$.

Getting there From I-35, get off at the Western Center Blvd. exit and drive to Club Gate Dr.

GLEN GARDEN GOLF & COUNTRY CLUB

The golf Glen Garden is old-school—a Texas classic where Byron Nelson and Ben Hogan learned the game as caddies back in the 1920s. One of Texas' oldest golf facilities, the old clubhouse that was built in 1912 has been replaced with a new $1.2 million facility complete with nostalgic memorabilia gracing the walls.

The Tom Bendelow-designed course offers numerous opportunities for birdie, with generous fairways that are friendly to the driver and well-conditioned greens of average speed that putt true. The layout ends with a strange twist, with four of the final five holes as par 3s. Nos. 14 and 15 are both over 200 yards, and No. 17 is the only easy par. No. 15 stands out among the group because of its blind shot to an elevated green.

Fortunately, the public can play on Mondays during the prime golf months of April to September.

In terms of nostalgia, imagine a 1927 *Caddyshack*-like Bushwood Caddy Tournament, but replace Denunzio and Danny with Hogan and Nelson. They say Nelson drained a long putt on the final hole to beat Hogan by one, and it's at least mildly humorous to imagine the crowd screaming "M..M...MISS IT!!!" as the lanky Nelson buried the clutch putt for the win.

The details 817-535-7582. 2916 Glen Garden Dr., Fort Worth, TX 76119

- 1912. Tom Bendelow. 18 holes. Par 71. Back – 6,166 (69.3/117). Middle – 5,936 (68.2/114). Forward – Par 75. 5,592 (72.1/120). Price - $$.

Getting there From I-35 south, exit Berry St. and head east to Glen Garden Dr. Turn south on Glen Garden and the course is on the right.

HAWKS CREEK GOLF COURSE

The golf The old Carswell Golf Club is renovated and boasts a new name, sporting new bent-grass greens, 419 Bermuda fairways and tees, and a new irrigation system that will hopefully keep it in the kind of superb condition that will make this a new favorite in Fort Worth. The course has been toughened

---

★

I've seen courses built on landfills, and they've ruined a
perfectly good garbage dump. Jay Moorish

up with the addition of sand and grass bunkers, as well as extensive moguls that often leave you with funky lies.

The course layout features narrow-tree lined fairways on the front, but a more generous back nine that is more susceptible to the wind. The most difficult hole is the 534-yard No. 16, a double-doglegging par 5 with a stream that winds across the fairway.

The details 817-738-8402. 6520 White Settlement Rd., Fort Worth, TX 76114

• www.hawkscreek.com

• 1950s. 18 holes. Par 71. Back – 6,568 (72.5/126). Middle – 6,189 (70.8/121). Forward – 5,586 (72.2/123). Price - $$.

Getting there Take I-35 W. south and exit 54A (TX 183). Turn right on NE 28th street and continue to White Settlement Rd. Turn left and look for the course.

IDEAL GOLF RANCH

The golf This relatively short but challenging course has been strategically laid out in and among some of the oldest oak trees in Texas. The scenic design offers two par 4s and seven par 3s, five of which have been routed between several 100-year-old oak trees. The course designer has left the natural beauty of this rugged terrain unscathed.

This course is fun, enjoyable and excellent for seniors, juniors, and ladies alike. The greens are small, medium-speed, and varying in undulation. Some are two-tiered and contain many subtle breaks. The fairways are tree-lined, extremely narrow, and vary between flat and rolling.

One of the two unique holes on this course is No. 2, a 108-yard, par 3 that requires a tee shot down a narrow, heavily tree-lined fairway to the green. The tee on this hole overlooks the course, the surrounding area, and the largest golf ball in Texas, which is this course's logo.

Hole 7 requires a tee shot to a well-protected, two-tiered green, which is set in the middle of many mature oak trees. This course truly offers target golf at its best.

The details 817-572-7312. 5151 Mansfield Hwy., Fort Worth, TX 76119.

• 1990s. Don Doherty. 18 holes. Par 70. 6,400 yards. Price - $.

Getting there From the Dallas/Fort Worth Airport, take Airport Frwy. to Loop 820 going south, exit at Mansfield Hwy., turn right, and proceed for approximately a quarter mile. The course is located just inside the loop where 820 and I-20 intersect. You can see the golf course from the 820 Frwy.

THE LINKS AT WATERCHASE

The golf Bring your best game to the Links at Waterchase—a long, difficult course that can be had if you get your mind right. Intimidating because of

---

In golf, when we hit a foul ball, we've got to go out there and play it. Sam Snead

its length (7,304 yards), much of the extra yardage comes from five excruciatingly long par 5s. The key here is to manage these holes, get on the green or close in three, then do what you have to do for your pars.

If you play regularly at a local par 3 course, you might want to work in a practice round before taking on The Links, since there's five par 3s.

Watch out for the enders on each side, which frame the scenic pond and waterfall that are sandwiched between the two greens. No. 9 is a 433-yard par 4, and requires a solid drive on the left side. Pay attention to the pin placement, as there is water behind the green. No. 18 goes 570 yards from the tips, and offers target golf at its best. You'll need to lay up at least 120 yards from the hole, and keep the approach below the pin to assure yourself of an uphill putt.

The details   817-861-4653. 8951 Creek Run Rd., Fort Worth, TX 76104

- www.linksatwaterchase.com
- Black – 7,304 (75.4/145). Gold – 7,006 (73.9/140). Blue – 6,661 (71.9/135). White – 6,175 (69.7/126). Green – 5,524 (67.5/123). Price - $$$.

Getting there Located on the east side of Fort Worth at I-30 and Eastchase Pkwy. Take the Eastchase exit and drive north to John T. White Rd. Turn right and drive a short distance, then take the first right on Randoll Mill Rd. Turn left on Creek Run Rd.

LOST CREEK GOLF CLUB

The golf   Although their mail is handled by the city of Aledo (Pop. 1,700), Lost Creek is actually located on the southwestern edge of Fort Worth and labels itself "the best golf value in Fort Worth." The course, designed by Leon Howard in 1971, has changed ownership too many times to count and is now a public course. Howard's design utilizes elevated tees and a tree-lined creek to add character to the course.

While there are two long par 4s, most holes play in the mid-300-yard range, making it a relatively short layout at only 6,388 yards. Holes of note are the 433-yard 13th, featuring a creek that crosses in front of the tee and pinches the fairway along the left side, and the difficult No. 18, where the creek cuts across the fairway twice, making it a long 526-yard hole.

The best tip for approach shots is to keep the ball below the hole, as most of the greens slope from back to front.

The details   817-244-3312. 4101 Lost Creek Blvd., Aledo, TX 76008

- 1971. Leon Howard. 18 holes. Par 71. 6,388 (70.6/115). Middle – 5,870 (69.2/113). Forward – 5,057 (68.2/110). Price - $.

Getting there From I-30 west, take the Link Crest exit and turn left. When you come to the stop sign, turn left, and drive over to Lost Creek Blvd. Turn right and follow the signs to the course.

MEADOWBROOK MUNICIPAL GOLF COURSE

The golf   Eight years before he built Colonial Country Club, John Bredemus came to Fort Worth to build Meadowbrook. The city bought the facility years later and brought Ralph Plummer in for renovations in 1962, when the creation of dams formed five new lakes and improved the irrigation system.

No. 5 should probably be a par 5 for most hackers–it plays 475 yards with water on the left of the dogleg, trees are on the right, and the approach must carry a creek. Don't worry about a bogey on this one. Hole 16 is another long par 4 that features an approach over water to the green.

The two best birdie opportunities are Nos. 7 and 14, both short par 4s that should leave you with only a short iron into the green.

The details   817-457-4616. 1815 Jenson Rd., Fort Worth, TX 76112

- www.fortworthgolf.org
- 1930. John Bredemus. 18 holes. Par 71. Back – 6,363 (70.2/126). Middle – 5,966 (68.0/118). Forward – 5,000 (68.4/116). Price - $$.

Getting there From I-30 east, take the Brent Wood Stair St. exit and turn left. When you reach Wilson Rd., turn right and look for the entrance off of Jensen Rd.

MIRA VISTA COUNTRY CLUB

The golf   Mira Vista CC opened in 1987 with a Tom Wieskopf/Jay Morrish design. The parkland-style layout rolls through hills of native grasses and wildflowers, sweeping around three lakes that spice up the course.

The duo's design isn't overly long, playing only 6,844 yards from the tips, but it boasts three par 4s over 450 yards and several long par 5s, including the 647-yard No. 6. This monster doglegs left inside a cliff that runs along the right side. Out-of-bounds is left, and a fairway bunker resides about a lob wedge from the narrow green, which is bolstered from behind by more bunkers.

No. 18 is one of the more interesting finishing holes that you'll come across, featuring two dogleg fairways, one right and one left, that both involve dealing with the creek that splits the two routes. The tee shot right is more favorable, since it is void of fairway bunkers like the ones on the left side. However, this option involves carrying two bunkers and the creek on the approach.

The details   817-294-6600. 6600 Mira Vista Blvd. Fort Worth, TX 76132

- Tournament – 6,844 (73.2/135). Champs – 6,545 (71.1/130). Member – 6,014 (68.9/119). Ladies' – 5,246 (71.0/124). Price - $$.

Getting there From I-20 west, take the Bryant/Irvin Rd. exit and turn left. Drive 2.5 miles to the course. The entrance is on the right side of the street.

It's not altogether to your advantage while standing over a 5-iron shot to be thinking, "I've got to remember to get some Freon in the Toyota." Dan Jenkins

PECAN VALLEY MUNICIPAL GOLF COURSE

The golf   The old Pecan Valley muni has evolved over the years as the successful culmination of work between the Army Corps of Engineer, the city of Fort Worth, and the Tarrant County Water Control District. When the city sold the old Worth Hills Golf Course to Texas Christian University, they were able to fund a deal to buy the 27-hole Benbrook Municipal below Lake Benbrook.

The **Hills Course** was rounded out in 1981 by Dave Bennett, who completed the addition to supplement this shorter, more wide-open course. The course is less lengthy now but water comes into play often, including the 375-yard 2nd hole that doglegs left around the water.

The **River Course**, the older of the two courses, was designed by Ralph Plummer, who made it playable for the average hack. Although two of the par 3s play well over 200 yards (Nos. 6 and 7), three of the par 5s are under 480 yards.

The details   817-249-1845. 6400 Pecan Valley Dr., Fort Worth, TX 76126

- www.fortworthgolf.com
- River: Ralph Plummer. 18 holes. Par 71. Back – 6,562 (71.3/124). Middle – 6,154 (69.7/119). Forward – Par 72. 5,419 (69.6/109). Price - $$.
- Hills: 1981. Dave Bennett. 18 holes. Par 72. Back – 6,577 (71.4/128). Middle – 6,005 (68.4/119). Forward – 5,275 (69.7/115). Price - $$.

Getting there This course is located on Lakeside Dr. in Fort Worth, just a few miles from I-10.

RIDGLEA COUNTRY CLUB

The golf   One of the state's largest country clubs, this facility offers two scenic courses that are quite challenging. The North Course is an old, traditional course that features narrow fairways and small greens. Both courses were updated in 1988 by Jay Morrish and are very well maintained

Designed by John Bredemus in 1928, the **North Course** features bent-grass greens and lush fairways, with natural streams throughout. Expect a difficult start with two long par 4s in the first five holes. The No. 4 hole plays into a green protected by water on the left and back sides.

The more difficult of the two courses, the **South Course** was designed by Ralph Plummer in 1955 and is reserved exclusively for use by men. Jay Morrish renovated the course in 1988. Hole 2 is guarded on the left by the Trinity River and is long at 450 yards. No. 10 is loaded with hazards–a lake guards the landing area that runs all the way to the back of the green. Drive it well on No. 12, where the river weaves across the fairway three times. The landing area off the tee is in a very small area at the corner of the dogleg. The Trinity affects No. 14 as well, winding across the fairway in front of the tee and again at 225 yards out.

The details 817-732-8111. 3700 Bernie Anderson Ave., Fort Worth, TX 76116

- www.ridgleacountryclub.com
- South: 1955. Ralph Plummer. 18 holes. Par 72. Back – 7,125 (73.6/131). Middle – 6,813 (72.1/127). Forward – 6,464 (70.4/124). Price - $$.
- North: 1928. John Bredemus. 18 holes. Par 71. Back – 6,467 (71.0/124). Middle – 6,097 (69.2/116). Forward – 5,527 (73.0/126). Price - $$$.

Getting there From I-30, get off at the Bernie Anderson Ave. exit and head south to the club.

RIVER CREST COUNTRY CLUB

The golf River Crest is the oldest course in Fort Worth, dating back to 1911 and preceded in the DFW area only by Dallas Country Club. Tom Bendelow, who also built the Dallas club, originally designed the course, which is relatively short by modern standards. In 1996 Williams & Gill upgraded the course and added a bit of length to the flat terrain. While there isn't much water, the narrow fairways are tough to hit consistently and the small greens are challenging targets on the approaches.

On the front nine, two of the longer holes are Nos. 3 and 5, both par 4s that go 430 and 458 yards, respectively.

Other notes: The 1984 white-columned clubhouse was honored by the Texas Society of Architects, and *Golf Magazine* once labeled the club "one of the snootiest clubs in America."

The details 817-738-9221. 1501 Western Ave., Fort Worth, TX 76107

- 1911. Tom Bendelow. 1996. Williams & Gill. 18 holes. Par 70. Back – 6,368 (70.8/132). Middle – 6,042 (69.1/128). Forward – Par 72. 5,584 (73.0/126). Price - $$.

Getting there From I-30, take the Hulen St. exit and go north. When the street dead-ends, turn right to the golf course.

ROCKWOOD MUNICIPAL GOLF COURSE

The golf The Rockwood muni dates back to the 1930s when John Bredemus added this course to his extensive design resume. Today 27 holes exist after Ralph Plummer came through for a renovation. Great examples of old-school architecture, all three nines are similar in design. The **Red** and **White Courses** are virtual twins, except that the Red Course is void of water. The **Blue Course**, considered the most difficult of the two, has the Trinity River coming into play on about seven holes and serves up one of the longest par 5s in Texas–the 667-yard No. 5.

✩

Golf is great exercise, particularly climbing in and out of the carts. Jack Berry

Other notes: The clubhouse includes a golf shop and snack shop with inside seating. A remote practice range is available, but is limited to hitting and retrieving your own golf balls.

The details   817-624-1771. 1851 Jacksboro Hwy., Fort Worth, TX 76114

- www.fortworthgolf.org
- Red/White: 18 holes. Par 71. Back – 6,340 (69.0). Middle – 6,070. Forward – Par 73. 5,566. Price - $.
- White/Blue: 18 holes. Par 71. Back – 6,794 (70.8). Middle – 6,418. Forward – Par 73. 5,778. Price - $.
- Blue/Red: 18 holes. Par 71. Back – 6,660 (69.8). Middle – 6,268. Par 73. Forward – 5,704. Price - $.

Getting there From Fort Worth, take Hwy. 199 (Jacksboro Hwy.) to the course.

SHADY OAKS COUNTRY CLUB

The golf   Home of the great Ben Hogan, and built by the famed Marvin Leonard, Shady Oaks is an exclusive club that was originally built for the average golfer. Leonard bought the land, known as the "Lone Oak Tract," from the Amon Carter Foundation and hired Robert Trent Jones to design the course over 200 acres of the 1,200-acre tract.

The signature feature of Shady Oaks is the large greens that are fast and average almost 200 feet in circumference. The bentgrass used for the greens came from Leonard's personal nursery.

The par 71 layout features two mean par 3s that play around 230 yards from the tips, as well as three impressive par 5s. No. 8 on the front goes 618 yards, and holes 14 and 15 on the back offer back-to-back par 5s that play 568 and 531 yards, respectively.

The details   817-732-1271. 320 Roaring Springs Rd., Fort Worth, TX 76114

- 1959. Robert Trent Jones, Sr. 18 holes. Par 71. Back – 6,916 (71.0/130). Middle – 6,308 (69.7/121). Forward – Par 73. 6,002 (74.5/123). Price - $$$.

Getting there From I-30 west, take the Horne St. exit and turn right. Drive a short distance to the course, and look for the entrance on the left side of the street.

SYCAMORE CREEK GOLF COURSE

The golf   Originally built in 1932, this longtime 9-hole favorite has been beloved by downtowners for ages because of its central location. The city purchased the course in 1977 and expanded the original 36 acres to 92 in the early 1990s. The remodel involved opening up the fairways and enlarging the

The game is not so easy as it seems. In the first place, the terrible inertia of the ball must be overcome. Lord Wellwood

greens. Trees and bunkers were added to give the old track even more character.

No. 1 is notable for its elevated tee, playing down to the fairway about 30 feet below. And No. 8 is the only par 5, a welcome birdie opportunity for the low handicapper.

The details 817-535-7241. 401 Martin Luther King Frwy., Fort Worth, TX 76104

- 1932. Pittman and Poe. 9 holes. Par 35. Back – 3,070 (34.4). Middle – 2,925 (33.7). Forward – Par 36. 2,786 (36.3/132). Price - $.

Getting there From Fort Worth, take Hwy. 287 north. The course is located just off 287 between Riverside and Vickery, on the right-hand side.

TIMBERVIEW GOLF COURSE

The golf In 1963 Fort Worth's Fouts family opened Timberview as a 9-hole facility that subsequently became very popular, providing impetus for an additional nine holes. The design features flat, tree-lined fairways with water in play on half the holes. The front nine is the more difficult of the two sides, primarily because it's not as open as the back.

Two par 5s stand out on the front nine. The 560-yard No. 4 bends right inside of two lakes on the left side, ending with a difficult approach into a multi-level, kidney-shaped green. The tunnel-like 517-yard No. 8 is lined by out-of-bounds on the left. In between the two, hole 5 is enjoyable because it plays only 296 yards, yet isn't quite drive-able because the green is small and elevated.

The details 817-478-3601. 4508 E. Enon Rd., Fort Worth, TX 76140

- 1963. Dan Fouts. 18 holes. Par 72. Back – 6,491 (70.4). Middle – 6,191 (69.0). Forward – 5,406 (70.0). Price - $$.

Getting there From I-20, take Exit 441 (W Anglin Dr.) and go south for about 2 miles to the course.

WOODHAVEN COUNTRY CLUB

The golf The ever-busy Leon Howard came to Woodhaven in 1969 to build this par 71 6,565-yard layout. Howard's traditional design features narrow-tree lined fairways, a significant amount of hills, out-of-bounds lining the fairways, and many challenging doglegs.

The best stretch of golf is on the front, with a genius combination of holes in Nos. 6-8. The par 3 No. 6 requires a carry of 200 yards to clear the water, and No. 7 takes plenty of strokes to reach the green 569 yards away. No. 8 is a 426-yard par 4 that plays uphill into a narrow fairway.

On the back, the 190-yard No. 17 features a lake along the left side of the hole–it's one of only a few holes on the course with water.

The details   817-457-5150. 913 Country Club Ln., Fort Worth, TX 76112

- 1969. Leon Howard. 18 holes. Par 71. Back – 6,465 (70.3/124). Middle – 6,083 (68.6/119). Forward – 5,431 (70.3/126). Price - $$.

Getting there From I-30 east, take the Oakland Blvd. exit and turn left. When you come to Bridge St., turn right and head over to Country Club Ln. Turn left and the course is just down the road.

Z BOAZ GOLF COURSE

The golf   Z Boaz has two separate lives–the pre-World War II layout, designed by John Bredemus, that was shut down for the war, and the post-war Ralph Plummer design that has been a staple for Fort Worth hacks for ages.

Byron Nelson helped promote the opening of the course in a 1950 exhibition match, back when green fees were under $1. Unlike most Plummer designs, this one is short, playing barely 6,000 yards from the tips and featuring several drive-able par 4s. No. 9 is the feature hole, playing 547 yards and doglegging left with a pond guarding the bend.

The details   817-738-6287. 3240 Lackland Rd., Fort Worth, TX 76116

- www.fortworthgolf.org
- 1930s. John Bredemus. 1950. Ralph Plummer. 18 holes. Par 70. Back – 6,033 (69.6/124). Middle – 5,655 (68.6/116). Forward – 4,782 (68.0/107). Price - $$.

Getting there From I-30 west, take the Green Oaks Rd. exit and turn left. The entrance is off Lackland Rd.

FORT WORTH NOTES   Cowtown's last gunfight occurred in 1887 in front of the **White Elephant Saloon,** and you can still have a beer and talk smack there today. Nearby are **Sundance Square** and the historic **Stockyards** area, both popular for shopping, dining, and carousing. Sundance, paved with red bricks and considered extremely hip due to the renovation of the historic buildings, is the best spot to pick a hotel. The western-themed Stockyards on the north side of downtown offers shopping, eats, and historical sidebars to go along with a few hotels.

Music-loving *touristas* might be interested in **Billy Bob's Texas,** "the world's largest honky-tonk," while the cultured set knows to plan ahead and find out if the likes of Lyle Lovett are entertaining at the venerable **Bass Hall.**

For grub near downtown you can get the best greasy Tex-Mex in Texas for under $5 per plate at places like **La Familia** on W. 7th St. and **Benito's** on Hemphill (Fort Worth natives still swear by **Joe T. Garcia's**). Closer to Colonial is the **Fiesta Mexican Restaurant,** also on Hemphill.

Meat lovers can go nuts at Fort Worth's old-school steak joints. **Massey's** serves up sloppy chicken-fried steak that might be the best in Texas, and **Kincaid's** is the best for burgers—a walk-up old-fashioned grocery store joint

A bad attitude is worse than a bad swing. Payne Stewart

where you pay on the 'honor system.' Also for meat look to the 1950s **Cattlemen's Steak House** on Main St., or out on Jacksboro Hwy. find the **Williams Ranch House.**

FRISCO

Elev. 703   Pop. 33,174

Frisco is the epitome of urban explosion, its population blowing up from a measly 1,100 in the 1960s to what some predict might reach 350,000 within the next few decades. The town booms around Preston Rd., the former Preston Trail and Shawnee Trail, which was used by wagon trains and cattle drives traveling between Oklahoma and Austin.

PLANTATION GOLF CLUB

The golf   Plantation was created for the average golfer–it's a user-friendly course where spectacular play is not required for a decent score. Playing only 6,400 yards from the tips and under 6,000 from the middle tees, the course isn't long, and it includes many par 4s that are nearly drive-able. Erratic, careless play is punished, however, with out-of-bounds lining the fairways and water coming into play on a few holes. Those short par 4s in particular are all guarded by water.

Two of the par 3s, the 148-yard No. 7 and the 188-yard No. 17, both require players to carry water.

Other notes: The speed of play is better than average because of the easier layout.

The details   972-335-4653. 4710 Plantation Ln., Frisco, TX 75035

- www.clubcorpgolf.com

- 1986. Richard Ellis. 18 holes. Back – 6,402 (70.9/122). Middle – 5,945 (68.1/117). Forward – 4,916 (70.4/113). Price - $$$.

Getting there From I-75 south, take Hwy. 121 west 7 miles to Hillcrest. Turn right and drive to Lebanon. Turn right and look for the entrance off of Plantation Ln.

STONEBRIAR COUNTRY CLUB

The golf   A demanding, modern course designed primarily by Ken Dye, with some input from Joe Finger and Byron Nelson, the private Stonebriar CC course is adjacent to the Westin Stonebriar Resort, which also offers a spectacular Tom Fazio course for club members and guests of the resort.

Dye's design routes around four interconnecting lakes that bring water into play on 13 of 18 holes. The fairways feature severe undulations, and the greens

If everybody could learn to hold his head still there wouldn't be any
golfers around still trying to break 100. Arnold Palmer

are extremely quick. Both Senior PGA and LPGA events have been held here, and participants confirmed that the most difficult hole is the 438-yard No. 9. Water squeezes the fairway on both sides, and the landing area narrows and eventually becomes all water at 230 yards out. This means that the long approach is going to be testy into the green protected by water on the right.

On the back, No. 15 is considered the most difficult–another long par 4 that rolls alongside a creek on the right. Interestingly, the green on No. 15 is shared with hole 7.

The details   972-625-8916. 5050 Country Club Dr., Frisco, TX 75034

- 1988. Dye, Finger, Nelson. Country Club Course: 1988. Ken Dye and Baxter Spann. 18 holes. Par 72. Back – 7,064 (74.8/140). Middle – 6,637 (72.6/132). Forward – 5,707 (74.1/130). Price - $$$$.

Getting there From Hwy. 121 north, take the Legacy exit west and the club-house is on the left side of the street.

THE TRAILS OF FRISCO

The golf   Semi-private but not for long, The Trails is one of Jeff Brauer's most unique designs—primarily because it doesn't fit the mold of his other courses. Brauer, who's known for his open, straight-forward courses, designed this one to tip out to a par 71 6,800 yards and loaded it with hidden creeks, scenic wetlands, extensive bunkering, and massive greens. In fact, first-timers will be confused here. They'll face intimidating views off the tee that leave doubt as to the problems that loom ahead, and it is definitely possible to lose all of your balls off the tee if you're struggling.

The course is just flat-out challenging, especially on the front nine. No. 1 opens up with a creek on the left that cuts in front of the green and generally makes its presence known on every shot. The play here is to stay right and stay away from its subtle presence on the left side. The creek comes into play on Nos. 2, 4, 5, and even No. 9, where it chutes from the fairway in front of the green and surrounds the green of this challenging par 4.

All told, water and waste areas are in play on 16 of 18 holes (including every par 3), and the creeks are enhanced by visible lakes and ponds on the back side, even though it is considered a bit easier than the front.

The details   972-668-4653. 10411 Teel Pkwy., Frisco, TX 75034

- www.americangolf.com
- 2000. Jeff Brauer. 18 holes. Par 71. Back – 6,800. Middle – 6,500. Forward – 5,900. Price - $$$.

Getting there From Hwy. 121, take the Dallas N. Tollway to FM 720, then drive west on 720 to and turn right on Teel.

I used to play golf with a guy who cheated so badly that he once
had a hole in one and wrote down a zero on the scorecard. Bob Brue

WESTIN STONEBRIAR RESORT COURSE

The golf   Located at what for now is the end of the north-bound Dallas Tollway is the Westin Stonebriar Resort, 30 minutes from downtown Dallas and an ideal business or resort getaway because of its convenient location near the generally fast-moving north-south thoroughfare. And in addition to the hotel-business conference amenities, there's the spectacular Tom Fazio route awaiting that is open for play only to resort guests and members of the adjoining Stonebriar Country Club.

This place embodies Dallas' northward surge. In the 1960s and 1970s, the new construction was further south in Richardson and Plano, when places like Preston Trails defined the suburbs' northern edge. However, these days the edge is up this way in Frisco. On this once-barren, extremely flat farmland that served primarily as a hayfield lies the still reasonably flat Fazio track (although he moved over 600,000 yards of earth during construction) that is famous for its lightning-fast, Augusta-like putting surfaces. Made up of the new heat-resistant A-4 bentgrass that was installed recently at Fort Worth's Colonial Country Club, these babies are certain three-jacks if you fail to pay attention to the pin placements with your approach.

The greens are the signature at the Westin Stonebriar, since Fazio's layout is surprisingly hacker-friendly, mostly void of forced carries with fairways framed by mounds that seem to push the ball back into the fairway. The mounding also has a pleasing aesthetic purpose, making it impossible to see the neighboring fairways and greens.

The best hole on the front is No. 2, a 407-yard doglegger that tees uphill over a wetland and involves an approach over a creek into a bunker-guarded green.

On the back Fazio dropped in a 5-acre lake that comes into play on Nos. 11 and 14, both 400-yard-plus par 4s. Bunkers line the fairway on No. 11, and the hole doglegs right against the wind. Besides the lake on No. 14, the deep, multi-level green is the problem most likely to drive your score up.

The details   972-625-8916. 5050 Country Club Dr., Frisco, TX 75034

• www.stonebriar.com

• Tom Fazio. 18 holes. Par 72. Back 7,045. Middle – 6,455. Forward – 5,125. Price - $$$$.

Getting there From Hwy. 121 north, take the Legacy Ave. exit and west. The clubhouse is on the left side of the street.

FRISCO NOTES   Picture massive new malls and immaculate shopping centers–sporting ways to spend your money on the latest fashion trends–as well as every option for food and drink. Trek into old Frisco for the dwindling remains of local eateries, where you might taste a little of the old-school charm

Few pleasures on earth match the feeling that comes from making a loud bodily-function noise just as a guy is about to putt. Dave Barry

at **Randy White's Hall of Fame BBQ,** probably the best option for the hungry golfer.

GAINESVILLE   Elev. 738   Pop. 14,760

Gainesville is the last town on I-35 before you reach Oklahoma. Back in the mid-1850s the town was on the edge of the frontier, convenient for hostile, raiding Indians who burdened the settlers. Fort Fitzhugh was nearby, and the community grew as a point on the California Trail. Cattle and cotton eventually fueled the economy, and Gainesville became known as a gateway to Texas because of its positioning on two major cross-country highways.

Most adventuring golf bums will encounter Gainesville on their way to Muenster and the unique Turtle Hill layout. However, the Ralph Plummer-designed Gainesville muni is worth a stop for a quick round.

GAINESVILLE MUNICIPAL GOLF COURSE

The golf   Gainesville's golf course is pretty much a simple muni-style layout that displays signs of being a links track, but definitely has some character with mature trees and frustrating, deceptive greens. These greens are tough on approach shots because they're small, and once you're on them the undulations can burn you for a three-jack. Ralph Plummer supposedly built this in the 1950s, and a creek runs through the course and comes into play several times. The course is fun because of its relaxing, rural setting, as well as the wide-open fairways that allow you to take full rips on just about every drive.

The details   940-668-4560. Hwy. 82. West, Gainesville, TX 76240

• 1950s. Ralph Plummer. 18 holes. Par 71. Back – 6,546 (71.3/123). Middle – 5,954 (68.4/116). Forward – Par 71. 5,012. Price - $$.

Getting there From I-35 north, take Hwy. 82 west. The course is about 3 miles down the road.

GAINESVILLE NOTES Historic homes are scattered throughout the town, so open your eyes and soak in the surroundings. **Miss Olivia's B&B Inn** is an exquisite Victorian home that is very much worthy of a night's stay. Downtown is filled with quaint shops and a friendly, bustling spirit. The **Historic Sante Fe Depot** is a popular starting point for Gainesville adventures, and the **Fried Pie Company** (940-665-7641) is one place you don't want to miss. For rural fare cruise east on US 82 and find **Catfish Louie's** (940-665-2779) or **The Neu Ranch House** (940-665-6789).

One very simple tip will infinitely improve the timing of most golfers. Merely pause briefly at the top of the backswing. Tommy Armour

GARLAND
Elev. 551 Pop. 215,768

Garland, another DFW bedroom community that covers the northeastern part of clustered Dallas County, is home to Duck Creek and the neighbor of Lake Ray Hubbard to the east. Duck Creek served as a station on the railroad and the community was once on its way to becoming a major shipping point for onions. The golf here consists of two private country clubs: an impressive city-owned facility with 63 holes and a quaint par 3 course.

EASTERN HILLS COUNTRY CLUB

The golf   Designed by John Bredemus protégé Ralph Plummer, whose laid-back, traditional style is evident on many Texas courses, Eastern Hills is an unusually hilly track for North Texas, providing lots of interesting lies that require some unique shot-making. Water hazards come into play on 6 or 7 holes, and the greens are extremely fast.

The back nine features two of the better holes–the 545-yard No. 14, which initially plays uphill off the tee before dropping down into a valley on the left, and the monster 219-yard No. 10, which might require a 3-wood into the wind and features a bunker-happy green with a creek on the right side.

The details   972-278-3051. 3000 S. Country Club Rd., Garland, TX 75043

• 1954. Ralph Plummer. 18 holes. Par 70. Back – 6,542 (71.0/128). Middle – 6,159 (69.2/124). Forward – Par 71. 5,361 (71.0/119). Price - $$.

Getting there From I-30 east, turn left on Beltline and drive to Centerville Rd. Turn right and head to Country Club Rd. Turn right again and look for the entrance on the left.

FIREWHEEL GOLF PARK

The golf   Firewheel is Texas' most impressive example of municipal golf. Owned and operated by the city of Garland, and extremely popular because of the fair price and number of available golf holes, Firewheel now sports 63 holes since the new Bridges course opened in the past few years. All three tracks can be challenging because they each incorporate a variety of hazards into their designs, including limestone that is scattered throughout the property.

The **Old Course** has water hazards that come into play throughout the design, such as on hole 18, a 400-yard, par 4 that requires a tee shot and an approach shot over the same creek, which winds through the hole. Hole 9 is the feature hole, a 552-yard par 5 that rolls downhill. The tee shot is into a narrow landing area carved out of trees, and on the approach you must be in perfect position because of the strategically placed pecan trees. No. 18 is challenging with both the tee shot and the approach over a creek that winds through the hole.

The **Lakes Course** is a links-style course that is loaded with water, and was a Dick Phelps creation on his return to Garland in 1987. Hole 7 is the most difficult–a long 549-yard par 5 that requires an approach over a pond.

The **Bridges Course** recently opened, featuring another 27 holes of Dick Phelps designed golf. This one has bent-grass greens, and two of the nines play about 3,500 yards from the tips, while the third nine is only 3,200 yards.

The details   972-205-2795. 600 W. Campbell Rd., Garland, TX 75044

- Old Course: 1983. Dick Phelps. Gold – 7,054 (74.1/129). Blue (71.6/125). White (69.7/119). Red (71.7/117). Price - $$.

- Lakes Course: 1987. Dick Phelps. Gold – 6,625 (72.0/126). Blue – 6,116 (69.5/119). White – 5,693 (67.3/114). Red - 5,215 (69.1/110). Price - $$.

- Bridges Course: 2002. Dick Phelps. 27 holes. Price - $$.

Getting there From Dallas, take Hwy. 75 north and exit Arapaho. Turn right and when you come to N. Garland Ave., turn left. Drive to W. Blackburn Rd. and turn west. The course is just down the road.

OAKRIDGE COUNTRY CLUB

The golf   The Oakridge CC is a short target course that plays only 6,516 from the tips (par 71) and a very hacker-friendly 6,089 yards from the white tees. Pesky Duck Creek winds through the course and comes into play on 13 holes. Water is the predominant hazard, with three other holes with ponds, and the greens can be testy because they are small, smooth, and fast.

No. 15 is the signature–a 354-yard par 4 with significant mounding and Duck Creek on the left. The approach is fun because the small green is nestled into a grove of oak trees.

The details   972-530-8008. 2800 Diamond Oaks Dr., Garland, TX 75044

- 1986. Jack Kidwell and Michael Hurdzan. 18 holes. Par 72. Back – 6,516 (71.3/125). Middle – 6,089 (69.2/119). Forward – 5,103 (70.7/118). Price - $$.

Getting there From I-75 going north, take Beltline going east, then get off at the Laurel Oaks Dr. exit and make a right. This road will lead you straight to the course.

UP TO PAR GOLF COURSE AND DRIVING RANGE

The golf   At this great little par 3 course, you can pay once and play all day, which is the best way to work out of the shanks. Up to Par has a few lakes that impact play. Ever since the course has been under new ownership, the layout and conditioning have improved dramatically.

The details   972-530-0585. 3015 N Shiloh Rd., Garland, TX 75044

• 9 holes. Par 27. 838 yards. Price - $.

Getting there Exit Shiloh Rd. off of Beltline.

MORE GARLAND GOLF

Dallas Golf 972-270-0989. 2118 Eastgate Dr., Garland, TX 75043

GARLAND NOTES   Try the **Dry Dock** (972-226-7440) on Marina Dr. for the lounge-bar type atmosphere. On Jupiter Rd. the old-school **Griff's Hamburgers** (972-530-7886) is popular. On Main St. there's **Big Man's East Texas** (972-276-6128) which serves damn good barbecue, and up the road in Sachse, TX you'll find **Lone Star Barbecue** (972-495-4929).

GLEN ROSE   Elev. 680   Pop. 2,122

Glen Rose is a charming little town located on US 67 between Cleburne and Stephenville. The town began as a trading post in 1849, an ideal spot because of its picturesque location at the confluence of the Brazos and Paluxy Rivers. Golfers know Glen Rose for its excellent Squaw Valley facility, which now boasts two 18-hole golf courses that are considered to be the best in the area. A great weekend road trip destination, Glen Rose offers B&B accommodations in its historic buildings and a vibrant downtown area, as well as the intriguing Dinosaur Valley State Park.

SQUAW VALLEY GOLF COURSE

The golf   The original course, Comanche Lakes, opened in 1992–a Jeff Brauer design that is open on the front and more densely wooded on the back. Brauer's work involved bringing in dirt to provide some mounding to the flat terrain, and he placed the course along a scenic creek that comes into play, mostly on the back.

No. 9 is the best hole on the front because of its split fairway. Macho men can go for the green by aiming over the lake–otherwise it plays a pedestrian 362 yards if you choose the left side, where it doglegs around the lake.

On the back, Nos. 15 and 16 are back-to-back par 4s that you'll be glad to get out of the way. The 15th rolls 462 yards and doglegs right, requiring a tee shot over the creek. The long approach is especially challenging due to the long row of trees at the corner of the green. Hole 16 features an elevated green above Squaw Creek. Play for position off the tee because the hole is not long.

The newer **Apache Links** course features more trees and massive undulating greens. Despite its name, it's is actually a bit more traditional in design that the Lakes course.

Other notes: Walking is permitted only on weekends.

The details   254-897-7956. 2439 E. Hwy. 67, Glen Rose, TX 76043

- Comanche Lakes Course: 1992. 18 holes. Par 72. Back – 6,731 (71.9/125). Middle – 6,284 (69.6/119). Forward – 5,014 (70.0/113). Price - $$.
- Apache Links Course: 18 holes. Par 72. Back – 7,063 (73.6/130). Price - $$.

Getting there Take Hwy. 67 from Dallas through Cleburne until you come to Glen Rose. Look for the signs to the course.

GLEN ROSE NOTES   For food, the options are impressive. **Two Grannies' Down Home Cookin'** (254-897-9773) is worth a shot just for the name, but also a place where great lunches are followed by perfect homemade peach cobbler. **Donna Kay's** is a catfish joint, **Ranchhouse BBQ** is popular, and the **MK Corral** is the place for steaks, while the **Lewis and Clark Cafe and Trading Co.** (254-898-2193) serves up quail filled with shrimp and wrapped in bacon (BYOB). There's lots of B&Bs in Glen Rose, including the **White Gables Inn** (254-897-2149) and the **Country Woods Inn** (817-279-3002). But the best option is outside of town on CR 2013 at the **Rough Creek Lodge** (254-918-2550). With their 40-foot limestone fireplace, spa, views of the lake, and an outstanding restaurant, this is the place to make a weekend of it.

GRAFORD
Elev. 954   Pop. 578

Graford, 12 miles east of Possum Kingdom Lake, takes its name from the towns of Graham and Weatherford, which it sits between in north-central Palo Pinto County. The town began in 1855 when G.R. Bevers established a home site at the Flat Rock Crossing of Big Keechi Creek. Road-trippers to Fort Belknap stopped here for supplies, and a store and post office were established.

Graford's place in the golf world stems from one of the most outstanding courses in the state: the demanding, spectacular Cliffs Country Club.

THE CLIFFS COUNTRY CLUB

The golf   One of the gems of Texas, The Cliffs is perched alongside the scenic Possum Kingdom Lake with its "18 signature holes" highlighted by 100-foot elevation changes, massive rock outcroppings, narrow, tree-lined fairways, and an infinite number of ways to destroy your golf round. Remove your expectations when "enjoying" The Cliffs, because it is a totally different golf experience. Hazard after hazard awaits from every angle, sometimes making it difficult to "enjoy" your golf vacation. Canyons, creeks, cedar and oak groves–everything imaginable gets in the way while you're hacking it toward the immaculate bent-grass greens.

The signature of signatures is the terrifying No. 15, a dicey par 3 that drops 100 feet over a cliff down to a miniscule green that is surrounded by the cliff wall to the left, water right, and sand in front.

The details   940-779-4040. 160 Cliffs Dr., Graford, TX 76449

- www.thecliffsresort.com

- 1989. Robert von Hagge and Bruce Devlin. Back – 6,808 (73.9/143). Middle – 6,469 (72.1/138). Forward – 4,876 (68.4/124). Price - $$$$.

Getting there This course is located on Star Route outside of Graford, 75 miles northwest of Fort Worth near Hwy. 16.

GRAFORD NOTES   Graford is out of the way so you'll want to consider taking advantage of the luxury resort accommodations, especially since you can package the golf fees for a discount. Graford is east of the lake, where you'll find **Lumpy's Barbecue** (940-779-3535) and **Char B's Grill** (940-779-3663). There's a semblance of night life at **Red Dawg's After Hours Club** (940-779-3399), but sometimes the preferred route involves touring south into the local drinking establishments of Palo Pinto, Strawn, Mingus, and Gordon.

GRANBURY Elev.725   Pop. 5,626

Granbury has character: it's located on beautiful Lake Granbury, serves as the seat of Hood County, and is loaded with historic buildings, fine dining, and charming B&Bs. And for a town of 5,600 residents, the amount of golf available in Granbury is astounding.

DE CORDOVA BEND COUNTRY CLUB

The golf   Fort Worth's Leonard family developed another part of their vast real-estate empire around Lake Granbury when they brought Leon Howard in to build this hacker-friendly club in 1968. The result is a modest 6,423-yard layout carved out of the rolling, mesquite-covered hills southwest of Fort Worth. The course is tight due to the trees and out-of-bounds stakes, and water and sand come into play frequently.

The details   817-326-4505. 5301 Country Club Dr., Granbury, TX 76049

- 1968. Leon Howard and Dave Bennett. 18 holes. Par 70. Back – 6,423 (70.2/119). Middle – 6,002 (68.3/113). Forward – 5,123 (70.8/118). Price - $$.

It seems to me that many courses are designed with an eye to difficulty alone, and that in the effort to construct an exacting course that will thwart the expert, the average golfer who pays the bills is entirely overlooked. Bobby Jones

Getting there From I-377 south, take Hwy. 167 left. When you reach the town of Acton, TX, turn around the sharp curve and then left onto Hwy. 4. Look for the security gate, then proceed to the course.

GRANBURY COUNTRY CLUB

The golf   After De Cordova Bend, Leon Howard came back in the early 1970s to build the 9-hole Granbury CC, a short course that features generous fairways and small greens. Howard's design is short at right around 3,000 yards, and the second set of tees play about the same the next time around. Water hazards pop up, but they're not prominent, and the real problems occur if you stray from the tree-lined fairways.

Two holes stand out: The skinny, 500-yard No. 8 and the tricky 360-yard No. 5, which doglegs left around a creek that cuts into the fairway.

The details   817-573-9912. County Rd. 430, Granbury, TX 76048

• 1971. Leon Howard. 9 holes. Par 36. Back – 3,016 (34.1/117). Forward – 2,396 (34.0). Price - $$.

Getting there From Fort Worth, take Hwy. 371 west for 30 miles into Granbury. Just south of town, take FM 430 and turn right, then find the course 1 mile down the road.

HARBOR LAKES ON LAKE GRANBURY

Opening 2003   Lake Granbury's newest addition is headed by Prime Golf, who also handles The Old Brickyard in Ennis as well as Stewart Peninsula in The Colony. Dick Phelps was hired to route this mid-range course through the Harbor Lakes residential community, and his design utilizes the lake and heavy bunkering to spice up the round. The course is designed for the big boys, tipping out at over 7,200 yards, and is slated for a June 2003 opening.

HIDDEN OAKS

The golf   Hidden oaks opened in 1998 and has gained a solid reputation due to its well-maintained conditions. Rex Worrel's 6,443-yard layout plays to the traditional par 72, offering generous, plush fairways and large, firm greens that roll true. And while there are a good amount of mature trees at Hidden Oaks, the struggling golfer will appreciate the frequency of open shots and the overall generous feel to the course.

No. 7 is the number one handicap. A 542-yarder from the tips, it's sandwiched between two relatively easy par 3s and is followed on No. 9 by a welcoming 472-yard par 5. The back side is inviting as well, offering short par 3s and average-length par 4s. In fact, the most difficult rated hole on the back is the 479-yard No. 17, which happens to be a par 5.

The details   817-279-1078. 2701 Hideaway Bay Ct., Granbury, TX 76049

That does look like very good exercise – but what is the little ball for? Ulysses S. Grant

- 1998. Rex Worrell. 18 holes. Par 72. Back – 6,443 (70.4/123). Middle – 6,111 (68.5/116). Forward – 5,741 (72.9/124). Price - $$.

Getting there Take Hwy. 377 south to Hwy. 167. In town, turn left on Granbury Rd. and find Meander Rd. Turn right, drive to Hideaway Bay Court Rd., and turn left to the course (on the left).

PECAN PLANTATION – OLD COURSE

The golf   Leon Howard laid this course out in 1971, and was given specific orders by developer Bob Leonard to take the environmentally sensitive route when designing the course. Cut out of a 3,000-acre former commercial pecan orchard in the floodplain of the Brazos River, Howard did his best to preserve trees and create a unique layout with good holes. His best work here is reflected in the difficult par 3s, all requiring long irons when playing from the 6,800-yard-plus tips.

The details   817-573-2645. 8650 Westover Ct., Granbury, TX 76049

- 1971. Leon Howard. 18 holes. Back – 6,830 (72.5/129). Middle – 6,566 (71.4/123). Senior – 5,947 (68.5/115). Forward – 5,466 (72.6/125). Price - $$$.

Getting there From Hwy. 377 west, take Hwy. 144 south to Granbury. In town look for signs to the course.

PECAN PLANTATION - NUTCRACKER COURSE

The golf   Fort Worth's sprawl and Granbury's growing population supported the addition of Pecan Plantation's Nutcracker Course. Lined with pecan trees, the design features flat terrain and a good combination of holes. The par 3s range from 150 to 225 yards, and the par 5s are all between 480 and 530 yards.

The details   817-279-0936. 9500 Orchard Dr., Granbury, TX 76049

- 1991. Lee Singletary. 18 holes. Par 72. Back – 6,743 (72.1/132). Middle – 6,161 (68.9/119). Forward – 5,044 (70.1/119). Price - $$.

Getting there Take Hwy. 377 south to Hwy. 144, then turn left and head to FM 2425. Turn left, and drive 6 miles to the back gate of the course.

MORE GOLF

Lake Country Driving Range: Hwy. 4, Granbury. 817-326-2320.

Golf Etc.: 5100 E. Hwy. 377, Granbury. 817-579-1515.

GRANBURY NOTES There's "bunches of BBQ" in Granbury, but if you need upscale try **The Nut House Restaurant** on the square. Other options are

Stringfellows , **Mi Familia** for chips and queso, or **Pearl Street Pasta**. For lodging consider the **Captain's House** (817-579-6664), which is only two blocks from the square, or the **Arbor House** (817-573-0073), which is near the lake. A good time to hit Granbury is in March when the **General Granbury's Birthday Celebration Bean and Rib Cook-Off** is cause for good times and carrying on.

GRAND PRAIRIE
Elev. 528 Pop. 127,427

At one time the prairie was in fact grand for this now-bustling suburb 12 miles west of Dallas. In the old days Fort Worth, Arlington, and Dallas didn't squeeze the town so hard, and Cottonwood, Fish, and Kirby Creeks all ran through the community more naturally. Today the town is also surrounded by Irving and Cedar Hill, and offers Mountain Creek Lake to its east and Joe Pool Lake to the south for some scenic respite amongst the growing industries. Six golf clubs currently call Grand Prairie home, but the golf world is buzzing about the new Wildflower Resort that's under construction on the shores of Joe Pool, slated for two Jack Nicklaus-designed tracks to accompany a Texas-sized world-class resort.

FUN CITY GOLF COURSE

The golf   This is a good course for beginners and seniors to play. Seniors enjoy the course because it is short and not too strenuous to walk. Beginners like it because it provides them with a challenge, but they don't feel overwhelmed. Water comes into play on only one hole. Ladies tee off from the same set as the men.

The details   972-262-0022. 3990 Westcliff Rd., Grand Prairie, TX 75052

• 1995. 17 holes. Par 51. Price - $.

Getting there From Arlington, take I-20 going east, get off at Exit 457 and turn left onto FM 1382, then proceed down to Fish Creek Rd. and make another left. Continue over to Westcliff and make a left again, drive 1 mile to the course, look for the entrance on the left side of the road.

GRAND PRAIRIE COUNTRY CLUB

The golf   The former Wood Crest Country Club opened in 1972. The Don January and Billy Martindale layout is built around a creek that meanders through 13 holes and is lined by a heavily wooded area of oaks and pecans. In 2001, the Mai family purchased the facility and renamed it Grand Prairie CC, and they've gone about improving the facility in recent years.

The best stretch of golf occurs right after the turn. Hole 10 starts it off with

*Golf seems to me an arduous way to go for a walk; I'd prefer
to take the dogs out.* Princess Anne of England

a 422-yard par 4, followed by the number one handicap hole, a 530-yard par 5, and the long, 210-yard No. 12.

The details 972-264-2974. 3502 Country Club Dr., Grand Prairie, TX 75052

• www.grandprairiecc.com

• 1972. Martindale - January. 18 holes. Par 72. Back – 6,360 970.6/113). Middle – 5,849 (67.8/108). Forward – Par 74. 5,278 (69.5/110). Price - $$.

Getting there From I-20 west, take the 1382 exit and turn right. When you come to Warrior Trail, turn left and drive to Southeast 8. Turn left again and go to Country Club Dr., where you'll turn left one more time and find the course down the road.

GREAT SOUTHWEST GOLF CLUB

The golf Ralph Plummer designed this course in 1965, incorporating three connected lakes into the layout. Dick Nugent came along in 1983 to lead a renovation effort that helped the course survive. The course has been known in recent years for its outstanding greens.

The best hole is the 223-yard No. 3, which plays downwind over water and is extremely difficult to stop on the small green. Interestingly, both nines end with very similar par 5s. Both are over 500 yards–No. 9 has water on the left side and in front of the green, while No. 18 features water on the right and in front of the green.

The details 972-647-0116. 612 E. Ave. J, Grand Prairie, TX 75050

• www.americangolf.com

• 1964. Ralph Plummer. 1983. Dick Nugent. 18 holes. Par 71. Back – 6,706 (72.7/127). Middle – 6,196 (69.9/123). Forward – 5,264 (71.6/125). Price - $$.

Getting there From Hwy. 360 south, take the Ave. J/Brown exit and turn left onto Ave J. Go over the bridge and the clubhouse is half a mile on the left.

PRAIRIE LAKES GOLF CLUB

The golf The former Grand Prairie Municipal Golf Course, which plays along the shores of Mountain Creek Lake, has been upgraded recently to give its loyal clientele a more modern, upscale golf experience. Sporting the new name of Prairie Lakes, the facility boasts new management that has implemented the course renovation, enlarged the clubhouse, and improved the pro shop.

Three nines help to handle the busy traffic, which numbers around 80,000 annually. Golfers come in droves to this Ralph Plummer design because of the outstanding condition. Water comes into play on 15 of the 27 holes, but the tree-lined fairways are generous even for the erratic golfer.

The details   972-263-0661. 3202 SE 14th St., Grand Prairie, TX 75052

- www.prairielakesgolf.com
- Red/White: 1963. Ralph Plummer. 18 holes. Par 71. Back – 6,219 (69.6/114). Middle – 5,759 (67.0/106). Forward – 5,176 (64.2/98). Price - $$.
- White/Blue: 18 holes. Par 72. Back – 6,309 (70.0/112). Middle – 5,884 (68.2/107). Forward – 5,253 (65.4/98). Price - $$.
- Blue/Red: Back – 18 holes. Par 72. 6,513 (71.2/118). Middle – 6,056 969.2/111). Forward – 5,488 966.5/102). Price - $$.

Getting there From I-20, exit Hwy. 138 and travel north to the 1st traffic light. At about 1 mile, turn right on SE 14th St.

RIVERSIDE GOLF CLUB

The golf   Riverside is appropriately named–it's set in a floodplain along the Trinity River with water in play on seemingly every hole. This is a combination links-style/traditional layout that is surprisingly difficult for a municipal course. Great holes abound on the Roger Packard layout, which requires the rarely found combination of length and accuracy when playing from the tips.

Holes 4-6 offer one of the better stretches of golf, starting with a 462-yard par 4 that is cut in the landing area by pesky fairway bunkers, and features a long approach into an elevated green that is surrounded by water and slopes back-to-front. Club less on No. 4 because leaving it short still offers the chance for an up-and-down.

No. 5 is a good par 3, especially from the middle tees where it generally plays as a short iron. Watch for the front pin placement, which can leave you with a long downhill putt if the tee shot is too long. Water looms to the right but it takes a bad shank to dunk it in the drink. No. 6 is one of the feature holes: it goes 543 yards, doglegging left along the Trinity with water fronting the green. The tee shot must be long and straight, and anything too far right leaves a precarious second shot around the bend.

The back side is the more fun of the two, taking you through good combinations of holes that offer excellent birdie opportunities if you're on your game. You'll need those birds when you come down the home stretch. The 18th is one of the most menacing in the area–a 438-yard par 4 with water along the left off the tee, and an approach over water to an elevated green that's surrounded by wet stuff. This ender requires two perfect golf shots to avoid a high number and reach the green in regulation.

Golf is a game of such monumental stupidity that anyone with a brain more active than a cantaloupe has difficulty gearing down to its demands. Peter Andrews

The details   817-640-7800. 3000 Riverside Dr., Grand Prairie, TX 75050

- 1984. Roger Packard. 18 holes. Par 72. Tiger – 7,025 (74.4/132). Champs – 6,433 (71.5/126). Regular – 5,785 (68.4/119). Ladies – 5,175 (69.5/113). Price - $$.

Getting there From I-30, travel 4 miles north to Hwy. 360. Take the Riverside exit, and the course is on the west side of the highway.

SUNSET GOLF CLUB

The golf   Sunset is a family-owned 9-holer that offers simple golf in a relaxed atmosphere, allowing you to play all day for one affordable green fee. The first hole is the only par 5 on this 3,305-yard par 35 layout. Water comes into play a few times, including the 437-yard par 4 No. 8, which features water off the tee and on the approach. From the tips, both par 3s play 175 yards and are rated amongst the easiest on the course.

The details   214-331-8057. 4906 E. Main St., Grand Prairie, TX 75050

- Chester B. Mims. 9 holes. Par 35. Back – 3,305 (35.5). Middle – 3,021 (34.4). Forward – 2,391 (33.4). Price - $$.

Getting there From I-30 east take Loop 12 south to Hwy. 180 (E. Main St). Turn right, and the course is on the right side of the road.

TANGLE RIDGE GOLF COURSE

The golf   Tangle Ridge's location near Joe Pool Lake is favorable because of the elevation changes that spice up this well-maintained public course. *Golf Digest* rated this 6,835-yard Jeff Brauer design as the 12th best in the state in 1998-99, and deservedly so. The course offers some outstanding holes, highlighted by impressive bent-grass greens that putt true.

In addition to the elevation changes, Brauer's design features generous fairways lined by thick brush and huge trees. Two holes grab your attention on the front side. The opener goes 469 yards and might be the most difficult on the course. While there aren't too many hazards, bunkers protect the fairway and green, and the thick rough lining the fairway makes it a difficult long approach if you miss the smooth stuff off the tee.

No. 8 is considered the signature: a 575-yarder that rolls downhill off the tee to a creek that cuts the fairway at 300 yards out. The approach on No. 8 must carry the creek to an elevated green protected by two massive mounds.

The details   972-299-6837. 818 Tangle Ridge Dr., Grand Prairie, TX 75052

- www.tangleridge.com
- 1995. Jeff Brauer. 18 holes. Par 72. Back – 6,835 (72.2/129). Middle – 6,337 (69.9/123). Forward – 5,187 (70.2/117). Price - $$.

⭐

Remember that the object of most greenside bunker shots is not to "blast" the ball out,
but to float it fairly gently from the trap on a cushion of sand,
by skimming the club easily just beneath the ball. John Jacobs

Getting there From I-20 east, turn right on Great Southwest Pkwy., then travel approximately 7 miles to Lake Ridge. Turn right and drive to Park Ridge, where you'll turn right and see the course.

THE WILDFLOWER RESORT

Opening 2004   Located on a 1,000-acre lakefront peninsula of Joe Pool Lake, The Wildflower Resort is slated to be a $200 million, 500-room Texas ranch-style luxury resort and conference center built around two Jack Nicklaus-designed courses. This one should be a good one. Troon Golf will manage the courses, which will feature Sergio Garcia's first foray into golf design–he'll use the support of Nicklaus' company to assist with his 18. Construction began in late 2002, with the opening scheduled for 2004.

GRAND PRAIRIE NOTES   The **Amerisuites** (972-988-6800) is on Hwy. 360, along with the **Hampton Inn** (982-988-8889). Everything to eat is on I-20–every chain you can imagine. Two good Italian joints are **Marsala Restaurante** (972-988-1101) and super-upscale **Fontana's** (972-263-1945) where you will need reservations on the weekends. And don't forget that you can bet on the ponies at **Lone Star Park**.

GRAPEVINE

Elev. 650   Pop. 42,059

The city of Grapevine is located smack dab in the middle of Dallas and Fort Worth on the northern side of the metroplex along the shores of Lake Grapevine. They say Sam Houston once negotiated the Treaty of Birds Fort here on the blackland prairie where wild mustang grapes once flourished. The town was sort of sleepy until the 1970s, when DFW Airport opened just south of town, spurring rapid growth and helping the city keep pace with the area's expansion. Grapevine is ideal for golfers visiting the DFW area because of its central location and outstanding public golf. Sandwiched between the lake and the new Bass Pro Outdoor World and adjoining hotel are three outstanding public facilities. The old Grapevine muni recently completed a renovation that resulted in 27 new holes, and Jerry Jones' Cowboys Golf Club has provided one of the better golf experiences in the state since it opened in 2001. And another is on the way, The Opryland Golf Club, which is part of the new Opryland Hotel Texas scheduled to open sometime in 2003.

COWBOYS GOLF CLUB

The golf   Definitely a must-play for the DFW-bound golfer, the Cowboys Golf Club is first-class all the way, and fortunately void of the cheese that you might suspect from an NFL-themed course. In this location next to the

---

Man blames fate for other accidents but feels personally responsible for a hole in one. Martha Beckman

Grapevine Municipal and the Lake Grapevine dam, Jeff Brauer created what might be his most impressive design.

Free of houses, the design rolls through some impressively wild terrain that is loaded with every species of tree imaginable, creeks, 100-foot elevation changes, and thick habitat that produced bobcats and cougars during construction. Fingered bunkering gives the track a MacKenzie-like look, which goes well with the natural setting and traditional design.

One of the better holes is No. 2, a skinny 376-yarder that plays over a creek and features a spectacularly difficult green that is bisected by a pesky ridge. Watch the pin placement here and keep the ball below the hole, or you'll end up with a 5-putt like I did.

On the back side No. 17 is the best par 3 on the course, and perhaps one of the best in the DFW area. Playing almost blindly uphill over a ravine and water hazard, the sloping green is difficult to hit because of the deceptive view from the tee.

This one is a first-class gem. We warmed up next to future NFL Hall of Famer Troy Aikman on the range and followed his group during our round, a nice complement to the plaques at each tee box commemorating the Cowboy organization's famous past.

The details   817-481-7277. 1600 Fairway Dr., Grapevine, TX 76051

- www.cowboysgolfclub.com
- 18 holes. Par 72. Back – 7,017 (74.2/140). Silver – 6,563 (71.7/130). Blue – 6,182 (69.9/127). White – 5,257 (71.6/130). Gold – 4,702 (68.9/114). Price - $$$$.

Getting there Located just north of DFW International Airport off Hwy. 26, .25 mile west of Grapevine Mills Mall and adjacent to the Opryland Hotel and Conference Center site.

GRAPEVINE MUNICIPAL GOLF COURSE

The golf   Nestled below the Lake Grapevine dam, one of the DFW-area's most popular courses now boasts a much-needed upgrade from its original 1978 Joe Finger/Byron Nelson design. After a few years of renovations, 27 new D.A. Weibring-designed holes are now open for play.

The newest nine, known as **Bluebonnet**, opened for play in 1999, highlighted by fast Tif-Eagle greens and some impressive elevation changes that often require blinds shots.

Mockingbird, the front nine of the old course, opened next, complementing Bluebonnet with a similar design. During the 2002 season the course was somewhat immature, but will be in prime shape for the 2003 season and beyond, especially since the course is so well-watered via its lakeside location.

The final renovation occurred on the **Pecan**, which runs closest to the dam

---

The wise man who has respect for the game before he plays it will take as much advice and coaching as he can get, and he will be content to begin in the most elementary way, and will not mind any amount of practice before he tries to make a complete round of the links. James Braid

and is scheduled to open for play sometime in the summer of 2003.

The details 817-410-3377. 3800 Fairway Dr., Grapevine, TX 76099

- Bluebonnet: 9 holes. Par 36. Black – 3,489. Blue – 3,196. White – 2,977. Red – 2,522. Price - $$.
- Mockingbird: 9 holes. Par 36. Black – 3,412. Blue – 3,188. White – 2,959. Red – 2,432. Price - $$.
- Pecan: Opening Spring 2003.

Getting there The course is located just north of DFW International Airport off State Hwy. 26, .25 mile west of Grapevine Mills Mall and adjacent to the Opryland Hotel and Conference Center site. Drive past the Cowboys Golf Club and over the dam, and you'll see the course below the dam on the right.

MORE GOLF

Former Texas Ranger owner Eddie Gaylord has been in the process of building the Opryland Hotel Texas, a 1,500-room hotel and convention center on Lake Grapevine that will feature a par 63, 18-hole executive course known as the **Opryland Golf Club**. The planned opening date is late 2003.

GRAPEVINE NOTES Check out the dinosaur bones, which were discovered during dam construction, on display in the nearby Corps of Engineers office. The best place to eat is **Esparza's** (817-481-4668), set in an old house and famous for its margaritas and Mexican food. The old-school joint is **Willhoit's** (817-481-7511), which is one of the best beer-joint grills in the DFW area. For lodging try the **Hilton DFW Lakes** (817-481-8444) or the **Embassy Suites** (972-724-2600) on Bass Pro Drive, which is adjacent to the outlet mall and **Bass Pro Outdoor World**.

GREENVILLE   Elev. 554 Pop. 25,051

Greenville, born of railroads and cotton but now home of industry, is sometimes called the "Gateway to Lake Tawakoni" even though others might argue. Outlet malls line the highway of this first major town on the way from Dallas to Texarkana. For the I-30-bound golfer there are two 9-hole courses that can make for a full day of golf in Greenville.

OAK CREEK COUNTRY CLUB

The golf   Oak Creek, which dates back to the 1950s, is known for its solid combination of holes and the frequency of water. The par 36 track plays to

---

If you want to have a flowing, rhythmic, and elegant putting stroke, the last thing to do is think about flow, rhythm, and elegance while you're putting. That will make your stroke tight and unstrained. Flow happens when you see it and do it. Dr. Bob Rotella

3,141 yards and features six par 4s under 400 yards. The par 3s, 201 and 155 yards respectively, are listed as the easiest holes on the course. The toughest is No. 3, a 542-yard par 5. Two sets of tees allow for an 18-hole round.

The details   903-454-6445. 969 FM 1570 W., Greenville, TX 75404

• 1953. 9 holes. Back – 3,141. Forward – 2,750. Price - $.

Getting there From I-30 south, take FM 1570 to Hwy. 34. Cross 34 and drive 3 miles to the course.

WRIGHT PARK GOLF COURSE

The golf   Wright Park, the older of the two courses in Greenville, has recently been improved under the guidance of Fort Worth-based architect Steve Plummer. The tees and greens have been replaced, and dirt was brought in to provide some mounding to the flat fairways. The design features mature trees that line most of the fairways; small, fast greens; and water that comes into play on four holes.

Three par 3s and four par 4s are sandwiched between two par 5s. The opener is longer at 486 yards, but No. 9 is considered the signature, playing only 437 yards but featuring a pond in the middle of the fairway. The most difficult par is probably the 218-yard No. 5.

The details   903-457-2996. 4903 Moulton St., Greenville, TX 75401.

• 1929. Dr. F. L. Young. 9 holes. Par 35. Back – 2,878 yards. Price - $.

Getting there From Dallas, take I-30 east and exit 94B. Drive south to the course.

GREENVILLE NOTES   The world-famous **Puddin' Hill Bakery** is here in Greenville, known for its tasty sandwiches and its scrumptious desserts. And the perfect place for golfers is **Cattyshack's Grill & Bar**. Sometimes the **Horseman's Club & Arena** has live music, but they always have cold beer. The only hotel is the **Comfort Inn**.

HASLET   Elev. 700   Pop. 1,134

Haslet is a little-known town just west of I-35, some 16 miles northwest of Fort Worth. Originally a railroad town, war-related employment in Fort Worth helped sustain the community. Today Haslet is another of the many bedroom communities to the DFW area and home to the 1966 Willow Springs Golf Course.

WILLOW SPRINGS GOLF COURSE

The golf   Willow Springs is famous for having two sets of greens for each hole, used to maintain the best possible conditions depending on the season–one for the winter, and one for the summer. This track plays just over 6,100 yards and offers a full 18 holes to the golfing public.

The opening hole is the most difficult–it's the only 400-yard-plus par 4 on the course. Nothing wrong with a bogey on this first hole, since it plays 446 yards. The back nine features two very birdie-able par 3s, as well as a 436-yard par 5 and a 280-yard par 4 that play back-to-back.

Other notes: They love greens here, so there's two to practice on near the clubhouse.

The details   817-439-1318. 1714 Avondale Haslet Rd., Haslet, TX 76052

- 1966. 18 holes. Par 72. Back – 6,158 (68.9). Middle – 5,882 (67.6). Forward – Par 70. 5,404 (65.5). Price - $.

Getting there From Hwy. 287 (Decatur) north, exit Willow Springs and drive past the stop sign. Turn right at the first right after the stop sign, then left on Avondale Haslet Rd. The entrance is on the right side.

HASLET NOTES   Haslet is a day trip, so grab lunch at **Lee's Barbecue** (817-439-5337) on Schoolhouse Rd. and head on down the road to the next town.

HILLSBORO

Elev. 634   Pop. 7,897

This outlet-center-world serves its purpose, but sometimes gets old. Lake Whitney is west, as are the Victorian homes downtown, and the city is known for its handsome Hill College. Lake Whitney receives the majority of attention in this part of the world, but the town of Hillsboro offers a 9-hole country club that's worth a look if you're touring the area.

HILLSBORO COUNTRY CLUB

The golf   The word on the Hillsboro CC is that it's just right for the average golfer. The design dates back to the 1930s, and is a traditional layout built around a creek that comes into play on a few holes. The greens are elevated, so take enough club.

Other notes: Depending on who you talk to, the course may or may not be open to the public, but we'll go with the Chamber of Commerce's friendly recommendation that out-of-towners are welcome at HCC. When we originally called to schedule a round that we ended up avoiding, we were abruptly told

Play the game, strategically, from the green back to the tee.
Design every shot for the easiest putt possible. Jackie Burke, Jr.

by the older gentleman who answered the phone that the course wasn't open to the public. Respect the locals and be on your best behavior when visiting Hillsboro's course.

The details 254-582-8211. 600 Country Club Dr., Hillsboro, TX 76645

- 1930s. 9 holes. Par 36. Back – 2,904 (35.0). Forward – 2,541. Price - $.

Getting there From I-35 south, take Exit 268 (Old Brandon Rd), turn right and go 4 blocks to Country Club Rd. Turn right again and head straight to the course.

HILLSBORO NOTES Southwest of town is **Lake Aquilla,** rumored to have outstanding fishing. Find B&B accommodations at the **Tarlton House** (254-582-7216). Out on the lake, the **Lake Whitney B&B** (254-694-7659) is the choice. For lunch, **El Conquistador** is sometimes called "the best in Texas." for Tex-Mex. **Up in Smoke BBQ** is just south of the city, next to the Knox service station. Downtown, the Italian joint on the square comes highly recommended.

IRVING
Elev. 470 Pop. 191,615

Originally just a watermelon farm around the turn of the century, Irving has surged into a thriving residential, commercial, and industrial city bordered by Dallas to the east and DFW Airport to the west. The Dallas Cowboys play football here, and the scenes around Texas Stadium have come to define the public's image of Irving's place in the Texas landscape. Ultramodern Las Colinas is next door, with its striking Williams Square and Mustangs exhibit. In terms of golf, three first-class country clubs contrast with the extremely hacker-friendly Twin Lakes municipal course. The TPC at Las Colinas resort is best known among the country clubs since it has been the home of the PGA Tour's Byron Nelson Golf Classic since 1983.

HACKBERRY CREEK COUNTRY CLUB

The golf Often overlooked in the DFW-area golf landscape, Hackberry Creek CC offers a 7,013-yard track in the northern reaches of Irving, surrounded by a residential community that actually complements the course quite well. Unlike other house-lined courses, the homes here are a reasonable distance from the course, allowing the golfer to focus on the task at hand.

This interesting track features a back nine loaded with three par 3s and three par 5s, extremely unique in this day and age. Overall, the fairways are generous, which is especially nice when playing from the 6,500-yard blue tees, but there is water throughout the design that often squeezes the target areas.

Only bullfighting and the water hole are left as vestigial evidence of what a bloody savage man used to be. Only in golf is this sort of contrived swindle allowed. Tommy Bolt

NORTH CENTRAL

If you get there early, take advantage of the solid practice facility that surrounds the pro shop, complete with a driving range and a putting and chipping green.

The details   972-869-2631. 1901 W. Royal Ln., Irving, TX 75063

- www.hackberrycreekcc.com
- 1986. B. Nelson. Gold – 7,013. (73.9/132). Blue – 6,562 (71.7/124). White – 6,259 (70.2/122). Red – 5,471 (71.4/119). Price - $$$.

Getting there From Hwy. 114 east, turn left onto the Beltline. When you come to Royal Ln., turn right and drive 1 mile to the course. The entrance is on the left side of the street.

LAS COLINAS COUNTRY CLUB

The golf   Las Colinas Country Club opened in 1963 with a Joe Finger design that took advantage of the rolling terrain between Dallas and Fort Worth. Finger's design features huge greens as well as fairways that are fairly wide, but never offer a level lie. The course rolls through beautiful oak, pecan, and mesquite trees, some of which must be the most magnificent in Texas. Overall, the course is old, well-tended, and spectacular.

On the front, the 437-yard hole 5 causes problems as it doglegs right over a creek that continues along the right side to the green.

On the back side, the later stretch of holes is the most challenging, starting with the 401-yard No. 15, which requires a longish approach over water into a peninsula green. Next comes the long No.16, which also doglegs right inside fairway bunkers that squeeze the landing area. And finally No. 18: a 550-yard par 5 that tees off over a creek and features a lake in the landing area. The approach on this signature hole plays into what is basically an island green.

The details   972-541-1141. 4400 N. O'Connor Rd., Irving, TX 75062

- www.lascolinascc.com
- 1963. Joe Finger. 18 holes. Par 71. Back – 6,809 (72.6/129). Middle – 6,359 (70.3/124). Forward – 5,222 (69.8/116). Price - $$$.

Getting there The course is located 15 minutes from the Dallas/Fort Worth Airport. Take 114 east for 10 miles and you'll see it on the south side of the highway.

TPC AT LAS COLINAS SPORTS CLUB

The golf   Big names have been involved from the beginning, including Robert Trent Jones, Jr., Jay Morrish, Ben Crenshaw, Tom Watson, and Byron Nelson, each of whom has collaborated to build the home of the PGA Tour's Byron Nelson Classic.

Humans love to play. You may have to work to teach a child to read or to convince her to pick up her room, but you generally won't have to work to teach her to play. Play comes naturally. You must quiet your mind and let yourself play. Dr. Bob Rotella

Mr. Nelson's tourney is held on the **TPC Course**, which has always been considered one of the top TPC courses and consistently features some of the best playing conditions of any tournament on tour. Playing to only a par 70, 6,850 yards from the tips, the design is highlighted by rolling fairways, extensive bunkering, and greens that are framed by grassy mounds.

On the front, No. 8 is one of the best holes: a 400-yarder with water along the left side and bunkers in play on right. Water surrounds the well-bunkered green. On the back No. 17 has been upgraded in recent years with the addition of a huge lake, creating an ominous view from the tee of this 217-yard par 3.

The **Cottonwood Valley Course** plays a role in the tournament every year during the first two rounds. Known for the opening hole featuring a Texas-shaped green bordered by an Oklahoma-like bunker, this course is usually not available for guests of the resort.

The details   972-717-2530. 4150 N. MacArthur Blvd., Irving, TX 75038

- www.fourseasons.com
- TPC Course: 1960s. Joe Finger. Back – 6,899 (73.5/135). Middle – 6,500 (71.4/129). Forward – 5,340 (70.6/116). Price - $$$$.
- Cottonwood Course: 1985. Robert Trent Jones, Jr. Back – 6,927 (73.4/133). Middle – 6,367 (70.5/126). Forward – 5,320 970.0/118). Price - $$$$.

Getting there From Hwy. 114 west, take the O'Connor exit and turn left. The clubhouse is on the left side of the street.

TWIN WELLS GOLF COURSE

The golf   From the fairways of Twin Wells, you can see the skyline of downtown Dallas–a nice aesthetic for this fun, user-friendly municipal. The course is mostly an open, links-style design, although a few holes that roll along the Trinity River favor a traditional-style on the back nine.

Hole 3 stands out on the front: a 437-yard dogleg left that is protected by fairway bunkers. On the back, No. 11 is the most difficult–another long par 4 at 451 yards.

The details   972-438-4340. 2000 E. Shady Grove Rd., Irving, TX 75060

- 1988. Par 72. Back – 6,636 (70.9 / 117). Middle – 6,259 (69.3/113). Forward – 5,056 (67.2/113). Price - $$.

Getting there From Hwy. 183 east, take Loop 12 south and exit Shady Grove Rd. Turn left, drive a short distance to the course, look for the clubhouse on the right side of the street.

Golf is a game to be played with two hands. Your left hand guides the club and keeps the face in the desired position for the hit, and power pours through the right hand and the club. Whack the hell out of the ball with the right hand. Tommy Armour

IRVING NOTES   The upscale **Mustang Cafe** in Las Colinas is the discerning golfers' first choice for either lunch or dinner. Taking the MacArthur exit off of 114 in either direction and will take you to the fast food joints and chains. Try the **Cool River Cafe** (972-888-4266) just of MacArthur on Hidden Ridge. For golfers, it's hard to pass up a **Hooters** (972-659-9464), and this one is on Belt Line Rd. We recommend that you stay at the TPC resort and go for the spa and golf treatments, but the **Omni Mandalay Hotel** (972-869-5511) is another solid option.

JACKSBORO   Elev. 1,074   Pop. 3,527

Jacksboro, the "Cross Roads of North Texas," is a prosperous little farming and ranching community located 60 miles northwest of Fort Worth in the heart of the Cross Timbers country. The town dates back to the mid-1800s, when it took root as a farming community in the pasturelands of the West Fork of Keechi Creek. Indian raids devastated the settlers until nearby Fort Richardson became established in the 1870s, about the same time the town became famous for hosting the murder trial of Kiowa chiefs Satanta and Big Tree.

JACKSBORO COUNTRY CLUB

The golf   The JCC, which supposedly dates back to the 1920s, is an old course that rolls through some hills and offers water hazards on only two holes. The 9 holes play to a par 35, and it's a stout 3,397 yards from the blue tees. The only par 5 is the opener, going 525 yards, but the remaining par 4s are all mostly long and challenging, including the 480-yard 2nd hole. The best birdie opportunities here are the par 3s: short irons from the whites, long irons from the blues, but really no major problems if you strike it well.

The details   940-567-3726. Hwy. 148 N., Jacksboro, TX 76458

- 1924. Henry Richards. 9 holes. Par 35. Back – 3,397 (35.5/112). Middle – 3,031 (34.7/111). Forward – Par 36. 2,445 (34.0/108). Price - $.

Getting there From Fort Worth, take Hwy. 199 west, then turn right on Hwy. 148 and head directly to the course.

JACKSBORO NOTES Visit the **Fort Richardson State Historical Park** south of town on US 281, a good place to camp if you're interested in roughing it. In town the **Butterfield Depot Motel** (940-567-5567) and **Jacksboro Inn** (940-567-3751) offer adequate accommodations. For lunch, how can you go wrong with the **Green Frog Restaurant** (940-567-5711), where they really do serve

---

☆

About the only positive contribution of uncontrolled pursuit of power is to make golf ball and equipment manufacturers rich. Jim Flick

"shrimp, hamburgers, Mexican food, rib-eyes, chicken-fried steak, sandwiches, pork chops, and anything else you might want."

JOSHUA   Elev. 928   Pop. 4,529

Located on Texas 174 between Burleson and Cleburne, Joshua is a small farming community that receives about 20,000 cars passing through its city limits each year. The countryside, spotted with dairy cows, horses, and cotton, pretty much says it all for this pass-through town that just happens to have an 18-hole golf course.

MOUNTAIN VALLEY COUNTRY CLUB

The golf   Mountain Valley, which opened in the 1960s, is laid out around two good-sized lakes, with a creek that rolls through the course and comes into play on four holes. Several of the tees are elevated, and while there are no sand bunkers, the course is spotted with grass bunkers that get in the way. The average-sized greens are well sloped and fast. Three of the tee boxes are elevated, and many of the fairways have dogleg configurations.

No. 3 is the most difficult hole on the front, a 523-yard par 5. On the back, No. 11 also measures well over 500 yards, and No. 18 is known as the signature, a long par 3 over a lake.

Other notes: The club doesn't have a formal driving range, but there's a warm-up area adequate for short irons only.

The details   817-295-7126. 395 Clubhouse Dr., Joshua, TX 76058

• 1965. 18 holes. Par 71. Back – 6,542 (70.4/118). Middle – 6,132 (68j.7/113). Forward – Par 72. 5,174 (68.5/113). Price - $.

Getting there Take 174 through Burleson. When you get to Joshua, look for the Mountain Valley Country Club Estates entrance. Turn left there and find the course.

JOSHUA NOTES   Joshua just isn't a weekend destination, so work it in one morning on the way to the Hill Country. For lunch, the **Dairy Queen** is always an option in Joshua, but the locals prefer **Laura & Sandy's Cutting Board Cafe** .

A rough should have high grass. When you go bowling they don't
give you anything for landing in the gutter, do they? Lee Trevino

KELLER

Elev. 704   Pop. 27,345

Located 15 miles north of Fort Worth, this up-and-coming commuter town sprang from the 1850s Double Springs settlement. The area marks the Eastern Cross Timbers region, with rangeland to the west and dense oak forests in the immediate region–perfect for rugged golf layouts such as Sky Creek Ranch. The area has grown tremendously, mainly because of its proximity to DFW International Airport, and most of Keller's residents work outside of the community.

SKY CREEK RANCH GOLF CLUB

The golf   One of the better public access courses in the state, Sky Creek Ranch boasts an immaculate Robert Trent Jones, Jr. design that is kept in immaculate condition by former Barton Creek Resort superintendent Steven Best. The clubhouse is perched atop the highest point in Tarrant County, and from this vantage point you'll have a great view of the fine 419 Bermuda fairways and the bent-grass greens that are framed by a forest of oak trees and carved by the frustrating Big Bear Creek.

The key to Sky Creek is playing from the correct set of tees. Water comes into play on 16 of 18 holes, and most of the greens are elevated and surrounded by trouble that will make your score skyrocket. From the tips, high handicappers will struggle with their inconsistency, since there is virtually no room for error at any point on this course. Rounds from the more forward tees are amazingly different, with hackers being able to hit 4 irons off the tee and mid-short irons in–a huge advantage on this course.

Jones, Jr.'s design features five par 5s that offer some intriguing risk-reward opportunities. Three of them have water fronting the green, forcing hacks to think about going for home in two. No. 5 might be the best of the bunch: a snaking 534-yard hole that requires a precise fade around the dogleg right, followed by a perfect layup to be in position for the regulation approach. The creek circles around the elevated green, and trees loom left of the fairway for layups that stray too far left. This hole requires some strategy.

Sky Creek also offers five par 3s–some very difficult, and others nice respites from the other challenging holes. No. 14 is probably the scariest hole on the course, a 212-yard par 3 that is lined by trees on the left and a huge lake along the right and beside the green. This hole, which has ruined many a round, has a small bail-out area left, but you'll need a perfect shot to keep the score reasonable.

A bit pricey for some North Texas golfers, Sky Creek is worth it for the diehards. In addition to the layout and condition, the practice facility is phenomenal–it features a driving range that plays downhill into an open valley with numerous target flags, as well as a large putting green that gives you a great feel for the round ahead. Chipping and pitching areas are available too.

The details 817-498-1414. 600 Promontory Dr., Keller, TX 76248

- www.skycreekranch.com

- 1999. Robert Trent Jones, Jr. Pro – 6,953 (73.4/136). Champ – 6,367 (70.8/127). Club – 5,940 (68.4/120). Forward – 5,390 (72.8/132). Price - $$$$.

Getting there From Ft. Worth, take I-35W north to Exit 64. Turn right on Golden Triangle Rd. and drive 7 miles. Turn right on Bear Creek Pkwy. and drive to the Hidden Lakes subdivision (west side of road). Turn right on Promontory Dr. to the course.

KELLER NOTES Chapp's Cafe (817-431-3888) has awesome burgers and a devoted local following. For Italian go to **Mezzaluna Restaurante** (817-431-3420), and for Mexican go to **El Paseo** (817-741-4100). All three are on Keller Pkwy.

KEMP
Elev. 382   Pop. 1,200

From Dallas, Kemp is the last town before you reach Cedar Creek Lake, an area bristling with enjoyable lakeside golf courses. The surrounding ranchlands are devoted to cattle production and most of the residents, if not retired, commute to jobs in the Dallas area.

CEDAR CREEK COUNTRY CLUB

The golf The first course developed along Cedar Creek Lake, this one opened in 1967 as part of a rural retirement community. The course's namesake waterway slinks its way through the course, coming into play six times as you wind your way through the tree-lined fairways.

Holes of note include the 470-yard, par 4 No. 6, which dives through a chute of trees to a large green. Thankfully, this monster is void of hazards. On the back No. 13 is feast or famine–a short par 5 at 483 yards, but a pond sits in the middle of the fairway. The ender at Cedar Creek goes 520 yards and is fairly manageable if you can keep it out of the trees.

The details 903-498-8419. 18392 Country Club Dr., Kemp, TX 75143

- 1967. 18 holes. Par 72. Back – 6,723 (72.2/122). Middle – 6,368 (70.4/120). Forward – 5,420 (71.2/123). Price - $$.

Getting there From Hwy. 175 east, take the Kemp exit and look for the signs to the course.

Amateur golf is a game of trouble shots and one-putt pars. It follows therefore that good scrambling is the amateur's fastest, most direct route to better golf. George Peper

INDIAN OAKS GOLF CLUB

The golf   Indian Oaks is a 30-hole golf course, offering "21 holes for the price of 18". Labeled in 1997 as "The Most Unique Golf Course in Texas" by the *Dallas Morning News*, they're nice enough to throw in a cheeseburger with chips and a drink with your green fee.

The course is tough not only because it is tight, but because there is water and sand on just about every hole. The greens are famous for the deceptive, fast undulations.

The details   903-498-3564. 7574 Lee Ln., Kemp, TX 75143

- www.indianoaksgolf.com
- 1990. Ken Andrews. 30 holes. 9-hole Red Course. 9-hole White Course. 12-hole Blue Course. Price - $$.

Getting there From Hwy. 175 east, take Exit 1388 and turn right. Continue down this road until it dead-ends, then turn left onto Hwy. 148. When you get to Hwy. 3094, go north. Follow the signs to the course.

KING'S CREEK GOLF CLUB

The golf   From the tips, King's Creek can play particularly tough because of the prevailing winds off the shores of Cedar Creek Lake. However, on calm days this course can be had, since the layout is fairly basic and features water on only six holes. In the late 1980s, the course became known for its improving condition, and that reputation has held true over the years.

The front nine is shorter and a little easier than the back, its toughest hole being the 200-yard No. 3 over water. No. 14 typifies the longer back: a 576-yard marathon with water on either side of the fairway.

The details   903-498-8888. 6025 Club Dr., Kemp, TX 75143

- 1980. 18 holes. Par 71. Back – 6,507 (72.0/124). Middle – 6,024 (69.4/118). Forward – 4,700 (68.0/113). Price - $$.

Getting there From Dallas, take I-175 south, then turn right on Hwy. 274. The course is 2 miles down the road.

KEMP NOTES   Kemp proper has no accommodations, so you'll need to head to Gun Barrel City, TX, the hub of Cedar Creek Lake commerce, where the coastal-feeling **Bait Bucket** serves up great food and even offers cabins for rent above the restaurant. For Italian find **Vitoni's**, or if you're in the mood for steaks, try **The Ranch House**. **Dock's Pub & Grille** (903-489-3627) is new and is gaining a reputation for its great sports-bar-type atmosphere.

Don't let the bad shots get to you. Don't let yourself become angry. The true scramblers are thick-skinned. And they always beat the whiners. Paul Runyan

Finally, on the other side of the lake, the town of Seven Points, TX has a family-style place called **McClain's** .

LAKE KIOWA

Elev. 754   Pop. 1,883

Lake Kiowa, established in 1967, is a private community located on a 600-acre lake 7 miles southeast of Gainesville. Of the 800-some-odd homes in the community, about half are occupied year round, with the others used as a quick vacation spot for north Texas families. The community has two sandy beaches and an 18-hole golf course, which you'll only get to play if you know a member or have enough savvy and desire to hustle your way on.

LAKE KIOWA GOLF COURSE

The golf   Leon Howard was hired in 1969 to build this private course for the Lake Kiowa community. His design is built around Lake Kiowa and two ponds that come into play on more than half the holes. Since the fairways meander through the houses, out-of-bounds is in play on most holes.

The front nine features three notable holes, all of which involve water. Hole 4 has character because the tee is surrounded by water, and the first shot plays over the lake. No. 8 is a long par 3 with water surrounding the green on three sides, and No. 9 is a short par 4 (318 yards) with an approach into an island green.

The most difficult hole on the back is the 418-yard No. 16, which doglegs around the lake and has an approach over water.

Other notes: The course was built on an old Kiowa Indian camp site, and various artifacts that were recovered during construction are featured in the clubhouse.

The details   940-668-7394. 100 Navajo Trail, Lake Kiowa, TX 76240

- Leon Howard. 18 holes. Par 72. Back – 6,605 (70.9/117). Middle – 6,217 (69.4/112). Forward – Par 73. 5,085 (69.0/110). Price - $.

Getting there From Dallas, take I-35 north to Hwy. 82. Head east on Hwy. 82 and follow the signs to the course. The course is next to Lake Kiowa.

LAKE KIOWA NOTES Seek spirited conversations at the nearby **Lake Kiowa Tavern** (940-612-2088), where a smile and a cold beer might win points with the locals, creating future opportunities to play their charming little course.

---

*The golfer obsessed with his putter or his grip is focusing on the
props, and not on the core of his performance. Dr. Bob Rotella*

LANCASTER

Elev. 512   Pop. 22,684

Lancaster ("Lankister" to the locals) has retained its small-town feel despite growing at the same rate as other DFW cities. Just a short drive south from Big D on I-35, you can veer off the main thoroughfare to find fine Victorian homes and a downtown area that has been completely renovated. Overlooked in the overgrown, upscale golf world of DFW, Lancaster boasts one of the better small-town courses in the state, and should definitely be considered because of its proximity to Dallas and minimal impact on the pocketbook.

COUNTRY VIEW GOLF COURSE

The golf   Ron Garl came by in 1989 and finally gave the city of Lancaster a golf course to be proud of. Billy Martindale's failed attempts to establish a course, followed by the city taking over the old Pecan Hollow Golf Club, eventually resulted in Garl coming in to build a truly unique course.

No. 7 is the most difficult hole–a long dogleg right with water in play off the tee and in the fairway. Also, get ready for No. 15, a unique par 3 that features a green completely surrounded by huge trees. Most of the tee boxes are elevated and there is water on over half of the holes.

The details   972-227-0995. 240 W. Belt Line Rd., Lancaster, TX 75146

- 1989. Ron Garl. 18 holes. Par 72. Back – 6,609 (71.0/128). Middle – 6,043 (68.6/122). Forward – 5,048 (68.2/120). Price - $$.

Getting there From I-35 south exit Belt Line Rd. and drive east 4 miles to the course. The course is on the right-hand side.

MORE LANCASTER GOLF

Check out the **David Royar Golf Shop** (972-227-0995) on W. Belt Line Rd. for used gear, repairs, and all things golf.

LANCASTER NOTES   This one is a day trip, so if you're passing through set up accommodations in Dallas or further south towards the Hill Country. If you must stay, roll into the **Country Rose B&B** (972-218-5017), Lancaster's only non-hotel lodging option. Your best bets for eats are **Amaya's Mexican Grill** (972-227-8911) on the historic town square, or **Hickory House Barbecue** (972-227-7322) on N. Dallas Ave.

LEWISVILLE

Elev. 490   Pop. 72,466

Lewisville offers a dynamic mix of urban sprawl and small-town charm, located minutes from Dallas. Its numerous residential subdivisions housing DFW commuters surround Old Town Lewisville and its charming store fronts, restaurants, and boutiques.

In terms of golf courses, Lewisville sometimes receives credit for the surrounding courses in Flower Mound and The Colony, which are all within a short drive. However, only three facilities officially call Lewisville home.

HANK HANEY GOLF RANCH AT VISTA RIDGE

The golf   Like Haney's signature facility in McKinney, Vista Ridge offers a 9-hole executive course with five lighted holes and a state-of-the-art teaching center complete with a lighted driving range over water, putting green, and short game area. The course is slated to open sometime in 2003, with four par 4s and five par 3s ranging from 80-170 yards. The longest par 4 is slated to go around 360 yards.

The details   972-315-5300. 2471 Stemmons Frwy., Lewisville, TX 75067.

• 2003. Hank Haney. 9 holes. Par 31. Price - $.

Getting there Take I-35 north from Dallas past 635 to Hwy. 121. Drive under the service road and look for the course on the right-hand side of the service road.

LAKE PARK GOLF COURSE

The golf   Lake Park is located below the Lake Lewisville dam, and was originally known as Oak Ridge Park. The city of Lewisville owned the course since its 1957 inception, but sold the facility to a partnership that includes former PGA Tour player Lanny Wadkins and his design partner Richard Watson.

Make sure that you warm up before your round, because No. 1 goes 465 yards with water in play off the tee. The next notable hole is No. 8, which offers a nice risk-reward situation with two small ponds protecting the green 312 yards away. With the wind it is definitely drive-able. On the back, No. 10 gives you the option to carry the lake with a 230-yard-plus drive, or lay up and leave yourself with a long approach over the water.

Other notes: There is a par 29 executive 9-hole course at Lake Park as well.

The details   972-219-5661. 6 Lake Park Rd., Lewisville, TX 75057

• 1996. 18 holes. Par 70. Back – 6,135 (68.3/108). Middle – 5,740 (66.5/103). Forward – 4,960. Price - $$.

• Executive Course: 1994. 9 holes. Par 29. Back – 1,724 (29.0). Middle – 1,552 (28.4). Forward – 1,363. Price - $.

The point is that it doesn't matter if you look like a beast before or after the hit, as long as you look like a beauty at the moment of impact. Seve Ballesteros

Getting there From Dallas, drive north on I-35 and take the Lake Park Rd. exit. Turn east, drive 1 mile to the course, and look for the entrance on the right side of the road.

THE GOLF CLUB AT CASTLE HILLS

The golf   Although Castle Hills is officially listed with a Lewisville address, the course borders Carrollton and North Dallas, on an unusually hilly piece of property for the usually flat Dallas area. The Morrish brothers designed this course, which tips out at a par 72 7,152 yards and features 419 Bermuda fairways, huge bent-grass greens, oaks, mesquites, and ponds and creeks that come into play on just over half the holes. The design incorporates significant elevation changes (up to 70 feet), and is highlighted by some unusual finger-like bunkers. Hacks will enjoy the generous fairways, which allow for aggressive plays off the tee since they're void of major hassles.

No. 7 is the highlight on the front—a 208-yarder that carries a rock-lined pond loaded with beautiful flowers. On the back, Nos. 11 and 12 are back-to-back testers, the first going 372 yards over a lake, and the second stretching to 601 yards with the old ranch's windmill and tank next to the green.

Also note that the club has a three-hole practice course featuring a 610-yard par 5, as well as a par 3 and par 4 hole. Tee times can be made up to 14 days in advance.

The details   972-899-7400. 699 Lady of the Lake Blvd., Lewisville, TX 75056

- www.thegolfclubch.com

- 1999. Jay Morrish. Back – 7,152. Middle – 6,607. Forward – 5,064. Price - $$$$.

Getting there From Dallas, drive north on I-35 to Hebron Pkwy., then turn right and proceed to Josey Ln. Turn left on Josey Ln.

LEWISVILLE NOTES   The Fairfield Inn (972-899-6900) is an option if you have to stay here instead of in Dallas or Fort Worth, as is the Courtyard by Marriott (972-316-3100). The nicest is the Homewood Suites by Hilton (972-315-6123). All up and down I-35 are the chains, but BJ's Restaurant & Brewhouse sort of offers a roadhouse experience. Clyde's Old Time Hamburgers is on Main St. in old downtown Lewisville. The best barbecue in town is Famous Dave's BBQ. And another burger option is the famous Texas Hamburger Factory (972-317-3603), which is unfortunately closed on Sundays.

If a putt looks straight, don't stare at the line for a long period of time trying to see if there's something you overlooked. Sooner or later, you'll invent a break that isn't there. Corey Pavin

LONE OAK
Elev. 562   Pop. 600

Lone Oak is on Hwy. 69 just south of Greenville, TX, and only 7 miles north of Lake Tawakoni. Named for a massive oak tree that dominated the grass-covered prairie, the community is soon to become known to North Texas golfers thanks to the unique residential development that will sprout around the Jeff Brauer-designed Mathews Bluff Golf Club.

MATHEWS BLUFF GOLF CLUB

The golf   In progress here at Lone Oak is the "early American" style Mathews Bluff Golf Club. The Jeff Brauer-designed course is set in the historical Rocky Ford area as part of a plan to capture the Dallas, Greenville, and Tyler golf markets.

The course will sit along the shores of Lake Tawakoni, nestled against 1,300 acres of Texas Parks and Wildlife land. A keenly sensitive environmental approach to design and construction will preserve the natural terrain and wildlife. Historically, the area was a crossing point of the Sabine River for settlers moving west; the Sabine was later dammed to create Lake Tawakoni. The land was purchased from 96-year-old Paul Mathews of Greenville who, as an avid hunter and golfer, stipulated that the land must be strictly preserved to the highest of standards.

From all indications, this one should be spectacular, as Brauer envisions tabletop greens, deep bunkers, holes fronting the lake, and an old rock quarry that will come into play. However, for now the project has been put on hold temporarily as the ownership group apparently awaits further financing.

LONE OAK NOTES   **Lone Oak Grocery** serves food until 9 p.m. (hamburgers and fajitas). **The Oak Café** on Hwy. 69 opens early for break but closes at 2 p.m.

MABANK
Elev. 393   Pop. 2,151

Mabank, like nearby Kaufman County neighbor Kemp, derives its simple existence from Cedar Creek Lake. Another former railroad town surrounded by cotton farms, its growth comes from the tourists, retirees, and young commuters who are attracted by the rural lake life away from the big-city hassles.

PINNACLE COUNTRY CLUB

The golf   Formerly known as Arrowhead Country Club, Pinnacle opened in 1970 as a 9-hole track nestled on the cozy banks of Cedar Creek Lake. Tough times descended and the course was shut down before reopening with

A bad grip has ruined more golf games than Ladies' Day. Lee Trevino

an additional nine and new ownership in the 1980s.

Dallas' eastward growth has turned many golfers onto the pleasant, rural atmosphere at Pinnacle Country Club. Every hole is lined with trees and, despite its short length, the course is particularly tough because of the numerous dogleg fairways. Not counting the par 3s, 11 of 14 holes have doglegs. Because of the trees it's recommended that you leave the driver in the bag.

The toughest hole is No. 15, a par 5 that goes 511 yards and offers a testy risk-reward decision. With a good drive into the wide-open fairway, going for it in two is possible by cutting the lake on the left side of the fairway.

The details 903-451-9797. 200 Pinnacle Club Dr., Mabank, TX 75147

- www.pinnaclegolfclub.com
- 1985. Don January. 18 holes. Par 71. Back – 6,441 (72.9/135). Middle – 5,943 (70.4/128). Forward – 5,195 (70.8/129). Price - $$.

Getting there From Hwy. 175 east, find the town of Eustace and turn right on Hwy. 316. Turn right and drive 5.5 miles to Clear Creek Rd. Turn right again and follow the signs to the course.

MABANK NOTES The **Birdhouse B&B** (903-887-1242) has been around since 1995, and is preferred because of its quiet setting. Out on the lake, the **Harbour Light Marina** (903-887-6656) can hook you up for lake excursions and provide provisions for weekend road tripping. On Mason St. there's the **Chattahoochie Smoke House** (903-432-2594), worthy if only for its name, and Tex-Mex cravers can dig into greasy portions at **El Plato De Oro** (903-880-9919) on Main St.

MANSFIELD
Elev. 596   Pop. 28,031

Located on US 287 about 15 minutes southwest of Fort Worth, Mansfield has transformed from a rural community into a bustling suburb. They say the state's first steam-powered gristmill operated here, bringing the town a little fame when flour was milled and delivered to the Confederate Army during the Civil War. Walnut Creek flows into nearby Joe Pool Lake to the east, and Mansfield's first country club is named after this longtime source of water. The public option for golf here is called Mansfield National–a new course that has received high praise since it opened in the late 1990s.

MANSFIELD NATIONAL GOLF CLUB

The golf John Colligan (Squaw Creek in Glen Rose) designed this par 72, 6,850-yard track around Low Branch Creek and a large 5-acre lake that

---

I've never known anyone to get from an average handicap to scratch in much less than two years. It may take you four to six years if you sustain a regular commitment to practice and playing. Dr. Bob Rotella

impacts play on the back nine. The tees range from 5,263 to 6,850 yards and the course plays to a par 72. The large, undulating greens make for inviting targets. The fairways are lined by every type of tree imaginable, with bunkers looming to suck in tee shots.

Scores can add up on holes 11 and 16, with the lake coming into play, but water comes into play on only four holes total.

The best hole is No. 5, considered one of the toughest par 3s in North Texas. It plays a very 3-wood-like 233 yards into a tough green that's hard to hold with the wind at your back.

The details   817-477-3366. 3750 National Pkwy., Mansfield, TX 76063

• www.mansfieldnational.com

• John Colligan. 18 holes. Par 72. Black – 6,850. Gold – 6,232. Brick – 5,263. Price - $$$.

Getting there From Dallas, take I-30 or I-20 west to Hwy. 360. Go south on Hwy. 360 all the way to National Pkwy. Turn east (left) on National Pkwy. and you can't miss the clubhouse (on your left).

WALNUT CREEK COUNTRY CLUB

The golf   Walnut Creek opened in 1968 with its original **Pecan Course**–a Don January - Billy Martindale design that is more traditional than its neighboring Oaks Course, and considered more challenging. While the course is not long at only 6,538 yards from the tips, the fairways are narrow and create the illusion of being longer than they actually are.

No. 1 is a solid starter, doglegging left for 378 yards from an elevated tee along a creek. The approach plays back uphill into an elevated green. No. 6 is another good hole, playing 440 yards with a long approach over water to an elevated green.

On the back, the best hole is No. 11. It's long at 438 yards but doglegs left downhill to a small green, providing the option of shortening the hole by cutting the corner and using the slope for extra distance.

The newer **Oak Course**, whose back nine was designed by PGA Tour pro Mark Brooks, is known more as a shot-maker's course. The best bets for birdies on the Oaks are the short par 3s, all of which are under 180 yards, and three of them playing 160 yards or less from the tips.

The details   817-473-6114. 1151 Country Club Dr., Mansfield, TX 76063

• www.walnutcreekcc.com

• Pecan Course: 1968. Martindale - January. 18 holes. Par 71. Back – 6,538 (71.9/129). Middle – 6,252 (70.6/127). Forward – 5,260 (72.1/124). Price - $$$.

• Oak Course: Mark Brooks. 18 holes. Par 72. Gold – 6,751 (74.1/128). Blue

Head-lifting is caused by fear and anxiety. You are seeking the result before you have struck the ball. You did not trust your swing. Ernest Jones

– 6,284 (72.0/124). White – 5,796 (69.6/119). Red – 4,823 (69.0/112). Price - $$$.

Getting there From I-20 east take Hwy. 287 south and, when you come to Walnut Creek Dr., turn left. Drive 2 blocks to Country Club Dr. and turn right.

MANSFIELD NOTES In Mansfield, which is generally a day trip from the DFW area, you have three solid dining options. **Stevens Garden & Grill** (817-473-8733) and **The Nut House Grill** (817-453-5166) serve more American-style fare, and **Cha Cha's** (817-473-8363) is Mansfield's most famous Mexican restaurant. When late-nighters require lodging, the **Comfort Inn** (817-453-8848) is clean, affordable, and convenient.

McKINNEY
Elev. 612   Pop. 40,404

McKinney exudes a Victorian charm with its vibrant courthouse square and shaded streets lined with historical buildings and homes. After mid-day excursions on the links it's the perfect place to meet the family, wind down, and enjoy a leisurely stroll around downtown for shopping and good eats.

And while it's not publicized enough, McKinney has become a virtual golf mecca with courses dotted all over the lush, blackland prairies east and west of I-75. With connections and time, one could easily spend a week here indulging in the outstanding golf courses.

ELDORADO COUNTRY CLUB

The golf   Designed by Gary Baird in 1981, Eldorado is situated in one of the most beautiful parts of McKinney, featuring a creek and an irrigation lake in addition to a multitude of trees. The course is known for its extremely sloped greens, which are often covered by heavy bunkering.

On the front, No. 5 is the toughest hole, going 433 yards with out-of-bounds on the right and a pond in the fairway at 200 yards from the tee. The approach must carry the bunker fronting the green.

The back nine features two mean par 5s–Nos. 11 and 15. The 11th is a narrow dogleg with a small pond looming right of the green. No. 15 is under 500 yards but features the creek cutting the fairway and riding the right side of the hole.

Other notes: The clubhouse burned to the ground in November of 1996 and was replaced in 1998.

The details   972-529-2770. 2604 Country Club Dr., McKinney, TX 75070

- 1982. Gary Baird. 18 holes. Par 72. Back – 6,770 (73.2/135). Middle –

The most important single move in establishing your tempo and rhythm is your takeaway. It sets the beat for everything that comes later. Strive on every shot to move the club back as deliberately as possible, consistent with swinging it back rather than taking it back. Jack Nicklaus

6,188 (70.5/126). Forward – 5,461 (71.8/122). Price - $$.

Getting there From I-75 north, take the Eldorado Pkwy. (Exit 39) and go west. When you come to Country Club Dr., turn right and look for the course on the left side of the street.

THE GOLF CLUB AT McKINNEY

The golf   Promoted as an affordable country club option, The Golf Club at McKinney is a new 18-hole daily fee course that measures 6,980 yards from the tips. We mention "daily fee" with a bit of hesitation, as it's clear the club would definitely prefer this to be a full-blown private facility. However, they will allow the public to play–preferably during the week and for a $60 green fee, which seems fairly hefty considering the other golf options available in that range in the DFW area.

The Lindsey Management Co. heads this one up via a joint venture between ex-NFL player Jim Lindsey and Dallas Cowboys owner Jerry Jones.

The details   972-540-6880. 3191 Medical Center Dr., McKinney, TX 75069

• Lyndy Lyndsey. 18 holes. Par 72. 4 sets of tees. Yardage ranges from 6,980 to 4,820 yards. Price - $$$.

Getting there From I-75 (Central Expy.), exit at Eldorado Pkwy. Turn right on Medical Center and proceed south to the club entrance on the left. Access is also available from Hwy. 5.

HANK HANEY GOLF RANCH

The golf   The result of a collaborative effort between big names Pete Dye and Hank Haney, this 9-hole facility opened in 1992 with Haney's signature practice facility located next to an impressive Dye 9-holer. This is about as good as it gets for a practice facility. The ranch's old barns and stables have been converted into the learning center, and Dye's course plays 3,000 yards to par 33.

The details   972-542-8800. 4101 S. Custer Rd., McKinney, TX 75070

• 1992. Hank Haney and Pete Dye. Par 33. Back – 2,516 yards. Forward – 2,108 yards. Price - $.

Getting there From Dallas, take the Dallas Tollway north for 20 miles to Hwy. 121. Turn right and drive 7 miles to Custer Rd. Next, turn left and drive 2.5 miles to the course.

No power on earth will deter men from using a ball that will add to the length of their drive. Golf Illustrated, 1902

McKINNEY COUNTRY CLUB

The golf   Considered among the top 10 in Texas 9-hole courses, McKinney CC is an old, traditional track that offers a very fair par 36 challenge. Playing to only 3,074 yards with every par 4 under 400 yards from the tips, there are plenty of chances to score well on this course. No. 2 is the longest hole and the number one handicap, a 507-yard par 5 sandwiched between the short 317-yard opening hole and the testy 185-yard No. 3. Holes 6 and 7 serve up a nice stretch of golf, starting with a 432-yard par 5 that's followed by a short par 3 and par 4.

The details   972-562-7731. FM 1378, McKinney, TX 75070

- 1920s. 9 holes. Par 36. Back – 3,074 (33.9/114). Forward – 2,703 (36.1/119). Price - $$.

Getting there Take I-75 north to Hwy. 5. Turn east down FM 1378, which turns into Country Club Rd. at about 2 miles. The entrance is on the left.

OAK HOLLOW GOLF COURSE

The golf   After 50 years, the old 9-hole McKinney Municipal Golf Course shut down to make room for the new 18-hole championship layout now known as Oak Hollow. This new layout, designed by Maury Miller, opened in 1998 and features rolling terrain that routes around six man-made lakes.

Miller's design is particularly friendly from the middle tees, playing a fair 6,277 yards with several short par 3s and many average-length par 5s. The number one handicap is No. 15, a 423-yard par 4.

The details   972-542-4523. 3005 N. McDonald St. #5, McKinney, TX 75070

- 1988. Maury Miller. 18 holes. Par 70. Back –6,879 (72.3/121). Middle – 6,277 (69.2/118). Forward – 5,280 (68.8/115). Price - $$

Getting there Take Hwy. 75 north to Hwy. 380, then head east to Hwy. 5 (McDonald St.). The road veers and leads you one mile to the course.

STONEBRIDGE RANCH HILLS COURSE

The golf   The second course created for the Stonebridge Ranch CC development is known as The Hills Course, for the famed Arthur Hills. Much more user-friendly than the neighboring Dye Course, this one offers 27 holes of generous fairways and fun golf.

Originally an 18-holer, 9 more holes have been added, creating three sets known as the Chisolm, Cimarron, and Saddleback nines. The **Saddleback** is the newest of the three.

Holes of note on the **Cimarron** nine are the 156-yard No. 11 that carries water, the 464-yard par 4 No. 14, which is the number one handicap, and the 549-yard No. 16 that has water in play on every shot.

⭐

Bobby Jones retired from active competition at age 28 in 1930, the year of his Grand Slam, and before the founding of Augusta National Golf Club.

On the **Chisolm** track the last two holes are the most challenging. No. 8 is a 168-yard par 3 over water to a green protected on three sides by the wet stuff. No. 9 goes 441 yards and carries water off the tee before forcing a long approach to a green fronted by bunkers.

The details   972-540-2000. 5901 Glen Oaks Dr., McKinney, TX 75070

- www.stonebridgeranch.com, Arthur Hills. 1988.
- Chisolm/Cimarron: Black – 7,087 (74.1/136). Blue – 6,675 (72.1/130). White - 6,203 (69.7/123). Red - 5,644 (76.8/133). Green – 5,053 (69.3/114). Price - $$$$.
- Cimarron/Saddleback: Black – 6,935 (73.2/133). Blue – 6,566 (71.3/128). White - 6,159 (69.1/120). Red - 5,719 (76.8/133). Green – 5,198 (70.0/117). Price - $$$$.
- Saddleback/Chisolm: Black – 7,004 (73.5/133). Blue – 6,571 (71.4/128). White – 6,208 (69.4/119). Red - 5,739 (76.8/133). Green – 5,213 (70.5/119). Price - $$$$.

Getting there From I-75 north turn west on Virginia Pkwy., then look for the signs to the course.

STONEBRIDGE RANCH DYE COURSE

The golf   Pete Dye certainly lived up to his reputation for building diabolical courses when he created the Stonebridge CC course. In fact, Dye himself claimed that the course is more challenging than his famed PGA West course in Palm Springs. If you're looking for a place to blow up your handicap before hitting the easier tracks, Stonebridge is the place.

Dye's design winds through the large lakes and rolling hills of a 6,700-acre residential complex with many amazing homes. The greens are large and fast, and the fairways are immaculate.

The last three holes are too much for the average golfer. Heading back to the clubhouse, they generally play into the prevailing wind. No. 16 is a par 5 at almost 600 yards. The par 3 No. 17 forces a carry of almost 200 yards, followed up with a 450-yard-plus par 4 that curves around a giant lake. Play this course from the white tees unless you're a 12 handicap or better.

Perhaps it was the 50-degree temperature and the extremely wet conditions, but rarely have we played a course where length off the tee was at such a premium. Every shot requires precision, and you will never look at an approach shot and think it's open and easy. Every green seems to be surrounded by danger, forcing the mentality that you must hit the perfect shot—which obviously makes it more difficult to relax and be loose with your game.

The details   972-529-5992. 7003 Beacon Hill Rd., McKinney, TX 75070

- www.clubsatstonebridgeranch.com
- 1988. Pete Dye. Black – 7,312 (75.9/146). Blue – 6,829 (73.5/137). White

– 6,359 (70.6/132). Green - 5,746 (72.5/123). Yellow – 5,222 (69.9/113). Price - $$$$.

Getting there From I-75 north, turn left on Virginia Pkwy. and drive about 4 miles to Stonebridge Dr. Turn left and head to Beacon Hill Rd., then take a right and look for the clubhouse on the left.

WESTRIDGE GOLF COURSE

The golf   The new Westridge is a unique Jeff Brauer design that is a welcome addition to McKinney golf because of its user-friendly layout. The design tips out at a standard looking 7,041 yards; however, its combination of six par 3s (none over water), six par 4s, and six par 5s is far from normal. Brauer incorporated deep bunkers, natural areas, and lakes to accompany the huge, undulating greens that await hacks who become lazy after getting home in regulation.

Other than the unique hole combination, the drive-able par 4s (Nos. 1 and 13) are notable during the summer months because they play downwind and are good birdie opportunities.

The details   972-346-2212. 9055 Cotton Ridge Rd. N., McKinney, TX 75070

* www.westridgegolfcourse.com

* 2001. Jeff Brauer. 18 holes. Par 72. Black – 7,041. Blue – 6,652. White – 6,004. Red – 5,293. Price - $$.

Getting there Located just south of Virginia Pkwy. and FM 2478 (Custer Rd.). From Hwy. 75, exit Virginia Pkwy. and head west to Custer Rd. Turn left, then right at Cotton Ridge.

MORE McKINNEY GOLF

Coming soon to Texas' fastest-growing county (spring 2004) is the world-class **TPC at Craig Ranch** (972-267-9229 or www.tpccraigranch.com), located at the northeast corner of Hwy. 121 and FM 2478. Tom Weiskopf has been hired to route this course along scenic Rowlett Creek, and he'll surely live up to his reputation for creating a natural track in building the newest addition to the PGA Tour's TPC series.

McKINNEY NOTES   Focus your efforts around the Courthouse Square, where there's enough shopping to burn a full day. When it's time to eat, head to the old hoosegow now known as **The Prison Bars and Grill** (972-542-5245), where you'll need reservations in the evening, and you can enjoy live music with your food on the weekends. Another nice spot is **Goodhues Wood Fired Grill** (972-562-7570), where steaks, lamb, duck, and pork are on the menu.

I've been squeezing the club so hard, the cow is screaming. J.C. Snead

For lodging, the town is loaded with B&Bs. The **Tartan Thistle** (972-548-4856) and **Bingham House** (972-529-1883) are beautiful old homes or, and for a more ranch-like feel, call the **Country Charm B&B** (972-529-9970).

MESQUITE
Elev. 491 Pop. 124,523

Around 1950, Mesquite sported 1,700 folks and the town's phones still required the Andy Griffith-style ring operator to push calls through. Then Big D boomed and the interstates opened, spurring growth at a ridiculous rate. Now the town has over 120,000 folks and is still growing. Surprisingly for such a substantial community, Mesquite offers the bare minimum in terms of golf–a basic 18-hole municipal and two nice par 3 tracks.

MESQUITE MUNICIPAL GOLF COURSE

The golf   Mesquite's muni, located in the Duck Creek floodplain, was built in the 1960s by Leon Howard. Playing only 6,280 yards from the tips and void of bunkers, it makes for a fun day on the links. In fact, water comes into play only seven times–not as much as you might think for a floodplain course that has been ravaged by floods over the years.

The most challenging hole, No. 13, has water. It's a 418-yard par 4 that doglegs right and features a tee shot over a creek, followed by a long approach to a tough, narrow green.

Other notes: Garrett Gill and George B. Williams redesigned this course.

The details   972-270-7457. 825 Hwy. 67, Mesquite, TX 75150

- 1965. Leon Howard. 18 holes. Par 71. Back – 6,280 (69.1/116). Middle – 5,907 (67.3/112). Forward – Par 72. 5,023 (73.2/114). Price - $.

Getting there From I-30 east, take Northwest Hwy. for half a mile to North Hwy. 67 and the course.

NORTH MESQUITE GOLF CENTER

The golf   Some have used the word "upscale" to describe this par 3 practice facility, and it is nice, but those terms are usually reserved for regulation courses. This one features mounding and bunkers, as well as water on four holes. The best hole plays over water into the wind: No. 6, which is only 134 yards but has bunkers around the green.

The details   972-686-6660. 2920 Gus Thommason Rd., Mesquite, TX 75150

- 1994. 9 holes. Par 27. Back – 1,223. Forward – 1,059. Price - $.

Getting there From I-30 east out of Dallas, take the Gus Thomasson Rd. exit

Above all, tempo is the great equalizer. It compensates for mechanical flaws in your swing, and will reduce your slices, hooks, and inconsistent contact. Bill Moretti

and the course is 2 miles away. The entrance is on the left side.

TOWN EAST GOLF CENTER

The golf   A picturesque little executive track on the fringes of Mesquite, Town East offers six par 3s, two par 4s, and one par 5. The course is loaded with water (8 of 9 holes), including the 80-yard No. 7 which plays into a sloping island green. The par 4s go 265 and 365 yards, and the par 5 is only 405 yards.

The details   972-226-8749. 3134 N. Belt Line Rd., Sunnyvale, TX 75182

• 9 holes. Par 31. Back – 1,827. Middle – 1,638. Forward – 1,550. Price - $.

Getting there Take I-30 east out of Dallas and exit Belt Line Rd. Turn right and drive 2 miles. The course is on the left.

MESQUITE NOTES   During the summer, the world-famous **Mesquite Championship Rodeo** (800-833-9339) is a big deal in these parts, with live shows on the weekends and all sorts of cowboy activities. **Eastwind BBQ** (972-222-2514) on Lawson Rd. is popular with the locals, and **Top Cat BBQ** (972-270-8870) offers another non-chain barbecue option. And there is an **El Fenix** (972-279-8900) here for traditional Tex-Mex fare. **Stacks Burger House** (972-270-6255) serves the best burger in Mesquite, but **Griff's Hamburgers** (972-288-6063) is a popular rival. And, as is typical for the burbs, you'll have a slew of options up and down the main highways when it comes to lodging. The **Hampton Inn & Suites** (972-329-3100) and the **Country Inn & Suites** (972-216-7460) are just a few of the dozens.

MIDLOTHIAN   Elev. 749   Pop. 7,155

Midlothian, The Cement and Steel Capital of Texas, is located on a musty, industrial-looking stretch of US 67 between Dallas and Cleburne. The railroad helped establish the town in the late 1880s, and farming was the long-time staple of the economy. Today, many residents commute to the DFW metroplex and live in the houses that have popped up on the surrounding farmland.

PECAN TRAILS GOLF COURSE

The golf   Unique in that it offers a 21-hole round, Pecan Trails lives up to its name by weaving through an old grove of pecan trees, with water coming into play on every hole. From the tips, the 6,028-yard layout plays to a par 80 and features nine par 4s, eight par 3s (including the last four holes), and four par 5s.

Even if you hit forty bad shots, you should still keep trying.
The other fellow might hit forty-one. Gary Player

The details 972-723-1376. 2651 Shiloh Rd., Midlothian, TX 76065

- www.pecantrails.com
- 1991. Tony Wells. 21 holes. Par 80. Back – 6,028. Forward – 5,578. Price - $$.

Getting there From Dallas, take I-67 south and exit Shiloh Rd. Turn left and follow the signs to the course.

MIDLOTHIAN NOTES Midlothian has good chow-down options, highlighted by **The Banana Boat's** great seafood and steaks. There's some semblance of a scene at **David's Plaza** –you can walk around and do a little shopping in places like the **J&H Card Shop** before strolling into **Plato Loco**, where you can bring your own beer. Another Tex-Mex best bet is **Campuzano's**. If BBQ sounds right, Midlothian has several spots. Overnighters should stay at the **Best Western** (972-775-1891).

MINERAL WELLS   Elev. 925   Pop. 16,946

Mineral Wells, a cool town that bustled in the 1920s, is dominated by the now-abandoned 14-story, sandstone-colored Baker Hotel. "Crazy Water" was found here in 1885, and was popular in the early 1900s for curing mental illnesses and other maladies. The Palo Pinto Mountains, the nearby Brazos River, the historic downtown scene, and the old Holiday Hills Country Club all combine to make Mineral Wells a worthwhile destination for the road-tripping hack.

HOLIDAY HILLS COUNTRY CLUB

The golf Holiday Hills is an old course that some say dates back to the 1920s. Its traditional layout features tree-lined fairways and is generally flat. The course is short at only 6,169 yards from the tips, and the club prides itself on the excellent condition of its undulating greens.

The front course features five par 3s, four of which play around 200 yards. The unique front nine features three par 3s and three par 5s, including the number one handicap No. 3, which goes a long 535 yards. If you're on a roll the final stretch of holes is welcome, featuring four par 4s under 400 yards.

The details 940-325-8403. 4801 Hwy. 180 E., Mineral Wells, TX 76067

- 1920. 18 holes. Par 71. Blue – 6,169 (69.0/123) White – 5,872 (67.1/118) Red - 5,002 (68.9/108). Price - $$.

Getting there From Fort Worth, take I-20 west to Hwy. 180. Then head west straight to the course.

Would you like to know the fastest way to take several strokes off your game? Spend two hours in a bunker. Greg Norman

MINERAL WELLS NOTES   The **Lodge on Lake Palo Pinto** (940-769-2600) is a great option for lodging when planning a lake and golf holiday. **Shotgun's Barbeque** (940-325-4242) is the best place to grab a quick sandwich. When in the mood for Tex-Mex, call on **Pulido's** (940-325-8664) on 2nd Ave. Down the road in Mingus, the **Smokestack** (254-672-5560) is a historic and popular place to eat. Starting in May, the **Famous Mineral Water Co.** (940-325-8870) features live music on Friday nights in their garden. And heading east takes you to Garner, TX, where the **Garner Store and Cafe** (940-682-7675) is supposedly the place where the domino game "42" was invented, as well as a home-style joint with fried catfish and such.

MUENSTER   Elev. 970   Pop. 1,534

Located west of Gainesville on US 82, Muenster is a tiny German town steeped in tradition, dominated by its steepled church tower whose bells can be heard for miles. Pump jacks from the 1930s oil boom dot the surrounding ranchlands, and the economy has always been driven by dairy farming and agriculture. You'll drive through Muenster on your way to Texas' finest off-the-beaten-path tracks–the immensely interesting Turtle Hill Golf Course.

TURTLE HILL GOLF COURSE

The golf   Former airline pilot and cattle rancher Dick Murphy turned his place eight miles north of Muenster, TX into one of the neatest 18-hole tracks in the state and, for around $30 on weekends, you can have the privilege of playing Murphy's self-designed and self-built masterpiece.

Mr. Murphy's design makes up for the lack of driving range by opening with several basic golf holes: the kind where you can relax, swing easy, and get into the flow of the round. Of those early holes No. 2 is the most challenging–it's a mid-length par 4 that doglegs right and requires a blind approach into an elevated green.

The back side continues with a solid mixture of holes highlighted by the spectacular par 3 No. 11, which is considered by many to be the most beautiful par 3 in Texas. The hole plays down into an amazingly deep ravine, and requires 2-3 clubs less than you would normally hit. If the tee shot isn't perfect here–tough with the wind and drop in elevation–you'll find yourself in the rugged Hill Country-like scrub that surrounds the green.

The bent-grass greens at Turtle Hill, surprising for a self-built ranch course, are large, roll true, and hold shots well.

You'll wonder where the heck you're going, and when you get there you'll know to expect the basic amenities. But even though there's no driving range, and the food and beverage service is limited, the Turtle Hill experience is definitely worth the trip.

The golf game isn't over till the last putt drops. Cary Middlecoff

The details   940-759-4896. Route 373 N., Muenster, TX 76252

- www.theturtle.com
- Gold – 6,742 (72.2/123). Blue – 6,272. White – 5,965. Red – 5,019. Price - $$.

Getting there From Gainesville, take Hwy. 82 west to Muenster. Turn north on Hwy. 373 and drive 8.5 miles to the course. The entrance is on the left.

MUENSTER NOTES   One of the true pleasures of playing Turtle Hill is knowing that on your way back, you can stop in the little town of Lindsay, TX and dig in for mouth-watering grub and cheap, ice-cold beer at **Deiter Brothers Restaurant** (940-665-5253). Also in Lindsay look for the **Silver Spur** for live Texas music in the evenings. In Muenster, there's **Rohmer's Restaurant** and **The Center**, two good German joints with home-style cooking. **The Picket Fence** (940-759-2942) is Muenster's only B&B.

NORTH RICHLAND HILLS   Elev. 650   Pop. 55,635

What can you say about North Richland Hills? Former dairy farm pastures were once home to the open range and blue skies, but now there's only the clustered chaos of urban middle-management-land, choked by the smog of new cars. Located at the junctions of US 183 and 820 just northwest of Fort Worth, middle-class residential neighborhoods bombarded with chain restaurants and truck dealerships are all that you'll see. It's worth a trip, though, for the Dick Phelps-designed Iron Horse Golf Course.

IRON HORSE GOLF COURSE

The golf   Iron Horse is laid out in the floodplain of Fossil Creek, an area loaded with woods and a railroad that divides the property into three tracts. When Dick Phelps designed the course he loaded it with par 4s that are over 400 yards. This track has only two par 5s, but you'll get your money's worth as they are virtually impossible to reach in two. The best hole is the 462-yard, par 4 No. 3, which is generally a bogey hole for the average golfer.

The details   817-485-6666. 6200 Skylark Circle, North Richland Hills, TX 76180

- www.ironhorsetx.com
- 18 holes. Par 70. Black – 6,580 (71.8/130). Green – 6,203 (69.8/122). White – 5,684 (66.9/114). Orange - 5,083 (69.6/119). Price - $$.

Getting there Take I-35 W. (US 287) north for 5 miles and merge on I-820 East (NE Loop 820) and go 2.4 miles. Take Exit 20 B and turn right (south) on Ruff

---

Snow Dr. Go one block and take a right on Meadow Lakes Dr. Continue on Meadow Lakes Dr. and follow the signs to the clubhouse.

NORTH RICHLAND HILLS NOTES   Take your time in the train depot-style clubhouse and enjoy post-round festivities there, or head to **Champ's BBQ** (817-281-2065) for a quick bite.

PLANO   Elev. 655 Pop. 219,486

Plano is Plano and there's a hell of a lot of people and a decent amount of golf. Dallas' premier and best-known satellite city has ballooned from 3,690 folks in 1960 to its current overpopulated mass of urban professionals numbering some 220,000.

CHASE OAKS GOLF CLUB

The golf   Chase Oaks is the centerpiece of a 900-acre residential and commercial development that dates back to the late 1980s. The club offers 27 holes of golf played as two totally different courses: the 18-hole Blackjack and the 9-hole Sawtooth.

Blackjack has received the most acclaim, at one point being ranked by the *Dallas Morning News* as the No. 1 public course in the state. The Bruce Devlin/Robert Von Hagge design plays 6,773 yards from the tips to a par 72, and their route features a good combination of blind shots, water carries, and doglegs.

In all, water comes into play on 12 holes, including the 187-yard No. 4, which is almost completely surrounded by water. In fact, all par 3s require fun shots over water. Holes 5 and 6 also stand out on the front. No. 5 plays 403 yards and requires a perfect drive to the right of the water. No. 6, the number one handicap hole, plays 450 yards into the wind, featuring an approach into a multi-level green.

On the back, No. 15 is notable for its dogleg right nature and tough because of the fairway bunker guarding the corner, as well as the approach shot over the creek into the small green.

The 9-hole **Sawtooth** offers two sets of tees, but only measures 6,016 yards.

The details   972-517-7777. 7201 Chase Oaks Dr., Plano, TX 75025

- www.chaseoaks.com
- Sawtooth Course: 1980s. Robert von Hagge and Bruce Devlin. 9 holes. Par 36. Back – 3,008 (35.1/130). Forward – 2,642 (36.0/124). Price - $$$.
- Blackjack Course: 1980s. Robert von Hagge and Bruce Devlin. 18 holes. Par 72. Back – 6,762 (74.4/139). Middle – 6,269 (71.5/134). Forward – 5,105 (70.0/128). Price - $$$.

Harvey Penick always wanted us to be good bunker players so we wouldn't be afraid to fire at a flag tucked next to one. Tom Kite

Getting there From Hwy. 75 north, take the Legacy exit west, and head to Chase Oaks Blvd. Turn north and drive to the course.

GLENEAGLES COUNTRY CLUB

The golf   Dallas golfers who have sampled them all claim that Gleneagles offers two of the toughest courses in the area. This private 36-hole club opened in the 1980s with two Robert von Hagge/Bruce Devlin layouts known as the King's and Queen's. Eldridge Miles, an old-school Dallas-area pro, once wrote to von Hagge that "I have played many of your courses and have always liked your work; however, I believe the Gleneagles course represents some of the most creative, interesting, and challenging work that you have every produced."

Ironically, the **Queen's Course** is the more difficult of the two because it lacks trees and is burdened by the wind. Bunkering is prominent on both courses, but is especially evident on the Queen's, which has numerous grass bunkers as well as deep sand bunkers. Water is everywhere, and if you spray the ball at all your score will add up quickly. The 190-yard No. 17, which usually plays like 210 with its headwind and full carry of water, and the 422-yard 18th, which features water on every shot, are considered two of the toughest holes in the state because there just isn't any margin for error.

The **King's Course** is considered the favorite among members. It's much like the Queens, with its links-style fairways framed by mounds, but it has more trees and water. The five pars are a real treat, with mens handicap ratings of 1, 3, 6 and 8.

The details   972-867-8888. 5401 W. Park Blvd., Plano, TX 75093

- www.gleneaglesclub.com

- King's Course: 1980s. Robert von Hagge and Bruce Devlin. Black – 6,806 (73.0/135). Blue – 6,425 (71.0/128). White – 6,096 (69.1/121). Green – 5,185 (70.4/121). Red – 4,913 (69.5/112). Price – $$$$.

- Queen's Course: 1980s. Robert von Hagge and Bruce Devlin. Black – 6,901 (74.0/136). Blue – 6,352 (71.3/129). White – 5,988 (69.2/122). Green – 5,270 (70.6/116). Red – 4,898 (69.3/114). Price – $$$$.

Getting there From downtown Dallas, take the Tollway north to Park Blvd. Turn east and drive 1 mile to the course. The entrance is on the left.

LOS RIOS COUNTRY CLUB

The golf   Los Rios opened in the early 1970s with a Don January and Billy Martindale design that takes advantage of eight small ponds and a creek that winds through the layout.

Water is in play on over half of the holes, including the opening 485-yard par 5 that features two ponds in play off the tee, and another fronting the green.

On the course, what is feared is like a magnet. Water, bunkers, trees, ravines, high grass – whatever you fear turns magnetic. Wiffi Smith

Two very difficult holes stand out on this narrow, shot-maker's course. No. 7 goes 431 yards but allows for a huge tee shot with a generous fairway, which will definitely help on the dicey approach over the creek into a shallow green. On the par 5 No. 14, water crosses the fairway three times from the back tees.

The details 972-424-4546. 1700 Country Club Dr., Plano, TX 75074

- www.irigolfgroup.com
- 1971. January-Martindale. 18 holes. Par 71. Back – 6,507 (70.7/127). Middle – 6,102 (69.2/119). Forward – 5,076 (70.1/122). Price - $$.

Getting there From I-75 north, take Plano Pkwy. east until it dead-ends at Los Rios Blvd. Turn left onto Los Rios Blvd. and continue on for 1 mile to Country Club Dr. Turn right and drive a short distance to the course–look for the entrance on the right side of the street.

PECAN HOLLOW COUNTRY CLUB

The golf One of the first courses in the growing 1970s Plano community, Pecan Hollow started out as the Plano Municipal Golf Course. Don January and Billy Martindale, who had recently completed their signature Royal Oaks course in Dallas, contracted with the city to help provide golf for Plano's growing population.

The terrain here is flat, and the fairways are mostly wide open. January used the standard bunkers, water hazards, and trees in his design to cause problems for the golfer. The greens are of medium size and speed, and the course is basically pretty standard until you reach the punishing final stretch of holes. Nos. 16-18 are all 445-yard-plus par 4s with water in play–one of the toughest tests of golf in the DFW area.

The details 972-941-7600. 4501 14th St., Plano, TX 75074

- 1972. January-Martindale. 18 holes. Par 72. Back – 6,772 (70.1/115). Middle – 6,231 (68.1/110). Forward – 5,320 (71.3/118). Price - $$.

Getting there From I-75 north, take Plano Pkwy. east, then exit at 14th St. Turn right, drive a short distance to the course, and look for the entrance on the left side of the street.

RIDGEVIEW RANCH GOLF CLUB

The golf Ridgeview Ranch is a Jeff Brauer design that opened in 1996. It's friendly to the average golfer because there are rarely forced carries of water or sand to reach the large greens, making short approaches good candidates for easy ups and downs.

The design rolls through hills and trees, incorporating two creeks that come into play. The fairways are average-sized and flat, although there are a few surprising elevation changes for this flat part of north Texas. The course rolls through a housing addition and some of the holes are very tight.

You have a perfect right to ask a golfer to hole out every single putt; and no golfer ought to take offense at your so asking him. Horace Hutchinson

Nos. 7 and 11 stand out in particular. The 7th goes 161 yards over White Rock Creek to a sloping green. No. 11 is tough because it plays well over 400 yards uphill into the prevailing wind.

Other notes: Carts are mandatory on weekends before 2 p.m. The cemetery next to the No. 3 green has graves dating back to 1800 and a historical marker commemorating the settlers that was commissioned by Stephen F. Austin.

The details 972-390-1039. 2701 Ridgeview Dr., Plano, TX 75025

- www.americangolf.com

- 1996. Jeff Brauer. 18 holes. Par 72. Copper – 7,025 (74.1/130). Blue – 6,529 (71.8/123). White – 6,135 (70.0/120). Red – 5,335 (70.4/117). Price - $$.

Getting there From Dallas, travel north on the Tollway and exit Spring Creek. Turn right and drive 5 miles to Independence. Turn left and drive north to Ridge View Dr., then take a right and the course is on the left.

PLANO NOTES   Avoid the chains for once if you can, with the possible exception of the neighborhood **Hooters**, and find yourself a local eatery with character. **Tino's Too** (972-881-9226) is Plano's favored Tex-Mex spot, offering only the best in greasy enchiladas, chips and salsa, cold beer, and frosty margs.

NORTH CENTRAL

POTTSBORO   Elev. 764   Pop. 1,579

The crusty lakeside town of Pottsboro, just south of the great Lake Texoma, was established in the 1870s, flourished from the railroad in the old days, and is able to hang on today as a result of nearby Denison and the goings-on at the lake. You'll pass through Pottsboro on your way to the tranquil golf resort on the wooded shores of Lake Texoma known as Tanglewood.

TANGLEWOOD RESORT

The golf   Ralph Plummer worked with Arnold Palmer on the original design back around 1970, and Ken Dye and Baxter Spann came along for an upgrade in 1988. This challenging course overlooking Lake Texoma is difficult because of the water and wind.

Be ready when you arrive, because the first two holes can ruin your day. Some say that No. 1 is the hardest on the course, playing 414 yards into a dogleg that's protected by a fairway bunker. No. 2 is longer at 444 yards–you'll need a monster tee shot to set up a reasonable approach into the bunkered green. This hole has a slight dogleg to the left as well.

On the back, No. 14 goes 230 yards with water on the right, and No. 18 is

---

Percentage golf is not so much the science of playing the game with the shots of which you are capable as it is of playing without the shot of which you are incapable. Jackie Burke, Jr.

a reachable par 5 with water in play on the first two shots.

Other notes: You either need to be a member or a guest of the resort to play.

The details   903-786-4140. Hwy. 120, Pottsboro, TX 75076

- www.tanglewoodresort.com
- 1970. Ralph Plummer (Ken Dye and Baxter Spann redesign in 1988). Champs – 6,993 (73.5/128). Back – 6,536 (71.1/113). Middle – 5,986 (68.3/107). Forward – 4,925 (67.5/104). Price - $$$.

Getting there From the Grayson Company Airport, head north on Hwy. 1417. Turn west on Hwy. 120 and drive into Pottsboro. In town, look for the signs to the course.

POTTSBORO NOTES For eats try **Huck's**, which specializes in tasty Lake Texoma catfish. You can generally strum up some action at **Grandpappy's Marina** , whether it's people-watching, hiring a fishing guide, or renting a boat for the afternoon. If you get a boat make sure you hit the islands, where you'll see people dancing around half-naked, playing horseshoes, barbecuing, and drinking beer. Next door is **The Point Restaurant,** overlooking the lake and sporting the typical lakeside atmosphere. Another good lakeside restaurant is **Low's Highport.** And you can kick off road trips into Oklahoma with a stop at **Wendy's Catfish** just on the other side of the dam.

PROSPER

Elev. 692   Pop. 2,097

Prosper, the last town established in Collin County, is next in line for an impressive population boom triggered by the Dallas Tollway's northward inching and Frisco's overflow. Located 10 miles northwest of McKinney near Texas 289, and due north of Dallas, it all began in 1902 when the railroad came through this agricultural area known as Elm Valley. The increasing rate of growth is evident in the numerous new residential communities, one of which houses the private D.A. Weibring track known as Gentle Creek Golf Club.

GENTLE CREEK GOLF CLUB

The golf   Gentle Creek opened in August of 2002 with a challenging D. A. Weibring design that serves as the centerpiece for Prosper's newest country club community. Although it is technically private, the public can play the course for the time being while they wait to fill the memberships.

Weibring's design tips out at over 7,300 yards, and features some excruciatingly long holes. Fortunately, there are alternative tees that make the course more playable for the average hack. First-timers out here should play from the 6,200-yard white tees to make the most of their day.

Putting is easy. All you need to do is roll a ball toward a hole. Remember, nothing rolls like a ball. Dr. Bob Rotella

The most spectacular hole is the Hill-Country-like par-3 No. 9, which is fronted by a huge pond, waterfall, and rock wall. Eight sets of tees give you options here, and there is sufficient bail-out room to the right, so plan accordingly on this tough mother.

The ender on the back side is a nice hole as well, with a 20-acre lake spanning the entire left side. If the wind is in your face, this hole's 560 yards is more like 660, and you'll need three full shots to get to the bunkered green that slopes back-to-front.

One design feature we noticed during our round here is that Weibring eliminated greenside rough, creating good opportunities for ups-and-downs if you can at least get the approach around the green in regulation.

The details   972-346-2500. 9712 Southern Hills Dr., Plano, TX 75025

- www.gentlecreek.com

- 18 holes. Par 72. Black – 7,317. Blue – 6,813. White – 6,203. Red – 5,003. Price - $$$.

Getting there Located on FM 1461 between Preston Rd. and FM 2478 (Custer Rd.), 1.5 miles east of Preston Rd.

PROSPER NOTES   When you're up this way, the best option is to track east or west on 289, where you'll run into all sorts of interesting restaurants. The original **Trail Dust Steakhouse** is out here. In the heart of old Prosper is the **Cotton Gin** , where they're gaining a reputation for big, juicy burgers. Finally, the town of Celina, TX is about 10 minutes due north–an interesting community with a few worthwhile local restaurants around the town square.

QUINLAN   Elev. 514   Pop. 1,370

The lake town of Quinlan, 45 miles east of Dallas, is just west of Lake Tawakoni–an outstanding lake that never gets any credit because of Lake Fork's famous reputation to the west. You can spend the night for a reasonable fee, hire a fishing guide to enjoy the lake, and spend the rest of your time on the Tawakoni Golf Course.

TAWAKONI GOLF COURSE

The golf   Tawakoni is a flat course, spotted by a few nice oaks, but especially difficult because of the stiff lake breeze that pounds the course. The design features tough approaches into greens that snake back into the trees.

Hole 7 is nice because of its location near the lake. The tee box offers a pleasing view of the water and the uphill, doglegging shot is perfect for a fade,

---

Comparatively few golfers ever show that they are aware that the golf architect tries to design a course that rewards an intelligent golfer and penalizes a stupid one. Tommy Armour

but dangerous because of the water right. The lake looms left, and the approach involves carrying the creek that fronts the green. This great hole goes 465 yards from the tips.

On the back, the final three holes offer a tough stretch of golf. Starting with the number one handicap, 425-yard No. 16, and followed by another long par 4 and a 530-yard par 5, you'll need to be on your game when you're heading to the clubhouse at Tawakoni.

The details 903-447-2981. 2104 W. State Hwy. 276, Quinlan, TX 75474

- 1971. John and Bill Lively. 18 holes. Par 72. Back – 6,691 (70.8/115). Middle – 6,295 (68.9/109). Forward – 5,021. Price - $$.

Getting there From I-30, take Hwy. 205 south, turn left on Hwy. 276, and travel 20 miles. Turn right on Hwy. 34, then turn left at the first traffic light (Hwy. 276). Drive 7 miles to the course, which is on the left.

QUINLAN NOTES　　Several interesting dining options can be found in Quinlan. The cleverly named **Willie's Westaurant** (903-356-4475) deserves mention at least for the name, but the place you must stop at is the **Hunt County Hamburger Co.** (903-356-0980), where you're guaranteed to be full and satisfied. Out on the lake, **Bedwell's Catfish Inn** (903-447-3631) can put you up for the night, and the **Grill On The Lake** (903-447-9988) is fun. Note that you'll pass through the town of West Tawakoni, TX known as the Catfish Capital of Texas.

RAVENNA   Elev. 597   Pop. 204

Sandwiched between the Red River and the city of Bonham, TX, the town of Ravenna is named after the deep ravine that runs through the middle of town. It is here, 70 miles from downtown Dallas and 32 miles north of McKinney, that you'll find the closest thing to Scotland in the Lone Star state.

ROYAL RAVENNA SCOTTISH LINKS GOLF CLUB

The golf　　Owner and course architect David Galvan has an affinity for the way golf was played in the beginning, and he's built one of the most unique golf experiences in Texas to prove his passion. This one is links-style all the way, from narrow fairways that might make you want to head home to the 3-foot high "heather" that frames the skinny targets. And while the course is short, tipping out at only 5,150 yards, the steady breezes force accurate shot-making, and you will definitely lose if you're determined to bang away for distance.

The short, flat course is favorable for walking, which you'll be forced to do

All swings have one thing in common: whatever the tempo, the speeds of the backswing and downswing are the same. Johnny Miller

just like in the old days. Pull carts are available, but we recommend that you carry your bag to really get into the mood.

Galvan designed the course so that most of the par 4s play against the prevailing wind, but both sides feature numerous short par 4s, and the longest par 4s (Nos. 6 and 15) are impacted only by cross winds.

From the No. 8 green you can see into Oklahoma, but you'd have to say that the 572-yard No. 5 is the signature since, according to Galvan, it has never been birdied. The two notable par 3s both play over water–No. 9 is 160 yards and No. 18 only goes 145 yards.

The greens are a mixture of savannah Bermuda and perennial rye grass, which apparently does well in these parts of Texas.

This course is a real treat that (for now) costs only $9 to play all day—however, that's bound to increase once the metroplex surges north and the course becomes more popular. Bring your own food and refreshments, as the pro shop is minimal at this stage in the club's development. Galvan has plans to add a grill that will overlook the entire 18th hole, but that's a few years away.

The details   903-640-2216. 2727 Texas Hwy. Ravenna, TX 75446

- 1999. David Galvan. Par 70. 5,150 yards. 3 sets of tees. Pull carts only. Price - $.

Getting there Southeast corner of Texas 1753 and Fannin 1410.

RAVENNA NOTES   Befriend the locals for down-home entertainment or head to Bonham—unless you think you might be able to strum up some action at the community center or volunteer fire department, which are about the only two things in Ravenna. **Lake Bonham** is 2 miles east and is a nice, quaint place to fish without the big crowds. The best place to eat in the area is in Bonham, TX at a new joint called **Schumardi's Restaurant**.

RED OAK
Elev. 608   Pop. 5,200

The small town of Red Oak, whose population has almost doubled since 1990, rests 35 miles south of Dallas, and is one of the last signs of urban sprawl as you drive south of Big D. Named after nearby Red Oak Creek, the town grew as a farming community that primarily harvested wheat and cotton. Farming is only part of the mix today, though, as the majority of residents commute to Dallas and its surrounding suburbs to earn their wages.

RED OAK VALLEY GOLF COURSE

The golf   Red Oak is a simple country course that you'll spot on the east side of I-35–with its lack of length and hazards, it's a good stop for the traveling hacker. Here you'll find birdie chances galore with many par 4s reachable

---

It is a law of nature that everybody plays a hole badly when going through. Bernard Darwin

by big hitters. The front nine has three par 3s that require long irons, but nothing else to cause real problems. The back nine sports a 440-yard par 4, but is balanced by the other short holes. Low scores are possible, as evidenced by the 1990 course record of 57.

The details   972-617-3249. Rural Route 5, Red Oak, TX 75154

- 1972. Leon Howard. 18 holes. Par 70. Back – 5,911 (67.7). Price - $.

Getting there From I-35 south, take the 408 exit and look for the course on the east side of the interstate.

RED OAK NOTES   This spot is a quick hit, so play it and move on. Play it early in the morning on the way out of Dallas. And since it's chain restaurants galore along I-35, the only viable local option is **Junior's Bar-B-Q** (972-617-5362) on Ovilla Rd. for lunch.

RICHARDSON   Elev. 630   Pop. 91,802

Richardson spans Dallas and Collin counties, bulging from Dallas' growth and fueled by the high-tech industry. Originally called Breckenridge, this once-rural village got its start from the railroad and is now home to one country club and a 36-hole municipal facility.

CANYON CREEK COUNTRY CLUB

The golf   One of the least-known courses in the Dallas area, Canyon Creek CC offers a 1963 Press Maxwell design that features tree-lined fairways and the meandering Canyon Creek. Set in the Canyon Creek subdivision, the course is hidden from the street and invisible to the curious golfer roaming the streets of Richardson. Tucked into the neighborhood, the colonial style-clubhouse overlooks the course from the highest point on the property. Canyon Creek is a challenging layout known for its massive, well-manicured greens.

The most difficult hole on the front is the 466-yard, par 4 No. 8, which rivals the 418-yard No. 11 as the signature. Hole 11 plays uphill into a fairway lined by the creek on the left, and features an approach shot over water to a well-bunkered green.

The details   972-231-1466. 625 W. Lookout Dr., Richardson, TX 75080

- www.canyoncreekclub.com
- 1963. Press Maxwell. Par 70. Back – 6,633 (71.5/124). Middle – 6,196 (69.4/119). Forward – Par 71. 5,491 (72.9/129). Price - $$.

Getting there From Dallas, take I-75 north to Campbell Rd. Turn west and drive to Custer Rd., then turn north and find Lookout Dr. Turn left to the course.

For an amateur, standing on the first hole of the Masters is the ultimate laxative. Trevor Homer

SHERRIL PARK GOLF COURSE

The golf   Leon Howard came along in 1972 to help bring golf to the city of Richardson. His first course, called **Course One**, is generally a fun-loving layout but serves up two mean, bitter holes. No. 1 is a slicer's delight, doglegging sharply to the right at 375 yards. Watch the trees that overhang the fairway. Later on, the 588-yard No. 14 is worthy of a deep breath and sip of cold beer–it plays into the wind with water along the right of the fairway and green.

North Dallas kept growing, so Howard was called in again to cram **Course Two** into a former landfill of about 120 acres. Like the first course, it has plenty of trees and creeks, but it plays much shorter. Water is present on 11 holes, including the most difficult No. 2, which doglegs left for 440 yards and involves the creek off the tee and on the approach. Thankfully, it's the only par 4 over 400 yards on the course.

Back-to-back par 5s provide good birdie chances on the front when you're hitting them well, and the 306-yard No. 9 can be managed if you are decisive in dealing with the water.

On the back, Nos. 17 and 18 are good finishers. The first plays 199 yards and is loaded with water, and the ender tees off over water but is only a 475-yard par 5.

The details   972-234-1416. 2001 E. Lookout Dr., Richardson, TX 75082

- Course One: 1973. Leon Howard. 18 holes. Par 72. Back – 6,899 (72.0/124). Middle – 6,245 (70.0/120). Forward – 5,182 (70.0/120). Price - $$.

- Course Two: 1980. Leon and Charles Howard. 18 holes. Par 70. Back – 5,632 (66.0/113). Middle – 5,337 (66.0/109). Forward – 4,974 (66.0/109). Price - $$.

Getting there From I-75 (Central), exit Renner Rd. and head east for 1 mile to Jupiter. Turn south and drive to E. Lookout Dr.

RICHARDSON NOTES   Consider the option of enjoying one of the great pleasures of muni golf–the post-round lunch with beers at the clubhouse grill. Otherwise we recommend two non-chain BBQ joints for lunch, both with names that smell of good barbecue. **Big Al's Bar-B-Que** (972-699-1521) is on Arapaho, and **Smokin' Tom's Texas Bar-B-Que** (972-231-7633) is on Campbell.

ROCKWALL   Elev. 596   Pop. 15,668

Rockwall is the seat of Texas' smallest county, located barely east of Dallas on the other side of Lake Ray Hubbard. In 1852 geologists discovered an

NORTH CENTRAL

impressive subterranean rock wall, up to 18 inches thick and stretching for over 4 miles, giving the town its name. A growing, bustling town populated by Dallas professionals, Rockwall has a golf scene that includes an older Ralph Plummer-designed country club and two new facilities: the much-bragged-about Buffalo Creek and a 9-hole par 3 known as the A-1 Golf Center.

A-1 GOLF CENTER

The golf   A 9-hole par 3 track, A-1 features holes ranging from 75-190 yards, with elevated tees and greens and water in play on three holes. No. 7 is considered the signature, about a 100-yard hole into an island green. While there are no bunkers, the lighted practice facility and driving range have everything you'll need to work on all aspects of your game. The club is also considering adding lights to the par 3 course.

The details   972-771-3996. 1805 I-30 E., Rockwall, TX 75087

• 2000. Doyle Anderson. 9 holes. Par 27. Price - $.

Getting there Take Exit 70 off of I-30, and the course is on the north side of the interstate.

BUFFALO CREEK GOLF CLUB

The golf   Highly touted Buffalo Creek has been praised for its layout, condition, and overall attention to detail. No matter who you talk to in the DFW area, they all seem to praise the superb condition of the course from tee to green. Offering a 7,018-yard par 71 Jay Morrish/Tom Weiskopf design, Buffalo Creek offers a good combination of holes: straight holes, dogleggers, uphill and downhill shots, and both long and short holes.

One of the best features is the club's method of using a pin location sheet to mark exactly where each pin is located on a particular day (up to six locations), which is unbelievably helpful to hacks who've never played the course before and have no feel for the look and contour of the greens.

The details   972-771-4003. 624 Country Club Dr., Rockwall, TX 75032

• www.americangolf.com

• Tom Weiskopf and Jay Morrish. 18 holes. Par 71. Back – 7,018 (73.8/133). Price - $$$.

Getting there Take I-30 east from Dallas and exit Ridge Rd. Turn right and find the course 1.6 miles down on the left.

THE SHORES COUNTRY CLUB

The golf   Laid out along the wind-swept shores of Lake Ray Hubbard, The Shores was designed in the late 1970s by Ralph Plummer, who served up

The good players are almost always the ones who ask me to watch them on the putting green. The high-handicappers, who need it the most, would rather do anything than have a putting lesson. Harvey Penick

his typical 7,000-yard-plus layout. Plummer's design involves the lake on five holes, as well as water on another seven. With its lack of trees, the main challenges are the water and the wind off the lake. Tees ranging from 5,200 to 7,100 yards allow an enjoyable day for any type of golfer.

Two holes stand out on the back nine, which is the most exciting since it rolls along the edge of the lake. No. 15 plays almost 600 yards from the tips and involves water on both the tee shot and approach. This one is especially difficult into the wind.

No. 18 is a 452-yard par 4, again with water in play off the tee and on the approach. The lake that cuts into the fairway squeezes the landing area, and a fairway bunker guards the corner of the slight dogleg left. The uphill approach involves carrying the water and hitting an accurate long iron or wood, something we're not always in the mood for at the end of a long round.

Other notes: Adjacent to the driving range there are three par 3 holes for practice.

The details 972-771-0301. 2600 Champions Dr., Rockwall, TX 75087

- www.irigolfgroup.com
- 1979. Ralph Plummer. 18 holes. Par 72. Back – 6,764 (72.5/121). Middle – 6,104 (69.1/116). Forward – 5,255 (70.2/116). Price - $$.

Getting there From I-30 east, exit Dalrock, turn left and head to Hwy. 66. At Lakeshore Dr., turn left and the clubhouse is just down the road.

MORE GOLF

Whittle Development has entertained the idea of expanding with another 18-hole course in the residential community on Lake Ray Hubbard. The course would be located on 560 acres 4 miles south of the existing course. Since the City of Dallas owns the water rights to Lake Ray Hubbard, water issues could impede this addition. Travis Ranch Lazarus Property Corporation has completed the land purchase for this 2,400-acre residential development, which will include a links-style golf course nestled in a 470-acre floodplain. Construction is a ways out, but Crenshaw, D.A. Weibring, and ClubCorp design officials have expressed interest in the project

---

ROCKWALL NOTES Besides the chains, **Soul Man's BBQ** on I-30 is the place to order a smooth sliced beef sandwich for lunch before the round. After the round, chips and queso goes well with frosty lime-quenched Corona at **El Trevino's**. Head to Dallas for the night, but if you must, there is a **Holiday Inn Express** (972-722-3265) in Rockwall.

A narrow plateau for a green, or a few hummocks in front of one,
will very likely cause just as much trouble and amusement to a player as
a gaping chasm stretching right across the course. Harry S. Colt, 1912

ROWLETT

Elev. 509   Pop. 44,503

Located just 4 miles east of Garland, Rowlett sprang to life when the Greenville and Dallas Railroad rolled through in 1889 and transformed the town into a thriving farm community. And while I-30 bypassed the town in the 1960s, the completion of Lake Ray Hubbard developed Rowlett into a lakefront community that's appealing for folks who don't mind the commute to Dallas for wages.

WATERVIEW GOLF CLUB

The golf   Rowlett's first course has been laid out over a flat range of pasture, supplemented by 15 acres of lakes and over 1,000 new trees. Designed to be hacker-friendly, the lack of mature trees provide an especially generous look and feel, tempting the mid-level handicapper to tee it up from the 7,191 yard tips and go long off the tee. Bent greens are the highlight of the round here–they roll true and provide solid opportunities to snake in a few long putts.

The details   972-463-8900. 9509 Waterview Pkwy., Rowlett, TX 75089

- www.waterviewdfw.com

- 18 holes. Back – 7,191. Slope 128. Price - $$$.

Getting there Off of I-30, exit Dalrock Rd. and drive north through Hwy. 66. A half-mile past 66 veer left on Princeton, which dead-ends at Liberty Grove. Turn right into the Waterview division and take Waterview Pkwy. to the clubhouse.

ROWLETT NOTES   Quite a few decent restaurants here, including **Nick's Sports Bar** , where you can have a few beers and watch a game. Another option is the highly recommended **Sammy Walker's BBQ**.

ROYSE CITY

Elev. 556   Pop. 2,957

Heading out of Dallas on I-30, you'll pass Rockwall before you roll into Royse City–a cotton town on the Blackland Prairie that dates back to 1886, when it was named after the man who platted the town, Mr. G.B. Royse. Here you'll find a funky 18-hole track known as Aaki Ranch.

AAKI RANCH INTERNATIONAL GOLF COURSE

The golf   Aaki Ranch is a basic, homemade 18-hole track that opened in 1997, featuring rolling Bermuda pastures, manmade lakes, and young trees.

Any golfer serious enough about his game to want to break 120 must learn to stop worrying about the last ten or twenty missed strokes. Stephen Baker

Playing only 6,487 yards from the tips with minimal trees lining the fairways, you'll be able to swing hard and let it rip.

The details   972-636-2254. 846 FM 2453, Royse City, TX 75189

- www.aakiranch.com

- 1997. Akira Ishikawa. 18 holes. Par 71. Blue – 6,487. White – 6,117. Red – 5,101. Price - $$.

Getting there From Dallas, head east on I-30 for about 25 miles to exit 77B (FM35). Turn right at the stop onto FM 35, then continue about 1 mile. Turn right onto FM 2453 and drive another half mile. The golf course is on your right.

ROYSE CITY NOTES Only low-budget motels to be found here, so head to Rockwall and find the **Country Inn & Suites** (800-456-4000). For grub in Royse City, try **Victoria's Restaurant** for home cooking, **Louie G's** for Italian, or the cozy little Tex-Mex spot on Main St. The locals drink at **Linda's Round Up** off of Hwy. 276, which sometimes has live music. A bigger option is the **Southern Junction** (972-771-2418): part dance hall, part steakhouse, and open Wed-Sat.

SHERMAN   Elev. 728   Pop. 34,044

First a stop on the stage line to San Francisco, then a railroad hub, Sherman originally grew due to transportation, but today is home to several Fortune 500 companies. The town is located just south of the Oklahoma border on I-75, and is handsomely shaded by giant trees, graced by old homes, and cultured by nostalgic Austin College.

Golf came to Sherman in the 1920s, when the Woodlawn Country Club opened for play. However, the new Champions Trail development has brought a modern alternative for the traveling golfer.

WOODLAWN COUNTRY CLUB

The golf   Once frequented by long-time pro Miller Barber, this old traditional track offers no real surprises on its rolling, tree-lined fairways. Water is in play on only a few holes, one of which is the 136-yard signature–a fun hole because of the peninsula green surrounded by water. The only par 5 plays 495 yards, but there are two 400-yard-plus par 4s on this 6,405-yard, par 71 layout.

I smoke a good deal, and once in a while some golf writer takes a crack at me about it. It's easy to say cigarettes are bad for you. But what about that stretching and stretching and stretching, inside your head? It's easy to prove cigarettes are all wrong for you physically. But championship golf is played mainly between the ears. If you don't smoke, I suppose you are better off – maybe. If you do smoke, I should say you were better off smoking in a hard round. Bobby Jones

The details   903-893-9657. 4046 Woodlawn Rd., Sherman, TX 75091

- 18 holes. Back – Par 71. 6,405 (70.2/119). Forward – 5,374 (69.7/120). Price - $.

Getting there From Dallas, take Hwy. 75 north for 75 miles, then take Exit 65. Follow Hwy. 691 east for 1 mile to the stoplight. Drive south on Hwy. 91 and turn left on Woodlake Rd.

MORE GOLF

The **Champions Trail Golf Course** is slated to open 9 holes in June 2003, with another 9 to follow in August. The facility is located 5 miles west of Sherman on Hwy. 82.

SHERMAN NOTES   Randy's **Bar-b-cue,** on the corner of Hwys. 691 and 1417, and the **OO Smokehouse** downtown are the spots for barbecue fans on the go. The **Kelly Square,** three stories high and impressively restored, houses restaurants, art galleries, and shopping. September is a good time to be in Sherman, not only for the weather but because of the bustling **Red River Valley Arts Fest** complete with arts, crafts, and picknicking evenings highlighted by live music. The active golfman might be interested in Texas' striped bass capital, **Lake Texoma,** which is surrounded by lodging, marinas, and great fun.

SOUTHLAKE   Elev. 632   Pop. 21,519

Nestled between Grapevine, Keller, and the DFW Airport, Southlake is the ultimate soccer mom community, booming since the 1980s as families have migrated away from the city to this charming rural area. While it is surrounded by outstanding golf courses, the only club that officially takes its mail from the Southlake post office is Timarron Country Club.

TIMARRON COUNTRY CLUB

The golf   Old Bear Creek meanders through the rolling terrain of Timarron, highlighting this par 72, 7,012-yard Byron Nelson/Baxter Spann design. The tree-lined fairways wind toward large, undulating greens that are considered faster than most.

The front offers the best birdie opportunity with the 185-yard No. 3. The signature hole is the last: a 540-yard downhiller that plays into the prevailing wind and features an approach over water to a bunker-guarded island green.

⭐

I have a classic case of the yips. You know, people say it's all in your
head, but it's not a mental thing with me. I have a physical problem. W
hen I sign my name, sometimes the pen jumps and there's nothing I can do. There's a
loose wire back there or something. There's nothing you can do. Johnny Miller

The details   817-481-7529. 1400 Byron Nelson Pkwy., Southlake, TX 76092

- 1994. Byron Nelson and Baxter Spann. 18 holes. Par 72. Black – 7,012 (74.2/137). Copper – 6,525 (71.5/130). White – 5,949 (68.9/126). Green – 5,309 (71.8/128). Price - $$$.

Getting there From Hwy. 114, exit White Chapel Blvd. and turn south. Drive to Continental Blvd. and turn left. This will take you to the main entrance to Timarron, then drive 1 mile to Byron Nelson Pkwy.

SOUTHLAKE NOTES The heart of Southlake is its impressive new **Town Square**, highlighted by the latest in shopping trends and a good variety of restaurants. The best strategy for weekend rounds is to talk the family into a mid-morning spree at the Town Square while you satisfy your golf addictions at a nearby course. Margaritas at **Mi Cocina** help calm feisty spouses and help lighten the load one may feel from expensive sprees on the square.

STEPHENVILLE   Elev. 1,283   Pop. 15,262

US 377 from Fort Worth takes you through Granbury, Tolar, and eventually to the cowboy dairy-town seat of Erath County known as Stephenville. Settlers came here in the 1850s and were pestered by Indians through the Civil War days. The 1899, red-bricked Tarleton State University is here, and the area is Texas' leading producer of Coastal Bermuda range grass, as well as the one of its largest dairy producers.

LEGENDS COUNTRY CLUB

The golf   Legends is the only 18-hole option in Stephenville. Known for its well-conditioned greens, this easy course is enjoyable because of its laid-back atmosphere.

Here you'll have the chance to start out strong, since the opening two holes consist of a 450-yard par 5 followed by a reasonably easy par 3. The most difficult par 4 and number one handicap is on the front in the 412-yard No. 4, but the remainder of the front poses little problems.

The same goes for the back nine–unlike many other courses today, it features two short par 4s to finish the round.

The details   254-968-2200. 137 Ben Hogan Dr., Stephenville, TX 76401

- 1978. 18 holes. Par 72. Back – 6,378 (70.2). Middle – 5,959 (68.8). Forward – 4,557 (70.8). Price - $$.

Getting there From Hwy. 377, turn right on Lingleville Hwy., then travel to Ben Hogan Dr. and make another right.

Much dripping wears away a stone, and continual fussing and fretting...wears away the golfer. Bernard Darwin, on too much waggle

TEJAS GOLF COURSE

The golf   Tejas is a fun 9-holer that allows you to play all day for one green fee, offering two sets of tees for a different look on round two. The par 36 layout plays to 2,957 yards, and features the standard mixture of par 3s, 4s, and 5s. The design features confidence-building par 4s, all barely over 300 yards, as well as a 433-yard par 5. The longest hole is No. 3, a 533-yard par 5. This one is a hacker's paradise–minimal hazards, short holes, all for a nice price.

The details   254-965-3904. 1089 Tejas Ln., Stephenville, TX 76401

• 1970. 9 holes. Par 36. Back – 2,957. Forward – 2,506. Price - $.

Getting there From Stephenville take Hwy. 281 north past the loop and Washington St. to Golf Course Rd. Turn left, drive a short distance to the course, and look for the entrance on the right side of the street.

STEPHENVILLE NOTES   Ask the locals about haunted **McDow Hole** on Green's Creek (FM 914), where the ghost of a young pioneer wife looms over the countryside. **Cafe Trifles** (254-918-0990) is a nice spot for lunch. In nearby Dublin, TX there's **Woody's** (254-445-3737) serving up pizzas, burgers, and BBQ plates that go well with cold beer and sports watching. The **Oxford House B&B** (254-965-6885) is the better lodging alternative to Stephenville's **Holiday Inn** (254-968-5256).

TERRELL   Elev. 530   Pop. 13,606

Located 30 miles east of Dallas on Hwy. 80, the town of Terrell was founded in 1873 when the railroad came through and put the town on the map as a bustling trade center. Today you may not notice Terrell unless you're looking for it on excursions into the Big Thicket, but golfers should consider a quick stop at the 9-hole Oak Grove Golf Course: a perfect warm-up before heading into the Texas woods for more golf.

OAK GROVE GOLF COURSE

The golf   One of Ralph Plummer's last projects, Oak Grove opened in 1979 and plays to a 3,187-yard par 36. Plummer's design features well-conditioned greens and narrow fairways lined by old trees.

The details   972-563-8553. 2000 Colquitt Rd., Terrell, TX 75160

• 1979. Ralph Plummer. 9 holes. Par 36. Back – 3,187 (34.4/106). Forward – 2,592 (33.8/103). Price - $.

Getting there From Dallas, take Hwy. 80 east 20 miles to Hwy. 205. Turn

---

Golf and wagering go together as smoothly as "double" and "bogey." James Y. Bartlett

north and drive 1.5 miles to Colquitt Rd., where you'll turn right to the course.

TERRELL NOTES   There are plenty of chains along the highway in Terrell, but look just a little farther east to Wills Point, TX and the **Rocking L Guest Ranch** (903-560-0246) for accommodations and outdoor excursions. For food, consider **Ranch Hand Barbecue** (972-563-9461) or the **Double T Steak & Grill Restaurant** (972-563-0511). Also don't forget that the marinas and restaurants of Lake Tawakoni aren't far away.

THE TEXAS TRAIL GOLF CLUB

Avid golfers are always looking for deals, and often want to avoid locking themselves in to a dues-paying club that restricts their freedom to roam and golf. By becoming a member of the Texas Trail Golf Club (www.thetexasgolftrail.com), Texas hackers can save up to 50% off normal green fees and earn 20 rounds of complimentary golf across Texas and Oklahoma. In addition, certain private clubs are available on "member-playdays." Check the Web site for further information. The annual fee is $299, but some claim to have negotiated rates around $250 by dealing directly with clubs who participate in the program. The DFW-area program is fully launched and achieving great success, while the Houston program is scheduled to get going in 2003.

TOLAR   Elev. 1,022   Pop. 504

Tolar, located on US 377 seven miles southwest of Granbury, has been famous in Texas golf since Marvin Leonard used his ranch to build the Augusta National of 9-hole Lone Star golf. The post office opened here in 1890 after the railroad chugged through, and the town quickly became established as a trade center for area ranchers and farmers.

STARR HOLLOW GOLF CLUB

The golf   This famous course, sometimes referred to as "Little Augusta," sits in the middle of a 3,000-acre ranch bought in 1965 by Colonial CC founder Marvin Leonard, who built the course primarily for his friends and a few area ranchers. Leonard never finished the back nine, but what was finished is considered one of the most interesting golf experiences in the state.

Most of the unusually small membership reside in Fort Worth and Dallas, so there's room in the gravel parking lot when you drive to this remote 9-hole

Consider, if you will, that on a par-72 course you can bogey 17 of the 18 holes and still break 90. Cliff McAdams

course. The clubhouse is the epitome of casual, exuding an old-school charm with walls covered by photos of Ben Hogan and aerials of the course.

The course bends around Leonard's manmade lake which, as legend has it, covers up the canyon where outlaw Belle Starr once stashed her stolen loot. Each hole, sporting its own unique Texas-like name, features two tees and two flags, enabling the complete 18-hole experience.

Given the charm described above, it's worth a shot at hustling your way onto this 9-hole Texas treasure.

The details   254-834-3464. 5717 Star Hollow Ct., Tolar, TX 76476

• 1969. Joe Finger. Back – Par 35. 2,980 yards (68.6). Forward – Par 36. 2,826 yards (71.7). Price - $$.

Getting there Tolar is southwest of Fort Worth between Granbury and Stephenville.

TOLAR NOTES   Starr Hollow's grill is famous for their juicy hamburgers, so don't miss em' post-round if you're ready to eat. Out on W. Hwy. 377 you'll run into **Billy Roys Bar-B-Que** (254-835-5075), the nearest joint for sloppy sliced beef sandwiches and a cold glass of iced tea. In town, the **Tolar Street Cafe** (254-835-4682) is the most popular place with the locals. For lodging, Granbury is a short drive northeast and is loaded with outstanding bed and breakfast accommodations.

TROPHY CLUB   Elev. 595   Pop. 6,350

Located 23 miles northeast of Fort Worth, the planned community of Trophy Club dates back to the 1970s when Arthur Hills and Ben Hogan collaborated on Hogan's only course project to create the centerpiece of the country club setting. Today the community is fully developed with grand homes and two 18-hole golf courses, and houses DFW professionals and their families in a scenic, almost Hill-Country-like setting.

TROPHY CLUB OF DALLAS

The golf   Trophy Club opened with nine holes in 1976, but is now the complete weekend experience with two 18-hole championship courses.

The original 9-hole **Hogan Course** is known as the only course that Ben Hogan designed, and was rounded out by Arthur Hills some 20 years later when he came in to add the second nine as well as his **Hills Course**.

Notable holes on the Hills include back-to-back toughies on the front–No. 6 at 395 yards is a mean par 4 with a fairway bunker, and No. 7 is a chal-

The primary concern of great golfers is performing as well as they can,
or as close to their potential as they can. If they do that and lose, they
shrug and move on. The wins will come. Dr. Bob Rotella

lenging par 5 at 516 yards. The best hole is the 18th, a 454-yard dogleg-left bruiser that bends around a lake guarding the fairway and green.

The details 817-430-0444. 500 Trophy Club Dr., Trophy Club, TX 76262

- www.trophyclub-dallas.com

- Hogan Course: 1976. Ben Hogan and Joe Lee. 18 holes. Par 72. Back – 6,953 (72.8/123). Middle – 6,441 (70.2/117). Forward – 5,598 (72.5/121). Price - $$$$.

- Hills Course: 1984. Arthur Hills. 18 holes. Par 72. Back – 6,942 (73.0/125). Middle – 6,291 (69.8/119). Forward – 5,304 (71.7/121). Price - $$$$.

Getting there From Dallas, take Hwy. 114 west through Grapevine. The entrance is 6 miles past Grapevine on the right side of the road.

TROPHY CLUB NOTES A weekend on the links out here isn't complete without a side trip into Roanoke for a meal at **Babe's Chicken Dinner House** (817-491-2900). Peruse the shop next door while you wait for a table, then clog your arteries with some of the most impressive home-style cooking in this part of the state. The menu features chicken-fried everything, sided by corn, biscuits, mashed potatoes and, of course, gravy.

WAXAHACHIE
Elev. 585   Pop. 22,038

Named after an Indian word that means "cow creek," Waxahachie was once smack in the middle of the Chisolm Trail and is now the seat of Ellis County, dotted with Victorian homes dating from the town's pre-eminence as a cotton hub. Also a commuter community to DFW, Waxahachie has but one golf course—the 18-hole country club.

WAXAHACHIE COUNTRY CLUB

The golf The WCC plays to a par 70, 6,120 yards from the tips, and is famous for its blind doglegs and hilly terrain. The design incorporates a good combination of golf holes, both long and short par 4s, and especially the solid par 5s that all play over 500 yards from the tips. The opening hole is one of the easiest–a short par 3 that is one of the better ways to start a round. But the next hole is the number one handicap, a 513-yard par 5.

The details 972-937-3521. 1920 W. Business 287, Waxahachie, TX 75165

- 18 holes. Par 70. Back – 6,120 (68.5/104). Middle – 5,840 (67.3/101). Forward – Par 71. 5,099 (68.3/118). Price - $$.

Getting there From I-35 south, take the Business 287 exit and turn left. Drive

---
☆

Directly, as I felt that it was about to jump (right hand), I would snatch at the ball in a desperate effort to play the shot before the involuntary movement could take effect. Up would go my head and body with a start and off would go the ball, anywhere but on the proper line. Harry Vardon

a short distance to the course, and look for the entrance on the left side of the street.

WAXAHACHIE NOTES   The action is downtown, where there's shopping and restaurants galore. The **1879 Townhouse Restaurant and Bakery** (972-937-7261) is across from the courthouse, specializing in roast beef and baked beans. Regulars to Waxahachie swear by the **Peel's Country Steakhouse** (972-938-3688), and the **Catfish Plantation** (972-937-9468) does its specialty better than most. Reserve your rooms at the newly remodeled **Rogers Hotel**, the **Rosemary Mansion B&B**, or the **Harrison B&B**.

WEATHERFORD   Elev. 1,052   Pop. 18,572

Weatherford, due west of Fort Worth, dates back to the mid-1800s, when it was a western frontier town that marked the beginning of Oliver Loving's organized cattle drives to the railheads in Kansas. Loving is buried in the Greenwood City Cemetery of this town, which boasts many magnificent Victorian homes that date back to the 1800s. Its proximity to Fort Worth drives a healthy golf market for Weatherford, with a total of four courses and 54 holes of golf.

CANYON WEST GOLF CLUB

The golf   The scenic ranchlands west of Fort Worth are full of rugged canyons, native wildflowers, and impressive elevation changes, all of which are incorporated into Canyon West's design. Located atop Parker County's highest summit, this 1997 18-holer incorporates all of those North Texas Hill Country features and more into its design. Waterfalls, miles of streams, exposed rocks, prairie grasses, wildflowers, and loads of oak, pecan, elm, and mesquite trees highlight the landscape.

Elevated tees offer views of the countryside. In addition to the scenery, golfers are welcomed by generous fairways that make this a fairly user-friendly course, especially given its reasonable yardage of 6,653 from the tips and the fact that water comes into play on only about half of the holes.

Other notes: During the week, the course offers seniors a two-for-one green fee. Walking is not allowed.

The details   817-596-4653. 200 Canyon West Dr., Weatherford, TX 76087

- www.canyonwestgolf.com
- 1997. Par 72. Back - 6,653 (71.0/124). Middle – 6,236 (68.7/116). Forward – 5,821 (66.9/112). Ladies – 5,433 (65.0/107). Price - $$$.

Golf is so much more fun when it is played well. I've always thought that if the game was worth playing at all, it was worth making some effort to play it correctly. Bobby Jones

Getting there From Ft. Worth, go west on I-20 and take exit 403. Cross left over the freeway and then make a quick right onto the service road. The entrance is 2.5 miles down the road.

CROWN VALLEY COUNTRY CLUB

The golf   One of Weatherford's newest residential developments, Crown Valley is open for public play right now, but eventually has plans to become private once the memberships have been filled. The course opened for play in late 2002 with a Steve Mrak-designed course that runs through a myriad of creeks, ponds, and lakes. Mrak ingeniously slated his No. 13 as an "unlucky" 250-yard par 3. From the tips, the course plays 7,100 yards to a par 72.

The details   817-596-7512. 1204 Mikus Rd., Weatherford, TX 76087.

• 2002, Steve Mrak. 18 holes. Par 72. 7,100 yards. Price - $$$.

Getting there The course is 1.5 miles north of I-20 on Milkus Rd.

HORSESHOE BEND COUNTRY CLUB

The golf   Horseshoe Bend is the other 9-hole course in Weatherford: a fun course with average-length par 3s and 4s, and a few 500-yard-plus par 5s. Oaks and pecans line the fairways of this flat course, which also has one lake that rarely comes into play.

The longest par 4 and number one handicap is the 393-yard No. 5. Nos. 3 and 8 are par 3s that play only 150 from the tips, both great birdie opportunities.

Two sets of tees allow for an 18-hole round.

The details   817-594-6454. 305 Lipan Trail, Weatherford, TX 76087

• 9 holes. Par 36. Back – 3,155 (35.0/110). Forward – 2,770 (34.8/108). Price - $.

Getting there From I-20 east, exit FM 1884 and turn left. Drive approximately 8 miles and turn right on Lipan Trail. The course is 4 miles down the road.

LIVE OAK COUNTRY CLUB

The golf   Live Oak is an old, semi-private course that originally opened in the 1930s with sand greens. Set in the pastures outside of Weatherford, it's a simple little layout with tree-lined fairways and small greens. Water impacts play on only 2 of 9 holes, so if you're hitting them straight it should be an enjoyable day.

Two par 3s stand out–the 5th hole because of the water around the green, and No. 7, which is lined by a ditch on the left and plays long over water. The ender is fun, going 518 yards with huge trees on either side of the fairway and a well-protected, bunker-infested green.

The details   817-594-7596. 1734 Bethel Rd., Weatherford, TX 76086

- 1930s. 9 holes. Par 35. Back – 3,051 (34.4/106). Middle – 2,888 (34.1/102). Forward – 2,439 (33.6/106). Price - $$.

Getting there From I-20 east, take Exit 407 and go north to Hwy. 51. At the first stop light, turn left on Bethel Rd. and then turn right again at the intersection with the blinking light.

SQUAW CREEK GOLF CLUB

The golf   Ralph Plummer built this course in the early 1970s for employees of the Lockheed Martin plant, but today Squaw Creek is open to the public. Its namesake creek runs through the property, and the course is popular because of its sloping, bent-grass greens. Walkers might have a rough go of it, as the terrain is fairly rugged and there are significant elevation changes.

Playing from the tips, you'll face quite a few 400-yard-plus par 4s, and a pair of par 3s that are over 200 yards. The number one handicap is the 595-yard No. 16.

The details   817-441-8185. 1605 Ranch House Rd., Weatherford, TX 76087

- 1971. Ralph Plummer. 18 holes. Par 71. Back – 6,749 (71.9/126). Middle – 6,124 (69.1/118). Forward – Par 72. 5,575 (71.5/119). Price - $$.

Getting there From I-30 west, take the 418 exit and turn right on Ranch House Rd. The entrance is on the left side of the road.

WEATHERFORD NOTES   **Montana's** has cold beer and chicken-fried steak bigger than the plates it's served on, and the **Mesquite Pit** is another good option for steaks. You can take your own cervezas into **La Playa Maya**, a nice touch when going for Tex-Mex. Weatherford offers a few nice B&B options in **Governor's Hill** (817-596-0534) and the unusually named **St. Sbotolph** (817-594-1455). The side trip down FM 51 north of town offers a glimpse of one of the state's oldest and largest pecan trees, estimated to be 300-1000 years old.

WESTLAKE   Elev. 667   Pop. 207

High-toned Westlake is located on the Tarrant and Denton county lines in the heart of the DFW metroplex. The community only houses about 250 residents, but is best known for the famous H. Ross Perot, Jr. Circle T Ranch development, as well as the high-profile corporate campus known as Solana. Solana's Village Circle is a mixture of office, retail, restaurant, and hotel space, and the Vaquero Club is the place to play golf.

--- ---

My partner always has a 1-iron in his bag; he has more than 37 tags hanging
from his bag; he has used the same putter since he was five years old; he's gone
if he tells me about his marital problems on the practice tee. Gary McCord

444 • *The Texas Golf Bible*

VAQUERO CLUB

The golf   The Vaquero Club is the centerpiece of the Discovery Land Company's vision to build an exclusive gated country club community similar to their earlier successes at Estancia in Scottsdale, AZ, and Iron Horse in Whitefish, MO. Lots go for around $1 million, the initiation fee is $75,000, and PGA Tour players such as Brian Watts, Brant Jobe, Harrison Frazar and Justin Leonard are making their presence known at this super-upscale golf facility.

Tom Fazio was hired to lay this one out amongst the rolling hills and groves of cedar and oak trees that are so prominent in this part of Texas. For aesthetics, the club has planted pistachio trees, which will sport their majestic red shades in the fall. Fazio's design features narrow fairways that are lined by thick, two-foot high coastal Bermuda rough. The pro-style bent-grass greens are slick, running an average of 10 on the stimpmeter. The best opportunities to score are early in the round, as the holes become increasingly more difficult as you work your way towards No. 18.

Fazio inserted an impressive waste-bunker on the 476-yard No. 6, covering almost 5 acres and creating an interesting look to the hole. The signature No. 16 goes almost 600 yards, but can be handled if you keep it in the fairway and out of the nasty rough. Watch for the huge bunker that borders the green.

Vaquero is first-class all the way, complete with Titleist Pro V1 range balls, uniformed caddies, a gourmet chef who prepares lunch at the turn, and a welcome no-cell-phone policy that is sure to be grossly violated by the deep-pocket execs who pay big bucks to play here.

The details   817-430-6600. 2300 Vaquero Club Dr., Westlake, TX 76262

• www.vaqueroclub.com

• 2002. Tom Fazio. 18 holes. Par 71. 7,064 yards. Price - $$$$.

Getting there On Hwy. 114 going west, you'll pass through Grapevine and Southlake and eventually reach the Solana office complex.

WESTLAKE NOTES   If you have the honor of gracing the fairways at Vaquero, you'll want to stay at the lavish, resort-like **Marriott Solana** (817-430-3848), an impressive architectural structure set among magnificent oak trees and beautiful wildflowers. This spot is 5 miles from historic Grapevine and truly in the heart of DFW, halfway between Dallas and Fort Worth and loaded with all of the non-golf activities you could possibly want. The workout facilities are plush, including an outdoor jogging track that is ideal for getting your heart rate up while enjoying the scenery.

NORTH CENTRAL

One bad shot does not make a losing score. Gay Brewer

WHITNEY

Elev. 585   Pop. 1,711

Gateway to Lake Whitney, due west of Hillsboro and I-35, Whitney popped up in 1879 when the railroad came through. Later it became a popular weekend destination when the lake won reknown for its clear, blue waters and outstanding fishing.

LAKE WHITNEY GOLF & TENNIS CLUB

The golf   Leon Howard built a par 70, 6,296-yard layout here in 1969 that features the rugged Hill Country terrain of the area, along with narrow, tree-lined fairways and some ponds that impact play. The most difficult hole is No. 10, a 235-yard par 3 that luckily plays downhill over a massive area of cattails.

The details   254-694-2313. 155 Country Club Rd., Whitney, TX 76692

- 1969. Leon Howard. 18 holes. Par 70. Back – 6,296 (69.8/113). Middle – 6,061 (67.6/113). Forward – 5,020 (67.6/113). Price - $.

Getting there From I-35 south, take Hwy. 22 west and exit Hwy. 22 Business. Drive north on FM 933 a few miles to Country Club Dr. Turn left and the course is 1.5 miles down the road.

WHITE BLUFF GOLF CLUB

The golf   White Bluff opened in the early 1990s along the shores of one of Texas' most productive fishing lake, Lake Whitney, and now sports two outstanding Bruce Lietzke-designed courses, plenty of accommodations, and the resources to make your lake time productive while on weekend excursions to the area.

The **Old Course,** considered the easier of the two tracks because of its generous fairways, still features the majestic oaks that are so prominent in this region of Texas. The front side is flat and allows you the chance to get warmed up for the scenic back nine. This back side, highlighted by views of Lake Whitney, offers more elevation changes and Hill Country scenery.

No. 12 (400 yards) is tough because is plays uphill and requires the tee shot to carry water, but No. 13 is the signature—a 160-yarder that overlooks a ravine and the lake and is the perfect introduction to the creek that impacts play on the next few holes.

The **New Course** tips out at 6,964 yards and features water on 16 of 18 holes. Plan your shots accordingly on this tricky track, as there are numerous blind water hazards that you will not know existed unless you've played the course before.

This course isn't as scenic as the Old Course, with no views of the lake, but offers one picturesque par 4 that plays almost 400 yards with a pond framed by a large rock bluff. Watch the finger of water that cuts in front of the green

I expect to make at least seven mistakes a round. Therefore, when I make a bad shot, I don't worry about it; it's just one of those seven. Walter Hagen

on the approach.

The details   254-694-3656. 22 Misty Valley Circle, Whitney, TX 76692

- www.whitebluffresort.com

- Old Course: 1993. Bruce Lietzke. 18 holes. Par 72. Gold – 6,866 (73.3/132). Blue – 6,424 (71.0/126). White – 5,878 (68.6/120). Red – 5,292 (72.4/128). Price - $$$.

- New Course: 1995. Bruce Lietzke. 18 holes. Par 72. Gold – 6,964 (73.9/139). Blue – 6,574 (71.9/132). White – 6,198 (70.2/129). Red – 5,589 (73.3/128). Price - $$$.

Getting there From I-35 going north, get off at Exit 368A, drive west for about 17 miles to Whitney, head north on FM 933 for 7 miles to the course.

WHITNEY NOTES   The outlet mall in Hillsboro helps keep punchy female family members at bay while you get your round(s) in. In the heart of Whitney is one of the best Mexican cafes anywhere, the popular **El Rancho** (254-694-5767), with its delicious beef fajitas. Quick, tasty lunches are served at **Cherokee Station BBQ Plus** (254-694-7873). On the lake, the **Light House** (888-944-8325) is spectacular and one of two spots for sunset gazing. The other is the **Arrowhead Resort** (254-694-3044), which can put you up and feed you at **Mel's Steakhouse** . Outdoorsmen will be drawn to the **W.B. Ranch** (254-694-4868), which offers guest rooms, ranch tours, and all sorts of hunting, in addition to lake and river fishing.

NORTH CENTRAL

WOLFE CITY Elev. 691   Pop. 1,566

One of the least-known golf destinations in Texas, Wolfe City is in the middle of nowhere on the Grassland Prairie, perched at the confluence of farm roads and generally void of civilization. There is really absolutely no reason in hell that the wayward golfer should end up in this remote part of Texas, but you never know where the road might lead you. This town is 70 miles northeast of Dallas, due north of Greenville's metropolis on the border of Hunt and Fannin counties. Typically these po-dunk towns pop up because they're associated with some sort of manmade reservoir and water recreation, yet this place is here in all its splendid glory–and somehow someone convinced Leon Howard and Dave Bennett to build a golf course here.

WEBB HILL COUNTRY CLUB

The golf   Funeral home man and golf fan Bobby Owens led the development of Webb Hill CC in 1969, and the Leon Howard-designed 18-hole course has served Wolfe City ever since. This course is heavily wooded, with narrow,

"Mrs. Crane! You're a little monkey woman, you know that?" Carl Spackler (Bill Murray) in *Caddyshack*

undulating fairways and a good combination of interesting tee shots. Howard's design involves a few blind tee shots that play uphill, as well as a few from elevated tees that offer good views of the holes ahead. Water comes into play on half the holes, and the large greens are of medium speed.

No. 8 is the signature, playing 590 yards and requiring two tough shots down a swerving fairway lined by a lake. The approach is nasty because of the skinny green that is covered by trees.

The details   903-496-2221. 438 FM 2358, Wolfe City, TX 75496

- 1969. Leon Howard and Dave Bennett. 18 holes. Par 72. Back – 6,808 (72.9/127). Middle – 6,379 (70.6/122). Forward – 5,193 (71.9/123). Price – $.

Getting there From I-30 east towards Greenville, take Hwy. 34 north to FM 2358. Turn left and the course is just down the road on the right side.

WOLFE CITY NOTES Walk around the town square and drop in for coffee talk at the local diner. Downtown **Temerario's** (903-886-4260) is known as the place for Tex-Mex, and on Monroe St., **Molina's** is another solid choice. For accommodations call the **Bodark B&B** (903-886-7705) or the **Chapin House B&B** (903-886-6713).

WYLIE

Wylie is heaven on earth for the folks who live there, sandwiched between Lake Lavon and Lake Ray Hubbard. It's rural enough to feel country, yet close enough to the urban confusion that is Plano and Garland. Wylie became known in the golf world in 1999 when the impressive Woodbridge Golf Club opened. Ever since, Woodbridge has been receiving acclaim as one of the top courses in Texas, hosting the Texas State Open as well as the qualifier for the Bank One Senior PGA Tour Championship.

WOODBRIDGE GOLF CLUB

The golf   Woodbridge's layout doglegs through some interesting terrain, with heavy woodlands, natural wetlands, streams, and meadows making the course scenic and fun. There are 15 doglegs in all, which makes for a tough, long 7,016 yards if you're playing from the tips.

Woodbridge's best feature is perfectly conditioned greens that vary in size and force you to think because of the heavy undulations.

One of the most challenging holes on the front nine is No. 5, a 429-yard par 4 that plays uphill through a tight chute of trees. The spectacular green is

The zone is the ability to give 110 percent of your attention and your focus to the shot. When I'm on the tee, I'll see a divot in the fairway and try to run my ball over that divot – and succeed.
That's the zone. Nick Price

guarded by a waterfall on the left, bunkers to the right and rear, and a pond in the front.

On the back, No. 16 is one of the nastiest, playing over water that wraps around the green. Overhanging trees get in the way off the tee, forcing you to work the ball if the pin is tucked right or left. Rather than getting fancy, the best play here is to get it on the green and work for the two-putt par.

The details 972-429-5100. 7400 Country Club Dr., Wylie, TX 75098

• www.visitwoodbridge.com

• 1999. Lee Singletary. 18 holes. Par 72. Back – 7,016 (72.8/141). Middle – 6,437 (72.1/131). Forward – 4,939 (67.0/109). Price - $$$.

Getting there From Dallas, take Hwy. 75 (Central Expressway) north to Hwy. 190 (George Bush Turnpike). Drive east to Hwy. 78, then north for 4 miles. The entrance to the subdivision is on the right, and there are signs to the course inside.

WYLIE NOTES After Woodbridge consider the **Ballard Street Cafe & Grill** (972-442-0453), where they serve chicken-fried steak North Texas style. If it needs to be a little quicker, pull in to **Outlaws Barbecue** (972-442-4568) for a quick lunch. For rendezvous that require immediate attention, slip into the **Campbell Heather B&B** (972-442-7707) and pretend you're in Fredericksburg.

NORTH CENTRAL TEXAS BORDER CROSSINGS

Not many Texans know it, but there's great golf to be had on the other side of Lake Texoma. Not only are the courses great, the prices are right—and there's just something neat about the charming little Oklahoma towns like Burneyville, Ardmore, Kingston, and Durant. And besides, if you didn't make it up this way your post round golf festivities couldn't include the rural blood sport of cockfighting, which is popular in seedy Oklahoma pits where locals gather to watch roosters shred each other to the death and to bet on their fates.

ARDMORE, OK   42 miles from Gainesville, TX

The **Dornick Hills Golf & Country Club** (508-223-2957) is a longtime top 10 track for Oklahoma. It's known for its doglegged fairways and the impressive No. 16 "cliff hole," which rolls 530 yards and involves an exciting approach over a 50-foot cliff to the green. The course is old, dating back to around 1920,

At the short hole bunkers should abound. They should be so numerous and so fearful in aspect that the player delivers his tee shot almost without hope of escape. John Low, 1903

and tips out to a par 70, 6,453 yards (72.7/130).

Short and hilly, the **Lake Murray State Park Golf Course** (580-223-4260) is known for offering numerous shot-making opportunities, even though water is in play on only a few holes. The best hole is the most scenic, the 140-yard No. 16 that plays over a waterfall.

The **Lakeview Golf Club** (580-223-4260) rolls around a lake and benefits from a few updates introduced in the mid-1990s, including the renovation of the clubhouse. You can see the lake on just about every hole of this 6,881-yarder (71.2/114), and par is supposed to be 71. No. 15 is the signature, a 360-yard par 4 that approaches over water.

BURNEYVILLE, OK   34 miles from Gainesville, TX

The **Falconhead Resort & Country Club** (508-564-3581) is a semi-private resort located in a gated residential community. Amazingly, the course was once a regular stop on the PGA Tour in the early 1960s. Known as the Poor Boy Open, the tourney was popular because of host Waco Turner's propensity to offer generous cash prizes. Robert Trent Jones, Sr. came though and shortened the par 72 track to 6,404 yards (70.2/125).

KINGSTON, OK   31 miles from Denison, TX

Some say the pro-like, bent-grass greens at the **Chichasaw Pointe Golf Course** (580-564-3581) are not only the best in Oklahoma, but the best in Texas. Randy Heckenkemper did this one in 1999, and since its opening it has been the favorite of North Texas golfers traveling over the border. Long at 7,047 yards, this scenic course offers views of Lake Texoma along with some impressive elevation changes. Watch out for the deep ravines that line some of the fairways—they are not always viewable from the tee—as well as the long-ass rough that looms around most greens, making it very difficult for up-and-down pars.

The 1970s-era **Lake Texoma State Park Golf Course** (580-564-3333) tips at 6,500 yards (71.4/126) and should be played in 71 strokes for the pros. Water is in play on over half the holes, and the flat front nine becomes a little more undulating on the back. Watch out for the pin placements on the multi-level greens.

DURANT, OK   22.3 miles from Denison, TX

Durant Country Club (580-875-3829) upgraded with an additional nine in the mid-1990s. This track goes about 6,500 yards in 72 strokes, and is known for its well-conditioned fairways.

✩

A narrow plateau for a green, or a few hummocks in front of one, will
very likely cause just as much trouble and amusement to a player as a
gaping chasm stretching right across the course. Harry S. Colt, 1912

★ NORTHEAST TEXAS ★

Non-Texans, and even die-hard Texans, often buy into the image of the Lone Star State as a dusty Western cowboy frontier. Northeast Texas, however, takes the traveling golfer into a world like no other. Boasting a forest bigger than the entire state of Indiana, this region is home to more than 23.4 million acres of lush, thick, emerald-green woods made up of tall ancient pines and old-ass cypress trees that are intermingled with impressively blooming ferns and dogwoods. Here you'll find giant lakes, cozy bed & breakfasts, and friendly country folk who take pride in their escape from the urban maelstrom.

An intense, flavorful Southern character flows through these towns. Pastel antebellum homes, lovingly restored with white Victorian trim, line the charming brick-paved streets of towns like Jefferson and Marshall. Fishing boats drift through the cypress swamps, bayous, and sloughs of Caddo Lake. A classic steam-powered locomotive with elegant passenger cars chugs into the station at Palestine. And flowers—acres and acres and acres of roses and azaleas fill the horizon outside Tyler. If you plopped most other Texans down in this region, they'd bet you money they'd been exported to Louisiana or Arkansas, or at least sent back in time to the turn of the century.

The area's verdant feel is literally heaven-sent. Northeast Texas gets an average of 40-55 inches of rainfall each year (more than say, Boston, Washington, D.C. or even Key West, Florida)—a major factor in producing the dense greenness of the Piney Woods. Like the majestic pines that surround them, families planted in East Texas tend to stay there, giving the region a love of history, tradition, and restoration. On any given side road, you're almost as likely to find an old-fashioned general store as a fast-food joint.

Tyler, the largest and most metropolitan city in the region, is home to only 85,000 people. And Longview isn't far behind with 75,000 folks. But for the most part, Northeast Texas is small-town, back-woods Texas, and only seven of the 42 cities with golf courses have populations exceeding 15,000. Play a few rounds here, and everyone will know your name.

NORTHEAST

★

Golf is the one game I know which becomes more and more difficult the longer one plays it. *Bobby Jones*

Northeast Mileage

	Athens	Atlanta	Big Sandy	Bullard	Canton	Carthage	Center	Clarksville	Cooper	Crockett	Daingerfd	Elkhart	Emory	Frankston	Gilmer	Gladewater	Hawkins	Hender.	Jacksonvl.	Jefferson	K
Athens		126	57	41	25	97	111	122	90	70	101	45	48	23	72	61	56	69	39	107	6
Atlanta	126		69	106	117	70	100	75	102	162	36	148	101	116	55	67	75	86	117	29	7
Big Sandy	57	69		37	50	57	86	83	76	103	44	79	45	46	15	10	6	41	49	54	2
Bullard	41	106	37		50	64	85	117	99	70	81	49	63	18	52	41	36	34	13	85	3
Canton	25	117	50	50		98	121	97	65	94	85	70	23	48	62	57	44	70	63	101	6
Carthage	97	70	57	64	98		30	125	131	100	72	92	103	77	57	47	63	29	61	41	3
Center	111	100	86	85	121	30		154	159	87	102	90	131	88	86	76	92	51	72	71	6
Clarksville	122	75	83	117	97	125	154		53	183	56	159	74	127	68	82	82	113	129	87	9
Cooper	90	102	76	99	65	131	159	53		159	73	135	42	107	73	86	71	117	111	104	10
Crockett	70	162	103	70	94	100	87	183	159		142	25	117	57	118	104	102	77	57	133	9
Daingerfield	101	36	44	81	85	72	102	56	73	142		122	66	90	29	43	49	67	93	32	5
Elkhart	45	148	79	49	70	92	90	159	135	25	122		93	32	93	83	77	68	36	124	7
Emory	48	101	45	63	23	103	131	74	42	117	66	93		71	51	55	40	82	75	91	6
Frankston	23	116	46	18	48	77	88	127	107	57	90	32	71		61	50	45	48	16	95	5
Gilmer	72	55	15	52	62	57	86	68	73	118	29	93	51	61		14	20	45	64	39	2
Gladewater	61	67	10	41	57	47	76	82	86	104	43	83	55	50	14		16	31	53	47	1
Hawkins	56	75	6	36	44	63	92	82	71	102	49	77	40	45	20	16		46	48	60	2
Henderson	69	86	41	34	70	29	51	113	117	77	67	68	82	48	45	31	46		33	57	1
Jacksonville	39	117	49	13	63	61	72	129	111	57	93	36	75	16	64	53	48	33		89	4
Jefferson	107	29	54	85	101	41	71	87	104	133	32	124	91	95	39	47	60	57	89		4
Kilgore	61	75	24	39	61	39	68	96	100	92	51	79	69	50	28	14	29	18	43	46	
Lindale	46	90	21	29	29	73	98	90	70	94	65	69	34	37	36	31	15	48	41	75	3
Longview	72	63	22	51	69	36	64	90	95	103	39	90	68	61	22	12	28	28	54	35	1
Malakoff	10	136	67	51	34	106	120	131	99	76	110	52	57	33	81	71	65	79	49	116	7
Marshall	94	45	45	72	91	26	56	102	113	117	47	108	90	83	39	35	50	41	72	16	3
Mineola	49	90	23	41	27	80	109	78	58	106	60	81	22	49	35	33	17	59	53	75	4
Mount Pleasant	101	51	45	82	78	87	116	38	55	148	18	123	57	91	30	44	50	75	94	49	5
Murchison	8	118	49	38	26	88	111	118	91	78	93	53	49	29	63	53	47	61	45	98	5
Nacogdoches	88	120	81	62	110	50	33	153	157	54	106	57	122	65	85	71	87	40	49	92	5
New Boston	139	36	82	119	119	95	125	39	84	181	39	161	98	128	67	81	88	105	131	55	8
Overton	57	86	31	27	58	42	65	104	105	83	62	67	69	44	36	21	37	14	31	58	1
Palestine	35	138	69	39	59	87	94	149	124	35	112	11	82	22	83	73	67	59	26	115	6
Paris	107	98	93	116	82	138	167	30	23	176	69	152	59	124	8	95	88	126	128	100	10
Pittsburg	91	51	33	70	70	76	104	49	62	136	15	112	50	80	19	33	39	64	82	45	4
Rusk	53	119	63	27	78	59	63	143	125	43	99	34	89	30	75	61	62	34	14	90	4
Scroggins	85	68	33	75	61	105	134	53	57	150	32	125	37	83	28	43	33	74	87	63	5
Sulphur Springs	69	87	55	78	45	110	139	53	21	139	55	114	22	86	53	65	50	96	90	86	7
Teague	56	182	113	85	80	133	137	177	145	63	156	47	103	68	127	117	117	111	104	72	161	11
Texarkana	151	26	94	131	140	95	125	60	105	188	57	173	119	141	80	92	100	111	142	54	10
Troup	53	100	39	14	55	50	71	117	102	69	76	53	67	30	49	35	39	21	17	72	2
Tyler	35	92	23	16	36	62	85	103	83	81	66	57	47	25	37	27	21	35	28	72	2
Yantis	62	90	40	63	38	98	126	68	36	127	55	103	15	71	43	51	35	81	75	82	6

Northeast Mileage

...ore	Lindale	Longview	Malakoff	Marshall	Mineola	Mt.Pleas.	Murchis.	Nacogdo.	New Boston	Overton	Palestine	Paris	Pittsburg	Rusk	Scroggins	Sulphur Sprg.	Teague	Texarkana	Troup	Tyler	Yantis
61	46	72	10	94	49	101	8	88	139	57	35	107	91	53	85	69	56	151	53	35	62
75	90	63	136	45	90	51	118	120	36	86	138	98	51	119	68	87	182	26	100	92	90
24	21	22	67	45	23	45	49	81	82	31	69	93	33	63	33	55	113	94	39	23	40
39	29	51	51	72	41	82	38	62	119	27	39	116	70	27	75	78	85	131	14	16	63
31	29	69	34	91	27	78	26	110	119	58	59	82	70	78	61	45	80	140	55	36	38
39	73	36	106	26	80	87	88	50	95	42	87	138	76	59	105	110	133	95	50	62	98
68	98	64	120	56	109	116	111	33	125	65	94	167	104	63	134	139	137	125	71	85	126
96	90	90	131	102	78	38	118	153	39	104	149	30	49	143	53	53	177	60	117	103	68
00	70	95	99	113	58	55	91	157	84	105	124	23	62	125	57	21	145	105	102	83	36
92	94	103	76	117	106	148	78	54	181	83	35	176	136	43	150	139	63	188	69	81	127
51	65	39	110	47	60	18	93	106	39	62	112	69	15	99	32	55	156	57	76	66	55
79	69	90	52	108	81	123	53	57	161	67	11	152	112	34	125	114	47	173	53	57	103
69	34	68	57	90	22	57	49	122	98	69	82	59	50	89	37	22	103	119	67	47	15
50	37	61	33	83	49	91	29	65	128	44	22	124	80	30	83	86	68	141	30	25	71
28	36	22	81	39	35	30	63	85	67	36	83	81	19	75	28	53	127	80	49	37	43
14	31	12	71	35	33	44	53	71	81	21	73	95	33	61	43	65	117	92	35	27	51
29	15	28	65	50	17	50	47	87	88	37	67	88	39	62	33	50	111	100	39	21	35
18	48	28	79	41	59	75	61	40	105	14	59	126	64	34	74	96	104	111	21	35	81
43	41	54	49	72	53	94	45	49	131	31	26	128	82	14	87	90	72	142	17	28	75
46	75	35	116	16	75	49	98	92	55	58	115	100	45	90	63	86	161	54	72	72	82
35	12	70	34	46	58	52	58	89	12	69	109	46	49	56	79	115	100	26	26	64	
35	43		81	22	45	52	63	67	77	23	80	103	41	60	56	75	126	88	37	37	63
70	55	81		103	58	111	18	98	149	66	41	116	100	63	94	79	52	161	63	44	72
34	65	22	103		68	64	85	76	70	45	98	115	54	74	78	92	144	71	59	59	82
46	12	45	58	68		53	40	100	94	47	71	75	45	67	33	37	104	115	45	25	22
58	65	52	111	64	53		93	115	40	66	113	51	11	106	23	37	157	62	79	67	46
52	37	63	18	85	40	93		94	131	48	43	108	82	59	73	71	64	143	45	26	57
58	88	67	98	76	100	115	94		144	55	64	166	104	35	115	136	104	146	55	75	121
89	103	77	149	70	94	40	131	144		100	151	69	52	138	70	76	195	21	114	105	87
12	35	23	66	45	47	66	48	55	100		57	117	54	40	64	84	103	111	14	22	69
69	59	80	41	98	71	113	43	64	151	57		141	102	30	113	104	46	163	44	47	93
09	87	103	116	115	75	51	108	166	69	117	141		62	142	63	38	162	90	119	100	53
46	54	41	100	54	45	11	82	104	52	54	102	62		94	16	44	146	71	68	56	39
49	55	60	63	74	67	106	59	35	138	40	30	142	94		101	104	76	145	26	42	89
56	45	56	94	78	33	23	73	115	70	64	113	63	16	101		38	159	92	77	58	27
79	49	75	79	92	37	37	71	136	76	84	104	38	44	104	38		125	97	81	62	15
15	101	126	52	144	104	157	64	104	195	103	46	162	146	76	159	125		207	89	90	118
00	115	88	161	71	115	62	143	146	21	111	163	90	71	145	92	97	207		125	117	108
26	33	37	63	59	45	79	45	55	114	14	44	119	68	26	77	81	89	125		20	67
26	13	37	44	59	25	67	26	75	105	22	47	100	56	42	58	62	90	117	20		47
64	34	63	72	82	22	46	57	121	87	69	93	53	39	89	27	15	118	108	67	47	

ATHENS
Elev. 490   Pop. 11,405

Athens, the county seat of Henderson County, is known as the Black-Eyed Pea Capital of the World and is located 35 miles west of Tyler. The town dates back to the 1850s, but didn't really become established until this part of Texas became an important part of the Cotton Belt. The Texas Parks and Wildlife's Texas Freshwater Fisheries Center in Athens is always an interesting spot for outdoorsmen, who can gaze at some of the huge bass that have been preserved by the Sharelunker program.

ATHENS COUNTRY CLUB

The golf   Athens Country Club is an 18-hole, semi-private course that dates back to the 1930s. On this short course (5,873 from the tips), you'll have the chance to hit short irons into every par 3, and have birdie opportunities at all four par 5s that play well under 500 yards. The front nine allows more room for wild tee shots, as it's more wide-open than the back. The feature hole is No. 13, a 427-yard par 4 highlighted by a blind approach shot to the green.

The details   903-677-3844. 500 Park Dr., Athens, TX 75751

- 1930. 18 holes. Par 71. Back – 5,873 (68.6/119). Middle – 5,681 (67.6/116). Forward – 4,870 (69.5/118). Price - $$.

Getting there From I-20 drive east and take Hwy. 19 south. Exit Athens Square, then drive west for one block and turn left on Prairieville Rd. At Park Ln. turn right, and the course is just up the road.

COUNTRY OAKS GOLF COURSE

The golf   Located in the small community of Cross Roads, TX about 14 miles southwest of Athens, Country Oaks is down-home golf at its finest, with super-friendly owners and laid-back golfers who make the day more enjoyable. The 18-hole layout is known for its numerous water hazards and excellent condition. In the spring, blooming dogwoods beautify the course.

The most difficult hole on this hilly track is the par 4 No. 13, which requires a long iron or fairway wood approach into an elevated green. However, the course also has a few long, challenging par 5s as well as great par 3s.

Another nice feature is that lunch is included with your green fee if you tee off in the morning.

The details   903-489-3325. RR 1. Athens, TX 75751.

- 18 holes. Par 70. Blue - 5,812. White - 5,419. Price - $.

Getting there Located 14 miles southwest of Athens at the intersection of FM 69 and 90.

ATHENS NOTES   The only place for cold beer is the **Athens Social Club.** Nearby **Lake Athens** is scenic and impressive, with majestic lake houses along its shaded shores. There's even a 150 lot with a private 4-hole course that appears Augusta-like from the water. Find the **Marina Restaurant** (903-677-8774) along the lake for eats. In town try **Danny's Smokehouse BBQ** (903-549-2716) for lunch, or maybe even the **Ole West Bean & Burger Co.** (903-675-8100). **Ochoa's, Felipe's,** and the **Cactus Cafe** all offer tasty Mexican food. For lodging the Best Western (903-675-9214) is just right, or you could try the **Pine Cone Country Inn** (903-449-7463) or **Avonlea** (903-675-5770) for B&B accomodations. Finally, if you're into people-watching, the **Old Fiddlers Reunion** in May and the **Black-Eyed Pea Jamboree** in July are the place to be.

ATLANTA   Elev. 264   Pop. 5,704

Just 10 miles west of the Arkansas border, Atlanta is the largest town and economic hub of Cass County. The railroad put the town on the map back in 1871, and lumber became the major industry until the Rodessa oil field helped pull Atlanta out of the Great Depression. These days hunting and fishing are popular activities outside of Atlanta, and the residents are very proud of their two excellent golf courses.

INDIAN HILLS COUNTRY CLUB

The golf   Indian Hills is a scenic course with a design that makes it extremely enjoyable to play. Only 2,700-some-odd yards from the back tees, this is a short course that features two par 4s under 300 yards, and a par 5 that plays only 420 yards. Walk the course, enjoy the scenery, and swing easy. The most difficult hole is No. 5, a 365-yard par 4 with a tree in the middle of the fairway that impacts the tee shot. Two sets of tees allow for an 18-hole round.

The details   903-796-4146. Ofarrel Rd., Atlanta, TX 75551

• 9 holes. Par 36. Back – 2,788 (34.4/111). Forward – 2,056 (36.5/108). Price - $$.

Getting there From Hwy. 59 south, turn left on Hwy. 77 (west). When you come to Ofarrel Rd., you are there.

SPRING CREEK GOLF COURSE

The golf   Spring Creek opened in 2000 as the second golf option in Atlanta. Built on a farm owned by one of the local residents, there's nothing fancy about this 9-hole public course. A few trees dot the landscape, but the layout is mostly wide open, offering simple golf with several interesting holes. Water impacts the design but there are no bunkers.

NORTHEAST

⭐

Television has proved that people will look at anything rather than each other. Ann Landers

Two par 3s stand out on this 3,000-yard layout. No. 6 plays 130 yards into an island green, and No. 4 is the most difficult, playing 165 yards uphill; the green rests on top of a bank. If you miss the green, your ball will roll back down the hill, leaving another precarious approach back up the bank.

Other notes: Locals claim it "plays tougher than it looks." The course serves food, but no alcohol. BYOB allowed.

The details   903-799-6500. 1500 Holly St., Atlanta, TX 75551

• Designed by local residents. 2000. 9 holes. Par 36. Blue – 3,000. White – 2,800. No ratings available. Carts available. Driving range. Price - $.

Getting there Located off of Hwy. 59 from Linden. At the four-way intersection you'll see Orr Chevrolet. Continue straight and the road turns into Main. Cross the railroad tracks, then turn left at the Brookshires store. Drive by the Texaco and State Highway Department, then turn right at the four-way stop. The course is on the right side of the road.

ATLANTA NOTES   Atlanta has a few motels, but we recommend the new **Atlantian B & B**, which recently opened in a restored old home. It's worth a stroll in the restored downtown, where you can grab a bite to eat at the **Main Street Diner**. Another option for eats is the **Catfish King** just outside of the US 59 loop. The country club serves alcohol, and Shreveport is only 100 miles away for the dedicated degenerate, but explorers should consider taking the farm roads east into Arkansas, then south into Louisiana to see if the back woods has any moonshine to offer.

BIG SANDY
Elev. 336   Pop. 1,331

The tiny town of Big Sandy is 10 miles north of I-20, about 20 miles from both Longview and Tyler, and approximately 90 miles from both Dallas and Shreveport, LA. Established in the 1870s, the town is named after the Big Sandy Creek to the south. Because of its location on US 80 and proximity to I-20, Big Sandy's quaint little 9-hole golf course is a convenient place to work in a no-hassle round when you're killing time in East Texas.

AMBASSADOR HILLS GOLF CLUB

The golf   Originally part of Ambassador University, this quaint little course is now open to the public. The design features hilly terrain, tight fairways, small greens of medium speed, and a few sand bunkers sprinkled throughout the design. This is a short course, with all of the par 4s well under 400 yards (No. 7 is 255 yards), two short par 3s, and a 438-yard par 5. Two sets of tees allow for an 18-hole round.

Writing is turning one's worst moments into money. J.P. Donleavy

The details   903-636-4653. RR 2, Big Sandy, TX 75755

- 1968. 9 holes. Par 35. 2,636 yards. Price - $.

Getting there From Dallas, take I-20 east to Longview. Take Hwy. 155 north, then turn east on Hwy. 80. Follow the signs leading to Ambassador University and the course.

BIG SANDY NOTES Big Sandy is home to a complex of beautifully restored Victorian homes. **Annie's B&B** (903-636-4355) is a nice country guest house. For side trips, **Lake Hawkins** is northwest of town, and 5 miles south on FM 1804 at Hoard lies the **Old Sabine Bottom** with an extensive set of hiking trails along the Sabine River.

BULLARD   Elev. 502   Pop. 1,380

This "suburb" of Tyler is nothing more than a four-way stop with a little gas and food and a whole lot of golf. Residents here work in Tyler and other large towns, or have interests in the goings-on around Lake Palestine. Because of its proximity to this scenic lake, Bullard is surrounded by quality golf clubs. The Emerald Bay, Eagle's Bluff, and Peach Tree clubs combine to offer 72 holes of golf, an amazing figure considering the size of Bullard.

EAGLE'S BLUFF COUNTRY CLUB

The golf   One of the longest courses in Texas that can play as long as 7,300 yards during tournament play, Eagle's Bluff features an Augusta National-like environment along the eastern shore of Lake Palestine. Native hardwood and dogwood trees line the fairways, and most tee shots will require a blast through a narrow tunnel out into a wide landing area.

The layout features dogleg fairways that result in tricky approach shots into huge greens (averaging over 8,400 square feet) that are protected by grass and sand bunkers, and very often water hazards. Both the front and back nines feature an island green—one of which is the signature par 3 No. 6, which plays 210 yards downhill into a green protected on all sides by water.

The details   903-825-2999. 99 Eagles Bluff Blvd., Bullard, TX 75757

- www.eaglesbluff.com
- 1999. Carlton Gipson. 18 holes. Par 71. Back – 7,035 (74.3/142). Middle – 6,421 (71.1/133). Forward – 4,967 (69.0/126). Price - $$$.

Getting there Out of Noonday, TX, drive about 3 miles to Texas 187 and look for the Eagle's Bluff sign on the right side of the road. From the sign the course entrance is 2 miles down the road.

NORTHEAST

✩

Secret disbelief in the enemy's play is useful. Sir Walter Simpson

EMERALD BAY COUNTRY CLUB

The golf   A private club nestled along the shores of Lake Palestine, this scenic course features narrow, tree-lined fairways and large, elevated greens. Surprisingly, there's not much water on the course, but three of the holes force a carry to the green.

The signature hole is No. 14, a 563-yard par 5 requiring a tee shot up a very narrow (20 yards wide), tree-lined fairway, then an approach shot over some oak and pecan trees to the green. The front nine features only one par 5–a 562-yard monster.

The details   903-825-3444. 208 Emerald Bay Dr., Bullard, TX 75757

- Par 71. 18 holes. Gold – 6,622 (70.9/121). Blue – 6,435 (69.7/117). White – 5,420 (64.8/107). Red – 5,074 (69.1/115). Price - $$.

Getting there From downtown Bullard, head southwest on Hwy. 344 until you come to a four-way stop. Drive 2 miles and look for the course on the left.

PEACH TREE GOLF CLUB

The golf   The Peach Tree Golf Club debuted in 1984 with their short, executive-style course, the **Peach Tree Course**. This simple track is popular with rookies and high handicappers.

In 1993, Carlton Gipson designed the highly acclaimed **Oak Hurst Course,** which has hosted numerous professional tournaments over the years. The *Dallas Morning News* has featured the course in their "Diamonds in the Rough" pieces about outstanding rural Texas courses.

Gipson's design is unique in that every hole appears different, requiring all sorts of shots and the use of every club in the bag. Oak Hurst is also well known for its large, well-bunkered, undulating greens and water that comes into play on over half of the holes.

The number-one-rated hole is No. 10, a challenging 595-yard par 5 that welcomes golfers who've allowed their concentration to wane at the turn. However, the most-talked-about hole is the par 4 16th, which plays around 400 yards and has been rated by the East Texas pros as the most difficult in the region.

Note that the course hosts weekly seniors days on Wednesdays and Fridays.

The details   903-894-7079. 6212 CR 152 W., Bullard, TX 75757

- www.easttexasgolf.com
- Peach Tree Course: 1984. C.R. Hurst and Buddy Bridges. 18 holes. Par 70. Back – 5,556 (65.7/109). Middle – 5,246 (64.1/106). Forward – 4,567 (66.0/111). Price - $$.
- Oak Hurst Course: 1993. Carlton Gipson. 18 holes. Par 72. Gold – 6,813 (72.3/126). Blue – 6,371 (70.1/120). White – 5,887 (67.5/114). Red – 5,086 (69.0/118). Price - $$$.

It's not whether you win or lose, but whether I win or lose. Sandy Lyle

NORTHEAST

Getting there From Tyler, take Hwy. 69 south and exit CR 145. Go west and follow the signs for 1 mile to the club.

BULLARD NOTES   Plan your weekend around activities on **Lake Palestine;** otherwise, Bullard is best experienced either as a day trip or passing through to play golf in Jacksonville, TX. In Bullard, you can eat at **Sue's Kitchen** and there's also a Mexican food cafe in town.

CANTON
Elev. 540   Pop. 3,357

Canton has always been known for its First Monday Trade Days. The tradition began with district court meetings, then grew as businesses traded surplus stock and neighbors bargained for more casual items. Today this market day is unbelievably huge, backing up traffic on nearby I-20 and covering over 100 acres with antiques, handmade goods, animals, and junk.

In past years, the planned weekend excursion to Canton by a loved one was a nightmare of epic proportions for any avid golfer looking to utilize weekend greens time wisely. However, now that the impressive Twin Lakes Golf Course has opened, harmony has been restored to the one-sided golf family. Now the golfer can experience a more balanced trip to Canton by working in 18 holes while the family shops, then hitting the market postround for an hour or two.

TWIN LAKES GOLF COURSE

The golf   Part of a large tree farm whose crop is irrigated by two lakes, Twin Lakes is one of the best golf values in the state. An outstanding, challenging track, despite the fact that it was designed by the landowner, the course is not crowded and the golf is spectacular. You'll notice how around half the holes play through the East Texas pines, while the other half play over and around the lakes. The course is long at 7,100 yards from the tips, and over 6,600 from the men's tees. Even the short holes are difficult, with strategically placed bunkers and difficult pin placements.

One of these is No. 9, perhaps one of the most difficult par 3s in the state. It rests along the lake with a huge tree to the left of the green that sucks in anything on that side. The wind howls off the lake and your subconscious tells you to aim right because of the tree. Anything less than perfect will find the water on the right. Less confident golfers sometimes lay up with a wedge, hoping to get their chip close enough for a one-putt. Considering the penalties that are possible on this hole, this isn't always a dumb move.

The details   903-567-1112. 1003 Van Zandt CR 4207, Canton, TX 75103.

• www.twinlakesgolfcourse.com

NORTHEAST

- 18 holes. Par 72. Champs – 7,171. Men's – 6,648. Forward – 5,739. Ladies' – 4,964. Price - $$.

Getting there From Dallas take I-20 east to Canton. Exit Hwy. 19 and drive south through town. The course is 8.5 miles farther on the east side of the highway.

VAN ZANDT COUNTRY CLUB

The golf Built by Leon Howard in the 1960s, this course is typical of his design approach: a fun, basic course that's not too difficult. The course is open to the public and the best time to play is during the week, when you'll often find that you're one of the only golfers on the course. On this fairly open course, the fairways and bent-grass greens are always in excellent condition and the staff is unbelievably friendly.

The details 903-567-2336. 172 N. I-20 Service Rd., Canton, TX 75103

- 1966. Leon Howard. 18 holes. Par 72. Back – 6,760 (71.8/124). Middle – 6,315 (69.5/118). Forward – 5,730 (71.3/116). Price - $.

Getting there From I-20 east, take Hwy. 19 north then drive a short distance to the course. The clubhouse is on the north side of the street.

CANTON NOTES Play golf, then meet the family after the round at **First Monday Trade Days,** the largest, most unbelievable market in the Southwest. The rural **Old Mill Cafe** (903-567-6241) is a good place for breakfast or lunch. Just up the road in Edgewood, TX in the back of Cousin's Produce is **Cowboy's Barbecue** (903-896-7444). The **Bed-and-Breakfast Country Style** (903-567-2899) is real close on FM 859 if you want to make it a weekend.

CARTHAGE   Elev. 249   Pop. 6,629

Here in the deepest, darkest portions of East Texas, only minutes from the Louisiana border in a county named after the Indian word for cotton (Panola), Tex Ritter and Jim Reeves were born. The town of Carthage is now home to the Texas Country Music Hall of Fame, but not known for much else. When in Carthage you'll be on your way to the excesses of Shreveport, or preparing to explore the depths of the Sabine National Forest. If you're a golfer, though, you'll want to stop by the Carthage Country Club before you head out of town.

CARTHAGE COUNTRY CLUB

The golf Carthage Country Club is a scenic little 9-hole country course that's open to the public. While most of the holes typify basic, small-town golf (par 4s well under 400 yards, a very short par 3), there are two holes that can

---

In spite of the high cost of living, it's still popular. Katherine Norris

stand up to the most accomplished golfer. The number one handicap is hole 3, a long, 554-yard par 5. And you'll need a fairway wood to reach No. 5, a 213-yard par 3.

Two sets of tees make for an 18-hole round. Pay once and play all day.

The details 903-693-9062. Route 79 N., Carthage, TX 75633

• 9 holes. Par 36. Back – 3,155. Forward – 2,473. Price - $.

Getting there From I-20 driving east, take Hwy. 59 south to Carthage. Find Hwy. 79 and drive east for 2 miles to the course.

LA-TEX GOLF COURSE

The golf   Hidden in the remote sticks of northeast Texas, the "latex" golf course was built about 30-35 years ago by employees of United Gas. Now the 9-hole course is owned by Gulf South Pipeline and known for its outstanding condition and its difficult, small greens.

There's a friendly debate in Carthage as to which is the better course. The thing the traveling golfer should remember is that this is far more than a non-maintained pasture golf course, yet it only costs $5 to play on the weekend. There is no pro shop and the green fees are dealt with via the honor system, with visitors dropping their payment in a drop box.

The short design is wide open and plays to a par 36. The two sets of tees allow for a second go-around, with the full 18 holes playing around 5,600 yards. The trick is in holding the small Bermuda greens, since approach shots must be perfect. Your short game will definitely get a workout here. There are no bunkers, and water comes into play only once (No. 8 with a carry over a pond).

The most difficult hole is No. 2, a dogleg left that requires a perfect tee shot to avoid the huge sycamore tree in the fairway. Perfect drives will leave you with a 50-60 yard approach, but again, the small greens are sometimes impossible to hold on any type of approach.

The details   903-766-3595. P.O. Box 261, Carthage, TX 75685.

• Circa 1965. 9 holes. Par 36. 2,800 yards. Price - $.

Getting there Take Hwy. 79 towards Shreveport for about 20 miles and look for the course on the right-hand side. If you reach the Wascomb turn-off, you've gone too far.

CARTHAGE NOTES   It's always worth a trip to DeBerry, TX for lunch at the **Stateline Bar-B-Que** (903-766-2541). Another rural joint with barbecue eats is **Lakeside Bar-B-Q** (903-693-5245) on FM 1970 near Lake Murvaul. In town, **Daddy Sam's** (903-693-7400) is known for catfish, and **T's Ribs** (903-693-8484) is a popular spot. The **Texas Country Music Hall of Fame** and the **Tex Ritter Museum** might interest you. For lodging there is a **Best Western** or

---

⭐

The secret's in the dirt. Dig it out like I did. Ben Hogan

Holiday Inn, as well as **Boone's B & B** (903-693-6298). Our recommendation is to stay at **Wiley's Lakeside Retreat** (903-693-3080) up by Lake Murvaul.

CENTER   Elev. 345   Pop. 5,660

The town of Center is in far, far East Texas, next door to the Sabine National Forest and the Sabine River, the boundary with Louisiana. Center is the seat of Shelby County, one of the original five Texas counties dating back to 1836 when the Republic of Texas gained independence from Mexico. Tobacco was once a big crop here, and timber and poultry have helped the locals earn a living since then.

CENTER COUNTRY CLUB

The golf   Center's little semi-private course is a flat, tree-lined track that can be challenging because of the tiny, elevated greens and the occasional water hazard. The wide fairways are lush and in good condition. The last hole is the feature hole, a 369-yard par 4 that requires an approach shot over water into a small green surrounded by trees.

The details   936-598-5513. Hwy. 96 N., Center, TX 75935

• 9 holes. Par 36. Back – 3,209 (35.1/121). Forward – 2,575. Price - $.

Getting there From I-20 south, exit Estes Pkwy. (Hwy. 149), then travel about 30 miles to Hwy. 59. Turn south until you hit Hwy. 96. Drive north on 96 to the course.

CENTER NOTES   Reserve a room at the **Best Western Inn** (936-598-3384) or **Rogers House B&B** (936-598-3971) check out the handsome, 110-year-old-plus **Shelby County Courthouse**, then head towards the **Sabine National Forest** for further explorations. Don't miss the **scenic drives** around the Shelbyville area on Texas 87 and FM 417 and 2694. Before you head out grab a bite at **Harry's Smoke House** (936-598-6445) or the extremely authentic **Dyes Kountry Katfish** (936-560-1316), where Thursdays is all-you-can-eat crawfish night.

CLARKSVILLE   Elev. 442   Pop. 3,879

Clarksville is located just 20 miles south of the Red River, just east of Paris, TX on US 82. A visit to this part of the state is worthwhile for its historical significance, if nothing else. This seat of one of the original Texas counties (Red River) dates back to 1834. In fact, Sam Houston Park just north on FM 410

⭐

I have a hunch that the yips is a result of years of competitive strain,
a sort of punch-nuttiness with the putter. Tommy Armour

hosts markers commemorating Sam Houston's entry into Texas, as well as the oldest known Anglo grave in the state.

CLARKSVILLE COUNTRY CLUB

The golf   Open to the public, the Clarksville Country Club is a quaint little course with narrow fairways lined with old trees. Nothing fancy here. This traditional, small-town layout features short par 4s, par 5s well under 500 yards, and par 3s that require no more than mid-irons. The medium-sized greens get the job done. Two sets of tees allow for an 18-hole round.

The details   903-427-3450. Hwy. 37 North, Clarksville, TX 75426

- 1965. 9 holes. Par 36. Back – 3,000. Forward – 2,345. Price - $.

Getting there From I-30 east, take Hwy. 37 north and drive until it dead-ends. Turn right and drive 5 miles to the course.

CLARKSVILLE NOTES   After the round enjoy a breezy lunch at **Coleman BBQ** (903-427-5131), then stop off at the 1885 **Red River County Courthouse** (903-427-3761), with its massive walls, impressive clock tower, and deed and marriage records from 1835. Another drive-by opportunity is the **Charles Demorse Home** north of the town square.

COOPER   Elev. 495   Pop. 2,150

Located 70 miles northeast of Dallas, Cooper is the county seat of Delta County, the fifth-smallest county in the state–it has only 261 acres and is home to a mere 5,000 residents. Today the town serves as the hub for the surrounding agricultural region and gateway to recreational activities on and around Cooper Lake.

DELTA COUNTRY CLUB

The golf   Delta Country Club is a 9-hole, semi-private track that offers an enjoyable round of golf for the average hacker, particularly the beginner who struggles with length off the tee. The short length of the course (2,548 yards with several par 4s under 300 yards), and the laid-back demeanor of the people make it the ideal place for the first-time golfer, as well as the traveler looking to enjoy the scenery along the Red River. Stray shots find big, mature trees. If you're spraying the ball at all, you'll find yourself short of the green, relying on your short game to get up and down for par. Only one set of tees here for golfers.

The details   903-395-4712. RR 1, Cooper, TX 75432

Sometimes you'd like to just stand there in the middle of the green and scream as loud as you can. But we're the perfect gentlemen. Ray Floyd

- 1930. 9 holes. Par 35. 2,548 yards. Price - $.

Getting there From Hwy. 19 north, turn left on FM 1529, then drive straight to the course.

COOPER NOTES   **Cooper Lake**, with over 10,000 acres of flooded timber, is just south of town, creating the perfect opportunity for a weekend of fishing and golf. Hire guide **Jason Hoffman** (903-395-3029, www.cooperlakeguideservice.com) to take you to the lunkers, and spend the night at the well-equipped **Fisherman's Landing** (903-395-4960; duck hunting also available). In town go for old-school grub at **Murray's Bar-B-Que** (903-395-4813), which looks more like a place to get your oil changed than a restaurant.

CROCKETT   Elev. 350   Pop. 7,191

Crocket was incorporated back in 1837 as the seat of Houston County, the third county seat in Texas. The Gossett family from Tennessee, veterans of the Battle of San Jacinto, donated the town site and named it after their old neighbor Davy Crockett, who reportedly stopped in Crockett to camp on his way to the Alamo.

This alluring little town is worth a trip for more than its historical significance. A trip to Crockett would not be complete without a visit to their beautiful 9-hole country club.

SPRING CREEK COUNTRY CLUB

The golf   Old-timers say that the course opened as the Orchard Golf Club in 1919, and had sand greens until the 1960s. Now known as Spring Creek, this is technically a private course, however the club has been known to allow out-of-towners access on occasion.

The design incorporates small, postage-stamp greens, water on 4 of 9 holes, and only one par 5. The most difficult hole is No. 2, a 210-yarder that plays into an extremely small green guarded by a bunker right-front.

Note that the traditional old clubhouse has some character, highlighted by a full bar and a great weekend menu.

The details   936-544-5444. RR 3, Crockett, TX 75835

- 1919. 9 holes. Par 35. Back – 2,885 (33.3/112). Forward – 2,489 (33.6/112). Price - $.

Getting there From Lufkin, take Hwy. 7 for 40 miles to Hwy. 27. Turn north and head to FM 2160. Turn west on 2160 and drive 3 miles to the course.

CROCKETT NOTES   For barbecue try **Smitty's** (936-544-2033) on 4th St., or **Thompson's** (936-544-5193) on Goliad. Another option for eats is the

NORTHEAST

Moosehead Cafe (936-544-5278). Drive around and ogle the historic homes in Crockett, then find **Davy Crockett Spring** where the colonel and his men stopped off on their way to the Alamo. For lodging consider the immaculate **Warfield House** (936-544-4037) on Houston Ave., which offers breakfast and other meals.

DAINGERFIELD
Elev. 403   Pop. 2,499

Daingerfield is about 60 miles southwest of Texarkana in the heart of northeast Texas. You'll find the town on US 259 twenty miles south of I-30. Europeans camped by a nearby spring around 1740, and the town formed in the 1840s. Years later Captain London Daingerfield's 100-man crew fought a gory battle with Indians near the spring.

BEAVER BROOK COUNTRY CLUB

The golf   Daingerfield's 9-hole, semi-private course is named after the creek that runs throughout the design, which seemingly comes into play on every hole. The course is open and generally plays pretty easy if you know how to negotiate the creek.

No. 7 is the most difficult even though it's only 326 yards. The key on hole 7 is to place the drive perfectly into the slanted fairway, then remember on the approach that the green slopes as well. No. 6 is fun because of the old oak trees in the middle of the fairway. And the ender is nice, a tricky little par 3 that plays alongside the creek.

The details   903-645-2976. RR 1, Daingerfield, TX 75638

- 9 holes. Par 36. Back – 2,948. Middle - 2,442. Forward – 2,148. Price - $.

Getting there From Dallas, take I-20 east to Hwy. 259. Go north past Mount Pleasant and over to Daingerfield. Turn left at the flashing red light, and the course is on the right 1 mile down the road.

NORTHEAST

DAINGERFIELD NOTES   The largest sweetgum tree in Texas is on Sue St. Check out the old courthouse that houses the **Morris County Museum**. Daingerfield is surrounded by lakes, including the pine-banked **Daingerfield State Park** a few miles southeast on TX 11. The only motel in town (**Daingerfield Motel**) is under new ownership and improving. Everyone in town raves about **Outlaw's BBQ**, and you can find Tex-Mex eats at a place called El Inca.

⭐

To play the golf of your dreams, you have to admit to yourself that you want to be good, and that you have the talent to play well. Dr. Bob Rotella

ELKHART   Elev. 390   Pop. 1,246

Named in honor of a friendly Indian who helped the early settlers establish their roots, Elkhart is located about 120 miles southeast of Dallas. You'll find this little town 10 miles south of Palestine on US 287. In the old days a mineral water spa attracted visitors, but now you won't find much more than a bank and a general store. Somewhat surprisingly for a town that seems to be lost in time, the community boasts one fairly modern facility, the Elkhart Golf Club.

ELKHART GOLF CLUB

The golf   Elkhart opened in 1992 with nine holes, then added another nine four years later. This 6,100- yard, par 70 layout features tight fairways lined with pine, oak, and elm trees, and the majority of greens are elevated.

You can pay once and play all day, a rare feature for an 18-hole course. And while some complain about the quality of golf you get for the money, the price is still inexpensive and you've got to consider that you're in Elkhart, TX. If the sun is shining and you're out on the golf course, you should have no problem with rough conditions and a bouncing putt every now and then.

The details   903-764-2461. FM 1817, Elkhart, TX 75839

• 1992. Garnett Beard. 18 holes. Par 70. Back – 6,100. Middle – 5,743. Forward – 4,665. Price - $$.

Getting there From Tyler, take Hwy. 155 south and drive 61 miles (toward Palestine) to Hwy. 287. Turn south and drive to Elkhart, then turn east onto FM 1817 and drive 1 mile to the course.

ELKHART NOTES   This small town has two solid lunch options: **Texas Real Pit BBQ** (903-764-0123) and **Joe Lee's Country Kitchen** (903-764-1229). Four miles south of town on FM 861 lies the reconstruction of the **Pilgrim Church,** supposedly the first Protestant church in Texas. Built in 1833, this might be a good spot to stop and pray for fairways and greens. The **Western Hotel** (903-764-2276) has rooms, but we recommend heading back up to Palestine for B&B accommodations.

EMORY   Elev. 478   Pop. 1,151

Emory, the seat of Rains County, was originally named Springville for the multitude of springs in the area. For the golfer and fisherman, Emory is a key destination because of its convenient location between the under-appreciated Lake

NORTHEAST

Tawakoni and the venerable Lake Fork, a world-class reservoir that not only produced the state record largemouth bass (18.18 lbs), but also over 75% of the top 50 bass that have ever been caught in Texas.

LAKE FORK GOLF CLUB

The golf An absolutely gorgeous course that is particularly inviting because of its short length, Lake Fork Golf Club features narrow fairways, medium-sized greens, and a welcome lack of bunkers.

While there are no bunkers, grass moguls frame the fairways, and the course is dotted with small ponds, four of which front greens. In addition to the many mature areas of foliage, the club planted over 4,000 new trees, including thousands of crape myrtles, in the late 1990s.

Two par 3s stand out–both Nos. 2 and 14 demand accurate long-iron approaches.

For course strategy, take the advice of one local who recommended his lifelong strategy of choking down and shortening the swing, emphasizing the importance of hitting them straight on this short course.

The details 903-473-3112. 252 Private Rd. 5937, Emory, TX 75440

- www.lakeforkgolfclub.com
- Ken Andrews. 18 holes. Par 72. Blue – 5,830. White – 5,536. Red – 4,353. Grill, pro shop, practice green. Price - $$.

Getting there Located approximately 8 miles from Emory. Take 515 to 2946, then turn left and drive 3 miles. The course is on the right.

EMORY NOTES Plan your trip by spending time on the Lake Fork Chamber of Commerce web site (www.lakeforkchamberofcommerce.com), which lists everything you need to know about restaurants, lodging, and guide services. Three golf courses surround the lake (see Mineola and Yantis), so there are plenty of opportunities to indulge yourself.

FRANKSTON   Elev. 389   Pop. 1,243

The town of Frankston sits within a 25-mile radius of Tyler, Jacksonville, Palestine, and Athens, and is just south of Lake Palestine. The lumber industry fueled Frankston in the beginning, but now the economy is based primarily on recreational income derived from Lake Palestine. Here in the rolling forest trails of East Texas, visitors are drawn to the peaceful setting, outstanding fishing, and world-class golf.

NORTHEAST

Most of the things that contribute to a bad shot in golf occur before you begin your backswing. Jim Flick

PINE DUNES RESORT & GOLF CLUB

The golf   Tell your buddies that you're planning a weekend of rural 9-hole golf out in the East Texas sticks, then take them to the little town of Frankston and surprise them with the astounding Pine Dunes Resort course. This new course is unlike anything in the state and must be played by anyone interested in the finer Texas tracks.

After Jodi Lutz purchased a rustic old course known as Dogwood Trails, PGA Tour veteran David Frost persuaded Lutz to develop the facility into a world-class layout. Jay Morrish did the design work here, and he created a superb variety of holes.

As the name implies, the course actually rests on top of some natural sand hills in the middle of the Piney Woods. The look is so unique that you will not believe you're in Texas. Anything out of the fairways results in sandy lies among the pine needles. The fairways are framed by both formal and natural bunkers that are reddish-brown in color. In fact when the course first opened, the natural sand framed most of the fairways, but the Bermuda has now grown into the sand, changing the rustic look. The club has even considered ways to eliminate the hardy Bermuda to re-establish the waste areas.

Of the notable holes, No. 5 stands out because of its alternate fairways, neither of which is very inviting. No. 6 is unique because it plays into a pit surrounded by bunkers and a nasty-looking lake on the left.

On the back, the sand is most evident on No. 11–a par 5 that forces a carry of the waste area on the second shot. Nos. 14 and 15 are separated only by a pond; Morrish eliminated the rough between the holes, creating the appearance of one massive fairway. The 15th hole plays downhill and is drive-able.

The ender goes 512 yards around a pond and a tight dogleg right. The approach is uphill to an interesting bowl-shaped green.

Wherever you go in Texas, make sure you hit Frankston. As resorts go, this one is a bit rustic but the golf is as good as anywhere in the state.

The details   903-876-4336. 159 Private Rd., Frankston, TX 75763

- www.pinedunes.com

- Jay Morrish. 18 holes. Par 72. Gold – 7,117 (74.4/131). Blue – 6,537 (71.3/126). White – 5,819 (68.1/119). Price - $$$.

Getting there   From Dallas take Hwy. 175 east to Frankston. Drive south on 155 for 6.2 miles to County Rd. 319. Turn right on 319 for 1.2 miles to the course.

FRANKSTON NOTES Since Frankston is small and out of the way, take advantage of the resort's newly opened condominiums and the **stay and play packages** for around $100 per person, an unbelievable value. For dining there is a little home-style restaurant in Frankston, but you'll probably head to Tyler or Palestine. Bring your own booze. While the course serves alcohol, the

Golf is not a game you can rush. For every stroke you try to force out
of her, she is going to extract two in return. Dave Hill

county is dry and the nearest place to buy cold beer for the condo is 15 miles away.

GILMER

Elev. 370   Pop. 4,932

Gilmer, the county seat of Upshur County, is on US 271 thirty-five miles northeast of Tyler. The town was originally settled in the 1830s when the area along Little Cypress Creek was filled with Cherokee Indians. This clean, friendly town has plenty to offer for a quick northeast Texas road trip. Affordable lodging, unique restaurants, and the Gilmer Country Club await weekend warriors looking for a convenient golf getaway.

GILMER COUNTRY CLUB

The golf   The GCC is an easy course that is generally flat and easy to walk. Here you'll find good-sized greens and three water holes: Nos. 6, 8, and 9. Hole 6 is a short par 3 that goes 138 yards, No. 8 is tough because of the length, playing 210 yards over a pond, and the last hole is a par 4 with a pond about 300 yards from the tee.

The details   903-734-4125. FM 2685, Gilmer, TX 75644

- 9 holes. Par 35. Back – 3,036. Middle – 2,936. Forward – 2,836. Closed Mondays. Price - $.

Getting there From Tyler, take Hwy. 155 north, then travel 35 miles to Gilmer. Drive 2 miles south to FM 2585 and turn right to reach the course.

GILMER NOTES   When making a weekend of it, reserve a room at the **Gilmer Inn** (903-843-3033) or **Executive Inn & Suites** (903-843-6099). Have coffee and breakfast at **Gotta Java** (903-843-4637), eat lunch at **Bodacious Bar-B-Q** (903-843-3481), then have dinner at **Catfish Junction** (903-843-5075).

GLADEWATER

Elev. 333   Pop. 6,113

Gladewater dates back to the 1870s when the town originated along Glade Creek in a unique, barren region called the Glades. Lumber and agriculture drive the economy, and the city is known for its numerous antique stores. Located on US 80 just 13 miles west of Longview, Gladewater should be known for its quality golf.

★

I am sure we shall have in Augusta a representative group of members from all over the world.
This club, as I hope, is to be a truly international club. Bobby Jones

GLADEWATER COUNTRY CLUB

The golf   Gladewater Country Club is a semi-private, 9-hole track that is known for its traditional design and well-manicured greens. The narrow fairways are lined with trees, and the design incorporates a few strategically placed trees that can alter your golf shots.

You'll have the chance to start strong here, with a 272-yard, par 4 opening hole, followed by a 157-yard par 3. The other par 4s average between 350-400 yards. Two sets of tees make for an 18-hole round. The number one handicap is No. 8, which plays an easier 450-yard par 5 on the front, but is a 400-yard par 4 the second time around.

Relax, have fun, and pay once to play all day.

The details   903-845-4566. 24345 County Rd. 3107, Gladewater, TX 75647

- 1930. 9 holes. Par 36. Back – 3,028 (34.0). Forward – 2,351. Price - $$.

Getting there From Hwy. 271 south drive through Gladewater, and proceed to Hwy. 135. Turn left (south), then make a right on Country Club Dr. The entrance is on the right side of the road.

SHALLOW CREEK COUNTRY CLUB

The golf   Also known as the Shallow Creek Golf & RV Resort (always good to know the RV part), this is an 18-hole, semi-private championship course. You'll have to decide if the words "RV" and "championship" go well together. The design incorporates fairways with generous landing areas, lots of natural hazards, and plenty of water.

Good golfers can be tested from the 7,000-yard-plus tips, but most hacks should place themselves at the gold tees and play from a much more reasonable 6,256 yards.

The most talked-about hole is the monstrous 16th, which plays a whopping 681 yards from the back tees, and a still-significant 600 yards from the gold tees. Take your time and you'll get there eventually.

Other notes: You can still make a weekend of it without the RV, as the course offers clean-looking "resort villas" for rent on a nightly or weekly basis. To complement the golf, the club offers a lighted driving range, miniature golf, an ATV park, fishing lake, volleyball court, and an equestrian center. What else could you possibly need?

The details   903-984-5335. 1204 Wilkins Rd., Gladewater, TX 75647

- www.shallowcreek.com
- 1989. Bill Webb. 18 holes. Par 71. Black – 7,070 (73.5/129). Gold – 6,256 (69.8/119). Blue – 5,464 (66.1/107). Red – 4,383 (65.6/114). Price - $$.

I don't think that hours and hours of putting practice are necessary to become a good putter or to maintain your skills. It is crucial to have a solid routine and a picture of yourself being a great putter. Dr. Bob Rotella

NORTHEAST

Getting there From I-20 east, take Hwy. 135 north and exit Wilkins Rd. Turn right and drive a short distance to the course.

GLADEWATER NOTES The **19th Hole at Shallow Creek** serves some of the best burgers around. Do lunch at **Calhoun's Bar-B-Q** (903-844-1906), and hit the antique shops downtown. Check into **Primrose Lane** (800-293-0195), a relaxing place to unwind after a day on the links, then drive into Winona, TX, where the romantic **O'Dells** (903-877-4488) is nestled into a renovated mercantile store. If you're craving Tex-Mex, stay in town and have chips and queso at **Guadalupe's Mexican Restaurant** (903-845-2318).

HAWKINS
Elev. 415 Pop. 1,337

Hawkins is another tiny East Texas town linked by US 80, I-20, and the web of farm roads that connect so many of these small communities–all of which seem to have great golf for the right price and without the crowds. After serving as an early port and stagecoach on the Sabine River, Hawkins became a railroad town in 1873, and oil has helped sustain the economy since then.

HOLLY LAKE RANCH GOLF CLUB

The golf Built by Leon Howard in the 1970s as the centerpiece of a rural residential community, this narrow course is loaded with trees and is known for its excellent greens. This 18-hole private track has a little bit of water, including the 425-yard No. 12 with a sharp dogleg left and a tee shot that must carry water.

The 13th hole is tough–a 560-yard dogleg left–and hole 16 is listed as the number one handicap at 423 yards. Most of the par 3s allow for a good chance at birdie, and are not too terribly long.

The details 903-769-2397. FM 2869, Hawkins, TX 75765

- 1977. Leon Howard. 18 holes. Par 72. Back – 6,705 (71.7/122). Middle – 6,385 (69.9/117). Forward – 5,437 (71.2/117). Closed Tuesdays. Price - $$.

Getting there From Tyler, take Hwy. 14 north through Hawkins. Turn right on FM 2869 and drive 6 miles to the gate on the right side of the road.

HAWKINS NOTES You'll find a few small restaurants around the Holly Lake area, but there's not too much to do in this rural area unless you have access to the community. **Petty's** is the best restaurant in Hawkins–nothing but the finest home cooking. Head to Tyler for lodging, as there is only one small motel in Hawkins.

---

*If golfers keep on playing so slowly, on the green particularly, one way
to correct the situation is to knock the ball into them. There will be a short delay while you have a
hell of a fight, but from then on you'll move faster.* Horace Hutchinson

HENDERSON
Elev. 505   Pop. 11,369

Henderson's story is pure Texas. Named after the first governor of Texas, it's the seat of the county that was named for Thomas Jefferson Rusk, who was a general during the Texas Revolution, developer of the Texas court system, and both senator and congressman.

Cherokee Indians were defeated here at the Battle of Neches around 1840, setting the stage for the formation of Rusk County. Cotton became the legal tender of the day until the business district was burned at the onset of the Civil War. More men from Rusk County fought in the war than any other county in Texas, and the city was eventually rebuilt. Then the oil boom came and changed the town forever.

Located on US 259 about 20 minutes south of Longview, this historic town is home to one of the very best 9-hole courses in the state, the Henderson Country Club.

HENDERSON COUNTRY CLUB

The golf   Rated as high as the fifth-best public 9-hole course by the *Dallas Morning News,* this is one of the tracks you don't want to miss when touring the Piney Woods. The course is known for being in great condition, but the lightning-fast greens will be what you talk about after the round. These greens are large, undulating, and easy to three-putt.

The details   903-657-6443. Hwy. 43, Henderson, TX 75652

• 1930. 9 holes. Par 35. Back – 2,958. Forward – 2,541. Short-iron-only driving range. Price - $.

Getting there From Tyler, take Hwy. 43 east and travel 35 miles to Henderson. In town turn onto Hwy. 43 and drive 1 mile to the course.

HENDERSON NOTES   Because Rusk County is dry, you'll need to drive the 18 miles to Kilgore for cold beer. For lodging, the best is the **Holiday Inn Express**. Driving around town, check the 15-plus historical markers, three of which are Texas historic landmark homes. The **Depot Museum** is worth a stop for those interested in the history of the area.

JACKSONVILLE
Elev. 516   Pop. 13,995

Because of its perfect size and ideal location, Jacksonville is one of the best spots to serve as the hub of an East Texas fandango. Smaller and easier to negotiate than Tyler, with more to offer than nearby Bullard, Frankston,

---

In golf you've got two continuously merciless competitors;
yourself and the course. Tommy Armour

or Rusk, this town is loaded with excellent restaurants, accommodations, and interesting history and surrounded by fantastic East Texas scenic drives.

CHEROKEE COUNTRY CLUB

The golf   Cherokee dates back to the 1930s, and its traditional, semi-private layout through the tall pines is known as a shot-maker's course. Playing only 6,208 yards from the tips, the course offers the option of hitting irons off the tee to keep it in the fairway. And since out-of-bounds comes into play frequently, conservative plays off the tee are recommended. Don't worry too much about water hazards though, since water comes into play only on holes 4, 15, and 18.

The most difficult hole is No. 14, a par 4 that doglegs left and involves an approach downhill over a creek.

Also note that the clubhouse is new, making it a nice place to hang out after the round.

The details   903-586-2141. Henderson Hwy., Jacksonville, TX 75766

- 1936. 18 holes. Par 71. Back – 6,208 (69.1/119). Middle – 5,794 (67.1/112). Forward – 5,145 (69.8/125). Price - $$.

Getting there From downtown Jacksonville, take Hwy. 79 east 4 miles to the course.

JACKSONVILLE NOTES   The scenic drives around Jacksonville are awesome (either way on US 69, and FMs 747 and 2138), including the breathtaking view at **Love's Lookout Park** (5 miles north on 69). The **Killough Monument** pays tribute to the victims of one of East Texas' worst Indian massacres. For lodging, stay in town at **The English Manor** (903-586-9821), or drive up to Lake Jacksonville and spend the night at the **Horseshoe Inn B & B** (903-586-4498). Both are solid B&B options in addition to the standard chain hotels in town. When it's time to eat, try the enchiladas at **El Plato De Oro** (903-589-3372), or order the melt-in-your-mouth ribs at **D.J.'s Smokehouse** (903-541-0802).

JEFFERSON   Elev. 200   Pop. 2,040

Located only 20 miles from Louisiana, Jefferson is one of the best destinations in the northeast Texas region. Once a booming river port town, Jefferson profited from a massive rechanneling of water that created a navigable route from the Big Cypress Bayou through Caddo Lake all the way to the Mississippi. Riverboat operations were extremely lucrative, with single shipments of cotton or locally brewed beer bringing in as much as $20,000 in profit.

This cozy town boasts more romantic bed and breakfasts and fabulous (as well as affordable) antique shops per capita than perhaps any other place in Texas. Charming red-brick streets, restored 19-century buildings, and majestic pine, oak, and maple trees grace Jefferson's quaint neighborhoods and downtown avenues. And if that isn't enough, Jefferson's 9-hole golf course is consistently rated as one of the best in Texas.

RUSTY RAIL GOLF CLUB

The golf   Rusty Rail has received a bit of acclaim in the past, including being named by the *Dallas Morning News* as one of the top 9-hole courses in Texas. The layout features straight, wide-open fairways, and the length of the holes is enough to create quite a challenge. Both par 3s will require long irons. No. 2 is the signature hole, playing 187 yards over water, while No. 5 plays 173 yards. The course has only one par 5, the 512-yard No. 8 hole. All six par 4s play around 350 yards, so if you can keep the ball in the fairway, you have a great shot at reaching the green in regulation.

The details   903-665-7245. Prospect Rd., Jefferson, TX 75657

• 1980. John Reeves. 9 holes. Par 35. Back – 3,015. Forward – 2,352. Price - $.

Getting there From Hwy. 59, turn right on Prospect Rd. and travel 6 miles north to the course.

JEFFERSON NOTES   Grab a bite at **Diamond Bessie's Saloon** (903-665-3956), where the meals are full of the flavor of old East Texas. Explore deep East Texas 12 miles east at **Caddo Lake**, where the scenery is spectacular, and you can take airboat tours to places that you would never expect to see in Texas. Back in Jefferson, spend the night in Texas' second-oldest continuously operating hotel, the 1852 **Excelsior House**. The award-winning **Hale House**, one of Jefferson's 46-some-odd bed and breakfasts, is another popular option for lodging.

KILGORE   Elev. 371   Pop. 11,524

Kilgore was settled by plantation owners before the Civil War, then became more established with the coming of the railroad in 1872. Timber was big and cotton was king until the town found itself smack dab in the middle of an oil field in the 1930s. At one time over 1,200 oil wells dug for the black gold within the city limits.

Gentlemen play golf. And if you aren't a gentleman when you start, after the crushing events of the game, you surely become one. Bing Crosby

Located just 18 miles southwest of Longview, and barely south of I-20, Kilgore is worth the stop for the curious golfer–it boasts a prominent little country club that dates back to 1935.

MEADOWBROOK COUNTRY CLUB

The golf   Formerly known as Roy H. Laird Country Club, this course was built in 1935 and has a solid reputation as one of the better 9-hole courses in the state. Meadowbrook's design features one par 5, one par 3, and seven par 4s, one of which is the 265-yard 7th hole.

The lone par 5 (No. 4) is a 520-yard dogleg right through a tight chute of trees. It's probably wise to under-club and pay attention to the wind on No. 6, the only par 3 that plays 150 yards and has out-of-bounds looming behind the green.

Every par 4 is under 400 yards, and other than a few holes with out-of-bounds behind the green, the primary cause of mounting scores has to do with the extremely deceptive greens, which feature dramatic undulations and are waiting for your three-putts.

Two sets of tees make for an 18-hole round.

The details   903-984-3387. 1306 Houston St., Kilgore, TX 75663

- 1935. 9 holes. Par 36. Back – 3,150 (35.0/123). Forward – 2,634 (35.3/115). Price - $$.

Getting there From Dallas, take I-20 east and turn south on Hwy. 259 to Kilgore. In town, turn left on Houston and drive 1 mile to the course.

KILGORE NOTES   Eat at the **Back Porch** (903-984-8141), where they serve basic East Texas fare. Stay at the **Kilgore Community Inn** (903-984-5501) near the college. Soak up Kilgore's history, where 1.2 acres of downtown (Main and Commerce Streets) once held the greatest concentration of oil wells in the world. The Kilgore National Bank even housed a well that was drilled through its terrazzo floor. Some say the world's best ribs are at the **Country Tavern** (903-984-9954) on Texas 31 west of town.

LINDALE   Elev. 576   Pop. 3,156

Lindale is located just north of I-20, in the middle of the rolling East Texas hills and forests that lead to the Lake Fork towns of Mineola and Yantis. Lindale's spot on the Texas golf map comes courtesy of two superb facilities that offer almost more golf than you can handle. The retirement community of Hide-A-Way Lake just west of town boasts 27 challenging holes carved out of the forest, and further west on I-20, Garden Valley offers one of the closest

NORTHEAST

When five up express, as is polite, regret at laying a stymie,
but rejoice in your heart. Sir Walter Simpson

experiences to Augusta National that you'll find in Texas. Here the soil is fertile, everything imaginable grows and blooms beautifully, and the peaceful presence of the majestic pines makes this a honey-hole of East Texas golf.

GARDEN VALLEY RESORT

The golf   Garden Valley, which is actually a few miles west of Lindale, offers 27 holes of lush East Texas golf.

The older **Hummingbird Course,** which has taken a back seat to the now-famous Dogwood Course, still offers adequate golf even though the quality is not up to the standards of its more popular brethren, and they've recently reduced the route to only 9-holes. Highlighted by extreme elevation changes, the course's signature hole is the 566-yard No. 2, which requires two shots over a hill followed by a tricky approach back downhill to the green.

In 1992 John Sanford was blessed with some amazing terrain for the **Dogwood Course** addition. Cut out of the thick East Texas forest with 100-foot-plus tall pines, this course is most often compared to the famed Augusta National because of the abundant crape myrtle, Carolina jasmine, hollies, and dogwoods–not to mention the more than 1,500 azaleas that bloom beautifully in the spring.

Although there are only two par 4s over 400 yards, the Dogwood is plenty difficult, playing to a 132 slope rating. Water is in play on 12 holes, the elevation changes are extremely confusing, and the bent-grass greens are lightning-fast.

The regulars know that a good start is imperative because the first four holes are the easiest on the course–two short par 4s and two easy par 3s over water. You'll need that momentum as the holes grow increasingly more difficult.

The par 3 9th hole plays 212 yards with an intimidating body of water lurking left. Hole 11 features a lake to the left and behind the green. No. 13 is the most difficult, featuring a testy drive through the chute of trees off the tee and a massive lake that protects the green.

Note that while the course is not known as a traditional golf resort, there are a few amenities to consider if you're making a weekend of it in East Texas. Garden Valley offers condos and lake houses for very reasonable fees. Perhaps the most appealing is the lake house on No. 12, which sleeps up to 10, features an outdoor grill, and even allows fishing off the pier for overnight guests.

The details   903-882-6107. 22049 FM 1995, Lindale, TX 75771

- www.gardenvalleygolfresort.com

- Hummingbird Course: 1976. Leon Howard. 9 holes. Par 35. Back – 3,195. Middle – 2,926. Forward – 2,570. Price - $$.

- Dogwood Course: 1992. John Sanford. 18 holes. Par 72. Back – 6,754 (72.4/132). Middle – 6,269 (70.1/126). Forward – 5,532 (72.5/130). Price - $$$.

I never kick my ball in the rough or improve my lie in a sand trap.
For that I have a caddie. Bob Hope

Getting there From I-20, take Hwy. 110 (Exit 548) south. After half a mile, turn right at the sign for the golf course. Travel about 1.5 miles and turn on FM 1995.

HIDE-A-WAY LAKE GOLF CLUB

The golf   Hide-A-Way Lake is a charming community centered around three outstanding bass fishing lakes and an impressive 27-hole golf course. Three 9-hole courses are played in 18-hole combinations, all of which feature tiny, elevated greens, various irrigation lakes, numerous dogleg holes, and fairways lined by the ever-present East Texas pine trees. The course is not long, but is extremely difficult if you fail to adapt your game to it.

The **West** nine, featuring three difficult par 3s, is the shortest and most unique of the three courses. The par 3s are all fairly long and, as is the case with every approach shot on this course, your irons must be dialed in if you want to avoid the dreaded carom off the side slope. Ups and downs are extremely tough if you miss on the wrong side. Pay particular attention to the slope of the greens and know where to bail-out. The most difficult hole on this side is No. 5, a long uphill double dogleg with a second shot over water and a very tricky green.

The **Central** nine is the longest and opens with a 561-yard monster. You'll need three solid shots to reach the green here, as the tee shot doglegs long and left, followed by two approaches up a steep hill. A huge oak tree blocks the green from about 40 yards out. This is an enjoyable nine with many challenging dogleg holes, as well as the typical elevated greens.

The newer **East** nine, like the Central, starts off with a pain-in-the-butt par 5. The tee shot needs to stay left to avoid the out-of-bounds and tall pines on the right. The second shot is key because you must lay up in front of the creek, and ensure you've got the perfect angle to the elevated green. The approach is intimidating–anywhere from a 5 iron to wedge over the creek into a multi-tiered green bordered by a lake on the right. Bogey is good here.

Note that the East greens aren't as strikingly elevated as the other two nines.

The details   903-882-8511. 302 Hide-A-Way Ln., Lindale, TX 75771

- Central-West: 18 holes. Par 71. 6,351 (70.8/122). Middle – 5,920 (69.7/113). Forward – 5,271 (69.4/115). Price - $$.

- Central-East: 18 holes. Par 71. Back – 6,632. Middle – 6,174. Forward – 5,417. Price - $$.

- East-West: 18 holes. Par 71. Back – 6,267. Middle – 5,962. Forward – 5,138. Price - $$.

Getting there Take the 849 exit off of I-20 and the community and course are on the north side of the road. You can see the driving range from the highway.

★

Few pleasures on earth match the feeling that comes from
making a loud bodily-function noise just as a guy is about to putt. Dave Barry

LINDALE NOTES   Lots of options for lunch in Lindale: **Catfish Heaven, Chew Chew Bar-B-Que, Jake's BBQ,** or **Juanita's Mexican Food.** Down the road in Edom, TX lies a rustic, rural artists' mecca–the place to eat is **The Shed Cafe** (903-852-7791). Sample East Texas fare like the rib-eye sandwich and green beans with buttered corn. For lodging call the nearby **Garden Valley Inn B&B** (903-882-7378), or check into one of the several chain hotels just off I-20.

LONGVIEW

Elev. 339   Pop. 74,021

The "long view" from nearby Rock Hill gave the town its name back in the 1870s when the railroad helped the lumber and agriculture industries prosper. Then the East Texas Oil Field hit and the town was well on its way to becoming the "Action Capital of East Texas," taking advantage of the oil boom and becoming a dynamic industrial force with over 200 manufacturing firms.

For a city its size, Longview is loaded with golf. Unfortunately for the traveling golfer, however, Longview's prosperous business history spurred the formation of private golf clubs, so the majority of golf courses here are closed to the unconnected hack. Of the seven golf facilities, only two regulation and one par 3 course are open to the public. Use some savvy, though–make some calls, plan ahead, bribe, beg, and plead. It's at least worth a shot to play some of the fabulous private courses in Longview.

ALPINE GOLF CLUB

The golf   The Alpine Golf Club is a fun little 18-hole public course, good for the beginner and loaded with birdie holes for even the average golfer. You'll need to hit it straight because of the tree-lined fairways, but nailing the driver off the tee is not a requirement and you'll be in good shape on many holes with a solid 4 or 5 iron.

Watch out for No. 9 when you play from the back tees, which you'll probably do instinctively when you see the measly 6,001 yards on the scorecard. At 240 yards, many will need to use the driver. In fact, shortening the hole would not only make it more forgiving, but allow for a more reasonable pace of play. This one is long, but the other par 3s play 120, 120, and 160 yards, respectively.

Bring a hard hat because the course is crammed together, making errant shots a real hazard for the leisurely hacker. However, the course is easy to walk, plays rather rapidly, and is in great condition, making it well worth the green fee for visiting golfers.

The details   903-753-4515. 2385 Smelly Rd. Longview, TX 75605

'   • 18 holes. Par 70. Back – 6,001 (67.4/108). Middle – 5,435 (66.0/107).

Golf is a game of motion and rhythm, not position and mechanics. Martin Hall

Forward – 4,795. Price - $$.

Getting there From I-20, take the Eastman exit (Hwy. 259), drive north over Hwy. 80, and turn right at the second traffic light (Alpine).

CHEROKEE COUNTY GOLF ASSOCIATION

The golf   Lake Cherokee, about 20 miles outside of Longview, is a 12-mile-long private lake with over 100 miles of shoreline. Residents and stockholders have the lake's recreational opportunities at their disposal, as well as the unique little 9-hole golf course designed in 1985 by Ed Stites.

While the course has three standard par 3s, Stites tricked up the course with 200-yard par 4s, including No. 2, listed at 187 yards, and par 5s that are barely over 400 yards. Members use two sets of tees to play 18 and, as you might imagine, it plays pretty fast.

The details   903-643-3571. NI33 Lake Cherokee, Longview, TX 75603

• 1985. Edward Stites. 9 holes. Par 35. Back – 2,168. Forward – 1,988. Price - $$.

Getting there From Shreveport, LA, take I-20 west to Hwy. 149. Turn left and drive 10 miles to the course. The entrance is off Lake Cherokee Rd. on the right side.

DIVINE NINE & ALPINE TARGET GOLF

The golf   This is the place to practice your short game in Longview. With holes ranging from 100 to 200 yards, this is a first-rate par 3 course that provides many interesting challenges. If you're off on the approach shots, the large, undulating greens are easy to three-putt. And if you're really spraying it, old oak and pine trees dot the landscape, knocking down errant shots. Water hazards impact five holes: two that require a carry of the hazard and three where water lines the hole.

If there's no time for the regulation courses, this is the place to kill some time if you're lounging around Longview.

The details   903-753-1415. 2695 Alpine Rd., Longview, TX 75605

• 1998. Mike Williams. 9 holes. Par 27. Back – 1,234. Middle – 1,042. Forward – 777. Price - $$.

Getting there From I-20 west to Loop 282, exit Alpine Rd. Turn right and proceed 1.5 miles to the course.

LONGVIEW COUNTRY CLUB

The golf   The LCC has been criticized over the years for its frequent flooding and poor condition; however, the club is back on track due to a slow process of improvement that is making this flat, wide-open course more enjoyable to play. An easy course that plays to an almost executive-like 5,800 yards, the only hazards to get in your way are the occasional water hazard and perhaps the poor conditions.

The average golfer will welcome the short par 4s and 5s, as well as the six par 3s. The toughest hole is the 396-yard, par 4 No. 7, difficult only because of its length.

Other notes: Senior discounts are offered on Tuesdays and Thursdays.

The details   903-759-9251. 2300 Hwy. 42, Longview, TX 75604

• Moore, Brewer, & Parvino. 18 holes. Par 70. Back – 5,497 (66.9/102). Middle – 5,072. Forward – 4,793 (70.1/113). Price - $$.

Getting there From I-20 east, take Hwy. 42 north, then drive 5.5 miles to the course. The entrance is on the right.

OAK FOREST COUNTRY CLUB

The golf   Oak Forest is the perfect combination of traditional and links-style designs. Set in a valley with mostly flat terrain, the front nine features water on every hole, subtle mounding, narrow fairways, and a welcome lack of trees. The trees come into play on the back nine and the greens are much smaller. A fun course in great condition, Oak Forest is known for its fast greens.

Holes of note include No. 8, considered the signature hole with a creek on the left and a grass bunker fronting the green. This is a challenging 182-yard par 3. No. 18 is a nice ender–playing 576 yards with huge fairway trees that affect the second shot, and a creek that cuts into the fairway in front of the green.

The details   903-297-3448. 601 Tomlinson Pkwy., Longview, TX 75605

• 1976. Billy Martindale. 18 holes. Par 72. Back – 6,367 (72.4/125). Middle – 6,082 (70.9/124). Forward – 4,899 (69.2/118). Price - $$.

Getting there From I-20 east, take Loop 281 north to Bill Owens Pkwy. Turn right on Oak Forest Country Club Dr. and the course is just down the road.

PINECREST COUNTRY CLUB

The golf   Pinecrest opened in 1921 as a 9-hole track with sand greens. One of the oldest courses in the state, it was updated in 1959 by Press Maxwell, making it a 6,400-yard par 70 layout. The design incorporates five or six water hazards and mounding around the greens.

The front is the more demanding of the nines, featuring many nasty holes. No. 2 is a long par 5 highlighted by a creek on the right that crosses the fairway at 220 yards from the tee. The same goes for hole 5, a 437-yard par 4 with a creek in the landing area. The par 5 No. 4 is rated the most difficult, but No. 9 is a 457-yard par 4 that requires two macho golf shots to get home in two.

There is no type of miracle that can't happen at least once on a golf course. Grantland Rice

The details   903-758-8000. 214 S. Club Dr., Longview, TX 75606

- 1921. Press Maxwell. 18 holes. Par 70. Back – 6,400 (70.9/122). Middle – 5,932 (68.1/112). Forward – 5,417 (70.6/118). Price - $$.

Getting there From I-20 east, take Hwy. 259 north for 4 miles to Cotton St. Turn right, drive a short distance to the course, and look for the entrance on the right side of the road.

WOOD HOLLOW GOLF CLUB

The golf   Some of the most memorable golf experiences don't necessarily come from the ultra-expensive resort courses with perfect, pristine conditions and astronomical slope ratings. Often it's the places like Wood Hollow, where the conditions are merely adequate but the wide-open fairways, large greens, and basic layout create opportunities for career-low rounds. At Wood Hollow, which opened in 1991, you can play confidently and shoot for the pins.

A few long par 5s, including the 605-yard No. 10, help push the course yardage over 6,000 yards. Otherwise it's average-length par 3s and short par 4s that await you. The best birdie opportunity is No. 13, playing 135 yards from the back and only 118 yards from the middle tees.

The details   903-663-4653. 5121 McCann Rd., Longview, TX 75605

- 1991. 18 holes. Par 70. Back – 6,102 (109). Middle – 5,603 (105). Forward – 4,942. Price - $.

Getting there From I-20 west to Loop 281, take the McCann Rd. exit, then drive 2 miles and you'll run right into the course.

LONGVIEW NOTES   Don't miss the experience of a meal at the part-bakery, part-meat-market **Butcher Shop** (903-758-6066), famous for sandwiches and burgers, as well as platters of juicy steaks and fries and scrumptious desserts. If you need to stay, Longview is packed with every possible chain hotel under the sun. **Papacitas** (903-663-1700) on W. Loop 281 is popular with the locals and travelers alike.

MALAKOFF   Elev. 377   Pop. 2,281

Malakoff is 8 miles west of Athens just south of Cedar Creek Lake. In the 1830s, nearby Wild Cat Creek was mined for silver, and in the 1930s the town gained prominence for the discovery of the "Malakoff Man," a large prehistoric carved head that was dug out of a gravel pit. Today the town serves folks looking for fun on Cedar Creek Lake, and provides the basics for members of the Star Harbor retirement community.

You will hit the ball farther more frequently when you don't try to hit it far. Sam Snead

STAR HARBOR GOLF CLUB

The golf   Typical of courses built for retirement communities, Star Harbor was designed with older golfers in mind. This 9-hole course plays just under 2,400 yards, with minimal hazards, wide-open fairways, and basic, medium-sized greens. Unless you find yourself in a grudge match with Grandpa, work on your game by playing Star Harbor with one club, say a 7 iron, and work on mastering different types of shots with that club.

The details   903-489-0091. 99 Sunset Blvd., Malakoff, TX 75148

• 1970. 9 holes. Par 34. Back – 2,373. Forward – 2,094. Price - $.

Getting there From Tyler, take Hwy. 31 west and drive 45 miles to Hwy. 198. Turn north, then proceed 2 miles to Star Harbor Rd. Turn left 4 miles into Malakoff and the course is just down the road. Note: Star Harbor Rd. turns into Sunset.

MALAKOFF NOTES   Plan the trip around activities at **Cedar Creek Lake** (call **Star Harbor Marina**, 903-489-0715), or simply experience this little town passing through to another destination. Either way, don't miss the outstanding **Ochoa's Mexican Restaurant** (903-489-1779).

MARSHALL
Elev. 375   Pop. 23,791

In the 1840s Pete Whetstone, after sharing his personal stash of moonshine, convinced the county commissioners that his land was the ideal location for the future seat of Harrison County. During the Civil War, the town played a significant role as a hub of activity for the Confederacy west of the Mississippi, producing saddles, clothing, and ammunition for the war effort.

Located barely west of the Louisiana border, Marshall is an interesting golf destination if you're traveling this way on I-20. The Marshall Lakeside Country Club dates back to the 1920s and has hosted some big-name guests over the years. Cypress Valley and Oak Lawn are quality courses, and the Point N Rise game bird preserve has a golf course in the planning stages.

CYPRESS VALLEY GOLF CLUB

The golf   Cypress Valley is a family-built and owned facility that offers the quality of a big city track for small-town prices. The design features lush conditions, subtle elevation changes, and some challenging holes with water-protected greens.

Hole 7 is famous locally–a 385-yard par 4 with a sharp dogleg right over a valley to the green. Another interesting hole is No. 15, where the green is sur-

A teaching professional should go back to the fundamentals frequently, and make certain that her pupil is executing them properly. Dr. Bob Rotella

rounded by a lake. The par 5 No. 18 is a tough finisher, playing 610 yards from the tips.

The details 903-938-4941. I-20 East, Marshall, TX 75671

- 1971. Clinton Howard Mace. 18 holes. Par 71. Back – 6,953 (72.8). Middle – 6,388 (69.0). Forward – 5,571 (65.0). Price - $$.

Getting there From I-20 east take Exit 628 and go west until you come to the course.

MARSHALL LAKESIDE COUNTRY CLUB

The golf   Lakeside is the oldest course in Marshall and one of the oldest in the state, dating back to the 1920s. This traditional course features tight, tree-lined fairways, tiny, swerving greens, and a good amount of water.

The most difficult hole is No. 2: a 431-yard par 4 that cuts 90 degrees left just 190 yards from the tee. Tee shots that fail to cut the corner perfectly leave a monstrous approach into the green.

Other notes: Celebrities such as Mickey Mantle, Y.A. Tittle, and Roy Clark have graced the fairways here. The course was renovated in the mid-1950s. Dallas-based architect Lee Singletary has done some work on the course over the years.

The details   903-938-4211. Hwy. 43 N., Marshall, TX 75671

- 1920. 9 holes. Par 36. Back – 3,131 (34.7/116). Forward – 2,622 (34.7/114). Price - $.

Getting there Lakeside is two miles north of Marshall on Hwy. 43.

OAK LAWN COUNTRY CLUB

The golf   Oak Lawn dates back to the 1940s, when it was laid out for the average golfer with generous fairways and basic, averaged-size greens. The design incorporates a creek and a lake.

The details   903-935-7555. 4307 Victory Dr., Marshall, TX 75672

- 1947. Elizabeth Handcock. 9 holes. Par 36. Back – 3,077 (33.8). Forward – 2,327. Price - $.

Getting there From Tyler, take I-20 east to Hwy. 59. Turn left, proceed to Hwy. 80, turn east, and drive 2 miles. Hwy. 80 becomes Victory and the course is just down the road.

NORTHEAST

MARSHALL NOTES   The **Point N Rise** (903-935-6878) game bird reserve offers hunting and lodging, and in the next year or so will open up a 9-hole golf course. For those with seediness in their soul, the lure of **Shreveport, LA** is difficult to overcome. Great food, music, drinking, and gambling are only 40 miles away. **Caddo Lake** is nearby for the outdoorsman. In Marshall, the

---

The loudest noise you hear on the golf course is the guy jangling coins to distract the player he bet against. Jim Murray

Ginocchio National Historic District in the heart of downtown offers the chance to dine and lodge where early Texas notables worked and played. The **Starr Family Home and State Historic Site** (903-935-3044) offer historical tours, dining, and lodging options inside the Texas Parks and Wildlife facility. Also consider lunch at **Porky's Smokehouse & Grill** (903-927-2144)on E. Carolanne St.

MINEOLA
Elev. 414   Pop. 4,694

Drive through Mineola in the spring, heading up US 69 to Lake Fork from I-20 and Lindale. This railroad town that originated in the 1840s sells itself as the "Gateway to East Texas Pine Country." The drive is spectacular with crimson clover, dogwoods, and bluebonnets blooming vibrantly over the carpeted meadows surrounded by majestic pines. If time permits, work in a round at the Mineola Country Club, which showcases that very same beauty.

MINEOLA COUNTRY CLUB

The golf   Mineola's semi-private, 9-hole course has long been considered one of the top small-town courses in the state. This old, traditional course is set in hilly East Texas terrain. Water comes into play on four holes, but the bunkering is minimal and not every fairway is lined by tall pines. The highlight of Mineola Country Club is the fast greens, which are considered among the best in East Texas.

The details   903-569-2472. 225 Country Club Dr., Mineola, TX 75773

• 1931. 9 holes. Par 35. Back – 3,331 (35.0/119). Middle – 3,164 (34.1/115). Forward – 2,631 (33.0/109). No driving range. Price - $.

Getting there Exit Country Club Rd. off of Hwy. 80 and drive north to the course.

MORE GOLF

The **Mineola Golf Practice Range** on NW Loop 564 offers the chance to loosen up if you need a break from long holiday family gatherings.

MINEOLA NOTES   Like the small towns of Emory and Yantis, Mineola is next to the world's best largemouth bass fishery. Call the **Lake Fork Lodge** (903-473-7326), which cleverly labels itself as a "bass and breakfast" resort. If you're looking around historic Mineola, have lunch at the **East Texas Burger Co.** (903-569-3140). **Two Senoritas** (903-569-1181) is a good dinner option if you're in the mood for greasy Tex-Mex.

Golf is very healthy; it is better to swat pills than to swallow them. Ted Osborne

MOUNT PLEASANT

Elev. 416   Pop. 14,139

Once labeled "One of the 100 Best Small Towns in America," Mount Pleasant is named for its scenic location in the beautifully wooded hills of upper northeast Texas. In the early 1900s the town attracted resort visitors to red mineral springs nearby. Today, it's a commercial center for farming, livestock, and oil. With plenty of lodging, restaurants, and shopping, as well as access to three nearby lakes, this is a golf destination worth investigating. The pristine Mount Pleasant Country Club, consistently rated one of the top 9-hole courses in the state, has recently added an additional nine, and the par 3 Shadow Lakes course is perhaps the finest of its kind in Texas.

MOUNT PLEASANT COUNTRY CLUB

The golf   Once rated as high as fifth by the *Dallas Morning News* for 9-hole courses in Texas, the course now offers the total experience, with an additional nine (Rausch Golf) opening in August 2002. Uneven lies, hilly terrain, narrow fairways, loads of trees, and immaculate greens are the features this semi-private country club is known for. The par 5s here are particularly tight off the tee, with No. 11 playing as the most difficult driving hole on the course.

The details   903-572-1804. 1000 Country Club Dr., Mount Pleasant, TX 79456

• 1940. 18 holes. Par 72. 6,500 yards. Price - $$.

Getting there On Hwy. 271 north, take the Green Hill Rd. exit. Turn right, and head down to Country Club Dr.

SHADOW LAKES GOLF COURSE

The golf   The folks behind the making of Shadow Lakes may have started a trend, since others are sure to try and duplicate the outstanding experience of playing a premier par 3 golf course. In immaculate condition, surrounded by majestic pines and laid out with extreme elevation changes, Shadow Lakes is far from the typical pitch-and-putt.

There aren't many easy holes at Shadow Lakes. The 4th hole, lined by huge pine trees on the right, plays 165 yards from an elevated tee with water fronting the green. Hole 9 will make you want to play again: a 104-yard shot into an island green with the only bail-out being two bunkers that guard the front of the green.

The course is lighted, allowing golfers to tee off as late as 11 pm.

The details   903-572-1288. RR 3, Mount Pleasant, TX 75455

• www.shadowlakescorp.com

• 9 holes. Blue – 1,186. White – 990. Red – 754. Price - $.

Getting there Take exit 162 off I-30.

First and foremost, when you practice with a ball and a hole,
always putt to make it. Dr. Bob Rotella

MOUNT PLEASANT NOTES   Pig out on golf in Mount Pleasant by playing all day at Mount Pleasant Country Club, then teeing off in the evening at Shadow Lakes. Take advantage of three nearby reservoirs famed for outstanding bass, crappie, and catfish fishing: Lakes Bob Sandlin, Monticello and Welsh. The **Kountry Korner** store at FM 127 and FM 2882 is a worthwhile stop with some 2,000 photographs displayed of bass caught weighing 7 lbs. or more. After dark, head to the **Orange Blossom Special** for beers and live music. For lodging there is a huge variety of chain hotels, but you're better off at the **Whitehouse B&B** (903-572-2264) 10 miles east of town.

MURCHISON
Elev. 455   Pop. 589

You can get there by turning south off of I-20 just outside of Canton onto rustic FM 773, which winds its way through the sticks to Ben Wheeler, TX and into the fork in the road at Murchison. Located 9 miles northeast of Athens, halfway between Cedar Creek Reservoir and Lake Palestine, Murchison is the place to refuel, load up on supplies, and pepper the locals with questions about fishing conditions, weather, and other possible hot spots to extend your road trip.

ECHO CREEK COUNTRY CLUB

The golf   Rusty Lambert purchased this old farmland from the Smith family in 1984 and proceeded to build a tough little 18-hole track that's loaded with lakes and tributaries winding their way through the design. The thick rough can get you, but fortunately there are no bunkers. Overall this is a great course for the money, with greens in outstanding shape and an extremely entertaining layout.

A few notes regarding the layout: Watch for the creek that impacts the tee shot and approach on No. 1, a 425-yard par 4. Hole 6 is a tough 500-yard par 5 because of the narrow fairway.

The 150-yard No. 7 is listed as the number one handicap because of the forced carry over the lake, but most agree that the 469-yard, par 4 No. 8 is the most difficult due to the creek in the fairway and the long approach shot.

On the back, hole 12 can be reached in two if you can cut the corner, but beware of the water hazard protecting the front left of the green. The green is hard to hold on No. 14, a 380-yard par 4 with an extremely tight fairway.

The greens are in good shape, the course is well tended, and the price is right. A road trip to Murchison for golf is definitely worth taking.

The details   903-852-7094. 6790 Ann Dr., Murchison, TX 75778

• 1989. Rusty Lambert. 18 holes. Par 71. Back – 6,200 (69.2/120). Middle –

*I never learned anything from a match that I won; I got my golf
education from drubbings.* Bobby Jones

5,676 (67.9/117). Forward – 4,770 (67.7/118). Beer available. Price - $$.

Getting there From Athens, drive east on Hwy. 31 to FM 317. Turn right and the course is 9 miles down on the left side of the road.

MURCHISON NOTES Playing Echo Creek is a day trip sort of thing, so grab lunch at **Piggy's BBQ** on Hwy. 31 and head on out of town. Athens is just 12 miles away.

NACOGDOCHES   Elev. 283   Pop. 30,037

The oldest town in Texas boasts some of the most colorful Texas history. Dating back to the La Salle expedition in 1687, then becoming somewhat established as a Spanish mission in 1716, this town was named after the Nacogdoches Indians and served as the major eastern gateway to Texas for over a hundred years.

Military commanders headquartered at the Old Stone Fort, the Battle of Nacogdoches drove Mexican troops out of East Texas for good, and Texas' first newspaper, millionaire, and oil well were produced here. The list goes on and on for this town of 30,000 that is home to Stephen F. Austin University and two wonderful golf courses.

PINEY WOODS COUNTRY CLUB

The golf   Piney Woods Country Club is a private, 18-hole facility that is known for the outstanding condition of its greens. As is typical of the terrain out here, pine trees line the fairways and if you fail to hit it straight, you'll find yourself in "jail."

The trick to scoring well here is learning the greens, which are small and feature subtle undulations. One of the most notable stretches of the layout is holes 10-14. Sandwiched between two par 5s that play about 450 yards from the back tees are the 270-yard par 4 No. 11, the short par 3 No. 12, and the 352-yard No. 13. Play conservatively on the front nine while you gain confidence on the greens, then be ready to attack this stretch of holes after the turn.

The details   936-569-9821. Hwy. 59 S., Nacogdoches, TX 75963

- 18 holes. Par 72. Back – 6,187 (69.5/125). Middle – 5,913 (68.2/121). Forward – 5,091 (69.0/116). Price - $$.

Getting there Take Hwy. 259 south through Nacogdoches and follow the signs to the course on the south side of town.

NORTHEAST

★

Golf is the hardest game in the world to play, and the easiest to cheat at. Dave Hill

WOODLAND HILLS GOLF COURSE

The golf   Perhaps the best way to give you an idea of the experience that awaits you at Woodland Hills is to mention that we were not able to find anyone who'd say anything bad about the facility. Some claim it's the best course they've played out of many, while others swear they'd pay significantly more than the posted fees. If they don't brag about the layout or the pristine condition of the course, they rave about the course management's attention to detail, particularly the tee time policies that effectively spread players out enough so that you rarely see other golfers. You never have to deal with the issue of playing behind slow golfers, or having another group rush you from behind.

An outstanding layout that has been upgraded over the past few years, combined with superb conditions, make this a must-play for the touring Texas hack. You'll need to hit the ball straight because of the tight fairways, but length is not a requirement here so consider using long irons off the tee. Although there are no bunkers, water hazards are prominent. The medium-sized greens are quick and in perfect condition.

The signature hole is No. 8, a 395-yard par 4 that features a tri-level fairway and an extremely elevated green.

The details   936-564-2767. 319 Woodland Hills Dr., Nacogdoches, TX 75964

- 1971. Don January. 18 holes. Par 72. Back – 6,620 (72.6/133). Middle – 6,162 (71.2/125). Forward – 5,069 (72.9/123). Price - $$.

Getting there From I-59 north, drive 15 miles to Lufkin and follow the signs to the course.

NACOGDOCHES NOTES   Wander around the 1837 **Oak Grove Cemetery**, which holds the remains of prominent characters in Texas history, such as Thomas J. Rusk. For eats, **Aubry's** on Main St. is popular for soul food, and you can watch the game and have a beer at the **Sport Shack**. Consider staying in one of the chain hotels on the south side, which is away from the college scene and closer to the courses. There are bed and breakfasts all around town, but **Anderson Point B&B** (409-569-7445), is worth the drive because of its spectacular setting near the lake.

NEW BOSTON   Elev. 352   Pop. 4,820

Here in the upper reaches of northeast Texas between the Red River and Sulphur River, macho man James Bowie established his Texas roots, eventually getting the county named in his honor after he added knife-fighting, ranching, Alamo hero-ing, and exploring to his resume.

In the past, New Boston has depended heavily on two military installations

It doesn't matter if you look like a beast before or after impact, as long as you look like a beauty at the moment of impact. Seve Ballesteros

for its prosperity. One of them, the former Red River Army Depot, now hosts a nice little park that features the Oak Grove Golf Club and Grill, as well as tennis and swimming facilities.

OAK GROVE GOLF CLUB

The golf   Since Jeffrey Prieskom purchased what was then an average 9-hole course in 1998, Oak Grove has rapidly become known as one of the finest courses in the area. With the addition of nine holes that opened for play in the fall of 2000, as well as continued improvements over the past few years (new greens on 7, 8, 14, and 16), this now borders on being a spectacular 18-hole course. Thanks to the choice of tees (ranging from 3,177 to 6,804 yards), anyone can enjoy a round here.

The details   903-223-8402. Red River Commerce Park, New Boston, TX 75570

• www.oakgrovegolf.com

• 18 holes. Par 72. Back – 6,804. Middle – 6,210. Forward – 4,632. Forward – 3,177. Price - $.

Getting there Located west of Texarkana off of I-30. Take the Red River Army Depot exit (No. 206) and proceed south to the main entrance of Red River Commerce Park. The golf club is located straight ahead. Turn right into the parking lot at the sign.

NEW BOSTON NOTES   After the round, grab a burger at the course (**Oak Grove Grill**), then drive the 8 miles north to the Red River. Fulfill a life-long dream and ask the locals to take you "noodling" for catfish (just do it). Explore for a while, then take the back roads (7 miles on 41 N, then 20 miles on 32 E) to Ashdown, AR and play one of their little 9-hole courses. If you stay in New Boston there are a few local motels, and the **Catfish King** (903-628-5502) will feed you.

OVERTON   Elev. 500   Pop. 2,383

Overton is another of the many small towns with 9-hole golf courses that you'll find bunched around I-20 and US 80 surrounding Tyler and Longview. The town was laid out in 1873 as a junction for two railroad lines and named after local landowner Frank Overton, who donated the land to establish the community. Since the only way to get into Overton is by taking farm roads, this is the off-the-beaten path trek into the sticks you've been looking for.

OVERTON MUNICIPAL GOLF COURSE

The golf   The Overton Muni offers a unique 9-hole experience, with four par 4s, three par 3s, and two par 5s. The fairways have mild undulations and can offer uneven lies.

Holes 2-8 can be fun, including the back-to-back par 4s under 300 yards (7 and 8), but watch out for the opening and finishing holes. No. 1 is a 530-yard par 5, with a creek coming into play in the fairway. No. 9 is a 175-yard hole with water between the tee and green.

The details   903-834-6414. South Lake Shore Dr., Overton, TX 75684

• 9 holes. Back – 2,816 (33.2/103). Middle – 2,735. Forward – 2,271 (32.2/103). Price - $.

Getting there Take Hwy. 64 east, and in downtown Overton turn left on Henderson Pass. Make another left on Lakeside Dr.

OVERTON NOTES   A dry county and a city course means no cerveza; however, they don't mind if you bring your own. **AJ's** serves chicken-fried steak "East Texas Style."

PALESTINE   Elev. 510   Pop. 17,632

Palestine dates back to the 1840s when it was established as the seat of Anderson County. Located 110 miles southeast of Dallas at the intersection of several major highways, the town serves as a hub for agriculture and oil and gas interests. The town is noted for its numerous historical attractions, including the 1853 Kolstad's Jewelers, now the oldest jewelry store in continuous operation in Texas. For golfers, "Palace-steen" offers its semi-private Meadowbrook Country Club as a diversion to historical tours of the city.

MEADOWBROOK COUNTRY CLUB

The golf   Nine-hole Meadowbrook serves up fairways lined with East Texas pines and a creek that impacts play on six of the nine holes. You will not be able to let it loose here, but instead will be thinking strategically about where you need to place the shot. Approaches are tricky because the greens are small and elevated. Bring a solid, short game to get up and down for par.

No. 1 plays only 300 yards, and there are a few other short holes. The most difficult is No. 7, a 218-yard par 3 that plays as a par 4 for the ladies. As always, two sets of tees offer an 18-hole round, and you can play all day for one green fee.

The details   903-723-7530. 2130 Country Club Rd., Palestine, TX 75802

• 9 holes. Par 36. Back – 2,937 (34.1/119). Forward – 2,471 (35.6/121). Price - $.

The golf swing is like a suitcase into which we are trying to pack one too many items. John Updike

Getting there From Tyler, take Hwy. 155 south for 40 miles. Take Loop 256 and turn north on Link St., then turn right on Country Club Rd.

PALESTINE NOTES Visit in March or April when the dogwood trees are in bloom. Reserve a room at the bed and breakfast of choice, the **Wiffletree Inn** (903-723-9565). Eat lunch at the **Caddo Creek Cafe** (903-729-1198), then stop in for dessert at the famous 1898 **Eilenberger's Butternut Baking Company** (903-729-2253). Twenty miles northwest on US 287, the **Engeling Wildlife Management** area offers 11,000 acres of wildlife habitat viewing and fishing.

PARIS
Elev. 592   Pop. 26,120

Located just 20 miles south of the Red River, Paris was settled in the 1840s by a diverse gaggle of frontier characters. Jesse James' brother Frank worked here, and West Point graduate and Confederate General Sam Maxey also had his hands in things. Famous female outlaw Belle Starr spent some nights in the local jail, and renowned cattle baron John Chisolm lived here as well. Unlike other old towns in this region, the downtown architecture features the styles of the 1920s because of two fires that burned the earlier structures to the ground.

Today Paris is the hub of one of Texas' most fertile agricultural regions. The terrain here is ideal for building beautiful golf courses, and the roving avid golfer has the opportunity to try three great courses, one dating back to 1918.

ELK HOLLOW GOLF COURSE

The golf Surprisingly for any course east of Dallas, Elk Hollow's 9-hole layout is void of the thick pine trees that typically line the fairways in East Texas. While there are a few trees that might randomly impact a shot, the course is wide open. Water only comes into play on a few holes.

The details 903-785-6585. 2200 36th St. NE, Paris, TX 75462

• 1971. 9 holes. Par 36. Back – 3,142. Forward – 2,487. Price - $.

Getting there In Sherman take Hwy. 82 east to Paris. Then take Hwy. 195 north and turn right on 36th St. The course is on the left side of the road.

PARIS GOLF & COUNTRY CLUB

The golf Dating all the way back to 1918, the Paris Golf and Country Club is one of the oldest courses in the state. The traditional design is considered more of a target course because of the curving nature of the fairways and the small greens, which are fast and usually in excellent condition. Because of

NORTHEAST

A golf swing is more than just a way of advancing the ball. It's a signature. Patty Sheehan

the creeks and ponds scattered throughout the course, you'll score higher than your normal handicap until you learn the layout.

Beware of the back nine. Hole 14 is the most difficult, at 423 yards with out-of-bounds and water along the left side of the fairway and behind the green. No. 15 plays tough also, with a fairway framed by out-of-bounds on the right and water on the left, and an approach into a long, narrow green. Even if you survive those holes, No. 18 awaits, testing you with an approach over water into a green surrounded by bunkers.

The details   903-785-6512. Hwy. 195, Paris, TX 75462

- 1921. 18 holes. Par 70. Back – 6,143 (67.6/117). Middle – 5,827. Forward – 4,983. Price - $.

Getting there From I-30 east, take Hwy. 24 north. When you come to Loop 286, turn northwest and head over to FM 195. Drive northeast and the course is on the left side of the road.

PINE RIDGE GOLF COURSE

The golf   Built in a gorgeous setting in 1986, Pine Ridge has gained a reputation for its ease and beauty over the years. This short course, which plays under 6,000 yards from the back tees, is wide open, void of bunkers, and has basic, medium-sized greens. There are a few trees to contend with but, if you can deal with the water hazards that impact a decent amount of holes, there's nothing else in the way of a career round.

Length is not an issue, so if you have any problems with your woods off the tee, don't hesitate to hit your irons. Longer hitters who keep it in the fairway will manhandle this course. Four of the five par 5s play around 450 yards from the back tees, three of which are on the par 37 front nine. The front also features two par 4s well under 300 yards. The back nine is a bit more difficult with a 526-yard, par 5, a 215-yard par 3, and two par 4s over 400 yards.

The details   903-785-8076. 5615 Pine Mill Rd., Paris, TX 75461

- 1986. Bruce Rainey. 18 holes. Par 72. Back – 5,855. Middle – 5,675. Forward – 4,462. Price - $$.

Getting there From Loop 286, travel 2 miles and turn up Pine Mill Rd. to the course.

PARIS NOTES   Cuss the fact that the Women's Christian Temperance Union was organized here by partaking of beers and music at **Dillons Bar & Grill** (903-784-3283). For fairly upscale food (grilled salmon, filet mignon) head for casual-yet-refined **Magel's Grill** (903-784-3186). Another option is to go for a beer and listen to blues and Cajun/Zydeco at the **Bayou Moon Cafe and Blues Emporium** (903-784-4249).

No statue has ever been erected for a critic. Jean Sibelius

PITTSBURG

Elev. 398   Pop. 4,461

Just a dozen miles south of Mount Pleasant, heavily timbered Pittsburg is the seat of Camp County and a commercial center for farming, poultry, and livestock. The headquarters for chicken king Bo Pilgrim are here, and growers of blueberries, blackberries, and peaches offer chances to pick your own produce. In fact, Camp County is one of the top 10 peach-producing counties in the state. This charming little town offers old-school grocery, hardware, drug stores, antique shops, and the quaint little 9-hole Princedale Golf Course.

PRINCEDALE GOLF COURSE

The golf   Princedale is an old, semi-private traditional layout set in the typical East Texas terrain of tall pine trees. Don't be surprised if you encounter a few uneven lies on the rolling fairways. The greens are in good condition, which always makes for an enjoyable day on the course.

The details   903-856-3737. Hwy. 11 East, Pittsburg, TX 75686

• 1928. 9 holes. Par 36. Back – 2,858. Forward – 2,235. Price - $.

Getting there Take Hwy. 271 north out of Tyler. When you come to Hwy. 11, turn right and drive less than a mile to the course. The entrance is on the right side of the highway.

PITTSBURG NOTES   Take in the small-town East Texas scene. Farm Roads 11, 49, and 155 offer scenic drives between the communities of Avinger, Linden, and Hughes Springs. Go for sausages on butcher paper at **Pittsburg Hot Links** (903-856-5765). For lodging, call **Mrs. B's Cottage Guesthouse** (903-856-6232) on Quitman St. Out on 271, look for **Blaylock's BBQ** for more good ole' East Texas grub.

RUSK

Elev. 489   Pop. 5,127

Rusk is a historic, charming town that's home to three state parks, loads of historical markers and beautiful old homes, and the longest footbridge in the world. Named after Thomas Jefferson Rusk, Major General of the Texas Republic, Chief Justice of the Supreme Court, attorney, judge, and general Renaissance man, the town is famed as the birthplace of James Hogg and Thomas Campbell, the first native Texans to serve as governor.

Golfers touring the area will be drawn into the rolling hills of the Piney Woods by two excellent 9-hole tracks–the Birmingham Golf Club and brand-new Rolling Hills Golf Course.

NORTHEAST

I don't know anything about music. In my line you don't have to. Elvis Presley

BIRMINGHAM GOLF CLUB

The golf   The Birmingham Golf Club is a 9-hole, semi-private course that features narrow fairways, pine trees, a good amount of hills and elevation changes, and average-sized, elevated greens.

The design incorporates a nice little lake that impacts play on two holes. One of them is the 155-yard par 3 finishing hole, which involves hitting over the lake. This is a very short course. The other par 3 is only 112 yards, and both par 5s play around 440 yards. Hole 8 is a 275-yard par 4.

Pay once and play all day, and use the second set of tees for an 18-hole round.

The details   903-683-9518. Hwy. 69, Rusk, TX 75785

• 1969. 9 holes. Par 36. Back – 2,773 (34.0/118). Forward – 2,515 (34.7/113). Price - $.

Getting there From Hwy. 175 south, take Hwy. 69 and drive south. When you come to Euclid St., turn left. The course is on the right side of the road.

ROLLING HILLS GOLF COURSE

The golf   Local entrepreneur Don Goff took this former salvage yard and turned it into a nice, easy little 9-hole track. The course opened for play in January 2002 and features short holes, small greens, and two big hills that spice up the layout.

Be careful with the opening hole, as you'll need to carry the pond to reach the green. Otherwise the course is pretty straightforward, with only two small bunkers.

Other notes: There is a practice putting green, but no driving range. The course serves sandwiches and burgers if you're interested in a quick bite.

The details   903-683-8442. Route 5, Rusk, TX 75785

• 2002. Don Goff. 9 holes. Par 34. 2,300 yards. Price - $$.

Getting there Take Hwy. 69 south from Tyler for 45 miles. The course is 6.5 miles south of Jacksonville on the right side of the highway. Look for the airport sign, and the course is to the right.

RUSK NOTES   The **scenic drives** around Rusk are spectacular, offering unparalleled woodland scenery. Both north and south on US 69, as well as FM 347 and FM 747 (not on most maps) are worth exploring. East of Rusk on US 84 are the friendly, interesting communities of **Sacul** and **Reklaw**. In town take a look at the **Bonner Bank Building**, built way back in 1865, then have lunch on the square at **Main St. Crossing** (903-683-4580). For lodging, the **Southern Motor Inn** (903-683-2688) gets the job done for the right price.

SCROGGINS
Elev. 360   Pop. 125

With a population that hovers around 100, Scroggins is the smallest town in the northeast region that has the privilege of having a golf course. The community dates back to the 1850s, when Mr. Milt Scroggins operated a sawmill. The railroad came through in the 1870s and the town has somehow subsisted ever since. Despite its small size and remote location, the diehard golfer who makes this a destination will be richly rewarded at the Cypress Creek Country Club.

CYPRESS CREEK COUNTRY CLUB

The golf   Cypress Creek is a 9-hole, semi-private track with four sets of tees, ranging in yardage from 3,204 to 2,352 yards. This course stands out compared to other rural 9-holers. The course is loaded with streams, creeks, and ponds, the fairways are plush, and the large greens feature undulations that make the dreaded three-jack a distinct possibility.

Hole 3 is a long par 4 (around 400 yards), and is listed as the number one handicap. Rather than a multitude of short holes like some small courses, the yardages at Cypress Creek have the more standard lengths of the modern game. The only exception is No. 2, a short par 5 under 450 yards.

The details   903-860-2154. 8102 FM 115, Scroggins, TX 75480

• 1970. 9 holes. Par 36. Back – 3,118. Forward – 2,358. Price - $$.

Getting there From I-30 exit Hwy. 37 to the right. Turn left on Hwy. 21, then take a right on Hwy. 115.

SCROGGINS NOTES   Make it a lake weekend and call the **Cypress Springs Marina Resort** (903-860-2891) for inexpensive lodging. Also on the lake is the **Tall Tree Marina**, with a restaurant and bar. Ten miles away is Mount Vernon, where you can dig in for good eats at **Barbecue Corral**. For tasty Mexican food, hit the **Cypress Glen Restaurant**.

SULPHUR SPRINGS
Elev. 530   Pop. 14,606

If you venture off I-30 about 85 miles from Dallas you'll get lost in the picturesque rolling hills of northeast Texas, where the pine trees start to grow and the dairy farms prosper. Almost 500 dairy farms dot the countryside, lending credence to the town's moniker "Dairy Capital of Texas." The town was named for the medicinal mineral springs once discovered here, but now the most therapeutic activity in Sulphur Springs is a round walking their lovely 18-hole country club.

Golf is so much more fun when it is played well. I've always thought that if the game was worth playing at all, it was worth making some effort to play it correctly. Bobby Jones

SULPHUR SPRINGS COUNTRY CLUB

The golf   Sulphur Springs CC is a short, semi-private track whose small greens require precision approach shots. The front nine is the easier of the two sides and offers plenty of birdie chances, including two short par 3s and a pair of par 5s that play under 500 yards.

The Billy Martindale-designed back features water on six of nine holes. The highlight is No. 18, a 335-yard par 4 that features water along the right side, including a portion that necks into the fairway at about 150 yards from the tee.

The details   903-885-4861. County Rd. 3451, Sulphur Springs, TX 75482

• 1940. 18 holes. Par 72. Blue – 6,107 (68.3/114). White – 5,880 (66.6/109). Gold – 5,203 (66.6/109). Price - $$.

Getting there From I-30 going east, take Exit 127 and go 3 miles down the access road. The course is on the right side of the road.

SULPHUR SPRINGS NOTES Begin a tour of the town at **Heritage Square**, highlighted by the handsome 1894 **Hopkins County Courthouse** which is surrounded by antique shops and restaurants. **Mossman Guitars** on Main St. builds guitars for musicians worldwide, and will show you the process. For fast, fresh Tex-Mex, hit the casual **TaMolly's** (903-885-0067) and sample the fajita nachos or pollo Monterey. **The Oaks B&B** (903-885-0434) is one minute from the Town Square.

TEAGUE   Elev. 499   Pop. 3,258

Teague sits in a strange spot, at least in terms of deciding which region of this book it belongs in. Located about 60 miles east of Waco and just a few miles west of the I-45 corridor that services Houston-Dallas traffic, you could make the argument that Freestone County could be in the North Central as well as the Central region. The line must be drawn somewhere, and Teague's proximity to I-45 makes it worthy of placement in Texas' Northeast region.

Teague is a railroad town; its railway was sometimes referred to as the "Boll Weevil Line" in the old days because of the multitude of trains heading to special conferences centered around the insect devastation in Texas cotton fields. Its railroad roots explain the brick-built look and feel of the town.

BIG CEDAR COUNTRY CLUB

The golf   Big Cedar is a nice place to play if you have realistic expectations. The dreaded bald spot rears its ugly head from time to time in the fair-

---

*I don't throw clubs anymore, in public, though once in a while I let one
fly, in a friendly round with Dad and Chick Ridley and Tess Bradshaw. I
get a great deal of relief from it, too, if you want to know the truth.* Bobby Jones

ways, and the greens are difficult to hold. When in doubt on club selection, play the shorter club and keep your approach below the hole, providing the chance for an easier up and down from below the pin.

The course has undergone quite a bit of construction recently, including the addition of new cart paths, and the removal of the old 9th hole (much to the chagrin of local golfers). The back nine is short and tight, and features a beautiful 10th hole that wraps around a lake.

The best feature at Big Cedar is the unbelievable hospitality of the staff. You never know what you might come across when facing the small town "country club" as an outsider, but this place is fun because the people are friendly.

The details   254-739-5600. Hwy. 84 East, Teague, TX 75860

- 18 holes. Par 72. Gold – 5,622 (67.8). Blue – 5,293 (66.5). White – 5,035 (65). Red – 4,430 (64.7). Price - $$.

Getting there From downtown Teague, go north on 4th St. to Hwy. 84. Turn right (east) and drive 4.5 miles to the course. The course is on the right-hand side.

TEAGUE NOTES   The county is dry, but the country club serves alcohol for a $3 membership. Here's the lowdown on food: **Sam's** is popular for the buffet. **Ponte's** is known for good burgers. The **I-45 Cafe** serves tasty truck-stop food. Everyone brags about **Cole's One Stop** and their BBQ, a Shell service station that "serves the best barbecue in the county." On 8th St., **Texas Pit Bar-B-Q** (254-739-5678) serves melt-in-your-mouth sliced beef sandwiches and thirst-quenching iced tea. If for some reason you must stay, the **Teague Motel** will get you through the night.

TEXARKANA   Elev. 295   Pop. 35,037

Half in Texas. Half in Arkansas. As they say: "Commercially and culturally one city, but two separate municipalities." Imagine the nation's only bi-state Justice Center housing courts and jails for two states, two counties, and two cities. The man who wrote the theme to the movie *The Sting*, Scott Joplin, did his thing here during rag-times. A mural here honors him, and there are numerous historical sites with classic architecture here. Golf-wise, Texarkana is the hometown of former British Open champion Bill Rogers as well as several excellent golf courses, particularly the new Hank Haney-designed Texarkana Golf Ranch. And as an added bonus, you have the quality tracks just across the border on the Arkansas side - the 1920s Texarkana CC and South Haven Golf Club, as well as the fantastic new Lindy Lindsey designed Links at Texarkana course.

NORTHEAST

⭐

Everyone who knows me knows I love music. I used my music to help me maintain my swing's rhythm. For me, waltz time, or 3/4 time, was perfect for the correct golf swing tempo. Sam Snead

NORTHRIDGE COUNTRY CLUB

The golf   PGA veteran and 1981 British Open champion Bill Rogers learned the game here on this tough track that is loaded with water hazards and trees. Other than the water, the course is known for its tricky, undulating greens. The signature hole is the 581-yard No. 5, which might require four shots to reach the green if you're not hitting them solid.

The details   903-792-9331. 120 Bill Rogers Dr., Texarkana, TX 75503

- 1962. 18 holes. Par 71. Back – 6,471 (70.4/127). Middle – 6,130 (69.5/124). Forward – 5,293 (70.0/113). Price - $$$.

Getting there From I-30 east, exit Summerhill Rd. and turn left. When you come to North Park Rd., turn right and proceed down to Bill Rogers. Turn left and the course is just down the road.

TEXARKANA GOLF RANCH

The golf   Set along the shores of beautiful Bringle Lake, the Texarkana Golf Ranch is one of the best new courses in the state, and some say the nation. With its thick forests, lush fairways, and significant elevation changes, this pristine course offers a peaceful golf experience for unbelievably affordable prices. Because the course was carved out of the natural East Texas terrain, they didn't have to move much dirt, and the low construction costs are passed on to the golfing public.

The design spreads out over 300-plus acres that could have easily supported the development of 36 holes. Instead there are only 18 holes, most of which are not adjacent; this means that you'll typically never see another group on the course.

You might even spy a celebrity or two. Those fortunate enough to attend the grand opening were able to attend a clinic from PGA Professional and Haney prodigy Mark O'Meara. Later that day you could also compete against him in the tournament that kicked off the course's grand opening.

The beauty here is unparalleled; every hole appears to be the signature hole. On the front Nos. 4 and 8 stand out a bit more than the others. No. 4 is the only hole where Bringle Lake is not visible, but because it features over 50 feet of elevation change over its 472 yards, it's one of the most spectacular holes.

No. 8 is almost comical, playing a devilish 666 yards from the tee–it's a double dogleg that requires two perfect shots to be in position to reach the green in regulation. Wayward approaches carom off the slopes beside the green, and ups and downs are not guaranteed.

The three finishing holes leave you drooling for more. No. 16 is over 500 yards and requires a tee shot over a lake into a tight landing area. The second shot is a lay-up into a sloping fairway. It can be impossible to get it close with the short approach because the green is perhaps the most undulating on the course.

─────────── ★ ───────────

No that I'm past my 25th birthday I prefer
"Bob" to "Bobby." "Bobby" is too kiddish. Bobby Jones

The beautiful No. 17 plays 214 yards on a long plateau beside the lake, and the spectacular ender plays 425 yards through the tall pines. It's tough to get the tee shot in the fairway because of the numerous bunkers, and especially because of the funky green. Surrounded by bunkers, this strange green is often a sure three-putt because the front slopes left to right, while the back does just the opposite.

The details   903-334-7401. 7401 Scott Wright Rd., Texarkana, TX 75503

- 2000. Hank Haney and Jim Fazio, Jr. 18 holes. Black – 7,369. Blue – 6,744. White – 6,157. Red – 5,118. Price - $$.

Getting there Take the Richmond Rd. exit north off of I-30, then turn right on Scott Wright Rd.

TEXARKANA GOLF CENTER

The golf   An interesting little 9-hole layout that offers a surprising variety of golf because of the terrain and multiple tees, Texarkana Golf Center is rumored to be one of the finest par 3 facilities in the nation.

Spread out over 40 acres, some of the terrain resembles the links-style prairie holes of Kansas or Scotland, while the others sport typical dense East Texas forestry. The holes average 168 yards from the back tees, with the longest playing 255 yards. Due to the multiple tees, however, the difficulty of the course can be adjusted to the appropriate skill of the golfer. From the forward tees, the holes average only 50 yards in length.

Elevation changes and five acres of water spice up the track. And the course is lighted to allow for nighttime play.

The details   870-774-4653. 3903 E. Broad St. (Hwy. 67), Texarkana, AR 71854

- 9 holes. Par 27. Four sets of tees measuring 1,500 from the back. Price - $$.

Getting there Located on Hwy. 67 just north of the Texarkana Regional Airport.

TEXARKANA NOTES   *Do not* get your picture taken at "photo island" with one foot in either state. Do go to **Big Jake's Smokehouse** (903-793-1169) for awesome East Texas barbecue. Texarkana has a lively cultural district with multiple museums worth touring if you're in the mood. The **Mansion on Main** (903-792-1835) is nice and puts you right downtown. Or call **Book-A-Bed-Ahead** (903-792-1835) for other lodging options. Also consider hopping across the border to check out the Arkansas golf scene.

Don't give anything and don't expect to be given anything. I've seen the best players in the world miss putts inside two feet, so no putt is a sure thing. If there's any kind of a sidehill or downhill contour, you'd be surprised how many "gimmes" can be missed. Sam Snead

TROUP

Elev. 494   Pop. 2,021

The railroad came through Troup in 1872, and by 1900, the town clearly had its priorities straight with a business community consisting of "eleven saloons and ten business houses." Although there are 100 businesses now, there's not one place to partake of spirits–so for recreation, everyone heads to the Hilltop Country Club.

HILLTOP COUNTRY CLUB

The golf   Playing under 2,700 yards, this 9-hole, semi-private track is a short course with tight, tree-lined fairways and small greens covered by bunkers. The design features many friendly holes, including the opening 420-yard par 5 and the 280-yard, par 4 finisher. Three par 3s are squeezed in between, two of which are barely over 100 yards. The feature hole is the "long" par 4 No. 7, which might require a longer iron into the small green if your drive is not solid.

Two sets of tees make for an 18-hole round.

The details   903-842-3516. Hwy. 135, Troup, TX 75789

• 1945. 9 holes. Par 35. Back – 2,650 (33.0). Forward – 2,278. Price - $.

Getting there From Tyler, take Hwy. 110 south through the town of Whitehouse all the way to Troup. Turn left on Hwy. 135 and drive to the Troup High School. The course is 1 mile behind the high school.

TROUP NOTES   Drive from Tyler, grab lunch and discuss local politics at the **Dairy Queen**, or track down the **People's Choice** (903-842-4008) catfish and crawfish house on Hwy. 110, then hit the course for an afternoon round. Drive back to Tyler for lodging or continue the road trip toward another nearby East Texas destination like **Overton** or **Bullard**.

TYLER

Elev. 558   Pop. 85,807

Pine trees, oil derricks, and roses. *Lots* of roses–30,000 rosebushes, in fact, in the world's largest municipal rose garden. It's not all roses, though. Tyler's unique combination of sandy soil, long growing seasons, and annual rainfall evenly spread throughout the year make it the ideal setting for Tyler's five beautiful golf courses, as well as the outstanding tracks that surround this basic city. While there isn't much to do in Tyler, the town has adequate lodging and facilities and can serve as the perfect hub for an East Texas golf orgy.

✦

If profanity had an influence on the flight of the ball, the game would be played far better than it is. Horace Hutchinson

BELLWOOD GOLF CLUB

The golf   Originally known as Cross Creek, this old course dates back to the early days of Texas golf. On this short, public course the narrow fairways roll through hilly East Texas terrain and are lined by tall, mature trees (pines and oaks). Water is not a predominant hazard here, with only a pond and a creek impacting two holes. The back nine is more difficult than the front, highlighted by the layout's two signature holes, Nos. 11 and 17.

Other notes: Locals brag about the pristine condition of the greens. Ladies receive discounts on Wednesdays.

The details   903-597-4871. 800 Bellwood Golf Club Rd., Tyler, TX 75709

- 1925. 18 holes. Par 70. Back – 6,200 (65.0). Forward – 5,054. Price - $$.

Getting there From Hwy. 31 or Loop 323, circle around Tyler. Merge back onto Hwy. 31 and head 1 mile west to the course.

BRIARWOOD GOLF CLUB

The golf   An outstanding course known for hosting past Southwest Conference championships, Briarwood is a challenging course that rolls through the tall East Texas pines.

The course opened in 1961 and was redesigned by Lee Singletary in 1985. The design is a bit unusual, with a front nine that features three par 3s, par 4s, and par 5s. No. 1 tests you early: a 515-yard par 5 that plays straightaway, but is difficult because of the fairway bunker and elevated green.

Two holes stand out on the back. Hole 15 is sort of reminiscent of Augusta—a par 3 over water to a small green framed by bunkers on either side and a flower garden in the back. The next hole is one of the most difficult: a 426-yard par 4 with a tee shot over water into an uphill, dogleg-right fairway.

Other notes: On Course Strategies of Austin has been managing the course since a July 2002 foreclosure. The course is now owned by a local real estate investor.

The details   903-593-7741. 4511 Briarwood Rd., Tyler, TX 75709

- 1961, 1985. Lee Singletary. 18 holes. Par 71. Back – 6,487 (70.6/118). Middle – 5,831 (67.3/112). Forward – 4,735 (66.1/111). Price - $$.

Getting there From Hwy. 155 south, turn left on Loop 323, then turn left again on Briarwood Rd. (which dead-ends at the course).

HOLLYTREE COUNTRY CLUB

The golf   Dating back to 1983, Hollytree features a demanding Bruce Devlin and Robert von Hagge design and has hosted collegiate events and top

NORTHEAST

Nobody thinks the way they should on every shot, nobody's that good. You were born human. Tom Kite

amateur tournaments over the years. It's known as a target course that features water hazards on almost every hole; you'll be faced with many risk-reward decisions throughout your round.

The design incorporates five par 3s and five par 5s. The tee shots can be intimidating, since nine of the holes require a carry over water off the tee. One of these is the signature par 4 No. 15, with water off the tee and along the left side of the fairway. If you survive the tee shot, you're still faced with a long approach into a multi-tiered green surrounded by sand.

Of the notable holes on the front, No. 3 is loaded with fairway bunkers and water, and holes 7 and 9 share a tee box and require solid drives to reach the fairway.

Other notes: While Hollytree is a private facility, the club allows USGA members who live at least 50 miles outside of Tyler to play.

The details 903-581-7723. 6700 Hollytree Dr., Tyler, TX 75703

- 1983. Bruce Devlin and Robert von Hagge. 18 holes. Par 72. Back – 6,690 (73.6/136). Middle – 6,273 (71.4/123). Forward – 5,168 (70.0/122). Price - $$.

Getting there From I-20 east, exit Tyler/Lindale and turn right. When you come to Loop 323, turn right, drive to South Broadway, then turn right again. When you reach Grande St., turn right, then turn left on Hollytree and drive to the course.

PINE SPRINGS GOLF COURSE

The golf   Pine Springs opened about three years ago and has gained the distinguished reputation of having unbelievably pure greens. This new course offers the benefits of modern design, featuring tough bunkering and water that gets in the way. A few holes feature ponds that must be carried on the approach. Hole 16 is one of the toughest, primarily because of the water.

The details 903-526-4653. 5630 Pine Springs Rd., Tyler, TX 75708

- 18 holes. Par 70. Blue – 6,256. White – 5,757. Yellow – 5,089. Forward – 4,373. Price - $$.

Getting there From I-20 exit 271 and head right for 3 miles. Turn right before the UT Health Center and drive 1 mile down the road. Turn left, then look for the course on the left side of the road.

WILLOWBROOK COUNTRY CLUB

The golf   Willowbrook dates back to the 1950s, when Ralph Plummer came through to put his mark on Tyler golf. In 1980, Joe Finger came along for a redesign of this hilly, tree-lined course.

I can guarantee that, if you stick with your improvement plan for three years, you will play the golf of your dreams. You'll also encounter periods when it all seems useless and you're tempted to give up, but this is the time to patiently persist. Dr. Bob Rotella

The design features fairways of average width, water on only a few holes, and fairly prominent bunkering. Play it smart and take an extra club on most approaches because of the elevated greens.

The most difficult hole is the 500-yard No. 16, a par 5 that forces two carries over water hazards and a green that is covered by bunkers.

The details   903-592-8229. 3205 W. Erwin St., Tyler, TX 75711

- 1953. Ralph Plummer. 1980. Joe Finger. 18 holes. Par 71. Back – 6,503 (72.1/126). Middle – 6,122 (70.4/122). Back – 5,329 (70.0/124). Price - $$.

Getting there From I-20, take Hwy. 69 south, then turn right on Loop 323. Turn left on Hwy. 64 to reach the course.

TYLER NOTES   **Bruno's Pizza** is famous locally for having the best pizza. The best spot for Mexican food is the crowded **Mercados** (903-534-1754). About the nicest sit-down meal you can find is at the **Mansion** (903-533-1628), an impressive old house at the intersection of Hwy. 64 and Spur 124. **The Radisson Hotel** is one of the nicer chains, and features the **Texas Steakhouse** (903-597-1301) in its lobby. The **Worldert-Spence Manor** (903-533-9057) is a nice bed and breakfast option if the chain hotels don't sound appealing. Also note that **Rudy's Country Store** (903-597-8391) serves outstanding barbecue out on Loop 323.

YANTIS   Elev. 499   Pop. 332

Yantis lies on the north side of famous Lake Fork. Like the town of Emory, it serves as a hub of activity for recreational outings on the lake. We know that sometime around 1885, the town was named after its first postmaster, George Yantis, a busy fellow who also ran a gristmill and cotton gin in the community of 35 residents. Lately the town of Yantis has received more acclaim because of the rave reviews showered on the new 18-hole golf course, which juts out onto two big peninsulas of Lake Fork.

LINKS AT LAND'S END

The golf   Lake Fork's premier golf facility is appropriately named–it's located in what seems like the middle of the lake. Half of the holes play along two peninsulas. Since October 2001 the course has had 18 holes.

The most difficult hole on the front nine, and the signature hole of the course, is the scenic par 5 No. 6, which takes you away from the trees and introduces you to the lake. Despite the average length, the hole plays long because of the wind, and is definitely a three-shot hole since you're forced to

---
★

I think it was Stevenson who said that bad men and fools eventually got what was coming to them, but the fools first. And when you feel so extremely a fool and a bad golfer to boot, what the deuce can you do, except throw the club away? Bobby Jones

lay up at about 150 yards out. Aim the tee shot to the right of the fairway, and beware of the deceptively uphill approach.

On the back be sure to manage your game on hole 11, a painstakingly long par 4 with the lake running down the left side of the fairway. The drive needs to be perfect here, with the lake looming left and any shot to the right being blocked by trees. Since the lake juts in front of the green, the safe play on the approach is to steer right. This isn't the hole to be aggressive on, so the average hacker should play for bogey.

Other notes: Complete with detailed tips for how to play every hole, along with pictures, hole diagrams, and yardages, the course's Web site is one of the most comprehensive you'll find. We definitely recommend spending a few minutes on the site before your trip.

The details   903-383-3290. 285 Private Rd. 5980, Yantis, TX 75497

- www.golflakefork.com

- 2001. Williams and Gill. 18 holes. Par 71. Champs – 6,664 (72.6/130). Member – 6,100 (70.2/129). Middle – 5,678 (67.6/122). Forward – 5,068. Price - $$.

Getting there From Dallas, take Hwy. 19 off 80 to Emory. Turn right toward Mineola on Hwy. 69. Look for the Lake Fork sign and FM 515 (bears right). Go 10 miles and cross the bridge. There's a Phillips 66 on the right 2 miles past bridge. Find County Rd. 1970, turn right, then turn left at the T. Follow 1970 and the course is on the left.

YANTIS NOTES   This is your chance to combine world-class bass fishing with excellent golf. Do your research and find the right guide to make your time on the lake adventurous and productive. **Fisherman's Cove Marina** (888-818-3675) is a good starting place. For lodging on the lake, call the **Lake Fork Lighthouse Resort** in Alba, TX (800-773-1085), or the **Oak Ridge Resort** (903-878-2529) in Quitman, TX. Between the fishing and golf, grab lunch at **Big Smith's Bar B Q** (903-383-2706) on day one, then **Billy Bo's Bar B Que** (903-383-7615) on day two. In the evenings, try **El Lago** (903-383-7056) for Mexican food.

NORTHEAST TEXAS BORDER CROSSINGS

The golf options in Northeast Texas expand significantly if you consider a jaunt across the border into the three adjacent states, Oklahoma, Arkansas and

---

Since it is beyond all reasonable expectations that a person may hole a chip shot, little will be gained by playing always for the hole . . . There are times when a four-foot uphill putt is a far less annoying proposition than one of half that length across a keen slope. Bobby Jones

Louisiana. Particularly with Shreveport, which might be the most underrated golf mecca in the United States, these forays are almost too good to be true for the restless golfer who enjoys gambling and golf. Note that the Texarkana courses in Louisiana are covered in the Texarkana, TX write-up.

BROKEN BOW, OK   46 miles from Clarksville, TX

A spectacular course located in the foothills of the Kiamichi Mountains, the **Cedar Creek Golf Course** (580-494-6456) is a must-play if you're traveling in the area. Extremely lush, lined with tall pine trees, and unusual because of the hilly terrain, this 6,600-yarder (71.3/128) should be played in 72 strokes, but is a real treat even at 100. The back nine was added in 1994 and features the signature No. 16, a 420-yard par 4 that plays to an island green in the middle of scenic Broken Bow Lake. More Texans should consider excursions to this under-appreciated part of Oklahoma, because it is truly spectacular.

IDABEL, OK   32 miles from Clarksville, TX

The **Idabel Country Club** (580-286-6836) is a nice 9-holer. Listed as a par 35 at 2,860 yards (34.1/116), it's known for being in excellent condition. The narrow, tree-lined fairways roll to small greens here. The best hole is No. 7, a roller-coaster par 4 that dives down off the tee, then back uphill beside water on the approach.

ASHDOWN, AR   20 miles from Texarkana, TX

The **Ashdown Golf Club** (870-898-5649) is relatively new, opening for play in 1989 with a 9-hole, 3,330-yard route that plays to a par 36. This one is modern as small-town 9-holers go, offering plenty of trees, bunches of bunkers, and water in play on 7 of 9 holes. The best hole is the ender, a 533-yarder that involves carrying water on the approach.

Nothing like touring the backwoods of Arkansas with the RV, and when you do, you can hook it up and pull out the clubs at the 18-hole **Millwood Landing Golf & RV Resort** (870-898-6674). Loaded with trees and an impressively hilly track, you'll rarely have an even lie in the fairway. The best hole is the par 3 No. 16, which plays 183 yards over water. The course is 6,413 yards, par 72, 70.4/118.

TEXARKANA, AR   Across the border from Texarkana, TX

The 9-hole **Links at Texarkana** (870-773-6154) tips out to a par 35, 2,600 yards, and is located in the middle of an apartment complex. Water is every-

NORTHEAST

The three things I fear most in golf are lightning, Ben Hogan, and a downhill putt. Sam Snead

506 • *The Texas Golf Bible*

where, the fairways leave little room for error, and you should bring your short game because the greens are real small.

The **South Haven Golf Course** (870-774-5771) is an old course that dates back to the 1920s, and features an updated back nine that was routed by John Rickman around 1990. Each nine is totally different. The front is flat and the back features more undulations. Water comes into play on half of the holes, and the design incorporates six dogleg fairways. No. 9 is one of the toughest–a 330-yard, par 4 that requires a tee shot over water into a dogleg-left fairway. The short distance of the hole and the dogleg force a perfect tee shot. From the tips, it rolls 6,227 yards in what should be 71 strokes (69.3/123).

The 1927 **Texarkana Country Club** (870-772-8221) was originally designed by Theodore Moreau, but updated in the late 1950s by Leon Howard. Consistently ranked as one of the top 10 courses in Arkansas, this track tips out at a par 72, 6,588 yards (71.5/126), and is known for its water and hills. No. 14 is the most notable hole, a 410 yarder that will make you beg for a bogey.

SHREVEPORT, LA

39 miles from Marshall, TX

Champion Links (318-865-7888) is a short, 1,150-yard par 3 track with holes ranging from 98 to 153 yards. Some of the holes are challenging because of the bayous that weave around the course, bringing water into play for wayward hacks. No. 3 is the signature, a 135-yarder that plays to a scenic green framed by water and trees.

The **East Ridge Country Club** (318-868-6571) is a 1950s Press Maxwell route that tips out at a par 72 6,696 yards (72.2/127). No. 16 (par 4, 361 yards) is the signature because of its approach over a creek to a bunker-protected green.

The popular **Huntington Park Golf Course** (318-673-7765) is long and demanding, tipping out at 7,294 yards (73.3). Often considered one of the top 10 public courses in Louisiana, its popularity comes from its affordable rate (around $25 with cart) rather than its playability. Even from the middle tees the track plays over 6,800 yards. The best hole is No. 14, a 460-yard par 4 that doglegs right and approaches over water.

The **Lakeside Park Golf Course** (318-673-7782) is a par 33, 2,502-yard track that plays up and down hills into small, sloped greens, and even offers a few dogleg fairways. Keep the ball below the hole here, as many of the greens slope back-to-front. The signature is No. 5, a 430-yarder that is tough because of the 220-yard forced carry off the tee. Perhaps it's because of that carry that

Golf has drawbacks. It is possible, by too much of it, to destroy the mind. Sir Walter Simpson

they allow old farts over 75 years old to play free during the week?

The **Northwood Country Club** (318-929-2380) expanded to 18 holes after Jeff Brauer came through in the late 1980s, and now tips out at 6,440 yards (69.6/116). This one is nice, featuring lush conditions, fast, immaculate greens, plenty of water, and tricky elevation changes. Brauer's No. 11 hole is the signature, a 550-yard par 5 that plays uphill from an elevated tee, then requires another uphill approach to a green framed by sand and water.

Old Querbes Park Golf Course (318-673-7773) is simple and entertaining, a par 71 route that tips out at only 6,207 yards. Generous fairways welcome drivers off the tee, and the course routes around one drainage ditch that comes into play every now and then. The only par 5 is No. 16, but you get your money's worth since it plays over 600 yards from the tips.

Over the years Leon Howard, Joe Finger, and Dave Bennett have all had a hand in shaping the **Shreveport Country Club** (318-631-1200), a narrow, tree-lined track that tips out to a par 71, 6,544 yards (71.9/130). The course is tricky because of the long, forced carries over the creeks and ditches that traverse the route. Once you successfully reach the green you have to deal with the lightning-fast putting surfaces. No. 9 is the toughest hole, playing 565 yards uphill all the way.

The venerable Arthur Hills-designed **Southern Trace Country Club** (318-798-8301) is a challenging 6,916-yard track that has been considered one of the finest in the state since it opened in 1989. This one is tough, with a slope of around 140, making it a viable venue for professional tournaments over the years. The signature at Southern Trace is the large, extremely quick greens.

The executive **Westwood Golf Course** (318-636-3162) has 18 holes that play 3,485 yards to a par 59. The fairways are wide open and friendly to beginning hacks even after dark, since 9 holes are lit until late into the evening.

BOSSIER CITY, LA   42 miles from Marshall, TX

The **Barksdale Air Force Base Golf Course** (318-456-3832) dates back to the 1940s, and plays to a meager par 70, 5,904-yard route (68.7/117). They say it's a shot-maker's course, with tight, tree-lined fairways and water in play on over half the holes. The greens here are large and welcome targets.

Freddy Couples had a hand in the new **Golf Club at Stonebridge** (318-747-2004), a 6,954-yard par 72 track that is loaded with water (17 of 18 holes). The fairways are narrow and lined with tons of trees, making it imperative to keep it in the fairway.

NORTHEAST

⭐

Husbands are like fires. They go out if unattended. Zsa Zsa Gabor

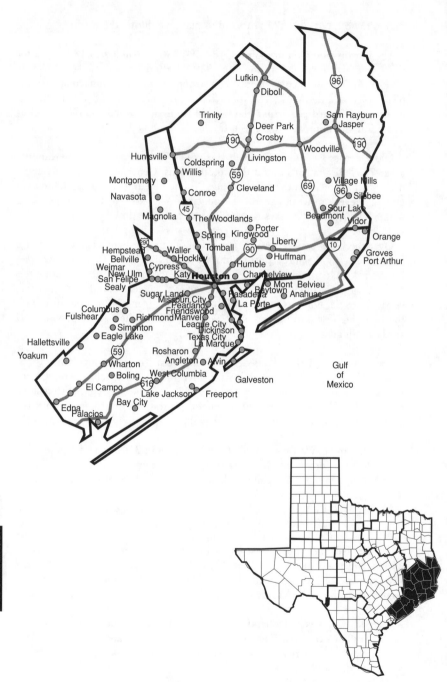

SOUTH EAST

SOUTHEAST TEXAS

In the 1980 film, Urban Cowboy, *a dull-witted roughneck and would-be* bull rider (John Travolta) finds himself in a swanky penthouse apartment in downtown Houston. The late night scene is dazzling: the lights of the nation's fourth-largest city are glittering far below him, while an oh-so-elegant cowgirl princess (Madelyn Smith) hands him a drink and fixes her beckoning brown eyes on his. The cowboy asks how her father could afford such a fancy place full of furnishings so fine they are beyond his comprehension. Without hesitation she answers, "Daddy's in oil . . . and all that that implies."

That scene summarizes Houston: its beauty, its swagger, and its lavish abundance borne of natural resources. Oil took a backwater marshland better known for shipwrecks and Indian uprisings and stood it on its head. In the 100 years after the famous "Lucas Gusher" at Spindletop in Beaumont, billions of dollars in oil wealth has flowed through the region. The money built spectacular hospitals, universities, museums, and cultural centers. It lured NASA, professional sports franchises, and world-class art into its embrace. It helped make Houston a truly sophisticated, international city.

Thankfully, it also built some fantastic golf courses. Houston is overgrown with golf, with more than 70 public courses available to the masses. Names like Palmer, Nicklaus, Norman, Fazio, Couples, Rees Jones, Arthur Hill, and Peter Jacobsen have all done their part to bring the game to Texas hacks. The result is that a golf trip through Houston (and its sprawling tangle of suburbs that seem to go on forever) is an exercise in judicious decision-making. How do you spend your time wisely when there are so many choices? *The Texas Golf Bible* is here to help.

Please don't forget that there is more to the Southeast than just Harris County. Up and down the Gulf Coast you'll find the salty-sea-air side of Texas, complete with shrimp boats and bikinis, battleships and Indian campgrounds, and even the finest greyhound racetrack in the South. Hurricanes, fires, and explosions of historic proportions have not quelled the spirit of this region--they've only strengthened its resolve. Throw into this rich mix elements of ethnic traditions from generations of Cajuns, Hispanics, French, and Caribbean cultures and you've got a taste of the Gulf Coast.

SOUTH EAST

⭐

If everybody could learn to hold his head still there wouldn't be any golfers around still trying to break 100. Arnold Palmer

Southeast Mileage

	Alvin	Anahuac	Bay City	Baytown	Beaumont	Bellville	Channelvw.	Cleveland	Coldspring	Columbus	Conroe	Crosby	Cypress	Deer Pk.
Alvin		57	59	31	94	81	30	70	87	88	66	41	59	24
Anahuac	57		116	26	46	109	33	57	76	120	78	34	74	38
Bay City	59	116		90	153	74	89	122	139	68	114	99	95	84
Baytown	31	26	90		63	87	11	50	68	98	59	16	52	12
Beaumont	94	46	153	63		140	70	67	85	155	90	63	111	75
Bellville	81	109	74	87	140		77	86	96	28	63	80	43	78
Channelview	30	33	89	11	70	77		49	66	88	52	12	41	9
Cleveland	70	57	122	50	67	86	49		19	113	23	37	58	55
Coldspring	87	76	139	68	85	96	66	19		124	34	55	76	72
Columbus	88	120	68	98	155	28	88	113	124		91	93	72	88
Conroe	66	78	114	59	90	63	52	23	34	91		44	40	55
Crosby	41	34	99	16	63	80	12	37	55	93	44		48	20
Cypress	59	74	95	52	111	42	41	58	76	72	40	48		46
Deer Park	24	38	84	12	75	78	9	55	72	88	55	20	46	
Diboll	132	110	184	113	99	147	111	63	62	175	86	100	121	117
Dickinson	12	49	71	23	86	90	28	71	89	100	69	36	61	22
Eagle Lake	75	118	58	96	165	32	84	111	128	16	103	91	66	85
Edna	102	146	43	122	183	88	114	143	160	64	133	120	114	111
El Campo	77	119	32	94	155	62	86	115	133	39	105	93	84	83
Freeport	37	94	43	68	131	98	68	103	120	101	98	78	86	62
Friendswood	8	51	68	25	88	83	22	65	83	91	61	33	57	17
Fulshear	47	82	60	60	118	34	50	78	96	43	64	56	37	49
Galveston	30	67	87	41	104	110	48	91	109	118	90	55	80	40
Ganado	95	137	38	113	174	80	105	134	151	56	124	112	104	102
Groves	99	51	159	69	17	152	76	83	102	163	106	77	126	81
Hallettsville	110	149	84	127	186	66	117	146	161	38	129	123	111	116
Hempstead	76	98	90	76	126	16	65	70	80	44	47	69	28	67
Hockley	68	84	105	62	121	33	51	68	80	65	45	58	10	56
Houston	25	49	76	27	85	62	17	45	63	73	41	23	28	16
Huffman	56	47	116	24	61	92	22	24	55	102	41	9	41	30
Humble	44	53	96	35	72	68	25	27	45	88	29	20	30	29
Huntsville	95	103	143	89	112	79	81	45	31	107	30	74	70	85
Jasper	158	112	210	127	67	174	130	89	88	202	111	118	148	137
Katy	49	76	70	55	112	34	44	70	87	44	54	49	26	45
Kingwood	49	60	101	41	78	74	31	25	43	93	27	26	36	35
La Marque	18	56	75	30	93	98	37	80	97	106	77	44	70	29
La Porte	24	34	83	8	71	85	17	58	75	96	63	21	53	8
Lake Jackson	32	89	38	63	126	92	62	97	115	94	92	73	79	56
League City	13	47	72	22	85	86	24	67	84	97	65	35	56	17
Liberty	60	25	119	29	43	97	32	32	50	112	54	20	67	39
Livingston	97	75	149	78	74	113	77	28	27	141	51	65	86	83
Lufkin	144	121	196	125	107	151	123	75	74	179	97	112	133	129
Madisonville	122	130	153	116	139	80	108	72	59	107	57	101	98	112
Magnolia	66	87	106	65	111	39	54	47	57	67	24	57	24	57
Manvel	8	63	62	38	101	74	33	67	85	81	63	43	50	28
Missouri City	25	63	64	38	100	60	31	60	78	67	53	38	33	27
Mont Belvieu	41	20	100	10	57	91	16	40	59	103	57	14	58	22
Montgomery	77	93	118	75	106	55	65	39	41	83	16	60	35	68
Navasota	94	114	111	93	132	37	82	65	65	64	42	85	46	84
New Ulm	65	110	26	88	146	63	76	103	121	65	95	84	68	75
Newgulf	65	110	26	88	146	64	76	103	121	65	95	84	68	75
Orange	116	68	175	85	24	164	92	90	108	179	113	87	137	97
Palacios	88	124	29	119	182	98	118	150	168	75	141	128	120	112
Pasadena	21	44	80	18	81	74	12	53	71	84	52	21	41	7
Pearland	10	54	69	28	91	77	23	60	77	85	56	33	47	18
Port Arthur	98	50	157	67	17	150	74	84	103	161	107	76	125	79
Porter	59	66	112	44	80	88	32	20	37	98	23	27	40	37
Richmond	35	77	51	52	113	46	44	73	91	53	63	51	36	41
Rosharon	16	73	48	47	110	78	45	74	92	84	69	52	58	40
Sam Rayburn	185	132	190	150	87	200	156	108	107	222	131	160	165	164
San Felipe	81	100	65	78	136	19	66	93	110	29	84	73	48	71
Sealy	82	100	62	78	136	14	66	93	110	25	85	73	48	71
Silsbee	110	83	169	79	21	146	82	60	70	163	83	71	130	90
Simonton	52	87	56	64	123	33	54	83	101	40	68	61	42	53
Sour Lake	86	40	145	55	20	128	62	47	65	143	70	51	97	67
Spring	49	65	98	45	84	60	34	38	51	82	18	32	25	38
Sugar Land	29	68	59	44	105	54	36	65	83	61	56	43	33	33
Texas City	23	56	80	30	94	102	38	80	98	111	80	44	72	29
The Woodlands	57	74	106	54	93	66	43	37	47	90	14	41	30	47
Tomball	55	75	96	54	98	45	43	46	56	73	23	45	14	46
Trinity	112	109	161	106	108	99	99	56	37	127	48	91	89	102
Vidor	100	53	160	70	7	146	77	72	91	162	95	69	118	81
Village Mills	137	80	217	97	35	183	103	55	60	193	78	79	143	111
Waller	66	88	86	67	117	25	56	65	75	53	42	59	16	57
Weimar	102	134	83	113	170	43	102	128	138	15	106	108	86	103
West Columbia	35	92	24	66	129	75	66	98	115	77	93	76	76	60
Wharton	64	106	25	82	142	49	74	102	120	43	93	80	68	71
Willis	73	84	122	67	94	70	59	27	26	98	9	52	49	63
Woodville	130	88	182	100	56	146	102	61	60	174	83	90	120	110
Yoakum	128	167	82	145	204	84	135	163	179	56	147	141	130	134

Southeast Mileage

	Eagle Lk.	Edna	El Campo	Freeport	Friendswood	Fulshear	Galveston	Ganado	Groves	Hallettsvl.	Hempstead	Hockley	Houston	Huffman	Humble	Huntsville	Jasper
	72	102	77	37	8	47	30	95	99	110	76	68	25	56	44	95	158
	118	146	119	94	51	82	67	137	51	149	98	84	49	47	53	103	112
	58	43	32	43	68	60	87	38	159	84	90	105	76	116	96	143	210
	96	122	94	68	25	60	41	113	69	127	76	62	27	24	35	89	127
	165	183	155	131	88	118	104	174	17	186	126	121	85	61	72	112	67
	32	88	62	98	83	34	110	80	152	66	16	33	62	92	68	79	174
	84	114	86	68	22	50	48	105	76	117	65	51	17	22	25	81	130
	111	143	115	103	65	78	91	134	83	146	70	68	45	24	27	45	89
	128	160	133	120	83	96	109	151	102	161	80	80	63	55	45	31	88
	16	64	39	101	91	43	118	56	163	38	44	65	73	102	88	107	202
	103	133	105	98	61	64	90	124	106	129	47	45	41	41	29	30	111
	91	120	93	78	33	56	55	112	77	123	69	58	23	9	20	74	118
	66	114	84	86	57	37	80	104	126	112	28	10	28	41	30	70	148
	85	111	83	62	17	49	40	102	81	116	67	56	16	30	29	85	137
	184	205	178	165	128	141	154	196	116	208	132	131	108	101	90	68	57
	86	114	89	48	12	60	21	107	92	122	79	71	28	51	45	98	150
Eagle Lk.		60	33	83	77	29	102	51	181	39	48	59	69	96	84	133	211
Edna	60		27	86	107	75	129	9	189	45	104	124	97	134	117	162	231
El Campo	33	27		72	80	48	106	19	161	52	77	94	70	105	89	135	203
Freeport	83	86	72		46	71	45	81	137	122	104	96	57	95	77	127	191
Friendswood	77	107	80	46		50	33	98	94	113	72	67	20	51	39	91	150
Fulshear	29	75	48	71	50		77	67	125	67	33	29	33	68	52	93	166
Galveston	102	129	106	45	33	77		125	110	139	100	91	49	70	66	119	169
Ganado	51	9	19	81	98	67	125		180	50	95	114	88	124	108	153	222
Groves	181	189	161	137	94	125	110	180		192	140	136	92	80	87	129	76
Hallettsvl.	39	45	52	122	113	67	139	50	192		81	104	100	142	120	140	234
Hempstead	48	104	77	104	72	33	100	95	140	81		18	51	69	54	64	158
Hockley	59	124	94	96	67	29	91	114	136	104	18		38	54	40	75	134
Houston	69	97	70	57	20	33	49	88	92	100	51	38		31	20	70	134
Huffman	96	134	105	95	51	68	70	124	80	141	69	54	31		11	71	128
Humble	84	117	89	77	39	52	66	108	87	120	54	40	20	11		59	115
Huntsville	133	162	135	127	91	93	119	153	129	140	64	75	70	71	59		103
Jasper	211	231	203	191	150	166	169	222	76	234	158	158	134	128	115	103	
	50	87	60	75	50	15	78	78	119	76	33	19	29	57	44	84	158
	89	123	95	82	45	58	72	114	93	125	60	46	25	16	7	57	113
	92	118	95	44	20	65	14	113	99	128	87	80	36	59	54	106	158
	93	117	90	62	19	56	35	109	76	122	74	63	23	30	36	92	135
	76	81	66	9	40	65	51	77	131	116	98	89	51	88	71	121	185
	82	115	88	51	8	56	25	106	90	120	75	66	24	46	41	94	149
	110	140	112	97	52	75	71	131	58	143	83	78	43	18	29	77	98
	139	171	143	130	93	106	119	162	91	173	98	96	73	66	55	43	60
	196	217	190	177	139	153	165	208	124	212	135	143	120	112	101	72	55
	111	167	141	154	118	97	146	158	156	140	64	104	97	98	86	28	131
	87	121	94	98	62	49	90	112	125	105	23	18	42	50	39	47	135
	66	97	70	42	16	40	37	88	106	103	72	60	22	59	41	92	155
	53	84	57	51	24	26	55	75	106	89	54	43	14	54	34	82	148
	102	129	101	78	35	65	51	120	63	132	79	68	32	23	33	86	118
	98	137	109	109	73	65	101	128	122	120	39	38	53	55	44	31	127
	69	125	99	125	90	54	118	116	148	97	21	36	69	87	66	43	147
	46	61	31	46	67	40	91	50	162	85	96	78	57	88	77	125	193
	46	61	31	46	67	40	91	50	162	85	96	78	57	88	77	125	193
	191	205	178	153	110	141	126	196	17	208	150	147	108	87	96	135	65
	69	42	36	69	96	84	113	38	187	87	113	130	105	141	124	170	238
	80	107	79	59	13	44	41	98	87	112	62	51	12	32	27	81	139
	70	101	74	47	6	44	39	92	96	107	66	57	15	43	34	85	148
	179	188	160	136	93	123	109	179	5	191	139	135	90	78	88	130	77
	91	131	100	86	53	54	76	121	99	138	64	50	27	19	8	53	110
	37	70	42	59	38	18	65	61	119	75	51	46	28	63	47	92	161
	75	89	62	29	24	44	45	80	115	106	75	68	29	67	48	98	162
	279	250	230	211	185	188	204	220	106	261	195	175	150	144	133	120	17
	22	83	53	109	79	20	103	73	152	61	28	40	51	78	77	115	182
	19	80	50	109	79	20	103	71	152	65	29	41	51	78	66	115	183
	184	190	163	148	103	126	121	181	38	193	130	140	93	80	80	101	51
	24	71	43	72	54	5	82	62	129	62	35	34	38	73	57	97	171
	142	170	143	123	80	106	96	161	37	173	114	108	73	49	60	92	74
	87	117	90	81	45	48	73	108	99	115	44	30	24	24	13	47	126
	45	78	51	55	30	20	59	69	111	83	52	43	19	54	39	85	153
	97	123	100	49	24	70	14	118	99	133	91	82	39	61	57	110	158
	93	124	97	89	53	55	81	115	108	122	50	36	32	31	21	43	125
	76	115	88	88	51	46	79	106	113	109	30	17	31	37	26	52	134
	152	180	152	145	108	110	136	171	125	160	83	94	88	90	77	20	94
	172	189	162	138	95	125	111	180	23	192	133	128	92	68	79	118	61
	220	216	187	177	132	158	152	178	55	230	170	153	117	77	81	97	50
	52	101	74	95	62	29	90	92	131	89	10	7	42	57	45	68	153
	31	62	53	115	105	58	132	65	177	25	58	79	87	116	102	120	216
	59	62	49	24	44	48	63	62	135	99	81	86	52	92	72	122	186
	31	40	13	59	67	35	93	32	149	64	64	78	57	89	77	122	191
	112	140	113	105	69	71	97	131	111	136	55	54	49	50	37	23	113
	183	203	176	163	123	139	141	194	73	206	130	130	106	99	87	75	28
	57	39	66	125	131	85	157	48	210	18	99	123	118	149	138	158	252

Southeast Mileage

	Katy	Kingwood	La Marque	La Porte	Lk. Jackson	League Cl.	Liberty	Livingston	Lufkin	Madisonvl.	Magnolia	Manvel	Missouri Cl.	Mt. Belvieu	Montgo...
Alvin	49	49	18	24	32	13	60	97	144	122	66	8	25	41	77
Anahuac	76	60	56	34	89	47	25	75	121	130	87	63	63	20	93
Bay City	70	101	75	83	38	72	119	149	196	153	106	62	64	100	11
Baytown	55	41	30	8	63	22	29	78	125	116	65	38	38	10	75
Beaumont	112	78	93	71	126	85	43	74	107	139	111	101	100	57	10
Bellville	34	74	98	85	92	86	97	113	151	80	39	74	60	91	55
Channelview	44	31	37	17	62	24	32	77	123	108	54	33	31	16	65
Cleveland	70	25	80	58	97	67	32	28	75	72	47	67	60	40	39
Coldspring	87	43	97	75	115	84	50	27	74	59	57	85	78	59	4
Columbus	44	93	106	96	94	97	112	141	179	107	67	81	67	103	83
Conroe	54	27	77	63	92	65	54	51	97	57	24	63	53	57	16
Crosby	49	26	44	21	73	35	20	65	112	101	57	43	38	14	60
Cypress	26	36	70	53	79	56	67	86	133	98	24	50	33	58	35
Deer Park	45	35	29	8	56	17	39	83	129	112	57	28	27	22	68
Diboll	132	88	142	120	160	129	85	35	12	90	109	130	123	103	98
Dickinson	57	51	9	16	43	4	52	99	145	125	70	20	35	33	81
Eagle Lake	40	89	92	93	76	82	110	139	196	111	87	66	53	103	98
Edna	87	123	118	117	81	115	140	171	217	167	121	97	84	129	13
El Campo	60	95	95	90	66	88	112	143	190	141	94	70	57	101	10
Freeport	75	82	44	62	9	51	97	130	177	154	98	42	51	78	10
Friendswood	50	45	20	19	40	8	52	93	139	118	62	16	24	35	73
Fulshear	15	58	65	56	65	56	75	106	153	97	49	40	26	65	65
Galveston	78	72	14	35	51	25	71	119	165	146	90	37	55	51	10
Ganado	78	114	113	109	77	106	131	162	208	158	112	88	75	120	12
Groves	119	93	99	76	131	90	58	91	124	156	125	106	106	63	12
Hallettsville	76	125	128	122	116	120	143	173	212	140	105	103	89	132	12
Hempstead	33	60	87	74	98	75	83	98	135	64	23	72	54	79	39
Hockley	19	46	80	63	89	66	78	96	143	103	18	60	43	68	38
Houston	29	25	36	23	51	24	43	73	120	97	42	22	14	32	53
Huffman	57	16	59	30	88	46	18	66	112	99	50	59	54	23	55
Humble	44	7	54	36	71	41	29	55	101	86	39	41	34	33	44
Huntsville	84	57	106	92	121	94	77	43	72	28	47	92	82	86	31
Jasper	158	113	158	135	185	149	98	60	55	131	135	155	148	118	12
Katy		50	65	52	69	53	69	98	144	97	46	42	27	59	57
Kingwood	50		60	42	77	47	36	53	99	84	44	47	40	39	43
La Marque	65	60		24	39	13	60	108	154	133	77	26	43	40	88
La Porte	52	42	24		56	15	37	86	132	119	64	31	34	18	75
Lake Jackson	69	77	39	56		45	92	125	171	148	93	36	45	72	10
League City	53	47	13	15	45		51	95	141	121	66	21	31	31	76
Liberty	69	36	60	37	92	51		50	96	104	68	62	57	20	69
Livingston	98	53	108	86	125	95	50		47	71	74	95	88	69	66
Lufkin	144	99	154	132	171	141	96	47		84	119	142	134	115	103
Madisonville	97	84	133	119	148	121	104	71	84		59	119	107	113	51
Magnolia	46	44	77	64	93	66	68	74	119	59		64	49	68	16
Manvel	42	47	26	31	36	21	62	95	142	119	64		18	47	75
Missouri City	27	40	43	34	45	31	57	88	134	107	49	18		46	60
Mont Belvieu	59	39	40	18	72	31	20	69	115	113	68	47	46		73
Montgomery	57	43	88	75	104	76	69	66	103	51	16	75	60	73	
Navasota	54	69	105	91	119	93	95	86	115	44	27	91	75	95	26
New Ulm	46	81	81	82	39	74	103	131	178	153	88	56	45	94	11
Newgulf	46	81	80	82	39	74	103	131	178	152	88	56	45	94	11
Orange	135	103	115	93	148	106	67	97	120	162	135	122	122	79	12
Palacios	95	130	101	112	64	101	147	178	225	176	129	90	92	128	14
Pasadena	40	33	28	13	53	15	41	81	127	108	53	23	23	27	64
Pearland	44	40	26	21	42	14	52	88	134	112	57	10	18	37	68
Port Arthur	118	94	98	75	130	89	58	92	124	157	126	105	105	62	12
Porter	53	6	66	45	79	52	37	48	94	80	46	49	46	49	38
Richmond	22	53	53	48	53	45	70	101	147	114	56	28	14	59	67
Rosharon	46	54	33	40	23	29	71	102	148	125	70	15	22	56	80
Sam Rayburn	177	131	193	157	204	180	125	77	57	147	153	174	171	142	154
San Felipe	22	71	92	79	102	79	92	121	167	93	69	72	52	83	79
Sealy	22	71	92	79	102	79	92	121	167	128	69	72	52	84	80
Silsbee	119	85	110	87	142	101	51	58	91	145	107	113	108	71	99
Simonton	18	63	70	60	66	61	80	111	157	98	51	45	31	69	66
Sour Lake	99	66	83	63	118	76	31	57	100	119	93	92	88	49	85
Spring	39	18	60	45	75	48	42	66	113	74	28	46	38	45	32
Sugar Land	22	45	47	40	49	37	62	93	139	107	48	22	6	51	60
Texas City	69	62	5	24	44	16	60	108	155	137	81	31	47	40	92
The Woodlands	46	27	68	54	84	56	50	64	111	70	26	54	45	54	28
Tomball	36	32	66	53	82	54	55	74	120	71	13	53	38	56	24
Trinity	101	75	123	110	139	111	84	34	52	45	67	110	100	96	51
Vidor	118	85	100	77	132	91	49	80	112	145	117	107	106	64	111
Village Mills	147	80	141	105	170	127	59	54	71	125	161	140	136	88	94
Waller	29	50	77	64	89	65	74	92	139	73	21	62	45	70	37
Weimar	58	108	121	110	109	111	127	156	192	121	82	95	82	117	79
West Columbia	54	78	51	60	18	49	95	126	172	144	90	38	46	76	102
Wharton	47	82	82	77	53	75	100	130	177	128	81	57	44	89	96
Willis	62	35	84	70	100	72	59	53	91	50	31	70	61	65	16
Woodville	130	85	130	108	157	121	71	32	51	103	107	128	120	90	99
Yoakum	94	143	146	140	120	138	161	191	230	158	123	121	107	150	138

Southeast Mileage

...sota	New Ulm	Newgulf	Orange	Palacios	Pasadena	Pearland	Pt. Arthur	Porter	Richmond	Rosharon	Sam Rayburn	San Felipe	Sealy	Silsbee	Simonton	Sour Lk.
4	106	65	116	88	21	10	98	59	35	16	185	81	82	110	52	86
14	125	110	68	144	44	54	50	66	77	73	132	100	100	63	87	40
1	84	26	175	29	80	69	157	112	51	48	190	65	62	169	56	145
3	103	88	85	119	18	28	67	44	52	47	150	78	78	79	64	55
32	161	146	24	182	81	91	17	80	113	110	87	136	136	21	123	20
7	18	63	164	98	74	77	150	88	46	78	212	19	146	33	128	60
2	91	76	92	118	12	23	74	32	44	45	156	66	66	82	54	62
5	118	103	90	150	53	60	84	20	73	74	108	93	93	60	83	47
5	135	121	108	168	71	77	103	37	91	92	107	110	110	70	101	65
4	16	65	179	75	84	85	161	98	53	84	222	29	163	40	143	82
2	92	95	113	141	52	56	107	23	63	69	131	84	85	83	68	70
5	99	84	87	128	21	33	76	27	51	52	160	73	73	71	61	51
5	65	68	137	120	41	47	125	40	36	58	165	48	48	130	42	97
4	96	75	97	112	7	18	79	37	41	40	164	71	71	90	53	67
1	181	166	122	213	116	122	117	83	136	137	68	155	156	83	146	91
7	109	79	108	99	19	18	90	57	47	28	185	84	84	102	64	78
9	28	46	191	69	80	70	179	92	37	75	279	22	19	184	24	142
25	85	61	205	42	107	101	188	131	70	89	250	83	80	190	71	170
9	56	31	178	36	79	74	160	100	42	62	230	53	50	163	43	143
25	134	46	153	69	59	47	136	86	59	29	211	109	109	148	72	123
0	104	67	110	96	13	6	93	53	38	24	185	79	79	103	54	80
4	45	40	141	84	44	44	123	54	18	44	188	20	20	126	5	106
18	128	91	126	113	41	39	109	76	65	45	204	103	103	121	82	96
16	74	50	196	38	98	92	179	121	61	80	220	73	71	181	62	161
48	174	162	17	187	87	96	5	99	119	115	106	152	152	38	129	37
7	58	85	208	87	112	107	191	137	75	106	261	61	193	62	173	115
1	41	96	150	113	62	66	139	64	51	75	195	28	29	130	35	114
6	55	78	147	130	51	57	135	50	46	68	175	40	41	140	34	108
9	76	57	108	105	12	15	90	27	28	29	150	51	51	93	38	73
7	103	88	87	141	32	43	78	19	63	67	144	78	78	80	73	49
6	91	77	96	124	27	34	88	8	47	48	133	78	66	80	57	60
3	90	125	135	170	81	85	130	53	92	98	120	115	115	101	97	92
47	208	193	65	238	139	148	77	110	161	162	17	182	183	51	171	74
4	47	46	135	95	40	44	118	53	22	46	177	22	22	119	18	99
9	96	81	103	130	33	40	94	6	53	54	131	71	71	85	63	66
05	117	81	115	101	28	26	98	66	53	33	193	92	92	110	70	85
1	104	82	93	112	13	21	75	45	48	40	157	79	79	87	60	63
19	127	39	148	64	53	42	130	79	53	23	204	102	102	142	66	118
3	104	74	106	101	15	14	89	52	45	29	180	79	79	101	61	76
5	118	103	67	147	41	52	58	37	70	71	125	92	92	51	80	31
36	146	131	97	178	81	88	92	48	101	102	77	121	121	58	111	57
15	192	178	120	225	127	134	124	94	147	148	57	167	167	91	157	100
4	90	153	162	176	108	112	157	81	114	125	148	93	128	98	119	74
27	64	88	135	129	53	57	126	46	56	70	153	69	69	107	51	93
1	97	56	122	90	23	10	105	49	28	15	174	72	72	113	45	92
5	77	45	122	92	23	18	105	46	14	22	171	52	52	108	31	88
5	109	94	79	128	27	37	62	49	59	56	142	83	84	71	69	49
26	74	110	129	145	64	68	123	38	67	80	154	79	80	99	66	85
	47	113	155	134	80	84	149	83	73	97	162	50	125	56	111	55
13		72	172	55	69	61	161	84	30	38	210	52	50	166	41	133
13	72		172	55	69	61	161	84	30	38	210	52	50	166	41	133
55	187	172		203	103	113	19	106	136	132	83	162	162	39	146	43
34	92	55	203		109	98	186	136	78	76	230	89	86	198	79	173
30	91	69	103	109		13	85	36	37	36	166	66	66	91	49	71
84	94	61	113	98	13		95	43	33	23	177	69	69	103	49	83
49	175	161	19	186	85	95		116	118	114	105	150	151	38	128	38
63	99	84	106	136	36	43	116		59	58	126	74	74	99	68	67
73	66	30	136	78	37	33	118	59		32	184	41	41	121	20	101
97	106	38	132	76	36	23	114	58	32		183	80	81	122	49	102
62	223	210	83	230	166	177	105	126	184	183		199	200	67	193	94
50	25	52	162	89	66	69	150	74	41	80	199		3	155	20	123
25	22	50	162	86	66	69	151	74	41	81	200	3		156	21	123
75	180	166	39	198	91	103	38	99	121	122	67	155	156		131	25
56	43	41	146	79	49	49	128	68	20	49	193	20	21	131		111
11	148	133	43	173	71	83	38	68	101	102	94	123	123	25	111	
55	94	80	108	125	34	39	100	20	47	52	145	69	70	92	52	72
73	68	38	127	86	29	24	110	49	8	26	174	43	43	113	25	93
09	119	89	115	106	31	30	98	67	58	38	179	94	94	110	75	85
54	100	85	117	132	43	47	109	27	55	61	152	75	75	97	60	81
40	69	78	122	123	42	46	113	33	46	59	158	58	59	106	50	86
63	159	144	131	188	99	103	126	72	110	116	113	134	134	92	115	91
37	169	154	18	188	88	97	24	88	119	116	77	143	144	24	130	26
0	194	178	60	217	112	124	53	74	153	148	66	168	169	20	163	28
31	50	84	141	109	53	56	130	53	47	66	184	34	34	124	30	104
77	32	86	193	89	99	100	176	112	67	99	236	43	178	54	158	97
02	84	22	151	52	56	45	134	83	36	24	207	65	62	145	49	121
86	57	15	165	49	66	61	147	85	29	49	210	38	35	150	31	130
42	118	104	117	148	59	63	112	32	71	77	140	93	94	87	76	74
19	179	164	79	210	111	120	74	81	133	134	45	154	154	40	143	49
15	76	103	226	81	130	125	209	156	93	124	280	79	211	80	191	133

SOUTH EAST

Southeast Mileage

	Spring	Sugar Land	Texas Ci.	The Woodlands	Tomball	Trinity	Vidor	Village Mills	Waller	Weimar	W. Columbia	Wharton	Willis	Woodville	Yoak
Alvin	49	29	23	57	55	112	100	137	66	102	35	64	73	130	12
Anahuac	65	68	56	74	75	109	53	80	88	134	92	106	84	88	16
Bay City	98	59	80	106	96	161	160	217	86	83	24	25	122	182	82
Baytown	45	44	30	54	54	106	70	97	67	113	66	82	67	100	14
Beaumont	84	105	94	93	98	108	7	35	117	170	129	142	94	56	20
Bellville	54	102	66	45	99	146	157	25	43	75	49	70	146	84	86
Channelview	34	36	38	43	43	99	77	103	56	102	66	74	59	102	13
Cleveland	38	65	80	37	46	56	72	55	65	128	98	102	27	61	16
Coldspring	51	83	98	47	56	37	91	60	75	138	115	120	26	60	17
Columbus	61	111	90	73	127	162	167	53	15	77	43	98	174	56	60
Conroe	18	56	80	14	23	48	95	78	42	106	93	93	9	83	14
Crosby	32	43	44	41	45	91	69	79	59	108	76	80	52	90	14
Cypress	25	33	72	30	14	89	118	143	16	86	76	68	49	120	13
Deer Park	38	33	29	47	46	102	81	111	57	103	60	71	63	110	134
Diboll	101	128	143	99	108	48	105	64	127	189	160	165	83	43	226
Dickinson	52	41	12	60	59	116	93	132	69	115	47	76	76	123	140
Eagle Lake	87	45	97	93	76	152	172	197	52	31	59	31	112	183	57
Edna	117	78	123	124	115	180	189	216	101	62	67	40	140	203	39
El Campo	90	51	100	97	88	152	162	187	74	53	49	13	113	176	66
Freeport	81	55	49	89	88	145	138	177	95	115	24	59	105	163	12
Friendswood	45	30	24	53	51	108	95	132	62	105	44	67	69	123	131
Fulshear	48	20	70	55	46	110	125	158	29	58	48	35	71	139	85
Galveston	73	59	14	81	79	136	111	152	90	132	63	93	97	141	15
Ganado	108	69	118	115	106	171	180	178	92	65	62	32	131	194	48
Groves	99	111	99	108	113	125	23	55	131	177	135	149	111	73	21
Hallettsville	83	133	122	109	160	192	207	89	25	99	64	136	206	18	19
Hempstead	44	52	91	50	30	83	133	170	10	58	81	64	55	130	99
Hockley	30	43	82	36	17	94	128	153	7	79	86	78	54	130	123
Houston	24	19	39	32	31	88	92	117	42	87	52	57	49	106	118
Huffman	24	54	61	31	37	90	68	77	57	116	92	89	50	99	149
Humble	13	39	57	21	26	77	79	81	45	102	72	77	37	87	138
Huntsville	47	85	110	43	52	20	118	97	68	120	122	122	23	75	158
Jasper	126	153	158	125	134	94	61	50	153	216	186	191	113	28	252
Katy	39	22	69	46	36	101	118	147	29	58	54	47	62	130	94
Kingwood	18	45	62	27	32	75	85	80	50	108	78	82	35	85	143
La Marque	60	47	5	68	66	123	100	141	77	121	51	82	84	130	146
La Porte	45	40	24	54	53	110	77	105	64	110	60	77	70	108	140
Lake Jackson	75	49	44	84	82	139	132	170	89	109	18	53	100	157	120
League City	48	37	16	56	54	111	91	127	65	111	49	75	72	121	138
Liberty	42	62	60	50	55	84	49	59	74	127	95	100	59	71	161
Livingston	66	93	108	64	74	34	80	54	92	156	126	130	53	32	191
Lufkin	113	139	155	111	120	52	112	71	139	192	172	177	91	51	230
Madisonville	107	137	70	71	45	145	187	73	121	144	128	50	103	158	158
Magnolia	28	48	81	26	13	67	117	161	21	82	90	81	31	107	123
Manvel	46	22	31	54	53	110	107	140	62	95	38	57	70	128	121
Missouri City	38	6	47	45	38	100	106	136	45	82	46	44	61	120	107
Mont Belvieu	45	51	40	54	56	96	64	88	70	117	76	89	65	90	150
Montgomery	32	60	92	28	24	51	111	94	37	97	102	96	16	99	138
Navasota	73	109	54	40	63	137	164	31	77	102	86	42	119	115	115
New Ulm	80	38	89	85	78	144	154	178	84	86	22	15	104	164	103
Newgulf	80	38	89	85	78	144	154	179	84	79	22	15	104	164	103
Orange	108	127	115	117	122	131	18	60	141	193	151	165	117	79	226
Palacios	125	86	106	132	123	188	188	217	109	89	52	49	148	210	81
Pasadena	34	29	31	43	42	99	88	113	53	99	56	66	59	111	130
Pearland	39	24	30	47	46	103	97	124	56	100	45	61	63	120	125
Port Arthur	100	110	98	109	113	126	24	53	130	176	134	147	112	74	209
Porter	20	49	67	27	33	72	88	74	53	112	83	85	32	81	156
Richmond	47	8	58	55	46	110	119	153	47	67	36	29	71	133	93
Rosharon	52	26	38	61	59	116	116	148	66	99	24	49	77	134	124
Sam Rayburn	145	174	179	152	158	113	77	66	184	236	207	210	140	45	279
San Felipe	69	43	94	75	58	134	143	168	34	43	65	38	93	154	79
Sealy	70	43	94	75	59	134	144	169	34	178	62	35	94	154	211
Silsbee	92	113	110	97	106	92	24	20	124	54	145	150	87	40	237
Simonton	52	25	75	60	50	115	130	163	30	158	49	31	76	143	80
Sour Lake	72	93	85	81	86	91	26	28	104	97	121	130	74	49	191
Spring		40	63	9	15	65	91	138	35	75	76	77	25	99	133
Sugar Land	40		52	47	38	103	111	143	42	125	43	38	63	125	101
Texas City	63	52		72	70	127	100	126	81	104	56	87	88	130	151
The Woodlands	9	47	72		22	61	99	144	42	88	84	84	22	97	140
Tomball	15	38	70	22		70	104	149	20	140	80	75	31	106	127
Trinity	65	103	127	61	70		114	89	88	176	140	140	39	66	178
Vidor	91	111	100	99	104	114		41	123	182	136	149	100	62	210
Village Mills	138	143	126	144	149	89	41		159	68	173	179	117	21	251
Waller	35	42	81	42	20	88	123	159		76	61	49	125	107	116
Weimar	75	125	104	88	140	176	182	68	76		58	64	132	193	43
West Columbia	76	43	56	84	80	140	136	173	76	58		36	100	158	106
Wharton	77	38	87	84	75	140	149	179	61	113	36		100	163	79
Willis	25	63	88	22	31	39	100	117	49	188	100	100		86	154
Woodville	99	125	130	97	106	66	62	21	125	193	158	163	86		224
Yoakum	101	151	140	127	178	210	225	251	116	43	106	79	154	224	

SOUTHEAST TEXAS
REGIONAL WEATHER

	Average Precipitation	Average Temperature (F)
January	3.29	50.4
February	2.96	53.9
March	2.92	60.6
April	3.21	68.3
May	5.24	74.5
June	4.96	80.4
July	3.6	82.6
August	3.49	82.3
September	4.89	78.2
October	4.27	69.6
November	3.79	61
December	3.45	53.5

ALVIN
Elev. 51   Pop. 20,797

Famous Texan Nolan Ryan's hometown sits among the rice fields and chemical plants southeast of Houston's metropolitan area and next door to NASA. The town sprouted in the 1870s when the railroad pushed through, and was burdened by catastrophe in the coming years as yellow fever, a disastrous fire, and two major hurricanes bombarded its residents. The beaches of Galveston are just down Hwy. 6, making Alvin a viable option for a quick 9-hole break on your way to the coast.

ALVIN GOLF & COUNTRY CLUB

The golf   Alvin's 1950s-style country club is built along the edge of Mustang Bayou. It features a short, flat track with wide-open fairways that you can play all day for one fee. The clubhouse, a former army barracks, was updated in the early 1990s, and the course was improved to bring it up to par with surrounding facilities.

Holes 5 and 6 stand out in the middle of the round. No. 5 is a par 4 that plays 425 yards, so average hacks will be faced with a long approach into the green. No. 6 is also tough because of the approach, since the green on No. 6 is fronted by two bunkers.

Other notes: The course is easy to walk, but the club allows it only on weekdays.

The details   281-331-4541. County Rd. 539, Alvin, TX 77512

- 1950s. 9 holes. Par 35. Back – 3,020 (34.9/117). Middle – 2,898 (34.2/114). Forward – 2,563 (34.5/112). Price - $.

Getting there From Hwy. 6 south, find County Rd. 146 and go north. Drive 2 blocks to County Rd. 539 and turn right. The road will dead-end at the course.

HILLCREST COUNTRY CLUB

The golf   Alvin's second country club opened in the 1960s, built by a man named Shorty Plaster who wanted to make the most of his land investment. Shorty was a hacker and his short course is designed to accommodate the lesser golfer with its executive-like 2,385-yard length.

Plaster's design opens up with three par 3s, followed by another on No. 5. Every par 4 plays 350 yards or less, and the sole par 5 is only 475 yards. Not many non-par-3 9-holers are blessed with lights, but this one is. The same goes for the driving range, so you can definitely spend some hours at this nice little country course.

The details   281-331-3505. 3401 Fairway Dr., Alvin, TX 77511

- 1960s. 9 holes. Par 33. Back – 2,385. Forward – 2,168. Price - $.

SOUTH EAST

Don't get into the habit of playing "winter rules." If you do, you'll never learn to play the shots you need to be a decent golfer. Winter rules are generally an amusing delusion. They aid neither in the development of the turf nor of the player. Tommy Armour

Getting there From I-45 south, exit Dixie Farm Rd. and turn right. Drive 8 miles to where it dead-ends, then turn on Hwy. 35. Drive 8 miles to Fairway Dr. and turn left.

ALVIN NOTES See if you run into Nolan Ryan at his favorite local hangout, **Joe's Barbecue** (281-331-9626) on Hwy. 6, where his cattle are cooked by owner Joe Saladino old-fashioned style. Joe starts every morning at 3 am., cooking away in four 15-foot-long pits and feeding 1,000 people daily.

ANAHUAC
Elev. 24   Pop. 2,011

The "Alligator Capital of Texas" is a weathered town that rests at the northeastern tip of Galveston Bay, due east of Houston and just south of I-10. Dating back to 1830 when Mexico established Fort Anahuac, the town became a prickly point of contention between colonists and the Mexican government. William Barret Travis was jailed here and Texans eventually drafted the Turtle Bayou Resolutions, considered a forerunner to their final declaration of independence. Today you can take in that history by camping at the remains of the old fort and touring the Chambers County Museum, two Texas road trip activities that go well with a round at the challenging Chambers County Golf Course.

CHAMBERS COUNTY GOLF COURSE

The golf Towns of 2,000 residents tend to offer the ultimate in confidence-building golf, which is definitely the case here at Chambers County. Most of those courses are only 9-holers, however. This 1960s-style track, built by county engineer R.T. Pinchback, boasts the full 18, which lays out over 180 acres of heavily wooded wetlands on the east side of Galveston Bay.

Pinchback's design is mostly open, although there are a few holes with narrow, tree-lined fairways. Bunkering is minimal, and the rough is manageable if you miss the fairway. Water comes into play on over half the holes.

Two holes stand out on each side. No. 6 is the most beautiful: a 428-yard tester that requires two shots over water before reaching the green. No. 18 features one of those narrow fairways, tight at only 25 yards and intimidating because it's generally into the wind. The hole bends and you'll need a 250-yard drive to reach the corner.

The details 409-267-8235. 1 Pinchback Dr., Anahuac, TX 77514

- 18 holes. Par 72. Back – 6,793 (71.8/116). Middle – 6,270 (69.5/111). Forward – Par 73 5,014 (67.7/110). Price - $$.

Getting there Take I-10 east from Houston and exit 812. Turn right, and the course is on the left down the road.

SOUTHEAST

The harder I practice, the luckier I get. Gary Player

ANAHUAC NOTES   The course does not serve beer, so stop at **DJ's Exxon** for provisions and barbecue to-go, which is more than adequate. The course allows you to bring your own beer. **RG's** also comes highly recommended for good local barbecue. The Tex-Mex option is off the Wallaceville exit, where you'll find the green-bluish building that houses **Fino's**. The one bar where you can wet your whistle down here is called the **Frontier Bar**. No lodging here, so head to the new hotel-motel in nearby Mont Belvieu, TX called the **Crystal Inn**.

BAY CITY Elev. 55   Pop. 18,386

A sleepy little town away from the big city of Houston (90 miles southwest), Bay City has an open, clean, prosperous feel. The rice lands have proved lucrative, as have the railroads, oil, and eventually the petrochemical industry. Named for its location on Bay Prairie, the town is the nation's leading rice producer thanks to the productive bottomlands of the Colorado River, which also frequently flooded the community until levees were installed in the 1920s.

The highlight of Bay City is the 1993 Gary Player design known as Rio Colorado, but the sport became popular during the 1930s with the opening of the Bay City CC, followed decades later by the company owned Bay-Cel G.C. opened by the Celanese Corporation.

BAY-CEL GOLF COURSE

The golf   Bay-Cel is a company-owned facility that offers 9 holes along the Colorado River.

The details   979-241-4243. FM 3057, Bay City, TX 77404

• 9 holes. Par 35. 3,200 yards. Price - $$.

Getting there Located southwest of Houston on Celanese Rd. off Hwy. 35.

BAY CITY COUNTRY CLUB

The golf   Bay City's original course dates back to the 1930s–it lays out along the Colorado River with giant old oak trees lining the fairways. In addition to the river, another creek winds through the layout, keeping water in play on just about every hole.

No. 6 is considered the signature not only for the stunning view of the countryside, but for its 185-yard poke over the water. The ender is tough as well,

There are many players in hot pursuit of the perfect putting stroke.
The more putts they miss, the more convinced they become that their stroke is to blame.
The more information they get about the stroke, the more lost they become in thoughts
of mechanics. The more lost they become, the worse they putt. Dr. Bob Rotella

featuring trees along the left, the river on the right, and that pesky creek that fronts the green.

Other notes: A tenth hole was added after the river temporarily swallowed No. 8. Walking is only allowed during the week.

The details   979-245-3990. Hwy. 35, Bay City, TX 77404

- 9 holes. Par 36. Back – 3,215 (35.4/117). Middle – 3,045 (34.4/115). Forward – 2,571 (34.9/122). Price - $.

Getting there From Hwy. 35, turn left on Latuelley, and the course is about a mile away.

RIO COLORADO GOLF COURSE

The golf   Designed by the Gary Player Design Company in 1993, Rio Colorado is a scenic course overlooking the Colorado River. The course is the result of Jim Hardy's vision–he pushed hard to create a facility that would rival any of the top layouts in Houston, yet be available to the public for a fraction of the cost. Almost 3 million dollars went into the clubhouse and the course is immaculate–well worth the drive to Bay City for those who are interested in adding this track to their golf resumes.

The most striking design aspect is the difference between the two nines. The front nine is more of a links-style route, wide open and susceptible to the coastal winds, while the back nine is carved out of the trees, with holes 13-17 rolling along the river.

No. 14 is one of the best holes, playing 322 yards doglegging 150 feet above the river. A 250-yard drive will cut the dogleg and carry across the river for an ideal birdie position.

Hole 18 is one demanding ender–playing 474 yards, it's not a welcome sight at the end of a long, hot summer day.

Other notes: Call ahead to ensure there isn't a tournament; otherwise, it's generally easy to walk on the course. The city park next to the course offers camping and fishing on the Colorado River. Watch the wetlands on the course, as alligators inhabit the swampy terrain. Supposedly there are two nudist colonies around Boling, so watch out if you're taking the back roads.

The details   979-244-2955. FM 2668, Bay City, TX 77404

- 1993. Gary Player. 18 holes. Par 72. Back – 6,835 (73.1/127). Middle – 6,258 (70.4/118). Forward – Par 71. 5,020 (69.1/116). Price - $$.

Getting there From Hwy. 60 west, travel through Bay City and then turn right on FM 2668. The course is on the right side.

BAY CITY NOTES   Only two roads in Matagorda County reach the Gulf of Mexico, and one of those is FM 2031, which disappears into the Gulf on an

To break 90, mentally remove every pin and instead concentrate on hitting greens. Take dead aim at the center of each green. Do this from every distance outside 50 yards. Jim McLean

isolated beach. In nearby Ashwood, TX, find the 1907 plantation-style **Caney House** (979-429-1973) surrounded by majestic pecans on the bank of Caney Creek. Road-trippers needing a place to crash cheaply can look to the **Cattlemen's Motel** (979-245-1751) or the always-reliable **South Texas Inn** (979-244-1432).

BAYTOWN
Elev. 20   Pop. 68,588

A town of massive industry, Baytown started up in 1822 with the Lynchburg Ferry and became a Confederate shipyard on the mouth of Goose Creek in 1864. With oil booming the economy, refineries and petrochemicals have given the community a unique new look. The great game here dates back to the 1920s, when the Goose Creek CC was opened by the Humble Oil Company. The traveler will have to hustle to work onto this old course, but there's golf to be had at the relatively new Evergreen Point course.

EVERGREEN POINT GOLF COURSE

The golf   Like most of the courses down this way, the sea-level elevation creates terrain that is loaded with water. Evergreen is no exception–several lakes and streams meander through this tree-lined course, creating water hazards on 15 holes.

This well-manicured design also features large, bunkered greens that are surrounded by magnolias, pines, and dogwoods.

The best hole is No. 3, a long, 462-yard par 4 that requires a long approach through tall magnolias into an elevated green.

The details   281-837-9000. 1530 Evergreen Rd., Baytown, TX 77520

- 1996. Dave Marr. 18 holes. Par 72. Champs – 6,969 (73.0/129). Regular – 6,389 (70.0/124). Senior – 5,955 (68.6.120). Forward – 5,348 (72.2/130). Price - $$$.

Getting there From the Houston Inter-Continental Airport, take Beltway 8 south to Beltway 225 east. Take Beltway 146 over the bridge (stay in the right lane). Next, take the Business 146 exit. Drive 2.5 miles and turn right on Spur 55. Take the first right and this will lead to the course.

GOOSE CREEK COUNTRY CLUB

The golf   Goose Creek was Baytown's first country club, organized in 1923 for employees of the Humble Oil Company. The course is known for its strange combination of holes, highlighted by five par 3s and five par 5s. The design rolls through a rice field with Goose Creek dominating the last five

Do you ever permit your fear of three-putting to dominate your love of one-putting ? Strive to have the love of one-putting be your stronger passion. Dr. Bob Rotella

holes of the water-infested front nine.

Holes of note on the front are No. 2, which forces a carry of water of the tee, and the long, 457-yard No. 4.

The back nine is more open, and also features a good amount of water. No. 17 is the most difficult with water lining the entire left side of the fairway.

The details   281-424-5565. 5000 Country Club, Baytown, TX 77521

- 18 holes. Par 72. Back – 6,500 (70.4/118). Middle – 6,111 (68.4/114). Forward – Par 73. 5,478 (70.7/124). Price - $$$.

Getting there From I-10 east, exit Garth Rd. and turn left. When you come to Baker, turn right and drive to Country Club Dr. Turn left and continue to the dead end. Turn right on Country Club View, then head to Muskogee Dr. and look for the parking lot.

BAYTOWN NOTES   The **Boardwalk Grill** (832-556-0486) is one you'll want to hit when touring this area after golf. Quick lunch can be had at **Bud's Barbeque** (281-422-5715). **O'Shays Tavern & Grill** (281-421-0571) is another good option. No eclectic lodging options, so you might as well go with one of the many new hotel/motels–be sure to call around and pit them against each other in a bidding war to obtain the best price. Try the **Best Western** (281-421-2233) or the **Holiday Inn Express** (281-421-7200). The oldest operating ferry in Texas is the 1824 **Lynchburg Ferry**, which still shuttles explorers across the San Jacinto River to see the **Battleship Texas** and the famous battlegrounds. Finally, the shores of **Goose Creek Stream** have been preserved for a greenbelt park that's a great place to exercise, bike, canoe, and play around.

BEAUMONT
Elev. 24 Pop. 109,841

You'll pass through lush, almost jungle-like Beaumont driving east from Houston on the way to Louisiana. The city dates back to the 1820s when trappers made use of the neighboring Big Thicket. It eventually became a center of commerce on the Neches River, with lumber and rice becoming prominent economic players. In 1901 the Spindletop Oilfield brought chaos, wealth, and 95% of Texas' oil production, yet today's metropolitan flavor didn't come about until three major oil refineries sprang up.

Despite the industry, Beaumont's flower-garden-like scenery is ideal for great-looking golf courses. In fact the town was one of the first in Texas to promote the game (the Beaumont CC dates from 1906), and today the community is loaded with five golf facilities.

Ranch hands of the Lazy C Ranch in Richmond, TX, divided
one acre of the property into 3,136,320 two-square-inch tracts to sell as
ranchettes. The ranch eventually became the site of the Old Orchard Golf Club.

SOUTH EAST

BAYOU DIN GOLF CLUB

The golf   Named after the Turkey Bayou that comes into play on a few holes, the original 18 opened for play in the late 1950s, and the club added an additional nine holes (the Links) in 1993.

All three nines are different, offering a good combination of traditional golf over wooded terrain and plenty of links-style golf with rolling hills and tall grasses. The original **Bayou Course** has tree-lined fairways and small greens, while the newer **Links Course** features more water (7 holes), the only bunkers of the entire 27 holes, and more elevated greens.

The best hole on the Links is No. 7, a long 585-yarder that plays like a par 6 into the wind. No. 12 on the Bayou is a 322-yard par 4 that's notable for its island green.

The details   409-796-1327. 8537 Labelle Rd., Beaumont, TX 77705

- www.aquilagolf.com
- Jimmy Witcher. 1958. 18 holes. Par 72. Blue – 6,285 (68.5/108). White – 5,836 (66.8/104). Gold – 5,523 (65.3/101). Red – 5,316 (64.4/98). Price - $$.
- Links Course: 1993. Warren Howard. Par 36. Back - 3,618 yards.

Getting there From I-10 east take the 845 exit and turn right on Major Dr. At the second stop sign (Labelle), turn right and you'll see the club.

BEAUMONT COUNTRY CLUB

The golf   Alex Findlay laid the BCC out in 1906, making it one of the oldest clubs in the state. He created what is now a short, old-school layout with narrow, tree-lined fairways and small, immaculately conditioned greens.

Findlay opens the course with some of the easiest holes of the 18, including the 291-yard par 4 No. 1. Another short par 4 and two par 3s follow, allowing the day to start right. Later on the front, the number one handicap 8th hole shows up, playing 520 yards and generally not reachable in two.

The back nine consists of short par 4s and 3s and offers plenty of birdie opportunities.

The details   409-898-7011. 5355 Pine St., Beaumont, TX 77704

- 1906. Alex Findlay. 18 holes. Par 72. Back – 6,414 (70.1/122). Middle – 6,093 (68.6/119). Forward – 5,412 (65.7/111). Price - $$$.

Getting there From I-10 east, take Hwy. 69 north to Lucas, then drive east to Pine St. Turn left and the course is a short distance down the road.

SOUTH EAST

Every golfer should establish his own par on a hole and play for that par. H.H. Ramsay

BELLE OAKS GOLF CLUB

The golf   Ralph Plummer laid out Belle Oaks in 1955, creating one of the longer courses around at the time. This 18-hole course serves up a few extremely long holes.

This scenic course is also very difficult to score well on. Several holes are extremely long, and water hazards come into play on five holes. Both par 3s on the front play over 200 yards, and four of the par 4s reach well into the 400-yard range, including the 461-yard No. 2.

And while the back features a 232-yard par 3, it's not as lengthy as the front. The best hole is No. 18, a 397-yard ender that features water in the landing area all the way to the green.

Although locals have complained about below-average course conditions in recent years, new management has brought the hope of much-needed improvements.

The details   409-796-1312. 15075 Country Club Dr., Beaumont, TX 77705

- 1955. Ralph Plummer. 18 holes. Par 71. Back – 6,755 (71.7/119). Middle – 6,301 (69.5/118). Forward – 5,493 (71.2/125). Price - $$$.

Getting there The course is located on Country Club Rd. halfway between the cities of Winnie and Port Arthur.

BRENTWOOD COUNTRY CLUB

The golf   Brentwood is a 1980s-style course with narrow fairways, loads of out-of-bounds, and water in play on more than half the holes.

Two par 5s stand out on the front: the opening 540-yard eye-opener, and the 517-yard No. 6, considered the toughest hole of the front nine.

On the back, the par 5 530-yard 15th hole is rated as the most difficult.

The details   409-840-9440. 4201 S. Major Dr., Beaumont, TX 77707

- 1984. 18 holes. Par 72. Back – 7,129 (73.8/129). Middle – 6,452 (72.0/123). Forward – 5,425 (70.6/112). Price - $$.

Getting there From I-10 east, take the Walden Rd. exit and turn left. Drive approximately 4 miles and turn left onto Major Dr. The course is .5 mile down the road, and the entrance is on the left side of the street.

HENRY HOMBERG GOLF COURSE

The golf   The Homberg is old-school golf at its finest. This course dates back to the 1930s and is named after the longtime Beaumont Municipal caddie who eventually became the head pro. Built by the Corps of Engineers, it has been Beaumont's most popular golf institution over the decades.

The design features two totally different nines. The front is more open than

From the roaring oceans to the majestic lakes, the rushing streams and quiet ponds and burns,
water adds a test to golf that entrances. Robert Trent Jones

the shorter, skinnier back, and boasts two notable par 4s. No. 4 plays into the wind at 445 yards, while No. 9 is known for its tight driving lane into a dog-leg-right fairway.

The details 409-842-3220. Tyrell Park Rd., Beaumont, TX 77720

- 1930. 18 holes. Par 72. Back – 6,786 (71.8/116). Middle – 6,449 (70.2/113). Forward – Par 73. 5,660 (71.8/117). Price - $$.

Getting there From I-10 east, take the Walden Rd. exit and go south. At the stoplight, Walden turns into Tyrrell Rd. and the course is on the left side.

RABBIT RUN AT BROOKS ROAD

The golf Beaumont's newest course opened in 1995, playing to an executive-like 5,792 yards from the middle tees. The flat fairways are not burdened by trees. Doglegs spice up the route, as do a few water hazards and the occasional bunker, and the course offers a good combination of various-sized greens. In fact, the greens might be the most challenging aspect at Rabbit Run–they feature severe undulations that make for very difficult two-putts.

The details 409-866-7545. Brooks Rd., Beaumont, TX 77720

- 1995. Johnny Barlow. 18 holes. Par 70. Back – 6,258. Middle – 5,792. Forward – Par 71. 4,773. Price - $$.

Getting there Take I-10 west to Houston and exit Brooks Rd. Travel west and cross Major Dr. then a third of a mile on the right is the entrance to the course.

BEAUMONT NOTES The outside deck at the **Tamale Company** (409-866-8033) is a good place for a cold beer, discussing the round, and planning the evening, which you're most likely to spend in the city's new entertainment district. Try the tasty Caribbean sirloin at **Spindletop** (409-833-9688), a noisy restaurant brimming with activity. A nice place to stay is the **Beaumont Holiday Inn Plaza** (409-842-5995). A little cheaper is **La Quinta** (409-842-0002). The best Mexican food in Beaumont is **Acapulco** (409-840-9840). **Sujiyama** (409-840-4414) is the place if Oriental food is what you need.

BELLVILLE   Elev. 220   Pop. 3,983

New Braunfels is known for its German-ness, but Bellville and the surrounding area was Texas' earliest center for intense German immigration in the 1830s. Located about an hour northwest of Houston, Bellville is the seat of one of the original Texas counties (Austin County), and is an ideal weekend destination when you're searching for charming small-town golf. Cattle farms

---

The chief reaction among amateurs to poor putting, it seems to me, is exasperation, combined with a sort of vague hope that, by some kind of mini-miracle, it will all have gotten better by the next time they play. Jack Nicklaus

dot the landscape and bluebonnets take over in the spring. Antique and craft shopping around the square keep the loved ones at bay, and "bed and breakfast accommodations offered in historic buildings" provide affordable, fun lodging.

BELLVILLE GOLF CLUB

The golf   Bellville offers a decent little 9-hole country course with wide-open fairways and small, mound-shaped greens that can be extremely tricky at times, depending on the condition. As with many small-town courses, the funds just are not available to maintain the course up to championship standards, so conditions vary depending on the weather. The trick here is to get used to the target greens and deal with the conditions–otherwise you might miss a few make-able putts. But we do that under the best of conditions, so does it really matter?

One pond comes into play on holes 6 and 7. Despite the greens, the tee boxes and fairways are generally in good condition.

The details   979-865-9058. Hwy. 36 N., Bellville, TX 77418

- 1940s. 9 holes. Par 36. Back – 3,131 (33.3/113). Forward – 2,490 (34.0/113). Price - $.

Getting there From I-10 east, take Hwy. 36 north to the course about 15 miles away.

BELLVILLE NOTES   Bass fishing is included with your stay at the **Bellville Ranch** (866-839-2705), which has restored old homes on its 1,100 acres. After the round, meet the shopping half of the family at the **Lemon Tree Cafe** (979-865-1552), housed in the old Dr Pepper building and popular because of their outstanding sandwiches complemented by thick home-style fries.

BOLING   Elev. 71   Pop. 1,297

The Boling post office has taken over for the former company town of Newgulf, which is now virtually a ghost town since the Texas Gulf Sulphur Company closed its doors. Amazingly, this area about an hour's drive southwest of Houston is as close to a living ghost town as you'll find. 7,000 acres of the old town sit in lonesome silence and there is absolutely nothing going on in these parts anymore. Yet the Newgulf Golf Club still exists, offering the perfect Twilight Zone golf road trip opportunity when you're venturing toward the coast in search of the Gulf and golf.

SOUTH EAST

☆

It is demonstrably more difficult to control a shot with a club of extreme loft than with one of moderate pitch. Therefore, the clubs of extreme loft should be left in the bag until the need for them becomes well defined. Bobby Jones

NEWGULF GOLF CLUB

The golf   Newgulf's 9-holer has two sets of tees to allow for a full day of golf. This traditional course, lined with trees along its generous fairways, features a creak that meanders through the layout as well as small, well-conditioned greens. Most of the holes are basic and offer good birdie opportunities for even the average golfer. A few holes present problems, however–for example, the par 5 No. 5, which plays 535 yards and requires three strokes to get there in regulation. The 391-yard par 4 No. 3 is rated the most difficult on the course.

The details   979-657-4639. Hwy. 131 Ave. J., Boling, TX 77420

- 9 holes. Par 36. Back – 3,091 (33.9/108). Forward – 2,501 (34.0/110). Price - $$.

Getting there From Horden, take FM 1301 south. When you see the sign for Newgulf, turn left and drive 3 miles to the course.

BOLING NOTES   Cruise the ghost town of Newgulf, which now boasts about a tenth of its former self. For a quick bite in Boling try the cafe-like **Mach's** or the small Mexican restaurant called **Amigo's**. Both serve beer, and are very inexpensive and good. **Wharton, TX** is 10 miles away (see Wharton entry) with more after-golf options.

CHANNELVIEW   Elev. 28   Pop. 29,685

Channelview is a blue-collar oil refinery suburb of Houston, named for its location on the northeastern bend of the Houston Ship Channel where the San Jacinto River forms Old River. Located just off I-10 and only minutes from Houston, it's an ideal golf destination because of its convenience and affordability. The eclectic Howard Hughes thought so in the 1940s when he built the original Channelview Golf Course, which has been totally replaced by the new River Terrace course.

RIVER TERRACE GOLF COURSE

The golf   Formerly known as Channelview Golf Course, which was built by Howard Hughes in the late 1940s, Channelview found a new location and built a brand-new course. Known for its immaculate, champion Bermuda greens that lean toward the fast side, the design features seven water holes and is mostly flat.

The details   281-452-2183. 16777 Wallisville Rd., Channelview, TX 77530

- 1999. 18 holes. 6,728 (70.7/118). Price $$.

All swings have one thing in common: whatever the tempo, the speeds of the backswing and downswing are the same. Johnny Miller

Getting there Drive north on Sheldon Rd. to Wallisville Rd. Turn left and drive about 1,000 yards to the course, which is on the right.

CHANNELVIEW NOTES The **Holiday Inn** (281-452-7304), **Best Value** (281-457-3000), and **Scottish Inn** (281-452-0400) round out all of your lodging options. On Sheldon Rd. there's fast food and also Tex-Mex–**Armenta's** and **El Tejano** both serve margaritas and cold beer with limes.

CLEVELAND

Elev. 160   Pop. 7,605

You'll pass through Cleveland on your way to the sticks of the Big Thicket north of Houston. The town was named after Kentucky native Charles Cleveland, who deeded the townsite for a whopping $1. Originally a lumber town dating back to the 1880s, Cleveland flourished after oil discoveries to the south. Nowadays, jaunts north of Houston to the east side of Sam Houston's forest can be accompanied by a quick 9-hole round at the Kirbywood Golf Club.

KIRBYWOOD GOLF CLUB

The golf Labeled as a confidence builder for the struggling hacker, or the perfect course for a beginner, Kirbywood is an affordable 9-hole course that's fun to play because of its excellent condition. Most of the holes are short, although a few play to a more standard length. Its ease makes it popular, so watch out for the summer afternoon rounds when the crowds come out to golf.

The details 281-432-0669. 904 Kirbywood Dr., Cleveland, TX 77327

• 9 holes. Par 36. Back – 2,837. Forward – 2,403. Price - $.

Getting there Take the Houston St. exit off of US 59 and drive east a few miles to Kirbywood. Turn left and it's a short drive to the clubhouse.

CLEVELAND NOTES Call the **Chain-O-Lakes Resort** (713-592-2150) for more information about their restaurant, lodging, and outdoor activities. The Sam Houston National Forest offers the **Lone Star Hiking Trail**, which begins 27 miles northwest of Cleveland on FM 1725. Hiking is the primary sporting interest. Another possible side trip involves taking Texas 105 to the town of Dolen, TX where you'll see the remnants of an old plantation river town, then further east on Texas 146 is Sam Houston's home during his second term of president (known as Grand Cane). For food there's a few Tex-Mex joints and **Hot Biscuit**, which features a buffet.

SOUTH EAST

Many players think the key to power is to swing the club past horizontal at the top of the backswing. Not true. It's much more important to have your right arm in a good position at the top. Butch Harmon

COLDSPRING

Elev. 356   Pop. 707

Sandwiched between the Sam Houston National Forest and Lake Livingston, Coldspring benefits from its outstanding location as a starting point of outdoor excursions, as well as its historic charm. The old Methodist Church here has been restored back to its 1848 splendor, the beautifully columned courthouse stands tall over the city, and visitors can lazily cruise the picturesque Old Town area. Golfers traveling to this town once known as Coonskin will want to know about the 18-hole Cape Royale Golf Course.

CAPE ROYALE GOLF COURSE

The golf   Originally a 9-hole course that opened in 1972, Cape Royal now offers 18 holes of golf over its rugged terrain. Numerous hills provide challenging elevation changes and a few unique holes.

From the tips the course plays to a par 70 6,088 yards, but offers holes of surprising length, especially on the front. This side features three long-iron par 3s and two 400-yard-plus par 4s, including the number one handicap No. 6.

The back side features only one par 5, the 11th hole, which plays 495 yards. The signature hole is the last, a 345-yard doglegger that plays uphill and offers a blind tee shot and a pond just beyond the landing area at the top of the hill.

The details   936-653-2388. Lake Livingston, Coldspring, TX 77331

• 1972. Bruce Litell. 18 holes. Par 70. Back – 6,088 (66.1/113). Middle – 5,628 (64.1/107). Forward – 4,941 (64.7/103). Price - $.

Getting there From I-45 north, exit Willis/1097 and turn right. Drive about 10 miles to Hwy. 150, then turn right and drive another 17 miles to Hwy. 156. Next turn left and head over to FM 224, where you'll make a right and drive 4 miles to the course. The clubhouse is on the right.

COLDSPRING NOTES   Call the **Holiday Shores Marina** (936-377-2696) since they have a waterfront cafe and cabins, and can point you in the right direction for Lake Livingston excursions. The **San Jacinto Inn** offers rooms. **Elaine's** has family-style dining and there's a good barbecue joint on Hwy. 156. On the courthouse square, find the **Coldspring Trading Co.** (936-653-4688) for shopping and general time-killing. Side-trip it deep into the forest and look for pristine **Double Lake** (Forest Rd. 210), and generally cruise through the Sam Houston National Forest for closer inspection of the Big Thicket.

SOUTH EAST

I had a prejudice against the British until I discovered that fifty percent of them were female.
Raymond Floyd

COLUMBUS

Elev. 201   Pop. 3,624

Old, historic Columbus begs Hill Country comparisons with its location along the bends of the Colorado River and the live oaks that shade its handsome homes. Laid out north of I-10 about 70 miles west of Houston, this tiny town slinks back into the shade away from the cars scurrying between San Antonio and Houston. Sam Houston burned the town in 1836 as he was buying time on his way to San Jacinto, and you can see where residents regrouped at the Columbus Court Oak just on the east side of the square.

COLUMBUS GOLF CLUB

The golf   The small town of Columbus offers a simple little 9-hole course that features tree-lined fairways and water on seven holes, as well as the chance to spot the white-tail deer that frequently roam the course.

The design incorporates a good mixture of holes: some play short, but others are of a more standard length. Three of the par 4s play around 300 yards, and the other two are 341 and 376 yards.

The details   979-732-5575. 1617 Walnut St., Columbus, TX 78934

- 1948. 9 holes. Par 36. Back – 2,943 (33.3/117). Forward – 2,617 (33.9/108). Price - $.

Getting there From I-10 driving east, take Hwy. 71 north. When you come to Walnut St., turn left and the course is 1.5 miles away.

COLUMBUS NOTES   Spend your pre- and post-golf hours killing time downtown searching for sidewalk cafes and friendly biergartens. Don't miss the 1883 **Old Water Tower**–interesting because of its architecture but also worthwhile as the home to the **Confederate Memorial Hall Museum**—and the impressive **Brunson Building**, now home to the **Live Oak Art Club**. On the square find **Of the Day/A Café** (979-732-6430) for a light lunch followed by belt-widening desert. If more golf is in order, don't forget that Columbus is sandwiched between the small 9-holers of San Felipe and Weimar on I-10.

CONROE

Elev. 213   Pop. 35,353

Rapidly expanding Conroe still has a lingering feel of the old South, with perfect-looking forestry that provides a peaceful, tranquil setting for commuters and retirees from Houston. Seven miles west of town Lake Conroe provides ample recreation, and the surrounding resort areas offer a wide variety of Montgomery County golf options. In fact some consider the Conroe area one of Texas' golf paradises, with some 300 holes available.

There is only one categorical imperative in golf. And that is to hit the ball. There are no minor absolutes. Sir Walter Simpson

CONROE COUNTRY CLUB

The golf   The Conroe CC is an old, traditional 9-hole course with tree-lined fairways and tiny greens. Majestic oaks and the original two-story frame clubhouse add character to the track, which originally opened as the San Jacinto Country Club back in 1935 to provide recreation for residents who were making good money in the oil business.

You'll notice the two challenging par 3s at CCC. No. 3 plays 179 yards over water to an elevated green, and No. 8 goes 200 yards over water to a small green.

The details   936-756-5222. Loop 336, Conroe, TX 77305

- 1935. 9 holes. Par 36. Blue – 3,176. White – 2,986 (70.0/126). Gold – 2,870. Red – 2,549 (69.4/114). Price - $$.

Getting there From Galveston, take I-45 north for 100 miles to Hwy. 105. Turn west and find Loop 336, then turn south and drive a short distance to the course.

PANORAMA COUNTRY CLUB

The golf   The Panorama CC offers three 9-hole combinations of friendly country club golf, featuring fairways of medium width and medium-sized greens that make it easy to avoid a three-jack. The original 18 holes were designed by Jay Riviere, and Jack Miller added the additional nine.

The **Red Course** is long and known for drastic elevation changes. Of the three, you'll be most squeezed by the fairways on the Red.

The scenic **Blue Course** is highlighted by several lakes. Its feature hole is the 184-yard No. 3, which requires a tee shot over water.

The **White Course** is the most hacker friendly, known for its short par 5s.

The details   936-756-5815. 73 Greenbriar Dr., Conroe, TX 77304

- 1960. Jay Riviere and Jack Miller.
- Red/White: Gold – 6,749 (72.5/129). Blue – 6,479 (70.6/126). White – 6,246 (69.4/121). Red – 5,631 (72.8/126). Price - $$$.
- White/Blue: Gold – 6,738 (72.1/128). Blue – 6,314 (69.7/125). White – 6,072 (68.5.122). Red – 5,326 (70.7/122). Price - $$$.
- Blue/Red: Gold – 6,875 (72.8/129). Blue – 6,483 (70.4/124). White – 6,226 (69.1/120). Red – 5,563 (72.3/126). Price - $$$.

Getting there From I-45, take the League Line Rd. exit and turn west. Drive 1.5 miles to the course and look for the entrance on the right side of the street.

From the roaring oceans to the majestic lakes, the rushing streams and quiet ponds and burns, water adds a test to golf that entrances. Robert Trent Jones

RIVER PLANTATION COUNTRY CLUB

The golf   River Plantation sports the laid-back demeanor of the Old South with its Southern Colonial style clubhouse and three 9-hole combinations named Augusta, Biloxi, and Charleston. Jay Riviere laid the course out around Stewart Creek in 1968–his design is traditional with skinny fairways and small greens.

The details   935-273-2611. 550 Country Club Dr., Conroe, TX 77302

- www.riverplantation.com
- 1968. Jay Riviere. Added nine holes by Jackson Bradley. 27 holes.
- Augusta/Biloxi: Back – 6,857 (73.2/130). Middle – 6,196 (70.2/118). Forward – 5,538 (72.8/130). Price - $$.
- Biloxi/Charleston: Back – 6,524 (71.8/123). Middle – 5,959 (68.9/115). Forward – 5,466 (72.8/129). Price - $$.
- Charleston/Augusta: Back – 6,509 (71.8/126). Middle – 5,885 (68.9/116). Forward – 5,318 (71.6/127). Price - $$.

Getting there From I-45, take Exit 83 and turn right. You can see the course from the interstate.

WEDGEWOOD GOLF COURSE

The golf   Wedgewood was originally destined for exclusivity–it was envisoned as a private club in the tradition of Augusta National and an extremely difficult course. Robert Von Hagge and Bruce Devlin began the project, moving on to make way for new blood when the economy went south. Bill Rogers and Ron Pritchard finished the design job, but the idea never took hold and the course eventually became public in 1989.

The design features water on many holes and numerous blind shots. In fact, you'll never be able to see the green from any tee box. No. 10 is a nice hole, playing 164 yards downhill to a well-guarded green. The best hole is the 451-yard No. 18, which requires a booming drive and a long, blind approach.

The details   281-353-1808. 5454 Hwy. 105 W., Conroe, TX 77304

- Bruce Devlin and Robert Von Hagge. 18 holes. Par 72. Champ – 6,817 (73.7/134). Tournament – 6,390 (71.8/128). Regular – 5,825 (70.2/122). Forward – 5,071 (70.6/128). Price - $$.

Getting there From I-45 north, take Hwy. 105 west for 3.5 miles until you see the course.

SOUTH EAST

CONROE NOTES   Hard to go wrong with a place like **Willie's Grill & Ice House** (936-321-0065) on S. I-45. Just 5 miles east is the eclectic community named **Cut and Shoot, TX** (pop. 1400), where flea markets prosper on the weekends. For barbecue try **Luther's Bar-B-Q** (281-363-2647) on I-45 N., or **McKenzie's BBQ** (936-539-4300) on N. Frazier. The eclectic **Alpenhaus** (936-321-4416) is also worthy of consideration. For lodging don't forget the resorts at The Woodlands and Montgomery are nearby, but more affordable digs can be found at the **Country Inn & Suites** (936-271-0110) or **Hampton Inn** (936-321-3800), both on I-45.

CROSBY

Elev. 43   Pop. 1,714

Deep in the bayous that define northeast Houston's limits lies Crosby, a railroad town that became a shipping center for agriculture and lumber back in 1865. Before the railroad the area was known as Lick Skillet, since passers-by supposedly enjoyed the sweet spring waters so much they licked their skillets clean. Humphrey Jackson, one of Texas' original 300 colonists, established roots here in the 1820s near what is now known as Jackson Bayou. Now this commuter community just east of Lake Houston serves as a more peaceful home to folks who earn their living in Houston.

INDIAN SHORES RECREATION CENTER

The golf   Indian Shores is a flat country course that's the perfect remedy for shaking the shanks and building back your golf confidence. With the exception of out-of-bounds on six holes and a few small ponds that get in the way on several holes, you can pretty much let it loose here and go low. Missed approaches can be recovered from, since the small, elevated greens roll true and are generally surrounded by terrain that is favorable for ups and downs.

The best hole is No. 7, a 203-yard par 3, but the course serves up a long par 5 as well as a few par 4s in the 400-yard range.

The details   281-324-2592. 2141 White Feather Trail, Crosby, TX 77532

- 1960. 9 holes. Par 36. Back – 3,305 (35.5/122). Forward – 2,822 (36.0/123). Price - $.

Getting there From Hwy. 90 east, turn right on FM 2100. Turn left 10 miles down the road on Indian Shores, which will turn into White Feather Trail. The course entrance is on the right

NEWPORT GOLF & COUNTRY CLUB

The golf   After operating as a private club for many years, this club changed ownership in 1999 and opened for public play after an extensive renovation. Despite the fact that it rolls through a housing development, the

*It is quite certain that, had the ground on which ordinary inland
golf is played today been the only available ground for the purpose,
the game would never have been invented at all.* Garden G. Smith, 1898

majestic trees of East Lake Houston help create a secluded feel. Out-of-bounds is prominent, and the tight fairways and 6,900-yard length dictate long, straight drives for success. Most of the greens are small and surrounded by bunkers.

The 190-yard No. 7 is a nice hole that plays a bit longer because it's into an elevated green. No. 18 is the signature–with water in play off the tee, the approach is into an island green.

Other notes: The course was once a stop on the LPGA Tour. The facility is adding nine holes that are currently under construction.

The details 281-328-3576. 16401 Country Club Dr., Crosby, TX 77532

- 1972. 18 holes. Par 72. Back – 6,497 (69.7/118). Middle – 5,860 (66.8/111). Forward – 5,171 (68.5/111). Price - $$.

Getting there From Hwy. 90 east, exit FM 2100 and head north. Go through Crosby and turn left on Diamondhead Blvd. Look for the signs to the course.

CROSBY NOTES   Other than the **Sonic,** you can choose between local faves **Straight off the Road BBQ** (281-328-1188), **Hector's Mexican Restaurant** (281-328-7780), or **Iguana Joe's Mexican Restaurant.** Stay at the **Baymont Inn** in Baytown instead of the **Crosby Motel,** which could use a little TLC. **Love's Marina** (281-328-2159) out on Lake Houston can get you started for lake-like excursions and marina lounging.

CYPRESS   Elev. 150   Pop. 18,527

Jaunts to Austin from Houston shoot road-trippers up US 290 past the veritable golf mecca of Cypress, whose four public facilities offer 63 holes. German settlers and American ranchers established roots here along Cypress Creek in the 1840s, and the town has always maintained strong farming roots. Oil helped the economy after 1900, and the city showed early signs of growing alongside Houston. For a time, the Houston Hotwell Sanitarium & Hotel helped hopeful settlers deal with the stresses of life via its hot artesian well with supposed healing powers. Today golf is the healing agent for this commuter community of subdivisions.

BLACK HORSE GOLF CLUB

The golf   The environmentally friendly Blackhorse Golf Club was designed by Peter Jacobsen and Jim Hardy, who teamed to build one of the best 36-hole daily fee facilities in Texas. Designed to maximize the natural setting, this beautiful complex is a perfect setting for golf with its huge variety of oaks, elms, and wetlands that provide habitat for a wide variety of bird species.

The **South Course** is known for the sand quarry that was ingeniously worked into the layout by the design team. Particularly on the back side, the wetlands and sand features come into play prominently and create a totally

SOUTH EAST

My parents didn't want to move to Florida, but they
turned sixty, and it was the law. Jerry Seinfeld

unique setting for golf.

The best stretch of the entire complex occurs on the **North Course**, where holes 4-6 generally get the best of high handicappers. Holes 4 and 5 route through massive trees and expansive wetlands, both playing over 400 yards. No. 6 is the signature: a 180-yarder that tees over the bend of the creek to an elevated green enhanced with railroad ties and framed by bunkers.

The details   281-304-1747. 12205 Fry Rd., Cypress, TX 77433

• www.blackhorsegolf.com

• North Course: 2000. Jacobsen-Hardy. 18 holes. Par 72. Tees ranging from 7,301-6,199 yards. (71.8/123). Price - $$$$.

• South Course: 18 holes.Par 72. Back - 6,936. Middle - 6,426. Forward - 6,069. Price $$$$.

Getting there Take Hwy. 290 west to the Spring Cypress exit. Go south (left) under Hwy. 290 to Old Hempstead Hwy. Turn right and drive half a mile. Turn left on House & Hahl Rd., then left on Mound Rd. and right on Fry Rd. The entrance is on the right.

CYPRESS GOLF CLUB

The golf   Designed and built by employees of the Panhandle Eastern Gas Company, the inspiration for the Cypress Golf Club came from a rustic 3-hole practice track built around the company's compressor station. Nine holes are available today for the course, which opened in the early 1990s for public play, and two sets of tees make for a completely different look the second time around.

The hacker-friendly design is short and flat, and while trees line the fairways, the landing areas are generous and the medium-sized greens are good, open targets. The course lays out beside Cypress Creek and two ponds impact play. The signature No. 3 hole is an 180-yarder that requires a carry of the water hazard. Note that from the second set of tees, No. 3 plays as a par 4. A few doglegs present challenging target golf opportunities, but the most difficult fairway to hit is on the 385-yard No. 9, which has a landing area of only about 25 yards.

The details   281-373-0727. 14914 Spring Cypress Rd., Cypress, TX 77410

• 1964. 9 holes. Back – 2,637 (33.5/107). Forward – 2,325 (33.2/106). Price - $$.

Getting there From Houston, take Hwy. 290 north 25 miles to the Spring Cypress Rd. exit. Turn east and drive 2.5 miles to the course. The entrance is on the left.

SOUTH EAST

⭐
Sometimes a particular hole will cause a choke – a choke hole...
Like the 18th at Cypress. It's like walking into a certain room in a big dark
house when you were a kid – you get this fear that hits you. Dave Marr

CYPRESS LAKES GOLF CLUB

The golf   One of the Houston area's newest courses, Cypress Lakes was designed by Jim Fazio, who carved the course out of the thick pine trees and used a significant number of lakes and bunkers to spice up this mounded track. Four sets of tees provide options ranging from 5,351 yards to 7,050 yards at the tips. In addition to the layout, the experience at Cypress Lakes is enhanced by the impressive driving range, which is complete with target greens guarded by bunkers–an unusual look for a basic driving range.

The details   281-304-8515. 18700 Cypresswood Dr., Cypress, TX 77429

- www.cypresslakesgc.com
- 18 holes. Champs – 7,050. Back – 6,566. Middle – 6,132. Forward – 5,351. Price - $$$.

Getting there Take 290 west to Cypress Rosehill Rd. Turn right and drive to the second entrance on your left, Cypresswood Dr. Turn left and you will find the Cypress Lakes entrance at the end of Cypresswood Dr.

LONGWOOD GOLF COURSE

The golf   Longwood is carved out of some unusually thick terrain for this area of the state–the dense underbrush runs through old oak and pine trees, making the course difficult to even walk through. Luckily, the fairways on this 27-hole route are wide enough to allow for less-than-perfect golf shots; otherwise, anything out of the fairway requires a hack back out just to get in play.

The **Pine Oak Course** is known for its signature No. 6 hole. It's only a short, 300-yard par 4 but unique because of the trees and terrain.

Best chances for birdie are holes 3 and 14. Toughest holes are Nos. 4 and 12.

The details   281-373-4100. 13300 Longwood Trace Dr., Cypress, TX 77429

- www.americangolf.com
- 1995. Keith Fergus and Harry Yewens. 18 holes. Par 72. Back – 6,925 (73.6/139). Middle – 6,468 (71.9/131). Forward – 5,094 (69.9/124). Price - $$.

Getting there From Houston, take Hwy. 290 west to Telge Rd. Turn north and travel 3.5 miles to Longwood Trace. Turn right and drive until you see the course on the left.

CYPRESS NOTES   True Texas dance halls are must-stops for the traveling golfer, and Cypress checks in with the 1890 **Tin Hall**, steeped in tradition and recently restored. For lodging the **Comfort Suites** (713-856-5005) is adequate, and the **Crown Plaza** (713-462-9977) or **Hampton Inn** (281-890-2299)

I work to the rule that if the green appears to be fast, I will aim my putt at an imaginary hole six to twelve inches short of the hole. Bobby Locke

are about the same. **Del Pueblo Mexican Restaurant** (281-970-1600) and **La Hacienda** (281-373-0300) offer Mexican fare and **Pallotta's** (281-807-1000) is the place for Italian food.

DEER PARK   Elev. 33   Pop. 28,520

The satellite community of Deer Park, located in an industrial section of Harris County just southeast of Houston, grew as a result of burgeoning businesses along the Houston Ship Channel. Amazingly, until 1996 this fast-growing city was void of public golf, with only the private Occidental Chemical course available for its employees. However, roving golfers have a reason to pass through this town now that the intriguing Battleground at Deer Park Golf Course has opened. Deer Park's proximity to the San Jacinto battlefield earned the name "The Birthplace of Texas," and the golf course plays off that theme with 18 holes named after some aspect of Texas history.

THE BATTLEGROUND AT DEER PARK

The golf   Created as a tribute to Texas' battle for independence, The Battleground is more of a links-style course that is burdened by the wind and tricky because of the abundance of water (14 holes). Despite its links flavor, the fairways are narrow, and they're lined by thick rough.

Providing sort of a golf experience/history lesson combined into one day, each hole is named after some significant person, item, or event in the Texas fight for independence. For example, one hole is named Sam Houston, while another is named after a pair of twin cannons: Twin Sisters.

No. 8 is one of the signature holes, a 175-yard poke over the water to a green that is shared with the par 5 No. 1. A waterfall accents the edge of the lake, providing a unique aesthetic.

On the back, the finishing hole is fun because you can play aggressively off the tee, free of major hazards in the landing area that is framed by mounding. The approach must carry water, and you'll need to take an extra club because the green is elevated.

The details   281-478-4653. 1600 Georgia Ave., Deer Park, TX 77536

- 1996. Tom Knickerbacker. 18 holes. Par 72. Back – 6,943 (73.6/130). Middle – 6,305 (70.8/125). Forward – 5,526 (73.1/134). Price - $$$.

Getting there From Houston, take Hwy. 610 and loop around the city to Hwy. 225 east. Take the first Deer Park exit and turn right onto Georgia St. Next, drive 1 mile to the course, and look for the entrance on the right side of the street.

My mother didn't breast-feed me. She said she liked me as a friend. Rodney Dangerfield

OCCIDENTAL CHEMICAL GOLF COURSE

The golf   This 9-holer is only open to Occidental's employees–a seemingly tight-knit group that takes a lot of pride in their golf course. A ditch runs through the course to allow for drainage, presenting the primary hazard on what is generally a very basic, user-friendly course.

The details   281-476-2101. 1000 Tidal Rd., Deer Park, TX 77536

• 9 holes. Par 35. 2,783 yards. Price - $.

Getting there Traveling from Houston on I-10 east, take Beltway 8 south to Hwy. 225. Drive on 225 west past Center St. until you reach Tidal Rd. Take Tidal north to the course.

DEER PARK NOTES   Consider getting into the true Texas spirit by touring the **San Jacinto Battleground State Park**, the once-bloodied site where Texas won its independence from Mexico in the defining Battle of San Jacinto. Next, track down **G's Icehouse** for beer and music. In terms of lodging, everything is in La Porte except for the **Best Western** (281-476-1900) in Deer Park. The best place for sit-down is **Antonio's** (281-479-0605). In La Porte, **The Monument Inn** (281-479-1521) on the ship channel is the place for seafood, and **Gringo's** (281-470-7424) has killer margs. In Kemah, TX, head for **Rock the Dock** on Thursdays with all sorts of fabulous local entertainment.

DIBOLL
Elev. 232   Pop. 5,250

Diboll is a sawmill and lumber town just north of the Neches River, just a short drive south of Lufkin, TX. Primarily known as the headquarters for the old Southern Pine Lumber Company, now known as Temple-Eastex, Diboll is a town you'll pass through on your way to excursions in the Davy Crockett National Forest or to play the outstanding Neches Pines Golf Course.

NECHES PINES GOLF COURSE

The golf   Often overshadowed by the nearby Crown Colony, Neches Pines definitely holds its own–not only in terms of the layout, but especially because of the price.

Paper magnate Arthur Temple donated the land in the 1960s, and Leon Howard designed the original nine that opened for play in 1967. Then Dave Bennett came along to add the second nine in 1990.

The front nine plays longer, but is more wide-open than the newer back. The feature hole is the 152-yard No. 14, considered by many to be one of the most difficult par 3s in Texas because of its severely sloping green. Do not miss this hole on the right side.

SOUTH EAST

⭐

There is no other sphere in which a belief in oneself has such immediate effects as it has in golf. P.G. Wodehouse

The details   936-829-5086. 900 Lumberjack Dr., Diboll, TX 75941

- 18 holes. Par 72. Blue – 7,014 (73.9/133). White – 6,535 (71.8/124). Red – 5,989 (71.4/123). Gold – 5,379 (69.2/119). Price - $.

Getting there From I-59 north, take the Diboll exit and look for signs in town to the course.

DIBOLL NOTES   For lodging in Diboll there is a **Best Western** (936-829-2055), which is new and quiet. For eats, **El Rancho Grande** is one of two Tex-Mex joints. The other, more Mom-and-Pop place is **Taqueria Nuevo Leon**, with huge portions and good prices. No beer at either, as the county is dry.

DICKINSON   Elev. 18   Pop. 17,093

Dickinson rests just outside the edge of Galveston, a product of the growth of Houston, Galveston, and NASA's LBJ Space Center in Webster. Its location along the bay drew settlers all the way back to the 1820s, when the Mexican government was handing out land grants along what eventually became known as Dickinson's Bayou. One of Texas' first railroads drove through in the 1850s, and the town became a hub for the Confederacy during the Civil War. Farmers took advantage of the soils, turning the town into a strawberry capital of sorts.

The traveling golfer has options in Dickinson, with two regulation 9-hole courses and a newish par 3 that all offer quick golf breaks while driving down Hwy. 3 between Galveston and Houston.

CHAPARRAL GOLF CLUB

The golf   Chaparral is one of two 9-hole tracks in Dickinson–another basic layout with water in play on five holes and noted for its extremely narrow fairways. The average-sized greens make for good targets when the wind is howling off the coast.

At Chaparral they start you off with the most difficult hole on the course, a 375-yard par 4, followed by the longest hole, a 520-yard par 5. All told, the course offers a good combination of holes, and none of the par 4s are over 400 yards.

The details   409-925-7800. 302 Ave. J., Dickinson, TX 77539

- 9 holes. Par 36. Back – 3,228. Middle – 3,093 (35.2/120). Forward – 2,805 (34.9/111). Price - $$.

Getting there From I-45 south, turn right Holland Dr., and the course is just south of Dickinson on Ave. J.

What an individual thinks of himself largely determines what
he will do and what he will be. William James

DICKINSON COUNTRY CLUB

The golf   Big Jim Ed Robbins built this 9-holer along the banks of Dickinson Bayou back in the 1940s, and this flat, easy course still survives and thrives today despite being surrounded by more modern tracks. Jim Ed's design features skinny, tree-lined fairways and well-conditioned greens. Water is in play on four or five holes, but not a major issue.

However, in the heart of the nine, Nos. 6 and 7–both par 5s–stand out because of the water. No. 6 requires a precarious tee shot over water to a landing area that backs into more water, so you don't have the luxury of missing a shot on this one. The 7th is a bit longer and also features an approach shot over the drink.

The club policy mandates members-only weekends, so call ahead to see if they might be open for a walk-on if the only time you're around is on a weekend. As always in the small towns, you can pay once and play all day, and they have two sets of tees for a different look the second time around.

The details   281-337-3031. 1 Country Club Dr., Dickinson, TX 77539

- 1940. Jim Ed Robbins. 9 holes. Par 36. Back – 3,178. Forward – 2,886. Price - $.

Getting there From Houston, take I-45 south and travel 20 miles Dickinson. Turn left onto Hwy. 517 south and drive 2.5 miles to the course.

GREEN RIVER GOLF CLUB

The golf   Green River is a challenging 9-hole par 3 that opened in 1996. The course features water on six holes, and large, fast, undulating greens. The best hole is the 123-yard No. 7–intimidating because of the approach into an island green. The course is lit, making it a great option for extended golf days when you run out of daylight at the other 9-holers in town.

The details   281-337-2021. 2100 Caroline, Dickinson, TX 77539

- 1996. Richard Luikens. 9 holes. Par 27. Back – 1,503. Middle – 1,298. Forward – 1,103. Price - $.

Getting there From I-45, exit Hwy. 646 and drive east for 4 miles to Caroline. The course is 1 mile south.

DICKINSON NOTES   Other than the fast-food chain stops, your only true local choice is **Roger's Malt Shop**. Don't stay in Dickinson–head to the bay town of **Kemah, TX**, where you'll find a boardwalk, good eats, and lodging along Galveston Bay.

Golf and wagering go together as
smoothly as "double" and "bogey." James Y. Bartlett

EAGLE LAKE

Elev. 174   Pop. 3,622

The wayward outdoorsman knows Eagle Lake, 50 miles southwest of Houston, as the "Goose Hunting Capital of the World"–a recreational area that became popular in the 1960s due to the numerous geese and ducks that wintered around the lake in the rice fields. Thankfully for sportsmen who've added golf to their hunting addiction, the Eagle Lake Golf Course offers a nice respite from the hours afield.

EAGLE LAKE GOLF COURSE

The golf   Despite the short length, the Eagle Lake Golf Course can play difficult because of the small greens. Bring your short game and get ready to put it to use, because your approaches must be honed in to have the chance to land on these tiny greens.

Two sets of tees make for an 18-hole round, and the look is surprisingly different on the back nine. There is only one par 5 on this course. The most difficult hole is No. 7 on the second go-round, which plays 215 yards with a creek that runs the length of the hole.

The details   979-234-5981. 200 Golf Course Rd., Eagle Lake, TX 77434

* 9 holes. Par 35. Back – 2,825 (33.8/110). Forward – 2,358 (34.0/113). Price - $.

Getting there From Houston, take I-90 west for 65 miles to the town of Eagle Lake. Drive through the center of town and you'll see the course.

EAGLE LAKE NOTES   This goose-hunter heaven boasts plenty of guide services to help you enjoy your time in Eagle Lake. Try **Tim Kelley's Waterfowl Outfitters** (979-234-3819), if for nothing more than the convenience they offer with their **Eagle Lake Lodge**. The **Sportsman's Lodge** (979-234-3159) can also put you up and help with contacts for outdoor excursions, as well as serve you good eats in their restaurant. Other dining options include the always-convenient **Dairy Delite** (979-234-7128), **Austin's Bar BQ** (979-234-5250) on Main St., or the **Blue Plate Cafe** (979-234-5224). Tex-Mex cravers need to check out **Taco Tony's Restaurant** (979-234-3984). Finally, restless gear-seekers can satisfy their needs for all things sporting-goods-related at **Johnny's Sport Shop** (979-234-3516), the place for forgotten provisions.

SOUTH EAST

EDNA

Elev. 90   Pop. 6,141

Edna is sort of the gateway to South Texas, just 24 miles northeast of Victoria, TX, and the seat of Jackson County. The town replaced the now-

---

Every day you don't hit balls is one day longer it takes you to get better. Ben Hogan flooded town of Texana, which is now covered by 11,000-acre Lake Texana. Centered around its modern courthouse, Edna sparkles from oil and agriculture prosperity and is worth a visit for the recreational opportunities on the lake, as well as the enjoyable Edna CC.

EDNA COUNTRY CLUB

The golf   Like many of the courses near the Gulf, the ECC is made difficult by the stiff ocean winds. Otherwise this is just another basic, fun small-town 9-hole track that allows you to pay once and play all day.

The details   361-782-3010. Hwy. 59, Edna, TX 77957

• 9 holes. Back – Par 36. 3,205. Forward – Par 37. 2,770. Price - $.

Getting there From Hwy. 59 south, turn left on Hwy. 111. Turn right at the first traffic light and travel to FM 1822. Turn left and the entrance is on the left side of the road.

EDNA NOTES   Two motels options are **The Jackson Inn** (361-782-0808) and the **Inns of Texas** (361-782-5276). For good Tex-Mex eats, **Dos Hermanos** takes care of business. The best spot for old-school burgers is **Triangle Treats** on Wells St. Also on Wells is **Frontier BBQ**. Festivities abound when the weather warms up–Fourth of July is huge at the lake, and **Texana Outback Day** happens in April with lots of Texas music and fun.

EL CAMPO   Elev. 110   Pop. 10,643

"The Camp," as Mexican cowboys called it around the turn of the century, is located along US 59 between Houston and Victoria in the middle of an area that's loaded with wintering waterfowl. The railroad came through in the 1880s, led by Italian count C.J. Telferner, whose "Macaroni Line" was developed by some 2,000 Italian laborers. El Campo, is at the center of the largest rice-producing county in the state, and is also driven by oil and gas production.

EL CAMPO COUNTRY CLUB

The golf   Jay Riviere came to "The Camp" in 1964 to build this links-style 9-holer. The main problem for golfers on this 3,190-yard track is the wind, since the course is fairly open and not protected by trees. The greens are rather large with subtle undulations, and like the rest of the course, are in excellent condition. This is also one where you can pay once and play all day.

The details   979-543-6592. FM 1300, El Campo, TX 77437

SOUTH EAST

Much dripping wears away a stone, and continual fussing and fretting...
wears away the golfer. Bernard Darwin (on too much waggle)

- 1964. Jay Riviere. 9 holes. Par 36. Back – 3,190 (34.6/117). Forward – 2,771 (35.5/118). Price - $$.

Getting there From Houston, take Hwy. 59 south for 75 miles to Hwy. 71. Turn north and exit FM Road 1300, where you'll turn left again and find the course just down the road.

EL CAMPO NOTES   The **Uptown Grill** (541-5195) is popular for weekend breakfast-goers, and **Mikeska's** (543-8252) on Hwy. 59 is a local tradition that shouldn't be passed up. There's live Texas honkytonk music at **Greek Brothers** (543-1757). Bring your gun and hunt geese and ducks via excursions via the **Paradise Hunting Co.** (979-543-6761), who can also feed you and give you a place to sleep. The **El Campo Museum** has some impressive big-game mounts from all over the world. For lodging there's a few local options in town, highlighted by the **Best Western** (979-543-7033).

FREEPORT
Elev. 15   Pop. 11,594

The sometimes-stinky deepwater port known as Freeport is newer than most Texas towns, dating back to 1912 when the Freeport Sulphur Company dug into the world's largest sulphur mine. More shrimp trawlers use Freeport as their home base than any other Gulf location, and the town is known as one of the finest places to fish in Texas. At times the Gulf of Mexico can look surprisingly blue, providing a great setting to hang out on the beach in sleepy towns like Surfside after your rounds at the Freeport muni course.

FREEPORT MUNICIPAL GOLF COURSE

The golf   Freeport's muni is more of a links-style track noted for its solid par 5 holes. Water comes into play in the form of rivers and lakes, but the course isn't overloaded with water. The par 5s in question each play well over 500 yards, and they're all rated as the most difficult holes on the course. No. 9 is the longest at 557 yards, but the most difficult is No. 7 at 520 yards.

The details   979-233-8311. 830 Slaughter Rd., Freeport, TX 77541

- 1976. 18 holes. Par 71. Back – 6,556 (70.5/113). Middle – 6,169 (69.0/112). Forward – 5,787 (71.2). Price - $.

Getting there Driving north on Hwy. 36, turn right at Slaughter Rd. You will see the course when Slaughter dead-ends.

FREEPORT NOTES   Find B&B accommodations at **Roses on the River** (800-610-1070) or Bankers Inn (979-233-4932). And you can call **Le Papillon Beach Rental** (281-852-8038) for a house on the beach, or go semi-seedy at a

---

A bad attitude is worse than a bad swing. Payne Stewart

few of the Surfside motels like **Anchor Motel** (979-239-3543) or **Cedar Sands Motel** (979-233-1942). The former resort town of Velasco, now Surfside, offers laid-back beach festivities such as pier fishing, surfing, and sunset watching. Nightlife is probably better found in Surfside, with the **Porthole Club & Grill** (979-233-6429) and the **Del's Lookout** (979-239-2666) both serving up beers and live music, with Del's favorable because of its beachfront location. In Freeport, **On the River** on 2nd St. serves a variety of excellent seafood. **B & B Cafe** is strictly steaks and seafood.

FRIENDSWOOD   Elev. 31   Pop. 29,037

The early Friendswood settlers were different from other Texas colonists–they were members of a Quaker colony from Kansas that briefly tried the rugged plains of the Llano Estacado before sending Indian fighter and buffalo hunter Jacob Brown down to South Texas to found a new community. South of Houston between Pearland and Alvin, and just west of Gulf-bound I-45, today the Quaker town of Friendswood is primarily a residential commuter community that grew in the 1960s as NASA employees chose the town as their home.

As for golf, Jay Riviere built the Friendswood CC in the 1970s to serve the burgeoning residential community, then returned more recently to create the public 27-hole Timber Creek Golf Club.

FRIENDSWOOD COUNTRY CLUB

The golf   Jay Riviere was invited down to the Meadows residential development in the 1960s to scope the possibilities of building a course around Chigger Creek. The course he created has homes lining its narrow, tree-lined fairways, which are bordered by a standard cut of rough. Water hazards come into play on 13 holes. The course was originally built in 1967 as a members-only club in the Sun Meadows residential development.

Since the course winds through the housing community, out-of-bounds is on every hole but one. Chigger Creek runs through the layout, which also features six lakes. The back nine is more wide open than the front.

No. 3 is one of the toughest holes, with a lake on the right side and in back of the green. Hole 15 is 204 yards and has a green surrounded on three sides by water. The longest par 4 is hole 18 (443 yards), but it is straight and is the only par 4 over 400 yards.

The details   281-482-4653. 3 Country Club Dr., Friendswood, TX 77546

- 1976. 18 holes. Par 72. Back – 6,721 (71.1/113). Middle – 6,412 (69.6/110). Forward – 5,807 (73.5/121). Price - $$.

"I smell varmint poontang, and the only good varmint poontang is dead varmint poontang, I think." Carl Spackler (Bill Murray) in Caddyshack

Getting there From I-45 south, take the NASA exit and turn right. Next drive 7 miles to the course, and look for the clubhouse on the right side of the road.

TIMBER CREEK GOLF CLUB

The golf   One of the best values in the Houston area, Timber Creek is popular for its great Jay Riviere layout and affordable price. In these days of impossible golf courses, where architects do their damndest to beat down the average hacks who form the true support system of the game, Riviere routed this one with generous fairways and holes of all levels of difficulties. He still held true, however, to his trademark of allowing an errant shot every now and then.

Riviere was blessed with some unique terrain for this 27-hole facility, much different than the typical links-style geography that is common to this area of tidal plains. Here oaks and pines line the fairways, and Clear Creek cuts through the rolling terrain so often that he had to install numerous bridges to span the hazard.

The **Creekside** nine is open, playing just over 3,100 yards from the tips to par 35. The game here is to flail away off the tee into the open landing areas. Then gear up for the difficult forced carries that are often found on approach, although one of the more difficult par 4s, the 422-yard No. 5, involves carrying the creek off the tee.

The **Pines** nine, while a bit tighter that Creekside, is still fairly generous off the tee, but almost 300 yards longer. This side features two monster par 5s that go over 550 yards from the big boy tees. No. 5 is the most difficult, a 427-yarder that doglegs left inside a lake, then approaches into a green protected by another water hazard on the right. Watch the closing stretch on this nine, which is made up of a long par 4, a par 3, and a 550-yard par 5.

The **Timber Trails** nine is the most difficult of the three tracks, and shows it early with a 480-yard opening par 4. On this one the fairways are more narrow, and you'll need a real game when playing from the tips, where the shortest par 4 is 412 yards. From the more forward tees, it's not as difficult, but either way it provides a good balance to the other two tracks.

The deal here is to play it smart, watch the yardages, and avoid major disasters. The course is set up to allow for good scoring, so hacks can walk away feeling right. Nothing fancy: just good golf, basic greens with standard slope and speed, and some fun holes.

The details   281-993-1140. 4554 FM 2351 Rd., Friendswood, TX 77546

- Creekside/Pines: Blue (70.8/121). White (68.0/119). Gold (65.5/114). Red (69.8/113). Price - $$$.

- Timber Trails/Creekside: Blue (71.8/119). White (69.0/119). Gold (66.2/115). Red (70.3/113). Price - $$$.

You can't catch a fish unless you keep your line in the water.
You have to be patient. A cold wind can be blowing and ice can be
forming on your eyebrows, but you have to keep at it. Sam Snead

SOUTH EAST

- Pines/Timber Trails: Blue (73.0/121). White (69.9/122). Gold (67.1/117). Red (72.1/113). Price - $$$.

Getting there Take I-45 south to Exit 29 and turn right on FM 2351. At the second light, turn right into the facility.

FRIENDSWOOD NOTES There's no place to stay here so look to Webster, TX and find **Howard Johnson** (281-316-2003) and a **Marriott** (281-486-2424). **Perry's** is a meat market and restaurant. The special is the smoked pork chop, and they cut the ribs for you at your table. **La Casita** is the place for Tex-Mex.

FULSHEAR
Elev. 129   Pop. 716

Fulshear is a small farm town west of Houston and south of I-10. The community developed around plantation man Churchill Fulshear, one of Texas' original settlers and the man who granted access to the railroad that eventually turned the town into a marketing center for local products. You'll need connections for golf here at the private Weston Lakes CC, so call ahead and check on the possibilities of their reciprocal policies.

WESTON LAKES COUNTRY CLUB

The golf The tiny town of Fulshear offers an impressive, Carlton Gipson/Hale Irwin-designed golf course for its membership. Ancient pecans line the fairways, and an extensive system of lakes sets the landscape for this long, difficult course. Out-of-bounds lines many holes, and frequent windy conditions make it a challenging task to keep the ball in play.

The front nine is highlighted by the mammoth 591-yard, par 5 8th hole, which starts the toughest stretch of golf around the turn. In fact, the top three most difficult rated holes encompass Nos. 8-10. No. 9 plays 412 yards into the clubhouse, followed by the unwelcome 453-yard par 4 No. 10 after your beer and hot dog at the turn.

The details 281-346-1228. 5627 Weston Dr., Fulshear, TX 77441

- www.wlakes.com
- 1985. Carton Gipson-Hale Irwin. 18 holes. Back – 7,064 (74.4/131). Middle – 6,495 (72.2/118). Forward – 5,576 (73.4/127). Price - $$.

Getting there From I-10 west, take the FM 359 exit and drive south. Head west on FM 1093 and drive 2 miles to the course where you'll see the clubhouse on the left side of the road.

SOUTH EAST

Consider, if you will, that on a par-72 course you can bogey
17 of the 18 holes and still break 90. Cliff McAdams

FULSHEAR NOTES   There are no B&Bs or hotels here, so get a room in **Brookshire, TX** if you're forced to shut it down for the night. There are three good places to dine after your round: **Las Floras** is Tex-Mex, **George T's** is more old-fashioned fast-food home-cooking, and **The Double Horn Grill**, located on 1093, is popular and usually crowded.

GALVESTON   Elev. 20   Pop. 59,567

One of Texas' most colorful and historical cities, Galveston is the most charming town on the Texas coast. This Victorian-gingerbread city is accentuated by its laidback demeanor, unusual shopping, and numerous cultural and historic attractions. Located 50 miles south of Houston, the island is part of a string of coastal sand barrier islands and is bordered by the natural harbor of Galveston Bay, historically the best port between New Orleans and Veracruz. Cabeza de Vaca likely shipwrecked here, and Pirate Jean Lafitte and the Karankawa Indians once roamed the coast. A 20-mile seawall protects the city from storms like the 1900 terror that wiped out the island and claimed 6,000 lives. In terms of golf, some argue that Galveston is the birthplace of Texas golf, with the 1898 Galveston Country Club rivaling only Dallas' old Dallas CC as the oldest in the state.

GALVESTON COUNTRY CLUB

The golf   The original Galveston CC dates back to 1898 as a 9-hole track with a membership of only 30; however, the hurricane of 1900 wiped out the facility. The club moved back and forth between the island and the mainland in the early 1900s–it was once known as the Oleander Country Club around 1912 before moving back onto the beach in 1918. That location on 61st Street remained intact until 1946, when John Bredemus was asked to design the new, short, water-infested, wind-burdened layout that exists today.

Ralph Plummer and Carlton Gipson had their hands in things over the years as developer George Mitchell obtained the facility's lease in exchange for promised long-term improvements.

Today mature palms and oleanders line the fairways, and much like the old days, the modern version is known for precise shot-making. Solid course management is mandatory for scoring well.

No. 7 is the most difficult, a 418-yarder that's lined by water on the left for the first half of the hole. Bogey is a good score when the wind is blowing. On the back side, the 180-yard No. 11 is a real treat. Virtually surrounded by water, the hole plays over the edge of the lake into a green framed by bunkers with water in the back.

There are no points for style when it comes to putting.
It's getting the ball in the cup that counts. Brian Swarbrick

The details 409-737-9830. 14228 Stewart Rd., Galveston, TX 77554

- www.galvestoncountryclub.com
- 1948. Gipson-Bredemus-Plummer. 18 holes. Par 72. Back – 6,437 (71.6/122). Middle – 5,996 (69.7/119). Forward – 5,292 (71.2/123). Price - $$$.

Getting there From I-45 south, take the 61st St. exit, then drive to Sea Wall Blvd. Turn right and head down to 12 Mile Rd. Turn right again and drive over to Stewart Rd., then turn left and drive a short distance to the course.

GALVESTON ISLAND MUNICIPAL GOLF COURSE

The golf Galveston residents finally got their municipal championship layout after years of bureaucratic wrangling. The course opened in 1974 after the city supposedly spent $1.8 million to build a facility that should have cost more in the neighborhood of $400,000.

It was worth it, though, to the avid golfer, since this Carlton-Gipson-redesigned track is one of the most difficult tracks in Texas, and is universally considered one of the top five municipals in the state. The Gulf winds pound the course and water comes into play on every hole. Even from the regular tees the route rolls 6,739 yards, so short knockers are truly at a disadvantage.

The details 409-744-2366. 1700 Sydnor Ln., Galveston, TX 77554

- www.galvestonmunigolf.com
- 18 holes. Par 72. Back – 6,969 (73.0/131). Middle – 6,739 (72.5/127). Forward – 5,407 (74.5/135). Price - $$.

Getting there From I-45 south, exit 61st St. and turn right. Find Stewart and turn right, then turn right again on 99th St. Drive to Sydnor Ln. Turn right, and you'll see the entrance on the right side of the road.

GALVESTON NOTES Known for its cozy, Old-World charm, Galveston has loads of eclectic B&B options, including the **1860 Rose Mansion** (409-763-1577) on Ave. M, and **The Mermaid and The Dolphin** (409-762-1561) on 33rd St. Both of these spots offer the basic $100-per-night accommodations, as well as some impressively upscale rooms/suites in the $300-$400 range. Learn more about all of the options at www.galvestonbedandbreakfast.com, a great site that offers maps, city info, and reviews of each inn. For some of the freshest Mexican food in Texas, track down **The Original Mexican Cafe** (409-762-6001), which serves breakfast, lunch, and dinner in a wonderful atmosphere. In the West End, find **JAX Cafe and Bar-B-Que** (409-744-7003) for mouthwatering crawfish sausage. Their rival is the family-owned **Queen's Bar-B-Que** (409-762-3151), a good option for dinner, but especially preferable for link sausage po-boy sandwiches to go. For history, Texas' earliest cultural mecca is

SOUTH EAST

No golfer can really play to the utmost of his game who is
discussing politics, the crops, the weather, and the grouse. Horace Hutchinson

loaded with historic homes and buildings, so don't miss the chance to soak up the architecture of this charming city.

GANADO
Elev. 64   Pop. 1,915

Originally called Mustang Settlement, Ganado popped up when early cattle ranchers who drove their herds to New Orleans established their camps along Mustang Creek. When the railroad came through, the prominence of cattle prompted the use of the Spanish word for herd, or ganado, to name the town that would eventually become a shipping center for Jackson County. Just 9 miles east of Edna, TX, separated by scenic Lake Texana, Ganado offers the traveling outdoorsman another 9-hole golf option to break up weekend hunting excursions.

GANADO GOLF & COUNTRY CLUB

The golf   Ganado CC offers 1950s-style 9-hole country golf–you can can play all day for one fee, avoid the intimidation of a championship course, and enjoy yourself among the abundant wildlife that roams the course. As you might expect, big trees line the fairways, and they've used water on a few occasions to spice things up. The best feature of this and any small-town course is the well-manicured greens that provide great targets and always roll true.

The details   361-771-2424. County Rd. 202, Ganado, TX 77962

• 1950s. 9 holes. Par 36. Back – 3,209. Forward – 2,732. Price - $.

Getting there Ganado is between Victoria and Houston on Hwy. 59. Driving west, take FM 202 and turn right, then drive past Ganado 3 miles to the course.

GANADO NOTES   There is no lodging in Ganado so make your reservations in El Campo or Edna. You have two dining options, both on Main St: **El Camino** and **Estella's**, both Tex-Mex joints with adequate food and atmosphere. **Lake Texana** and its state park are just west.

GROVES
Elev. 11   Pop. 15,733

This suburb of Port Arthur, TX, originally called Pecan Grove, is located just north of Port Arthur in the farthest southeastern corner of Texas. Refineries, petrochemical plants, and shipbuilding define the economy, and the folks who

We can't all be heroes, because somebody has to sit on the curb and clap as they go by. Will Rogers

SOUTH EAST

reside here have the pleasure of playing at the unique 1930s Port Groves Golf Club.

PORT GROVES GOLF CLUB

The golf   This flat course features small, elevated greens and narrow fairways. The course's signature hole is No. 3, a 390-yard par 4 that requires an approach shot over water to a green framed in back by out-of-bounds stakes. There are additional sets of tees that can be used when playing an 18-hole round on this course, which has few trees and no bunkers.

Legend has it that Byron Nelson once intentionally three-jacked the 18th hole to avoid breaking the course record of 60 so that a local golfer could retain the record. This is a links-style layout with lots of moguls and small undulating greens. You'll find yourself hitting lots of bump-and-run shots.

The details   409-962-4030. 5721 Monroe St., Groves, TX 77619

- 1932. A. Aames. 9 holes. Back – 2,650. Par 35 (33.5). Forward – 2,650. Par 36 (33.5). Price - $.

Getting there Drive toward Port Arthur on the Twin City Hwy., then turn left onto Monroe St.

GROVES NOTES   Consider all goings-on and lodging in Port Arthur, TX, but specific to Groves you'll find **The Rib Cage** (409-962-7427) for meaty portions and **Larry's Cajun Restaurant** (409-962-3381) for Creole cooking and live music. Before golf, hit **Jivin' Java** (409-962-2431) for coffee and breakfast. Drive down to where the road ends at Sabine Pass, TX and go for seafood at **The Shrimp Dock** (409-971-0014). There are a few local motels with clean, affordable lodging in Groves.

HALLETTSVILLE   Elev. 232   Pop. 2,770

Located along the Lavaca River just south of I-10 halfway between Houston and San Antonio, the tranquil Czech and German town of Hallettsville spreads out from its courthouse square. Frontier machisma Margaret Hallet–wife of John, trading post proprietor, and speaker of numerous Indian dialects–donated the land for the town, which is now comfortable and brick-fronted. Like nearby Shiner and Gonzales, Hallettsville is a great touring town for the Texas traveler.

SOUTHEAST

I'll always remember the day I broke ninety. I had a few beers in the clubhouse and was so excited
I forgot to play the back nine. Bruce Lansky

HALLETTSVILLE GOLF COURSE

The golf   Located in the city park, Hallettsville's quaint little 9-hole course starts off fairly simply with four par 4s, but then takes you on an interesting ride over the final five holes. The sequence offers two birdie chances in the 139-yard No. 5 and the 290-yard, par 4 hole 6. A 221-yard, par 3 is next, followed by a 306-yard par 4 and the 507-yard finisher.

There are two sets of tees for an 18-hole round.

The details   361-798-9908. La Grange St., Hallettsville, TX 77964

- 1960s. 9 holes. Par 35. Back – 2,985 (33.1/107). Forward – 2,480 (34.3/108). Price - $.

Getting there From I-10, take Hwy. 77 south 18 miles to La Grange St.

HALLETTSVILLE NOTES   The **Texas Championship Domino Hall of Fame** (tournament held every January) shares space with **The Texas Fiddler's Hall of Fame** (Fiddler's Frolic held fourth week of April) at the **Knights of Columbus Hall**, Hwy. 77 South. Both are open Mon-Fri 9 am. to 11 am. Other noteworthy buildings on the square include the one now occupied by the **Hallettsville Florist**. This was the photography studio of J. Braunig and offers the absolute best view of a courthouse anywhere in the state. Above the florist is a tearoom where the ceiling was built of glass to let in the northern light for photographs. Stick around for dusk and watch the bats fly off for their nourishment. Other dining options include **Hermes Country Market** (361-798-4891) or **Kolacny's BBQ House** (361-798-4400) for smoked-cooking type fares, and the **Hinze's Country Cafe** (361-798-7198) takes the cake for home cooking. For lodging, contact **Enchanted Oaks Lodge** (361-798-4410).

HEMPSTEAD
Elev. 251   Pop. 4,198

Here at Hempstead, 50 miles from Houston, the Coastal Plain begins to pucker with swells among the former plantations, one of which housed Texas' first cotton gin and was the site of the state's first cotton and corn seedlings. Close enough to Houston to offer great big-city golf, but far enough away to offer small-town charm, Hempstead is a mandatory stop for the restless golfer–it sports two nice facilities and the quaint courses of Brenham, Weimar, Bellville, and Navasota all just short drives away.

FOX CREEK GOLF COURSE

The golf   Fox Creek is a traditional, blue-collar course that has improved since the late 1990s, when ownership began improving the conditions. The

The older you get the stronger the wind gets–and it's always in your face. Jack Nicklaus

price is right and it's fun to play, with a wide-open front nine that allows you to warm up, followed by a back nine that offers a little more of a challenge.

Holes 5-8 are considered the most difficult stretch at Fox Creek, consisting of three of the toughest holes on the course. This stretch features two long par 4s, a long par 3, and the number one handicap, 525-yard No. 8.

The course doesn't have any bunkers, so it's advisable to practice your short game out of thick rough to be ready for ups-and-downs after approach misses.

The details   979-826-2131. 15120 FM 359 Rd., Hempstead, TX 77445

- 18 holes. Par 71. Back – 6,130. Middle – 5,630. Forward – 4,590. Price - $$.

Getting there From Hwy. 290 west, turn right on 359 and drive 7 miles to the course. The clubhouse is on the left.

LEGENDARY OAKS

The golf   In the 1960s, Leon Howard designed this scenic little track, then known as Lawrence Marshal, around a lake; however, the traditional layout was revamped in the late 1990s when Jay Riviere came through and added nine holes. Now the facility is part of a new 280-acre master-planned community. The course weaves its way through majestic old oak trees and tips out at just over 6,500 yards.

Note that as of press time the course is on the market for $2.5 million.

The details   979-826-4001. Urban Rd. at Hwy. 290, Hempstead, TX 77445

- 1963. Leon Howard. 1998 Jay Riviere. 18 holes. Par 71. 6,500 yards. Price - $$.

Getting there From Houston, take Hwy. 290 west 45 miles to Hempstead. Turn left on Urban Rd., and drive half a mile to the course.

HEMPSTEAD NOTES Deep down the back roads of 529/359 you can find the **Monaville Store and Icehouse**, where provisions and cold beverages are available to replenish the road trip supplies. Watch for nesting geese in the fall and winter and bluebonnets in the spring, and don't forget to stop off at one of the roadside watermelon stands. A trip this way can be enhanced with a trip to **Peckerwood Garden**, where you'll see many impressive botanical explorations, including a fine collection of Mexican oak trees (look for the Peckerwood Foundation sign). For lodging consider the **Hempstead Inn**, an attractive spot with solid food that pays tribute to Hempstead's label of "Six Shooter Junction," a name earned when post-Civil War shootouts were commonplace.

SOUTH EAST

⭐

Every rock'n'roll band I know, guys with long hair and tattoos, plays golf now. Alice Cooper

HOCKLEY
Elev. 220   Pop. 300

At one time, the rambling golfer would never have stopped off in Hockley, since the Tennwood Country Club course was open only to employees of the Tenneco Corporation. However, in 1998 the facility was sold to a California company that hired Tom Fazio to redesign the course, which was then renamed Houston Oaks and opened to the public. That put this otherwise nondescript town just 36 miles northwest of Houston on the Texas golf map.

HOUSTON OAKS GOLF CLUB

The golf   The Tenneco Corporation hired Ralph Plummer to build this course as the centerpiece of a recreational facility for their employees. The course remained private until 1998, when a California company bought the facility, renamed it, and opened its 36 holes to the public.

The original **Oaks Course** is considered to be the most scenic; however, locals prefer the Tom Fazio-designed **Links Course** for its numerous challenges.

The Links is flat, dotted by massive, majestic oak trees, loaded with huge bunkers, and features water on about half of the holes. The front side is more of an open, links-style track with significant mounding, and it opens with a few friendly birdie opportunities.

No. 18 is a fine finishing hole: a long par 4 framed by fairway bunkers that features an approach into a multi-level green.

Afterwards, consider touring the grounds and possibly even wetting a line in one of the 16 acres fishing lakes.

The details   936-931-2917. 22602 Hegar Rd., Hockley, TX 77447

* www.houstonoaks.com

* Oaks: 1950s. Ralph Plummer. Back – 6,420 (70.5/121). Middle – 6,093 (69.3/118). Forward – Par 72. 5,396 (70.9/118). Price - $$.

* Links: 1984. Tom Fazio. 18 holes. Par 72. Back – 6,397 (70.8/120). Middle – 5,902 (68.9/112). Forward – 5,011 (68.3/109). Price - $$.

Getting there From Hwy. 290 west take the Hegar Rd. exit and turn right. Drive 4.5 miles to the course and look for the clubhouse on the right.

HOCKLEY NOTES   The **Stockman's Restaurant** in Waller, TX is the closest sit-down joint–a popular steakhouse and the best option if you don't hang around the Houston Oaks grill for post-round festivities. And if Houston isn't in the cards for nightlife, make the relatively new **Super 8 Motel** (979-826-4700) on US 290 your home away from home.

Golf - the second best pastime that any sinner on this earth can have. R.H. Lyttleton

HOUSTON
Elev. 55   Pop. 1,786,691

Want to know how great Houston is? Just ask any longtime resident. Houstonians love to brag about their city, and that civic pride is one of the town's best assets.

The swagger was apparent early on. When two brothers, John and Augustus Allen, set up a trading post on Buffalo Bayou in 1836, they boasted that Houston would become the next New Orleans. For a while, the cotton trade helped Houston reign supreme. But the Civil War slowed things down and Houston languished until the coming of the railroads. The discovery of oil at nearby Spindletop in 1901 created another boom as investors, speculators, and oilfield workers swarmed in. During World War II, Houston became a major center for shipbuilding, steel, and petrochemicals.

Houston's oil dependency backfired in the 1980s, when a decline in oil prices threw the city into a downward spiral. Medical research, aerospace, high-tech, and international banking have helped even out the boom/bust cycle somewhat and today Houston is on the upswing with a population of more than 4.8 million in the CMSA (the city and its central suburbs) and growing.

For most people, Houston means NASA, the Astrodome, the center of cancer and heart transplant medicine, and the world's largest rodeo. Forgotten is the awesome influence of shipping; the Port of Houston is now the sixth largest in the world. The port makes Houston a truly international city, and the effects of foreign influence and investment are felt everywhere, from the art galleries to the restaurants to even the golf courses.

Variety is the byword of Houston area links. Whatever you want, it's there; so keep turning the pages of *The Texas Golf Bible* until you find it. Don't forget that, like Dallas, the city offers a myriad of recreational activities for the wife and family, so make this part of your road trip a family affair.

BAY OAKS COUNTRY CLUB

The golf   Bay Oaks CC features a challenging Arthur Hills design that lays out along Horsepen Bayou, offering a good combination of traditional and links-style holes. Man-made lakes and the bayou bring water into play on 14 of 18 holes

The more traditional front nine is highlighted by the 531-yard No. 5, which bends right around a lake that comes into play on every shot.

The more open back nine features more notable holes, including the best par 3, a 184-yard No. 12 over water, and two outstanding finishing holes. No. 17 doglegs right 435 yards to a green that is bordered by water on the right, and No. 18 plays 450 yards over a swale to a green bordered by water on the left.

From the tips, the par 4s are long, ranging from 429 to 459 yards, and every par 5 is over 500 yards, including the 569-yard No. 16.

The details   281-488-9753. 14545 Bay Oaks Blvd., Houston, TX 77059

SOUTH EAST

★

If you drink, don't drive. Don't even putt. Dean Martin

- www.bayoakscountryclub.com
- Par 72. Gold – 7,011 (74.7/134). Blue – 6,626 (72.7/126). White – 6,112 (70.4/121). Red – 5,289 (71.9/128). Price - $$$.

Getting there From Houston, take I-45 to the Clear Lake exit and turn left. Drive about 3 miles, then turn right on Bay Oaks Blvd.

BEAR CREEK GOLF WORLD

The golf The floodplain of Addicks Reservoir hosts the 54-hole Bear Creek Golf World, a facility that is symbolic of Houston's golf boom 25 years ago. Long-time Houston pro Dick Forester headed the project in an attempt to capitalize on Houston's growing need for public golf facilities.

The original **Presidents Course** features par 4s around 350 yards and several short par 5s in the 470-yard range. Of the three courses, this is the only one without water, and is much more hacker-friendly than the Masters.

The **Masters Course** provides the best challenge for the single-digit handicapper. Measuring over 7,100 yards from the tips, its length and narrow fairways demand long, accurate golf shots. Nos. 9 and 18 are indicative of the design–both are long par 4s that route back to the golf shop.

The **Challenger Course** is the easiest of the three and recommended for beginners.

Other notes: The greens and tees were renovated in the early 1990s after American Golf bought the facility.

The details 281-859-8188. 16001 Clay Rd., Houston, TX 77084

- Presidents Course: 1968. Jay Riviere and Dick Forester. 18 holes. Par 72. Blue – 6,562 (69.5/1115). White – 6,115 (68.1/109). Forward – 5,728 (70.6/111). Price - $$.
- Masters Course: 1973. Jay Riviere. 18 holes. Black – 7,131 (74.1/133). Blue – 6,739 (72.9/128). White – 6,188 (68.9/123). Red – 5,544 (72.1/125). Price - $$$.
- Challenger Course: 1978. Bruce Little. 18 holes. Par 66. Blue – 5,295 (65.5/105). White – 4,907 (62.5/99). Red – 4,432 (64.7/103). Price - $$.

Getting there From I-10 west, take Hwy. 6 north for 4 miles to Golf Course Rd., then turn right and drive a short ways to the course.

BLAKETREE NATIONAL GOLF CLUB

The golf The Blaketree National Golf Club is a 7,236-yard, par 71 daily fee track located on the late Thomas W. Blake's former Sandy Branch Ranch 7 miles northwest of Houston. Blake, a former Rice University golfer who belonged to the Southwest Conference Championship teams of 1929 and 1930, was also a successful attorney and oilman.

Nobody asked how you looked, just what you shot. Sam Snead

Blake's vision began to take hold in 1985 when he hired Ben Crenshaw and Bill Coore to route the course. After completing 11 holes, the oil bust took hold and put the brakes on the project, which laid dormant until 1999 when Blake supervised the construction himself.

Tall pines line the fairways, and golfers face native wetlands, bunkering, subtle elevation changes, and lightning-fast greens throughout the round. While there are a few forced carries, many approaches offer the chance to run the shot onto the putting surface.

The front side features a few long par 4s, including the opening 444-yard No. 1 and the uphill holes 3 and 4. No. 4 is lined by water on the left the entire length of the fairway. Those are tough, but not near as difficult as No. 8–a ridiculous dogleg left that bends to a green with water on the left, and can at times play longer than 500 yards! Work your draw off the tee and cut the corner on No. 8.

The back side is actually tighter–it opens up with the signature hole, the 195-yard No. 10 that plays from an elevated tee over a lake. No. 12 can really piss you off–another almost 500-yard par 4 that plays uphill, featuring an approach over water. At that point you'll be smiling at Blaketree's reputation for not being tricked up as you limp to No. 18, only to find a 657-yarder staring you in the face.

Note that lodging is available for those interested in a weekend get-away to Blaketree–a four-bedroom cottage sits on the first fairway and is available for rentals.

The details   936-449-4907. 4430 S. FM 1486 Rd., Houston, TX 77019

- 18 holes. Par 71. Back – 7,326 (74.6/134). Men's – 6,600 (72.1/130). Price - $$$.

Getting there After traveling down the mile-long road off FM 1486, take 290 into the Beltway 8. Take 249 off Beltway 8 to Magnolia, TX to the intersection at 1488 (road ends). Turn right, go over the tracks and turn left to FM 1774. Go one mile to 1486 (flashing light), turn right, and the course is 6.5 miles down on the left.

BRAEBURN COUNTRY CLUB

The golf   The fourth oldest and one of the most elite clubs in Houston, Braeburn CC dates back to the 1920s when John Bredemus was hired to build what was supposed to be called the Colonial Country Club. The club was foreclosed upon in 1929, but was brought back to life in 1931 by a group headed by Houston's legendary Jack Burke, Sr.

Braeburn has long been known as a shot-maker's course because of the predominance of trees. Carlton Gipson rolled through in the early 1990s to update the course and add elevation changes.

SOUTH EAST

Can you name me one single case where devotion to this pestilential pastime has done a man any practical good? P.G. Wodehouse

The details 713-774-2586. 8101 Bissonnet St., Houston, TX 77074

- www.braeburncc.com
- 1926. John Bredemus. 18 holes. Par 72. Green – 6,808 (72.8/131). Blue – 6,324 (70.2/122). White – 5,647 (67.0/113). Red – 5,054 (72.0/126). (69.7/122). Price - $$$.

Getting there From Hwy. 59 south, exit Bissonnet St. and turn left. Drive under the highway through the second traffic light, and the course is less than a mile away

BROCK PARK GOLF COURSE

The golf Brock Park opened in the late 1940s next to the old Acme Brick Company, one of Houston's most beautiful areas because of its wooded location along Greens Bayou. They called it Lake Forest Country Club back then when the Elks Lodge showed an interest in owning the property. Finally in the 1960s, the city purchased the course in an effort to help meet the demand for public golf.

The best hole on the front is the 222-yard No. 2, a difficult par 3 that plays through a narrow chute of trees. On the back, Nos. 11 and 12 are both driveable par 4s where you'll need to ensure par or better, since the number one handicap No. 14 looms close by. No. 14 goes 220 yards over Greens Bayou, and it's all carry.

The details 281-458-1350. 8201 John Ralston Rd., Houston, TX 77044

- 1953. 18 holes. Par 72. Back – 6,427 (70.6/114). Forward – 5,245. Price - $$.

Getting there From I-10 east, take the McCarty St. exit, and drive north for 6 miles until you come to John Ralston Rd. Turn left and head straight to the course.

CHAMPIONS GOLF CLUB

The golf Founded by golf legends Jimmy Demaret and Jack Burke in 1957, Champions is the site of the 1967 Ryder Cup, as well as the 1969 US Open (won by Orville Moody) and the 1993 US Amateur. The club offers two impeccable 18-hole courses that feature narrow, tree-lined fairways and large, quick greens.

The **Cypress Creek Course**, considered the more difficult of the two, is famous for its 236-yard No. 4, which hammered Ben Hogan for a 9 in 1971 and literally took him to his knees when he injured himself scrambling down the bank of Cypress Creek.

The **Jack Rabbit Course**, often overshadowed by the Cypress course, actually has a higher slope rating for its George Fazio design that features small

Champions Golf Club in Houston has listed as many as 250 single-digit handicappers among its membership.

greens and numerous out-of-bounds. You'll notice the par 3s, all of which play longer than 190 yards. You'll also notice the par 5s, all of which play greater than 540 yards. No. 9 is the longest at 602 yards.

The signature hole is the shortest par 5. The 540-yard dogleg left No. 10 is tough because of its tiny green surrounded by water on three sides.

The details   281-444-6449. 13722 Champions Dr., Houston, TX 77069•
   Cypress: 1959. Ralph Plummer. 18 holes. Par 71. Back – 7,200 (74.6/131). Middle – 6,513 (71.4/124). Forward – 6,103 (68.9/120). Price - $$$$.

• Jack Rabbit: 1957. George and Tom Fazio. 18 holes. Back – 7,089 (74.2/131). Middle – 6,493 (71.4/124). Forward – 6,287 (69.8/123). Price - $$$$.

Getting there From Hwy. 249 north, take Hwy. 1960 east and the course is 1 mile down on the left.

CLASSIC 3 GOLF COURSE

The golf   Labeled as the premier training facility in Texas, Classic 3 features almost three acres of water over its 9 holes, which results in numerous tee shots over the wet stuff. Pines and oaks line the fairways and the medium-sized greens have some subtle undulations.

The details   281-440-1308. 6224 Theall Rd., Houston, TX 77066.

• Derrell Witt. 9 holes. Par 27. Back – 1,245. Forward – 1,029. Price - $$.

Getting there From downtown Houston, take Hwy. 290 going west to the Sam Houston Tollway and proceed north. Take the 249 exit, drive north to the 1960 intersection, and turn right to Cutten Rd. Continue for approximately a half mile to Theall Rd. and turn right–the course is visible from the road.

CLEAR CREEK GOLF COURSE

The golf   The Clear Creek Golf Course is a flat, wide-open links-style track loaded with water and bunkers. The only sort of elevation changes you'll experience come from the ravines that route through the course and the undulating greens.

The back nine is the more challenging, spiced up by some interesting par 3s and two outstanding par 5s. No. 11 goes 555 yards and involves an approach over a ravine, and No. 13 is a 584-yard monster that double-doglegs to a skinny green framed by bunkers.

The details   713-738-8000. 3902 Fellows Rd., Houston, TX 77047

• www.clearcreekclub.com

• 1987. B. Spann, K. Dye, and J. Finger. 18 holes. Par 72. Back – 6,758

*Golf is a game in which one endeavors to control a ball with
implements ill adapted for the purpose.* Woodrow Wilson

(71.4/120). Middle – 6,110 (69.0/113). Forward – 5,263 (70.0/111). Price
- $$.

Getting there The course is located in the Tom Bass Park at the corner of Hwy.
288 and the Sam Houston Tollway. From the Astrodome, take Hwy. 288 south
for 7 miles to the course. Look for the entrance off Fellows Rd.

CLEAR LAKE GOLF COURSE

The golf   Little-known Milt Coggins was hired in the early 1960s to design
9 holes for one of the nation's first master-planned communities. Then Jay
Riviere came along for his first solo project to add the second nine in 1967.
Back then there were no trees–the ones that were planted on the open prairie
have finally matured, providing some character to this flat course. Out-of-
bounds is prominent because of the houses, and water comes into play on a
few holes. However, the most difficult aspect of a round at Clear Lake is in
dealing with the small, mound-shaped greens.

The details   281-488-0252. 1202 Reseda Dr., Houston, TX 77062

• 1963. Jay Riviere. 18 holes. Par 72. Back – 6,757 (71.7/113). Middle –
  6,419 (70.0/111). Forward – 5,735 (72.9/116). Price - $$$.

Getting there From I-45 south, get off at the El Dorado St. exit and turn right
on El Camino Rd. When you come to Reseda Rd., turn left and look for the
clubhouse on the right side.

GLENBROOK GOLF COURSE

The golf   Imagine the 1920s when golf courses were built by hand and the
sand greens were rolled smooth with oil. Historic Glenbrook was around in
those days–this 9-holer opened in 1926. In the 1980s Houston reworked Sims
Bayou into a flood relief project and changed the routing of the course.
However, Robert McKinney was able to redesign the course and involve the
bayou on seven holes.

   The most noticeable problem facing golfers at this Houston muni is the tee
shots that require carries of up to 200 yards.

The details   713-649-8089. 8205 North Bayou, Houston, TX 77017

• 18 holes. Par 71. Blue – 5,923 (70.5/120). White – 5,579 (67.5/116).
  Yellow – 5,220. Red – 4,861. Price - $$.

Getting there From I-45 north, take the Monroe exit and turn right on
Howard Dr. Find Arizona St. and turn left. The course is off of Bayou Dr.

SOUTH EAST

---

*Love and putting are mysteries for the philosopher
to solve. Both subjects are beyond golfers.* Tommy Armour

THE GOLF CLUB AT WESTWOOD

The golf   Located near downtown Houston, Westwood was built by John Bredemus in 1929 and is one of Houston's most historic courses. The original 9-hole Bredemus track survived until the 1950s, when the bayou was rerouted through the course as part of a flood control project. Club members hired Joe Finger, whose father designed the original clubhouse, to oversee the construction of the new course.

Finger's layout is burdened by the wind, and features small greens and water in play on 15 holes. Flowers line the lush course, creating a garden-like setting that has hosted the likes of the PGA Tour's Houston Open in 1972.

The feature hole is No. 13, a 437-yard challenge with an extremely narrow fairway.

Other notes: In 1990 the club spent $1 million to improve the course, including a complete greens renovation that created what many consider the most undulating greens in Houston.

The details   713-774-2521. 8888 Country Creek Dr., Houston, TX 77036

- Blue – 6,989 (73.4/122). White – 6,506 (70.8/117). Yellow – 6,238 (70.0/114). Red – 5,657 (73.8/133). Price - $$$.

Getting there From Hwy. 59 south, take the Bissonnet St. exit and turn right. When you come to Country Creek Dr., turn right and the road will take you to the course.

GUS WORTHAM PARK GOLF COURSE

The golf   Texas' oldest existing 18-hole track was originally built in 1908 to serve members of Houston Country Club. When the club found a new location in the 1950s, Gus Wortham bought the facility and opened it to the public with $60 annual dues. The city of Houston took over in 1973, and it's been one of the busiest courses in the state ever since.

The unique design features a trio of par 5s on holes 2-4, a rarity in golf. One of the better birdie opportunities is the 293-yard No. 9. On the back, one of Texas' signature par 3s awaits in the 250-yard No. 16.

The details   713-921-3227. 7000 Capitol St., Houston, TX 77223

- 1908. 18 holes. Par 72. Back – 6,314 (69.5/113). Forward – 5,904 (73.0/117). Price - $$.

Getting there From I-45, take the Wakeside Blvd. exit and travel 1 mile north to Capitol St.

SOUTH EAST

Perhaps the most fatal beam of all that can float over your mental vision is the vision of a past hole played badly which you are filled with some insane notion of "making up for." The idea of "making up," by present extra exertions, for past deficiencies is one of the most deadly and besetting delusions that is prone to affect the golfing mind. Its results are inevitably ruinous. Horace Hutchinson

HEARTHSTONE GOLF & COUNTRY CLUB

The golf   The original 18 opened in 1977 after Jay Riviere brought in over 2,000 trees to line the fairways, and a third nine was added in 1986 by Joe Finger. Each nine features some impressive, difficult par 3 holes and plenty of bunkers throughout the design.

The **Wolf Corner Course** is the shortest of the three nines, and is more wide open. Its famous par 3 is No. 6, which plays only 106 yards but features a green surrounded by water on three sides.

The **Jackrabbit Course** is the most difficult, featuring tight fairways, frequent out-of-bounds, and numerous water hazards. Nos. 4 and 8 are both over 200 yards and feature water.

The **Horsepen Course** is flat and wide open, spotted by a few ravines located by the greens. No. 3 goes 232 yards, and No. 5 is 198 yards with a lake to the right of the green.

The details   281-463-2204. 7615 Ameswood Rd., Houston, TX 77095

- Wolf Corner/Horsepen: Gold – 6,493 (71.1/120). Blue – 6,140 (70.0/117). White – 5,706 (67.1/112). Red – 5,044 (69.8/118). Price - $$$.
- Horsepen/Jackrabbit: Gold – 6,548 (71.8/124). Blue – 6,229 (70.7/122). White – 5,885 (68.6/117). Red – 5,182 (70.7/127). Price - $$$.
- Jackrabbit/Wolf Corner: Gold – 6,631 (72.3/123). Blue – 6,293 (71.3/120). White – 5,863 (68.7/118). Red – 5,218 (70.7/123). Price - $$$.

Getting there From Hwy. 90, exit Eldridge and turn north. When you come to FM 529, head west, find Huffmeister, and turn west again.

HERMANN PARK GOLF COURSE

The golf   Another of Houston's old-school golf courses, Hermann was built by John Bredemus and became the playground of Tommy Bolt, Jack Burke, Jr., and Jimmy Demaret, among others. After shutting down in 1997 for extensive renovations, the facility has become one of the finest municipals in the Harris County area.

Today you'll encounter prominent fairway mounding and huge, multi-tiered greens. The best hole is No. 13, a 458-yard par 5 that doglegs right. While short, the hole requires strategy with a set of trees in the fairway.

The details   713-526-0077. 2155 N. MacGregor Dr., Houston, TX 77030

- 1999. 18 holes. Par 71. Back – 6,014 (67.9/117). Middle – 5,294 (65.8/109). Forward – 4,724 (63.7/99). Price - $$.

Getting there Take I-45 south from Houston and roll down Hwy. 288 south. Exit McGregor Dr. and turn right. The entrance is on the right.

Golf is a day spent in a round of strenuous idleness. William Wordsworth

HERON LAKES GOLF COURSE

The golf   Heron Lakes makes for a fine weekend when you're looking to combine hacker-friendly golf with post-round horse race wagering. Located across the highway from the Sam Houston Racepark, Heron Lakes serves up 18 holes of relatively easy golf where length isn't required to score well.

The details   281-807-4653. 7910 N. Sam Houston Pkwy W., Houston, TX 77064

* www.heronlakesgc.com
* 18 holes. Par 69. Blue – 5,171. White – 4,827. Price – $$.

Getting there The course is located 5 minutes from Willowbrook Mall and just across the tollway from the Sam Houston Racepark.

Houston Country Club back in the day. Check out the two old Model T's.

HOUSTON COUNTRY CLUB

The golf   Around the turn of the century Houston had no golf to speak of, unlike today where over 130 courses can be found in the Greater Houston area. It all began to change when prospective HCC members started to contribute $25 each– eventually, the money was used to lease 45 acres from Rice University. Nine holes sprang up, the golf craze began, and the overloaded facility was forced to move outside the city limits.

⭐

All men make mistakes, but married men find out about them sooner. Red Skelton

From 1914 to the mid-1950s, the 18-hole A.W. Pollard design hosted Houston's elite. And when Houston's growth squeezed the club yet again, HCC found a new home and hired Robert Trent Jones to build his first Houston course.

Incidentally, Gus Wortham bought the original 18-hole track, which is now one of Houston's six municipal courses.

Jones' layout lasted until the late 1980s when Ben Crenshaw and his partner, Bill Coore, were hired to to renovate the greens and work on the grasses. The master's course was mostly left in place.

The course design features lots of trees, open fairways, prominent bunkering, and elevated greens. Water is surprisingly not that prevalent. The opening holes are among the best, with two long and challenging par 4s. Two par 3s stand out in the middle of the round–Nos. 9 and 14 both play over 220 yards.

The details   713-465-8381. 1 Potomac Dr., Houston, TX 77227

• www.houstoncc.com

• 1914. 18 holes. Tips – 6,971 (72.9/122). Back – 6,569 (70.8/118). Middle – 5,991 (67.5/115). Forward – 5,522 (70.3/14). Price - $$$$.

Getting there From Hwy. 290 west, take the 610 Loop west and look for the signs leading to the course.

HOUSTON HILLS GOLF COURSE

The golf   Houston Hills is a links-style course built by Chuck Berson in 1988. Although some of the fairways are lined by trees, the course is mostly open and routes around several irrigation lakes that come into play. Berson created small greens with mild undulations that make for challenging targets.

The front side boasts the two best holes. No. 5 goes 202 yards over a lake, but plays into one of the largest greens on the course. No. 9 is the signature because it requires a mid-iron approach over water to an island green.

The details   281-933-2300. 9720 Ruffino Rd., Houston, TX 77031

• 1988. Chuck Berson. Back – 6,707 (67.9/104). Middle – 6,270 (66.0/100). Forward – 5,253 (69.8/117). Price - $$.

Getting there From Hwy. 59, take Beltway 8 going south. Later you'll need to make a U-turn on the Beltway toward Hwy. 59–turn off on the first road on the right.

HOUSTON NATIONAL GOLF CLUB

The golf   With the addition of nine new holes in 2002, Houston National is now a 27-hole links-style track that is long, loaded with water, and known for its small greens. With hardly an even lie on the course due to the extensive

Never putt for a three-foot circle. If you aren't trying to hole every putt you have, you are going to lose to someone who is. Dr. Bob Rotella

mounding and reshaping, Robert von Hagge created a true test of golf.

The highlight hole is the 647-yard par 5 that came with the most recent nine–it's long and brutal into the wind. You'll need three impressive golf shots to reach the green in elevation, which is no guarantee since the unique green connects each level with only a small strip of grass.

The details   281-304-1400. 16500 Houston National Blvd., Houston, TX 77095

• 2002. Robert Von Hagge. 18 holes. Par 72. 7.337 (75.8/133). Price - $$$.

Getting there Take US 290 north to the Barker-Cypress exit. Turn left and look for the Stone Gate development.

INWOOD FOREST GOLF CLUB

The golf   Jay Riviere, Jackson Bradley, and Don Collet combined to build this 27-hole facility, which serves as the centerpiece for the middle-class Inwood Forest residential community. Tracks that run through housing developments are usually loaded with out-of-bounds, and this one is no exception–the potential for a big number looms on every hole if your misses cross to the other side of the stakes. Water is prominent as well, with Vogel Creek, White Oak Bayou, and 11 manmade lakes spotting the landscape.

The longest of the three is the **East Course**, which is highlighted by No. 2–a 447-yard par 4 that tees over the creek that runs along the entire left side.

The 2nd hole is the signature on the **West Course**–a 180-yard par 3 that plays to a wooded green fronted by the creek. No. 9 is the toughest, a 454-yard dogleg right with water on the left side and beside the green.

The **North Course** is the local favorite and receives the majority of play, primarily because it's considered the easiest of the three.

The details   281-448-0223. 7603 Antoine Dr., Houston, TX 77088

• www.inwoodgolf.com

• North/West: 1970. Jay Riviere. 18 holes. Par 72. Back – 6,546 (71.3/130). Middle – 6,194 (69.6/127). Forward – 5,639 (71.9/123). Price - $$$.

• West/East: 18 holes. Par 71. Back – 6,734 (72.3/129). Middle – 6,278 (70.2/124). Forward – 5,459 (71.3/123). Price - $$$.

• East/North: 18 holes. Par 71. Back – 6,614 (71.6/125). Middle – 6,222 (69.6/122). Forward – 5,484 (71.2/121). Price - $$$.

Getting there From Hwy. 290, get off at the Antoine Dr. exit and turn north. Drive 3 miles to the course and look for the entrance on the left side of the road.

SOUTH EAST

Never make a golf bet where you have to shoot even par (with your handicap strokes) to win.
Always figure you're going to shoot three or four over par. Sam Snead

JERSEY MEADOW GOLF COURSE

The golf   This facility has three separate 9-hole courses that are played in three 18-hole combinations. They are traditional Atlantic coast-style golf courses. Although ownership has changed frequently over the years, it is now a solid public facility for Houston.

The **White Course** is the toughest nine, with the tightness of the fairways making it a difficult course. This track does not have much water.

The **Red Course** is tree-lined with some water coming into play on a few holes. The fairways were built on rolling terrain and the greens are large.

In 1991 Carlton Gipson added the 9-hole **Blue Course**, a links-style target course to go along with the club's new driving range and miniature golf course. There are several bunkers and numerous holes with water in play throughout its design, although the trees are still fairly immature. On this one, good drives will leave you with short irons into the greens.

In 1991 Carlton Gipson added another 9 holes, a new driving range, and a miniature golf course. For the most part, if you are driving it well you'll have medium to short iron approaches. The new course is more of a links style course with a lot of fairly immature trees that don't really affect play.

Three lakes come into play on 6 holes. No. 1 is nice because it's a par 5 and only 464 yards. No. 2 is only 300 yards but has water in front of the green forcing a full 300-yard carry if you want to reach the green off the tee.

The details   713-896-0900. 8502 Rio Grande St., Houston, TX 77040

- www.jerseymeadow.homestead.com
- 1953. Joe Finger. 18 holes. Par 71. Price - $$$.
- Red/White: Back – 6,434 (70.5/117). Middle – 6,055 (68.7/115). Forward – 5,183 (67.9/112).
- White/Blue: Back – 6,275 (70.4/119). Middle – 5,745 (68.0/114). Forward – 5,015 (65.8/108).
- Blue/Red: 1992. Gipson, Finger. Par 72. Back – 6,343 (68.9/115). Middle – 5,850 (66.3/111). Forward – 4,898 (64.1/106).

Getting there Take Hwy. 290 going west, turn right on Jones Rd., go .25 mile, and turn right at the Jersey Meadow Fun Center. Drive through the parking lot and take the road to the course.

LAKESIDE COUNTRY CLUB

The golf   In 1951, Lakeside was born when a group of prominent Houston businessmen bought this area west of town known as Pine Lakes Farms. Ralph Plummer came in and designed the layout, which was modernized by Ron Pritchard in 1990. Pritchard added new grass and some mound-

If one has not learned enough of golf by the time he steps on to the first tee, then he has run out of time. Bobby Jones

ing to the flat layout but kept Plummer's traditional design.

Two par 5s stand out–the almost 600-yard par 5 hole 3 with its L-shaped green, and the 503-yard 18th, which requires a tough tee shot and an approach over water. No. 3 goes well with the four 400-yard-plus par 4s on the front.

The details   281-497-2222. 100 Wilcrest Dr., Houston, TX 77042

• www.lakesidecc.com

• 1951. Ralph Plummer-Ron Pritchard. 18 holes. Champs – 6,983 73.7/132). Reg – 6,574 (71.2/126). Middle – 5,939 (67.9/120). Forward – 5,373 (70.8/120). Price - $$$.

Getting there From Beltway south, take I-10 west and exit Wilcrest Dr. Turn left, drive a short distance to the course, and look for the entrance on the right side of the street.

LOCHINVAR COUNTRY CLUB

The golf   Named after a hero of the Sir Walter Scott poem "Marmion," the ultimate male chauvinist, Lochinvar is an exclusive, all-male golf club patterned after Dallas' Preston Trail. In the late 1970s, Houston businessman Curtis Hankamer developed the property and hired Jack Nicklaus to come in and design one of his few Texas courses.

The result is a unique course carved out of the tall pines and oaks near Houston's Intercontinental Airport–it features a few links-style features with grass bunkers and numerous undulations. The fairways are mostly generous and the greens are sloped and fast. The signature hole is No. 12, a 393-yard par 4 that requires a perfect drive and an approach over a scenic, rock-lined stream.

The original pro here was the legendary Claude Harmon, whose son Butch assumed the reins as golf director until the late 1990s.

The details   281-821-0220. 2000 Farrel Rd., Houston, TX 77073

• 1980. Jack Nicklaus. 18 holes. Par 72. Tips – 7,066 (73.4/133). Men's – 6,503 (71.2/130). Price - $$$$.

Getting there From I-45 south, take the Rankon exit and turn left. Drive to Hardy Ave. and turn left. At Farrel Rd. turn right and the course is just ahead.

MELROSE GOLF COURSE

The golf   One of eight muni tracks inside the Houston city limits, Melrose is a lighted par 3 course that is ideal for cold beers and late-night practice rounds.

The details   281-847-1214. 401 Canino Rd. Houston, TX 77076.

• 18 holes. Par 54. 1,917 yards. Price - $.

SOUTH EAST

If conversation was fertilizer, Trevino would be up to his neck in grass all the time. Lee Trevino

Getting there From I-45 north drive past Little York and take the Canino Rd. exit. Drive east for 3 miles past Airline Dr.

Jackie Burke playing Memorial Park circa 1960.

MEMORIAL PARK GOLF COURSE

The golf One of Texas' classics, Memorial Park dates back to the 1930s when John Bredemus utilized work crews from the Civilian Conservation Corps to build what was one of the nation's best courses at the time. Jimmy Demaret, Dave Marr, and Tommy Bolt learned the game here, and the Houston Open was hosted at various times during the 1940s,'50s, and '60s.

Amazingly, the course Houstonites refer to as "The Old Grand Dame" became neglected over the years, with storms and disease wiping out trees and a general lack of care taking its toll. However, in the 1990s the city partnered with several private companies to infuse $4.5 million into renovating the course and expanding the clubhouse.

Pines and oaks line the generous fairways and the large greens are of average speed. The best hole is the scenic No. 15, a 180-yarder that plays over a rock-framed pond.

Note that the course is closed on Tuesdays, and on Mondays, Wednesdays, and Thursdays, the course closes after 1:30 pm. because it sanctions that time for high schoolers.

The details 713-862-4033. 1001 E. Memorial Loop, Houston, TX 77007

• www.memorialparkgolf.com

Good players handle pressure putts by developing a strong
routine and relying on it in the clutch. Dr. Bob Rotella

- 1936. John Bredemus. 18 holes. Par 72. Blue (73.0/122). White (70.3/116). Red (70.7/114). Price - $$.

Getting there Go west on Memorial Dr. past Westcott St. into Memorial Park (just west of downtown). Turn right at the first entrance inside the park.

MULLIGAN'S GOLF PAR 3

The golf   Mulligan's is a lighted 9-hole par 3 course located in the middle of Houston. Water comes into play on 4 of 9 holes, including the signature No. 9, which features a full carry of water to the green 132 yards away. The course is void of bunkers, but the greens are first-class and in great condition for a par 3 facility.

The details   281-890-6026. 11010 Jones Rd. Houston, TX 77070

- 1998. Derrell Witt. 9 holes. Par 27. Back – 1,224. Forward – 1,058. Price - $.

Getting there Located half a block from the intersection of Hwy. 1960 and Jones Rd.

NORTHGATE COUNTRY CLUB

The golf   As the centerpiece of a small, upscale housing community, Northgate is crammed into an area of land that's dominated by huge trees. Labeled a shot-maker's course because of the super-tight fairways and small, testy greens, the course offers 27 holes of golf that many consider some of the toughest in Houston.

The **Bridges Course** is the most recent addition, featuring wider fairways than the other nines and offering some interesting risk-reward decisions. The 427-yard No. 3 stands out because of its three-tiered fairways.

The **Bunkers Course** is named appropriately, featuring loads of sand in the design. They say No. 1 is the toughest opener in Texas, playing 417 yards with two extremely dangerous shots. The tee shot must be perfectly placed and the approach must carry 200 yards over water.

The **Creek Course** is narrow and loaded with water. The best hole is No. 8, a 200-yard-plus par 3 from an elevated tee box. A creek looms right, and the green features a ridge in the middle and bunkers on either side.

The details   281-440-1223. 17110 Northgate Forest Dr., Houston, TX 77068

- www.northgatecountryclub.com
- Creek/Bunkers: Black – 6,540 (71.5/132). Blue – 6,226 (69.6/126). White – 5,648 (67.4/120). Red – 4,714 (67.9/118). Price - $$$.
- Bunkers/Bridges: Black – 6,867 (72.7/133). Blue – 6,406 (70.2/125). White

SOUTH EAST

My divorce came as a complete surprise to me. That will happen
when you haven't been home in 18 years. Lee Trevino

– 5,803 (67.5/119). Red – 4,983 (69.1/119). Price – $$$.

- Bridges/Creek: Black – 6,839 (72.6/133). Blue – 6,447 (70.6/129). White –5,839 (67.7/121). Red – 5,037 (69.0/120). Price - $$$.

Getting there From I-45 north, exit 1960 and turn left. When you come to Northgate Forest Dr., turn right and the course will be on the right side of the road.

PASADENA MUNICIPAL GOLF COURSE

The golf   On the grounds of the old Ellington Air Force Base that shut down in the 1970s lies the 18-hole Pasadena Muni, upgraded by Jay Riviere in 1981 with an additional nine. Water and out-of-bound comes into play on every hole of this links-style track. The fairways are narrow and the small greens are elevated.

Water is everywhere, with some holes having wet stuff on either side of the fairway. No. 7 is the signature, a 437-yarder with water crossing the fairway and requiring a huge tee shot to carry.

The details   281-481-0834. 1000 Duffer Ln., Houston, TX 77034

- 1971. Jay Riviere. 18 holes. Par 72. Blue – 6,750 (72.2/118). White – 6,225 (69.7/113). Gold – 5,456 (66.1/108). Red – 4,910 (67.9/108). Price - $$.

Getting there From I-45 south, take the Beltway east and look for the course on the right side.

PINE CREST GOLF CLUB

The golf   Derrell Witt had a hand in many of Carlton Gipson's successes, including Houston-area tracks like Greatwood and the impressive renovations at BraeBurn Country Club. Pine Crest was his first solo project, and he was able to use his background in landscape architecture to move over 250,000 cubic feet of dirt to create 13 lakes that form the basis of this semi-private course. The water helps the crew keep it in lush condition compared to other courses in the area.

The best hole is the last one, playing 571 yards into a narrow, tree-lined fairway with an approach over water to the green.

The details   713-462-4914. 3080 Gessner Dr., Houston, TX 77080

- 1992. Derrell Witt. Yellow – 6,907 (72.5/124). Blue – 6,570 (71.8/123). White – 6,181 (69.3/121). Forward – 5,482 (71.5/125). Price - $$.

Getting there From Beltway 8 south take the Clay St. exit and turn left. Look for the course on the right side.

SOUTH EAST

Women with pasts interest men because they hope history will repeat itself. Mae West

PINE FOREST COUNTRY CLUB

The golf   Pine Forest was originally a John Bredemus-designed course located just north of Loop 610 in the middle of Houston Heights. When the club moved west in 1974 to avoid Houston's sprawl, they hired Jay Riviere to come in and build three 9-hole tracks.

Riviere implemented a chain of lakes that bring water into play on all but 6 or 7 holes. All three courses feature plush fairways and giant greens.

The most challenging combination is the White/Green route, featuring the most difficult hole at Pine Forest: the 435-yard No. 15 which doglegs left around the trees to a green fronted by a lake.

On the Gold Nine, the 3rd hole stands out because it plays well over 400 yards and features water in play on both the tee shot and approach.

Other notes: The course is known for the annual Three Amigos tournament hosted by Fred Couples, Blaine McCallister, and CBS broadcaster Jim Nantz.

The details   281-463-1234. 18003 Clay Rd., Houston, TX 77084

- Green/Gold: 1975. Jay Riviere. 18 holes. Par 72. Back – 6,813 (72.9/129). Middle – 6,432 (70.7/125). Forward – 5,583 (66.9/117). Price - $$.
- Gold/White: 1975. Jay Riviere. 18 holes. Par 72. Back - 6,706 (72.3/128). Middle - 6,317 (70.0/123). Forward - 5,496 (66.8/117). Price - $$.
- White/Green: 1983. Jay Riviere. 18 holes. Par 72. Back - 6,835 (73.0/127). Middle - 6,465 (70.5/125). Forward - 5,575 (66.7/118). Price - $$.

Getting there From I-10 east take the Addicks exit and turn north onto Hwy. 6. When you come to Clay Rd. turn left–the course is on the left side of the street just down the road.

REDSTONE GOLF CLUB

The golf   Located on the site of the former George Fazio-designed El Dorado Country Club, Redstone will serve as the new home of the Shell Houston Open through 2012, as well as the centerpiece for the Fall Creek residential development. The facility will include a hotel and conference center and serve as the home for the Houston Golf Association.

Slated as the longest course in the state (7,500 yards), the course was designed by Peter Jacobsen and Jim Hardy, who used four of El Dorado's holes. Trees are everywhere, so much so that the design is void of fairway bunkers–a particularly unusual feature for a PGA-caliber course.

Future plans include an addition 18 holes designed by Rees Jones and routed around Greens Bayou (opening 2005), as well as a 9-hole par 3 course.

The details   281-454-6590 Hwy. 59 at Beltway, Houston, TX 77030

- 2003. Peter Jacobsen and Jim Hardy. 7,250 yards. Price - $$$$.

Getting there From downtown Houston, follow 59 north to Beltway 8 East.

SOUTH EAST

A woman drove me to drink, and I never even had the courtesy to thank her. W.C. Fields

Find the Fall Creek subdivision—about 1.5 miles from 59—and turn right on Mesa Dr. Turn left on Fall Creek Bend through the subdivision and follow the signs.

RIVER OAKS COUNTRY CLUB

The golf   River Oaks isn't the oldest, but it's definitely one of the preeminent names in Houston golf. Dating back to 1925 when Houston was hardly exposed to the game of golf, Philadelphian Jack Burke Sr. became the first head pro, no long before Sam Snead and Ben Hogan began coming to the club to work on their game. A new generation of golfers like Jimmy Demaret and Claude Harmon, Sr. (Butch's dad) came along, and River Oaks earned a reputation as the hub of Houston golf.

Designed by the legendary Donald Ross, River Oaks is a timeless, traditional layout that is one of the most exclusive in the country. The high-dollar real estate that Ross had to work with was small, but covered with stately old oak trees and ancient pines all nestled along the banks of Buffalo Bayou.

The layout features some of the area's best short holes–distance isn't an issue, but accuracy is imperative. In addition to the oaks and pines, the skinny fairways are lined with azaleas, magnolias, and dogwoods. The greens are small, slick, and make for challenging targets.

Other notes: Joe Finger came along in 1967 to initiate improvements of the greens, tees, and the rerouting of a few holes.

The details   713-529-4321. 1600 River Oaks Blvd., Houston, TX 77019

- 1923. Donald Ross. 18 holes. Par 72. Blue – 6,868 (72.1/126). White – 6,458 (70.5/123). Red – 5,990 (68.3/120). Forward – 5,547 (72.5/118). Price - $$$$.

Getting there From I-45 south take the Hwy. 610 exit west and find Westheimer Rd. Turn right and look for River Oaks Blvd., where you'll turn left–it will lead to the clubhouse.

ROYAL OAKS COUNTRY CLUB

The golf   The Royal Oaks CC serves up an unparalleled Fred Couples signature course that tips out to a 7,007-yard, par 72, highlighted by the superb features of the country's finest golf clubs: tall Texas pines, scenic waterfalls, undulating, multi-level greens, and even a few island holes. Couples clearly favors traditional golf designs, as this one is pure old-school. A whopping six sets of tees allow just about anyone to enjoy the game at this exclusive club.

The front side features the most difficult rated hole–the 473-yard No. 7, which tees over water and involves a tricky approach into a green protected by

Armed with ignorance, golfers shell out hundreds, sometimes thousands of dollars on new clubs, believing that their investment is going to help them play better. You can spend a million dollars, if your clubs don't fit, you're not going to play good golf. Jonathan Abrahams

water left and back. The fairway snakes on No. 7, which creates some deceptive angles from which to approach the hole.

On the back, Couples mixed it up well by offering an easier stretch of golf on holes 13-16, which consist of two relatively short par 4s and a pair of reasonable par 3s.

The details 713-914-0014. 3039 Rosemary Park Ln., Houston, TX 77082

- www.royaloakscc.com

- Fred Couples. 18 holes. Par 72. Medal – 7,033. Champ – 6,715. Tourney – 6,383. Regular – 6,075. Forward – 5,452. Fairway – 4,841. Price - $$$$.

Getting there Take Beltway 8 south from I-10 to Westheimer. Turn right and drive to Rosemary Park Ln., where you'll turn left into the club.

SHARPSTOWN MUNICIPAL GOLF COURSE

The golf After shutting down for most of 2002 for a $1.2 million renovation project, the Sharpstown Muni opened for play in August 2002 sporting new cart paths, an upgraded irrigation system based on lake expansion, less cross-fairway drainage, and an overall more natural look.

Originally known as the Sharpstown Country Club back in the 1950s and '60s and former host of the Houston Open, the course shut down amid financial turmoil until the city of Houston scooped it up in the late 1970s and hired Jay Riviere to renovate the layout.

With its generous fairways, the course is primarily known as a hacker-friendly track. Wayward tee shots are recoverable because of the relatively sparse tree-lined fairways. Even though there are some rather long par 4s, you'll be able to fire away with your driver on the straightaway holes.

The final stretch of golf is the best, with a few short par 4s and 3s as well as a birdie-able par 5.

Note that they refer to the net along No. 6 as the Zindler Net–it's a wire contraption installed to protect the home of local newsman Marvin Zindler, who lived near the course in the 1970s and '80s. Houstonites know Zindler for his infamous association with the famed La Grange, TX chicken ranch.

The details 713-988-2099. 6600 Harbor Town Dr., Houston, TX 77036

- www.houstonmunicipalgolf.com

- Jay Riviere. 18 holes. Par 70. Back – 6,670 yards (69.7/113). Middle – 6,396 (68.2/112). Forward – 5,883 (72.0/113). Price - $$.

Getting there From Hwy. 59 south take the Bell Aire Blvd. exit and turn right. When you come to Harbor Town Dr., turn right and the course is just down the road on the left side.

SOUTH EAST

I didn't touch a drop of liquor until I was in my 60s. I never saw the point in starting. When I was young I saw drinking ruin a lot of golfers and celebrities. Today, though, a Diet Coke with some dark rum in it takes away some of my aches and pains. Sam Snead

SUGAR HILL GOLF COURSE

The golf   Built atop the site of the former Doty Landfill, which was originally covered by 4 feet of dirt and then molded with an additional 2,000,000 cubic yards of earth, Sugar Hill is a mounded, roller-coaster-like links-style track set amid the flatlands of Houston. The challenge here is dealing with the uneven lies. In fact the hills are so prominent that it's often impossible to see the adjoining holes. Water comes into play on only 4 holes, and while they've incorporated the use of bunkers, it's not as prominent a feature as you might expect for a Scottish-like track.

No. 2 is the number one handicap–a 406-yarder that bends right around a lake and requires a perfect tee shot to set up for the approach.

The details   281-561-5252. 12000 Bissonnet St., Houston, TX 77099

• www.sugarhillgolfcourse.com

• 2001. 18 holes. Par 72. 6,700 yards. Price - $$.

Getting there Take the US 59 Kirkwood exit north and turn left on Bissonnet.

TEXACO COUNTRY CLUB

The golf   Originally opened as a 9-holer in 1924 for the Texas Co., TCC is the oldest existing private course in Houston that is still in its current location. Another nine was added in 1938, creating the full golf experience with a design that incorporated the unusual Cypress Pond. The pond is loaded with lily pads and cypress trees, which complements this traditional track quite well. The greens are small and undulating–difficult targets but fairly reasonable two-putts.

No. 11 is the toughest hole at 563 yards. Considered one of the best holes in the Houston area, it's a double dogleg that has lots of trees and Greens Bayou to boot.

The details   713-453-7501. 12800 Texaco Rd., Houston, TX 77229

• www.texacocc.com

• 1930s. 18 holes. Par 72. Back – 6,254 (69.9/119). Middle – 5,965 (68.6/117). Forward – 5,453 (70.5/122). Price - $$.

Getting there From I-10 going east, get off at the Federal Rd. exit and make a left. Travel about 2 miles to Texaco Rd. and make a right.

TEXAS PAR GOLF ACADEMY

The golf   Texas Par is a 9-hole executive track with a good combination of open and wooded holes. Water comes into play a few times, but its signature is its small, undulating greens. No. 8 is the longest and most likely to blow up

SOUTH EAST

your round–a 470-yard par 5 that bends left and features an approach into a green bordered by water on the left.

The details 281-493-3276. 4035 Hwy. 6 S., Houston, TX 77082

- 1976. Ruben Lopez. 9 holes. Par 32. Back – 2,252. Middle – 1,984. Forward – 1,714. Price - $$.

Getting there From downtown Houston, take Hwy. 6 south 1.5 miles past Westheimer St. to the course. The entrance is on the right side of the road.

WILDCAT GOLF CLUB

The golf Architect Roy Case created both courses on this new 36-hole, daily-fee facility that is located only 10 minutes from downtown Houston. In addition to the views of the skyline, Case had at his disposal a touch of Hill Country terrain with dramatic elevation changes, as well as the typical Houston-area prairie lands. From this he was able to carve the links-style Highlands Course and the more traditional Lakes Course.

As its name implies, the **Lakes Course**, which tips out at a par 72 7,016 yards, is loaded with water. The best hole is the 539-yard No. 7, which is listed as the number one handicap. Interestingly, the four easiest holes are the par 3s, which range from 165 to 218 yards.

The **Highlands Course** is probably the more stimulating of the two, offering better views of the city, natural wetlands and grasses, and some intriguing flat sand bunkers. Case must have an affinity for the number 7, because like the Lakes track, the 421-yard, par 4 hole 7 is the most difficult rated hole. Watch out for the par 5s on this one, three of which play at or above 570 yards from the tips.

The details 713-413-3400. 12000 Almeda Rd., Houston, TX 77045

- www.wildcatgolfclub.com
- Highlands Course: 2001. Roy Case.
- Lakes Course: 2002. Roy Case. 18 holes. Par 72. Black – 7,016 (73.2/135). Gold – 6,535 (71.2/131). Blue – 6,045 (68.9/114). White – 5,482 (66.3/103). Price - $$$.

Getting there From downtown, take Hwy. 288 south for 5 miles to Loop 610. Head west and find the Fannin exit, where you'll U-turn under 610 and drive east on the access road to Almeda Rd. Turn right on Almeda and the course is 3 miles further.

SOUTH EAST

WORLD HOUSTON GOLF COURSE

The golf This cow-pasture course was formerly known as H&H, for the H&H Guest Ranch. Developers came along in the 1980s and provided the

Serious sport has nothing to do with fair play. It is bound up with hatred jealousy, boastfulness. It is war minus the shooting. George Orwell

funding needed to improve the course. In 1984, American Golf took over and continued to improve the course into the 1990s.

The course is well-conditioned, wide-open, and relatively short, with only one par 4 playing over 400 yards (No. 12). Small lakes dot the landscape, bringing water into play on 14 holes. The course's signature is its excellent greens.

The details   281-449-8384. 4000 Greens Rd., Houston, TX 77032

• www.worldhoustongolf.com

• Jay Riviere. 18 holes. Par 72. Back – 6,642 (71.2/117). Middle – 6,075 (69.5/108). Forward – 5,204 (71.4/123). Price - $$$.

Getting there From Houston, take US 59 north to Greens Rd., then turn left 2 miles to the course entrance on the right.

HOUSTON NOTES   Line up your lodging first, and consider taking advantage of downtown Houston's new boutique accommodations like **The Sam Houston Hotel** and **The Magnolia Hotel**, both unique because of the historic locations. Also consider timing your evenings around the great game of baseball at the new **Minute Maid Park** (formerly Enron Field), where you can reserve a room at the **Inn at the Ballpark** next door. Also downtown find the **Doubletree Hotel at Allen Center**, **Four Seasons Hotel**, and others. Houston's oldest buildings, some dating back to the 1860s, are on the north side of downtown. Today they house shops, restaurants, and clubs.

The family can have fun around the **Uptown/Galleria** area, where loads of restaurants and shopping are available. Try the **Hotel Derek** or **Marriott Courtyard** when down this way.

Museum-goers can stay at **The Patrician B&B** and around The Heights area, there's the **Angel Arbor B&B**, and **Sara's B&B**.

For action hit **Kenneally's** on South Shephers, an Irish pub with live music and lots of character. And for views of the city and smooth jazz, hit **Scott Gertner's Skybar**. Those spots are perfect after a juicy steak at River Oaks' **The Stables**, a quaint, locally-owned Houston tradition that sports hunting trophies, horse racing paraphernalia, and a classy décor.

For late night bar-hopping there's the fast-laned **Mercury Room** on Prairie, which is next door to the **Boaka Bar**. However hardcore drinkers will prefer the more toned down **Kay's Lounge**, a dive that has served the locals with cold bottles of beer, jukebox tunes, and a pool table since Prohibition.

SOUTH EAST

Sudden success in golf is like the sudden acquisition of wealth. It is apt to unsettle and deteriorate the character. P.G. Wodehouse

HUFFMAN

Elev. 63   Pop. 250

A half hour from Houston on the other side of Lake Houston and the scenic FM 1960 bridge lies Huffman, an extremely small lakeside community that was named for its original settler, David Huffman, way back in 1839. Nothing much has ever surfaced here except for the farthest edges of Houston's growth, with residential communities housing Houston commuters who enjoy the lake and don't mind the drive. However, Houston-area golfers know that one of the region's best-kept secrets resides just north of town in the new and improved Red Wolf Run Golf Club. Long the victim of poor conditions and a lengthy drive, the course is seeing a resurgence now that Baytown's Harrington family has invested in the fabulous Jay Riviere design and created an unbelievable golf value for the touring hack.

RED WOLF RUN GOLF CLUB

The golf   After new ownership and a $1.5 million cash infusion, the former Bear Creek East and Lake Houston Golf Club is worthy of the praise it's starting to receive in the Houston golf circles. Now known as the Red Wolf Run Golf Club, this 6,949-yard Jay Riviere track sports new Bermuda 419 fairways, Tifdwarf greens, and new trees to go along with the new management's policy of offering customer service-oriented amenities to make this a first-class golf destination.

There's no doubt that this is a Texas-themed facility, complete with holes named after the Harrington's bulls (they are providers of bulls for professional rodeos) and a Southwestern-styled clubhouse.

As for the golf course, Riviere's design has always been considered a fine layout. However, years of neglect helped perpetuate the belief that it just wasn't worth the drive out to Huffman to play this heavily-wooded track loaded with long par 4s.

Take advantage of the easier front nine by scoring well on the opening holes, where four of the shortest par 4s range from 370 to 420 yards. No. 9 is the most difficult hole on the course, a 453-yarder that chutes through a narrow opening uphill into the sloped fairway. This one is mean–it was formerly a par 5 on the old course–and requires a long approach over a lake.

The par 3s are challenging at Red Wolf, ranging from mid to long irons, but it's the longer holes that eat you alive. The back opens with two long par 4s, including the 456-yard No. 11, and average golfers will be grateful that some of Riviere's generosity is still in play, because you'll want to take advantage of the open greens that present chances to run the ball onto the putting surface.

The last two holes are particularly difficult, with the 524-yard No. 17 requiring two carries of water, and the 420-yard No. 18 playing alongside a creek that borders right and cuts in front of the green.

The details   281-324-1842. 27350 Afton Way, Huffman, TX 77336

Television: the bland leading the bland. Fred Allen

- 18 holes. Par 72. 7,080 yards. Price - $$.

Getting there From US 59 north, take FM 1960 east to FM 2100. Turn left and drive 3 miles to Afton Way. Turn right on Afton.

HUFFMAN NOTES Give the **Cedar Landing Restaurant** (281-324-1113) a try if you're taking your time in the area–seafood is the specialty. The **Lake Houston State Park** offers the chance to hike, camp, and generally become one with nature if you're itching to get outdoors. The park also has a few dining halls and lodges for large groups.

HUMBLE

Elev. 65   Pop. 13,341

Once a lazy sawmill town, Humble boomed after the 1904 oil gushers and subsequently grew around the Humble Oil & Refining Company, now known as Exxon. Located where the Big Thicket runs into the coastal plains, Humble's location 15 miles north of Houston and due east of the Intercontinental airport make it a bustling metro community loaded with golf.

THE ATOSCOCITA CLUB OF HOUSTON

The golf Named after the Indian word for "swampland," Atascocita rolls around the shores of Lake Houston and features three 9-hole courses. The golf here is of good quality, and the course has a bit of character with some palm-tree-lined fairways.

The **Pinehurst Course** tips out at 3,238 yards and is mostly straightaway. Although there are several 400-yard-plus par 4s, the most difficult rated hole is the opener, a 385-yarder. This par 35 nine-hole course only has one par 5: the 502-yard No. 5.

The **Shores Course** offers a few more uneven lies at it rolls through the hilliest part of the property. Like Pinehurst, its opening hole is perhaps the toughest: a 555-yard par 5 that is particularly mean into the wind. This track is probably the toughest of the three, with long par 4s and a 220-yard par 3 (No. 8).

No. 6, the signature hole on the **Point Course,** starts a tough stretch of holes as a 404-yarder that involves a longish approach into a green surrounded by bunkers. No. 6 is followed by a 550-yard par 5 and two more 400-yard-plus par 4s.

The details 281-852-8111. 20114 Pinehurst Dr., Humble, TX 77346

- www.atascocitaclub.com, 1957. Ralph Plummer. 1985. Redesigned by Don January-Billy Martindale.

- 1956. Ralph Plummer. 18 holes. Par 71. Back – 6,661 (71.7/121). Middle – 6,341 (70.2/117). Forward – 5,575 (72.3/125). Price - $$$.

Putting: It's not how, but how many. My sidesaddle style wasn't pretty to look at, but I would have putted standing on my head if it would have helped. Sam Snead

- 1956. Ralph Plummer. 18 holes. Par 71. Back – 6,754 (72.0/121). Middle – 6,400 (69.7/118). Forward – 5,433 (71.4/127). Price - $$$.
- 1956. Ralph Plummer. 18 holes. Par 70. Back – 6,569 (71.0/116). Middle – 6,183 (68.7/115). Forward – 5,288 (70.5/122). Price - $$$.

Getting there From I-59, take FM 1960 east to Pinehurst Trails. Turn left, look for the course sign, then turn right into the parking lot.

EL DORADO GOLF CLUB

The golf   El Dorado is an older Houston course, built in 1964 on the Ginther family's homestead dating back to the turn of the century. Big names George Fazio and Jay Riviere collaborated on the design, which is known for its long, skinny fairways and tiny, fast greens.

The duo created a circular route with parallel fairways. The course rolls to clockwise on the front, then turns back to the left for the second nine.

No. 5 is the longest of several mammoth par 4s on the front. This tough hole plays 474 yards and doglegs left, featuring a long approach into a green fronted by a bunker.

The details   281-458-1010. 7900 Old N. Belt Dr. E, Humble, TX 77396

- 1964. George Fazio-Jay Riviere. 18 holes. Par 72. Back – 7,118 (73.8/125). Middle – 6,583 (71.4/119). Forward – 5,957 (72.7/114). Price - $$$.

Getting there From Hwy. 59 north, take the Beltway 8 exit and turn right. The course is 1.5 miles down the road, and the entrance is on the right side.

HUMBLE OIL PATCH GOLF CENTER

The golf   Cheap and affordable, Humble's newest par 3 nine-holer offers short holes (all under 100 yards) and a quick fix for the addicted golfer who doesn't have time to work in a full round.

The details   713-548-7273. 2107 N. Houston Ave., Humble, TX 77338

- 2002. 9 holes. Walking only. Price - $.

Getting there Take US 59 north to Humble, then turn east on FM 1960. Drive to North Houston Ave. and the course is 1 mile down on the left.

TOUR 18 - HOUSTON

The golf   Parlaying the successes of the Dallas-area Tour 18, Houston's version of America's greatest holes has become one of Harris County's most popular golf destinations. This one takes advantage of the Southeast Texas pines, with towering trees lining every hole, and the impressive conditions that have made both Tour 18s popular with the public.

SOUTH EAST

Fall in love with the stroke you have. It's more than good enough to get the ball into the hole if you can see the ball go in the hole. Dr. Bob Rotella

Two holes stand out on the front side, and they're not the replicas of Augusta's Amen Corner (5-7 on this track). No. 1 is perhaps the most difficult on the course, intimidating off the tee because it is surrounded by wetlands. You'll need a solid drive to start well on this narrow, 440-yard hole. Bay Hill, La Costa, Inverness, and Pinehurst are also modeled, but the other great hole on the front is No. 9, a version of TPC Sawgrass's island hole.

Texas' own Colonial's third hole makes a showing on No. 12, and you'll get to see what Pebble Beach might feel like on No. 13. And those who've played the Dallas track know that the crew can sometimes get diabolical with their stimp-meter readings and pin placements, which is similar to what happens on No. 15–a replica of Shinnecock Hills' 8th hole. The green on this one slopes so heavily toward the front that a three-jack is almost certain.

Doral rears its head on No. 18, the perfect finishing hole for this track. Play the approach to the right side of the green, away from the water left, just like the pros do when they're protecting that precious lead.

The details   281-540-0404. 3102 FM 1960 Rd. E., Humble, TX 77338

• www.tour18golf.com

• 1992. Dave Edsall. 18 holes. Par 72. Back – 6,807 (72.2/126). Middle – 6,335 (70.3/121). Forward – 5,583 (66.6/113). Price - $$$$.

Getting there From US 59 north, turn right on FM 1960 and drive east for about 2 miles to the course entrance.

WALDEN ON LAKE HOUSTON

The golf   Patterned after the successful Robert Von Hagge-Bruce Devlin-designed Walden on Lake Conroe, this course opened in 1982 and immediately became known for its numerous bunkers and lakes. Considered a shot-maker's course, this layout features over 100 bunkers and requires precise play throughout.

Holes of note are the intimidating opening hole–a long, bending par 4 with a lake guarding the right side. Beware of the pin placement on this multi-tiered green. No. 8 is a 429-yard par 4 that requires a long drive and perfect approach because of the channel that guards the tiny, bunker-loaded green. On the back No. 14 is the best, dominated by a large lake in the fairway. At 444 yards it also requires a challengingly long approach into a small green.

The details   281-852-3551. 18100 Walden Forest Dr., Humble, TX 77346

• www.americangolf.com

• 1985. Bruce Devlin and Robert Von Hagge. 18 holes. Par 72. Back – 6,781 (73.0/133). Middle – 6,476 (71.8/132). Forward – 5,211 (70.3/125). Price - $$$.

Golf is an art form, not a science. You don't have to conform to some mechanical model of a perfect swing. You just have to remember your goal – to have a bunch of fun by making a little white ball go from the ground here in front of you into a target area over there. Jim Flick

Getting there From U.S. Hwy. 59 north, take the FM 1960 exit and go east for 8 miles to the course. The clubhouse is on the right side of the road.

HUMBLE NOTES   We'll try and point out a few dining options with character, such as **Mo's BBQ** and **Humble City Cafe & Bakery** (281-319-0200), the best place in the area for home cooking. Quick lunches can be had at **Trigg's Cafe** (281-540-2700), the **Humble Deli** (281-446-8544), or even **Tin Roof BBQ** (281-852-5577). Other BBQ joints are **Luther's Barbecue** (281-446-0441), **Mo's Original BBQ** (281-548-3777), or **Bobby Mac's BBQ** (281-328-1074). Good food and live music can be had at the **Cactus Moon Blues Cafe** (281-446-2202). Nothing special to recommend here for lodging–if you're flying into Houston Intercontinental, you might consider the **Marriott Hotels Resorts Suites** (281-443-2310). Otherwise, there are plenty of chains.

HUNTSVILLE
Elev. 400   Pop. 31,706

Sam Houston's town started as an Indian trading post in 1836, and was one of Texas' earliest and most prominent cities. Restored homes dot the city, and the downtown area offers arts and antique shopping galore. Sam Houston State University makes its home here, and the town serves as headquarters for the state prison system. This "Jewel of the Big Thicket" offers a nice variety of golf for a town of only 31,000 folks. The Elkins Lake, Country Campus, and Outlaw Gap courses offer a more affordable alternative to the spectacular Waterwood Resort. And now that Tripp Davis' new course, Ravens Nest, has opened, this charming town boasts almost 100 holes of golf.

COUNTRY CAMPUS GOLF COURSE

The golf   Sam Houston State University's course is known as Country Campus, and it plays around a winding creek that rolls through the layout. The tree-lined fairways slope up and down and take you to some particularly small greens.

The details   936-291-0008. Hwy. 19, Huntsville, TX 77320

• 9 holes. Back – 3,250. Middle – 2,900. Forward – 2,610. Price - $$.

Getting there From Huntsville, take Hwy. 19 north for 10 miles to the course. The entrance is on the right side of the road.

ELKINS LAKE RECREATION ASSOCIATION

The golf   As the name implies, Elkins Lake provides the landscape for this

SOUTH EAST

The practice tee is the place to try things out and to work hard; the golf course is the place to let things go, free yourself up. Don't try harder on the golf course. Try less hard. Davis Love, Jr.

now 27-hole facility. Ralph Plummer designed the original 18 in the 1960s, and Jeff Blume just recently came through to complete the third nine, which opened for play in the fall 2002. The fairways roll through the woods bordered by the Sam Houston National Forest on the west and Huntsville State Park to the north. Another unique aspect of the course is the way the design incorporates the old homestead's original equipment barns and bathhouse.

The details   936-295-4312. 282 Elkins Lake, Huntsville, TX 77340

- 1967. Ralph Plummer. 18 holes. Par 72. Back – 6,640 (71.6/120). Middle – 6,404 (69.8/121). Forward – Par 73. 5,657 (73.2/130). Price - $$.

Getting there From I-45 north, take exit 112 and drive a short distance to the course. The clubhouse is on the left.

OUTLAW GAP GOLF CLUB

The golf   Huntsville's par 3 course is named after owner and designer, Ray Outlaw, who opened the facility in 1984. The 9 holes play 1,370 yards from the back tee, and feature two manmade lakes that come into play on four holes. Outlaw's design has character for a par 3, built atop a hill with bunkers coming into play on most holes.

The details   409-295-5525. Route 4, Huntsville, TX 77340

- 1984. R. Outlaw. 9 holes. Par 27. Back – 1,370. Forward – 1,174. Price - $.

Getting there From Houston, take I-45 north to the Huntsville State Park exit. Turn right. When you come to Old Hwy. 75, make another right and drive 1 mile to the course.

RAVEN NEST GOLF COURSE

The golf   If architect Tripp Davis can pull off what he accomplished at The Tribute north of Dallas, golfers traveling to Huntsville will be extremely pleased to make the trip into the East Texas pines. Davis' design features extensive bunkering, severe fairway undulations, and the good ole East Texas pine trees. Raven Nest is the new home course for the Sam Houston State golf teams.

The details   936-438-8588. 457 Hwy. 45 S., Huntsville, TX 77340

- 2002. Tripp Davis. Par 71. 7,001 yards. Price - $$$.

Getting there The course is located on the west side of I-45.

If you can only sneak a little time each week to practice, work on your alignment. Lay some clubs on the ground to use as a guide; that way your swing can develop around a solid setup position.

Billy Ray Brown

SOUTH EAST

WATERWOOD NATIONAL RESORT & COUNTRY CLUB

The golf The diabolical Pete Dye, known for his ridiculously difficult courses, was somehow selected as the man to design Waterwood's resort course. The railroad ties and bulkhead water hazards are here, as are the tight fairways, long carries over water, and small greens. Every hole is ruthless, and the course rating ranks Waterwood as one of the 50 most difficult courses in the nation. In fact, the PGA Tour Q-School tourney has been held here three times.

The 14th hole overlooks Lake Livingston and is nicknamed "The Cliffs." At 225 yards you'll feel like you're hitting over the entire lake, which isn't the mental imagery you need when you're getting ready to fire a 3 wood or driver into a green that has virtually no bail-out area.

The details 936-891-5050. 1 Waterwood Pkwy., Huntsville, TX 77320

- www.waterwoodnational.com
- 1975. Pete Dye. 18 holes. Par 72. Gold – 6,872 (73.7/142). Blue – 6,233 (70.6/132). White – 5,400 (67.2/121). Red – 5,029 (68.0/117). Price - $$.

Getting there From I-45 in Huntsville, take Hwy. 190 east for 18 miles to Waterwood Pkwy. Next drive 7 miles north, crossing FM 980 to the clubhouse.

HUNTSVILLE NOTES Some say that Texas' best barbecue is done up at the **New Zion Barbecue House** (409-295-7394), where the ribs are the specialty but the messy chicken melts in your mouth. Old man Houston's burial site is at the **Oakwood Cemetery**, and his home and law office are open and available for tours. The rambling traveler will enjoy the scenic drives through the **Sam Houston National Forest**. FM 1374 heads to the **Stubblefield Lake** area, and FM 1375 rolls through **New Waverly** and to the **Walker Lake** area. For B&B accommodations try the **Pine Prairie B&B** (936-291-2423), the **Longhorn House Ranch B&B** (936-295-1844), or **The Whistler B&B** (936-295-7173).

JASPER

Elev. 221   Pop. 7,838

They say Jasper is the "Jewel of the Forest"–a sawmill town with a stench of pine, it's surrounded by lakes and a paradise for the touring sportsman. The old town dates back to 1824, when it was known as Bevil and housed future leaders of the Texas Revolution, and eventually became a Confederate stronghold during the Civil War. Today adventurists searching for action can hit lakes Sam Rayburn or Toledo Bend, which are loaded with outstanding options for

Typically, players who don't have a consistent preshot routine hit their shots okay in practice, but struggle in competition. Dr. Bob Rotella

the golfer, and round out weekends spent in Jasper and its 9-hole country club.

JASPER COUNTRY CLUB

The golf   Jasper's 9-hole country club dates back to the 1940s, offering the typical narrow, tree-lined fairways and two-sets of tees for a full day of golf. Water impacts play on only a few holes, and greenside bunkering is not prominent. The best feature is the well-maintained Tifdwarf greens which hold shots and putt true.

The 2nd hole is the longest par 4 and most difficult rated hole on the course, playing a testy 399 yards the first time and an easier 369 yards the next. The other tough hole, No. 5, a short par 5 on the front, plays to a 409-yard par 5 the next time around.

The details   409-384-4342. Hwy. 96, Jasper, TX 75951

- 1940s. 9 holes. Par 36. Back – 3,221 (34.8/114). Forward – 2,648 (35.3/112). Price - $.

Getting there Located on Hwy. 96 three miles north of Jasper.

JASPER NOTES   For lodging, you can try the restored 1901 historic **Swann Hotel Bed & Breakfast** (877-489-9717) on Lake Sam Rayburn. Sit-down meals can be had at the **Cedar Tree** (409-384-8832), where the seafood spread is impressive and should be followed by the scrumptious pecan pie. Explorers can side-trip to the **Angelina National Forest** just 13 miles northwest on Texas 3.

KATY   Elev. 145   Pop. 11,775

On top of a massive gas field 30 miles west of Houston rests the town of Katy, once home to an open, grass-covered prairie that was ideal for farming. Now it's home to a small, flourishing metropolis that is loaded with subdivisions and golf courses.

THE CLUB AT FALCON POINT

The golf   Falcon Point features a Bruce Devlin and Robert Von Hagge design that is known for its immaculate bent-grass greens and insanely difficult course layout. The duo's links-style design rolls through Katy's countryside with water in play on virtually every hole, thanks to the 10 interconnecting lakes that were built for flood control.

No. 5 is the signature. Not difficult due to its 475-yard length, it's tricky

---

The shorter the club, the shorter the backswing, the shorter the follow-through. There's no need to drop the wedge down your back at the completion of the swing, as you might the driver. Let the club stop at whatever point in the follow-through it runs out of momentum. Jack Nicklaus

because water is in play on every shot and is especially present on the approach shot, with an elevated green covered in trees and water in the front and to the side.

On the back side, Nos. 17 and 18 present a great pair of finishing holes. The first is a 163-yarder into a green protected left by water and bunkers to the right. The 18th is the most difficult on the course: a 429-yarder that requires a tee shot over water and an approach into the wind into an elevated green.

The details   281-392-7888. 24503 Falcon Point Dr., Katy, TX 77494

• www.falconpoint.com

• 1985. Bruce Devlin and Robert Von Hagge. 18 holes. Gold – 6,771 (73.4/134). Blue – 6,467 (71.2/125). White – 6,145 (69.1/118). Red – 5,008 (70.6/128). Price - $$$.

Getting there From I-10 west, take the Katy/Fort Bend County Rd. exit and drive south to the course. The clubhouse is on the right side of the road.

GOLF CLUB AT CINCO RANCH

The golf   Carlton Gipson designed Cinco Ranch in the early 1990s. This highly touted residential project was named the National Project of the Year for 1993 by the National Association of Home Builders Institute.

The centerpiece of the community is Gipson's 7,044-yard golf course, which features an ocean of water that impacts play on 16 of 18 holes. For the most part, the holes are straight and open, with minimal trees framing the paths to the greens. The greens are unique because of the unusually shaped bunkers that create very different short game challenges from what one normally finds.

One of the best holes is No. 4, a 557-yard par 5 that features an approach shot over water into an elevated green. In addition to the water, the green is fronted by a bunker that is at least 10 feet below the hole. This requires a phenomenal, blind bunker shot for an up-and-down.

The details   281-395-4653. 23030 Cinco Ranch Blvd., Katy, TX 77450

• www.clubcorpgolf.com

• 1993. Carlton Gipson. 18 holes. Par 71. Cinco – 7,044 (73.7/132). Tourney – 6,503 (70.6/128). Regular – 5,940 (68.5/122). Forward – 5,263 (70.3/118). Price - $$$.

Getting there From I-10 west, take Cinco Ranch Blvd. and head south to the course.

SOUTH EAST

Chip shots require visualization too. See the ball landing on the green and making its roll to the hole. Then gear your thoughts and setup toward making the ball hit that landing spot. Greg Norman

GREEN MEADOWS GOLF CLUB

The golf   Local boys Ward Stanberry and M.L. Scott opened Green Meadows in 1968 as a 9-holer on their families' land, then followed a few years later with an additional nine.

This old route is known as the **East Course**–it was re-routed after the newer West Course opened, and now opens with a unique par 3-5-3-5 combination that has a tendency to slow down play. Despite the opening 231-yarder, the East is a short course with eight par 4s under 350 yards and no bunkers. However, you'll need to ensure some accuracy off the tee, as not every fairway is generous, and the mature trees that overhang the fairway will grab errant shots. The par 5 No. 18 is the signature, featuring a tee shot over a ravine and a sharp dogleg left.

The newer **West Course** is longer at 6,700 yards, but opens up quite a bit and could even be considered more of a links-style track.

Other notes: The routing takes you by the old clubhouse several times, so it's generally convenient to pull in for a quick break to stock up on food and drink or use the restroom. Also note that there are snakes on the course, particularly around the water hazards.

The details   281-391-3670. 6450 Franz Rd., Katy, TX 77492

- East Course: 1968. 18 holes. Par 70. Back – 5,688 yards (63.3/104). Forward – 4,935 (67.6/109). Price - $$.

- West Course: 18 holes. 6,702 yards. Price - $$.

Getting there From I-10 west, take Exit 742, drive to the third traffic light, then turn right on Ave. D. Head 1 mile until you see the sign to the course. Turn left on Franz Rd., a few hundred yards up the street.

MEADOWBROOK FARMS GOLF CLUB

The golf   Sculpted by Greg Norman out of the tall grassland prairies and rice fields west of Houston, Meadowbrook Farms is part of a planned 800-acre residential development headed by Landmark National. Norman's layout includes deep-faced sod bunkers, Lil Prong Creek, and a multitude of oaks, pecans, and sycamores that take the golfer toward greens that are extremely hard.

The lack of parallel holes allows for an open, natural setting that is perfect for golf, especially since Norman didn't favor much reshaping–instead, he used the natural topography of the former rice farm.

Holes of note on the front are the 160-yard No. 6 and the 420-yard No. 9, both accented by the tall native grasses. No. 9 involves wetlands in front of the green, which is tough considering the longish approach.

Several holes on the back can destroy your round, including the narrow, doglegging 395-yard No. 10. It's imperative to find the fairway on this one.

SOUTH EAST

It's a good backstop if I chip the ball too hard, and it often helps my depth perception. Even putting from the fringe, I leave the pin in-especially going downhill. Tom Watson

And No. 15 is short (340 yards), but is loaded with bunkers that are difficult for the high-handicapped hack.

The best hole of the bunch is perhaps No. 18, a 545-yarder that involves a layup of a canal off the tee and two solid shots to reach the green in regulation.

All told, this one is worth the investment. The bag drop service is friendly and prompt, and the clubhouse offers affordable amenities, including a great little bar and grill.

The details   281-693-4653. 9595 S. Fry Rd., Katy, TX 77494

- 1999. Greg Norman. 18 holes. Par 72. Back – 7,100 (74.2/137). Middle – 6,600 (71.3/126). Forward – 5,000 (64.1/108). Price - $$$.

Getting there From downtown Houston on I-10, drive west to Grand Parkway (Hwy. 99). Take Grand Parkway south to Fry Rd., then turn right. Take Fry Rd. west for approximately 1.3 miles, and the entrance is on the left.

WILLOW FORK COUNTRY CLUB

The golf   Jay Riviere was hired to build Willow Fork, which opened in 1990 and lays out over an open prairie that once harvested rice and cattle. His links-style terrain features some of the natural wetlands as well as additional water hazards.

These wetlands are evident on holes 4-6, a picturesque stretch where alligators roam and errant balls are usually gone forever. No. 9 is the most challenging, a 447-yard par 4 lined on the left by the bayou. It features an approach over a lake that fronts the green.

The details   281-579-6262. 21055 Westheimer Pkwy., Katy, TX 77450

- 1990. Jay Riviere. 18 holes. Par 72. Back – 6,954 (72.4/126). Middle – 6,550 (70.6/120). Forward – 5,703 (72.0/123). Price - $$$.

Getting there From I-10 west, take the Fry Rd. exit and turn left. Drive 3.5 miles to Westheimer and turn right, then you'll see the club on the left.

KATY NOTES Try lunch at **Gerard's Sidewalk Grill** (281-450-2572). Smack talk about your round at **Bryant's Ice House** (281-392-5741) or the aptly named **Ice House** (281-391-5012). For lodging the **Best Western** (281-392-9800) highlights a slate of chain options that also include a **Holiday Inn** and a **Marriott**.

SOUTHEAST

If you're like most players, you'll find that you hit the ball solid, straighter and farther with a swing that's considerably slower and easier than your maximum. It should be your goal to keep that tempo on the course. Butch Harmon

KINGWOOD
Elev. 64   Pop. 44,952

Just north of Houston on US 59, Kingwood is a suburban residential community that resulted from the joint efforts of the King Ranch and the Exxon subsidiary Friendswood Development Company. Amazingly, the population boomed from 50 to almost 20,000 in a span of four years from 1986 to 1990, and the area is now home to upwards of 40,000 people. Lake Houston is nearby, and this tidy community benefits from the new money that has created schools, churches, shopping centers, and greenbelts.

THE DEERWOOD CLUB OF KINGWOOD

The golf   Deerwood came along in 1981 featuring a long, demanding track created by Joe Finger and Byron Nelson. Lake Houston lines the course and its water provides hazards on every hole but two. Tee shots demand length and accuracy, and the greens feature some of the most severe undulations in the Houston area.

This quality course hosted the second stage of the PGA Tour's Qualifying Tourney in 1994, and is known for its signature 13th hole, which plays 170 yards into an island green. However, many claim the 453-yard No. 4 is the most difficult around: an almost impossible hole that requires a huge drive and a long carry over water to reach the green in regulation.

The details   281-360-1065. 1717 Forest Garden Dr., Kingwood, TX 77345

• www.kingwoodclub.com

• 1981. Finger-Nelson-Dye. 18 holes. Par 72. Gold – 7,108 (74.0/139). Blue – 6,576 (72.3/132). White – 6,139 (70.2/128). Red – Par 74. 5,622 (73.7/120). Price - $$.

Getting there From Hwy. 59 north, take the Kingwood Dr. exit and turn right. Drive 5 miles to Forest Garden and turn right, then another mile to the course. The entrance is on the right.

KINGWOOD COVE GOLF CLUB

The golf   One of the earliest courses in the Kingwood area, this shotmaker's course rolls through a dense forest along the north bank of the San Jacinto River and has long been one of the best golf values around Houston.

At Kingwood you have the chance to start off strong, with 8 of the first 9 holes being wide open, straight, and having minimal hazards. The most difficult hole on the front is the impressive, doglegging 360-yard No. 8, which curls around the lake and plays into a severely sloping, two-tiered green.

The more difficult back nine, which is longer and more narrow, starts off with a 527-yard par 5 that doglegs left at 225 yards off the tee. Play a cautious

Swinging a weighted practice club will do more for your swing than a hundred swing-training gizmos combined. Bob Toski

shot into the dogleg, as water is on the right side of the fairway and will catch booming drives.

The late 1990s ushered in renovations that have improved the course significantly, including tee box improvements and a new irrigation system.

The details   281-358-1155. 805 Hamblen Rd., Kingwood, TX 77339

- www.kingwoodcove.com
- 1960s. 18 holes. Par 71. Back – 6,722 (71.9/118). Middle – 6,211 (69.8/114). Forward – 5,601 (73.2/114). Price - $$.

Getting there From Hwy. 59 north, take Loop 494/Townsend north over the San Jacinto River bridge, then turn right on Hamblen. Drive a short distance to the course and look for the clubhouse on the left side of the street.

KINGWOOD COUNTRY CLUB

The golf   Hailed as one of the "World's Largest Private Country Clubs," the umbrella of the Kingwood clubs includes four courses at the main facility, as well as a fifth nearby known as Deerwood.

The **Island Course**, built in 1974 and considered to be one of architect Joe Finger's greatest courses, is this club's signature course because of its length and small, fast greens. In the course's first year of operation, the American Society of Golf Course Architects named the 573-yard No. 6 the Hole of the Year.

Two years later *Golf Digest* noted No. 18 as the toughest finishing hole in golf. This nightmare hole plays 576 yards with a lake on the left and around the green, as well as water in the middle of the fairway and on the right. If you survive the tee shot, you'll need a perfect second shot to avoid having to pull out your calculator and add up the disaster.

The **Marsh Course** came along 7 years after the original Island Course and was Finger's last imprint on the facility. The course plays through the marshlands around Lake Houston with water coming into play 12 times off the tee, making the tee shot critical to the round.

The first hole, a 406-yard par 4, doglegs right around a lake that cuts into the middle of the fairway. The par 5 No. 9 doglegs left and has water in play off the tee and on the approach. No. 15 is the most demanding hole–a 443-yard par 4 that involves cutting the corner of a long lake off the tee.

You can't overlook the par 3s on the Marsh Course, two of which require long irons and carry over water, and another that plays 205 yards into a green protected by a pond.

The **Lake Course**, much like the Marsh Course, places a premium on accuracy. Lakes, ponds, and creeks all come into play here. The 549-yard No. 5 doglegs to the right around a lake. No. 10 is similar in design except that it turns to the left and has water in play on every shot. The most difficult par 4 goes 459 yards and has a lake fronting the green.

Make a longer swing for a longer bunker shot. Swing smoothly, not violently. A rehearsal swing outside the bunker will give you the feel. Butch Harmon

SOUTH EAST

Ken Dye's **Forest Course**, known as the most demanding track at KCC, spreads out through Lake Houston's marshy backwaters and is actually 6-8 feet below the surrounding terrain. The eeriness of being eye-level with the surrounding tree trunks makes for a unique round, especially since Dye used such extensive mounding to mold this water-resistant course. The track also features deep, massive bunkers, skinny fairways, and small greens. Lake Houston borders three holes, offering some respite from the below-ground sensations.

The signature of the Forest Course is the outstanding final stretch of holes that starts with the imposing 473-yard No. 15. Play it like a par 5, and consider laying up with the second shot to give yourself a reasonable chance at a short-chip up-and-down for par. Otherwise you'll be hitting a fairway wood into a green surround by water and bunkers. If you do go for it, miss it right and bail out into the bunkers.

Dye has spoke highly of this course, calling it "the best course we've done in Houston." *Golf Digest* was impressed enough to rate it the 16th best course in the state in 1998.

The details   281-358-2171. 1700 Lake Kingwood Trail, Kingwood, TX 77339

- www.kingwoodclub.com
- Island Course: 1974. Joe Finger. 18 holes. Par 72. Back – 7,309 (74.2/134). Middle – 6,802 (72.2/125). Forward – Par 74. 6,064 (75.1/129). Price - $$$$.
- Marsh Course: 1976. Joe Finger. 18 holes. Par 72. Back – 6,935 (72.7/130). Middle – 6,114 (70.2/115). Forward – 5,351 (71.7/123). Price - $$$$.
- Lake Course: 1977. Bruce Littell. 18 holes. Par 72. Back – 7,089 (72.3/126). Middle –6,289 (69.3/117). Forward – 5,303 (71.8/122). Price - $$$$.
- Forest Course: 1992. Ken Dye. 18 holes. Par 72. Back – 7,092 (74.6/138). Middle – 6,583 (72.2/129). Forward – 5,597 (74.4/138). Price - $$$$.

Getting there From I-59 north, take the Kingwood Dr. exit and turn right. At Lake Kingwood Trail Dr., turn right and you will see the course.

KINGWOOD FAMILY GOLF CENTER

The golf   As its name implies, this new par 3 is created for the family. It's a great place to kill an afternoon piddling around the 5,000-square-foot pro shop for odds and ends, practicing on the driving range or putting green, or dallying late into the night on the lighted par 3 course.

This one is challenging, featuring some swamp that comes into play as well as a lake that impacts three holes. Bunkers, both sand and grass, dot the 60 acres.

✦

A good designer makes sure the cartpath runs along the right-hand side of the women's tee. Ladies don't like showing their behinds to the rest of the foursome when they bend over to tee their ball. Pete Dye

The best hole is the last: a 214-yarder over the swamp to a shallow green.

The details   281-359-3995. 22601 Hwy. 59 N., Kingwood, TX 77339

- 1996. Sean Brown. 9 holes. Par 27. Back – 1,484. Middle – 1,332. Forward – 928. Price - $.

Getting there From I-10, take Hwy. 59 north to the Kingwood Dr. exit. Make a U-turn and look for the entrance on the right side of the road.

KINGWOOD NOTES Give **Cliff's CMC** (281-359-2934) a try before you look to the more robust Humble area for further dining options. In Kingwood, off of Hwy. 59 there's a **Holiday Inn Express** (281-359-2700) if you need to pull it over for the night.

LA MARQUE   Elev. 15   Pop. 13,682

Once known as Highlands, and then as Buttermilk Station, this residential community southeast of Houston is en route for Galveston-bound golfers passing through on their way to vacations on the coast. Here among the massive plants that dominate the skyline is a 1940s-style country club known as Lakeview, the only golf course that calls La Marque home.

LAKEVIEW COUNTRY CLUB

The golf   Lakeview opened in 1949, built on old Camp Wallace after World War II with the old army barracks still serving as the clubhouse. The course is flat and void of bunkers, but is loaded with water hazards created by the more than 20 acres of lakes.

The funky design of the front nine involves three par 5s, playing about 650 yards longer than the back nine. The front nine also has the signature hole, the 410-yard No. 8, which is particularly difficult because of two lakes that impact strategy.

On the back, short holes abound, including the 258-yard par 4 No. 15 as well as several short par 3s. The last two holes are par 5s, going 474 and 522 yards respectively.

The details   409-935-6811. 1219 Palm St., La Marque, TX 77568

- 1940s. 18 holes. Par 72. Back – 6,127. Middle – 5,707 (69.4/113). Forward – 5,137 (68.1/107). Price - $$.

Getting there From I-45 south, take Exit 10 and drive under the overpass. Stay right and look for the signs to the course about 2 miles away.

SOUTH EAST

What any good teacher likes is a pupil who's committed to doing the right things for an extended period of time. Dr. Bob Rotella

LA MARQUE NOTES Texas City and La Marque share a chamber of commerce, so consider both locales as one when determining post-golf action. For lodging look to Hwy. 146, where a **Days Inn** (409-945-9900) and a **La Quinta** (409-948-3101) offer affordable rooms. In La Marque there's **Benito's** (409-935-9018) on First St. Also remember that Galveston awaits in all its splendor just over the causeway.

LAKE JACKSON
Elev. 14 Pop. 23,412

About 50 miles southwest of Galveston, Lake Jackson rests along a small oxbow lake that was once part of a pre-Civil War plantation. In the 1940s, the Dow Chemical Company created the community for employees working on war projects, and the city has grown into Brazoria County's largest. The game of golf surfaced here in the 1950s when Ralph Plummer was commissioned to design the private Riverside Country Club on the shores of Brazoria Lake. And now, after years of delays due to environmental concerns, golf will be available to the masses when the Jeff Brauer-designed Wilderness Golf Course opens sometime in 2003.

RIVERSIDE COUNTRY CLUB

The golf   Riverside is flat with narrow, tree-lined fairways and average-sized greens. The highlight here is the spectacular, peaceful setting on the shores of Brazoria Lake and the Brazos River. Spanish moss covers the trees and the lake divides the course in half, coming into play on 10 holes. The course is loaded with bridges that enable golfers to traverse the lakes, jumping from tee to green hole after hole.

The toughest hole is No. 16. Ironically, it doesn't involve water, but doglegs left for 432 yards and requires back-to-back "A-game" shots to reach the green in two.

The details   979-798-2101. Hwy. 392, Lake Jackson, TX 77566

- www.riversidecountry.com
- Private. 1957 by Ralph Plummer. Par 72. Back – 6,556 (70.5/126). Middle – 6,141 (68.9/115). Forward – 5,588 (72.5/129). Price - $$.

Getting there From Hwy. 521, turn left on Hwy. 332 and drive straight to the course.

WILDERNESS GOLF COURSE

Opening 2003   Voters approved $6 million in funding for Lake Jackson's

If you're a youngster growing up putting on bad greens, be patient. Eventually you'll see some nice, smooth surfaces, and when you do, you'll hole everything. Bob Rosburg

new daily-fee course back in 1997, but environmental concerns have delayed the project since then. However. the city council has recently given the green light for Jeff Brauer to get to work, and the Wilderness Golf Course will in fact become a reality sometime in 2003.

LAKE JACKSON NOTES   Road-trip west to Brazoria and the **Armadillo Ballroom & Club** (979-798-8500). Afterwards, crash at the **Ramada Inn** on US 332. Dining options involve the **Redtop Texas Style Burger** (979-297-3079), **Smithhart's Downtown Grill** (979-297-0082), and **Tortuga's Cantina** (979-297-2700).

LAPORTE   Elev. 28   Pop. 28,538

"The Door" is a deepwater port town of petrochemical companies with pleasing bayside facilities and residential subdivisions. In the big-band days of the 1920s and 1930s, the Sylvan Beach resort/dance pavilion gained notoriety. Today the modern park offers numerous recreational opportunities along Galveston Bay, all of which blend in nicely with rounds at La Porte's 1988 Jay Riviere-designed municipal golf course.

BAY FOREST GOLF COURSE

The golf   Amongst the chemical plants, refinery towers, and wood-lined waterways of LaPorte lies the 18-hole Bay Forest, which features a tight front nine that opens up on the lake-dominated back side. Water is in play on 16 of 18 holes. Because of LaPorte's proximity to the Gulf, the coastal winds make this a long course.

Despite its tight nature, the front nine offers a few nice birdie opportunities, including the short par 3 No. 6. This hole generally only requires a 9 iron to carry the bunker fronting the green.

On the back, the par 5 No. 10 is one of the most birdie-friendly holes on the course. It's followed by the signature No. 11–a great-looking dogleg right that bends around a pond to a well-bunkered green. The play with the approach on 11 is to leave it below the hole.

The par 5 No. 18 is a challenging finisher that requires good golf shots into the wind and the accuracy to avoid the water that sneaks into the fairway in the landing area from the right. The second shot must carry water and a bunker, and the recommended play on the approach is to keep it on the right side of the green.

The details   281-471-4653. 201 Bay Forest Dr., LaPorte, TX 77571

SOUTH EAST

Very few golfers actually watch how the ball is spinning, how high it's flying, where it lands on the green, how far it rolls. They rake another ball in front of them before the one they just hit is halfway to the hole. Concentrate. Watch the ball. The feedback will tell you what to do next. Phil Rodgers

- 1988. Jay Riviere. 18 holes. Par 72. Back – 6,756 (72.4/126). Middle – 6,235 (69.9/122). Forward – 5,094 (69.3/113). Price - $$.

Getting there From Hwy. 45 south, take the 610 Loop north. When you come to Hwy. 225 head east and take the Pasadena exit. Turn right, find Hwy. 146 and go south (right). Next, get off at the Fairmont Pkwy. exit and turn left. When you get to South Broadway St., turn right and drive 1 mile to the course. The clubhouse is on the right side of the street.

LAPORTE NOTES All three Mexican local restaurants are outstanding. **El Toro** (281-471-2505), **Gringo's** (281-470-7424), and **Las Hadas** (281-471-0538) are all toss-ups food-wise with subtle differences in scene. There are no B&Bs so you'll have to make do with the chains–the **Best Western** and **La Quinta** are both on Hwy. 146.

LEAGUE CITY

Elev. 20   Pop. 45,444

J.C. League rolled into town and assumed ownership of the community that was known as both Butler's Ranch and Clear Creek. Formerly a Karankawa Indian village on Magnolia Bayou and Clear Creek, old man League brought modern industry by deeding the land for the railroad. Saloons and general stores popped up around the depot and a place known as Straggler's Hall. Cattle and farming became prominent, and the city was entrenched enough to hang on until it could become the commuter community that it is today. Golf was blessed upon the city in 1983 with the South Shore Harbour facility, and has recently made its timeless presence known again with the opening of the spectacular Magnolia Creek course.

MAGNOLIA CREEK GOLF LINKS

The golf Magnolia Creek is a true links-style track developed by a local investment group that appears to be doing everything right. From the course design and the preferred players program to the yardage books on every cart and even the web site, everything is first-class and they've gone the extra mile to create an outstanding golf experience.

Patterned after the links courses of Britain and Ireland that rest along the sea, this course is dominated by the Gulf Coast winds, which persist to push wayward drives away from the generous landing areas and into the tall, native grasses. You'll find your drives rolling far, as the fairways are firm. This makes play tricky due to the pot bunkers that dot the fairway and suck in rolling shots.

Note that the course has a great practice facility, and there's more to come here. The planned addition of the Wales nine will break ground once the facil-

SOUTH EAST

Reverse every natural instinct and do the opposite of what you are inclined to do, and you will probably come very close to having a perfect golf swing. Ben Hogan

ity reaches a certain benchmark for rounds played.

The details   281-557-0555. 1501 Bay Area Blvd., League City, TX

- www.magnoliacreekgolf.com
- Thomas E. Clark. 18 holes. Price - $$$.
- England/Scotland: Varden (75.1/133). Old Tom (72.3/126). Willie (69.5/119). Vare (66.1/115).
- England/Ireland: Varden (74.9/137). Old Tom (72.2/127). Willie (69.6/122). Vare (66.1/113).
- Scotland/Ireland: Varden (75.2/137). Old Tom (72.9/128). Willie (70.3/122). Vare (66.6/114).

Getting there From downtown, take Hwy. 288 south for approximately 5 miles. Exit Loop 610 West and take the Fannin exit. Make a U-turn under Loop 610 and proceed east on the access road to Almeda Rd. Turn right on Almeda and go 3 miles to the Wildcat entrance.

SOUTH SHORE HARBOUR GOLF CLUB

The golf   South Shore was the first course tackled by the design team of Jay Riviere and Dave Marr. The course opened with 18 holes in 1983, and Carlton Gipson stopped by in 1994 to add a third nine.

Laid out over some extremely flat land not far from the Gulf, South Shore's main obstacle is the persistent coastal winds. The architects did their best to mold the flat terrain by incorporating elevated greens and tees and bringing in enough earth to create some elevation changes, so the course has a little character.

Nos. 4 and 12 stand out on the old course because of the peninsula greens guarded by bunkers.

The details   281-334-0525. 4300 S. Shore Blvd., League City, TX 77573

- 1983. Dave Marr and Jay Riviere. 18 holes.
- Admiral – 6,882 (73.0/129). Champs – 6,432 (70.9/123). Regular – 5,918 (68.2/114). Forward – 5,446 (72.7/128). Price - $$.

Getting there From Houston, take I-45 south to FM 518. Head east for 9 miles, then look for the course on the left side of the road.

LEAGUE CITY NOTES   There are only two hotels–the **Super 8** is on the freeway, and further down toward Kemah, TX is the fantastic **South Shore Harbor Resort** (281-334-1000 or www.sshr.com), a beautiful facility more amenable to the discerning golfer. There are restaurants in the resort. Next to the hotel is **Brothers Petronella** (281-334-2444). For barbecue call **Red River BBQ** (281-332-8086) and **Esteban's** (281-332-4195) is the place for Mexican

---

If you accelerate the putter, your contact will be more
consistent, even on mis-hits. Tom Watson

SOUTH EAST

food. For live jazz find **Dolphin Street** (281-291-8300) in Clear Lake, or head to the **Kemah Crab House** on the boardwalk in Kemah for seaside atmosphere and outstanding food.

LIBERTY   Elev. 30   Pop. 8,173

Equidistant from Beaumont and Houston on US 90, Liberty is one of the oldest settled communities in Texas–the town was laid out in 1831. It's an intriguing place with a fascinating history: many of its citizens fought for Texas Independence at San Jacinto, the town became a bustling river port for steamboats traversing northward on the Trinity, and none other than William Travis and Sam Houston practiced law here. Today this seat of Liberty County is a farming and ranching community that has received economic stimulus over the years from substantial oil production.

MAGNOLIA RIDGE COUNTRY CLUB

The golf   Golfing residents of Liberty live a charmed existence, having the pleasure of playing one of the best 9-hole tracks in the state. In 1951, an aspiring young architect named Ralph Plummer, who at the time specialized in 9-hole courses, was lured to Liberty by Milton Demaret (Jimmy's brother), the head pro.

Plummer made the most of the opportunity, creating a masterpiece out of the giant magnolias, oaks, and pines on the site. Abbots Creek runs through the layout and is featured on the difficult 364-yard No. 6. The creek looms right and cuts in front of the green, and out-of-bounds looms left. If you survive the tee shot, you'll need more accuracy for the approach into the multi-leveled green.

The details   936-336-3551. 100 Country Club Ln., Liberty, TX 77575

• 1950s. 9 holes. Par 36. Back – 3,245 (36.0/108). Forward – 2,675. Price - $.

Getting there Take I-10 south out of Houston, and exit Liberty, which turns into Hwy. 90. Get on the loop and turn right on the road by the car dealership. Follow the signs to the course.ro.

LIBERTY NOTES   Stroll around the square and find **Deardon's** (936-334-1010). **Mas Amigos Mexican Restaurant** (936-336-2725) is where the locals will point you for tasty enchiladas, and another good sit-down option is **Sam's Steak & Seafood** (936-334-8860). Your bed and breakfast of choice

The average caddie can find five balls while looking for
yours—which he can't find. Robinson Murray

should be the **Magnolia House** (936-334-0188). Soak up the history by touring the town for interesting-looking old homes and Sam Houston's law office.

LIVINGSTON

Elev. 194   Pop. 7,699

Resort-minded Livingston appears more modern since its buildings were razed after a disastrous turn-of-the-century fire. This lumber town on the edge of the Big Thicket gained some prosperity due to oil. Lake Livingston is just west, with its state park offering recreation, as well as the delightful Mill Ridge Golf Club.

MILL RIDGE GOLF CLUB

The golf   Long a 9-hole favorite of visitors to Lake Livingston, Mill Ridge took over the neighboring municipal track in 1999 to create a new 18-hole layout that is lined by giant pine trees on the grounds of the historic Ogletree Sawmill.

This hillside course often presents nice views of the East Texas countryside, and a winding creek that rolls through the new nine creates a few more water hazards.

Visitors used to the old 9-holer are in for a surprise after holes 1-5. Nos. 6-14 play across the railroad tracks on the new property, bringing the golfer back to the original course for the finishing holes 15-18.

The details   936-327-3607. 1501 Mill Ridge Dr., Livingston, TX 77351

- www.millridgegolf.com
- 1999. 18 holes. Par 70. Back – 6,108 (69.3/116). Middle – 5,733 (67.5/112). Forward – 4,679 (64.0/102). Price - $$$.

Getting there Take Hwy. 59 north out of Houston. Outside of Livingston take the Mill Ridge Dr. exit and the course is just ahead on the right.

LIVINGSTON NOTES   Check out the **Milam Home B&B** (936-327-1173) for the basic wrap-around porch type accommodation, or go for something a little different at the **Healing Waters Retreat** (936-329-8865), where you can take advantage of the luxurious setting built around a bubbling spring and eat a fine meal at any time of the day. The basic hotel option is the **Econo Lodge** (409-327-2451). In town for meals, look to the corner of the square for the **Courthouse Whistle Stop Cafe** (936-327-3222), where the crawfish étoufée lunch special can be followed up by fattening desserts and antique shopping.

SOUTH EAST

Many players think the key to power is to swing the club past horizontal at the top of the backswing. Not true. It's much more important to have your right arm in a good position at the top. Butch Harmon

LAKE LIVINGSTON GOLF TRAIL

In the rolling hills and shadows of the East Texas Piney Woods, the Trinity River is captured to form Lake Livingston, the second-largest lake in Texas. Less than an hour north of Houston, the southern end of this 93,000-acre "oasis in the pines" is home to two distinct golf courses, **Mill Ridge Golf Club** in Livingston and **Cape Royale Golf Course** in Coldspring

These two unique courses have joined to offer you a golf package unlike any other in the Houston area. The Lake Livingston Golf Trail provides golfers almost unlimited golf for one set price. No daily limits on the number of rounds–no mandatory twilight round the first day–no extra fees for carts, hotel rooms, meals, and taxes.

We say *almost* unlimited because you are limited to one course per day. You can start the trail on either Mill Ridge or Cape Royale. Call 800-410-5495 for more information.

LUFKIN
Elev. 326   Pop. 32,353

Sandwiched between the Davy Crockett and Angelina national forests, Lufkin is a blue-collar lumber town with two phenomenal private golf courses. Recreational opportunities abound here deep in the Piney Woods, in particular with the huge Sam Rayburn Reservoir to the east. However, golfers traveling in this neck of the woods will want to pull out all the stops and figure out how to work their way on the famous Crown Colony CC, often considered the premier golf experience in Texas.

CROWN COLONY COUNTRY CLUB

The golf   Perhaps one day the greatness that is Crown Colony will finally supplant Fort Worth's Colonial Country Club as Texas' finest golf course. For now this course, which opened in the late 1970s, may have to wait a few more decades for its legend to grow. The course is certainly worthy, offering immaculate conditions paired with demanding target golf. Water is in play on 13 holes, the pine-lined fairways feature numerous elevation changes, and the greens are small targets.

The best hole on the front is No. 4, about a 180-yarder all over water, but you're bound to notice the opening set of holes that feature two monster par 5s. The 583-yard No. 3 bends left around a lake and plays to a tricky little green nestled against water's edge.

On the back, you'll remember the ender–an almost 600-yard tree-lined monster. And the preceding 203-yard No. 17 isn't the way to build confidence for the finisher. Together the two finishing holes can absolutely destroy your round.

If your back hurts from playing golf, you're not swinging correctly. If you shift your weight to the left on the downswing, and let your right heel come off the ground, you should be able to play forever. Bob Toski

The details   936-637-8800. 900 Crown Colony Dr., Lufkin, TX 75901

- www.crowncolonycc.net
- 1979. Devlin and von Hagge. 18 holes. Par 72. Blue – 6,785 (73.4/141). White – 6,250 (70.1/134). Gold – 5,304 (65.2/117). Red – 4,831 (68.6/122). Price - $$.

Getting there From Houston, take Hwy. 59 north. Exit Champions Dr. and you will see the course.

LUFKIN COUNTRY CLUB

The golf   The LCC is an old course, dating back to the 1920s, that features a heavily wooded layout with a very interesting set of holes. Hills provide fun elevation changes and water comes into play on several holes, but the most interesting feature is that the front nine plays to a par 37 with three par 5s.

Hole 6 offers one of the better birdie chances–a short par 5 at 448 yards with a creek that cuts the fairway about 100 yards from the green. No. 8 is another reachable par 5, but this time it involves the creek crossing the fairway twice.

Rarely do you find a drive-able par 4 on a finishing hole, but LCC offers up a 298-yard test with out-of-bounds on the right as the ender.

The details   936-639-3664. 1624 Sayers St., Lufkin, TX 75902

- 1920s. 18 holes. Par 72. Back – 6,347 (70.4/128). Middle – 6,131 (69.5/126). Forward – 5,042 (68.0/115). Price - $$.

Getting there Exit Sayers St. off of State Loop 287, and drive south to the course.

LUFKIN NOTES   Rolling around the east Texas woods you may run into one of two no-nonsense burger joints that must be experienced: **Ray's Drive-In and Cafe** (936-634-3262) on Timberland, and **Ray's West** (936-637-2525) on S. John Redditt, where they serve big juicy burgers, catfish, and even a little barbecue. Lufkin's **Holiday Inn** (936-639-3333) is on US 59 south, and B&B accommodations can be found at the **Wisteria Hideaway B&B** (936-875-2914).

MADISONVILLE   Elev. 278   Pop. 3,825

Quiet Madisonville, a town centered by its stately courthouse, rests just west of I-45 about 100 miles northwest of Houston. Known as the location for one of Sam Houston's most famous diatribes against secession, as well as the handsome 1904 Woodbine Hotel, Madisonville is a worthy break point on week-

---

I adore the game of golf. I won't ever retire. I'll play until I die. Then I want them to roll me into a bunker, cover me with sand, and make sure nobody's ball lands in there for a while. Lee Trevino

end excursions along the interstate–especially if you can work your way on the 1967 Leon Howard-designed Oakridge CC.

OAK RIDGE COUNTRY CLUB

The golf   Oak ridge was reopened by the Cobblestone Golf Group after the IRS shut it down in the late 1980s for unpaid back taxes.

The course originally opened in 1982 with a design by Jack Kidwell and Michael Hurdzan. They made the most of Duck Creek, which comes into play on 13 of 18 holes. In fact, every hole on the back nine has water in play.

If you're striking the ball well, No. 3 is reachable in two at only 475 yards. However, this par 5 has water in play off the tee and on the approach. The best hole is No. 18, a 393-yard dogleg left with water in play on both shots because of the creek that crisscrosses the green.

The details   936-348-6264. FM 1452, Madisonville, TX 77864

* 1967. Leon Howard. 9 holes. Par 36. Back – 3,408 (35.9/125). Middle – 3,209 (34.5/120). Forward – 2,758 (38.2/113). Price - $.

Getting there On I-45 north out of Houston, exit Hwy. 21 and turn left. When you come to FM 1452, make another left, then drive 1 mile to the course. The entrance is on the right side of the road.

MADISONVILLE NOTES   The **Baker House** (936-348-2280) is one lodging option, and the historic **Woodbine Hotel** also offers a B&B setting in addition to its museum and restaurant. For the casual, beaten-down golfer who just needs greasy Tex-Mex and cold beers, the laid-back **El Jardin Mexican Restaurant** (936-348-2367) is the place to park yourself for the evening.

MAGNOLIA   Elev. 271   Pop. 1,220

Magnolia is way the hell outside of Houston, 40 miles northwest but still within range of the urban sprawl. Here in this community that was named for the magnolia trees at the base of Mill Creek, big-city golf has put this town of 1,220 on the map for traveling Texans. Two first-class golf courses have been carved out of the pine forest here. High Meadow Ranch is often considered the best public course in the Houston area, while Lake Windcrest is considered the best value.

HIGH MEADOW RANCH GOLF CLUB

The golf   Upscale and daily-fee, High Meadow Ranch was designed by

I think of driving the ball through an imaginary goal post,
especially when the landing area is tight. Tom Watson

PGA Tour pro David Ogrin in cahoots with Nugent Golf Associates as part of a housing development. Tipping out at over 7,400 yards, the course plays to a par 72 and rolls through some intriguing hardwood terrain that's highlighted by several natural ravines. The course is routed in three 6-hole "loops," each offering different golf experiences.

The oak-laden **Forest** loop routes over the ravines, which come into play on 5 of the 6 holes. The **Pine Barrens** loop, lined by majestic pines, features generous fairways, native grass areas, and large greens. And fittingly, the **Signature** loop is the perfect combination of the first two, offering a more dramatic stretch of holes. The highlight is the signature No. 18. This memorable ender plays 440 yards into a green fronted by a creek and protected by an 8-foot rock wall, meaning that a huge drive is necessary to avoid an impossible carry on the approach.

The details 281-356-7700. 37300 Golf Club Trail, Magnolia, TX 77355

- www.highmeadowranchgolf.com
- 1999. 18 holes. Par 72. Back – 7,400 (75.7/133). Middle – 6,000 (73.3/124). Forward – 4,800 (72.0/120). Price - $$$.

Getting there The course is located 40 miles northwest of Houston between Tomball and Magnolia. Drive north of Beltway 8 on Hwy. 249. Five miles north of Tomball, Hwy. 249 becomes FM 1774. The club is on the left.

LAKE WINDCREST GOLF CLUB

The golf Lake Windcrest is an aesthetic, shot-maker's course carved out of Magnolia's surrounding hardwood forests. Mostly hacker-friendly, this course has four sets of tees give you some options depending on how you're feeling–the clever design allows for multiple strategies to obtain par.

Designed by Thomas Walker, who thankfully created wide fairways with generous landing areas, the design offers a good combination of holes with all sorts of doglegs, uphill and downhill plays, and both long and short holes. In fact, even if your game is off, there are ample up-and-down opportunities for par, with plenty of bail-out areas around the greens.

The details 281-259-2279. 10941 Clubhouse Circle, Magnolia, TX 77354

- www.lakewindcrestgolf.com
- Thomas E. Walker. Tips - 7,470 (75.7/133). Price - $$$.

Getting there From Magnolia, take the 3rd Lake Windcrest entrance. From I-45 north, take 242 west (left) until it dead-ends into 1488. Go west (left) on 1488 to the first Lake Windcrest entrance on the left.

SOUTHEAST

If you can throw a wadded-up piece of paper into a garbage can, or toss a golf ball to a person 10 feet away, you've got touch. Don't sell yourself short. Phil Rodgers

MAGNOLIA NOTES Stay at the **Magnolia Inn Suites** (281-259-6119). The main drag downtown has **Hot Dogs & More,** highly recommended for its down-home flavor. **El Rancho Grande** serves Tex-Mex and icy margies, as does **Las Fuentes.** Some will point you towards **Hickory Hollow BBQ** for lunch, and the place for pre-round breakfast is a great little bakery that opens early on the main drag, the **Mayflower Bakery.**

MANVEL
Elev. 54   Pop. 3,046

The outlying Houston suburb of Manvel, home of the prominent oil and rice production so common to the area, waits patiently in line to become the area's next bustling residential community. Here, just a few miles northwest of Alvin on Hwy. 6 lies a unique Palm Springs-style development known as Rodeo Palms, whose new golf course will serve as the centerpiece of this private community when it opens in late 2003.

RODEO PALMS COUNTRY CLUB

The golf This course ramped up construction again in 2002 after a six-month delay due to funding issues. Derrell Witt is handling the design work, with plans for a par 72 7,100-yard track that will be dominated by its signature palm trees. Residents of the private Rodeo Palms community will benefit from a 25,000-square-foot-clubhouse and a spa/fitness facility. The existing project plan calls for the course to open sometime in summer 2003.

The details Rodeo Dr., Manvel, TX 77578

• Summer 2003. 18 holes. Par 72. 7,100 yards. Private. Price - $$$$.

Getting there Located at Hwy. 288 and Rodeo Palms Pkwy. just north of Hwy. 6, just 20 minutes from downtown Houston.

MANVEL NOTES All of your dining needs can be satisfied along Hwy. 6, where the seasoned traveler will avoid the Burger Kings and look to places like **Daddy's Money Ice Bar & Grill** (281-489-1777) or **La Matita** (281-489-9392) for food and drink. Afterwards you'll either be heading to Houston for nightlife or rambling down to the coast for the weekend. Seek lodging elsewhere.

The real test of golf—and life—is not keeping out of the rough,
but getting out after we are in. Henry Lash

MISSOURI CITY
Elev. 79   Pop. 52,913

Just outside Houston's loop, about 20 miles southwest of town, rests another one of the many commuter communities. This one was once known as the "Land of Genial Sunshine and Eternal Summer." The history is typical–investors laid out the town and promoted sales based on the coming of the railroad, which eventually opened markets to farmers and ranchers. Oil came after 1900, then gas and eventually even a salt mine. Today it's all about houses and folks who work in and around Houston, as well as three private country clubs.

QUAIL VALLEY COUNTRY CLUB

The golf   Developers eventually had their way with this cow pasture on the fringe of Houston. Loaded with native pecans and oaks and supplemented with even more transplanted trees, the terrain is ideal for golf, with two creeks and five natural lakes on the property. In fact, it's good enough to host the PGA Tour's Houston Open in 1973 and 1974.

The traditional **El Dorado Course** plays to a par 70 and features five par 3s that go 190-yards-plus from the tips. Jay Riviere designed the back nine.

La Quinta Course is a typical regulation course, slightly more difficult than El Dorado because of the water in play on 10 holes.

For overflow traffic and short-game work, the **Executive Course** has even more water that is complemented by small greens. It's the most demanding track at Quail Valley.

The details   281-437-8277. 2880 La Quinta Dr., Missouri City, TX 77459

- www.quailvalleycc.com
- La Quinta Course: 1980. Jack Miller. 18 holes. Par 72. Back – 6,816 (72.3/130). Middle – 6,290 (69.9/126). Forward – 5,552 (71.4/116). Price - $$$.
- El Dorado Course: 18 holes. Jack Miller. Par 70. Back – 6,680 (71.8/129). Middle – 6,116 (70.1/124). Forward – Par 71. 5,243 (70.2/115). Price - $$$.
- Executive Course: 1984. Jay Riviere. 9 holes. Par 32. Back – 2,145. Forward – 1,830. Price - $$$.
- Par 3 Course: 9 holes. Par 27. 1,500 yards. Price - $.

Getting there From Hwy. 59 south, take the Bellfort/Murphy Rd. exit and turn left. Drive under the freeway onto Murphy Rd., past Hwy. 90 and Cartwright Rd., the turn left on El Dorado. The entrance is on the left.

SOUTH EAST

I've studied golf for almost 50 years now and know a hell of a lot about nothing. Why did Jack Nicklaus, the greatest player in history, change his swing every other week? We're always chopping and changing. Golf is a puzzle without an answer. Gary Player

WILLOWISP COUNTRY CLUB

The golf   Willowisp sports a shady past. Originally known as the Glenhaven Country Club, it was developed by a group of Dallas hustlers who sold $1,000 lifetime memberships out of a temporary office. The course went bankrupt after the developers bailed, delaying the fruition of Joe Finger's vision.

After extensive renovation, the course opened in 1964 after almost 1,000 trees were brought in to complement the 40,000 plants that were added to spice up the design. The course is flat, and water comes into play on about half of the holes. The best stretch occurs on Nos. 6-11, which features two 450-yard par 4s, two par 5s that are impossible to reach in two, and a monster 230-yard par 3.

These days the club sports a new set of greens, which were renovated in 2002.

The details   281-437-8210. 14502 Fondren Rd., Missouri City, TX 77489

- www.willowispcc.com

- 1960s. Joe Finger. 18 holes. Par 71. Blue (71.8/122). White (70.3/113). Red (69.8/115). Gold (66.4/104). Price - $$$.

Getting there From Hwy. 59, take the Fondren exit and travel 5 miles south to S. Main St. The course is 1 mile away.

SIENNA PLANTATION COUNTRY CLUB

The golf   The new Arthur Hills/Mike Dasher-designed Sienna Plantation is a flat, wooded course that has been enhanced to provide elevation changes. The result is a challenging track that rolls between lakes, creeks, and the native hardwoods that dominate the landscape.

In terms of playability, you'll primarily notice the abundance of risk-reward decisions that are required throughout the round on this course, which tips out at 7,154 yards.

Out of the chute you'll be challenged immediately–the opening two holes play as a 427-yard par 4 and a 601-yard par 5. It lightens up a bit on holes 3-4 with a reasonably short par 3 and a short par 4, but holes 5-8 can blow your score up quickly if you're not on your game. No. 6 is a monster 251-yard par 3 sandwiched between two 450-yard par 4s.

On the back it's more of the same, with the nine opening with four 400-yard-plus par 4s. Both par 3s are over 200 yards, and the par 5s are each well over 500 yards. The only real birdie opportunity for the average handicapper is the 320-yard No. 16.

The first time I quit, I was playing in a tournament at Industry Hills in California. I shot 45 on the front nine. I told my caddie to go to the refreshment stand and get some cigarettes, the strongest kind they had. He came back with a pack of Pall Malls, and I shot 32 on the back. For me, smoking and golf go together. JoAnne Carner

The details   281-778-4653. 1 Waters Lake Blvd., Missouri City, TX 77459

- www.siennagolf.com
- Arthur Hills-Mike Dasher. 18 holes. Par 72. Black – 7,154. Blue – 6,624. White – 6,024. Green – 5,239. Price - $$$.

Getting there Take Hwy. 59 south to the Williams Trace exit. Turn left on Williams Trace to Hwy. 6. Turn left and drive 5.5 miles to the Sienna Plantation main entrance.

MISSOURI CITY NOTES   No place to stay here, so head to Sugar Land for the night. **Bravo's Mexican Food,** on the border of Sugar Land and Missouri City, is your best bet to relax at the end of the day.

MONT BELVIEU
Elev. 48   Pop. 2,324

About 30 miles east of Houston just barely north of I-10 lies the small salt-domed community of Mont Belvieu, originally known as Barbers Hill. Farming and cattle were the mainstays until oil was discovered, and the town has survived by associating with Houston and Baytown. The golf here is worthy of derailing a pilgrimage–the 1999 Eagle Pointe Golf Club is a tough temptation to pass up on road trips east to the further reaches of the bayous.

EAGLE POINTE GOLF CLUB

The golf   Rick Forester built this course in 1999, taking advantage of the distinctive natural terrain that includes abundant elevation changes and the snaking Old River. The pine-lined fairways roll through bunkers and water hazards to reach some impressive, well-conditioned greens.

The front features the most difficult rated hole in the 438-yard No. 6, which plays 419 yards from the tips and allows you to become intimate with the Old River. You'll need a solid tee shot to get in position for a decent approach and avoid the river on the left. The longish approach goes into a green surrounded on three sides by the Old River.

The back side boasts the course's signature hole. No. 18 is a 429-yard par 4 that requires a lengthy approach into a green surrounded by water.

The details   281-385-6666. 12440 Eagle Pointe Dr., Mont Belvieu, TX 77580

- 1999. Rick Forester. 18 holes. Par 72. Back – 6,893 (72.2/128). Middle – 6,176 (68.8/120). Forward – 4,916 (67.4/113). Price - $$$.

Getting there 30 miles east of Houston. Take I-10 east to Exit 800, turn left, proceed 3.5 miles and turn right on Eagle Pointe Dr.

SOUTH EAST

After every round, ask yourself if you feel as though you just played a game that you love. Dr. Bob Rotella

MONT BELVIEU NOTES   Eagle Pointe's grill is worth prolonging your stay–you can enjoy cold beers and fill up on their above-average grub. Down the road where 146 and I-10 merge, head south about 2-3 miles for a stop at **Steve's BBQ**, followed by lounging with locals at the cantina-like **Lime Light**. That's about it for local stuff. Baytown is 5-10 minutes away with more upscale action and lodging.

MONTGOMERY   Elev. 291   Pop. 489

The golf   The golf mecca of Montgomery, with its listed population of under 500, is often overlooked, but it's one of the most beautiful, outstanding locations in Texas for a golf orgy. The town is historic, dating back to its days as the seat of Texas' third-oldest county, but it was soon surpassed by burgeoning Conroe. Nestled here in the Piney Woods along Lake Conroe you'll find no less than six first-class golf facilities.

APRIL SOUND GOLF COURSE

The golf   April Sound, a resort known for its eminently playable track, offers an 18-hole track that tips out at 6,200 yards and an executive 9-holer.

The **Lakeview Course** is dogleg-heavy, forcing a few precise shot-making opportunities. Its back nine is the favorite–a challenging, tighter track with a better set of holes. The best hole is No. 15, a long, 430-yarder that involves water off the tee and a creek that impacts the approach on the left.

The executive **Inland Course** has one water hazard and several sand bunkers incorporated into its design.

The details   936-588-1101. 1000 April Sound Blvd., Montgomery, TX 77356

- www.april-sound.com

- White-Blue: 1971. Carlton Gipson. 18 holes. Par 71. Back – 6,207 (69.5/112). Middle – 5,807 (67.7/110). Forward – 5,333 (71.6/124). Price - $$.

- Inland Course: 1971. Carlton Gipson. 9 holes. Par 32. Back 2,311. Middle - 2,160. Forward - 2,002. Price - $.

Getting there From Houston, take I-45 north to Hwy. 105. Drive west 9 miles to the course on the right.

*Water holes are sacrificial waters where you make a steady gift of
your pride and high-priced balls.* Tommy Bolt

BENTWATER COUNTRY CLUB

The golf   Located on the shores of the beautiful 10,000-acre Lake Conroe and bounded by 158,000 acres of national forest, Bentwater has two outstanding courses that feature spectacular views and impressive golf holes.

The **Weiskopf Course** front nine features one of the toughest par 4s around–the 470-yard No. 6, which plays uphill into the wind.

On the back, considered one of the most scenic back nines anywhere, you'll encounter one of Weiskopf's all-time favorite holes, the 434-yard par 4 No. 12 with its split fairway and approach into a green protected by water left and back. Two holes later No. 14 is another great hole, a 200-yard par 3 perched on the edge of the lake.

The **Miller Course** is quite different from Weiskopf's design. Architect Jack Miller, who worked as a designer under Jack Nicklaus for 10 years, bragged that the terrain "is absolutely the finest piece of land I've ever been able to work on." His parkland-style track features lush fairways, virtually no rough, pine needles sprinkled about the course, and Champion Bermuda greens that are surrounded by huge swales.

No. 14 is bordered by the blue waters of Lake Conroe, and is annually selected as one of the best par 3s in Texas.

The details   936-597-6224. 800 Bentwater Dr., Montgomery, TX 77356

- www.bentwater.com
- Miller Course: Gold – 6,809 (71.4/125). Blue – 6,353 (69.3/122). White – 5,943 (67.6/121). Red – 5,459 (71.5/121).Price - $$$.
- Weiskopf Course: Gold – 6,920 (72.4/124). Blue – 6,500 (70.2/117). White – 6,217 (68.9/115). Red – 5,818 (71.8/128). Price - $$$.

Getting there From I-45, take Exit 94 and turn right. Travel about 7.5 miles then look for Bentwater Dr. and the course on the left.

DEL LAGO RESORT GOLF CLUB

The golf   Nestled along Lake Conroe, Del Lago is a self-contained retreat that offers outstanding golf, a variety of lake activities, and lodging in its 21-story hotel complex overlooking the lake.

Formerly tipped out at 6,794 yards, the Dave Marr-designed golf course has been lengthened with a new set of tees, now playing around 7,100 yards. Pines and oaks line the fairways and the bunker-laden track is spiced up with waterfalls, fountains, lakes, and even an island tee box.

The front side features one of Texas' most scenic holes: a 458-yard par 4 that approaches over water to a green that's lined by a spectacular waterfall on the left.

*You must keep the clubface open in soft sand. I simply cannot
stress enough the importance of this. My father used to make me
imagine that I had a glass balanced on the clubface. The only way it could stay there was if the
clubface remained open through the hitting area.* Johnny Miller

On the back, No. 12 stands out because of its undulating fairway, huge bunkers, and its hourglass-shaped green. However, No. 18 is the one to watch out for–a long par 4 that plays into the wind. A water hazard fronts the green, which, by the way, is all of 10,000 square feet.

The course can play particularly tough if the greenskeeper is coming to work after a tough night on the town. Watch out for some diabolical pin placements.

In terms of accommodations, Del Lago offers 310 suites with impressive views of Lake Conroe, as well as 35 cottages and 13 lakeside villas.

The details   936-582-7417. 500 La Costa Dr., Montgomery, TX 77356

- www.dellago.com
- 1981. Dave Marr. 18 holes. Par 72. Back – 6,794 (72.6/131). Middle – 6,402 (69.5/129). Forward – 5,180 (71.7/122). Price – $$.

Getting there From I-45 north, exit Hwy. 105 (exit 87) and turn west. Drive 12 miles to Walden Rd. and turn right. The course is a short distance down the road.

FISH CREEK GOLF CLUB

The golf   This course features gently rolling fairways bordered by mature oaks and pines. The well-placed bunkers and meandering Fish Creek call for precise, strategic play. Compared to the other top public courses in Houston, this is a great golf value that offers top-notch conditions as well as an excellent practice facility. Frequent elevation changes spice up your round–the course lays out with the natural terrain, and will develop more character as it matures. The excellent service here makes the higher fee and drive from Houston worth it.

Fish Creek in Montgomery has also unveiled its third nine holes.

The details   936-588-8800. 6201 Mulligan Dr., Montgomery, TX 77356

- www.fishcreekgolf.com
- Steve Elkington. 18 holes. Par 72. 6,834 (73.4/130). Middle - 6,197 (71.6/124). forward - 5,293 (72.8/127). Price - $$$$.

Getting there 35 miles north of Houston.

GRAND LAKE ESTATES

Opening 2003   Gary Player's new, private Grand Lake Estates course opened nine holes for play in October 2002, and is slated to open the second nine sometime in the first half of 2003. Located on an unusual piece of land in Montgomery County that rests 300 feet above sea level, Player has created an impressive signature course with 100-foot elevation changes that are atypical to the area. The 7,100-yard track winds through loads of scenic waterfalls and

"Keep your left arm straight" is a myth. It's more important to keep your muscles free from tension. Loose muscles let you make a bigger turn and swing the club faster. Gale Peterson

eight spring-fed lakes. Bent-grass greens have been installed and the course features two island greens (936-447-4636).

WALDEN GOLF & COUNTRY CLUB

The golf Long considered the best course in the Houston area, Walden rolls through a spectacular setting on the southwest shores of Lake Conroe and offers one of the most memorable golf experiences in Texas.

The course was designed by Robert von Hagge and Bruce Devlin, who moved over 300,000 cubic yards of earth to extend the lakefront property. This famous spot is now home to the unforgettable 589-yard double dogleg, which rounds out the impressive stretch of par 5 holes that make up Nos. 9-11.

More about No. 11: A draw is preferable off the tee, avoiding the trees and out-of-bounds that guard the left side. The key second shot should be a fairway wood left, avoiding Lake Conroe that comes into play on the right. If that shot is solid you'll face a 120-150-yard approach over the lake to a green that slopes back to front. Watch the wind and don't be afraid to take a bogey, as this is one of the finest, most difficult holes in Texas.

The details 936-448-4668. 13101 Walden Rd., Montgomery, TX 77356

- www.waldengolf.com
- 1976. Bruce Devlin and Robert von Hagge. 18 holes. Blue – 6,756 (73.1/140). White – 6,248 (70.7/133). Gold – 5,751 (69.6/123). Red – 4,993 (70.6/124). Price - $$$$.

Getting there From I-45 north, take Hwy. 105 (Exit 87) and head west. When you come to Walden Rd., turn right and drive 3 miles to the course.

MONTGOMERY NOTES Other than the Del Lago Resort, which has full accommodations, consider **The Heritage House** (936-597-6100) or **Shepphard Hill B&B** (936-344-9212).**The Grill** (936-582-7888) sits right on the lake. On Main St. find the **Moonstruck Cafe** (936-756-5282). The steakhouse in town is called the **Old Montgomery Steakhouse** (936-597-5155), and **Mexican Chefs** (936-597-6633) is the place for Tex-Mex. **Cielito Lindo** (936-597-6633) has "fine Mexican food." **King's Cafe** (936-597-6028) for casual outdoor breakfasts when the weather is good. **Izzy's Ice House** is a fun new bar and **Papa's on the Lake** (936-447-2500) has live music and good food.

SOUTH EAST

Go find some stimulating, fulfilling, challenging human endeavor
that, unlike golf, does not require a commitment of time and effort
to realize maximum enjoyment. And call me when you find it. Jim Flick

NAVASOTA
Elev. 215   Pop. 7,816

South of Bryan-College Station on Hwy. 6 lies the former plantation town of Navasota. Old homes around town and along the highway offer a historic feel, highlighted by a picturesque downtown loaded with shops. Cotton was king here before the Civil War for this Confederate haven, yet unpaid soldiers burned the city, only to rebuild it just before yellow fever wiped it out just a few years later. The city's first muni opened in the 1950s, and two more facilities have followed over the years: one country club and an upscale course named Pecan Lakes that should be your first priority when hitting the links in Navasota.

NAVASOTA MUNICIPAL GOLF COURSE

The golf   The Navasota muni is a 1950s-style traditional layout that is the place to play for a career-low round. The track is flat, with some occasional mounding and non-menacing grass bunkers that line the fairways and cover some greens. Three holes are doglegs, creating some interesting opportunities to get aggressive on this very short course.

The round starts off with two par 4s under 300 yards, followed by a 426-yard par 5 that is sandwiched between two gimme par 3s. The toughest holes are back to back: the "long" 178-yard No. 7 followed by the most realistic par 4 No. 8, which goes 387 yards.

The details   936-825-7284. 108 August Horst Dr., Navasota, TX 77868

• 1952. 9 holes. Par 36. 2,723 yards. Price - $.

Getting there From Houston, take Hwy. 290 north to Hwy. 6. Turn north again, and travel 25 miles to Anderson Rd. Turn right again and find Washington St. (Hwy. 105). This road will take you to the course, which is on the left side of the road.

BLUEBONNET COUNTRY CLUB

The golf   Once labeled as "one of the greatest second shot courses in the country" by original pro Jay Hebert (captain of the 1971 Ryder Cup team), this bluebonnet-laden track is the highlight of a 2,200-acre development between Houston and College Station.

Jay Riviere designed this one, and he incorporated lakes, ponds, and creeks on 14 of 18 holes, as well as some impressive elevation changes. Rick Forester came through for a redesign in 1983 to spice up the layout. At Bluebonnet CC you'll find good birdie chances in the short 500-yard par 5s, as well as a few tough pars in the long par 4s that approach the 450-yard range.

No. 11 is the best hole, a 360-yarder with water on either side of the dogleg

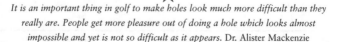

It is an important thing in golf to make holes look much more difficult than they really are. People get more pleasure out of doing a hole which looks almost impossible and yet is not so difficult as it appears. Dr. Alister Mackenzie

fairway. The approach is into a green surrounded by bunkers.

The details 936-894-2207. 4505 Old Bridge Rd., Navasota, TX 77868.

- www.bluebonnetcc.com

- 1970s. Jay Riviere. 18 holes. Par 72. Back – 6,495 (71.0/129). Middle – 6,150 (69.5/125). Forward – 5,159 (70.4/129). Price - $$.

Getting there From I-45 north, take Hwy. 105 west to FM 2445. Turn north and drive about 3.5 miles to the course. The entrance is on the left.

PECAN LAKES GOLF CLUB

The golf   Jay Riviere added another of his many southeast Texas course designs to his resume with the new Pecan Lakes Golf Club. Par 72 and tipping out at 6,922 yards, this water-infested track plays around a 20-acre lake and waterway system.

Water is the primary difficulty, coming into play on 17 of 18 holes, but the course is mostly hacker-friendly with most par 4s ranging from 300 to 400 yards.

The round starts off into the wind and rolls through groves of pecans, oaks, and elms. No. 8 is the best hole–a tough par 4 that plays between trees on the right and water along the left side. The long approach on No.8 must carry a bunker, and is particularly difficult because of the small green.

Like the front, the back opens up playing into the wind, with No. 10 playing 400 yards beside water. No. 11 goes 560 yards with a tricky approach that must carry a greenside water hazard. No. 18 is the longest par 4 (452 yards) and doglegs left around two bunkers, with water along the right.

The details   936-870-3889. 2001 Fairway Ln., Navasota, TX 77868

- www.pecanlakesgolfclub.com

- 18 holes. Par 72. Champ – 6,922 (71.8/119). Middle – 6,354 (69.1/116). Intermediate – 5,748 (69.5/112). Forward – 5,114. Price - $$.

Getting there The course is southeast of town on Hwy. 105 toward Brenham, on the left side of the road.

NAVASOTA NOTES   When in Navasota, stay at **The Castle Inn** (409-825-8051) if a bed and breakfast outing is in order. Otherwise, look to the **Best Western** (409-825-7775) or the **Cedar Creek Inn** (409-825-8000) for more basic accommodations. Two restaurants to recommend here–**Arargarita's Mexican Restaurant** (409-825-2284) on Washington, or the always-crowded **Cow Talk Steakhouse** (409-825-6993) on E. Hwy. 90. For history, consider the monument honoring the wayward French explorer La Salle, who was mur-

Certainly when you're playing for a lot of dough, you should hole everything. From four feet to two feet to one inch – putt it into the hole. It only takes a moment and it avoids all arguments. Sam Snead

dered near Navasota after missing his goal of finding the mouth of the Mississippi River. A statue is on Texas 90 downtown.

NEW ULM
Elev. 402   Pop. 650

New Ulm is another of the many quaint German villages that are so predominant in the heart of south central Texas. Your visit to this town of less than 700 residents will center around activities at The Falls Resort. Because of its midpoint location between towns like Columbus, Bellville, Brenham, and Sealy, Falls Resort might be your best option to set up headquarters for golf excursions in this part of Texas.

THE FALLS RESORT & CLUB

The golf   The Falls is located 90 minutes west of Houston in some impressive golf terrain. Dense forests, clear-water lakes, and waterfalls combine to make this place a special golf experience.

Despite its opening during the economic downturn of the mid-1980s, resulting in frequent ownership changes, the course has persevered because of the way designers Jay Riviere and Dave Marr took advantage of the natural terrain to build a spectacular golf course.

Holes of note include the famous 209-yard No. 3, which is known because of the dicey front pin placement protected by little green, as well as sand and water. Another tough hole on the front is No. 6, which plays 407 yards and features a fairway framed by water and bunkers. On the elevated approach, it's hard to hole the green because of the severe slope towards the water. If you're short, the multi-level bunkers will suck in the shot and leave you with a blind beach shot to the green.

On the back, the best hole is the 448-yard No. 17. You can't afford to hit it too long because of the water and woods looming right, and the approach is tough because of the creek in play by the green.

The details   979-992-3123. 1750 N. Falls Dr., New Ulm, TX 78950.

- www.thefallsresort.com
- Jay Riviere and Dave Marr. 18 holes. Par 72. Blue – 6,757 (72.3/133). White – 6,173 (69.5/126). Gold – 5,709. Red – Par 73. 5,326 (70.0/123). Orange – 4,654. Price - $$$.

Getting there From I-10 west, take the second Sealy exit and head north on Hwy. 36. Turn left on FM 109, travel 22 miles to New Ulm, then turn left where the road dead-ends. The course is 3 miles down the road.

If the green appears to be slow, and particularly if durin g the last two or three feet to the hole the ground is uphill, I hit it firmly for the back of the hole. Bobby Locke

NEW ULM NOTES   Your trip to New Ulm should center around your reservations at the resort, so check their web site and call for the different varieties of stay-and-play packages. The resort has a grill, or if you rent a vacation home you can bring your own groceries and cook out on your private grill. Other than the resort, stop by **Schulz General Store** (409-992-3342) for groceries, booze, hardware, and any other provision you might need, and meals can be had at the **Voskamp Diner & Bakery** (409-992-3388). Another lodging option is the quaint **Peacock Cottage** (979-992-3704).

ORANGE   Elev. 20   Pop. 18,643

The city of Orange has character. This isolated community on the Louisiana border has a shady history filled with outlaws, gambling, bootlegging, and whorehouses. Located at the junction of the Gulf Intracoastal Waterway and the Sabine River, this gateway city grew up around the steam sawmills prior to the Civil War. Clever hustlers made money, built elaborate homes, and enjoyed the social scene around Orange's opera house and hotel. Eventually a channel was dug and the city became a deepwater port before oil boomed the economy. Imagine the days of the famous Silver Slipper and Show Boat nightclubs, with the venerable Donald Ross rolling into town to build one of the only two courses he ever created in Texas: the Sunset Grove Country Club.

DUPONT EMPLOYEE RECREATION CENTER

The golf   The DuPont employee course plays only 6,385 yards, but it is burdened by the wind and known for making a golfer use every club in his bag. The front nine seems to offer more birdie opportunities than the back, with two medium range par 3s, short par 5s, and par 4s that play under 400 yards. The toughest hole on the front is the 409-yard, par 4 No. 5. The back nine plays to a par 35 and features only one par 5, which follows the number one handicap hole. No. 4 is the longest par 4 at 454 yards, and is sure to leave you with a long iron into the green.

The details   409-886-1779. 2601 Irving St., Orange, TX 77630

- 1965. 18 holes. Par 71. Back – 6,385 (69.8/114). Middle – 6,057 (68.1/111). Forward – 5,672 (72.2/120). Price - $$.

Getting there Heading into Orange on I-10, turn south on Hwy. 62 and drive to Hwy. 105 (Western Ave.). Take Western east to Irving and turn right (south).

✩

Practice in ways that build confidence. Dr. Bob Rotella

SUNSET GROVE COUNTRY CLUB

The golf   There are only two Donald Ross Courses in Texas–one is Houston's prestigious River Oaks, and the other is Sunset Grove. Ross made the most of the swamplands and hardwoods here in Orange, creating another masterpiece that has stood the test of time.

Originally known as Pea Vine Country Club, the club opened in 1925. The course plays like many other Ross designs–if you miss the elevated greens, ups-and-downs are extremely difficult.

Other notes: The club allows USGA members to play if they can provide the proper identification.

The details   409-883-9454. 2900 W. Sunset Dr., Orange, TX 77630

- 1920s. Donald Ross. 18 holes. Par 71. Back – 6,394 (70.4/117). Middle – 6,188 (69.7/117). Forward – Par 73. 5,491 (72.5/122). Price - $$.

Getting there From I-10 east, take the 16th St. exit and turn right. When you come to Sunset Dr., turn right and look for the course on the right side.

MORE GOLF

The daily-fee **Starwood Golf Course** is in the planning stages, an 18-holer that will serve as the centerpiece of a new residential community in the Little Cypress area off of Hwy. 87. Construction should begin in 2003 and the course should open in the summer of 2004.

ORANGE NOTES   Van Choate's **Cajun Cookery** (409-886-0990) serves buffet-style boudin balls, étouffée, gumbo, and anything else Cajun for lunch. The dinner menu is astounding, and the peach cobbler even washes down well with cold beer. Stay at the B&B next door to the **Old Orange Cafe** (409-886-3222), **Nimitz's B&B** (409-886-2911). **The Ramada Inn** (409-883-0231) has an outstanding seafood buffet on the weekends. **Casa Ole** has good margaritas, **Cody's** specializes in steaks, and **Crazy Jose's** is in nearby Pinehurst, TX.

PALACIOS   Elev. 17   Pop. 4,379

Warm sea breezes and palm trees greet you in this "City by the Sea," a sleepy fishing village founded in 1903 by shipwrecked Spaniards. Nestled along Tres Palacios Bay, this town of some 4,000 residents sports an extreme laid-back demeanor that's perfect for outdoorsmen seeking adventures on the water or via hunting expeditions. And thankfully for the traveling golfman, the great game can be played at Palacios' 9-hole golf course, making the perfect late-afternoon activity before hitting the bayside bars and restaurants for evening entertainment.

Fairway: A narrow strip of mown grass that separates two groups of golfers looking for lost balls in the rough. Henry Beard

PALACIOS GOLF COURSE

The golf   Palacios Golf Course is a typical small-town track with wide-open fairways, water in play on a few holes, and the always-nice policy of being able to play all day for one fee.

The details   361-972-5947. Hwy. 35, Palacios, TX 77465

- 1960s. 9 holes. Par 36. Back – 3,178 (33.9/117). Forward – 3,088 (32.5/114). Price - $.

Getting there From Houston, take Hwy. 59 south. When you come to Hwy. 35 south, the course is just down the road on the right.

PALACIOS NOTES   There's more lodging in this city by the sea than you could ever imagine, highlighted by the historic 1903 **Luther Hotel** (361-972-2312), which once served as headquarters for early land developers. B&Bs like **Moonlight Bay** and the **Le Jardin de le Mer B&B** are two of the many, many solid options. Walk along the lighted seawall and gaze at the shrimp fleets returning. Tour the **La Salle Shipwreck Excavation Headquarters**. You can fish on the lighted piers at night. **The Outrigger** (361-972-1479) specializes in seafood and steaks, and the same goes for the new **Wagon Wheel**, which sometimes has live music. **Palacios Mexican Restaurant** (361-972-2766) is the place for Tex-Mex.

PASADENA   Elev. 35 Pop. 133,964

Perhaps the largest of Houston's industrial suburbs, Pasadena is a residential community closely associated with the massive industries along the Houston Ship Channel. Its Spanish name, "Land of Flowers," doesn't necessarily apply anymore, since the industrialization has sapped some of the beauty from the flowering meadows along Vince's Bayou. San Jacinto Junior College is here, with a 1960s-style 9-hole golf course that offers some respite from the smog. The same can be said for Pasadena's other two golf facilities–the Baywood CC and the Chemlake Golf Club.

BAYWOOD COUNTRY CLUB

The golf   Employees of the Humble Oil Company (now Exxon) built Baywood in 1946. Surprisingly for a course constructed by untrained architects, it has become a Southeast Houston golf institution. Accuracy is required because some of the fairways are narrow with sharp doglegs. Water hazards come into play on seven holes.

SOUTH EAST

★

The chief reaction among amateurs to poor putting, it seems to me,
is exasperation, combined with a sort of vague hope that, by some kind of mini-miracle, it will all
have gotten better by the next time they play. Jack Nicklaus

No. 4 requires an accurate long iron off the tee into the dogleg right. Because of a creek on the left and the corner of the dogleg on the right, an iron is a smart play on No. 5. Hole 10 is a long par 4 with out-of-bounds on the left and trees on the right.

The details   281-487-0050. 5500 Genoa Red Bluff Rd., Pasadena, TX 77505

• 1946. Champs – 6,574 (71.0/118). Regular – 6,308 (69.6/117). Senior – 5,852 (67.0/113). Ladies Champs – 5,733 (72.8/127). Ladies Regular – 5,204 (70.1/119). Price - $$$.

Getting there From I-45 south, take the Fuqua St. exit to Beltway 8. Turn left on Beltway 8 and drive to Genoa Red Bluff Rd. Turn right, drive 5 miles to the course, then look for the entrance on the right side of the road.

CHEMLAKE GOLF CLUB

The golf   Wouldn't it be nice if all companies built golf courses for their employees? This course is owned by Celanese Chemical Corporation and was built for the sole use of their employees and their guests. Find one of those folks and talk them into getting you on.

The details   281-474-6402. 9502 Bayport Rd., Pasadena, TX 77505

• 1970s. 9 holes. Par 36. Back – 3,190. Forward – 2,574. Price - $$.

Getting there From Hwy. 225 east, take Red Bluff Rd. southwest to Bayport Rd. and turn left.

SAN JACINTO COLLEGE GOLF COURSE

The golf   On this college course that is open to the public, the main problems are the small, undulating greens and water, which comes into play on six holes. Trees get in the way when you spray it, so play your irons off the tee on this extremely short 9-holer that features five par 4s under 300 yards. Both par 3s play under 160 yards, and the longest hole is No. 8, a 520-yard par 5.

The details   281-476-1880. 8060 Spencer Hwy., Pasadena, TX 77505

• 1960s. 9 holes. Par 36. Back – 2,638. Middle – 2,512. Forward – 2,386. Price - $$.

Getting there From I-10, take Beltway 8 east and turn left on Fairmont. Drive 4 miles passed Red Bluff, and look for Spencer Hwy. Take a left to the course.

PASADENA NOTES   The **Best Western** (281-476-1900), the **Budget Host Inn** (281-487-8877) and the **Great Western** (281-998-8888) are about it for lodging. For eats try the **Cowboy Ranch** (281-479-1950), which gets a lot of play from tourists, or **Gilley's Restaurant** (281-991-4100).

Always keep in mind that if God didn't want a man to have mulligans,
golf balls wouldn't come three to a sleeve. Dan Jenkins

SOUTH EAST

PEARLAND

Elev. 55   Pop. 37,640

When Pearland was founded as a railroad switch back in the 1890s, developers promoted the area by boasting of its "perfect climate—fertile, and easily cultivated." Brazoria County's northernmost and fastest-growing city, which was named for the abundance of pear trees back in the old days, has doubled in population during the last decade. Subdivisions house Houston commuters who take advantage of the good housing values and proximity to both downtown and the Gulf Coast. The great game made it to Pearland in the 1920s, with the opening of the Golfcrest CC. However, public golf has just recently become a pastime, with two relatively new courses opening since 1988.

COUNTRY PLACE GOLF CLUB

The golf   Country Place opened in 1982 after Jay Riviere was brought in to build the course as the centerpiece of a residential development for senior citizens. Mike Hoelzer rolled through in the late 1990s for a redesign on this fairly basic 18-hole course. The short design features generous fairways and prominent bunkering around the undulating greens. Lakes and ponds have been added over the years and impact play on most holes. Trees have also been added over the years to spice up the flat, prairie-like course.

No. 9 is one of the toughest holes, a 440-yard par 4 that doglegs and has water. No. 16 is considered the signature—a 554-yard par 5 that also doglegs and has water in play.

The details   713-436-1533. 3123 Flower Field Ln., Pearland, TX 77584

- 18 holes. Par 72. Back – 6,802 (72.8/125). Middle – 6,391 (70.1/121). Forward – 5,399 (71.8/121). Price - $$.

Getting there Take Hwy. 59 south from Houston to Hwy. 288. Turn left on the McHard Rd. exit and drive to the course.

GOLFCREST COUNTRY CLUB

The golf   Golfcrest originally opened in 1927 as the alternative to the old-money course of Houston's River Oaks, located just south of town. The facility moved to Pearland in 1965 and hired Joe Finger to rebuild the course in 1971.

Finger moved a significant amount of dirt and integrated mounding and bunkering into the predominantly flat terrain. Lakes are placed throughout the design, coming into play on 13 holes, and the greens are extremely fast with sneaky undulations. The main trick to playing Golfcrest is dealing with the wind.

Other notes: In 1932, Golfcrest experimented with night golf by installing floodlights on the front nine.

SOUTH EAST

Remember that you do not so often win holes as the result of your own brilliant play as by the mistakes that the other man makes. James Braid

The details   281-485-4593. 2509 Country Club Dr., Pearland, TX 77581

- 1927. 1971. Joe Finger. Blue – 7,044 (74.2/131). White – 6,584 (71.9/128). Gold – 6,020 (69.8/124). Red – 5,632 (72.8/124). Price - $$$.

Getting there From Hwy. 288 south take Hwy. 18 east to Country Club Dr. Turn left, drive 1 mile to the course, and look for the entrance on the right side of the street.

SOUTHWYCK GOLF CLUB

The golf   Southwyck is new and improved after re-opening in the summer of 2002 with new fairways, tees, and greens. This links-style track features prominent bunkering, water in play on 14 holes, and is known for its difficult back nine.

Southwyck first opened in 1988 on the prairie lands east of downtown Houston–at the time, it was the only true links-style track in the area. Like the Scottish courses, this track is susceptible to the wind, and Kavanaugh did a nice job of confusing golfers off the tee, as it's difficult to determine exactly where you want to hit the shot. Depth perception is difficult, and local knowledge is helpful.

The course once served as the home course for the famous University of Houston golf team, and it served them well with its difficulty. Large mounding prevents level lies, and water comes into play on 13 holes. Tall native grasses line the fairway and require desperate hacks into the fairway when errant shots become buried in the heather.

No. 5 is a monster par 3 at 250 yards, but the par 3 No. 11 might be more difficult because of the long carry of a ravine down to the green 212 yards away. No. 3 might be the toughest in Houston. It rolls 467 yards into the wind with fairway bunkers lining the right side.

The details   713-436-1448. 2901 Clubhouse Dr., Pearland, TX 77584

- 1988. Ken Kavanaugh. 18 holes. Par 72. Champs – 6,914 (73.2/127). Back – 6,394 (70.6/118). Middle – 5,867 (68.4/115). Forward – 5,145 (66.2/112). Price - $$.

Getting there From Hwy. 288 south find the Hwy. 518/Pearland exit. Turn left and look for the Silver Lake subdivision. Take that road to the course.

PEARLAND NOTES   Hampton Inn (832-736-9977) and the **Best Western** (281-997-2000) have rooms. Italian food is best at **Big Humphrey's Pizza** (281-485-0392) and you can find basic down-home fare at **Kelly's Country Cookin'** (281-997-0044). The **Pearland Classic Cafe** (281-997-9007) offers a bar, laid-back atmosphere, and some great food. There's not all that much to do in

On the golf course, a man may be the dogged victim of inexorable fate,
be struck down by an appalling stroke of tragedy, become the hero of unbelievable melodrama, aor
the clown in a side-splitting comedy. Bobby Jones

Pearland, but the location is ideal because you'll be relatively close to just about anywhere you'll want to go. Galveston is 45 minutes away and downtown Houston is only 20 minutes away.

PORT ARTHUR   Elev. 18   Pop. 56,827

The slogan for Port Arthur has been "We Oil the World," which definitely applies to this city that has become one of the world's largest oil refining and petrochemical centers. It all began back in the 1890s when Arthur Stillwell laid out the city and combined the railroad's inland connection with a 12-mile canal from saltwater Lake Sabine to the sea. Today Port Arthur mixes its rustic old sea-worn homes and buildings with newer, more modern structures. Abundant outdoor opportunities greet the outdoorsman, with excellent fresh and deepwater fishing to be found, along with bird sanctuaries and other activities centered around 3,500-acre Pleasure Island and its huge marina. The island boasts Port Arthur's newest course, and two other facilities are available to the avid golfman who seeks the great game down this way.

BABE ZAHARIAS GOLF CLUB

The golf   This course was named after Mildred "Babe" Didriksen Zaharias, who is considered one of the greatest athletes of all time-she won two gold medals in the 1932 Olympics and excelled in every sport she ever tried. This Leon Howard-designed 18-holer is burdened by the Gulf winds but is generally hacker-friendly, tipping out at only 6,700 yards and offering minimal water hazards.

The details   409-722-8286. 3500 Jimmy Johnson Blvd., Port Arthur, TX 77642

• www.aquilagolf.com

• 1979. Leon Howard. 18 holes. Par 72. Back – 6,687 (70.5/109). Middle – 6,333 (67.9/102). Forward – 5,568 (64.4/93). Price - $$.

Getting there From Port Arthur, take Hwy. 69 to Jimmy Johnson Blvd. and turn right.

THE PALMS GOLF COURSE

The golf   Pleasure Island is now home to a new links-style track that opened for play in 2002, replacing the old course that faded away around 1980. With its unique location on the island of pleasure in the intercoastal waterway and Lake Sabine, this 6,900-yard track has a bit of character, with loads of donated Florida palm trees as well as uncharacteristic elevation

The road to improvement is filled with moments of great joy and satisfaction, as well as with plateaus and setbacks. Dr. Bob Rotella

Babe Zaharias posing in the slick garb of the day.

changes that were the result of the dredged ship channel. In fact, the island itself came about in the early 1900s as the U.S. Army Corps of Engineers cut the ship channel and piled mud from the bottom of Sabine Lake.

The details   409-984-5000. 1901 T.B. Ellison Pkwy., Port Arthur, TX 77642

• 2002. 18 holes. 6,900 yards. Price - $$.

Getting there Once on Pleasure Island, look for the water tower that looks like a golf ball sitting on a tee.

PORT ARTHUR NOTES   The **Cajun Cabins** (409-982-6050) on Pleasure Island are the unique, local place to stay. **Esther's** (409-962-6268) does seafood and is under Rainbow Bridge. **Schooner Restaurant** (409-722-2323) has seafood but also serves other items.

PORTER
Elev. 107   Pop. 1,490

Porter is next in line once Kingwood overflows from the city slickers who crave more affordable suburban housing and are willing to put up with the painstaking drives into Houston. The town is located on US 59 about 26 miles north of Houston, and boasts one of the Houston area's best-kept golf secrets in its semi-private Bentwood Country Club. For now, the club remains open to the public until the subdivision can sell enough homes.

BENTWOOD COUNTRY CLUB

The golf   The formerly private Bentwood CC opened to the public in 1997 when the development failed to sell enough houses, and for now it remains that way. The Dave Marr/Jay Riviere design rolls through the towering pines and features impressive undulations due to the 500,000 cubic yards of dirt moved during construction.

Other than the mounding, the most notable design feature is the huge greens, which are well-manicured and around 7,500 square feet. The course is nicely balanced–challenging, but not too tough. The fairways are of medium size and water comes into play on less than half the holes.

The best hole is No. 17, a 200-yard par 3 with water along the right. The green on 17 is protected by a huge bunker on the left.

Other notes: The course and development are owned by the country of Nauru.

The details   281-354-4653. 19980 Bentwood Oaks Dr., Porter, TX 77365

• www.bentwoodcountryclub.com

• 1994. Dave Marr and Jay Riviere. Champs – 7,002 (71.4/125). Bentwood

---

Mulligan: Invented by an Irishman who wanted to hit one more twenty-yard grounder. Jim Bishop

– 6242 (69.0/119). Exec – 5,647 (66.3/115). Forward – 5,188 (70.1/120). Price - $$$.

Getting there Take Hwy. 59 north out of Houston to Exit 13-14. Drive south on the access road and the course is on the west side of the road.

PORTER NOTES   There's no beer in Porter so go to Humble, which you'll probably do anyway since there's more to do in the bigger cities south of here. Look for the small barbecue place next to **Ricardo's Mexican Restaurant** on FM 1314. Also try **La Casita**. No B&Bs in Porter but there are chain motels along the highway.

RICHMOND   Elev. 104   Pop. 14,307

Originally the hub of a pre-Civil War cattle empire that made use of the fertile lands between the Brazos and Colorado rivers, the Richmond-Rosenberg area became one of Houston's bedroom communities in the 1940s. The trend continues today as the area's growth mirrors that of other Houston suburbs, and the trend is perhaps most evident in the abundance of golf courses that have sprung up in the last decade. Richmond boasts no less than six golf facilities. The highlight is the high-end Houstonian Golf Club and Resort, which can serve as the perfect hub for a golf vacation down this way.

FORT BEND COUNTRY CLUB

The golf   Leon Roberts upgraded this 9-hole facility in the 1960s, adding an additional nine to the former cattle lands on the outskirts of Houston. Roberts' design is short but difficult, loaded with pecan trees and known for its signature small greens and tough finishing holes that route around Rabbs Bayou.

Get your birdies on the more generous and open front side, because you'll need some room for error on the final stretch home. No. 16 involved the bayou looming left, and requires an accurate tee shot to a narrow landing area. No. 17 bends hard right and requires a 220-yard carry of the bayou. And No. 18 offers a similar challenge–a 394-yard par 4 highlighted by another long carry of the bayou.

The details   281-342-8368. 2627 FM 762, Richmond, TX 77406

- 18 holes. Par 71. Back – 6,346 (69.2/114). Middle – 6,116 (68.5/112). Forward – 5,575 (72.5/123). Price - $$$.

Getting there From US 59 west, take Exit 762 and turn right. Drive 1.5 miles to the course. The entrance is on the right.

Bunkers are not placed on a course haphazard, but they are made at particular places to catch particular kinds of defective shots. James Braid

HOUSTONIAN GOLF & COUNTRY CLUB

The golf   After all these years, weekend visitors to The Houstonian Hotel, Spa, and Club can now enjoy the new Rees Jones-designed Houstonian Golf Club. Designed to be free from the dreaded course-lining housing developments, the course tips out at around 7,100 yards and offers several sets of tees for the average golfer. Twelve holes feature water, and elevated tees offer great views of the pecan-lined fairways below.

The back side is the better of the two, highlighted by the picturesque No. 14–a short 350-yarder that overlooks three lakes and involves a testy approach into a green surrounded by wet stuff.

No. 15 is a nice par 3 with water right, but only plays 167 yards. No. 17 is a bit more challenging with no room for error, playing 207 yards into an elevated green.

The ender plays into the wind at 464 yards, and is unfortunately listed as a par 4. The highlight on No. 18 is the 150-yard bunker that lines the right side of the hole.

First-timers should consider hiring one of the club's caddies. Outfitted in full white garb, they'll make you feel like you're in the thick of it at Augusta National.

The facility is also the home of the Dick Harmon School of Golf, so there's plenty to do when you make a weekend of it here. The hunting-themed lodge, highlighted by game mounts and a fireplace, creates a great setting for relaxation. The Grille and Bar is available for post-round revelry as well. Package the trip with luxury accommodations at The Houstonian Hotel, which comes with access to the exclusive Houstonian Fitness Club and Spa as well as shuttle service to and from the course.

The details   281-494-4246. 12610 FM 1464, Richmond, TX 77469

- www.houstoniangolf.com
- 18 holes. 7,100 yards. Price - $$$$.

Getting there Take I-10 to Hwy. 6 and head south toward Westheimer. Turn right on Westheimer (west), then left on FM 1464. The club is 5.6 miles down the road on the right.

OLD ORCHARD GOLF CLUB

The golf   Building on one of the world's most famous horse farms, the Lazy C Ranch, architect Carlton Gipson used the scenic natural setting in conjunction with eight man-made lakes to create an impressive 27-hole golf course. In all, 17 of the 27 holes have water in play, and the ambiance of the old ranch is still in place–the nines are named Stables, Barn, and Range. The main ranch house became the restaurant and the foreman's house now serves as the pro shop.

There were two things that made golf appealing to the average man: Arnold Palmer and the invention of mulligans. Bob Hope

SOUTH EAST

Most of the courses run through an old pecan orchard and feature tight fairways. However, the Range nine is more open and resembles a links-style layout.

The most challenging hole on the course is the Barn's last 460-yard par 4. This mean hole is not only worthy of par 5 status, but has water in play along the right side of the fairway.

The details   281-277-3300. 13134 FM 1464 Rd., Richmond, TX 77469

- www.oldorchardgolf.com, 1990. Keith Fergus-Harry Yewens. Price - $$$.

- Stables/Barn: 18 holes. Par 72. Back – 6,888 (73.5/130). Middle – 6,291 (70.4/120). Forward – 5,035 (69.0/113).

- Barn/Range: 18 holes. Par 72. Back – 6,927 (73.6/127). Middle – 6,309 (71.4/115). Forward – 5,167 (69.4/114).

- Range/Stables: 18 holes. Par 72. Back – 6,687 (71.7/124). Middle – 6,148 (69.0/115). Forward – 5,020 (68.1/111).

Getting there From I-10 west, turn left onto Hwy. 6 and drive 2 miles to Westheimer Rd. Turn right, then turn left on FM 1464. The course is on the right 6.5 miles down the road.

PECAN GROVE PLANTATION COUNTRY CLUB

The golf   Pecan Grove came along in the late 1970s when J.B. Belin brought Carlton Gipson in to help him mold this country setting into a golf course community. As the name implies, pecan trees are prevalent, as well as oaks and other thick forestry. Gipson's layout is carved out of this terrain and winds through the residential community.

The course was 18 holes when it opened in 1979; Gipson added a third nine in 1988.

The **Plantation Course** features five ponds that impact play on six holes, in addition to heavy bunkering and a good amount of out-of-bounds. The best hole is No. 2, a long par 4 that doglegs right with bunkers covering both the bend in the fairway and each side of the green.

The **Grove Course** features flat, narrow fairways and is the longest of the three courses. No. 5 stands out because of its length (436 yards) and the fact that it's almost mandatory to cut the corner of the dogleg to avoid a monstrous approach shot.

The **Pecan Course** is known for having more water than the other two. Its feature hole is No. 9, and like the other courses, is another long par 4 dogleg into an elevated green.

The details   281-342-9940. 3000 Plantation Dr., Richmond, TX 77469

- 1978. Carlton Gipson. Price - $$$.

- Pecan/Grove: 18 holes. Par 72. Back – 6,776 (72.6/121). Middle – 6,219

Pain and suffering are inevitable in our lives, but misery is an option. Chip Beck

(69.9/118). Forward – 5,415 (70.8/120).

- Grove/Plantation: 18 holes. Par 72. Back – 6,981 (73.7/125). Middle – 6,458 (71.2/119). Forward – 5,457 (70.9/120).

- Plantation/Pecan: 18 holes. Par 72. Back – 6,907 (73.1/126). Middle – 6,309 (70.3/119). Forward – 5,336 (70.5/118).

Getting there From Houston, travel south on US 59 and take Hwy. 6. Turn left on Hwy. 90 west and drive 8 miles until you reach FM 359. Turn right onto Plantation Dr. and take the first left into the club parking lot.

RIVER POINTE GOLF CLUB

The golf   River Pointe lays out beside the Brazos River offering plenty of challenges, particularly from its numerous water hazards that come into play on just about every hole. The signature is No. 18, a nice par 4 that tees over water and approaches into an island green.

The details   281-343-9995. 11207 FM 2759, Richmond, TX 77469

- www.riverpointegolfclub.com
- Carlton Gipson. 18 holes. Par 71. 6,908 yards. Price - $$.

Getting there From Houston take 59 south to Richmond, exit Crab River Rd. Grand Pkwy., over 59 on overpass, straight to FM 2759, turn left and go 4.5 miles until you see the course on the left side.

SHADOWHAWK GOLF CLUB

The golf   The 1999 Rees Jones Shadowhawk GC is a traditional course that routes around a 70-acre irrigation lake and is highlighted by numerous pecan trees. For the most part this one is hacker-friendly, with generous landing areas. However, the challenge lies in dealing with the small, elevated greens. Bring your short game when you come to Shadowhawk.

The signature is the 540-yard No. 18, a great finishing hole that is bordered by a lake and offers a great risk-reward decision with its severe dogleg right.

The details   281-340-7205. 4100 Shadow Hawk Dr., Richmond, TX 77469

- www.shadowhawkgolfclub.com
- 1999. Rees Jones. 18 holes. Par 72. Back – 7,207 (74.7/133). Middle – 6,726 (72.5/128). Forward – 5,248 (70.0/120). Price - $$$.

Getting there Take US 59 south and find Grand Pkwy. north. Turn right on FM 1464, and the course is 2 miles down on the left.

RICHMOND NOTES   Track down the BYOB, open-air **Trading Post** (281-937-9204), which can accommodate big crowds and has iced cold beer

---

If a great golf swing put you high on the money list, there'd be
some of us who would be broke. Raymond Floyd

and set-ups. Texans crave places like **The Swinging Door** (281-342-4758), both for the atmosphere and sticky Southern barbecue. For traditional Tex-Mex, call on **Rancho Grande Mexican Restaurant** (281-344-0886).

ROSHARON
Elev. 50   Pop. 435

The "Rose of Sharon Garden Ranch" is now called Rosharon, a town of just 400 residents that was settled before the Civil War by sugar planters. Today, like Manvel to the north, the area's surrounding farmlands await Houston's expansion. But for now it's still empty and laid-back out in these parts of Brazoria County, making it a nice pass-through destination for the rambler looking for secluded, no-hassle golf.

BRAZORIA BEND GOLF COURSE

The golf   Originally built by Houstonian Frank Cope around 1970, Brazoria Bend lays out in the Oyster Creek floodplain surrounded by rice fields and pine trees. The Reiser family purchased the property in the 1990s, and their improvements have molded this into a modern, first-class course known for its immaculate condition.

Old man Cope's design features wide fairways, elevated greens, and water in play on four holes. All par 4s are under 400 yards, including the 297-yard No. 7. All told, the quiet country setting and the play-all-day-for-one fee policy make Rosharon a worthwhile day trip.

The details   281-431-2954. 2315 County Rd. 57, Rosharon, TX 77583

- 1960s. Frank Cope. 9 holes. Par 36. Back – 3,240 (34.8/115). Middle – 2,941 (33.5/109). Forward – 2,740 (35.3/106). Price - $$.

Getting there Take Hwy. 288 south out of Houston for 20 miles. Go two exits south of Hwy. 6 and turn right on CR 57. The course is 1 mile down on the right.

ROSHARON NOTES   Not much here, really. The closest place to stay is **Alvin, TX,** and there's nothing to eat in Rosharon. Have a hot dog at the clubhouse or drive into **Manvel, TX** for good eats.

SAM RAYBURN
Elev. 138   Pop. 600

The label of Sam Rayburn, TX applies only to this secluded resort about 3 miles southeast of the Lake Sam Rayburn–it's not an official incorporated

---

If you are in the top twenty on Sunday, a birdie will make you twice what a bogey will cost you. Mark Brooks

town. You'll come here to enjoy the resort and the lake, and that's about it. The nearest town is Jasper, 12-15 miles away, and the Twin Dykes Marina is about 3 minutes from the resort. When you reserve your rooms at the resort, ask them to hook you up with a fishing guide on the lake and add that to your portfolio of adventures.

RAYBURN RESORT & COUNTRY CLUB

The golf   Adjacent to the Big Thicket and the shores of lake Sam Rayburn, this secluded course is located halfway between Dallas and Houston and offers 27 holes designed by three big-name architects. Bruce Devlin and Jay Riviere designed one nine, as did Robert von Hagge and Robert Trent Jones, Jr.

Riviere designed the original **Gold Nine**, which lacks the elevation changes of the other two and has water on only one hole. The **Blue Nine**, designed by Jones, Jr. is the easiest of the three, featuring generous landing areas off the tee. The **Green Nine** is considered the most difficult because of the tight fairways and challenging approaches.

The Green is also the most enjoyable, opening up with a tough 370-yard dogleg left into a fairway that chutes downhill and a blind approach into an elevated green.

The dreaded 600-yard double dogleg rears its ugly head on the No. 4 hole, bending right, then back downhill to the left and eventually into an elevated green. Bogey is good here because a ravine dominates the left side, and water is behind the green.

The details   409-698-2271. 601 Country Club Dr., Sam Rayburn, TX 75951

- www.rayburnresort.com
- Blue/Gold: 18 holes. Par 72. Back – 6,731 (71.3/116). Middle – 6,244 (69.3/112). Forward – 5,524 (72.2/126). Price - $$$.
- Green/Gold: 1967. Back – 6,728 (72.2/124). Middle – 6,220 (69.6/121). Forward – 5,301 (71.0/118). Price - $$$.
- Blue/Green: 18 holes. Par 72. Back – 6,719 (72.5/129). Middle – 6,184 (70.1/125). Forward – 5,237 (71.0/123). Price - $$$.

Getting there From Jasper, take Hwy. 96 north to Hwy. 255. Turn left and drive for 3.5 miles to Hwy. 1007. Turn right, go 1 more mile, then turn right on Wingate Blvd.

SAM RAYBURN NOTES   As part of the resort's offerings, the **Rayburn Country Hotel** offers rooms for around $50 per night, as well as condos that offer more amenities in the $100 range. Call 800-882-1442 to make reservations and obtain reduced rates via the offered golf packages. Other activities include a 25-meter swimming pool, lighted tennis courts, and water sports

Golf and masturbation have at least one thing in common. Both are a lot more satisfying to do than they are to watch. Anonymous

available on Lake Sam Rayburn next door. The **Hidden Falls Ranch** offers horseback riding. For breaks from the resort head to Hwy. 255 (which crosses the dam) and find **The Stump**, a grill/lounge/beer joint place.

SAN FELIPE   Elev. 150   Pop. 740

San Felipe is one of Texas' most unique travel-golf experiences because of its quiet natural setting and its impressive history. Known as the "Birthplace of Anglo-American Settlement in Texas," this historic little town was home to Texas' first colonists in 1823 and was the location for many important meetings that led to the Texas Declaration of Independence. Santa Anna's Mexican army invaded and demolished this strategic site, which was eventually rebuilt after the victory at San Jacinto. There's more–the early roots of the Texas Rangers started here, and the postal system began here as well. The traveling Texan can soak all of this in and enjoy the 9-hole golf course (which is next to the state park with full facilities all in one weekend.

STEPHEN F. AUSTIN COUNTRY CLUB

The golf   Nature lovers and golfers who take particular pride in spending time outdoors will love this course. Loaded with wildlife and featuring fairways that weave through native pecan trees, Stephen F. is a beautiful 18-hole course set near the Brazos River.

The course originally opened in 1955, with both the design and construction being done by local golfers. The course has been ravaged by floods over the years, but continues to be one of the favorite rural courses of those who have played it.

Put your driver in the bag and play for accuracy. The course is under 5,900 yards from the back tees, and on many holes even drives that find the fairway will not result in a clear view of the green. Only one par 5 is over 500 yards, and most of the par 4s are under 400 yards. Bollinger Creek runs throughout the course and forces carries on four occasions. The back nine, built in 1970, is a little more open than the front nine.

The details   979-885-2811. Park Rd. 38, San Felipe, TX 77473

- 18 holes. Blue – 5,800 (120/67.3). White – 5,505 (66.2/114). Red – 5,137 (69.7/116). Price - $$.

Getting there From I-10 driving north, take a left on Park Rd. 38, then proceed less than a mile to the course.

SAN FELIPE NOTES   The course is adjacent to the 664-acre **Stephen F. Austin State Park**, which offers camping, nature trails, and fishing in the

A good straight drive or a soft chip stiff to the pin gives him the bliss that used to come thinking of women, imagining if only you and she were alone on some desert island. John Updike

Brazos River. Check out the replica of Austin's dog-run log cabin near the old ferry crossing at the river. The park store can help you with your provisions, and there's a few small grocery stores in San Felipe, but not much else. Look to **Sealy, TX** for lodging (**Holiday Inn Express**, 979-885-2121), as well as dining if you're not picnicking in the park. In nearby Cat Spring, TX find the **Blisswood B&B** (979-865-5594) as an alternative lodging option.

SEALY
Elev. 203   Pop. 5,461

Drive into Sealy from the north (Texas 36) in the spring and its beauty is stunning. Road-tripping through rolling farm country with oak trees and bluebonnets in bloom is a much better route than the less colorful and more congested I-10. Sealy is known for its charming downtown area highlighted by several intriguing buildings and old homes. One of those is the original Sealy Mattress Factory. Though the town was amazingly void of golf until 1998, hacks can now get their fill in Sealy at the 27-hole River Ridge course by Jay Riviere.

RIVER RIDGE GOLF CLUB

The golf   Sealy's golf course opened in 1998 with an open, Jay Riviere-designed 27 holes that utilize the unique terrain along the Brazos River. Rolling hills, plentiful pecan trees, immaculate greens, and impressive elevation changes greet golfers, and each 9-hole tract spreads out over more than 120 acres, creating a natural setting that's perfect for golf.

No. 2 on the River Course is one of the better holes–a par 4 that bends left and involves water off the tee and on the approach. The smart play is to aim at the bunkers towards the right side of the fairway and avoid Lake Victoria on the left. Par-able because it's not a long hole, it's a definite confidence booster to negotiate the water and reach the green in regulation.

The details   979-885-3333. 31333 Brazos Oak Ln., Sealy, TX 77474.

• 1998. Jay Riviere. 18 holes. Par 72. Back – 6,946 (71.5/129). Middle – 6,426 (69.7/124). Forward – 5,929 (74.3/135). Price - $$.

Getting there On I-10 driving west, take Exit 725 and turn right. Circle under the bridge, proceed to Chew St., and turn right. The course is half a mile on the right.

SEALY NOTES   Sealy's traditional favorite is **Hinze BBQ** (979-885-7808) on Hwy. 36, but **Los Amigos** (979-885-1126) and **Tony's** (979-885-4140) offer Tex-Mex alternatives. For accommodations check out the **J Bar J Guest Ranch** (979-885-2554), or **Sealy's B&B** option, **Sunshine Farms** (979-865-5000).

You can talk to a fade, but a hook won't listen. Lee Trevino

SILSBEE

Elev. 85   Pop. 6,393

The sawmill town of Silsbee is just north of Beaumont, TX, and is known for the giant Kirby Forest Industries. Oil and agriculture supplement the lumber interests here in Hardin County's most important town. Hunting and fishing are extremely popular in these parts, and can be supplemented by rounds at the 9-hole Silsbee CC.

SILSBEE COUNTRY CLUB

The golf   Mostly a flat course, the SCC has some mounding that comes into play as it rolls through the tree-lined fairways featuring water in play on 4 of 9 holes. The landscape is dotted with bunkers–some are strategically placed in fairways but most are found around the small, sloped greens, which are usually quite firm.

They saved the best for last here, with a 9th hole par 4 that plays 360 yards slightly uphill into a skinny fairway, followed by an approach to a front-to-back sloping green. Keep it below the hole!

The details   409-385-4372. FM 418, Silsbee, TX 77656

• 9 holes. Par 36. Back – 3,203 (35.0/120). Forward – 2,542 (35.1/118). Price - $.

Getting there Take Hwy. 69 east out of Beaumont, then turn left on FM 418. Drive 5 miles to the course.

SILSBEE NOTES   Explore the **Neches River** by hiring a guide (409-246-3107) to take you boating and fishing through the forested swamps of the **Big Thicket biosphere**. Canoe outfitters specialize in float trips in the **Village Creek State Park**, which is named for the 63-mile long creek that flows through the heart of the forest. There are no B&Bs, so crash at the **Pinewood Inn** (409-385-5593), which is the newer of the three hotel/motels. The unusually named **West Texas BBQ** on US 96 north to Jasper, TX is famous locally for the quality grub they throw at you. For really good old-fashioned cooking find **The Cottage** in a little white house, where home-cut fries and real, man-made macho burgers leave you feeling full.

SIMONTON

Elev. 118   Pop. 718

Simonton is south of I-10 about 45 minutes west of Houston, and connected to the greater Houston area via FM 1093. Formerly a plantation along the Brazos River settled by James Simonton before the Civil War, it was eventually broken up and sold. The railroad came through in the 1880s. After the turn of the century, investors from Kansas bought the land to grow potatoes, and the area became one of the leading producers of potatoes in the country. Now the town awaits the continued westward sprawl of Houston.

VALLEY LODGE/WHISPERING OAKS GOLF COURSE

The golf   Unfortunately, hard times have fallen on golf in Simonton, as their relatively new 18-hole golf course has been foreclosed upon by the mortgage company.

After opening in the early 1990s, Simonton's first course re-opened in 1992 after being washed away by massive flooding. The greens were goners, and it took some time to get the course back in shape. However, now the 5,697-yard layout along the Brazos River is better from the experience. It's a shame that this one appears to be out of the picture for a while–the fairways were in good condition and sculpted by moguls, and the river views made it a pleasing day at the course.

The feature hole was, and might someday still be, the 211-yard par 3 No. 8. Keep an eye on this one, as someone will surely fulfill their dream of owning a golf course and bring this one back to life.

The details   N/A. 614 Horseshoe, Simonton, TX 77476

• 1992. David Sloane. 18 holes. Par 71. Back – 5,697 (69.0/128). Middle – 5,396. Forward – 5,063. Price - $$.

Getting there From I-10 east, take FM 1489 and turn right. Travel to FM 1093 (Horseshoe Rd.) and turn right, and the entrance is on the right side of the road.

SIMONTON NOTES   In this very small town, the place to grab a bite is **Big Little Scotty's Cafe**, which serves burgers, fries, and other home-style fare.

SOUR LAKE   Elev. 49   Pop. 1,667

Just a stone's throw northwest of Beaumont, TX, the former Sour Lake Springs is is the oldest existing town in Hardin County. Named for the prominent mineral springs, it was originally settled in the 1830s. Health seekers flocked to the community for the curative aspects of the waters and the town became somewhat of a health resort, with early entrepreneurs bottling the magic liquid for sale–an Indian named Dr. Mud became famous for his treatments. In modern times, Texaco began here and ended up owning the lake and giving life to the area.

SOUTH EAST

They say some men are good putters or chippers. Nonsense. The whole secret of golf is to choose the right club for the right shot. Gary Player

IDYLWILD GOLF CLUB

The golf   The little-known Henry Ransom turned this from a mineral lake into a 6,727-yard, par 72 layout in 1962. His tight design slinks through the tree-lined fairways–it's tough because of the numerous water hazards on the bayou, which house friendly alligators.

Hole 7 doglegs right over 400 yards and involves a risky approach over the bayou. The opener on the back is another long par 4 (410 yards) that doglegs left and requires a long, accurate approach to the green.

The details   409-753-2521. 1100 E. Pineshadows Dr., Sour Lake, TX 77659

- 1960s. Henry Ransom. 18 holes. Par 72. Back – 6,727. Middle – 6,251 (69.7/120). Forward – 5,200 (70.0/115). Price - $$$.

Getting there From I-10 east in Beaumont, find the Lufkin sign (Hwys. 96, 287, and 69), and drive north. Take Hwy. 105 west about 8 miles and the course is on the right.

SOUR LAKE NOTES   Venture around the bayou and find the town of Lumberton, TX, where the famous **Catfish Cabin Seafood Restaurant** (409-755-6800) serves some of the freshest seafood in the South. Also down the road in Kountze, TX you'll run into the homestyle **Mama Jack's** (409-246-3450) for buffet fixins, which works well when you've made reservations at either the **Pelt Farm B&B** (409-287-3300) or the **Ethridge Farm Log Cabin B&B** (409-898-2710).

SPRING   Elev. 101   Pop. 36,885

Another of Houston's bustling suburbs, Spring was settled by German immigrants in the 1840s and barely survived as a railroad center until Houston sucked it in with its northern expansions. Subdivisions popped up, golf course construction surged, and old houses were restored and opened as shops. Now when you're in this neck of the woods, you can tour the over 80 unique shops and restaurants in Old Town Spring before and after your golf outings.

AUGUSTA PINES GOLF CLUB

The golf   Created by Tour 18, Inc., Augusta Pines is a new 7,000-yard track located at the southern edge of The Woodlands. The lush setting is perfect for golf, highlighted by over 30 acres of lakes and creeks and loads of oaks, pines, and dogwoods. The highlight of the course is the two finishing holes: a par 3 and par 5 that both feature island greens.

After your round, consider spirits and food at **Savannah's Steak & Seafood Co.** inside the club.

If you break 100, watch your golf. If you break 80, watch your business. Joey Adams

The details 832-381-1000. 18 Augusta Pines Dr., Spring, TX 77389

- www.tour18.com
- 18 holes. Par 72. Pro - 7,041. Masters - 6,446. Members - 6,140. Forward - 5,606. First - 5,007. Price - $$$$.

Getting there From Houston drive north on I-45 and exit FM 2920. Turn left and drive 5 miles west to Kuykendahl. At mile 7, turn right on Augusta Pines and drive to the course.

CYPRESSWOOD GOLF CLUB

The golf Cypresswood started the trend toward high-quality daily-fee golf clubs in the Houston area, and now features three regulation 18-hole courses in the floodplains of the Cypress and Spring Creeks. Towering trees, no nearby homes, and no out-of-bounds are just a few of the features of this Pinehurst-like experience.

The original **Cypress Course** is a little tougher than the Creek course. The meandering fairways offer uneven lies, and it's considered more of a target course because it has more water and dogleg fairways than its brethren. In fact, water comes into play on 16 holes.

Cypress features two mean holes–one par 4 and one par 5. No. 9 doglegs 427 yards and requires a solid drive to be in position for a green-in-regulation approach. No. 15 goes almost 600 yards, and has a creek that cuts into the fairway in front of the green.

The 18th can be a demanding ender, sometimes playing as much as 450 yards when the pin is in the back of the large green.

The **Creek Course** was the second to open, again receiving some acclaim from *Golf Digest* as one of the best in 1989. Known for its large greens and sometimes difficult pin placements, it lays out similar to Cypress, though the fairways are a bit more generous.

On the front, holes 5 and 6 are both par 5s that are reachable in two for the average golfer when playing from the middle tees. On the back, two par 4s stand out as probably the most demanding holes on the course. The par 4 No. 13 plays 469 yards and sometimes longer if you take the wide turn around the dogleg right. Hole 16 goes over 400 yards and requires a 230-yard carry off the tee.

The **Tradition Course** opened for play in 1998, and might be the best of the three tracks. A traditional, Donald Ross-like design with rolling fairways and links-style bunkers, the course also features large greens. Architect Keith Foster has claimed that the terrain of this course is some of the best he's seen in Texas.

No. 4 is the most-difficult-rated hole. On this 448-yard par 4 you'll need a good tee shot to get over the hill, which sets you up for a downhill approach into a green framed by bunkers and water.

SOUTH EAST

Talking to a golf ball won't do you any good. Unless you do it
while your opponent is teeing off. Bruce Lansky

Hole 12 is also considered one of the better holes—a 543-yard par 5 that features a fairway bunker in the landing area off the tee and a fairway that slopes downhill after the bunker. A good drive over the bunker is ideal because of the roll. Watch out for the creek that runs the length of the hole.

No. 18 is somewhat similar to the 12th–another long par 5 with fairway bunkers on the left and a creek that crosses the fairway on the approach, as well as a lake that runs the length of the left side.

The details 281-821-6300. 21602 Cypresswood Dr., Spring, TX 77373

- www.cypresswood.com
- Creek: 1988. Rick Forester. 18 holes. Par 72. Back - 6,937 (72/124) Price - $$$.
- Tradition: 1998. Rick Forester. 18 holes. Par 72. Back - 7,220 (74.4/134). Price - $$$.
- Cypress: 1987. Rick Forester. 18 holes. Par 72. Back - 6,906 (71.8/123). Price - $$$.

Getting there From I-45 south, turn left on FM 1960 and travel about 6 miles. Turn left again on Cypresswood Dr. (you'll see a Shell gas station). Turn right at the next light.

GLEANNLOCH FARMS GOLF CLUB

The golf One of Houston's top-rated public courses, Gleannloch Farms features a Jay Riviere 27-hole track on the site of the formerly world-famous Gleannloch Arabian Horse Farm. Loaded with rural charm, the gently rolling terrain snakes through the tall pines highlighted by strategically placed lakes, sand bunkers, and grass bunkers. While houses are nearby, the dense woods keeps the course secluded and peaceful-feeling.

The **Paddock** nine opens up with a 580-yard par 5 and offers a four long par 4s along the way—three of them make up the final stretch of holes 6-9, which are all par 4s.

The **Gleann** nine is a bit more user friendly, only tipping out at 3,355 yards since it sports three long-iron par 3s. Hole 9 is the longest, a 598-yard par 5.

The **Lock** nine opens up with one of the most difficult holes on the course, a 459-yard par 4 that will leave you satisfied with a bogey. The best birdie chance is No. 6, which only plays 143 yards from the gold tees.

The details 281-225-1200. 19393 Champion Forest Dr., Spring, TX 77379

- www.golfgleannloch.com
- Paddock-Gleann: 18 holes. Par 71. Black – 7,050 (73.4/131). Green – 6,391 (70.3/124). Gold – 5,717 (67.2/118). Red – 5,079 (69.9/117). Price - $$$.

When I hear a man censured for collapsing in the last round of a competition
when he apparently had it won, I always want to ask the critic if he has ever had
three 5s to beat his own best score and if he got them. Whether the score be 70
or 100 is of little moment. It's all a question of what it means. Bobby Jones

- Gleann-Loch: Black – 6,959 (72.9/129). Green – 6,354 (70.0/120) Gold – 5,775 (67.4/116). Red – 4,979 (69.5/114). Price - $$$.

- Loch-Paddock: Black – 7,299 (74.7/131). Green – 6,657 (71.7/123). Gold – 6,086 (69.2/121). Red – 5,332 (71.3/117). Price - $$$.

Getting there Glennloch Farms is located 28.7 miles (40 minutes) NW of downtown Houston, situated east of Hwy. 249 and north of FM 1960.

RAVENEAUX COUNTRY CLUB

The golf   Robert von Hagge and Bruce Devlin turned their attention to Raveneaux once Walden on Lake Conroe was completed in 1974. The two were excited to mold this part of Champions Forest into another upscale classic on the northwest side of town, closer to Houston.

The **Old Course** is the longer of the two, with more trees and water coming into play on 14 of 18 holes. Two par 5s stand out on the Old Course. No. 2 plays a whopping 618 yards, and the 18th goes 511 yards with water all along the right side and four bunkers protecting the green. This final hole marks the end of an extremely tough finish to the course, since water is in play on the final five holes.

The **New Course** opened seven years later to accommodate the demand created by new residents. Known as a shot-maker's track, the design features heavy bunkering, impressive lakes, and demanding, elevated greens. This course has as much or more water than its older brother.

You'll need precision tee shots during the round, especially on the 331-yard No. 16–it plays into a dogleg-left fairway and features an approach over a huge bunker in front of the green.

Other notes: Raveneaux is the name of the place where Napoleon took time to relax. The course experienced a 100-year flood during construction, washing away much of the newly shaped course. Both courses were renovated in the 1980s by Ken Kavanaugh.

The details   281-370-6370. 9415 Cypresswood Dr., Spring, TX 77379

- 1978. Robert von Hagge and Bruce Devlin. 18 holes. Par 71. Back - 6,703 (72.0/133). Middle - 6,202 (69.8/127). Forward - 5,095 (70.1/129).

Getting there From Hwy. 249, take the Champions Dr. exit and turn left. The course is just down the road.

SPRING VALLEY GOLF CLUB

The golf   Spring Valley is the realization of the late, great Texan Vernon A. Roland, who grew up on the land, served the country in World War II, and became a successful businessman by running Houston's Roland Cleaners. A man who knew the land intimately, he originally purchased it to run a sawmill

Always putt to one-putt. Never putt not to three-putt. Dr. Bob Rotella

but then fell in love with the great game of golf, which inspired him to build this charming little 9-holer.

Roland opened this par 34, executive-like track in 1993 amid the tranquil beauty around Spring Creek. Roland's course is fun, sporting five par 4s well under 300 yards, three short-iron-only par 3s, and a reachable par 5 as the opening hole, which also happens to be the number one handicap.

The details   281-351-8628. 25110 Gosling Rd., Spring, TX 77389

- www.springvalleygolfclub.com
- 9 holes. Par 34. Blue – 2,142. Red – 1,936. Price - $$.

Getting there From Houston take I-45 north to FM 2920, then turn left under the freeway. Take 2920 to Rhodes Rd. and turn left on Spring Stuebner. Gosling Rd. is ahead, where you'll turn right and drive 3 miles to the course.

WILLOW CREEK GOLF CLUB

The golf   Once a relatively unknown secret where Houston-area pros stopped by for casual rounds on their days off, Willow Creek is a difficult track that's definitely worthy of challenging the world's best golfers. The club is named after the creek that meanders through the layout, which Robert von Hagge and Bruce Devlin built in 1981. Their design incorporates the tall pines and dogwoods for aesthetics and is a magnificent course.

Much of Willow Creek's difficulty lies in the fact that water is in play on just about every hole. The narrow fairways are lined with trees, and out-of-bounds comes into play on a few holes. The best hole is the par 3 No. 12, which features water near the tee and a partially hidden green that rests 222 yards away.

The details   281-376-4061. 24525 Northcrest Dr., Spring, TX 77389

- www.willowcreekclub.com
- 1981. Von Hagge-Devlin. 18 holes. Par 72. Back - 6,811 (71.1/132). Middle - 6,331 (69.6/124). Forward - 5,012 (69.5/122). Price - $$$.

Getting there From I-45 going north, get off at Exit 2920 and stay on the feeder road until it loops back under the interstate. When you come to Spring/Stuebner St. make a right, drive 4.5 miles to Northcrest and make a right, continue down this road until you see the course. Look for the clubhouse on the left side of the North Hampton Estates.

WINDROSE GOLF CLUB

The golf   Windrose is a fun golf course that rolls through the wetlands, lined by oaks and pines and spotted by lakes that come into play on about half of the holes. On this relatively easy course, most of the greens are open and do not require forced carries. The large greens make for welcome targets, and they roll fast and true.

I don't enjoy playing video golf because there's nothing to throw. Paul Azinger

The best hole is the lone 458-yard par 4 No. 13, which is dominated by impressive old oak trees and plays into a well-bunkered green that is bordered from behind by a lake.

The details   281-370-8900. 6235 Pinelakes Blvd., Spring, TX 77379

- www.windrosegolfclub.com
- 18 holes. Par 72. Black – 7,203. Middle – 6,608. Senior – 6,069. Front – 5,355. Price - $$.

Getting there Take I-45 north from Houston to FM 2920, then turn left and drive to Kuykendahl. Turn left and find Windrose half a mile down on the right side.

SPRING NOTES   Don't miss the eclectic, down-home **Wunsche Bros. Cafe** (281-350-1902), where they'll get you fed and liquored up in the old 1902 hotel and saloon. The chicken-fry comes highly recommended. Also of note are **Papa's Social Club** (281-362-8371) and the **Inwood Grill** (281-681-3838). The best option for lodging is the **Holiday Inn Express** (281-681-8088).

SUGAR LAND   Elev. 82   Pop. 51,725

Sugarland has sure become popular for a sugarcane field town plagued by epidemics and fevers that was once called the "Hell Hole on the Brazos." Just 20 years ago, Sugar Land was home to a mere 5,000 residents, but has boomed incredibly as a satellite community to Houston. Once one of Stephen F. Austin's secretaries was granted land in the area, he founded a plantation that succeeded primarily from the production of sucarcane. After the railroad established the means to ship the refined sugar, the famous Imperial Sugar Company took off and the community thrived as a company town. Where there's urban sprawl, there's golf, and this town of some 50,000 is jammed with four country clubs and 126 holes of golf.

GREATWOOD GOLF CLUB

The golf   Greatwood is known for its white sand bunkers and impressive par 3s, three of which play right at or over 200 yards. The 1989 Carlton Gipson design features elevated tees and greens that sandwich plush fairways and are contoured with mounds.

The 434-yard par 4 hole 5 is one difficult par, featuring fairways loaded with bunkers and involves water on the approach. No. 18 goes 576-yards. While the tee shot is fairly standard, the second shot must land short of a plateau and might involve a blind approach shot if placed too far to the left. The intimidating approach plays into a green surrounded by water on three sides.

SOUTHEAST

⭐

The secret of golf is to turn three shots into two. Bobby Jones

The details   281-343-9999. 6767 Greatwood Pkwy., Sugar Land, TX 77479

- www.greatwoodgolfclub.com
- 1989. Carlton Gipson. 18 holes. Par 72. Black – 6,829 (72.6/130). Blue – 6,387 (69.4/128). White – 6,003 (67.7/124). Red – 5,290 (70.0/125). Price - $$.

Getting there From Hwy. 59 south, turn left on Crab River Rd., then make a left onto the other side of Hwy. 59. Look for Greatwood Pkwy. and make another left when you get there.

RIVERBEND COUNTRY CLUB

The golf   Press Maxwell came along in 1957 with the goal of building one of Houston's most prestigious courses on the southwest edge of the city limits. The terrain he was given to work with was ideal–void of housing developments, it sat in the middle of a cattle farm on the north shore of Oyster Creek. Maxwell carved the course out of a pecan orchard and created a course to stand the test of time.

Joe Finger came along in 1972 to reconfigure a few holes, and Carlton Gipson helped modernize the layout in 1988. The layout features mature trees in play on every hole and a significant amount of water (approx. 14 holes).

The details   281-491-2500. 1214 Dulles Ave., Sugar Land, TX 77478

- 1957. Press Maxwell. 18 holes. Gold – 6,677 (72.0/125). Blue – 6,360 (70.3/122). White – 5,944 (68.5/118). Red - 5,387 (72.5/129). Price - $.

Getting there From Hwy. 59 south, take the Kirkwood Blvd exit. Drive 3 miles to the course. The entrance is on the right side of the street.

SUGAR CREEK COUNTRY CLUB

The golf   One of only five Texas courses built by the legendary, original Robert Trent Jones, this club has three separate 9-hole tracks named Robert, Trent, and Jones. The flat course lays out in the Oyster Creek watershed, and is loaded with pecan, oak, and elm trees.

The Robert/Trent 18 plays easier because of its generous fairways, short length, and lack of water (only one hazard). The other two tracks squeeze the tee shots a bit more and have more water. All of the greens are of average size and speed, and a few are elevated.

Other notes: Jones came back in 1992 for a $1.5 million renovation.

The details   281-494-9131. 2400 Country Club Blvd., Sugar Land, TX 77478

- Robert/Trent: 18 holes. Par 72. Back – 6,546 (71.3/120). Middle – 5,978

It is demonstrably more difficult to control a shot with a club of extreme loft than with one of moderate pitch. Therefore, the clubs of extreme loft should be left in the bag until the need for them becomes well defined. Bobby Jones

(68.3/117). Forward – 5,339 (70.2/122). Price - $$$.

- Trent/Jones: 18 holes. Par 72. Back – 6,676 (72.0/125). Middle – 6,162 (69.3/119). Forward – 5,512 (71.6/126). Price - $$$.
- Jones/Robert: 18 holes. Par 72. Back – 6,553 (71.3/123). Middle – 6,068 (69.2/118). Forward – 5,265 (70.6/124). Price - $$$.

Getting there Take Hwy. 59 south to Sugar Creek Blvd. Turn left and drive to the first four-way stop sign and the course.

SWEETWATER COUNTRY CLUB

The golf   Roger Packard came to Texas from Chicago in the early 1980s to build what was originally three 9-hole tracks built for the LPGA and their Hall of Fame. Packard returned in 1990 to add a fourth nine, leaving the course with two 18-hole layouts.

Both are short courses that put a premium on accuracy. The **Pecan Course** is more traditional and longer than the Cypress Course, with water in play on 12 holes. The **Cypress Course** features more mounding in the fairways.

The details   281-980-4100. 4400 Palm Royale Blvd., Sugar Land, TX 77479

- Pecan Course: 18 holes. Blue (74.5/131). White (72.7/126). Gold (70.6/123). Red (73.6/131). Price - $.
- Cypress Course: 18 holes. Blue – 6,687 (72.3/126). White – 6,268 (70.0/122). Gold - 5,893 (68.5/119). Red – 5,407 (72.1/131). Price - $.

Getting there From Hwy. 59 south, take the Sweetwater Blvd. exit and turn left. When you come to Palm Royale Blvd., turn right and drive a short distance to the course. The entrance is on the left.

SUGAR LAND NOTES   **Brookstreet Barbecue** (281-313-4000) serves St. Louis-style ribs and other messy specialties. On the other side of 59 in Stafford, TX, give the long-time Houston area tradition **Otto's** (281-313-6886) a try–they've been serving burgers and barbecue for over 50 years. Also in Stafford is the famous 1928 **Avalon Diner III** (281-240-0213), where the blue plate special is done to perfection and they serve breakfast all day. For lodging the **Drury Inn** is down and dirty in a good way.

TEXAS CITY   Elev. 12   Pop. 42,488

Texas City and its twin sister La Marque are both areas of massive industrial activity, jammed with giant plants and scenic only to the most die-hard locals. This "Port of Industrial Opportunity" does, however, offer a productive 5-mile

The fact is that the ball is round and it's going to roll in the direction in which you hit it. High-speed video of golfers' putting strokes confirms this. Dr. Bob Rotella

SOUTH EAST

jetty into Galveston Bay, with various recreational activities that are highlighted by spectacular fishing and the 18-hole Bayou Golf Club.

BAYOU GOLF CLUB

The golf   Joe Finger laid the Bayou out in the 1970s. The links-style course he carved out of the 200 acres along Moses Bayou has plenty of water and elevated tees and greens. The Galveston Bay winds affect this open course, so the 6,665-yard par 72 plays significantly longer. Every par 5 is over 500 yards, and four of the par 4s are over 400 yards.

On the front, the long par 4 No. 6 is tough because the approach must carry the bayou to a tiny green. And No. 10 involves a lake off the tee and on the approach.

The back is what really tears into the soul of a golfer, though, presenting a 580-yard double dogleg on No. 15 followed just a short while later by the ridiculous 475-yard par 4 17th. This hole is lined on the left by old Moses, and water hazards creep into the fairway. The inevitably long approach goes into an elevated green guarded by water.

The details   409-643-5850. 2800 Ted Dudley Dr., Texas City, TX 77592

- 1970s. Joe Finger. 18 holes. Par 72. Back – 6,665 (71.0/114). Middle – 6,251 (69.4/111). Forward – Par 73. 5,448 (70.0/118). Price - $$.

Getting there From Hwy. 146 south, turn right on Loop 197, and head over to Ted Dudley Dr. Turn right, and the course is on the right side of the street.

TEXAS CITY NOTES Sometimes dog racing is actually an appropriate activity after a day on the links, so cruise into the **Gulf Greyhound Park** and take advantage of their air-conditioned grandstand and solid dining, while making a few investments in the speedy canine species. **Grand Prize BBQ** (409-948-6501) is a solid lunch option. **El Nopalito Restaurant** (409-948-4499) offers sit-down Tex-Mex. No real interesting lodging options to recommend–just the chains.

TOMBALL   Elev. 196   Pop. 9,089

Located at the northern end of Harris County, Tomball still maintains something of a small-town feel despite the persistent nudge of Houston's sprawl. The town was named around the turn of the century for prominent Houston attorney and U.S. Congressman Thomas H. Ball, who helped route the railroad through the town. The discovery of oil created "Oil Town U.S.A." and the city

I've been really stressed. Pressure never bothered me until I was sober. John Daly

negotiated a contract with Humble Oil (now Exxon) that secured free water and gas for its residents in exchange for drilling rights within the city. The golf here consists of the private 9-hole Tomball CC and the extremely popular 1950s Treeline Golf Club.

TOMBALL COUNTRY CLUB

The golf   The TCC goes 3,140 yards over 9 holes, with tight fairways and unbelievable greens. The oil hands needed a place to play so Humble Oil took care of their folk, carving a 9-holer out of the tall pines. Nos. 6 and 9 stand out–the first because of its 601-yard length, the second because of its approach over water.

Ask for the "Tomball special" where you can play the two sets of tees for an 18-hole round. Note the significant difference in distance when playing from the next set of tees.

The details   281-351-5102. 22303 Walden Way, Tomball, TX 77375

- 9 holes. Par 35. Back – 3,140 (34.2/113). Forward – 2,607 (34.1/113). Price - $$.

Getting there Take Hwy. 45 north out of Houston, then FM 2920 north for 6 miles to the Walden Woods subdivision. Turn left on Walden Way and drive a short distance to the course.

TREELINE GOLF CLUB

The golf   Treeline started back in the 1950s when the Hodges family built a 3-hole pasture course on their dairy farm. Friends persuaded them to add an additional 6 holes, and the popular Tomball track eventually added the full 18-hole experience.

The layout is short and sweet, playing just over 6,000 yards from the tips. Water comes into play on 12 holes, and the numerous trees cause all kinds of problems. No. 4 is the most difficult par 4 due to its 450-yard length. Of the par 3s, Nos. 3 and 17 both play a good ways over water. No. 9 is the best par 5, playing 498 yards with an approach shot into a peninsula green.

The details   281-376-1542. 17505 N. Eldridge Pkwy., Tomball, TX 77375

- www.treelinegolf.com
- 1950s. 18 holes. Par 70. Back – 6,010 (68.4/117). Middle – 5,425 (65.8/108). Forward – 4,752 (62.3/99). Price - $$.

Getting there From FM 1960, take Hwy. 249 north to Spring Cypress Rd. Turn left, then 1 mile away turn right on N. Eldridge Pkwy.

SOUTH EAST

If you thought about merely walking down the street the way
you think about golf, you'd wind up falling off the curb. John Updike

TOMBALL NOTES   The premier dining option is the intimate **La Tavola** (281-357-0999), where Italian specialties go well with the atmosphere (liquor license pending–consider bringing a bottle of wine). For more laid-back barbecue fare try **The Rib Tickler** (281-255-9431) or **Tomball Bar-B-Q** (281-351-0929). Another easy to-go option is **Hobo's Sandwich Shop** (281-351-5082). There's a **Best Western** and **Holiday Inn Express**, but for B&B accommodations try **Lucy's Garden** (281-357-4070 or www.lucysgarden.com).

TRINITY
Elev. 211   Pop. 2,715

One of the gateways to recreation on nearby Lake Livingston, Trinity is a longtime lumbering center that now hums as a result of tourism. With the coming of the railroad, its role as one of the transportation hubs for the East Texas lumber industry supported over 30 sawmills at one time. You'll be here for the lake and the golf along the lake, as either a guest of a Westwood Shores CC member as a paying customer of the Jack Nicklaus-designed Whispering Pines Golf Club.

LAKE ESTATES GOLF COURSE

The golf   Formerly known as the Crow Hallow Golf Club, this 9-hole track is now under new ownership and on the road to improvement. No. 1 plays over water, which is a testy way to start, and you have to watch for out-of-bounds. Other holes take on more of a links-style look, and are open and friendly to the average golfer.

The details   936-594-2583. FM 3453, Trinity, TX 75862

• 9 holes. 3,200 yards. Par 36. Price - $$.

Getting there Located off of FM 3453.

WESTWOOD SHORES COUNTRY CLUB

The golf   The track here along Lake Livingston weaves around eight manmade lakes, with holes that roll through skinny, pine-tree lined fairways routing to averaged-sized greens.

The par 5s stand out for their length, one on each side. No. 8 is ranked number two in terms of difficulty, but plays 590 yards, while the toughest hole is No. 12 at a mere 569 yards.

The details   936-594-9172. RR 4, Trinity, TX 75862

• 18 holes. Par 72. Back – 6,791 (72.3/124). Middle – 6,337 (70.1/118). Forward – 5,138 (69.5/113). Price - $$.

The rules invite cheating...It's like trying to keep up with the tax code. Peter Andrews

Getting there From I-45 north, take Hwy. 19 toward Trinity. When you come to Hwy. 94, turn right, drive down FM 356, then turn right again and drive 3 miles to the course. The course is on the left side.

WHISPERING PINES GOLF CLUB

The golf   Located in the piney woods near Lake Livingston, Whispering Pines is now open year-round as a wonderful golf vacation destination that sports a Jack Nicklaus-designed championship track and abundant recreational opportunities.

Tipping out at over 7,300 yards, this course offers plenty of length for the low handicapper, as well as a more reasonable 6,700-yard set of tees.

The number one handicap is No. 4, a 443-yard par 4, and the best birdie opportunity is the 178-yard No. 15, which plays only 136 yards from the middle tees.

Other notes: Mainly for First Tee Program participants, the facility serves up a 3-hole par 3 course.

The details   936-594-4980. 1532 Whispering Pines Dr., Trinity, TX 75862

• www.whisperingpinesgolfclub.com

• Jack Nicklaus. 18 holes. 7,330 (75.8/134). 6,695 (72.0/132). 6,064 (70.2/130). 5,021 (67.5/120). Price - $$.

Getting there Located in Trinity, TX, Whispering Pines is approximately 88 miles north of Houston.

TRINITY NOTES   Cottages are available for overnight stays at the rate of $125 at Whispering Pines. The Parker House (936-594-3260) offers water skiing and river tours in addition to lodging, and the Sanderson B&B (936-594-3986) is first-class on Hwy. 19. Also across the lake in Riverside, TX there's the Bethy Creek Resort (936-594-2511), where they'll rent you a boat and put you up for the night. The Riverside Cafe or Talent's BBQ, both in Riverside, are good places to eat, and there's also a cafe on the lake just outside of Riverside toward Trinity. Also cruise through the former ghost town of Sebastopol–it was once a major river port before dying out, and eventually became revitalized by lake-goers.

VIDOR   Elev. 26   Pop. 10,956

The city of Vidor, 6 miles east of Beaumont, is a company town of lumber and steel. It was named after entrepreneur Charles Vidor, who acquired the old Beaumont Sawmill Co. and eventually opened the Miller-Vidor Lumber Co. While Vidor is not one of the more likely golf destinations, if you find yourself

---

Golf is a game everybody quits, but nobody stops playing. Bill Davis

cruising on I-10 coming back from a long weekend in New Orleans it might be possible to rid the shakes with a round at Riverwood Golf Course.

RIVERWOOD GOLF COURSE

The golf   Riverwood opened in the 1970s, designed and built by the Barlow family. As you might expect, the par 71, 6,771-yard track is carved out of the thick East Texas pine forest. The best feature of this 18-holer is that you can pay once and play all day, cart included.

The details   409-768-1710. 657 Eagle St., Vidor, TX 77670

- 1970s. Johnny Barlow. 18 holes. Par 71. Back – 6,771. Middle – 6,410. Forward – 5,114. Price - $$.

Getting there From I-10 east in Vidor, exit Hwy. 105 and turn right. Drive about 5 miles over two sets of tracks, then the road veers right. Continue straight down the narrow road and turn left and the intersection. Drive to Eagle St and turn right.

VIDOR NOTES   **Burr's Country Store Bar-B-Q** (409-769-2309) is outside of Vidor on I-10 toward Orange, TX, loaded with sausage, boudin, and all things barbecue (except longnecks). Two Mexican restaurants are **Casa Ole House** and the newer **El Toro House**. Deli sandwiches and hamburgers can be had at **Novrozky's**. **BBQ Depot House** and **Wright's BBQ House** serves the smoked stuff in town. Surprisingly there are no B&Bs, but there is a **Budget Inn** on I-10, and Orange, TX has better accommodations. Vidor itself is dry, but a short drive south on Main St. (to a different precinct) there is a club called **Field House** with local bands and suds.

VILLAGE MILLS   Elev. 103   Pop. 1,700

Another of the old lumber towns in the thick of the Big Thicket, Village Mills is 42 miles north of Beaumont on US 69. You'll perhaps experience this town in conjunction with a weekend in the Big Thicket National Preserve, which is just a few miles due east. The community, named for nearby Village Creek, used the railroad to ship lumber out of the area. In the 1940s, oil was discovered and the town hung on for the next 30-some-odd years. More recently, the Wildwood Resort has contributed to the local economy, which is why the traveling Texas golfer will find himself in this remote part of the state.

WILDWOOD GOLF COURSE

The golf   Wildwood was designed in 1966 by Leon Howard, who was

---

SOUTH EAST

able to use this impressive terrain near the Big Thicket National Preserve to his advantage as he turned this par 71, 6,696-yard layout into the centerpiece of a resort community. His design features two large lakes that come into play on about half the holes, as well as wide fairways and good-sized, mounded greens.

Hackers can enjoy themselves at Wildwood because it takes unusually bad tee shots to get into trouble here. Each nine ends with an impressive hole. The front nine's ender is only a 455-yard par 5, but has a creek cutting across the fairway around 260 yards from the tee. No. 18 involves carrying a drainage ditch off the tee, then plays uphill into a dogleg fairway that is lined by trees.

In between, No. 12 presents some problems because it plays 221 yards and requires a carry over a creek.

The details   409-834-2940. Hwy. 69, Village Mills, TX 77663

- www.wildwoodresortcity.com
- 1960s. Leon Howard. 18 holes. Par 72. Back – 6,696 (71.9/121). Middle – 6,227 (69.9/116). Forward – 5,340 (69.7/115). Price - $$.

Getting there From Hwy. 69 south, turn right on Button Willow Dr. The course is on the right side of the street.

VILLAGE MILLS NOTES   Consider a stay at the **Triple D Guest Ranch** (409-457-2248) outside of Village Mills. And at the resort there's plenty to do, including bass fishing on 365-acre **Lake Kimble**, campgrounds on **Village Creek**, tennis and other miscellaneous sporting activities, and a lakeside cafe with burgers, seafood, and steaks.

WALLER
Elev. 244   Pop. 2,092

Waller, like Hockley and Hempstead, is another Texas 6/US 290 Houston commuter community just 40 miles west of the mother city. Its history is typical of small-town Texas: farming, ranching, and the railroad. When cotton was prominent, the Boettcher Cotton Gin functioned as a marketing cooperative for area farmers as well as a place to hang out. Thankfully, the weekend drives between Austin and Houston can sometimes be spiced up by excursions in the tiny towns along 290, and Waller offers that opportunity with its Jimmy-Demaret-designed 9-hole country club.

WALLER COUNTRY CLUB

The golf   Jimmy Demaret laid this one out in the early 1970s, and his jewel of a design features the ubiquitous pine trees as well as a winding creek, two lakes, and a few small ponds that impact play.

Sandwiched between two 530-yard par 5s are three par 3s and four par 4s.

SOUTH EAST

⭐

Practice ought to focus your mind in the same way in which you want to focus it on the golf course. That is quality practice. Dr. Bob Rotella

The par 3s are considered the easiest holes on the course; however, one plays 223 yards. The par 4s play just under 400 yards, including the number one handicap at 370 yards.

Other notes: Walk-ons are welcome here, as it never takes too much time to get on the course. Discounts are offered early in the week. The clubhouse is new and offers good options for food and drink.

The details   936-991-3335. 15357 Penick Rd., Waller, TX 77484

- 1972. Jimmy Demaret. 9 holes. Par 35. Back – 3,114 (34.1/113). Middle – 2,974 (33.7/108). Forward – 2,349 (33.3/100). Price - $.

Getting there Located 3 miles south of SH 290 on FM 362 in Waller on Penick Rd.

WALLER NOTES   Hit the backroads to the **Cedar Creek Cafe** on Hwy. 6 and FM 2979. For lodging look south of Hempstead, TX for the new **Oak Shadows Cottage** (979-826-2690), which sits on 20 scenic acres and is ideal for romance and antiquing. The touring golfer might plan the trip to Waller for the first part of the week, as the club offers discounts Monday through Wednesday. Find the middle-of-nowhere town of **Fetzer, TX** and see if anyone worthwhile is playing music at **Henry's Hideout**.

WEIMAR
Elev. 408   Pop. 1,981

You could argue that the metropolis of Weimar is Hill Country all the way, but its location east of north-south US 77 helps affiliate this history-rich little German town more with Houston. After Stephen F.'s colonists settled the area, the community blossomed as an agricultural center. This one is worth a stop when rambling between Houston and San Antonio–downtown has character with its interesting architecture and charming shops, and the Weimar Golf Club gives the golfer time to play while the rest of the family shops.

WEIMAR GOLF CLUB

The golf   Weimar's golf club is a short, well-maintained course that features one lake and a good amount of trees. Some have complained of the increased green fees in recent years, but it's hard to find fault with such a well-maintained country course in such a small town. You'll enjoy the hospitality and the golf in Weimar.

The details   979-725-8624. Hwy. 98 E., Weimar, TX 78962

- 9 holes. Par 36. Back – 3,041 (34.0/115). Forward – 2,488 (34.5/115). Price - $$.

There are several good ways to swing at a golf ball, but only one good way to play golf...aggressively! Greg Norman

Getting there Take I-10 north out of Houston to Hwy. 155. Turn right (west), then continue for 4 blocks to Hwy. 90. Turn east and drive to the course.

WEIMAR NOTES   Tour the picturesque downtown, where you can piddle around in the shops, find some great eateries, and hole up in **The Tavern** (979-725-8799) for dominoes and cards with the locals. Folks come from all over the state to load up on **Kaspar's** jerky and homemade sausage. A stop by the **Fishbeck's Texaco** (979-725-6240) for barbecue lunch is always timely when you need other provisions for the road. For lodging call **The Weimar Inn** (979-725-8990), which is located downtown in an old bank building, or **The Phoenix** (979-733-0304), located on 75 acres outside of town. Convince your honey to enter the beauty pageant for the **Weimar Gederke** celebration held annually on the Saturday before Mother's Day.

WEST COLUMBIA   Elev. 40   Pop. 4,520

It's funny how fate plays out. At one time it was in the cards for West Columbia (formerly Columbia) to serve as Texas' capital. Sam Houston was sworn in here as the first President of the Republic of Texas, and the first congress was held here in this 1824 establishment that was one of the first Anglo settlements in Texas. The history is strong here and there is plenty to see and do in this town where Texas began, especially for the golf addict who can plan his trip around action at the Columbia Lakes Resort.

COLUMBIA LAKES RESORT

The golf   Originally developed by the Tenneco company as a place for executives to discuss strategy, the course owners ended up caving in to the economic possibilities of the valuable real estate and hiring Jack Miller to create the course as the centerpiece of a subdivision in the early 1970s.

Tall Texas oak trees covered in moss, dogleg fairways, lagoons, and winding, clear-blue lakes highlight the golf course on this 2,000-acre resort. Many of the holes have been nominated as some of the most difficult in Houston, including the 533-yard No. 5, which doglegs right around a lake that impacts play on every shot. No. 18, a long par 4, requires a perfect drive to the right side of the fairway in order to have a chance to fire away at the long approach. This approach must carry water and avoid the overhanging trees, and the green is extremely shallow, less than 50 feet deep.

Tom Fazio redesigned this impressive resort course in the early 1980s. It was his first assignment in Texas before working on his famous Barton Creek layout.

SOUTHEAST

It doesn't matter what kind of club head is on one end of that
shiny metal shaft if a fat head is on the other end. Robinson Murray

The details   979-345-5151. 188 Freeman Blvd., West Columbia, TX 77486

- www.columbia-lakes.com

- 1973. Tom Fazio and Jack Miller. 18 holes. Par 72. Back – 6,967 (75.7/131). Middle – 6,300 (72.2/125). Forward – 72.3/132). Price - $$$.

Getting there From Hwy. 288 south, take Hwy. 35 west and turn right on Columbia Lakes Blvd. The course is just down the road on the left side of the street.

WEST COLUMBIA NOTES Indulge in the resort and take advantage of their 300-acre stocked trophy bass lake. If you don't stay there, make your reservations at the **Country Hearth Inn** (979-345-2399). For eats try **J & C B-B-Que** (979-345-6391), which is carry-out only. **Scott's BBQ** (979-345-6162) is solid, and **SB's Cafe** (979-345-6282) offers another local sit-down option. Possible side trips include a cruise by the **Masonic** and **Orozimbo Oaks**, the latter of which marks the site where Santa Anna was once held prisoner after the Battle of San Jacinto. Also look for the **Varner Hogg Plantation** and the state historic park, where the impressive mansion once housed former Texas governor James Hogg.

WHARTON
Elev. 111   Pop. 9,237

An hour southwest of Houston on US 59, and only 45 minutes from the Gulf, Old South relic Wharton is near the Colorado River with majestic Victorian homes, pristine lawns, and moss-covered oaks. This seat of Wharton County sprang to life as part of the Caney Run mail route that was set up by the Republic of Texas in 1838. Named after the Wharton brothers who were leaders in the revolution, the town has served as home base for CBS newsman Dan Rather as well as the infamous Robert "Three-Legged Willie" Williamson, one of the earliest Texans to spout the popular frontier rhetoric calling for Texas' independence.

WHARTON COUNTRY CLUB

The golf   The WCC upgraded in the late 1990s by renovating their bunkers and greens. The terrain is varied here, with numerous ravines and creeks that come into play.

Three par 3s are highlights of the round, mostly because they are all reasonably short and definite birdie opportunities. The toughest hole is the par 4 No. 3 at 429 yards, but every other par 4 is under 400 yards and both par 5s are reachable in two.

Two sets of tees make for an 18-hole round.

I like to see players turn putting practice into a game. Putting contests with a friend are far more beneficial than working on your stroke on the putting green. Dr. Bob Rotella

SOUTH EAST

The details   979-532-5940. 126 Country Club Dr., Wharton, TX 77488

- 9 holes. Back – Par 35. 2,895 (34.9/111). Forward – Par 36. 2,709 (36.4/117). Price - $$.

Getting there Take Hwy. 59 south out of Houston and exit Wharton. Drive south and look for Boling Hwy. Turn left and drive to Alabama Rd., where you'll turn right and drive to Hwy. 60. Turn left on 60 and travel 1 mile to Old Lane City Hwy. 1. Turn left and the course is 3 miles down the road. Turn left at the course sign.

WHARTON NOTES   Stay at the **Johansen House B&B** (979-532-8988) or the **Caney Creek B&B** (979-532-5856), which also has a lodge for larger groups. **Heinz's BBQ** (979-532-2710) is on the loop, and there's **Los Cucos Mexican Cafe** for Tex-Mex. On the square in search of nightlife, hit the **Innkeeper Ale House and Martini Bar** (979-531-0105) for spirits and live music. **Fibber's** has a buffet and **Square Meals** serves good sandwiches and burgers on the square. Also on the square is the pressed-tin-ceiling **Pat-A-Cake** (979-282-8000), which serves a huge Cobb sandwich with avocados and blue cheese.

WILLIS
Elev. 384   Pop. 3,985

Houston and Conroe spill into forested Willis, but not too much. A tidy town once known for its fine tobacco, Willis is located just off I-45 north of Conroe, sandwiched between Lake Conroe to the west and the Sam Houston National Forest to the east. The high-tech industry has made its mark here but lumber still plays a role in the economy, as do a few other minor cash crops. Conveniently located in this small town away from urbanity, Willis' Texas National Golf Club tempts Dallas-bound travelers who are cruising north on I-45.

TEXAS NATIONAL GOLF CLUB

The golf   The terrain around Willis is loaded with forests of dogwood, holly, and pine trees, creating the perfect environment for an Augusta National imitation. Jack Miller created just that in the 1970s, coming up with one of the most unusual courses in the Houston area and one of the closest comparisons to the Master's layout you'll find in Texas.

Recent renovations at the course include new cart paths and additional bridges on the course, as well as an update to the 11,000-square-foot clubhouse.

Miller's secluded layout features water on 12 holes, and the elevation

SOUTH EAST

Golf is a game that creates emotions that sometimes cannot be endured with the club still in your hands. Bobby Jones

changes are reminiscent of the Hill Country. The best hole is No. 2, a 222-yard par 3 that plays over a pond.

Other notes: Walking is only allowed during the week.

The details 936-856-4233. 8720 Club House Dr., Willis, TX 77378

- Par 72. Gold – 6,806 (71.4 / 127). Blue – 6,313 (69.1/121). White – 5,640 (67.0/112). Red – 4,964 (68.5/122). Price - $$$.

Getting there The course is 2 miles east of Willis on FM 2432. From Houston, take I-45 north toward Dallas and pass through Conroe. Take the Seven Coves exit (FM 830) and turn right at the light. Turn left on Hwy. 75, then right on FM 2432. The course is on the left 2 miles down the road.

WILLIS NOTES Try the **Best Western** (936-856-1904) off of I-45. A couple of Tex-Mex joints–**Los Pericos** and **La Hacienda Mexican Restaurant** –both serve cold beer and margaritas. Locals brag about the **Pizza Shack**. Also don't forget about **Blackie's Barbecue** (936-856-5867) on Danville.

THE WOODLANDS
Elev. 98   Pop. 55,649

The Woodlands is a 27,000-acre incorporated city created by visionary George Mitchell to be a housing and recreational hot spot for Houston-area residents. The Woodlands Corporation has spent impressively here, building golf course after golf course out of the thick forest and eventually bringing the PGA Tour's Houston Open to their facility in 1975. The master-planned community itself was one of the first of its kind in the nation. It now features eight charming communities with beautiful homes, loads of shopping and restaurants, and more than 100 miles of hike and bike trails to go with the 80-some-odd neighborhood parks.

The traveling Texan will be most interested in The Woodlands Resort & Conference Center, a spectacular leisure destination nestled in the forests north of Houston that is complete with championship golf, outdoor activities, shopping, fine dining, and even the full-blown spa experience.

THE CLUB AT CARLTON WOODS

The golf Located in the Carlton Woods residential community, with a separate address, pro shop, and phone number, The Club at Carlton Woods is a 7,385-yard, par 72 Jack-Nicklaus-designed route that opened for play in June 2001 and has quickly earned acclaim as one of the finest in Texas.

This is the place where the game of golf is taken to a new level. Members walk and have caddies, and there's minimal signage and fluff to ensure the ultimate natural setting. Even the course is straightforward, with the design man-

SOUTH EAST

Some guys get so nervous playing for their own money, the greens don't need fertilizing for a year. Dave Hill

aged by The Bear himself. He had at his disposal an impressive piece of property with unusual elevation changes for the area.

As with other Nicklaus tracks, this one is fair off the tee, yet challenging on the approaches. The key here is to pay attention to the pin location on the small greens, and generally keep it below the hole. A few water hazards require forced carries, but those are few and far between.

The best hole on the front is No. 9, a 455-yard par 4 that rolls along a beautiful lake, but the number one handicap is the 470-yard No. 2, which plays uphill into an elevated green.

On the back side, watch out for the 192-yard, all-carry-over-water No. 12, which precedes a 580-yard par 5. No. 17 is another good par 3, playing 222 yards into an elevated green protected by water. Then the ender: a 548-yard dogleg right that swerves between the tall pines and a lake.

Carlton Woods is a must-play if you can swing it. Call your doctor and attorney friends who might've forked over the almost six-figure initiation fee and see if they can help. Otherwise, this one is only for members.

The details   281-863-5820. 1 Carlton Woods Dr., The Woodlands, TX 77382

• www.theclubatcarltonwoods.com

• 2001. Jack Nicklaus. 18 holes. Par 72. Back – 7,385 (75.3/185). Middle - 6,917 (72.7/130). Forward – 5,496 (71.2/127). Price – $$$$.

Getting there From I-45 north, exit Woodlands Pkwy. and turn left. When you come to Grogan's Mill Rd., turn left, and drive to South Mill Bend Rd. and turn left again. The entrance is a short way down on the left.

MONTGOMERY COUNTY GOLF CENTER

The golf   This confidence-building 9-hole par 3 course plays just over 1,000 yards and features minimal bunkering and a few water hazards. With a lighted driving range, it's the perfect place to practice the night before your big rounds at the resort courses.

The details   409-273-4002. 1780 I-45 South, The Woodlands, TX 77387

• 9 holes. Par 27. 1,037 yards. Price - $.

Getting there From Conroe, take I-45 south 1 mile to the course.

THE WOODLANDS RESORT AND COUNTRY CLUB

The golf   Known for its reputation as a business conference center, The Woodlands has been plugging its resort as a family destination. It serves up almost 500 rooms, five restaurants, a full-service spa, and everything else you might need to persuade the wife and kids to make it a weekend in the forests north of Houston.

For the average guy visiting the resort, you'll have two golf options: The

SOUTHEAST

famous Tournament Players Course and the new and improved Pines Course. However, for those with country club connections, a call from your local pro can generally get you onto the private 27-hole Palmer Course, the Jay Morrish-designed Oaks course, and even the new Gary Player track. If that works out, you'll be shuttling from your room to the private fairways of these exclusive courses, feeling satisfied about the funds you're dropping at the resort.

The **TPC Course** opened in 1978 as a member and resort course. It was designed by Bruce Devlin and Robert von Hagge to be the course to host the Houston Open. In those days the TPC concept was not in place, but when PGA Tour commissioner Deane Beman toured the track, he was convinced of its worthiness as the first TPC conversion. After minor revisions the former East Course was renamed the TPC, and immediately became one of the most popular courses on tour.

The last two holes can bring the average resort golfer to his knees. Both 17 and 18 require approaches over water, the latter being more challenging because of its 437-yard length.

The **Pines Course** opened in 1982, added by Robert von Hagge and Bruce Devlin as part of the expansion that moved the Houston Open to the also-new TPC Course. Redesigned in 2002-2003 by Roy Case, this one is shorter than the others, and the easiest of them all. Only two par 4s venture into the 400-yard range. However, the par 5s are in the mid-550 range, including two in the first four holes and back-to-back on the back nine.

The par 4s are the most demanding holes. No. 6 doglegs right around a pond and plays 426 yards, while No. 15 goes 448 yards, bending left by a fairway bunker and featuring an approach over a creek.

The Palmer Course features more rolling terrain, moguls, and grass bunkers than the other Woodlands courses, and is unique because even though it has generous fairways, golfers need to be in just the right position to go for the greens in regulation. The King & General nines opened in 1990, and the Deacon nine opened in 1995.

The 7,200-yard **Player Course** opened in 2001, and has earned a reputation as the most difficult course on the property.

The **Oaks Course** was upgraded in the late 1990s by Jay Morrish, and was renamed to account for the impressive variety of oaks that dot the landscape. The undulating greens here can be challenging, especially when they're the target on holes like No. 6, with its peninsula green, and on the signature No. 18, where the putting surface juts out into Lake Harrison.

The details   281-367-1100. 2301 N. Millbend Dr., The Woodlands, TX 77380

- www.thewoodlands.com

- TPC Course: 1978. Bruce Devlin and Robert von Hagge. Back – 7,018 (73.1/136). Middle – 6,295 (70.3/128). Forward – 5,326 (72.1/128). Price - $$$$.

The pressure gets worse the older you get. The hole starts to look the size of a Bayer aspirin. Gary Player

- Pines Course: Under construction and scheduled to open in spring 2003.
- Palmer Course: 1990, Arnold Palmer and Ed Seay. 27 holes. Price - $$$$.
- Player Course: 2001. Gary Player. 18 holes. Par 72. 7,200 yards. Price - $$$$.
- Oaks Course: Jay Morrish. 18 holes. Par 72. Over 7,000 yards. Price - $$$$.

Getting there Take I-45 30 miles north of Houston and take the Woodlands Pkwy. exit. Turn right and when you come to Grogan's Mill Rd., turn left. At N. Millbend Dr. turn right, and the next left is the entrance to the club.

THE WOODLANDS NOTES Take advantage of this world-class resort destination by sampling the five spectacular restaurants, the facility's spa, or any of the outdoor activities that are available. The **Silver, Gold,** and **Platinum Escapes** are available specifically for golfers, but you can package all sorts of romance and spa experiences as well. Rates vary depending on availability and time of year, so do your due diligence and visit the web site or call them (800-433-2624 or www.thewoodlands.com).

Outside the resort, look for **Tom's Texas Smokehouse** (281-465-4820) for lip-smacking barbecue and ice-cold bottles of beer. **Louie's Raw Bar & Grill** (281-296-2722) has fresh fish and lots of character. Or for Italian, **Amerigo's Grille** (281-362-0808) is fancy and known for its Wild Boar Chop. The preferred spot for lodging other than the resort is the new **Woodlands Waterway Marriott Hotel** (281-367-9767).

WOODVILLE   Elev. 232   Pop. 2,415

Woodville is another small, far east Texas sawmill town that boasts a 9-hole track carved out of the thick piney forest. This county seat is beautiful, set in an area of springs and hills, highlighted by thousands of wildflowers and hundreds of unique trees–specifically the beautiful dogwood, which is celebrated in the spring with the annual Dogwood Festival. Not far from the Texas border, Woodville is southeast of Lufkin between Livingston and Jasper on US 190. They're new to the golf landscape with their fancy Dogwood Hills CC.

DOGWOOD HILLS COUNTRY CLUB

The golf   Dogwood Hills opened in the early 1990s and has gained a reputation as one of the nicest 9-hole courses around. The layout is a bit tricked up, with several blind tee shots, but that seems to blend in well with the overall golf experience without detracting from the round. The design is extremely tight, with quite a few hills.

The best hole is No. 5–a 374-yard, par 4 that features a huge oak tree in the middle of the fairway that impacts the tee shot.

The details 409-283-8725. 150 US 190 W., Woodville, TX 75979

- 1992. 9 holes. Back – Par 36. 3,010 yards. Forward – Par 37. 2,568 yards. Price - $.

Getting there Take Hwy. 59 north out of Houston to Livingston. Next, take Hwy. 190 east to Woodville, and continue on 190 about 3 miles to the course. The entrance is on the left.

WOODVILLE NOTES With lots of interesting spots, it's tough to choose where to eat here. The **Dogwood Cafe** (409-283-2903) might edge **The Highlander** (409-283-7572) just a little, but the best option is probably **Jimmy's Burger & Steak House** (409-283-2863), where red meat is served to make the rambling golfman whole. Down the road in **Hillster, TX,** find the always-reliable **The Tree Restaurant & Grill** (409-283-8040). Overnighters should know about **The Woodville Inn** (409-283-3741), but romantic endeavors are best pursued up the highway in **Colmesneil, TX** at the **Clear Creek B&B** (409-837-9047).

YOAKUM
Elev. 322   Pop. 5,517

Yoakum, a tweener town on the edge of our Southeast, Central, and South regions, was founded in 1887 and was once the main spot for northbound cattle drives up the Chisolm Trail. Today the "Leather Capital of the World" boasts 12 leather goods firms and some 16 factory locations. Cowboy culture is strong, and Lavaca and DeWitt counties are among the top cow-calf producers in Texas. Golfers here can get their kicks at the Yoakum muni golf course, where stay-and-play packages help keep expenses to favorable weekend road-trip levels.

YOAKUM MUNICIPAL GOLF COURSE

The golf Yoakum's 9-hole course features narrow fairways and small, quick greens. Two ponds wreak havoc on three holes. The yardage here suits the average golfer–the layout features two par 5s that play around 450 yards, two par 3s that require only short irons, and five par 4s that all play well under 400 yards. Pay once and play all day.

The details 361-293-5682. 703 Southwell St., Yoakum, TX 77995

- www.viptx.net/lamancha

- 1936. 9 holes. Par 36. Back – 2,960 (33.7/110). Forward – 2,506. Price - $.

---

*Actually, the only time I ever took out a one-iron was
to kill a tarantula. And I took a 7 to do that.* Jim Murray

Getting there From Hwy. 111 south, turn left on Hwy. 77. When you reach Hwy. 95, turn left again and drive to Southwell St. Turn right and the entrance is on the left side of the street.

YOAKUM NOTES   Make sure you check out the golf packages at **La Mancha Inn** in Yoakum. The **Heritage Museum** on Simpson St. displays leather wares as well as artifacts of area history. Lots of dining options: **Cervantes** (361-293-6262) and **Mi Casa** (361-293-7262) allow you to get greasy, and the **Downtown Deli** (361-293-5490) serves fabulous sandwiches. Locals love the sit-down **Hilltop Restaurant** (361-293-6261). Road-trippers can make the 19th hole 11 miles north in **Shiner, TX** at the Spoetzl Brewery, where you can tour the famous Texas landmark beer shop as well as the great local shops, restaurants, and beer joints.

SOUTHEAST TEXAS BORDER CROSSINGS

We've counted a grand total of nine coon-ass golf tracks within an hour's drive of a Southeast Texas town that has golf. See below and enjoy your adventures into the swampland backwoods of Looziana.

SULPHUR, LA   25 miles from Orange, TX

The **Bayou Oaks Country Club** (318- 583-7129) is a flat, simple 18-hole course, tipping out at 6,203 yards (par 72). Though void of bunkers, it's spiced up just a little with water on about seven holes. The signature here is the large greens, which are welcome targets for approach shots.

The beautiful 1950s **Frasch Park Golf Club** (318-527-2515) goes almost 6,300 yards (70.3/126) from the back tees, and plays to a par 72. Built around a canal that impacts play on numerous holes, the fairways wind through mature trees that grab errant shots.

LAKE CHARLES, LA   35 miles from Orange, TX

The relatively new **Eagles & Birdies** (318-478-1160) par 3 track opened in 1999 sporting 9 holes; it rolls around 1,800 yards from one set of tees. They did a nice job of incorporating water into the design, including one hole that features an island green.

The **Lake Charles Country Club** (318-477-0047) routes 6,656 yards along Lake Charles (72.2/128), and is one of the old-school tracks that is susceptible to low scores if you can keep the ball in the tight fairways. The opening hole might be the toughest—a long par 5 that goes 560 yards.

Located on the Chenault Air Base, the **Mallard Cove Golf Course** (318-491-1204) has been rated as one of the top public courses in the state over the

SOUTH EAST

---

years. James Wall designed the course in the 1970s, and he incorporated a decent amount of water over the 6,903-yard route (72.4/125). The back nine is a bit more difficult, since the fairways are skinny and lined by more trees.

Pine Shadows (318-433-8681) is desirable for its affordability, but is also a well-conditioned track. This one tips out at a par 72, 6,494 yards (70.3/110).

DE RIDDER, LA   54 miles from Jasper, TX

The Beauregard Country Club (318-463-4444) routes just over 6,300 yards (68.9/113), and is a friendly little country club course that plays to a par 72. The best hole is No. 11, a short par 4 that rides alongside a lake to the well-bunkered green.

LEESVILLE, LA   51 miles from Jasper, TX

The Leesville Municipal Golf Course (318-239-2526) is a rolling course with generous fairways and fast greens. A few bunkers spot the course, but you can generally go for it on every hole with the driver. This 1930s-style track plays 2,821 yards and is a par 35.

FORT POLK, LA   70 miles from Jasper, TX

The Warrior Hills Golf Course (318-531-4661) is a flat, 6,500-yard (71.0/129) route that doesn't cost much, but serves up a nice round of golf if you're touring the back roads out this way.

SOUTH EAST

☆

Golf is like love. One day you think you're too old, and the next
you can't wait to do it again. Roberto de Vicenzo

Jimmy Demaret shaking hands with Lawson Little.

SOUTH TEXAS
REGIONAL WEATHER

	Average Precipitation	Average Temperature (F)
January	1.71	49.3
February	1.81	53.5
March	1.52	61.7
April	2.5	69.3
May	4.22	75.5
June	3.81	82.2
July	2.16	85
August	2.54	84.9
September	3.41	79.3
October	3.17	70.2
November	2.62	60.4
December	1.51	52.2

SOUTH TEXAS

First things first: a National Golf Foundation poll concluded that the Rio Grande Valley has more playable days of golf (less than 25 days lost to bad weather) per year than anywhere else in the United States. That alone is reason to consult your travel agent. But South Texas has a deeper, more exotic appeal than climate.

It begins with a perceptible change in pace. From San Antonio south to the Mexico border, time moves slower. Except for some portions of New Mexico, there is really nothing like it anywhere else in the US. Especially when compared with the ambitious, build-and-conquer mentality of the major cities, life in South Texas has a more placid, contented feel. The spirit of mañana ("tomorrow," as in, "I'll get it done tomorrow, instead") pervades everything, providing good therapy for Type A personalities who need to slow down and savor life's pleasures.

You'll have to drive a bit before you can begin savoring. The flat, dry desert peppered with mesquite trees and prickly pear cacti stretches on for miles, and when someone says to you, "Let's run over to the next town and get some lunch," keep in mind that the next town may be 75 miles away. Again, you have to change your way of looking at things. While you may consider driving time an inconvenience, locals see it as time to talk with friends, reflect, listen to music, and enjoy the open sky above.

The sweltering summer heat of this region would be unbearable if not for the cooling breezes that blow in off the Gulf. Some breezes are not only cool, they knock the hat off your head, as winds sweep through with very little standing in their way. Like Scots on the fabled links of the sport's ancestry, Valley golfers hone their skills playing against the wind. Most courses have even been designed to factor in these predominant southeast winds that can easily blow your score up 10 strokes or more.

The South Texas golf experience has San Antonio to the north, and the eclectic border towns that cling to the Rio Grande along the south. There's not much in the middle, but almost every little town big enough to have a Dairy Queen has at least one golf course. Wherever you roam in South Texas, you'll surely be within close range of a game, and it won't cost you much when you get there. The region makes its money off agriculture (mostly citrus) and ranching, not golf. Green fees can be laughably low, even when the quality of the course is high. "Good value" is a major draw for South Texas.

With all the agriculture and ranching in the area, people know how to grow things around here. That means the Bermudas are rugged and "wear resistant," but smooth—a delight to play on. The greens here will surprise you with their quality, and the landscaping of the courses is often inspired and quite

SOUTH

*The golfing area of the brain is a fragile thing that is
terribly susceptible to suggestion.* Harvey Penick

lush.

Before or after a round, make the distinctive food part of your "borderplex" adventure. We've highlighted many spots to try, most of which are independents with the owner in the kitchen and his wife out front. Oh, and leave your tony Ralph Lauren golf attire at home; the look and the mood in South Texas is always laid-back.

The average golfer would rather play above 100 than face
what he thinks is the drudgery of practice. Grantland Rice

90 Uvalde
Bracketville
90
Helotes
San Antonio
La Vernia
183
Devine Hondo
Castroville
181
Cuero
77
57
Yorktown
Eagle Pass
Pleasanton
37
Victor
277
Kenedy
Goliad
Carrizo
Springs
83
Beeville
77
35
Sinton
Refugi
Port Lava
181
Rockpor
Port A
59
Portland
Corpus C
Alice
Laredo
281
Bishop
Kingville
359
Gulf
Falfurrias
of
Zapata
Mexico
83
281
77
Raymondville
Edinburg
Harlingen
R. Viejo/
McAllen
Port Is
Mission
S. Pad
Pharr
Weslaco
Alamo Mercedes
Brownsville

SOUTH

South Mileage

	Alamo	Alice	Beeville	Bishop	Brackettville	Brownsville	Carrizo Springs	Castroville	Corpus Christi	Cuero	Devine	Eagle Pass	Edinburg	Falfurrias	Goliad	Harlingen	Helotes	Hondo	Kenedy	King...
Alamo		112	167	118	318	49	230	246	151	226	234	272	11	77	195	28	261	255	210	1
Alice	112		55	27	216	147	137	135	44	115	123	179	101	37	84	122	149	144	97	2
Beeville	167	55		65	194	188	144	111	56	61	100	186	156	101	29	163	128	121	33	7
Bishop	118	27	65		239	124	164	157	33	119	145	206	109	46	87	99	173	166	99	6
Brackettville	318	216	194	239		360	89	98	235	206	103	47	310	284	210	335	124	82	183	24
Brownsville	49	147	188	124	360		280	280	157	243	269	322	57	129	212	25	300	289	225	11
Carrizo Springs	230	137	144	164	89	280		102	174	180	82	42	230	171	173	255	134	92	180	16
Castroville	246	135	111	157	98	280	102		153	108	19	115	235	171	113	256	26	16	81	1
Corpus Christi	151	44	56	33	235	157	174	153		99	141	216	141	84	68	132	167	162	92	3
Cuero	226	115	61	119	206	243	180	108	99		115	221	215	161	31	218	113	124	42	12
Devine	234	123	100	145	103	269	82	19	141	115		108	223	161	114	244	42	21	87	15
Eagle Pass	272	179	186	206	47	322	42	115	216	221	108		272	215	214	297	150	100	197	20
Edinburg	11	101	156	109	310	57	230	235	141	215	223	272		66	184	32	250	244	199	10
Falfurrias	77	37	101	46	284	129	171	171	84	161	161	215	66		131	104	184	202	133	36
Goliad	195	84	29	87	210	212	173	113	68	31	114	214	184	131		187	115	128	31	94
Harlingen	28	122	163	99	335	25	255	256	132	218	244	297	32	104	187		274	265	199	93
Helotes	261	149	128	173	124	300	134	26	167	113	42	150	250	184	115	274		43	83	18
Hondo	255	144	121	166	82	289	92	16	162	124	21	100	244	202	128	265	43		101	17
Kenedy	210	97	33	99	183	225	180	81	92	42	87	197	199	133	31	199	83	101		10
Kingsville	111	29	70	6	242	118	162	162	39	125	151	204	102	38	94	93	181	171	106	
La Vernia	239	127	75	139	145	263	137	48	131	61	55	163	228	175	73	238	51	63	51	14
Laredo	150	97	131	125	168	200	81	141	142	191	121	123	152	90	160	177	168	138	162	11
McAllen	7	110	166	118	311	56	223	245	151	225	233	265	10	75	194	34	259	254	208	11
Mercedes	13	121	172	108	331	36	244	256	141	226	244	286	23	91	195	14	275	265	224	10
Mission	13	117	172	125	305	62	217	251	157	231	237	259	16	83	200	40	267	258	216	11
Pharr	4	108	163	116	314	53	226	243	149	223	231	268	8	73	192	31	257	252	206	11
Pleasanton	203	91	69	114	132	237	94	44	110	85	33	136	192	129	84	212	59	54	57	11
Port Aransas	179	72	64	61	254	185	202	172	28	101	160	244	169	111	70	160	200	181	96	67
Port Isabel	62	157	198	134	370	23	290	290	167	253	278	332	67	138	222	35	318	299	243	12
Port Lavaca	227	120	81	110	258	234	225	160	80	54	167	267	218	159	52	209	169	176	85	11
Portland	158	52	49	40	239	165	181	157	8	91	145	223	149	90	60	140	173	166	81	47
Rancho Viejo	42	137	179	115	350	10	270	271	148	233	259	312	48	79	202	15	263	280	211	10
Raymondville	41	100	142	78	313	47	233	234	111	196	222	275	34	70	165	22	253	243	178	72
Refugio	179	71	33	61	227	185	177	139	41	57	133	219	170	107	26	160	184	154	59	67
Rockport	180	74	62	63	252	187	201	170	30	90	158	243	171	113	63	162	196	179	97	69
San Antonio	235	124	89	146	122	269	115	24	142	85	33	139	224	162	91	245	22	40	61	15
Sinton	155	47	30	37	220	162	170	138	26	81	126	212	146	84	50	137	161	147	62	44
Uvalde	279	176	155	199	40	320	50	58	195	166	63	57	270	205	170	295	85	42	143	202
Victoria	221	110	56	104	232	228	199	134	84	28	141	241	210	151	26	203	142	150	58	110
Weslaco	9	117	172	111	326	41	239	251	144	229	240	281	19	87	198	19	271	260	220	10
Yorktown	219	108	54	112	193	236	165	96	92	17	102	207	208	155	24	211	100	111	25	11
Zapata	101	104	159	120	217	150	129	190	148	219	170	171	104	87	188	128	217	187	213	11

SOUTH TEXAS • 661

South Mileage

	Laredo	McAllen	Mercedes	Mission	Pharr	Pleasanton	Port Aransas	Port Isabel	Port Lavaca	Portland	Rancho Viejo	Raymondville	Refugio	Rockport	San Antonio	Sinton	Uvalde	Victoria	Weslaco	Yorktown	Zapata
	150	7	13	13	4	203	179	62	227	158	42	41	179	180	235	155	279	221	9	219	101
	97	110	121	117	108	91	72	157	120	52	137	100	71	74	124	47	176	110	117	108	104
	131	166	172	172	163	69	64	198	81	49	179	142	33	62	89	30	155	56	172	54	159
	125	118	108	125	116	114	61	134	110	40	115	78	61	63	146	37	199	104	111	112	120
	168	311	331	305	314	132	254	370	258	239	350	313	227	252	122	220	40	232	326	193	217
	200	56	36	62	53	237	185	23	234	165	10	47	185	187	269	162	320	228	41	236	150
	81	223	244	217	226	94	202	290	225	181	270	233	177	201	115	170	50	199	239	165	129
	141	245	256	251	243	44	172	290	160	157	271	234	139	170	24	138	58	134	251	96	190
	142	151	141	157	149	110	28	167	80	8	148	111	41	30	142	26	195	84	144	92	148
	191	225	226	231	223	85	101	253	54	91	233	196	57	90	85	81	166	28	229	17	219
	121	233	244	237	231	33	160	278	167	145	259	222	133	158	33	126	63	141	240	102	170
	123	265	286	259	268	136	244	332	267	223	312	275	219	243	139	212	57	241	281	207	171
	152	10	23	16	8	192	169	67	218	149	48	34	170	171	224	146	270	210	19	208	104
	90	75	91	83	73	129	111	138	159	90	79	70	107	113	162	84	205	151	87	155	87
	160	194	195	200	192	84	70	222	52	60	202	165	26	63	91	50	170	26	198	24	188
	177	34	14	40	31	212	160	35	209	140	15	22	160	162	245	137	295	203	19	211	128
	168	259	275	267	257	59	200	318	169	173	263	253	184	196	22	161	85	142	271	100	217
	138	254	265	258	252	54	181	299	176	166	280	243	154	179	40	147	42	150	260	111	187
	162	208	224	216	206	57	96	243	85	81	211	178	59	97	61	62	143	58	220	25	213
	119	112	102	118	110	119	67	128	116	47	108	72	67	69	151	44	202	110	104	118	114
	175	237	246	244	235	42	138	273	114	123	253	216	99	136	25	105	106	87	244	49	212
McAllen	143		20	6	3	202	179	69	228	159	49	45	179	181	234	156	272	220	15	218	94
Mercedes	163	20		26	17	213	169	49	217	148	29	30	169	170	245	145	291	212	5	219	114
Mission	137	6	26		9	208	185	75	234	165	55	51	186	187	240	162	266	226	22	224	88
Pharr	146	3	17	9		199	177	66	225	156	46	42	177	178	232	153	275	218	12	216	97
Pleasanton	133	202	213	208	199		129	247	136	114	228	191	102	127	32	95	92	110	208	72	169
Port Aransas	170	179	169	185	177	129		195	68	21	176	139	44	18	153	34	214	81	172	94	176
Port Isabel	212	69	49	75	66	247	195		244	174	24	56	195	197	279	171	330	238	54	246	163
Port Lavaca	212	228	217	234	225	136	68	244		73	224	187	50	51	138	72	218	26	220	65	223
Portland	149	159	148	165	156	114	21	174	73		155	118	34	22	138	19	199	76	151	84	156
Rancho Viejo	192	49	29	55	46	228	176	24	224	155		37	176	177	260	152	310	219	34	226	143
Raymondville	158	45	30	51	42	191	139	56	187	118	37		139	140	223	115	273	182	34	189	124
Refugio	163	179	169	186	177	102	44	195	50	34	176	139		36	117	24	187	43	172	51	175
Rockport	171	181	170	187	178	127	18	197	51	22	177	140	36		151	32	212	63	173	87	178
San Antonio	154	234	245	240	232	32	153	279	138	138	260	223	117	151		119	82	112	240	73	201
Sinton	145	156	145	162	153	95	34	171	72	19	152	115	24	32	119		181	67	148	74	151
Uvalde	130	272	291	266	275	92	214	330	218	199	310	273	187	212	82	181		192	286	153	178
Victoria	187	220	212	226	218	110	81	238	26	76	219	182	43	63	112	67	192		215	39	214
Weslaco	159	15	5	22	12	208	172	54	220	151	34	34	172	173	240	148	286	215		222	109
Yorktown	175	218	219	224	216	72	94	246	65	84	226	189	51	87	73	74	153	39	222		204
Zapata	49	94	114	88	97	169	176	163	223	156	143	124	175	178	201	151	178	214	109	204	

SOUTH

ALAMO

Elev. 98 Pop. 15,456

The city of Alamo blends in with Pharr and San Juan on US 83 nine miles southeast of McAllen. Originally called Agostadero de Alamo ("Pasture of Cottonwood Trees"), the area was cleared of brush and cattle in the early 1900s and opened to settlement by farmers from the Midwest and homesteaders from Mexico.

ALAMO COUNTRY CLUB

The golf   Alamo Country Club is a 9-hole private course that is very well-maintained. The lush fairways are lined with palm trees and water hazards come into play on several holes.

The details   956-787-0910. 438 Alamo Country Club, Alamo, TX 78516

- 9 holes. Par 35. 2,192 yards. Price - $$.

Getting there Take the city of Alamo exit off of 83, then travel 1 mile north to Tower Rd.

ALAMO NOTES   For no-frills barbecue try **Original Willie's Bar-B-Q** (956-702-1370), where the specialty is the tender smoked chicken. On Main St. you'll find the **Alamo Inn Magic Valley B&B** (956-453-3899).

ALICE

Elev. 205 Pop. 19,156

The dividing point between the brush country and the coastal plains, Alice is sometimes referred to as the "Hub City of South Texas." Originally called Bandana, then Kleberg, then finally named Alice after the daughter of Captain Richard King of the King Ranch, Alice was the world's largest cattle shipping point from 1888 to 1893, and today is a center for the petroleum industry, agribusiness, and tourism in South Texas. A great place for the outdoorsman, Alice serves as a base for hunting deer, javelina, turkey, dove, and quail and has two 18-hole golf courses.

ALICE COUNTRY CLUB

The golf   Alice Country Club is a private club with a Ralph Plummer-designed 9-hole course that opened for play in the early 1950s. Rugged South Texas mesquite trees line the narrow fairways. The signature hole is No. 3, which requires a tee shot into a dogleg fairway and an approach shot over a creek.

The details   361-664-3723. Country Club Rd., Alice, TX 78332

SOUTH

If you think a guy is trying to hustle you, just make two bets. One match, one medal. It's real hard to lose both. Lee Trevino

- 1952. Ralph Plummer. 9 holes. Par 36. Back – 3,325 (35.3/116). Forward – 2,695 (34.8/105). Grill with alcohol available. Driving range with chipping and putting practice areas. Closed Mondays. Price - $$.

Getting there From Corpus Christi take Hwy. 44 east, then turn left at Country Club Rd.

ALICE MUNICIPAL GOLF COURSE

The golf Alice's flat, 18-hole public course is a short, basic course that plays barely over 6,000 yards. No bunkers. Wide fairways. Normal greens.

The details 361-664-7033. Texas Blvd., Alice, TX 78332

- 18 holes. Par 71. Back – 6,099 (67.8/108). Forward – 5,066 (65.6/100). Price - $$.

Getting there Off of I-281 driving south, turn left on Commerce Rd., then travel until you see Texas Blvd. Turn right and head south to Anderson Park St.

ALICE NOTES You can find tasty, fresh Mexican food at **Chentes Restaurant**. Learn more about the staples of South Texas history, cattle and law enforcement, at the **South Texas Museum** in Alice, which resides in the former headquarters of the McGill cattle ranching business. The two-story 1941 marble and stone building is a designated landmark.

BEEVILLE
Elev. 214   Pop. 13,118

The Indians came through and massacred Mary Hefferman's family in 1853, but that tragic event wasn't enough to inspire community leaders to keep the name Maryville–this seat of Bee County took the name of Beeville in 1860.

This clean, relaxed little town of 13,000 is only 60 miles from Corpus Christi and 90 miles from San Antonio, and rests at the crossroads of two major highways, US 181 and US 59.

BEEVILLE COUNTRY CLUB

The golf Beeville Country Club is a private course that offers narrow, tree-lined fairways and small greens. No need to bring your sand wedge, as there are no bunkers, but water comes into play on many holes.

The 509-yard par 5 No. 2 hole features a tee shot into a dogleg-right fairway and an approach that must carry the pond fronting the green. Water also protects the front of the greens on holes 5, 7 and 8. Another notable hole is No. 3, a 229-yard par 3.

A hazard placed in the exact position where a player would naturally go is frequently the most interesting situation, as then a special effort is needed to get over or avoid it. Dr. Alister Mackenzie

The details 361-358-2136. Hwy. 181, Beeville, TX 78104

- 9 holes. Par 36. Back – 3,191 (35.5/119). Forward – 2,600 (34.7/106). Price – $.

Getting there Located off the Hwy. 181 bypass just outside Beeville.

JOHN C. BEASLEY MUNICIPAL GOLF COURSE

The golf You can't play here on Tuesdays, as this is the day dedicated to the maintenance man who goes about his duties and takes care of the large, well-conditioned greens. Leon Howard designed this 9-hole course in the early 1980s, and his track features narrow, tree-lined fairways, water on four of the nine holes (2, 3, 4, and 5), and no bunkers. Out-of-bounds comes into play on holes 1 and 9.

No. 5 is the feature hole, playing about 170 yards with a pond fronting the green. Hole 3 is also challenging, with water on both sides of the fairway and a landing area only 40 yards wide.

The details 361-362-7618. 400 N. Washington St., Beeville, TX 78102

- 1983. Leon Howard. 9 holes. Par 36. Back – 3,272 (35.4). Forward – 2,922. Closed Tuesdays. Price - $.

Getting there From Hwy. 59 west, turn right at the Dairy Queen on Route 351, then drive 5 blocks to the course.

BEEVILLE NOTES Beeville sports the stately **Beeville County Courthouse,** and local artisans display their work in the **Beeville Art Museum and Gallery,** as well as quaint little shops around town. In nearby Oakville try the down-home **Van's Bar-B-Que** (361-786-3995), a roadside joint whose walls covered with celebrity photos.

BISHOP   Elev. 59   Pop. 3,320

Because of the "mighty good cotton and corn land" of the surrounding blackland prairies, early entrepreneur F.Z. Bishop set his sights on developing 2,300 acres of the Driscoll Ranch into a burgeoning little agricultural town.

Farming is still important, but the discovery of oil and gas in the area resulted in the development of new industries. In 1945 the Celanese Corporation of America entered the chemical industry by opening their Bishop plant along Highway 77 south of town. Over the years the plant has employed an average of 750 workers, who've been fortunate enough to have at their disposal a place to play the hallowed game.

As a kid I was always pretty focused when I played. I loved being in my own little world and concentrating, but I also enjoyed talking to my playing competitors. I enjoyed their company. Even if it was a person I didn't particularly care for, I still talked to them. Tiger Woods

SOUTH

CHEMCEL GOLF CLUB

The golf   The devoted golfer must be creative in order to work his way onto what is usually an inaccessible facility. Since Chemcel is private and open only to employees and their guests, the smart play is to befriend someone in town and share your passion for the sport.

If you can work your way on, you'll encounter an unusually long layout for a 9-hole track (over 3,500 yards), and a design featuring a creek that impacts play on three holes, as well as a few out-of-bounds areas.

The details   361-584-6156, Celanese Chemical Plant, Bishop, TX 78343

• 9 holes. Par 36. 3,503 yards. Price - $.

Getting there 3 miles south of town on Hwy. 77. The course is behind the Celanese Chemical Plant.

BISHOP NOTES   Chemcel is private, and Bishop is small, so even though this is an unlikely golf destination, you should know that your best available meal is probably a burger at the **Dairy Queen**. If you're broken down and must stay, you can buy a six-pack at the **Super S** and lounge in your room at the **Days Inn** (512-584-4444). Otherwise keep in mind that **Baffin Bay** is only 25 miles away, and you're in the heart of South Texas' best hunting country.

BRACKETTVILLE   Elev. 1,110   Pop. 1,902

This seat of Kinney County rests on US 90 between San Antonio and Del Rio. The town became established as a supply post for Fort Clark, one of the most historic military posts in the Southwest. The fort deactivated in 1944 and the community subsisted by serving as a trade center for surrounding ranches and farms. Hunting is popular in the area, and Fort Clark has recently become popular as a resort for Winter Texans who enjoy the mild winter weather.

FORT CLARK SPRINGS GOLF COURSE

The golf   Fort Clark Springs is a residential and resort community that offers a short 18-hole regulation course and a 9-hole par 3 course, both of which are open for public play. Las Moras Creek meanders through the picturesque community of about 750 households, and the population swells a bit during the winter as retirees move in and take advantage of the warm weather.

One of the great features of this course is that it offers the chance to play from the tips and score very well, as the back tees are just over 5,700 yards.

SOUTH

Just knock the hell out of it with your right hand. Tommy Armour

Most of the par 4s are barely over 300 yards, making length off the tee a non-issue. Only the par 4 No. 16 at 357 yards resembles anything close to what you might see back home. Hole 12 has some length at 566 yards, and is the number one handicap hole.

Plan accordingly if you're in the area, as the course is popular with the locals and can get very crowded. Call ahead. Tee times are required on the weekends. One option is to get there early and walk on the par 3 course as a warm-up for your round on the big course.

The details   830-563-9204. Hwy. 90, Brackettville, TX 78832

- Regulation Course: 1983. Horris Woods Smith. 18 holes. Par 70. Back – 5,752 (64.4/97). Middle – 5,413 (64.4/93). Forward – 4,694 (65.0/100). Price - $$.

- Par 3 Course: 9 holes. No charge to play.

Getting there The course is on Hwy. 90 on the north side of the road.

BRACKETTVILLE NOTES   The **Fort Clark Springs Motel** (830-563-9210) has 36 rooms and is within walking distance of the **Las Moras Inn Restaurant** and historic district. Check out the **historic buildings** dating back to the 1870s downtown (St. Mary Catholic Church and the Masonic Lodge). The vistas north of town show the beautiful Hill Country and the wild game of the area. Take these routes (Ranch Roads 674 or 334) late in the day to combine the setting sun with views of the West Nueces River winding among the steep cliffs.

BROWNSVILLE   Elev. 35 Pop. 147,545

Established in 1846 after General Zachary Taylor built Fort Brown as then-national boundary to Mexico, Brownsville is the Rio Grande Valley's largest–and Texas' southernmost–city. In Brownsville the traveling golfer can take advantage of the sub-tropical climate, proximity to Mexico, and excellent golf courses.

BROWNSVILLE MUNICIPAL GOLF COURSE

The golf   The Brownsville Muni is the perfect place to build your confidence and work on your game, especially in this day and age of championship layouts that torture the average hacker. The fairways are wide open and the large greens, although fast, offer a generous target for the wayward approach shot. The only catch is that water comes into play on most holes.

Hole 2 (only 328 yards) is one of those holes, and with an approach needing to carry about 100 yards of water, is considered one of the most challeng-

SOUTH

---

*I may go for it or I may not. It all depends on what
I elect to do on my backswing.* Billy Joe Patton

SOUTH TEXAS • 667

ing. Despite this testy second hole, the front nine is where you have the best opportunity to go low. The front is void of par 5s, and features seven par 4s, most of which are under 330 yards. In fact, No. 8 is only 278 yards. The back can hurt you with longer par 4s and three par 5s, including the monster 18th hole at 626 yards.

The details 956-541-2582. 1800 W. San Marcelo Blvd., Brownsville, TX 78526

• 1977. Donald Sechrest. 18 holes. Par 70. Back – 6,049 (69.3/113). Middle – 5,226 (65.2/103). Forward – 4,846 (67.3/107). Price - $

Getting there From Hwy. 77 driving south, exit FM 802 and turn left. Travel to Jose Marti and turn left again. When you reach San Marcelo, turn left. The entrance is on the right side of the road.

FORT BROWN MEMORIAL GOLF COURSE

The golf This short, charming 18-hole public course was built on the historic grounds of Fort Brown in the 1950s. We recommend that you take in the atmosphere by walking this course, as the terrain is flat and easy to negotiate. Fort Brown serves up a 230-yard par 3 as its finishing hole, which generally plays into the prevailing wind.

Be sure to take advantage of the one-night Paradise Golf Package at the **Holiday Inn Fort Brown** (956-546-2201), which features breakfast and 18 holes with a cart.

The details 956-541-0394. 300 River Levy Dr., Brownsville, TX 78523

• 1958. 18 holes. Par 72. Back – 6,072 (67.0/108). Forward – 4,803 (65.0/108). Price - $$.

Getting there From Hwy. 77 south, drive until the road ends and turn right on International Blvd. Proceed over the International Bridge and make a left on Ft Brown Rd. Go to the end of Ft. Brown Rd. and turn left on River Levee (Little League Park).

RIVER BEND RESORT & COUNTRY CLUB

The golf Set along the Rio Grande River, this is a scenic course with spectacular views. The front nine was built in 1987, and the back nine followed in 1992. The highlight of the course is the longest water hazard in Texas, the Rio Grande River, which flows along holes 5 through 13 on the left side of the fairway.

Narrow fairways and grass bunkers make the course tough, especially when the wind is howling, as it is tough to hit the small, firm greens. Water is everywhere. No. 14 is the only hole without water. The par 3 17th hole, with its island greens, headlines a series of demanding par 3 holes. The last hole plays 434 yards into the wind and has out-of-bounds on either side of the fairway.

SOUTH

Let your left heel come off the ground if that helps you make a full backswing. Butch Harmon

The details   956-548-0192. Rural Route 8, Box 649, Brownsville, TX 78520

- 1987. 18 holes. Par 72. Back – 6,735 (72.6/119). Middle – 6,276 (71.0/115). Forward – 5,067 (68.6/110). Price - $$.

Getting there From Harlingen, take Hwy. 77 south. When you come to Hwy. 802 turn right, then continue until you reach Hwy. 281. Turn right again and drive approximately 2.5 miles to the course.

VALLEY INTERNATIONAL COUNTRY CLUB

The golf   Set among the tall palm trees and tropical conditions, this 18-hole course was one of the first tracks in the Rio Grande Valley. Built on both sides of the coastal tributary, water comes into play on 12 holes. Beware of the wind, but when it's calm your tee shots will find wide fairways and generous landing areas, and the approaches are into medium-sized greens with an average speed. Get to know the speed of these fair greens and you will start rolling in 10-20 footers with confidence.

Hole 4 is the number one handicap and plays 422 yards from the tips, where water crosses the fairway in the landing area and menaces over the right side of the hole. Other notable holes are the long par 3 10th hole with its peninsula green, as well as the 17th (512-yard par 5), which is loaded with water on the right that crosses in front of the green.

The **Par 3 Course** (1,052 yards) features small greens and narrow fairways lined by houses. These tiny greens are difficult to hit, so your short irons must be on or you'll be working on your up and downs. Like the big course, this layout incorporates several small lakes. Ladies and men play from the same set of tees on this course.

The details   956-546-5331. FM 802, Brownsville, TX 78523

- Main Course: 18 holes. Par 70. Back – 6,538 (72.3/125). Middle – 6,130 (70.3/120). Forward – 4,924 (69.7/116). Price - $$.

- Par 3 Course: 9 holes. Par 27. 1,052 yards. Price - $.

Getting there On south Hwy. 77, exit FM 802 and turn right. Proceed to McAllen Rd. and turn left, where the road eventually dead-ends at the parking lot.

BROWNSVILLE NOTES   Reserve your room at the **Holiday Inn Fort Brown**, which is convenient if you decide to cross the border. But before you venture to Matamoros, consider the tasty fried shrimp at the old-fashioned **Oyster Bar** (956-542-9786), or chile con queso at **Antonio's Mexican Village** (956-542-6504). For gringo fun in old Mexico, **Garcia's** is more high-toned and closer to the **Caliente off-track betting bar**, but **Blanca White's** tends to get

Your arms should hang under your shoulders and feel relaxed. Your wrists will already be semi-cocked, so you can simply maintain that wrist cock as you swing back. Your hands are closer to your body for leverage. Tom Watson

a little rowdier. The **Drive Inn** has been around since 1916 and is still the best place to eat in Matamoros.

CARRIZO SPRINGS

Elev. 602   Pop. 5,624

Set on a desolate stretch of Hwy. 277 between Eagle Pass and Laredo, this area grew in the late 1800s when cattle ranching prospered. With the line of springs that named the town, combined with good soil and a long growing season, farming is what spurs the economy here in Carrizo Springs.

CARRIZO SPRINGS MUNICIPAL GOLF COURSE

The golf   Carrizo Springs offers up an interesting 9-hole golf course that plays to a long 3,420 yards. The length is the only major obstacle as the fairways are wide, there are no bunkers, and the water hazards are minimal. Since the region is dry, the fairways are very firm and your ball will roll more than it normally would on a lush fairway. However, this course makes up for the lack of watering the fairways with a reputation for outstanding greens.

The 440-yard par 4 No. 4 is the number one handicap, and hole 6 is a long par 5 at 565 yards. Both par 3s are close to 200 yards. Your best chance for birdies are the 500-yard No. 1 and No. 5, the 360-yard par 4. The course offers two sets of tees for an 18-hole round. The course is more crowded in the afternoon, but if you show up early you'll often have the course to yourself.

The details   830-876-2596. Rural Route 2, Box 44, Carrizo Springs, TX 78834

- 9 holes. Par 36. Back – 3,420 (35.7/114). Forward – 2,620 (36.0/117). Price - $$.

Getting there From I-35 south, take Hwy. 85 west and the course is on the left side.

CARRIZO SPRINGS NOTES   Downtown Carrizo Springs is colorful and festive, and you'll find a few unique shops along the sidewalks. **Mi Casa Steak House** (830-876-3778) is a local favorite. Southeast on US 83 is the town of Catarina, TX and the historic **Catarina Hotel** (830-999-3677). This 100-year-old building was key during the town's growth, and housed a cafe and bank in the bottom of the building. You can still grab a bite at the cafe today.

SOUTH

What any good teacher likes is a pupil who's committed to doing the right things for an extended period of time. Dr. Bob Rotella

CASTROVILLE
Elev. 787   Pop. 2,792

On Hwy. 90 west, just on the other side of San Antonio's Loop 1604, the setting is half Hill Country, half South Texas scrub. This little slice of Texas Alsace was settled along the Medina River in 1844 by Henri Castro and a band of colonists from Alsace, France.

When making the drive from Austin to Del Rio via San Antonio, we often push through the big city and stop in this little town that offers fine dining, cozy lodging, and a few shops worth visiting.

ALSATIAN GOLF CLUB

The golf   Known as one of the best golf values in the San Antonio area, the Alsatian Golf Club offers an outstanding golf experience for a town of 2,700. This well-designed links-style track takes full advantage of the terrain, making use of every possible variation in elevation.

The club's reputation for having two completely different nines is well deserved. In fact, some say that every hole appears to have been built by a different architect. While the front nine is flat with fairways lined by immature trees, the back nine features mounded fairways lined with mature oaks and a creek bed that comes into play throughout the design.

After a standard opening hole, the challenge picks up with the long, par 4 No. 2. The tee shot on this hole forces you to lay up behind the fairway lake, leaving you with a 180-yard approach over the water and into the wind.

No. 13 on the back takes you for a ride: a 570-yard par 5 with an elevated tee shot down into the creek bottom, followed by an approach through a narrow fairway into an elevated green.

More course notes: The greens average about 5,000 square feet in size, are firm, and putt true. The clubhouse is small and simple, serving basic foods and canned beer. A bucket of balls and a cart are included with the full green fee. While walking is allowed, club personnel strongly suggest that you ride, and the green fee will not be reduced for walkers. The facility offers completely closed golf carts for use during the winter months.

The details   830-931-3100. 1339 County Rd. 4516, Castroville, TX 78009

- 1995. Steve Mrak. Par 72. Black – 6,882 (72.3/127). Blue – 6,325 (69.6/119). Gold – 5,647 (66.6/109). Red – 4,920. Price - $$.

Getting there From San Antonio, take Hwy. 90 west for 35 miles through Castroville. Find County Rd. 4516 (located at the top of a hill) and turn right. Look for the signs to the course.

CASTROVILLE NOTES   Historic downtown is worth a look, and **La Normandie Restaurant** off Houston Square offers a lunch buffet of Alsatian specialties. Plan your trip for a Saturday afternoon of golf, followed by spirits and live music at **The Quihi Gun Club,** a building that stands six feet off the ground because it's surrounded by the Quihi and Elm Creeks. This legendary Texas dance hall is the longest-running gun club in the US and was originally built to help defend against Indian attacks. Spend the night at the **Landmark Inn,** a mid-1800s general store that now boasts squeaky-clean rooms.

CORPUS CHRISTI
Elev. 35 Pop. 281,453

Corpus Christi hasn't always been known as the Texas Riviera, nor as a sought-after travel or golf destination. Serving briefly as a supply point during the Mexican War, Corpus struggled to grow until Richard King and Mifflin Kenedy invested money in the community.

Sometimes called "The Sparkling City by the Sea," Corpus sprawls out close to the bay with the small resort area of North Beach nestled above. The golf in Corpus is plentiful, from the historic Corpus Christi Country Club and the scenic Padre Isles Country Club to the long-time municipal favorites Gabe Lozano and Oso Beach courses.

CORPUS CHRISTI COUNTRY CLUB

The golf   Big-name architects have left their mark on Corpus Christi Country Club over the years. Fred McLeod, then the winter professional at Maryland's Columbia Country Club, built the course in 1909, followed by a redesign at the hands of John Bredemus in 1921 and a rare visit by Robert Trent Jones in the mid-1960s. This beautiful links-style course offers open fairways and undulating greens where stiff winds can interfere with drives and cause high shots to blow wildly off course.

When the 9-hole course originally opened on the high-toned North Beach, President William Howard Taft was in Texas to visit his brother, who owned a ranch across Nueces Bay. Taft participated in the opening ceremonies in front of the green wooden building that's distinguished by its white trim and veranda on all four sides.

The course fell victim to the 1919 hurricane, and club members didn't reorganize until 1921. John Bredemus came down from Del Rio after the completion of the San Felipe Springs Country Club and immediately put crewmen to work clearing and grading for $1.50 a day. The fairways and greens were fertilized with cottonseed meal, and the first shot was fired on Labor Day, 1922. At the time, this course on the Texas Riviera was considered one of the finest in the country.

At the end of the Depression, oil was discovered under the course and wells produced from 1936 to 1943, increasing revenues but creating some interesting man-made hazards in the layout. By 1938, the club expanded the course to 18 holes. The existing Robert Trent Jones design opened in 1963 on Everhart Rd.

SOUTH

★

Of all the hazards, fear is the worst. Sam Snead

The details 361-991-7870. 6300 Everhart Rd., Corpus Christi, TX 78413

- 1963. Robert Trent Jones, Sr. 18 holes. Par 72. Back – 6,506 (71.6/124). Middle – 6,105 (69.8/121). Forward – 5,299 (70.4/114). Price - $$$.

Getting there Exit the Crosstown Expressway off of I-37 and head south to South Padre Island Dr. Continue south and exit Everhart, then proceed for 3.5 miles to the course. The clubhouse is on the left side of the road.

GABE LOZANO SR. GOLF CENTER

The golf The Gabe Lozano facility, named after the original owner, is home to an 18-hole regulation course and a 9-hole executive course. Traditionally the most popular course in Corpus Christi, this public course hosts upwards of 70,000 rounds per year.

The course was built by Leon Howard in 1965 and renovated in 1983. It's a long course that features water hazards on most holes, as well as bunkers in the fairways and around the greens. Despite these hazards, the fairways have wide landing areas and the layout is pretty much wide open, which helps when the wind is blowing hard off the Gulf.

Hole 10 is the most difficult–a dogleg left with water on either side of the fairway and green.

The 9-hole **Executive Course** consists of six par 3s and three par 4s, and has water in play on holes 1, 3, and 4.

The details 361-883-3696. 4401 Old Brownsville Rd., Corpus Christi, TX 78405

- 1965. Leon Howard. 18 holes. Par 72. Back – 6,953 (72.6/128). Middle – 6,503 (70.5/121). Forward – 5,149 (68.8/112). Price - $$.

- Executive Course: 9 holes. Par 30. Back - 1,947 yards. Price - $.

Getting there Driving south on I-37, exit Padre Island and drive straight to Old Brownsville Dr. Turn left and the entrance is on the right side of the street.

GULF WINDS GOLF COURSE

The golf On the grounds of the Naval Air Station, this military facility started out as a rudimentary 6-hole course that opened in 1955 and eventually became a first-class 18-hole layout. Prior to the final expansion in 1985, the course had 12 holes, with hackers playing six of the holes twice for a full round of golf.

The military personnel, some of whom maintain the course in exchange for green fees, keep this simple track in excellent condition. The course has forgiving, wide-open fairways–if your approaches are accurate into the small greens, only a true butcher could three-putt. Two ponds and a creek impact

SOUTH

---

play on six holes. At only 5,700 yards, the course is very susceptible to low scores without the wind.

Hole 18 is a good finisher, playing 420 yards into the wind with out-of-bounds looming left.

The details 361-961-3250. Bldg. 1272, Naval Air Station, Corpus Christi, TX 78419

- 18 holes. Par 71. Back – 6,319 (70.4/114). Middle – 5,700 (67.3/107). Forward – 4,865 (66.6/108). Price - $$.

Getting there From I-37 south exit South Padre Island Dr. and turn onto NAS Drive. Follow the signs to the naval base and the course.

KINGS CROSSING COUNTRY CLUB

The golf This links-style country club course was designed by Bill Coore in 1986. The layout features Oso Creek, manmade lakes, and many bunkers, along with mounding in the fairways and around the greens. Many holes involve doglegs with bunkers and mounds protecting the corners. With no trees and the Gulf nearby, wind is always a major factor.

The signature hole is the 393-yard par 4 No. 14, with water along the left side of the fairway. The back nine starts out with a challenging 633-yard par 5 with water on either side of the fairway. The finishing hole is also tough–a long par 4 with a tee shot over the water into a fairway that slopes toward the lake.

The details 361-994-1300. 6201 Oso Pkwy., Corpus Christi, TX 78414

- www.kingscrossingcc.com
- 1986. Bill Coore. 18 holes. Par 71. Back – 6,804 (72.0/117). Middle – 6,164 (69.0/112). Forward – 5,465 (69.0/113). Price - $$$.

Getting there Driving south on Padre Island Dr., turn right on Staples, then proceed another 4 miles to Oso Pkwy.

OSO BEACH MUNICIPAL GOLF COURSE

The golf The Oso Beach Golf & Country Club opened in 1939 with an 18-hole John Bredemus design along the Cayo de Oso watershed, where the bay wind blows incessantly. The course opened to the public in 1946, and the Corpus Christi Golf Association promoted the facility with its "World Championship Four-Ball Match" featuring the golf dream team of Ben Hogan, Byron Nelson, Sam Snead, and Jimmy Demaret.

The course plays out over flat terrain, but the fairways are lined by trees and bunkers impact play throughout. Water is the main issue on the back, coming into play much more than on the front. The toughest hole is the 180-yard par 3 No. 13–it plays directly into the prevailing south wind, with an intimidating

SOUTH

Every hole should be a difficult par and a comfortable bogey. Robert Trent Jones

tee shot over water that is often too much to handle.

The details 361-991-5351. 5601 Alameda St., Corpus Christi, TX 78412

- 1938. 18 holes. Par 70. Back – 6,223 (69.9/119). Middle – 5,728 (67.2/112). Forward – 4,994 (68.3/114). Price - $$.

Getting there From Hwy. 358 driving east, exit Shoreline Dr. and turn left. When you come to Airline turn right, then proceed over to Alameda and turn left. The clubhouse is on the right side of the street.

PADRE ISLES COUNTRY CLUB

The golf The "St. Andrews of Padre Island" opened in the 1970s, featuring a Bruce Littell links-style design with water on 15 of 18 holes. With stiff sea breezes and sand dunes covered in thick grasses, along with the nasty "heather" that borders most holes, Padre Isles is one tough mother.

Besides the difficult layout, the greens are tricky because the grain grows downwind, eliminating the slope from the equation–not something the inland golfer becomes easily accustomed to. Remember: when putting, consider the wind first.

Hole 4 is rated the most difficult, a long par 5 that plays 509 yards from the middle tees.

The details 361-949-8056. 14353 Commodores Dr., Corpus Christi, TX 78418

- www.padreislescc.com
- 1971. Bruce Littell. 18 holes. Par 72. Back – 6,590 (72.2/124). Middle – 6,150 (69.8/118). Forward – 5,516 (71.2/122). Price - $$$.

Getting there Look for signs in Corpus Christi. Take the two bridges over to South Padre Island Dr.

PHAROAHS COUNTRY CLUB

The golf Pharoahs is built on flat terrain, making it easy to walk and enjoyable to play. Water hazards (lakes, ponds, and streams) come into play on 15 holes.

Each nine plays to a par 35, featuring only one par 5 on each side. On the front, the par 5 No. 7 plays only 476 yards from the tips, but is listed as the number one handicap. Most of the par 4s play in the mid-300-yard range, except for the 412-yard No. 9 and the 400-yard No. 14.

If you're hitting the ball well from the middle tees, low scores are definitely possible because you'll be hitting short irons into most holes. In fact, the white tees play under 6,800 yards, and a 200-yard long iron or fairway wood will often get you in great position off the tee.

SOUTH

⭐

Bobby Jones stands to the ball as if engaged in conversation. Anonymous

The details   361-991-2477. 7111 Pharaoh Dr., Corpus Christi, TX 78412

- 1969. Ralph Plummer. 18 holes. Par 70. Back – 6,187 (69.0/110). Middle – 5,796 (67.2/103). Forward – 5,400 (70.9/116). Price - $$.

Getting there From Hwy. 358 west, exit Nile and turn left. When you come to Pharaohs Dr., turn right and the entrance is on the right side of the street.

RIVER HILLS COUNTRY CLUB

The golf   Originally, River Hills was a 9-hole layout designed by Warren Cantrell. Leon Howard came along and added another nine in 1965. Laid out along the Nueces River, River Hills is a short course with water hazards coming into play on almost half the holes. The design features narrow fairways and average-sized greens of medium speed.

The 382-yard par 4 No. 2 is listed as the most difficult, but the next two most difficult-rated holes also await you on the front nine. If you can survive the front, the back nine features a few short par 4s and two par 3s that require no more than a wedge or 9 iron.

The details   361-387-3563. FM 624, Corpus Christi, TX 78426

- 1960. Warren Cantrell. 18 holes. Par 70. Back – 6,096 (69.2/116). Middle – 5,712 (67.2/113). Forward – 5,201 (68.2/118). Price - $$$.

Getting there From I-37 south take I-77 south and exit FM 624. Turn right, then drive 1.5 miles to the course. The clubhouse is on the right side of the street.

CORPUS CHRISTI NOTES   When you're not golfing, spend some time fishing and people-watching on **Mustang Island** 10 miles south of town. If the course doesn't offer enough action, the **Greyhound Race Track** offers investment opportunities. When it's time to eat, take in the sunset at **Snoopy's Pier** (361-949-8815) or partake of the traditional South Texas atmosphere at **Joe Cotten's Barbecue** (361-767-9973) on Hwy. 77 in nearby Robstown, TX, where you can stuff your face with sliced pork and sausage served on white butcher paper. Either rent a condo or beach house, or stay at the **Best Western Sandy Shores** or **Holiday Inn North Padre Island**.

SOUTH

A former world-class player who can barely break 80 now, and whose name I won't mention, pulled me aside at Westchester a couple of years ago. He told me, "I used to cry when I walked off the 18th green, because there was no more golf to play. Now I cry when I walk off the ninth green, because I have to play nine more." Dr. Bob Rotella

CUERO
Elev. 177   Pop. 6,607

Named for Cuero Creek, also referred to as Arroyo del Cuero because of the Indian's practice of killing wild cattle stuck in the quicksand of the creekbed, Cuero is halfway between San Antonio and the Gulf Coast on US 87. The town is known for turkeys and its annual Gobbler Gallop, a tradition that dates back to the early 1900s when turkey growers herded their flocks down country roads and through the city streets to the packing house.

Cuero played a role in the development of golf in Texas. The South Texas Golf Association was formed here in 1925, largely due to the efforts of members of the old Cuero Country Club.

CUERO PARK MUNICIPAL GOLF COURSE

The golf   Cuero's 9-hole public golf course dates back to the 1920s. This is a small-town course, characterized by seven par 4s with open fairways that allow for wildness off the tees. Two sets of tees make for an 18-hole round. The easiest hole is the 132-yard par 3 No. 3. The only par 5 is only 503 yards. Of the seven par 4s, No. 2 is the longest at 390 yards and is the number one handicap.

The details   361-275-3233. 1200 E. Main St., Cuero, TX 77954

- 1920s. 9 holes. Par 36. Back – 3,140 (34.8/103). Forward – 2,609 (35.2/110). Price - $.

Getting there From Hwy. 87 driving north, the course is in town across the street from the Wal-Mart. Look for the rock gate.

CUERO NOTES   Cuero is home to three BBQ and four Tex-Mex joints, but the **Doll House Cafe** (361-275-2627) is an institution and the **Landmark** (361-275-2166) is popular as well. Shops are everywhere on Main and Esplanade streets, and the city offers a driver's guide to historic homes. There are several decent motels, but we recommend one of the three bed and breakfasts: **Broadway House** (361-275-3088), **Clayton Street Guest House** (361-275-3232), or the **Wildflower Inn** (361-275-0250). The liveliest time to be in Cuero is every October for **Turkeyfest** (www.turkeyfest.org).

DEVINE
Elev. 670   Pop. 4,171

Devine sits just 30 miles southwest of San Antonio on I-35, home to a peanut shipping center and noted for its production of white corn used to make tortillas. The town was named after an attorney for the railroad, Thomas

---

⭐

*Good golfing temperament falls between taking it with a grin
or shrug and throwing a fit.* Sam Snead

Jefferson Devine, who had his hands in the business of the day back in 1881 when the railroad made it down this way.

DEVINE GOLF COURSE

The golf   Nestled in the foothills south of San Antonio, this 18-hole public course was labeled by *Golf Digest* as "one of the best-kept secrets in South Texas." Built in 1967, the course is covered with centuries-old majestic oaks that frame lush fairways and multi-tiered greens. Water comes into play on six holes.

Start off well with the short, 332-yard par 4 No. 1, and the 527-yard par 5 No. 2. Decent scores on those two holes can help your confidence for No. 3, the number one handicap at 410 yards.

The details   830-665-9943. 116 Malone Dr., Devine, TX 78016

- 1967. 18 holes. Par 72. Back – 6,596 (70.4/119). Middle – 6,247 (68.8/115). Forward – 5,075 (67.9/105). Price - $.

Getting there From I-35 south, exit Big Foot and go straight past the stop sign. When you get to Libold, turn right and look for the signs to the course.

DEVINE NOTES   This is the place to play on your way to Laredo. Drive through San Antonio early and work in a mid-morning round in Devine. Grab a sandwich to go at **Bob's BBQ** (830-633-5415), or sit down for lunch at the **Triple C Restaurant** (830-663-8414), which is popular with locals and tourists driving through. If you're having trouble determining the next stage of your road trip, linger late at **Ruthie's Lounge**, a local bar perfect for discussing the road ahead.

EAGLE PASS   Elev. 726   Pop. 23,450

Eagle Pass is a unique town–unlike other border cities of South Texas, it has a more western, wild, and remote feel to it. Eagle Pass was a military camp in the Mexican War, dating back to 1849. The outpost evolved into Fort Duncan, which became an active Confederate base and trading post for Mexico.

EAGLE PASS GOLF CLUB

The golf   Set along the Mexican border, this rugged, flat course dates back to the 1940s. If you're passing through town and have the urge, it's worth your while to walk the course and take in the scenery. Play as many holes as you like, because the minimal green fee allows you to play all day and there are two sets of tees that allow for an 18-hole round.

The opening hole is the only par 3 (191 yards). The remaining eight holes consist of seven par 4s and a par 5 that measures only 469 yards. If you're driv-

SOUTH

⭐

A good golf swing is simply useless in any other human pursuit. Bernard Suits

ing well and feeling confident, flail away at the 278-yard par 4 finishing hole, which is the easiest on the course.

The details   830-773-9761. 483 Bliss St., Eagle Pass, TX 78852

• 1946. 9 holes. Par 36. 2,980 yards. Price - $.

Getting there On Hwy. 277 going south, turn right on Main St. in the city. Drive to Bliss St. and turn right, where you will see the entrance on the right side of the street.

EAGLE PASS NOTES   **Fort Duncan** is now a city park with accompanying museum, and the old buildings are still in decent shape. If you're really into exploring, head across the river into Mexico and find the old towns of **Guerrero** and **San Juan Bautista** (45 minutes down Hwy. 2), where you'll see the missions (est. 1700) that served as Spain's base point for the occupation of Texas. In **Piedras Negras**, the bustling **Zaragosa Market Square** has some old-Mexico charm, with trinkets galore, and there are a few gringo-friendly restaurants that offer outstanding food and cold beer for very reasonable prices. Finally, we feel compelled to mention the **Kickapoo Lucky Eagle Casino**, the only casino in Texas, which offers a very different gambling experience (6.5 miles south of town).

EDINBURG
Elev. 91   Pop. 51,935

Edinburg is the first city you'll encounter as you drive though the vast citrus and vegetable fields on your way down US 281 into the heart of the Lower Rio Grande Valley. The town's original location on the Rio Grande River washed away, so officials moved the county records to nearby Hidalgo, and then eventually further inland to its present location. In addition to agriculture, the influx of winter Texans and other tourism helps drive the economy. For these tourists, Edinburg offers two solid 18-hole facilities and a 9-hole course, all of which are open to the public.

EBONY HILLS PUBLIC GOLF COURSE

The golf   Highlighted by a canal than runs through the layout, this is a simple 9-hole public course with palm and ebony trees lining the fairways. Ebony Hills offers three sets of tees, ranging from the 3,022-yard tips to 2,549 yards.

The details   956-292-2144. 300 W. Palm Dr., Edinburg, TX 78539

• 9 holes. Par 35. Back – 3,022 (34.9/111). Middle – 2,785 (34.1/106). Forward – 2,549 (32.9/102). Price - $.

It is better to smash your clubs than to lose your temper. Lord Balfour (1890)

Getting there On Hwy 281 driving south, exit at Freddy Gonzalez and turn right. When you get to Closner Rd. (Business 281) turn left, followed by a right at the first signal light (Palm Drive). Palm Drive dead-ends at the course.

LOS LAGOS GOLF CLUB

The golf   Taking advantage of the Rio Grande Valley's growing reputation as a burgeoning golf destination, the city of Edinburg invested over $6 million to produce what is touted as one of the best courses in the Valley.

Eleven acres of lakes highlight this Robert von Hagge design, which leans more towards a links-style layout. The signature hole is the intimidating par 3 No. 14, which plays anywhere from 130 to 160 yards depending on the tee and pin placements. The southeast wind impacts your shot into a kidney-shaped green that is guarded by water on the left and a large pot bunker on the front right. The green is a tough two-putt, and if you miss the approach back right, you're faced with a tough chip back downhill toward the hole.

Los Lagos is a well-balanced course with equal yardage on both nines. Your best birdie chance is the 12th hole, which plays only 342 yards from the blue tees and has no major hazards. Water is in play on 12 of the 18 holes.

The open-air pavilion is a great place to enjoy your post-round beverages.

The details   956-316-0444. 1720 S. Raul Longoria Rd., Edinburg, TX 78539

- www.loslagosgolfclub.com

- 18 holes. Par 72. Black – 7,188 (74.7/132). Blue – 6,789 (72.8/127). White – 6,211 (70.1/122). Red – 5,561 (67.0/115). Price - $$.

Getting there From 281 north, exit on Freddy Gonalez and turn right. Drive down until you see Super Splash and turn right on Raul Longoria. The course is on the left side of the road next to Super Splash.

PALACIO GOLF COURSE

The golf   Until the new Los Lagos club opened recently, Palacio was the only 18-hole course in Edinburg. The name of the game here is dealing with the wind, which seems to always blow from the Gulf and makes the course much more difficult.

The details   956-381-0964. RR 18, Box 985, Edinburg, TX 78539

- 1976. 18 holes. Par 71. Back – 6,204 (70.4/115). Middle – 5,492 (68.3/111). Forward – 4,550. Price - $.

Getting there Exit Monte Cristo off 281 south, then turn left and drive 2.5 miles to the course.

EDINBURG NOTES   Go for beers at the **Glasscock Brewing Company**

SOUTH

✦

As far as swing techniques are concerned, I don't know diddly-squat. When I'm playing well, I don't even take aim. Freddy Couples

(956-386-0091), the only microbrewery in South Texas. The botanas platter at **Casa Del Taco** (956-383-0521) has been labeled sinful. When craving action, find the **Sheriff's Posse Rodeo** where among other rodeo activities, pesos are often wagered on quarter horse races. Lots of lodging-take your pick of the chain hotels.

FALFURRIAS Elev. 125 Pop. 6,300

The ranch town of Falfurrias, once famous for the largest Jersey cattle herd in the world, is on the US 281 route to the Valley, about halfway between San Antonio and Harlingen. Big Ed Lasater named the town after the Spanish word for "heart's delight," although it's more fun to think of the Mexican slang "filfarrias": a grungy, unkempt person. An old shepherd named Don Filfarrias apparently provided the inspiration for the word back when Lasater was establishing his Falfurrias Ranch. Today Falfurrias is renowned for its sweet cream butter and serves as a shipping and business hub for Brooks County's agricultural, dairy, and oil industries. In addition to the Kingsville, TX 9-holer, the Falfurrias Golf Course is the other golf option when passing through this area en route to the Valley or to Baffin Bay for weekend fishing trips.

FALFURRIAS GOLF COURSE

The golf An interesting little course known for its pesky, elevated greens, the conditions here are better than average as small-town 9-holers go. Somewhat testy from the tips, there are no bunkers, so don't worry about playing from the beach.

Every green on this course is elevated, and the fairways are plush. There are no sand bunkers on the course

The details 361-325-5348. 401 E. Travis, Falfurrias, TX 78355

• 1985. 9 holes. Par 36. Back – 3,227. Forward – 2,700. Price - $.

Getting there From Hwy. 281 south, turn left on Travis and you'll see the course.

FALFURRIAS NOTES The **Days Inn** (361-325-2515) and the brand-new **Best Western** (361-325-4848) serve a free continental breakfast to start the day. The local eateries are **Strickland's** (361-325-5222), mainly for barbecue, **El Jardin** (361-325-3722) for Tex-Mex, and the **Side Door Cafe** (361-325-5151) for just about anything you want. Evening beers and music can be had at **The Corral Club** (361-325-3553) or the **VFW** (361-325-3198), which also happens to have a pool table. In October the thing to do here is celebrate the **Fiesta del Campo**, a 3-day event that attracts upwards of 20,000 folks and is generally just a good excuse to have fun.

GOLIAD

Elev. 167   Pop. 2,041

The serene Goliad of today conceals its historic, tumultuous past. This old town was founded as a colony of New Spain back in the early 1700s and has played an important role in the development of Texas over the years. Mission Espiritu Santo lasted longer than any other in Texas and was responsible for Goliad's development into a cattle ranching center. The Hanging Tree is here, and the Presidio la Bahia was the most fought-over fort in Texas. Once an important trade center when Indianola was the major Texas port, Goliad's importance as a market declined and ranching and agriculture have carried the economy.

GOLIAD COUNTY GOLF COURSE

The golf   Scores can add up on this little 9-hole course if your game is not on. Although there are no bunkers, the fairways are squeezed by mature trees and there seem to be water hazards on just about every hole. Approach shots require accuracy because the greens are small. This is a good course to walk because of the flat terrain.

The details   361-645-8322. 1103 E. Fannin St., Goliad, TX 77963

• 1970. Par 36. Back – 3,163. Forward – 2,595. Price - $.

Getting there From Victoria, take Hwy. 59 south then exit on Fannin St. Turn left and drive 1 mile to the course. The entrance is on the left side of the road.

GOLIAD NOTES   Eat at the excellent **Empresario Restaurant** (361-645-2347) on the courthouse square, and reserve a room at the **Antler's Inn** (361-645-8215), a popular stop for hunters. Fifteen miles from Goliad at the intersection of FM 622 and 2987 lies the 1890 **Schroeder Dance Hall**, a landmark Saturday night dancehall where Roy Clark, Hank Thompson, Ray Price, Mel Tillis, Ernest Tubb, and many more have played. The notable historic sites, in addition to **Mission Espiritu** and **Presidio la Bahia**, are the **Mission Rosario**, the famous Mexican General Zaragoza's birthplace, and the burial site of Colonel James Fannin and his men, who were executed by Santa Anna in the Mexican War.

⭐

Everybody has two swings: the one he uses during the last three holes of a tournament and the one he uses the rest of the time. Tony Penna

HARLINGEN

Elev. 36   Pop. 59,253

Harlingen dates back to 1905, and from the beginning has been a transportation and distribution hub for the subtropical tip of Texas. Palm trees dot the landscape, romantic Old Mexico is nearby, some sort of harvest is always in progress, and the surf-sloshed Gulf beaches are only miles away.

Golf came to Harlingen with the opening of the 9-hole country club in 1929. While some of the facilities cater specifically to winter Texans and retirement communities, there is affordable, quality golf to be found here.

COTTONWOOD CREEK GOLF COURSE

The golf   Cottonwood is a public par 3 course with small, undulating greens that have a reputation for being quick. The feature hole is the 175-yard No. 5 because of the tee shot over a creek.

The details   956-428-7758. 1001 S. Ed Carey, Harlingen, TX 78550.

• 9 holes. Joe Finger-Ken Dye. Par 27. Back – 1,245. Forward – 1,060. Price - $.

Getting there From Brownsville, drive north on Hwy. 177 until you reach Harlingen.

FAIR WINDS GOLF COURSE

The golf   An older par 3 course with attached driving range, Fair Winds' layout features elevated Bermuda greens, the always-welcome lack of bunkers, and sometimes the occasional pond after it rains. A little more that your standard pitch-and-putt, the longest hole plays 190 yards. Old palm and mesquite trees line the layout. The hardest hole is the longest–No. 7 plays almost 200 yards into a stiff cross wind.

Beware of the winter Texans who partake in league play and frequently bombard the course with groups 30-40 strong during morning sessions. The course is popular because it's a quick challenge.

The details   956-423-2010. 1001 S. Ed Cary Dr. Harlingen, TX 78552.

• 1967. 9 holes. Par 27. 1,306 yards. Price - $.

Getting there Take the Expressway and exit Ed Carey. Turn right and the course is 1 mile down the road from Home Depot.

HARLINGEN COUNTRY CLUB

The golf   The original HCC facility is now known as the Tony Butler Municipal Golf Course, a course that dates back to a 1920s John Bredemus design. Members hired Leon Howard and Dave Bennett in the 1960s to give

SOUTH

The arc of your swing doesn't have a thing to do with the size of your heart. Carol Mann

new life to Harlingen CC by laying out this water-infested track, with a subsequent update in 1985 by Dick Nugent. On this flat course with plush dogleg fairways, water comes into play on 14 of 18 holes.

The details 956-412-4110. 5500 El Camino Real, Harlingen, TX 78552

• 1968. Leon Howard. 18 holes. Par 72. Back – 6,541 (71.6/126). Middle – 6,261 (70.4/122). Forward – 5,625 (6.9/130). Price - $$$.

Getting there From I-77 south, take I-83 west and exit Stewart. Turn right and drive 1 mile to the course. The entrance is on the right side of the street.

STUART PLACE COUNTRY CLUB

The golf Formerly just a par 3 course, Stuart Place is a 9-hole golf course that has been lengthened recently to a regulation par 36 layout.

The details 956-428-2000. 1111 Stuart Place Rd. Harlingen, TX 78552.

• 9 holes. Par 36. No carts rented after 4:30 pm. Price - $$.

Getting there On 83 towards McAllen, exit Stuart Place and turn right; the course is on the right side of the street.

SUNSHINE COUNTRY CLUB ESTATES

The golf Sunshine is a private course located in a retirement community that has been open for about 20 years. Of the par 3 courses in the Valley, this is considered one of the best. The course lays out over flat terrain and several lakes come into play, making water hazards the most prominent cause of difficulty.

The course wanders through the housing community with a few trees spread throughout the course. Six of the nine holes have water, which is dyed blue for aesthetics. The greens are large and elevated, and grass berms are incorporated into the design to add character.

The most difficult hole is No. 9, mainly because it is the longest at 161 yards. Also, there's water to the right and behind the green, as well as a large tree beside the lake that catches errant shots. The best birdie opportunity is No. 8.

Other notes: There is no formal pro shop. Guest fees are voluntary and there is a box to slip the payment in.

The details 956-425-1420. 4110 N. Expwy. 77-7000, Harlingen, TX 78550.

• 9 holes. Par 27. 1,033 yards. Price - $.

Getting there From McAllen, take Hwy. 83 east to Hwy. 77. Turn north and drive 3 miles to the course. The entrance is on the right.

SOUTH

Thinking instead of acting is the number one disease in golf. Sam Snead

TONY BUTLER MUNICIPAL GOLF COURSE

The golf   Harlingen's long-time favorite course, named after local golf pro legend Tony Butler, dates back to 1929 when John Bredemus built what was then known as the Harlingen Country Club.

In those days Harlingen was just a sleepy little village, void of winter Texans, and the Rio Grande Valley Open was a stop on the pro tour, hosting the likes of Walter Hagen.

Bredemus built a tough one, featuring three tough opening holes that brought the Haig to his heels. No. 1 in particular, with its gnarly rough to the left, forced Hagen to play back toward the tee box after his opening shot hooked into this rough, leaving him unable to play toward the green. On the second hole Hagen had to carry a ravine to reach the par 3, and with his confidence a bit shaken after the bad start he surely wasn't pleased to see No. 3, a par 4 with the Rio Grande on the right and water on the left.

Now the facility boasts 27 holes, with Dennis Arp of Rancho Viejo fame adding an 18-hole championship layout that has recently been updated with a new irrigation system.

Both courses are short, which is preferred in the sometimes-blustery conditions, and feature narrow fairways lined by mesquite trees. A lake snakes its way through the designs and impacts play on several holes. The greens are large and fast, and usually surrounded by bunkers. While the terrain is predominantly flat, there are a few hills to spice things up.

On the big course, the consensus is that the front nine plays more difficult than the back because of its length combined with the predominance of water hazards. Yet the back features the signature hole–the 170-yard, par 3 15th hole.

The details   956-430-6685. 2640 S. M St., Harlingen, TX 78552

- 1920s. John Bredemus. Big course: 18 holes. Par 71. Back – 6,320 (69.1/113). Middle – 5,837 (66.7/106). Forward – 5,123 (69.1/112). Price - $$.

- 9-hole course: Par 35. Back – 2,881. Forward – 2,467. Price - $.

Getting there From Hwy. 77 south, exit M St., then turn right. The clubhouse is on the right side of the road.

TREASURE HILLS COUNTRY CLUB

The golf   One of the better layouts in the Rio Grande Valley has just gotten even better with the recent renovation of the golf course and clubhouse. The greens have been replaced and the fairways have been treated with herbicides that have significantly improved their condition.

Built on rolling terrain, the wide fairways present nice targets off the tee, and

SOUTH

The practice tee is the place to try things out and to work hard; the golf course is the place to let things go, free yourself up. Don't try harder on the golf course. Try less hard. Davis Love, Jr.

the elevated greens require taking an extra club every now and then. While not an overbearing factor, water hazards come into play throughout the design. Get your rounds in now on this scenic course, as there is word that the facility has aspirations of becoming private in the future.

The details 956-425-1700. 3009 N. Augusta Ntl. Dr., Harlingen, TX 78550

• 1986. Dick Watson. 18 holes. Par 72. Back – 6,960 (73.5/124). Middle – 6,424 (71.0/119). Forward – 5,230 (71.0/118). Price - $$$.

Getting there From Hwy. 77 driving south, exit on Ed Carey and turn left. When you come to Business 77 turn right, drive down to Trailer Hills Blvd. and turn left. Veer right at the split in the road and turn left on Pinehurst, where you'll see signs to the course.

HARLINGEN NOTES   Gamble at the **Valley Greyhound Racetrack** then spend your winnings across the border in **Nuevo Progreso,** where you can shop, drink, and eat the time away. **Arturo's** over there is high-toned and serves good meals. The **Longhorn Cattle Company** (956-399-4400) in San Benito is a great little barbecue joint that serves awesome sausage and cold beer. For rooms try the convenient **Harlingen Inn** (956-425-7070), or the **Ross Haus B&B** (956-425-1717), which is in one of the Valley's oldest homes. Enchilada lovers from all over the Valley cram into **Los Asados** (956-421-3074) for the steak and enchiladas plate.

HELOTES   Elev. 1,035   Pop. 1,600

The "green roasting ear of corn," as the Spanish meaning for Helotes implies, is 17 miles northwest of downtown San Antonio, and the first road-trip stop on the way to and from Bandera, TX. The town has been around since the 1850s when Mexican and Apache Indian communities intermingled here, and San Antonians moved this way for country living beginning in the 1980s. Helotes is best known for Mr. John T. Floore and his country store, the longtime favorite of locals and road-trippers passing through this part of Texas. Whether you're playing at nearby La Cantera, at Helotes' Oak Valley par 3, or even in Bandera, it's tough to pass up good times in Helotes.

OAK VALLEY DRIVING RANGE & PAR 3

The golf   The only quick place in the area to work on your game "par 3 style", Oak Valley offers a driving range to accompany its lighted 9-hole pitch-and-putt. Nice trees line the course and the longest hole is 150 yards.

The details   210-695-2606. 18632 Bandera Rd., Helotes, TX 78023

• 1989. Adam Morales. 9 holes. Par 27. Back – 1,075. Forward – 810. Price - $.

Slow is long. Fast is short. Don January

Getting there From San Antonio, take Bandera Rd. west and drive 8 miles to the course

---

HELOTES NOTES Dining options include **El Chaparral** for Tex-Mex, **Bobby K's** for burgers, and the **Hickory Hut** for barbecue. But the best is the tree-shaded **Grey Moss Inn** (210-695-8301) for awesome steaks. There are no lodging options in Helotes, so look to San Antonio or Bandera if you need to spend the night. The highlight of Helotes is the world-famous **John T. Floore's** (210-695-8827) beer joint/honkytonk/tamale house, where live Texas music has been a tradition for over 60 years. Dance and drink the night away during one of their patio weekend concerts or simply hang out in the late afternoons over beers and pool.

HONDO
Elev. 901   Pop. 8,065

North of Hondo the Hill Country starts to show with bumpy baby versions of the thicker hills ahead. Hondo, the seat of Medina County, dates back to the 1880s and still shows its age with Old West-style downtown buildings bunched north of the railroad tracks that ride beside Hwy. 90. The town's name comes from Hondo Creek, hondo being Spanish for "deep."

HONDO GOLF COURSE

The golf This old 9-hole course resides at the Hondo Air Base and dates back to the 1930s. It's a traditional small-town layout featuring tight fairways and tiny greens. Two sets of tees allow for an 18-hole round. Under 3,000 yards in length, the layout features five par 4s, two par 3s, and two par 4s.

The details 830-426-2331. Hondo Air Base, Hondo, TX 78861

- 1930. 9 holes. Par 36. Back – 2,937 (35.0). Forward – 2,595 (34.6). Price - $.

Getting there From San Antonio, take US 90 west through Hondo. When you come to the flashing yellow light, turn left and drive half a mile to the course.

HONDO NOTES The best way to experience golf in Hondo is to make your reservations at the **777 Exotic Game Ranch**, where hunting, fishing for lunkers, and lodging are all available. Work the golf in around your activities on this ranch. If passing through, take the scenic drive north on FM 462 about 24 miles, where 40-foot dinosaur tracks are found in the bed of Hondo Creek. The restored 1897 Southern Pacific depot houses the **Medina County Museum** and a bit of the area's history. Tune into 1460 on the AM dial (KCWM) for

SOUTH

Natural golfers are bad golfers, but natural putters are good putters. Percy Boomer vintage country music. West of Hondo near the village of D'Hanis, TX is the 1906 **Koch Hotel B&B** (830-363-7500), with five private rooms.

KENEDY
Elev. 271   Pop. 3,567

Named after Mifflin Kenedy, well-known business partner of King Ranch honcho Richard King, Kenedy established itself during the railroad era as a trade and business center. Frequent gunfighting earned the town the nickname of "Six Shooter Junction." When hot mineral water was discovered in 1915, the Hot Wells Hotel and Bath House became popular with travelers. Today Kenedy continues to serve as the economic center for the surrounding agricultural area and is the only place to play golf in Karnes County.

KARNES COUNTY COUNTRY CLUB

The golf   Karnes County is an old course that dates back to the 1920s. This 9-hole country course is built on 160 acres of mesquite-covered rolling hills. Water only comes into play on the 5th hole, a 425-yard par 5. The toughest hole is the finisher, a 450-yard par 4 that ironically follows a 425-yard par 5.

The course is open to the public and annual memberships are available, which might be of interest if you travel to the area to hunt and fish frequently. Golf cart sheds are available for hackers who tote their own ride.

The details   830-583-3200. Hwy. 181, Kenedy, TX 78119

• 9 holes. Par 36. Back – 3,150. Forward – Par 37. 2,570. Price - $.

Getting there From San Antonio, take Hwy. 181 south through Kenedy. The course is 2 miles south of town.

KENEDY NOTES   Find the old-school diner **Barth's** (830-583-2468) and try the Chicken Ranchero followed by cinnamon nut bread for desert. Sixteen miles north in Falls City is **Shorty's** (830-254-3322), where they serve up grilled sirloin in butter with black-eyed peas and Texas Toast. For lodging, the local **Days Inn** is your best bet.

KINGSVILLE
Elev. 66   Pop. 25,427

Founded in 1904 forty miles southwest of Corpus Christi, Kingsville is the dusty company town of the King Ranch. After Captain Richard King died, his widow put up considerable acreage to help finance railroad expansion, and part of the provision was that Kingsville become the headquarters for the rail-

The more time I have to think about a shot, the worse I'm going to hit it. Larry Laoretti

road. Today the city is a center for agriculture, oil, and banking. Texas A&M at Kingsville is located here, as well as a US Naval Air Station.

L.E. RAMEY GOLF COURSE

The golf   Loaded with water hazards, bunkers, and mesquite trees, L.E. Ramey is a tough little course that was one of the best courses in the state when it was built in the 1970s. This is a solid design with tree-lined fairways and large greens in outstanding condition. The course was named after Kingsville doctor and avid golfer Lindell Ramey.

The course has changed management many times over the years, fluctuating back and forth between private owners and Kleberg County. The course suffers during drought conditions with dried-out fairways that cannot be helped by the aging irrigation system. Locals have pushed for private ownership to ensure that the course is well maintained, but no takers have surfaced.

From the middle tees this course plays to a reasonable 6,185 yards, highlighted by par 3s that can be reached with a 6 iron or less. From the tips the course is much, much longer (almost 7,000 yards).

The details   361-592-1101. FM 3320, Kingsville, TX 78364

- www.kingsvilletxedc.org/golfcours.html
- 1970. 18 holes. Par 72. Back – 6,995 (72.5/128). Middle – 6,185 (68.8/122). Forward – 5,540 (71.3/107). Price - $.

Getting there From Hwy. 77 south, exit Prant Rd. and turn left. Follow the signs to the course.

KINGSVILLE NOTES Stroll through downtown and find the **King Ranch Saddle Shop** in the historic Raglands Building, which has outfitted dignitaries for 120 years, then take a tour of the ranch to learn more about its truly fascinating history. The **Mesquite Grill** and the **Barn Door** are popular eateries. Just 16 miles south on **Baffin Bay,** you can hire a guide for fishing and stay at **Bailey's Lodge** (361-595-4666).

LA VERNIA   Elev. 474   Pop. 976

Originally named Live Oak Grove for the abundance of majestic live oak trees in this area just east of San Antonio, La Vernia was established in 1850 by settlers from Mississippi. The name La Vernia comes from the Spanish word *la verde*, or "the green," but this fertile region is also referred to as the Glass

Go find some stimulating, fulfilling, challenging human endeavor that, unlike golf, does not require a commitment of time and effort to realize maximum enjoyment. And call me when you find it. Jim Flick

League after a fellow named Glass who divided and sold his property into separate farms. The countryside around La Vernia still sustains about a dozen productive farms, all over 100 acres each, and is the ideal setting for the beautiful Las Palomas Country Club.

LAS PALOMAS COUNTRY CLUB

The golf   Located in the rolling hills of a former ranch only 25 miles east of San Antonio, Las Palomas is a links-style course built in 1997. Bert Buehler laid the course out with minimal trees, rolling fairways, undulating greens, bunkers, and water hazards, which all combine to make this one of the more difficult courses in the area. It plays long because of the wind (over 7,000 from the tips).

The signature hole is the 210-yard par 3 No. 16, which plays downhill to a two-tiered green that is protected by bunkers. Despite the length, avoid using the driver off the tee because the rough is coastal and averages about 4-6 inches.

The details   830-379-8825. 120 Las Palomas Dr., La Vernia, TX 78121

• 1997. Bert Buehler. 18 holes. Par 72. Back – 7,018 (72.5/122). Middle – 6,307 (69.3/115). Forward – 5,278 (70.2/117). Price - $$.

Getting there Take Hwy. 87 east for 30 miles to FM 539. Drive north 5 miles to the course, which is on the right side of the road.

LA VERNIA NOTES   You can have lunch at the **South Texas Steakhouse**, but that's about it for La Vernia–there's no shopping, lodging, or attractions to speak of. Head to San Antonio if you have plans, otherwise fill up the cooler and buy gas at one of La Vernia's convenience stores and work your way south for further adventures.

LAREDO   Elev. 438 Pop. 188,135

Driving the 150 miles southwest to Laredo from San Antonio, the flat plains are blanketed with the dense scrub of prickly pear, dwarf oak, mesquite, huisache, blackbrush, and cenizo. Located on the Rio Grande River, Laredo is the largest port of entry anywhere on the US-Mexico border, and is South Texas' main business center. Traveling Texans cross the river here to shop and party in Nuevo Laredo.

Unfortunately for the avid linksman, golf options in Laredo are surprisingly limited for a town that's the fastest-growing city in the U.S. and home to almost 200,000 residents.

The game would be nothing without the troublesome business round the hole. Joyce Wethered

CASABLANCA GOLF COURSE

The golf   Unfortunately for the citizens of Laredo and those visiting this bustling border city, the only option for public golf is the very average 18-hole Casa Blanca Golf Course. Although a new clubhouse was added in 1996, the overall condition of the course is below average and locals complain the most about the greens.

Leon Howard built this course in the 1960s. While his front nine is a decent layout that can be challenging, the back nine doesn't seem to flow with the remainder of the design. Water comes into play on only three holes. The hard-pan fairways allow your ball to roll well.

Your best birdie opportunity is the 130-yard No. 8. And if you score well on the front, you'll be delighted to see the first two holes on the back, which are both par 5s under 500 yards from the back tees. The number one handicap is 524-yard No. 4 hole.

The details   956-791-7262. 3302 Winsome Ct., Laredo, TX 78045

- 1967. Leon Howard. 18 holes. Par 72. Back – 6,590. Middle – 6,267. Forward – 5,631. Price - $$.

Getting there Driving east on Hwy. 59, exit on Lake Casa Blanca. Proceed to the dead-end, then turn south on Dakota. You will be able to see the course straight ahead.

LAREDO COUNTRY CLUB

The golf   Do what you can to get on this course–it's one of the finest in the state. Joe Finger, whose resume includes many courses in Mexico, built this course in the early 1980s along the banks of the Rio Grande River. Finger's design features tree-lined fairways edged with demanding rough, water hazards, and sand bunkers throughout, and undulating Bermuda greens that are very fast.

One hole of note is the number one handicap No. 3, a 455-yard par 4 that requires a tee shot into a fairway bordered by water on the left and out-of-bounds on the right. Play it safe and be happy with a bogey on No. 18, a long dogleg left with water along the entire length of the hole, topped off by an approach into a peninsula green.

The details   956-727-0183. 1415 Country Club Dr., Laredo, TX 78045

- 1983. Joe Finger. Par 72. Back – 7,125 (74.6/133). Middle – 6,520 (71.6/125). Forward – 5,740 (74.8/128). Price - $$$.

Getting there Take I-35 south and exit Del Mar Blvd. Turn left, and when you get to McPherson, make another left. Drive to Plantation Blvd. and turn right, then turn left on Country Club Dr. and head to the course entrance.

SOUTH

One of the best practice drills from sand is to tee the ball low and then play the shot. Your goal is to try to break the tee in half. Corey Pavin

LAREDO NOTES   On your way to the early tee time, stop at **Cotulla-Style Pit Bar-B-Q** (956-724-5747) for the best breakfast tacos in the world (they call 'em mariachis). It's difficult to recommend anything other than **La Posada** (956-722-1701) for lodging. Very convenient because it is right on the border, has excellent rooms, and is next door to the **Tack Room**, where you can sit at the bar and order a great steak. Work in an adventure across the bridge to Nuevo Laredo and belly up to the bar at the **Cadillac Bar** for cigars and beers, then wander next door into the noisy **off-track betting joint** and pretend you're a degenerate Mexican vagabond.

McALLEN
Elev. 122 Pop. 112,395

Another of the mishmash of Valley towns that rest on US 83, McAllen has perked up recently with its revitalized downtown. Old-school street lamps and immaculate landscaping line the avenues where small shops sell typical border fare.

ADOBE WELLS COUNTRY CLUB

The golf   One day we might be privileged enough to work our way onto the hallowed grounds of the Adobe Wells Country Club, but for now this destination is only the stuff golf dreams are made of. With Augusta-like secrecy, this club guards its most hidden treasures as if it were the most exclusive club in the world. When querying for basic course information to offer the reader perspective on Adobe Wells' place in the golf universe, we were politely informed "This is a private facility and we would not want to give that information out to the public." That's an amazing statement considering that this is an 18-hole par 3 course located in a friendly retirement community.

The details   956-686-8801. 4901 Daffodil, McAllen, TX

• 18 holes. Par 54. 2,237 yards. Price - $.

Getting there Located at the corner of Hwy. 495 and Taylor Rd.

MCALLEN COUNTRY CLUB

The golf   For over 20 years, McAllen Country Club was an average 9-hole layout. Then Jay Riviere came along in 1968, added nine more holes, and molded the course into a first-class layout. And now with the recent completion of a massive irrigation project, the course is in the best condition of its 55-year existence.

The design features plush fairways lined by oak trees, and small, elevated greens. Because of the tight fairways, locals are in the habit of using irons off

I prefer practicing alone to playing for nothing. Raymond Floyd

the tee. The feature hole is No. 7, a 400-yard par 4 with an approach shot over water. Hole 17 is also tough, playing 222 yards from the back tees over water.

The details   956-686-0923. 615 Wichita Ave., McAllen, TX 78505

• 1968. Jay Riviere. Par 71. Back – 6,454 (70.8/118). Middle – 5,946 (66.7/113). Forward – 5,325 (69.6/113). Price - $$.

Getting there From the McAllen Airport, take Wichita Ave. east. Once you cross the street next to the airport, you should be able to see the course.

PALM VIEW GOLF COURSE

The golf   McAllen's 27-hole public facility recently completed a $4 million renovation that involved a complete re-landscaping of the existing flat terrain. Recent addition include lakes, new greens, new trees, a state-of-the-art practice facility, and a new irrigation system similar to what was installed at McAllen Country Club.

The details   956-687-9591. 2701 S. Ware Rd., McAllen, TX 78503

• 2000. Charles Howard. 18 holes. Par 72. Back – 6615 (72.4/121). Middle – 5779 (68.3/113). Forward – (67.8/107). Price - $$$.

Getting there From Hwy. 83 west, exit Ware Rd. and drive under the overpass. Continue on for almost a mile to the course, then look for the entrance on the left side of the road.

MCALLEN NOTES   Reserve your room at the pink Spanish Colonial-style **Renaissance Casa de Palmas** (956-631-1101), which has more character than the others with its shady courtyard and peaceful fountain. If you're tired of Tex-Mex, **Espana** is a yellow-stuccoed Mediterranean restaurant a few blocks away. **Los Arrieros Mexican Restaurant**, a lively joint popular with the locals, is the place for calories before the early tee times. On the border **Hidalgo** has some old buildings that are worth a look (the old post office, Rodriguez General Store, old courthouse, and jail), and the bustling market in **Reynosa**, followed by queso flameado at **La Fogata**, is a great way to finish the day.

MERCEDES
Elev. 61   Pop. 14,016

Lush with citrus groves and palm trees, Mercedes is 25 miles east of McAllen on US 83. Farming, cotton, and livestock were big here in the 1960s, but the town has recently become recognized nationally for its custom bootmakers.

SOUTH

There are three ways of learning golf: by study, which is the most wearisome; by imitation, which is the most fallacious; and by experience, which is the most bitter. Robert Browning

LA FLORESTA GOLF CLUB

The golf   La Floresta rolls through some interesting terrain that offers scenic views of the countryside, but you won't get to see it unless you are a guest or resident of this retirement community. This par 3 course features mostly basic holes that are great for your short iron game. However, there is one hidden hole with a blind tee shot over trees to the green.

The details   956-565-6314. RR 4, Mercedes, TX 78750

• 1981. 9 holes. Par 27. 2,218 yards. Price - $$.

Getting there From Mercedes, take Route 491 south for 3.5 miles. The course is located on the left-hand side of the street.

LLANO GRANDE GOLF COURSE

The golf   Llano Grande Resort is surrounded by palm trees and citrus groves. But no matter how you paint the picture, it's still an 81-acre mobile home and travel trailer park for winter Texans that features an 18-hole "championship" layout with four sets of tees.

While the tips plays at a reasonable 6,781 yards, we recommend that you play the course from the blue tees, which still plays at a respectable 6,387 yards but cuts the par 3s down to mid-short iron range and makes the par 4s very enjoyable. This track gives you the opportunity to start well with a mid-range par 3, but follows it up with one of the most difficult holes on the course, a 416-yard par 4.

The details   956-565-3351. 489 Yolanda St., Mercedes, TX 78570

• www.llanogra022deresort.com

• 18 holes. Par 72. Gold – 6,781. Blue – 6,387. White – 6,075. Price - $$.

Getting there Take Hwy. 83 west and proceed 15 miles to West Rd. Take the only turn you can and drive 1.5 miles to Golf Course Rd.

THE PALMS AT MID VALLEY

The golf   The Palms is an 18-hole public course that sits at the northern edge of Mercedes in a floodplain. This is a long, intimidating links-style course with plenty of bunkers, elevated greens, thick rough, and even a few palm trees. Four sets of tees offer drastically different rounds. The tips (black) play from 7,114 yards, while the forward men's tees (white) play from only 5,694 yards.

I never quite understood the idea of those seeking to standardize
golf instruction throughout the world. It was perhaps in theory a
worthwhile idea, but one destined to fail. While I am prepared to concede there are certain funda-
mentals in the golf swing, I believe the whole art of teaching golf lies in helping the pupil to trans-
late the fundamental principles via his own physique. Henry Cotton

The 446-yard par 4 No. 5 is the number one handicap, but the signature hole is the 11th, a 393-yard par 4 that requires a tee shot over water to a narrow fairway with out-of-bounds stakes on either side of the fairway. Even once you get it on the green you're not home for good, as it is severely sloped from back to front.

The details   956-565-3211. North of FM 491, Mercedes, TX 78570

- 1995. John Aguillon. 18 holes. Par 72. Back – 7,114 (74.3/120). Middle – 6,570 (71.2/115). Forward – 5,493 (72.1/115). Price - $$.

Getting there From Harlingen, take the 77/83 Expwy. west toward McAllen. When you come to FM 491, exit and turn north. Then drive 2.5 miles to the course and look for the entrance on the right side of the road.

MERCEDES NOTES   The **Howard Johnson Victoria Palms** (956-464-7801) is the place to crash before an early morning tee time in Mercedes. For lunch, try **Wild Bill's** (956-757-4002) in La Feria, TX, where brisket and fried okra is a specialty, then roll into **Camargo's Hand Made Boots** to check out their classic work and see if they'll make you a pair of custom leather golf boots. History and architecture buffs should find the town of **Santa Maria** interesting with its mid-1800s Gothic style church.

MISSION
Elev. 134   Pop. 40,083

More small-town than its neighbor McAllen, home of former Dallas Cowboy coach, Tom Landry (and the grapefruit), Mission is the midway point between South Padre Island and Lake Falcon. To the east the Valley is clogged with cars, but to the west the landscape turns into rolling country covered with mesquite and prickly pear.

THE CLUB AT CIMMARON

The golf   Originally designed by Dave Bennett in 1982 and considered one of the premier courses in the Valley, Cimarron implemented a membership program in 1999 that earmarked funds to improve the facility. In the past few years, the greens have been replaced and the irrigation has been improved.

This tough layout features water on 16 holes, plush fairways, and elevated greens. The 532-yard par 5 opener stands out on the front, but the back is the more difficult of the two nines, with several challenging holes.

No. 13 plays the most difficult: a 434-yard par 4 that plays uphill into the wind. The average hack will be satisfied with a bogey. No. 16 is another long par 4, playing 423 yards. The signature hole is the finisher–it features an island tee box and water along the left side of the fairway that impacts all three shots.

"One cannot think well, love well, sleep well, if one has not dined well." – Virginia Woolf

The details   956-581-7408. 1200 S. Shary Rd., Mission, TX 78572

- www.clubatcimarron.com
- 1982. Dave Bennett. 18 holes. Par 72. Back – 6,821 (71.9/129). Middle – 6,464 (69.7/123). Forward – 5,374. Price - $$$.

Getting there From 83 west, exit Shary Rd. and turn north. Look for the signs to the course.

MARTIN'S VALLEY RANCH GOLF COURSE

The golf   Martin's Valley was built for the winter Texan, offering 27 holes of golf along with garden homes, mobile homes, and recreational vehicles available next to the course. Set in the rolling terrain of the South Texas countryside, the wide fairways are bordered by mesquite trees and the large greens are well maintained.

The details   956-585-6330. 7400 W. Hwy. 83, Mission, TX 78572

- 1984. 27 holes. Price - $$.
- A-B: 1984. Par 72. Back – 6,695 (71.4/112). Middle – 5,928 (67.9/108). Forward – 5,237 (69.0/109).
- B-C: 1994. 18 holes. Par 72. Back – 6,843 (72.2/114). Middle – 6,249 (69.4/110). Forward – 5,542 (70.4/110).
- C-A: 1994. 18 holes. Par 72. Back – 6,770 (71.4/112). Middle – 6,081 (68.2/106). Forward – 5,636 (70.8/112).

Getting there Located 6 miles west of Mission on Hwy. 83.

SEVEN OAKS RESORT & COUNTRY CLUB

The golf   Seven Oaks is an 18-hole, semi-private facility that offers golf packages and two differing nines laid out in a scenic portion of the Rio Grande Valley. While there is no water on the front nine, the back nine has eight lakes that come into play.

The hole to watch out for is the 485-yard, par 5 No. 16, featuring a pond in the middle of a dogleg-left fairway.

The details   956-581-6267. 1300 Circle Dr., Mission, TX 78572

- 18 holes. Par 70. Back – 6,032 (69.3/113). Middle – 5,438 (66.9/108). Forward – 4,864 (69.0/111). Price - $$.

Getting there From Hwy. 83 west, turn right on Los Ebones Rd., then head back across the overpass south. Look for the signs to the course.

SOUTH

SHARY MUNICIPAL GOLF COURSE

The golf   Originally a short, 9-hole course with open fairways and slow, average-sized greens, Shary has opened a new 18-hole course in recent years.

The big course is challenging because the fairways are narrow and lined by out-of-bounds. Water hazards impact several holes as well. Play it safe off the tee with a 3-wood or long iron to avoid big numbers.

The signature hole for the small course is No. 4, a 355-yard par 4 that features an approach shot over water to the green.

The details   956-580-8770. 2201 N. Mayberry St., Mission, TX 78572

- 18-hole course: Par 71. Back – 6,025 (69.9/118). Middle – 5,672 (68.2/115). Forward – 4,893 (68.7/117). Price - $$.
- 9-hole course: 1929. Price - $.

Getting there From 83 west, exit Brian Rd. and drive north. When you come to FM 495, turn left and drive to Mayberry, then turn left again. The course is on the right side.

MISSION NOTES   The diner-like atmosphere at **Taco Olé** (956-581-7431) is the best spot to satisfy your Tex-Mex cravings, however some locals will argue that **El Patio** (956-519-8575) is the best Mexican food in the entire valley. You could get it to-go and drive south to the **La Lomita Mission** for a picnic. Originally built in 1866 by Oblate padres, the tiny structure still has the original brick floors and beamed ceilings shaped from native trees. For lodging, the **Comfort Inn** is nice and new, and **El Rocio** (956-584-7432) is sort of a retreat-B&B where you might sometimes have the entire place to yourself.

PHARR   Elev. 111   Pop. 49,655

While it's hard to distinguish the conglomeration of cities crammed into the tip of Texas, Pharr still boasts of itself as the "Crossroads of the Rio Grande Valley." Located at the junction of US 281 and 83, Pharr dates back to 1909 when Henry Pharr bought 20,000 acres for $17.50 an acre to pursue the sugarcane craze.

One way to know it's Pharr, the "RV Park Capital of Texas," is to keep your eyes peeled for caravanning winter Texans who come to enjoy the warmer climes and partake in the game of golf.

TIERRA DEL SOL

The golf   Of the three golf venues available in Pharr, the best option is the recently renovated Tierra Del Sol. In the summer of 1999, the course upgraded

When you hit an iron shot, you want to take as long a divot as you can. You want it to be long and thin, like a big strip of bacon. You have to apply equal force with both hands to do it. If your divots are short and deep, it's because you're using too much right hand. Tommy Bolt

the irrigation system, replaced the grass on the fairways and greens, and added 25 new bunkers.

Wind and water are the primary hazards. In fact, water comes into play on most holes. The signature hole is No. 5, a 400-yard-plus par 4 with water along the right and out-of-bounds on the left. If you catch this one into the wind, you can bet on no better than a bogey.

The details   956-702-2320. 700 E. Hall Acres Rd., Pharr, TX 78577

• 18 holes. Par 72. 6,767 yards. Price - $$.

Getting there From Pharr, take Hwy. 281 south for 2 miles to the course.

TROPIC STAR

The golf   This is your chance to make your dreams come true and play a golf course located in an RV park. The listed policy is "closed to the public," but don't let that minor hindrance force you to miss the opportunity of a life-time. Beg, hustle, bribe, whatever . . . just work your way on and enjoy the round. The pitch-and-putt design is flat, and easy for the winter Texans to walk and get the old heart pumping.

The details   956-787-5957. 1401 S. Cage, Pharr, TX 78577

• 1977. 9 holes. Par 27. 1,450 yards. Price - $.

Getting there From McAllen, take Hwy. 83 east. When you come to US 281, turn south (S. Cage Blvd). Drive 2 miles and look for the entrance on the left side of the road.

PHARR NOTES   The original **Poncho's Nuevo Mexico Restaurant** (956-782-9991) and **Garza's Cafe** (956-787-9051) are the places to drive up the grease factor in your diet and have a little fun. Crash at the newly remod-eled **San Juan Hotel**.

PLEASANTON   Elev. 374   Pop. 8,589

When time is on your side and your eye is on the Coastal Bend of South Texas, take US 281 south out of San Antonio instead of I-37. You'll have a bet-ter view of the South Texas landscape, as well as the chance to see the cattle, peanut, and petroleum town of Pleasanton. The locals here claim that their town is the birthplace of the cowboy, and they commemorate that distinction each August with the Cowboy Homecoming Festival.

Pleasanton's country club is the only place to play for residents of Atascosa

Babe Zaharias was not only a great golfer, she was a tremendous Indian wrestler. She challenged me to a match in 1946, just after I got out of the parachute infantry. As we joined hands and stood toe to toe, I thought, "This will be easy." Ten seconds later, I was flat on my back. Pete Dye

SOUTH

County, which includes the nearby towns of Poteet, Jourdanton, Charlotte, Christine, and Campbellton.

PLEASANTON COUNTRY CLUB

The golf   Pleasanton's semi-private country club features 18 holes of tree-lined fairways and large greens. The course is flat, and the layout makes it enjoyable to walk. Watch out for the mature oak trees that can impact your shots. Water comes into play on only five holes.

The number one handicap is the par 5, 534-yard 13th hole; however, three of the four par 3s play over 175 yards from the back tees. In fact, even the average golfer can manage this course from the back tees because there is a good mixture of average-length holes with a few longer ones thrown in. Two solid birdie chances are Nos. 6 and 10. Hole 6 requires no more than a 9 iron, and No. 10 is a 300-yard par 4.

The details   830-281-3486. 1801 McGuffin Dr., Pleasanton, TX 78064.

• 1960. Steve Mark. 18 holes. Par 72. Back – 6,529. Middle – 6,198. Forward – 5,160. Price - $.

Getting there From I-37 driving south, take Hwy. 97 west, then drive a short distance to the course.

PLEASANTON NOTES   On the way to the course, grab a sandwich at **McBee's Barbecue** (830-569-2602), then after the round, make it a point to stop in at the **Bar K Ice House** or **Dalton's** and order an ice-cold Lone Star Beer. If you have too many "national beers of Texas" we've counted at least seven local motels in town. However, you're better off reserving a room or your own cabin at **La Estrellita B&B** (866-668-7139), where Belinda's Authentic Texas King Ranch Chicken is served in generous portions.

PORT ARANSAS   Elev. 20   Pop. 3,486

Port Aransas is a somewhat laid-back resort and fishing community located on Mustang Island 24 miles northeast of Corpus Christi. Unlike South Padre, with its high-rise condos and sometimes overwhelming crowds, Port A has faded wood beach houses, quaint shops, and unique lodging reminiscent of the old days.

With the opening of the Grand Caribbean 9-hole course in summer 2002, vacationing golfers no longer have to venture into Corpus for a quick golf fix.

SOUTH

GRAND CARIBBEAN AT DUNE CREST

The golf   Part of a rental condominium complex for vacationers, Grand Caribbean is a 9-hole, par 3 course that opened in 2002. Located near the beach, this is a links-style layout with the longest hole playing 143 yards. Carts are available, but we recommend that you get your exercise in and walk the course, as the green fee is $20 to play 9 holes with a cart (guests receive $5 off the green fee).

The details   361-749-1974. 5495 SH 361. Port Aransas, TX 78373.

• 2002. 9 holes. Par 27. About 1,500 yards. Price - $.

Getting there Located 5 miles south of Port Aransas on Mustang Island on Hwy. 361.

MORE GOLF   530 acres were recently set aside for a planned $290-million resort at the junction of Mustang Island and Padre Island. The Port Aransas Planning Commission has approved the first part of the development, which includes a marina, homes, and a golf course.

PORT ARANSAS NOTES   Port Aransas offers 18 miles of uncrowded beaches for surf-fishing and roaming before and after golf. **The Other Guy's** (361-749-4972), is a casual seafood joint, specializing in crab cakes, where you order your food at the register and they bring it out to you. There are countless condos, bed and breakfasts, and beach-side rentals, but the vintage **Tarpon Inn** (361-749-5555) has history dating back to 1886 and served as a secret retreat for Franklin D. Roosevelt.

PORT ISABEL &
SOUTH PADRE ISLAND   Elev. 15   Pop. 5,067

Port Isabel is a tiny, picturesque village on the Laguna Madre, the body of water between the Texas mainland and South Padre Island. The port served as a supply base during the Mexican war and hosted gold seekers who landed here to begin the trek to California during the Gold Rush.

South Padre is famous for the warm, clear-green Gulf waters and miles of isolated sandy beaches. Legendary for its spring break debauchery, the island serves itself up as a more traditional vacation venue the remainder of the year. With premier resorts, bay and Gulf-side dining, great fishing, and shopping, South Padre is Texas' finest spot to take in the seaside atmosphere.

Here at the tip of Texas, 984 miles away from Texas' northernmost golf course in Booker, TX, the avid golfer can break away from family beach activities on Padre with two golf options, both on the mainland in Port Isabel. The

SOUTH

"Any hole which must keep its green concealed from all parts of the fairway is open to severe criticism." A.W. Tillinghast

par 3 Jim Paul Golf Course is the best option if time is an issue or if you need to work on your short game. But the spot you don't want to miss is the ultra-unique South Padre Island Golf Club.

JIM PAUL GOLF COURSE

The golf   Jim Paul is an 18-hole par 3 course that consists of holes ranging from 44 to 146 yards, with most holes being under 100 yards. The design incorporates a few water hazards, and the course is a solid challenge when the wind is blowing off the Gulf.

The details   956-943-7520. 950 S Garcia St., Port Isabel, TX 78578

• 18 holes. Par 54. 1,405 yards. Price - $.

Getting there This course is located on Garcia St. in Port Isabel.

SOUTH PADRE ISLAND GOLF CLUB

The golf   This southernmost course in Texas, despite its name, is actually situated on the mainland in Port Isabel. Architects Chris Cole and Stephen Caplinger carved an outstanding layout out of the wild native Gulf coast vegetation, with several holes bordering the Laguna Madre. The club has hosted the Texas Senior Open and the South Texas PGA Southern Championship since its opening in 1997.

The design features wide fairways bordered by native yucca, mesquite, and cactus, and the windy conditions often make it challenging to keep it in the fairway. Errant shots will be lost for sure. Others that fail to find the fairway will bury in waste areas and deep rough.

For the most part, the longer holes seem to play more downwind, while the shorter ones play into the wind. The large greens are of championship quality. Three of them are multi-tiered.

No. 5 is the feature hole, a picturesque, 335-yard, par 4 with a tee shot that must carry the Laguna Madre into a sharp dogleg-right fairway. On the back, No. 11 is unique because of the giant mesquite tree that dominates the middle of the fairway. Hole 12 can be interesting: it's a short par 3 that is completely surrounded by water.

The facility has plans for slow expansion based on how quickly the residential lots are developed. A second 18-hole course is under construction, with three holes complete. Designed by Chris Cole and Jeff Potts, this layout will feature only par 3 and par 4 holes and play to 5,400 yards.

The details   956-943-5678. 1 Gulf House Rd., Port Isabel, TX 78578

• www.spigolf.com

• 1997. Chris Cole and Stephen Caplinger. 18 holes. Par 72. Back – 6,931

Golf architects make me sick. They can't play golf, so they try and rig the courses so that nobody else can play either. Sam Snead

(73.0/130). Middle – 6,291 (69.9/123). Forward – 5,406 (66.0/108). Price - $$$.

Getting there The club is on Hwy. 100 before you cross over the causeway onto the island of South Padre. Turn right on FM 520 and continue for 2.5 miles to the course.

PORT ISABEL NOTES Investigate the golf packages offered by many of the hotels and resorts, then call **Jim's Pier** (956-761-2865) to reserve a guide to take you to the speckled trout and redfish in the Laguna Madre. Fish in the mornings, play golf in the afternoons, then watch the sunset with cold beers at **Scampi's** (956-761-1755). For the lazy man's mid-day breakfast, **Isabel's Cafe** (956-943-5082) is a hole in the wall with coffee and papas con huevos, and **Ted's** (956-761-5327) is laid-back, friendly, and the perfect place for migas and the morning paper.

PORT LAVACA
Elev. 19   Pop. 11,978

Port Lavaca, the county seat of Calhoun County, is a little fishing community on the west coast of Lavaca Bay. In 1840 Comanches raided Linnville and burned the town, prompting the residents to move to what is now Port Lavaca.

HATCH BEND COUNTRY CLUB

The golf Since Port Lavaca often gets lost in the shuffle of the more popular Gulf Coast destinations, the semi-private Hatch Bend Country Club is overlooked by golfers looking to get their rounds in. One of the best features of this course is the lack of people, which make it easy to play quickly and keeps the course in solid condition.

This 9-hole course, built in 1958, was laid out with two sets of tees to enable a different look on your second round. The fairways are fairly open and the greens are of average size and speed. Nothing fancy. Birdie opportunities abound here with many short par 4s, two par 5s just over 500 yards, and two short par 3s. The toughest hole is the 537-yard No 5.

The details 361-552-3037. Meadowview Ln., Port Lavaca, TX 77979

• 1958. 9 holes. Par 36. Back – 3,036 (34.9). Forward – 2,489 (34.8). Price - $$$.

Getting there From Port Lavaca, take Hwy. 35 south towards Corpus Christi about 6 miles to the course.

PORT LAVACA NOTES Throw a line in the water, or better yet, hire a guide to take you fishing. Sip on cold beer and gaze at the bay while you wait

SOUTH

⭐
The real trick to golf course architecture is to lure the golfer into false sense of security. Pete Dye

for your grilled shrimp cilantro at **Captain Joe's Seafood and Grill** (361-552-2900). Stay at the brand-spanking-new **Best Western**.

PORTLAND
Elev. 21   Pop. 15,033

Portland lies on a bluff overlooking Corpus Christi Bay, and is just 11 miles across the causeway bridge from its larger, neighboring city. Hurricanes destroyed the dreams of early speculators who hoped to turn the town into a major port and shipping center, and today Portland survives as more of a suburb of Corpus Christi. Portland's claim to fame is their spectacular seaside links course laid out along the bay–the North Shore Country Club.

NORTH SHORE COUNTRY CLUB

The golf   Long considered the jewel of the Gulf Coast, North Shore is known for its famous stretch of holes on the back nine (13-16) set against the backdrop of the bay. Built in 1985 by Bruce Devlin and Robert von Hagge, this private course is thankfully available to the public due to reciprocal arrangements with several Coastal Bend hotels.

The course is not particularly long (6,805 yards), and there are not many trees, but winds often blow 20-40 mph on good days, and the design is loaded with bunkers, water hazards, and side-hill lies. The fairways are 419 Bermuda, and the slick, elevated Tifdwarf greens are known for being in excellent condition year-round.

Course knowledge makes a difference here, so it's to your advantage to play with a member or schedule multiple rounds while you're in the area. The design features several blind tee shots. The more difficult back nine, while more open, is considered more of a position golf course.

Some have compared the famous stretch on the back nine to playing on a resort course in Hawaii. It starts with the signature 13th hole, which plays from a spectacular tee over an inlet of the bay down to a massive green cuddled up against the sand and surf. Watch out for the wind and the ocean spray while you're putting.

Nos. 14 and 15 play along the bay. Keep your tee shot left on the 531-yard 14th to avoid the cliffs looming right on the second shot. The 352-yard 15th hole doglegs right and plays over an inlet just past the turn. The green here isn't an inviting target–it's tiny, elevated, and surrounding by waste areas and a bunker.

You might be able to finally take a breath after No. 16, a long par 3 into a deep green with the Gulf on the left.

Roberto De Vicenzo was a magnificent ball-striker who acquired an almost fatal case of the yips.
Years ago I was paired with Roberto and another player, Mario Gonzalez, who had the yips even
worse than Roberto. Mario would flinch and miss a two-footer, and Roberto would giggle.
Nothing is funnier to someone with the yips than watching someone else with the yips try to stab
the ball into the hole. Tony Jacklin

The details   361-643-6057. 801 E. Broadway St., Portland, TX 78374

- 1985. Bruce Devlin and Robert von Hagge. 18 holes. Par 72. Back – 6,805 (73.5/135). Middle – 6,297 (71.7/126). Forward – 4,975 (70.3/122). Price - $$$.

Getting there From I-37 south, take Hwy. 181 north. Exit at North Shore Blvd. and turn right. Drive a short distance and look for the course entrance off of Broadway.

PORTLAND NOTES   Portland's recently renovated **Days Inn** sits beside Nueces Bay, making it the best spot in Portland to stay by the water. **Abigail's**, a nice little restaurant in the hotel, is one spot in this dry town where you can have a cold bottle of beer. There are also several tasty Tex-Mex restaurants in town. For lunch drive up the road to Gregory, TX and find **Mack's BBQ**. For nightlife, drive the 6 miles over the bridge to Corpus.

RANCHO VIEJO
Elev. 37   Pop. 1,734

Founded as the first settlement via the Espiritu Land Grant by the king of Spain in 1771, Rancho Viejo has become a golf paradise for travelers in the Lower Rio Grande Valley. This relaxed community and resort covers 1,400 tropical acres carved out of the citrus groves and resacas of the Rio Grande Delta. Spanish tiled roofs, lush gardens, and fountains reflect the Spanish influence. Mexico is 15 minutes away, and the beaches of South Padre are just a bit further.

Two excellent golf courses, combined with 2-3 bedroom villas, excellent dining, as well as other resort activities, make Rancho Viejo one of the best travel destinations for golf in this southernmost portion of Texas.

RANCHO VIEJO RESORT & COUNTRY CLUB

The golf   When Dennis Arp sculpted the El Diablo course out of the vast citrus orchards, golf became the thing to do in Rancho Viejo. This full-service resort boasts two excellent 18-hole courses of championship quality that have played host to the PGA Tour Qualifying School for Curtis Strange, Craig Stadler, and Peter Jacobson, as well as the likes of Willie Nelson and Dean Martin who have participated in the club's annual Hacker's Tournament.

El Diablo (the devil) is the most demanding of the two layouts and earns its name with a design that features water on nine holes, ten dogleg holes, and large, undulating greens that are easy three-putts. Palm trees and tropical vegetation provide problems and out-of-bounds is always a factor, since the course sometimes routes between houses.

Start each hole with an awareness that there may be subtle or mysterious elements waiting to saboobtage your game. Robert Trent Jones, Jr.

Hole 3 is one of the most difficult, a 440-yard dogleg left with water affecting both the drive and the approach. No. 14 is a long par 5 that doglegs twice around a lake, and the par 3 No. 16 plays 224 yards from the tips. The tee shot on 16 carries 120 yards of what was once part of the Rio Grande River. The large green is protected by bunkers, but is difficult to hit because of the wind. The smart player knows that the bail-out area short offers the chance for an up-and-down par.

El Angel, the easier course, is a links-style layout that features mounding to go with loads of water and bunkers. On the back, get your birdie on the short, par 5 No. 16 by avoiding the water on either side of the fairway, because you might need an extra stroke on the 465-yard, par 4 17th hole.

Aside from the courses, the resort is home to the famous **John Jacobs Golf School**, his only site in Texas. For those wanting the full-blown instructional experience followed by practice rounds, Rancho Viejo is the place to get lost in the game for the weekend.

The details   956-350-4359. 1 Rancho Viejo, TX 78575.

- www.playrancho.com
- El Angel Course: 1971. Dennis Arp. 18 holes. Par 70. Back – 6,301 (71.5/120). Middle – 5,900 (68.6/114). Forward – 5,087 (69.6/113). Price - $$$.
- El Diablo Course: 1971. Dennis Arp. 18 holes. Par 70. Back – 6,847 (73.7/129). Middle – 6,315 (71.2/122). Forward – 5,979 (75.5/131). Price - $$$.

Getting there From Hwy. 100 west, take Hwy. 77 south and drive for about 15 miles. Turn right on Carman, then drive to Rancho Viejo Dr.

RANCHO VIEJO NOTES   Rancho Viejo is the perfect place to set up headquarters while vacationing in the Valley. Everything you could possibly need is here: quality rooms, two restaurants, tennis, swimming pools, and a quaint workout facility. During the peak season, golf packages include breakfast, range balls, and unlimited golf for $255 per night per couple. Even better deals are available in the summer.

RAYMONDVILLE   Elev. 40   Pop. 9,596

Raymondville, the Onion Capital of Texas, is generally just a pit stop for vacationers driving to and from the tip of Texas. Here at the southernmost edge of the Wild Horse Desert, a barbed wire fence once ran down the middle of what is now Raymondville's main street (Hidalgo Ave.). The fence separated

SOUTH

Ben Hogan had no calluses on his hands. The first time I shook his hand I was amazed. His skin was tough as rawhide, but there was no buildup anywhere. That's a sign of how perfect his grip was. The fact he didn't wear a glove makes it even more amazing. Tom Weiskopf

the hundreds of thousands of King Ranch acreage to the north and the 24,000 acres owned by Edward Burleson Raymond to the south.

RAYMONDVILLE MUNICIPAL GOLF COURSE

The golf   A 9-hole muni with minimal hazards, this track is good for the high handicapper and a nice place to play if you need a break on your way to South Padre. The design features wide fairways and minimal trees, so you'll be able to let it loose. The only water hazard is on No. 9, which also has a few grass bunkers protecting the green.

The details   956-689-9904. 142 S. 7th St., Raymondville, TX 78580

• 9 holes. Par 36. Back – 2,990. Forward – 2,747. Price - $.

Getting there From San Antonio, take Hwy. 77 south past Corpus Christi. Drive through Raymondville and look for the course signs about 2.5 miles outside of town.

RAYMONDVILLE NOTES   While you'll probably play golf in Raymondville while passing to and from the Valley, the **Inn at El Canelo** (956-689-5042) is an outstanding bed and breakfast on a remote, private ranch outside of town. Given the lack of crowds in Raymondville, this might be one of the most unique golf getaways available in Texas. If you need a meal for take-out, call Cornerstone (956-689-5167), and for sit-down look to the **Mesquite Restaurant** for all kinds of food (956-689-9316), or **Casa Blanca** (956-689-3230) for straight up Tex-Mex.

REFUGIO   Elev. 49   Pop. 2,886

Back in the 1700s, Karankawa Indians and Spanish explorers grew accustomed to this spot on the Mission River, just 43 miles inland from Corpus Christi Bay. Early settlers acquired the rights to the mission and town in 1831, and the battle of Refugio was fought here during the Texas Revolution. The rich history, proximity to the Gulf, and a scenic 9-hole golf course make Refugio an ideal spot for Coastal Bend road-trippers looking to work in a quick round of golf.

REFUGIO COUNTY COUNTRY CLUB

The golf   Typical of the region, Refugio County Country Club is covered with large oak trees and even a few pecans. The design winds through the hilly terrain and features small greens that are slower than average. The layout also

SOUTH

Every player has his or her own tempo. There are good players who swing slow, like Fred Couples and Ernies Els. And there are good players who swing fast, like Lanny Wadkins and Nick Price.

Butch Harmon

features a ditch that comes into play on five holes, and a water hazard that impacts Nos. 6 and 7.

The only par 5 is the short 455-yard No. 3. Most of the holes are of standard length. The most difficult is the 375-yard No. 6, although some argue that the next hole, a 211-yard par 3, is actually the toughest test of golf.

The details   512-526-5554. Woodsboro Hwy., TX 78377

- 1940. 9 holes. Par 35. Back – 2,779 (33.8). Forward – 2,218 (32.5). Price - $.

Getting there From Hwy. 77 north, drive through Refugio 2 miles. The course is on the right side of the road.

REFUGIO NOTES   Take in the history of the Texas Revolution and the famous battle that was fought here in 1836. The way to get away in Refugio is to schedule lodging and excursions at the **Dos Vaqueros** (361-543-4905), a historic cattle ranch that offers deluxe accommodations as well as hunting, fishing and other activities. For eats in town, try **Maria's Gypsy Ice** (361-526-1948) for a burger.

ROCKPORT
Elev. 20   Pop. 7,940

Rockport dates back to the Civil War era, where it was established as a shipping point and slaughterhouse town. Thirty miles northeast of Corpus Christi, the Rockport-Fulton area sports a laid-back demeanor characterized by seafood vendors, wooden fishing piers, quaint shops, restaurants, and art galleries that boast the works of the largest per-capita artist's colony in the state.

BUCCANEER BAY RESORT GOLF COURSE

The golf   Lined with beautiful live oak trees and a series of scenic lakes and ponds, Rockport's only public golf course is perfect–it offers a quick place to play when vacationing in the area with family, and is also a great place for a practice round the day before your round at Live Oak Country Club.

The holes on this 9-hole track average about 160 yards. After your round, have a beer in the charming, two-story clubhouse, then cruise around scenic and historic Lamar St.

Note that the course is closed on Wednesdays through the end of November, then opens seven days a week to accommodate the winter Texan crowd.

The details   361-790-7513. 1024 8th St., Rockport, Texas 78382

- 9 holes. Par 27. 1,474 yards. Price - $.

To be good around the greens, you need a mind-set where you
can accept failure. If you're facing a lob shot over a bunker to a tightly cut
pin, you can't think of the consequences of missing. Phil Rodgers

Getting there Located on Lamar Peninsula near Goose Island State Park. Go through Rockport / Fulton toward Tivoli and go over the causeway. Turn on Park Rd. 13 at the Exxon station, then left on Bois d' Arc.

LIVE OAK COUNTRY CLUB

The golf   Live Oak is a private 9-hole course, named appropriately for the ancient live oak trees that line the fairways. This short layout (2,878 yards) is flat, making it perfect for the walking golfer. Nothing too fancy here–just a few water hazards and some random bunkers scattered throughout.

The design features one par 5 that plays 500 yards (No. 3), but the longest par 4 is 335 yards (No. 4 is only 277 yards), so you can afford to hit an iron off the tee and avoid the large oaks to either side.

The details   361-729-7311. 318 Country Club, Aransas Pass, TX 78335

• 1953. 9 holes. Par 36. Back – 2,878 (33.7/116). Forward – 2,468 (33.4/98). Price - $$.

Getting there Exit 1069 off of I-35 and turn left. Travel about 7 miles to the course and look for the entrance on the right side of the road.

ROCKPORT COUNTRY CLUB

The golf   RCC is the best place to play in Rockport, an outstanding championship Bill Coore design that opened in 1984, and considered one of the best courses in South Texas. And while it is technically a private facility, their policy is to reciprocate with USGA members.

Coore's layout rolls over very scenic terrain, with views of the coast and the accompanying wildlife. There is water on 12 holes and the fairways are dominated by huge bunkers, including one that stretches an impressive 400 yards. The fairways are mostly slim and the dogleg holes are short, requiring precise shot-making. The course's signature is its phenomenal greens.

The best hole is No. 14, a 550-yard-plus eye-opener that requires numerous shots over water.

The details   361-729-8324. 101 Champions Dr., Rockport, TX 78381

• 1984. Bill Coore. Par 71. Back – 6,469 (72.0/123). Middle – 5,933 (69.1/118). Forward – 5,117 (68.3/117). Price - $$$.

Getting there From Hwy. 35 north drive into Rockport. When you come to Traylor, turn left and it will lead you directly to the course.

ROCKPORT NOTES   Check for golf packages at **Laguna Reef on the Bay** (800-248-1057). Go for shrimp quesadillas or duck gumbo at laid-back

I've studied golf for almost 50 years now and know a hell of a lot about nothing. Why did Jack Nicklaus, the greatest player in history, change his swing every other week? We're always chopping and changing. Golf is a puzzle without an answer. Gary Player

AransaZu (361-727-1105). For the high-toned, hit **Hemingway's Bar and Grill** (361-729-7555), a classy restaurant with an elegant mahogany-and-brass bar and a first-class kitchen. On Fulton Rd., the **Fulton Mansion State Historical Site** shows off the three-story 1870s mansion built by cattle baron George Fulton.

SAN ANTONIO
Elev. 701 Pop. 1,182,840

If Dallas and Houston are the two loud brawling brothers of Texas, San Antonio is the precious little sister. Quiet, cultured, and certainly more beautiful than her metropolitan siblings, San Antonio hides its booming Americanism under a delicately stitched shawl of Hispanic serenity. Travel to this South Texas jewel of a city and you will truly feel like you've been away on vacation. Well known outside of Texas as the state's premier golf destination, San Antonio lives up to that reputation, charming visitors with its Mexican heritage, Hill Country scenery, rich history, and fabulous golf courses.

For Texans, much of the city's mythic power emanates from the smaller-than-expected Spanish mission known as the Alamo. No matter which version of history you subscribe to, these facts remain: a small band of men fought valiantly and gave their lives for the cause of Texas Independence, and for that the 300-year-old structure, now encircled by office towers and hotels, has become a shrine to all that is noble about the Lone Star State.

Just past the Alamo (and everything you'll want to see in downtown San Antonio is within walking distance) the Riverwalk of shops and restaurants meanders along what remains of the San Antonio River. At night it becomes a festival of lights, laughter, and mariachi music, a fiesta where everyone's invited. Hispanic and Anglo culture co-exist easily and intermingle in San Antonio, to their mutual benefit. That combination of aesthetics carries over into all areas of life in the Alamo City, from food to architecture to music. You can even feel the blending in the golf courses as you sense how the land and the history influence everything. This rare treasure of a city is a "must visit" for golfers and travel lovers alike.

ALAMO GOLF CENTER

The golf   Executive courses are often overlooked, yet they offer affordable golf and the chance to walk away feeling really good about your game. The courses are not difficult and the atmosphere is usually very casual, allowing average hacks the chance to relax and have fun, one of the best ways to get your swing in a groove.

Alamo Golf Center is the perfect example of such a place. A full-service prac-

When your hands get too close to your head,, you can't create power. Keep some space between your head and your hands. Butch Harmon

tice facility with an attached par 65 executive course, this peaceful little course is a great way to hone in your irons and work on your up-and-downs. Alamo's layout features trees, ponds, and greens that are just challenging enough to keep it interesting, but easy enough to build your confidence.

Hole 15 is one of the better tests, a 321-yard, par 4 that features a pond resting behind the green.

The details   210-696-4000. 9700 Rochelle St., San Antonio, TX 78240

- 1993. T.R. Terrell. 18 holes. Par 65. Back – 4,515 (65.0/118). Middle – 4,259. Forward – 3,830 (64.8/111). Price - $$.

Getting there From I-10, take the Prue Rd. exit and turn left. When you come to Babcock, turn left again, then turn right on Pembroke Ln. The entrance is just down the road off of Rochelle.

BRACKENRIDGE PARK GOLF COURSE

The golf   One of the all-time classics of Texas golf, Brackenridge Park was designed by the venerable A.W. Tillinghast in 1916, and is the oldest public course in the state. Whether it's the old limestone starters shack, the commemorative plaques that date the course, the stories of the old Texas Open tourneys played here from 1922 to 1959, or the massive, museum-like, Tudor rock clubhouse with its Champions Boards hanging on the walls, this course must be played by every Texan golfer.

Imagine old man Brackenridge hunting bear on this property back in the early days of Texas. Imagine Ben Hogan, Walter Hagen, Sam Snead, Arnold Palmer, and Byron Nelson gracing the fairways. Imagine the great game of golf working its way into the consciousness of old-time Texas, while the mastermind behind revered Bethpage, Baltustrol, Winged Foot, and San Francisco CC strutted into town to put his mark on Texas along the San Antonio River.

The flat, old course is not known for its difficulty, although the majestic oaks and pecans that line the narrow fairways have their ways of reaching out and sucking in shots that aren't perfectly straight. There's even the random palm tree here at Brackenridge. The one you'll most likely notice affects the approach on No. 4.

The river comes into play on several holes. In fact, on the back nine creeks and ponds come into play on 7 of 9 holes, complementing the straightforward front nine, which has only one pond.

In 1968, Brackenridge underwent extensive renovation due to highway construction on 281 and I-35. The course lost 10 acres, and a few of the long par 4s on the back were shortened.

The par 3s on the back are memorable. Hole 16 plays over a creek into an elevated green, and the 18th plays 166 yards over a pond.

After the round, lounge in the historic clubhouse before heading to

Good posture at address is crucial. Bend from the waist, flex your knees and stick out your backside. Your eyes should be outside your hands. Tom Watson

Tomatillos Cafe & Cantina for dinner, then try the popular **Liberty Bar**, a neat joint that leans so much you'll think it's about to collapse.

The details 210-226-5612. 2315 Ave. B, San Antonio, TX 78215

- 1917. A.W. Tillinghast. 18 holes. Par 72. Back – 6,185 (70.1/122). Middle – 5,767 (67.7/118). Forward – 5,216 (68.0/112). Price - $$.

Getting there From Broadway driving north, turn left on Mill Race St., which leads directly to the course.

BRIGGS RANCH GOLF CLUB

The golf The die-hard golfer always appreciates the old-school, machismo aura of a golf-only facility created solely for the purpose of offering the most complete golf experience possible. Briggs Ranch is one of those, the first and only in San Antonio, a $10 million project designed by Tom Fazio and requiring an initiation fee upwards of $50,000 limited to only 300 men and women.

Along with Fazio, longtime San Antonio golf celebs Bill Rogers and Buddy Cook are part of the team that created the par 72, 7,308-yard layout, which happens to be one of the only solid-sodded courses in the country. Imagine sodding over 100 acres at around $15,000 per acre!

The course features bent-grass greens, fancy Zeon Zoysia fairways (the only one in Texas), and supreme Hill Country terrain that, despite being only 20 minutes from downtown San Antonio, is surprisingly void of urban sprawl.

Suffice it to say that this is one you'll want to pull the strings to get on. Pristine, private golf courses are the dreams of every golfer, especially when after-round festivities include cold beers at a giant 40-foot antique bar imported from "a famous South Texas ranch."

The details 210-670-9400. 2818 Rustlers Trail, San Antonio, TX 78245

- 2001. Tom Fazio. Gold – 7,206 (74.0/132). Blue – 6,869 (72.4/126). Silver – 6,404 (70.2/120). Red – 5,279 (71.5/128). Price - $$$$.

Getting there Take 90 toward Castroville, then take exit 211 to the right. After another right, the course entrance is across from the Golf Club of Texas.

BROOKS AIR FORCE BASE GOLF COURSE

The golf The Brooks AFB course opened in 1971, and has remained a 9-hole course ever since, but two sets of tees make this challenging, wind-burdened course play to a par 72, 6,700-yards for a full 18 holes. In addition to the wind, bunkers dot the hilly design, spotting the rolling fairways and elevated greens. Water comes into play on 6 of 9 holes.

No. 4 is called the signature because it requires a tee shot over water, and its length leaves you with a long iron into the green. No. 7 is a tough par 3, long and into a small, elevated green that slopes back to the fairway.

SOUTH

The thing that hurt my putting worst was thinking too much about how I was making the stroke, and not enough about getting the ball in the hole. Bobby Jones

The details   210-536-2636. 8003 18th St., San Antonio, TX 78235

- 1971. 9 holes. Par 36. Back – 3,387 (36.2/118). Middle – 3,290 (35.2/117). Forward – 2,892 (36.2/125). Price - $$.

Getting there From downtown San Antonio, take I-37 south and exit Military Dr. Turn right, then follow the signs to the course.

CANYON SPRINGS GOLF CLUB

The golf   Despite not remaining a premier resort as originally planned, Canyon Springs still offers 18 holes of spectacular public golf that wind through several residential communities. Gary Player protégé Thomas Walker laid this one out, and he's received accolades for the course's natural feel, despite the route through the homes. His design features giant oak trees; huge, undulating greens; prominent bunkering; and elevated tees. Throughout the round you'll face a good combination of split fairways, forced carries, and fairways that are both generous and unforgiving. Rock formations dot the landscape, and thick, gnarly rough awaits anything off the fairway.

Each side's finishing hole features a waterfall. The 18th is the most talked about–a 400-yard par 4 that plays from an elevated tee down to a fairway bordered by a creek and waterfalls.

The most intriguing hole is No. 18, a 400-yard par 4 featuring an elevated tee box and a fairway punctuated by a creek and waterfall.

Other notes: Both *Golf Digest* and *Golf Magazine* lauded Canyon Springs as one of America's best new public courses in 1998.

The details   210-497-1770. 24400 Canyon Golf Rd., San Antonio, TX 78258

- www.canyonspringscc.com

- Thomas Walker. 18 holes. Par 72. Back – 7,077 (72.8/130). Middle – 6,677 (70.7/123). Forward – 5,234 (70.0/115). Price - $$.

Getting there From San Antonio, take US 281 north to Evans. Turn left on Evans and find the course 3.5 miles away.

CEDAR CREEK GOLF COURSE

The golf   San Antonio's newest and most scenic municipal course opened in 1989 after Ken Dye created his 7,150-yard par72 layout out of this rugged Hill Country terrain. The course features wild elevation changes and incredibly craggy terrain–you'll know that you're about to experience something special when you overlook the surrounding countryside from the clubhouse before the round. Old oak trees and cedar elms line the fairways, five of which dogleg; expect to encounter blind shots and uneven lies. The greens mirror the

The worst way to try to make a great stroke is by thinking about its mechanics when you putt the ball. It's something best left to your subconscious. Dr. Bob Rotella

course layout, with frequent undulations, and many have two and three levels. Don't forget to pay attention to the pin placement on these tricky greens.

The first hole is one of the most scenic, dropping 70 feet off the tee and sloping down to a green that slides to the right. Aim left on the approach. Also on the front, No. 9 plays downhill to the tune of 565 yards, and features an approach into a green protected by water.

On the back, No. 14 offers the dreaded double-doglegger, and the view from the 210-yard 17th hole is nice. In between those is the flattest hole on the course, a 380-yarder that bends hard right and tempts you to cut the corner. Beware of the pond on the left side of the green.

The details   210-695-5050. 8250 Vista Colina, San Antonio, TX 78255

• 1989. B. Spann, K. Dye, & Joe Finger. 18 holes. Par 72. Gold – 7,158 (73.4/132). Blue – 6,650 (71.3/125). White – 6,130 (68.9/118). Red – 5,535 (70.8/113). Price - $$.

Getting there From I-10 west, take Loop 1604 and drive 3 miles to the Kyle Seale Pkwy. Turn right and drive 2 miles to the course, which is on the left.

THE CLUB AT SONTERRA

The golf   Sonterra is private, and features two 18-hole tracks on opposite sides of Loop 1604. The club got its start in 1985 when Bruce Devlin and Robert von Hagge completed a 7,070-yard layout that features three famously difficult holes, then expanded when ownership acquired the old Canyon Creek Country Club across the highway.

The **North Course**, also known as Sunburst, features outstanding bent-grass greens and some extremely impressive terrain. Unlike many courses in the area, this one lacks numerous trees, but makes up for it with loads of fairway bunkers. The course opens with a monster dogleg-right, 571-yard par 5, which features a mean approach into an elevated green fronted by bunkers. No. 5 is another tough par 5, but fun because of the blind tee shot. The most scenic hole is No. 6, which plays 165 yards over a waterfall and lake to a small green.

The **South Course**, also known as Deer Canyon, plays down in a valley through large oaks, its signature being the numerous rock walls that come into play. Those walls are most prominent on holes 1 and 17. For the most part, this one is a traditional layout with small, mound-shaped greens. There is no water on the South Course.

The details   210-496-1560. 901 Sonterra. Blvd, San Antonio, TX 78258

• North/Sunburst Course: 1985. Robert von Hagge-Bruce Devlin. 18 holes. Gold – 7,070 (74.5/137). Blue – 6,601 (72.3/131). White – 6,156 (70.1/119). Red – 4,883 (68.7/120). Price - $$$$.

• South/Deer Canyon Course: Reese Maxwell-Joe Finger. 18 holes. Par 72. Back – 6,535 (71.1/123). Middle – 6,299 (69.9/120). Forward – 5,602 (71.1/122). Price - $$$$.

Last week I made a double bogey and didn't even get mad. Now, that's bad. Jack Nicklaus

Getting there Driving west on Loop 1604, turn right (north) on Shore Oak Pkwy., then turn left on Sonterra a few miles up the road.

THE DOMINION COUNTRY CLUB

The golf   Bill Johnston designed this difficult course, which opened in 1984 and rolls through the lush Hill Country setting near Leon Creek.

Ancient oaks squeeze the fairways, Leon Creek winds through the layout, and the fast, sloping greens make this one tough mother. The back nine is considered more difficult, but the front has its share of challenging holes.

No. 2 requires a layup off the tee of about 180 yards for the average golfer, since only a 300-yard drive could carry the creek. The creek is also in play on the par 5 No. 7, which features a deceptive fairway that slopes towards the water. No. 9 is another difficult par 5 highlighted by a drainage ditch on the left and green-side pond.

Two holes stand out on the back. No. 16 plays 440 yards into the wind, with water on the right and trees on the left. The length of the hole inevitably leaves you with a monstrous approach shot, which might be over the water if you're too far right off the tee.

The genius design on 18 makes it a great finishing hole. Playing well over 500 yards from the tips, it goes uphill left into the dogleg and generally requires three full shots, with the last one hazardous because of the water left and behind the green.

Other notes: The homes of George Strait and NBA superstar David Robinson grace the fairways of Dominion. The club hosted the Senior PGA Tour's SBC tournament for years. Ralph Bender had $17 million at his disposal when he built the clubhouse, which is considered one of the finest in the state.

The details   210-698-1146. 1 Dominion Dr., San Antonio, TX 78257

- 1984. Bill Johnston. 18 holes. Par 72. Gold – 6,827 (72.8/130). Blue – 6,447 (71.2/123). White – 6,055 (69.1/118). Red - 5,392 (71.3/120). Price - $$.

Getting there Take I-10 west past Loop 1604, and exit Camp Bullis. Stay on the access road, and look for the Dominion entrance on the right side of the road.

FORT SAM HOUSTON GOLF COURSE

The golf   Fort Sam has more character and history than any other Texas military course, sporting a 1937 A.W. Tillinghast design that hosted the Texas Open back in the 1950s and 60s, and is the only military course ever to host a PGA event.

Old man Tillie's course is known as **La Loma**, and it's laid out near the giant

You know those two-foot downhill putts with a break? I'd rather see a rattlesnake. Sam Snead

national cemetery. Its colorful history includes Sam Snead's 1950 Texas Open victory, as well as a win by Arnold Palmer before the event was moved across town to the Oak Hills Country Club.

The **Salado Course,** named after the creek that runs through the layout, is considered the more scenic, featuring more water hazards and an unusual amount of blind shots. Construction was completed on the full 18 holes back in 1965. The layout features a front nine dominated by seven par 4s and a back nine with three par 3s and three par 5s. Salado plays 6,725 yards from the tips, and while most of the par 4s are under 400 yards, the par 3s are in the 200-yard range. The best hole is the 611-yard No. 5.

The details 210-222-9386. 1212 Stanley Rd., Fort Sam Houston, TX 78234

- La Loma Course: 1937. A.W. Tillinghast. 18 holes. Par 72. Back – 6,774 (72.5/124). Middle – 6,270 (70.2/117). Forward – 5,446 (70.8/115). Price - $$$.

- Salado Course: 18 holes. Par 72. Back – 6,725 (72.7). Middle – 6,248 (70.3/117). Forward – 5,390 (70.1/113). Price - $$$.

Getting there From I-35 south, take the Rittiman Rd. exit to Harry Wurzbach. Turn left, and the course is on the left.

GATEWAY HILLS GOLF CLUB

The golf Another one of San Antonio's many military courses, Gateway dates back to 1946 when it opened with a traditional 9-hole layout. The second nine was added in the 1950s, providing military personnel with a full day of tight, hilly fairways and blind golf shots. Water comes into play on only two holes, and the greens are mostly flat with the rare undulation.

On the front, No. 4 is the best hole, playing 454 yards over a small ravine and into an elevated, bunker-protected green. The back side opens well with the signature 577-yard No. 10, a unique hole because of the scenery and its secluded green surrounded by oak and mesquite trees.

The details 210-671-2517. Bldg. 2901, Lackland AFB, 78236

- 18 holes. Par 72. Blue – 6,917 (73.1/125). White – 6,544 (71.2/122). Gold – 5,818 (67.7/113). Red – 5,437 (71.5/116). Price - $$.

Getting there From Hwy. 90 west, take the Military Dr. exit and turn left. When you come to the second gate, turn in and follow the signs to the clubhouse.

The majority of right-handed golfers prefer putts that break from right to left. That's something of a mystery, as physics doesn't play favorites with an object rolling along the ground. But my theory is that right-to-left breakers are easier because of the way the face of the putter behaves during the stroke. Johnny Miller

THE GOLF CLUB OF TEXAS

The golf   The Golf Club is Lee Trevino's only Texas signature course, located in the historic Briggs Ranch and created to be friendly for the average golfer. This open course rolls through a nice Hill Country setting, is loaded with oaks, yuccas, and wildflowers, and features water on 11 holes.

One both sides of the course, the second hole is the most difficult rated hole. No. 2 goes 398 yards from the tips and features a pesky fairway bunker and generally plays into the wind. The approach is into a green guarded by deep bunkers to the left and water in back. No. 11 plays 458 yards and is lined on the right by Lucas Creek, which makes it risky to cut the corner of the dogleg right fairway. You'll inevitably be left with a long approach, so remember that the bail-out area is to the left of the green.

The details   210-677-0027. 13600 Briggs Ranch, San Antonio, TX 78245

• www.thegolfcluboftexas.com

• 1999. Lee Trevino. Par 72. Back – 7,022 (73.1/135). Middle – 6,467 (70.3/129). Forward – 4,823 (67.9/109). Price - $$$$.

Getting there Located at the corner of Hwy. 90 and Hwy. 211 north. From 410 or 1604, take Hwy. 90 west to Hwy. 211. Take 211 north and look for the entrance on the right.

HYATT HILL COUNTRY RESORT

The golf   The Hyatt Hill Country Resort, the first destination resort inside the city limits, kicked off the 1990s San Antonio golf boom that is still going strong today. The resort is located across from Sea World, whose success helped convince Hyatt that this part of Texas was prime for resort developments. Arthur Hills was hired to come in and mold the former Wiseman Ranch, and the result is a lush course in perfect condition that offers four sets of tees for every type of golfer. With its limestone walls and metal roofs, the hotel reeks of Hill Country style, and is accentuated by Hills' challenging, but fair design.

The front nine boasts the signature hole, the long par 4 No. 5 that plays downhill and features an approach over water, but is better known for its two difficult finishing par 5s. No. 8 goes 563 yards and involves water crossing the fairway on two occasions, as well as an approach into a tough green surrounded by a mound on the left and water and sand on the right. Hole 9 plays 554 yards and requires a perfect drive downhill to a large lake that fronts the double green.

The back is loaded with long par 4s that play around 450 yards, and like the front, ends with a difficult par 5. No. 18 plays around 550 yards and features an approach into a green surrounded by water and sand.

If your concentration is getting bad, take up bass fishing. It will really improve your ability to focus. If you aren't ready when that fish hits, you can't set the hook. Lee Trevino

Other notes: *Golf Magazine* once named this club one of its "Top 10 You Can Play." The club is entertaining ideas of a 9-hole addition. After the round, have cold beers in Charlie's Long Bar, an eclectic saloon with a long copper bar.

The details   210-520-4040. 9800 Hyatt Resort Dr., San Antonio, TX 78251

• 1993. Arthur Hills. 18 holes. Par 72. Back – 6,913 (73.9/136). Middle – 6,481 (72.0/130). Forward – 4,781 (67.8/114). Price - $$$$.

Getting there From downtown, take I-35 south to Hwy. 90, then west to the Sea World exit. Drive past Loop 410, then 3.5 miles to the resort where the club is on the right.

KELLY AIR FORCE BASE GOLF COURSE

The golf   Set in the hills of southern San Antonio, the Kelly AFB Golf Course was originally built by military employees and volunteers as a 9-hole course in 1969, with a second nine added shortly thereafter. Water hazards come into play on 14 of 18 holes, and the plush fairways roll to greens that are pretty quick. Afterwards, players always remember the huge hill that offers an outstanding view of the city from the 9th and 18th tee boxes.

The design is known for its solid par 3s and difficult finishing holes. The two par 3s that stand out the most are the 200-yard No. 2, which requires a full carry of water to a green surrounded by sand and more wet stuff. No. 16 is 190 yards and plays to the smallest green on the course.

No. 16 is followed by the 275-yard No. 17, which plays straight uphill into a green that slopes drastically back towards the fairway.

The details   210-977-5100. Golf Shop, Bldg. 8, San Antonio, TX 78236

• 1968. 18 holes. Par 72. Back – 6,869 (73.0/123). Middle – 6,422 (70.5/117). Forward – Par 74. 5,354 (71.0/117). Price - $$.

Getting there From Hwy. 90 west, take the General McMullen Dr. exit and turn left. Drive a short distance to the military base, then ask the sentry for directions to the clubhouse.

LA CANTERA GOLF CLUB

The golf   Home of the PGA's Texas Open since 1995, La Cantera features two truly spectacular golf courses that roller-coaster through the hills west of San Antonio.

The original **Resort Course** is a Tom Weiskopf/Jay Morrish collaboration that is cut out of a limestone quarry, playing 7,001 yards from the tips but offering another four sets of tees for any sort of hack. White bunkers and majestic oaks dot the plush fairways, and streams weave in and out of the

SOUTH

What separates the great players from the good players or the 15-handicap player from the 20-handicap player is not so much ability as brainpower and emotional equilibrium. Arnold Palmer

design. Many holes offer panoramic views of the city and countryside, where you'll be able to look down over the hole ahead and see the huge, undulating greens in the distance.

Every hole seems like a signature hole, even the 600-yard-plus opener, but the best hole is the 415-yard No. 12. It features a fairway loaded with stair-stepped bunkers and a green guarded by a natural waterfall. The approach shot on 12 is one of the most scenic in Texas.

The new **Palmer Course** is virtually impossible to walk because of the hilly terrain, and it features plenty of blind shots. The most difficult hole is the 426-yard No. 5, which requires an impressive long iron to carry the dry creek bed.

The resort and golf are pricey, but the twilight rate is phenomenal and generally allows you to play without the crowds. We were able to walk on with no wait at a fraction of the prime rate on a late September Sunday afternoon.

The details   210-558-4653. 16641 La Cantera Pkwy., San Antonio, TX 78256

• www.lacanteragolfclub.com

• Resort Course: Black – 7,001 (72.5/134). Gold – 6,406 (69.6/127). Copper – 6,026 (68.2/119). Silver – 5,581 (66.1/113). Jade – 4,993 (67.1/108). Price - $$$$.

• Palmer: Black – 6,929 (74.2/142). Gold – 6,535 (72.4/139). Copper – 6,115 (70.6/134). Silver – 5,684 (69.3/128). Jade – 5,066 (65.3/116). Price - $$$$.

Getting there From San Antonio, take I-10 west to the La Cantera Pkwy. exit. Turn left and the course is about 1 mile down on the right side of the road.

MISSION DEL LAGO MUNICIPAL GOLF COURSE

The golf   This is one of San Antonio's six municipal courses, and perhaps the toughest, playing a mean 7,208 yards from the tips and featuring 10 water holes and stiff winds off of Lake Mitchell.

The clubhouse has a bit of charm, with sort of an old Texas mission look. The fairways are lush, the greens roll true, and there are a few holes that make it a memorable round of golf.

Hole 6 is the most difficult–it doglegs left and plays up hill at 435 yards. The green is tough because of its severe slope. Also on the front, the long par 5 No. 9 can get you because it's bordered by out-of-bounds on either side of the fairway.

On the back, No. 16 rivals the 18th as the signature hole. You may need a fairway wood to reach this long par 3, and there is water behind the hole if you're too strong. The 18th is the longest par 4 and plays up a steep hill to a blind green that is protected by a huge bunker.

The property dictates what you put there, the topography, the drainage. A lot of designers get caught up in building for the pros, but the supporters of golf are the guys shooting in the 80s and 90s. You have build so it's challenging for good players, but the average player isn't going back if he shoots too far over his handicap. Jay Riviere

Other notes: The course allows fivesomes on the weekends, but we didn't find too many who complained about slow play. Golfers had positive things to say about the frequent beverage cart sightings.

The details 210-627-2522. 1250 Mission Grande, San Antonio, TX 78221

• 18 holes. Par 72. Back – 7,004 (72.6/127). Middle – 6,210 (68.9/116). Forward – 5,301 (69.2/113). Price - $$.

Getting there From US 281 south, take Loop 410 west, then exit Roosevelt Ave. Turn left and drive 2 miles to the course. The clubhouse is on the right.

NORTHERN HILLS COUNTRY CLUB

The golf Northern Hills opened in 1969 with a Joe Behlau design that plays to a par 71, 6,536-yards from the tips, featuring small, multi-level greens and tree-lined fairways.

Behlau didn't have much room to work with on this centrally-located facility, so you'll notice that the front side rolls to the right, while the back nine works back to the opposite direction. Consequently, if your misses off the tee are flying in the right direction, you'll be able to keep it in play and avoid big numbers. Slices and fades work on the front, and draws and hooks survive on the back.

Everyone talks about the difficult par 3s, all of which require long irons. With the exception of two dogleg par 5s, the remainder of the holes play straightaway, providing the opportunity to flail away if you're hitting them straight.

The details 210-655-8026. 13202 Scarsdale St., San Antonio, TX 78217

• 1969. Joe Behlau. Par 71. Back – 6,536 (70.8/118). Middle – 6,117 (68.6/111). Forward – 5,076 (69.7/117). Price - $$.

Getting there From Hwy. 410 east, take the Nacogdoches exit and turn left. Drive approximately 4 miles and the street turns into Bulverde. Bulverde changes into Scarsdale, and you will eventually see the course on the right.

OAK HILLS COUNTRY CLUB

The golf Oak Hills has as much character as any storied, private, member-owned country club in the world. This one dates back to the early 1920s when it was built by the famed A.W. Tillinghast, and has hosted 24 PGA Tour events won by every big name in the book. Guys like Arnold Palmer, Ben Crenshaw, Tom Watson, and Lee Trevino have won here, just to name a few.

Tillinghast's design was modified in 1984 by Jay Morrish, but it still retains the characteristic features created by the master. Tight, tree-lined fairways,

When undecided, use the longer club. You are smack in between clubs for your approach shot.
What should you do? I take the longer club and make one of two adjustments: I shorten my swing
or I grip down on the club. Either way, you don't have to try to overpower the shot. You can
swing firmly but smoothly, with a clear mind. Tom Watson

large sand bunkers, strategically placed grass bunkers, and challenging doglegs all combine to require every golf shot imaginable. The course is immaculate, with perfectly trimmed old oak trees accented by meadow-like grass along the fairways, greens that roll smooth and fast, and fairways that are as lush as they come.

The course is known for its signature finishing holes on each side. Nos. 9 and 18 are both par 3s that involve elevated tee shots over water to well-guarded greens that are also somewhat elevated.

The details   210-349-5151. 5403 Fredericksburg Rd., San Antonio, TX 78229

• 1922. A.W. Tillinghast. 18 holes. Par 71. Back – 6,650 (71.8/128). Middle – 6,125 (69.0/123). Forward – 5,423 (72.0/125). Price - $$.

Getting there From Loop 410 west, take the Fredericksburg Rd. exit and turn right. When you pass Callahan Rd., turn left into the clubhouse parking lot.

OLMOS BASIN MUNICIPAL GOLF COURSE

The golf   One of San Antonio's most popular munis, Olmos Basin opened in the early 1960s and has thrived despite its flood-ravaged locale and sometimes questionable condition. The city renovated the course in 1994, but conditions never became laudable until recent commitments from the city's senior-level management. Nevertheless, it's hard to stand up to some of San Antonio's spectacular tracks, and no matter what you say, you pay for what you get. Olmos serves its purpose well, providing a challenging golf course for the right price. A quaint, old-school clubhouse and grill with tasty food enhance the experience. Watch out for crowds, especially on the weekends, as walk-up play sometimes requires up to a 2-hour wait.

The details   210-826-4041. 7022 McCullough Ave., San Antonio, TX 78216

• 1963. George Hoffman. 18 holes. Par 72. Back – 6,896 (71.0/123). Middle – 6,526 (70.0/118). Forward – 5,748 (71.0/120). Price - $$.

Getting there From US 281 north, take the Basse St. exit and turn west. When you come to McCullough, turn right and look for the entrance on the right-hand side.

OLYMPIA HILLS GOLF & CONFERENCE CENTER

The golf   Located in an area of San Antonio known as Universal City, Olympia Hills opened in 2000 and quickly gained a reputation for its outstanding greens, which feature tricky undulations and putt extremely fast due to the hybrid Flora Dwarf Bermuda, which allows a lower mowing height. The layout offers dramatic elevation changes of 50 feet or more on holes 8 and 11,

Only bad golfers are lucky. They're the ones bouncing balls off trees, curbs, turtles and cars.
Good golfers have bad luck. When you hit the ball straight, a
funny bounce is bound to be unlucky. Lee Trevino

which are considered the most scenic for good reason. The longest hole is No. 6, a 575-yard par 5 that is impossible to reach in two.

The details 210-945-4653. 12900 Mount Olympus, Universal City, TX 78148

• www.olympiahillsgolf.com

• 18 holes. Par 72. Blue – 6,923 (73.4/132). White – 6,553. Gold – 6,023. Green – 5,534. Price - $$$.

Getting there Located just south of I-35, outside of Loop 1604 in the Olympia Hills subdivision.

PECAN VALLEY GOLF CLUB

The golf   Pecan Valley, now considered one of Texas' top public courses, is distinguished by its storied past and traditional layout. The 1968 PGA Championship was held here on its 50th anniversary, and this Press Maxwell design has also hosted several Texas Opens. Maxwell's layout, which features majestic oaks and pecans along with meandering Salado Creek, was updated to the tune of $6 million in 1998 by Bob Cupp.

The front side is highlighted by the difficult par 3 No. 3, which was thankfully shortened by 60 yards during Cupp's renovation. The hole drops 60 feet and is guarded by a ball-sucking pond on the right side. Make sure you watch the wind on this hole.

The back side is known for its tough finishing holes, which some consider the toughest ending holes in Texas. The 14th is the signature, a mean, 460-yard dogleg right that requires a monster drive to the corner to have a reasonable chance to get home in two. Both par 3s on the back play 200-yards-plus from the tips (Nos. 12 and 16), and the famous 18th hole is known for its role in determining the 1968 PGA champion.

After hooking his tee shot, Palmer drilled his 3-wood uphill within 10 feet from the pin, giving himself the chance for his eventual playoff-forcing birdie putt miss. A plaque honors the spot where he hit the shot, and his 3-wood is on display in the clubhouse. During that same tournament, Jack Nicklaus missed the cut and complained of the course's difficulty, comparing it to a hayfield.

The details   210-333-9018. 4700 Pecan Valley Dr., San Antonio, TX 78233

• www.agpa.com

• 1964. Press Maxwell. 18 holes. Par 71. Back – 7,010. Middle – 6,530. Forward – 5,335. Price - $$.

Getting there From US 281 south, exit South Cross Blvd. and drive east to Pecan Valley Dr. The entrance to the club is on the left-hand side of the road.

You'll see the hole and putt better if you have someone tend the flag on everything outside 15 feet. Tommy Bolt

THE QUARRY GOLF CLUB

The golf   A piece of San Antonio was beautified in the early 1990s when Keith Foster drew the assignment to convert the old Alamo Cement plant from an abandoned eyesore into one of the most unique courses in Texas.

Foster's 6,740-yard, par 72 layout opens up with a true links-style front nine, void of trees and featuring tall grasses and several creeks. It is the easier and more basic of the two sides. The front is fun and is an adequate warm-up for the roller-coaster ride that starts on No. 10. The back nine plays entirely in an abandoned rock quarry with 100-foot-plus walls rising on three sides.

Nos. 12 and 13 both feature a quarry lake and involve spanning the 90-foot bridge over the water. No. 13 is a 362-yarder that doglegs left along the lake. Hole 15 plays 520-yards-plus into a green that lies at the base of a huge stone wall, offering the always-entertaining option of banking the approach onto the green. No. 17 is the most dramatic, requiring a tee shot over a deep ravine highlighted by a 40-foot waterfall, then doglegging left over the quarry wall.

The details   210-824-4500. 444 E. Basse Rd., San Antonio, TX 78209

• www.quarrygolf.com
• 1992. Keith Foster. Pro – 6,740 (72.4/128). Champs – 6,128 (69.2/120). Regular – 5,576 (66.7/111). Forward – 4,897 (67.4/115). Price - $$$$.

Getting there From downtown San Antonio, take US 281 north 4 miles to East Basse Rd. Turn right, and drive 1 mile to the course. The course is located about 2 minutes from the airport and about 6 minutes from downtown San Antonio.

RANDOLPH OAKS GOLF COURSE

The golf   This Air Force course dates back to the 1950s. Joe Finger took over the design duties from Ralph Plummer, who was supposedly tired of dealing with the military red tape during construction. Their collaboration resulted in a long, flat course that is known for its wide fairways and small, elevated greens. Bunkers are in play, and a few water hazards dot the design, but they are not prominent features.

You'll sense the length on the par 3s, since two are over 200 yards, and the others play over 180. The par 5s are long as well, averaging 550 yards in length. No. 5 is notable because the approach is surrounded by water, and No. 12 is considered the toughest because of its long, 589-yard dogleg that turns sharply off the tee.

The details   210-652-4653. Bldg. 1300, Randolph AFB, 78148

• 1950. Joe Finger. 18 holes. Par 72. Champs – 7,172 (74.5/125). Regular – 6,744 (72.4/120). Forward – 5,873 (68.1/116). Ladies – 5,486 (71.2/118). Price - $$.

A firm handshake doesn't reveal a thing about character.
All it tells me is, you're probably going to hold the club too tight. Bob Toski

Getting there From I-35 north, turn right on Loop 1604. When you come to FM 78, turn left (east), and the road will take you to the main gate.

THE REPUBLIC GOLF CLUB

The golf   The Republic is new and makes the perfect "tweener" course, since it's considered a fair-priced, quality alternative to the high-priced $100 layouts and the super-cheap, overcrowded munis. With wide fairways and huge greens, hackers can get their kicks and have the chance for a decent round on this 7,007-yard, par 71 layout, which plays to a manageable 6,622 or 6,147 yards from the forward tees.

The design features many risk-reward shots over ravines and water hazards, tough par 3s, and a few drive-able par 4s. From the tips, two of the par 3s play 220-yards-plus, including the 243-yard No. 17.

The details   210-359-0000. 4226 SE Military Dr., San Antonio, TX 78222

• 18 holes. Par 71. Golf - 7007 (73.5/131). Forest – 6,622 (71.6/125). Blue – 6,147 (69.1/118). Stone – 5,540 (65.5/109). Red – 4,683 (66.9/109). Price - $$$.

Getting there The course is on S.E. Military Dr. bounded by South I-410 and W.W. White. Take US 281 (same road as I-37) south from downtown and look for the Brooks AFB sign. Get off at the second exit onto SE Military Dr. The course is about a mile north on your right.

RIVERSIDE GOLF COURSE

The golf   Old Riverside has some character, as it was once the site of Roosevelt's Rough Riders' preparation before the Spanish American War. The facility dates back to the 1930s, when George Hoffman designed the course around the San Antonio River with good views of San Antonio's skyline. While Riverside offers the standard muni benefits to San Antonio's hacks, the added feature of a 9-hole par 3 course makes it stand out from the rest.

Hoffman's front nine rolls through giant pecan trees and the back nine features the river more prominently. Nos. 16 and 17 are the best holes: the first plays 600 yards, followed by a mean 230-yard par 3 that generally plays into the wind.

Note that walking is mandatory on the 9-hole course.

The details   210-533-8371. 203 McDonald, San Antonio, TX 78210

• 18-hole course: 1974. Vern Scmidt-Harold Henk. 18 holes. Par 72. Back – 6,729 (72.0/128). Middle – 6,211 (69.6/123). Forward – 5,730 (72.0/121). Price - $$.

When I feel myself tightening up under the pressure, I shake my hands at the wrists like a swimmer who's on the mark ready to start a race. I will often do it before I putt. Any tightness in my body eases, so I can make my best effort without forcing the stroke. Tom Watson

- 9-hole course: Par 27. 920 yards. Price - $.

Getting there From I-37 south, take the South Cross Blvd. exit and turn west. When you come to Roosevelt Blvd., turn right and the course is on the left side of the street.

SAN ANTONIO COUNTRY CLUB

The golf   SACC dates back to 1907 and was designed by golf pioneer Alex Findlay, who opened what is now the back nine. Findlay's short design was lined by the big homes of the Alamo Heights area. He added the second nine in 1913, and the revered A.W. Tillinghast came along in the 1920s for some minor updates while he was working on Oak Hills Country Club. Other updates over the years include Joe Finger's work on the greens, and Jay Morrish reworking a few holes in the 1980s.

This beautiful old course is a pleasure, offering only the basics with gently rolling fairways and superb greens.

Other notes: SACC was one of the first in the nation to use golf carts (1946).

The details   210-824-8861. 4100 N. New Braunfels, San Antonio, TX 78209

- 1908. Alex Findlay. 18 holes. Par 72. Gold – 6,774 (72.7/128). Blue – 6,329 (70.1/122). White – 5,992 (68.6/116). Red – Par 74. 5,599 (72.7/127). Price - $$.

Getting there From the San Antonio Airport, take US 281 south to Hildebrand. Turn left and drive straight to the course.

SAN PEDRO PAR 3 GOLF COURSE

The golf   An old par 3 course that opened in the 1950s, this is simply a place to work on your game when you're in the area. Only one set of tees here, so your honey can compete straight up.

The details   210-349-5113. 6102 San Pedro Ave., San Antonio, TX 78216

- 1950. Chuck Klein. 9 holes. Par 27. 944 yards. Price - $.

Getting there From US 281 south, take Loop 14 west. When you come to San Pedro, turn south and the course is on your left 3.5 miles.

SEVEN OAKS HOTEL AND SPORTS CLUB

The golf   An extremely short par 3 course, the design features one set of tees, bunkers, ponds, and outstanding views of the countryside.

The details   210-824-5371. 1400 Austin Hwy., San Antonio, TX 78209

SOUTH

Don't be discouraged by three-putting [from long range]. If you were playing miniature golf, a hole 60 feet long would carry a par of 3. Consider a two-putt from long range a birdie of sorts, and move on. Johnny Miller

• 1970. 9 holes. Par 27. 768 yards. Price - $.

Getting there From downtown, take I-35 north and exit Eisenhauer. Turn left, and drive 1.5 miles to the Austin Hwy. intersection. Turn right, drive .25 mile to the course, and look for the hotel on the right just across the street from the course.

SILVERHORN GOLF CLUB

The golf   Silverhorn opened in 1996, patterned after the successful Silverhorn track in Oklahoma City. It was designed by Randy Heckenkemper with the help of PGA Tour veterans Scott Verplank and Willie Wood.

The design incorporates elevated greens and a significant number of dry creeks that criss-cross the fairways and front many greens–particularly on the back, where the dry creeks come into play on just about every hole.

The opening hole is difficult because it plays 578 yards, and another tough par 5 on the front is No. 6, a 542-yard dogleg left with a lake in play on every shot. The next hole also skirts the lake, playing 175 yards to the green.

On the more wooded back, No. 18 is the highlight: an uphill, dogleg-right hole dominated by a giant oak tree and one of the dry creeks that fronts the green.

Other notes: Range balls are included with the green fee.

The details   210-545-5300. 1100 Bitters Rd., San Antonio, TX 78216

• 1996. Randy Heckenkemper. Gold – 6,922 (73.1/129). Black – 6,333 (70.6/125). Silver – 5,831 (68.2/116). Green – 5,271 (66.4/109). Price - $$$.

Getting there From downtown San Antonio, take US 281 north to Bitters Rd. Turn left, travel 1.5 miles to Partridge Trail, then make another left to the course.

WILLOW SPRINGS GOLF COURSE

The golf   Laid out in the 1920s along east San Antonio's Salado Creek, Willow Springs is a long course that features generous fairways and extremely large greens. Emil Loeffler designed the original nine in 1923, and John Bredemus added the second in 1925 for this 7,221-yard layout that eventually hosted the Texas Open in 1940.

Although a few holes offer great opportunities to hit the driver on open fairways, the layout also features a few doglegs that will make you think twice about nailing the big dog. No. 2 is ridiculously long at 663 yards.

The details   210-226-6721. 202 Coliseum Rd., San Antonio, TX 78219

• www.wsgolf.com

• 1923. Emil Loeffler. John Bredemus. Gold – 7,221 (73.9/134). Blue – 6,979

If there is larceny in a man, golf will bring it out. Paul Gallico

(72.1/129). White – 6,392 (70.4/121). Red–- 5,443 (72.5/120). Price - $$.

Getting there From I-35 north, take the Coliseum Rd. exit and turn right. The course is a few miles down on the left.

WINDCREST GOLF CLUB

The golf　Windcrest is not as well known in San Antonio's golf portfolio, but offers a relaxing, simple place to play in the midst of all of the difficult championship courses. This 1960s-style 9-hole private executive track features averaged-sized fairways, water on a few holes, and two sets of tees to allow for an 18-hole round. Of the nine holes, three are par 3s, five are par 4s, and there is only one par 5, which is the 491-yard 9th hole.

The details　210-655-1421. 8600 Midcrown Dr., San Antonio, TX 78239

• 1964. 9 holes. Par 34. Back – 2,295 (31.6/104). Forward – 2,014 (32.2/34). Price - $.

Getting there From San Antonio, take Hwy. 10 east to Hwy. 410. Turn north and exit Walsum St., then turn east and proceed .5 mile to Midcrown Dr. Turn north and drive 6 blocks to the course. The entrance is on the right.

WOODLAKE GOLF & COUNTRY CLUB

The golf　Built by the fiery Scotsman Desmond Muirhead, Woodlake hosted the PGA Tour's Texas Open from 1972-76 and was the site of Ben Crenshaw's first tour victory, which happened to be his first professional start out of college.

Muirhead was a landscape planner who became one of the game's most controversial architects, and his Woodlake design is known for its narrow fairways and well-protected greens that put a premium on shot-making. Although not always the most aesthetically pleasing feature, parallel fairways offer the chance to recover from wayward shots and are especially nice on the long par 4s, since you can try to drive it far without losing a stroke.

No. 5 is one of two notable par 5s, playing 515 yards with an approach into a green fronted by water and framed by sand. The 557-yard 18th is the signature hole, playing into the wind and bending to the right with water right, out-of-bounds left, and a creek that fronts the green.

The details　210-661-6124. 6500 Woodlake Pkwy., San Antonio, TX 78244

• 1972. Desmond Muirhead. 18 holes. Par 72. Back – 6,691 (71.6/129). Middle – 6,228 (69.4/126). Forward – 5,305 (70.8/121). Price - $$.

Getting there From I-35 north, take the Binz-Engleman exit and turn right. When you come to FM 78, turn left and drive 3 miles to Woodlake Pkwy. Turn

SOUTH

Men, your wife appreciates that you are a better golfer than she is. She also suspects you don't understand the golf swing as well as you think you do, and she's right. So, for the sake of world peace, keep your advice to yourself. Bob Toski

right, proceed a short distance to the course, and look for the entrance on the left side of the street.

SAN ANTONIO NOTES   When close to downtown, before you pay tribute to your Texas roots at **The Alamo,** have a beer and check out the museum at the old **Lone Star Beer Brewery.** The now world-famous **River Walk** is practically next door with more dining and drinking options than you can imagine. Reserve a room at **La Mansion Del Rio** (800-292-7300), the river's oldest and most distinguished hotel, take a good look at the design of any of the **35 historic bridges** that span the river, then pick a place to settle in for the evening festivities. The more macho should hit the **Esquire Bar,** a rowdy, local establishment on Commerce St. Also on Commerce find **Schilo's Delicatessen** (210-223-6692), a San Antonio landmark that has been around for 100 years. Some of the famous Mexican restaurants in San Antonio include **El Mirador** (210-225-9444) on S. St. Mary's, **Los Barrios** (210-732-6017) on Blanco Rd., and **Paloma Blanca Mexican Cuisine** (210-822-6151) on Broadway.

SINTON
Elev. 43   Pop. 6,625

Sinton, only 28 miles from Corpus Christi, is the San Patricio County seat and rests at the intersection of US 77 and 181. The town was established on 640 acres on the south bank of Chiltipin Creek and was named after David Sinton, one of the stockholders of the Coleman-Fulton Pasture Company that founded the town.

Sinton has a rich history in cattle ranching, oil and gas, and has recently become a popular destination for birding and antique shopping. Welder Park, named after a local rancher and oilman named Robert M. Welder, who gave generously to the community, is home to Sinton's 18-hole municipal golf course. The park and the course offer a nice place to stop off when touring this part of the Coastal Bend.

SINTON MUNICIPAL GOLF COURSE

The golf   This 18-hole course is known for the strong prevailing winds that make proper club selection crucial. While the fairways are mostly wide open, there are trees that can alter shots. The greens are small and there are no bunkers.

From the middle tees, every par 5 is under 500 yards, and every par 4 with the exception of No. 18 is under 400 yards. Hole 18 is the signature hole and number one handicap, playing 455 yards as a par 4.

The details   361-364-9013. Robert Welder Park, Sinton, TX 78387

Here's irony for you: The driver goes the shortest distance when you throw it. The putter flies farthest, followed by the sand wedge. Tommy Bolt

- 18 holes. Par 72. Back – 6,572 (71.1/116). Middle – 6,331 (69.9/114). Forward – 5,412 (71.0/118). Price - $.

Getting there From Hwy. 77 east, take Hwy. 181 north 2.5 miles to the course.

SINTON NOTES   With the salty smell of the coast luring you for adventures on the beach, it's hard to justify making it a weekend in Sinton. Play the course on your way to Corpus, Port Aransas, or Rockport. If it's lunchtime, grab a sandwich at **Harvey's Bar-B-Que** (512-364-4200).

UVALDE
Elev. 913   Pop. 15,144

Uvalde, a unique little town at the border between South Texas and the rugged Hill Country, sits at the crossroads of the nation's two longest highways: US 90 and US 83. Former Texas governor Dolph Briscoe called Uvalde home, as did notorious frontier outlaw J. King Fisher and FDR's vice president, Cactus Jack Garner. A charming community that maintains an ordinance to protect oak trees growing in the middle of its streets, today Uvalde is a retail center for cattle, sheep, and goat ranching.

UVALDE MEMORIAL PARK GOLF COURSE

The golf   Originally opened around 1950, Uvalde's fun little 9-hole course has recently been upgraded to offer the complete 18-hole experience. It makes for an interesting combination, as architect Jep Willies reworked the hole combinations to integrate the new construction rather than tacking on a separate addition. The new areas are more modern and have immature trees, giving the course a links-style feel–the old areas have mature trees that get in the way, making it a more traditional, keep-it-in-the-fairway type of course. The new holes have bigger greens as well.

On the front, No. 2 is a 400-yard par 4 with trees on the left and lined by thick rough. A good tee shot is imperative on this hole if you have hopes of reaching the green in regulation.

On the back, No. 10 has a big lake coming into play off the tee, and No. 11 has a small pond in the fairway about 250 yards from the tee. You'll need to hit them well here. Hole 16 is the most difficult: a gnarly dogleg par 4 with a severely sloping green.

Other notes: During the recent build-out, archaeologists discovered Indian artifacts. PGA Tour veteran Miller Barber stopped by one year and won the annual Fourth of July Tournament. The pro shop is small and handles the basics. There is no grill–only snack foods are available. The course does not serve alcohol but allows golfers to bring their own until they start selling cold beer again.

✯

I know of no recreation which is a better character builder than golf. Tony Jacklin

The details   830-278-6155. 329 East Garden St., Uvalde, TX 78802

- Circa 1950. 2001. Jep Willies. 18 holes. Par 71. Champs – 6,238 (69.9/121). Blue – 5,828 (67.5/115). White 5,073 (63.8/107). Forward – 5,028 (63.8/107). Price - $$.

Getting there This course is located on Garden St. in Uvalde.

UVALDE NOTES   A long-time tradition in Uvalde is **Evett's Barbecue** (830-278-6204), or you might try the **Lone Star Saloon** for live music. The restored **Grand Opera House** (1890) has tours and performances throughout the year. For lodging call **Casa de Leona B&B** (830-278-8550) just outside of town. Don't miss the scenic drives offering some of the most impressive views in the Texas Hill Country: US 83 north through Concan, past Garner State Park to Leakey, then west on FM 337 (also south on Texas 55). Or at Leakey, east on FM 337 to Vanderpool and south on FM 187 to Sabinal.

VICTORIA
Elev. 93   Pop. 61,579

Take US 181 southeast of San Antonio for 60 miles to Kenedy, then wind your way through a variety of roads through Goliad and then on to Victoria. Once there, drive around "Old Victoria" and admire the beautiful restored homes, many of which are national landmarks.

The city was a crossroads for early explorers Cabeza de Vaca and la Salle, and in 1824 Martin De Leon received permission Mexico to establish a settlement between the Guadalupe River and the Lavaca River. Originally named Nuestra De Guadalupe De Victoria, the name was shorted to Victoria after the Texas Revolution. Agriculture, oil, and gas are the primary industries.

COLONY CREEK COUNTRY CLUB

The golf   The feel to this course is that of European links, with strong winds and open greens that allow for just about any type of shot on your approach. Water comes into play on 15 holes, and you'll need accuracy off the tee to keep the ball in the tight fairways. Your best bet to score well here is to gear up for the five par 3s, which are some of the easier holes on the course. The 354-yard, par 4 No. 7 is listed as the number one handicap.

The details   361-576-0018. 301 Colony Creek Dr., Victoria, TX 77904

- 1985. Dick Watson. Back – 6,413 (70.9 / 121). Middle – 6,009 (69 / 119). Forward – 5,036 (68.7 / 112). Food and drink available. Rental clubs also. Price - $$.

SOUTH

Practicing all the time helps my confidence more than it does my swing. Knowing you've paid a price gives you a give advantage. Lee Trevino

Getting there From Hwy. 59, take the Victoria exit. When you come to the first traffic light, turn right on John Stockbauer. Turn right again on Colony Creek Dr. and head straight to the course.

RIVERSIDE GOLF COURSE

The golf   Victoria's muni course offers 27 holes of golf that are played in three 18-hole combinations. The design for the three nines is very similar, as the holes lay out over very flat terrain. The Blue Course, which is considered the most difficult, also has the facility's toughest hole. No. 5 is a 194-yard, par 3 with an intimidating tee shot over water. Finally, it's no guarantee to dominate the par 5s here, as each one plays over 500 yards from the back tees.

The details   361-573-4521. 302 McCright Dr., Victoria, TX 77901

• 1945. Ralph Plummer. 18 holes. Par 72. Back – 6,606 (71.1/113). Forward – 5,497 (69.2/119). Price - $$.

Getting there From US 59 south, exit Navarra and turn left. Drive to Red River, then turn left again and find McCright Dr.

VICTORIA COUNTRY CLUB

The golf   Victoria Country Club is a private, 18-hole facility originally designed in the 1930s by John Bredemus, and redesigned in 1985 by Joe Finger and Baxter Spann. Their design features large greens and generous fairways, along with a few lakes that impact play. This is a fair test of golf: challenging, but not difficult enough to cause the average golfer to have a miserable round.

Longer hitters have the opportunity to birdie No. 1, a 471-yard par 5 from the white tees, but this opener is followed by two long par 4s. No. 3 is the signature, a 427-yard par 4 that plays straightaway into a green that is protected by bunkers.

The back nine opens up with a long par 4 (390 yards), but is more noted for its difficult finishing holes. From the back tees, 16 and 17 are par 4s that play well over 400 yards, followed by the almost 600-yard par 5 finishing hole that plays the toughest on the course when the wind is blowing hard.

The details   361-575-6161. 14 Spring Creek Rd., Victoria, TX 77904

• 1935. John Bredemus. 18 holes. Par 72. Blue – 6,870 (72.2/119). White – 6,327 (69.7/116). Gold (67.9/113). Red – 5,279 (71.7/117). Price - $$$.

Getting there From Hwy. 59 south, exit Loop 463 and turn right. When you come to Navarro, turn left and proceed to Whispering Creek. Turn right, and after you reach Country Club Dr., turn left.

MORE GOLF   You can hit balls at the **Northside Golf Range** on Navarro (512-573-1229).

SOUTH

Some players have short putting drills they perform as faithfully each day as they do brushing their teeth. Dr. Bob Rotella

VICTORIA NOTES   Plan your visit in late October for the **International Armadillo Confab and Exposition,** complete with dillo racing and a chili cook-off. **Coleto Creek Lake** and **Lake Texana State Park** are nearby. If you're hungry, the popular spot is the **Rosebud Fountain and Grill** (361-573-5111), where a ham-and-cheese sandwich might hit the spot. Also try Tex-Mex at **Siesta** (361-578-9927), or track down the oldest deli in Texas, **Fosatti's,** established in 1882. One of a few motels on the way to Houston is the **Westerner Motor Hotel** (361-575-4531).

WESLACO   Elev. 70   Pop. 28,007

Located just south of US 83, only 7 miles from the border city of Nuevo Progreso and centered between Harlingen to the east and McAllen to the west, Weslaco is the hidden gem of the Rio Grande Valley. It's less crowded than Harlingen and McAllen, close to the action in Progreso, and has a revitalized downtown that is rich in 1930s Spanish architecture and Texas historic sites. Furthermore, Weslaco boasts perhaps the Valley's finest golf course, the spectacular Tierra Santa Golf Club, as well as a peculiar 9-hole layout named the Village Executive Golf Course.

TIERRA SANTA GOLF CLUB

The golf   The first daily-fee course built in the Rio Grande Valley, Tierra Santa opened in 1997 as the centerpiece of a residential community. This challenging 18-hole track was designed by Jeff Brauer, who consulted with PGA Tour pro Steve Elkington to sculpt the flat farmland into undulating fairways that wind through a total of 14 lakes.

The course is very challenging, with water on most holes, significant length, and wind that always seems to blow strong. The lush fairways are covered in bunkers, and most holes are finished off with extremely large, fast greens that reek of championship quality. The trick here is to know where to bail out, as many "safe" bailout areas were incorporated into the layout.

Five of the par 4s are over 430 yards. The 3rd hole offers a risk-reward decision with a double fairway that tempts you with a 200-yard carry over water on one side, and a safe landing area to the right. The most difficult hole on the course is the 443-yard No. 5, which features a 200-yard carry off the tee and water on the left of the fairway and beside the green. No. 9 can get you as well–it's a 460-yard monster with bunkers all over the fairway.

The scenic 18th is the signature hole at 451 yards with water along the left

One time at Chattanooga I hit a real pretty iron to the green, and danged if my ball didn't hit a bobwhite in the air and knock it dead. My ball stopped about a foot from the cup and I knocked it in. Only time I ever made two birdies on one hole. Sam Snead

side and bunkers on the right. Your approach shot must carry the waterfall fronting the green.

The details   956-973-1811. 3701 S. Westgate Dr., Weslaco, TX 78596

- 1997. Jeff Brauer. 18 holes. Par 72. Back – 7,100 (74.1/125). Middle – 6,601 (71.7/120). Forward – 5,283 (71.3/121). Price - $$.

Getting there From Harlingen or McAllen, take Hwy. 83 to the Westgate exit. Drive 3.5 miles to the end of the road where the course is located.

VILLAGE EXECUTIVE GOLF COURSE

The golf   This is the place to practice your short game before heading to Tierra Santa. The design features five par 3s and two legitimate par 4s, plus two "pseudo" par 4s that are actually par 3s. The yardage for the par 4s goes 303, 143, 147, and 282, respectively. One of them is a severe dogleg and the other is over water. One large pond comes into play on two holes.

The details   956-968-6516. 3300 S. International Blvd., Weslaco, TX 78596.

- 1980. Larry Dittburner. 9 holes. Par 31. 1,531 yards. Pull carts available. Price - $.

Getting there Two miles south of Business 83 on FM 1015.

WESLACO NOTES   The best choice for lodging when playing Tierra Santa or any of the upper Valley courses is the **Best Western Palm Aire** (800-248-6511). For a nice meal, find **Ciro's** (956-969-2236), which features a multitude of unusual shrimp dishes, among other tasty choices. **Fat Daddy's** (956-969-3668) a home-cooking joint with a sign over the kitchen warning "Never trust a skinny cook," is the place to dig into sausage, chicken-fried steak, and peach cobbler.

YORKTOWN   Elev. 266   Pop. 2,299

Yorktown is a very old town located about 70 miles southwest of San Antonio and 35 miles northwest of Victoria. Indian fighter and ranchman Captain John York settled on Coleto Creek back in 1846, and partnered with land speculator Charles Eckhardt to establish the Old Indianola Trail.

⭐

A guy I caddied for, a gambler and bookmaker named LoBall Johnny Wilson, told me, "You're playing too many good players. There are plenty of people around who aren't as good as you." Gambling at golf is all about using psychology and human nature to your advantage, and by age 13 these things were instinctive to me. Phil Rodgers

YORKTOWN COUNTRY CLUB

The golf   Established in 1923, YCC has a 9-hole course situated on 42 acres of land about 2 miles outside of Yorktown. The design features a creek that runs throughout the course, and tight fairways that are lined with trees and out-of-bounds. There are no bunkers on the course.

The details   361-564-9191. Country Club Rd., Yorktown, TX 78164

• 9 holes. Par 35. Price - $.

Getting there Southwest of Cuero on Hwy. 72.

YORKTOWN NOTES After your round roll into **El Sombrero Cafe** (361-564-3644) for tasty Tex-Mex, then stroll historic downtown before retreating to **The Pecan Tree Inn B&B** (361-564-3223). This convenient spot is just north of Main St. within walking distance to the shopping and historic sites of Yorktown. The restored 1920s house is nestled in a grove of pecan trees and has a wrap-around porch that's perfect for reading.

ZAPATA   Elev. 311   Pop. 5,056

Named in honor of Antonio Zapata, a tough Mexican pioneer and Indian fighter, Zapata is the county seat and headquarters for a large ranching area as well as the base for activities on Lake Falcon.

LOS EBANOS GOLF CLUB

The golf   Laid out in a pasture of rolling hills, this picturesque course provides a little of everything. Valleys, trees, and water hazards provide challenging shots. The signature hole is No. 2 (382 yards, par 4) with out-of-bounds on the left side of the fairway.

The first nine plays to a distance of 2,964 yards and the second round is at 3,139. There are actually 10 holes here, with a separate tee and green for No. 18. All told, 18 holes play to a par 71.

The club has recently installed a totally automated sprinkler system, an improvement that should make a big difference in the overall condition of the course. Out-of-towners bringing foursomes benefit from a promotion allowing the fourth member to play for free. During the summer $10 gets you a half cart and unlimited play after 4:30 pm on weekdays.

The details   956-765-8336. 701 Lincoln St., Zapata, TX 78076

• www.losebanosgolf.com

• 1986. 9 holes. Par 35. Back – 2,964. Middle – 2,815. Forward – 2,206. Price: $.

SOUTH

When you cross that border, man, you in another country. U.S. Border Patrolman

Getting there Located downtown, three blocks due west of the Civic Center. From Hwy. 83 north, turn right at the 1st block after the Post Office. Look for the signs to the course.

ZAPATA NOTES   Zapata serves as home base for adventures on **Lake Falcon** and, given the small size and remote location of the town, you'll either play the course passing through or in conjunction with a fishing trip on Falcon. Hire **Jim Murray** (956-848-5630) or **Mike Perez** (956-584-9887) to take you fishing, reserve a room at the **Redwood Lodge** (956-765-4371), **Best Western Inn** (956-765-8403), or any of the other decent accommodations in Zapata, then golf and fish the weekend away. For the ultimate side trip, grab tacos to-go after touring historical **Roma, TX**, then drive to the ruins of **Guerrero Viejo** for a picnic. The town was submerged when Falcon Dam was built in 1953, but is dry again now that Falcon has receded due to drought. Pick up Hwy. 2 after you pass the dam, then drive 23 miles to the marked turnoff and then another 9 miles to the ruins.

SOUTH TEXAS BORDER CROSSINGS

For the immensely curious, super-restless golfer, wayward excursions are available across the line in select Mexican border cities. Proceed with caution, take your old set of clubs, generally dress down, be ready for anything, and have fun.

MATAMOROS, MEXICO   Across the border from Brownsville, TX

The impressively named **El Sausito de Matamoros Club** (88-129259) is private and only available to the well-connected gringo. For access, start by spending heavily in the turista shops just across the border and asking store management for possible references to those in the know.

NUEVO LAREDO, MEXICO   Across the border from Laredo, TX

Ventures to Nuevo Laredo's infamous La Zona Rosa can be preceded by golf adventures at one of two 9-hole courses: the **Club Campestre de Nuevo Laredo** (871-42334) or the **Club Campestre Riviera Del Bravo** (871-42334), which tips out at a par 72, 6,325 yards (rating 71.1) when you play it twice and offers caddies to make up for their lack of carts–a good thing, given the way the natives drive over there.

SOUTH

It is easier to replace the turf than to returf the place. Anonymous

734 • *The Texas Golf Bible*

REYNOSA, MEXICO   10 miles from McAllen, TX

Gringos call it the **Reynosa Country Club,** but the locals know it as the more fancy-sounding **Club Campestre Reynosa** (89-120848). It's a 9-holer that plays to par 72, 6,640 yards (rating 71.1) when you play it twice. It is listed as private but you never know what the actual policy may be. Check it out and let us know.

There is no surer nor more painful way to learn a rule than to be penalized for breaking it. Tom Watson

From left to right, Johnny Weismuller, Jimmy Demaret,
Byron Nelson, and Bing Crosby in a tournament to help sell
war bonds during WWII. Check out the musicians.

THE TEXAS SWING: PGA TOURNEYS IN TEXAS

The Texas Open

Pro golf came to Texas in 1922 with the birth of the Texas Open in San Antonio. The tourney that is now the fifth oldest event on the PGA Tour began on the oldest public course in the state: San Antonio's Brackenridge Park. San Antonio resident John Bredemus, the father of Texas golf, and San Antonio News sports editor Jack O'Brien founded the Texas Professional Golfers Association that same year. They both played a key role in raising the projected $5,000 in prize money, which at the time was a phenomenal purse compared to the $500 offered by the US Open.

As many as 4,000 golf fans came to Texas' first pro tournament and watched Scotsman Bob MacDonald fire a total of 281 to win the prize money. MacDonald received the full sum after O'Brien passed the hat around to make up for his miscalculation of the estimated prize amount.

The tournament struggled for survival in those early years, and playing conditions were definitely not up to the high standards of today's pro golf. However, the 1923 event captured national headlines when British Open champion Walter Hagen stormed to victory from a six-shot deficit, drawing attention to pro golf in Texas.

Harvey Penick, who played as many as 20 early Texas Opens, wrote, "Some people don't realize this was the tournament which helped launch the PGA Tour." Bredemus and O'Brien got the ball rolling for greater things to come in San Antonio. In 1928 Tommy Armour, the players' association president, drew up the articles of incorporation for the Professional Touring Golfers Association, which just happens to be today's PGA Tour.

PAST TEXAS OPEN CHAMPIONS

2002 Loren Roberts 261	1974 Terry Diehl 269	1947 Ed Oliver 265
2001 Justin Leonard 266	1973 Ben Crenshaw 270	1946 Ben Hogan 264
2000 Justin Leonard 261	1972 Mike Hill 273	1945 Sam Byrd 268
1999 Duffy Waldorf 270	1971 No Tournament	1944 Johnny Revolta 273
1998 Hal Sutton 270	1970 Ron Cerrudo 273	1943 No Tournament
1997 Tim Herron 271	1969 Deane Beman 274	1942 Chick Harbert 272
1996 David Ogrin 275	1968 No Tournament	1941 Lawson Little
1995 Duffy Waldorf 268	1967 Chi Chi Rodriguez 277	1940 Byron Nelson 271
1994 Bob Estes 265	1966 Harold Henning	1939 Dutch Harrison 271
1993 Jay Haas 263	1965 Frank Beard 270	1938 No Tournament
1992 Nick Price 263	1964 Bruce Crampton 273	1937 No Tournament
1991 Blaine McCalister 269	1963 Phil Rodgers 268	1936 No Tournament
1990 Mark O'Meara 261	1962 Arnold Palmer 273	1935 No Tournament
1989 Donnie Hammond 258	1961 Arnold Palmer 270	1934 Wiffy Cox 283
1988 Corey Pavin 259	1960 Arnold Palmer 276	1933 No Tournament
1986 Ben Crenshaw 196	1959 Wes Ellis 276	1932 Clarence Clark 287
1985 John Mahaffey 268	1958 Bill Johnston 274	1931 Abe Espinosa 281
1984 Calvin Peete 266	1957 Jay Hebert 271	1930 Denny Shute 277
1983 Jim Colbert 261	1956 Gene Littler 276	1929 Bill Mehlhorn 277
1982 Jay Haas 262	1955 Mike Souchak 257	1928 Bill Mehlhorn 297
1981 Bill Rogers 266	1954 Chandler Harper 259	1927 Bobby Cruickshank 272
1980 Lee Trevino 265	1953 Tony Holguin 264	1926 Mac Smith 288
1979 Lou Graham 268	1952 Jack Burke, Jr. 260	1925 Joe Turnesa 284
1978 Ron Streck 265	1951 Dutch Harrison 265	1924 Joe Kirkwood 279
1977 Hale Irwin 266	1950 Sam Snead 265	1923 Walter Hagen 279
1976 Butch Baird 273	1949 Dave Douglas 268	1922 Bob MacDonald 281
1975 Don January 275	1948 Sam Snead 264	

COLONIAL NATIONAL INVITATIONAL

John Bredemus designed Fort Worth's Colonial Country Club in 1935, and in 1941 the club hosted the first US Open to be held in a Southern state. In 1946 the course hosted the Colonial National Invitational, an invitation-only format in the tradition of the Masters, and the event has been held there ever since. In addition to being the only tournament that has been played at the same site through its history, Colonial is the only PGA tournament with the course's name in its event.

Ben Hogan, a local boy who grew up poor in Fort Worth and learned the game as a caddie, won the first event in 1946 by firing a course record 65 and taking home the $3,000 winner's check. This was before the course became known as Hogan's Alley—Hogan ended up winning the event five times. His last PGA Tour victory occurred at Colonial in 1959. Amazingly, he finished in the top 10 four times after he turned 50. In 1970, at the age of 58, he fired an opening round 69 before pulling out of the tournament due to illness.

The Wall of Champions near the first tee features a plaque for each one of the winners since 1946. A trophy room in the clubhouse celebrates the many achievements of Hogan, displaying awards, prizes, and mementos from his competitive years.

PAST COLONIAL CHAMPIONS

2002 Nick Price 267	1983 Jim Colbert 278	1964 Billy Casper 279
2001 Sergio Garcia 267	1982 Jack Nicklaus 273	1963 Julius Boros 279
2000 Phil Mickelson 268	1981 Fuzzy Zoeller 274	1962 Arnold Palmer 281
1999 Olin Browne 272	1980 Bruce Lietzke 271	1961 Doug Sanders 281
1998 Tom Watson 265	1979 Al Geiberger 274	1960 Julius Boros 280
1997 David Frost 265	1978 Lee Trevino 268	1959 Ben Hogan 285
1996 Corey Pavin 272	1977 Ben Crenshaw 272	1958 Tommy Bolt 282
1995 Tom Lehman 271	1976 Lee Trevino 273	1957 Roberto deVincenzo 284
1994 Nick Price 266	1975 No Tournament	1956 Mike Souchak 280
1993 Fulton Allem 264	1974 Rod Curl 276	1955 Chandler Harper 276
1992 Bruce Lietzke 267	1973 Tom Weiskopf 276	1954 Johnny Palmer 280
1991 Tom Purtzer 267	1972 Jerry Heard 275	1953 Ben Hogan 282
1990 Ben Crenshaw 272	1971 Gene Littler 283	1952 Ben Hogan 279
1989 Ian Baker Finch 270	1970 Homero Blancas 283	1951 Cary Middlecoff 282
1988 Lanny Wadkins 270	1969 Gardner Dickinson 278	1950 Sam Snead 277
1987 Keith Clearwater 266	1968 Billy Casper 275	1949 No tournament
1986 Dan Pohl 205	1967 Dave Stockton 278	1948 Clayton Heafner 272
1985 Corey Pavin 266	1966 Bruce Devlin 280	1947 Ben Hogan 279
1984 Peter Jacobsen 270	1965 Bruce Crampton 276	1946 Ben Hogan 279

BYRON NELSON TOURNAMENT

Originally called the Dallas Open, the tournament dates back to 1944 when the modern pros of the day came to Dallas' Lakewood Country Club to hack it out. Nelson, "the tall Texan with the huge hands," won the first event by 10 strokes and went on to one of the most impressive streaks in sports history: 11 consecutive tournament victories in 1945. Nelson is the only player to have a tournament named in his honor. Sam Snead won it the next year before the tourney was moved to Brook Hollow Golf Club. That 1946 event was won by Ben Hogan.

After a 10-year absence, the tournament picked back up again in 1959 at the Oak Cliff Country Club, with Sam Snead taking home the prize. And in 1961, Dallas' Earl Stewart Jr. became the PGA Tour's first hometown winner.

Eventually, the tournament became the Byron Nelson Golf Classic, was rescheduled from the fall to the spring, and moved to Preston Trail, where it was held for 15 years. In the early 1980s, the Las Colinas Sports Club started hosting the event and has done so ever since, now raising more than $3 million annually for local youth programs.

PAST BYRON NELSON CHAMPIONS

2002 Shigeki Maruyama 266

2001 Robert Damron 263	1983 Ben Crenshaw 273	1963 No Tournament 277
2000 Jesper Parnevik 269	1982 Bob Gilder 266	1962 Billy Maxwell 277
1999 Loren Roberts 262	1981 Bruce Lietzke 281	1961 Earl Stewart, Jr. 278
1998 John Cook 265	1980 Tom Watson 274	1960 Johnny Pott 275
1997 Tiger Woods 263	1979 Tom Watson 275	1959 Julius Boros 274
1996 Phil Mickelson 265	1978 Tom Watson 272	1958 Sam Snead 272
1995 D.A. Weibring 263	1977 Raymond Floyd 276	1957 Sam Snead 264
1995 Robin Freeman 263	1976 Mark Hayes 273	1956 Don January 268
1995 Ernie Els 263	1975 Tom Watson 269	1955 No Tournament
1994 Neal Lancaster 132	1974 Brian Allin 269	1954 No Tournament
1993 Corey Pavin 270	1973 Lanny Wadkins 277	1953 No Tournament
1992 Billy Ray Brown 199	1972 Chi Chi Rodriguez 273	1952 No Tournament
1991 Nick Price 270	1971 Jack Nicklaus 274	1951 No Tournament
1990 Payne Stewart 202	1970 Jack Nicklaus 274	1950 No Tournament
1989 Jodie Mudd 265	1969 Bruce Devlin 277	1949 No Tournament
1988 Bruce Lietzke 271	1968 Miller Barber 270	1948 No Tournament
1987 Fred Couples 266	1967 Bert Yancey 274	1947 No Tournament
1986 Andy Bean 269	1966 Roberto De Vicenzo 276	1946 Ben Hogan 284
1985 Bob Eastwood 272	1965 No Tournament	1945 Sam Snead 276
1984 Craig Stadler 276	1964 Charles Coody	1944 Byron Nelson 276

THE HOUSTON OPEN

On the drive back from San Antonio's Texas Open, a group of Houston businessmen dreamed up the idea of creating their own pro tournament, the Houston Open. They formed the Houston Golf Association and held the first tourney in 1946 at River Oaks Country Club for a purse of $10,000. 1946 was the year of Byron Nelson's phenomenal string of 11 tournament wins, and he charged from behind to win the event in a dramatic Sunday finish.

Until the Houston Open found a permanent home at The Woodlands in 1975, the tournament moved around a variety of Houston locales. River Oaks, Memorial Park, Pine Forest, BraeBurn, Sharpstown, Champions Golf Club, Quail Valley, and Westwood all hosted the tournament. Eventually the event became a huge fundraiser for charity, ranking second only to the Byron Nelson.

The Woodlands' TPC course hosted the event in 1985, quickly becoming one of the favorite tracks of PGA Tour players. With its exciting series of finishing holes, the tournament is famous for exciting Sundays, with winners coming from as far back as seven shots to take the lead.

PAST HOUSTON OPEN CHAMPIONS

2003 Fred Couples	1983 David Graham 275	1963 Bob Charles 268
2002 Vijay Singh 266	1982 Ed Sneed 275	1962 Bobby Nichols 278
2001 Hal Sutton 278	1981 Ron Streck 198	1961 Jay Hebert 276
2000 Robert Allenby 275	1980 Curtis Strange 266	1960 Bill Collins 280
1999 Stuart Appleby 279	1979 Wayne Levi 268	1959 Jack Burke, Jr. 277
1998 David Duval 276	1978 Gary Player 270	1958 Ed Oliver 281
1997 Phil Blackmar 276	1977 Gene Littler 276	1957 Arnold Palmer 279
1996 Mark Brooks 274	1976 Lee Elder 278	1956 Ted Kroll 277
1995 Payne Stewart 276	1975 Bruce Crampton 273	1955 Mike Souchak 273
1994 Mike Heinen 272	1974 Dave Hill 276	1954 Dave Douglas 277
1993 Jim McGovern 199	1973 Bruce Crampton 277	1953 Cary Middlecoff 283
1992 Fred Funk 272	1972 Bruce Devlin 278	1952 Jack Burke, Jr. 277
1991 Fulton Allem 273	1971 Hubert Green 280	1951 Marty Furgol 277
1990 Tony Sills 204	1970 Gibby Gilbert 282	1950 Cary Middlecoff 277
1989 Mike Sullivan 280	1969 No Tournament	1949 John Palmer 272
1988 Curtis Strange 270	1968 Roberto De Vicenzo 274	1948 No Tournament
1987 Jay Haas 276	1967 Frank Beard 274	1947 Bobby Locke 277
1986 Curtis Strange 274	1966 Arnold Palmer 275	1946 Byron Nelson 274
1985 Raymond Floyd 277	1965 Bobby Nichols 273	
1984 Corey Pavin 274	1964 Mike Souchak 278	

GOLF & TEXAS WEATHER

Talk about things that constantly change, and Texas weather ranks right up there with stock prices, your wife's mood, and the political views of the average U.S. congressman. For reasons that confuse even reasonably competent meteorologists, it's very difficult to predict what will happen in God's heaven from day to day over the Lone Star State. For the most part, though, the terms "warm" and "dry" abound, meaning perfect for golf.

When It's Cold

Let's begin our discussion with winter. Be thankful that unlike our Northern counterparts, Texas hacks can generally play the game in some form all year round. We don't have to come up with wild games of ice golf on frozen ponds. December days in Texas can reach the 70s, and for some families living on or near a golf course, an afternoon round is part of their Christmas Day tradition.

Playing in the chill of winter not only means fewer golfers on the course, but substantial savings as well, plus a great way to keep your game sharp all year. Generally, winter mornings in Texas can be frosty but the sun comes out in the afternoon to make conditions reasonable, especially when you can deflect the wind.

The key is proper attire. Use a layered clothing strategy so you can easily add or remove items as needed. Watch out for the dreaded "Nanook of the North" syndrome that can leave you looking like a Pillsbury Doughboy, totally unable to swing a golf club. The best single investment is a shell—either a vest or windbreaker—made with tough but light GoreTex fabric to block the cold, wind, and wet. Some of these clothing items can be expensive, but think of it as good equipment rather than fancy apparel. When wearing layers, do as Tom Watson says and "Swing more slowly, so the sequence of the motion in the swing stays intact." That's good advice even on a warm day.

The fast-changing Texas weather means that you have to be prepared. In winter, a clear, 60-degree day can turn nasty in less than an hour, with temperatures dropping a good 20 degrees as the diabolical wind and slashing rain that usually accompany a cold front rush in. Have the right gear on hand (and focus on staying dry, since cold can generally be managed until you get soaked) and you can still finish your round.

On cold days, 75% of your body heat can be lost through your head, so wear a winter hat, preferably fleece that covers your ears. Special winter gloves are also available at retail stores around the state. Gloves take bit of an adjustment but are well worth it if you're determined to brave the elements, especially since your hands are how you connect with the club.

The next piece is knowing how to play winter golf. First, have the right attitude. Remove your expectations of low rounds, since it's just not the same. Take a macho approach and be ready to toughen up to the elements rather than complain about the conditions. And carefully select your playing partners, since it's easier to handle tough weather conditions when you're out there having fun with your non-whining golf companions.

Be sure to warm up more than you normally would for a summer round. Extra stretching can loosen the muscles up and make cold temps bearable. Once you've teed off, don't forget to hit "more club." The ball isn't going to carry as much when it's cold. Also, practice "knock-down" shots to keep the ball out of the swirling winds. The advantage is twofold here: You're never going to manhandle the wind, and less spin means less margin for wayward shots. Secondly, fairways that are not overseeded will be firm with dead grass, and you can take advantage of the extra roll with a lower trajectory shot.

With a little preparation, dealing with the Texas weather can be a breeze. Tote the right gear so you can avoid miserable rounds and keep the weather from ruining your day.

When It's Hot

Four simple rules: first, remain hydrated with water. That's right, water, not beer. Only water gives your body what it really needs to stay loose and cool during a sweltering day. Beer, while very enjoyable, is an extra beverage, not a water substitute. Second, wear light-colored, lightweight fabrics; dark colors absorb sunlight, light colors reflect it. Third, use plenty, and I mean plenty of SPF 30 or higher sunscreen all over before facing the sun. Fourth, seek shade wherever you can find it. Even a moment or two under a tree or canopy will help cool you down.

When It's Wet

The negatives are obvious: your hands are wet and you can't grip the club, the course plays much longer since the fairways are wet and the ball doesn't roll, and for the low handicapper, the ball refuses to spin when it's wet. However, if you make it a point to gear up and stay reasonably dry, the one true benefit to playing in the rain is that approach shots stick like darts. Also don't forget that putts roll more slowly.

When It's Windy

Accept the fact that when the Texas winds pick up, your score is going to soar. Shots with side spin will blow wildly off course. Long holes are longer, and it's impossible to stop the ball on approaches when it's at your back. Other than following the common-sense rules of adjusting your aim and striving for less trajectory, the best thing you can do is to focus on swinging slowly and smoothly. Choke up and consider taking a three-quarter swing.

Lightning

Despite what Lee Trevino said, God actually can hit a 1-iron. And he proved it to Trevino in June 1975 when a lightning bolt struck the Merry Mex, permanently damaging the vertebrae in his lower back. Luckily for Trevino, he was able to recover somewhat after a series of operations, but his days of total dominance on the PGA Tour were lost forever.

Anyone who's watched a Texas spring or summer storm blow through knows that lightning is serious stuff. Statistics prove that most lightning fatalities occur during the turbulent spring and summer months when thunderstorms and golf outings peak. Over the past 30 years, lightning has killed an average of 73 Americans and injured another 300, and five percent of these deaths occur on golf courses.

Thankfully, golf is the only sport that has regulations related to lightning. In the USGA Rules of Golf, Rule 6-8 allows players to discontinue play if they believe there is a danger from lightning.

Golfers caught off guard by a fast-moving storm should quickly determine the nearest safe place. Avoid trees, which attract lightning, and look for a large permanent building or enclosed metal vehicle.

GOLF GEAR – TEXAS WEATHER
SURVIVAL CHECKLIST

Rain suit

Gloves or mittens

Extra towels

Lip balm

Fleece hat

Umbrella

Extra socks

Extra shoes

Sunscreen

The right attitude

Golf hat

Golf bag cover

Beverages – Water and light beer when it's hot.
A nip of Schnapps when it's cold.

HUNTING, FISHING & GOLF

Once upon a March weekend, I made the drive down to the new Bear Ridge Golf Course just outside of Waco to meet a buddy from Austin. Our agenda? Play golf and catch up on lost time. We started the round at 9:00 a.m., and like giddy schoolgirls off to shop for a prom dress, excitedly weighed our afternoon post-golf options while we played. Should we fish the afternoon away at a nearby private tank, or stretch the limits of daylight (and our cash) by hacking and wagering through an additional 18 holes?

We were young men on the road with a six-pack for fuel, and the day was shining and fine like a vintage sports car. We decided to push the pedal to the floor and fit everything in. The beautifully forested course was empty for the afternoon round, so we were able to make good time. The only sounds were the rushing water of the nearby Bosque River and the squeals of my whining over hole after hole of lost bets. Once the 36-hole marathon was complete, we made a local convenience store our 19th hole and loaded up on gas, CDs, burritos, and more beer before hitting the back roads to find our fishing hole. At sundown, the sky turned orange, then purple, then blue-gray as a menacing storm front appeared: perfect Hill Country fishing weather. We hit the tank with our light tackle to cast poppers. The action was furious over the next two hours as the front blew through and the black bass danced. You could almost hear a drum roll and cymbal crash before our final cast, when my partner landed a 12-pound hefty. Afterwards, the bed of my pickup truck became our private porch—the perfect place to sit back, discuss the day's adventures, and watch the storm roll off and reveal a starry Texas sky. We talked the way old friends talk, deep into the night, and reluctantly said goodbye only when the silent alarm of responsibility sounded. He headed south and I headed north, back to our wives and jobs and cityscapes. Even the arched eyebrow of my spouse, cocked and ready like a pistol as I crept in past 3:00 a.m., could not diminish my reverie. It was a mission accomplished: golf, fishing, and friendship merged together for an unforgettable one-day adventure.

FISHING & GOLF

Texas has much to offer the sports-minded gentleman. When it comes to fishing, Texas boasts more than 5,000 square miles of inland freshwater and hundreds of creeks, rivers, and lakes, along with 624 miles of shoreline along the Gulf of Mexico. In between, many of Texas' 900-plus golf courses are routed around small ponds that serve as sanctuaries for Texas lunkers.

You won't find brochures for it, but diehard sportsmen have fished golf course irrigation lakes for ages. My West Texas youth was filled with late night/early morning incursions onto private golf courses, accompanied by a motley crew of burly buddies with coolers, tobacco, stink bait, and gear. The most successful exploits concluded with spirited late-afternoon rounds on those same courses. The fish in those country club tanks (perhaps taking after the clubs' privileged membership) were fat and satisfied, and we reeled in "golf course catfish" by the dozens. Some were filleted and prepared for the next night's fish fry, while others suffered the fate of trying to survive the chlorine in our parents' pools.

For years we've heard stories of PGA pros heading back onto the course post-round with their rods and reels to enjoy the pre-sunset solitude. Imagine Tiger and Phil kicking back with a cold one while wetting a line at some of the most prestigious courses in America.

Golf courses and water go hand in hand, so what makes for a better road trip than golf and fishing? Fishing and golf. Golf and fishing. They sound great together and complement each other so well that it's hard to resist working in a few casts during an early-morning or late-evening round. Have you ever strolled up to a clear pond hoping to retrieve the ball you just dunked into the drink, only to be dumbfounded by the size of the largemouth just floating at the surface, laughing at you? When the course is empty and the time is right, consider taking your revenge. A few casts can be had with a lightweight, pre-rigged, multi-piece rod that can be assembled and taken apart quickly and stowed in your golf bag.

A more realistic approach is to take advantage of the unbelievable benefits offered by The Great American Bass Club (214-871-0044). Formerly the Great Texas Bass Club, this association offers daily-fee tanks and lakes all over the state, and most are within a reasonable distance of anywhere you might be playing golf. Their web site, www.gtbc.com, is the perfect starting point for planning a fishing/golf road trip, with a statewide map of the possible fishing locations, a directory of lodging options, and many other fishing-related links.

HUNTING & GOLF

Hunting and golf are a perfect marriage of outdoor activities. What better way to unwind from the frustrations of golf than going out and shooting something?

Seriously, there's no better way for the modern man to celebrate the great outdoors than with a combination trip of hunting and golf. Golf represents our civilized side—a game of infinite changes executed within a clear set of rules. Modern golf courses are methodically designed and attentively manicured to keep us in line. Hunting, on the other hand, evokes our primal nature and takes us back to the wild. Stalking your game through the woods, you never know what you'll find as you spend your day immersed in country that still bears God's original signature.

And the rhythms of the two activities mesh quite well. Deer and dove hunting are best in the very early morning or late afternoons, at feeding time. What better way to spend the middle portion of your day than with a relaxed round of golf?

Hunting has always been a wildly popular pastime for outdoor-loving Texans. With more than 913,000 hunters listed we rank second nationally, spending over a billion dollars annually on the sport. This popularity, combined with the plentitude of golf courses, means it's easier than ever to plan a hunting/golf getaway. The Internet is a good starting point. We recommend the

Texas Parks & Wildlife Department's "Public Hunting Pages" at www.tpwd.state.tx.us/hunt.

Since 97% of Texas is privately owned, the use of lease agreements with private landowners is a very popular means of access to hunting. If you're not invited to a private spot, here are some ways of obtaining access to private hunting leases:

• Watch your local newspapers, which will typically have an outdoors column and carry ads for hunting leases in their classified sections.
• Call the Chamber of Commerce for the towns you'll be visiting and ask for hunting points of contact in the community.
• When driving through small-town Texas on your way to play golf, make it a point to visit the local feed or sporting goods stores and inquire about nearby hunting areas.

Starting Points for Hunting/Fishing & Golf Combinations

About 20 miles south of Junction, TX you'll run into the **Rio Bonito Ranch** (800-864-4303), a 1930s-style hacienda retreat that offers catch-and-release opportunities on several creek-fed lakes, as well as meals and lodging in a macho ranch house on a bluff that overlooks the fishing grounds. This place is an outdoorsman's dream, giving you great accommodations and access to secluded Hill Country fishing—plus it's close to some of Texas' most remote, unique golf. Rocksprings, Junction, Sonora, Menard, Mason, and Kerrville all offer small-town golf that you can play quickly and affordably, allowing you to balance all your manly activities.

The now world-famous **Lake Fork** in East Texas offers over 27,000 acres of flooded timbers, grass beds, and rocky points. It's lunker heaven for sportsmen pursuing the Texas largemouth bass. Seventeen of Texas' 25 largest hogs have been hauled from this lake. Make your tee times at The Links at Land's End in Emory and reserve a room at the **Lake Fork Lodge** (903-473-7236, www.lakeforklodge.com). The Bass and Breakfast plan runs under $100 per night, and the guide service is $275 per day.

Way out east on the Texas-Louisiana border you'll find the **Toledo Bend** and **Sam Rayburn Reservoirs**, both within an hour's drive of the outstanding courses around Lufkin and Nacogdoches. Also nearby are the **Rayburn Resort** course and the **Jasper Country Club**, as well as Carthage and Henderson if you look to the north. Call **DW's Guide Service** (409-625-4585), with facilities on both sides of Toledo Bend. Owner Darrell Lyons can hook you up in a "bass or pontoon boat for fishing and duck hunting, golf, sightseeing, and photography."

If the weekend doesn't lend itself to road-tripping, don't forget the urban option. Stay in town and fish local streams, ponds, rivers, and lakes in the morning, then golf all afternoon. Or vice versa. One example that I've used successfully in Dallas is to stalk the mutant black bass of **Bachman Creek** southeast of the Northwest Highway and Midway intersection. Park at the church on the west side of Midway and cross over the bridge on your way to the creek. Springtime is best, since the water is cool and somewhat fresh from frequent rains. Believe me, there are pools in there that hold dumb Dallas bass up to 3 pounds. There's nothing better than casting to fat Dallas-bred lunkers in the middle of the city just minutes from home. And if you don't get your fill, take your multi-piece rod to the course. Once the course clears in the late summer afternoons, you'll have the ponds all to yourself.

Finally, in addition to your web searches for possible starting points of wayward outdoors excursions, the following books are must-buys for anyone planning outdoor time in Texas.

Recommended Reading

The Roads of Texas (Shearer Publishing, 800-458-3808). This is the ultimate resource if you're looking to stimulate the road-trip-drool. Over 25,000 state and county highways and byways, as well as historical and travel information.

Flyfisher's Guide to Texas by Phil H. Shook (Wilderness Adventures Press). Similar to *The Texas Golf Bible* but written for the fly fishermen and women of Texas, this book is dry, but impressively fact-filled and complete. It's a must-have for road-trippers looking for off-the-beaten path honey holes in between golf outings.

Fly Fishing the Texas Hill Country by Bud Priddy (W. Thomas Taylor, Barksdale, TX). This grassroots-style book grew from the notes of the man who was once considered the most knowledgeable fly fisherman in the Hill Country. It goes down and dirty with all sorts of great spots where you can pull over and dig in for Texas fish. In addition to the 14 rivers and detailed access points, the newest version has commentaries by well-versed Texas contributors who offer strategies, times, and even food and lodging options.

Fly Fishing the Texas Coast by Chuck Scates and Phil H. Shook (Pruett Publishing Company). Another Texas masterpiece written by die-hard fishermen who've spent their lives on Texas waters. This book covers the entire Texas coastline in impressive detail.

Fly Shops and Guide Services

Amarillo
- •RiverFields (806-351-0980. 2465 I-40 W.)
- •Top Notch Outfitters (806-353-9468. 2617 Wolfin Village)

Austin
- •Austin Angler (512-472-4553. 312 N. Congress Ave.)
- •Orvis Austin (512-231-1645. 9333 Research Blvd.)
- •Austin Outfitters (512-329-6061. 2901 Capital of Texas Hwy.)

Dallas
- •Backwoods (972-671-0372. 1453 W. Campbell Rd., Richardson)

•Barlow's Tackle Shop (972-231-5982. 451 N. Central Expressway in Richardson)
•Dallas Flyfishers (972-618-6714)
•Orvis (214-265-1600. 10720 Preston Rd.)
•Pocket Sports Company (214-553-0347. 7235 Syracuse Dr.)
•Blue Drake Outfitters (214-350-4665. Inwood Village on Lovers Lane)

Del Rio
•Devils River Outfitters (800-7DEVILS)

Fort Worth
•Main Street Outfitters (817-332-4144. 501 Main St.)
•Backwoods (817-332-2423. 3212 Camp Bowie)

Gruene
•Gurene Outfitters (830-625-4440. 1629 Hunters Rd.)

Houston
•Angler's Edge (713-993-0208. 1141-5 Uptown Park Blvd.)
•Bass Pro Shop (281-644-2200. 500 Katy Mills Circle, Katy, TX)
•Canoesport (713-660-7000. 5808 S. Rice Ave.)
•Cut Rate Sporting Goods Inc. (713-827-7762. 10551 Telephone Rd.)
•Flywater Outfitters – Cut Rate Sporting Goods (713-827-7762. 8933 Katy Freeway)
•Orvis Houston (713-783-2111. 5848 Westheimer)
•Westbank Angler (713-961-3474. 5000 Westheimer)
•Tackle Hut (713-694-8008. 216 W. Little York Rd.)

Fredericksburg
•Hill Country Outfitters (830-997-3761. 109 E. Main St.)

Kerrville
•Pico Outdoor Company (830-895-4348. 1600 Harper Rd.)

McAllen
•Rio Grande Outfitters (956-682-0104. 905 Dove Ave.)

San Antonio
•Hill Country Outfitters (210-491-4416. 18030 Hwy. 281 North)
•Tackle Box Outfitters (210-821-5806)
•One Shot Outfitters (210-402-5344. 1870 Stone Oak Pkwy.)

Tyler
•Jones Creek (903-526-3474. 2301 S. Broadway)

A golfer fishing in a pond on a Dallas-area country club golf course.

CAMPING & GOLF

Admit it: this is one recreational combo you haven't thought of before. That's because you're locked into the mentality of golf as strictly a "means-to-an-end" activity—something you set out to do, rather than something you experience along the way. So free your mind and go with me on this theme.

Golf is often considered an uppity pursuit. This is largely because the cost to play continues to escalate, a result of rising real estate values throughout most parts of the country. Happily, these factors have very little effect in Texas, which I hence officially name "The Mecca of Affordable Golf." So, unlike denizens of the other 49 states, Texans and those smart enough to vacation here can consider the notion of combining the great game with a camping excursion. Discard your mental images of security-obsessed country club gates swinging open and shut, "Proper Attire Required" signs everywhere, and scowling golf course marshals following you suspiciously in their carts. Think open, friendly, fun. Think freedom!

Of the 428 cities and towns covered in this book, almost 300 of them have populations of under 15,000; this means that golf in Texas is much more rural than you might think. The path to the great outdoors leads through these small towns out onto the back roads. For the layman, this means affordable, low-stress golf without the crowds, allowing you to kick back "camping trip-style" and play the game as a common man, rather than as a country club snoot.

Imagine sleeping under the stars next to a rolling river, cooking steaks over a campfire, sipping a nice bottle of wine or digging into a cold, crowded cooler of ice and beer, and discussing the day's 36- or 54-hole golf marathon. And how often on a weekend camping trip are you looking for some action during the day? If there's one point that this book should hammer home, it's that wherever you go in Texas, a golf course somewhere nearby is just waiting to spice up your getaway.

All over the state, from El Paso to Texarkana, from Amarillo to South Padre, Texas is dotted with hundreds of state parks and RV parks offering the opportunity to get away and enjoy the outdoors. So don't hatch a migraine with hours and hours of advance planning. Personally, when the siren calls, I don't even spend time organizing my gear; I simply grab my clubs, a few changes of clothes (if that) and head out spontaneously down the road. Part of my adventurer's psyche is wondering where I'll find a hotel room, while the other hopes that I'll be sleeping sporadically in the car in true golf bum style. Call it a "camping & golf trip" and you can sleep in the car, haul an RV or pop-up camper, or pitch a tent and roll out the sleeping bag. You're free!

Do your homework via the Texas Parks & Wildlife Department web site (www.tpwd.state.tx.us), a veritable encyclopedia of state park information that even includes a link to parks that have golf nearby. In fact, the 9-hole Lockhart State Park Golf Course is owned by the state, and there are agreements in place with the Stephen F. Austin State Park course in San Felipe (see Southeast region) and the Lost Pines Golf Course in Bastrop State Park.

Every true golfman is a gear nut, so imagine the joy of being able to add more items to your shopping list. Instead of rolling into your local sporting goods store only for golf equipment, you can really go nuts and fill your truck with camping gear as well!

Many state parks have electrical hook-ups and showers, but if you're really packing into the sticks, consider just bringing along a few main clubs (3-wood, 6-iron, wedge, putter), so you can tape them together and carry them easily. This also makes for an interesting round that will help improve your game.

Be thinking of your general route and where you might need to stock up for supplies along the way, since you'll inevitably leave behind valuable gear. Secretly, that's always been one of the hidden pleasures for me–realizing that I've forgotten my favorite knife, but damn, now I have to stop off and pick up another one.

A few tips for your camping & golf adventures:

- Watch your clubs and keep them in a safe spot.

- Take good care of your clubs when you travel. Consider buying a hard case to protect your golf club investment.

- Gear up. Watch the weather and be ready for anything–especially in Texas. Bring multiple pairs of golf shoes or at least running shoes to serve as replacements if your main digs get wet.

- After checking the TPWD site, call their reservations number (512-389-8900) to lock in your spot, and think through the weekend and holiday issues so you avoid ridiculous crowds.

Below we've listed a few recommended camping & golf locales, all of which can be found in the appropriate region of *The Texas Golf Bible*. Also, don't forget to check the lakes around Texas. Many of them offer camping and RV facilities that are close to golf courses.

Bastrop State Park: Now offering 18 holes, the park course is improved and very affordable, and the other fine Bastrop courses are close by (ColoVista and Pine Forest).

Boone RV Park, Lampasas: This RV park is the perfect home base for all-day golf marathons at the wonderful Hancock Park Golf Course.

Fort Clark Springs, Bracketville: Complete with an 84-space RV and tent camping park, as well as hiking trails and miles of creekfront fishing, this popular Winter Texan retreat west of San Antonio is a good place to stay on the way to Del Rio, which has two 9-holers, as well as Uvalde's new and improved 18-hole track.

Guadalupe River State Park: About 15 miles east of Boerne, this park is near Tapatio Springs and Comfort's Buckhorn course.

Martin Dies State Park, Jasper: You can canoe on Steinhagen Lake, and since this one is in the sticks, far from civilization, there aren't many folks. Try to work onto the Jasper Country Club, and the Rayburn Country Resort golf course is nearby.

New Braunfels: Loaded with RV parks, Guadalupe River frontage camping locations, and other Canyon Lake locales, this is a hotspot for camping and golf. And it's not too far out in the boonies if you start itching for city life again.

Riverside Park, Bay City: This city-run park with RV hook-ups and showers is on the banks of the Colorado River, with the 18-hole Rio Colorado Golf Course next door.

Stephen F. Austin State Park: Near Sealy in the town of San Felipe, TX, and less than an hour from Houston and San Antonio, this park is a great place to bring your mountain bike, and you can also work in a little fishing in the Brazos River.

Schreiner State Park, Kerrville: With the Guadalupe River rolling through, fishing and canoeing are popular breaks from golf time on one of Kerrville's tracks, the Lady Bird Johnson Golf Course in Fredericksburg, or even the goat track in Rocksprings.

CAMPING & GOLF SURVIVAL LIST

Toilet paper

Sunscreen

Coolers, large and small

Insect repellent

First aid kit

Blocks of ice for keeping food and beverages cold

Music

Flashlights

Extra towels for cleaning purposes

Compasses

Folding chairs

Clothesline for hanging up wet clothing

Tarps for covering stuff and a poncho

Camp cooking set, with pots, frying pan, small plates, and cups

Fold-out picnic tables and chairs

GOLF & THE ROMANTIC WEEKEND

OPEN with you, in a smoking jacket, holding a flute of fine champagne. The lights are low and a fire crackles in the fireplace. You have a devious grin on your face, as if you know something diabolical. ENTER your wife (or girlfriend) in a satin teddy. CUT to you ogling her, and her looking back at you. ZOOM in to the red rose, plucked from your pocket and now in your mouth as you pull her close and begin a slow tango. You dance. The scent of love is in the air. Finally, as you execute a dramatic dip, we DISSOLVE to a CLOSE UP of you whispering into her ear, "Darling, I love you. I must have you. Let's go play golf!"

Okay, so the script needs a little work.

The truth is, it's not easy to combine golf and romance in a way that will satisfy both parties, so most couples don't even try. What a mistake! I'm here to report that it can be done. It has been done!

The essence of a romantic weekend is shared happiness. Guys, that's sharing as in give-and-take. Use your brain pan and put her needs first. You've already decided on golf as the central activity, so plan the rest of the trip around what she likes, even if that means antique shopping. Balance is the key for all aspects of the romantic golf weekend.

A romantic getaway warrants special accommodations, a place that invites you to linger with your loved one. It doesn't have to be a four-star resort, but a place with lots of atmosphere, like a cabin hidden in the woods. The more character, the better.

Next, consider what she will do while you're playing golf. The best option by far is a menu of nurturing spa treatments: massage, manicure, hydrotherapy, facials, etc. As she basks in the pampering most women dream about, you are free to drink in the glories of the great game, and perhaps a nice steam afterward, with total impunity.

While there is something to be said for spontaneity, the best romantic/golf getaway requires thoughtful preparation. As your Juliet sees the weekend unfold, she will appreciate the time you spent attending to special touches (booking treatments in advance, having flowers in the room, putting a special card on her pillow). Sure, discussing what each of you want can be helpful; still, some of my greatest romantic successes have been the result of secretive planning and ingenious surprise. One planning tip: be sure to let your partner know what to bring. As we all know, clothing is important to the ladies, and they like to know what sort of social situation they're getting into. Leaving them unprepared is a major mood-killer. If the trip is a secret, then contact her best friend and pack accordingly.

The bottom line: If you work hard to make sure she feels pampered and loved, she will not begrudge you some time on the links. And if you're an avid golfer, one of the best things you can do is take her along in the cart and show her what you love about golf. Let her experience the game from your perspective. Women eat that stuff up. That sharing stuff.

A romantic golf excursion should be a mix of outdoor and indoor fun. It should challenge and restore you, leaving an imprint on your souls forever as well as creating fun, intimate memories that the two of you can re-live over and over.

For specific golf and romance packages, check the "Golf Schools and Resorts" chapter for the various locales around the state. Contact the resorts or do some searching on their web sites for details on how you might combine your love of golf with your love of spouse. If you can't find specific information, then make the call and ask pointed questions about how to set the weekend up for love.

THE SINGLES GOLF ASSOCIATION

Based in the Dallas-Fort Worth Area, the Singles Golf Association is an impressive 120-member group of avid single golfers that get together for 18 formal tournaments per year, and dozens of other casual golf outings. And it isn't a meat market – these folks stress the traditional aspects of the game and require that prospective members have a legitimate golf game as well as a good understanding of the rules and etiquette. "Mulligan money" from their tournament outings goes towards Junior Golf donations. After starting out with two female members and their group of guy friends, their eight years of existence have resulted in about ten marriages and countless other hookups. And while most of them range in age from 30-50, they just recently booted out a 70-plus-year-old member who fell in love and tied the knot. For information, call 972-867-2313.

BUSINESS & GOLF

Civilization may be falling apart, the ozone is disappearing, and culture is in the crapper. But for the business person who loves golf, there's never been a better time to be alive. More than ever, even the bean counters in Accounting are willing to admit that a round of golf is a small but very powerful tool of goodwill in the battle to gain new clients. In the old days, taking a client out for 18 holes involved faking a major illness; today, no Watergate-style cover-up is necessary. The smart executive who secures "face time" with the client over a round of golf is lauded as an example of "hustle"...even if he's really a hustler!

Golf and business go hand in hand, sure, but not everyone understands the art of blending the two. This brand of golf is more about fellowship than score. Call it "golf with a purpose"—a game to help achieve other social and financial ends. If your playing partner is sizing up a 20-foot putt while you're trying to negotiate a tricky lie in the bunker, you quickly become comrades in pursuit of a common goal: a respectable score. Later, when it's time to close the deal, you'll have a deeper understanding of each other.

Where else but a golf course can executives spend a leisurely four hours in such a private, sociable setting? What better way to cement a relationship with a client than lifting a glass together after a round? Believe it or not, there is solid behavioral science to back up the fact that men open up and share more freely when they engage in an activity, such as golf, as opposed to a formal conversational environment, like a meeting.

There is a distinct difference between playing golf with your buddies versus playing golf in a business setting, and you'll need some savvy when dealing with employees, partners, or customers on the golf course. How well you comport yourself over those 18 holes—balancing business and friendship, dealing with competition and success—suggests to others how you might behave in the boardroom or around the bargaining table. Since your actions will speak volumes, here are some suggestions on how to send the right message and make it through the round.

Learn the etiquette

Follow the basic protocols: stay quiet when your partners are hitting and always treat the course with the utmost respect. Don't make your partners lose face because you've stepped in their putting line or failed to rake a bunker. The bumbling hack who finds himself (dis)gracing the fairways of an upscale private club will embarrass himself and lose the deal.

Gracefully engage your partners

Don't worry about closing the deal during a round. Instead, focus on getting to know your partners. Be sure to find out personal things like the names of their spouse and children, and what they like to do away from the office. Also, know when it's appropriate to talk business. Avoid diving into your core business conversations right away, and play close attention to your golf partners' moods while looking for the signals of opportunistic timing.

Relax and be low-key

Don't be intimidated by the situation. Show clients you can handle the pressure with good humor; otherwise, you'll tense up and doom your chances of pulling off an effective golf swing. Golf is difficult enough as it is! If you start hacking it around, prove your mettle by keeping your composure and taking it like a man. Announce your high score with a smile. Besides, your partners might not even notice since they'll be so focused on their own games.

You want people to remember how enjoyable it was playing with you, so watch how you react to bad bounces and swing crises. If you lose your temper, you're done. If you get used to dealing calmly with struggles on the course, it will help your overall game even in casual golf situations.

Don't offer advice

It's okay to talk shop and discuss the latest swing fads, but if your partner is hacking away, refrain from opening your mouth with inappropriate swing tips. You don't know what the hell you're talking about, anyway. Just play and have fun.

Learn to read people

The best approach to the dicey details of business and golf is to learn how to read people on the golf course. Are they serious about the game, and how do they approach their decisions during the round? Knowing the answers to those questions helps you feel easier in the setting, and can even clue you in to the appropriate timing to initiate that important business discussion you've been waiting for.

Golf nuts avoid business discussions on the course. They love the game and want to soak it all in, and would probably prefer playing golf on vacation rather than in a business setting.

Power executives, on the other hand, strongly associate golf with business. They love the camaraderie of the game as well as the competition. Be ready to gamble a dollar or two since they believe it makes the game more enjoyable. Risk is everything to the gambling golfer and he'll do anything to get an edge, sometimes pushing it too hard to form a true bond with a more emotionally balanced golfer.

Then there's the non-serious golfer—the one who doesn't compete or track his handicap. This is the guy who plays the game for fun and relaxation, and enjoys the camaraderie more than anything else.

THE ESSENCE OF GOLF MACHISMO
Handicapping, Scoring, Statistics, Rules, Etiquette, Statistics, Gamesmanship, Wagering, Games, Style, Etc.

machismo: 1. A strong or exaggerated sense of masculinity stressing attributes such as physical courage, virility, domination of women, and aggressiveness; 2. An exaggerated sense of strength or toughness

Follow me on this one if you will. For the purposes of this chapter, machismo, used in a light-hearted yet somewhat serious sense, is a term used to describe someone who has the savvy and experience to handle themselves confidently and effectively in every situation. Clint Eastwood's characters always smoothly deals with outlaws, James Bond always handles things better than we would, and Harrison Ford's Indiana Jones always efficiently takes care of business.

The bottom line: Knowing the intricacies of the often misunderstood aspects of the game such as rules and etiquette, or gamesmanship and wagering, sets you apart from the layman. It breeds confidence. It is machismo.

EXAMPLES OF GOLF MACHISMO

A few years back when the Ryder Cup came to Brookline, Phil Mickelson and Jarmo Sandelin found themselves dueling at the par 3 No. 2 hole. After sticking his shot close to the pin, the diminutive Sandelin looked at Mickelson in anticipation of him conceding the putt. In what might be considered a rare macho gesture for the happy-go-lucky non-major champion, Mickelson reached into his pocket and pulled out a ball marker for Sandelin, who subsequently missed the putt.

Slammin' Sam Snead never won the PGA Tournament, but he definitely had the chance in 1947. In those days the championship was decided by match play, and Snead and Lew Worsham went toe to toe for 36 holes, with Worsham routinely giving the Slammer the short gimmes. Yet on the final hole, Worsham waxed machismo and stared in silence after Snead lagged his putt within the leather. Flustered, Snead butchered the putt and lost the match. Another story says that Snead left the putt way short, then as he set up to putt again, Worsham interrupted by asking Snead "Are you sure you're away?"—upsetting the Slammer enough to blow the putt. Either way, history shows that golf machismo was the order of the day, resulting in the edge Worsham needed to overcome the favored golfer.

The 2002 U.S. Open at Bethpage, NY was marred by nasty weather, and conditions became virtually unplayable despite the USGA's insistence on continuance of play. Tiger Woods persevered and kept his mouth shut. Sergio Garcia whined like a baby about the unfair conditions. Tiger followed the creed of the golf macho and won the tournament. Sergio, a fiery Spaniard, uncharacteristically avoided the machismo option and proved that he was the lesser man.

HANDICAPPING

I have a few degenerate buddies who will immediately flip to this chapter expecting tips on how to handle horse (or even dog) wagering at one of the eclectic Texas tracks. Sorry, guys, but this isn't about picking a winner. This section is here because for every avid golfer who uses the handicap system effectively, there are a dozen weekend hacks who have no idea of how the system works.

While the USGA has done an admirable job of designing and promoting the handicap system, many of us don't take the time to use it, so keeping an accurate handicap falls by the wayside. Some of us use the system sporadically and make a guess at our handicap level when asked. Others never use it and don't care. It doesn't have to be that way. Knowledge is power, my friends, and knowing your actual handicap will help you in a variety of ways.

Without getting into the details of how course ratings and slope are computed, understand that the United States Golf Association uses those figures to determine how many strokes a given hack should get in an attempt to level the playing field for everyone. Because of this system, any two players can theoretically go out and compete against one another. Think about it. You can't do that in any other sport.

TEXAS HANDICAP NETWORK

In an effort to improve handicapping, the Texas Golf Association and the South Texas Amateur Golf Association have joined forces to market and support the Golfers Handicap and Information Network (GHIN) by creating the Texas Handicap Network. The Texas aura of having a multitude of quality players has been tainted by the image of players with mystery handicaps. This effort will help get all golfers on the same system and allow for consistent handicap administration, while also providing additional technical support at the club level.

In another classic scene from Caddyshack, the Judge asks: "You don't keep score? Then how do you measure yourself against other golfers?" Ty (Chevy Chase): "By height." That's funny, but it's a shame because a golfer without a handicap really can't compete at any meaningful level. Establishing a handicap is easy: Simply play ten or more rounds, keep your score, and turn in the score-cards with two signatures: yours and one of your partner's.

Many public facilities have their own handicap computers, so choose a convenient area course where you play frequently to turn in your scores. You don't have to be a member of a club, which is nice for the roving golfer. At any given time, your handicap is the average of the 10 best scores of your previous 20 rounds. As a general rule, your handicap is the number of strokes over par it should take you each time out. Thus, a 10 handicapper should shoot an 82 on a par 72 course.

The most important point to this entire discussion is that handicapping is imperative when you're playing for cash. Most of your golf will typically be matches with other players. If the computer posts you as a 12 and your buddy as a 17, you'll give him 5 strokes a round. Circle the five most difficult holes on the card, and don't forget that you're spotting him a stroke on those holes.

In order to reach the next level and give yourself a huge advantage over 98% of all other golfers, there are certain rules you need to follow every time you play:

- Know the rules of golf and play by them. If you don't know them, start learning.

- Eliminate the psychological crutch of needing to improve your lie. Always play the ball as it lies. That's the way the game is meant to be played.

- Get into the habit of knocking down the short putts to finish a hole. If you start relying on your buddies to give you the "gimmes," you're in trouble when it counts the most.

- Start counting every shot. None of what I've mentioned above applies until you follow this basic tenet. Swallow your pride and write your real score down every time—even the quadruples that so often ruin a decent round.

KEEPING SCORE

While keeping score helps you measure your progress against the game, the courses, and even other golfers, it's easy to get too caught up in how many shots it takes you to make it through the day. Have some perspective and remember that scoring isn't everything. Many times you'll be playing matches against other players or teams, and the only thing that matters is how you come out compared to your opponents. Remember both sides of it and balance your approach to achieve the most enjoyment from the game. If you're having a bad hole, concede it and move on.

RULES

The rules of golf, while important, can sometimes be totally overwhelming, and are often too much to grasp for the average golfman. Understand that your knowledge of the rules of golf will develop over time. The best approach is to start becoming aware of certain scenarios while you play, then over time you'll patiently absorb the intricacies of the game. Watch more accomplished golfers on the tee and on the green to see how they behave. When they lose a golf ball, how do they handle it? Eventually you'll get the hang of the basics, and if you start playing frequently the rest will fall into place. Below we've included a few important rules from the United States Golf Association's *The Rules of Golf*.

- Dropping the ball: Lift and clean the ball, find the nearest spot where you have complete relief and mark it with a tee, measure one club length from that mark (use your driver), then naturally drop the ball.

- Off the tee: Tee it up between the markers, not in front, and no more than two club lengths behind them.

- The lost ball: You have five minutes to find it, then you must return to the tee or to the point from which you last hit the ball and play another. It'll cost you stroke and distance. If you slice it wildly off the tee but you think it might still be in, hit a provisional to avoid the long walk back. When it's lost in a water hazard, drop behind the hazard keeping the point where the ball last crossed the hazard between you and the hole. And don't forget to add a one-stroke penalty.

- Unplayable lie: You can play from where you hit your last shot, drop within two club lengths of where the ball is (no closer to the hole), or you can go back as much as you like, provided that you keep the same line to the hole. Whatever you decide, give yourself a one-stroke penalty.

- Play it as it lies: It's a hard thing to get in the hang of, but once you do you'll never play another way.

- Ball in a hazard: Remember that when you're in a hazard (bunker, water, etc.), you cannot touch the ground or water with your club before impact.

ETIQUETTE

Similar to grasping the rules, learning the ins and outs of proper golf etiquette takes time, and is something you should patiently pursue as you succumb to the lures of the game. Entire books have been written about golf etiquette, and we've included a few pointers below, but just remember that the golf machismo knows how to handle himself on the course.

- As a general rule, smile and keep your mouth shut. Don't go crazy in complimenting every shot your partner hits. Don't immediately dive into questioning your partners about what they do for a living, where they live, etc. The quiet golfman is a more confident golfman. It will help you in match play and make you more likable to other players. Rare men like Lee Trevino can pull it off, but most of us are better off in zipping it shut. Another point that goes along with keeping quite is to avoid giving advice to other golfers.

- Respect the course and the Golf Gods, and repair divots and ball marks.

- For general hacks, "ready golf," which means forgetting about whose honor it is, is the best way to play. Even if you don't play that way, be ready to hit at all times.

- If you hack it into another group, always, always, always yell "FORE!"

- Don't lollygag at the turn. Get your stuff and go.

- When you're done on a hole, get the hell off the green. Write your scores down elsewhere and make room for the duffers behind you.

- Avoid the drunk-college-guy trick of tearing ass all over the course with your cart. Keep it away from the greens and on the cart path at all times. Watch for the group in front of you and refrain from slamming on the brakes while they're on the tee.

STATISTICS

The number of stats kept for PGA Tour players is amazing: average driving distance, sand saves, trips to the bathroom. While tracking all of your golf statistics is burdensome, the dedicated hack will enjoy the game much more by keeping a few basic statistics in addition to score. Things like how many greens you hit in regulation (G.I.R.), how many fairways hit off the tee, how many putts averaged, and how many strokes it takes to get down from a greenside bunker help you detect strengths and weaknesses in your game. And if you wisely elect to invest in golf instruction, these stats are extremely beneficial to your pro.

GAMESMANSHIP AND WAGERING

The USGA's "Policy on Gambling" section within its Rules of Golf states that: "The USGA does not object to informal wagering among individual golfers or teams of golfers when the players in general know each other. Participation in the wagering is optional...and the amount of money involved is such that the primary purpose is playing the game for enjoyment." Translation: bet away, boys!

In fact, nowhere is betting more popular than on the PGA Tour. During Tuesday practice rounds, pros bet thousands with each other. And when you see two pros lining up putts on the practice green before a round, you can count on the fact that there's money on the line. Indeed, the PGA Tour itself is really a gamble: every week, 156 players pay to tee it up on Thursday knowing that almost half of them will miss the cut and go home without making a penny. The other half will stay and compete for purses of up to $6 million. "Golf is just a gambling sport," says Dallas' Harrison Frazar, a UT grad and tour player since 1996. "We spend $3,000 to $5,000 a week just to come out and see if we can make more money. In a sense, we're betting on ourselves."

For the rest of us, golf is recreation, a way to have fun. We get plenty of stress at the office, so that added pressure of a hefty bet can ruin the whole enterprise. What we're talking about is betting for fun—a small, reasonable amount—to enhance the experience and build camaraderie. Some old codgers even play for dimes. In other words, it's not the amount, it's the bragging rights, and the chance to slap a friend on the back and say, "Hey, I just got into your wallet!"

There are a million games and types of wagers invented just for golf. We've chosen just a handful that are popular at courses around Texas. Try them out the next time you and the gang get together. By the way, in most of these games, you need to take handicaps into consideration and figure out who gets strokes from whom on each hole. An extra stroke can make a huge difference to the outcome.

GOLF BETTING GAMES

BINGO, BANGO, BONGO: A simple game that can be played with two, three, or four players. Each hole has three available points, with each point equaling, say, a dollar. The first ball hit on the green—"Bingo"—wins a dollar. The person closest to the pin after every player's ball is on the green— "Bango"—is the second point. "Bongo," the first ball in the hole, earns the last buck.

HAMMER: A popular country club game that also is a favorite of tour players during practice rounds. The "hammer" is open at the start of each hole. If at any point of playing the hole a player believes he has the other player beat, he can "hammer" his opponent. That player has a choice of conceding the hole or accepting the hammer, which doubles the bet. If that player believes he gains the upper hand on the next shot, he can hammer back. So a bet can be doubled multiple times. Beware overusing the hammer late in the round: this can get expensive.

HONEST JOHN: On the first tee, each player predicts what score he will shoot that day. The player who finishes closest to his prediction without going over wins the pot.

LAS VEGAS: Play this game with four players divided into two teams. On each hole, each team combines its score to come up with the lowest possible two-digit number. In other words, if one teammate gets a 3 and the other gets a 4, their score is 34. If the other team posts two 4s, its score is 44 and it loses the hole by 10 points.

NASSAU: The classic golf betting game involves three match-play wagers: front nine, back nine and entire round. Perfect for two guys just having a leisurely round.

NINES: The perfect three-man game, probably invented by guys who could never scare up a foursome. Each hole has a total value of nine points. The player with the lowest score earns five points, the second lowest earns three points, and the highest earns one point. When there is a two-way tie for lowest score, those players get four points. When two players tie for the high score, they get two points each. A three-way tie is worth three points.

QUARTERS: A game designed to pass the time while you're standing on the tee box waiting to hit. Using only their drivers, players "tee off" from the tee marker of the men's tees and must hit to the tee marker of the ladies tees, striking it, then hitting back up to the men's tee marker. Each shot is worth a quarter, with the loser paying the winner 25 cents (or whatever amount) for every stroke above the winning total.

SKINS: You've probably seen the big-money version of this on TV. Players place a dollar value per hole. If one player gets the lowest score on a hole, he wins one skin. If two or more players tie for low score, the skin is carried over to the next hole, and so on, until a hole is won outright.

THOUSAND-DOLLAR-NO-BOGEY: A popular game among pros during British Open and Masters practice rounds. A foursome decides before the round that if anyone in the group plays bogey-free, he gets $1,000 from each of his playing partners.

TREES: A game made popular by Dallasite Lee Trevino and his buddies. Each time a player hit a tree, he had to pay the others in the foursome $10. If a ball bounced off one tree and hit another, each playing partner got $20.

WOLF: Players take turns on each tee being the designated "wolf." The wolf hits first and then watches the tee shots of the other players. The wolf then chooses one as his partner to play against the others. Or, the wolf may choose to play the others on his own. Some call that "pigging it."

GOLF BETTING LINGO

FORT WORTH RULES: This rather crude rule states that "Any male golfer whose tee shot does not go further than the ladies tees must play the rest of the hole with his manhood exposed from his trousers."

PRESS: A bet made by a player who is behind in a match. Many match bets have automatic presses. For example, if a player is one or two holes down, an additional bet will begin from that hole onward. Often, on the 9th or 18th hole there is a get-even bet that enables the player who is behind to recoup his losses.

SANDBAGGER: A golfer who exaggerates his handicap or purposely plays poorly the first hole in an attempt to lure an unsuspecting opponent into a higher bet.

TRASH: Sometimes referred to as "garbage" or "junk," these are smaller side bets. Players earn money for getting up and down from a greenside bunker ("sandies"), hitting the green off the tee on a par 3 ("greenies"), making par despite hitting a tree ("woodies"), or sinking a putt longer than two flag sticks ("polies"). Reverse-trash means loss of money for three-putts, hitting a ball into a bunker or water, or making worse than a bogey.

STYLE

These days a few professional golfers have made it a point to dress uniquely in an attempt to create their own special brand, thus capitalizing on the advertising and sponsorship dollars that often follow being a celebrity along the lines of Dennis Rodman or Deion Sanders. Jesper Parnevik wears his hat pointed to the sky and tight, colorful clothes, and is perhaps the only one who call pull off his different look. Charles Howell goes too far with his tight pants and ridiculous colors, and Aaron Baddeley isn't much different, combining outrageous threads with a white belt. However how can one argue with the suave, casual look of Freddy Couples, or the classic Polo-draped Davis Love III? Yet no matter what you wear, the important thing is how you wear it, so we've included a few suggestions on how you can ensure a decent look on the course.

- Wear your pants on your waist for a balanced look. The belt buckle should always be visible.

- Be sure that your pants aren't too short, and that the cuffs have a slight break that rests on your shoes. A nice-fitting pair of pants will not allow your fans to see your socks.

- The proper shirt-sleeve length is right at the elbow, and should not hang down any further on your arms.

- The shoulder seam should rest just off the shoulder blade.

- Avoid Dork Syndrome and refrain from buttoning your shirt all the way to the top. A little bit of a gap is best.

- Avoid the David Duval look and refrain from wearing shades on the course. It just doesn't work.

APPENDICES

GOLF ORGANIZATIONS

American Junior Golf Association . . . . .770-998-4653 . . . . .www.ajga.org
American Society of Golf Course Architects . . . . .312-372-7090 . . . . .www.golfdesign.org
Association of Disabled American Golfers . . . . . . .303-922-5228 . . .www.discovercolorado.com
Golf Writers Association of America . . . . .313-442-1481 . . . . .www.gwaa.com
Ladies Professional Golf Association . . . . .904-254-8800 . . . . .www.lpga.com
Minority Golf Association of America . . . . .516-288-8255 . . . . .www.mgaa.com
National Association of Left-Handed Golfers . . . . .800-844-6254 . . . . .www.dca.net/golf
National Golf Foundation . . . . .800-NGF-2500 . . . . .www.ngf.org
PGA Tour . . . . .904-285-3700 . . . . .www.pgatour.com
Professional Clubmakers Society . . . . .800-548-6094 . . . . .www.proclubmakers.org
Professional Golfers' Association (PGA) . . . . .407-624-8400 . . . . .www.pga.com
Royal Canadian Golf Association . . . . .905-849-9700 . . . . .www.rcga.com
Texas Golf Association . . . . .214-468-8942 . . . . .www.txga.org
United States Golf Association (USGA) . . . . .908-234-2300 . . . . .www.usga.com

MAGAZINES

Avid Golfer Magazine . . . . .972-550-5000 . . .www.avidgolferonline.com
Austin Golf Magazine . . . . .www.austingolfmag.com
Golf Digest . . . . .800-727-4653 . . . . .www.golfdigest.com
Golf Illustrated . . . . .918-491-6100 . . . . .www.golfillustrated.com
Golf Magazine . . . . .www.golfmagazine.com
Golf Tips . . . . .319-820-1500 . . . . . . .www.golftipsmag.com
Golfweek . . . . .407-345-5500 . . . . .www.golfweek.com
Golf World 800-727-4653
Scratch Golfer Magazine . . . . .469-384-0061 . . . . . .www.scratch.golfer.com
Texas Golfer Magazine . . . . .713-623-4613 .www.texasgolfermagazine.com

TEXAS TRAVEL BOOKS

Backroads of Texas In it's fourth edition, this book has loads of information
and recommended itineraries for Texas travel. Lone Star Books. Copyright
2000 by Gulf Publishing Co.

The Roads of Texas Better than any atlas you'll reference when traveling in
Texas, this amazing publication has every road in Texas. Shearer Publishing
(800-458-3808).

GOLF ON THE WEB

Of the thousands of available golf sites, here are a few that stand out. Many
of these are specific to Texas.

americangolf.com   Check it out for discounts for American Golf courses
in Texas and throughout the US.

austingolfmag.com   A new magazine focused on Texas' greatest city and
its golf.

avidgolferonline.com DFW-based *Avid Golfer Magazine's* online version of
their entertaining publication.

buygolf.com	A huge online retail store, they also provide PGA Tour information and a fantasy golf game.
clubcorpgolf.com	Offers discounts for Club Corp courses in Texas and throughout the US.
DFW4golf.com	Look for deals in the Dallas-Fort Worth area.
eaglgolf.com	Offers discounts for courses in Texas and throughout the US.
edwinwatts.com	One of the best online retail sites with a massive inventory of equipment, clothing, and all things golf.
global.fitness.com	Great site for all sorts of fitness topics that can help you with your golf game.
globalgolfguide.com	A worldwide golf course locator that allows you to make travel plans on the site.
gogogolf.net	An internet tee time service that also offers discounts.
golf.com	Huge site with anything and everything golf related.
golfball.com	Find articles, equipment information, and golf tips on this site.
golfcircuit.com	Great site that provides a search engine specifically geared to golf sites.
golfcourse.com	While they still don't have all of the Texas courses, they have information on thousands of courses in the US.
golfcpons.com	Another site that offers discounts via coupons for all kinds of courses.
golfdigest.com	Excellent web version of *Golf Digest* magazine.
golfdirect.com	North American Golf Directory list of golf courses, resorts, and schools across the US.
golfinDallas.net	A site specifically for City of Dallas courses. Discounts offered here as well.
golfQ-com	Great place for discounts, including a frequent-player program and a venue for earning points towards free rounds.
golfquesttexas.com	A great site with outstanding photography of Texas golf courses.
golfsmith.com	An awesome retail online site that often offers web discounts for their already reasonably-priced items.
golfsocietyUSA.com	A fee-based site that offers discounts throughout the US.
golfTexas.com	Part of the world-wide travelgolf.com umbrella, the folks who write about Texas courses here do a phenomenal job.
golf-Golfing.com	Member site that offers discounted fees for 12 area courses.
golfpassbook.com	Lots of deals here on Texas courses (green fees, schools, and travel).
golfresorts.com	More than 600 links to golf resorts around the world.

golfweek.com	The country's premiere online golf magazine. Get this and the print version if you are a golf fan.
lpga.com	The official site of the LPGA Tour, where the ladies are slowly becoming more and more attractive.
mrgolf.com	A golf etiquette page that is a great resource for freshening up on your golf savvy every now and then.
NTPGA.com	For $50 you can buy a LinksPass that provides discounts across North Texas.
pelzgolf.com	Master Dave Pelz' web site with great instruction and advice on the short game and putting.
pga.com	The official site of the PGA of America, complete with tournament information, player profiles, and other tidbits.
STPGA.com	Receive discounts for South Texas with their GolfPass.
teachkidsgolf.com	Great site for dads like me who want their kids to learn the game. Not bad for adults who need to learn, either.
texasgolfnetwork.com	A member site that provides discounts for about 40 DFW-area courses.
TXGA.org	Texas Golf Association web site.
USGA.com	The official site of the United States Golf Association, complete with rules, handicap information, and much more.

TEXAS STAY & PLAY RESORT DESTINATIONS

April Sound Country Club and Resort	Montgomery	409-588-1101
Barton Creek Conference Resort and Country Club	Austin	800-336-6157
Columbia Lakes Resort and Conference Center	West Columbia	800-231-1030
Del Lago Resort Hotel and Conference Center	Montgomery	800-335-5246
The Falls Resort	New Ulm	409-992-3123
Flying L Guest Ranch	Bandera	800-292-5134
Four Seasons Resort and Club at Las Colinas	Irving	972-717-0700
Horseshoe Bay Resort and Conference	Horseshoe Bay	800-252-9363
The Houstonian Hotel Club and Spa	Houston	713-680-2626
Hyatt Bear Creek Resort	D/FW Airport	972-453-1234
Hyatt Regency Hill Country Resort	San Antonio	210-647-1234
Lago Vista Clubs and Resort	Lago Vista	800-288-1882
Lajitas Resort and Golf Club	Lajitas	877-525-4287
Columbia Lakes Resort and Conference Center	West Columbia	800-231-1030
Lakeway Inn	Austin	800-525-3929
Mill Creek Resort and Country Club	Salado	254-947-5141
Rancho Viejo Resort and Country Club	Brownsville	800-531-7400
The Radison Hotel and Conference Center	Denton	940-565-8499
Rayburn Country Resort and Country Club	Sam Rayburn	800-882-1442
Tanglewood Resort	Pottsboro	800-833-6569
Tapatio Springs Resort and Country Club	Boerne	800-999-3299
Waterwood National Resort and Country Club	Huntsville	409-891-5211
White Bluff on Lake Whitney	Whitney	888-944-8325
The Woodlands Resort	The Woodlands	281-367-1100
Westin La Cantera	San Antonio	800-446-5387

TEXAS GOLF RETAIL STORES

Abilene	West Texas Discount Golf	(915) 695-2241
Abilene	Evans Golf	(915) 691-9607
Abilene	Golf Etc. Abilene	(915) 698-4653
Addison	Dallas Golf Company	(972) 866-0007
Allen	Golf Etc. Allen	(972) 396-0029
Amarillo	Golf USA of Amarillo	(806) 358-9932
Amarillo	Golf Headquarters	(806) 358-1385
Arlington	Wally's Discount Golf Shops	(817) 261-9301
Arlington	Edwin Watts Golf	(817) 861-6677
Arlington	Custom Craft Golf	(817) 543-1936
Arlington	Golfsmith Golf Center	(817) 557-5077
Arlington	Burton & Associates	(817) 460-2268
Austin	Golfsmith International	(512) 837-4810
Austin	Instant Replay Golf	(512) 454-6111
Austin	Golfsmith Golf Center	(512) 502-9231
Austin	Golfsmith Golf Center	(512) 821-4050
Austin		igogolf-com
Austin	Fairways Women's Golf	(512) 330-0015
Bee Cave	Golf USA of Austin	(512) 402-9666
Brownsville	Golf Headquarters	(956) 541-2952
Bryan	Pro Golf Discount	(979) 776-4653
Carrollton	Lou's Golf Shop	(972) 446-1418
Cedar Hill	Golf USA of Cedar Hill	(469) 272-9500
College Station	Golf Etc. College Station	(979) 696-2733
Copperas Cove	C C Golf	(254) 547-1999
Corpus Christi	Edwin Watts Golf	(361) 852-0358
Corpus Christi	Golf Shop	(361) 991-8101
Corpus Christi	Pro Golf Discount	(361) 985-9944
Crosby	Golf Ball Warehouse	(281) 328-7851
Dallas	Edwin Watts Golf	(214) 352-9431
Dallas	Wally's Discount Golf Shops	(214) 637-2944
Dallas	Edwin Watts Golf	(972) 404-4424
Dallas	Golfsmith	(972) 991-9255
Dallas	PGA Tour Shop Dallas	(972) 574-3600
Dallas	GolfTEC	(972) 239-4700
Deer Park	Swede Discount Golf	(281) 479-0982
Denton	Second Hand Sports	(940) 898-8733
Eagle Lake	Johnny's Sport Shop	(979) 234-3516
El Paso	K & W Golf Shop	(915) 755-2500
El Paso	Ramons Golf Shop	(915) 566-0449
El Paso	Go Golf	(915) 771-9460
Flower Mound	Just Golf	(972) 691-2582
Fort Worth	Tour Line Golf	(817) 560-4700
Fort Worth	Golfworld Unlimited, Inc-	(817) 457-9345
Fort Worth	Supreme Golf	(817) 731-4441
Fort Worth	Target Golf	(817) 451-1967
Fort Worth	Supreme Golf	(817) 877-5484
Fort Worth	Golf Etc. City View	(817) 731-3098
Fort Worth	Golf Etc. Lake Worth	(817) 238-1333
Frisco	Golf Etc. Frisco	(972) 668-8033
Gainesville	Second Hand Sports	(940) 668-8343
Garland	Dallas Golf Company	(972) 270-0989
Garland	Wally's Discount Golf Shops	(972) 494-2226
Georgetown	Golf on the Square	(512) 869-8714
Granbury	Golf Etc. of America, Inc-	(817) 279-7888
Granbury	North Texas Golf World	(817) 579-0432

Grapevine	MacBirdie Golf Gifts	(972) 874-8565
Harlingen	Golf Headquarters	(956) 423-7182
Harlingen	Elliott's Custom Golf	(956) 428-5448
Houston	Edwin Watts Golf	(281) 890-3340
Houston	Joe's Golf & Tennis	(713) 977-7575
Houston	Golf & Tennis Etc-	(281) 444-4090
Houston	Golf Superstore	(713) 910-2888
Houston	Golf Superstore	(281) 893-8020
Houston	Golf Warehouse	(281) 596-9090
Houston	Bob's Golf	(713) 783-6224
Houston	Strictly Golf	(713) 623-4282
Houston	The Sport Shoppe	(281) 879-0929
Houston	Edwin Watts Golf	(713) 627-2411
Houston	Golfsmith Golf Center	(281) 537-0101
Houston	Golfsmith	(713) 334-3334
Houston	Golf Warehouse Main Store	(281) 596-9090
Houston	Golf Superstore	(713) 532-8888
Houston	Big O's Golf	(713) 941-0095
Houston	Wood Arts Golf Inc	(281) 440-8581
Houston	Golf Crafters	(281) 440-4343
Houston	Joe's Golf & Tennis	(713) 464-1661
Houston	Oshman's Sporting Goods, Inc-	(713) 928-3171
Houston	Golf Warehouse	(281) 443-2828
Humble	Niblett's Golf	(281) 359-2627
Hurst	Supreme Golf	(817) 465-7700
Hurst	Golf Etc. Mid-Cities	(817) 577-1999
Irving	Dallas Golf Company	(972) 255-3639
Irving	GolfTEC	(972) 580-3600
Irving	Golf USA of Euless	(817) 545-2648
Kerrville	Golf USA of Kerrville	(830) 896-3330
Laredo	Driver Golf	(956) 791-1001
Lubbock	Golf USA of Lubbock	(806) 795-6906
Lubbock	Golf Headquarters	(806) 795-6730
Lufkin	Golf USA of Lufkin	(936) 639-2500
Mc Kinney	Golf Etc. McKinney	(214) 733-8273
McAllen	Golf Headquarters	(956) 687-3942
Mesquite	Wally's Discount Golf Shops	(972) 270-6602
Midland	Golf Headquarters	(915) 686-7367
New Braunfels	Golf USA of New Braunfels	(830) 626-3455
Odessa	Golf Etc. Odessa	(915) 363-8000
Odessa	Legends Golf	(915) 332-0357
Pharr	Mulligan's Golf Superstore	(956) 787-9464
Plano	Wally's Discount Golf Shops	(972) 612-9422
Plano	Golfsmith	(972) 424-4823
Plano	Clubfinders Golf	(972) 633-1033
Plano	Golf Etc. Plano	(972) 608-8782
Richardson	Dallas Golf Company	(972) 231-9399
Richardson	Wally's Discount Golf Shops	(972) 437-6655
San Angelo	Golf Plus	(915) 944-7654
San Antonio	Golf Emporium Super Store	(210) 828-2626
San Antonio	J & P Golf Discount	(210) 377-3847
San Antonio	Jon's Golf Shop	(210) 821-6207
San Antonio	McCarter's Golf Shop	(210) 684-4222
San Antonio	SA Golf Supply	(210) 490-6200
San Antonio	Golf Craft	(210) 349-7575
San Antonio	Edwin Watts Golf	(210) 822-4060
Southlake	Supreme Golf	(817) 251-0808
Southlake	Golf Etc. Southlake	(817) 416-5886
Spring	Golf Etc. the Woodlands	(281) 419-7888

Stafford	Golf Superstore	(281) 879-8884
Texarkana	Golf USA of Texarkana	(903) 832-2698
Texarkana	Texarkana Golf Shops	(903) 793-4394
Tyler	Edwin Watts Golf	(903) 561-8851
Tyler	International Golf	(903) 561-1635
Waco	Clubhouse Golf	(254) 776-4653
Waco	Tees Discount Golf	(254) 776-1815
Weatherford	Golf Etc. Weatherford	(817) 613-1122
Webster	T P G Discount Golf	(281) 332-8687
Wichita Falls	Arnie Golf	(940) 766-2661
Wichita Falls	Second Hand Sports	(940) 855-1401

TEXAS PRACTICE AND DRIVING RANGES

Amarillo
Driver's Driving Range ......4601 S Osage St ....(806) 379-6565

Angleton
Double Eagle Golf ....RR 1 ....(979) 849-2984

Arlington
Family Golf Center ....1301 NE Green Oaks Blvd ....(817) 261-6312
Westpark Golf ....3210 W Pioneer Pkwy ....(817) 469-1146

Austin
Oak Hill Golf ....5243 W Highway 290 ....(512) 892-5634
Ben White Golf Center ......714 E Ben White Blvd ....(512) 462-2104
Mister Tee ....13910 Ranch Road 620 N ....(512) 335-4444
Hank Haney Golf Ranch .....10515 N Mo Pac Expy ....(512) 345-2013
Tejas Golf ....5721 Taylor Draper Cv ....(512) 331-7079

Bastrop
Cedar Creek Driving Range ....West Highway 71 ....(512) 332-0100

Beaumont
Games People Play ....5945 College St ....(409) 866-3883
All American Golf Center .....4600 Jerry Ware Dr ....(409) 727-4045
Golden Triangle Golf Center ...8310 Eastter Freeway ....(409) 899-5243

Carrollton
Carrollton Golf Center ......2351 FM 544 ....(972) 492-7677
Cowboys Golf Range ....1659 W Belt Line Rd ....(972) 242-0700
Golden Bear Golf Center ....2538 Golden Bear Dr ....(972) 733-4111

Colleyville
Bob Moore's Sports Center ....6113 Colleyville Blvd ....(817) 481-5237

Commerce
Chile's Driving Range ....PO Box 2190 ....(903) 886-6405

Conroe
Herridge Pratice Center ......5851 W Davis St ....(936) 756-8687

Corpus Christi
Cimarron Golf Driving Range ..3752 Cimarron Blvd ....(361) 993-8180

Dallas
Preston Golf Center ....4700 Alliance Blvd ....(972) 596-6060
Hank Haney Golf Ranch ......8787 Park Ln ....(214) 341-9600

Hank Haney City Pointe . . . . . .12121 N Stemmons Fwy . . . .(972) 247-5622
Hank Haney Glf Ctr . . . . .3636 McKinney Ave . . . .(214) 520-7275
Big Tee Indoor Golf . . . . .2529 Royal Ln Ste 235 . . . .(972) 247-9064

Diana
Evening Shade Golf Center . . . .Highway 259 . . . .(903) 968-6924

El Paso
Desert East Driving Range . . . . .1351 N Lee Trevino Dr . . . .(915) 591-4653

Euless
Cooper's Golf Park . . . . .1200 S Pipeline Rd W . . . .(817) 283-2222

Flower Mound
Vista Ridge Golf Center . . . . . . .132 Flower Mound Rd . . . .(972) 539-9197

Fort Worth
Golf World . . . . .9521 South Fwy . . . .(817) 551-0990
Master Tech Golf . . . . .3715 NE 28th St . . . .(817) 831-4653
Family Golf Center . . . . .3200 Chapel Creek Blvd . . . .(817) 560-0200

Friendswood
Championship Golf Center . . . .1730 Broadway St . . . .(281) 992-5652

Fulton
Caddy Shack Golf Center . . . . .3451 Highway 35 South . . . .(361) 790-5115

Garland
Hit N Go . . . . .226 W Centerville Rd . . . .(972) 864-4653

Georgetown
Shell Road Golf Center . . . . . .2200 Shell Rd . . . .(512) 868-8098

Granbury
Lake Country Driving Range . . .3801 Acton Hwy . . . .(817) 326-2320

Grand Prairie
Practice Practice, Inc- . . . . .5720 Lake Ridge Pkwy . . . .(817) 640-1750

Harker Heights
Bravo Golf Range . . . . .3701 Oakridge Blvd . . . .(254) 337-4904

Houston
Southwest Golf Center . . . . . . .10400 Bissonnet St . . . .(281) 933-4447
Houston Golf Practice Range . . .13049 Westheimer Rd . . . .(281) 531-7285
Tee Time Golf Range . . . . . . .14441 Stuebner Airline Rd . . . .(281) 444-6301
Championship Family Golf . . . .15650 Kuykendahl Rd . . . .(281) 580-7892
Stop & Sock Range . . . . .13255 Scarsdale Blvd . . . .(281) 484-4010
Marti Golf Center . . . . .8003 S Dairy Ashford St . . . .(713) 568-5297
Bushwood Golf Center . . . . . .9210 Highway 6 N . . . .(281) 550-6236
Brown's Golf World . . . . .17002 1/2 North Fwy . . . .(281) 443-8548
Antoine Golf . . . . .5000 W Tidwell Rd . . . .(713) 683-7888
Eaglequest At Houston . . . . . .3601 Wilcrest Dr . . . .(713) 789-1010

Humble
Caddy Shack Golf Range . . . . . .2324 FM 1960 Rd E . . . .(281) 446-2425

Irving
Irving Golf Range . . . . .5310 W Airport Fwy . . . .(972) 513-0004
Las Colinas Golf . . . . .3755 Carbon Rd . . . .(972) 570-0596

Katy
Houston Golf Practice Range . . .1100 Westgreen Blvd . . . .(281) 579-9595

Keller
Keller Practice Tee . . . . .4720 Keller Hicks Rd . . . .(817) 431-9402

Kemah
South Shores Golf Center . . . . .1425 Marina Bay Dr . . . .(281) 334-6147

Kennedale
Golf Driving Range . . . . .1101 N Bowman Springs Rd . . . .(817) 572-3120

Kingsville
The Ballpark Kingsville . . . . . . .2520 E Santa Gertrudis St . . . .(361) 592-2444

Lewisville
Timbercreek Golf Center . . . . . .280 E Corporate Dr . . . .(972) 219-0550

Longview
Alpine Target Golf Center . . . . .2695 Alpine St . . . .(903) 753-1415

Lubbock
Golf Station . . . . .114th and Indiana Avenue . . . .(806) 745-0336

McKinney
Fairview Golf Center . . . . .321 Stacy Rd . . . .(972) 727-4024

Midlothian
Sweetspot Driving Range . . . . . .4191 N Highway 67 . . . .(972) 723-1150

Mission
The Practice Tee . . . . .1/4 Mile South Cherry Road . . . .(956) 585-1614

Nacogdoches
Your Tee Time . . . . .2227 N Stallings Dr . . . .(936) 560-4300

N. Richland Hills
Southwest Golf . . . . .8707 Grapevine Hwy . . . .(817) 428-8919

Odessa
Legacy Golf Center . . . . .3033 NE Loop 338 . . . .(915) 550-7525

Orange
Par 3 Driving Range . . . . .Hwy 87 Rt 5 Box 1480 . . . .(409) 886-1944

Plano
The Golf Center of Plano . . . . .4401 14th St . . . .(972) 423-3449

Port Arthur
Divots .5801 N Twin City Hwy . . . .(409) 962-7700

Richardson
Hit or Miss Driving Range . . . .2005 Willingham Dr . . . .(972) 234-4653

Rosharon
The Golf Camp . . . . .3510 County Road 63 . . . .(281) 369-2441

Round Rock
Emerald Green Golf Complex . .3301 Highway 35 . . . .(512) 251-7273

San Antonio

Eaglequest At Precision . . . . . . .450 Ira Lee Rd . . . .(210) 822-9412
Blossom Golf Center . . . . .13800 Jones Maltsberger Rd . . . .(210) 494-0002
Polo Field Driving Range . . . . . .915 E Mulberry Ave . . . .(210) 736-9592
T C's Golf Academy . . . . .16900 Blanco Rd . . . .(210) 492-7888
Ten Cup Golf . . . . .10865 W Loop 1604 N . . . .(210) 695-5163

San Marcos

Southwest Golf Range . . . . .1301 Highway 80 . . . .(512) 754-0077

Spring

Tee Time . . . . .602 Pruitt Rd . . . .(281) 298-1186
Cypress Creek Golf Co. . . . . . . .8830 Louetta Rd . . . .(281) 376-1006
Spring Golf Center . . . . .4535 Fm 2920 Rd . . . .(281) 288-8685

Temple

Caddy Shack Golf Range . . . . . .2901 Kegley Ln . . . .(254) 771-3303

The Colony

Texas Legends Golf Center . . .6001 Main St . . . .(972) 625-8333

Tyler

Westwood Driving Range . . . . .Spur 364 . . . .(903) 592-2506
Practice Tee . . . . .5052 Troup Hwy . . . .(903) 561-3146
Tyler Family Golf Center . . . . . .800 Bellwood Golf Club Rd . . . .(903) 597-2100

Victoria

Northside Golf Range . . . . .9404 N Navarro St . . . .(361) 573-1229
Riverside Driving Range . . . . . .1407 W Red River St . . . .(361) 572-4221

Waco

Brazus Golf . . . . .251 East Interstate I-35 . . . .(254) 753-8522

Wichita Falls

Loop 11 Driving Range . . . . . . .3200 Northwest Hwy . . . .(940) 855-9070

Wolfforth

Bullseye Driving Range . . . . . .9506 Upland Ave . . . .(806) 866-2194

Alphabetical by Course

Texas Golf Courses By City

Border Crossings: Courses In Adjoining States And Mexico

ABOUT THE AUTHOR

JASON STONE is a 31-year-old native Texan and a graduate of
The University of Texas at Austin who has played literally "hundreds" of golf courses in the Lone Star State. A self-described
"washed-up athlete who is addicted to sports," Stone balances
his passion for the outdoors with a love for reading, especially
biographies and history. Stone and his wife Robin live in Dallas
with their two sons—super toddler Sam and newborn Charlie—
and their needy black labrador retriever, Hank. The fish above
was caught on a golf-fish road trip.

COMING SOON – MORE GOLF BIBLES

The Alabama Golf Bible

The Arizona Golf Bible

The Arkansas Golf Bible

The Colorado Golf Bible

The Florida Golf Bible

The Louisiana Golf Bible

The Mississippi Golf Bible

The New Mexico Golf Bible

The Oklahoma Golf Bible

Check out www.golfbibles.com
for updates, new books, and more!

QUICK ORDER FORM

Telephone Orders: Call 866-357-2122 toll free. Have your credit card ready.

Online Orders: www.texasgolfbible.com

Email Orders: orders@texasgolfbible.com

Postal Orders: Fandango Publishing Co.,
                  P.O. Box 7776, Dallas, TX 75209

Please send the following books:

_____

_____

_____

_____

_____

_____

Name: _____

Address: _____

City: _____

Telephone: _____

Email address: _____

Sales tax: Please add 8.25% for products shipped to Texas addresses.

Shipping:
U.S.: $4.00 for the first book and $2.00 for each additional product.
International: $9.00 for first book and $5.00 for each additional product.

Payment: Check____   Credit Card____

Visa____   MasterCard____   Discover____   AMEX____

Card number: _____

Name on Card: _____

Exp. Date: _____